The Modern Tradition

The Modern Tradition

BACKGROUNDS OF MODERN LITERATURE

EDITED BY

RICHARD ELLMANN
NORTHWESTERN UNIVERSITY

AND

CHARLES FEIDELSON, JR.
YALE UNIVERSITY

New York OXFORD UNIVERSITY PRESS 1965

Printed in the United States of America

PREFACE

We have grown accustomed to speak offhandedly of "modern literature," of the "modern temper," and even of "the modern," but until recently we have not made much effort to analyze the meaning of this term that we find so useful. We have postponed the task of defining it for the same reason we feel it to be important—it refers to something intimate and elusive, not objective and easily analyzed. The modern is not like the reassuring landscape of the past, open and invadable everywhere. It is at once more immediate and more obscure: a blur of book titles, a mood of impatience with anachronisms, a diffuse feeling of difference. Or it is a voice to which we intuitively respond, a language that gives new valences to words long enrolled in the dictionary, including "modern" itself.

Intellectual and cultural historians and historians of art seem to have been more inquisitive in this respect than students of modern literature. Criticism has certainly not neglected the literature of the twentieth century, but most of the comprehensive studies have not been very analytic, and most of the analytic studies have not been very comprehensive. The last volume of the *Oxford History of English Literature,* an extreme example, makes no attempt at general definition—indeed, offers no broad consideration of the period at all—but consists of separate essays on *Eight Modern Writers.* Yet it is clear that "modern" amounts to more than a chronological description. The term designates a distinctive kind of imagination—themes and forms, conditions and modes of creation, that are interrelated and comprise an imaginative whole. One characteristic of works we call modern is that they positively insist on a general frame of reference within and beyond themselves. They claim modernity; they profess modernism. That is what we vaguely acknowledge when we invoke the word to describe them. However difficult to objectify, therefore, the modern awaits definition, and there is reason to think that the study of modern literature will increasingly become a study of the modern in general. Criticism is growing bolder in method and more philosophic in purpose, responding to the breadth of intention that we perceive in modern writing.

Moreover, we no longer completely identify the modern with the contemporary—the immediate literary world in which we live without much hope of defining it. Harry Levin's recent essay, "What Was Modernism?", makes explicit what everyone has begun to realize, that the great age of the century's literature, the age of Yeats, Joyce, Eliot, and Lawrence, of Proust, Valéry, and Gide, of Mann, Rilke, and Kafka, has already passed into history. Looking back upon that age historically, we are able to see it in historical depth. We become aware of what we must call a "modern tradition," which reaches well back into the romantic era and even beyond. And the more we extend our perspective in time, the less inclined we are to see this tradition as narrowly literary. What comes to mind is rather something broadly imaginative, a large spiritual enterprise including philosophic, social, and scientific thought, and aesthetic and literary theories and manifestoes, as well as poems, novels, dramas.

If we can postulate a modern tradition, we must add that it is a paradoxically untraditional tradition. Modernism strongly implies some sort of historical discontinuity, either a liberation from inherited patterns or, at another extreme, deprivation and disinheritance. In an essay on "The Modern Element in Modern Literature," Lionel Trilling singles out a radically anti-cultural bias as the most important attribute of the modern imagination. Committed to everything in human experience that militates against custom, abstract order, and even reason itself, modern literature has elevated individual existence over social man, unconscious feeling over self-conscious perception, passion and will over intellection and systematic morals, dynamic vision over the static image, dense actuality over practical reality. In these and other ways, it has made the most of its break with the past, its inborn challenge to established culture. Concurrently, it has been what Henry James called an "imagination of disaster." Interwoven with the access of knowledge, the experimental verve, and the personal urgency of the modern masters is, as Trilling also finds, a sense of loss, alienation, and despair. These are the two faces, positive and negative, of the modern as the anti-traditional: freedom and deprivation, a living present and a dead past.

Yet the concept of a modern tradition is not simply the invention of historically minded critics. The modernists have been as much imbued with a feeling for their historical role, their relation to the past, as with a feeling of historical discontinuity. They have had a sense of an ancestral line, even if it is often an underground stream. Their suspicion of old forms has made them search for kinsmen in old rebellions. Or, striving to locate their disinheritance in the course of history, they have constantly been searching for and never quite finding their starting-point—the end of Victorianism, the beginning of romanticism, the mid-seventeenth century, the end of the Middle Ages. The paradoxical task of the modern imagination, whether liberated or alienated, has been to stand both inside and outside itself, to articulate its own formlessness, to encompass its own extravagant possibilities.

That undertaking is what Stephen Spender, in *The Struggle of the Modern*, formulates as "the vision of a whole situation." The modern, according to Spender, finds its character by confronting the past and including this confrontation within itself as part of a single total experience. It is more than a cultivation of immediacy, of free or fragmented awareness; it is the embodiment in current imagery of a situation always larger than the present, and as such it is also a containment of the resources and perils of the present by rediscovery of a relevant past. In this sense, modernism is synthetic in its very indeterminacy. Modern writers, working often without established models and bent on originality, have at the same time been classicists, custodians of language, communicators, traditionalists in their fashion.

Assuming that there is a "modern tradition" and that the phrase conveys something of the ambiguous essence of modernity, this book sets out to describe the modern movement with as much of its real complexity, and with as much depth in time and intellectual breadth, as are possible within a single volume. The purpose of the book is exploratory. It is not designed to argue a general theory of modernism but to represent the various factors that any theory will be obliged to take into account. The representation is by direct quotation. Each section is introduced by a brief prospectus, but the editors have avoided extensive paraphrase and interpretation, their object being not a simplified restatement but a manageable epitome of the writers speaking for themselves.

Specifically, the materials, with rare exceptions, consist of discursive statements by writers, artists, philosophers, and scientists. The choice of the discursive is deliberate. No attempt has been made to seek out the dominant images, the obsessive concretions of character, action, and language that doubtless count for more in the actual making of literature than any conscious programs or explicit ideas. Social and economic factors and external historical events have also been largely omitted. Given the scope of this book, such exclusions are necessary; but they have a certain value as well. By preserving this level of abstraction, one may often glimpse more readily the structures common to both image and idea, artistic purpose and historical cause—the basic modes of being that are syncretized in art on the one hand and in thought or life on the other. The central literary exhibits, from Wordsworth to Proust, from Flaubert to Joyce, are easily available. In effect, this book seeks to present the universe of discourse to which they belong.

The arrangement is by themes, not by individuals. The aim is to represent these themes either by classic statements or at least by important and lucid statements. Some writers appear more than once; they are the men who talk about what they are doing as well as doing it, men of letters as well as creators. Sometimes they will contradict themselves or appear in unexpected guises; and the declarations of different writers, or even of the same writer, will not always have the same assertive weight. But this kind of unevenness is in the nature of the case. Ranging from momentary crystallizations of attitude through more elaborate hypotheses to confirmed beliefs and scientific doctrines, these statements are testimony of minds at work, at once creating and responding to an imaginative situation. However abstract in language, in another sense they are part of a concrete emergent vision.

Without professing to establish a set of first principles or criteria of modernism, it is possible to find some convenient landmarks or measuring points in this fluid intellectual world. The nine topics into which the book is divided have not chosen themselves, of course, yet they have arisen fairly directly from the materials, do not reflect any strong prejudices on the part of the editors, and have about them an accessibility that is in their favor. Their arrangement does not imply any strict system of logical subordination, nor are the topics to be regarded as exactly equal in importance. They have presented themselves as centers around which modern thinking whirls or clings. While each is a kind of spectrum of possibilities, the word spectrum itself is too prescriptive. These ideas jut out of their confines; they blend into each other in the way of montage, or come round upon each other, or otherwise intersect and parallel. A complete purview is out of the question, and would be if this book were twice as long. If each topic helps to lead the reader through the dense world of modernism, which is the common medium of all, the book will have served its purpose.

Since the introductions to the various sections explain the plan and range of each, and also suggest ways in which the topics are related to one another, no extended discussion is necessary here. The first two sections are mainly literary and aesthetic in emphasis. *Symbolism* is centered in art itself: the concept of imagination, the autonomy of the work of art, formalism, the creative process, and the heroic role of the artist. *Realism* has to do with art as a function of environment: historical determinants and social action, the pressures of experience and the responsibility of truthfulness. There follow two sections of a more philosophic cast. In *Nature*, several romantic and post-romantic theories are represented—worlds of organic harmony, of biological struggle, of mechanistic force, and of human or scientific experiment. Under *Cultural History* are included both the theme of human freedom in historical experience and a number of patterns—dialectical, repetitive, symbolic, or religious—by which the historical process has been schematized.

Moving to a primarily psychological plane, the next two sections are concerned with non-intellectual modes of thought. In *The Unconscious*, the center is Freudian psychology, but the topic also embraces pre-Freudian ideas of psychic energy and post-Freudian programs for the liberation of impulse. *Myth* includes both anthropological and Jungian versions of the myth-making mind, along with more properly literary doctrines of mythic imagination. The final sections turn toward the world of consciousness, toward individual subjective experience, and toward ethical and religious questions. *Self-*

Consciousness, as the title indicates, groups together various kinds of self-definition and self-assessment—such themes as self-realization, the situation and process of consciousness, the inner divisions of the self, and the pursuit of personal freedom. The existentialist analysis of these and related aspects of selfhood is presented separately under *Existence.* The concluding section, entitled *Faith,* is a survey of religious postures that have been adopted in the decline of Christianity—attitudes of attack, of reinterpretation, and of embattled orthodoxy.

In addition to this general topical arrangement, a certain structure has also been brought out within the materials of each section. But the reader is invited to look through and beyond the overt plan of the book. He will find that the selections are usually of sufficient scope to stand on their own, and that their meaning often overflows the particular categories in which they have been placed. One passage will frequently comment upon another in a far subtler way than any system of topics and subheadings can indicate. A motif that is dominant in one section will be powerfully latent in others. What is not formulated may occupy the reader fully as much as what is. The editors offer the book in the hope that it will give body to the concept of modernism and convey some of the life as well as the form of the modern imagination.

A great number of writers and publishers have contributed to this volume. Permissions to reprint are acknowledged in each case, but so large-scale an indebtedness requires a general expression of gratitude. The editors thank George Cohen for his guidance among many documents of modern art. We also wish to thank the staff of Oxford University Press for their aid and encouragement; and Adele Dalsimer and Susan Holahan for invaluable assistance.

Evanston, Illinois   R. E.
New Haven, Connecticut   C. F., JR.
18 October 1964

CONTENTS

xi

Indeterminacy

4 CULTURAL HISTORY

Introduction, 453

Idealism

Patterns of Repetition

History and Imagination

Religion and History

Primitive Survivals

5 THE UNCONSCIOUS

Introduction, 539

Unreason and Reason

The Freudian Unconscious

Liberation of the Unconscious

6 MYTH

Myth in Primitive Thought

The Collective Unconscious

Myth and Literature

7 SELF-CONSCIOUSNESS

Introduction, 685

Self-Realization

The Field of Consciousness

The Divided Self

Freedom

8 EXISTENCE

Introduction, 803

The Definition of Existence

Moments of Existence

Value in Existence

9 FAITH

Introduction, 883

Christianity and Christendom

Deified Man

Poetized Religion

Paganized Christianity

Orthodoxy

The State of Doubt

The Modern Tradition

1
SYMBOLISM

Imagination and Nature

The Revolt Against Nature

OSCAR WILDE: The Priority of Art
RAINER MARIA RILKE: The Unnatural Will to Art
PABLO PICASSO: Art as Individual Idea
ANDRÉ MALRAUX: Art as the Modern Absolute

The Interaction of Imagination and Nature

IMMANUEL KANT: The Imaginative Faculty and the Function of Art
SAMUEL TAYLOR COLERIDGE: The Coalescence of Mind and Nature
RAINER MARIA RILKE: The Penetration of Things
HANS ARP: Concrete Art

Symbolic Nature

WILLIAM BLAKE: The Eternal World of Vision
WILLIAM WORDSWORTH: Natural Apocalypse
CHARLES BAUDELAIRE: The Temple of Nature
W. B. YEATS: Symbol as Revelation
PAUL KLEE: Eternal Genesis

Imagination and Thought

The State of Doubt

JOHANN WOLFGANG VON GOETHE: Escape from Ideas
JOHN KEATS: Negative Capability
GUSTAVE FLAUBERT: Art without Conclusions

Introduction

Though not all romantics are symbolists, the symbolist is a kind of romantic, one who singles out and develops the romantic doctrine of creative imagination. Whatever else he may affirm, the symbolist holds that human imagination actively constructs the world we perceive or at least meets it more than halfway, and does not merely reflect the given forms of external objects. Not only like the romantics but also like Kant, on whose idealism he often leans for philosophic support, he is a deliberate innovator, experimenting with a new human perspective. He is exploring the possibility of a basic shift in emphasis—from physical to mental reality, from the multiplicity of sense experience to unifying ideas, from the objects of knowledge to the processes of knowing. But he is not systematically idealistic. As an exponent of imagination, the symbolist tends to be defiantly aesthetic in his view of the mind, of "ideas," and of knowledge itself; he is likely to be impatient with abstract Reason, the god of philosophic idealism, and to disparage all mental powers except the concrete Imagination. At his most extreme, he would say that logic is mere police work and memory is mere bookkeeping (though there may be a more profound mythic memory, which is nothing less than the cumulative imagination of mankind). He would contend that the artistic image or symbol—and especially the verbal symbol, the language of a poem—is the key to the relation of mind and nature; that it is the salvation of thought; that it possesses an absolute autonomy; and that its maker, the artist, is the truly heroic man.

The relation between the imaginative mind and nature obviously depends somewhat upon whether "nature" is taken to mean the physical landscape of fields and trees, the force animating that landscape, the external world in general, or unconscious life as opposed to conscious fabrication.[1] But many symbolists look at nature askance in all these senses, as a kind of brutal, massive, and crude encroachment of the non-human and sub-human. Their rebellion against it leads to Wilde's paradox that art holds no mirror up to nature, but is rather man's protest against nature's ineptitudes, his substitu-

[1] On nature in general, see Section 3.

7

tion of perfect imaginative forms for rudimentary natural ones. Nature, always outdone, can at best provide enfeebled copies of what artists have conceived more perfectly. When we fancy we are admiring nature, we are actually admiring (with eyes that have been taught by imaginative artists what to look for) nature's approximation to these prior forms. Wilde reverses Taine's contention that art is shaped by its age;[2] instead, art creates the age.

Rilke also maintains that art is contrary to nature, not so much by forging perfect patterns, however, as by uncovering a hidden reality that nature, especially our own human nature, urges us to ignore. Outward events and circumstances are so engrossing that most people gladly dwell among them; but the artist turns away into the "abyss" of his own being to learn what is there and to become reconciled with his own latent powers. In this way he is able to surpass his ordinary self, to achieve a preternatural level of being and perception.[3] This sense of a secret reality leads Picasso, in a rare statement about his art, to say that the artist expresses "what nature is not." He does so by granting forms a life of their own, independent of their function or appearance in external nature. Judged in terms of nature, these forms are lies; but they are valid imaginative expressions, manifesting the distinctive world of the artist. When people objected to his portrait of Gertrude Stein on the grounds that it did not resemble her, Picasso replied, "It will." Malraux agrees that the ruling passion of modern art has been to dominate appearances, to create—by rejection and distortion—another world. With a touch of regret that Picasso does not share, Malraux finds that individual artists have severed their own consciousness from all public expectations. They have substituted the value of art itself for the accepted values—the presumed "nature of things"—to which in other ages art has usually been subordinated. Art thereby becomes the modern absolute, but at the same time, rejecting so much of "the estate of man," it is anxious and perplexed, uneasily assertive, and even moves toward a kind of modern barbarism.[4]

To distinguish between nature and imagination is often only a step toward reconciling the two. This *rapprochement* is apparent in Kantian idealism. Kant postulates a "transcendental faculty of imagination," an a priori unifying or "synthetic" power of the mind without which we could never reproduce the image of an object (its "representation"), just as we would never have possessed any image at all without an earlier "synthesis of apprehension." In effect, Kant regards aesthetic creation (or "genius") as a special case of the generic imagination. Unlike mere "taste," which is an awareness of the beautiful things that are present in our initial apprehension of nature, genius is active and constructive. It is the *"beautiful representation* of a thing." The world of aesthetic ideas, the products of genius, is like a second

[2] See Section 2.
[3] In addition to later passages in this section, related selections from Rilke appear in Sections 3 and 7.
[4] A related selection from Malraux appears in Section 4.

8

nature built out of the first, the "actual nature" that we grasp through the synthesis of apprehension, and recall through the synthesis of reproduction. The aesthetic world also differs from the nature that is known through concepts. Though both are constructs, aesthetic nature has a richness of content that no abstract rational scheme can ever encompass. Yet the aesthetic world is truly a world of thought. It has the ideal quality of intellectual forms and the intuitive, untranslatable immediacy of sensory perception.

In a development typical of the post-Kantian era, Coleridge focuses upon this mid-point of the ideal and actual, the intellectual and empirical. He pictures art as an interaction or "coalescence" of mind and nature, a process in which the original terms are altered. Imagination is not a mere duplication of nature, nor is it a propounding of human thought; it is an activity or function that lies between, a union and reconcilement of nature with what is distinctively human. By means of this vital force, which "dissolves, diffuses, dissipates in order to re-create," man joins his mind (itself responsive to laws of nature) to the spirit of nature, and both are symbolically articulated in the form of the highest art. Since it is genuinely creative, imagination is quite distinct from "fancy," which does no more than shuffle the "fixities and definites" of practical experience. In the same way, Coleridge sharply distinguishes between allegorical art, which constructs a parallel between imagination and nature, and symbolical art, which makes one tune out of two.[5]

Rilke's term for "coalescence" is less philosophical; he calls it "penetration into the confidence of things." Those things that are outside us in daily life are absorbed into the artist's mind, where, without surrendering their material reality, they acquire a spiritual one as well. They now can take on a life of their own, and become tutelary to man like angels. To undergo this experience is to attain, in "a single violent gasp of feeling," what Coleridge more abstractly described. For Hans Arp, the relation of imagination to nature is a kind of sexual congress, an impregnation of objects. Unlike Picasso, Mondrian, and others who sponsor art against nature, Arp wants man to recognize his own naturalness. He calls for a "concrete art" in which imagination, the engendering power, is part of the natural world that it quickens.

A third symbolist attitude toward nature hinges on belief in an eternal language which the symbolic imagination can read within or behind natural objects. To William Blake, nature is a deception and a delusion when seen only by the corporeal eye and its confederate, memory, for which "the vanities of space and time" are all in all. But when properly apprehended by the visionary eye, nature *is* imagination; that is, it embodies realities. The whole world, including the perceiver, is understood by Blake to be a primal and eternal unity, which he depicts under the figure of a single radiant man, a Christ. To separate, as allegory does, the human from the natural, or the temporal from the eternal, is to dismember. Symbolism presents the unity behind these misleading divisions, and what the symbolic artist knows now,

[5] Compare Cassirer's account of mythical thought in Section 6.

9

all will perceive at the Last Judgment.[6] In *The Prelude* Wordsworth recounts a vision comparable to Blake's, which he experienced on crossing the Alps. Woods, streams, cliffs, and clouds alike presented themselves in their permanent aspect, as symbols of eternity.[7]

For Baudelaire nature at times becomes a "temple" in which one can perceive the mysterious correspondence of natural forms to each other and to qualities of one's own mind. Such correspondences suggest permanent essences, which Yeats considers to be "disembodied powers." By the use of emotional and intellectual symbols, the poet frees the essences of things from the "crude circumstances" in which they are hidden. These circumstances are themselves confused remnants of the buried reality which imaginative men have summoned into existence in the past.[8] Paul Klee regards nature as only one possible product of the "heart of creation," a kind of primal imagination which is the eternal generating force. The artist struggles to participate in that force by depicting it rather than its secondary manifestations in natural objects.[9]

The symbolist state of mind, at its creative pitch, has become a main preoccupation of symbolist writers. They seek to define the difference between their artistic processes and ordinary habit-ridden and opinion-ridden consciousness. "Ideas," which play so prominent a part in daily life, will probably be of no use here, for, as Goethe says, the poet deals with impressions. Art is not aimed at the reader's understanding, according to Goethe, and later poets as diverse as Coleridge and Eliot have agreed that art is perhaps most effective when imperfectly understood. Whatever claims religion and philosophy have outside art, within art they have no claim except as artistic materials.

From a similar vantage point, John Keats defines the mood of artistic creation by his term "negative capability," meaning the acceptance of uncertainties, mysteries, and doubts, without any compulsion to resolve them in rational terms or to weigh them by factual probability. The "cold philosophy" of abstract ideas can only destroy the surmises and intuitions from which creative art is born. Flaubert also lays stress on the negative aspect of imagination. According to him, *not to conclude* is a characteristic of the creative mind which is reflected in the work itself; just as the artist renounces clear-cut opinions, so the absence of them is one of the marks of great works of literature.[10]

These theories do not imply that art is the purely emotional creature of inspiration. Rather, as Paul Valéry is at pains to show in his critical essays, poetical feeling is one thing, and a poem, or the artificial synthesis of this

[6] For related selections from Blake, see Sections 5, 6, and 7.
[7] Compare Whitehead's comment on Wordsworth's visionary experience (Section 3).
[8] For related selections from Yeats, see Sections 4 and 7.
[9] For other examples of romantic attitudes toward nature that tend in the direction of symbolism, see "Organicism" in Section 3.
[10] In addition to later passages in this section, related selections from Flaubert appear in Section 2.

state in some work, is quite another. Valéry asserts that a poem is a "machine" for producing poetic feeling in a reader, and to construct the machine an immense amount of abstract thought is required. There must be efforts of will and analysis, choices and delimitations of material. The language must be freed from irrelevancies, and the artist's inner speech, his "drama of mental images," is bound to take account even of "ideas." While these cannot appear in discursive form, their influence may be felt as a pressure upon the poet's manner of performing the act of thought. For granted that poetry exceeds prose, as dancing exceeds walking, the same limbs are exercised.

To differentiate between propositions as they occur in poetry and prose, I. A. Richards offers the term *pseudo-statements*. Poetic propositions, though they look like statements, are not to be judged by truth or falsity, but only by their effect in releasing or organizing many impulses and attitudes. What Coleridge called the "willing suspension of disbelief" induced by a poem is simply our recognition that a different mode of assertion is involved. While T. S. Eliot has not always taken the same position on this question, especially as applied to religious verse, his essay on the metaphysical poets agrees that, when philosophy enters poetry, its truth or falsity as philosophy does not matter. He particularly admires the "mechanism of sensibility" which enabled seventeenth-century writers to encompass thought and emotion alike and turn them into poetry. Modern poetry must try to recover this lost capacity.[11]

Another face of poetic inconclusiveness and non-assertion is poetic affirmation, which is equally indifferent to objective tests of truth. Nietzsche finds that "untruth" is a condition of life; opinions, ideas, and beliefs are unavoidably false, yet they are necessary to gauge reality against imagined standards without which life would be arid. Affirmations, however fictional, are life-furthering because they extend man's sway over things and also provide necessary food for the passions, which crave attachments. Consequently skeptics, including Zarathustra himself, employ convictions as expressive material.[12] Yeats, in espousing what might be called affirmative capability, emphasizes the usefulness of affirmations in giving free play to the mind. Every affirmation which can engage us thoroughly, even though briefly, has some validity. In his essay, *Symbolism in Poetry*, Yeats argues against Goethe's view that the poet should know all philosophy, but keep it out of his work. According to Yeats, philosophy may enter poetry in the form of fragments which are a kind of intellectual reflection of emotions. Nietzsche regards affirmations as life-furthering but illusory; Yeats sees them instead as inevitably partial. Their imaginative reach toward Truth is more important than their factual truth or error.[13]

[11] A related selection from Eliot appears in Section 6.
[12] For related selections from Nietzsche, see Sections 4, 5, 7, 8, 9, and especially the selection from *The Birth of Tragedy* in Section 5.
[13] The symbolist problem of the relation between imagination and abstract thought is

The main bent of symbolist theory, whether in relation to nature or to abstract thought, is to preserve the autonomy of art. So as to make sure that art is its own master, symbolists discard "impure" elements, such as didacticism, which have sometimes appeared in the works of earlier artists. Baudelaire proclaims that art demands the suppression of outside motives; moral teaching violates the aesthetic effect. Art may indeed, if it wishes, disdain vice, though because of disharmony rather than evil, and art may result in the uplifting of men's minds. But these are not its purpose, which is to create beauty, or more largely, to satisfy the longing for heaven on earth in the only way available. Oscar Wilde enlarges the list of proscribed elements to include persuasion, autobiography, and practical utility. With reckless single-mindedness, art expresses nothing but itself.

As the model for artistic form, Wilde names music, and this analogy is part of the symbolist effort to establish the autonomy of poetry. Pater's declaration, "All art constantly aspires to the condition of music," concurs with Richard Wagner's view that literature must become like music by immediately presenting, rather than describing or analyzing, its subject, and by finding an alogical language that will dissolve ideas into feelings. Wagner thought these aims had been perfectly attained in music-drama.[14] Practitioners of other arts have not completely shared this enthusiasm. Mallarmé bows courteously to Wagner and praises music for its incantatory qualities, but he thinks that music has its source in relationships that words have established, and that poetry can become a higher music. By invoking, alluding, suggesting, never speaking with prose directness, its language moving always toward a life of its own, the poem will begin to express what is beyond speech. The poet's task is not to change from one art to another, but by denuding language of prose tatters, to restore it to its original purity in "the mind's native land."

In cubism, Apollinaire thought painting had achieved a comparable purification by disengaging beauty from all that was conventionally human. Paintings were no longer to be given objects for titles; they were simply to be called "paintings." Marcel Duchamp finds even this kind of title an impurity. He therefore proposes to name one of his works a "delay," so that it will no longer be thought of as a picture. Painters vie with each other, as Yeats said symbolist poets did, in finding things to exclude.

The doctrine of purity has influenced even the theory of prose fiction, the art that traditionally has been most receptive to extra-artistic motives.[15] Virginia Woolf held that the novel should not imitate objective life by means of a plot, but rather should present the "luminous halo" or "semi-transparent

---

analogous in some ways to the existentialist problem of concrete thinking in relation to abstract or objective truth. Compare the selections from Kierkegaard and Nietzsche under "The Definition of Existence" in Section 8, as well as Kierkegaard's idea of "indirection" (Section 7).

[14] For a related selection from Wagner, see Section 6.

[15] Compare the controversies of Henry James with H. G. Wells, and of Flaubert with George Sand, in Section 2.

envelope" of consciousness, the unsequential and perhaps irrational form in which life is really experienced. Events are no more than small islands in a mental sea.[16] Flaubert remarked to the brothers Goncourt that neither plot nor character interested him; *Madame Bovary*, he said, was intended only to convey a gray color. (It had, nevertheless, a pronounced and steady plot, and a profound study of character.) He aspired to write a book without a subject, held together by style alone—the one element which is peculiar to art. In that direction, he was persuaded, lay the future. As if to bear out this prophecy, André Gide's hero in *The Counterfeiters* offers to strip the novel of virtually all its customary elements. His pure novel is to be a fugue; all that will be left in it is the interplay between objective reality and the effort to stylize reality into art. Not the book, but the act of writing it, is the real subject.[17] In order to prevent any dilution of vision, these artists search for novels, poems, and pictures indefinable except as themselves.

This search leads to a symbolist axiom: the artist disappears in his artifact.[18] Though art does not reproduce the objective world, the work itself must be objective, not subjective. Flaubert would have the writer be like God, implicitly present everywhere in his creation but totally invisible as a person. Rilke's praise of his favorite painter, Cézanne, for his "unlimited objectivity," aloof from private memories and immediate concerns, falls into the same pattern. T. S. Eliot theorizes that a work of art is successful insofar as it is the "objective correlative" of the writer's emotion; it fails if it is only a confession. James Joyce traces a logical development in the relation between the artist and his material. The objective image becomes increasingly palpable until it reaches the stage of epiphany or complete aesthetic existence, while by a reverse process the artist's personality recedes from sight. The perfect literary artifact is static, as against the dynamic experience of ordinary life, and it is objectively dramatic, as against the lyrical expression of more naïve art.

The depersonalization of art, emphasizing the hard and objective thing which the artist is to produce, is related to Imagism, an effort to find concrete images that instantaneously present things and participate in their objective solidity. The image, writes Ezra Pound, is the poet's pigment; it is his primary material. Later Pound altered the term "image" to "vortex," so as to indicate a less passive, more substantial and self-propelling quality in his medium. An analogous development in painting is Dubuffet's conception of the paste he uses as having claims of its own. The paste brings subjects along with it: a cat, a trout, or a bull. The artist's medium takes control, leaving him, as Eliot once wrote in a related context, no more than a catalytic agent.

[16] Compare Henry James's fictional device of the "center of consciousness" (Section 7). But for James, "consciousness" implies order, and his work is non-objective because for him objective life implies irrationality.
[17] For related selections from Gide, see Sections 3, 7, and 9.
[18] Compare the concept of the mask in Section 7 (Nietzsche and Yeats).

13

The peculiar status of a symbolist work—neither a description of the world nor a direct expression of the artist himself—entails an equally distinctive structure, which may be characterized as alogical. Its language is set apart from that of everyday communication; the "dialect of the tribe" (as Mallarmé called it) is purified, and as Valéry says, "a language within a language" is created. Every word, Rilke declares, takes on a new and unique meaning when it enters into a poem. The symbolist endeavor to deal with problems of form alogically is well illustrated by Joyce's use of language in *Finnegans Wake:* words are suddenly made plastic, shaped and reshaped like Dubuffet's paste, and their lingual fusions parallel and evoke similar fusions of incident and character. Many symbolist poems, including Rimbaud's "Bateau ivre," Yeats's "Sailing to Byzantium," and Valéry's "Le Cimetière marin," are voyages through imagery, with a progression not explicable in purely logical terms. Dylan Thomas, to describe the structure of his poems, says that he seeks an extreme metamorphic form, in which one image is allowed to breed others, often contradictory, and all the images co-exist or try to destroy each other in dialectical profusion, the total work being a peace beyond their small wars. His theory denies any sequence to the poem's life; a match is struck to image after image. Hart Crane also sees in the poem a kind of internal dynamism, yet he repudiates the idea that this is illogical. It has instead a "higher logic"; metaphors may seem hyperbolical, but they particularize states of feeling in a precise and accurate way. The poem's system of connections has an order which is psychologically if not scientifically valid. In painting, Max Ernst tells how multiple and contradictory images make their unexpected appearances on his canvases. And Eisenstein, in writing about the film, celebrates montage for splicing heterogeneous images together to achieve an effect not paraphrasable or in any other way attainable.[19]

One result of the symbolist movement has been to create out of the artist a new hero. While he does not champion conventional moral patterns in his work, his way of life has its own morality about it. The artist-hero descends into the mind, Yeats thinks, as other heroes enter physical combat. Although Flaubert chafes at the self-sacrifice, the quasi-religious asceticism, that art imposes upon him, he accepts and welcomes it too. Rilke attests that an artist surrenders love and friendship to carry on his embattled search for the understanding of things. Artistic heroism is epitomized by Paul Valéry in his figure of Leonardo da Vinci, a type of the artist as universal man. Exploring the night of consciousness, the artist discovers that the reality to which we are accustomed is but one solution out of many possible ones. He is able to divest objects of their peculiarities and, at the same time, to sense what con-

[19] On poetic alogicality, compare the programs of Dadaism and Surrealism (Section 5), as well as Gide's cultivation of inconsistency and Schlegel's concept of irony (Section 7). Whitehead's account of the structure of nature (Section 2) and Cassirer's account of the structure of mythical thought (Section 6) are close in many ways to the symbolist theory of poetic structure.

sciousness is apart from its objects, to reach "the deep note of existence itself." Such a man is interested in everything, yet always seems to be thinking of something else, for his mental life is double, a drama of mental images proceeding concurrently with an awareness of the movements of thought itself. He takes responsibility for his perceptions in a way that others do not, and he is concerned not with results but with the exercise of creative power.[20]

Insofar as the artist takes risks and suffers in order to create, his life may serve as an exemplar for human behavior. But beyond this kind of imitation of the man, we may model ourselves upon his work. On this principle, life itself may come to be a kind of artifact. So Walter Pater wishes us to give the highest quality to every moment as though each were an intense artistic image. Huysmans' hero Des Esseintes, convinced that his life must be as little natural as possible if it is to have artistic shape, cultivates wholly artificial sensations. André Gide also discovers life to be a process of aesthetic creation, the formulation of a single image in which is reflected all we have done. The artist, unnaturally vigilant of this process, lives his life as he will recount it, yet in recounting it he is changed. Yeats, in the last letter he wrote, suggested that his life was an image which his death would complete, a kind of total symbolic embodiment in which his works and actions alike would have part. Going beyond Des Esseintes' conviction that to make one's life into a work of art is a fine outrage to nature, Yeats regards this process as a vindication of imagination against determinism. Rilke offers art a further purpose, to transform the earth by bringing it inside the mind instead of leaving it frighteningly aloof. Not only may we subdue life by our art, but death too, for that loses its terrors as our consciousness embraces it.[21]

Deviously but surely, then, symbolist art moves toward a recognition of the artist's role in his society. Even Flaubert sketches tentatively, and almost in desperation, an "aesthetic mysticism." There are hints in his letters that he envisages humanity as ultimately awaking, uniting, and finding a higher morality in art. Flaubert argues that, since artistic form has an intrinsic virtue, perhaps it evinces an eternal principle, a divine order. Meanwhile we may love each other in art. E. M. Forster adopts art for art's sake without this metaphysical hope. Too rashly attributing chaos to nature on the basis of Einstein's discoveries, Forster declares that works of art are the only objects in the universe that possess internal order. They are lighthouses among "the thankless seas."[22]

Flaubert and Forster are brought to make their claims for a social value in art because, it seems, they can find nothing else to uphold. A writer like Rimbaud takes the artist's part much more fiercely. For him the poet is a Promethean criminal who at infinite risk explores the unknown. A seer, or even a

[20] In connection with artistic heroism, see the expressionist credo of Kandinsky and Nietzsche's moral ideal of self-overcoming in Section 7.
[21] The idea of life as art is developed by Yeats into a vision of history as art (see Section 4).
[22] Compare Malraux on the triumph of art over history (Section 4).

god, he assumes responsibility for man and the lower creatures, and by his painfully won discoveries enables humanity to progress. Mallarmé is by temperament more reserved: for him art is an aristocratic mystery, too sacred for the vulgar to penetrate. Yet it is an indispensable renewal of the highest human power, that of penetrating nature's façade; and Mallarmé extols it the more to the degree that he finds it undiscussable.

In opposition to the almost magical view of art that Mallarmé takes, W. H. Auden used to speak of art as an impersonal game, though a game of knowledge. It makes nothing happen, but is a way of naming hidden relationships. More recently, Auden has offered a conception of art as a rite which celebrates reality. It subtly remakes for man the relations of the sacred and profane, the ideal and the real, the one and the many. Unlike religion in dwelling upon the created world rather than the creator, it is characterized by a similar awe. Wallace Stevens sees poetry, somewhat as Matthew Arnold did,[23] replacing religion rather than companioning it. In an age of disbelief, poetry must supply the satisfactions of belief; it must help people to live by lending life its savor, by enabling them to perceive order in disorder, and so replacing with a human glory the lost glory of the gods. Stevens denies that the poet has any social or moral obligations, yet, without being obliged, the poet wishes to convey his imagination of things to others. He does so by forming those "supreme fictions" without which we cannot conceive of life, just as we cannot conceive of the universe without solar light.[24]

[23] See Section 9.
[24] In connection with the social and quasi-religious function of symbolist art, see Section 6 (*Myth*) and the selections from Arnold and Santayana in Section 9.

OSCAR WILDE

The Priority of Art

A Dialogue

PERSONS: *Cyril and Vivian.* SCENE: *the library of a country house in Notting-hamshire.*

CYRIL (*coming in through the open window from the terrace*): My dear Vivian, don't coop yourself up all day in the library. It is a perfectly lovely afternoon. The air is exquisite. There is a mist upon the woods, like the purple bloom upon a plum. Let us go and lie on the grass and smoke cigarettes and enjoy Nature.

VIVIAN: Enjoy Nature! I am glad to say that I have entirely lost that faculty. People tell us that Art makes us love Nature more than we loved her before; that it reveals her secrets to us; and that after a careful study of Corot and Constable we see things in her that had escaped our observation. My own experience is that the more we study Art, the less we care for Nature. What Art really reveals to us is Nature's lack of design, her curious crudities, her extraordinary monotony, her absolutely unfinished condition. Nature has good intentions, of course, but, as Aristotle once said, she cannot carry them out. When I look at a landscape I cannot help seeing all its defects. It is fortunate for us, however, that Nature is so imperfect, as otherwise we should have no art at all. Art is our spirited protest, our gallant attempt to teach Nature her proper place. As for the infinite variety of Nature, that is a pure myth. It is not to be found in Nature herself. It resides in the imagination, or fancy, or cultivated blindness of the man who looks at her. . . . Now, if you promise not to interrupt too often, I will read you my article.

CYRIL: You will find me all attention.

VIVIAN (*reading in a very clear voice*): "THE DECAY OF LYING: A PROTEST.—One of the chief causes that can be assigned for the curiously commonplace character of most of the literature of our age is undoubtedly the decay of Lying as an art, a science, and a social pleasure. The ancient historians gave us delightful fiction in the form of fact; the modern novelist presents us with dull facts under the guise of fiction. The Blue-Book is rapidly becoming his ideal both for method and manner.

From "The Decay of Lying" [1889], *The Works of Oscar Wilde*, ed. G. F. Maine, London, 1948, pp. 909, 911-12, 916-17, 918, 921-2, 924-6, 930-31.

17

He has his tedious *document humain,* his miserable little *coin de la création,* into which he peers with his microscope. He is to be found at the Librairie Nationale, or at the British Museum, shamelessly reading up his subject. He has not even the courage of other people's ideas, but insists on going directly to life for everything, and ultimately, between encyclopaedias and personal experience, he comes to the ground, having drawn his types from the family circle or from the weekly washerwoman, and having acquired an amount of useful information from which never, even in his most meditative moments, can he thoroughly free himself.

"The loss that results to literature in general from this false ideal of our time can hardly be overestimated. People have a careless way of talking about a 'born liar,' just as they talk about a born poet. But in both cases they are wrong. Lying and poetry are arts—arts, as Plato saw, not unconnected with each other—and they require the most careful study, the most disinterested devotion. Indeed, they have their technique, just as the more material arts of painting and sculpture have their subtle secrets of form and colour, their craft-mysteries, their deliberate artistic methods. As one knows the poet by his fine music, so one can recognize the liar by his rich rhythmic utterance, and in neither case will the casual inspiration of the moment suffice. Here, as elsewhere, practice must precede perfection. But in modern days while the fashion of writing poetry has become far too common, and should, if possible, be discouraged, the fashion of lying has almost fallen into disrepute. Many a young man starts in life with a natural gift for exaggeration which, if nurtured in congenial and sympathetic surroundings, or by the imitation of the best models, might grow into something really great and wonderful. But, as a rule, he comes to nothing. He either falls into careless habits of accuracy——"

CYRIL: My dear fellow!

VIVIAN: Please don't interrupt in the middle of a sentence. "He either falls into careless habits of accuracy, or takes to frequenting the society of the aged and the well-informed. Both things are equally fatal to his imagination, as indeed they would be fatal to the imagination of anybody, and in a short time he develops a morbid and unhealthy faculty of truth-telling, begins to verify all statements made in his presence, has no hesitation in contradicting people who are much younger than himself, and often ends by writing novels which are so life-like that no one can possibly believe in their probability. This is no isolated instance that we are giving. It is simply one example out of many; and if something cannot be done to check, or at least to modify, our monstrous worship of facts, Art will become sterile and beauty will pass away from the land. . . ." I do not know anything in the whole history of literature sadder than the artistic career of Charles Reade. He wrote one beautiful book, *The Cloister and the Hearth,* a book as much above *Romola* as *Romola* is above *Daniel Deronda,* and wasted the rest of his life in a foolish attempt to be modern, to draw public attention to the state of our convict prisons, and the management of our private lunatic asylums. Charles Dickens was depressing enough in all conscience when he tried to arouse our sympathy for the victims of the poor-law administration; but Charles Reade, an artist, a scholar, a man with a true sense of beauty, raging and roaring over the abuses of contemporary life like a common pamphleteer or a sensational journalist, is really a sight for the angels to weep over. Believe me, my dear Cyril, modernity of form and modernity of subject-matter are entirely and absolutely wrong. We have mistaken the common livery of the age for the vesture of the Muses, and spend our days in the sordid streets and hideous suburbs of our vile cities when we should be out on the hillside with Apollo. Certainly we are a degraded race, and have sold our birthright for a mess of facts.

CYRIL: There is something in what you say, and there is no doubt that whatever amusement we may find in reading a purely modern novel, we have rarely any artistic pleasure in re-reading it. And this is perhaps the best rough test of what is literature and what is not. If one cannot enjoy reading a book over and over again, there is no use reading it at all. But what do you say about the return to Life and Nature? This is the panacea that is always being recommended to us.

VIVIAN: I will read you what I say on that subject. The passage comes later on in the article, but I may as well give it to you now:—

"The popular cry of our time is 'Let us return to Life and Nature; they will recreate Art for us, and send the red blood coursing through her veins; they will shoe her feet with swiftness and make her hand strong.' But, alas! we are mistaken in our amiable and well-meaning efforts. Nature is always behind the age. And as for Life, she is the solvent that breaks up Art, the enemy that lays waste her house."

CYRIL: What do you mean by saying that Nature is always behind the age?

VIVIAN: Well, perhaps that is rather cryptic. What I mean is this. If we take Nature to mean natural simple instinct as opposed to self-conscious culture, the work produced under this influence is always old-fashioned, antiquated, and out of date. One touch of Nature may make the whole world kin, but two touches of Nature will destroy any work of Art. If, on the other hand, we regard Nature as the collection of phenomena external to man, people only discover in her what they bring to her. She has no suggestions of her own. Wordsworth went to the lakes, but he was never a lake poet. He found in stones the sermons he had already hidden there. He went moralising about the district, but his good work was produced when he returned, not to Nature but to poetry. Poetry gave him "Laodamia," and the fine sonnets, and the great Ode such as it is. Nature gave him "Martha Ray" and "Peter Bell," and the address to Mr. Wilkinson's spade.

CYRIL: I think that view might be questioned. I am rather inclined to believe in "the impulse from a vernal wood," though of course the artistic value of such an impulse depends entirely on the kind of temperament that receives it, so that the return to Nature would come to mean simply the advance to a great personality. You would agree with that, I fancy. However, proceed with your article.

VIVIAN (reading): "Art begins with abstract decoration, with purely imaginative and pleasurable work dealing with what is unreal and non-existent. This is the first stage. Then Life becomes fascinated with this new wonder, and asks to be admitted into the charmed circle. Art takes life as part of her rough material, re-creates it, and refashions it in fresh forms, is absolutely indifferent to fact, invents, imagines, dreams, and keeps between herself and reality the impenetrable barrier of beautiful style, of decorative or ideal treatment. The third stage is when Life gets the upper hand, and drives Art out into the wilderness. This is the true decadence, and it is from this that we are now suffering. . . . The whole history of these arts in Europe is the record of the struggle between Orientalism, with its frank rejection of imitation, its love of artistic convention, its dislike to the actual representation of any object in Nature, and our own imitative spirit. Wherever the former has been paramount, as in Byzantium, Sicily and Spain, by actual contact or in the rest of Europe by the influence of the Crusades, we have had beautiful and imaginative work in which the visible things of life are transmuted into artistic conventions, and the things that Life has not are invented and fashioned for her delight. But wherever we have returned to Life and Nature, our work has always become vulgar, common and uninteresting. . . .

"Art finds her own perfection within, and not outside of, herself. She is not to be judged by any external standard of resemblance. She is a veil, rather than a mirror. She has flowers that no forests know of, birds that no woodland possesses. She makes and unmakes many worlds, and can draw the moon from heaven with a scarlet thread. Hers are the 'forms more real than living man,' and hers the great archetypes of which things that have existence are but unfinished copies. Nature has, in her eyes, no laws, no uniformity. She can work miracles at her will, and when she calls monsters from the deep they come. She can bid the almond-tree blossom in winter, and send the snow upon the ripe cornfield. . . ."

CYRIL: . . . I should like to ask you a question. What do you mean by saying that life, "poor, probable, uninteresting human life," will try to reproduce the marvels of art? I can quite understand your objection to art being treated as a mirror. You think it would reduce genius to the position of a cracked looking-glass. But you don't mean to say that you seriously believe that Life imitates Art, that Life in fact is the mirror, and Art the reality?

VIVIAN: Certainly I do. Paradox though it may seem—and paradoxes are always dangerous things—it is none the less true that Life imitates art far more than Art imitates life. We have all seen in our own day in England how a certain curious and fascinating type of beauty, invented and emphasised by two imaginative painters, has so influenced Life that whenever one goes to a private view or to an artistic salon one sees, here the mystic eyes of Rossetti's dream, the long ivory throat, the strange square-cut jaw, the loosened shadowy hair that he so ardently loved, there the sweet maidenhood of "The Golden Stair," the blossom-like mouth and weary loveliness of the "Laus Amoris," the passion-pale face of Andromeda, the thin hands and lithe beauty of the Vivian in "Merlin's Dream." And it has always been so. A great artist invents a type, and Life tries to copy it, to reproduce it in a popular form, like an enterprising publisher. Neither Holbein nor Vandyck found in England what they have given us. They brought their types with them, and Life with her keen imitative faculty set herself to supply the master with models. The Greeks, with their quick artistic instinct, understood this, and set in the bride's chamber the statue of Hermes or of Apollo, that she might bear children as lovely as the works of art that she looked at in her rapture or her pain. They knew that Life gains from art not merely spirituality, depth of thought and feeling, soul-turmoil or soul-peace, but that she can form herself on the very lines and colours of art, and can reproduce the dignity of Pheidias as well as the grace of Praxiteles. Hence came their objection to realism. They disliked it on purely social grounds. They felt that it inevitably makes people ugly, and they were perfectly right. We try to improve the conditions of the race by means of good air, free sunlight, wholesome water, and hideous bare buildings for the better housing of the lower orders. But these things merely produce health, they do not produce beauty. For this, Art is required, and the true disciples of the great artist are not his studio-imitators, but those who become like his works of art, be they plastic as in Greek days, or pictorial as in modern times; in a word, Life is Art's best, Art's only pupil.

As it is with the visible arts, so it is with literature. The most obvious and the vulgarest form in which this is shown is in the case of the silly boys who, after reading the adventures of Jack Sheppard or Dick Turpin, pillage the stalls of unfortunate apple-women, break into sweet-shops at night, and alarm old gentlemen who are returning home from the city by leaping out on them in suburban lanes, with black masks and unloaded revolvers. This interesting phenomenon, which always occurs after the appearance of a new edition of either of the books I have alluded to, is usually attributed to the influence of literature on the imagination. But this is a mistake. The imagination is essentially creative, and always seeks for a new form. The boy burglar is simply the inevitable result of life's imitative instinct. He is Fact, occupied as Fact usually is, with trying to reproduce Fiction, and what we see in him is repeated on an extended scale throughout the whole of life. Schopenhauer has analysed the pessimism that characterises modern thought, but Hamlet invented it. The world has become sad because a puppet was once melancholy. . . .

CYRIL: The theory is certainly a very curious one, but to make it complete you must show that Nature, no less than Life, is an imitation of Art. Are you prepared to prove that?

VIVIAN: My dear fellow, I am prepared to prove anything.

CYRIL: Nature follows the landscape painter, then, and takes her effects from him?

VIVIAN: Certainly. Where, if not from the Impressionists, do we get those wonderful brown fogs that come creeping down our streets, blurring the gas-lamps and changing the houses into monstrous shadows? To whom, if not to them and their master, do we owe the lovely silver mists that brood over our river, and turn to faint forms of fading grace curved bridge and swaying barge? The extraordinary change that has taken place in the climate of London during the last ten years is entirely due to a particular school of Art. You smile. Consider the matter from a scientific or a metaphysical point of view, and you will find that I am right. For what is Nature? Nature is no great mother who has borne us. She is our creation. It is in our brain that she quickens to life. Things are because we see them, and what we see, and how we see it, depends on the Arts that have influenced us. To look at a thing is very different from seeing a thing. One does not see anything until one sees its beauty. Then, and then only, does it come into existence. At present, people see fogs, not because there are fogs, but because poets and painters have taught them the mysterious loveliness of such effects. There may have been fogs for centuries in London. I dare say there were. But no one saw them, and so we do not know anything about them. They did not exist till Art had invented them. Now, it must be admitted, fogs are carried to excess. They have be-

come the mere mannerism of a clique, and the exaggerated realism of their method gives dull people bronchitis. Where the cultured catch an effect, the uncultured catch cold. And so, let us be humane, and invite Art to turn her wonderful eyes elsewhere. She has done so already, indeed. That white quivering sunlight that one sees now in France, with its strange blotches of mauve, and its restless violet shadows, is her latest fancy, and, on the whole, Nature reproduces it quite admi- · ·
rably. Where she used to give us Corots and Daubignys, she gives us now exquisite Monets and entrancing Pissaros. Indeed there are moments, rare, it is true, but still to be observed from time to time, when Nature becomes absolutely modern. Of course she is not always to be relied upon. The fact is that she is in this unfortunate position. Art creates an incomparable and unique effect, and, having done so, passes on to other things. Nature, upon the other hand, forgetting that imitation can be made the sincerest form of insult, keeps on repeating this effect until we all become absolutely wearied of it. Nobody of any real culture, for instance, ever talks nowadays about the beauty of a sunset. Sunsets are quite old-fashioned. They belong to the time when Turner was the last note in art. To admire them is a distinct sign of provincialism of temperament. Upon the other hand they go on. Yesterday evening Mrs. Arundel insisted on my going to the window and looking at the glorious sky, as she called it. Of course I had to look at it. She is one of those absurdly pretty Philistines to whom one can deny nothing. And what was it? It was simply a very second-rate Turner, a Turner of a bad period, with all the painter's worst faults exaggerated and over-emphasized. Of course I am quite ready to admit that Life very often commits the same error. She produces her false Renés and her sham Vautrins, just as Nature gives us, on one day a doubtful Cuyp, and on another a more than questionable Rousseau. Still, Nature irritates one more when she does things of that kind. It seems so stupid, so obvious, so unnecessary. A false Vautrin might be delightful. A doubtful Cuyp is unbearable. However, I don't want to be too hard on Nature. I wish the Channel, especially at Hastings, did not look quite so often like a Henry Moore, grey pearl with yellow lights, but then, when Art is more varied, Nature will, no doubt, be more varied also. That she imitates Art, I don't think even her worst enemy would deny now. It is the one thing that keeps her in touch with civilised man. But have I proved my theory to your satisfaction?

CYRIL: You have proved it to my dissatisfaction, which is better. But even admitting this strange imitative instinct in Life and Nature, surely you would acknowledge that Art expresses the temper of its age, the spirit of its time, the moral and social conditions that surround it, and under whose influence it is produced.

VIVIAN: Certainly not! Art never expresses anything but itself. This is the principle of my new aesthetics; and it is this, more than that vital connection between form and substance, on which Mr. Pater dwells, that makes basic the type of all the arts. Of course, nations and individuals, with that healthy natural vanity which is the secret of existence, are always under the impression that it is of them that the Muses are talking, always trying to find in the calm dignity of imaginative art some mirror of their own turbid passions, always forgetting that the singer of life is not Apollo but Marsyas. Remote from reality and with her eyes turned away from the shadows of the cave, Art reveals her own perfection, and the wondering crowd that watches the opening of the marvellous many-petalled rose fancies that it is its own history that is being told to it, its own spirit that is finding expression in a new form. But it is not so. The highest art rejects the burden of the human spirit, and gains more from a new medium or a fresh material than she does from any enthusiasm for art, or from any lofty passion, or from any great awakening of the human consciousness. She develops purely on her own lines. She is not symbolic of any age. It is the ages that are her symbols. . . .

CYRIL: . . . But in order to avoid making any error I want you to tell me briefly the doctrines of the new aesthetics.

VIVIAN: Briefly, then, they are these. Art never expresses anything but itself. It has an independent life, just as Thought has, and develops purely on its own lines. It is not necessarily realistic in an age of realism, nor spiritual in an age of faith. So far from being the creation of its time, it is usually in direct opposition to it, and the only history that it preserves for us is the history of its own progress. Sometimes it returns upon its footsteps, and revives some antique form, as happened in the archaistic movement of late Greek Art, and in the pre-Raphaelite movement of our own day. At other times it entirely anticipates its age, and produces in one century work that it takes another century to understand, to appreciate, and to enjoy. In no case does it reproduce its age. To pass from the art of a time to the time itself is the great mistake that all historians commit.

The second doctrine is this. All bad art comes from returning to Life and Nature, and elevating them into ideals. Life and Nature may sometimes be used as part of Art's rough material, but before they are of any real service to Art they must be translated into artistic conventions. The moment Art surrenders its imaginative medium it surrenders everything. As a method Realism is a complete failure, and the two things that every artist should avoid are modernity of form and modernity of subject-matter. To us, who live in the nineteenth century, any century is a suitable subject for art except our own. The only beautiful things are the things that do not concern us. It is, to have the pleasure of quoting myself, exactly because Hecuba is nothing to us that her sorrows are so suitable a motive for a tragedy. Besides, it is only the modern that ever becomes old-fashioned. M. Zola sits down to give us a picture of the Second Empire. Who cares for the Second Empire now? It is out of date. Life goes faster than Realism, but Romanticism is always in front of Life.

The third doctrine is that Life imitates Art far more than Art imitates Life. This results not merely from Life's imitative instinct, but from the fact that the self-conscious aim of Life is to find expression, and that Art offers it certain beautiful forms through which it may realize that energy. It is a theory that has never been put forward before, but it is extremely fruitful, and throws an entirely new light upon the history of Art.

It follows, as a corollary from this, that external Nature also imitates Art. The only effects that she can show us are effects that we have already seen through poetry, or in paintings. This is the secret of Nature's charm, as well as the explanation of Nature's weakness.

The final revelation is that Lying, the telling of beautiful untrue things, is the proper aim of Art. But of this I think I have spoken at sufficient length. And now let us go out on the terrace, where "droops the milk-white peacock like a ghost," while the evening star "washes the dusk with silver." At twilight nature becomes a wonderfully suggestive effect, and is not without loveliness, though perhaps its chief use is to illustrate quotations from the poets. Come! We have talked long enough.

RAINER MARIA RILKE

The Unnatural Will to Art

Do not expect me to talk about my interior effort,—I must be silent on that score; it would be unwise to render account, even to myself, of all the changes of fortune I shall have to undergo in my struggle towards concentration. This reversal of all one's forces, this changed direction of soul can never be accomplished without a number of crises; most artists avoid it by means of diversions, but that is just why they never again succeed in touching their center of production, from which they started at the moment of their purest impulse. Always when you begin to work you must recreate this first innocence, you must return to the ingenuous place where the Angel discovered you when he brought you the first binding message; you must find once more the couch behind the briars where you were then asleep: this time you will not sleep there: you will have to pray and groan,—no matter: if the Angel deigns to appear, it will be because you have convinced him, not by tears but by your humble resolve to be always beginning—to be a Beginner!

Oh, Dear, how many times in my life—and never so much as now—have I told myself that Art, as I conceive it, is a movement contrary to nature. No doubt God never foresaw that any one of us would turn inwards upon himself in this way, which can only be permitted to the Saint because he seeks to besiege his God by attacking him from this unexpected and badly defended quarter. But for the rest of us, whom do we approach when we turn our back on events, on our future even, in order to throw ourselves into the abyss of our being, which would engulf us were it not for the sort of trustfulness that we bring to it, and which seems stronger even than the gravitation of our nature? If the meaning of sacrifice is that the moment of greatest danger coincides with that when one is saved, then certainly nothing resembles sacrifice more than this terrible will to Art. How tenacious it is, how insensate! All that the rest forget in order to make their life possible, we are always bent on discovering, on magnifying even; it is we who are the real awakeners of our monsters, to which we are not hostile enough to become their conquerors; for in a certain sense we are at one with them; it is they, the monsters, that hold the surplus strength which is indispensable to those that must surpass themselves. Unless one assigns to the act of victory a mysterious and far deeper meaning, it is not for us to consider ourselves the tamers of our internal lions. But suddenly we feel ourselves walking beside them, as in a Triumph, without being able to remember the exact moment when this inconceivable reconciliation took place (bridge barely curved that connects the terrible with the tender . . .).

Letter [1920], *Letters to Merline*, translated by Violet M. MacDonald, London, 1952, pp. 47-9, 62-4; reprinted by permission of Methuen & Co. Ltd. and Éditions du Seuil.

PABLO PICASSO

Art as Individual Idea

I can hardly understand the importance given to the word *research* in connection with modern painting. In my opinion to search means nothing in painting. To find, is the thing. Nobody is interested in following a man who, with his eyes fixed on the ground, spends his life looking for the pocketbook that fortune should put in his path. The one who finds something no matter what it might be, even if his intention were not to search for it, at least arouses our curiosity, if not our admiration.

Among the several sins that I have been accused of committing, none is more false than the one that I have, as the principal objective in my work, the spirit of research. When I paint my object is to show what I have found and not what I am looking for. In art intentions are not sufficient and, as we say in Spanish: love must be proved by facts and not by reasons. What one does is what counts and not what one had the intention of doing.

We all know that art is not truth. Art is a lie that makes us realize truth, at least the truth that is given us to understand. The artist must know the manner whereby to convince others of the truthfulness of his lies. If he only shows in his work that he has searched, and re-searched, for the way to put over his lies, he would never accomplish anything.

The idea of research has often made painting go astray, and made the artist lose himself in mental lucubrations. Perhaps this has been the principal fault of modern art. The spirit of research has poisoned those who have not fully understood all the positive and conclusive elements in modern art and has made them attempt to paint the invisible and, therefore, the unpaintable.

They speak of naturalism in opposition to modern painting. I would like to know if anyone has ever seen a natural work of art. Nature and art, being two different things, cannot be the same thing. Through art we express our conception of what nature is not.

Velasquez left us his idea of the people of his epoch. Undoubtedly they were different from what he painted them, but we cannot conceive a Philip IV in any other way than the one Velasquez painted. Rubens also made a portrait of the same king and in Rubens' portrait he seems to be quite another person. We believe in the one painted by Velasquez, for he convinces us by his right of might.

From the painters of the origins, the primitives, whose work is obviously different from nature, down to those artists who, like David, Ingres and even Bouguereau, believed in painting nature as it is, art has always been art and not nature. And from the point of view of art there are no concrete or abstract forms, but only forms which are more or less convincing lies. That those lies are necessary to our mental selves is beyond any doubt, as it is through them that we form our esthetic point of view of life.

Cubism is no different from any other school of painting. The same principles and the same elements are common to all. The fact that for a long time cubism

Statement, first published in *The Arts*, III, May 1923, pp. 315-26. Text here is from *Picasso: Fifty Years of his Art*, by Alfred H. Barr, Jr., New York, 1946, pp. 270-71. Copyright 1946 by The Museum of Modern Art, New York, and reprinted with its permission.

25

has not been understood and that even today there are people who cannot see anything in it, means nothing. I do not read English, an English book is a blank book to me. This does not mean that the English language does not exist, and why should I blame anybody else but myself if I cannot understand what I know nothing about?

I also often hear the word evolution. Repeatedly I am asked to explain how my painting evolved. To me there is no past or future in art. If a work of art cannot live always in the present it must not be considered at all. The art of the Greeks, of the Egyptians, of the great painters who lived in other times, is not an art of the past; perhaps it is more alive today than it ever was. Art does not evolve by itself, the ideas of people change and with them their mode of expression. When I hear people speak of the evolution of an artist, it seems to me that they are considering him standing between two mirrors that face each other and reproduce his image an infinite number of times, and that they contemplate the successive images of one mirror as his past, and the images of the other mirror as his future, while his real image is taken as his present. They do not consider that they all are the same images in different planes.

Variation does not mean evolution. If an artist varies his mode of expression this only means that he has changed his manner of thinking, and in changing, it might be for the better or it might be for the worse.

The several manners I have used in my art must not be considered as an evolution, or as steps toward an unknown ideal of painting. All I have ever made was made for the present and with the hope that it will always remain in the present. I have never taken into consideration the spirit of research. When I have found something to express, I have done it without thinking of the past or of the future. I do not believe I have used radically different elements in the different manners I have used in painting. If the subjects I have wanted to express have suggested different ways of expression I have never hesitated to adopt them. I have never made trials nor experiments. Whenever I had something to say, I have said it in the manner in which I have felt it ought to be said. Different motives inevitably require different methods of expression. This does not imply either evolution or progress, but an adaptation of the idea one wants to express and the means to express that idea.

Arts of transition do not exist. In the chronological history of art there are periods which are more positive, more complete than others. This means that there are periods in which there are better artists than in others. If the history of art could be graphically represented, as in a chart used by a nurse to mark the changes of temperature of her patient, the same silhouettes of mountains would be shown, proving that in art there is no ascendant progress, but that it follows certain ups and downs that might occur at any time. The same occurs with the work of an individual artist.

Many think that cubism is an art of transition, an experiment which is to bring ulterior results. Those who think that way have not understood it. Cubism is not either a seed or a foetus, but an art dealing primarily with forms, and when a form is realized it is there to live its own life. A mineral substance, having geometric formation, is not made so for transitory purposes, it is to remain what it is and will always have its own form. But if we are to apply the law of evolution and transformism to art, then we have to admit that all art is transitory. On the contrary, art does not enter into these philosophic absolutisms. If cubism is an art of transition I am sure that the only thing that will come out of it is another form of cubism.

Mathematics, trigonometry, chemistry, psychoanalysis, music, and whatnot, have been related to cubism to give it an easier interpretation. All this has been pure literature, not to say nonsense, which brought bad results, blinding people with theories.

Cubism has kept itself within the limits and limitations of painting, never pretending to go beyond it. Drawing, design and color are understood and practiced in cubism in the same spirit and manner that they are understood and practiced in all other schools. Our subjects might be different, as we have introduced into painting objects and forms that were formerly ignored. We have kept our eyes open to our surroundings, and also our brains.

We give to form and color all their individual significance, as far as we can see it; in our subjects we keep the joy of discovery, the pleasure of the unexpected; our subject itself must be a source of interest. But of what use is it to say what we do when everybody can see it if he wants to?

ANDRÉ MALRAUX

Art as the Modern Absolute

What exactly is a modern picture? That compendious term "easel picture" covers a wide field: a Braque still life obviously differs *toto coelo* from one by a Dutch little master; indeed a Cézanne still life is equally remote from it; and many of Manet's were something unique in painting when he made them and as unlike Chardin's as they were unlike the Dutch still lifes of foodstuffs. Modern pictures are not objects intended to be hung on a drawing-room wall to ornament it— even if we do hang them there. It is possible that, thanks to the process of metamorphosis, Picasso may come to be aligned, in the year 2200, with the Persian ceramists; but this will happen only if people of that day have ceased to understand the first thing about his art. The gestures we make when handling pictures we admire (not only masterpieces) are those befitting precious objects: but also, let us not forget, objects claiming veneration. Once a mere collection, the art museum is by way of becoming a sort of shrine, the only one of the modern age; the man who looks at an *Annunciation* in the National Gallery of Washington is moved by it no less profoundly than the man who sees it in an Italian church. True, a Braque still life is not a sacred object; nevertheless, though not a Byzantine miniature, it, too, belongs to another world and it is hallowed by its association with a vague deity known as Art, as the miniature was hallowed by its association with Christ Pantocrator.

From *The Voices of Silence* [1951], translated from the French by Stuart Gilbert, New York, 1953, pp. 600-607. Published by Doubleday & Co., Inc.; reprinted by permission of Doubleday & Co., Inc. and Martin Secker & Warburg Ltd.

In this context the religious vocabulary may jar on us; but unhappily we have no other. Though this art is not a god, but an absolute, it has, like a god, its fanatics and its martyrs and is far from being an abstraction. The Independents who spoke so charily of their art, so rarely laid down the law, and whose favorite mode of expression was the more or less witty repartee, saw in the function attributed to art by their official adversaries (more than in their works, at which they merely mocked) not only a misconception but something positively revolting. The most fanatical went so far as to frown on even purely personal gestures which looked like truckling to the enemy; thus Renoir's break with Degas was the result of an insulting letter Degas sent him when he was awarded the Cross of the Legion of Honor (which he had never solicited). How could they have regarded an Impressionist who reverted to academic painting as other than a renegade? And how, then, could an indictment of the contemporary world fail to have a certain kinship with the religious sentiment?

From the Romantic period onward art became more and more the object of a cult; the indignation felt at Jan Van Eyck's having been employed to design stucco decorations came from a feeling that this was nothing short of sacrilege. Else why be so much distressed at the thought that the great Italian Masters painted the figures on marriage coffers, but not by the fact that they painted those on the predellas? The artist's personal life had come to be regarded as the mere vehicle of his art. Such men as Velazquez and Leonardo who painted only when commissioned were very different from Cézanne for whom painting was a *vocation*. Though it may not convey a precise idea of human significance at its highest level, modern art often illustrates a precise conception of the artist.

There was no longer any question of an unavowed absolute like Vermeer's: our moderns made no secret of their intention to dominate appearances and build anew the world that had vanished from Europe, a world that had known and venerated supreme values. Less and less hampered by the "lifelike," the artist's vision harked back to the sacrosanct figures of that autonomous world which had passed away.

This would have been better understood had not the religious element in art been confused, from the time of the Romantics (and by them most of all), with the powerful expression of some vague religious emotion. Nothing has misled our art historians more than the "artistic" Masses celebrated by violinists in concert-halls beneath Beethoven's mask and facing plaster casts of Michelangelo. Art is not a dream and those dreamlike figures dear to the Pre-Raphaelites, to Puvis and to Gustave Moreau are being more and more obliterated by the advance of modern art, which does not sponsor any makeshift absolute but, at least in the artist's eyes, has stepped into its—the absolute's—place.

It is not a religion, but a faith. Not a sacrament, but the negation of a tainted world. Its rejection of appearances and its distortions derive from an impulse very different from that behind the art of savages and even Romanesque art, yet akin to these by reason of the intimate relation they create between the painter and the thing created. Hence the curious mingling of acceptance and rejection of the world that we find in the art of the late nineteenth-century masters. Cézanne, Renoir and Van Gogh did not reject it as did Ivan Karamazov, but they rejected more than the social order of their day. Van Gogh's art in his best period had become no more than indirectly Christian; indeed, it was a substitute for his faith. If Cézanne, the good Catholic, had painted Crucifixions, they would have been Cézannesque, and that is doubtless why he painted none. As against representation of the visible world, artists try to create another world (not only another representation) for their personal use. Talk of a modern art "of the masses" is mere wishful thinking: the expression of a desire to combine a taste for art with one for human brotherhood. An art acts on the masses only when it is at the service of *their* absolute and inseparable from it; when it creates Virgins, not just statues. Though, needless to say, the Byzantine artist did not see people in the street like figures in ikons, any more than Braque sees fruit-dishes in fragments, the forms of Braque cannot mean to twentieth-century France what the forms of Daphni meant to Macedonian Byzantium. If Picasso had painted Stalin in Russia, he would have had to do so in a style repudiating that of all his pictures, including *Guernica*. For a modern artist any genuine attempt to appeal to the masses would necessitate his "conversion," a change of absolute. Sacred art and religious art can exist only in a community, a social group swayed by the same belief, and if that group dies out or is dispersed, these arts are forced to undergo a metamorphosis. The only "community" available to the artist consists of those who more or less are of his own kind (their number nowadays is on the increase). At the same time as it is gaining ground, modern art is growing more and more indifferent to the perpetuation of that realm of art which sponsored it from the days of Sumer to the time when the first rifts developed in Christendom: the realm of the gods, living or dead, of scriptures and of legends. The sculptors of the Old Kingdom and the Empire, of the Acropolis, of the Chinese figures hewn in the rock-face, of Angkor and Elephanta, no less than the painters of the Villeneuve *Pietà* and the Nara frescoes and, later, Michelangelo, Titian, Rubens and Rembrandt linked men up with the universe; as did even Goya, flinging them his gifts of darkness. As for the art of today—does it not tend to bring to men only that scission of the consciousness, whence it took its rise? . . .

It is the high place assigned in our culture to the spirit of enquiry that differentiates it from all the cultures of the past with the exception of the Greek, and it is to this spirit that modern science owes the alarming power it now possesses. Our art, too, is becoming an uneasy questioning of the scheme of things.

Never indeed since the Renaissance has this spirit relaxed its supremacy, save in appearance. The ornate shadow of Versailles, lengthening out across the whole of the seventeenth century, tends to hide from us its harassed soul; beneath the rich profusion of the Jesuit churches the rifts in Christendom were ever widening. Leonardo had been interrogation incarnate, yet this enabled him to come to terms with the universe on Far-Eastern lines—a solution of which his drawings of clouds may be regarded as the symbol. Later, when that spirit of questioning probed deeper, until man no longer was an ally of the outside world but its foe—when, with the factory replacing the cathedral, the artist felt himself shut out from this new world man had conquered—the history of our art seemed to be that of a conquest of the world by the individual, acting alone. We are told that our individualist art has touched its limit, and its expression can go no farther. That has often been said; but if it cannot go farther, it still may go elsewhere. The great Christian art did not die because all possible forms had been used up; it died because faith was being transformed into piety. Now, the same conquest of the outside world that brought in our modern individualism, so different from that of the Renaissance, is by way of relativizing the individual. It is plain to see that man's faculty of transformation, which began by a remaking of the natural world, has ended by calling man himself in question. Still too strong to be a slave, and not strong enough to remain the lord of creation, the individual man, while by no means willing to renounce his conquests, is ceasing to find in them his *raison d'être*; the devalued individual of the five-year plans and the Tennessee Valley is losing nothing of his strength, but individualist art is losing its power to annex the world.

Thus it is that a Picasso steps into the place of a Cézanne and the sense of conquest, of man triumphant, is replaced by a spirit of questioning, sometimes serene, but usually anxious and perplexed. And thus it is that the *negative values* which bulk so large in our civilization as well as in our art come to the fore and the fetishes force their way into our culture. For the men who made them, these fetishes were not necessarily disturbing elements, but for us, when we discover them, they are. All our art, even the least denunciatory, Renoir's or Braque's for instance, contains a challenge of a world that it disowns, and we refuse, no less emphatically than Byzantium, to be dominated by the world of visual experience. Whereas Van Gogh saw himself as the pioneer of the art of the future, an art in which the lost plenitude of the art of the past would reappear, Picasso has learnt that were it to re-emerge it would re-emerge *against* him. But for the painter always his art comes first; inseparable from the will to art, his questioning serves him as a means of furthering it, as it furthers that of the great poets. Shakespeare's interrogation of the meaning of life is the source of his noblest poetry; however passionate the denunciation of the scheme of things in Dostoevski's novels, it changes its nature and becomes art in the scene where Muishkin and Rogojin are keeping vigil over Nastasia Philippovna's dead body. Indeed Dostoevski himself wrote: "The great thing is to make my *Brothers Karamazov* a work of art." Despite the insatiable questioning basic to Greek thought, the impression Greek art made on the world for many centuries was one of a triumphant affirmation.

Our Museum without Walls is taking form while the long struggle between official art and forward-looking art is drawing to a close. Everywhere except in Soviet Russia the "banned" art is triumphant; official teaching has become irrelevant and the Prix de Rome an obsolete survival. But this triumph, that of the individual, is coming to look to us as precarious as it is spectacular. Seconded by the Museum without Walls which it called into being, modern art confirms the autonomy of painting. For a tradition—that is to say a culture conscious of its claims on every field of human activity—it has substituted a culture that sets up no such claim: a culture that is not categorical but explorative. In this quest the artist, and perhaps modern man in general, knows only his starting-point, his methods and his bearings, and follows the uncharted path of the great sea-venturers.

But even today, can we conceive of a culture on the lines of the great voyages of discovery? Haunted by a mythical past and imbued with a religious faith that had lost nothing of its hold on the minds of men, the Renaissance had only fleeting glimpses of this possibility.

Victorious as it is, our modern art fears it may not outlast its victory without undergoing a metamorphosis; foreseeing that painting may very well cease following the graph begun by Manet and passing through Cézanne to Picasso, it is persistently scanning the horizon for its successor. How far does contemporary art reflect contemporary culture? It is quite possible that the successor of the art we call "modern" will be still more individualist; and it is not impossible that it will assume, to begin with, the form of a resuscitation before developing into a new art, vaster in scope and deeper, born of this resuscitation.

For our art has brought to us not only those arts which are akin to it. Every art that greatly differs from its predecessor involves a transformation of taste and this is often the point of departure for further changes. We have seen how it led in cultures mindful of the past to the re-emergence of forms seemingly or actually akin to its own; but this resuscitation was due not to any specifically artistic quality in those earlier works but to values of another order, and often of a national order. Thus certain revivals of the past in Persia and the Far East, and even the Italian Renaissance, suggest a harking back to racial traditions and glorious memories in order to efface from art the traces of a foreign conqueror. Sometimes these values were of a subtler nature. Thus sixteenth-century Rome took over all the forms of the past which seemed to contain intimations of the Christian harmony she sponsored. This harmony was by way of replacing the earlier Christian values in a realm which was not that of art alone, since art did not as yet exist in its own right, but was dedicated primarily to the service of that communion which was the Christian ideal.

Modern art, by substituting art's *specific* value for the values to which hitherto art had been subordinated, is bringing about a resuscitation whose various elements seem to be superimposed one on the other. The most obvious of these, if perhaps the most superficial, caters to our contemporary taste. It is not always concerned with forms, yet is sometimes of a wholly plastic order, and in such cases corresponds to an element of our art whose mode of expression, or symbol, is the patch of color irrelevant both to the structure of the picture and to its composition (in the traditional meaning of the term). It does not serve as an accent stressing any detail of the execution nor, as in Japan, some feature of the thing portrayed; rather it seems to exist capriciously, as though it had been put in for its own sake only.

Nevertheless, in the work of those who make use of the patch we can almost always see that it has a certain relevance: in the case of Picasso with a passionate constructivism; in Bonnard's, then in Braque's, with an effect of harmony; in Léger's, with an architectural lay-out. Sometimes, too, the patch sounds a high-pitched note keyed to the calligraphy (from Dufy onwards to the blood-red splashes of André Masson). But in the art of Miro, as formerly in that of Kandinsky and as in the art of Klee, the patch often exists in its own right, apart from any reference to the picture's content, and we are tempted to speak of a one-dimensional art. Often this obsession with the patch seems to incite the painter to blot out the picture itself, as does the calligraphy in some of Picasso's works. Indeed in Picasso's case as in Miro's it pointed the way to ceramics; as though the artists were groping for some pictorial outlet other than the easel picture. But there is no question here of decorative art; it is a far cry from these earthenware objects to what some gay vase painted by Renoir might have been, or to the tapestry cartoons of Poussin, or Goya's in his first period. "You can eat off them," Picasso says, pointing to his plates, knowing quite well that most of them are calculated to prevent one's eating off them. This unpredictable, dazzling, tempestuous art of his, the Baroque of individualism, brings to mind the darkly glowing patches on some Persian crockery, above all when it comes to us in fragments. Like that of the Kumishah vases, the modern patch is combined with a delicate naïve calligraphy, seemingly quite alien to it, yet in fact developing its full value when brought in contact with the patch. Actually, the Persian patches made their impression without reference to the objects to which they belonged, and which no one would have thought of likening to pictures. None the less they have much to tell us about the picture; and not, appearances notwithstanding, about the *objet d'art*.

The frontiers of art have often been modified and there are colors other than those of oil painting. However, we have not here an entirely new departure like the invention of the stained-glass window. What we have is simply the extreme limit (for the time being) of modern painting: something that stands in much the same relation to our art culture as does the "savage" feather cloak, which in fact is sponsored by the patch; for the annexation of the fetish has been the work of the modernist, who integrates it in his art. (An "absolutely free" art does not lead to the picture or to statuary, but to *objects*.) Our modern use of the patch goes much farther than the splashes of color in folk art (which were not always due to carelessness on the part of the stenciler or colorer) and those on the white-ground lecythi; it suggests a form of "pure painting" in which certain works of the past would seem to have participated to a greater or a less extent. For we must not forget that the triumph of modern art was also the triumph of color: Impressionists, Expressionists and Fauves successively promoted it and the analytic Cubism of Léger, Picasso and even Braque (despite a good many quiet, almost monochrome compositions) ended up in a blaze of color. Shadows were eliminated and with them broken colors, and everything opposed to these came back into favor: from Haïda "objects" to Coptic fabrics, from the household gods of the Hopis to Gallic coins. In the plastic arts, as in music, literature, and the theater, stridency had become the order of the day.

Works of this order would figure prominently amongst our present-day rediscoveries, were it *only* color that we were rediscovering, and did we tend to substitute the occasional "lucky fluke" for conscious mastery. But the "thrills" of Haïda art soon began to pall, and the Hopis are far from being Sumerians. We describe the New Hebridean ancestors as effigies ("paintings" would fit them quite as well) but we do not call them statues. Whilst certain arts that ours has resuscitated have been so thoroughly integrated into our culture as to transform it, others merely strike us as new schools and, like all new schools, either hold their ground or pass away. Thus our resuscitations sometimes answer to a desire for strong sensations, for works which engender new dialogues with new interlocutors; sometimes to an atavistic yearning for the mysterious; and sometimes to the modern appreciation of all arts which, like the work of our great European painters, give rise to a dialogue that strikes ever deeper, and indeed seems inexhaustible.

If we could picture a great artist acquainted, in addition to contemporary works, with only the specifically plastic qualities of the works of the past, such a man would seem to us the superior type of the modern barbarian: one whose barbarianism is not, as in an earlier age, definable by his rejection of the status of citizen, but by his rejection of the estate of Man. Were our culture to be restricted solely to our response (lively though it is) to forms and colors, and their vivid expression in contemporary art—surely the name of "culture" could hardly be applied to it! But it is far from being thus restricted. For alongside the resuscitation of works akin to those of our own art another factor is coming into play: one whose consequences it is as yet impossible to foresee. Though some artists and aestheticians still maintain that modern art, the arts of savages and certain ancient forms are incompatible, the general public finds no difficulty in feeling a like enthusiasm for them all; its taste for modern painting leads it to crowd the Louvre, not to desert it.

IMMANUEL KANT

The Imaginative Faculty and the Function of Art

Whatever the origin of our representations may be, whether they be due to the influence of external things or to internal causes, whether they have arisen *a priori* or empirically as phenomena, as modifications of the mind they must always belong to the internal sense, and all our knowledge must therefore finally be subject to the formal condition of that internal sense, namely, time, in which they are all arranged, joined, and brought into certain relations to each other. This is a general remark which must never be forgotten in all that follows.

Every representation contains something manifold, which could not be represented as such, unless the mind distinguished the time in the succession of one impression after another; for as contained in one moment, each representation can never be anything but absolute unity. In order to change this manifold into a unity of intuition (as, for instance, in the representation of space), it is necessary first to run through the manifold and then to hold it together. It is this act which I call the synthesis of apprehension, because it refers directly to intuition which no doubt offers something manifold, but which, without a synthesis, can never make it such, as it is contained in *one* representation.

This synthesis of apprehension must itself be carried out *a priori* also, that is, with reference to representations which are not empirical. For without it we should never be able to have the representations either of space or time *a priori*, because these cannot be produced except by a synthesis of the manifold which the senses offer in their original receptivity. It follows therefore that we have a pure synthesis of apprehension. . . .

It is no doubt nothing but an empirical law according to which representations which have often followed or accompanied one another, become associated in the end and so closely united that, even without the presence of the object, one of these representations will, according to an invariable law, produce a transition of the mind to the other. This law of reproduction, however, presupposes that the phenomena themselves are really subject to such a rule, and that there is in the variety of these representations a sequence and concomitancy subject to certain

From *The Critique of Pure Reason* [1781], translated from the German by F. Max Müller, New York and London, 1907, pp. 82-5.
From *The Critique of Judgment* [1790], translated from the German by J. C. Meredith, Oxford, 1952, pp. 172-9; reprinted by permission of the Oxford University Press.

rules; for without this the faculty of empirical imagination would never find anything to do that it is able to do, and remain therefore buried within our mind as a dead faculty, unknown to ourselves. If cinnabar were sometimes red and sometimes black, sometimes light and sometimes heavy, if a man could be changed now into this, now into another animal shape, if on the longest day the fields were sometimes covered with fruit, sometimes with ice and snow, the faculty of my empirical imagination would never be in a position, when representing red colour, to think of heavy cinnabar. Nor, if a certain name could be given sometimes to this, sometimes to that object, or if the same object could sometimes be called by one, and sometimes by another name, without any rule to which representations are subject by themselves, would it be possible that any empirical synthesis of reproduction should ever take place.

There must therefore be something to make this reproduction of phenomena possible by being itself the foundation *a priori* of a necessary synthetical unity of them. This becomes clear if we only remember that all phenomena are not things by themselves, but only the play of our representations, all of which are in the end determinations only of the internal sense. If therefore we could prove that even our purest intuitions *a priori* give us no knowledge, unless they contain such a combination of the manifold as to render a constant synthesis of reproduction possible, it would follow that this synthesis of the imagination is, before all experience, founded on principles *a priori*, and that we must admit a pure transcendental synthesis of imagination which forms even the foundation of the possibility of all experience, such experience being impossible without the reproductibility of phenomena. Now, when I draw a line in thought, or if I think the time from one noon to another, or if I only represent to myself a certain number, it is clear that I must first necessarily apprehend one of these manifold representations after another. If I were to lose from my thoughts what precedes, whether the first parts of a line or the antecedent portions of time, or the numerical unities representing one after the other, and if, while I proceed to what follows, I were unable to reproduce what came before, there would never be a complete representation, and none of the before-mentioned thoughts, not even the first and purest representations of space and time, could ever arise within us.

The synthesis of apprehension is therefore inseparably connected with the synthesis of reproduction, and as the former constitutes the transcendental ground of the possibility of all knowledge in general (not only of empirical, but also of pure *a priori* knowledge), it follows that a reproductive synthesis of imagination belongs to the transcendental acts of the soul. We may therefore call this faculty the transcendental faculty of imagination.

THE RELATION OF GENIUS TO TASTE

For *estimating* beautiful objects, as such, what is required is *taste*; but for fine art, i.e. the *production* of such objects, one needs *genius*.

If we consider genius as the talent for fine art (which the proper signification of the word imports), and if we would analyse it from this point of view into the faculties which must concur to constitute such a talent, it is imperative at the outset accurately to determine the difference between beauty of nature, which it only requires taste to estimate, and beauty of art, which requires genius for its possibility (a possibility to which regard must also be paid in estimating such an object).

A beauty of nature is a *beautiful thing*; beauty of art is a *beautiful representation* of a thing.

To enable me to estimate a beauty of nature, as such, I do not need to be previously possessed of a concept of what sort of a thing the object is intended to be, i.e. I am not obliged to know its material finality (the end), but, rather, in forming an estimate of it apart from any knowledge of the end, the mere form pleases on its own account. If, however, the object is presented as a product of art, and is as such to be declared beautiful, then, seeing that art always presupposes an end in the cause (and its causality) a concept of what the thing is intended to be must first of all be laid at its basis. And, since the agreement of the manifold in a thing with an inner character belonging to it as its end constitutes the perfection of the thing, it follows that in estimating beauty of art the perfection of the thing must be also taken into account—a matter which in estimating a beauty of nature, as beautiful, is quite irrelevant.—It is true that in forming an estimate, especially of animate objects of nature, e.g. of a man or a horse, objective finality is also commonly taken into account with a view to judgement upon their beauty; but then the judgement also ceases to be purely aesthetic, i.e. a mere judgement of taste. Nature is no longer estimated as it appears like art, but rather in so far as it actually *is* art, though superhuman art; and the teleological judgement serves as basis and condition of the aesthetic, and one which the latter must regard. In such a case, where one says, for example, "that is a beautiful woman," what one in fact thinks is only this, that in her form nature excellently portrays the ends present in the female figure. For one has to extend one's view beyond the mere form to a concept, to enable the object to be thought in such manner by means of an aesthetic judgement logically conditioned.

Where fine art evidences its superiority is in the beautiful descriptions it gives of things that in nature would be ugly or displeasing. The Furies, diseases, devastations of war, and the like, can (as evils) be very beautifully described, nay even represented in pictures. One kind of ugliness alone is incapable of being represented conformably to nature without destroying all aesthetic delight, and consequently artistic beauty, namely, that which excites *disgust*. For, as in this strange sensation, which depends purely on the imagination, the object is represented as insisting, as it were, upon our enjoying it, while we still set our face against it, the artificial representation of the object is no longer distinguishable from the nature of the object itself in our sensation, and so it cannot possibly be regarded as beautiful. The art of sculpture, again, since in its products art is almost confused with nature, has excluded from its creations the direct representation of ugly objects, and, instead, only sanctions, for example, the representation of death (in a beautiful genius), or of the warlike spirit (in Mars), by means of an allegory, or attributes which wear a pleasant guise, and so only indirectly, through an interpretation on the part of reason, and not for the pure aesthetic judgement.

So much for the beautiful representation of an object, which is properly only the form of the presentation of a concept, and the means by which the latter is universally communicated. To give this form, however, to the product of fine art, taste merely is required. By this the artist, having practised and corrected his taste by a variety of examples from nature or art, controls his work and, after many, and often laborious, attempts to satisfy taste, finds the form which commends itself to him. Hence this form is not, as it were, a matter of inspiration, or of a free swing of the mental powers, but rather of a slow and even painful process of improvement, directed to making the form adequate to his thought without prejudice to the freedom in the play of those powers.

Taste is, however, merely a critical, not a productive faculty; and what conforms to it is not, merely on that account, a work of fine art. It may belong to useful and mechanical art, or even to science, as a product following definite rules which are capable of being learned and which must be closely followed. But the pleasing form imparted to the work is only the vehicle of communication and a mode, as it were, of execution, in respect of which one remains to a certain extent free, notwithstanding being otherwise tied down to a definite end. So we demand that table appointments, or even a moral dissertation, and, indeed, a sermon, must bear this form of fine art, yet without its appearing *studied*. But one would not call them on this account works of fine art. A poem, a musical composition, a picture-gallery, and so forth, would, however, be placed under this head; and so in a would-be work of fine art we may frequently recognize genius without taste, and in another taste without genius.

THE FACULTIES OF THE MIND WHICH CONSTITUTE GENIUS

Of certain products which are expected, partly at least, to stand on the footing of fine art, we say they are *soulless*; and this, although we find nothing to censure in them as far as taste goes. A poem may be very pretty and elegant, but is soulless. A narrative has precision and method, but is soulless. A speech on some festive occasion may be good in substance and ornate withal, but may be soulless. Conversation frequently is not devoid of entertainment, but yet soulless. Even of a woman we may well say, she is pretty, affable, and refined, but soulless. Now what do we here mean by "soul"?

"Soul" (*Geist*) in an aesthetical sense, signifies the animating principle in the mind. But that whereby this principle animates the psychic substance (*Seele*)— the material which it employs for that purpose—is that which sets the mental powers into a swing that is final, i.e. into a play which is self-maintaining and which strengthens those powers for such activity.

Now my proposition is that this principle is nothing else than the faculty of presenting *aesthetic ideas*. But, by an aesthetic idea I mean that representation of the imagination which induces much thought, yet without the possibility of any definite thought whatever, i.e. *concept*, being adequate to it, and which language, consequently, can never get quite on level terms with or render completely intelligible.—It is easily seen, that an aesthetic idea is the counterpart (pendant) of a *rational idea*, which, conversely, is a concept, to which no *intuition* (representation of the imagination) can be adequate.

The imagination (as a productive faculty of cognition) is a powerful agent for creating, as it were, a second nature out of the material supplied to it by actual nature. It affords us entertainment where experience proves too commonplace; and we even use it to remodel experience, always following, no doubt, laws that are based on analogy, but still also following principles which have a higher seat in reason (and which are every whit as natural to us as those followed by the understanding in laying hold of empirical nature). By this means we get a sense of our freedom from the law of association (which attaches to the empirical employment of the imagination), with the result that the material can be borrowed by us from nature in accordance with that law, but be worked up by us into something else—namely, what surpasses nature.

Such representations of the imagination may be termed *ideas*. This is partly because they at least strain after something lying out beyond the confines of experience, and so seek to approximate to a presentation of rational concepts (i.e. intellectual ideas), thus giving to these concepts the semblance of an objective reality. But, on the other hand, there is this most important reason, that no concept can be wholly adequate to them as internal intuitions. The poet essays the task of interpreting to sense the rational ideas of invisible beings, the kingdom of the blessed, hell, eternity, creation, &c. Or, again, as to things of which examples occur in experience, e.g. death, envy, and all vices, as also love, fame, and the like, transgressing the limits of experience he attempts with the aid of an imagination which emulates the display of reason in its attainment of a maximum, to body them forth to sense with a completeness of which nature affords no parallel; and it is in fact precisely in the poetic art that the faculty of aesthetic ideas can show itself to full advantage. This faculty, however, regarded solely on its own account, is properly no more than a talent (of the imagination).

If, now, we attach to a concept a representation of the imagination belonging to its presentation, but inducing solely on its own account such a wealth of thought as would never admit of comprehension in a definite concept, and, as a consequence, giving aesthetically an unbounded expansion to the concept itself, then the imagination here displays a creative activity, and it puts the faculty of intellectual ideas (reason) into motion—a motion, at the instance of a representation, towards an extension of thought, that, while germane, no doubt, to the concept of the object, exceeds what can be laid hold of in that representation or clearly expressed.

Those forms which do not constitute the presentation of a given concept itself, but which, as secondary representations of the imagination, express the derivatives connected with it, and its kinship with other concepts, are called (aesthetic) *attributes* of an object, the concept of which, as an idea of reason, cannot be adequately presented. In this way Jupiter's eagle, with the lightning in its claws, is an attribute of the mighty king of heaven, and the peacock of its stately queen. They do not, like *logical attributes*, represent what lies in our concepts of the sublimity and majesty of creation, but rather something else—something that gives the imagination an incentive to spread its flight over a whole host of kindred representations that provoke more thought than admits of expression in a concept determined by words. They furnish an *aesthetic idea*, which serves the above rational idea as a substitute for logical presentation, but with the proper function, however, of animating the mind by opening out for it a prospect into a field of kindred representations stretching beyond its ken. But it is not alone in the arts of painting or sculpture, where the name of attribute is customarily employed, that fine art acts in this way; poetry and rhetoric also derive the soul that animates their works wholly from the aesthetic attributes of the objects—attributes which go hand in hand with the logical, and give the imagination an impetus to bring more thought into play in the matter, though in an undeveloped manner, than allows of being brought within the embrace of a concept, or, therefore, of being definitely formulated in language.—For the sake of brevity I must confine myself to a few examples only. When the great king expresses himself in one of his poems by saying:

> Oui, finissons sans trouble, et mourons sans regrets,
> En laissant l'Univers comblé de nos bienfaits.
> Ainsi l'Astre du jour, au bout de sa carrière,
> Répand sur l'horizon une douce lumière,
> Et les derniers rayons qu'il darde dans les airs
> Sont les derniers soupirs qu'il donne à l'Univers;

he kindles in this way his rational idea of a cosmopolitan sentiment even at the close of life, with the help of an attribute which the imagination (in remembering all the pleasures of a fair summer's day that is over and gone—a memory of which pleasures is suggested by a serene evening) annexes to that representation, and which stirs up a crowd of sensations and secondary representations for which no expression can be found. On the other hand, even an intellectual concept may serve, conversely, as attribute for a representation of sense, and so animate the latter with the idea of the supersensible; but only by the aesthetic factor subjectively attaching to the consciousness of the supersensible being employed for the purpose. So, for example, a certain poet says in his description of a beautiful morning: "The sun arose, as out of virtue rises peace." The consciousness of virtue, even where we put ourselves only in thought in the position of a virtuous man, diffuses in the mind a multitude of sublime and tranquillizing feelings, and gives a boundless outlook into a happy future, such as no expression within the compass of a definite concept completely attains.

In a word, the aesthetic idea is a representation of the imagination, annexed to a given concept, with which, in the free employment of imagination, such a multiplicity of partial representations are bound up, that no expression indicating a definite concept can be found for it—one which on that account allows a concept to be supplemented in thought by much that is indefinable in words, and the feeling of which quickens the cognitive faculties, and with language, as a mere thing of the letter, binds up the spirit (soul) also.

SAMUEL TAYLOR COLERIDGE
The Coalescence of Mind and Nature

The postulate of philosophy and at the same time the test of philosophic capacity, is no other than the heaven-descended KNOW THYSELF! (E cœlo descendit, Γνῶθι

From *Biographia Literaria* [1817], ed. J. Shawcross, Oxford, 1907, Vol. I, pp. 162-7, 189-90.
From "On Poesy or Art" [1818], *Miscellanies*, ed. T. Ashe, London, 1885, pp. 42-9.
From "The Statesman's Manual" [1817], *Complete Works*, ed. W. G. T. Shedd, New York, 1884, Vol. I, pp. 465, 437-8.

σεαυτόν). And this at once practically and speculatively. For as philosophy is neither a science of the reason or understanding only, nor merely a science of morals, but the science of BEING altogether, its primary ground can be neither merely speculative nor merely practical, but both in one. All knowledge rests on the coincidence of an object with a subject. (My readers have been warned in a former chapter that, for their convenience as well as the writer's, the term, subject, is used by me in its scholastic sense as equivalent to mind or sentient being, and as the necessary correlative of object or *quicquid objicitur menti*.) For we can *know* that only which is true: and the truth is universally placed in the coincidence of the thought with the thing, of the representation with the object represented.

Now the sum of all that is merely OBJECTIVE, we will henceforth call NATURE, confining the term to its passive and material sense, as comprising all the *phaenomena* by which its existence is made known to us. On the other hand the sum of all that is SUBJECTIVE, we may comprehend in the name of the SELF or INTELLIGENCE. Both conceptions are in necessary antithesis. Intelligence is conceived of as exclusively representative, nature as exclusively represented; the one as conscious, the other as without consciousness. Now in all acts of positive knowledge there is required a reciprocal concurrence of both, namely of the conscious being, and of that which is in itself unconscious. Our problem is to explain this concurrence, its possibility and its necessity.

During the act of knowledge itself, the objective and subjective are so instantly united, that we cannot determine to which of the two the priority belongs. There is here no first, and no second; both are coinstantaneous and one. While I am attempting to explain this intimate coalition, I must suppose it dissolved. I must necessarily set out from the one, to which therefore I give hypothetical antecedence, in order to arrive at the other. But as there are but two factors or elements in the problem, subject and object, and as it is left indeterminate from which of them I should commence, there are two cases equally possible.

I. EITHER THE OBJECTIVE IS TAKEN AS THE FIRST, AND THEN WE HAVE TO ACCOUNT FOR THE SUPERVENTION OF THE SUBJECTIVE, WHICH COALESCES WITH IT.

The notion of the subjective is not contained in the notion of the objective. On the contrary they mutually exclude each other. The subjective therefore must supervene to the objective. The conception of nature does not apparently involve the co-presence of an intelligence making an ideal duplicate of it, that is, representing it. This desk for instance would (according to our natural notions) be, though there should exist no sentient being to look at it. This then is the problem of natural philosophy. It assumes the objective or unconscious nature as the first, and has therefore to explain how intelligence can supervene to it, or how itself can grow into intelligence. If it should appear, that all enlightened naturalists, without having distinctly proposed the problem to themselves, have yet constantly moved in the line of its solution, it must afford a strong presumption that the problem itself is founded in nature. For if all knowledge has, as it were, two poles reciprocally required and presupposed, all sciences must proceed from the one or the other, and must tend toward the opposite as far as the equatorial point in which both are reconciled and become identical. The necessary tendence therefore of all natural philosophy is from nature to intelligence; and this, and no other is the true ground and occasion of the instinctive striving to introduce theory into our views of natural *phænomena*. The highest perfection of natural philosophy would consist in the perfect spiritualization of all the laws of nature into laws of intuition and intellect. The *phænomena* (*the material*) must wholly disappear, and the laws alone (*the formal*) must remain. Thence it comes, that in nature itself the more the principle of law breaks forth, the more does the *husk* drop off, the *phænomena* themselves become more spiritual and at length cease altogether in our consciousness. The optical *phænomena* are but a geometry, the lines of which are drawn by light, and the materiality of this light itself has already become matter of doubt. In the appearances of magnetism all trace of matter is lost, and of the *phænomena* of gravitation, which not a few among the most illustrious Newtonians have declared no otherwise comprehensible than as an immediate spiritual influence, there remains nothing but its law, the execution of which on a vast scale is the mechanism of the heavenly motions. The theory of natural philosophy would then be completed, when all nature was demonstrated to be identical in essence with that, which in its highest known power exists in man as intelligence and self-consciousness; when the heavens and the earth shall declare not only the power of their maker, but the glory and the presence of their God, even as he appeared to the great prophet during the vision of the mount in the skirts of his divinity.

This may suffice to show, that even natural science, which commences with the material *phænomenon* as the reality and substance of things existing, does yet by the necessity of theorizing unconsciously, and as it were instinctively, end in nature as an intelligence; and by this tendency the science of nature becomes finally natural philosophy, the one of the two poles of fundamental science.

2. OR THE SUBJECTIVE IS TAKEN AS THE FIRST, AND THE PROBLEM THEN IS, HOW THERE SUPERVENES TO IT A COINCIDENT OBJECTIVE.

In the pursuit of these sciences, our success in each, depends on an austere and faithful adherence to its own principles, with a careful separation and exclusion of those, which appertain to the opposite science. As the natural philosopher, who directs his views to the objective, avoids above all things the intermixture of the subjective in his knowledge, as for instance, arbitrary suppositions or rather sufficients, occult qualities, spiritual agents, and the substitution of final for efficient causes; so on the other hand, the transcendental or intelligential philosopher is equally anxious to preclude all interpellation of the objective into the subjective principles of his science, as for instance the assumption of impresses or configurations in the brain, correspondent to miniature pictures of the *retina* painted by rays of light from supposed originals, which are not the immediate and real objects of vision, but deductions from it for the purposes of explanation. This purification of the mind is effected by an absolute and scientific scepticism, to which the mind voluntarily determines itself for the specific purpose of future certainty. Des Cartes who (in his meditations) himself first, at least of the moderns, gave a beautiful example of this voluntary doubt, this self-determined indetermination, happily expresses its utter difference from the scepticism of vanity or irreligion: *Nec tamen in eo Scepticos imitabar, qui dubitant tantum ut dubitent, et præter incertitudinem ipsam nihil quærunt. Nam contra totus in eo eram ut aliquid certi reperirem.*[1] Nor is it less distinct in its motives and final aim, than in its proper objects, which are not as in ordinary scepticism the prejudices of education and circumstance, but those original and innate prejudices which nature herself has planted in all men, and which to all but the philosopher are the first principles of knowledge, and the final test of truth.

Now these essential prejudices are all reducible to the one fundamental presumption, THAT THERE EXIST THINGS WITHOUT US. As this on the one hand originates, neither in grounds nor arguments, and yet on the other hand remains proof against all attempts to remove it by grounds or arguments (*naturam furca expellas tamen usque redibit*); on the one hand lays claim to IMMEDIATE certainty as a position at once indemonstrable and irresistible, and yet on the other hand, inasmuch as it refers to something essentially different from ourselves, nay even in opposition to ourselves, leaves it inconceivable how it could possibly become a part of our immediate consciousness; (in other words how that, which *ex hypothesi* is and continues to be extrinsic and alien to our being, should become a modification of our being) the philosopher therefore compels himself to treat this faith as nothing more than a prejudice, innate indeed and connatural, but still a prejudice.

The other position, which not only claims but necessitates the admission of its immediate certainty, equally for the scientific reason of the philosopher as for the common sense of mankind at large, namely, I AM, cannot so properly be entitled a prejudice. It is groundless indeed; but then in the very idea it precludes all ground, and separated from the immediate consciousness loses its whole sense and import. It is groundless; but only because it is itself the ground of all other certainty. Now the apparent contradiction, that the former position, namely, the existence of things without us, which from its nature cannot be immediately certain, should be received as blindly and as independently of all grounds as the existence of our own being, the Transcendental philosopher can solve only by the supposition, that the former is unconsciously involved in the latter; that it is not only coherent but identical, and one and the same thing with our own immediate self consciousness. To demonstrate this identity is the office and object of his philosophy.

The Imagination then I consider either as primary, or secondary. The primary Imagination I hold to be the living power and prime agent of all human perception, and as a repetition in the finite mind of the eternal act of creation in the infinite I AM. The secondary Imagination I consider as an echo of the former, coexisting with the conscious will, yet still as identical with the primary in the *kind* of its agency, and differing only in *degree*, and in the *mode* of its operation. It dissolves, diffuses, dissipates, in order to recreate: or where this process is rendered impossible, yet at all events it struggles to idealize and to unify. It is essentially *vital*, even as all objects (*as* objects) are essentially fixed and dead.

FANCY, on the contrary, has no other counters to play with, but fixities and

[1] Des Cartes, *Diss. de Methodo.* AUTHOR'S NOTE.

definites. The fancy is indeed no other than a mode of memory emancipated from the order of time and space; while it is blended with, and modified by that empirical phenomenon of the will, which we express by the word Choice. But equally with the ordinary memory the Fancy must receive all its materials ready made from the law of association.

Man communicates by articulation of sounds, and paramountly by the memory in the ear; nature by the impression of bounds and surfaces on the eye, and through the eye it gives significance and appropriation, and thus the conditions of memory, or the capability of being remembered, to sounds, smells, &c. Now Art, used collectively for painting, sculpture, architecture and music, is the mediatress between, and reconciler of, nature and man. It is, therefore, the power of humanizing nature, of infusing the thoughts and passions of man into every thing which is the object of his contemplation; colour, form, motion, and sound, are the elements which it combines, and it stamps them into unity in the mould of a moral idea.

The primary art is writing;—primary, if we regard the purpose abstracted from the different modes of realizing it, those steps of progression of which the instances are still visible in the lower degrees of civilization. First, there is mere gesticulation; then rosaries or *wampun*; then picture-language; then hieroglyphics, and finally alphabetic letters. These all consist of a translation of man into nature, of a substitution of the visible for the audible.

The so called music of savage tribes as little deserves the name of art for the understanding as the ear warrants it for music. Its lowest state is a mere expression of passion by sounds which the passion itself necessitates;—the highest amounts to no more than a voluntary reproduction of these sounds in the absence of the occasioning causes, so as to give the pleasure of contrast,—for example, by the various outcries of battle in the song of security and triumph. Poetry also is purely human; for all its materials are from the mind, and all its products are for the mind. But it is the apotheosis of the former state, in which by excitement of the associative power passion itself imitates order, and the order resulting produces a pleasurable passion, and thus it elevates the mind by making its feelings the object of its reflexion. So likewise, whilst it recalls the sights and sounds that had accompanied the occasions of the original passions, poetry impregnates them with an interest not their own by means of the passions, and yet tempers the passion by the calming power which all distinct images exert on the human soul. In this way poetry is the preparation for art, inasmuch as it avails itself of the forms of nature to recall, to express, and to modify the thoughts and feelings of the mind. Still, however, poetry can only act through the intervention of articulate speech, which is so peculiarly human, that in all languages it constitutes the ordinary phrase by which man and nature are contradistinguished. It is the original force of the word "brute," and even "mute," and "dumb," [they] do not convey the absence of sound, but the absence of articulated sounds.

As soon as the human mind is intelligibly addressed by an outward image exclusively of articulate speech, so soon does art commence. But please to observe that I have laid particular stress on the words "human mind,"—meaning to exclude thereby all results common to man and all other sentient creatures, and consequently confining myself to the effect produced by the congruity of the animal impression with the reflective powers of the mind; so that not the thing presented, but that which is re-presented by the thing, shall be the source of the pleasure. In this sense nature itself is to a religious observer the art of God; and for the same cause art itself might be defined as of a middle quality between a thought and a thing, or as I said before, the union and reconciliation of that which is nature with that which is exclusively human. It is the figured language of thought, and is distinguished from nature by the unity of all the parts in one thought or idea. Hence nature itself would give us the impression of a work of art, if we could see the thought which is present at once in the whole and in every part; and a work of art will be just in proportion as it adequately conveys the thought, and rich in proportion to the variety of parts which it holds in unity.

If, therefore, the term "mute" be taken as opposed not to sound but to articulate speech, the old definition of painting will in fact be the true and best definition of the Fine Arts in general, that is, *muta poesis*, mute poesy, and so of course poesy. And, as all languages perfect themselves by a gradual process of desynonymizing words originally equivalent, I have cherished the wish to use the word "poesy" as the generic or common term, and to distinguish that species of poesy which is not *muta poesis* by its usual name "poetry"; while of all the other species which collectively form the Fine Arts, there would remain this as the common definition,—that they all, like poetry, are to express intellectual purposes, thoughts, conceptions, and sentiments which have their origin in the human mind,—not, however, as poetry does, by means of articulate speech, but as nature or the divine art does, by form, color, magnitude, proportion, or by sound, that is, silently or musically.

Well! it may be said—but who has ever thought otherwise? We all know that art is the imitatress of nature. And, doubtless, the truths which I hope to convey would be barren truisms, if all men meant the same by the words "imitate" and "nature." But it would be flattering mankind at large, to presume that such is the fact. First, to imitate. The impression on the wax is not an imitation, but a copy, of the seal; the seal itself is an imitation. But, further, in order to form a philosophic conception, we must seek for the kind, as the heat in ice, invisible light, &c., whilst, for practical purposes, we must have reference to the degree. It is sufficient that philosophically we understand that in all imitation two elements must coexist, and not only coexist, but must be perceived as coexisting. These two constituent elements are likeness and unlikeness, or sameness and difference, and in all genuine creations of art there must be a union of these disparates. The artist may take his point of view where he pleases, provided that the desired effect be perceptibly produced,—that there be likeness in the difference, difference in the likeness, and a reconcilement of both in one. If there be likeness to nature without any check of difference, the result is disgusting, and the more complete the delusion, the more loathsome the effect. Why are such simulations of nature, as waxwork figures of men and women, so disagreeable? Because, not finding the motion and the life which we expected, we are shocked as by a falsehood, every circumstance of detail, which before induced us to be interested, making the distance from truth more palpable. You set out with a supposed reality and are disappointed and disgusted with the deception; whilst, in respect to a work of genuine imitation, you begin with an acknowledged total difference, and then every touch of nature gives you the pleasure of an approximation to truth. The fundamental principle of all this is undoubtedly the horror of falsehood and the love of truth inherent in the human breast. The Greek tragic dance rested on these principles, and I can deeply sympathize in imagination with the Greeks in this favourite part of their theatrical exhibitions, when I call to mind the pleasure I felt in beholding the combat of the Horatii and Curiatii most exquisitely danced in Italy to the music of Cimarosa.

Secondly, as to nature. We must imitate nature! yes, but what in nature,—all and everything? No, the beautiful in nature. And what then is the beautiful? What is beauty? It is, in the abstract, the unity of the manifold, the coalescence of the diverse; in the concrete, it is the union of the shapely (*formosum*) with the vital. In the dead organic it depends on regularity of form, the first and lowest species of which is the triangle with all its modifications as in crystals, architecture, &c.; in the living organic it is not mere regularity of form, which would produce a sense of formality; neither is it subservient to any thing beside itself. It may be present in a disagreeable object, in which the proportion of the parts constitutes a whole; it does not arise from association, as the agreeable does, but sometimes lies in the rupture of association; it is not different to different individuals and nations, as has been said, nor is it connected with the ideas of the good, or the fit, or the useful. The sense of beauty is intuitive, and beauty itself is all that inspires pleasure without, and aloof from, and even contrarily to, interest.

If the artist copies the mere nature, the *natura naturata*, what idle rivalry! If he proceeds only from a given form, which is supposed to answer to the notion of beauty, what an emptiness, what an unreality there always is in his productions, as in Cipriani's pictures! Believe me, you must master the essence, the *natura naturans*, which presupposes a bond between nature in the higher sense and the soul of man.

The wisdom in nature is distinguished from that in man by the co-instantaneity of the plan and the execution; the thought and the product are one, or are given at once; but there is no reflex act, and hence there is no moral responsibility. In man there is reflexion, freedom, and choice; he is, therefore, the head of the visible creation. In the objects of nature are presented, as in a mirror, all the possible elements, steps, and processes of intellect antecedent to consciousness, and therefore to the full development of the intelligential act; and man's mind is the very focus of all the rays of intellect which are scattered throughout the images of nature. Now so to place these images, totalized, and fitted to the limits of the human mind, as to elicit from, and to superinduce upon, the forms themselves the moral reflexions to which they approximate, to make the external internal, the internal external, to make nature thought, and thought nature,—this is the mystery of genius in the Fine Arts. Dare I add that the genius must act on the feeling, that body is but a striving to become mind,—that it is mind in its essence!

In every work of art there is a reconcilement of the external with the internal; the conscious is so impressed on the unconscious as to appear in it; as compare mere letters inscribed on a tomb with figures themselves constituting the tomb. He who combines the two is the man of genius; and for that reason he must partake of both. Hence there is in genius itself an unconscious activity; nay, that is the genius in the man of genius. And this is the true exposition of the rule that the artist must first eloign himself from nature in order to return to her with full effect. Why this? Because if he were to begin by mere painful copying, he would produce masks only, not forms breathing life. He must out of his own mind create forms according to the severe laws of the intellect, in order to generate in himself that co-ordination of freedom and law, that involution of obedience in the prescript, and of the prescript in the impulse to obey, which assimilates him to nature, and enables him to understand her. He merely absents himself for a season from her, that his own spirit, which has the same ground with nature, may learn her unspoken language in its main radicals, before he approaches to her endless compositions of them. Yes, not to acquire cold notions—lifeless technical rules—but living and life-producing ideas, which shall contain their own evidence, the certainty that they are essentially one with the germinal causes in nature,— his consciousness being the focus and mirror of both,—for this does the artist for a time abandon the external real in order to return to it with a complete sympathy with its internal and actual. For of all we see, hear, feel and touch the substance is and must be in ourselves; and therefore there is no alternative in reason between the dreary (and thank heaven! almost impossible) belief that every thing around us is but a phantom, or that the life which is in us is in them likewise; and that to know is to resemble, when we speak of objects out of ourselves, even as within ourselves to learn is, according to Plato, only to recollect; —the only effective answer to which, that I have been fortunate to meet with, is that which Pope has consecrated for future use in the line—

And coxcombs vanquish Berkeley with a grin!

The artist must imitate that which is within the thing, that which is active through form and figure, and discourses to us by symbols—the *Natur-geist*, or spirit of nature, as we unconsciously imitate those whom we love; for so only can he hope to produce any work truly natural in the object and truly human in the effect. The idea which puts the form together cannot itself be the form. It is above form, and is its essence, the universal in the individual, or the individuality itself,—the glance and the exponent of the indwelling power.

Each thing that lives has its moment of self-exposition, and so has each period of each thing, if we remove the disturbing forces of accident. To do this is the business of ideal art, whether in images of childhood, youth, or age, in man or in woman. Hence a good portrait is the abstract of the personal; it is not the likeness for actual comparison, but for recollection. This explains why the likeness of a very good portrait is not always recognized; because some persons never abstract, and amongst these are especially to be numbered the near relations and friends of the subject, in consequence of the constant pressure and check exercised on their minds by the actual presence of the original. And each thing that only appears to live has also its possible position of relation to life, as nature herself testifies, who, where she cannot be, prophesies her being in the crystallized metal, or the inhaling plant.

————————

The fact . . . that the mind of man in its own primary and constitutional forms represents the laws of nature, is a mystery which of itself should suffice to make us religious: for it is a problem of which God is the only solution, God, the one before all, and of all, and through all!—True natural philosophy is comprized in the study of the science and language of *symbols*. The power delegated to nature is all in every part: and by a symbol I mean, not a metaphor or allegory or any other figure of speech or form of fancy, but an actual and essential part of that, the whole of which it represents. Thus our Lord speaks symbolically when he says that "the eye is the light of the body." The genuine naturalist is a dramatic poet in his own line, and such as our myriad-minded Shakespeare is, compared with the Racines and Metastasios, such and by a similar process of self-transformation would the man be, compared with the Doctors of the mechanic school, who should construct his physiology on the heaven-descended Know Thyself. . . .

Eheu! paupertina philosophia in paupertinam religionem ducit:—A hunger-bitten and idea-less philosophy naturally produces a starveling and comfortless religion. It is among the miseries of the present age that it recognizes no *medium* between literal and metaphorical. Faith is either to be buried in the dead letter, or its name and honors usurped by a counterfeit product of the mechanical understanding, which in the blindness of self-complacency confounds symbols with allegories. Now an allegory is but a translation of abstract notions into a picture-language, which is itself nothing but an abstraction from objects of the senses; the principal being more worthless even than its phantom proxy, both alike unsubstantial, and the former shapeless to boot. On the other hand a symbol . . . is characterized by a translucence of the special in the individual, or of the general in the special or of the universal in the general; above all by the translucence of the eternal through and in the temporal. It always partakes of the reality which it renders intelligible; and while it enunciates the whole, abides itself as a living part in that unity of which it is the representative. The others are but empty echoes which the fancy arbitrarily associates with apparitions of matter, less beautiful but not less shadowy than the sloping orchard of hillside pasture-field seen in the transparent lake below. Alas, for the flocks that are to be led forth to such pastures!

RAINER MARIA RILKE

The Penetration of Things

Malte's experience obliges me at times to reply to these cries from the unknown; he would have done so if ever such voices had reached him,—and he has left me a sort of legacy of action which I am not free to divert from a charitable purpose. It is he too that obliges me to continue in the infinite devotion which requires me to love all the things I want to give shape to, with all my faculties of loving; that was his own irresistible force, of which he has left me the life-interest. Imagine Malte, in that Paris that was so terrible to him, having a lover, or even

Letter [1920], *Letters to Merline*, translated by Violet M. MacDonald, London, 1952, pp. 273-5; reprinted by permission of Methuen & Co. Ltd. and Éditions du Seuil.

a friend! Would he ever have penetrated so far into the confidence of things? For (as he repeatedly told me in our few intimate conversations) the things whose essential life you wish to express, begin by asking you: "Are you free? Are you prepared to devote *all* your love to me, to lie with me as St. Julian the Hospitaller lay beside the leper, giving him the supreme embrace that no simple, passing charity could accomplish, because its motive is love, the whole of love, all the love that exists on earth?" And if the thing sees (said Malte), if the thing sees that you are preoccupied, with even a mere particle of your interest, it shuts itself up again; it may perhaps give you a countersign, it may make a little, faintly friendly sign (and even that is a good deal for a human being imprisoned among others obstinately pursuing a meaningless eloquence) but it refuses to give you its heart, to disclose to you its patient being, its sweet sidereal constancy that makes it so like the constellations! If a thing is to speak to you, you must regard it for a certain time *as the only one that exists*, as the one and only phenomenon, which, thanks to your laborious and exclusive love, is now placed at the center of the Universe, and there, in that incomparable place, is this day attended by the Angels.

What you have just read, my loving Friend, is a chapter from the lessons I received from Malte (my only friend for so many years of suffering and temptation)—and I see that you say the same thing, absolutely, when you speak of your drawings and paintings as seeming valid to you only because of the amorous entanglement, of which the brush or pencil executes the embrace, the caressing and voluptuous act of possession. The *dormeuse*, and certain parts of the *jeune fille au balcon rouge du printemps*, as well as the vision of the other girl in the tragic embrasure of the eternal window—gave me palpitations, not merely sensuous but *infinite* ones; you know, the sort of palpitations that could come from running fast, and from the advent of the lover, and from the terror of happiness that the influences of spring sometimes assail us with: it was like an emotion *caused by all that at the same time*—and I leave you to imagine how powerful it was. This was what I meant, actually, when I wrote that, in every one of the pastels, what astonishes me most is the unity of consciousness with which the object is always apprehended; a single violent gasp of feeling, a single gesture of passion has dragged it in, close to the heart, as a single whole; there is never any sense of one thing having been grasped after another. It is Merline again—oh, in love with earth and heaven—that I sing! Again the power of your arms, and their ineffable glory in rendering such obedience to your sovereign heart, your heart old and new, your spring and summer heart, your heart which, if it had not blossomed out in this dazzling fashion, would long ago have been a star, not as terribly great as Venus, but of the same fire, the same celestial conflagration!

Concrete Art

I BECAME MORE AND MORE REMOVED FROM AESTHETICS

I became more and more removed from aesthetics. I wanted to find another order, another value for man in nature. He was no longer to be the measure of all things, no longer to reduce everything to his own measure, but on the contrary, all things and man were to be like nature, without measure. I wanted to create new appearances, extract new forms from man. This tendency took shape in 1917 in my "objects." Alexandre Partens wrote of them in the *Almanach Dada*: "It was the distinction of Jean Arp to have at a certain moment discovered the true problem of the craft itself. This allowed him to feed it with a new, spiritual imagination. He was no longer interested in improving, formulating, specifying an aesthetic system. He wanted immediate and direct production, like a stone breaking away from a cliff, a bud bursting, an animal reproducing. He wanted objects impregnated with imagination and not museum pieces, he wanted animalesque objects with wild intensities and colors, he wanted a new body among us which would suffice unto itself, an object which would be just as well off squatting on the corners of tables as nestling in the depths of the garden or staring at us from the wall. . . . To him the frame and later the pedestal seemed to be useless crutches. . . ."

Even in my childhood, the pedestal enabling a statue to stand, the frame enclosing the picture like a window, were for me occasions for merriment and mischief, moving me to all sorts of tricks. One day I attempted to paint on a windowpane a blue sky under the houses that I saw through the window. Thus the houses seemed to hang in mid-air. Sometimes I took our pictures out of their frames and looked with pleasure at these windows hanging on the wall. Another time I hung up a frame in a little wooden shack, and sawed a hole in the wall behind the frame, disclosing a charming landscape animated by men and cattle. I asked my father for his opinion of the work I had just completed. He gave me a strange, somewhat surprised look. As a child I also took pleasure in standing on the pedestal of a statue that had collapsed and mimicking the attitude of a modest nymph.

Here are a few of the names of my Dadaist objects: Adam's Head, Articulating Comma, Parrot Imitating the Thunder, Mountain with Shirtfront of Ice, Spelling Furniture, Eggboard, Navel Bottle. The fragility of life and human works was converted with the Dadaists into black humor. No sooner is a building, a monument completed than it begins to decay, fall apart, decompose, crumble. The pyramids, temples, cathedrals, the paintings of the masters, are convincing proof of this. And the buzzing of man does not last much longer than the buzzing of the fly spiraling so enthusiastically around my *baba au rhum*.

Dada aimed to destroy the reasonable deceptions of man and recover the natural and unreasonable order. Dada wanted to replace the logical nonsense of the men of today by the illogically senseless. That is why we pounded with all

From *On My Way, Poetry and Essays* 1912-47, New York, 1948, pp. 47-51, 70-72; reprinted by permission of George Wittenborn, Inc., Publishers, 1018 Madison Avenue, New York 21, N.Y.

our might on the big drum of Dada and trumpeted the praises of unreason. Dada gave the Venus de Milo an enema and permitted Laocoon and his sons to relieve themselves after thousands of years of struggle with the good sausage Python. Philosophies have less value for Dada than an old abandoned toothbrush, and Dada abandons them to the great world leaders. Dada denounces the infernal ruses of the official vocabulary of wisdom. Dada is for the senseless, which does not mean nonsense. Dada is senseless like nature. Dada is for nature and against art. Dada is direct like nature. Dada is for infinite sense and definite means.

THE NAVEL BOTTLE

The bourgeois regarded the Dadaist as a dissolute monster, a revolutionary villain, a barbarous Asiatic, plotting against his bells, his safe-deposits, his honors. The Dadaist thought up tricks to rob the bourgeois of his sleep. He sent false reports to the newspapers of hair-raising Dada duels, in which his favorite author, the "King of Bernina," was said to be involved. The Dadaist gave the bourgeois a sense of confusion and distant, yet mighty rumbling, so that his bells began to buzz, his safes frowned, and his honors broke out in spots. "The Eggboard," a game for the upper ten thousand, in which the participants leave the arena covered with egg yolk from top to toe; "The Navel Bottle," a monstrous home furnishing in which bicycle, whale, brassière and absinthe spoon are combined; "The Glove," which can be worn in place of the old-fashioned head—were devised to show the bourgeois the unreality of his world, the nullity of his endeavors, even of his extremely profitable patrioteerings. This of course was a naive undertaking on our part, since actually the bourgeois has less imagination than a worm, and in place of a heart has an over-life-size corn which twitches in times of approaching storm—on the stock exchange.

TALK

When Dada revealed its eternal wisdom to man, man laughed indulgently and went on talking. Man talks enough to make the very rats sick to their stomach. While his voracity forces him to stuff into his mouth everything that fails to evade his claws, he still manages to talk. He talks so much that the day darkens and the night pales with fright. He talks so much that the sea runs dry and the desert turns to swamp. The main thing for him is to talk, for talk is healthy ventilation. After a fine speech he feels very hungry and changes his mind. At the same time he assumes the noble attitude of rotten meat. Man declares red what he called green the day before and what in reality is black. He is forever making definitive statements on life, man and art, and he has no more idea than the mushroom what life, man and art actually are.

SON OF LIGHT

Man hidden away in his vanity like a mole in his hill no longer understands the language of light which fills the sky with its inconceivable immensity. Man believes himself to be the summit of creation. The face of light does not perturb him. He confounds himself with light. This toad likes to call himself the son of light.

Man owes it to his incongruously developed reason that he is grotesque and ugly. He has broken away from nature. He thinks that he dominates nature. He thinks he is the measure of all things. Engendering in opposition to the laws of nature, man creates monstrosities. He desires that of which he is incapable, and despises what is within his powers. The artificial and monstrous seem to him the goal of perfection. Whatever he can achieve, he covers with blood and mud. Only in the monstrous is man creative; those unfit for this work compose verses, strum the lyre or brandish the paint brush. This last group devote themselves with enigmatic frenzy to the painting of still-lives, landscapes, nudes. Since the days of the caves, man has been painting still-lives, landscapes, and nudes. Since the days of the caves, man has glorified and deified himself, and has brought about human catastrophe by his monstrous vanity. Art has collaborated in his false development. To me the conception of art that has upheld the vanity of man is sickening.

MAN LOVES WHAT IS VAIN AND DEAD

In art also man loves what is vain and dead. He cannot understand that painting is something other than a landscape prepared with oil and vinegar, and sculpture something other than a woman's thigh made out of marble or bronze. Any living transformation of art seems to him as detestable as the eternal metamorphoses of life. Straight lines and honest colors exasperate him above all. Man doesn't want to get to the bottom of things. The radiance of the universe makes his degeneration and ugliness too apparent. That is why man clings desperately to graceful garlands and makes himself a specialist in values. Out of his nine openings framed in curls, man exhales blue vapor, gray fog, blue smoke. Sometimes he tries like a fly to walk on the ceiling, but he always fails and falls with a crash on the table covered with the best crockery.

Man calls the concrete abstract. This is not surprising, for he commonly confuses front and back even when using his nose, his mouth, his ears, that is to say, five of his nine openings. I understand that a cubist painting might be called abstract, for parts of the object serving as model for the picture have been abstracted. But in my opinion a picture or a sculpture without any object for model is just as concrete and sensual as a leaf or a stone.

ART IS A FRUIT

Art is a fruit that grows in man, like a fruit on a plant, or a child in its mother's womb. But whereas the fruit of the plant, the fruit of the animal, the fruit in the mother's womb, assume autonomous and natural forms, art, the spiritual fruit of man, usually shows an absurd resemblance to the aspect of something else. Only in our own epoch have painting and sculpture been liberated from the aspect of a mandolin, a president in a Prince Albert, a battle, a landscape. I love nature, but not its substitutes. Naturalist, illusionist art is a substitute for nature.

I remember a discussion with Mondrian in which he distinguished between art and nature, saying that art is artificial and nature natural. I do not share his opinion. I believe that nature is not in opposition to art. Art is of natural origin and is sublimated and spiritualized through the sublimation of man.

A FEW LINES OF PLOTINUS

For those among men whose souls have gone beyond that of centipedes, spiders, snails, flies, leeches, bankers, politicians, and who wish to approach beauty and light, I quote these few lines of Plotinus: "It is first of all necessary to make the organ of vision analogous and similar to the object to be contemplated. Never would the eye have perceived the sun if it had not first taken the form of the sun; likewise, the soul cannot see beauty unless it first becomes beautiful itself, and every man must make himself beautiful and divine in order to attain the right of beauty and divinity." . . .

THE GERM OF A NEW PLASTIC WORK

A small fragment of one of my plastic works presenting a curve or a contrast that moves me, is often the germ of a new work. I intensify the curve or the contrast, and this determines new forms. Among the new forms two grow with special intensity. I let these two continue to grow until the original forms have become secondary and almost expressionless. Finally I suppress one of the secondary, expressionless forms so that the others become more apparent. One work often requires months, years. I work until enough of my life has flowed into its body. Each of these bodies has a spiritual content, but only on completion of the work do I interpret this content and give it a name. In this way my works have received names such as "Black cloud-arrow and white points," "Plant escutcheon," "Arabic eight," "Plant pendulum at rest," "Leaves arranged according to the law of chance."

CONCRETE ART

we do not want to copy nature. we do not want to reproduce, we want to produce. we want to produce like a plant that produces a fruit and not to reproduce. we want to produce directly and not through interpretation.

as there is not the slightest trace of abstraction in this art, we call it: concrete art.

the works of concrete art should not be signed by their creators. these paintings, these sculptures, these objects, should remain anonymous in the great studio of nature like clouds, mountains, seas, animals, men. yes, men should return to nature, artists should work in community like the artists of the middle ages. in 1915 o. van rees, c. van rees, freundlich, s. taeuber and myself, made an attempt of this kind.

in 1915 I wrote: "these works are constructed with lines, surfaces, forms and colors. they strive to surpass the human and achieve the infinite and the eternal. they are a negation of man's egotism. . . . the hands of our brothers, instead of serving us as our own hands, have become enemy hands. instead of anonymity there was celebrity and the masterpiece, wisdom was dead. . . . to reproduce is to imitate, to play a comedy, to walk the tightrope. . . ."

the renaissance puffed up human reason with pride. modern times with their science and technology have made man a megalomaniac. the atrocious confusion of our epoch is the consequence of this overestimation of reason.

the evolution of traditional painting towards concrete art, beginning with cézanne and via the cubists has often been explained, and these historical explanations have confused the problem. abruptly, "according to the laws of chance," the human mind underwent a transformation about the year 1914: an ethical problem presented itself. most of these works were not exhibited until about 1920. there was a blossoming of all the colors and all the forms in the world. these paintings, these sculptures, these objects, were liberated from conventional element. in every country adepts of this new art arose.—concrete art influenced architecture, furniture, cinema, typography.

certain "surrealist objects" are also concrete works. without any descriptive content, they seem to me exceedingly important for the evolution of concrete art, for, by allusion, they succeed in introducing into this art the psychic emotion that makes it live.

concrete art aims to transform the world. it aims to make existence more bearable. it aims to save man from the most dangerous folly: vanity. it aims to simplify man's life. it aims to identify him with nature. reason uproots man and causes him to lead a tragic existence. concrete art is an elemental, natural, healthy art, which causes the stars of peace, love and poetry to grow in the head and the heart. where concrete art enters, melancholy departs, dragging with it its gray suitcases full of black sighs.

WILLIAM BLAKE
The Eternal World of Vision

REVD. SIR,

I really am sorry that you are fall'n out with the Spiritual World, Especially if I should have to answer for it. I feel very sorry that your Ideas & Mine on Moral Painting differ so much as to have made you angry with my method of study. If I am wrong, I am wrong in good company. I had hoped your plan comprehended All Species of this Art, & Expecially that you would not regret that Species which gives Existence to Every other, namely, Visions of Eternity. You say that I want somebody to Elucidate my Ideas. But you ought to know that What is Grand is necessarily obscure to Weak men. That which can be made Explicit to the Idiot is not worth my care. The wisest of the Ancients consider'd what is not too Explicit as the fittest for Instruction, because it rouzes the faculties to act. I name Moses, Solomon, Esop, Homer, Plato. . . .

I have therefore proved your Reasonings Ill proportion'd, which you can never prove my figures to be; they are those of Michael Angelo, Rafael & the Antique, & of the best living Models. I perceive that your Eye is perverted by Caricature Prints, which ought not to abound so much as they do. Fun I love, but too much Fun is of all things the most loathsom. Mirth is better than Fun, & Happiness is better than Mirth. I feel that a Man may be happy in This World. And I know that This World Is a World of Imagination & Vision. I see Every thing I paint In This World, but Every body does not see alike. To the Eyes of a Miser a Guinea is far more beautiful than the Sun, & a bag worn with the use of Money has more beautiful proportions than a Vine filled with Grapes. The tree which moves some to tears of joy is in the Eyes of others only a Green thing which stands in the way. Some see Nature all Ridicule & Deformity, & by these I shall not regulate my proportions; & some scarce see Nature at all. But to the Eyes of the Man of Imagination, Nature is Imagination itself. As a man is, so he sees. As the Eye is formed, such are its Powers. You certainly Mistake, when you say that the Visions of Fancy are not to be found in This World. To Me This World is all One continued Vision of Fancy or Imagination, & I feel Flatter'd when I am told so. What is it sets Homer, Virgil & Milton in so high a rank of Art? Why is the Bible more Entertaining & Instructive than any other book? Is

Letter to the Rev. Dr. Trusler [1799] and from "A Vision of the Last Judgment" [1810], *Complete Writings*, ed. Geoffrey Keynes, London and New York, 1957, pp. 793-4, 604-17; reprinted by permission of the Nonesuch Press.

54

it not because they are addressed to the Imagination, which is Spiritual Sensation, & but mediately to the Understanding or Reason? Such is True Painting, and such was alone valued by the Greeks & the best modern Artists. Consider what Lord Bacon says: "Sense sends over to Imagination before Reason have judged, & Reason sends over to Imagination before the Decree can be acted." See Advancemt. of Learning, Part 2 P. 47 of first Edition.

But I am happy to find a Great Majority of Fellow Mortals who can Elucidate My Visions, & Particularly they have been Elucidated by Children, who have taken a greater delight in contemplating my Pictures than I even hoped. Neither Youth nor Childhood is Folly or Incapacity. Some Children are Fools & so are some Old Men. But There is a vast Majority on the side of Imagination or Spiritual Sensation. . . .

I am, Revd. Sir, your very obedient servant,

WILLIAM BLAKE.

————————

The Last Judgment [will be] when all those are Cast away who trouble Religion with Questions concerning Good & Evil or Eating of the Tree of those Knowledges or Reasonings which hinder the Vision of God, turning all into a Consuming Fire. When Imagination, Art & Science & all Intellectual Gifts, all the Gifts of the Holy Ghost, are look'd upon as of no use & only Contention remains to Man, then the Last Judgment begins, & its Vision is seen by the Imaginative Eye of Every one according to the situation he holds.

The Last Judgment is not Fable or Allegory, but Vision. Fable or Allegory are a totally distinct & inferior kind of Poetry. Vision or Imagination is a Representation of what Eternally Exists, Really & Unchangeably. Fable or Allegory is Form'd by the daughters of Memory. Imagination is surrounded by the daughters of Inspiration, who in the aggregate are call'd Jerusalem. Fable is allegory, but what Critics call The Fable, is Vision itself. The Hebrew Bible & the Gospel of Jesus are not Allegory, but Eternal Vision or Imagination of All that Exists. Note here that Fable or Allegory is seldom without some Vision. Pilgrim's Progress is full of it, the Greek Poets the same; but Allegory & Vision ought to be known as Two Distinct Things, & so call'd for the Sake of Eternal Life. Plato has made Socrates say that Poets & Prophets do not know or Understand what they write or Utter; this is a most Pernicious Falshood. If they do not, pray is an inferior kind to be call'd Knowing? Plato confutes himself.

The Last Judgment is one of these Stupendous Visions. I have represented it as I saw it; to different People it appears differently as every thing else does; for tho' on Earth things seem Permanent, they are less permanent than a Shadow, as we all know too well.

The Nature of Visionary Fancy, or Imagination, is very little known, & the Eternal nature & permanence of its ever Existent Images is consider'd as less permanent than the things of Vegetative & Generative Nature; yet the Oak dies as well as the Lettuce, but Its Eternal Image & Individuality never dies, but renews by its seed; just so the Imaginative Image returns by the seed of Contemplative Thought; the Writings of the Prophets illustrate these conceptions of the Visionary Fancy by their various sublime & Divine Images as seen in the Worlds of Vision.

The Learned m . . . or Heroes; this is an . . . & not Spiritual . . . while the Bible . . . of Virtue & Vice . . . as they are Ex . . . is the Real Di . . . Things. The . . . when they Assert that Jupiter usurped the Throne of his Father, Saturn, &.brought on an Iron Age & Begat on Mnemosyne, or Memory, The Greek Muses, which are not Inspiration as the Bible is. Reality was Forgot, & the Vanities of Time & Space only Remember'd & call'd Reality. Such is the Mighty difference between Allegoric Fable & Spiritual Mystery. Let it here be Noted that the Greek Fables originated in Spiritual Mystery & Real Visions, which are lost & clouded in Fable & Allegory, while the Hebrew Bible & the Greek Gospel are Genuine, Preserv'd by the Saviour's Mercy. The Nature of my Work is Visionary or Imaginative; it is an Endeavour to Restore what the Ancients call'd the Golden Age.

This world of Imagination is the world of Eternity; it is the divine bosom into which we shall all go after the death of the Vegetated body. This World of Imagination is Infinite & Eternal, whereas the world of Generation, or Vegetation, is Finite & Temporal. There Exist in that Eternal World the Permanent Realities of Every Thing which we see reflected in this Vegetable Glass of Nature. All Things are comprehended in their Eternal Forms in the divine body of the Saviour, the True Vine of Eternity, The Human Imagination, who appear'd to Me as Coming to Judgment among his Saints & throwing off the Temporal that the Eternal might be Establish'd; around him were seen the Images of Existences according to a certain order Suited to my Imaginative Eye as follows. . . .

In Eternity one Thing never Changes into another Thing. Each Identity is Eternal: consequently Apuleius's Golden Ass & Ovid's Metamorphosis & others of the like kind are Fable; yet they contain Vision in a sublime degree, being derived from real Vision in More ancient Writings. Lot's Wife being Changed into [a] Pillar of Salt alludes to the Mortal Body being render'd a Permanent Statue, but not Changed or Transformed into Another Identity while it retains its own Individuality. A Man can never become Ass nor Horse; some are born with shapes of Men, who may be both, but Eternal Identity is one thing & Corporeal Vegetation is another thing. Changing Water into Wine by Jesus & into Blood by Moses relates to Vegetable Nature also. . . .

It ought to be understood that the Persons, Moses & Abraham, are not here meant, but the States Signified by those Names, the Individuals being representatives or Visions of those States as they were reveal'd to Mortal Man in the Series of Divine Revelations as they are written in the Bible; these various States I have seen in my Imagination; when distant they appear as One Man, but as you approach they appear Multitudes of Nations. . . .

If the Spectator could enter into these Images in his Imagination, approaching them on the Fiery Chariot of his Contemplative Thought, if he could Enter into Noah's Rainbow or into his bosom, or could make a Friend & Companion of one of these Images of wonder, which always intreats him to leave mortal things (as he must know), then would he arise from his Grave, then would he meet the Lord in the Air & then he would be happy. General Knowledge is Remote Knowledge; it is in Particulars that Wisdom consists & Happiness too. Both in Art & in Life, General Masses are as Much Art as a Pasteboard Man in Human. Every Man has Eyes, Nose & Mouth; this Every Idiot knows, but he who enters into & discriminates most minutely the Manners & Intentions, the Characters in all their branches, is the alone Wise or Sensible Man, & on this discrimination All Art is founded. I intreat, then, that the Spectator will attend to the Hands & Feet, to the Lineaments of the Countenances; they are all descripive of Character, & not a line is drawn without intention, & that most discriminate & particular. As Poetry admits not a Letter that is Insignificant, so Painting admits not a Grain of Sand or a Blade of Grass Insignificant—much less an Insignificant Blur or Mark. . . .

The Last Judgment is an Overwhelming of Bad Art & Science. Mental Things are alone Real; what is call'd Corporeal, Nobody Knows of its Dwelling Place: it is in Fallacy, & its Existence an Imposture. Where is the Existence Out of Mind or Thought? Where is it but in the Mind of a Food? Some People flatter themselves that there will be No Last Judgment & that Bad Art will be adopted & mixed with Good Art, That Error or Experiment will make a Part of Truth, & they Boast that it is its Foundation; these People flatter themselves: I will not Flatter them. Error is Created. Truth is Eternal. Error, or Creation, will be Burned up, & then, & not till Then, Truth or Eternity will appear. It is Burnt up the Moment Men cease to behold it. I assert for My Self that I do not behold the outward Creation & that to me it is hindrance & not Action; it is as the dirt upon my feet, No part of Me. "What," it will be Question'd, "When the Sun rises, do you not see a round disk of fire somewhat like a Guinea?" O no, no, I see an Innumerable company of the Heavenly host crying, "Holy, Holy, Holy is the Lord God Almighty." I question not my Corporeal or Vegetative Eye any more than I would Question a Window concerning a Sight. I look thro' it & not with it.

WILLIAM WORDSWORTH

Natural Apocalypse

Yet still in me with those soft luxuries
Mixed something of stern mood, an underthirst
Of vigour seldom utterly allayed:
And from that source how different a sadness
Would issue, let one incident make known.
When from the Vallois we had turned, and clomb
Along the Simplon's steep and rugged road,
Following a band of muleteers, we reached
A halting-place, where all together took
Their noon-tide meal. Hastily rose our guide,
Leaving us at the board; awhile we lingered,
Then paced the beaten downward way that led
Right to a rough stream's edge. and there broke off;

From *The Prelude* [1803; 1850], Book VI, lines 557-640.

The only track now visible was one
That from the torrent's further brink held forth
Conspicuous invitation to ascend
A lofty mountain. After brief delay
Crossing the unbridged stream, that road we took,
And clomb with eagerness, till anxious fears
Intruded, for we failed to overtake
Our comrades gone before. By fortunate chance,
While every moment added doubt to doubt,
A peasant met us, from whose mouth we learned
That to the spot which had perplexed us first
We must descend, and there should find the road,
Which in the stony channel of the stream
Lay a few steps, and then along its banks;
And, that our future course, all plain to sight,
Was downwards, with the current of that stream.
Loth to believe what we so grieved to hear,
For still we had hopes that pointed to the clouds,
We questioned him again, and yet again;
But every word that from the peasant's lips
Came in reply, translated by our feelings,
Ended in this,—*that we had crossed the Alps.*
   Imagination—here the Power so called
Through sad incompetence of human speech,
That awful Power rose from the mind's abyss
Like an unfathered vapour that enwraps,
At once, some lonely traveller. I was lost;
Halted without an effort to break through;
But to my conscious soul I now can say—
"I recognise thy glory;" in such strength
Of usurpation, when the light of sense
Goes out, but with a flash that has revealed
The invisible world, doth greatness make abode,
There harbours; whether we be young or old,
Our destiny, our being's heart and home,
Is with infinitude, and only there;
With hope it is, hope that can never die,
Effort, and expectation, and desire,
And something evermore about to be.
Under such banners militant, the soul
Seeks for no trophies, struggles for no spoils
That may attest her prowess, blest in thoughts
That are their own perfection and reward,
Strong in herself and in beatitude
That hides her, like the mighty flood of Nile
Poured from his fount of Abyssinian clouds
To fertilise the whole Egyptian plain.
   The melancholy slackening that ensued

Upon those tidings by the peasant given
Was soon dislodged. Downwards we hurried fast,
And with the half-shaped road which we had missed,
Entered a narrow chasm. The brook and road
Were fellow-travellers in this gloomy strait,
And with them did we journey several hours
At a slow pace. The immeasurable height
Of woods decaying, never to be decayed,
The stationary blasts of waterfalls,
And in the narrow rent at every turn
Winds thwarting winds, bewildered and forlorn,
The torrents shooting from the clear blue sky,
The rocks that muttered close upon our ears,
Black drizzling crags that spake by the way-side
As if a voice were in them, the sick sight
And giddy prospect of the raving stream,
The unfettered clouds and region of the Heavens,
Tumult and peace, the darkness and the light—
Were all like workings of one mind, the features
Of the same face, blossoms upon one tree;
Characters of the great Apocalypse,
The types and symbols of Eternity,
Of first, and last, and midst, and without end.

CHARLES BAUDELAIRE

The Temple of Nature

CORRESPONDANCES

La Nature est un temple où de vivants piliers
Laissent parfois sortir de confuses paroles;
L'homme y passe à travers des forêts de symboles
Qui l'observent avec des regards familiers.
Comme de longs échos qui de loin se confondent
Dans une ténébreuse et profonde unité,
Vaste comme la nuit et comme la clarté,
Les parfums, les couleurs et les sons se répondent.
Il est des parfums frais comme des chairs d'enfants,
Doux comme les hautbois, verts comme les prairies,
—Et d'autres, corrompus, riches et triomphants,
Ayant l'expansion des choses infinies,
Comme l'ambre, le musc, le benjoin et l'encens,
Qui chantent les transports de l'esprit et des sens.

"Correspondances" [1857], *Selected Verse*, translated from the French by Francis Scarfe, 1961, pp. 36-7, reprinted by permission of Penguin Books, Inc.

(Nature is a temple, in which living pillars sometimes utter a babel of words; man traverses it through forests of symbols, that watch him with knowing eyes.

Like prolonged echoes which merge far away in an opaque, deep oneness, as vast as darkness, as vast as light, perfumes, sounds, and colours answer each to each.

There are perfumes fresh and cool as the bodies of children, mellow as oboes, green as fields; and others that are perverse, rich, and triumphant,

that have the infinite expansion of infinite things—such as amber, musk, benjamin, and incense, which chant the ecstasies of the mind and senses.)

W. B. YEATS

Symbol as Revelation

I

"Symbolism, as seen in the writers of our day, would have no value if it were not seen also, under one disguise or another, in every great imaginative writer," writes Mr. Arthur Symons in *The Symbolist Movement in Literature*, a subtle book which I cannot praise as I would, because it has been dedicated to me; and he goes on to show how many profound writers have in the last few years sought for a philosophy of poetry in the doctrine of symbolism, and how even in countries where it is almost scandalous to seek for any philosophy of poetry, new writers are following them in their search. We do not know what the writers of ancient times talked of among themselves, and one bull is all that remains of Shakespeare's talk, who was on the edge of modern times; and the journalist is convinced, it seems, that they talked of wine and women and politics, but never about their art, or never quite seriously about their art. He is certain that no one, who had a philosophy of his art or a theory of how he should write, has ever made a work of art, that people have no imagination who do not write without forethought and afterthought as he writes his own articles. He says this with enthusiasm, because he has heard it at so many comfortable dinner-tables, where some one had mentioned through carelessness, or foolish zeal, a book whose difficulty had offended indolence, or a man who had not forgotten that beauty is an accusation. These formulas and generalisations, in which a hidden sergeant has drilled the ideas of journalists and through them the ideas of all but all the modern world, have created in their turn a forgetfulness like that of soldiers in battle, so that journalists and their readers have forgotten, among many like events, that Wagner spent seven years arranging and explaining his ideas before he began his most characteristic music; that opera, and with

"The Symbolism of Poetry" [1900], from *Essays and Introductions*, New York, 1961, pp. 153-64. Copyright © 1961 by Mrs. W. B. Yeats; reprinted by permission of The Macmillan Company, New York, The Macmillan Company of Canada Ltd., Messrs. Macmillan & Co. Ltd. of London, and Mrs. W. B. Yeats.

it modern music, arose from certain talks at the house of one Giovanni Bardi of Florence; and that the Pleiade laid the foundations of modern French literature with a pamphlet. Goethe has said, "a poet needs all philosophy, but he must keep it out of his work," though that is not always necessary; and almost certainly no great art, outside England, where journalists are more powerful and ideas less plentiful than elsewhere, has arisen without a great criticism, for its herald or its interpreter and protector, and it may be for this reason that great art, now that vulgarity has armed itself and multiplied itself, is perhaps dead in England.

All writers, all artists of any kind, in so far as they have had any philosophical or critical power, perhaps just in so far as they have been deliberate artists at all, have had some philosophy, some criticism of their art; and it has often been this philosophy, or this criticism, that has evoked their most startling inspiration, calling into outer life some portion of the divine life, or of the buried reality, which could alone extinguish in the emotions what their philosophy or their criticism would extinguish in the intellect. They have sought for no new thing, it may be, but only to understand and to copy the pure inspiration of early times, but because the divine life wars upon our outer life, and must needs change its weapons and its movements as we change ours, inspiration has come to them in beautiful startling shapes. The scientific movement brought with it a literature, which was always tending to lose itself in externalities of all kinds, in opinion, in declamation, in picturesque writing, in word painting, or in what Mr. Symons has called an attempt "to build in brick and mortar inside the covers of a book"; and now writers have begun to dwell upon the element of evocation, of suggestion, upon what we call the symbolism in great writers.

II

In "Symbolism in Painting," I tried to describe the element of symbolism that is in pictures and sculpture, and described a little the symbolism in poetry, but did not describe at all the continuous indefinable symbolism which is the substance of all style.

There are no lines with more melancholy beauty than these by Burns—

> The white moon is setting behind the white wave,
> And Time is setting with me, O!

and these lines are perfectly symbolical. Take from them the whiteness of the moon and of the wave, whose relation to the setting of Time is too subtle for the intellect, and you take from them their beauty. But, when all are together, moon and wave and whiteness and setting Time and the last melancholy cry, they evoke an emotion which cannot be evoked by any other arrangement of colours and sounds and forms. We may call this metaphorical writing, but it is better to call it symbolical writing because metaphors are not profound enough to be moving, when they are not symbols, and when they are symbols they are the most perfect of all, because the most subtle, outside of pure sound, and through them one can the best find out what symbols are. If one begins the reverie with any beautiful lines that one can remember, one finds they are like those by Burns. Begin with this line by Blake—

> The gay fishes on the wave when the moon sucks up the dew;

or these lines by Nash—

> Queens have died young and fair,
> Brightness falls from the air,
> Dust hath closed Helen's eye;

or these lines by Shakespeare—

> Timon hath made his everlasting mansion
> Upon the beached verge of the salt flood;
> Who once a day with his embossed froth
> The turbulent surge shall cover;

or take some line that is quite simple, that gets its beauty from its place in a story, and see how it flickers with the light of the many symbols that have given the story its beauty, as a sword-blade may flicker with the light of burning towers.

All sounds, all colours, all forms, either because of their pre-ordained energies or because of long association, evoke indefinable and yet precise emotions, or, as I prefer to think, call down among us certain disembodied powers, whose footsteps over our hearts we call emotions; and when sound, and colour, and form are in a musical relation, a beautiful relation to one another, they become as it were one sound, one colour, one form, and evoke an emotion that is made out of their distinct evocations and yet is one emotion. The same relation exists between all portions of every work of art, whether it be an epic or a song, and the more perfect it is, and the more various and numerous the elements that have flowed into its perfection, the more powerful will be the emotion, the power, the god it calls among us. Because an emotion does not exist, or does not become perceptible and active among us, till it has found its expression, in colour or in sound or in form, or in all of these, and because no two modulations or arrangements of these evoke the same emotion, poets and painters and musicians, and in a less degree because their effects are momentary, day and night and cloud and shadow, are continually making and un-making mankind. It is indeed only those things which seem useless or very feeble that have any power, and all those things that seem useful or strong, armies, moving wheels, modes of architecture, modes of government, speculations of the reason, would have been a little different if some mind long ago had not given itself to some emotion, as a woman gives herself to her lover, and shaped sounds or colours or forms, or all of these, into a musical relation, that their emotion might live in other minds. A little lyric evokes an emotion, and this emotion gathers others about it and melts into their being in the making of some great epic; and at last, needing an always less delicate body, or symbol, as it grows more powerful, it flows out, with all it has gathered, among the blind instincts of daily life, where it moves a power within powers, as one sees ring within ring in the stem of an old tree. This is maybe what Arthur O'Shaughnessy meant when he made his poets say they had built Nineveh with their sighing; and I am certainly never certain, when I hear of some war, or of some religious excitement or of some new manufacture, or of anything else that fills the ear of the world, that it has not all happened because of something that a boy piped in Thessaly. I remember once telling a seer to ask one among the gods who, as she believed, were standing about her in their symbolic bodies, what would come of a charming but seeming trivial labour of a friend, and the form answering, "the devastation of peoples and the over-whelming of cities." I doubt indeed if the crude circumstance of the world, which seems to create all our emotions, does more than reflect, as in multiplying mirrors, the emotions that have come to solitary men in moments of poetical contemplation; or that love itself would be more than an animal hunger but for the poet and his shadow the priest, for unless we believe that outer things are the reality, we must believe that the gross is the shadow of the subtle, that things are wise before they become foolish, and secret before they cry out in the market-place. Solitary men in moments of contemplation receive, as I think, the creative impulse from the lowest of the Nine Hierarchies, and so make and unmake mankind, and even the world itself, for does not "the eye altering alter all"?

> Our towns are copied fragments from our breast;
> And all man's Babylons strive but to impart
> The grandeurs of his Babylonian heart.

III

The purpose of rhythm, it has always seemed to me, is to prolong the moment of contemplation, the moment when we are both asleep and awake, which is the one moment of creation, by hushing us with an alluring monotony, while it holds us waking by variety, to keep us in that state of perhaps real trance, in which the mind liberated from the pressure of the will is unfolded in symbols. If certain sensitive persons listen persistently to the ticking of a watch, or gaze persistently on the monotonous flashing of a light, they fall into the hypnotic trance; and rhythm is but the ticking of a watch made softer, that one must needs listen, and various, that one may not be swept beyond memory or grow weary of listening; while the patterns of the artist are but the monotonous flash woven to take the eyes in a subtler enchantment. I have heard in meditation voices that were forgotten the moment they had spoken; and I have been swept, when in more profound meditation, beyond all memory but of those things that came from beyond the threshold of waking life. I was writing once at a very symbolical and abstract poem, when my pen fell on the ground; and as I stooped to pick it up, I remembered some phantastic adventure that yet did not seem phantastic, and then another like adventure, and when I asked myself when these things had happened, I found that I was remembering my dreams for many nights. I tried to remember what I had done the day before, and then what I had done that morning; but all my waking life had perished from me, and it was only after a struggle that I came to remember it again, and as I did so that more powerful and startling life perished in its turn. Had my pen not fallen on the ground and so made me turn from the images that I was weaving into verse, I would never have known that meditation had become trance, for I would have been like one who does not know that he is passing through a wood because his eyes are on the pathway. So I think that in the making and in the understanding of a work of art, and the more easily if it is full of patterns and symbols and music, we are lured to the threshold of sleep, and it may be far beyond it, without knowing that we have ever set our feet upon the steps of horn or of ivory.

IV

Besides emotional symbols, symbols that evoke emotions alone,—and in this sense all alluring or hateful things are symbols, although their relations with one another are too subtle to delight us fully, away from rhythm and pattern,—there are intellectual symbols, symbols that evoke ideas alone, or ideas mingled with emotions; and outside the very definite traditions of mysticism and the less definite criticism of certain modern poets, these alone are called symbols. Most things belong to one or another kind, according to the way we speak of them and the companions we give them, for symbols, associated with ideas that are more than fragments of the shadows thrown upon the intellect by the emotions they evoke, are the playthings of the allegorist or the pedant, and soon pass away. If I say "white" or "purple" in an ordinary line of poetry, they evoke emotions so exclusively that I cannot say why they move me; but if I bring them into the same sentence with such obvious intellectual symbols as a cross or a crown of thorns, I think of purity and sovereignty. Furthermore, innumerable meanings, which are held to "white" or to "purple" by bonds of subtle suggestion, and alike in the emotions and in the intellect, move visibly through my mind, and move invisibly beyond the threshold of sleep, casting lights and shadows of an indefinable wisdom on what had seemed before, it may be, but sterility and noisy violence. It is the intellect that decides where the reader shall ponder over the procession of the symbols, and if the symbols are merely emotional, he gazes from amid the accidents and destinies of the world; but if the symbols are intellectual too, he becomes himself a part of pure intellect, and he is himself mingled with the procession. If I watch a rushy pool in the moonlight, my emotion at its beauty is mixed with memories of the man that I have seen ploughing by its margin, or of the lovers I saw there a night ago; but if I look at the moon herself and remember any of her ancient names and meanings, I move among divine people, and things that have shaken off our mortality, the tower of ivory, the queen of waters, the shining stag among enchanted woods, the white hare sitting upon the hilltop, the fool of faery with his shining cup full of dreams, and it may be "make a friend of one of these images of wonder," and "meet the Lord in the air." So, too, if one is moved by Shakespeare, who is content with emotional symbols that he may come the nearer to our sympathy, one is mixed with the whole spectacle of the world; while if one is moved by Dante, or by the myth of Demeter, one is mixed into the shadow of God or of a goddess. So too one is furthest from symbols when one is busy doing this or that, but the soul moves among symbols and unfolds in symbols when trance, or madness, or deep meditation has withdrawn it from every impulse but its own. "I then saw," wrote Gérard de Nerval of his madness, "vaguely drifting into form, plastic images of antiquity, which outlined themselves, became definite, and seemed to represent symbols of which I only seized the idea with difficulty." In an earlier time he would have been of that multitude, whose souls austerity withdrew, even more perfectly than madness could withdraw his soul, from hope and memory, from desire and regret, that they might reveal those processions of symbols that men bow to before altars, and woo with incense and offerings. But being of our time, he has been like Maeterlinck, like Villiers de l'Isle Adam in *Axël*, like all who are preoccupied with intellectual symbols in our time, a foreshadower of the new sacred book, of which all the arts, as somebody has said, are beginning to dream. How can the arts overcome the slow dying of men's hearts that we call the progress of the world, and lay their hands upon men's heartstrings again, without becoming the garment of religion as in old times?

V

If people were to accept the theory that poetry moves us because of its symbolism, what change should one look for in the manner of our poetry? A return to the way of our fathers, a casting out of descriptions of nature for the sake of nature, of the moral law for the sake of the moral law, a casting out of all anecdotes and of that brooding over scientific opinion that so often extinguished the central flame in Tennyson, and of that vehemence that would make us do or not do certain things; or, in other words, we should come to understand that the beryl stone was enchanted by our fathers that it might unfold the pictures in its heart, and not to mirror our own excited faces, or the boughs waving outside the window. With this change of substance, this return to imagination, this understanding that the laws of art, which are the hidden laws of the world, can alone bind the imagination, would come a change of style, and we would cast out of serious poetry those energetic rhythms, as of a man running, which are the invention of the will with its eyes always on something to be done or undone; and we would seek out those wavering, meditative, organic rhythms, which are the embodiment of the imagination, that neither desires nor hates, because it has done with time, and only wishes to gaze upon some reality, some beauty; nor would it be any longer possible for anybody to deny the importance of form, in all its kinds, for although you can expound an opinion, or describe a thing when your words are not quite well chosen, you cannot give a body to something that moves beyond the senses, unless your words are as subtle, as complex, as full of mysterious life, as the body of a flower or of a woman. The form of sincere poetry, unlike the form of the popular poetry, may indeed be sometimes obscure, or ungrammatical as in some of the best of the Songs of Innocence and Experience, but it must have the perfections that escape analysis, the subtleties that have a new meaning every day, and it must have all this whether it be but a little song made out of a moment of dreamy indolence, or some great epic made out of the dreams of one poet and of a hundred generations whose hands were never weary of the sword.

Eternal Genesis

I would like now to examine the dimensions of the object in a new light and so try to show how it is that the artist frequently arrives at what appears to be such an arbitrary "deformation" of natural forms.

First, he does not attach such intense importance to natural form as do so many realist critics, because, for him, these final forms are not the real stuff of the process of natural creation. For he places more value on the powers which do the forming than on the final forms themselves.

He is, perhaps unintentionally, a philosopher, and if he does not, with the optimists, hold this world to be the best of all possible worlds, nor to be so bad that it is unfit to serve as a model, yet he says:

"In its present shape it is not the only possible world."

Thus he surveys with penetrating eye the finished forms which nature places before him.

The deeper he looks, the more readily he can extend his view from the present to the past, the more deeply he is impressed by the one essential image of creation itself, as Genesis, rather than by the image of nature, the finished product.

Then he permits himself the thought that the process of creation can today hardly be complete and he sees the act of world creation stretching from the past to the future. Genesis eternal!

He goes still further!

He says to himself, thinking of life around him: this world at one time looked different and, in the future, will look different again.

Then, flying off to the infinite, he thinks: it is very probable that, on other stars, creation has produced a completely different result.

Such mobility of thought on the process of natural creation is good training for creative work.

It has the power to move the artist fundamentally, and since he is himself mobile, he may be relied upon to maintain freedom of development of his own creative methods.

This being so, the artist must be forgiven if he regards the present state of outward appearances in his own particular world as accidentally fixed in time and space. And as altogether inadequate compared with his penetrating vision and intense depth of feeling.

And is it not true that even the small step of a glimpse through the microscope reveals to us images which we should deem fantastic and over-imaginative if we

From *On Modern Art* [1945], translated from the German by Paul Findlay, London, 1948, pp. 43, 45, 47, 49, 51, 53-5; reprinted by permission of Faber & Faber Ltd.

were to see them somewhere accidentally, and lacked the sense to understand them?

Your realist, however, coming across such an illustration in a sensational magazine, would exclaim in great indignation: "Is that supposed to be nature? I call it bad drawing."

Does then the artist concern himself with microscopy? History? Palaeontology?

Only for purposes of comparison, only in the exercise of his mobility of mind. And not to provide a scientific check on the truth of nature.

Only in the sense of freedom.
In the sense of a freedom, which does not lead to fixed phases of development, representing exactly what nature once was, or will be, or could be on another star (as perhaps may one day be proved).

But in the sense of a freedom which merely demands its rights, the right to develop, as great Nature herself develops.

From type to prototype.

Presumptuous is the artist who does not follow his road through to the end. But chosen are those artists who penetrate to the region of that secret place where primeval power nurtures all evolution.

There, where the power-house of all time and space—call it brain or heart of creation—activates every function; who is the artist who would not dwell there? In the womb of nature, at the source of creation, where the secret key to all lies guarded.

But not all can enter. Each should follow where the pulse of his own heart leads.

So, in their time, the Impressionists—our opposites of yesterday—had every right to dwell within the matted undergrowth of every-day vision.

But our pounding heart drives us down, deep down to the source of all.

What springs from this source, whatever it may be called, dream, idea or phantasy—must be taken seriously only if it unites with the proper creative means to form a work of art.

Then those curiosities become realities—realities of art which help to lift life out of its mediocrity.

For not only do they, to some extent, add more spirit to the seen, but they also make secret visions visible.

I said "with the proper creative means." For at this stage is decided whether pictures or something different will be born. At this stage, also, is decided the kind of pictures.

These unsettled times have brought chaos and confusion (or so it seems, if we are not too near to judge).

But among artists, even among the youngest of them, one urge seems to be gradually gaining ground:

The urge to the culture of these creative means, to their pure cultivation, to their pure use.

The legend of the childishness of my drawing must have originated from those linear compositions of mine in which I tried to combine a concrete image, say that of a man, with the pure representation of the linear element.

Had I wished to present the man "as he is," then I should have had to use such a bewildering confusion of line that pure elementary representation would have been out of the question. The result would have been vagueness beyond recognition.

And anyway, I do not wish to represent the man as he is, but only as he might be.

And thus I could arrive at a happy association between my vision of life (Weltanschauung) and pure artistic craftsmanship.

And so it is over the whole field of use of the formal means: in all things, even in colours, must all trace of vagueness be avoided.

This then is what is called the untrue colouring in modern art.

As you can see from this example of "childishness" I concern myself with work on the partial processes of art. I am also a draughtsman.

I have tried pure drawing, I have tried painting in pure tone values. In colour, I have tried all partial methods to which I have been led by my sense of direction in the colour circle. As a result, I have worked out methods of painting in coloured tone values, in complementary colours, in multicolours and methods of total colour painting.

Always combined with the more subconscious dimensions of the picture.

Then I tried all possible syntheses of two methods. Combining and again combining, but, of course, always preserving the culture of the pure element.

Sometimes I dream of a work of really great breadth, ranging through the whole region of element, object, meaning and style.

This, I fear, will remain a dream, but it is a good thing even now to bear the possibility occasionally in mind.

Nothing can be rushed. It must grow, it should grow of itself, and if the time ever comes for that work—then so much the better!

> We must go on seeking it!
> We have found parts, but not the whole!
> We still lack the ultimate power, for:
> the people are not with us.

But we seek a people. We began over there in the Bauhaus. We began there with a community to which each one of us gave what he had.
More we cannot do.

JOHANN WOLFGANG VON GOETHE

Escape from Ideas

The conversation now turned upon "Tasso," and the idea which Goethe had endeavoured to represent by it.

"Idea!" said Goethe, "not that I know of! I had the life of Tasso, I had my own life; and whilst I brought together two odd figures with their peculiarities, the image of Tasso arose in my mind, to which I opposed, as a prosaic contrast, that of Antonio, for whom also I did not lack models. The further particulars of court life and love affairs were at Weimar as they were in Ferrara; and I can truly say of my production, *it is bone of my bone, and flesh of my flesh.*

"The Germans are, certainly, strange people. By their deep thoughts and ideas, which they seek in everything and fix upon everything, they make life much more burdensome than is necessary. Only have the courage to give yourself up to your impressions, allow yourself to be delighted, moved, elevated, nay, instructed and inspired for something great; but do not imagine all is vanity, if it is not abstract thought and idea.

"Then they come and ask, 'What idea I meant to embody in my Faust?' as if I knew myself and could inform them. *From heaven, through the world, to hell,* would indeed be something; but this is no idea, only a course of action. And further, that the devil loses the wager, and that a man, continually struggling from difficult errors towards something better, should be redeemed, is an effective, and to many, a good enlightening thought; but it is no idea which lies at the foundation of the whole, and of every individual scene. It would have been a fine thing, indeed, if I had strung so rich, varied, and highly diversified a life as I have brought to view in Faust upon the slender string of one pervading idea.

"It was, in short," continued Goethe, "not in my line, as a poet, to strive to embody anything *abstract.* I received in my mind impressions, and those of a sensual, animated, charming, varied, hundredfold kind, just as a lively imagination presented them; and I had, as a poet, nothing more to do than artistically to round off and elaborate such views and impressions, and by means of a lively representation so to bring them forward that others might receive the same impression in hearing or reading my representation of them.

"If I still wished, as a poet, to represent any idea, I would do it in short poems, where a decided unity could prevail, and where a complete survey would be easy,

From J. P. Eckermann, *Conversations of Goethe* [1836], translated from the German by John Oxenford, London, 1850, Vol. I, pp. 415-16, 160-61.

as, for instance, in the Metamorphosis of Animals, that of the plants, the poem 'Bequest' (Vermächtniss), and many others. The only production of greater extent, in which I am conscious of having laboured to set forth a pervading idea, is probably my 'Wahlverwandtschaften.' This novel has thus become comprehensible to the understanding; but I will not say that it is therefore better. I am rather of the opinion, that the more incommensurable, and the more incomprehensible to the understanding, a poetic production is, so much the better it is."

After some slight discussion of other topics, we came upon the mistake of those artists who made religion art, while for them art should be religion. "Religion," said Goethe, "stands in the same relation to art as any other of the higher interests in life. It is merely to be looked upon as a material, with similar claims to any other vital material. Faith and want of faith are not the organs with which a work of art is to be apprehended. On the contrary, human powers and capacities of a totally different character are required. Art must address itself to those organs with which we apprehend it; otherwise it misses its effect. A religious material may be a good subject for art, but only in so far as it possesses general human interest. The Virgin with the Child is on this account an excellent subject, and one that may be treated a hundred times, and always seen again with pleasure."

JOHN KEATS

Negative Capability

My dear Brothers, . . .

I dined with Haydon the Sunday after you left, and had a very pleasant day. I dined too (for I have been out too much lately) with Horace Smith, and met his two brothers, with Hill and Kingston, and one Du Bois. They only served to convince me how superior humour is to wit, in respect to enjoyment. These men say things which make one start, without making one feel; they are all alike; their manners are alike; they all know fashionables; they have all a mannerism in their very eating and drinking, in their mere handling a decanter. They talked of Kean and his low company. "Would I were with that company instead of yours," said I to myself! I know such like acquaintance will never do for me, and yet I am going to Reynolds on Wednesday. Brown and Dilke walked with me and back to the Christmas pantomime. I had not a dispute, but a disquisition, with Dilke upon various subjects; several things dove-tailed in my mind, and at once it struck me what quality went to form a man of achievement, especially in literature, and which Shakespeare possessed so enormously—I mean *Negative*

Letter to George and Thomas Keats [1817], *Letters*, ed. Maurice Buxton Forman, London, 1935 (2nd edition), pp. 71-2; reprinted by permission of Oxford University Press.

Capability, that is, when a man is capable of being in uncertainties, mysteries, doubts, without any irritable reaching after fact and reason. Coleridge, for instance, would let go by a fine isolated verisimilitude caught from the Penetralium of mystery, from being incapable of remaining content with half-knowledge. This pursued through volumes would perhaps take us no further than this, that with a great poet the sense of Beauty overcomes every other consideration, or rather obliterates all consideration.

Shelley's poem is out, and there are words about its being objected to as much as "Queen Mab" was. Poor Shelley, I think he has his Quota of good qualities, in sooth la!! Write soon to your most sincere friend and affectionate Brother,

JOHN.

GUSTAVE FLAUBERT
Art without Conclusions

I am very behind hand with you, my dear fellow-writer and reader. Do not take the rarity of my letters as a criterion of my affection. Put it down merely to the trials of Paris life, to the publication of my book, and the archaeological reading in which I am at present engaged. But now I am back in the country again with more time to myself, and now we are going to spend the evening together. Let us talk first of ourselves, then of your books, and finally of certain social and political ideas on which we differ.

You ask me how I cured myself of the nervous delusions from which I once suffered. In two ways: (1) by examining them scientifically—that is to say by trying to understand them—and (2) *by force of will*. I often felt the onset of madness. There was a whirl of ideas and images in my poor mind, and my consciousness, my ego, seemed to be foundering like a ship in a storm. But I clung tight to my reason. Though battered and beaten, it kept the upper hand. At other times I tried to reconstruct my appalling sufferings in my imagination. I played with fantasy and madness, as Mithridates did with his poisons. I was sustained by an intense pride, and conquered the disease by grappling with it hand to hand. There is one quality, or rather a habit, which you seem to lack, I mean *the love of contemplation*. Take life, the passions and yourself as a subject for intellectual exercise. You are in revolt against the injustice of the world, against its baseness, its tyranny and all the vileness and corruption of life. But do you thoroughly understand them? Have you fully studied them? Are you God? Who informed you that your human judgment is infallible, that your feelings do not lead you astray? How can we, with our limited senses and our circumscribed intelligence, attain to absolute knowledge of truth and goodness? Shall we ever grasp the absolute? In order to survive, one must give up having clear-cut opinions about

Letter to Mlle. Leroyer de Chantepie [1857], *Letters*, ed. Richard Rumbold and translated from the French by J. M. Cohen, London, 1950, pp. 106-10; reprinted by permission of George Weidenfeld & Nicolson Ltd. and Philosophical Library, New York.

anything at all. *Humanity is like that*; it is not a question of changing it, but of knowing it. *Think less about yourself.* Give up all hope of a solution. The answer is in our Father's heart. He alone possesses it, and does not communicate it. But there are in the *ardours of learning* pleasures of the mind befitting noble souls. Make mental contact with your brothers of three thousand years ago; relive all their sufferings, all their dreams, and you will feel your heart and your mind expanding together till every phantom and every being is enveloped in the cloak of a deep and boundless sympathy. *Do try to cease living subjectively.* Do some deep reading. Draw up a plan of study; make it strenuous and consistent. Read history, especially ancient history. *Compel yourself to regular, exhausting work.* Life is such a hideous business that the only method of bearing it is to avoid it. And one does avoid it by living in Art, in the ceaseless quest for Truth presented by Beauty. When you read the great masters, try to grasp their method, to draw near to the heart of them, and you will rise from your studies dazzled with joy. You will be like Moses descending Sinai, with the light shining from his face because he had seen God.

What is all this about remorse and guilt, and vague apprehensions and confession? Forget it all, my poor soul, for your own good. Since you feel your conscience entirely clear, you can stand before the Eternal Being and say "Here am I." If one is guiltless what has one to fear? And what can we humans be guilty of, inadequate as we are for evil as for good! All your troubles arise from too much idle thinking. Lacking external food, your greedy mind has turned in on itself and gnawed itself to the bone. You must *build it up again*, fatten it and, what is more, keep it from straying. Here is an example; you are greatly preoccupied with the injustices of this world, with socialism and politics. All right. Then start by reading *everyone* who has had the same ideals. Dig into the Utopians and the dry-as-dust dreamers. And next, before allowing yourself a definite opinion, you will have to study a new science, more discussed than studied— Political Economy, I mean. You will be amazed to find yourself changing your ideas like a shirt, every day. No matter. There will be nothing bitter about your scepticism. It will be like watching the human drama, with History seeming to pass across the stage for your eyes alone.

Superficial, limited creatures, rash, feather-brained souls, demand a conclusion from everything; they want to know the purpose of life and the dimensions of the infinite. Picking up a handful of sand in their poor, puny grasp, they say to the Ocean: "I shall now count the grains on your shores." But when the sand slips through their fingers and the sum proves long, they stamp and burst into tears. Do you know what we should do on that shore? Either kneel down or walk. You must walk.

No great genius has come to final conclusions; no great book ever does so, because humanity itself is forever on the march and can arrive at no goal. Homer comes to no conclusions, nor does Shakespeare, nor Goethe, nor even the Bible. That is why I am so deeply revolted by that fashionable term, the *Social Problem*. The day on which the answer is found will be this planet's last. Life is an eternal problem; so is history and everything else. Fresh figures are always being added to the sum. How can you count the spokes of a turning wheel? The nineteenth century is like a slave so proud of his newly-won freedom that he imagines it is he that has discovered the sun. It is said, for example, that the Reformation was the prelude to the French Revolution. That would be true enough if matters could rest there; but the Revolution itself was a prelude to a different state of things, and so on, and so on. Our most advanced ideas will look very silly and out of date when people come to look back on them. I will wager that in a bare fifty years, the terms, Social Problem, raising the morals of the masses, progress and democracy, will have passed into the realm of dead catch-words, and will seem as grotesque as Sensibility, nature, crotchets and sweet ties of affection, that were so fashionable towards the end of the eighteenth century.

I believe in the perpetual evolution of humanity and in its ever-changing forms, and consequently I abominate all those frames which men try to cram it into by main force, all the formulas by which they define it, and all the plans they devise for it. Democracy is no more man's last word than was slavery, or feudalism, or monarchy. No horizon perceived by human eyes is ever the shore, because beyond that horizon lies another, and so on for ever. Therefore it seems idiotic to me to seek the best religion or the best government. For me, the one on its deathbed is the best, since it is then making way for another.

I am rather cross with you for saying, in one of your earlier letters, that you are in favour of compulsory education for all. I loathe everything compulsory, all laws, governments and regulations. What is society, that it should force me to do anything at all? What God made it my master? See how it falls back into the old injustices of the past. It will no longer be a despot that oppresses the individual, but the masses, the public safety, the state that is always right, the universal catchword, Robespierre's maxim. I prefer the desert, and I shall return to the Bedouin who are free.

PAUL VALÉRY

Poetry, Language and Thought

The idea of Poetry is often contrasted with that of Thought, and particularly "Abstract Thought." People say "Poetry and Abstract Thought" as they say Good and Evil, Vice and Virtue, Hot and Cold. Most people, without thinking any further, believe that the analytical work of the intellect, the efforts of will and precision in which it implicates the mind, are incompatible with that freshness of inspiration, that flow of expression, that grace and fancy which are the signs of poetry and which reveal it at its very first words. If a poet's work is judged profound, its profundity seems to be of a quite different order from that of a philosopher or a scientist. Some people go so far as to think that even meditation on his art, the kind of exact reasoning applied to the cultivation of roses, can only harm a poet, since the principal and most charming object of his desire must be to communicate the impression of a newly and happily born state of creative emotion which, through surprise and pleasure, has the power to remove the poem once and for all from any further criticism.

This opinion may possibly contain a grain of truth, though its simplicity makes me suspect it to be of scholarly origin. I feel we have learned and adopted this antithesis without reflection, and that we now find it firmly fixed in our mind, as a verbal contrast, as though it represented a clear and real relationship between well-defined notions. It must be admitted that that character always in a hurry to have done, whom we call *our mind*, has a weakness for this kind of simplification, which freely enables him to form all kinds of combinations and judgments, to display his logic, and to develop his rhetorical resources—in short, to carry out as brilliantly as possible his business of being a mind.

At all events, this classic contrast, crystallized, as it were, by language, has always seemed to me too abrupt, and at the same time too facile, not to provoke me to examine the things themselves more closely. . . .

For my part I have the strange and dangerous habit, in every subject, of wanting to begin at the beginning (that is, at my *own* beginning), which entails beginning again, going back over the whole road, just as though many others had not already mapped and traveled it. . . .

This is the road offered to us, or imposed on us, by *language*.

From "Poetry and Abstract Thought" [1938], in *The Art of Poetry*, translated from the French by Denise Folliot, *Collected Works*, ed. Jackson Matthews, Bollingen Series, Vol. VII, New York, 1958, pp. 52-3, 53-4, 56, 57-60, 63-6, 67-70, 70-74, 75-81; reprinted by permission of the Bollingen Foundation and Routledge & Kegan Paul Ltd.

With every question, before making any deep examination of the content, I take a look at the language; I generally proceed like a surgeon who sterilizes his hands and prepares the area to be operated on. This is what I call *cleaning up the verbal situation*. You must excuse this expression equating the words and forms of speech with the hands and instruments of a surgeon. . . .

I shall . . . take care not to accept what the words *Poetry* and *Abstract Thought* suggest to me the moment they are pronounced. But I shall look into myself. There I shall seek my real difficulties and my actual observations of my real states; there I shall find my own sense of the rational and the irrational; I shall see whether the alleged antithesis exists and how it exists in a living condition. . . .

I have, then, noticed in myself certain states which I may well call *poetic*, since some of them were finally realized in poems. They came about from no apparent cause, arising from some accident or other; they developed according to their own nature, and consequently I found myself for a time jolted out of my habitual state of mind. Then, the cycle completed, I returned to the rule of ordinary exchanges between my life and my thought. But meanwhile *a poem had been made*, and in completing itself the cycle left something behind. This closed cycle is the cycle of an act which has, as it were, aroused and given external form to a poetic power. . . .

On other occasions I have noticed that some no less insignificant incident caused—or seemed to cause—a quite different excursion, a digression of another nature and with another result. For example, a sudden concatenation of ideas, an analogy, would strike me in much the way the sound of a horn in the heart of a forest makes one prick up one's ears, and virtually directs the co-ordinated attention of all one's muscles toward some point in the distance, among the leafy depths. But this time, instead of a poem, it was an analysis of the sudden intellectual sensation that was taking hold of me. It was not verses that were being formed more or less easily during this phase, but some proposition or other that was destined to be incorporated among my habits of thought, some formula that would henceforward serve as an instrument for further researches. . . .

I apologize for thus revealing myself to you; but in my opinion it is more useful to speak of what one has experienced than to pretend to a knowledge that is entirely impersonal, an observation with no observer. In fact there is no theory that is not a fragment, carefully prepared, of some autobiography.

I do not pretend to be teaching you anything at all. I will say nothing you do not already know; but I will, perhaps, say it in a different order. You do not need to be told that a poet is not always incapable of solving a *rule of three*; or that a logician is not always incapable of seeing in words something other than concepts, categories, and mere pretexts for syllogisms.

On this point I would add this paradoxical remark: if the logician could never be other than a logician, he would not, and could not, be a logician; and if the poet were never anything but a poet, without the slightest hope of being able to reason abstractly, he would leave no poetic traces behind him. I believe in all sincerity that if each man were not able to live a number of other lives besides his own, he would not be able to live his own life.

My experience has thus shown me that the same *self* can take very different forms, can become an abstract thinker or a poet, by successive specializations, each of which is a deviation from that entirely unattached state which is super-ficially in accord with exterior surroundings and which is the average state of our existence, the state of undifferentiated exchanges.

Let us first see in what may consist that initial and *invariably accidental* shock which will construct the poetic instrument within us, and above all, what are its effects. The problem can be put in this way: Poetry is an art of Language; cer-tain combinations of words can produce an emotion that others do not produce, and which we shall call *poetic*. What kind of emotion is this?

I recognize it in myself by this: that all possible objects of the ordinary world, external or internal, beings, events, feelings, and actions, while keeping their usual appearance, are suddenly placed in an indefinable but wonderfully fitting relationship with the modes of our general sensibility. That is to say that these well-known things and beings—or rather the ideas that represent them—somehow change in value. They attract one another, they are connected in ways quite different from the ordinary; they become (if you will permit the expression) *musicalized, resonant,* and, as it were, harmonically related. The poetic universe, thus defined, offers extensive analogies with what we can postulate of the dream world.

Since the word *dream* has found its way into this talk, I shall say in passing that in modern times, beginning with Romanticism, there has arisen a fairly understandable confusion between the notion of the dream and that of poetry. Neither the dream nor the daydream is necessarily poetic; it may be so: but fig-ures formed *by chance* are only *by chance* harmonious figures.

In any case, our memories of dreams teach us, by frequent and common ex-perience, that our consciousness can be invaded, filled, entirely absorbed by the production of an *existence* in which objects and beings seem the same as those in the waking state; but their meanings, relationships, modes of variation and of substitution are quite different and doubtless represent, like symbols or alle-gories, the immediate fluctuations of our *general* sensibility uncontrolled by the sensitivities of our *specialized* senses. In very much the same way the *poetic state* takes hold of us, develops, and finally disintegrates.

This is to say that the *state of poetry* is completely irregular, inconstant, in-voluntary, and fragile, and that we lose it, as we find it, *by accident*. But this state is not enough to make a poet, any more than it is enough to see a treasure in a dream to find it, on waking, sparkling at the foot of one's bed.

A poet's function—do not be startled by this remark—is not to experience the poetic state: that is a private affair. His function is to create it in others. The poet is recognized—or at least everyone recognizes his own poet—by the simple fact that he causes his reader to become "inspired." Positively speaking, inspiration is a graceful attribute with which the reader endows his poet: the reader sees in us the transcendent merits of virtues and graces that develop in him. He seeks and finds in us the wondrous cause of his own wonder.

But poetic feeling and the artificial synthesis of this state in some work are two quite distinct things, as different as sensation and action. A sustained action is much more complex than any spontaneous production, particularly when it has to be carried out in a sphere as conventional as that of language. Here you see emerging through my explanations the famous ABSTRACT THOUGHT which cus-tom opposes to POETRY. . . .

The great painter Degas often repeated to me a very true and simple remark by Mallarmé. Degas occasionally wrote verses, and some of those he left were delightful. But he often found great difficulty in this work accessory to his painting. (He was, by the way, the kind of man who would bring all possible difficulty to any art whatever.) One day he said to Mallarmé: "Yours is a hellish craft. I can't manage to say what I want, and yet I'm full of ideas. . . ." And Mallarmé answered: "My dear Degas, one does not make poetry with ideas, but with *words*."

Mallarmé was right. But when Degas spoke of ideas, he was, after all, thinking of inner speech or of images, which might have been expressed in *words*. But these words, these secret phrases which he called ideas, all these intentions and perceptions of the mind, do not make verses. There is something else, then, a modification, or a transformation, sudden or not, spontaneous or not, laborious or not, which must necessarily intervene between the thought that produces ideas—that activity and multiplicity of inner questions and solutions—and, on the other hand, that discourse, so different from ordinary speech, which is verse, which is so curiously ordered, which answers no need *unless it be the need it must itself create*, which never speaks but of absent things or of things profoundly and secretly felt: strange discourse, as though made by someone *other* than the speaker and addressed to someone *other* than the listener. In short, it is a *language within a language.*

Let us look into these mysteries.

Poetry is an art of language. But language is a practical creation. It may be observed that in all communication between men, certainty comes only from practical acts and from the verification which practical acts give us. *I ask you for a light, You give me a light:* you have understood me.

But in asking me for a light, you were able to speak those few unimportant words with a certain intonation, a certain tone of voice, a certain inflection, a certain languor or briskness perceptible to me. I have understood your words, since without even thinking I handed you what you asked for—a light. But the matter does not end there. The strange thing: the sound and as it were the features of your little sentence come back to me, echo within me, as though they were pleased to be there; I, too, like to hear myself repeat this little phrase, which has almost lost its meaning, which has stopped being of use, and which can yet go on living, though with quite another life. It has acquired a value; and has acquired it *at the expense of its finite significance.* It has created the need to be heard again. . . . Here we are on the very threshold of the poetic state. This tiny experience will help us to the discovery of more than one truth.

It has shown us that language can produce effects of two quite different kinds. One of them tends to bring about the complete negation of language itself. I speak to you, and if you have understood my words, those very words are abolished. If you have understood, it means that the words have vanished from your minds and are replaced by their counterpart, by images, relationships, impulses; so that you have within you the means to retransmit these ideas and images in a language that may be very different from the one you received. *Understanding* consists in the more or less rapid replacement of a system of sounds, intervals, and signs by something quite different, which is, in short, a modification or interior reorganization of the person to whom one is speaking. And here is the counterproof of this proposition: the person who does not understand *repeats* the words, or *has them repeated* to him.

Consequently, the perfection of a discourse whose sole aim is comprehension obviously consists in the ease with which the words forming it are transformed into something quite different: the *language* is transformed first into *non-language* and then, if we wish, into a form of language differing from the original form.

In other terms, in practical or abstract uses of language, the form—that is the physical, the concrete part, the very act of speech—does not last; it does not out-live understanding; it dissolves in the light; it has acted; it has done its work; it has brought about understanding; it has lived.

But on the other hand, the moment this concrete form takes on, by an effect of its own, such importance that it asserts itself and makes itself, as it were, respected; and not only remarked and respected, but desired and therefore re-peated—then something new happens: we are insensibly transformed and ready to live, breathe, and think in accordance with a rule and under laws which are no longer of the practical order—that is, nothing that may occur in this state will be resolved, finished, or abolished by a specific act. We are entering the poetic universe.

Permit me to support this notion of a *poetic universe* by referring to a similar notion that, being much simpler, is easier to explain: the notion of a *musical universe*. I would ask you to make a small sacrifice: limit yourselves for a moment to your faculty of hearing. One simple sense, like that of hearing, will offer us all we need for our definition and will absolve us from entering into all the diffi-culties and subtleties to which the conventional structure and historical com-plexities of ordinary language would lead us. We live by ear in the world of noises. Taken as a whole, it is generally incoherent and irregularly supplied by all the mechanical incidents which the ear may interpret as it can. But the same ear isolates from this chaos a group of noises particularly remarkable and simple—that is, easily recognizable by our sense of hearing and furnishing it with points of reference. These elements have relations with one another which we sense as we do the elements themselves. The interval between two of these privileged noises is as clear to us as each of them. These are the *sounds*, and these units of sonority tend to form clear combinations, successive or simultaneous implications, series, and intersections which one may term *intelligible*: this is why abstract pos-sibilities exist in music. But I must return to my subject.

I will confine myself to saying that the contrast between noise and sound is the contrast between pure and impure, order and disorder; that this differentiation between pure sensations and others has permitted the constitution of music; that it has been possible to control, unify, and codify this constitution, thanks to the intervention of physical science, which knows how to adjust measure to sensation so as to obtain the important result of teaching us to produce this sonorous sen-sation consistently, and in a continuous and identical fashion, by instruments that are, in reality, *measuring instruments*. . . .

The poetic universe is not created so powerfully or so easily. It exists, but the poet is deprived of the immense advantages possessed by the musician. He does not have before him, ready for the uses of beauty, a body of resources expressly made for his art. He has to borrow *language*—the voice of the public, that collection of traditional and irrational terms and rules, oddly created and transformed, oddly codified, and very variedly understood and pronounced. Here there is no physicist who has determined the relations between these elements; no tuning forks, no metronomes, no inventors of scales or theoreticians of harmony. Rather, on the contrary, the phonetic and semantic fluctuations of vocabulary. Nothing pure; but a mixture of completely incoherent auditive and psychic stimuli. Each word is an instantaneous coupling of a *sound* and a *sense* that have no connection with each other. Each sentence is an act so complex that I doubt whether anyone has yet been able to provide a tolerable definition of it. As for the use of the resources of language and the modes of this action, you know what diversity there is, and what confusion sometimes results. A discourse can be logical, packed with sense, but devoid of rhythm and measure. It can be pleasing to the ear, yet completely absurd or insignificant; it can be clear, yet useless; vague, yet delightful. But to grasp its strange multiplicity, which is no more than the multiplicity of life itself, it suffices to name all the sciences which have been created to deal with this diversity, each to study one of its aspects. One can analyze a text in many different ways, for it falls successively under the jurisdiction of phonetics, semantics, syntax, logic, rhetoric, philology, not to mention metrics, prosody, and etymology. . . .

So the poet is at grips with this verbal matter, obliged to speculate on sound and sense at once, and to satisfy not only harmony and musical timing but all the various intellectual and aesthetic conditions, not to mention the conventional rules. . . .

You can see what an effort the poet's undertaking would require if he had *consciously* to solve all these problems. . . .

It is always interesting to try to reconstruct one of our complex activities, one of those complete actions which demand a specialization at once mental, sensuous, and motor, supposing that in order to accomplish this act we were obliged to understand and organize all the functions that we know play their part in it. Even if this attempt, at once imaginative and analytical, is clumsy, it will always teach us something. As for myself, who am, I admit, much more attentive to the formation or fabrication of works than to the works themselves, I have a habit, or obsession, of appreciating works only as actions. In my eyes a poet is a man who, as a result of a certain incident, undergoes a hidden transformation. He leaves his ordinary condition of general disposability, and I see taking shape in him an agent, a living system for producing verses. As among animals one suddenly sees emerging a capable hunter, a nest maker, a bridge builder, a digger of tunnels and galleries, so in a man one sees a composite organization declare itself, bending its functions to a specific piece of work. Think of a very small child: the child we have all been bore many possibilities within him. After a few months of life he has learned, at the same or almost the same time, to speak and to walk. He has acquired two types of action. That is to say that he now possesses two kinds of potentiality from which the accidental circumstances of each moment will draw what they can, in answer to his varying needs and imaginings.

Having learned to use his legs, he will discover that he can not only walk, but run; and not only walk and run, but dance. This is a great event. He has at that moment both invented and discovered a kind of *secondary use* for his limbs, a generalization of his formula of movement. In fact, whereas walking is after all a rather dull and not easily perfectible action, this new form of action, the Dance, admits of an infinite number of creations and variations or *figures*.

But will he not find an analogous development in speech? He will explore the possibilities of his faculty of speech; he will discover that more can be done with it than to ask for jam and deny his little sins. He will grasp the power of reasoning; he will invent stories to amuse himself when he is alone; he will repeat to himself words that he loves for their strangeness and mystery.

So, parallel with *Walking* and *Dancing*, he will acquire and distinguish the divergent types, *Prose and Poetry*. . . .

Walking, like prose, has a definite aim. It is an act directed at something we wish to reach. Actual circumstances, such as the need for some object, the impulse of my desire, the state of my body, my sight, the terrain, etc., which order the manner of walking, prescribe its direction and its speed, and give it a *definite end*. All the characteristics of walking derive from these instantaneous conditions, which combine *in a novel way* each time. There are no movements in walking that are not special adaptations, but, each time, they are abolished and, as it were, absorbed by the accomplishment of the act, by the attainment of the goal.

The dance is quite another matter. It is, of course, a system of actions; but of actions whose end is in themselves. It goes nowhere. If it pursues an object, it is only an ideal object, a state, an enchantment, the phantom of a flower, an extreme of life, a smile—which forms at last on the face of the one who summoned it from empty space.

It is therefore not a question of carrying out a limited operation whose end is situated somewhere in our surroundings, but rather of creating, maintaining, and exalting a certain *state*, by a periodic movement that can be executed on the spot; a movement which is almost entirely dissociated from sight, but which is stimulated and regulated by auditive rhythms.

But please note this very simple observation, that however different the dance may be from walking and utilitarian movements, it uses the same organs, the same bones, the same muscles, only differently co-ordinated and aroused.

Here we come again to the contrast between prose and poetry. Prose and poetry use the same words, the same syntax, the same forms, and the same sounds or tones, but differently co-ordinated and differently aroused. Prose and poetry are therefore distinguished by the difference between certain links and associations which form and dissolve in our psychic and nervous organism, whereas the components of these modes of functioning are identical. This is why one should guard against reasoning about poetry as one does about prose. What is true of one very often has no meaning when it is sought in the other. But here is the great and decisive difference. When the man who is walking has reached his goal —as I said—when he has reached the place, book, fruit, the object of his desire (which desire drew him from his repose), this possession at once entirely annuls his whole act; the effect swallows up the cause, the end absorbs the means; and, whatever the act, only the result remains. It is the same with utilitarian language: the language I use to express my design, my desire, my command, my opinion; this language, when it has served its purpose, evaporates almost as it is heard. I have given it forth to perish, to be radically transformed into something else in your mind; and I shall know that I was *understood* by the remarkable fact that my speech no longer exists: it has been completely replaced by its *meaning*—that is, by images, impulses, reactions, or acts that belong to you: in short, by an interior modification in you.

As a result the perfection of this kind of language, whose sole end is to be understood, obviously consists in the ease with which it is transformed into something altogether different.

The poem, on the other hand, does not die for having lived: it is expressly designed to be born again from its ashes and to become endlessly what it has just been. Poetry can be recognized by this property, that it tends to get itself reproduced in its own form: it stimulates us to reconstruct it identically.

That is an admirable and uniquely characteristic property.

I should like to give you a simple illustration. Think of a pendulum oscillating between two symmetrical points. Suppose that one of these extremes represents *form*: the concrete characteristics of the language, sound, rhythm, accent, tone, movement—in a word, the Voice in action. Then associate with the other point, the acnode of the first, all significant values, images and ideas, stimuli of feeling, and memory, virtual impulses and structures of understanding—in short, everything that makes the *content*, the meaning of a discourse. Now observe the effect of poetry on yourself. You will find that at each line the meaning produced within you, far from destroying the musical form communicated to you, recalls it. The living pendulum that has swung from *sound* to *sense* swings back to its felt point of departure, as though the very sense which is present to your mind can find no other outlet or expression, no other answer, than the very music which gave it birth.

So between the form and the content, between the sound and the sense, between the poem and the state of poetry, a symmetry is revealed, an equality between importance, value, and power, which does not exist in prose; which is contrary to the law of prose—the law which ordains the inequality of the two constituents of language. The essential principal of the mechanics of poetry—that is, of the conditions for producing the poetic state by words—seems to me to be this harmonious exchange between expression and impression.

I introduce here a slight observation which I shall call "philosophical," meaning simply that we could do without it.

Our poetic pendulum travels from our sensation toward some idea or some sentiment, and returns toward some memory of the sensation and toward the potential act which could reproduce the sensation. Now, whatever is sensation is essentially *present*. There is no other definition of the present except sensation itself, which includes, perhaps, the impulse to action that would modify that sensation. On the other hand, whatever is properly thought, image, sentiment, is always, in some way, a production of absent things. Memory is the substance of all thought. Anticipation and its gropings, desire, planning, the projection of our hopes, of our fears, are the main interior activity of our being.

Thought is, in short, the activity which causes what does not exist to come alive in us, lending to it, whether we will or no, our present powers, making us take the part for the whole, the image for reality, and giving us the illusion of seeing, acting, suffering, and possessing independently of our dear old body, which we leave with its cigarette in an armchair until we suddenly retrieve it when the telephone rings or, no less strangely, when our stomach demands provender. . . .

Between Voice and Thought, between Thought and Voice, between Presence and Absence, oscillates the poetic pendulum.

The result of this analysis is to show that the value of a poem resides in the indissolubility of sound and sense. Now this is a condition that seems to demand the impossible. There is no relation between the sound and the meaning of a word. The same thing is called HORSE in English, HIPPOS in Greek, EQUUS in Latin, and CHEVAL in French; but no manipulation of any of these terms will give me an idea of the animal in question; and no manipulation of the idea will yield me any of these words—otherwise, we should easily know all languages, beginning with our own.

Yet it is the poet's business to give us the feeling of an intimate union between the word and the mind. . . . The state in which the inseparability of sound and sense, in which the desire, the expectation, the possibility of their intimate and indissoluble fusion are required and sought or given, and sometimes anxiously awaited, is a comparatively rare state. It is rare, firstly because all the exigencies of life are against it; secondly because it is opposed to the crude simplifying and specializing of verbal notations.

But this state of inner modification, in which all the properties of our language are indistinctly but harmoniously summoned, is not enough to produce that complete object, that compound of beauties, that collection of happy chances for the mind which a noble poem offers us.

From this state we obtain only fragments. All the precious things that are found in the earth, gold, diamonds, uncut stones, are there scattered, strewn, grudgingly hidden in a quantity of rock or sand, where chance may sometimes uncover them. These riches would be nothing without the human labor that draws them from the massive night where they were sleeping, assembles them, alters and organizes them into ornaments. These fragments of metal embedded in formless matter, these oddly shaped crystals, must owe all their luster to intelligent labor. It is a labor of this kind that the true poet accomplishes. Faced with a beautiful poem, one can indeed feel that it is most unlikely that any man, however gifted, could have improvised without a backward glance, with no other effort than that of writing or dictating, such a simultaneous and complete system of lucky finds. Since the traces of effort, the second thoughts, the changes, the amount of time, the bad days, and the distaste have now vanished, effaced by the supreme return of a mind over its work, some people, seeing only the perfection of the result, will look on it as due to a sort of magic that they call INSPIRATION. They thus make of the poet a kind of temporary *medium*. If one were strictly to develop this doctrine of pure inspiration, one would arrive at some very strange results. For example, one would conclude that the poet, since he merely transmits what he receives, merely delivers to unknown people what he has taken from the unknown, has no need to understand what he writes, which is dictated by a mysterious voice. He could write poems in a language he did not know. . . .

In fact, the poet has indeed a kind of spiritual energy of a special nature: it is manifested in him and reveals him to himself in certain moments of infinite worth. Infinite for him. . . . I say, *infinite for him*, for, alas, experience shows us that these moments which seem to us to have a universal value are sometimes without a future, and in the end make us ponder on this maxim: *what is of value for one person only has no value*. This is the iron law of Literature.

But every true poet is necessarily a first-rate critic. If one doubts this, one can have no idea of what the work of the mind is: that struggle with the inequality of moments, with chance associations, lapses of attention, external distractions. The mind is terribly variable, deceptive and self-deceiving, fertile in insoluble problems and illusory solutions. How could a remarkable work emerge from this chaos if this chaos that contains everything did not also contain some serious chances to know oneself and to choose within oneself whatever is worth taking from each moment and using carefully?

That is not all. Every true poet is much more capable than is generally known of right reasoning and abstract thought.

But one must not look for his real philosophy in his more or less philosophical utterances. In my opinion, the most authentic philosophy lies not so much in the objects of our reflection as in the very act of thought and in its handling. Take from metaphysics all its pet or special terms, all its traditional vocabulary, and you may realize that you have not impoverished the thought. Indeed, you may perhaps have eased and freshened it, and you will have got rid of other people's problems, so as to deal only with your own difficulties, your surprises that owe nothing to anyone, and whose intellectual spur you feel actually and directly.

It has often happened, however, as literary history tells us, that poetry has been made to enunciate theses or hypotheses and that the *complete* language which is its own—the language whose *form*, that is to say the action and sensation of the Voice, is of the same power as the *content*, that is to say the eventual modification of a *mind*—has been used to communicate "abstract" ideas, which are on the contrary independent of their form, or so we believe. Some very great poets have occasionally attempted this. But whatever may be the talent which exerts itself in this very noble undertaking, it cannot prevent the attention given to following the ideas from competing with the attention that follows the song. The DE RERUM NATURA is here in conflict with the nature of things. The state of mind of the reader of poems is not the state of mind of the reader of pure thought. The state of mind of a man dancing is not that of a man advancing through difficult country of which he is making a topographical survey or a geological prospectus.

I have said, nevertheless, that the poet has his abstract thought and, if you like, his philosophy; and I have said that it is at work in his very activity as a poet. I said this because I have observed it, in myself and in several others. Here, as elsewhere, I have no other reference, no other claim or excuse, than recourse to my own experience or to the most common observation.

Well, every time I have worked as a poet, I have noticed that my work exacted of me not only that presence of the poetic universe I have spoken of, but many reflections, decisions, choices, and combinations, without which all possible gifts of the Muses, or of Chance, would have remained like precious materials in a workshop without an architect. Now an architect is not himself necessarily built of precious materials. In so far as he is an architect of poems, a poet is quite different from what he is as a producer of those precious elements of which all poetry should be composed, but whose composition is separate and requires an entirely different mental effort.

One day someone told me that lyricism is enthusiasm, and that the odes of the great lyricists were written at a single stroke, at the speed of the voice of delirium, and with the wind of inspiration blowing a gale. . . .

I replied that he was quite right; but that this was not a privilege of poetry alone, and that everyone knew that in building a locomotive it is indispensable for the builder to work at eighty miles an hour in order to do his job.

A poem is really a kind of machine for producing the poetic state of mind by means of words. The effect of this machine is uncertain, for nothing is certain about action on other minds. But whatever may be the result, in its uncertainty, the construction of the machine demands the solution of many problems. If the term *machine* shocks you, if my mechanical comparison seems crude, please notice that while the composition of even a very short poem may absorb years, the action of the poem on the reader will take only a few minutes. In a few minutes the reader will receive his shock from discoveries, connections, glimmers of expression that have been accumulated during months of research, waiting, patience, and impatience. He may attribute much more to inspiration than it can give. He will imagine the kind of person it would take to create, without pause, hesitation, or revision, this powerful and perfect work which transports him into a world where things and people, passions and thoughts, sonorities and meanings proceed from the same energy, are transformed one into another, and correspond according to exceptional laws of harmony, for it can only be an exceptional form of stimulus that simultaneously produces the exaltation of our sensibility, our intellect, our memory, and our powers of verbal action, so rarely granted to us in the ordinary course of life.

Perhaps I should remark here that the execution of a poetic work—if one considers it as the engineer just mentioned would consider the conception and construction of his locomotive, that is, making explicit the problems to be solved—would appear impossible. In no other art is the number of conditions and independent functions to be co-ordinated so large. I will not inflict on you a detailed demonstration of this proposition. It is enough for me to remind you of what I said regarding sound and sense, which are linked only by pure convention, but which must be made to collaborate as effectively as possible. From their double nature words often make me think of those complex quantities which geometricians take such pleasure in manipulating.

Fortunately, some strange virtue resides in certain moments in certain people's lives which simplifies things and reduces the insurmountable difficulties I spoke of to the scale of human energies.

The poet awakes within man at an unexpected event, an outward or inward incident: a tree, a face, a "subject," an emotion, a word. Sometimes it is the will to expression that starts the game, a need to translate what one feels; another time, on the contrary, it is an element of form, the outline of an expression which seeks its origin, seeks a meaning within the space of my mind. . . . Note this possible duality in ways of getting started: either something wants to express itself, or some means of expression wants to be used.

My poem *Le Cimetière marin* began in me by a rhythm, that of a French line . . . of ten syllables, divided into four and six. I had as yet no idea with which to

fill out this form. Gradually a few hovering words settled in it, little by little determining the subject, and my labor (a very long labor) was before me. Another
poem, *La Pythie*, first appeared as an eight-syllable line whose sound came of its
own accord. But this line implied a sentence, of which it was part, and this sentence, if it existed, implied many other sentences. A problem of this kind has an
infinite number of solutions. But with poetry the musical and metrical conditions
greatly restrict the indefiniteness. Here is what happened: my fragment acted
like a living fragment, since, plunged in the (no doubt nourishing) surroundings
of my desire and waiting thought, it proliferated, and engendered all that was
lacking: several lines before and a great many lines after.

I apologize for having chosen my examples from my own little story: but I
could hardly have taken them elsewhere.

Perhaps you think my conception of the poet and the poem rather singular.
Try to imagine, however, what the least of our acts implies. Think of everything
that must go on inside a man who utters the smallest intelligible sentence, and
then calculate all that is needed for a poem by Keats or Baudelaire to be formed
on an empty page in front of the poet.

Think, too, that of all the arts, ours is perhaps that which co-ordinates the
greatest number of independent parts or factors: sound, sense, the real and the
imaginary, logic, syntax, and the double invention of content and form . . .
and all this by means of a medium essentially practical, perpetually changing,
soiled, a maid of all work, *everyday language*, from which we must draw a pure,
ideal Voice, capable of communicating without weakness, without apparent effort, without offense to the ear, and without breaking the ephemeral sphere of
the poetic universe, an idea of some *self* miraculously superior to Myself.

I. A. RICHARDS
Pseudo-Statements

The business of the poet, as we have seen, is to give order and coherence, and so
freedom, to a body of experience. To do so through words which act as its skeleton, as a structure by which the impulses which make up the experience are adjusted to one another and act together. The means by which words do this are
many and varied. To work them out is a problem for linguistic psychology, that
embarrassed young heir to philosophy. What little can be done shows already
that most critical dogmas of the past are either false or nonsense. A little knowledge is not here a danger, but clears the air in a remarkable way.

Roughly and inadequately, even in the light of present knowledge, we can say
that words work in the poem in two main fashions. As sensory stimuli and as (in
the *widest* sense) symbols. We must refrain from considering the sensory side of
the poem, remarking only that it is *not* in the least independent of the other
side, and that it has for definite reasons prior importance in most poetry. We

From "Poetry and Beliefs," *Science and Poetry* [1926], New York and London, 1935 (2nd
edition), pp. 61-74, 92-4; reprinted by permission of the author, and executors of C. K.
Ogden.

must confine ourselves to the other function of words in the poem, or rather, omitting much that is of secondary relevance, to one form of that function, let me call it *pseudo-statement*.

It will be admitted—by those who distinguish between scientific statement, where truth is ultimately a matter of verification as this is understood in the laboratory, and emotive utterance, where "truth" is primarily acceptability *by* some attitude, and more remotely is the acceptability *of* this attitude itself—that it is *not* the poet's business to make scientific statements. Yet poetry has constantly the air of making statements, and important ones; which is one reason why some mathematicians cannot read it. They find the alleged statements to be *false*. It will be agreed that their approach to poetry and their expectations from it are mistaken. But what exactly is the other, the right, the poetic, approach and how does it differ from the mathematical?

The poetic approach evidently limits the framework of possible consequences into which the pseudo-statement is taken. For the scientific approach this framework is unlimited. Any and every consequence is relevant. If any of the consequences of a statement conflicts with acknowledged fact then so much the worse for the statement. Not so with the pseudo-statement when poetically approached. The problem is—just how does the limitation work? One tempting account is in terms of a supposed universe of discourse, a world of make-believe, of imagination, of recognised fictions common to the poet and his readers. A pseudo-statement which fits into this system of assumptions would be regarded as "poetically true"; one which does not, as "poetically false." This attempt to treat "poetic truth" on the model of general "coherence theories" is very natural for certain schools of logicians but is inadequate, on the wrong lines from the outset. To mention two objections, out of many; there is no means of discovering what the "universe of discourse" is on any occasion, and the kind of coherence which must hold within it, supposing it to be discoverable, is not an affair of logical relations. Attempt to define the system of propositions into which

O Rose, thou art sick!

must fit, and the logical relations which must hold between them if it is to be "poetically true"; the absurdity of the theory becomes evident.

We must look further. In the poetic approach the relevant consequences are not logical or to be arrived at by a partial relaxation of logic. Except occasionally and by accident logic does not enter at all. They are the consequences which arise through our emotional organisation. The acceptance which a pseudo-statement receives is entirely governed by its effects upon our feelings and attitudes. Logic only comes in, if at all, in subordination, as a servant to our emotional response. It is an unruly servant, however, as poets and readers are constantly discovering. A pseudo-statement is "true" if it suits and serves some attitude or links together attitudes which on other grounds are desirable. This kind of "truth" is so opposed to scientific "truth" that it is a pity to use so similar a word, but at the present it is difficult to avoid the malpractice.[1]

This brief analysis may be sufficient to indicate the fundamental disparity and

[1] A pseudo-statement, as I use the term, is not necessarily false in any sense. It is merely a form of words whose scientific truth or falsity is irrelevant to the purpose at hand.

"Logic" in this paragraph is, of course, being used in a limited and conventional, or popular sense.

opposition between pseudo-statements as they occur in poetry and statements as they occur in science. A pseudo-statement is a form of words which is justified entirely by its effect in releasing or organising our impulses and attitudes (due regard being had for the better or worse organisations of these *inter se*); a statement, on the other hand, is justified by its truth, *i.e.*, its correspondence, in a highly technical sense, with the fact to which it points.

Statements true and false alike do, of course, constantly touch off attitudes and action. Our daily practical existence is largely guided by them. On the whole true statements are of more service to us than false ones. None the less we do not and, at present, cannot order our emotions and attitudes by true statements alone. Nor is there any probability that we ever shall contrive to do so. This is one of the great new dangers to which civilisation is exposed. Countless pseudo-statements—about God, about the universe, about human nature, the relations of mind to mind, about the soul, its rank and destiny—pseudo-statements which are pivotal points in the organisation of the mind, vital to its well-being, have suddenly become, for sincere, honest and informal minds, impossible to believe as for centuries they have been believed.[2] The accustomed incidences of the modes of believing are changed irrecoverably; and the knowledge which has displaced them is not of a kind upon which an equally fine organisation of the mind can be based.

This is the contemporary situation. The remedy, since there is no prospect of our gaining adequate knowledge, and since indeed it is fairly clear that genuine knowledge cannot meet this need, is to cut our pseudo-statements free from that kind of belief which is appropriate to verified statements. So released they will be changed, of course, but they can still be the main instruments by which we order our attitudes to one another and to the world. This is not a desperate remedy, for, as poetry conclusively shows, even the most important among our attitudes can be aroused and maintained without any believing of a factual or verifiable order entering in at all. We need no such beliefs, and indeed we must have none, if we are to read *King Lear*. Pseudo-statements to which we attach no belief and statements proper, such as science provides, cannot conflict. It is only when we introduce inappropriate kinds of believing into poetry that danger arises. To do so is from this point of view a profanation of poetry.

Yet an important branch of criticism which has attracted the best talents from prehistoric times until to-day consists of the endeavour to persuade men that the functions of science and poetry are identical, or that the one is a "higher form" of the other, or that they conflict and we must choose between them.

The root of this persistent endeavour has still to be mentioned; it is the same as that from which the Magical View of the world arose. If we give to a pseudo-statement the kind of unqualified acceptance which belongs by right only to certified scientific statements—and those judgments of the routine of perception

---

2 For the mind I am considering here, the question "Do I believe x?" is no longer the same. Not only the "What" that is to be believed but the "How" of the believing has changed—through the segregation of science and its clarification of the techniques of proof. This is the danger; and the remedy suggested is a further differentiation of the "Hows." To these differences correspond differences in the sense of "is so" and "being" where, as is commonly the case, "is so" and "being" assert believings. As we admit this, the world that "is" divides into worlds commensurable in respect of so-called "degrees of reality." Yet, and this is all-important, these worlds have an order, with regard to one another, which is the order of the mind; and interference between them imperils sanity.

and action from which science derives—, if we can contrive to do this, the impulses and attitudes with which we respond to it gain a notable stability and vigour. Briefly, if we can contrive to believe poetry, then the world *seems*, while we do so, to be transfigured. It used to be comparatively easy to do this, and the habit has become well established. With the extension of science and the neutralisation of nature it has become difficult as well as dangerous. Yet it is still alluring; it has many analogies with drug-taking. Hence the endeavours of the critics referred to. Various subterfuges have been devised along the lines of regarding Poetic Truth as figurative, symbolic; or as more immediate, as a truth of Intuition transcending human knowledge; or as a higher form of the same truth as reason yields. Such attempts to use poetry as a denial or as a corrective of science are very common. One point can be made against them all: they are never worked out in detail. There is no equivalent of Mill's *Logic* expounding any of them. The language in which they are framed is usually a blend of obsolete psychology and emotive exclamations.

The long-established and much-encouraged habit of giving to emotive utterances—whether pseudo-statements simple, or looser and larger wholes taken as saying something figuratively—the kind of assent which we give to unescapable facts, has for most people debilitated a wide range of their responses. A few scientists, caught young and brought up in the laboratory, are free from it; but then, as a rule, they pay no *serious* attention to poetry. For most men the recognition of the neutrality of nature brings about—through this habit—a divorce from poetry. They are so used to having their responses propped up by beliefs, however vague, that when those shadowy supports are removed they are no longer able to respond. Their attitudes to so many things have been forced in the past, overencouraged. And when the world-picture ceases to assist there is a collapse. Over whole tracts of natural emotional response we are to-day like a bed of dahlias whose sticks have been removed. And this effect of the neutralisation of nature is only in its beginnings. However, human nature has a prodigious resilience. Love poetry seems able to out-play psychoanalysis.

A sense of desolation, of uncertainty, of futility, of the groundlessness of aspirations, of the vanity of endeavour, and a thirst for a life-giving water which seems suddenly to have failed, are the signs in consciousness of this necessary reorganisation of our lives.[3] Our attitudes and impulses are being compelled to be-

[3] My debt to *The Waste Land* here will be evident. The original footnote seems to have puzzled Mr. Eliot and some other readers. Well it might! In saying, though, that he "had effected a complete severance between his poetry and all beliefs" I was referring not to the poet's own history, but to the technical detachment of the poetry. And the way in which he then seemed to me to have "realized what might otherwise have remained a speculative possibility" was by finding a new order through the contemplation and exhibition of disorder.

"Yes! Very funny this terrible thing is. A man that is born falls into a dream like a man falls into the sea. If he tries to climb out into the air as inexperienced people endeavour to do, he drowns—*nicht wahr?* . . . No! I tell you! The way is to the destructive element submit yourself, and with the exertions of your hands and feet in the water make the deep, deep, sea keep you up. So if you ask me how to be? In the destructive element immerse . . . that was the way." *Lord Jim*, p. 216. Mr. Eliot's later verse has sometimes shown still less "dread of the unknown depths." That, at least, seems in part to explain to me why *Ash Wednesday* is better poetry than even the best sections of *The Waste Land*.

come self-supporting; they are being driven back upon their biological justification, made once again sufficient to themselves. And the only impulses which
seem strong enough to continue unflagging are commonly so crude that, to more
finely developed individuals, they hardly seem worth having. Such people cannot
live by warmth, food, fighting, drink, and sex alone. Those who are least affected
by the change are those who are emotionally least removed from the animals. As
we shall see at the close of this essay, even a considerable poet may attempt to
find relief by a reversion to primitive mentality.

It is important to diagnose the disease correctly and to put the blame in the
right quarter. Usually it is some alleged "materialism" of science which is denounced. This mistake is due partly to clumsy thinking, but chiefly to relics of
the Magical View. For even if the Universe were "spiritual" all through (whatever that assertion might mean; all such assertions are probably nonsense), that
would not make it any more accordant to human attitudes. It is not what the
universe is made of but how it works, the law it follows, which makes knowledge
of it incapable of spurring on our emotional responses, and further, the nature
of knowledge itself makes it inadequate. The contact with things which we
therein establish is too sketchy and indirect to help us. We are beginning to
know too much about the bond which unites the mind to its object in knowledge [4] for that old dream of a perfect knowledge which would guarantee perfect
life to retain its sanction. What was thought to be pure knowledge, we see now
to have been shot through with hope and desire, with fear and wonder; and these
intrusive elements indeed gave it all its power to support our lives. In knowledge,
in the "How?" of events, we can find hints by which to take advantage of circumstances in our favour and avoid mischances. But we cannot get from it a
raison d'être or a justification of more than a relatively lowly kind of life.

The justification, or the reverse, of any attitude lies, not in the object, but in
itself, in its serviceableness to the whole personality. Upon its place in the whole
system of attitudes, which is the personality, all its worth depends. This is true
equally for the subtle, finely compounded attitudes of the civilised individual as
for the simpler attitudes of the child.

In brief, the imaginative life is its own justification; and this fact must be
faced, although sometimes—by a lover, for example—it may be very difficult to
accept. When it is faced, it is apparent that all the attitudes to other human
beings and to the world in all its aspects, which have been serviceable to humanity, remain as they were, as valuable as ever. Hesitation felt in admitting this is a
measure of the strength of the evil habit I have been describing. But many of
these attitudes, valuable as ever, are, now that they are being set free, more difficult to maintain, because we still hunger after a basis in belief.

APPENDIX

Two chief words seem likely occasions of misunderstanding in the above: and
they have in fact misled some readers. One is *Nature*, the other is *Belief*.

[4] Verifiable scientific knowledge, of course. Shift the sense of "knowledge" to include
hope and desire and fear as well as reference, and what I am saying would no longer be
true. But the relevant sense of "true" would have changed too. Its sanction would no
longer be verifiability.

Nature is evidently as variable a word as can be used. Its senses range from the mere inconclusive THAT, in which we live and of which we are a part, to whatever would correspond to the most detailed and interconnected account we could attain of this. Or we omit ourselves (and other minds) and make Nature *either* what influences us (in which case we should not forget our metabolism), *or* an object we apprehend (in which case there are as many Natures as there are types of apprehension we care to distinguish). And what is "natural" to one culture is strange and artificial to another. (See *Mencius on the Mind*, chap III.) More deceptively, the view here being inseparable from the eye, and this being a matter of habitual speculation, we may talk, as we think, the same language, and yet put very different things into Nature; and what we then find will not be unconnected with what we have put in.

I have attempted some further discussion of these questions in Chapters VI and VII of *Coleridge on Imagination*.

Belief. Two "beliefs" may differ from one another: (1) In their objects (2) In their statements or expressions (3) In their modes (4) In their grounds (5) In their occasions (6) In their connections with other "beliefs" (7) In their links with possible action (8) And in other ways. Our chief evidence usually for the beliefs of other people (and often for our own) must be some statement or other expression. But very different beliefs may fittingly receive the same expression. Most words used in stating any speculative opinion are as ambiguous as "Belief"; and yet by such words belief-objects must be distinguished.

But in the case of "belief" there is an additional difficulty. Neither it nor its partial synonyms suggest the great variety of attitudes (3) that are commonly covered (and confused) by the term. They are often treated as though they were mere variations in degree. Of what? Of belief, it would be said. But this is no better than the parallel trick of treating varieties of love as a mere more or less only further differentiated by their objects. Such crude over-simplifications distort the structure of the mind, and, although favorite suasive devices with some well-intentioned teachers, are disastrous.

There is an ample field here awaiting a type of dispassionate inquiry which it has seldom received. A world threatened with ever more and more leisure should not be too impatient of important and explorable subtleties.

Meanwhile, as with "Nature," misunderstandings should neither provoke nor surprise. I should not be much less at my reader's mercy if I were to add notes doubling the length of this little book. On so vast a matter, even the largest book could contain no more than a sketch of how things have seemed to be sometimes to the writer.

Sensibility and Thought in Metaphysical Poetry

By collecting these poems[1] from the work of a generation more often named than read, and more often read than profitably studied, Professor Grierson has rendered a service of some importance. Certainly the reader will meet with many poems already preserved in other anthologies, at the same time that he discovers poems such as those of Aurelian Townshend or Lord Herbert of Cherbury here included. But the function of such an anthology as this is neither that of Professor Saintsbury's admirable edition of Caroline poets nor that of the *Oxford Book of English Verse*. Mr. Grierson's book is in itself a piece of criticism and a provocation of criticism; and we think that he was right in including so many poems of Donne, elsewhere (though not in many editions) accessible, as documents in the case of "metaphysical poetry." The phrase has long done duty as a term of abuse or as the label of a quaint and pleasant taste. The question is to what extent the so-called metaphysicals formed a school (in our own time we should say a "movement"), and how far this so-called school or movement is a digression from the main current.

Not only is it extremely difficult to define metaphysical poetry, but difficult to decide what poets practice it and in which of their verses. The poetry of Donne (to whom Marvell and Bishop King are sometimes nearer than any of the other authors) is late Elizabethan, its feeling often very close to that of Chapman. The "courtly" poetry is derivative from Jonson, who borrowed liberally from the Latin; it expires in the next century with the sentiment and witticism of Prior. There is finally the devotional verse of Herbert, Vaughan, and Crashaw (echoed long after by Christina Rossetti and Francis Thompson); Crashaw, sometimes more profound and less sectarian than the others, has a quality which returns through the Elizabethan period to the early Italians. It is difficult to find any precise use of metaphor, simile, or other conceit, which is common to all the poets and at the same time important enough as an element of style to isolate these poets as a group. Donne, and often Cowley, employ a device which is sometimes considered characteristically "metaphysical"; the elaboration (contrasted with the condensation) of a figure of speech to the farthest stage to which ingenuity can carry it. Thus Cowley develops the commonplace comparison of the world to a chessboard through long stanzas (*To Destiny*), and Donne, with more grace, in A *Valediction*, the comparison of two lovers to a pair of compasses. But elsewhere we find, instead of the mere explication of the content of a comparison, a development by rapid association of thought which requires considerable agility on the part of the reader.

> On a round ball
> A workman that hath copies by, can lay

---

[1] *Metaphysical Lyrics and Poems of the Seventeenth Century*: Donne to Butler. Selected and edited, with an Essay, by Herbert J. C. Grierson (Oxford: Clarendon Press. London: Milford) AUTHOR'S NOTE.

"The Metaphysical Poets" [1921], *Selected Essays*: New Edition, by T. S. Eliot, copyright 1932, 1936, 1950 by Harcourt, Brace & World Inc. © 1960 by T. S. Eliot. Reprinted by permission of Harcourt, Brace & World Inc. and Faber & Faber Ltd.

> An Europe, Afrique, and an Asia,
> And quickly make that, which was nothing, All,
>> So doth each teare,
>> Which thee doth weare,
> A globe, yea, world by that impression grow,
> Till thy tears mixt with mine doe overflow
> This world, by waters sent from thee, my heaven dissolved so.

Here we find at least two connections which are not implicit in the first figure, but are forced upon it by the poet: from the geographer's globe to the tear, and the tear to the deluge. On the other hand, some of Donne's most successful and characteristic effects are secured by brief words and sudden contrasts:

> A bracelet of bright hair about the bone,

where the most powerful effect is produced by the sudden contrast of associations of "bright hair" and of "bone." This telescoping of images and multiplied associations is characteristic of the phrase of some of the dramatists of the period which Donne knew: not to mention Shakespeare, it is frequent in Middleton, Webster, and Tourneur, and is one of the sources of the vitality of their language.

Johnson, who employed the term "metaphysical poets," apparently having Donne, Cleveland, and Cowley chiefly in mind, remarks of them that "the most heterogeneous ideas are yoked by violence together." The force of this impeachment lies in the failure of the conjunction, the fact that often the ideas are yoked but not united; and if we are to judge of styles of poetry by their abuse, enough examples may be found in Cleveland to justify Johnson's condemnation. But a degree of heterogeneity of material compelled into unity by the operation of the poet's mind is omnipresent in poetry. We need not select for illustration such a line as:

> Notre âme est un trois-mâts cherchant son Icarie;

we may find it in some of the best lines of Johnson himself (*The Vanity of Human Wishes*):

> His fate was destined to a barren strand,
> A petty fortress, and a dubious hand;
> He left a name at which the world grew pale,
> To point a moral, or adorn a tale—

where the effect is due to a contrast of ideas, different in degree but the same in principle, as that which Johnson mildly reprehended. And in one of the finest poems of the age (a poem which could not have been written in any other age), the *Exequy* of Bishop King, the extended comparison is used with perfect success: the idea and the simile become one, in the passage in which the Bishop illustrates his impatience to see his dead wife, under the figure of a journey:

> Stay for me there; I will not faile
> To meet thee in that hollow Vale.
> And think not much of my delay;
> I am already on the way,
> And follow thee with all the speed

Desire can make, or sorrows breed.
Each minute is a short degree,
And ev'ry houre a step towards thee.
At night when I betake to rest,
Next morn I rise nearer my West
Of life, almost by eight houres sail,
Than when sleep breath'd his drowsy gale . . .
But heark! My Pulse, like a soft Drum
Beats my approach, tells Thee I come;
And slow howere my marches be,
I shall at last sit down by Thee.

(In the last few lines there is that effect of terror which is several times attained by one of Bishop King's admirers, Edgar Poe.) Again, we may justly take these quatrains from Lord Herbert's Ode, stanzas which would, we think, be immediately pronounced to be of the metaphysical school:

So when from hence we shall be gone,
  And be no more, nor you, nor I,
  As one another's mystery,
Each shall be both, yet both but one.

This said, in her up-lifted face,
  Her eyes, which did the beauty crown,
  Were like two starrs, that having faln down,
Look up again to find their place:

While such a moveless silent peace
  Did seize on their becalmed sense,
  One would have thought some influence
Their ravished spirits did possess.

There is nothing in these lines (with the possible exception of the stars, a simile not at once grasped, but lovely and justified) which fits Johnson's general observations on the metaphysical poets in his essay on Cowley. A good deal resides in the richness of association which is at the same time borrowed from and given to the word "becalmed"; but the meaning is clear, the language simple and elegant. It is to be observed that the language of these poets is as a rule simple and pure; in the verse of George Herbert this simplicity is carried as far as it can go—a simplicity emulated without success by numerous modern poets. The *structure* of the sentences, on the other hand, is sometimes far from simple, but this is not a vice; it is a fidelity to thought and feeling. The effect, at its best, is far less artificial than that of an ode by Gray. And as this fidelity induces variety of thought and feeling, so it induces variety of music. We doubt whether, in the eighteenth century, could be found two poems in nominally the same metre, so dissimilar as Marvell's *Coy Mistress* and Crashaw's *Saint Teresa*; the one producing an effect of great speed by the use of short syllables, and the other an ecclesiastical solemnity by the use of long ones:

Love, thou art absolute sole lord
Of life and death.

If so shrewd and sensitive (though so limited) a critic as Johnson failed to define metaphysical poetry by its faults, it is worth while to inquire whether we may not have more success by adopting the opposite method: by assuming that the poets of the seventeenth century (up to the Revolution) were the direct and normal development of the precedent age; and, without prejudicing their case by the adjective "metaphysical," consider whether their virtue was not something permanently valuable, which subsequently disappeared, but ought not to have disappeared. Johnson has hit, perhaps by accident, on one of their peculiarities, when he observes that "their attempts were always analytic"; he would not agree that, after the dissociation, they put the material together again in a new unity.

It is certain that the dramatic verse of the later Elizabethan and early Jacobean poets expresses a degree of development of sensibility which is not found in any of the prose, good as it often is. If we except Marlowe, a man of prodigious intelligence, these dramatists were directly or indirectly (it is at least a tenable theory) affected by Montaigne. Even if we except also Jonson and Chapman, these two were notably erudite, and were notably men who incorporated their erudition into their sensibility: their mode of feeling was directly and freshly altered by their reading and thought. In Chapman especially there is a direct sensuous apprehension of thought, or a re-creation of thought into feeling, which is exactly what we find in Donne:

> . . . in this one thing, all the discipline
> Of manners and of manhood is contained;
> A man to join himself with th' Universe
> In his main sway, and make in all things fit
> One with that All, and go on, round as it;
> Not plucking from the whole his wretched part,
> And into straits, or into nought revert,
> Wishing the complete Universe might be
> Subject to such a rag of it as he;
> But to consider great Necessity.

We compare this with some modern passage:

> No, when the fight begins within himself,
> A man's worth something. God stoops o'er his head,
> Satan looks up between his feet—both tug—
> He's left, himself, i' the middle; the soul wakes
> And grows. Prolong that battle through his life!

It is perhaps somewhat less fair, though very tempting (as both poets are concerned with the perpetuation of love by offspring), to compare with the stanzas already quoted from Lord Herbert's Ode the following from Tennyson:

> One walked between his wife and child,
> With measured footfall firm and mild,
> And now and then he gravely smiled.
>   The prudent partner of his blood
>   Leaned on him, faithful, gentle, good,
>   Wearing the rose of womanhood.

And in their double love secure,
The little maiden walked demure,
Pacing with downward eyelids pure.
These three made unity so sweet,
My frozen heart began to beat,
Remembering its ancient heat.

The difference is not a simple difference of degree between poets. It is something which had happened to the mind of England between the time of Donne or Lord Herbert of Cherbury and the time of Tennyson and Browning; it is the difference between the intellectual poet and the reflective poet. Tennyson and Browning are poets, and they think; but they do not feel their thought as immediately as the odour of a rose. A thought to Donne was an experience; it modified his sensibility. When a poet's mind is perfectly equipped for its work, it is constantly amalgamating disparate experience; the ordinary man's experience is chaotic, irregular, fragmentary. The latter falls in love, or reads Spinoza, and these two experiences have nothing to do with each other, or with the noise of the typewriter or the smell of cooking; in the mind of the poet these experiences are always forming new wholes.

We may express the difference by the following theory: The poets of the seventeenth century, the successors of the dramatists of the sixteenth, possessed a mechanism of sensibility which could devour any kind of experience. They are simple, artificial, difficult, or fantastic, as their predecessors were; no less nor more than Dante, Guido Cavalcanti, Guinizelli, or Cino. In the seventeenth century a dissociation of sensibility set in, from which we have never recovered; and this dissociation, as is natural, was aggravated by the influence of the two most powerful poets of the century, Milton and Dryden. Each of these men performed certain poetic functions so magnificently well that the magnitude of the effect concealed the absence of others. The language went on and in some respects improved; the best verse of Collins, Gray, Johnson, and even Goldsmith satisfies some of our fastidious demands better than that of Donne or Marvell or King. But while the language became more refined, the feeling became more crude. The feeling, the sensibility, expressed in the Country Churchyard (to say nothing of Tennyson and Browning) is cruder than that in the Coy Mistress.

The second effect of the influence of Milton and Dryden followed from the first, and was therefore slow in manifestation. The sentimental age began early in the eighteenth century, and continued. The poets revolted against the ratiocinative, the descriptive; they thought and felt by fits, unbalanced; they reflected. In one or two passages of Shelley's Triumph of Life, in the second Hyperion, there are traces of a struggle toward unification of sensibility. But Keats and Shelley died, and Tennyson and Browning ruminated.

After this brief exposition of a theory—too brief, perhaps, to carry conviction—we may ask, what would have been the fate of the "metaphysical" had the current of poetry descended in a direct line from them, as it descended in a direct line to them? They would not, certainly, be classified as metaphysical. The possible interests of a poet are unlimited; the more intelligent he is the better; the more intelligent he is the more likely that he will have interests: our only condition is that he turn them into poetry, and not merely meditate on them poetically. A philosophical theory which has entered into poetry is established, for its truth or falsity in one sense ceases to matter, and its truth in another sense is proved. The poets in question have, like other poets, various faults. But they were, at best, engaged in the task of trying to find the verbal equivalent for states of mind and feeling. And this means both that they are more mature, and that they wear better, than later poets of certainly not less literary ability.

It is not a permanent necessity that poets should be interested in philosophy, or in any other subject. We can only say that it appears likely that poets in our civilization, as it exists at present, must be *difficult*. Our civilization comprehends great variety and complexity, and this variety and complexity, playing upon a refined sensibility, must produce various and complex results. The poet must become more and more comprehensive, more allusive, more indirect, in order to force, to dislocate if necessary, language into his meaning. (A brilliant and extreme statement of this view, with which it is not requisite to associate oneself, is that of M. Jean Epstein, *La Poésie d'aujourd'hui.*) Hence we get something which looks very much like the conceit—we get, in fact, a method curiously similar to that of the "metaphysical poets," similar also in its use of obscure words and of simple phrasing.

> O géraniums diaphanes, guerroyeurs sortilèges,
> Sacrilèges monomanes!
> Emballages, dévergondages, douches! O pressoirs
> Des vendanges des grands soirs!
> Layettes aux abois,
> Thyrses au fond des bois!
> Transfusions, représailles,
> Relevailles, compresses et l'éternal potion,
> Angélus! n'en pouvoir plus
> De débâcles nuptiales! de débâcles nuptiales!

The same poet could write also simply:

> Elle est bien loin, elle pleure,
> Le grand vent se lamente aussi . . .

Jules Laforgue, and Tristan Corbière in many of his poems, are nearer to the "school of Donne" than any modern English poet. But poets more classical than they have the same essential quality of transmuting ideas into sensations, of transforming an observation into a state of mind.

> Pour l'enfant, amoureux de cartes et d'estampes,
> L'univers est égal à son vaste appétit.
> Ah, que le monde est grand à la clarté des lampes!
> Aux yeux du souvenir que le monde est petit!

In French literature the great master of the seventeenth century—Racine—and the great master of the nineteenth—Baudelaire—are in some ways more like each other than they are like any one else. The greatest two masters of diction are also the greatest two psychologists, the most curious explorers of the soul. It is interesting to speculate whether it is not a misfortune that two of the greatest masters of diction in our language, Milton and Dryden, triumph with a dazzling disregard of the soul. If we continued to produce Miltons and Drydens it might not so much matter, but as things are it is a pity that English poetry has remained so incomplete. Those who object to the "artificiality" of Milton or Dryden sometimes tell us to "look into our hearts and write." But that is not looking deep enough; Racine or Donne looked into a good deal more than the heart. One must look into the cerebral cortex, the nervous system, and the digestive tracts.

May we not conclude, then, that Donne, Crashaw, Vaughan, Herbert and Lord Herbert, Marvell, King, Cowley at his best, are in the direct current of English poetry, and that their faults should be reprimanded by this standard rather than coddled by antiquarian affection? They have been enough praised in terms which are implicit limitations because they are "metaphysical" or "witty," "quaint" or "obscure," though at their best they have not these attributes more than other serious poets. On the other hand, we must not reject the criticism of Johnson (a dangerous person to disagree with) without having mastered it, without having assimilated the Johnsonian canons of taste. In reading the celebrated passage in his essay on Cowley we must remember that by wit he clearly means something more serious than we usually mean today; in his criticism of their versification we must remember in what a narrow discipline he was trained, but also how well trained; we must remember that Johnson tortures chiefly the chief offenders, Cowley and Cleveland. It would be a fruitful work, and one requiring a substantial book, to break up the classification of Johnson (for there has been none since) and exhibit these poets in all their difference of kind and of degree, from the massive music of Donne to the faint, pleasing tinkle of Aurelian Townshend—whose Dialogue Between a Pilgrim and Time is one of the few regrettable omissions from the excellent anthology of Professor Grierson.

FRIEDRICH NIETZSCHE

The Acceptance of Untruth

Our Ultimate Gratitude to Art.—If we had not approved of the Arts and invented this sort of cult of the untrue, the insight into the general untruth and falsity of things now given us by science—an insight into delusion and error as conditions of intelligent and sentient existence—would be quite unendurable. *Honesty* would have disgust and suicide in its train. Now, however, our honesty has a counterpoise which helps us to escape such consequences;—namely, Art, as the *good-will* to illusion. We do not always restrain our eyes from rounding off and perfecting in imagination: and then it is no longer the eternal imperfection that we carry over the river of Becoming—for we think we carry a *goddess,* and are proud and artless in rendering this service. As an aesthetic phenomenon existence is still *endurable* to us; and by Art, eye and hand and above all the good conscience are given to us, *to be able* to make such a phenomenon out of ourselves. We must rest from ourselves occasionally by contemplating and looking down upon ourselves, and by laughing or weeping *over* ourselves from an artistic remoteness: we must discover the *hero,* and likewise the *fool,* that is hidden in our passion for knowledge; we must now and then be joyful in our folly, that we may continue to be joyful in our wisdom! And just because we are heavy and serious men in our ultimate depth, and are rather weights than men, there is nothing that does us so much good as the *fool's cap and bells:* we need them in presence of ourselves—we need all arrogant, soaring, dancing, mocking, childish and blessed Art, in order not to lose the *free dominion over things* which our ideal demands of us.

One should not be deceived: great spirits are skeptics. Zarathustra is a skeptic. Strength, *freedom* which is born of the strength and overstrength of the spirit, proves itself by skepticism. Men of conviction are not worthy of the least consideration in fundamental questions of value and disvalue. Convictions are

From *The Joyful Wisdom* [1882], translated from the German by Thomas Common, Edinburgh and London, 1910, pp. 145-7.
From *The Antichrist* [1895], translated from the German by Walter Kaufmann, *The Portable Nietzsche,* ed. Walter Kaufmann, New York, 1954, p. 638; reprinted by permission of The Viking Press Inc.

prisons. Such men do not look far enough, they do not look *beneath* themselves: but to be permitted to join in the discussion of value and disvalue, one must see five hundred convictions *beneath* oneself—*behind* oneself.

A spirit who wants great things, who also wants the means to them, is necessarily a skeptic. Freedom from all kinds of convictions, to be able to see freely, is part of strength. Great passion, the ground and the power of his existence, even more enlightened, even more despotic than he is himself, employs his whole intellect; it makes him unhesitating; it gives him courage even for unholy means; under certain circumstances it does not begrudge him convictions. Conviction as a *means:* many things are attained only by means of a conviction. Great passion uses and uses up convictions, it does not succumb to them—it knows itself sovereign.

W. B. YEATS

The Conquest of Scepticism

Ezra Pound bases his scepticism upon the statement, that we know nothing but sequences. "If I touch the button the electric lamp will light up—all our knowledge is like that." But this statement, which is true of science, which implies an object beyond the mind and therefore unknown, is not true of any kind of philosophy. Some Church father said, "We can never think nor know anything of the Gospel"; some Arian, "I know God as He is known to Himself." The Church father had like Ezra a transcendent object of thought; his arose out of self-surrender, Ezra's out of search for complete undisturbed self-possession. In Eliot, and perhaps in [Wyndham] Lewis, bred in the same scepticism, there is a tendency to exchange search for submission. Blake denounced both nature and God considered external like Nature as mystery; he was enraged with Wordsworth for passing Jehovah "unafraid," not because Jehovah is mystery but because the passage from potential to actual man can only come in terror. "I have been always an insect in the roots of the grass"—my form of it perhaps.

I agree with Ezra in his dislike of the word belief. Belief implies an unknown object, a covenant attested with a name or signed with blood, and being more emotional than intellectual may pride itself on lack of proof. But if I affirm that such and such is so, the more complete the affirmation, the more complete the proof, and even when incomplete, it remains valid within some limit. I must kill scepticism in myself, except in so far as it is mere acknowledgement of a limit, gradually, in so far as politeness permits, rid my style of turns of phrase that employ it. Even the politeness should be ejected when charm takes its place as in poetry. I have felt when re-writing every poem—"The Sorrow of Love" for instance—that by assuming a self of past years, as remote from that of today as some dramatic creation, I touched a stronger passion, a greater confidence than

Journal [1929], quoted by Richard Ellmann in *The Identity of Yeats*, New York, 1951, pp. 239-40; reprinted by permission of Mrs. W. B. Yeats.

I possess, or ever did possess. Ezra when he re-creates Propertius or some Chinese poet escapes his scepticism. The one reason for putting our actual situation into our art is that the struggle for complete affirmation may be, often must be, that art's chief poignancy. I must, though [the] world shriek at me, admit no act beyond my power, nor thing beyond my knowledge, yet because my divinity is far off I blanch and tremble.

We, even more than Eliot, require tradition and though it may include much that is his, it is not a belief or submission, but exposition of intellectual needs. I recall a passage in some Hermetic writer on the increased power that a God feels on getting into a statue. I feel as neither Eliot nor Ezra do the need of old forms, old situations that, as when I re-create some early poem of my own, I may escape from scepticism. For years past I have associated the first unique [?] impulse to any kind of lyric poetry that has the quality of a ballad ("The Tower," for instance) with an imagination of myself awaiting in some small seaside inn the hour of embarking upon some eighteenth or seventeenth century merchant ship, a scene perhaps read of in boyhood, that returns with simpler rhythms and emotions. Nor do I think that I differ from others except in so far as my preoccupation with poetry makes me different. The men sitting opposite me, in the Rapallo restaurant where some days ago the sound of a fiddle made me remember the old situation, are to my eyes modern but only a perverted art makes them modern to themselves. The "modern man" is a term invented by modern poetry to dignify our scepticism.

CHARLES BAUDELAIRE

The Didactic Heresy

There is another heresy, an error which has a more persistent life, I mean the heresy of didacticism, with its inevitable corollaries, the heresies of passion, truth, and morality. Most people assume that the object of poetry is some kind of teaching, that it must now fortify conscience, now perfect manners, now, in sum, demonstrate something useful. Poetry, however little one descends into oneself, interrogates one's soul, recalls one's memories of enthusiasm, has no object but itself: it can have no other, and no poem will be so great, so noble, so truly worthy of the name of poem as that which has been written solely for the pleasure of writing a poem.

I do not mean that poetry may not ennoble manners—let this be understood —or that its final result may not be to raise men above the level of common interests; that would be an obvious absurdity. I say that if the poet has pursued a moral end, he has diminished his poetical power; and it is not risky to bet that his work will be poor. Poetry cannot, on pain of death or dethronement, be assimilated into science or morality; it does not have truth for its object, but only itself. The means of demonstrating truths are altogether different. Truth has nothing to do with songs. Everything that makes a song charming, gracious, irresistible, would steal from truth its authority and power. Cold, calm, and impassive, the spirit of demonstration rebuffs the Muse's diamonds and flowers, and so is the exact contrary of the poetical temper.

Pure intellect aims at truth, taste discloses beauty to us, and the moral sense teaches us duty. It is true that the mean has connections with both extremes, and is separated from the moral sense by only a slight difference which Aristotle has not hesitated to number among the several virtues of its delicate operations. Moreover, what particularly exasperates the man of taste in the spectacle of vice is its deformity, its disproportion. Vice strikes a blow against the right and true, and revolts the intellect and conscience; but as an outrage to harmony, as a dissonance, it will especially offend certain poetical natures; and I do not think it would be scandalizing to consider every infraction of morality, of moral beauty, as an offense against universal rhythm and prosody.

This is the admirable, immortal instinct of beauty which makes us consider the earth and its sights as a glimpse of heaven, a correspondence with it. The

From "Theophile Gautier" [1861], *L'Art romantique* [1868], in *Oeuvres Complètes*, ed. Jacques Crépet, Paris, 1925, III, 157-60; translated by the editors.

101

unquenchable thirst for everything that is beyond and everything that life reveals, is the most living proof of our immortality. It is at once through poetry and *across* poetry, through music and *across* music, that the soul catches a glimpse of the splendors situated beyond the tomb; and when an exquisite poem brings tears to the eyelids, these tears are not proof of an excess of joy, but witness rather of a roused melancholy, of nervous strain, of a nature, exiled in the imperfect, which would like to take possession at once, on this very earth, of a heaven that has been made manifest.

So the first principle of poetry is, strictly and simply, the human aspiration towards a superior beauty, and the principle declares itself in an enthusiasm, a carrying off of the soul; enthusiasm quite independent of passion, which is the heart's drunkenness, and of truth, which is the reason's pasture. For passion is a natural thing, too natural not to introduce a marring, discordant tone into the domain of pure beauty; too intimate and too violent not to scandalize the pure desires, gracious melancholies, and noble despairs which dwell in the supernatural regions of poetry.

OSCAR WILDE

The Improvidence of Art

The artist is the creator of beautiful things.
To reveal art and conceal the artist is art's aim.
The critic is he who can translate into another manner or a new material his impression of beautiful things.
The highest, as the lowest, form of criticism is a mode of autobiography.
Those who find ugly meanings in beautiful things are corrupt without being charming. This is a fault.
Those who find beautiful meanings in beautiful things are the cultivated.
For these there is hope.
They are the elect to whom beautiful things mean only Beauty.
There is no such thing as a moral or an immoral book. Books are well written, or badly written. That is all.
The nineteenth century dislike of Realism is the rage of Caliban seeing his own face in a glass.
The nineteenth century dislike of Romanticism is the rage of Caliban not seeing his own face in a glass.
The moral life of man forms part of the subject-matter of the artist, but the morality of art consists in the perfect use of an imperfect medium. No artist desires to prove anything. Even things that are true can be proved.
No artist has ethical sympathies. An ethical sympathy in an artist is an unpardonable mannerism of style.

Preface to *The Picture of Dorian Gray* [1891], *The Works of Oscar Wilde*, ed. G. F. Maine, London, 1948, p. 17.

No artist is ever morbid. The artist can express everything.

Thought and language are to the artist instruments of an art.

Vice and virtue are to the artist materials for an art.

From the point of view of form, the type of all the arts is the art of the musician.

From the point of view of feeling, the actor's craft is the type.

All art is at once surface and symbol.

Those who go beneath the surface do so at their peril.

Those who read the symbol do so at their peril.

It is the spectator, and not life, that art really mirrors.

Diversity of opinion about a work of art shows that the work is new, complex, and vital.

When critics disagree the artist is in accord with himself.

We can forgive a man for making a useful thing as long as he does not admire it. The only excuse for making a useless thing is that one admires it intensely.

All art is quite useless.

RICHARD WAGNER

Literature as Music-Drama

And in fact there *must* of necessity arise in the German musician some *ideal* aim in regard to the opera—that form of artistic production that is for him so problematical, that continually attracts and as constantly repels him,—that so entirely fails to satisfy him in the way in which it is actually brought before him:—and in this fact lies the peculiar significance of German efforts in art, not only in this but in almost every artistic field. Permit me to point out the characteristics of this significance a little more closely.

The Latin nations of Europe indisputably attained, at an early period, to one great point of advantage over the Germanic—namely, in the development of *Form*. While Italy, Spain, and France made for themselves that pleasing and appropriate form which soon gained a general and proper adoption for all outward expression in life and art, Germany remained in this respect in a state of undeniable anarchy, which could not be concealed, but was rather increased, by the fact that it sought to make use of the already perfect form employed by foreigners. The obvious disadvantage under which the German nation labored on this account in all which concerned outward form (and how much this includes!), retarded the development of German art and literature so long, that it has only been since the latter half of the last century that such a movement showed itself in Germany, as the Latin nations had experienced ever since the beginning of the period of the Renaissance.

This German movement could at first assume little character but that of a reaction against the foreign, distorted, and therefore distorting Latinized forms;

From "The Music of the Future" [1860], *Art, Life and Theories*, translated from the German by Edward L. Burlingame, New York, 1889 (2nd edition), pp. 139-41, 146-7, 150-51, 157-61.

yet as this could not act favorably to a German form that had not been *re-pressed*, but had in reality *never existed*, the movement tended strongly toward the discovery of some method of expression of a purely ideal *human* nature,— not to one that should belong to this one nation alone. The influence of the two leading German poets, Goethe and Schiller, peculiar, new, and unprecedented as it was in art-history, shows itself in this,—that now for the first time this problem of an ideal, purely human art-form in its fullest meaning became the object of investigation; and the search for this form was almost the most important element of their labors. Rebelling against the force of that method of expression that still passed for a law among the Latin nations, they succeeded in looking upon this method objectively, in comprehending its disadvantages as well as its advantages, in going back from it to the origin of all European art-form— the Greek; and finally, grasping the antique form with the requisite freedom, to proceed from it to an ideal art-expression which, as one purely human and freed from narrow national customs, could develop these customs into a form that should be human in the truest sense, and only obey eternal laws.

The disadvantage under which the German had thus far labored as opposed to the Latin, was thus converted into an advantage. For while the Frenchman, for example, contented himself with an entirely developed, congruous form, and, willingly subjecting himself to its apparently unalterable laws, devoted himself only to continual reproductions of it, and thus felt himself committed to what was, in a higher sense, a stagnation of his productiveness,—the German, with a full recognition of the advantageous elements of such a position, nevertheless saw its disadvantageous elements as well. The lack of freedom in it did not escape him, and the prospect opened to him of an ideal art-form in which what was always valuable in every method of expression should have representation, freed from the fetters of the purely fortuitous and the false. The immeasurable importance of such a form must consist in this, that, putting aside the limiting factor of narrow national influence, it should be one universally intelligible and open to every people.

If, in the matter of literature, the differences of the European languages would act as an obstacle to this, it must be in music, that language intelligible to all men, that the great equalizing power is to be found, which, converting the language of ideas into the language of the feelings, would bring the deepest secrets of the artistic conception to general comprehension, especially if this comprehension can be made distinct through the plastic expression of dramatic representation,—can be given such a distinctness as up to this time painting alone has been able to claim as its peculiar influence.

You see here, hastily sketched, the plan of that work of art which always presented itself to me as the ideal one, and which I at one time felt impelled to describe in its theoretic features. It was at a period when a gradually increasing distaste for that school of art which, when compared with the ideal I had conceived, had only the repulsive resemblance to it that an ape has to a man,—it was at a time when distaste for this had so gained possession of me that I longed to flee before it and hide myself in the most complete retirement. . . .

But the investigation into the character of the lamentable destruction of the great Greek art-work attracted me still more strongly. Here I was first struck by the remarkable phenomenon of the division and separation of those individual branches of art which had formerly been united in the perfect and complete drama. The special art-ingredients detached themselves from that omnipotent union in which they, working for a single object, had rendered it possible to make intelligible to the whole people the noblest and deepest purposes of humanity,— detached themselves from it to become no longer the inspired teachers of the public, but the consoling pastime of special art-lovers; so that while gladiatorial combats and battles of wild beasts were exhibited to the populace, the educated man occupied himself in solitude with literature and painting. It was important for me, above all things, that I thought myself forced to recognize that the special, separately developed branches of art, however much their capabilities of expression might finally be brought out and heightened by great geniuses, nevertheless, without falling into unnaturalness and decided error, could never aim to supply in any way the place of that all-powerful work of art which was only possible through a union of their forces.

Having at hand the opinions of the greatest critics,—the investigations, for instance, of a Lessing into the limits of painting and poetry,—I believed that I might form the theory that every *individual* branch of art follows out a development of its powers that finally leads it to their limits; and that it cannot pass these limits without the danger of losing itself in the unintelligible and absolutely fantastic—even in the absurd. I thought that I saw in this point the necessity for it to join companionship at this stage with another class of art, related to it, and the only one capable of going on from this position. And as I was of necessity keenly interested (having regard to my own ideal) in following out this tendency in each special kind of art, I finally believed that I could recognize it most distinctly in the relation of poetry to music,—especially considering the remarkable importance modern music has assumed. And as I thus endeavored to imagine that work of art in which all branches of art could unite in their highest perfection, I came as a matter of course to the *conscious* contemplation of that ideal which had *unconsciously* gradually formed within me, and had hovered before the seeking artist. . . .

In order to gain a proper conception of this part to be taken by the poet— a part so important for the influence of the whole; in order to conceive of it as a voluntary one, and as wished for by the poet himself, I considered first of all those repeated and earnestly expressed hopes and wishes of great poets, such as I have already mentioned, to see in the opera an ideal branch of art. I sought to explain to myself the motive of this wish, and thought I found it in that natural desire of the poet, which decides him, in conception as well as in form, to use language, the materialization of abstract ideas, in such a way as to work immediately upon the feelings themselves. As this tendency is a controlling one even in the *invention* of the poetic subject, and only that life-picture of humanity is called poetic in which all motives attributable to abstract reason disappear in favor of the representation of motives of pure human feeling, so it is also the only criterion for the *form* and *expression* of the poetic recital. The poet seeks, in his language, to make the abstract, conventional meaning of words subordinate to their original, sensible one; and to secure, by rhythmic order, as well as by the almost musical dressing of words in versification, an effect for his phraseology which shall gain possession of and influence the feelings as though by enchantment.

In this course of the poet, so necessary to his very nature, we see him finally come to the limits of his branch of art, where it already seems to touch music; and thus the most successful work of the poet must be, for us, that which should be, in its perfection, entirely musical. . . .

Beethoven received the rich and promising heritage of both these masters. He developed the symphonic form to such a comprehensive breadth, and filled it with contents of such unprecedentedly various and ravishing melody, that we stand to-day before the symphony of Beethoven as before the stone that marks the boundary of an entirely new period in the general history of art; for in it there came into the world a phenomenon, nothing even approaching which is to be found in the art of any age or any nation.

For in this symphony there is spoken by musical instruments a language of which no one in any preceding age had any knowledge, inasmuch as the pure musical expression in it enchains the hearer with a lasting effect hitherto unknown, in the most inconceivably varied shades of tone, and moves his inmost nature with a strength unattainable by any other art; revealing to him in its variety so free and audacious a regularity, that it must seem to us more powerful than all logical sequence, yet without in the least containing in itself the laws of logic. Indeed, that purely logical mental process which followed the guidance of cause and effect, finds nothing here to cling to. The symphony must needs appear to us a revelation from another world; and in very truth it does discover to us a connection between the phenomena of existence, which differs entirely from the ordinary logical *nexus*, and in regard to which one thing is undeniable—that it forces itself upon us in the most overwhelmingly convincing manner, and takes possession of our feelings with such positiveness that the reasoning faculty is entirely confused and disarmed by it.

The metaphysical necessity for the discovery of this entirely new power of language precisely in our own age, seems to me to lie in the increasingly conventional development of modern tongues. If we look more closely at the development of these languages, we shall find in the so-called roots of words an origin which shows us distinctly how in its first beginning the formation of the *idea* from the *thing*, was almost entirely coincident with the subjective conception with regard to the latter; and the assumption that the first language of mankind must have had a great resemblance to singing, need not perhaps appear ridiculous.

Human speech certainly developed from a purely sensuous, subjectively-felt signification of words, into a more abstract sense, in such a way that at length these words had only a conventional meaning left, which deprived the feelings of all part in the understanding of them, and made their very connection and construction entirely dependent on certain rules that could be learned. Conventionality developed in language, in necessary accord with the moral development of the race; a conventionality whose laws were no longer comprehensible to the purely natural feelings, but were incorporated in rules of education intelligible only to the reflective powers. And since the modern European languages, further divided into different classes, began to follow their purely conventional development with an increasingly obvious tendency, music has developed, on the other hand, into a hitherto unknown capability of expression.

It seems as though purely human feeling, grown stronger by its very repression on the side of conventional civilization, had sought out a means of bringing into use some laws of language peculiar to itself, by means of which it could express itself intelligibly, freed from the trammels of logical rules of thought. The extraordinary popularity of music in our age, the ever-increasing participation (extending through all classes of society) in the production of music of the deepest character, the growing desire to make of musical culture a necessary part of every education,—all these things which are certainly obvious and undeniable, distinctly prove the justice of the assumption that a deeply-rooted and earnest need of humanity finds expression in modern musical development; and that music, unintelligible as its language is when tried by the laws of logic, must bear within it a more convincing means of making itself understood, than even those laws contain.

In the light of this unavoidable acknowledgment, there remain but two ways of development open to poetry. Either it must entirely pass over into the field of pure abstraction—of combinations of meanings, and the representation of things by the explanation of the logical laws of thought;—and this is what, in its guise as *philosophy*, it already does. Or it must become intimately bound up with music, and with such music as that whose endless power is revealed to us by the symphony of Beethoven.

Poetry will easily find its way to this, and will recognize its strongest, inmost longing in its final culmination in music, so soon as it appreciates a want in it, which only poetry in its turn can supply. To explain this want, let us first establish that ineradicable quality of the human perceptive process, which impelled man to the discovery of the laws of causality, and because of which he involuntarily asks himself, in the presence of every impressive phenomenon—"*Why is this?*"

The hearing of a symphonic musical composition does not, it is true, entirely silence this question; but rather, since it cannot answer it, it produces a confusion in the capability of logical presentation, which may not only disturb it, but can even be the cause of an entirely erroneous judgment. To answer this disturbing yet unavoidable question in such a way as to elude it, in a certain sense, by appeasing it at the beginning—this is something that can only be the work of the *poet*. But only that poet can succeed in it, who fully appreciates the tendency of music, and its inexhaustible power of expression, and therefore so composes his poem that it can penetrate into the finest fibres of musical texture, and completely dissolve the spoken idea in feeling. Obviously, therefore, no poetic form is fitted for his use but that in which the poet no longer *describes*, but brings his subject into actual representation, that is convincing to the senses;—and this form is nothing but—the drama.

The drama, at the moment of its realistic, scenic presentation, awakens in the spectator real participation in the action presented to him; and this is so faithfully imitated from real life (or at least from the possibilities of it), that the sympathetic human feeling passes through such participation into a state of ecstasy which forgets that momentous question "*Why?*" and willingly yields itself up to the guidance of those new laws through which music makes itself so strangely intelligible, and at the same time—in the deepest sense—gives the only correct answer to that very "*Why?*"

Poetry as Incantation

A fundamental and fascinating crisis in literature is now at hand.

Such is the plain and present truth in the eyes of all those for whom literature is of primary importance. What we are witnessing as the finale of our own century is not upheaval (as was the case a hundred years ago), but rather a fluttering in the temple's veil—meaningful folds and even a little tearing.

This is disconcerting for the French reading public, whose habits were interrupted by the death of Victor Hugo. Pursuing his mysterious task, Hugo reduced all prose—philosophy, oratory, history—to poetry; and since he was himself poetry personified, he nearly abolished the philosopher's, speaker's, or historian's right to self-expression. In that wasteland, with silence all around, he was a monument. Yet in a crypt of equal silence lay the divinity of this majestic, unconscious idea: namely, that the form we call verse is itself, quite simply, literature; that we have verse so long as we have diction, rhythm so long as we have style. Poetry, I think, waited patiently and respectfully until this giant (whose ever more grasping, ever firmer blacksmith's hand was coming to be the definition of verse) had disappeared; then it broke up. The entire language was fitted out for prosody, and therein it re-discovered its vital sense of pause. Now it could fly off, freely scattering its numberless and irreducible elements. Or we might well compare it to the multiple sounds issuing from a purely verbal orchestration.

That was the beginning of the change in poetry which Verlaine, with his fluid verse, had secretly and unexpectedly prepared when he returned to certain primitive resources in language.

I was witness to this adventure. And although my role in it was not so influential as has been claimed (for no single person was responsible), I did at least take great interest in it. It is time to discuss it, and it seems better to do so at a distance, or, so to speak, anonymously.

It will be agreed that because of the priority on magic power which is given to rhyme, French poetry has been intermittent ever since its evolution. It shines for a moment, dies out, and waits. There is extinction—or rather wear and tear which reveal the weft; there is repetition. After an almost century-long period of poetic orgy and excess which can be compared only to the Renaissance, the latest poetic urge (counteracting a number of different circumstances) is being fulfilled not by a darkening or cooling off process, but, on the contrary, by a variation in continuing brilliance. The retempering of verse, ordinarily a secret affair, is now being done openly: poets are resorting to delightful approximations.

The kind of treatment that has been given to the hieratic canon of verse can, I think, be divided into three graduated parts.

Official prosody has cut and dried rules; there lies its obstinacy. It gives its official approval to such "wise" procedures as the observance of the hemistich, and pronounces judgment on the slightest effort to simulate versification. It is like the law which states, for example, that abstinence from theft is the essence

From "Crisis in Poetry" [1886-95], *Selected Prose Poems, Essays, and Letters*, translated from the French by Bradford Cook, Baltimore, 1956, pp. 34-6, 37-43; reprinted by permission of the Johns Hopkins University Press.

of honesty. But this is precisely what we need least to learn; for if we have not understood it by ourselves from the first, it is useless to obey it.

Those who are still faithful to the alexandrine, i.e., to the modern hexameter, have gone inside it and loosened this rigid, childish metrical mechanism; and so, now that such artificial metronomes have been abolished, there is joy for our ears alone in perceiving all possible combinations and interrelationships of twelve tones. . . .

But the truly remarkable fact is this: for the first time in the literary history of any nation, along with the general and traditional great organ of orthodox verse which finds its ecstasy on an ever-ready keyboard, any poet with an individual technique and ear can build his own instrument, so long as his fluting, bowing, or drumming are accomplished—play that instrument and dedicate it, along with others, to Language.

Thus we have won a great new freedom; and it is my firm belief that no beauty of the past has been destroyed as a result. I am convinced that the solemn poetic tradition which was mainly established by our classical genius will continue to be observed on all important occasions. But whenever it shall seem unfitting to disturb the echoes of that venerable past for sentimental or narrative purposes, we shall be careful to avoid such disturbance. Each soul is a melody; its strands must be bound up. Each poet has his flute or viol, with which to do so.

In my opinion, we have been late in finding the true condition and possibility not only of poetic self-expression, but of free and individual modulation.

Languages are imperfect because multiple; the supreme language is missing. Inasmuch as thought consists of writing without pen and paper, without whispering even, without the sound of the immortal Word, the diversity of languages on earth means that no one can utter words which would bear the miraculous stamp of Truth Herself Incarnate. This is clearly nature's law—we stumble on it with a smile of resignation—to the effect that we have no sufficient reason for equating ourselves with God. But then, esthetically, I am disappointed when I consider how impossible it is for language to express things by means of certain keys which would reproduce their brilliance and aura—keys which do exist as a part of the instrument of the human voice, or among languages, or sometimes even in one language. When compared to the opacity of the word *ombre*, the word *ténèbres* does not seem very dark; and how frustrating the perverseness and contradiction which lend dark tones to *jour*, bright tones to *nuit!* We dream of words brilliant at once in meaning and sound, or darkening in meaning and so in sound, luminously and elementally self-succeeding. *But,* let us remember that if our dream were fulfilled, *verse would not exist*—verse which, in all its wisdom, atones for the sins of languages, comes nobly to their aid.

Strange mystery—and so, equally mysterious and meaningful, prosody sprang forth in primitive times.

The ideal would be a reasonable number of words stretched beneath our mastering glance, arranged in enduring figures, and followed by silence.

Granted that individual inventiveness, in the case of a French poet, need not outweigh the influence of his poetic heritage; still it would be highly annoying if he were not able to follow his own paths, walk through their numberless little flowers, and gather up whatever notes his voice might find. The attempt to do so has been made just recently, and poets are still conducting learned research in the direction of syllable stressing, for example. But apart from that, there is the fascinating pastime of breaking the old alexandrine into still recognizable fragments, alternately elusive or revealing. This is preferable to total and sudden novelty. It was good to relax the rules, but the ardor which got the new school too far out of tune should now be cooled. Most delightfully out of tune, yes; but to go further, as a result of that liberation, and to suppose that every poet henceforth should invent his own prosody and base it on his own special musical gift— to say nothing of his own spelling system—is simply ridiculous. That kind of thing is cannon fodder for the newspaper boys. Verses will always be similar, and the old proportions and regularity will be observed, because the poetic act consists of our sudden realization that an idea is naturally fractionized into several motifs of equal value which must be assembled. They rhyme; and their outward stamp of authenticity is that common meter which the final stress establishes.

But the crisis in poetry lies less in the very interesting interregnum or rest treatment undergone by versification, than in certain new states of our poetic mind.

We now *hear* undeniable rays of light, like arrows gilding and piercing the meanderings of song. I mean that, since Wagner appeared, Music and Verse have combined to form Poetry.

Either one of these two elements, of course, may profitably stand apart in triumph and integrity, in a quiet concert of its own if it chooses not to speak distinctly. Or else the poem can tell of their reassociation and restrengthening: the instrumentation is brightened to the point of perfect clarity beneath the orchestral veil, while verse flies down into the evening darkness of the sound. That modern meteor—the symphony—approaches thought with the consent or ignorance of the musician. And thought itself is no longer expressed merely in common language.

Thus Mystery bursts forth ineffably throughout the heavens of Its own impersonal magnificence, wherein it was ordained that the orchestra should complement our age-old effort to make the spoken word our only form of music.

Twin symbols interrelated.

The Decadent or Mystic Schools (as they call themselves or as they were hastily labeled by the public press) find their common meeting-ground in an Idealism which (as in the case of fugues and sonatas) shuns the materials in nature, avoids any thought that might tend to arrange them too directly or precisely, and retains only the suggestiveness of things. The poet must establish a careful relationship between two images, from which a third element, clear and fusible, will be distilled and caught by our imagination. We renounce that erroneous esthetic (even though it has been responsible for certain masterpieces) which would have the poet fill the delicate pages of his book with the actual and palpable wood of trees, rather than with the forest's shuddering or the silent scattering of thunder through the foliage. A few well-chosen sounds blown heavenward on the trumpet of true majesty will suffice to conjure up the architecture of the ideal and only habitable palace—palace of no palpable stone, else the book could not be properly closed. . . .

It is not *description* which can unveil the efficacy and beauty of monuments, seas, or the human face in all their maturity and native state, but rather evocation, *allusion, suggestion.* These somewhat arbitrary terms reveal what may well be a very decisive tendency in modern literature, a tendency which limits literature and yet sets it free. For what is the magic charm of art, if not this: that, beyond the confines of a fistful of dust or of all other reality, beyond the book itself, beyond the very text, it delivers up that volatile scattering which we call the Spirit, Who cares for nothing save universal musicality.

Speech is no more than a commercial approach to reality. In literature, allusion is sufficient: essences are distilled and then embodied in Idea.

Song, when it becomes impalpable joy, will rise to heaven.

This is the ideal I would call Transposition; Structure is something else.

If the poem is to be pure, the poet's voice must be stilled and the initiative taken by the words themselves, which will be set in motion as they meet unequally in collision. And in an exchange of gleams they will flame out like some glittering swath of fire sweeping over precious stones, and thus replace the audible breathing in lyric poetry of old—replace the poet's own personal and passionate control of verse.

The inner structures of a book of verse must be inborn; in this way, chance will be totally eliminated and the poet will be absent. From each theme, itself predestined, a given harmony will be born somewhere in the parts of the total poem and take its proper place within the volume; because, for every sound, there is an echo. Motifs of like pattern will move in balance from point to point. There will be none of the sublime incoherence found in the page-settings of the Romantics, none of the artificial unity that used to be based on the square measurements of the book. Everything will be hesitation, disposition of parts, their alternations and relationships—all this contributing to the rhythmic totality, which will be the very silence of the poem, in its blank spaces, as that silence is translated by each structural element in its own way. (Certain recent publications have heralded this sort of book; and if we may admit their ideals as complements to our own, it must then be granted that young poets have seen what an overwhelming and harmonious totality a poem must be, and have stammered out the magic concept of the Great Work.) Then again, the perfect symmetry of verses within the poem, of poems within the volume, will extend even beyond the volume itself; and this will be the creation of many poets who will inscribe, on spiritual space, the expanded signature of genius—as anonymous and perfect as a work of art.

Chimaera, yes! And yet the mere thought of it is proof (reflected from Her scales) that during the last twenty-five years poetry has been visited by some nameless and absolute flash of lightning—like the muddied, dripping gleams on my windowpane which are washed away and brightened by streaming showers of rain—revealing that, in general, all books contain the amalgamation of a certain number of age-old truths; that actually there is only one book on earth, that it is the law of the earth, the earth's true Bible. The difference between individual works is simply the difference between individual interpretations of one true and established text, which are proposed in a mighty gathering of those ages we call civilized or literary.

Certainly, whenever I sit at concerts, amid the obscurity and ecstasy of sound, I always perceive the nascent form of some one of those poems which have their origin and dwelling in human life—a poem more understandable because unheard, because the composer, in his desire to portray its majestic lines, was not even *tempted* to "explain everything." My feeling—or my doubtlessly ineradicable prejudice as a writer—is that nothing will endure if it remains unspoken; that our present task, precisely (now that the great literary rhythms I spoke of are being broken up and scattered in a series of distinct and almost orchestrated shiverings), is to find a way of transposing the symphony to the Book: in short, to regain our rightful due. For, undeniably, the true source of Music must not be the elemental sound of brasses, strings, or wood winds, but the intellectual and written word in all its glory—Music of perfect fulness and clarity, the totality of universal relationships.

One of the undeniable ideals of our time is to divide words into two different categories: first, for vulgar or immediate, second, for essential purposes.

The first is for narrative, instruction, or description (even though an adequate exchange of human thoughts might well be achieved through the silent exchange of money). The elementary use of language involves that universal *journalistic style* which characterizes all kinds of contemporary writing, with the exception of literature.

Why should we perform the miracle by which a natural object is almost made to disappear beneath the magic waving wand of the written word, if not to divorce that object from the direct and the palpable, and so conjure up its *essence* in all purity?

When I say: "a flower!" then from that forgetfulness to which my voice consigns all floral form, something different from the usual calyces arises, something all music, essence, and softness: the flower which is absent from all bouquets.

Language, in the hands of the mob, leads to the same facility and directness as does money. But, in the Poet's hands, it is turned, above all, to dream and song; and, by the constituent virtue and necessity of an art which lives on fiction, it achieves its full efficacy.

Out of a number of words, poetry fashions a single new word which is total in itself and foreign to the language—a kind of incantation. Thus the desired isolation of language is effected; and chance (which might still have governed these elements, despite their artful and alternating renewal through meaning and sound) is thereby instantly and thoroughly abolished. Then we realize, to our amazement, that we had never truly heard this or that ordinary poetic fragment; and, at the same time, our recollection of the object thus conjured up bathes in a totally new atmosphere.

GUILLAUME APOLLINAIRE

Pure Painting

The plastic virtues: purity, unity, and truth, keep nature in subjection.

The rainbow is bent, the seasons quiver, the crowds push on to death, science undoes and remakes what already exists, whole worlds disappear forever from our

"On Painting" [1913], translated from the French by Lionel Abel, *Cubist Painters, Aesthetic Meditations,* New York, 1944, pp. 9-16, 17-18; reprinted by permission of George Wittenborn, Inc., Publishers, 1018 Madison Avenue, New York 21, N.Y.

understanding, our mobile images repeat themselves, or revive their vagueness, and the colors, the odors, and the sounds to which we are sensitive astonish us, then disappear from nature—all to no purpose.

This monster beauty is not eternal.

We know that our breath has had no beginning and will never cease, but our first conceptions are of the creation and the end of the world.

However too many painters still adore plants, stones, the sea, or men.

We quickly get used to the bondage of the mysterious. And servitude ends by creating real delights.

Workers are allowed to control the universe, yet gardeners have even less respect for nature than have artists.

The time has come for us to be the masters. And good will is not enough to make victory certain.

On this side of eternity dance the mortal forms of love, whose accursed discipline is summed up by the name "nature."

Flame is the symbol of painting, and the three plastic virtues burn with radiance.

Flame has a purity which tolerates nothing alien, and cruelly transforms in its image whatever it touches.

Flame has a magical unity; if it is divided, each fork will be like the single flame.

Finally it has the sublime and incontestable truth of its own light.

Good western painters of this period hold to their purity, without regard to natural forces.

Purity is a forgetting after study. And for a single pure artist to die, it would be necessary for all pure artists of past ages to have never existed.

Painting purifies itself in Europe with the ideal logic which the older painters handed on to the new ones, as if giving them life.

And that is all.

This painter finds pleasure, that one, pain; one squanders his inheritance, another becomes rich, and still others have nothing but life.

And that is all.

You cannot carry around on your back the corpse of your father. You leave him with the other dead. You remember him, miss him, speak of him with admiration. And if you become a father yourself, you cannot expect one of your children to be willing to split in two for the sake of your corpse.

But in vain do our feet relinquish the soil which holds the dead.

To insist on purity is to baptize instinct, to humanize art, and to deify personality.

The root, the stem and the flower of the lily instance the development of purity to its symbolical blossoming.

All bodies stand equal before light, and their modifications are determined by this dazzling power, which molds them according to its will.

We do not know all the colors. Each of us invents new ones.

But above all, the painter must contemplate his own divinity, and the pictures which he offers to the admiration of men will confer upon them, likewise, the glory of exercising their divinity—if only for a moment. To achieve this, it is necessary to encompass in one glance the past, the present, and the future.

The canvas should present that essential unity which alone can elicit ecstasy.

Then nothing unstable will send us off half-cocked. We will not be suddenly turning back. Free spectators, we will not sacrifice our lives to our curiosity. The smugglers of appearances will not be able to get their contraband past the salt statues before our customs house of reason.

We will not go astray in the unknown future, which, severed from eternity, is but a word fated to tempt man.

We will not waste our strength on the too fugitive present; the fashionable, for the artist, can only be the mask of death.

The pictures will exist ineluctably. The vision will be entire, complete, and its infinity, instead of indicating some imperfection, will simply express the relation between a newly created thing and a new creator, nothing more. Otherwise there would be no unity, and the connection which the different points of the canvas have with various dispositions, objects, and lights, would reveal only an assemblage of odds and ends, lacking all harmony.

For while an infinite number of creatures, each testifying to its creator, can exist without any one creation encroaching on the space of the others, yet it is impossible to conceive them all at once, and death results from their juxtaposition, their union, their love.

Each god creates in his own image, and so do painters. Only photographers manufacture duplicates of nature.

Neither purity nor unity count without truth, which cannot be compared to reality, since it is always the same, subsisting beyond the scope of nature, which strives to imprison us in that fatal order of things limiting us to the merely animal.

Artists are above all men who want to become inhuman.

Painfully they search for traces of inhumanity, traces which are to be found nowhere in nature.

These traces are clues to truth, aside from which there is no reality we can know.

But reality will never be discovered once and for all. Truth is always new. Otherwise truth would be a system even more wretched than nature itself.

But such pitiful truth, more distant, less distinct, less real each day, would reduce painting to a sort of plastic writing, intended simply to facilitate communication between people of the same race.

In our times, a machine to reproduce such signs would be quickly invented.

———————

Many new painters limit themselves to pictures which have no real subjects. And the titles which we find in the catalogues are like proper names, which designate men without characterizing them.

There are men named Stout who are in fact quite thin, and others named White who are very dark; well now, I have seen pictures entitled *Solitude* containing many human figures.

In the cases in question, the artists even condescend at times to use vaguely explanatory words such as *Portrait, Landscape, Still-life*; however, many young painters use as a title only the very general term *Painting*.

These painters, while they still look at nature, no longer imitate it, and carefully avoid any representation of natural scenes which they may have observed, and then reconstructed from preliminary studies.

Real resemblance no longer has any importance, since everything is sacrificed by the artist to truth, to the necessities of a higher nature whose existence he assumes, but does not lay bare. The subject has little or no importance any more.

Generally speaking, modern art repudiates most of the techniques of pleasing devised by the great artists of the past.

While the goal of painting is today, as always, the pleasure of the eye, the art-lover is henceforth asked to expect delights other than those which looking at natural objects can easily provide.

Thus we are moving towards an entirely new art which will stand, with respect to painting as envisaged heretofore, as music stands to literature.

It will be pure painting, just as music is pure literature.

The music-lover experiences, in listening to a concert, a joy of a different order from the joy given by natural sounds, such as the murmur of the brook, the uproar of a torrent, the whistling of the wind in a forest, or the harmonies of human speech based on reason rather than on aesthetics.

In the same way the new painters will provide their admirers with artistic sensations by concentrating exclusively on the problem of creating harmony with unequal lights.

Everybody knows the story told by Pliny about Apelles and Protogenes. It clearly illustrates the asethetic pleasure resulting solely from the contradictory harmonies referred to above.

Apelles landed, one day, on the Isle of Rhodes, and went to see the work of Protogenes, who lived there. Protogenes was not in the studio when Apelles arrived. An old woman was there, looking after a large canvas which the painter had prepared. Instead of leaving his name, Apelles drew on the canvas a line so subtle that nothing happier could be conceived.

Returning, Protogenes saw the line, recognized the hand of Apelles, and drew on the latter's line another line of another color, one even more subtle, so that it seemed as if there were three lines.

Apelles came back the next day, and again did not find his man; the subtlety of the line which he drew this time caused Protogenes to despair. The sketch aroused for many years the admiration of connoisseurs, who contemplated it with as much pleasure as if it had depicted gods and goddesses, instead of almost invisible lines.

The secret aim of the young painters of the extremist schools is to produce pure painting. Theirs is an entirely new plastic art. It is still in its beginnings, and is not yet as abstract as it would like to be. Most of the new painters depend a good deal on mathematics, without knowing it; but they have not yet abandoned nature, which they still question patiently, hoping to learn the right answers to the questions raised by life.

A man like Picasso studies an object as a surgeon dissects a cadaver.

This art of pure painting, if it succeeds in freeing itself from the art of the past, will not necessarily cause the latter to disappear; the development of music has not brought in its train the abandonment of the various genres of literature, nor has the acridity of tobacco replaced the savoriness of food.

The new artists have beeen violently attacked for their preoccupation with geometry. Yet geometrical figures are the essence of drawing. Geometry, the science of space, its dimensions and relations, has always determined the norms and rules of painting.

Until now, the three dimensions of Euclid's geometry were sufficient to the restiveness felt by great artists yearning for the infinite.

The new painters do not propose, any more than did their predecessors, to be geometers. But it may be said that geometry is to the plastic arts what grammar is to the art of the writer. Today, scientists no longer limit themselves to the three dimensions of Euclid. The painters have been led quite naturally, one might say by intuition, to preoccupy themselves with the new possibilities of spatial measurement which, in the language of the modern studios, are designated by the term: the fourth dimension.

Regarded from the plastic point of view, the fourth dimension appears to spring from the three known dimensions: it represents the immensity of space eternalizing itself in all directions at any given moment. It is space itself, the dimension of the infinite; the fourth dimension endows objects with plasticity. It gives the object its right proportions on the whole, whereas in Greek art, for instance, a somewhat mechanical rhythm constantly destroys the proportions.

Greek art had a purely human conception of beauty. It took man as the measure of perfection. But the art of the new painters takes the infinite universe as its ideal, and it is to this ideal that we owe a new norm of the perfect, one which permits the painter to proportion objects in accordance with the degree of plasticity he desires them to have.

Nietzsche divined the possibility of such an art:

"O divine Dionysius, why pull my ears?" Ariadne asks her philosophical lover in one of the celebrated dialogues on the Isle of Naxos. "I find something pleasant and delightful in your ears, Ariadne; why are they not even longer?"

Nietzsche, in relating this anecdote, puts in the mouth of Dionysius an implied condemnation of all Greek art.

Finally, I must point out that the fourth dimension—this utopian expression should be analyzed and explained, so that nothing more than historical interest may be attached to it—has come to stand for the aspirations and premonitions of the many young artists who contemplate Egyptian, negro, and oceanic sculptures, meditate on various scientific works, and live in the anticipation of a sublime art.

Wishing to attain the proportions of the ideal, to be no longer limited to the human, the young painters offer us works which are more cerebral than sensual. They discard more and more the old art of optical illusion and local proportion, in order to express the grandeur of metaphysical forms. This is why contemporary art, even if it does not directly stem from specific religious beliefs, nonetheless possesses some of the characteristics of great, that is to say, religious art.

It is the social function of great poets and artists to renew continually the appearance nature has for the eyes of men.

Without poets, without artists, men would soon weary of nature's monotony. The sublime idea men have of the universe would collapse with dizzying speed. The order which we find in nature, and which is only an effect of art, would at once vanish. Everything would break up in chaos. There would be no seasons, no civilization, no thought, no humanity; even life would give way, and the impotent void would reign everywhere.

Poets and artists plot the characteristics of their epoch, and the future docilely falls in with their desires.

The general form of an Egyptian mummy is in conformity with the figures drawn by Egyptian artists, and yet the ancient Egyptians were far from being all alike. They simply conformed to the art of their time.

To create the illusion of the typical is the social role and peculiar end of art. God knows how the pictures of Monet and Renoir were abused! Very well! But one has only to glance at some photographs of the period to see how closely people and things conformed to the pictures of them by these great painters.

Since of all the plastic products of an epoch, works of art have the most energy, this illusion seems to me quite natural. The energy of art imposes itself on men, and becomes for them the plastic standard of the period. Thus, those who mock the new painters are actually laughing at their own features, for people in the future will portray the men of today to be as they are represented in the most alive, which is to say, the newest art of our time. And do not tell me there are today various other schools of painting in whose images humanity will be able to recognize itself. All the art works of an epoch end by resembling the most energetic, the most expressive, and the most typical works of the period. Dolls belong to popular art; yet they always seem to be inspired by the great art of the same epoch. This is a truth which can easily be verified. Yet who would dare to say that the dolls which were sold at bargain counters, around 1880, were shaped by a sentiment akin to what Renoir felt when he painted his portraits? No one perceived the relationship then. But this only means that Renoir's art was sufficiently energetic to take hold of our senses, even though to the general public of the epoch in which he made his debut, his conceptions seemed absurd and foolish.

There has been a certain amount of suspicion, notably in the case of the most recent painters, of some collective hoax or error.

But in all the history of art there is not a single instance of such general collaboration in artistic fraud or error. There are, indeed, isolated cases of mystification and blundering. But the conventional elements of which works of art are to a great extent composed guarantee the impossibility of such instances becoming general.

If the new school of painting were indeed an exception to this rule, it would be so extraordinary as to verge on the miraculous. As readily imagine all the children of some country born without heads, legs or arms, an obvious absurdity. There are no collective errors or hoaxes in art; there are only various epochs and dissimilar schools. Even if the aims pursued by these schools are not all equally elevated or equally pure, all are equally respectable, and, according to the ideas one has of beauty, each artistic school is successively admired, despised, and admired once more.

_____

The new school of painting is known as cubism, a name first applied to it in the fall of 1908 in a spirit of derision by Henri Matisse, who had just seen a picture of some houses, whose cube-like appearance had greatly struck him.

The new aesthetics was first elaborated in the mind of André Derain, but the most important and audacious works the movement at once produced were those of a great artist, Pablo Picasso, who must also be considered one of the founders: his inventions, corroborated by the good sense of Georges Braque, who exhibited a cubist picture at the *Salon des Indépendants* as early as 1908, were envisaged in the studies of Jean Metzinger, who exhibited the first cubist portrait (a portrait of myself) at the *Salon des Indépendants* in 1910, and who in the same year managed to induce the jury of the *Salon d'Automne* to admit some cubist paintings. It was also in 1910 that pictures by Robert Delaunay, Marie Laurencin, and Le Fauconnier, who all belonged to the same school, were exhibited at the *Indépendants*. . . .

Cubism differs from the old schools of painting in that it aims, not at an art of imitation, but at an art of conception, which tends to rise to the height of creation.

In representing conceptualized reality or creative reality, the painter can give the effect of three dimensions. He can to a certain extent cube. But not by simply rendering reality as seen, unless he indulges in *trompe-l'oeil*, in foreshortening, or in perspective, thus distorting the quality of the forms conceived or created.

I can discriminate four trends in cubism. Of these, two are pure, and along parallel lines.

Scientific cubism is one of the pure tendencies. It is the art of painting new structures out of elements borrowed not from the reality of sight, but from the reality of insight. All men have a sense of this interior reality. A man does not have to be cultivated in order to conceive, for example, of a round form.

The geometrical aspect, which made such an impression on those who saw the first canvases of the scientific cubists, came from the fact that the essential reality was rendered with great purity, while visual accidents and anecdotes had been eliminated. The painters who follow this tendency are: Picasso, whose luminous art also belongs to the other pure tendency of cubism, Georges Braque, Albert Gleizes, Marie Laurencin, and Juan Gris.

Physical cubism is the art of painting new structures with elements borrowed, for the most part, from visual reality. This art, however, belongs in the cubist movement because of its constructive discipline. It has a great future as historical painting. Its social role is very clear, but it is not a pure art. It confuses what is properly the subject with images. The painter-physicist who created this trend is Le Fauconnier.

Orphic cubism is the other important trend of the new art school. It is the art of painting new structures out of elements which have not been borrowed from the visual sphere, but have been created entirely by the artist himself, and been endowed by him with fullness of reality. The works of the orphic artist must simultanously give a pure aesthetic pleasure, a structure which is self-evident, and a sublime meaning, that is, a subject. This is pure art. The light in Picasso's paintings is based on this conception, to which Robert Delaunay's inventions have contributed much, and towards which Fernand Léger, Francis Picabia, and Marcel Duchamp are also addressing themselves.

Instinctive cubism, the art of painting new structures of elements which are not borrowed from visual reality, but are suggested to the artist by instinct and intuition, has long tended towards orphism. The instinctive artist lacks lucidity and an aesthetic doctrine; instinctive cubism includes a large number of artists. Born of French impressionism, this movement has now spread all over Europe.

Cézanne's last paintings and his water-colors belong to cubism, but Courbet is the father of the new painters; and André Derain, whom I propose to discuss some other time, was the eldest of his beloved sons, for we find him at the beginning of the fauvist movement, which was a kind of introduction to cubism, and also at the beginnings of this great subjective movement; but it would be too difficult today to write discerningly of a man who so willfully stands apart from everyone and everything.

The modern school of painting seems to me the most audacious that has ever appeared. It has posed the question of what is beautiful in itself.

It wants to visualize beauty disengaged from whatever charm man has for man, and until now, no European artist has dared attempt this. The new artists demand an ideal beauty, which will be, not merely the proud expression of the species, but the expression of the universe, to the degree that it has been humanized by light.

The new art clothes its creations with a grandiose and monumental appearance which surpasses anything else conceived by the artists of our time. Ardent in its search for beauty, it is noble and energetic, and the reality it brings us is marvelously clear. I love the art of today because above all else I love the light, for man loves light more than anything; it was he who invented fire.

MARCEL DUCHAMP

The Non-Picture

KIND OF SUB-TITLE
DELAY IN GLASS

Use "delay" instead of "picture" or
"painting"; "picture on glass" becomes
"delay in glass"—but "delay in
glass" does not mean "picture
on glass"—
   It's merely a way
of succeeding in no longer thinking
that the thing in question is
a picture—to make a "delay" of it
in the most general way possible,
not so much in the different meanings
in which "delay" can be taken, but
rather in their indecisive reunion
"delay"—a "delay in glass"
      as you would say a "poem in prose"
      or a spittoon in silver

"Kind of Sub-Title," *The Green Box*, translated from the French by George Heard Hamilton, New Haven, 1957, unpaged; reprinted by permission of George Heard Hamilton and Marcel Duchamp.

VIRGINIA WOOLF

The Novel of Consciousness

In making any survey, even the freest and loosest, of modern fiction, it is difficult not to take it for granted that the modern practice of the art is somehow an improvement upon the old. With their simple tools and primitive materials, it might be said, Fielding did well and Jane Austen even better, but compare their opportunities with ours! Their masterpieces certainly have a strange air of simplicity. And yet the analogy between literature and the process, to choose an example, of making motor cars scarcely holds good beyond the first glance. It is doubtful whether in the course of the centuries, though we have learnt much about making machines, we have learnt anything about making literature. We do not come to write better; all that we can be said to do is to keep moving, now a little in this direction, now in that, but with a circular tendency should the whole course of the track be viewed from a sufficiently lofty pinnacle. It need scarcely be said that we make no claim to stand, even momentarily, upon that vantage ground. On the flat, in the crowd, half blind with dust, we look back with envy to those happier warriors, whose battle is won and whose achievements wear so serene an air of accomplishment that we can scarcely refrain from whispering that the fight was not so fierce for them as for us. It is for the historian of literature to decide; for him to say if we are now beginning or ending or standing in the middle of a great period of prose fiction, for down in the plain little is visible. We only know that certain gratitudes and hostilities inspire us; that certain paths seem to lead to fertile land, others to the dust and the desert; and of this perhaps it may be worth while to attempt some account.

Our quarrel, then, is not with the classics, and if we speak of quarrelling with Mr. Wells, Mr. Bennett, and Mr. Galsworthy, it is partly that by the mere fact of their existence in the flesh their work has a living, breathing, everyday imperfection which bids us take what liberties with it we choose. But it is also true that, while we thank them for a thousand gifts, we reserve our unconditional gratitude for Mr. Hardy, for Mr. Conrad, and in a much lesser degree for the Mr. Hudson of *The Purple Land, Green Mansions,* and *Far Away and Long Ago.* Mr. Wells, Mr. Bennett, and Mr. Galsworthy have excited so many hopes and

"Modern Fiction" [1919], from *The Common Reader* (I), London and New York, 1925, pp. 184-95. Copyright 1925 by Harcourt, Brace & World, Inc.; renewed 1953 by Leonard Woolf; reprinted by permission of Harcourt, Brace & World Inc., The Hogarth Press, and Leonard Woolf.

disappointed them so persistently that our gratitude largely takes the form of thanking them for having shown us what they might have done but have not done; what we certainly could not do, but as certainly, perhaps, do not wish to do. No single phrase will sum up the charge or grievance which we have to bring against a mass of work so large in its volume and embodying so many qualities, both admirable and the reverse. If we tried to formulate our meaning in one word we should say that these three writers are materialists. It is because they are concerned not with the spirit but with the body that they have disappointed us, and left us with the feeling that the sooner English fiction turns its back upon them, as politely as may be, and marches, if only into the desert, the better for its soul. Naturally, no single word reaches the centre of three separate targets. In the case of Mr. Wells it falls notably wide of the mark. And yet even with him it indicates to our thinking the fatal alloy in his genius, the great clod of clay that has got itself mixed up with the purity of his inspiration. But Mr. Bennett is perhaps the worst culprit of the three, inasmuch as he is by far the best workman. He can make a book so well constructed and solid in its craftsmanship that it is difficult for the most exacting of critics to see through what chink or crevice decay can creep in. There is not so much as a draught between the frames of the windows, or a crack in the boards. And yet—if life should refuse to live there? That is a risk which the creator of *The Old Wives' Tale*, George Cannon, Edwin Clayhanger, and hosts of other figures, may well claim to have surmounted. His characters live abundantly, even unexpectedly, but it remains to ask how do they live, and what do they live for? More and more they seem to us, deserting even the well-built villa in the Five Towns, to spend their time in some softly padded first-class railway carriage, pressing bells and buttons innumerable; and the destiny to which they travel so luxuriously becomes more and more unquestionably an eternity of bliss spent in the very best hotel in Brighton. It can scarcely be said of Mr. Wells that he is a materialist in the sense that he takes too much delight in the solidity of his fabric. His mind is too generous in its sympathies to allow him to spend much time in making things shipshape and substantial. He is a materialist from sheer goodness of heart, taking upon his shoulders the work that ought to have been discharged by Government officials, and in the plethora of his ideas and facts scarcely having leisure to realise, or forgetting to think important, the crudity and coarseness of his human beings. Yet what more damaging criticism can there be both of his earth and of his Heaven than that they are to be inhabited here and hereafter by his Joans and his Peters? Does not the inferiority of their natures tarnish whatever institutions and ideals may be provided for them by the generosity of their creator? Nor, profoundly though we respect the integrity and humanity of Mr. Galsworthy, shall we find what we seek in his pages.

If we fasten, then, one label on all these books, on which is one word, materialists, we mean by it that they write of unimportant things; that they spend immense skill and immense industry making the trivial and the transitory appear the true and the enduring.

We have to admit that we are exacting, and, further, that we find it difficult to justify our discontent by explaining what it is that we exact. We frame our question differently at different times. But it reappears most persistently as we drop the finished novel on the crest of a sigh—Is it worth while? What is the point of it all? Can it be that, owing to one of those little deviations which the human spirit seems to make from time to time, Mr. Bennett has come down with his magnificent apparatus for catching life just an inch or two on the wrong side? Life escapes; and perhaps without life nothing else is worth while. It is a confession of vagueness to have to make use of such a figure as this, but we scarcely better the matter by speaking, as critics are prone to do, of reality. Admitting the vagueness which afflicts all criticism of novels, let us hazard the opinion that for us at this moment the form of fiction most in vogue more often misses than secures the thing we seek. Whether we call it life or spirit, truth or reality, this, the essential thing, has moved off, or on, and refuses to be contained any longer in such ill-fitting vestments as we provide. Nevertheless, we go on perseveringly, conscientiously, constructing our two and thirty chapters after a design which more and more ceases to resemble the vision in our minds. So much of the enormous labour of proving the solidity, the likeness to life, of the story is not merely labour thrown away but labour misplaced to the extent of obscuring and blotting out the light of the conception. The writer seems constrained, not by his own free will but by some powerful and unscrupulous tyrant who has him in thrall, to provide a plot, to provide comedy, tragedy, love interest, and an air of probability embalming the whole so impeccable that if all his figures were to come to life they would find themselves dressed down to the last button of their coats in the fashion of the hour. The tyrant is obeyed; the novel is done to a turn. But sometimes, more and more often as time goes by, we suspect a momentary doubt, a spasm of rebellion, as the pages fill themselves in the customary way. Is life like this? Must novels be like this?

Look within and life, it seems, is very far from being "like this." Examine for a moment an ordinary mind on an ordinary day. The mind receives a myriad impressions—trivial, fantastic, evanescent, or engraved with the sharpness of steel. From all sides they come, an incessant shower of innumerable atoms; and as they fall, as they shape themselves into the life of Monday or Tuesday, the accent falls differently from of old; the moment of importance came not here but there; so that, if a writer were a free man and not a slave, if he could write what he chose, not what he must, if he could base his work upon his own feeling and not upon convention, there would be no plot, no comedy, no tragedy, no love interest or catastrophe in the accepted style, and perhaps not a single button sewn on as the Bond Street tailors would have it. Life is not a series of gig lamps symmetrically arranged; life is a luminous halo, a semi-transparent envelope surrounding us from the beginning of consciousness to the end. Is it not the task of the novelist to convey this varying, this unknown and uncircumscribed spirit, whatever aberration or complexity it may display, with as little mixture of the alien and external as possible? We are not pleading merely for courage and sincerity; we are suggesting that the proper stuff of fiction is a little other than custom would have us believe it.

It is, at any rate, in some such fashion as this that we seek to define the quality which distinguishes the work of several young writers, among whom Mr. James Joyce is the most notable, from that of their predecessors. They attempt to come closer to life, and to preserve more sincerely and exactly what interests and moves them, even if to do so they must discard most of the conventions which are commonly observed by the novelist. Let us record the atoms as they fall upon the

mind in the order in which they fall, let us trace the pattern, however disconnected and incoherent in appearance, which each sight or incident scores upon
the consciousness. Let us not take it for granted that life exists more fully in what
is commonly thought big than in what is commonly thought small. Any one who
has read *The Portrait of the Artist as a Young Man* or, what promises to be a
far more interesting work, *Ulysses*, now appearing in the *Little Review*, will have
hazarded some theory of this nature as to Mr. Joyce's intention. On our part,
with such a fragment before us, it is hazarded rather than affirmed; but whatever
the intention of the whole, there can be no question but that it is of the utmost
sincerity and that the result, difficult or unpleasant as we may judge it, is undeniably important. In contrast with those whom we have called materialists,
Mr. Joyce is spiritual; he is concerned at all costs to reveal the flickerings of that
innermost flame which flashes its messages through the brain, and in order to
preserve it he disregards with complete courage whatever seems to him adven-
titious, whether it be probability, or coherence, or any other of these signposts
which for generations have served to support the imagination of a reader when
called upon to imagine what he can neither touch nor see. The scene in the
cemetery, for instance, with its brilliancy, its sordidity, its incoherence, its sudden lightning flashes of significance, does undoubtedly come so close to the quick
of the mind that, on a first reading at any rate, it is difficult not to acclaim a
masterpiece. If we want life itself, here surely we have it. Indeed, we find ourselves fumbling rather awkwardly if we try to say what else we wish, and for what
reason a work of such originality yet fails to compare, for we must take high
examples, with *Youth* or *The Mayor of Casterbridge*. It fails because of the
comparative poverty of the writer's mind, we might say simply and have done
with it. But it is possible to press a little further and wonder whether we may
not refer our sense of being in a bright yet narrow room, confined and shut in,
rather than enlarged and set free, to some limitation imposed by the method as
well as by the mind. Is it the method that inhibits the creative power? Is it due
to the method that we feel neither jovial nor magnanimous, but centred in a self
which, in spite of its tremor of susceptibility, never embraces or creates what is
outside itself and beyond? Does the emphasis laid, perhaps didactically, upon
indecency, contribute to the effect of something angular and isolated? Or is it
merely that in any effort of such originality it is much easier, for contemporaries
especially, to feel what it lacks than to name what it gives? In any case it is a
mistake to stand outside examining "methods." Any method is right, every
method is right, that expresses what we wish to express, if we are writers; that
brings us closer to the novelist's intention if we are readers. This method has
the merit of bringing us closer to what we were prepared to call life itself; did
not the reading of *Ulysses* suggest how much of life is excluded or ignored, and
did it not come with a shock to open *Tristram Shandy* or even *Pendennis* and be
by them convinced that there are not only other aspects of life, but more important ones into the bargain.

However this may be, the problem before the novelist at present, as we suppose it to have been in the past, is to contrive means of being free to set down
what he chooses. He has to have the courage to say that what interests him is no
longer "this" but "that": out of "that" alone must he construct his work. For
the moderns "that," the point of interest, lies very likely in the dark places of

psychology. At once, therefore, the accent falls a little differently; the emphasis is upon something hitherto ignored; at once a different outline of form becomes necessary, difficult for us to grasp, incomprehensible to our predecessors. No one but a modern, no one perhaps but a Russian, would have felt the interest of the situation which Tchekov has made into the short story which he calls "Gusev." Some Russian soldiers lie ill on board a ship which is taking them back to Russia. We are given a few scraps of their talk and some of their thoughts; then one of them dies and is carried away; the talk goes on among the others for a time, until Gusev himself dies, and looking "like a carrot or a radish" is thrown overboard. The emphasis is laid upon such unexpected places that at first it seems as if there were no emphasis at all; and then, as the eyes accustom themselves to twilight and discern the shapes of things in a room we see how complete the story is, how profound, and how truly in obedience to his vision Tchekov has chosen this, that, and the other, and placed them together to compose something new. But it is impossible to say "this is comic," or "that is tragic," nor are we certain, since short stories, we have been taught, should be brief and conclusive, whether this, which is vague and inconclusive, should be called a short story at all.

The most elementary remarks upon modern English fiction can hardly avoid some mention of the Russian influence, and if the Russians are mentioned one runs the risk of feeling that to write of any fiction save theirs is waste of time. If we want understanding of the soul and heart where else shall we find it of comparable profundity? If we are sick of our own materialism the least considerable of their novelists has by right of birth a natural reverence for the human spirit. "Learn to make yourself akin to people. . . . But let this sympathy be not with the mind—for it is easy with the mind—but with the heart, with love towards them." In every great Russian writer we seem to discern the features of a saint, if sympathy for the sufferings of others, love towards them, endeavour to reach some goal worthy of the most exacting demands of the spirit constitute saintliness. It is the saint in them which confounds us with a feeling of our own irreligious triviality, and turns so many of our famous novels to tinsel and trickery. The conclusions of the Russian mind, thus comprehensive and compassionate, are inevitably, perhaps, of the utmost sadness. More accurately indeed we might speak of the inconclusiveness of the Russian mind. It is the sense that there is no answer, that if honestly examined life presents question after question which must be left to sound on and on after the story is over in hopeless interrogation that fills us with a deep, and finally it may be with a resentful, despair. They are right perhaps; unquestionably they see further than we do and without our gross impediments of vision. But perhaps we see something that escapes them, or why should this voice of protest mix itself with our gloom? The voice of protest is the voice of another and an ancient civilisation which seems to have bred in us the instinct to enjoy and fight rather than to suffer and understand. English fiction from Sterne to Meredith bears witness to our natural delight in humour and comedy, in the beauty of earth, in the activities of the intellect, and in the splendour of the body. But any deductions that we may draw from the comparison of two fictions so immeasurably far apart are futile save indeed as they flood us with a view of the infinite possibilities of the art and remind us that there is no limit to the horizon, and that nothing—no "method," no experiment, even of the wildest—is forbidden, but only falsity and pretence. "The proper stuff of fiction" does not exist; everything is the proper stuff of fiction, every feeling, every thought; every quality of brain and spirit is drawn upon; no perception comes amiss. And if we can imagine the art of fiction come alive and standing in our midst, she would undoubtedly bid us break her and bully her, as well as honour and love her, for so her youth is renewed and her sovereignty assured.

GUSTAVE FLAUBERT
Style as Absolute

17 March 1861

Flaubert said to us today: "The story, the plot of a novel is of no interest to me. When I write a novel I aim at rendering a color, a shade. For instance, in my Carthaginian novel, I want to do something purple. The rest, the characters and the plot, is a mere detail. In *Madame Bovary*, all I wanted to do was to render a grey color, the mouldy color of a wood-louse's existence. The story of the novel mattered so little to me that a few days before starting on it I still had in mind a very different Madame Bovary from the one I created: the setting and the overall tone were the same, but she was to have been a chaste and devout old maid. And then I realized that she would have been an impossible character."

There are in me, literally speaking, two distinct persons: one who is infatuated with bombast, lyricism, eagle flights, sonorities of phrase and the high points of ideas; and another who digs and burrows into the truth as deeply as he can, who likes to treat a humble fact as respectfully as a big one, who would like to make you feel almost *physically* the things he reproduces; this latter person likes to laugh, and enjoys the animal sides of man. . . .

What seems beautiful to me, what I should like to write, is a book about nothing, a book dependent on nothing external, which would be held together by the strength of its style, just as the earth, suspended in the void, depends on nothing external for its support; a book which would have almost no subject, or at least in which the subject would be almost invisible, if such a thing is possible. The finest works are those that contain the least matter; the closer expression comes to thought, the closer language comes to coinciding and merging with it, the finer the result. I believe that the future of Art lies in this direction. I

From Edmond and Jules de Goncourt, *Pages from the Goncourt Journal*, ed. and translated from the French by Robert Baldick, London and New York, 1962, p. 58; reprinted by permission of the copyright holders and Oxford University Press.
Letter to Louise Colet [1852] *Selected Letters*, translated from the French by Francis Steegmuller, London, 1954, pp. 127-8. Copyright 1953 by Francis Steegmuller; reprinted by permission of Farrar, Straus & Co. and Hamish Hamilton Ltd.

see it, as it has developed from its beginnings, growing progressively more ethereal, from the Egyptian pylons to Gothic lancets, from the 20,000-line Hindu poems to the effusions of Byron. Form, as it is mastered, becomes attenuated; it becomes dissociated from any liturgy, rule, yardstick; the epic is discarded in favor of the novel, verse in favor of prose; there is no longer any orthodoxy, and form is as free as the will of its creator. This emancipation from matter can be observed everywhere: governments have gone through similar evolution, from the oriental despotisms to the socialisms of the future.

It is for this reason that there are no noble subjects or ignoble subjects; from the standpoint of pure Art one might almost establish the axiom that there is no such thing as subject, style in itself being an absolute manner of seeing things.

ANDRÉ GIDE

The Pure Novel

I should like to strip the novel of every element that does not specifically belong to the novel. Just as photography in the past freed painting from its concern for a certain sort of accuracy, so the phonograph will eventually no doubt rid the novel of the kind of dialogue which is drawn from the life and which realists take so much pride in. Outward events, accidents, traumatisms, belong to the cinema. The novel should leave them to it. Even the description of the characters does not seem to me properly to belong to the *genre*. No; this does not seem to me the business of the *pure* novel (and in art, as in everything else, purity is the only thing I care about). No more than it is the business of the drama. And don't let it be argued that the dramatist does not describe his characters because the spectator is intended to see them transposed alive on the stage; for how often on the stage an actor irritates and baffles us because he is so unlike the person our own imagination had figured better without him. The novelist does not as a rule rely sufficiently on the reader's imagination.

———————

"Is it because the novel, of all literary *genres*, is the freest, the most *lawless*," held forth Edouard, ". . . is it for that very reason, for fear of that very liberty (the artists who are always sighing after liberty are often the most bewildered when they get it), that the novel has always clung to reality with such timidity? And I am not speaking only of the French novel. It is the same with the English novel; and the Russian novel, for all its throwing off of constraints, is a slave to resemblance. The only progress it looks to is to get still nearer to nature. The

From *The Counterfeiters* [1925], with Journal of "The Counterfeiters" by André Gide, translated by Dorothy Bussy, New York, 1927, pp. 67, 171-7; copyright 1927, 1955 by Alfred A. Knopf, Inc. Reprinted by permission of Alfred A. Knopf, Inc. and Martin Secker & Warburg Ltd.

novel has never known that 'formidable erosion of contours,' as Nietzsche calls
it; that deliberate avoidance of life, which gave style to the works of the Greek
dramatists, for instance, or to the tragedies of the French XVIIth century. Is
there anything more perfectly and deeply human than these works? But that's
just it—they are human only in their depths; they don't pride themselves on appearing so—or, at any rate, on appearing real. They remain works of art."

Edouard had got up, and, for fear of seeming to give a lecture, began to pour
out the tea as he spoke; then he moved up and down, then squeezed a lemon into
his cup, but, nevertheless, continued speaking:

"Because Balzac was a genius, and because every genius seems to bring to his
art a final and conclusive solution, it has been decreed that the proper function
of the novel is to rival the *état-civil*. Balzac constructed his work; he never
claimed to codify the novel; his article on Stendhal proves it. Rival the *état-civil!*
As if there weren't enough fools and boors in the world as it is! What have I to
do with the *état-civil? L'état c'est moi!* I, the artist; civil or not, my work
doesn't pretend to rival anything."

Edouard, who was getting excited—a little factitiously, perhaps—sat down. He
affected not to look at Bernard; but it was for him that he was speaking. If he
had been alone with him, he would not have been able to say a word; he was
grateful to the two women for setting him on.

"Sometimes it seems to me there is nothing in all literature I admire so much
as, for instance, the discussion between Mithridate and his two sons in Racine;
it's a scene in which the characters speak in a way we know perfectly well no
father and no sons could ever have spoken in, and yet (I ought to say for that
very reason) it's a scene in which all fathers and all sons can see themselves.
By localizing and specifying one restricts. It is true that there is no psychological
truth unless it be particular; but on the other hand there is no art unless it be
general. The whole problem lies just in that—how to express the general by the
particular—how to make the particular express the general. May I light my pipe?"

"Do, do," said Sophroniska.

"Well, I should like a novel which should be at the same time as true and as
far from reality, as particular and at the same time as general, as human and as
fictitious as *Athalie*, or *Tartuffe* or *Cinna*."

"And . . . the subject of this novel?"

"It hasn't got one," answered Edouard brusquely, "and perhaps that's the most
astonishing thing about it. My novel hasn't got a subject. Yes, I know, it sounds
stupid. Let's say, if you prefer it, it hasn't got *one* subject . . . 'a slice of life,'
the naturalist school said. The great defect of that school is that it always cuts its
slice in the same direction; in time, lengthwise. Why not in breadth? Or in
depth? As for me I should like not to cut at all. Please understand; I should like
to put everything into my novel. I don't want any cut of the scissors to limit its
substance at one point rather than at another. For more than a year now that
I have been working at it, nothing happens to me that I don't put into it—everything I see, everything I know, everything that other people's lives and my own
teach me. . . ."

And the whole thing stylized into art?" said Sophroniska, feigning the most
lively attention, but no doubt a little ironically. Laura could not suppress a smile.
Edouard shrugged his shoulders slightly and went **on:**

"And even that isn't what I want to do. What I want is to represent reality on the one hand, and on the other that effort to stylize it into art of which I have just been speaking."

"My poor dear friend, you will make your readers die of boredom," said Laura; as she could no longer hide her smile, she had made up her mind to laugh outright.

"Not at all. In order to arrive at this effect—do you follow me?—I invent the character of a novelist, whom I make my central figure; and the subject of the book, if you must have one, is just that very struggle between what reality offers him and what he himself desires to make of it."

"Yes, yes; I'm beginning to see," said Sophroniska politely, though Laura's laugh was very near conquering her. "But you know it's always dangerous to represent intellectuals in novels. The public is bored by them; one only manages to make them say absurdities and they give an air of abstraction to everything they touch."

"And then I see exactly what will happen," cried Laura; "in this novelist of yours you won't be able to help painting yourself."

She had lately adopted in talking to Edouard a jeering tone which astonished herself and upset Edouard all the more that he saw a reflection of it in Bernard's mocking eyes. Edouard protested:

"No, no. I shall take care to make him very disagreeable."

Laura was fairly started.

"That's just it; everybody will recognize you," she said, bursting into such hearty laughter that the others were caught by its infection.

"And is the plan of the book made up?" enquired Sophroniska, trying to regain her seriousness.

"Of course not."

"What do you mean? Of course not!"

"You ought to understand that it's essentially out of the question for a book of this kind to have a plan. Everything would be falsified if anything were settled beforehand. I wait for reality to dictate to me."

"But I thought you wanted to abandon reality."

"My novelist wants to abandon it; but I shall continually bring him back to it. In fact that will be the subject; the struggle between the facts presented by reality and the ideal reality."

The illogical nature of his remarks was flagrant—painfully obvious to everyone. It was clear that Edouard housed in his brain two incompatible requirements and that he was wearing himself out in the desire to reconcile them.

"Have you got on far with it?" asked Sophroniska politely.

"It depends on what you mean by far. To tell the truth, of the actual book not a line has been written. But I have worked at it a great deal. I think of it every day and incessantly. I work at it in a very odd manner, as I'll tell you. Day by day in a note-book, I note the state of the novel in my mind; yes, it's a kind of diary that I keep as one might do of a child. . . . That is to say, that instead of contenting myself with resolving each difficulty as it presents itself (and every work of art is only the sum or the product of the solutions of a quantity of small difficulties), I set forth each of these difficulties and study it. My note-book contains, as it were, a running criticism of my novel—or rather of the novel in general. Just think how interesting such a note-book kept by Dickens or Balzac would be; if we had the diary of the *Education Sentimentale* or of *The Brothers Kara-mazof!*—the story of the work—of its gestation! How thrilling it would be . . . more interesting than the work itself. . . ."

Edouard vaguely hoped that someone would ask him to read these notes. But not one of the three showed the slightest curiosity. Instead:

"My poor friend," said Laura, with a touch of sadness, "it's quite clear that you'll never write this novel of yours."

"Well, let me tell you," cried Edouard impetuously, "that I don't care. Yes, if I don't succeed in writing the book, it'll be because the history of the book will have interested me more than the book itself—taken the book's place; and it'll be a very good thing."

"Aren't you afraid, when you abandon reality in this way, of losing yourself in regions of deadly abstraction and of making a novel about ideas instead of about human beings?" asked Sophroniska kindly.

"And even so!" cried Edouard with redoubled energy. "Must we condemn the novel of ideas because of the groping and stumbling of the incapable people who have tried their hands at it? Up till now we have been given nothing but novels with a purpose parading as novels of ideas. But that's not it at all, as you may imagine. Ideas . . . ideas, I must confess, interest me more than men—interest me more than anything. They live; they fight; they perish like men. Of course it may be said that our only knowledge of them is through men, just as our only knowledge of the wind is through the reeds that it bends; but all the same the wind is of more importance than the reeds."

"The wind exists independently of the reed," ventured Bernard. His intervention made Edouard, who had long been waiting for it, start afresh with renewed spirit:

"Yes, I know; ideas exist only because of men; but that's what's so pathetic; they live at their expense."

Bernard had listened to all this with great attention; he was full of scepticism and very near taking Edouard for a mere dreamer; but during the last few moments he had been touched by his eloquence and had felt his mind waver in its breath; "But," thought Bernard, "the reed lifts its head again as soon as the wind has passed." He remembered what he had been taught at school—that man is swayed by his passions and not by ideas. In the meantime Edouard was going on:

"What I should like to do is something like the art of fugue writing. And I can't see why what was possible in music should be impossible in literature. . . ."

To which Sophroniska rejoined that music is a mathematical art, and moreover that Bach, by dealing only with figures and by banishing all pathos and all humanity, had achieved an abstract *chef d'œuvre* of boredom, a kind of astronomical temple, open only to the few rare initiated. Edouard at once protested that, for his part, he thought the temple admirable, and considered it the apex and crowning point of all Bach's career.

"After which," added Laura, "people were cured of the fugue for a long time to come. Human emotion, when it could no longer inhabit it, sought a dwelling place elsewhere."

The discussion tailed off in an unprofitable argument. Bernard, who until then had kept silent, but who was beginning to fidget on his chair, at last could bear it no longer; with extreme, even exaggerated deference, as was his habit whenever he spoke to Edouard, but with a kind of sprightliness, which seemed to make a jest of his deference:

"Forgive me, sir," said he, "for knowing the title of your book, since I learnt it through my own indiscretion—which however you have been kind enough to pass over. But the title seemed to me to announce a story."

"Oh, tell us what the title is!" said Laura.

"Certainly, my dear Laura, if you wish it. . . . But I warn you that I may possibly change it. I am afraid it's rather deceptive. . . . Well, tell it them, Bernard."

"May I? . . . *The Counterfeiters*," said Bernard. "But now *you* tell us—who are these Counterfeiters?"

"Oh dear! I don't know," said Edouard.

Bernard and Laura looked at each other and then looked at Sophroniska. There was a long sigh; I think it was drawn by Laura.

In reality, Edouard had in the first place been thinking of certain of his fellow novelists when he began to think of *The Counterfeiters*, and in particular of the Comte de Passavant. But this attribution had been considerably widened; according as the wind blew from Rome or from elsewhere, his heroes became in turn either priests or free-masons. If he allowed his mind to follow its bent, it soon tumbled headlong into abstractions, where it was as comfortable as a fish in water. Ideas of exchange, of depreciation, of inflation, etc., gradually invaded his book (like the theory of clothes in Carlyle's *Sartor Resartus*) and usurped the place of the characters. As it was impossible for Edouard to speak of this, he kept silent in the most awkward manner, and his silence, which seemed like an admission of penury, began to make the other three very uncomfortable.

"Has it ever happened to you to hold a counterfeit coin in your hands?" he asked at last.

"Yes," said Bernard; but the two women's "No" drowned his voice.

"Well, imagine a false ten-franc gold piece. In reality it's not worth two sous. But it will be worth ten francs as long as no one recognizes it to be false. So if I start from the idea that . . ."

"But why start from an idea?" interrupted Bernard impatiently. "If you were to start from a fact and make a good exposition of it, the idea would come of its own accord to inhabit it. If I were writing *The Counterfeiters* I should begin by showing the counterfeit coin—the little ten-franc piece you were speaking of just now."

So saying, he pulled out of his pocket a small coin, which he flung on to the table.

"Just hear how true it rings. Almost the same sound as the real one. One would swear it was gold. I was taken in by it this morning, just as the grocer who passed it on to me had been taken in himself, he told me. It isn't quite the same weight, I think; but it has the brightness and the sound of a real piece; it is coated with gold, so that, all the same, it is worth a little more than two sous; but it's made of glass. It'll wear transparent. No; don't rub it; you'll spoil it. One can almost see through it, as it is."

GUSTAVE FLAUBERT

The Impersonality of Art

I hasten to thank you; I have received everything you sent. Thank you for the letter, the books, and above all for the portrait. I am touched by this delicate attention.

I am going to read your three volumes slowly and attentively—that is (I am sure in advance), as they deserve.

But I am prevented from doing so for the moment, since before returning to the country I have to do some archaeological work in one of the least-known periods of antiquity—a task which is preparation for another task. I am going to write a novel whose action will take place three centuries before Christ. I feel the need of taking leave of the modern world: my pen has been steeped in it too long, and I am as weary of portraying it as I am disgusted by the sight of it.

With a reader such as you, Madame, one who is so understanding, frankness is a duty. I therefore answer your questions: *Madame Bovary* is based on no actual occurrence. It is a *totally fictitious* story; it contains none of my feelings and no details from my own life. The illusion of truth (if there is one) comes, on the contrary, from the book's impersonality. It is one of my principles that a writer should not be his own theme. An artist must be in his work like God in creation, invisible and all-powerful; he should be everywhere felt, but nowhere seen.

Furthermore, Art must rise above personal emotions and nervous suscepti- bilities. It is time to endow it with pitiless method, with the exactness of the physical sciences. Still, for me the capital difficulty remains style, form, that indefinable Beauty implicit in the conception and representing, as Plato said, the splendor of Truth.

For a long time, Madame, I led a life like yours. I too spent several years completely alone in the country, hearing in winter no sound but the rustle of the wind in the trees and the cracking of the drift-ice on the Seine under my window. If I have arrived at some understanding of life, it is because I have lived little in the ordinary sense of the word; I have eaten meagerly, but ruminated much; I have seen all kinds of people, and visited various countries. I have traveled on foot and on camel-back. I am acquainted with Parisian speculators and Damascus

Letter to Mlle. Leroyer de Chantepie [1857] *Selected Letters,* translated from the French by Francis Steegmuller, London, 1954, pp. 195-6. Copyright 1953 by Francis Steegmuller; reprinted by permission of Farrar, Straus & Co. and Hamish Hamilton Ltd.

Jews, with Italian ruffians and Negro mountebanks. I made a pilgrimage to the Holy Land and was lost in the snows of Parnassus—which may be taken symbolically.

Do not complain; I have been here and there in the world and have a thorough knowledge of that Paris you dream of; there is nothing to equal a good book at your fireside, the reading of *Hamlet* or *Faust* on a day when your responses are keen. My own dream is to buy a little palace in Venice, on the Grand Canal.

So there, Madame—part of your curiosity is gratified. To complete my portrait and biography, add only this: I am thirty-five, five feet eight, with the shoulders of a stevedore and the nervous irritability of a young lady of fashion. I am a bachelor and a recluse.

In closing, let me thank you again for sending me the picture. It will be framed and hung between those of loved ones. I suppress a compliment which is at the tip of my pen, and beg you to believe me your affectionate colleague.

If all you needed to be a poet were to have sensitive nerves, I should be greater than Shakespeare—or Homer either, for I imagine he was without nerves. But this is blasphemy. . . .

You often find children who are upset by music. They show great talent and remember tunes at a single hearing. When they play the piano they grow excited and their hearts beat faster. They get thin and pale, and fall ill; and like dogs they feel their nerves shrivel with pain at the very sound of music. It is not they that are the future Mozarts. Their *vocation* has been displaced; the spirit has passed into the flesh where it remains sterile, and the flesh decays; the result is neither genius nor good health.

It is the same with art. Feeling does not make poetry; and the more personal you are, the poorer you will be. That has always been my sin; I have always put myself into everything I have done. There I am, for instance, in Saint Anthony's place; the *Temptation* was mine and not the reader's. *The less one feels a thing, the more fit one is to express it in its true nature* (as it always is, in itself, in its generic being and divorced from all ephemeral conditions). But one must have the faculty for *making oneself feel*. This faculty is neither more nor less than genius; *which is*, to have the object posed in front of one.

RAINER MARIA RILKE

Artistic Objectivity

That is why I must be cautious in trying to write about Cézanne, which naturally tempts me greatly now. Not the person (I really ought to see that at last)

Letter to Clara Rilke [1907], *Letters*, translated from the German by Jane Bannard Greene and M. D. Herter Norton, New York, 1945-48, Vol. I, pp. 313-14. Copyright 1947 and 1948 by W. W. Norton & Co., Inc.; reprinted by permission of W. W. Norton & Co.

who takes in pictures from so private an angle is justified in writing about them; one who could quietly confirm them in their existence, without experiencing through them more or other than facts, would surely be fairest to them. But within my own life this unexpected contact, coming and making a place for itself as it did, is full of confirmation and pertinence. Another poor man. And what progress in poverty since Verlaine (if Verlaine wasn't already a relapse), who under *"Mon Testament"* wrote: *Je ne donne rien aux pauvres parce que je suis un pauvre moi-même,* and in almost all of whose work this not-giving was, this embittered displaying of empty hands, for which Cézanne during the last thirty years had no time. When should he have shown his hands? Malicious glances did often find them, whenever he was on his way, and lewdly uncovered their indigence; we, however, are given to know from the pictures only how massive and genuine the work lay in them to the end. This work, which had no preferences any more, no inclinations, no fastidious indulgences; whose smallest component had been tested on the scales of an infinitely sensitive conscience and which with such integrity reduced the existent to its color content that it began, beyond color, a new existence, without earlier memories. It is this unlimited objectivity, which declines to interfere in any other sphere, that makes Cézanne's portraits so outrageous and absurd to people. They apprehend, without realizing, that he was reproducing apples, onions, and oranges with sheer color (which to them may still seem a subordinate device of pictorial practice), but when they come to landscape, they miss interpretation, judgment, superiority, and where portraiture is concerned, why, the rumor of intellectual conception has been passed on even to the most bourgeois, and so successfully that something of the kind is already noticeable even in Sunday photographs of engaged couples and families. And here Cézanne naturally seems to them quite inadequate and not worth discussing at all. He is actually as alone in this salon as he was in life, and even the painters, the young painters, already pass him by more quickly because they see the dealers on his side.

T. S. ELIOT

The Objective Correlative

The only way of expressing emotion in the form of art is by finding an "ob-jective correlative"; in other words, a set of objects, a situation, a chain of events which shall be the formula of that *particular* emotion; such that when the ex-ternal facts, which must terminate in sensory experience, are given, the emotion is immediately evoked. If you examine any of Shakespeare's more successful tragedies, you will find this exact equivalence; you will find that the state of mind of Lady Macbeth walking in her sleep has been communicated to you by a skil-

From "Hamlet" [1919], in *Selected Essays:* New Edition, by T. S. Eliot, copyright 1932, 1936, 1950, by Harcourt, Brace & World Inc., pp. 124-5. © 1960 by T. S. Eliot. Reprinted by permission of Harcourt, Brace & World Inc. and Faber & Faber Ltd.

ful accumulation of imagined sensory impressions; the words of Macbeth on hearing of his wife's death strike us as if, given the sequence of events, these words were automatically released by the last event in the series. The artistic "inevitability" lies in this complete adequacy of the external to the emotion; and this is precisely what is deficient in *Hamlet*. Hamlet (the man) is dominated by an emotion which is inexpressible, because it is in *excess* of the facts as they appear. And the supposed identity of Hamlet with his author is genuine to this point: that Hamlet's bafflement at the absence of objective equivalent to his feelings is a prolongation of the bafflement of his creator in the face of his artistic problem. Hamlet is up against the difficulty that his disgust is occasioned by his mother, but that his mother is not an adequate equivalent for it; his disgust envelops and exceeds her. It is thus a feeling which he cannot understand; he cannot objectify it, and it therefore remains to poison life and obstruct action. None of the possible actions can satisfy it; and nothing that Shakespeare can do with the plot can express Hamlet for him. And it must be noticed that the very nature of the *données* of the problem precludes objective equivalence. To have heightened the criminality of Gertrude would have been to provide the formula for a totally different emotion in Hamlet; it is just *because* her character is so negative and insignificant that she arouses in Hamlet the feeling which she is incapable of representing.

JAMES JOYCE

Stasis and Objective Form

He was passing through Eccles' St one evening, one misty evening, with all these thoughts dancing the dance of unrest in his brain when a trivial incident set him composing some ardent verses which he entitled a "Vilanelle of the Temptress." A young lady was standing on the steps of one of those brown brick houses which seem the very incarnation of Irish paralysis. A young gentleman was leaning on the rusty railings of the area. Stephen as he passed on his quest heard the following fragment of colloquy out of which he received an impression keen enough to afflict his sensitiveness very severely.

The Young Lady—(drawling discreetly) . . . O, yes . . . I was . . . at the . . . cha . . . pel. . . .
The Young Gentleman—(inaudibly) . . . I . . . (again inaudibly) . . . I . . .
The Young Lady—(softly) . . . O . . . but you're . . . ve . . . ry . . . wick . . . ed. . . .

Stephen Hero, London and New York, 1944, p. 188. Copyright 1944 © 1955 by New Directions; reprinted by permission of New Directions and Jonathan Cape.
A Portrait of the Artist as a Young Man [1916], *The Portable Joyce*, ed. Harry Levin, New York, 1947, pp. 469-76, 477-82; reprinted by permission of The Viking Press Inc. and Jonathan Cape.

This triviality made him think of collecting many such moments together in a book of epiphanies. By an epiphany he meant a sudden spiritual manifestation, whether in the vulgarity of speech or of gesture or in a memorable phase of the mind itself. He believed that it was for the man of letters to record these epiphanies with extreme care, seeing that they themselves are the most delicate and evanescent of moments. He told Cranly that the clock of the Ballast Office was capable of an epiphany. Cranly questioned the inscrutable dial of the Ballast Office with his no less inscrutable countenance.

—Yes, said Stephen. I will pass it time after time, allude to it, refer to it, catch a glimpse of it. It is only an item in the catalogue of Dublin's street furniture. Then all at once I see it and I know at once what it is: epiphany—

—What?—

—Imagine my glimpses at that clock as the gropings of a spiritual eye which seeks to adjust its vision to an exact focus. The moment the focus is reached the object is epiphanised.

They lit their cigarettes and turned to the right. After a pause Stephen began:

—Aristotle has not defined pity and terror. I have. I say . . .

Lynch halted and said bluntly:

—Stop! I won't listen! I am sick. I was out last night on a yellow drunk with Horan and Goggins.

Stephen went on:

—Pity is the feeling which arrests the mind in the presence of whatsoever is grave and constant in human sufferings and unites it with the human sufferer. Terror is the feeling which arrests the mind in the presence of whatsoever is grave and constant in human sufferings and unites it with the secret cause.

—Repeat, said Lynch.

Stephen repeated the definitions slowly.

—A girl got into a hansom a few days ago, he went on, in London. She was on her way to meet her mother whom she had not seen for many years. At the corner of a street the shaft of a lorry shivered the window of the hansom in the shape of a star. A long fine needle of the shivered glass pierced her heart. She died on the instant. The reporter called it a tragic death. It is not. It is remote from terror and pity according to the terms of my definitions.

—The tragic emotion, in fact, is a face looking two ways, towards terror and towards pity, both of which are phrases of it. You see I use the word *arrest*. I mean that the tragic emotion is static. Or rather the dramatic emotion is. The feelings excited by improper art are kinetic, desire or loathing. Desire urges us to possess, to go to something; loathing urges us to abandon, to go from something. The arts which excite them, pornographical or didactic, are therefore improper arts. The esthetic emotion (I used the general term) is therefore static. The mind is arrested and raised above desire and loathing.

—You say that art must not excite desire, said Lynch, I told you that one day I wrote my name in pencil on the backside of the Venus of Praxiteles in the Museum. Was that not desire?

—I speak of normal natures, said Stephen. You also told me that when you were a boy in that charming carmelite school you ate pieces of dried cowdung.

Lynch broke again into a whinny of laughter and again rubbed both his hands over his groins but without taking them from his pockets.

—O, I did! I did! he cried.

Stephen turned towards his companion and looked at him for a moment boldly in the eyes. Lynch, recovering from his laughter, answered his look from his humbled eyes. The long slender flattened skull beneath the long pointed cap brought before Stephen's mind the image of a hooded reptile. The eyes, too, were reptile-like in glint and gaze. Yet at that instant, humbled and alert in their look, they were lit by one tiny human point, the window of a shrivelled soul, poignant and self-embittered.

—As for that, Stephen said in polite parenthesis, we are all animals. I also am an animal.

—You are, said Lynch.

—But we are just now in a mental world, Stephen continued. The desire and loathing excited by improper esthetic means are really not esthetic emotions not only because they are kinetic in character but also because they are not more than physical. Our flesh shrinks from what it dreads and responds to the stimulus of what it desires by a purely reflex action of the nervous system. Our eyelid closes before we are aware that the fly is about to enter our eve.

—Not always, said Lynch critically.

—In the same way, said Stephen, your flesh responded to the stimulus of a naked statue but it was, I say, simply a reflex action of the nerves. Beauty expressed by the artist cannot awaken in us an emotion which is kinetic or a sensation which is purely physical. It awakens, or ought to awaken, or induces, or ought to induce, an esthetic stasis, an ideal pity or an ideal terror, a stasis called forth, prolonged and at last dissolved by what I call the rhythm of beauty.

—What is that exactly? asked Lynch.

—Rhythm, said Stephen, is the first formal esthetic relation of part to part in any esthetic whole or of an esthetic whole to its part or parts or of any part to the esthetic whole of which it is a part.

—If that is rhythm, said Lynch, let me hear what you call beauty: and, please remember, though I did eat a cake of cowdung once, that I admire only beauty.

Stephen raised his cap as if in greeting. Then, blushing slightly, he laid his hand on Lynch's thick tweed sleeve.

—We are right, he said, and the others are wrong. To speak of these things and to try to understand their nature and, having understood it, to try slowly and humbly and constantly to express, to press out again, from the gross earth or what it brings forth, from sound and shape and colour which are the prison gates of our soul, an image of the beauty we have come to understand—that is art.

They had reached the canal bridge and, turning from their course, went on by the trees. A crude grey light, mirrored in the sluggish water, and a smell of wet branches over their heads seemed to war against the course of Stephen's thought.

—But you have not answered my question, said Lynch. What is art? What is the beauty it expresses?

—That was the first definition I gave you, you sleepy-headed wretch, said Stephen, when I began to try to think out the matter for myself. Do you remember the night? Cranly lost his temper and began to talk about Wicklow bacon.

—I remember, said Lynch. He told us about them flaming fat devils of pigs.

—Art, said Stephen, is the human disposition of sensible or intelligible matter for an esthetic end. You remember the pigs and forgot that. You are a distressing pair, you and Cranly.

Lynch made a grimace at the raw grey sky and said:

—If I am to listen to your esthetic philosophy give me at least another cigarette. I don't care about it. I don't even care about women. Damn you and damn everything. I want a job of five hundred a year. You can't get me one.

Stephen handed him the packet of cigarettes. Lynch took the last one that remained, saying simply:

—Proceed!

—Aquinas, said Stephen, says that is beautiful the apprehension of which pleases. Lynch nodded.

—I remember that, he said, *Pulcra sunt quæ visa placent.*

—He uses the word *visa*, said Stephen, to cover esthetic apprehensions of all kinds, whether through sight or hearing or through any other avenue of apprehension. This word, though it is vague, is clear enough to keep away good and evil, which excite desire and loathing. It means certainly a stasis and not a kinesis. How about the true? It produces also a stasis of the mind. You would not write your name in pencil across the hypothenuse of a rightangled triangle.

—No, said Lynch, give me the hypothenuse of the Venus of Praxiteles.

—Static therefore, said Stephen. Plato, I believe, said that beauty is the splendour of truth. I don't think that it has a meaning but the true and the beautiful are akin. Truth is beheld by the intellect which is appeased by the most satisfying relations of the intelligible: beauty is beheld by the imagination which is appeased by the most satisfying relations of the sensible. The first step in the direction of truth is to understand the frame and scope of the intellect itself, to comprehend the act itself of intellection. Aristotle's entire system of philosophy rests upon his book of psychology and that, I think, rests on his statement that the same attribute cannot at the same time and in the same connexion belong to and not belong to the same subject. The first step in the direction of beauty is to understand the frame and scope of the imagination, to comprehend the act itself of esthetic apprehension. Is that clear?

—But what is beauty? asked Lynch impatiently. Out with another definition. Something we see and like! Is that the best you and Aquinas can do?

—Let us take woman, said Stephen.

—Let us take her! said Lynch fervently.

—The Greek, the Turk, the Chinese, the Copt, the Hottentot, said Stephen, all admire a different type of female beauty. That seems to be a maze out of which we cannot escape. I see, however, two ways out. One is this hypothesis: that every physical quality admired by men in women is in direct connexion with the manifold functions of women for the propagation of the species. It may be so. The world, it seems, is drearier than even you, Lynch, imagined. For my part I dislike that way out. It leads to eugenics rather than to esthetic. It leads you out of the maze into a new gaudy lectureroom where MacCann, with one hand on *The Origin of Species* and the other hand on the new testament, tells you that you admire the great flanks of Venus because you felt that she would bear you burly offspring and admired her great breasts because you felt that she would give good milk to her children and yours.

—Then MacCann is a sulphuryellow liar, said Lynch energetically.

—There remains another way out, said Stephen, laughing.

—To wit? said Lynch.

—This hypothesis, Stephen began.

A long dray laden with old iron came round the corner of Sir Patrick Dun's hospital covering the end of Stephen's speech with the harsh roar of jangled and rattling metal. Lynch closed his ears and gave out oath after oath till the dray had passed. Then he turned on his heel rudely. Stephen turned also and waited for a few moments till his companion's illhumour had had its vent.

—This hypothesis, Stephen repeated, is the other way out: that, though the same object may not seem beautiful to all people, all people who admire a beautiful object find in it certain relations which satisfy and coincide with the stages themselves of all esthetic apprehension. These relations of the sensible, visible to you through one form and to me through another, must be therefore the necessary qualities of beauty. Now, we can return to our old friend Saint Thomas for another pennyworth of wisdom.

Lynch laughed.

—It amuses me vastly, he said, to hear you quoting him time after time like a jolly round friar. Are you laughing in your sleeve?

—MacAlister, answered Stephen, would call my esthetic theory applied Aquinas. So far as this side of esthetic philosophy extends Aquinas will carry me all along the line. When we come to the phenomena of artistic conception, artistic gestation and artistic reproduction, I require a new terminology and a new personal experience.

—Of course, said Lynch. After all Aquinas, in spite of his intellect, was exactly a good round friar. But you will tell me about the new personal experience and new terminology some other day. Hurry up and finish the first part.

—Who knows? said Stephen, smiling. Perhaps Aquinas would understand me better than you. He was a poet himself. He wrote a hymn for Maundy Thursday. It begins with the words *Pange lingua gloriosi*. They say it is the highest glory of the hymnal. It is an intricate and soothing hymn. I like it: but there is no hymn that can be put beside that mournful and majestic processional song, the *Vexilla Regis* of Venantius Fortunatus.

Lynch began to sing softly and solemnly in a deep bass voice:

> Impleta sunt quæ concinit
> David fideli carmine
> Dicendo nationibus
> Regnavit a ligno Deus.

—That's great! he said, well pleased. Great music! . . .

They turned their faces towards Merrion Square and went on for a little in silence.

—To finish what I was saying about beauty, said Stephen, the most satisfying relations of the sensible must therefore correspond to the necessary phases of artistic apprehension. Find these and you find the qualities of universal beauty. Aquinas says: *Ad pulcritudinem tria requiruntur integritas, consonantia, claritas.* I translate it so: *Three things are needed for beauty, wholeness, harmony and radiance.* Do these correspond to the phases of apprehension? Are you following?

—Of course, I am, said Lynch. If you think I have an excrementitious intelligence run after Donovan and ask him to listen to you.

Stephen pointed to a basket which a butcher's boy had slung inverted on his head.

—Look at that basket, he said.

—I see it, said Lynch.

—In order to see that basket, said Stephen, your mind first of all separates the basket from the rest of the visible universe which is not the basket. The first phase of apprehension is a bounding line drawn about the object to be apprehended. An esthetic image is presented to us either in space or in time. What is audible is presented in time, what is visible is presented in space. But temporal or spatial, the esthetic image is first luminously apprehended as selfbounded and selfcontained upon the immeasurable background of space or time which is not it. You apprehended it as *one* thing. You see it as one whole. You apprehend its wholeness. That is *integritas.*

—Bull's eye! said Lynch, laughing. Go on.

—Then, said Stephen, you pass from point to point, led by its formal lines; you apprehend it as balanced part against part within its limits; you feel the rhythm of its structure. In other words, the synthesis of immediate perception is followed by the analysis of apprehension. Having first felt that it is *one* thing you feel now that it is a *thing.* You apprehend it as complex, multiple, divisible, separable, made up of its parts, the result of its parts and their sum, harmonious. That is *consonantia.*

—Bull's eye again! said Lynch wittily. Tell me now what is *claritas* and you win the cigar.

—The connotation of the word, Stephen said, is rather vague. Aquinas uses a term which seems to be inexact. It baffled me for a long time. It would lead you to believe that he had in mind symbolism or idealism, the supreme quality of beauty being a light from some other world, the idea of which the matter was but the shadow, the reality of which it was but the symbol. I thought he might mean that *claritas* was the artistic discovery and representation of the divine purpose in anything or a force of generalization which would make the esthetic image a universal one, make it outshine its proper conditions. But that is literary talk. I understand it so. When you have apprehended that basket as one thing and have then analysed it according to its form and apprehended it as a thing you make the only synthesis which is logically and esthetically permissible. You see that it is that thing which it is and no other thing. The radiance of which he speaks is the scholastic *quidditas,* the *whatness* of a thing. This supreme quality is felt by the artist when the esthetic image is first conceived in his imagination. The mind in that mysterious instant Shelley likened beautifully to a fading coal. The instant wherein that supreme quality of beauty, the clear radiance of the esthetic image, is apprehended luminously by the mind which has been arrested by its wholeness and fascinated by its harmony is the luminous silent stasis of esthetic pleasure, a spiritual state very like to that cardiac condition which the Italian physiologist

Luigi Galvani, using a phrase almost as beautiful as Shelley's, called the enchantment of the heart.

Stephen paused and, though his companion did not speak, felt that his words had called up around them a thought enchanted silence.

—What I have said, he began again, refers to beauty in the wider sense of the word, in the sense which the word has in the literary tradition. In the marketplace it has another sense. When we speak of beauty in the second sense of the term our judgment is influenced in the first place by the art itself and by the form of that art. The image, it is clear, must be set between the mind or senses of the artist himself and the mind or senses of others. If you bear this in memory you will see that art necessarily divides itself into three forms progressing from one to the next. These forms are: the lyrical form, the form wherein the artist presents his image in immediate relation to himself; the epical form, the form wherein he presents his image in mediate relation to himself and to others; the dramatic form, the form wherein he presents his image in immediate relation to others.

—That you told me a few nights ago, said Lynch, and we began the famous discussion.

—I have a book at home, said Stephen, in which I have written down questions which are more amusing than yours were. In finding the answers to them I found the theory of the esthetic which I am trying to explain. Here are some questions I set myself: *Is a chair finely made tragic or comic? Is the portrait of Mona Lisa good if I desire to see it? Is the bust of Sir Philip Crampton lyrical, epical or dramatic? If not, why not?*

—Why not, indeed? said Lynch, laughing.

—*If a man hacking in fury at a block of wood*, Stephen continued, *make there an image of a cow, is that image a work of art? If not, why not?*

—That's a lovely one, said Lynch, laughing again. That has the true scholastic stink.

—Lessing, said Stephen, should not have taken a group of statues to write of. The art, being inferior, does not present the forms I spoke of distinguished clearly one from another. Even in literature, the highest and most spiritual art, the forms are often confused. The lyrical form is in fact the simplest verbal vesture of an instant of emotion, a rhythmical cry such as ages ago cheered on the man who pulled at the oar or dragged stones up a slope. He who utters it is more conscious of the instant of emotion than of himself as feeling emotion. The simplest epical form is seen emerging out of lyrical literature when the artist prolongs and broods upon himself as the centre of an epical event and this form progresses till the centre of emotional gravity is equidistant from the artist himself and from others. The narrative is no longer purely personal. The personality of the artist passes into the narration itself, flowing round and round the persons and the action like a vital sea. This progress you will see easily in that old English ballad *Turpin Hero* which begins in the first person and ends in the third person. The dramatic form is reached when the vitality which has flowed and eddied round each person fills every person with such vital force that he or she assumes a proper and intangible esthetic life. The personality of the artist, at first a cry or a cadence or a mood and then a fluid and lambent narrative, finally refines itself out of existence, impersonalises itself, so to speak. The esthetic image in the dramatic form is life purified in and reprojected from the human imagination. The mystery of esthetic like that of material creation is accomplished. The artist, like the God of the creation, remains within or behind or beyond or above his handiwork, invisible, refined out of existence, indifferent, paring his fingernails.

—Trying to refine them also out of existence, said Lynch.

F. S. FLINT AND EZRA POUND
Imagism

Some curiosity has been aroused concerning *Imagisme,* and as I was unable to find anything definite about it in print, I sought out an *imagiste,* with intent to discover whether the group itself knew anything about the "movement." I gleaned these facts.

The *imagistes* admitted that they were contemporaries of the Post Impressionists and the Futurists; but they had nothing in common with these schools. They had not published a manifesto. They were not a revolutionary school; their only endeavor was to write in accordance with the best tradition, as they found it in the best writers of all time,—in Sappho, Catullus, Villon. They seemed to be absolutely intolerant of all poetry that was not written in such endeavor, ignorance of the best tradition forming no excuse. They had a few rules, drawn up for their own satisfaction only, and they had not published them. They were:

1. Direct treatment of the "thing," whether subjective or objective.

2. To use absolutely no word that did not contribute to the presentation.

3. As regarding rhythm: to compose in sequence of the musical phrase, not in sequence of a metronome.

By these standards they judged all poetry, and found most of it wanting. They held also a certain "Doctrine of the Image," which they had not committed to writing; they said that it did not concern the public, and would provoke useless discussion.

The devices whereby they persuaded approaching poetasters to attend their instruction were:

1. They showed him his own thought already splendidly expressed in some classic (and the school musters altogether a most formidable erudition).

2. They re-wrote his verses before his eyes, using about ten words to his fifty.

Even their opponents admit of them—ruefully—"At least they do keep bad poets from writing!"

I found among them an earnestness that is amazing to one accustomed to the usual London air of poetic dilettantism. They consider that Art is all science, all religion, philosophy and metaphysic. It is true that *snobisme* may be urged

F. S. Flint, "Imagisme," and Ezra Pound, "A Few Don'ts by an Imagiste," *Poetry* (Chicago), I [1913], pp. 198-206. The statement by Pound appears also in *Pavannes and Divagations,* New York, 1958. © 1958 by Ezra Pound and reprinted with permission of New Directions and the author.

against them; but it is at least *snobisme* in its most dynamic form, with a great deal of sound sense and energy behind it; and they are stricter with themselves than with any outsider.   F. S. FLINT

An "Image" is that which presents an intellectual and emotional complex in an instant of time. I use the term "complex" rather in the technical sense employed by the newer psychologists, such as Hart, though we might not agree absolutely in our application.

It is the presentation of such a "complex" instantaneously which gives that sense of sudden liberation; that sense of freedom from time limits and space limits; that sense of sudden growth, which we experience in the presence of the greatest works of art.

It is better to present one Image in a lifetime than to produce voluminous works.

All this, however, some may consider open to debate. The immediate necessity is to tabulate A LIST OF DONT's for those beginning to write verses. But I can not put all of them into Mosaic negative.

To begin with, consider the three rules recorded by Mr. Flint, not as dogma—never consider anything as dogma—but as the result of long contemplation, which, even if it is some one else's contemplation, may be worth consideration.

Pay no attention to the criticism of men who have never themselves written a notable work. Consider the discrepancies between the actual writing of the Greek poets and dramatists, and the theories of the Graeco-Roman grammarians, concocted to explain their metres.

LANGUAGE

Use no superfluous word, no adjective, which does not reveal something.

Don't use such an expression as "dim lands *of peace*." It dulls the image. It mixes an abstraction with the concrete. It comes from the writer's not realizing that the natural object is always the *adequate* symbol.

Go in fear of abstractions. Don't retell in mediocre verse what has already been done in good prose. Don't think any intelligent person is going to be deceived when you try to shirk all the difficulties of the unspeakably difficult art of good prose by chopping your composition into line lengths.

What the expert is tired of today the public will be tired of tomorrow.

Don't imagine that the art of poetry is any simpler than the art of music, or that you can please the expert before you have spent at least as much effort on the art of verse as the average piano teacher spends on the art of music.

Be influenced by as many great artists as you can, but have the decency either to acknowledge the debt outright, or to try to conceal it.

Don't allow "influence" to mean merely that you mop up the particular decorative vocabulary of some one or two poets whom you happen to admire. A Turkish war correspondent was recently caught red-handed babbling in his dispatches of "dove-gray" hills, or else it was "pearl-pale," I can not remember.

Use either no ornament or good ornament.

RHYTHM AND RHYME

Let the candidate fill his mind with the finest cadences he can discover, preferably in a foreign language so that the meaning of the words may be less likely to divert his attention from the movement; e.g., Saxon charms, Hebridean Folk Songs, the verse of Dante, and the lyrics of Shakespeare—if he can dissociate the vocabulary from the cadence. Let him dissect the lyrics of Goethe coldly into their component sound values, syllables long and short, stressed and unstressed, into vowels and consonants.

It is not necessary that a poem should rely on its music, but if it does rely on its music that music must be such as will delight the expert.

Let the neophyte know assonance and alliteration, rhyme immediate and delayed, simple and polyphonic, as a musician would expect to know harmony and counterpoint and all the minutiae of his craft. No time is too great to give to these matters or to any one of them, even if the artist seldom have need of them.

Don't imagine that a thing will "go" in verse just because it's too dull to go in prose.

Don't be "viewy"—leave that to the writers of pretty little philosophic essays. Don't be descriptive; remember that the painter can describe a landscape much better than you can, and that he has to know a deal more about it.

When Shakespeare talks of the "Dawn in russet mantle clad" he presents something which the painter does not present. There is in this line of his nothing that one can call description; he presents.

Consider the way of the scientists rather than the way of an advertising agent for a new soap.

The scientist does not expect to be acclaimed as a great scientist until he has *discovered* something. He begins by learning what has been discovered already. He goes from that point onward. He does not bank on being a charming fellow personally. He does not expect his friends to applaud the results of his freshman class work. Freshmen in poetry are unfortunately not confined to a definite and recognizable class room. They are "all over the shop." Is it any wonder "the public is indifferent to poetry"?

Don't chop your stuff into separate *iambs*. Don't make each line stop dead at the end, and then begin every next line with a heave. Let the beginning of the next line catch the rise of the rhythm wave, unless you want a definite longish pause.

In short, behave as a musician, a good musician, when dealing with that phase of your art which has exact parallels in music. The same laws govern, and you are bound by no others.

Naturally, your rhythmic structure should not destroy the shape of your words, or their natural sound, or their meaning. It is improbable that, at the start, you will be able to get a rhythm-structure strong enough to affect them very much, though you may fall a victim to all sorts of false stopping due to line ends and caesurae.

The musician can rely on pitch and the volume of the orchestra. You can not. The term harmony is misapplied to poetry; it refers to simultaneous sounds of different pitch. There is, however, in the best verse a sort of residue of sound which remains in the ear of the hearer and acts more or less as an organ-base. A rhyme must have in it some slight element of surprise if it is to give pleasure; it need not be bizarre or curious, but it must be well used if used at all.

Vide further Vildrac and Duhamel's notes on rhyme in *"Technique Poétique."*

That part of your poetry which strikes upon the imaginative *eye* of the reader will lose nothing by translation into a foreign tongue; that which appeals to the ear can reach only those who take it in the original.

Consider the definiteness of Dante's presentation, as compared with Milton's rhetoric. Read as much of Wordsworth as does not seem too unutterably dull.

If you want the gist of the matter go to Sappho, Catullus, Villon, Heine when he is in the vein, Gautier when he is not too frigid; or, if you have not the tongues, seek out the leisurely Chaucer. Good prose will do you no harm, and there is good discipline to be had by trying to write it.

Translation is likewise good training, if you find that your original matter "wobbles" when you try to rewrite it. The meaning of the poem to be translated can not "wobble."

If you are using a symmetrical form, don't put in what you want to say and then fill up the remaining vacuums with slush.

Don't mess up the perception of one sense by trying to define it in terms of another. This is usually only the result of being too lazy to find the exact word. To this clause there are possibly exceptions.

The first three simple proscriptions will throw out nine-tenths of all the bad poetry now accepted as standard and classic; and will prevent you from many a crime of production.

". . . *Mais d'abord il faut être un poète,*" as MM. Duhamel and Vildrac have said at the end of their little book, *"Notes sur la Technique Poétique"*; but in an American one takes that at least for granted, otherwise why does one get born upon that august continent!   EZRA POUND

EZRA POUND

Vorticism

"It is no more ridiculous that a person should receive or convey an emotion by means of an arrangement of shapes, or planes, or colours, than that they should receive or convey such emotion by an arrangement of musical notes."

I suppose this proposition is self-evident. Whistler said as much, some years ago, and Pater proclaimed that "All arts approach the condition of music."

Whenever I say this I am greeted with a storm of "Yes, but" . . . s. "But why isn't this art futurism?" "Why isn't?" "Why don't?" and above all: "What, in Heaven's name, has it got to do with your Imagiste poetry?"

Let me explain at leisure, and in nice, orderly, old-fashioned prose.

We are all futurists to the extent of believing with Guillaume Apollinaire that

"On ne peut pas porter *partout* avec soi le cadavre de son père." But "futurism," when it gets into art, is, for the most part, a descendant of impressionism. It is a sort of accelerated impressionism.

There is another artistic descent *via* Picasso and Kandinsky; *via* cubism and expressionism. One does not complain of neo-impressionism or of accelerated impressionism and "simultaneity," but one is not wholly satisfied by them. One has perhaps other needs.

It is very difficult to make generalities about three arts at once. I shall be, perhaps, more lucid if I give, briefly, the history of the vorticist art with which I am most intimately connected, that is to say, vorticist poetry. Vorticism has been announced as including such and such painting and sculpture and "Imagisme" in verse. I shall explain "Imagisme," and then proceed to show its inner relation to certain modern paintings and sculpture.

Imagisme, in so far as it has been known at all, has been known chiefly as a stylistic movement, as a movement of criticism rather than of creation. This is natural, for, despite all possible celerity of publication, the public is always, and of necessity, some years behind the artists' actual thought. Nearly anyone is ready to accept "Imagisme" as a department of poetry, just as one accepts "lyricism" as a department of poetry.

There is a sort of poetry where music, sheer melody, seems as if it were just bursting into speech.

There is another sort of poetry where painting or sculpture seems as if it were "just coming over into speech."

The first sort of poetry has long been called "lyric." One is accustomed to distinguish easily between "lyric" and "epic" and "didactic." One is capable of finding the "lyric" passages in a drama or in a long poem not otherwise "lyric." This division is in the grammars and school books, and one has been brought up to it.

The other sort of poetry is as old as the lyric and as honourable, but, until recently, no one had named it. Ibycus and Liu Ch'e presented the "Image." Dante is a great poet by reason of this faculty, and Milton is a wind-bag because of his lack of it. The "image" is the furthest possible remove from rhetoric. Rhetoric is the art of dressing up some unimportant matter so as to fool the audience for the time being. So much for the general category. Even Aristotle distinguishes between rhetoric, "which is persuasion," and the analytical examination of truth. As a "critical" movement, the "Imagisme" of 1912 to '14 set out "to bring poetry up to the level of prose." No one is so quixotic as to believe that contemporary poetry holds any such position. . . . Stendhal formulated the need in his *De L'Amour:*—

"La poésie avec ses comparaisons obligées, sa mythologie que ne croit pas le poète, sa dignité de style à la Louis XIV et tout l'attirail de ses ornements appelés poétique, est bien au dessous de la prose dès qu'il s'agit de donner une idée claire et précise des mouvements de coeur, or dans ce genre on n'émeut que par la clarté."

Flaubert and De Maupassant lifted prose to the rank of a finer art, and one has no patience with contemporary poets who escape from all the difficulties of the infinitely difficult art of good prose by pouring themselves into loose verses.

The tenets of the Imagiste faith were published in March, 1913, as follows:—

I. Direct treatment of the "thing," whether subjective or objective.

II. To use absolutely no word that does not contribute to the presentation.

III. As regarding rhythm: to compose in sequence of the musical phrase, not in sequence of the metronome.

There followed a series of about forty cautions to beginners, which need not concern us here.

The arts have indeed "some sort of common bond, some inter-recognition." Yet certain emotions or subjects find their most appropriate expression in some one particular art. The work of art which is most "worth while" is the work which would need a hundred works of any other kind of art to explain it. A fine statue is the core of a hundred poems. A fine poem is a score of symphonies. There is music which would need a hundred paintings to express it. There is no synonym for the *Victory of Samothrace* or for Mr. Epstein's flenites. There is no painting of Villon's *Frères Humains*. Such works are what we call works of the "first intensity."

A given subject or emotion belongs to that artist, or to that sort of artist who must know it most intimately and most intensely before he can render it adequately in his art. A painter must know much more about a sunset than a writer, if he is to put it on canvas. But when the poet speaks of "Dawn in russet mantle clad," he presents something which the painter cannot present.

I said in the preface to my *Guido Cavalcanti* that I believed in an absolute rhythm. I believe that every emotion and every phase of emotion has some toneless phrase, some rhythm-phrase to express it.

(This belief leads to *vers libre* and to experiments in quantitative verse.)

To hold a like belief in a sort of permanent metaphor is, as I understand it, "symbolism" in its profounder sense. It is not necessarily a belief in a permanent world, but it is a belief in that direction.

Imagisme is not symbolism. The symbolists dealt in "association," that is, in a sort of allusion, almost of allegory. They degraded the symbol to the status of a word. They made it a form of metonomy. One can be grossly "symbolic," for example, by using the term "cross" to mean "trial." The symbolist's *symbols* have a fixed value, like numbers in arithmetic, like 1, 2, and 7. The imagiste's images have a variable significance, like the signs *a*, *b*, and *x* in algebra.

Moreover, one does not want to be called a symbolist, because symbolism has usually been associated with mushy technique.

On the other hand, Imagisme is not Impressionism, though one borrows, or could borrow, much from the impressionist method of presentation. But this is only negative definition. If I am to give a psychological or philosophical definition "from the inside," I can only do so autobiographically. The precise statement of such a matter must be based on one's own experience.

In the "search for oneself," in the search for "sincere self-expression," one gropes, one finds some seeming verity. One says "I am" this, that, or the other, and with the words scarcely uttered one ceases to be that thing.

I began this search for the real in a book called *Personæ*, casting off, as it were, complete masks of the self in each poem. I continued in long series of translations, which were but more elaborate masks.

Secondly, I made poems like "The Return," which is an objective reality and has a complicated sort of significance, like Mr. Epstein's "Sun God," or Mr.

Brzeska's "Boy with a Coney." Thirdly, I have written "Heather," which represents a state of consciousness, or "implies," or "implicates" it.

A Russian correspondent, after having called it a symbolist poem, and having been convinced that it was not symbolism, said slowly: "I see, you wish to give people new eyes, not to make them see some new particular thing."

These two latter sorts of poems are impersonal, and that fact brings us back to what I said about absolute metaphor. They are Imagisme, and in so far as they are Imagisme, they fall in with the new pictures and the new sculpture.

Whistler said somewhere in the *Gentle Art*: "The picture is interesting not because it is Trotty Veg, but because it is an arrangement in colour." The minute you have admitted that, you let in the jungle, you let in nature and truth and abundance and cubism and Kandinsky, and the lot of us. Whistler and Kandinsky and some cubists were set to getting extraneous matter out of their art; they were ousting literary values. The Flaubertians talk a good deal about "constatation." "The 'nineties" saw a movement against rhetoric. I think all these things move together, though they do not, of course, move in step.

The painters realise that what matters is form and colour. Musicians long ago learned that programme music was not the ultimate music. Almost anyone can realize that to use a symbol *with an ascribed or intended meaning* is, usually, to produce very bad art. We all remember crowns, and crosses, and rainbows, and what not in atrociously mumbled colour.

The Image is the poet's pigment.[1] The painter should use his colour because he sees it or feels it. I don't much care whether he is representative or non-representative. He should *depend*, of course, on the creative, not upon the mimetic or representational part in his work. It is the same in writing poems, the author must use his *image* because he sees it or feels it, *not* because he thinks he can use it to back up some creed or some system of ethics or economics.

An *image*, in our sense, is real because we know it directly. If it have an age-old traditional meaning this may serve as proof to the professional student of symbology that we have stood in the deathless light, or that we have walked in some particular arbour of his traditional paradiso, but that is not our affair. It is our affair to render the *image* as we have perceived or conceived it.

Browning's "Sordello" is one of the finest *masks* ever presented. Dante's "Paradiso" is the most wonderful *image*. By that I do not mean that it is a perseveringly imagistic performance. The permanent part is Imagisme, the rest, the discourses with the calendar of saints and the discussions about the nature of the moon, are philology. The form of sphere above sphere, the varying reaches of light, the minutiæ of pearls upon foreheads, all these are parts of the Image. The image is the poet's pigment; with that in mind you can go ahead and apply Kandinsky, you can transpose his chapter on the language of form and colour and apply it to the writing of verse. As I cannot rely on your having read Kandinsky's *Ueber das Geistige in der Kunst*, I must go on with my autobiography.

Three years ago in Paris I got out of a "metro" train at La Concorde, and saw suddenly a beautiful face, and then another and another, and then a beautiful child's face, and then another beautiful woman, and I tried all that day to find words for what this had meant to me, and I could not find any words that seemed

[1] The image has been defined as "that which presents an intellectual and emotional complex in an instant of time." AUTHOR'S NOTE.

to me worthy, or as lovely as that sudden emotion. And that evening, as I went home along the Rue Raynouard, I was still trying and I found, suddenly, the expression. I do not mean that I found words, but there came an equation . . . not in speech, but in little splotches of colour. It was just that—a "pattern," or hardly a pattern, if by "pattern" you mean something with a "repeat" in it. But it was a word, the beginning, for me, of a language in colour. I do not mean that I was unfamiliar with the kindergarten stories about colours being like tones in music. I think that sort of thing is nonsense. If you try to make notes permanently correspond with particular colours, it is like tying narrow meanings to symbols.

That evening, in the Rue Raynouard, I realized quite vividly that if I were a painter, or if I had, often, *that kind* of emotion, or even if I had the energy to get paints and brushes and keep at it, I might found a new school of painting, of "non-representative" painting, a painting that would speak only by arrangements in colour.

And so, when I came to read Kandinsky's chapter on the language of form and colour, I found little that was new to me. I only felt that some one else understood what I understood, and had written it out very clearly. It seems quite natural to me that an artist should have just as much pleasure in an arrangement of planes or in a pattern of figures, as in painting portraits of fine ladies, or in portraying the Mother of God as the symbolists bid us.

When I find people ridiculing the new arts, or making fun of the clumsy odd terms that we use in trying to talk of them amongst ourselves; when they laugh at our talking about the "ice-block quality" in Picasso, I think it is only because they do not know what thought is like, and that they are familiar only with argument and gibe and opinion. That is to say, they can only enjoy what they have been brought up to consider enjoyable, or what some essayist has talked about in mellifluous phrases. They think only "the shells of thought," as De Gourmont calls them; the thoughts that have been already thought out by others.

Any mind that is worth calling a mind must have needs beyond the existing categories of language, just as a painter must have pigments or shades more numerous than the existing names of the colours.

Perhaps this is enough to explain the words in my "Vortex":—

"Every concept, every emotion, presents itself to the vivid consciousness in some primary form. It belongs to the art of this form."

That is to say, my experience in Paris should have gone into paint. If instead of colour I had perceived sound or planes in relation, I should have expressed it in music or in sculpture. Colour was, in that instance, the "primary pigment"; I mean that it was the first adequate equation that came into consciousness. The Vorticist uses the "primary pigment." Vorticism is art before it has spread itself into flaccidity, into elaboration and secondary applications.

What I have said of one vorticist art can be transposed for another vorticist art. But let me go on then with my own branch of vorticism, about which I can probably speak with greater clarity. All poetic language is the language of exploration. Since the beginning of bad writing, writers have used images as ornaments. The point of Imagisme is that it does not use images *as ornaments*. The image is itself the speech. The image is the word beyond formulated language.

I once saw a small child go to an electric light switch and say, "Mamma, can

I *open* the light?" She was using the age-old language of exploration, the language of art. It was a sort of metaphor, but she was not using it as ornamentation.

One is tired of ornamentations, they are all a trick, and any sharp person can learn them.

The Japanese have had the sense of exploration. They have understood the beauty of this sort of knowing. A Chinaman said long ago that if a man can't say what he has to say in twelve lines he had better keep quiet. The Japanese have evolved the still shorter form of the *hokku*.

> The fallen blossom flies back to its branch:
> A butterfly.

That is the substance of a very well-known *hokku*. Victor Plarr tells me that once, when he was walking over snow with a Japanese naval officer, they came to a place where a cat had crossed the path, and the officer said, "Stop, I am making a poem." Which poem was, roughly, as follows:—

> The footsteps of the cat upon the snow:
> (are like) plum-blossoms.

The words "are like" would not occur in the original, but I add them for clarity.

The "one image poem" is a form of super-position, that is to say, it is one idea set on top of another. I found it useful in getting out of the impasse in which I had been left by my metro emotion. I wrote a thirty-line poem, and destroyed it because it was what we call work "of second intensity." Six months later I made a poem half that length; a year later I made the following *hokku*-like sentence:—

> The apparition of these faces in the crowd:
> Petals, on a wet, black bough.

I dare say it is meaningless unless one has drifted into a certain vein of thought.[2] In a poem of this sort one is trying to record the precise instant when a thing outward and objective transforms itself, or darts into a thing inward and subjective.

This particular sort of consciousness has not been identified with impressionist art. I think it is worthy of attention.

The logical end of impressionist art is the cinematograph. The state of mind of the impressionist tends to become cinematographical. Or, to put it another way, the cinematograph does away with the need of a lot of impressionist art.

There are two opposed ways of thinking of a man: firstly, you may think of him as that toward which perception moves, as the toy of circumstance, as the plastic substance *receiving* impressions; secondly, you may think of him as directing a certain fluid force against circumstance, as *conceiving* instead of merely reflecting and observing. One does not claim that one way is better than the other, one notes a diversity of the temperament. The two camps always exist.

[2] Mr. Flint and Mr. Rodker have made longer poems depending on a similar presentation of matter. So also have Richard Aldington, in his *In Via Sestina*, and "H. D." in her *Oread*, which latter poems express much stronger emotions than that in my lines here given. Mr. Hueffer gives an interesting account of a similar adventure of his own in his review of the Imagiste anthology.

In the 'eighties there were symbolists opposed to impressionists, now you have vorticism, which is, roughly speaking, expressionism, neo-cubism, and imagism gathered together in one camp and futurism in the other. Futurism is descended from impressionism. It is, in so far as it is an art movement, a kind of accelerated impressionism. It is a spreading, or surface art, as opposed to vorticism, which is intensive.

The vorticist has not this curious tic for destroying past glories. I have no doubt that Italy needed Mr. Marinetti, but he did not set on the egg that hatched me, and as I am wholly opposed to his aesthetic principles I see no reason why I, and various men who agree with me, should be expected to call ourselves futurists. We do not desire to evade comparison with the past. We prefer that the comparison be made by some intelligent person whose idea of "the tradition" is not limited by the conventional taste of four or five centuries and one continent.

Vorticism is an intensive art. I mean by this, that one is concerned with the relative intensity, or relative significance of different sorts of expression. One desires the most intense, for certain forms of expression *are* "more intense" than others. They are more dynamic. I do not mean they are more emphatic, or that they are yelled louder. I can explain my meaning best by mathematics.

There are four different intensities of mathematical expression known to the ordinarily intelligent undergraduate, namely: the arithmetical, the algebraic, the geometrical, and that of analytical geometry.

For instance, you can write

$$3 \times 3 + 4 \times 4 = 5 \times 5,$$
or, differently, $3^2 + 4^2 = 5^2$.

That is merely conversation or "ordinary common sense." It is a simple statement of one fact and does not implicate any other.

Secondly, it is true that

$$3^2 + 4^2 = 5^2, 6^2 + 8^2 = 10^2, 9^2 + 12^2 = 15^2, 39^2 + 52^2 = 65^2.$$

These are all separate facts, one may wish to mention their underlying similarity; it is a bore to speak about each one in turn. One expresses their "algebraic relation" as

$$a^2 + b^2 = c^2.$$

That is the language of philosophy. It MAKES NO PICTURE. This kind of statement applies to a lot of facts, but it does not grip hold of Heaven.

Thirdly, when one studies Euclid one finds that the relation of $a^2 + b^2 = c^2$ applies to the ratio between the squares on the two sides of a right-angled triangle and the square on the hypotenuse. One still writes it $a^2 + b^2 = c^2$, but one has begun to talk about form. Another property or quality of life has crept into one's matter. Until then one had dealt only with numbers. But even this statement does not *create* form. The picture is given you in the proposition about the square on the hypotenuse of the right-angled triangle being equal to the sum of the squares on the two other sides. Statements in plane and descriptive geometry are like talk about art. They are a criticism of the form. The form is not created by them.

Fourthly, we come to Descartian or "analytical geometry." Space is conceived as separated by two or by three axes (depending on whether one is treating form in one or more planes). One refers points to these axes by a series of co-ordinates. Given the idiom, one is able *actually to create.*

Thus, we learn that the equation $(x - a)^2 + (y - b)^2 = r^2$ governs the circle. It is the circle. It is not a particular circle, it is any circle and all circles. It is nothing that is not a circle. It is the circle free of space and time limits. It is the universal, existing in perfection, in freedom from space and time. Mathematics is dull ditchwater until one reaches analytics. But in analytics we come upon a new way of dealing with form. It is in this way that art handles life. The difference between art and analytical geometry is the difference of subject-matter only. Art is more interesting in proportion as life and the human consciousness are more complex and more interesting than forms and numbers.

This statement does not interfere in the least with "spontaneity" and "intuition," or with their function in art. I passed my last *exam.* in mathematics on sheer intuition. I saw where the line *had* to go, as clearly as I ever saw an image, or felt *caelestem intus vigorem.*

The statements of "analytics" are "lords" over fact. They are the thrones and dominations that rule over form and recurrence. And in like manner are great works of art lords over fact, over race-long recurrent moods, and over to-morrow.

Great works of art contain this fourth sort of equation. They cause form to come into being. By the "image" I mean such an equation; not an equation of mathematics, not something about *a*, *b*, and *c*, having something to do with form, but about *sea, cliffs, night,* having something to do with mood.

The image is not an idea. It is a radiant node or cluster; it is what I can, and must perforce, call a VORTEX, from which, and through which, and into which, ideas are constantly rushing. In decency one can only call it a VORTEX. And from this necessity came the name "vorticism." *Nomina sunt consequentia rerum,* and never was that statement of Aquinas more true than in the case of the vorticist movement. . . .

NOTE

I am often asked whether there can be a long imagiste or vorticist poem. The Japanese, who evolved the *hokku,* evolved also the Noh plays. In the best "Noh" the whole play may consist of one image. I mean it is gathered about one image. Its unity consists in one image, enforced by movement and music. I see nothing against a long vorticist poem.

On the other hand, no artist can possibly get a vortex into every poem or picture he does. One would like to do so, but it is beyond one. Certain things seem to demand metrical expression, or expression in a rhythm more agitated than the rhythms acceptable to prose, and these subjects, though they do not contain a vortex, may have some interest, an interest as "criticism of life" or of art. It is natural to express these things, and a vorticist or imagiste writer may be justified in presenting a certain amount of work which is not vorticism or imagisme, just as he might be justified in printing a purely didactic prose article. Unfinished sketches and drawings have a similar interest; they are trials and attempts toward a vortex.

The Value of Materials

The pictures done in 1950 and 1951 are closely linked, like all my works of these last years, to the specific behavior of the material used, and, if you will, to its disposition. I say its disposition in the sense one speaks of the disposition of an animal, for I should say right off that I see no great difference (metaphysically, that is) between the paste I spread and a cat, a trout or a bull. My paste is a being as these are. Less circumscribed, to be sure, and more emulsified; its ordinance is stranger, much stranger certainly; I mean foreign to us, humans, who are so very circumscribed, so far from the formless (or, at least, think ourselves to be). All the more interesting then, being the bearer of a knowledge to which, without its aid, one could not aspire. Capable of bringing to us astonishing news from the country of the non-circumscribed, from the country of the formless—far better than a cat, or a trout. Those who imagine that these kinds of pastes are something inert make a grave mistake. Formless does not mean inert, far from it! My connection with the material I use is like the bond of the dancer with his partner, the rider with his horse, the fortune teller with her cards. One can now understand how I feel in coming upon a new kind of coating, and with what eagerness I try it out.

I handled for a long time, this year, a paste which I made myself at the time I used it (it dries very quickly); I mixed zinc oxide with a lean but viscous varnish, rich in gum, very much like the one sold in New York under the name of damar varnish. This paste, while still fresh, repels the oil, and the glazes one applies on it organize themselves into enigmatic branchings. Gradually, as it dries, its resistance to the fat colored sauces weakens, and it assembles them differently. Its behavior changes every fifteen minutes.

These branched facts, running trees, by which I saw my figures suddenly illuminated, have transported me into an invisible world of fluids circulating in the bodies and around them, and have revealed to me a whole active theater of facts, which perform, I am certain, on some level of life. Half revealed, of course, in some sphinx's tongue, very different from our articulated languages: one expects such a tongue from a being as different from ourselves as gum-varnish. I must say my feeling is—always has been—very strong that the key to things must not be as we imagine it, but that the world must be ruled by strange systems of which we have not the slightest inkling. This is why I rush towards strange things. I am quite convinced that truth is strange; it is at the far end of strangeness that one has a chance to find the key to things.

Having been attached for such a long time—a whole year—to the particular theme of the body of the naked woman, it was to this theme again that I first linked my experiments with new techniques, and you will find examples in such paintings as *The Tree of Fluids*. When I ask myself what has brought me to this subject, so typical of the worst painting, I think it is, in part, because the female body, of all the objects in the world, is the one that has long been associated (for

"Landscaped Tables, Landscapes of the Mind, Stones of Philosophy," quoted in Peter Selz, *The Work of Jean Dubuffet*, New York, 1962, pp. 63-4; reprinted by permission of The Museum of Modern Art.

153

Occidentals) with a very specious notion of beauty (inherited from the Greeks and cultivated by the magazine covers); now it pleases me to protest against this aesthetic, which I find miserable and most depressing. Surely I aim for a beauty, but not that one. The idea that there are beautiful objects and ugly objects, people endowed with beauty and others who cannot claim it, has surely no other foundation than convention—old poppycock—and I declare that convention unhealthy. I enjoy, at any rate, dissociating, to begin with, this pretense of beauty from any object I undertake to paint, starting again from this naught. Very often this cleaning suffices for the object to emerge suddenly wonderful—as it is in fact, as any object can be. The beauty of an object depends on how we look at it and not at all on its proper proportions. It is my inclination in this direction that has made certain people believe the mood of my art to be bitter. These people have seen that I intend to sweep away everything we have been taught to consider— without question—as grace and beauty; but have overlooked my work to substitute another and vaster beauty, touching all objects and beings, not excluding the most despised—and, because of that, all the more exhilarating. The beauty for which I aim needs little to appear—unbelievably little. Any place—the most destitute—is good enough for it. I would like people to look at my work as an enterprise for the rehabilitation of scorned values, and, in any case, make no mistake, a work of ardent celebration.

RAINER MARIA RILKE

Language within Language

No one would think of thrusting a ropemaker, cabinetmaker or shoemaker away from his craft "into life," in order that he may be a better ropemaker, cabinetmaker or shoemaker; also the musician, the painter, the sculptor one would rather let carry on theirs. Only, with regard to him who writes, the craft seems to be so lowly, so naturally accomplished (everyone can write), that some (and among them at times also Dehmel) were of the opinion that the person occupied with writing would immediately fall into empty play if he were left alone too much with his craft! But what a fallacy! To be able to write is, God knows, no less "difficult a craft," all the more since the material of the other arts is removed as a matter of course from daily use, while the poet's task is increased by the strange obligation to set apart his word from the words of everyday life and communication thoroughly and fundamentally. No word in the poem (I mean here every "and" or "the") is identical with the same-sounding word in common use and conversation; the purer conformity with the law, the great relationship, the constellation it occupies in verse or artistic prose, changes it to the core of its nature, renders it useless, unserviceable for mere everyday use, untouchable and permanent: a transformation as it takes place, incredibly, splendidly, sometimes in Goethe (*Harz Journey in Winter*), often in George.

Letter to Countess Margot Sizzo-Crouz [1922], translated from the German by Eva Rennie, *Selected Letters*, ed. Harry T. Moore, New York, 1960, pp. 325-6. Reprinted by permission of Doubleday and Co.

JAMES JOYCE

Plastic Language

brings us back to Howth Castle & Environs. Sir Tristram, violer d'amores, had passencore rearrived on the scraggy isthmus from North Armorica

Letter to Harriet Shaw Weaver [1926], *Letters*, ed. Stuart Gilbert, London and New York, 1955, pp. 247-8; reprinted by permission of the Viking Press Inc. and Faber & Faber Ltd.

to wielderfight his penisolate war; nor had stream rocks by the Oconee exaggerated themselse to Laurens County, Ga, doublin all the time; nor avoice from afire bellowsed mishe to tauftauf thuartpeatrick; not yet, though venisoon after, had a Kidscad buttended a bland old isaac; not yet, though all's fair in vanessy, were sosie sesthers wroth with twone jonathan. Rot a peck of pa's malt had Shem or Shen brewed by arclight and rory end to the regginbrow was to be seen ringsome on the waterface.   JAMES JOYCE

Paris. 15/xi/926

Dear Madam: Above please find prosepiece ordered in sample form. Also key to same. Hoping said sample meets with your approval

yrs trly
Jeems Joker

Howth (pron Hoaeth) = Dan Hoved (head)
Sir Amory Tristram 1st earl of Howth changed his name to Saint Lawrence, b[orn] in Brittany (North Armorica)
Tristan et Iseult, passim
viola in all moods and senses
Dublin, Laurens Co, Georgia, founded by a Dubliner, Peter Sawyer, on r. Oconee. Its motto: Doubling all the time.
The flame of Christianity kindled by S. Patrick on Holy Saturday in defiance of royal orders
Mishe = I am (Irish) i.e. Christian
Tauf = baptise (German)
Thou art Peter and upon this rock etc (a pun in the original aramaic)
Lat: Tu es Petrus et super hanc petram
Parnell ousted Isaac Butt from leadership
The venison purveyor Jacob got the blessing meant for Esau
Miss Vanhomrigh and Miss Johnson had the same christian name
Sosie = double
Willy brewed a peck of maut
Noah planted the vine and was drunk
John Jameson is the greatest Dublin distiller
Arthur Guinness „ „   „   „   brewer
rory = Irish = red
rory = Latin, roridus = dewy
At the rainbow's end are dew and the colour red: bloody end to the lie in Anglo-Irish = no lie
regginbrow = German regenbogen + rainbow
ringsome = German ringsum, around
When all vegetation is covered by the flood there are no eyebrows on the face of the Waterworld
exaggerare = to mound up
themselse = another dublin 5000 inhabitants
Isthmus of Sutton a neck of land between Howth head and the plain

Howth = an island for old geographers
passencore = pas encore and *ricorsi storici* of Vico
rearrived = idem
wielderfight = wiederfechten = refight
bellowed = the response of the peatfire of faith to the windy words of the apostle

DYLAN THOMAS

A Battle of Images

When you say that I have not [Norman] Cameron's or [Charles] Madge's "concentric movement round a central image," you are not accounting for the fact that it consciously is not my method to move concentrically round a central image. A poem by Cameron *needs* no more than one image; it moves around one idea, from one logical point to another, making a full circle. A poem by myself *needs* a host of images, because its centre is a host of images. I make one image—though "make" is not the word; I let, perhaps, an image be "made" emotionally in me and then apply to it what intellectual and critical forces I possess—let it breed another, let that image contradict the first, make, of the third image bred out of the other two together, a fourth contradictory image, and let them all, within my imposed formal limits, conflict. Each image holds within it the seed of its own destruction, and my dialectal [dialectical?] method, as I understand it, is a constant building up and breaking down of the images that come out of the central seed, which is itself destructive and constructive at the same time.

What I want to try to explain—and it's necessarily vague to me—is that the *life* in any poem of mine cannot move concentrically round a central image; the life must come out of the centre; an image must be born and die in another; and any sequence of my images must be a sequence of creations, recreations, destructions, contradictions. I cannot, either—as Cameron does, and as others do, and this primarily explains his and their writing round the central image—make a poem out of a single motivating experience; I believe in the simple thread of action through a poem, but that is an intellectual thing aimed at lucidity through narrative. My object is, as you say, conventionally "to get things straight." Out of the inevitable conflict of images—inevitable, because of the creative, recreative, destructive and contradictory nature of the motivating centre, the womb of war —I try to make that momentary peace which is a poem. I do not want a poem of mine to be, nor can it be, a circular piece of experience placed nearly outside the living stream of time from which it came; a poem of mine is, or should be, a watertight section of the stream that is flowing all ways, all warring images within it should be reconciled for that small stop of time. I agree that each of my earlier poems might appear to constitute a section from one long poem; that is because I was not successful in making a momentary peace with my images at

Letter to Henry Treece, from Henry Treece, *Dylan Thomas*, London, 1956, p. 37; reprinted by permission of Ernest Benn Ltd.

the correct moment; images were left dangling over the formal limits, and dragged the poem into another; the warring stream ran on over the insecure barriers, the fullstop armistice was pulled and twisted raggedly on into a conflicting series of dots and dashes.

HART CRANE

The Dynamics of Metaphor

Apropos of the poem *At Melville's Tomb*, printed in the verse section of this number, the following correspondence between its author and the editor, printed with the consent of both, may be of interest to our readers.

FROM THE EDITOR TO MR. CRANE:

Take me for a hard-boiled unimaginative unpoetic reader, and tell me how *dice* can *bequeath an embassy* (or anything else); and how a calyx (*of death's bounty* or anything else) can give back a *scattered chapter, livid hieroglyph;* and how, if it does such a *portent* can be *wound in corridors* (of shells or anything else).

And so on. I find your image of *frosted eyes lifting altars* difficult to visualize. Nor do compass, quadrant and sextant *contrive* tides, they merely record them, I believe.

All this may seem impertinent, but is not so intended. Your ideas and rhythms interest me, and I am wondering by what process of reasoning you would justify this poem's succession of champion mixed metaphors, of which you must be conscious. The packed line should pack its phrases in orderly relation, it seems to me, in a manner tending to clear confusion instead of making it worse confounded.

But pardon me—you didn't ask for criticism. Of course I should not venture upon these remarks if I were not much interested.

FROM MR. CRANE TO THE EDITOR:

Your good nature and manifest interest in writing me about the obscurities apparent in my Melville poem certainly prompt a wish to clarify my intentions in that poem as much as possible. But I realize that my explanations will not be very convincing. For a paraphrase is generally a poor substitute for any organized conception that one has fancied he has put into the more essentialized form of the poem itself.

At any rate, and though I imagine us to have considerable differences of opinion regarding the relationship of poetic metaphor to ordinary logic (I judge this from the angle of approach you use toward portions of the poem), I hope my

A discussion with Harriet Monroe in *Poetry* (Chicago), xxix (Oct. 1926), pp. 34-41; reprinted by permission of *Poetry* (Chicago) and the estates of Hart Crane and Harriet Monroe.

answers will not be taken as a defense of merely certain faulty lines. I am really much more interested in certain theories of metaphor and technique involved generally in poetics, than I am concerned in vindicating any particular perpetrations of my own.

My poem may well be elliptical and actually obscure in the ordering of its content, but in your criticism of this very possible deficiency you have stated your objections in terms that allow me, at least for the moment, the privilege of claiming your ideas and ideals as theoretically, at least, quite outside the issues of my own aspirations. To put it more plainly, as a poet I may very possibly be more interested in the so-called illogical impingements of the connotations of words on the consciousness (and their combinations and interplay in metaphor on this basis) than I am interested in the preservation of their logically rigid significations at the cost of limiting my subject matter and perceptions involved in the poem.

This may sound as though I merely fancied juggling words and images until I found something novel, or esoteric; but the process is much more predetermined and objectified than that. The nuances of feeling and observation in a poem may well call for certain liberties which you claim the poet has no right to take. I am simply making the claim that the poet does have that authority, and that to deny it is to limit the scope of the medium so considerably as to outlaw some of the richest genius of the past.

This argument over the dynamics of metaphor promises as active a future as has been evinced in the past. Partaking so extensively as it does of the issues involved in the propriety or non-propriety of certain attitudes toward subject matter, etc., it enters the critical distinctions usually made between "romantic," "classic" as an organic factor. It is a problem that would require many pages to state adequately—merely from my own limited standpoint on the issues. Even this limited statement may prove onerous reading, and I hope you will pardon me if my own interest in the matter carries me to the point of presumption.

Its paradox, of course, is that its apparent illogic operates so logically in conjunction with its context in the poem as to establish its claim to another logic, quite independent of the original definition of the word or phrase or image thus employed. It implies (this *inflection* of language) a previous or prepared receptivity to its stimulus on the part of the reader. The reader's sensibility simply responds by identifying this inflection of experience with some event in his own history or perceptions—or rejects it altogether. The logic of metaphor is so organically entrenched in pure sensibility that it can't be thoroughly traced or explained outside of historical sciences, like philology and anthropology. This "pseudo-statement," as I. A. Richards calls it in an admirable essay touching our contentions in last July's *Criterion*, demands completely other faculties of recognition than the pure rationalistic associations permit. Much fine poetry may be completely rationalistic in its use of symbols, but there is much great poetry of another order which will yield the reader very little when inspected under the limitation of such arbitrary concerns as are manifested in your judgment of the Melville poem, especially when you constitute such requirements of ordinary logical relationship between word and word as irreducible.

I don't wish to enter here defense of the particular symbols in my own poem, because, as I said, I may well have failed to supply the necessary emotional connectives to the content featured. But I would like to counter a question or so of yours with a similar question. Here the poem is less dubious in quality than my own, and as far as the abstract pertinacity of question and its immediate consequences are concerned the point I'm arguing about can't be better demonstrated. Both quotations are familiar to you, I'm sure.

You ask me how a *portent* can possibly be wound in a *shell*. Without attempting to answer this for the moment, I ask you how Blake could possibly say that "a *sigh* is a *sword* of an Angel King." You ask me how *compass, quadrant and sextant* "*contrive*" tides. I ask you how Eliot can possibly believe that "Every street *lamp* that I pass *beats* like a fatalistic *drum!*" Both of my metaphors may fall down completely. I'm not defending their actual value in themselves, but your criticism of them in each case was leveled at an illogicality of relationship between symbols, which similar fault you must have either overlooked in case you have ever admired the Blake and Eliot lines, or have there condoned them on account of some more ultimate convictions pressed on you by the impact of the poems in their entirety.

It all comes to the recognition that emotional dynamics are not to be confused with any absolute order of rationalized definitions; ergo, in poetry the *rationale* of metaphor belongs to another order of experience than science, and is not to be limited by a scientific and arbitrary code of relationships either in verbal inflections or concepts.

There are plenty of people who have never accumulated a sufficient series of reflections (and these of a rather special nature) to perceive the relation between a *drum* and a *street lamp*—*via* the *unmentioned* throbbing of the heart and nerves in a distraught man which *tacitly* creates the reason and "logic" of the Eliot metaphor. They will always have a perfect justification for ignoring those lines and to claim them obscure, excessive, etc., until by some experience of their own the words accumulate the necessary connotations to complete their connection. It is the same with the "patient etherized upon a table," isn't it? Surely that line must lack all eloquence to many people who, for instance, would delight in agreeing that the sky was like a dome of many-colored glass.

If one can't count on some such bases in the reader now and then, I don't see how the poet has any chance to ever get beyond the simplest conceptions of emotion and thought, of sensation and lyrical sequence. If the poet is to be held completely to the already evolved and exploited sequences of imagery and logic —what field of added consciousness and increased perceptions (the actual province of poetry, if not lullabys) can be expected when one has to relatively return to the alphabet every breath or so? In the minds of people who have sensitively read, seen and experienced a great deal, isn't there a terminology something like short-hand as compared to usual description and dialectics, which the artist ought to be right in trusting as a reasonable connective agent toward fresh concepts, more inclusive evalutions? The question is more important to me than it perhaps ought to be; but as long as poetry is written, an audience, however small, is implied, and there remains the question of an active or an inactive imagination as its characteristic.

It is of course understood that a street-lamp simply can't beat with a sound like a drum; but it often happens that images, themselves totally dissociated, when joined in the circuit of a particular emotion located with specific relation to both of them, conduce to great vividness and accuracy of statement in defining that emotion.

Not to rant on forever I'll beg your indulgence and come at once to the explanations you requested on the Melville poem:

> The dice of drowned men's bones he saw bequeath
> An embassy.

Dice bequeath an embassy, in the first place, by being ground (in this connection only, of course) in little cubes from the bones of drowned men by the action of the sea, and are finally thrown up on the sand, having "numbers" but no identification. These being the bones of dead men who never completed their voyage, it seems legitimate to refer to them as the only surviving evidence of certain messages undelivered, mute evidence of certain things, experiences that the dead mariners might have had to deliver. Dice as a symbol of chance and circumstance is also implied.

> The calyx of death's bounty giving back, *etc.*

This calyx refers in a double ironic sense both to a cornucopia and the vortex made by a sinking vessel. As soon as the water has closed over a ship this whirlpool sends up broken spars, wreckage, etc., which can be alluded to as *livid hieroglyphs*, making a *scattered chapter* so far as any complete record of the recent ship and her crew is concerned. In fact, about as much definite knowledge might come from all this as anyone might gain from the roar of his own veins, which is easily heard (haven't you ever done it?) by holding a shell close to one's ear.

> Frosted eyes lift altars.

Refers simply to a conviction that a man, not knowing perhaps a definite god yet being endowed with a reverence for deity—such a man naturally postulates a deity somehow, and the altar of that deity by the very *action* of the eyes *lifted* in searching.

> Compass, quadrant and sextant contrive no farther tides.

Hasn't it often occurred that instruments originally invented for record and computation have inadvertently so extended the concepts of the entity they were invented to measure (concepts of space etc.) in the mind and imagination that employed them, that they may metaphorically be said to have extended the original boundaries of the entity measured? This little bit of "relativity" ought not to be discredited in poetry now that scientists are proceeding to measure the universe on principles of pure *ratio*, quite as metaphorical, so far as previous standards of scientific methods extended, as some of the axioms in *Job*.

I may have completely failed to provide any clear interpretation of these symbols in their context. And you will no doubt feel that I have rather heatedly explained them for anyone who professed no claims for their particular value. I hope, at any rate, that I have clarified them enough to suppress any suspicion that their obscurity derives from a lack of definite intentions in the subject-matter of the poem. The execution is another matter, and you must be accorded a superior judgment to mine in that regard.

FROM THE EDITOR TO MR. CRANE:

No doubt our theories and ideals in the art differ more or less fundamentally, yet I would not deny to the poet the right to take certain of the liberties you claim. I think he can take as many as he succeeds with without mystifying his particular audience; for mystery is good, but not mystification.

I think that in your poem certain phrases carry to an excessive degree the "dynamics of metaphor"—they telescope three or four images together by mental leaps (I fear my own metaphors are getting mixed!) which the poet, knowing his ground, can take safely, but which the most sympathetic reader cannot take unless the poet leads him by the hand with some such explanation as I find in your letter. I refer to such phrases as my letter quoted, except that I think I was over-exacting in criticizing the "quadrant and sextant" line. Accepting as I do much of what you say about "the illogical impingements of the connotations of words on the consciousness, and their combinations and interplay in metaphor," I must admit that these phrases in your poem are for me too elliptical to produce any effect but mystification (this until you explained them).

I don't get this effect from Blake or Eliot in the lines you quote or others that I have read. I am not familiar with Blake's symbolic poems but now, opening Prof. Pierce's volume of selections from them, I find in their use of metaphor a singular simplicity and clarity. He deals with magnificient mysteries, but presents them in flaming images like

> what time I bound my sandals
> On to walk forward through eternity.

I find here no crowded and tortured lines.

My argument comes down, I suppose, rather to your practice than your theory. Or, more specifically, your practice strains your theory by carrying it with relentless logic, to a remote and exaggerated extreme. You find me testing metaphors, and poetic concept in general, too much by logic, whereas I find you pushing logic to the limit in a painfully intellectual search for emotion, for poetic motive. Your poem reeks with brains—it is thought out, worked out, sweated out. And the beauty which it seems entitled to is tortured and lost.

In all this I may be entirely wrong, and I am aware that a number of poets and critics would think so. Yvor Winters for example, in a recent letter, speaks of your *Marriage of Faustus and Helen* in *Secession 7* as "one of the great poems of our time, as great as the best of Stevens or Pound or Eliot." Well, I cannot grant it such a rank.

The editor would rather not have the last word, but as Mr. Crane contributes no further to the discussion, we must pass it on to our readers.   H. M.

MAX ERNST
Multiple Vision

One rainy day in 1919, finding myself in a village on the Rhine, I was struck by the obsession which held under my gaze the pages of an illustrated catalogue showing objects designed for anthropologic, microscopic, psychologic, mineralogic, and paleontologic demonstration. There I found brought together elements of figuration so remote that the sheer absurdity of that collection provoked a sudden intensification of the visionary faculties in me and brought forth an illusive succession of contradictory images, double, triple and multiple images, piling up on each other with the persistence and rapidity which are peculiar to love memories and visions of half-sleep.

These visions called themselves new planes, because of their meeting in a new unknown (the plane of non-agreement). It was enough at that time to embellish these catalogue pages, in painting or drawing, and thereby in gently reproducing only that which *saw itself in me*, a color, a pencil mark, a landscape foreign to the represented objects, the desert, a tempest, a geological cross-section, a floor, a single straight line signifying the horizon . . . thus I obtained a faithful fixed image of my hallucination and transformed into revealing dramas my most secret desires—from what had been before only some banal pages of advertising.

Under the title "La Mise sous Whisky-Marin" I assembled and exhibited in Paris (May 1920) the first results obtained by this procedure, from the *Phallustrade* to *The Wet Nurse of the Stars*.

From *Beyond Painting*, New York, 1948, p. 14; reprinted by permission of George Wittenborn, Inc., Publishers, 1018 Madison Avenue, New York 21, N.Y.

SERGEI EISENSTEIN
The Image in Process

. . . The juxtaposition of two separate shots by splicing them together resembles not so much a simple sum of one shot plus another shot—as it does a *creation*. . . .

What is essentially involved in such an understanding of montage? In such a case, each montage piece exists no longer as something unrelated, but as a given *particular representation* of the general theme that in equal measure penetrates *all* the shot-pieces. The juxtaposition of these partial details in a given montage construction calls to life and forces into the light that *general* quality in which each detail has participated and which binds together all the details

From *The Film Sense* [1938], translated from the Russian by Jay Leyda, New York, 1947, pp. 7, 11-19, 30-32, 33, 34-6. Copyright 1942 by Harcourt, Brace & World Inc.; reprinted by permission of Harcourt, Brace & World Inc.

into a *whole*, namely, into that generalized *image*, wherein the creator, followed by the spectator, experiences the theme.

If *now* we consider two pieces of film placed together, we appreciate their juxtaposition in a rather different light. Namely:

Piece A (derived from the elements of the theme being developed) and piece B (derived from the same source) in juxtaposition give birth to the image in which the thematic matter is most clearly embodied.

Expressed in the imperative, for the sake of stating a more exact working formula, this proposition would read:

Representation A and *representation* B must be so selected from all the possible features within the theme that is being developed, must be so sought for, that their *juxtaposition*—that is, the juxtaposition of *those very elements* and not of alternative ones—shall evoke in the perception and feelings of the spectator the most complete *image of the theme itself*.

Into our discussion of montage two new terms have entered: "representation" and "image." I want to define the demarcation between these terms before we proceed further.

We turn to an example for demonstration. Take a white circular disc of average size and smooth surface, its circumference divided into sixty equal parts. At every fifth division is set a figure in the order of succession of 1 to 12. At the center of the disc are fixed two metal rods, moving freely on their fixed ends, pointed at their free ends, one being equal to the radius of the disc, the other rather shorter. Let the longer pointed rod have its free end resting at the figure 12, and the shorter, in succession, have its free end pointing toward the figures 1, 2, 3, and so on up to 12. This will comprise a series of *geometrical* representations of successive relations of the two metal rods to one another expressed in the dimensions 30, 60, 90 degrees, and so on up to 360 degrees.

If, however, this disc be provided with a mechanism that imparts steady movement to the metal rods, the geometrical figure formed on its surface acquires a special meaning: it is now not simply a *representation*, it is an *image* of time.

In this instance, the representation and the image it evokes in our perception are so completely fused that only under special conditions do we distinguish the geometrical figure formed by the hands on the dial of the clock from the concept of time. Yet this can happen to any one of us, given, admittedly, the unusual circumstances.

It happened to Vronsky after Anna Karenina tells him that she is pregnant:

> When Vronsky looked at his watch on the Karenins' verandah he was so agitated and so preoccupied that he saw the hands and the face of the watch without realizing the time.

In his case, the *image* of time created by the watch did not arise. He saw only the geometrical representation formed by the watch dial and the hands.

As we can see in even so simple an instance, where the question touches only astronomical time, the hour, the representation formed by the clock dial is insufficient in itself. It is not enough merely to see—something has to happen to the representation, something more has to be done with it, before it can cease to be perceived as no more than a simple geometrical figure and can become perceptible as the image of some particular "time" at which the event is occurring. Tolstoy points out to us what happens when this process does not take place.

What exactly is this process? A given order of hands on the dial of a clock invokes a host of representations associated with the time that corresponds to the given order. Suppose, for example, the given figure be five. Our imagination is trained to respond to this figure by calling to mind pictures of all sorts of events that occur at that hour. Perhaps tea, the end of the day's work, the beginning of rush hour on the subway, perhaps shops closing, or the peculiar late afternoon light . . . In any case we will automatically recall a series of pictures (representations) of what happens at five o'clock.

The image of five o'clock is compounded of all these individual pictures.

This is the full sequence of the process, and it is such at the point of assimilating the representations formed by the figures which evoke the images of the times of day and night.

Thereafter the laws of economy of psychic energy come into force. There occurs "condensation" within the process above described: the chain of intervening links falls away, and there is produced instantaneous connection between the figure and our perception of the time to which it corresponds. The example of Vronsky shows us that a sharp mental disturbance can cause this connection to be destroyed, and the representation and the image become severed from each other.

We are considering here the *full* presentation of the process which takes place when an image is formed from a representation, as described above.

These "mechanics" of the formation of an image interest us because the mechanics of its formation in *life* turn out to be the prototype of the method of creating images in art.

To recapitulate: between the representation of an hour on the dial of the clock and our perception of the image of that hour, there lies a long chain of linked representations of separate characteristic aspects of that hour. And we repeat: that psychological habit tends to reduce this intervening chain to a minimum, so that only the beginning and the end of the process are perceived.

But as soon as we need, for any reason, to establish a connection between a representation and the image to be evoked by it in the consciousness and feelings, we are inevitably compelled to resort again to a chain of intervening representations, which, in aggregate, form the image.

Consider first an example approximating closely the other example from everyday life.

In New York City most of the streets have no names. Instead, they are distinguished by numbers—Fif:h Avenue, Forty-second Street, and so on. Strangers find this method of designating streets extraordinarily difficult to remember at first. We are used to streets with names, which is much easier for us, because each name at once brings up an image of the given street, i.e., when you hear the street name, this evokes a particular complex of sensations and, together with them, the image.

I found it very difficult to remember the *images* of New York's streets and, consequently, to recognize the streets themselves. Their designations, neutral numbers like "Forty-second" or "Forty-fifth," failed to produce images in my mind that would concentrate my perception on the general features of one or the other street. To produce these images, I had to fix in my memory a set of objects characteristic of one or another street, a set of objects aroused in my consciousness in answer to the signal "Forty-second," and quite distinct from those aroused by the signal "Forty-fifth." My memory assembled the theaters, stores and buildings, characteristic of each of the streets I had to remember. This process went through definite stages. Two of these stages should be noted: in the first, at the verbal designation: "Forty-second Street," my memory with great difficulty responded by enumerating the whole chain of characteristic elements, but I still obtained no true perception of the street because the various elements had not yet been consolidated into a single image. Only in the second stage did all the elements begin to fuse into a single, emerging image: at the mention of the street's "number," *there still arose this whole host of its separate elements, but now not as a chain, but as something single—*as a whole character-ization of the street, *as its whole image.*

Only after this stage could one say that one had really *memorized* the street. The image of the given street began to emerge and live in the consciousness and perception exactly as, in the course of creating a work of art, its single, recog-nizable whole image is gradually composed out of its elements.

In both cases—whether it be a question of memorizing or the process of per-ceiving a work of art—the procedure of entering the consciousness and feelings through the whole, the whole *through the image,* remains obedient to this law.

Further, though the image enters the consciousness and perception *through aggregation,* every detail is preserved in the sensations and memory *as part of the whole.* This obtains whether it be a sound image—some rhythmic or melodic sequence of sounds, or whether it be a plastic, a visual image, embracing in pictorial form a remembered series of separate elements.

In one way or another, the series of ideas is built up in the perception and consciousness into a whole image, storing up the separate elements.

We have seen that in the process of remembering there are two very essential stages: the first is the *assembling* of the image, while the second consists in the *result* of this assembly and its significance for the memory. In this latter stage it is important that the memory should pay as little attention as possible to the first stage, and reach the result after passing through the stage of assembling as swiftly as possible. Such is practice in life in contrast to practice in art. For when we proceed into the sphere of art, we discover a marked displacement of empha-sis. Actually, to achieve its result, a work of art directs all the refinement of its methods to the *process.*

A work of art, understood dynamically, is just this process of arranging images in the feelings and mind of the spectator.[1] It is this that constitutes the peculiar-ity of a truly vital work of art and distinguishes it from a lifeless one, in which the spectator receives the represented result of a given consummated process of creation, instead of being drawn into the process as it occurs.

This condition obtains everywhere and always, no matter what the art form under discussion. For example, the lifelike acting of an actor is built, not on his

[1] Later we shall see that this same dynamic principle lies at the base of all truly vital images, even in such an apparently immobile and static medium as, for example, painting.

representing the copied results of feelings, but on his causing the feelings to *arise, develop, grow into other feelings—to live before the spectator.*

Hence the image of a scene, a sequence, of a whole creation, exists not as something fixed and ready-made. It has to rise, to unfold before the senses of the spectator.

In the same way a character (both in the writing and in the performing of a rôle), if it is to produce a genuinely living impression, must be built up for the spectator in the course of the action, and not be presented as a clockwork figure with set *a priori* characteristics.

In drama it is particularly important that the course of the action should not only build up an *idea* of the character, but also should build up, should "image," *the character itself.*

Consequently, in the actual method of creating images, a work of art must reproduce that process whereby, *in life itself*, new images are built up in the human consciousness and feelings.

We have just shown the nature of this in our example of the numbered streets. And we should be correct in expecting an artist, faced with the task of expressing a given image by factual representation, to resort to a method precisely like this "assimilation" of the streets of New York.

We also used the example of the representation formed by the dial of a clock, and revealed the process whereby the image of time arises in consequence of this representation. To create an image, a work of art must rely upon a precisely analogous method, the construction of a chain of representations.

Let us examine more broadly this example of time.

With Vronsky, above, the geometrical figure failed to come to life as an image of time. But there are cases when what is important is not to perceive the hour of twelve midnight chronometrically, but to experience midnight in all the associations and sensations the author chooses to evoke in pursuance of his plot. It may be an hour of the anxious awaiting of a midnight assignation, an hour of death at midnight, the hour of a fateful midnight elopement, in other words it may well be far from a simple representation of the chronometrical hour of twelve midnight.

In such a case, *from a representation of the twelve strokes* must emerge the image of midnight as a kind of "hour of fate," charged with significance. . . .

Montage has a realistic significance when the separate pieces produce, in juxtaposition, the generality, the synthesis of one's theme. This is the image, incorporating the theme.

Turning from this definition to the creative process, we shall see that it proceeds in the following manner. Before the inner vision, before the perception of the creator, hovers a given image, emotionally embodying his theme. The task that confronts him is to transform this image into a few basic *partial representations* which, in their combination and juxtaposition, shall evoke in the consciousness and feelings of the spectator, reader, or auditor, that same initial general image which originally hovered before the creative artist.

This applies both to the image of the work of art as a whole and the image of each separate scene or part. This holds true in precisely the same sense for the actor's creation of an image.

The actor is confronted with exactly the same task: to express, in two, three, or four features of a character or of a mode of behavior, those basic elements which in juxtaposition create the integral image that was worked out by the author, director and the actor himself.

What is most noteworthy in such a method? First and foremost, its dynamism. This rests primarily in the fact that the desired image is *not fixed or ready-made, but arises—is born.* The image planned by author, director and actor is concretized by them in separate representational elements, and is assembled—again and finally —in the spectator's perception. This is actually the final aim of every artist's creative endeavor.

Gorky put this eloquently in a letter to Konstantin Fedin:

> You say: You are worried by the question, "how to write?" I have been watching for 25 years how that question worries people . . . Yes, it is a serious question; I have worried about it myself, I do worry about it, and I shall go on worrying about it to the end of my days. But for me the question is formulated: How must I write so that the man, no matter who he may be, shall emerge from the pages of the story about him with that strength of physical palpability of his existence, with that cogency of his *half-imaginary* reality, with which I see and feel him? That is the point as I understand it, that is the secret of the matter. . . .

Montage helps in the resolution of this task. The strength of montage resides in this, that it includes in the creative process the emotions and mind of the spectator. The spectator is compelled to proceed along that selfsame creative road that the author traveled in creating the image. The spectator not only sees the represented elements of the finished work, but also experiences the dynamic process of the emergence and assembly of the image just as it was experienced by the author. And this is, obviously, the highest possible degree of approximation to transmitting visually the author's perceptions and intention in all their fullness, to transmitting them with "that strength of physical palpability" with which they arose before the author in his creative work and his creative vision. . . .

The strength of the method resides also in the circumstance that the spectator is drawn into a creative act in which his individuality is not subordinated to the author's individuality, but is opened up throughout the process of fusion with the author's intention, just as the individuality of a great actor is fused with the individuality of a great playwright in the creation of a classic scenic image. In fact, every spectator, in correspondence with his individuality, and in his own way and out of his own experience—out of the womb of his fantasy, out of the warp and weft of his associations, all conditioned by the premises of his character, habits and social appurtenances, creates an image in accordance with the representational guidance suggested by the author, leading him to understanding and experience of the author's theme. This is the same image that was planned and created by the author, but this image is at the same time created also by the spectator himself. . . .

The image planned by the author has become flesh of the flesh of the spectator's risen image. . . . Within me, as a spectator, this image is born and grown. Not only the author has created, but I also—the creating spectator—have participated.

At the beginning of this chapter I spoke of an emotionally exciting and moving story as distinguished from a logical exposition of facts—as much difference as there is between an experience and an affidavit.

An *affidavit-exposition* would be the corresponding *non-montage* construction in each of the examples that have been cited. In the case of Leonardo da Vinci's notes for The Deluge, an affidavit-exposition would not have taken into consideration as he did the various scales and perspectives to be distributed over the surface of the finished picture, according to his calculations of the trajectory of the spectator's eyes. It would have been satisfied by a mere display of the dial of a clock telling the exact time of the overthrow of the Provisional Government. If Maupassant had used such a method in the passage of Duroy's appointment, it would have been a curt item of information that the hour of twelve struck. In other words such an approach conveys bare documentary information, not raised by means of art to a created exciting force and emotional affect. As affidavit-expositions, these examples would all be, in film terms, *representations shot from a single set-up*. But, as fashioned by artists, they constitute *images*, brought to life by means of *montage construction*.

And now we can say that it is precisely the *montage principle*, as distinguished from that of *representation*, which obliges spectators themselves to *create* and the montage principle, by this means, achieves that great power of inner creative excitement[2] in the *spectator* which distinguishes an emotionally exciting work from one that stops without going further than giving information or recording events.

Examining this distinction we discover that the montage principle in films is only a sectional application of the *montage principle in general*, a principle which, if fully understood, passes far beyond the limits of splicing bits of film together.

[2] It is quite obvious that the *theme as such* is capable of exciting emotionally, independently of the form in which it is presented. A brief newspaper report of the victory of the Spanish Republicans at Guadalajara is more moving than a work by Beethoven. But we are discussing here how, by means of art, to raise a given theme or subject, that may already be exciting "in itself," to a maximum degree of affectiveness. It is further quite obvious that montage, as such, is in no way an exhaustive means in this field, though a tremendously powerful one.

W. B. YEATS

The Courage of the Artist

[LIONEL JOHNSON]

I am speaking of him very candidly; probably he would not [wish] to be spoken of in this way, but I would wish to be spoken of with just such candour when I am dead. I have no sympathy with the mid-Victorian thought to which Tennyson gave his support, that a poet's life concerns nobody but himself. A poet is by the very nature of things a man who lives with entire sincerity, or rather, the better his poetry the more sincere his life. His life is an experiment in living and those that come after have a right to know it. Above all it is necessary that the lyric poet's life should be known, that we should understand that his poetry is no rootless flower but the speech of a man, [that it is no little thing] to achieve anything in any art, to stand alone perhaps for many years, to go a path no other man has gone, to accept one's own thought when the thought of others has the authority of the world behind it, . . . to give one's life as well as one's words which are so much nearer to one's soul to the criticism of the world. . . . Why should we honor those that die upon the field of battle, a man may show as reckless a courage in entering into the abyss of himself.

An unpublished speech [1907], quoted by Richard Ellmann, in *Yeats: The Man and the Masks*, New York, 1948, pp. 5-6; reprinted by permission of Mrs. W. B. Yeats.

GUSTAVE FLAUBERT

Art as Ascetic Religion

Tonight I finished scribbling the first draft of my young girl's dreams. I'll spend another fortnight sailing on these blue lakes, after which I'll go to a ball and then spend a rainy winter, which I'll end with a pregnancy. And about a third of my book will be done. . . .

Letter to Louise Colet [1852], *Selected Letters*, translated from the French by Francis Steegmuller, London, 1954, pp. 131-3. Copyright 1953 by Francis Steegmuller; reprinted by permission of Farrar, Straus & Co. and Hamish Hamilton Ltd.

If I haven't written sooner in reply to your sorrowful and discouraged-sounding letter, it is because I have been in a great fit of work. The day before yesterday I went to bed at five in the morning and yesterday at three. Since last Monday I have put everything else aside, and have done nothing all week but sweat over my *Bovary*, disgruntled at making such slow progress. I have now reached my ball, which I will begin Monday. I hope that may go better. Since you last saw me I have written 25 pages in all (25 pages in six weeks). They were tough. Tomorrow I shall read them to Bouilhet. As for myself, I have gone over them so much, recopied them, changed them, handled them, that for the time being I can't make head or tail of them. But I think they will stand up. You speak of your discouragements: if you could see mine! Sometimes I don't understand why my arms don't drop from my body with fatigue, why my brains don't melt away. I am leading a stern existence, stripped of all external pleasure, and am sustained only by a kind of permanent rage, which sometimes makes me weep tears of impotence but which never abates. I love my work with a love that is frenzied and perverted, as an ascetic loves the hair shirt that scratches his belly. Sometimes, when I am empty, when words don't come, when I find I haven't written a single sentence after scribbling whole pages, I collapse on my couch and lie there dazed, bogged in a swamp of despair, hating myself and blaming myself for this demented pride which makes me pant after a chimera. A quarter of an hour later everything changes; my heart is pounding with joy. Last Wednesday I had to get up and fetch my handkerchief; tears were streaming down my face. I had been moved by my own writing; the emotion I had conceived, the phrase that rendered it, and the satisfaction of having found the phrase—all were causing me to experience the most exquisite pleasure. At least I believe that all those elements were present in this emotion, which after all was predominantly a matter of nerves. There exist even higher emotions of this same kind: those which are devoid of the sensory element. These are superior, in moral beauty, to virtue—so independent are they of any personal factor, of any human implication. Occasionally (at great moments of illumination) I have had glimpses, in the glow of an enthusiasm that made me thrill from head to foot, of such a state of mind, superior to life itself, a state in which fame counts for nothing and even happiness is superfluous. If everything around us, instead of permanently conspiring to drown us in a slough of mud, contributed rather to keep our spirits healthy, who can tell whether we might not be able to do for aesthetics what stoicism did for morals? Greek art was not an art; it was the very constitution of an entire people, of an entire race, of the country itself. In Greece the profile of the mountains was different from elsewhere, and they were composed of marble, which was thus available to the sculptors, etc.

The time for Beauty is over. Mankind may return to it, but it has no use for it at present. The more Art develops, the more scientific it will be, just as science will become artistic. Separated in their early stages, the two will become one again when both reach their culmination. It is beyond the power of human thought today to foresee in what a dazzling intellectual light the works of the future will flower. Meanwhile we are in a shadowy corridor, groping in the dark. We are without a lever; the ground is slipping under our feet; we all lack a basis—literati and scribblers that we are. What's the good of all this? Is our chatter the answer to any need? Between the crowd and ourselves no bond exists. Alas for the crowd; alas for us, especially. But since there is a reason for everything, and since the fancy of one individual seems to me just as valid as the appetite of a million men and can occupy an equal place in the world, we must (regardless of material things and of mankind, which disavows us) live for our vocation, climb into our ivory tower, and dwell there along with our dreams. At times I have feelings of great despair and emptiness—doubts that taunt me at my moments of naïvest satisfaction. And yet I would not exchange all this for anything, because my conscience tells me that I am fulfilling my duty, obeying a decree of fate—that I am doing what is Good, that I am in the Right.

RAINER MARIA RILKE

The Mission of the Artist

With every day it becomes clearer to me that I was right in setting myself from the start against the phrase my relatives like: Art is something one just cultivates on the side in free hours, when one leaves the government office, etc.—That to me is a fearful sentence. I feel that this is my belief: Whoever does not conse-crate himself wholly to art with all his wishes and values can never reach the highest goal. He is not an artist at all. And now it can be no presumption if I confess that I feel myself to be an artist, weak and wavering in strength and boldness, yet aware of bright goals, and hence to me every creative activity is serious, glorious, and true. Not as martyrdom do I regard art—but as a battle the chosen one has to wage with himself and his environment in order to go forward with a pure heart to the greatest goal, the one day of celebration, and with full hands to give to all successors of the rich reconciliation finally achieved. But that needs a whole man! Not a few weary leisure hours.

Letter to Ludwig Ganghofer [1897], *Letters*, translated from the German by Jane Bannard Greene and M. D. Herter Norton, New York, 1945-48, Vol. I, pp. 27-8. Copyright 1947 and 1948 by W. W. Norton & Co., Inc.; reprinted by permission of W. W. Norton & Co.

PAUL VALÉRY

The Artist as Universal Man

Since mind has found no limit to its activity, and since no idea marks the end of the business of consciousness, it must most likely perish in some incomprehen-

"Introduction to the Method of Leonardo da Vinci" [1895], translated from the French by Thomas McGreevy, *Selected Writings*, New York, 1950, pp. 89-101. Copyright 1950 by New Directions; reprinted by permission of New Directions and Peter Owen Ltd.

sible climax foreshadowed and prepared by those terrors and odd sensations of which I have spoken; they give us glimpses of worlds that are unstable and incompatible with fullness of life: inhuman worlds, feeble worlds, worlds comparable to those that the mathematician calls forth when he plays with axioms, the physicist when he postulates *constants*, other than those admitted. Between the clarity of life and the simplicity of death, dreams, anxieties, ecstasies, all the semi-impossible values and transcendental or irrational solutions into the equation of knowledge, all these form curious stages, variations, phases that it is beyond words to describe—for there are no names for those things amongst which one is completely alone.

As the elusive art of music unites the liberties of sleep with the development and consistency of extreme attention and makes a synthesis of intimate things which last only a moment, so the fluctuations of the psychic equilibrium give one a glimpse of deviating modes of existence. We have in us forms of sensibility which, though they may be born, may not develop. They are instants snatched from the implacable criticism of the passage of time; they cannot survive if our being is to function fully: either we perish or they disperse. But they are monsters full of lessons for us, these monsters of the intelligence, these transitory stages, these spaces in which the continuity, the relation, the mobility we know, are altered; empires in which illumination is associated with sorrow; powerhouses where the orientation of fears and desires sends us on strange circuits; matter which consists of time; abysses literally of sorrow, or love, or quietude; regions curiously attached to themselves; non-Archimedean realms which defy movement; perpetuities in a flash of lightning; surfaces that shape themselves to our nausea, bend under our lightest decisions. . . . One cannot say that they are real; one cannot say that they are not real. Who has not experience of them does not know the value of natural intelligence and of even the most ordinary environment; he does not understand the true fragility of the world—which has no relation to so simple a thing as our alternative of being or not being. The wonder is not that things should be; it is that there should be such things and not such other things. *The image of this world* is part of a family of images, an infinite group, all the elements of which we possess—but unconsciously—consciousness of possession is the secret of the inventors.

I

The consciousness as it emerges from these gaps, these personal deviations in which weakness and the presence of poisons in the nervous system, but also the power as well as the subtlety of the attention and a most exquisite logic, a cultivated mysticism, all, severally, direct it, the consciousness, then, comes to suspect all accustomed reality of being only one solution amongst many others of universal problems. It tells itself that things should be somewhat different from what they are without its being very different from itself. It dares to consider its body and its world as almost arbitrary restrictions imposed on the range of its functions. It sees itself as corresponding, or as responding, not to a world, but to some system of a higher order the elements of which may themselves be worlds. It is capable of more interior combinations than are necessary for living; it judges itself deeper than the abyss of physical life and death. And this attitude to its own position cannot react back on itself, so far is it withdrawn, placed beyond all things, so much has it applied itself to the task *of never figuring in anything that it might imagine or agree to.* It has become no more than a dark body which absorbs everything and gives out nothing.

Drawing from these exact observations and from these inevitable pretensions a dangerous boldness; strong in this type of independence and unchangingness that it has to admit it possesses, it postulates itself in the end as the direct heir and image of that being that has no form, no origin, on which devolves, to which is related, the whole effort of the cosmos. A little more and it will admit as necessary existences only two entities, both of them essentially unknown: itself and X; both of them abstracted from everything, implicated in everything, implicating everything; equal and consubstantial.

The man who has been led by a mind that works tirelessly to this contact with living shadows, to this point of pure being, sees himself naked and destitute, reduced to the supreme poverty of power without a purpose, victim, masterpiece, perfection of simplification and dialectic order; his state comparable to that reached by the richest mind when it has become assimilated to itself, when it has recognized itself and consummated itself in a little group of characters and symbols. The work which we devote to the object of our reflections he has expended on the subject which reflects.

He is no longer concerned to choose or to create, to maintain or to develop himself. There is nothing to conquer. There cannot even be question of destroying himself. Genius is now entirely consumed, cannot be used to any further purpose. It was no more than a means to attain to the last simplicity. There is no act of genius which would not be *less* than the act of being. An imbecile is created and informed by a magnificent law; the most powerful mind finds nothing better than itself.

To sum up, being constrained to define itself by the sum of things and excess of knowledge over the sum of things, this perfected consciousness, which, to establish itself, has to begin by denying an infinite number of faiths, an infinite number of elements, and by exhausting the objects of its force without exhausting the force itself, this perfected consciousness differs as little as could be wished from nothingness. It reminds one absurdly of an audience invisible in the darkness of a theater which cannot see itself, which can see only the spectacle before it, and which, yet, all the time, invincibly feels itself the center of a breathlessly interesting evening. It is complete, impenetrable, absolute night; but filled with things, eager, secretly organized, made up of organisms which limit and compress themselves; a compact night, its shadows packed with organisms which live, breathe, warm themselves and which defend, each according to its nature, their places and functions. Before this intense, mysterious assembly, are all the things of sensibility, intelligibility, possibility, glittering and moving in an enclosed framework. Nothing can be born, die, or exist in any degree, or have time, place, form or meaning, except on this stage which the fates have circumscribed, and having separated which, from nobody knows what primordial confusion, as on the first day darkness was separated from light, they have opposed and subordinated to the condition of *being seen.* . . . .

If I have brought the reader to this solitude and to this desperate clarity, it is because it was very necessary to carry the idea that I have formed of intellectual power to its ultimate consequences. The human characteristic is consciousness; the characteristic of consciousness is a process of perpetual exhaustion, of detachment without rest or exclusion from everything that comes before it, whatever that thing may be—an inexhaustible activity, independent of the quality as of the quantity of the things which appear and by means of which the man of intellect must at last bring himself deliberately to an unqualified refusal to be anything whatsoever.

All phenomena being thus regarded with a sort of equal repulsion and as rejected successively by an identical gesture, appear to be, in a certain sense, equivalent to each other. Feelings and thoughts are included in the uniform condemnation extended to all that can be perceived. It must be quite understood that nothing is exempted from the rigor of this exhaustion, that our attention should suffice to put our most intimate feelings on the same plane as exterior objects and events; from the moment that they become observable they go to join the rest of observed things.

Color, grief, memories; surprises and things expected; the tree outside, the rustling of its leaves, its yearly change, its shadow as well as its substance, its accidents of shape and position, the far-off thoughts that it brings back to my wandering attention—*all these things are equal.* . . . All things are replaceable by all things—may not this be the definition of *things?*

It is impossible that the activity of the mind should not in the end force it to this ultimate, elementary consideration. Its multiplied movements, its intimate struggles, its perturbations, its analytic returns on itself—do these leave anything unchanged? Is there anything that resists the lure of the senses, the dissipation of ideas, the fading of memories, the slow variation of the organism, the incessant and multiform activities of the universe? There is only this consciousness, and this consciousness only at its most abstract.

Our *personality* itself, which, stupidly, we take to be our most intimate and deepest *possession*, our sovereign good, is only a thing, and mutable and accidental in comparison with this other most naked ego; since we can think about it, calculate its interests, even lose sight of them a little, it is therefore no more than a secondary psychological divinity that lives in our looking-glass and answers to our name. It belongs to the order of Penates. It is subject to pain, greedy for incense like false gods; and, like them, it is food for worms. It expands when praised. It does not resist the power of wine, the charm of words, the sorcery of music. It admires itself, and through self-admiration becomes docile and easily led. It is lost in the masquerade and yields itself strangely to the anamorphosis of sleep. And further, it is painfully obliged to recognize that it has equals, to admit that it is *inferior* to some—a bitter and inexplicable experience for it, this.

Besides, everything convinces it that it is a mere phenomenon; that it must figure with all the accidental facts of the world amongst statistics and tables; that it had its beginning in a seminal chance, a microscopic incident; that it has run thousands of millions of risks; that it has been shaped by a number of happenings and that, however much it may be admirable, free, acknowledged, brilliant, it is, in sum, the effect of an incalculable disorder.

Each person being a sport of nature, a *jeu de l'amour et du hasard*, the most beautiful purpose and even the most learned thought of this recreated creature inevitably recall his origin. His activities are always relative, his masterpieces are fortuitous. He thinks mortally, individually, by fits and starts; and he finds the best of his ideas in casual and secret circumstances which he refrains from making public. Besides, he is not sure of being positively *some one*, he disguises and denies, more easily than he affirms, himself. Drawing from his own inconsistency some strength and much vanity, he puts his most cherished moments into fictions. He lives by romance, sees himself in a thousand roles. . . . His hero is never himself. . . .

And finally he passes nine-tenths of his time in what has yet to happen, in that which no longer is, in what cannot possibly be; to such an extent that our true *present* has nine chances out of ten of never being.

But all the time each private life possesses, deep down as a treasure, the fundamental permanence of consciousness which depends on nothing. And as the ear catches and loses and catches again, and loses again through all the varying movement of a symphony some grave and persistent *motif* which ceases to be heard from moment to moment, but which never ceases to be there—so the pure *ego*, the unique and continuous element in each being in the world, rediscovering itself and then losing itself again, inhabits our intelligence eternally; this deep *note* of existence itself dominates the whole complication of circumstance and change in existence from the moment that it is heard.

Is it not the chief and secret achievement of the greatest mind to isolate this substantial permanence from the strife of everyday truths? Is it not essential that in spite of everything he shall arrive at self-definition by means of this pure relationship, changeless amongst the most diverse objects, which will give him an almost inconceivable universality, give him, in a sense, the power of a corresponding universe? It is not his cherished self that he elevates to so high a degree, since by thinking about it he has renounced it, and has substituted for it in the place of subject this *ego* which is unqualified, which has no name, no history, which is no more sensitive, no less real than the center of gravity of a planetary system or ring, but which is a result of the whole—whatever that whole may be. . . .

A moment since, and the obvious purpose of this wonderful intellectual life was still to astonish itself. Its preoccupation was to produce offspring that it could admire; it limited itself to what is most beautiful, most sweet, most bright, most substantial; and it was untroubled—save for its resemblance to other existing organisms, the strangest problem that one can propound to oneself; which is put to us by the existence of those who resemble us, and which consists simply in the possible existence of other intelligences, in the plurality of the singular, in the contradictory coexistence of lives independent amongst themselves *tot capita, tot tempora*—a problem comparable to the physical problems of *relativity* but infinitely more difficult.

But now, carried away by his anxiety to be unique and guided by his ardor for omnipotence, this same being has passed beyond all creations, all works, beyond even his greatest designs at the same time that he has put away from him all tenderness for himself and all preference for his own desires. He immolates, in one instant, his individuality. He feels himself pure consciousness; and two of that cannot exist. He is the I, the pronoun of universality, the name of *that* which has no relation to appearance. Oh, to what a point has pride been trans-

formed! How it has arrived at a position that it did not even know it was seeking! How temperate the reward of its triumphs! A life so firmly directed, and
which has treated as obstacles to be avoided or to be mastered all the objects it
could propose to itself, must, after all, have attained an unassailable end, not an
end to its duration, but an end within itself. Its pride has brought it as far as
this. And here its pride is consumed. Pride, which conducted it, leaves it, astonished, naked, infinitely simple at the pole of its treasures.

II

I propose to imagine a man whose activities seem so distant from each other that
if I can find a unifying idea of them it may well seem more comprehensive than
all other ideas. I wish him to have an abnormally lively perception of the difference between things—the adventures of such a perception could well be described
as analysis. Everything interests him. It is of the universe that he thinks always.
And he thinks of rigor.[1] He is so made that he misses nothing of all that enters
into the tangle of what exists—not a single shrub. He goes down into the depth
of that which is for all men to see, but there he wanders away and studies himself. He learns the habits and organizations of nature, works on them from every
angle. And he comes to be the only man who constructs, calculates, sets in
motion. He leaves behind him churches and fortresses; he fashions ornaments—
full of sweetness and strength—and a thousand machines; and he makes rigorous
calculation along many unsurveyed lines. He leaves the remains of no one knows
what great playthings. In these pastimes mixed up with his scientific studies—
themselves constituting something not distinguishable from passion—he has the
charm of always seeming to be thinking of something else. I shall follow him
through the rude unity and density of the world, where he will become so familiar with nature that, in order to keep in contact with it he will imitate it, and
will finish by finding it difficult to conceive an object which is not in nature.

It remains to give a name to this creature of thought in order to set a limit to
the elaboration of terms ordinarily too far apart and likely to escape from any
attempt to associate them. No name seems to me more suitable than that of
Leonardo da Vinci. Whoever imagines a tree to himself must also imagine a sky
or a background against which to see it standing. That is logic of a kind that is
almost self-evident and almost unrealized. The figure I imagine reduces himself
to an inference of this nature. Little of what I say of him must be considered as
applicable to the man who has made the name illustrious: I am not following
up a coincidence that seems to me impossible to make clear. I am trying to
express a point of view with regard to the detail of an intellectual life, to make
one suggestion as to the methods which every discovery implies, one chosen
amongst the multitude of things that may be imagined, a model, that may well
be thought a rough one but in every way preferable to strings of doubtful anecdotes, to commentaries in the catalogues of art collections, to dates—erudition of
that sort would only falsify the purely hypothetical aim of this essay. I am not
altogether ignorant of such matters, but them, above all, I must refrain from
discussing, in order not to cause confusion between a surmise as to conditions
that are quite general and the outward fragments of a personality which has

[1] *Hostinato rigore*, obstinate rigor. Leonardo's motto. AUTHOR'S NOTE.

vanished to a point where we are given—by the fragments—the certitude that we can never know it better.

Many an error which distorts the judgements made on human achievements is due to a singular forgetfulness of their genesis. One forgets often that they have not always been in existence. From which has arisen a kind of reciprocal coquetry of silence on the part of artists as to the origins of their work—to the extent of too carefully hiding them even. We fear that they are humble, these origins, even that they are mere nature. And though very few artists have the courage to say how they produced their work, I believe that there are not many more who take the risk of understanding it themselves. Such understanding commences with the very difficult abandonment of the notion of glory, of the laudatory epithet; it tolerates no idea of superiority, no delusion of greatness. It leads to the discovery of the relative beneath the apparent perfection. And it is necessary if we are not to believe that minds are as profoundly different as their products make them appear. For example, certain works of science, and mathematical works in particular, show such clarity in their construction that one would say that they were not the work of any person at all. There is something *unhuman* about them. And this quality has had the effect of making people suppose so great a difference between certain studies, as, for instance, between the sciences and the arts, that, owing to it, opinion has also assumed a separation between the minds devoted to each, as complete as that which seems to exist between the results of their labors. These labors, however, only differ as variations from a common basis, differ in what of it they include and what of it they leave out in forming their languages and their symbols. One must, therefore, have some distrust of books and explanations that seem too clear. We are deceived by what is definite; and then what is made specially to be looked at changes its aspects in our eyes and takes on a nobler air. It is when working on movements which are still irresolute, unstilled, which may not either be called diversions or laws, works of art or theorems, movements which, when completed, lose their likeness to each other, that the operations of the mind can be of use to us.

Interiorly there is a drama. "Drama," "adventure," "agitation," all words of this kind may be used, provided that they be numerous and that one is corrected by the other. This drama, like the plays of Menander, is often lost. Nevertheless we have the manuscripts of Leonardo, the celebrated notes of Pascal. These fragments command attention. They help us to divine through what intellectual somersaults, what odd intrusion of human affairs, what repeated sensations, after what immense passages of languor, the shadows, the specters that presage their future works, show themselves to men. It suffices, without resorting to such outstanding examples as might imply the possibility of making the mistakes that attach to the study of exceptions, to study someone who believes himself alone and abandons himself to himself, who *recoils* before an idea; grasps it; denies, smiles or shrinks back—acting, as it were, the curious character of his own variety. It is the way madmen behave before the world.

Such examples relate definite, measurable, physical movements immediately to the personal comedy of which I spoke. The actors in this drama are mental images, and it is easy to understand that if the peculiarities of these images be eliminated, and if only their succession, frequency, periodicity, their diverse capacities for association, and, finally, their duration, be studied, one is at once tempted to find analogies in what is called the material world, to compare them with scientific analyses, to give them an environment, a continuity, properties of displacement, of speed, and then mass and energy. One comes to the conclusion that many such systems are possible, that no one of them is worth more than another, and that the use of them—which is important since it always throws light on something—ought to be at every instant under supervision and its purely verbal role kept in mind. For, in reality, analogy is only the faculty of varying the images, of combining them, of making part of one coexist with part of another and perceiving, voluntarily or otherwise, the similarities in their construction. And that renders it impossible to describe the mind which is their world. Here words lose their virtue. It is here that they are formed and spring to the mind's eye—it is the mind that describes words to us.

In this way man comes to have *visions* whose power is his power. He relates his history to them. They bind it geometrically. And from that come those decisions which surprise, the perspectives, the blinding divinations, precisions of judgment, illuminations, and also the incomprehensible anxieties, the stupidities. In certain outstanding cases one invokes abstract gods, genius and inspiration and a thousand others, and asks oneself with stupefaction how these accidents arise. And once more one believes that something has created itself—for man adores mystery and the marvelous precisely as he likes to shut his eyes to what is going on behind the scenes at the theater. One treats what is logical as if it were a miracle. But the "inspired" author has been ready to perform his task a year before it was done, had been ripe, had been thinking of it always, perhaps without being conscious of the fact, and while others could not yet see, he had studied, arranged, and now had only read what was already in his mind. The secret—Leonardo's and Buonaparte's, as that which all highest intelligences possess once—is, and can only be, in the relationship that they can find—that they were forced to find—*between things whose laws of continuity escape us*. It is certain that at the decisive moment they had only to perform some definite acts. And the achievement that impressed the world, the supreme achievement, was quite a simple affair—like comparing two lengths.

This attitude makes it possible to grasp the unity of method with which we are so concerned. Here it is natural, elementary. It is life and the explanation of life. And thinkers as powerful as he of whom I think as I write these words, having mastered the resources implicit in this method, may well write at this clearer and more conscious point: *Facil cosa e farsi universale*—it is easy to make oneself universal! They can for a moment admire the prodigious instruments that they are, though the next moment they must deny anything in the nature of prodigy.

This final clarity, however, is only found after long wanderings, inevitable idolatries. The consciousness of the operations of thought, the unrecognized logic of which I have spoken, exists but rarely, even in the most powerful minds. The number of conceptions, the power to extend them, and the abundance of discoveries made, are another thing and are produced independently of any judgement that one may make as to their nature. This judgement is, notwithstanding, of easily realized importance. A flower, a proposition, a noise, can be imagined almost simultaneously: one can make them follow each other at what distance one pleases; any of these subjects of thought can also be changed, distorted, made to lose its initial aspect following the will of the mind that holds it; but it is the knowledge of this power of the mind alone that gives the thing its value. This alone permits one to criticize such *formations*, to interpret them, to find in them only what they contain, and not to stretch them to the point of confusing their various stages with those of reality. With this knowledge commences the analysis of all intellectual phases, of all that itself will have the power to classify as folly, idolatry, discovery—hitherto mere nuances, not to be distinguished from each other. They were equivalent variations from a common substance, comparable one to the other, carelessly, as it were, finding indefinite levels, sometimes nameable but all belonging to the same category. Consciousness of the thoughts that one has, to the extent to which they are thoughts, is awareness of this equality or homogeneity: the feeling that all combinations of the kind are legitimate, natural, and that the method consists in exciting them, in seeing them with precision, in searching for their implications.

At a point in this awareness or double mental life which reduces ordinary thought to something like the illusions of a waking sleeper, it seems that the sequence of these illusions, the cloud of combinations, of contrasts, of perceptions, which group themselves about some study or which float on indeterminately, at pleasure, develop with a regularity that is *perceptible*, with the evident continuity of a machine. Then emerges the idea or the wish to precipitate the movement of this progress, to carry its terms to their *limit*, the limit of their imaginable expression—*after which all shall be changed*. And if this mode of being conscious becomes habitual, one will come to consider at once all the possible results of a contemplated act, all the implications of a conceived object, and in this way to achieve their annihilation, to achieve the faculty of divining always a thing more intense or more exact than the thing allowed, to attain the power of shaking oneself free of any thought that has lasted too long. No matter what it be, a thought that has become fixed takes on the characteristics of hypnosis and becomes, in the language of logic, an idol; in the domain of poetic construction and art, a sterile monotony. The sense of which I speak, which leads the mind to foresee its own activities, to imagine the structure of what has to be imagined in detail as a whole, and the effect of the sequence thus calculated, this sense is the condition of all generalization. It is that which in certain individuals appears as a veritable passion, and with an energy that is remarkable; which, in the arts, permits of progress and explains the more and more frequent employment of concentrated terms, abridgements and violent contrasts; and it exists implicitly in its rational form as the basis of all mathematical conceptions. It is an operation very similar to it which under the name of reasoning by recurrence, extends the range of these analyses, and which, from simple addition to infinitesimal, achieves something more than merely to spare the necessity for an indefinite number of useless experiments; achieves existences more complex—for the conscious imitation of an act is a new act which comprehends all possible modifications of the first.

This picture, drama, whirl, clarity, opposes itself naturally to other movements and other stages which we call "nature" or "the world," things that we do not know what to do with, except distinguish ourselves from them—and then we immediately reincorporate ourselves in them.

Philosophers have generally ended by implicating our existence in this notion and it inversely in our notion of ourselves; yet they rarely go farther; we know that their business is to contend against the thought of their predecessors rather than to look into it for themselves. Scientists and artists have used the notion of nature variously: scientists finishing by measuring and then constructing themselves; artists by constructing as if they had already measured. Everything that they have made takes its place of itself in the sum of things and plays its part there, continuing things through the new shapes it gives to the materials that constitute them. But, before considering and building, one observes; the characters of the sense, their different ways of accommodation, distinguish and choose, amongst the qualities offered in the aggregate, those which are to be retained and developed by the individual. The process is at first submitted to, almost without thinking, with a feeling of letting oneself be filled, of slow circulation, as of happiness; then one begins to be interested and to give different values to things that had seemed settled, simple; one adds to them, takes more pleasure in isolated details, explains them to oneself, and what happens is as the re-emergence of an energy that the senses had absorbed; soon this distorts the aspect of things in its turn, using for the purpose the considered thought of a human being.

The universal man begins also by simple contemplation, but he always returns to be impregnated by what he sees, returns to the intoxication of the particular instinct and to the emotion which the least of things real arouses if one keeps in mind the two, thing and instinct, in every way separate from each other and yet combining, in so many ways, so many different qualities.

III

He who has never completed—be it but in dream—the sketch for some project that he is free to abandon; who has never felt the sense of adventure in working on some composition which he knows finished when others only see it commencing; who has not known the enthusiasm that burns away a minute of his very self; or the poison of conception, the scruple, the cold breath of objection coming from within; and the struggle with alternative ideas when the strongest and most universal should naturally triumph over both what is normal and what is novel; he who has not seen the image on the whiteness of his paper distorted by other possible images, by his regret for all the images that will not be chosen; or seen in limpid air a building that is not there; he who is not haunted by fear of the giddiness caused by the receding of the goal before him; by anxiety as to means; by foreknowledge of delays and despairs, calculation of progressive phases, reasoning about the future—even about things that should not, when the time comes, be reasoned about—that man does not know either—and it does not matter how much he knows besides—the riches and resources, the domains of the spirit, that are illuminated by the conscious act of *construction*. The gods have received from the human mind the gift of the power to create because that mind, being cyclical and abstract, may aggrandize what it has imagined to such a point that it is no longer capable of imagining it.

WALTER PATER

The Intensity of the Moment

Δέγει που 'Ηράκλειτος ότι πάντα χωρεῖ καὶ οὐδὲν μένει

To regard all things and principles of things as inconstant modes or fashions has more and more become the tendency of modern thought. Let us begin with that which is without—our physical life. Fix upon it in one of its more exquisite intervals, the moment, for instance, of delicious recoil from the flood of water in summer heat. What is the whole physical life in that moment but a combination of natural elements to which science gives their names? But those elements, phosphorus and lime and delicate fibres, are present not in the human body alone: we detect them in places most remote from it. Our physical life is a perpetual motion of them—the passage of the blood, the waste and repairing of the lenses of the eye, the modification of the tissues of the brain under every ray of light and sound—processes which science reduces to simpler and more elementary forces. Like the elements of which we are composed, the action of these forces extends beyond us: it rusts iron and ripens corn. Far out on every side of us those elements are broadcast, driven in many currents; and birth and gesture and death and the springing of violets from the grave are but a few out of ten thousand resultant combinations. That clear, perpetual outline of face and limb is but an image of ours, under which we group them—a design in a web, the actual threads of which pass out beyond it. This at least of flame-like our life has, that it is but the concurrence, renewed from moment to moment, of forces parting sooner or later on their ways.

Or, if we begin with the inward world of thought and feeling, the whirlpool is still more rapid, the flame more eager and devouring. There it is no longer the gradual darkening of the eye, the gradual fading of colour from the wall—movements of the shore-side, where the water flows down indeed, though in apparent rest—but the race of the mid-stream, a drift of momentary acts of sight and passion and thought. At first sight experience seems to bury us under a flood of external objects, pressing upon us with a sharp and importunate reality, calling us out of ourselves in a thousand forms of action. But when reflexion begins to play upon those objects they are dissipated under its influence; the cohesive force seems suspended like some trick of magic; each object is loosed into a group of impressions—colour, odour, texture—in the mind of the observer. And if we

"Conclusion" [1868] in Studies in the History of the Renaissance [1873], New York, 1919, pp. 194-9; and from Marius the Epicurean [1885], New York, 1921, pp. 121-4.

continue to dwell in thought on this world, not of objects in the solidity with which language invests them, but of impressions, unstable, flickering, inconsistent, which burn and are extinguished with our consciousness of them, it contracts still further: the whole scope of observation is dwarfed into the narrow chamber of the individual mind. Experience, already reduced to a group of impressions, is ringed round for each one of us by the thick wall of personality through which no real voice has ever pierced on its way to us, or from us to that which we can only conjecture to be without. Every one of those impressions is the impression of the individual in his isolation, each mind keeping as a solitary prisoner its own dream of a world. Analysis goes a step farther still, and assures us that those impressions of the individual mind to which, for each one of us, experience dwindles down, are in perpetual flight; that each of them is limited by time, and that as time is infinitely divisible, each of them is infinitely divisible also; all that is actual in it being a single moment, gone while we try to apprehend it, of which it may ever be more truly said that it has ceased to be than that it is. To such a tremulous wisp constantly re-forming itself on the stream, to a single sharp impression, with a sense in it, a relic more or less fleeting, of such moments gone by, what is real in our life fines itself down. It is with this movement, with the passage and dissolution of impressions, images, sensations, that analysis leaves off— that continual vanishing away, that strange, perpetual weaving and unweaving of ourselves.

Philosophiren, says Novalis, *ist dephlegmatisiren, vivificiren.* The service of philosophy, of speculative culture, towards the human spirit, is to rouse, to startle it to a life of constant and eager observation. Every moment some form grows perfect in hand or face; some tone on the hills or the sea is choicer than the rest; some mood of passion or insight or intellectual excitement is irresistibly real and attractive to us,—for that moment only. Not the fruit of experience, but experience itself, is the end. A counted number of pulses only is given to us of a variegated, dramatic life. How may we see in them all that is to be seen in them by the finest senses? How shall we pass most swiftly from point to point, and be present always at the focus where the greatest number of vital forces unite in their purest energy?

To burn always with this hard, gemlike flame, to maintain this ecstasy, is success in life. In a sense it might even be said that our failure is to form habits: for, after all, habit is relative to a stereotyped world, and meantime it is only the roughness of the eye that makes any two persons, things, situations, seem alike. While all melts under our feet, we may well grasp at any exquisite passion, or any contribution to knowledge that seems by a lifted horizon to set the spirit free for a moment, or any stirring of the senses, strange dyes, strange colours, and curious odours, or work of the artist's hands, or the face of one's friend. Not to discriminate every moment some passionate attitude in those about us, and in the very brilliancy of their gifts some tragic dividing of forces on their ways, is, on this short day of frost and sun, to sleep before evening. With this sense of the splendour of our experience and of its awful brevity, gathering all we are into one desperate effort to see and touch, we shall hardly have time to make theories about the things we see and touch. What we have to do is to be for ever curiously testing new opinions and courting new impressions, never acquiescing in a facile orthodoxy of Comte, or of Hegel, or of our own. Philosophical theories or ideas, as points of view, instruments of criticism, may help us to gather up what might otherwise pass unregarded by us. "Philosophy is the microscope of thought." The theory or idea or system which requires of us the sacrifice of any part of this experience, in consideration of some interest into which we cannot enter, or some abstract theory we have not identified with ourselves, or of what is only conventional, has no real claim upon us.

One of the most beautiful passages of Rousseau is that in the sixth book of the *Confessions*, where he describes the awakening in him of the literary sense. An undefinable taint of death had clung always about him, and now in early manhood he believed himself smitten by mortal disease. He asked himself how he might make as much as possible of the interval that remained; and he was not biassed by anything in his previous life when he decided that it must be by intellectual excitement, which he found just then in the clear, fresh writings of Voltaire. Well! we are all *condamnés* as Victor Hugo says: we are all under sentence of death but with a sort of indefinite reprieve—*les hommes sont tous condamnés à mort avec des sursis indéfinis:* we have an interval, and then our place knows us no more. Some spend this interval in listlessness, some in high passions, the wisest, at least among "the children of this world," in art and song. For our one chance lies in expanding that interval, in getting as many pulsations as possible into the given time. Great passions may give us this quickened sense of life, ecstasy and sorrow of love, the various forms of enthusiastic activity, disinterested or otherwise, which come naturally to many of us. Only be sure it is passion—that it does yield you this fruit of a quickened, multipled consciousness. Of such wisdom, the poetic passion, the desire of beauty, the love of art for its own sake, has most. For art comes to you proposing frankly to give nothing but the highest quality to your moments as they pass, and simply for those moments' sake.

———

With this view he would demand culture, παιδεία, as the Cyrenaics said, or, in other words, a wide, a complete, education—an education partly negative, as ascertaining the true limits of man's capacities, but for the most part positive, and directed especially to the expansion and refinement of the power of reception; of those powers, above all, which are immediately relative to fleeting phenomena, the powers of emotion and sense. In such an education, an "esthetic" education, as it might now be termed, and certainly occupied very largely with those aspects of things which affect us pleasurably through sensation, art, of course, including all the finer sorts of literature, would have a great part to play. The study of music, in that wider Platonic sense, according to which, *music* comprehends all those matters over which the Muses of Greek mythology preside, would conduct one to an exquisite appreciation of all the finer traits of nature and of man. Nay! the products of the imagination must themselves be held to present the most perfect forms of life—spirit and matter alike under their purest and most perfect conditions—the most strictly appropriate objects of that impassioned contemplation, which, in the world of intellectual discipline, as in the highest forms of morality and religion, must be held to be the essential function of the "perfect." Such manner of life might come even to seem a kind of religion—an inward, visionary, mystic piety, or religion, by virtue of its effort to live days "lovely and pleasant" in themselves, here and now, and with an all-sufficiency of well-being in the immediate sense of the object contemplated, in-dependently of any faith, or hope that might be entertained as to their ulterior tendency. In this way, the true esthetic culture would be realizable as a new form of the contemplative life, founding its claim on the intrinsic "blessedness" of "vision"—the vision of perfect men and things. One's human nature, indeed, would fain reckon on an assured and endless future, pleasing itself with the dream of a final home, to be attained at some still remote date, yet with a conscious, delightful home-coming at last, as depicted in many an old poetic Elysium. On the other hand, the world of perfected sensation, intelligence, emotion, is so close to us, and so attractive, that the most visionary of spirits must needs rep-resent the world unseen in colors, and under a form really borrowed from it. Let me be sure then—might he not plausibly say?—that I miss no detail of this life of realized consciousness in the present! Here at least is a vision, a theory, $\theta\epsilon\omega\rho\iota\alpha$, which reposes on no basis of unverified hypothesis, which makes no call upon a future after all somewhat problematic; as it would be unaffected by any discovery of an Empedocles (improving on the old story of Prometheus) as to what had really been the origin, and course of development, of man's actually attained faculties and that seemingly divine particle of reason or spirit in him. Such a doctrine, at more leisurable moments, would of course have its precepts to de-liver on the embellishment, generally, of what is near at hand, on the adornment of life, till, in a not impracticable rule of conduct, one's existence, from day to day, came to be like a well-executed piece of music; that "perpetual motion" in things (so Marius figured the matter to himself, under the old Greek imageries) according itself to a kind of cadence or harmony.

It was intelligible that this "esthetic" philosophy might find itself (theoreti-cally, at least, and by way of a curious question in casuistry, legitimate from its own point of view) weighing the claims of that eager, concentrated, impassioned realization of experience, against those of the received morality. Conceiving its own function in a somewhat desperate temper, and becoming, as every high-strung form of sentiment, as the religious sentiment itself, may become, some-what antinomian, when, in its effort towards the order of experiences it prefers, it is confronted with the traditional and popular morality, at points where that morality may look very like a convention, or a mere stage-property of the world, it would be found, from time to time, breaking beyond the limits of the actual moral order; perhaps not without some pleasurable excitement in so bold a venture.

JORIS-KARL HUYSMANS
Artificial Sensation

Sometimes of an afternoon, when Des Esseintes happened to be already up and about, he would set in action the system of pipes and conduits which emptied the aquarium and refilled it with fresh water, and then pour in a few drops of

From *Against Nature* [1884], translated from the French by Robert Baldick, 1959, pp. 34-5, 35-7, 58-9; reprinted by permission of Penguin Books Inc.

coloured essences, thus producing at will the various tints, green or grey, opaline or silvery, which real rivers take on according to the colour of the sky, the greater or less brilliance of the sun's rays, the more or less imminent threat of rain—in a word, according to the season and the weather.

He could then imagine himself between-decks in a brig, and gazed inquisitively at some ingenious mechanical fishes driven by clockwork, which moved backwards and forwards behind the port-hole window and got entangled in artificial seaweed. At other times, while he was inhaling the smell of tar which had been introduced into the room before he entered it, he would examine a series of colour-prints on the walls, such as you see in packet-boat offices and Lloyd's agencies, representing steamers bound for Valparaiso and the River Plate, alongside framed notices giving the itineraries of the Royal Mail Steam Packet Line and the Lopez and Valéry Companies, as well as the freight charges and ports of call of the transatlantic mail-boats.

Then, when he was tired of consulting these time-tables, he would rest his eyes by looking at the chronometers and compasses, the sextants and dividers, the binoculars and charts scattered about on a side-table which was dominated by a single book, bound in sea-calf leather: the *Narrative of Arthur Gordon Pym*, specially printed for him on laid paper of pure linen, hand-picked and bearing a seagull water-mark.

Finally he could take stock of the fishing-rods, the brown-tanned nets, the rolls of russet-coloured sails and the miniature anchor made of cork painted black, all piled higgledy-piggledy beside the door that led to the kitchen by way of a corridor padded, like the passage between dining-room and study, in such a way as to absorb any noises and smells.

By these means he was able to enjoy quickly, almost simultaneously, all the sensations of a long sea-voyage, without ever leaving home; the pleasure of moving from place to place, a pleasure which in fact exists only in recollection of the past and hardly ever in experience of the present, this pleasure he could savour in full and in comfort, without fatigue or worry, in this cabin whose deliberate disorder, impermanent appearance, and makeshift appointments corresponded fairly closely to the flying visits he paid it and the limited time he gave his meals, while it offered a complete contrast to his study, a permanent, orderly, well-established room, admirably equipped to maintain and uphold a stay-at-home existence.

Travel, indeed, struck him as being a waste of time, since he believed that the imagination could provide a more-than-adequate substitute for the vulgar reality of actual experience. In his opinion it was perfectly possible to fulfil those desires commonly supposed to be the most difficult to satisfy under normal conditions, and this by the trifling subterfuge of producing a fair imitation of the object of those desires. Thus it is well known that nowadays, in restaurants famed for the excellence of their cellars, the gourmets go into raptures over rare vintages manufactured out of cheap wines treated according to Monsieur Pasteur's method. Now, whether they are genuine or faked, these wines have the same aroma, the same colour, the same bouquet; and consequently the pleasure experienced in tasting these factitious, sophisticated beverages is absolutely identical with that which would be afforded by the pure, unadulterated wine, now unobtainable at any price. . . .

As a matter of fact, artifice was considered by Des Esseintes to be the distinctive mark of human genius.

Nature, he used to say, has had her day; she has finally and utterly exhausted the patience of sensitive observers by the revolting uniformity of her landscapes and skyscapes. After all, what platitudinous limitations she imposes, like a tradesman specializing in a single line of business; what petty-minded restrictions, like a shopkeeper stocking one article to the exclusion of all others; what a monotonous store of meadows and trees, what a commonplace display of mountains and seas!

In fact, there is not a single one of her inventions, deemed so subtle and sublime, that human ingenuity cannot manufacture; no moonlit Forest of Fontainebleau that cannot be reproduced by stage scenery under floodlighting; no cascade that cannot be imitated to perfection by hydraulic engineering; no rock that papier-mâché cannot counterfeit; no flower that carefully chosen taffeta and delicately coloured paper cannot match!

There can be no shadow of doubt that with her never-ending platitudes the old crone has by now exhausted the good-humoured admiration of all true artists, and the time has surely come for artifice to take her place whenever possible. . . .

He made his way to the dining-room, where there was a cupboard built into one of the walls containing a row of little barrels, resting side-by-side on tiny sandalwood stands and each broached at the bottom with a silver spigot.

This collection of liqueur casks he called his mouth organ.

A rod could be connected to all the spigots, enabling them to be turned by one and the same movement, so that once the apparatus was in position it was only necessary to press a button concealed in the wainscoting to open all the conduits simultaneously and so fill with liqueur the minute cups underneath the taps.

The organ was then open. The stops labelled "flute," "horn," and "vox angelica" were pulled out, ready for use. Des Esseintes would drink a drop here, another there, playing internal symphonies to himself, and providing his palate with sensations analogous to those which music dispenses to the ear.

Indeed, each and every liqueur, in his opinion, corresponded in taste with the sound of a particular instrument. Dry curaçao, for instance, was like the clarinet with its piercing, velvety note; kümmel like the oboe with its sonorous, nasal timbre; crème de menthe and anisette like the flute, at once sweet and tart, soft and shrill. Then to complete the orchestra there was kirsch, blowing a wild trumpet blast; gin and whisky raising the roof of the mouth with the blare of their cornets and trombones; marc-brandy matching the tubas with its deafening din; while peals of thunder came from the cymbal and the bass drum, which arak and mastic were banging and beating with all their might.

He considered that this analogy could be pushed still further and that string quartets might play under the palatal arch, with the violin represented by an old brandy, choice and heady, biting and delicate; with the viola simulated by rum, which was stronger, heavier, and quieter; with vespetro as poignant, drawn-out, sad, and tender as a violoncello; and with the double-bass a fine old bitter, full-bodied, solid, and dark. One might even form a quintet, if this were thought desirable, by adding a fifth instrument, the harp, imitated to near perfection by the vibrant savour, the clear, sharp, silvery note of dry cumin.

The similarity did not end there, for the music of liqueurs had its own scheme of interrelated tones; thus, to quote only one example, Benedictine represents, so to speak, the minor key corresponding to the major key of those alcohols which wine-merchants' scores indicate by the name of green Chartreuse.

Once these principles had been established, and thanks to a series of erudite experiments, he had been able to perform upon his tongue silent melodies and mute funeral marches; to hear inside his mouth crème-de-menthe solos and rum-and-vespetro duets.

He even succeeded in transferring specific pieces of music to his palate, following the composer step by step, rendering his intentions, his effects, his shades of expression, by mixing or contrasting related liqueurs, by subtle approximations and cunning combinations.

At other times he would compose melodies of his own, executing pastorals with the sweet blackcurrant liqueur that filled his throat with the warbling song of a nightingale; or with the delicious cacaochouva that hummed sugary bergerets like the *Romances of Estelle* and the *"Ah! vous dirai-je, maman"* of olden days.

ANDRÉ GIDE

The Reflexive Image

[1892]
1 JANUARY

Wilde, I believe, did me nothing but harm. In his company I had lost the habit of thinking. I had more varied emotions, but had forgotten how to bring order into them. Above all, I could no longer follow the deductions of others. A few thoughts from time to time, but my clumsiness in handling them made me give them up. I return now, with difficulty but also with great delight, to my history of philosophy, where I am studying the problem of language (which I shall take up with Müller and Renan).

3 JANUARY

Shall I always torment myself thus and will my mind never, O Lord, come to rest in any certainty? Like an invalid turning over in his bed in search of sleep, I am restless from morning till night, and at night my anxiety awakens me.

I am anxious to know what I shall be; I do not even know what I want to be, but I do know that I must choose. I should like to progress on safe and sure roads that lead only to the point where I have decided to go. But I don't know; I don't know what I ought to want. I am aware of a thousand possibilities in me, but I cannot resign myself to want to be only one of them. And every moment, at every word I write, at each gesture I make, I am terrified at the thought that this

From *The Journals of André Gide, 1889-1913*, translated by Justin O'Brien, New York, 1947-51, Vol. I, pp. 18-19, 29. Copyright 1947 by Alfred A. Knopf, Inc. Reprinted by permission of Alfred A. Knopf, Inc. and Martin Secker & Warburg Ltd.

is one more ineradicable feature of my physiognomy becoming fixed: a hesitant, impersonal physiognomy, an amorphous physiognomy, since I have not been capable of choosing and tracing its contours confidently.

O Lord, permit me to want only one thing and to want it constantly.

A man's life is his image. At the hour of death we shall be reflected in the past, and leaning over the mirror of our acts, our souls will recognize *what we are*. Our whole life is spent in sketching an ineradicable portrait of ourselves. The terrible thing is that we don't know this: we do not think of beautifying ourselves. We think of it in speaking of ourselves; we flatter ourselves; but later our terrible portrait will not flatter us. We recount our lives and lie to ourselves, but our life will not lie; it will recount our soul, which will stand before God in its usual posture.

This can therefore be said, which strikes me as a kind of reverse sincerity (on the part of the artist):

Rather than recounting his life as he has lived it, he must live his life as he will recount it. In other words, the portrait of him formed by his life must identify itself with the ideal portrait he desires. And, in still simpler terms, he must be as he wishes to be. . . .

11 JANUARY

I am torn by a conflict between the rules of morality and the rules of sincerity.

Morality consists in substituting for the natural creature (the old Adam) a fiction that you prefer. But then you are no longer sincere. The old Adam is the sincere man.

This occurs to me: the old Adam is the poet. The new man, whom you prefer, is the artist. The artist must take the place of the poet. From the struggle between the two is born the work of art. . . .

La Roque

I wanted to suggest, in the *Tentative amoureuse*, the influence of the book upon the one who is writing it, and during that very writing. As the book issues from us it changes us, modifying the course of our life, just as in physics those free-hanging vases, full of liquid, are seen, as they empty, to receive an impulse in the opposite direction from that of the liquid's flow. Our acts exercise a retroaction upon us. "Our deeds act upon us as much as we act upon them," said George Eliot.

In my case I was sad because a dream of irrealizable joy was tormenting me. I relate that dream and, isolating the joy from the dream, I make it mine; my dream has broken the spell and I am full of joy.

No action upon an object without retroaction of that object upon the subject. I wanted to indicate that reciprocity, not in one's relations with others, but with oneself. The subject that acts is oneself; the object that retroacts is a literary subject arising in the imagination. This is consequently an indirect method of acting upon oneself that I have outlined; and it is also, more directly, a tale.

The Completed Image

I know for certain that my time will not be long. I have put away everything that can be put away that I may speak what I have to speak, and I find "expression" is a part of "study." In two or three weeks—I am now idle that I may rest after writing much verse—I will begin to write my most fundamental thoughts and the arrangement of thought which I am convinced will complete my studies. I am happy, and I think full of an energy, of an energy I had despaired of. It seems to me that I have found what I wanted. When I try to put all into a phrase I say, "Man can embody truth but he cannot know it." I must embody it in the completion of my life. The abstract is not life and everywhere draws out its contradictions. You can refute Hegel but not the Saint or the Song of Sixpence.

Letter to Lady Elizabeth Pelham [1939], from *The Letters of W. B. Yeats*, ed. Allan Wade, New York, 1955, p. 922; reprinted by permission of Rupert Hart-Davis Ltd.

RAINER MARIA RILKE

The Aesthetic Transformation of the Earth

And am I the one to give the *Elegies* their proper explanation? They reach out infinitely beyond me. I regard them as a further elaboration of those essential premises that were already given in the *Book of Hours*, that in the two parts of the *New Poems* tentatively played with the image of the world and that then in the *Malte*, contracted in conflict, strike back into life and there almost lead to the proof that this life so suspended in the bottomless is impossible. In the *Elegies*, starting from the same postulates, life becomes possible again, indeed, it experiences here that ultimate *affirmation* to which young Malte, though on the difficult right path *des longues études*, was as yet unable to conduct it. *Affirmation of life-AND-death appears as one in the Elegies.* To grant one without the other is, so it is here learned and celebrated, a limitation which in the end shuts out all that is infinite. *Death* is the *side of life* averted from us, unshone upon by us: we must try to achieve the greatest consciousness of our existence which is at home in *both unbounded realms, inexhaustibly nourished from both.* . . . The true figure of life extended through *both* spheres, the blood of the mightiest circulation flows through *both: there is neither a here nor a beyond, but the great unity* in which the beings that surpass us, the "angels," are at home. And now the place of the love problem, in this world extended by its greater half, in this world only now *whole*, only now *sound.* I am amazed that the *Sonnets to Orpheus*, which are at least as *"difficult,"* filled with the same essence, are not more

Letter to Witold von Hulewicz [1925], *Letters*, translated from the German by Jane Bannard Greene and M. D. Herter Norton, New York, 1945-48, Vol. II, pp. 372-6. Copyright 1947 and 1948 by W. W. Norton & Co., Inc.; reprinted by permission of W. W. Norton & Co.

helpful to you in the understanding of the *Elegies*. These latter were begun in 1912 (at Duino), continued in Spain and Paris—fragmentarily—until 1914; the War interrupted this my greatest work altogether; when in 1922 I ventured to take them up again (here), the new elegies and their conclusion were preceded, in a few days, by the *Sonnets to Orpheus*, which imposed themselves tempestuously (and which had *not* been in my plan). They are, as could not have been otherwise, of the same "birth" as the *Elegies*, and their springing up, without my willing it, in connection with a girl who had died young, moves them even closer to the source of their origin: this connection being one more relation toward the center of *that* realm whose depth and influence we share, everywhere unboundaried, with the dead and those to come. We of the here and now are not for a moment hedged in the time-world, nor confined within it; we are incessantly flowing over and over to those who preceded us, to our origins and to those who seemingly come after us. In that greatest *"open"* world all *are*, one cannot say "simultaneous," for the very falling away of time determines that they all *are*. Transiency everywhere plunges into a deep being. And so all the configurations of the here and now are to be used not in a time-bound way only, but, as far as we are able, to be placed in those superior significances in which we have a share. But *not in the Christian sense* (from which I am more and more passionately moving away), but, in a purely earthly, blissfully earthly consciousness, we must introduce what is *here* seen and touched into the wider, into the widest orbit. Not into a beyond whose shadow darkens the earth, but into a whole, into *the whole*. Nature, the things of our intercourse and use, are provisional and perishable; but they are, as long as we are here, *our* property and our friendship, co-knowers of our distress and gladness, as they have already been the familiars of our forebears. So it is important not only not to run down and degrade all that is here, but just because of its provisionalness, which it shares with us, these phenomena and things should be understood and transformed by us in a most fervent sense. Transformed? Yes, for it is our task to imprint this provisional, perishable earth so deeply, so patiently and passionately in ourselves that its reality shall arise in us again "invisibly." *We are the bees of the invisible. Nous butinons éperdument le miel du visible, pour l'accumuler dans la grande ruche d'or de l'Invisible.* The *Elegies* show us at this work, at the work of these continual conversions of the beloved visible and tangible into the invisible vibrations and excitation of our own nature, which introduces new vibration-frequencies into the vibration-spheres of the universe. (Since different elements in the cosmos are only different vibration-exponents, we prepare for ourselves in this way not only intensities of a spiritual nature but also, who knows, new bodies, metals, nebulae and constellations.) And this activity is curiously supported and urged on by the even more rapid fading away of so much of the visible that will no longer be replaced. Even for our grandparents a "house," a "well," a familiar tower, their very clothes, their coat: were infinitely more, infinitely more intimate; almost everything a vessel in which they found the human and added to the store of the human. Now, from America, empty indifferent things are pouring across, sham things, *dummy life.* . . . A house, in the American sense, an American apple or a grapevine over there, has *nothing* in common with the house, the fruit, the grape into which went the hopes and reflections of our forefathers. . . . Live things, things lived and conscient of us, are running out and can no longer be replaced. *We are perhaps the last still to have known such things.* On us rests the responsibility not alone of preserving *their* memory (that would be little and unreliable), but their human and laral value. ("Laral" in the sense of the household gods.) The earth has no way out other than to become invisible: *in* us who with a part of our natures partake of the invisible, have (at least) stock in it, and can increase our holdings in the invisible during our sojourn here,—*in* us alone can be consummated this intimate and lasting conversion of the visible into an invisible no longer dependent upon being visible and tangible, as our own destiny continually *grows at the same time* MORE PRESENT AND INVISIBLE in us. The *Elegies* set up this norm of existence: they assure, they celebrate this consciousness. They cautiously fit it into its traditions, in that they claim for this supposition ancient traditions and rumors of traditions and even in the Egyptian cult of the dead evoke a foreknowledge of such relationships. (Although the "Land of Lamentation" through which the older "lamentation" leads the young dead is *not to be identified with* Egypt, but is only, in a sense, a mirroring of the Nile country in the desert clarity of the consciousness of the dead.) When one makes the mistake of holding up to the *Elegies* or *Sonnets* Catholic conceptions of death, of the beyond and of eternity, one is getting entirely away from their point of departure and preparing for oneself a more and more basic misunderstanding. The "angel" of the *Elegies* has nothing to do with the angel of the Christian heaven (rather with the angel figures of Islam). . . . The angel of the *Elegies* is that creature in whom the transformation of the visible into the invisible, which we are accomplishing, appears already consummated. For the angel of the *Elegies* all past towers and palaces are existent, *because* long invisible, and the still standing towers and bridges of our existence *already* invisible, although (for us) still persisting physically. The angel of the *Elegies* is that being who vouches for the recognition in the invisible of a higher order of reality.—Hence "terrible" to us, because we, its lovers and transformers, do still cling to the visible.—All the worlds of the universe are plunging into the invisible as into their next deepest reality; *a few stars immediately intensify and pass away in the infinite consciousness of the angels—, others are dependent upon beings who slowly and laboriously transform them, in whose terrors and ecstasies they attain their next invisible realization. We are,* let it be emphasized once more, *in the sense of the* Elegies, *we are these transformers of the earth; our entire existence, the flights and plunges of our love, everything qualifies us for this task* (beside which there exists, essentially, no other). (The *Sonnets* show details from this activity which here appears placed under the name and protection of a dead girl whose incompletion and innocence holds open the gate of the grave so that, gone from us, she belongs to those powers that keep the one half of life fresh and open toward the other wound-open half.) *Elegies* and *Sonnets* support each other constantly—, and I see an infinite grace in the fact that, with the same breath, I was permitted to fill both these sails: the little rust-colored sail of the *Sonnets* and the *Elegies'* gigantic white canvas.

May you, dear friend, perceive here some advice and elucidation and, for the rest, help yourself along. For: I do not know whether I ever could say more.

GUSTAVE FLAUBERT

An Aesthetic Mysticism

[TO GUY DE MAUPASSANT]

You are living an absolute hell of a life, I know, and I pity you from the bottom of my heart. But all your time from 5 in the evening till 10 in the morning can be devoted to the Muse, who is still the best wench of the lot. Come, old chap, put your chin up. What is the good of brooding on your misery? You must face up to yourself like a brave man; that is the way to become one. A little more pride, for goodness' sake! The "lad" used to have more conceit of himself. What you need are "principles." But that is easily said; the question is, what principles? Well, for an artist there is only one: to sacrifice everything to Art. Life for him must be no more than a means to an end, and the last person he must consider is himself.

[TO MAXIME DU CAMP]

You seem to have some sort of interfering mania about me. Not that it worries me, never fear. My mind has been made up on these matters for a long time.

I shall only say that all these expressions: *make haste, now is the time, the moment has come, filling a place, taking up a position, ultra vires*, etc., are to me a meaningless language. You might just as well be speaking to a Red Indian. Don't you understand?

To *get there*, but where? To the position of Messrs. Murger, Feuillet, Monselet, etc., Arsène Houssaye, Taxile Delord, Hippolyte Lucas and seventy-two more of them. Thank you very much.

Letters to Guy de Maupassant [1875] and Maxime du Camp [1852], *Letters*, ed. Richard Rumbold and translated from the French by J. M. Cohen, London, 1950, pp. 218, 67-9; reprinted by permission of George Weidenfeld and Nicolson Ltd. and Philosophical Library, New York.
    Letter to Louise Colet [1853], *Selected Letters*, translated from the French by Francis Steegmuller, London, 1954, pp. 161-2. Copyright 1953 by Francis Steegmuller. Reprinted by permission of Farrar, Straus & Co. and Hamish Hamilton Ltd.
    Letters to Louise Colet [1852, 1853] and to George Sand [1876], *Letters*, ed. Richard Rumbold and translated from the French by J. M. Cohen, London, 1950, pp. 72-3, 83-4, 84-5, 201-2; reprinted by permission of George Weidenfeld and Nicolson Ltd. and Philosophical Library, New York.

To be well known is not my main business; it can only be entirely satisfying to those with a poor conceit of themselves. Besides, even then does one ever know when to rest content? The utmost renown never slakes a man's appetite and, unless he is a fool, he almost always dies uncertain of his own fame. For prominence is no more help towards a true self-estimate than obscurity.

I am aiming at something better, at pleasing myself. To me success appears to be a by-product, not a goal. Now I have been marching on this goal for what seems to me a long time, without the slightest deflection; nor have I ever stopped to pay court to ladies by the wayside, or to sleep on the greensward. If it is an illusion I am pursuing, at least I prefer the highest illusions.

I had rather see the whole United States perish than sacrifice a single principle. I would sooner die like a dog than hurry my sentence by so much as a second before it is ripe.

I have in my head the method of writing and the choice of language that I wish to attain. When I think I have plucked the fruit, I shall not refuse to sell it, nor reject the world's applause if it is good. But, in the meantime, I do not want to diddle the public. There it is.

And if when that time comes it is too late and people have lost their appetite, that will be too bad. Believe me, I wish I were much more facile, and could draw larger profits for much less work. But I can see no remedy.

There may well be favourable moments in business, a lucky run on such and such an article, a passing craze which sends up the price of rubber or printed cottons. Let would-be manufacturers of such goods hurry to put their factories up, of course. But if your work of art is good, if it is *right*, it will evoke its response, it will find its place, in six months time, in six years or when you are dead. What does it matter?

You talk of finding the *breath of life* in Paris. To my mind your breath of life very often stinks of decayed teeth. You invite me to breathe the air of that Parnassus, but I find it rather noxious than heady. The laurels plucked there are, you must agree, a little dung-spattered.

What is more, I am sorry to see a man like you going one better than the Marquis d'Escarbagnas with her "there was no climate outside Paris for honest men." That seems to me a pretty provincial point of view itself—a narrow one, I mean. Humanity is everywhere, my dear man, but there is more humbug in Paris than elsewhere, I grant you.

There is certainly one thing you gain in Paris, and that is cheek. But it costs you a few grey hairs.

Anyone who has turned out to be a man of real strength, despite a Paris upbringing, must have been born a demi-god. He will have grown up with his ribs compressed and a weight on his head; whereas a man has to be absolutely devoid of native originality, if solitude, concentration, and years of work do not finally make something of him.

As for your bitter outcry at the stultifying nature of my life, you might as well blame a cobbler for making shoes, or a blacksmith for hammering his iron, as reproach an artist for living in his workshop. As I work every day from one in the afternoon till one in the morning, except for an interval between six and eight, I can hardly see anything to spend the remainder of my time on. If I really lived in the provinces or in the country, and spent my days playing dominoes or growing melons, I should understand your criticism. But if I am becoming stupid, it is Lucian, Shakespeare and the writing of a novel that are the cause.

I told you that I should come and live in Paris when my book was finished, and that I should publish it if I were satisfied with it. I have not altered my decision. That is all I can say, nothing more.

Really, old chap, one must take things as they come. I don't care about any fresh literary disputes that may arise. I care even less for Augier's success, and I don't give a damn if Vacquerie and Ponsard spread themselves till they have crowded me right out. I shall not come and push them from my place.

And here I send you my love.

[TO LOUISE COLET]

Yes, I maintain (and in my opinion this should be a rule of conduct for an artist) that one's existence should be in two parts: one should live like a bourgeois and think like a demi-god. Physical and intellectual gratifications have nothing in common. If they happen to coincide, hold fast to them. But do not *try* to combine them: that would be factitious. And this idea of "happiness," incidentally, is the almost exclusive cause of all human misfortunes. We must store up our hearts' marrow and give of it only in small doses; and the innermost sap of our passions we must preserve in precious flasks. These essences of ourselves must be reserved as sublime nourishment for posterity. Who can tell how much is wasted every day in emotional outpourings?

We marvel at the mystics, but what I have just said explains their secret. Their love, like mountain streams, ran in a single bed—narrow, deep, and steep; that is why it carried everything before it.

If you seek happiness and beauty simultaneously, you will attain neither one nor the other, for the price of beauty is self-denial. Art, like the Jewish God, wallows in sacrifices. So tear yourself to pieces, mortify your flesh, roll in ashes, smear yourself with filth and spittle, wrench out your heart! You will be alone, your feet will bleed, an infernal disgust will be with you throughout your pilgrimage, what gives joy to others will give none to you, what to them are but pinpricks will cut you to the quick, and you will be lost in the hurricane with only beauty's faint glow visible on the horizon. But it will grow, grow like the sun, its golden rays will bathe your face, penetrate into you, you will be illumined within, ethereal, all spiritualized, and after each bleeding the flesh will be less burdensome. Let us therefore seek only tranquillity; let us ask of life only an armchair, not a throne; only water to quench our thirst, not drunkenness. Passion is not compatible with the long patience that is a requisite of our calling. Art is vast enough to take complete possession of a man. To divert anything from it is almost a crime; it is a sin against the Idea, a dereliction of duty. But we are weak, the flesh is soft, and the heart, like a branch heavy with rain, trembles at the slightest tremor of the earth. We pant for air like a prisoner, an infinite weakness comes over us, we feel that we are dying. Wisdom consists in jettisoning the smallest possible part of the cargo, that the vessel may keep safely afloat. . . .

[TO LOUISE COLET]

I am turning to a kind of aesthetic mysticism (if the two words can be used together), and I wish my faith were stronger. When no encouragement comes from others, when the external world disgusts, weakens and corrupts, *honest* and *sensitive* people are forced to look within themselves for a fitter dwelling place. If society continues on its present course, we shall see mystics again, I think, as we have done in every dark age. Denied an outlet, the soul will retire into itself. Very soon we shall see the reappearance of universal apathy, of beliefs in the end of the world, of Messianic claims. But lacking a theological foundation, where can this unconscious fervour find a basis? Some will seek it in the flesh, others in the old religions, and yet others in Art; and like the Children of Israel in the desert, humanity will adore all sorts of idols. Our kind have come a little too early; in twenty-five years' time the nodal point will respond magnificently to an artist's touch. Then prose (prose especially, the younger medium) will be capable of a grand humanitarian symphony. There may be a return to books like the *Satyricon* and the *Golden Ass*, but in place of their abounding sensuality, their successors will have an equally abounding psychological wealth.

This is what the world's socialists, with their eternal materialistic prophecies, have refused to see. They have denied *pain*; they have blasphemed against three-quarters of modern poetry, the blood of Christ which runs in our veins. Nothing will exhaust it or dry it up. The problem is not to drain it away, but to make it flow in a stream. If the consciousness of human insufficiency, of the vanity of life, were to perish (which would result from their hypothesis) we should be sillier than the birds, who at least perch on the trees. At present man's soul is asleep, drugged by the words she has heard; but she will have a frenzied awakening, and give herself over to the joys of liberty; for she will have no restraints left to hold her back, no government, no religion, no principles of any sort. Republicans of all complexions are to me the cruellest pedagogues in the world, with their dreams of organisation, legislation, and a monastically rigid society. I believe, on the other hand, that rules of all kinds are breaking down, that barriers are tumbling, and the earth falling to a dead level. This vast disorder may perhaps bring liberty. At least Art, which is always in the vanguard, has followed this road. What is the prevalent poetic form nowadays? Broad construction itself is becoming more and more impossible, with our limited and precise vocabulary and our vague, confused and fugitive ideas. All that we can do then is, out of sheer virtuosity, to tighten the strings of the overstrummed guitar and become primarily virtuosi, seeing that simplicity in our age is an illusion. At this point the picturesque has almost completely died out. Poetry, however, will not die, but where poetry will come into things in future I can hardly see. Who knows? Perhaps beauty will become a useless quality to humanity, and Art will be something halfway between algebra and music.

[TO LOUISE COLET]

Nature cares precious little for us—the trees, the grass and the waves present us with a cruelly impassive front. The Havre steamship's bell is ringing so furiously that I must stop. What a din industry does make in the world! The machine is a rowdy object. Talking of industry, have you ever thought of the number of stupid professions it gives rise to, and of the mass of inanity it will eventually produce? That would be an alarming piece of research. What can you expect from a population which, like Manchester's, spends its life making pins? And the making of a single pin requires five or six different processes. As the work is split up, you get, beside the machines proper, a quantity of human machines. Think of the job of a railway car attendant or a feeder in a printing works, etc. Man is indeed becoming an animal. Leconte is right; the way he set that theory out I shall never forget. The *contemplatives* of the Middle Ages were very different men from our modern *men of action*.

Humanity hates us; we do not minister to it and we hate it because it wounds us. Therefore, we must love one another in *Art*, as the mystics love one another *in God*, and everything must grow pale before that love. Let all life's other lamps (which stink, one and all) vanish before this great sun. In an age when all common bonds are snapped, and when Society is just one huge brigandage (to use official parlance) more or less well organised, when the interests of flesh and spirit draw apart like wolves and howl in solitude, one must act like everyone else, cultivate an ego (a more beautiful one naturally) and live in one's den. The distance between myself and my fellow men widens every day. I feel this process working in my heart and I am glad, for my sensitivity towards all that I find sympathetic continually increases, as a result of this very withdrawal.

[TO LOUISE COLET]

Remarks on morals and aesthetics: a local man, who has been mayor for *forty years*, told me that all that time he had only known *two* convictions for theft, out of a population of more than three thousand. That strikes me as illuminating. If sailors and workmen are of a different kidney, what is the reason? I believe that it arises from *contact with greatness*. A man who has always before his eyes as wide a stretch as human sight can cover must derive from that very familiarity a scornful habit of equanimity (think of the wastefulness of sailors of all sorts, of how little they care for their lives or their money). I believe that is the direction in which to look for the *moral effect of Art*. Its intrinsic sublimity, like nature's, will lead to a higher morality; by virtue of its very superiority it will serve a useful purpose. The sight of a cornfield brings more joy to a philanthropist's heart than a view of the Ocean, for everyone agrees that Agriculture encourages good habits. But what a poor creature a carter is beside a sailor! The ideal is like the sun; it sucks up all the filth in the world.

[TO GEORGE SAND]

I do not agree with Turgenev's severity towards *Jack*, nor with his immense admiration for *Rougon*. Daudet's book has charm, Zola's strength. But neither of them is *primarily* concerned with what is for me the purpose of Art: Beauty. I remember how violently my heart leapt at the sight of one wall of the Acropolis, a mere bare wall (the one on the left as you go up to the Propylaea). Well, I wonder whether a book, independent of its subject matter, may not produce the same effect. Is not there an intrinsic virtue, a kind of divine impulse in the precision of the grouping, the perfection of the parts, the surface polish, the total harmony? Is there not (I speak as a Platonist) something of an eternal principle here? Why else is there an inevitable relationship between the right word and the right sound? Why else do one's over-compressed thoughts always take the shape of verse? The law of numbers governs both feelings and imagery, and what appears merely superficial is, in point of fact, the heart of the matter. If I were to go on for long in this strain I should soon be all at sea. For, to look at it another way, Art ought to be simple. Art, really, is whatever one can make it. We are not free to choose. Each man, willy-nilly, follows his natural course. Really, your old Cruchard does not know whether he is on his head or his heels.

E. M. FORSTER

Art as Evidence of Order

I believe in art for art's sake. It is an unfashionable belief, and some of my statements must be of the nature of an apology. Sixty years ago I should have faced you with more confidence. A writer or a speaker who chose "Art for Art's Sake" for his theme sixty years ago could be sure of being in the swim, and could feel so confident of success that he sometimes dressed himself in aesthetic costumes suitable to the occasion—in an embroidered dressing-gown, perhaps, or a blue velvet suit with a Lord Fauntleroy collar; or a toga, or a kimono, and carried a poppy or a lily or a long peacock's feather in his mediaeval hand. Times have changed. Not thus can I present either myself or my theme to-day. My aim rather is to ask you quietly to reconsider for a few minutes a phrase which has been much misused and much abused, but which has, I believe, great importance for us—has, indeed, eternal importance.

Now we can easily dismiss those peacock's feathers and other affectations—they are but trifles—but I want also to dismiss a more dangerous heresy, namely the silly idea that only art matters, an idea which has somehow got mixed up with the idea of art for art's sake, and has helped to discredit it. Many things, besides art, matter. It is merely one of the things that matter, and high though the claims are that I make for it, I want to keep them in proportion. No one can spend his or her life entirely in the creation or the appreciation of masterpieces. Man lives, and ought to live, in a complex world, full of conflicting claims, and if we simplified them down into the aesthetic he would be sterilised. Art for art's sake does not mean that only art matters and I would also like to rule out such phrases as, "The Life of Art," "Living for Art," and "Art's High Mission." They confuse and mislead.

"Art for Art's Sake" [1949], from *Two Cheers for Democracy*, London and New York, 1951, pp. 88-94. Copyright 1949 by E. M. Forster; reprinted by permission of Harcourt, Brace & World, Inc. and Edward Arnold & Co.

What does the phrase mean? Instead of generalising, let us take a specific instance—Shakespeare's *Macbeth*, for example, and pronounce the words, "*Macbeth for Macbeth's sake*." What does that mean? Well, the play has several aspects—it is educational, it teaches us something about legendary Scotland, something about Jacobean England, and a good deal about human nature and its perils. We can study its origins, and study and enjoy its dramatic technique and the music of its diction. All that is true. But *Macbeth* is furthermore a world of its own, created by Shakespeare and existing in virtue of its own poetry. It is in this aspect *Macbeth* for *Macbeth's* sake, and that is what I intend by the phrase "art for art's sake." A work of art—whatever else it may be—is a self-contained entity, with a life of its own imposed on it by its creator. It has internal order. It may have external form. That is how we recognise it.

Take for another example that picture of Seurat's which I saw two years ago in Chicago—"*La Grande Jatte*." Here again there is much to study and to enjoy: the pointillism, the charming face of the seated girl, the nineteenth-century Parisian Sunday sunlight, the sense of motion in immobility. But here again there is something more; "*La Grande Jatte*" forms a world of its own, created by Seurat and existing by virtue of its own poetry: "*La Grande Jatte*" *pour* "*La Grande Jatte*": *l'art pour l'art*. Like *Macbeth* it has internal order and internal life.

It is to the conception of order that I would now turn. This is important to my argument, and I want to make a digression, and glance at order in daily life, before I come to order in art.

In the world of daily life, the world which we perforce inhabit, there is much talk about order, particularly from statesmen and politicians. They tend, however, to confuse order with orders, just as they confuse creation with regulations. Order, I suggest, is something evolved from within, not something imposed from without; it is an internal stability, a vital harmony, and in the social and political category it has never existed except for the convenience of historians. Viewed realistically, the past is really a series of *dis*orders, succeeding one another by discoverable laws, no doubt, and certainly marked by an increasing growth of human interference, but disorders all the same. So that, speaking as a writer, what I hope for to-day is a disorder which will be more favourable to artists than is the present one, and which will provide them with fuller inspirations and better material conditions. It will not last—nothing lasts—but there have been some advantageous disorders in the past—for instance, in ancient Athens, in Renaissance Italy, eighteenth-century France, periods in China and Persia—and we may do something to accelerate the next one. But let us not again fix our hearts where true joys are not to be found. We were promised a new order after the first world war through the League of Nations. It did not come, nor have I faith in present promises, by whomsoever endorsed. The implacable offensive of Science forbids. We cannot reach social and political stability for the reason that we continue to make scientific discoveries and to apply them, and thus to destroy the arrangements which were based on more elementary discoveries. If Science would discover rather than apply—if, in other words, men were more interested in knowledge than in power—mankind would be in a far safer position, the stability statesmen talk about would be a possibility, there could be a new order based on vital harmony, and the earthly millennium might approach. But Science shows no signs of doing this: she gave us the internal combusion engine, and before we had digested and assimilated it with terrible pains into our social system, she harnessed the atom, and destroyed any new order that seemed to be evolving. How can man get into harmony with his surroundings when he is constantly altering them? The future of our race is, in this direction, more unpleasant than we care to admit, and it has sometimes seemed to me that its best chance lies through apathy, uninventiveness, and inertia. Universal exhaustion might promote that Change of Heart which is at present so briskly recommended from a thousand pulpits. Universal exhaustion would certainly be a new experience. The human race has never undergone it, and is still too perky to admit that it may be coming and might result in a sprouting of new growth through the decay.

I must not pursue these speculations any further—they lead me too far from my terms of reference and maybe from yours. But I do want to emphasize that order in daily life and in history, order in the social and political category, is unattainable under our present psychology.

Where is it attainable? Not in the astronomical category, where it was for many years enthroned. The heavens and the earth have become terribly alike since Einstein. No longer can we find a reassuring contrast to chaos in the night sky and look up with George Meredith to the stars, the army of unalterable law, or listen for the music of the spheres. Order is not there. In the entire universe there seem to be only two possibilities for it. The first of them—which again lies outside my terms of reference—is the divine order, the mystic harmony, which according to all religions is available for those who can contemplate it. We must admit its possibility, on the evidence of the adepts, and we must believe them when they say that it is attained, if attainable, by prayer. "O thou who changest not, abide with me," said one of its poets. "*Ordina questo amor, o tu che m'ami,*" said another: "Set love in order thou who lovest me." The existence of a divine order, though it cannot be tested, has never been disproved.

The second possibility for order lies in the aesthetic category, which is my subject here: the order which an artist can create in his own work, and to that we must now return. A work of art, we are all agreed, is a unique product. But why? It is unique not because it is clever or noble or beautiful or enlightened or original or sincere or idealistic or useful or educational—it may embody any of those qualities—but because it is the only material object in the universe which may possess internal harmony. All the others have been pressed into shape from outside, and when their mould is removed they collapse. The work of art stands up by itself, and nothing else does. It achieves something which has often been promised by society, but always delusively. Ancient Athens made a mess—but the *Antigone* stands up. Renaissance Rome made a mess—but the ceiling of the Sistine got painted. James I made a mess—but there was *Macbeth*. Louis XIV— but there was *Phèdre*. Art for art's sake? I should just think so, and more so than ever at the present time. It is the one orderly product which our muddling race has produced. It is the cry of a thousand sentinels, the echo from a thousand labyrinths; it is the lighthouse which cannot be hidden: *c'est le meilleur témoignage que nous puissions donner de notre dignité.* Antigone for Antigone's sake, Macbeth for Macbeth's, "La Grande Jatte" pour "La Grande Jatte."

If this line of argument is correct, it follows that the artist will tend to be an outsider in the society to which he has been born, and that the nineteenth century conception of him as a Bohemian was not inaccurate. The conception erred in three particulars: it postulated an economic system where art could be a full-time job, it introduced the fallacy that only art matters, and it overstressed idiosyncracy and waywardness—the peacock-feather aspect—rather than order. But it is a truer conception than the one which prevails in official circles on my side of the Atlantic—I don't know about yours: the conception which treats the artist as if he were a particularly bright government advertiser and encourages him to be friendly and matey with his fellow citizens, and not to give himself airs.

Estimable is mateyness, and the man who achieves it gives many a pleasant little drink to himself and to others. But it has no traceable connection with the creative impulse, and probably acts as an inhibition on it. The artist who is seduced by mateyness may stop himself from doing the one thing which he, and he alone, can do—the making of something out of words or sounds or paint or clay or marble or steel or film which has internal harmony and presents order to a permanently disarranged planet. This seems worth doing, even at the risk of being called uppish by journalists. I have in mind an article which was published some years ago in the London *Times*, an article called "The Eclipse of the Highbrow," in which the "Average Man" was exalted, and all contemporary literature was censured if it did not toe the line, the precise position of the line being naturally known to the writer of the article. Sir Kenneth Clark, who was at that time director of our National Gallery, commented on this pernicious doctrine in a letter which cannot be too often quoted. "The poet and the artist," wrote Clark, "are important precisely because they are not average men; because in sensibility, intelligence, and power of invention they far exceed the average." These memorable words, and particularly the words "power of invention," are the Bohemian's passport. Furnished with it, he slinks about society, saluted now by a brickbat and now by a penny, and accepting either of them with equanimity. He does not consider too anxiously what his relations with society may be, for he is aware of something more important than that—namely the invitation to invent, to create order, and he believes he will be better placed for doing this if he attempts detachment. So round and round he slouches, with his hat pulled over his eyes, and maybe with a louse in his beard, and—if he really wants one—with a peacock's feather in his hand.

If our present society should disintegrate—and who dare prophesy that it won't?—this old-fashioned and démodé figure will become clearer: the Bohemian, the outsider, the parasite, the rat—one of those figures which have at present no function either in a warring or a peaceful world. It may not be dignified to be a rat, but many of the ships are sinking, which is not dignified either—the officials did not build them properly. Myself, I would sooner be a swimming rat than a sinking ship—at all events I can look around me for a little longer—and I remember how one of us, a rat with particularly bright eyes called Shelley, squeaked out, "Poets are the unacknowledged legislators of the world," before he vanished into the waters of the Mediterranean.

What laws did Shelley propose to pass? None. The legislation of the artist is never formulated at the time, though it is sometimes discerned by future generations. He legislates through creating. And he creates through his sensitiveness and his power to impose form. Without form the sensitiveness vanishes. And form is as important to-day, when the human race is trying to ride the whirlwind, as it ever was in those less agitating days of the past, when the earth seemed solid and the stars fixed, and the discoveries of science were made slowly, slowly. Form is not tradition. It alters from generation to generation. Artists always seek a new technique, and will continue to do so as long as their work excites them. But form of some kind is imperative. It is the surface crust of the internal harmony, it is the outward evidence of order.

My remarks about society may have seemed too pessimistic, but I believe that society can only represent a fragment of the human spirit, and that another fragment can only get expressed through art. And I wanted to take this opportunity, this vantage ground, to assert not only the existence of art, but its pertinacity. Looking back into the past, it seems to me that that is all there has ever been: vantage grounds for discussion and creation, little vantage grounds in the changing chaos, where bubbles have been blown and webs spun, and the desire to create order has found temporary gratification, and the sentinels have managed to utter their challenges, and the huntsmen, though lost individually, have heard each other's calls through the impenetrable wood, and the lighthouses have never ceased sweeping the thankless seas. In this pertinacity there seems to me, as I grow older, something more and more profound, something which does in fact concern people who do not care about art at all.

In conclusion, let me summarise the various categories that have laid claim to the possession of Order.

(1) The social and political category. Claim disallowed on the evidence of history and of our own experience. If man altered psychologically, order here might be attainable: not otherwise.

(2) The astronomical category. Claim allowed up to the present century, but now disallowed on the evidence of the physicists.

(3) The religious category. Claim allowed on the evidence of the mystics.

(4) The aesthetic category. Claim allowed on the evidence of various works of art, and on the evidence of our own creative impulses, however weak these may be, or however imperfectly they may function. Works of art, in my opinion, are the only objects in the material universe to possess internal order, and that is why, though I don't believe that only art matters, I do believe in Art for Art's Sake.

ARTHUR RIMBAUD

The Poet as Revolutionary Seer

My Dear Sir!

So you are a teacher again. One owes a duty to Society, you have told me; you belong to the teaching body: you are running along the right track—I too follow the principle: I am cynically getting myself *kept*. I dig up old imbeciles from our

Letters to Georges Izambard and Paul Demeny [1871], from *Selected Verse*, ed. and translated from the French by Oliver Bernard, 1962, pp. 5-16; reprinted by permission of Penguin Books Inc.

school: I serve up to them the stupidest, dirtiest, nastiest things I can think of in word and deed: I am paid in small beers and bottles of wine. *Stat mater dolorosa, dum pendet filius*—My duty is to Society, quite true—and I'm right—You too are right, for the present. At bottom, all you see in your principle is subjective poetry: your obstinacy in going back to the pedagogical trough—excuse me—proves that. But you'll still end up self-satisfied, having done nothing, and never having wanted to do anything. Not to mention that your subjective poetry will always be disgustingly tepid. Some day I hope—many other people hope, too—that I shall see objective poetry in your principle. I shall see it more sincerely than you would! —I shall be a worker: that is the idea that holds me back when mad rage drives me towards the battle of Paris—where so many workers are still dying as I write to you! Work now?—never, never; I'm on strike.

I'm lousing myself up as much as I can these days. Why? I want to be a poet, and I am working to make myself a *seer*: you won't understand this at all, and I hardly know how to explain it to you. The point is, to arrive at the unknown by the disordering of *all the senses*. The sufferings are enormous, but one has to be strong, to be born a poet, and I have discovered I *am* a poet. It is not my fault at all. It is a mistake to say: I think. One ought to say: I am thought. Pardon the pun.

I is someone else. So much the worse for the wood if it find itself a violin, and contempt to the heedless who argue about something they know nothing about!

I've decided to give you an hour of modern literature . . .

—And now here is a discourse in prose on the future of poetry:

All ancient poetry culminated in Greek poetry, harmonious Life.

—From Greece to the romantic movement—in the Middle Ages—there are men of letters, versifiers. From Ennius to Theroldus, from Theroldus to Casimir Delavigne, it's all rhymed prose, a game, the enfeeblement and glory of countless idiotic generations: Racine is the pure, strong, great man—If his rhymes had been effaced, and his hemistitches got mixed up, today the Divine Fool would be as unknown as any old author of *Origins*. After Racine the game gets crumby. It has been going on for two thousand years!

Neither joke nor paradox. My reason inspires me with more certitude on this subject than any *Young-France* ever had with rage. Besides, *newcomers* are free to condemn their ancestors: one is at home, and there's plenty of time.

Romanticism has never been properly judged. Who was there to judge it? The Critics!! The Romantics? who proved so clearly that the song is very seldom the work, that is to say, the idea sung and intended by the singer.

For *I* is someone else. If brass wakes up a trumpet, it is not its fault. To me this is obvious: I witness the unfolding of my own thought: I watch it, I listen to it: I make a stroke of the bow: the symphony begins to stir in the depths, or springs on to the stage.

If the old fools had not discovered only the *false* significance of the Ego, we should not now be having to sweep away those millions of skeletons which, since time immemorial, have been piling up the fruits of their one-eyed intellects, and claiming themselves to be the authors of them!

In Greece, I say, verses and lyres give rhythm to action. After that, music and rhymes are a game, a pastime. The curious are charmed with the study of this past: many of them delight in reviving these antiquities—that's their affair. Universal mind has always thrown out its ideas naturally; men would pick up a part of these fruits of the brain: they acted through them, they wrote books through them: and so things went on, since man did not work on himself, either not yet being awake, or not yet in the fullness of the great dream. Writers, civil servants: author, creator, poet, *that* man never existed!

The first study for a man who wants to be a poet is the knowledge of himself, complete. He looks for his soul, inspects it, puts it to the test, learns it. As soon as he knows it, he must cultivate it! It seems simple: in every brain a natural development takes place; so many *egoists* proclaim themselves authors; there are plenty of others who attribute their intellectual progress to themselves!—But the soul has to be made monstrous, that's the point: after the fashion of the *comprachicos*, if you like! Imagine a man planting and cultivating warts on his face.

I say that one must be a *seer*, make onself a *seer*.

The poet makes himself a *seer* by a long, prodigious, and rational *disordering* of *all the senses*. Every form of love, of suffering, of madness; he searches himself, he consumes all the poisons in him, and keeps only their quintessences. This is an unspeakable torture during which he needs all his faith and superhuman strength, and during which he becomes the great patient, the great criminal, the great accursed—and the great learned one!—among men.—For he arrives at the *unknown*! Because he has cultivated his own soul—which was rich to begin with— more than any other man! He reaches the unknown, and even if, crazed, he ends up by losing the understanding of his visions, at least he has seen them! Let him die charging through those unutterable, unnameable things: other horrible workers will come; they will begin from the horizons where he has succumbed! . . .

—To continue:

So, then, the poet really is the thief of fire.

He is responsible for humanity, even for the *animals*; he must see to it that his inventions can be smelt, felt, heard. If what he brings back from *down there* has form, he brings forth form; if it is formless, he brings forth formlessness. A language has to be found—for that matter, every word being an idea, the time of the universal languages will come! One has to be an academician—deader than a fossil—to finish a dictionary of any language. Weak-minded people, beginning by *thinking about* the first letter of the alphabet, would soon rush into madness!

This [new] language would be of the soul, for the soul, containing everything, smells, sounds, colours; thought latching on to thought and pulling. The poet would define the amount of the unknown awakening in the universal soul in his own time: he would produce more than the formulation of his thought or the measurement *of his march towards Progress*! An enormity who has become normal, absorbed by everyone, he would really be a *multiplier of progress*!

This future will, as you see, be materialistic—Always filled with *Number* and *Harmony*, these poems will be made to endure. Essentially, it will be Greek poetry again, in a way.

Eternal art will have its function, since poets are citizens. Poetry will no longer rhyme with action; *it will be ahead of it*!

Poets like this will exist! When the unending servitude of woman is broken, when she lives by and for herself, when man—hitherto abominable—has given her her freedom, she too will be a poet! Woman will discover part of the unknown! Will her world of ideas be different from ours? She will discover things strange and unfathomable, repulsive and delicious. We shall take them unto ourselves, we shall understand them.

Meanwhile let us ask the *poet* for the *new*—in ideas and in forms. All the bright boys will imagine they can soon satisfy this demand:—it is not so!

The first romantics were *seers* without quite realizing it: the cultivation of their souls began accidentally: abandoned locomotives, but with their fires still alight, which the rails still carry along for a while.—Sometimes Lamartine is a *seer*, but strangled by the old form. Hugo, who is *too ham*, really has VISION in his last works: *Les Misérables* is a real *poem*. I have *Les Châtiments* with me; *Stella* shows the limit of Hugo's *vision*. Too many Belmontets and Lamennais, Jehovahs and columns, old cracked enormities.

Musset is fourteen times execrable to us suffering generations carried away by visions—to whom his angelic cloth is an insult! O! the insipid tales and proverbs! O the *Nuits*! O *Rolla*, O *Namouna*, O *the Chalice*! it is all French, that is, detestable to the highest degree; French, not Parisian! More work of the evil genius that inspired Rabelais, Voltaire, Jean La Fontaine, with M. Taine's commentary! Springlike, the wit of Musset! Charming, his love! There's enamel painting and solid poetry for you! *French* poetry will be enjoyed for a long time—but in France. Every grocer's boy can reel off a Rollaesque speech, every budding priest has the five hundred rhymes hidden away in the secrecy of a notebook. At fifteen, these outbursts of passion make boys lecherous, at sixteen they are already content to recite them with *feeling*; at eighteen, even at seventeen, every schoolboy who has the ability does a Rolla, writes a Rolla! Perhaps some still die of it. Musset could not do anything: there were visions behind the gauze of the curtains: he closed his eyes. French, sloppy, dragged from barroom to schoolroom desk, the fine corpse is dead, and henceforth let us not even bother to awaken it with our execrations!

The second Romantics are very *seeing*: Théophile Gautier, Leconte de Lisle, Théodore de Banville. But because examining the invisible and hearing the unheard-of is quite different from recapturing the spirit of dead things, Baudelaire is the first *seer*, king of poets, *a real God!* Unluckily he lived in too artistic a circle; and the form which is so much praised in him is trivial. Inventions from the unknown demand new forms.

Broken-in to the old forms, among the simpletons, A. Renaud—has done his Rolla—L. Grandet—has done his Rolla; the Gauls and the Mussets, G. Lafenestre, Coran, Cl. Popelin, Soulary, L. Salles; the scholars, Marc, Aicard, Theuriet; the dead and the imbeciles, Autran, Barbier, L. Pichat, Lemoyne, the Deschamps, the Des Essarts; the journalists, L. Cladel, Robert Luzarches, X. de Ricard; the fantasists, C. Mendès; the bohemians; the women; the talents, Léon Dierx and Sully-Prudhomme, Coppée—the new school, called Parnassian, possesses two seers: Albert Mérat and Paul Verlaine, a real poet.—So there you are.

Art as Aristocratic Mystery

Whatever is sacred, whatever is to remain sacred, must be clothed in mystery. All religions take shelter behind arcana which they unveil only to the predestined. Art has its own mysteries.

We can find an example of this in music. If we open any work of Mozart, Beethoven, or Wagner and glance quickly at the first page, we will be overcome with religious astonishment at the sight of those macabre processions of rigid, chaste, and undeciphered signs. Then we will shut the missal, and it will still remain untouched by any profane thought.

I have often wondered why one art in particular, the greatest of arts, has been refused this necessary characteristic; an art which faces hypocritical curiosity without mystery, blasphemy without terror, and suffers the smiles and grimaces of the ignorant and the hostile.

That art is poetry. *Flowers of Evil*, for example, is printed with the sort of type which burgeons forth every morning in the flowerbeds of some utilitarian tirade, and it is sold in black and white books which are exactly the same as those filled with the viscount of Terrail's prose or Mr. Legouvé's poetry.

Thus those who are first in line go right into a masterpiece; and ever since the beginning of poetry, no one has kept these intruders away by inventing an immaculate language, a series of sacred formulae which would blind the common eye with dull study, but arouse the patience of the predestined. And to think that the admission ticket of these intruders consists of a page of the alphabet which they have learned to read!

Oh, golden clasps of ancient missals! Oh, immaculate hieroglyphs of papyrus rolls!

What is the result of this absence of mystery?

Poetry, like all things of perfect beauty, is perforce admired. But the admiration is distant, vague—a stupid admiration since it is the mob's. Then, because of this general reaction, a fantastic, preposterous idea occurs to these minds: namely, that poetry must be *taught* in school; and so, like anything else that is taught to the many, poetry is inevitably reduced to the level of a science. It is explained to all alike, democratically. For it is difficult to tell in advance which tousled head contains the white sibylline star.

Therefore, since nobody can be fairly called a complete person if he does not know history (i.e., a science), if he misunderstands physics (i.e., a science), so nobody has received a *solid* education if he cannot *judge* Homer and *read* Hugo (i.e., men of science).

A man (I mean one of those men, who has received the empty title of "citizen" from modern vanity, since the latter is hard up for flattering names), a citizen, (and this has sometimes made me think, and proudly confess, that music, which is an aroma breathed out by the censer of dreams, is yet different from more palpable aromas in the sense that it brings with it no ecstatic delight), this

"Art for All" [1862], *Prose Poems, Essays, and Letters*, translated from the French by Bradford Cook, Baltimore, 1956, pp. 9-13; reprinted by permission of the Johns Hopkins University Press.

man, as I was saying, or rather this citizen, strides through our museums with a careless freedom and an absent-minded frigidity which he would not dare exhibit even in a church. For there he would know that he must at least pretend to be interested in some way. From time to time he turns to Rubens and Delacroix with a glance reeking of vulgarity. If we whisper the names of Shakespeare or Goethe as quietly as we can, this character lifts his head as if to say: "That's for me."

The fact is that, since music is an art, since painting is an art, since sculpture is an art in everybody's mind; and since poetry is no longer an art in anybody's mind (and notice that people would be ashamed if they were not *acquainted* with poetry; yet I don't know anyone who has to be ashamed of not being an expert in art), music, painting, and sculpture are therefore left to "those who are in the business," whereas people *learn* poetry because they want to appear educated.

It should be said here that certain awkwardly heroic writers are wrong to call the mob to account for its inept taste and nonexistent imagination. "To insult the mob is to degrade oneself," as Charles Baudelaire rightly observed; and, in any case, the artist should scorn to attack the Philistines. However glorious and saintly the exception may be, he still proves the rule. And who will deny that the rule is the absence of ideal? Then again, it is not only the serenity of scorn that impels us to avoid these recriminations; reason teaches us that they can only be useless or harmful: useless if the Philistine pays no attention to them; harmful if he becomes irritated with the widespread stupidity of the mob, clings to the poets, and thus swells the army of false admirers. I prefer the profane to the profaner. Let us remember that the poet (whether he rhymes, sings, paints, or sculptures) is not on a level beneath which other men crawl; the mob is a level and the poet flies above it. Seriously, has the Bible ever told us that angels mock man because he has no wings?

Men must be made to believe that they can be complete even if they have not read Hugo's poetry, just as they believe that they are complete even if they have not read Verdi's music at sight. The educational bases of the multitude need not include art; that is, a mystery accessible only to the very few. The multitude would profit in that they would no longer waste time dozing over Virgil, and could devote that time to action and to a practical purpose. Poetry, on its side, would profit because it would no longer be irritated (only a slight irritation, it must be admitted, for something which is immortal) by the barking sounds of a pursuing pack of creatures who, simply because they are educated and intelligent, think they have the right to judge it or, even worse, dictate to it.

But, after all, poets, and even the greatest poets, are perfectly acquainted with that difficulty.

In other words, I congratulate any *philosopher* who seeks popularity. He is not supposed to close his hand irrevocably upon the fistful of radiant truths that it holds; he scatters them, and it is proper that each of his fingers should leave them in its luminous wake. But when a *poet*, a worshipper of beauty which is inaccessible to the mob, is not content with the Sanhedrin of art, then I am bothered and I simply don't understand.

Let man be democratic; the artist must separate and remain an aristocrat.

And yet this is precisely what does not happen. Cheap editions of the poets' work are increased with the consent and even the blessing of the poets themselves. Oh, dreamers, oh, singers, do you suppose that this is the way to win glory? When the artist alone possessed your work you had a true admirer, even though he had to spend his last cent for the most recent of your gems. But does this mob understand you now that it has *bought* you because you were cheap? One last barrier—the seven francs it would have to spend—still separated you from the mob's desires (desires already cheapened by teaching), and now you foolishly knock that barrier down! Oh, enemies to yourself! Why do you encourage (even more through your doctrines than through the price of your books, which is not entirely in your own hands), why do you preach that blasphemy which is the popularization of art? So then, are you going to walk in the company of those who blot out music's mysterious notes (this is not a laughing matter, for the idea has spread everywhere), who unveil its mysteries to the crowd? Or in the company of those who spread it to the countryside, at any price; who care not whether the playing is out of tune, so long as there is playing? What will come of this on some future day, on the day of judgment? You too will be *taught*, like those great martyrs Homer, Lucretius, and Juvenal!

You may say: "What of Corneille, Molière, and Racine? They are popular and glorious:" No, they are not popular. Their names are popular, perhaps; but their poetry is not. The mob has read them once, that is true; and without understanding them. But who rereads them? Only artists.

You have already had to pay the penalty: for in the midst of your exquisite and dazzling works you have occasionally scattered verses which lack that high aroma of supreme distinction which usually hovers about them. And *these* are the verses which the mob will admire. You will stand by helplessly and see that your true masterpieces are accessible only to exceptional spirits and neglected by this mob which never should have seen them at all. If this were not already true, if the masses had not already withered his poems, it is certain that the truly radiant works of Hugo would not be *Moses* or *Pray, my child,* as the masses think they are, but *Faun* or *Tears in the night.*

The present hour is a grave one. The people are being educated and great doctrines are going to be spread. If there is a popularization, let us make sure that it is a popularization of the good, not of the beautiful; that your efforts do not tend—and I trust that they have not tended in that direction—to make you a *workers' poet,* which would be grotesque, if it were not pitiful, for the truly superior artist.

Let the masses read works on moral conduct; but please don't let them ruin our poetry.

Oh, poets, you have always been proud; now be more than proud, be scornful!

W. H. AUDEN

Poetry as a Game of Knowledge

A poet is, before anything else, a person who is passionately in love with language. Whether this love is a sign of his poetic gift or the gift itself—for falling in love is given not chosen—I don't know, but it is certainly the sign by which one recognizes whether a young man is potentially a poet or not.

"Why do you want to write poetry?" If the young man answers: "I have important things I want to say," then he is not a poet. If he answers: "I like hanging around words listening to what they say," then maybe he is going to be a poet.

As T. S. Eliot has said in one of his essays, the sign of promise in a young writer is not originality of idea or emotion, but technical competence. The subject matter of promising juvenilia is as a rule slight and unimportant, the style derivative, but this slight derivative thing is completely said.

In the first stages of his development, before he has found his distinctive style, the poet is, as it were, engaged to language and, like any young man who is courting, it is right and proper that he should play the chivalrous servant, carry parcels, submit to tests and humiliations, wait hours at street corners, and defer to his beloved's slightest whims, but once he has proved his love and been accepted, then it is another matter. Once he is married, he must be master in his own house and be responsible for their relationship.

The poet is the father who begets the poem which the language bears. At first sight this would seem to give the poet too little to do and the language too much till one remembers that, as the husband, it is he, not the language, who is responsible for the success of their marriage which differs from natural marriage in that in this relationship there is no loveless lovemaking, no accidental pregnancies.

Poets, like husbands, are good, bad and indifferent. Some are Victorian tyrants who treat language like a doormat, some are dreadfully hen-pecked, some bored, some unfaithful. For all of them, there are periods of tension, brawls, sulky silences, and, for many, divorce after a few passionate years.

In the course of many centuries a few labor-saving devices have been introduced into the mental kitchen—alcohol, coffee, tobacco, benzedrine—but these mechanisms are very crude, liable to injure the cook, and constantly breaking down. Writing poetry in the twentieth century A.D. is pretty much the same as it was in the twentieth century B.C.: nearly everything has still to be done by hand.

Rhymes, meters, stanza-forms, etc., are like servants. If the master is just enough to win their affection and firm enough to command their respect, the result is

"Squares and Oblongs," from *Poets at Work*, ed. Charles D. Abbott, New York, 1948, pp. 171-81. Copyright 1948 by Harcourt, Brace & World, Inc.; reprinted by permission of Harcourt, Brace & World, Inc.

an orderly happy household. If he is too tyrannical, they give notice; if he lacks authority, they become slovenly, impertinent, drunken and dishonest.

The poet who writes "free" verse is like Robinson Crusoe on his desert island: he must do all his cooking, laundry, darning, etc., for himself. In a few exceptional cases this manly independence produces something original and impressive, but as a rule the result is squalor—empty bottles on the unswept floor and dirty sheets on the unmade bed.

Milton's intuition in his *Ode on the Nativity* gives the lie to his personal overestimation of the poet's importance. If the Fall made man conscious of the difference between good and evil, then the Incarnation made him conscious of the difference between seriousness and frivolity and exorcised the world. Before that, one might say that only children, i.e. those in whom the consciousness of good and evil was not yet fully developed, could play games. The adult had to take frivolity seriously, i.e., turn games into magic, and in consequence could never wholeheartedly enjoy them because necessarily he was always anxious as to whether the magic would work this time.

Two theories of poetry. Poetry as a magical means for inducing desirable emotions and repelling undesirable emotions in oneself and others, or Poetry as a game of knowledge, a bringing to consciousness, by naming them, of emotions and their hidden relationships.

The first view was held by the Greeks, and is now held by MGM, Agit-Prop, and the collective public of the world. They are wrong.

Being ignorant of the difference between seriousness and frivolity, the Greeks confused art with religion. In spite of this, they produced great works of art. This was possible because in reality, like all pagans, they were frivolous people who took nothing seriously. Their religion was just a camp.

But we, whether Christians or not, cannot escape our consciousness of what is serious and what is not. Consequently, if we try to treat art as magic, we produce, not great works of art, but only dishonest and insufferably earnest and boring Agit-Prop for Christianity, Communism, Free Enterprise or what have you.

How can I know what I think till I see what I say? A poet writes "The chestnut's comfortable root" and then changes this to "The chestnut's customary root." In this alteration there is no question of replacing one emotion by another, or of strengthening an emotion, but of discovering what the emotion is. The emotion is unchanged, but waiting to be identified like a telephone number one cannot remember. "8357. No. that's not it. 8557, 8457, no, it's on the tip of my tongue, wait a moment, I've got it, 8657. That's it."

There are events which arouse such simple and obvious emotions that an AP cable or a photograph in *Life* magazine are enough and poetic comment is impossible. If one reads through the mass of versified trash inspired, for instance, by the Lidice Massacre, one cannot avoid the conclusion that what was really bothering the versifiers was a feeling of guilt at not feeling horrorstruck enough. Could a good poem have been written on such a subject? Possibly. One that revealed this lack of feeling, that told how when he read the news, the poet, like you and I, dear reader, went on thinking about his fame or his lunch, and how glad he was that he was not one of the victims.

Christianity knows of only one predestined life like the lives of the mythical heroes of Greek tragedy and this life is (a) not a myth, (b) not a tragedy. Further, esthetic values have nothing to do with its ritual representation; whether the Mass is well or badly sung is irrelevant.

If I understand what Aristotle means when he speaks of catharsis, I can only say he is wrong. It is an effect produced, not by works of art, but by bull-fights, professional football matches, bad movies and, in those who can stand that sort of thing, monster rallies at which ten thousand girl guides form themselves into the national flag.

If art were magic, then love lyrics would be love charms which made the Cruel Fair give one her latch key. In that case a magnum of champagne would be more artistic than a sonnet.

The girl whose boy-friend starts writing her love poems should be on her guard. Perhaps he really does love her, but one thing is certain: while he was writing his poems he was not thinking of her but of his own feelings about her, and that is suspicious. Let her remember St. Augustine's confession of his feelings after the death of someone he loved very much: "I would rather have been deprived of my friend than of my grief."

Everyone in his heart of hearts agrees with Baudelaire: "To be a useful person has always seemed to me something particularly horrible," for, subjectively, to be useful means to be doing not what one wants to do, but what someone else insists on one's doing. But at the same time, everyone is ashamed to admit in public that he is useless. Thus if a poet gets into conversation with a stranger in a railway coach and the latter asks him: "What is your job?," he will think quickly and say: "A schoolteacher, a beekeeper, a bootlegger," because to tell the truth would cause an incredulous and embarrassing silence.

The day of the Master's study with its vast mahogany desk on which the blotting paper is changed every day, its busts of Daunty, Gouty and Shopkeeper, its walls lined with indexed bookshelves, one of which is reserved for calf-bound copies of the Master's own works, is over for ever. From now on the poet will be lucky if he can have the general living room to himself for a few hours or a corner of the kitchen table on which to keep his papers. The soft carpets, the big desks, will all be reserved by the Management for the whopping liars.

Over too, the day of the salon and the café, the select group of enthusiastic rebels. No more movements. No more manifestoes. Every poet stands alone. This does not mean that he sulks mysteriously in a corner by himself; on the contrary he may, perhaps, lead a more social life than before, but as a neighbor like his neighbors, not as a poet. Where his gift is concerned, he stands alone and joins nobody, least of all his contemporary brother poets.

The ideal audience the poet imagines consists of the beautiful who go to bed with him, the powerful who invite him to dinner and tell him secrets of state, and his fellow-poets. The actual audience he gets consists of myopic school-teachers, pimply young men who eat in cafeterias, and his fellow-poets. This means that, in fact, he writes for his fellow-poets.

Happy the lot of the pure mathematician. He is judged solely by his peers and the standard is so high that no colleague can ever win a reputation he does not deserve. No cashier writes articles in the Sunday *Times* complaining about the incomprehensibility of Modern Mathematics and comparing it unfavorably with the good old days when mathematicians were content to paper irregularly shaped rooms or fill bath-tubs with the waste-pipe open. Better still, since engineers and physicists have occasionally been able to put his equations to destructive use, he is even given a chair in a State University.

The poet is capable of every form of conceit but that of the social worker:— "We are all here on earth to help others; what on earth the others are here for I don't know."

How glad I am that the silliest remark ever made about poets, "the unacknowl-edged legislators of the world," was made by a poet whose work I detest. Sounds more like the secret police to me.

The Prophet says to men: "Thus saith the Lord."
    The Poet says firstly to God: "Lord, do I mean what I say?" and secondly to men: "Do you mean what I mean?"
    Agit-Prop says to men: "You mean what I say and to hell with the Lord who, even if he exists, is rotten with liberalism anyway."

From now on the only popular art will be comic art, like Groucho Marx or Li'l Abner, and this will be unpopular with the Management. Whatever their dif-ferences, highbrows and lowbrows have a common enemy, The Law (the Divine as well as the secular), and it is the Law which it cannot alter which is the sub-ject of all comic art. What is not comic will either be highbrow art, or popular or official magic.

It is a sobering experience for any poet to read the last page of the Book Section of the Sunday *Times* where correspondents seek to identify poems which have meant much to them. He is forced to realize that it is not his work, not even the work of Dante or Shakespeare, that most people treasure as magic talismans in times of trouble, but grotesquely bad verses written by maiden ladies in local newspapers; that millions in their bereavements, heartbreaks, agonies, depres-sions, have been comforted and perhaps saved from despair by appalling trash while poetry stood helplessly and incompetently by.

The frightful falsehood which obsessed the Greeks and Romans and for which mankind has suffered ever since, was that government is a similar activity to art, that human beings are a medium like language out of which the gifted politician creates a good society as the gifted poet creates a good poem.

A society which really was like a poem and embodied all the esthetic values of beauty, order, economy, subordination of detail to the whole effect, would be a nightmare of horror, based on selective breeding, extermination of the physically or mentally unfit, absolute obedience to its Director, and a large slave class kept out of sight in cellars.

The poet writes:

> The mast-high anchor dives through a cleft

changes it to

> The anchor dives through closing paths

then to

> The anchor dives among hayricks

finally to

> The anchor dives through the floors of a church.

The cleft and the closing paths have been liquidated and the hayricks deported to another stanza.
  There's Creative Politics and Scientific Government for you.

All poets adore explosions, thunderstorms, tornadoes, conflagrations, ruins, scenes of spectacular carnage. The poetic imagination is therefore not at all a desirable quality in a chief of state.

The democratic idea that anyone should be able to become president is right. For to talk of the profession of politics or a gifted politician ought to be non-sense. A good politician ought to mean someone who loves his neighbor and, with God's help, anyone can do that if he choose.

If God were a poet or took poetry seriously (or science too for that matter), he would never have given man free will.

The old superstition that it is dangerous to love a poet is perhaps not without some foundation. Given the opportunity, a poet is perhaps more tempted than others to drop his old innocent game of playing God with words, and take up that much more exciting but forbidden game of creating a human being, that game which starts off with such terrific gusto but always ends sooner or later in white faces and a fatal accident.

His life was like a poem. If so, he was a very great scoundrel who said to himself early in life: "I will explore every possibility of sinning and then repent on my death-bed." Faust? Exactly. Marlowe was not as intelligent as Goethe but he had more common sense. At least he knew that Faust went to hell. Faust is damned, not because he has sinned, but because he made a pact with the Devil, that is, like a poet he planned a life of sin beforehand.

The low-brow says: "I don't like poetry. It requires too much effort to understand and I'm afraid that if I learnt exactly what I feel, it would make me most uncomfortable." He is in the wrong, of course, but not so much in the wrong as the highbrow whose gifts make the effort to understand very little and who, having learned what he feels, is not at all uncomfortable, only interested.

Orpheus who moved stones is the archetype, not of the poet, but of Goebbels. The archetype, not of the poet as such, but of the poet who loses his soul for poetry, is Narcissus.

Being esthetes, the Greeks were naïve psychologists. Narcissus does not fall in love with his reflection because it is beautiful but because it is like himself. In a later version of the myth, it is a hydrocephalic idiot who gazes entranced into the pool, saying: "On me it looks good." In another, still more sophisticated version, Narcissus is neither beautiful nor ugly but as completely average as a Thurber husband, and instead of addressing his image with the declarative "I love you," he puts to it over and over again the same question, "Haven't we met before someplace?"

The present state of the world is so miserable and degraded that if anyone were to say to the poet: "For God's sake, stop humming and put the kettle on or fetch bandages. The patient's dying," I do not know how he could justifiably refuse. (There is, of course, an inner voice which says exactly this to most of us, and our only reply is to pretend to be extremely hard of hearing.) But no one says this. The self-appointed unqualified Nurse says: "Stop humming this instant and sing the Patient a song which will make him fall in love with me. In return I'll give you extra ration-cards and a passport"; and the poor Patient in his delirium cries: "Please stop humming and sing me a song which will make me believe I am free from pain and perfectly well. In return I'll give you a penthouse apartment in New York and a ranch in Arizona."

To such requests and to the bribes that go with them, the poet can only pray that he will always have the courage to stick out his tongue, say, like Olaf the conscientious objector in Cummings' poem,—"There is some s. I will not eat,"— and go on humming quietly to himself.

Poetry as Rite

The impulse to create a work of art is felt when, in certain persons, the passive awe provoked by sacred beings or events is transformed into a desire to express that awe in a rite of worship or homage, and to be fit homage this rite must be beautiful. This rite has no magical or idolatrous intention; nothing is expected in return. Nor is it, in a Christian sense, an act of devotion. If it praises the Creator, it does so indirectly by praising His creatures—among which may be human notions of the Divine Nature. With God as redeemer, it has, so far as I can see, little if anything to do.

In poetry the rite is verbal; it pays homage by naming. I suspect that the predisposition of a mind towards the poetic medium may have its origin in an error. A nurse, let us suppose, says to a child, "Look at the moon!" The child looks and for him this is a sacred encounter. In his mind the word *moon* is not a name of a sacred object but one of its most important properties and, therefore, numinous. The notion of writing poetry cannot occur to him, of course, until he has realized that names and things are not identical and that there cannot be an intelligible sacred language, but I wonder if, when he has discovered the social nature of language, he would attach such importance to one of its uses, that of naming, if he had not previously made this false identification.

The pure poem, in the French sense of *la poésie pure* would be, I suppose, a celebration of the numinous-in-itself in abstraction from all cases and devoid of any profane reference whatsoever—a sort of *sanctus, sanctus, sanctus*. If it could be written, which is doubtful, it would not necessarily be the best poem.

A poem is a rite; hence its formal and ritualistic character. Its use of language is deliberately and ostentatiously different from talk. Even when it employs the diction and rhythms of conversation, it employs them as a deliberate informality, presupposing the norm with which they are intended to contrast.

The form of a rite must be beautiful, exhibiting, for example, balance, closure and aptness to that which it is the form of. It is over this last quality of aptness that most of our aesthetic quarrels arise, and must arise, whenever our sacred and profane worlds differ.

> To the Eyes of a Miser, a Guinea is far more beautiful than the Sun & a bag worn with the use of Money has more beautiful proportions than a Vine filled with Grapes.

Blake, it will be noticed, does not accuse the Miser of lacking imagination.

The value of a profane thing lies in what it usefully does, the value of a sacred thing lies in what it *is*; a sacred thing may also have a function but it does not have to. The apt name for a profane being, therefore, is the word or words that accurately describe his function—a Mr. Smith, a Mr. Weaver. The apt name for a sacred being is the word or words which worthily express his importance—Son of Thunder, The Well-Wishing One.

From "Making, Knowing, and Judging" [1956], *The Dyer's Hand*, New York, 1962, pp. 57-60. © Copyright 1946 by W. H. Auden; reprinted by permission of Random House, Inc. and Faber & Faber Ltd.

Great changes in artistic style always reflect some alteration in the frontier between the sacred and profane in the imagination of a society. Thus, to take an architectural example, a seventeenth-century monarch had the same function as that of a modern State official—he had to govern. But in designing his palace, the Baroque architect did not aim, as a modern architect aims when designing a government building, at making an office in which the king could govern as easily and efficiently as possible; he was trying to make a home fit for God's earthly representative to inhabit; in so far as he thought at all about what the king would do in it as a ruler, he thought of his ceremonial not his practical actions.

Even today few people find a functionally furnished living-room beautiful because, to most of us, a sitting-room is not merely a place to sit in; it is also a shrine for father's chair.

Thanks to the social nature of language, a poet can relate any one sacred being or event to any other. The relation may be harmonious, an ironic contrast or a tragic contradiction like the great man or the beloved and death; he can relate them to every other concern of the mind, the demands of desire, reason and conscience, and he can bring them into contact and contrast with the profane. Again the consequences can be happy, ironic, tragic and, in relation to the profane, comic. How many poems have been written, for example, upon one of these three themes:

This was sacred but now it is profane. Alas, or thank goodness!

This is sacred but ought it to be?

This is sacred but is that so important?

But it is from the sacred encounters of his imagination that a poet's impulse to write a poem arises. Thanks to language, he need not name them directly unless he wishes; he can describe one in terms of another and translate those that are private or irrational or socially unacceptable into such as are acceptable to reason and society. Some poems are directly *about* the sacred beings they were written *for*; others are not, and in that case no reader can tell what was the original encounter which provided the impulse for the poem. Nor, probably, can the poet himself. Every poem he writes involves his whole past. Every love-poem, for instance, is hung with trophies of lovers gone, and among these there may be some very peculiar objects indeed. The lovely lady of the present may number among her predecessors an overshot water-wheel. But the encounter, be it novel or renewed by recollection from the past, must be suffered by a poet before he can write a genuine poem.

Whatever its actual content and overt interest, every poem is rooted in imaginative awe. Poetry can do a hundred and one things, delight, sadden, disturb, amuse, instruct—it may express every possible shade of emotion, and describe every conceivable kind of event, but there is only one thing that all poetry must do; it must praise all it can for being and for happening.

Art as Establisher of Value

In an age of disbelief, or, what is the same thing, in a time that is largely humanistic, in one sense or another, it is for the poet to supply the satisfactions of belief, in his measure and in his style. I say in his measure to indicate that the
figures of the philosopher, the artist, the teacher, the moralist and other figures,
including the poet, find themselves, in such a time, to be figures of an importance
greatly enhanced by the requirements both of the individual and of society; and
I say in his style by way of confining the poet to his role and thereby of intensi-
fying that role. It is this that I want to talk about today. I want to try to formulate a conception of perfection in poetry with reference to the present time and
the near future and to speculate on the activities possible to it as it deploys itself
throughout the lives of men and women. I think of it as a role of the utmost
seriousness. It is, for one thing, a spiritual role. One might stop to draw an ideal
portrait of the poet. But that would be parenthetical. In any case, we do not say
that the philosopher, the artist or the teacher is to take the place of the gods. Just
so, we do not say that the poet is to take the place of the gods.

To see the gods dispelled in mid-air and dissolve like clouds is one of the great
human experiences. It is not as if they had gone over the horizon to disappear
for a time; nor as if they had been overcome by other gods of greater power and
profounder knowledge. It is simply that they came to nothing. Since we have
always shared all things with them and have always had a part of their strength
and, certainly, all of their knowledge, we shared likewise this experience of annihilation. It was their annihilation, not ours, and yet it left us feeling that in a
measure, we, too, had been annihilated. It left us feeling dispossessed and alone
in a solitude, like children without parents, in a home that seemed deserted, in
which the amical rooms and halls had taken on a look of hardness and emptiness.
What was most extraordinary is that they left no mementoes behind, no thrones,
no mystic rings, no texts either of the soil or of the soul. It was as if they had
never inhabited the earth. There was no crying out for their return. They were
not forgotten because they had been a part of the glory of the earth. At the same
time, no man ever muttered a petition in his heart for the restoration of those
unreal shapes. There was always in every man the increasingly human self, which
instead of remaining the observer, the non-participant, the delinquent, became
constantly more and more all there was or so it seemed; and whether it was so or
merely seemed so still left it for him to resolve life and the world in his own
terms.

Thinking about the end of the gods creates singular attitudes in the mind of
the thinker. One attitude is that the gods of classical mythology were merely
aesthetic projections. They were not the objects of belief. They were expressions
of delight. Perhaps delight is too active a word. It is true that they were engaged

From "Two or Three Ideas," *Opus Posthumous*, ed. Samuel French Morse, New York,
1957, pp. 206-9. Copyright 1957 by Elsie Stevens and Holly Stevens. Reprinted by permission of Alfred A. Knopf, Inc. and Faber & Faber Ltd.

From "The Noble Rider and the Sound of Words" [1942], pp. 27-33, "Imagination as
Value" [1949], pp. 138-9, 153-5, and "The Figure of the Youth as Virile Poet" [1944], pp.
40-43, 60-62, *The Necessary Angel*, New York, 1951. Copyright 1942, 1944, 1949 by
Wallace Stevens. Reprinted by permission of Alfred A. Knopf, Inc. and Faber & Faber Ltd.

with the future world and the immortality of the soul. It is true, also, that they were the objects of veneration and therefore of religious dignity and sanctity. But in the blue air of the Mediterranean these white and a little colossal figures had a special propriety, a special felicity. Could they have been created for that propriety, that felicity? Notwithstanding their divinity, they were close to the people among whom they moved. Is it one of the normal activities of humanity, in the solitude of reality and in the unworthy treatment of solitude, to create companions, a little colossal as I have said, who, if not superficially explicative, are, at least, assumed to be full of the secret of things and who in any event bear in themselves even, if they do not always wear it, the peculiar majesty of mankind's sense of worth, neither too much nor too little? To a people of high intelligence, whose gods have benefited by having been accepted and addressed by the superior minds of a superior world, the symbolic paraphernalia of the very great becomes unnecessary and the very great become the very natural. However all that may be, the celestial atmosphere of these deities, their ultimate remote celestial residences are not matters of chance. Their fundamental glory is the fundamental glory of men and women, who being in need of it create it, elevate it, without too much searching of its identity.

The people, not the priests, made the gods. The personages of immortality were something more than the conceptions of priests, although they may have picked up many of the conceits of priests. Who were the priests? Who have always been the high priests of any of the gods? Certainly not those officials or generations of officials who administered rites and observed rituals. The great and true priest of Apollo was he that composed the most moving of Apollo's hymns. The really illustrious archimandrite of Zeus was the one that made the being of Zeus people the whole of Olympus and the Olympian land, just as the only marvelous bishops of heaven have always been those that made it seem like heaven. I said a moment ago that we had not forgotten the gods. What is it that we remember of them? In the case of those masculine do we remember their ethics or is it their port and mien, their size, their color, not to speak of their adventures, that we remember? In the case of those feminine do we remember, as in the case of Diana, their fabulous chastity or their beauty? Do we remember those masculine in any way differently from the way in which we remember Ulysses and other men of supreme interest and excellence? In the case of those feminine do we remember Venus in any way differently from the way in which we remember Penelope and other women of much mark and feeling? In short, while the priests helped to realize the gods, it was the people that spoke of them and to them and heard their replies.

Let us stop now and restate the ideas which we are considering in relation to one another. The first is that the style of a poem and the poem itself are one; the second is that the style of the gods and the gods themselves are one; the third is that in an age of disbelief, when the gods have come to an end, when we think of them as the aesthetic projections of a time that has passed, men turn to a fundamental glory of their own and from that create a style of bearing themselves in reality. They create a new style of a new bearing in a new reality. This third idea, then, may be made to conform to the way in which the other two have been expressed by saying that the style of men and men themselves are one.

I am interested in the nature of poetry and I have stated its nature, from one of the many points of view from which it is possible to state it. It is an inter-dependence of the imagination and reality as equals. This is not a definition, since it is incomplete. But it states the nature of poetry. Then I am interested in the role of the poet and this is paramount. In this area of my subject I might be expected to speak of the social, that is to say sociological or political, obligation of the poet. He has none. That he must be contemporaneous is as old as Longi-nus and I dare say older. But that he *is* contemporaneous is almost inevitable. How contemporaneous in the direct sense in which being contemporaneous is in-tended were the four great poets of whom I spoke a moment ago? I do not think that a poet owes any more as a social obligation than he owes as a moral obliga-tion, and if there is anything concerning poetry about which people agree it is that the role of the poet is not to be found in morals. I cannot say what that wide agreement amounts to because the agreement (in which I do not join) that the poet is under a social obligation is equally wide. Reality is life and life is society and the imagination and reality; that is to say, the imagination and society are inseparable. That is pre-eminently true in the case of the poetic drama. The poetic drama needs a terrible genius before it is anything more than a literary relic. Besides the theater has forgotten that it could ever be terrible. It is not one of the instruments of fate, decidedly. Yes: the all-commanding subject-matter of poetry is life, the never-ceasing source. But it is not a social obligation. One does not love and go back to one's ancient mother as a social obligation. One goes back out of a suasion not to be denied. Unquestionably if a social movement moved one deeply enough, its moving poems would follow. No politician can command the imagination, directing it to do this or that. Stalin might grind his teeth the whole of a Russian winter and yet all the poets in the Soviets might remain silent the following spring. He might excite their imaginations by some-thing he said or did. He would not command them. He is singularly free from that "cult of pomp," which is the comic side of the European disaster; and that means as much as anything to us. The truth is that the social obligation so closely urged is a phase of the pressure of reality which a poet (in the absence of dra-matic poets) is bound to resist or evade today. Dante in Purgatory and Paradise was still the voice of the Middle Ages but not through fulfilling any social obli-gation. Since that is the role most frequently urged, if that role is eliminated, and if a possible poet is left facing life without any categorical exactions upon him, what then? What is his function? Certainly it is not to lead people out of the confusion in which they find themselves. Nor is it, I think, to comfort them while they follow their readers to and fro. I think that his function is to make his imagination theirs and that he fulfills himself only as he sees his imagination be-come the light in the minds of others. His role, in short, is to help people to live their lives. Time and time again it has been said that he may not address him-self to an élite. I think he may. There is not a poet whom we prize living today that does not address himself to an élite. The poet will continue to do this: to address himself to an élite even in a classless society, unless, perhaps, this ex-poses him to imprisonment or exile. In that event he is likely not to address him-self to anyone at all. He may, like Shostakovich, content himself with pretence. He will, nevertheless, still be addressing himself to an élite, for all poets address themselves to someone and it is of the essence of that instinct, and it seems to amount to an instinct, that it should be to an élite, not to a drab but to a woman with the hair of a pythoness, not to a chamber of commerce but to a gallery of one's own, if there are enough of one's own to fill a gallery. And that élite, if it responds, not out of complaisance, but because the poet has quickened it, because he has educed from it that for which it was searching in itself and in the life around it and which it had not yet quite found, will thereafter do for the poet what he cannot do for himself, that is to say, receive his poetry.

I repeat that his role is to help people to live their lives. He has had immensely to do with giving life whatever savor it possesses. He has had to do with whatever the imagination and the senses have made of the world. He has, in fact, had to do with life except as the intellect has had to do with it and, as to that, no one is needed to tell us that poetry and philosophy are akin. I want to repeat for two reasons a number of observations made by Charles Mauron. The first reason is that these observations tell us what it is that a poet does to help people to live their lives and the second is that they prepare the way for a word concerning escapism. They are: that the artist transforms us into epicures; that he has to discover the possible work of art in the real world, then to extract it, when he does not himself compose it entirely; that he is *un amoureux perpétuel* of the world that he contemplates and thereby enriches; that art sets out to express the human soul; and finally that everything like a firm grasp of reality is eliminated from the aesthetic field. With these aphorisms in mind, how is it possible to condemn escapism? The poetic process is psychologically an escapist process. The chatter about escapism is, to my way of thinking, merely common cant. My own remarks about resisting or evading the pressure of reality mean escapism, if analyzed. Escapism has a pejorative sense, which it cannot be supposed that I include in the sense in which I use the word. The pejorative sense applies where the poet is not attached to reality, where the imagination does not adhere to reality, which, for my part, I regard as fundamental. If we go back to the collection of solid, static objects extended in space, which Dr. Joad posited, and if we say that the space is blank space, nowhere, without color, and that the objects, though solid, have no shadows and, though static, exert a mournful power, and, without elaborating this complete poverty, if suddenly we hear a different and familiar description of the place:

> This City now doth, like a garment, wear
> The beauty of the morning, silent, bare,
> Ships, towers, domes, theatres, and temples lie
> Open unto the fields, and to the sky;
> All bright and glittering in the smokeless air;

if we have this experience, we know how poets help people to live their lives. This illustration must serve for all the rest. There is, in fact, a world of poetry indistinguishable from the world in which we live, or, I ought to say, no doubt, from the world in which we shall come to live, since what makes the poet the potent figure that he is, or was, or ought to be, is that he creates the world to which we turn incessantly and without knowing it and that he gives to life the supreme fictions without which we are unable to conceive of it.

And what about the sound of words? What about nobility, of which the fortunes were to be a kind of test of the value of the poet? I do not know of anything that will appear to have suffered more from the passage of time than the music of poetry and that has suffered less. The deepening need for words to express our thoughts and feelings which, we are sure, are all the truth that we shall ever experience, having no illusions, makes us listen to words when we hear them, loving them and feeling them, makes us search the sound of them, for a finality, a perfection, an unalterable vibration, which it is only within the power of the acutest poet to give them. Those of us who may have been thinking of the path of poetry, those who understand that words are thoughts and not only our own thoughts but the thoughts of men and women ignorant of what it is that they are thinking, must be conscious of this: that, above everything else, poetry is words; and that words, above everything else, are, in poetry, sounds. This being so, my time and yours might have been better spent if I had been less interested in trying to give our possible poet an identity and less interested in trying to appoint him to his place. But unless I had done these things, it might have been thought that I was rhetorical, when I was speaking in the simplest way about things of such importance that nothing is more so. A poet's words are of things that do not exist without the words. Thus, the image of the charioteer and of the winged horses, which has been held to be precious for all of time that matters, was created by words of things that never existed without the words. A description of Verrocchio's statue could be the integration of an illusion equal to the statue itself. Poetry is a revelation in words by means of the words. Croce was not speaking of poetry in particular when he said that language is perpetual creation. About nobility I cannot be sure that the decline, not to say the disappearance of nobility is anything more than a maladjustment between the imagination and reality. We have been a little insane about the truth. We have had an obsession. In its ultimate extension, the truth about which we have been insane will lead us to look beyond the truth to something in which the imagination will be the dominant complement. It is not only that the imagination adheres to reality, but, also, that reality adheres to the imagination and that the interdependence is essential. We may emerge from our *bassesse* and, if we do, how would it happen if not by the intervention of some fortune of the mind? And what would that fortune of the mind happen to be? It might be only commonsense but even that, a commonsense beyond the truth, would be a nobility of long descent.

If these expressions speak for any considerable number of people and, therefore, if any considerable number of people feel this way about the truth and about what may be called the official view of being (since philosophic truth may be said to be the official view), we cannot expect much in respect to poetry, assuming that we define poetry as an unofficial view of being. This is a much larger definition of poetry than it is usual to make. But just as the nature of the truth changes, perhaps for no more significant reason than that philosophers live and die, so the nature of poetry changes, perhaps for no more significant reason than that poets come and go. It is so easy to say in a universe of life and death that the reason itself lives and dies and, if so, that the imagination lives and dies no less.

Once on a packet on his way to Germany Coleridge was asked to join a party of Danes and drink with them. He says:

> I went, and found some excellent wines and a dessert of grapes with a pineapple. The Danes had christened me Doctor Teology, and dressed as I was all in black, with large shoes and black worsted stockings, I might certainly have passed very well for a Methodist missionary. However I disclaimed my title. What then may you be . . . Un philosophe, perhaps? It was at that time in my life in which of all possible names and characters I had the greatest disgust to that of un philosophe. . . . The Dane then informed me that all in the present party were Philosophers likewise. . . . We drank and talked and sung, till we talked and sung altogether; and then we rose and danced on the deck a set of dances.

As poetry goes, as the imagination goes, as the approach to truth, or, say, to being by way of the imagination goes, Coleridge is one of the great figures. Even so, just as William James found in Bergson a persistent euphony, so we find in Coleridge, dressed in black, with large shoes and black worsted stockings, dancing on the deck of a Hamburg packet, a man who may be said to have been defining poetry all his life in definitions that are valid enough but which no longer impress us primarily by their validity.

To define poetry as an unofficial view of being places it in contrast with philosophy and at the same time establishes the relationship between the two. In philosophy we attempt to approach truth through the reason. Obviously this is a statement of convenience. If we say that in poetry we attempt to approach truth through the imagination, this, too, is a statement of convenience. We must conceive of poetry as at least the equal of philosophy. If truth is the object of both and if any considerable number of people feel very sceptical of all philosophers, then, to be brief about it, a still more considerable number of people must feel very sceptical of all poets. Since we expect rational ideas to satisfy the reason and imaginative ideas to satisfy the imagination, it follows that if we are sceptical of rational ideas it is because they do not satisfy the reason and if we are sceptical of imaginative ideas it is because they do not satisfy the imagination. If a rational idea does not satisfy the imagination, it may, nevertheless, satisfy the reason. If an imaginative idea does not satisfy the reason, we regard the fact as in the nature of things. If an imaginative idea does not satisfy the imagination, our expectation of it is not fulfilled. On the other hand, and finally, if an imaginative idea satisfies the imagination, we are indifferent to the fact that it does not satisfy the reason, although we concede that it would be complete, as an idea, if, in addition to satisfying the imagination, it also satisfied the reason. From this analysis, we deduce that an idea that satisfies both the reason and the imagination, if it happened, for instance, to be an idea of God, would establish a divine beginning and end for us which, at the moment, the reason, singly, at best proposes and on which, at the moment, the imagination, singly, merely meditates. This is an illustration. It seems to be elementary, from this point of view, that the poet, in order to fulfill himself, must accomplish a poetry that satisfies both the reason and the imagination. It does not follow that in the long run the poet will find himself in the position in which the philosopher now finds himself. On the contrary, if the end of the philosopher is despair, the end of the poet is fulfillment, since the poet finds a sanction for life in poetry that satisfies the imagination. Thus, the poetry, which we have been thinking of as at least the equal of philosophy, may be its superior. Yet the area of definition is almost an area of apologetics. The look of it may change a little if we consider not that the definition has not yet been found but that there is none. . . .

What we have called elevation and elation on the part of the poet, which he communicates to the reader, may be not so much elevation as an incandescence of the intelligence and so more than ever a triumph over the incredible. Here as part of the purification that all of us undergo as we approach any central purity, and that we feel in its presence, we can say:

> No longer do I believe that there is a mystic muse, sister of the Minotaur. This is another of the monsters I had for nurse, whom I have wasted. I am myself a part of what is real, and it is my own speech and the strength of it, this only, that I hear or ever shall.

These words may very well be an inscription above the portal to what lies ahead. But if poetic truth means fact and if fact includes the whole of it as it is between the extreme poles of sensibility, we are talking about a thing as extensible as it is ambiguous. We have excluded absolute fact as an element of poetic truth. But this has been done arbitrarily and with a sense of absolute fact as fact destitute of any imaginative aspect whatever. Unhappily the more destitute it becomes the more it begins to be precious. We must limit ourselves to saying that there are so many things which, as they are, and without any intervention of the imagination, seem to be imaginative objects that it is no doubt true that absolute fact includes everything that the imagination includes. This is our intimidating thesis.

One sees demonstrations of this everywhere. For example, if we close our eyes and think of a place where it would be pleasant to spend a holiday, and if there slide across the black eyes, like a setting on a stage, a rock that sparkles, a blue sea that lashes, and hemlocks in which the sun can merely fumble, this inevitably demonstrates, since the rock and sea, the wood and sun are those that have been familiar to us in Maine, that much of the world of fact is the equivalent of the world of the imagination, because it looks like it. Here we are on the border of the question of the relationship of the imagination and memory, which we avoid. It is important to believe that the visible is the equivalent of the invisible; and once we believe it, we have destroyed the imagination; that is to say, we have destroyed the false imagination, the false conception of the imagination as some incalculable *vates* within us, unhappy Rodomontade. One is often tempted to say that the best definition of poetry is that poetry is the sum of its attributes. So, here, we may say that the best definition of true imagination is that it is the sum of our faculties. Poetry is the scholar's art. The acute intelligence of the imagination, the illimitable resources of its memory, its power to possess the moment it perceives—if we were speaking of light itself, and thinking of the relationship between objects and light, no further demonstration would be necessary. Like light, it adds nothing, except itself. What light requires a day to do, and by day I mean a kind of Biblical revolution of time, the imagination does in the twinkling of an eye. It colors, increases, brings to a beginning and end, invents languages, crushes men and, for that matter, gods in its hands, it says to women more than it is possible to say, it rescues all of us from what we have called absolute fact and while it does these things, and more, it makes sure that

. . . la mandoline jase,
Parmi les frissons de brise.

Having identified poetic truth as the truth of fact, since fact includes poetic fact, that is to say: the indefinite number of actual things that are indistinguishable from objects of the imagination; and having, as we hope, washed the imagination clean, we may now return, once again, to the figure of the youth as virile poet and join him, or try to do so, in coming to the decision, on which, for him and for us, too, so much depends. At what level of the truth shall he compose his poems? That is the question on which he is reflecting, as he sits in the radiant and productive atmosphere, which is his life, surrounded not only by double characters and metaphysicians, but by many men and many kinds of men, by many women and many children and many kinds of women and of children. The question concerns the function of the poet today and tomorrow, but makes no pretence beyond.

———————

Then, too, before going on, we must somehow cleanse the imagination of the romantic. We feel, without being particularly intelligent about it, that the imagination as metaphysics will survive logical positivism unscathed. At the same time, we feel, and with the sharpest possible intelligence, that it is not worthy to survive if it is to be identified with the romantic. The imagination is one of the great human powers. The romantic belittles it. The imagination is the liberty of the mind. The romantic is a failure to make use of that liberty. It is to the imagination what sentimentality is to feeling. It is a failure of the imagination precisely as sentimentality is a failure of feeling. The imagination is the only genius. It is intrepid and eager and the extreme of its achievement lies in abstraction. The achievement of the romantic, on the contrary, lies in minor wish-fulfillments and it is incapable of abstraction. In any case and without continuing to contrast the two things, one wants to elicit a sense of the imagination as something vital. In that sense one must deal with it as metaphysics.

If we escape destruction at the hands of the logical positivists and if we cleanse the imagination of the taint of the romantic, we still face Freud. What would he have said of the imagination as the clue to reality and of a culture based on the imagination? Before jumping to the conclusion that at last there is no escape, is it not possible that he might have said that in a civilization based on science there could be a science of illusions? He does in fact say that "So long as a man's early years are influenced by the religious thought-inhibition . . . as well as by the sexual one, we cannot really say what he is actually like." If when the primacy of the intelligence has been achieved, one can really say what a man is actually like, what could be more natural than a science of illusions? Moreover, if the imagination is not quite the clue to reality now, might it not become so then? As for the present, what have we, if we do not have science, except the imagination? And who is to say of its deliberate fictions arising out of the contemporary mind that they are not the forerunners of some such science? . . .

My final point, then, is that the imagination is the power that enables us to perceive the normal in the abnormal, the opposite of chaos in chaos. It does this every day in arts and letters. This may seem to be a merely capricious statement; for ordinarily we regard the imagination as abnormal per se. That point of view was approached in the reference to the academic struggle between reason and the imagination and again in the reference to the relation between the imagination and social form. The disposition toward a point of view derogatory to the imgination is an aversion to the abnormal. We see it in the common attitude toward modern arts and letters. The exploits of Rimbaud in poetry, if Rimbaud can any longer be called modern, and of Kafka in prose are deliberate exploits of the abnormal. It is natural for us to identify the imagination with those that extend its abnormality. It is like identifying liberty with those that abuse it. A literature overfull of abnormality and, certainly, present-day European literature, as one knows it, seems to be a literature full of abnormality, gives the reason an appearance of normality to which it is not, solely, entitled. The truth seems to be that we live in concepts of the imagination before the reason has established them. If this is true, then reason is simply the methodizer of the imagination. It may be that the imagination is a miracle of logic and that its exquisite divinations are calculations beyond analysis, as the conclusions of the reason are calculations wholly within analysis. If so, one understands perfectly the remark that "in the service of love and imagination nothing can be too lavish, too sublime or too festive." In the statement that we live in concepts of the imagination before the reason has established them, the word "concepts" means concepts of normality. Further, the statement that the imagination is the power that enables us to perceive the normal in the abnormal is a form of repetition of this statement. One statement does not demonstrate the other. The two statements together imply that the instantaneous disclosures of living are disclosures of the normal. This will seem absurd to those that insist on the solitude and misery and terror of the world. They will ask of what value is the imagination to them: and if their experience is to be considered, how is it possible to deny that they live in an imagination of evil? Is evil normal or abnormal? And how do the exquisite divinations of the poets and for that matter even the "aureoles of the saints" help them? But when we speak of perceiving the normal we have in mind the instinctive integrations which are the reason for living. Of what value is anything to the solitary and those that live in misery and terror, except the imagination?

2

REALISM

Objectivity

GEORGE ELIOT: A Realism of Love
BERNARD SHAW: False Ideals Exposed
GUSTAVE FLAUBERT: Heroic Honesty
ANTON CHEKHOV: Dunghills as Artistic Material

Historical Determinism

HONORÉ DE BALZAC: Society as Historical Organism
HIPPOLYTE TAINE: Art as Historical Product
GUSTAVE FLAUBERT: Shortcomings of Taine's Theory
LEO TOLSTOY: Man as the Creature of History

Naturalistic Determinism

THEODORE DREISER: Man as Natural Mechanism
EDMOND AND JULES DE GONCOURT: The Fad of Naturalism
EMILE ZOLA: The Novel as Social Science
AUGUST STRINDBERG: A Naturalistic Manifesto
EDMOND AND JULES DE GONCOURT: The Fad of Naturalism

Melioristic Realism

LEO TOLSTOY: Art as Ethical Communication
F. M. DOSTOEVSKY: Prophetic Realism
GEORGE SAND AND GUSTAVE FLAUBERT: The Counter-Religions of
Humanity and Art
H. G. WELLS AND HENRY JAMES: The Counter-Claims of
Content and Form

Socialist Realism

A New Realism

Introduction

In all schools of realism objectivity of some kind is a main tenet. The realist, in his most elementary guise, wishes to present "reality" by allowing characters and events to appear in his work with as little sign of his personal intervention as possible. While he does not deny the imaginative faculty, he often minimizes its importance. Opposing symbolist predilections for an esoteric subject-matter, for perfection of form, and for an elite audience, the realist offers his work as a means of communication among men, dealing with large subjects in a comprehensible way, form subordinated to content. Frequently he upholds a theory of historical or natural determination to explain the objective conditions that control both his characters and himself as writer.

George Eliot proclaims the duty of the novel to describe the commonplace, even though that may be unbeautiful, because the only thing worth portraying is what really is. She commends the Dutch painters for their affectionate interest in homely scenes. Her form of realism may be considered one of love in that it offers its attention and sympathy particularly to imperfect beings, those neglected by "romantic" art. Bernard Shaw asserts with more impatience the writer's obligation to expose the falsity of ideals—glorified conventions which, though some may have had an original usefulness, are now coercive and destructive. Responding strongly to Ibsen's influence, Shaw instructs the artist to let in fresh air by unmasking pretense, by freeing himself and his readers from allegiances which are the more absurd the more high-minded they pretend to be. Flaubert and Chekhov are less polemical than Shaw in their advocacy of realism. Flaubert affirms that the writer must describe what he detests with utter accuracy and, since society will be sure to object, heroic honesty. Chekhov agrees that the dunghill may be a necessary subject for the artist, who must always defeat the inclination in himself and others to prettify and conceal. Instead of the social conscience which underlies Shaw's attitude, Flaubert and Chekhov have a kind of aesthetic conscience which obliges them to be realists.[1]

A conception of man as the prey of circumstances has had an imaginative

[1] For related selections from Flaubert, see Section 1. Compare Rousseau's heroic self-revelation in Section 7.

attraction for modern writers, including both artists and critics. Balzac framed his *Human Comedy* as an almost scientific classification of human types, comparable to zoological varieties among the lower animals. Men are modified by a combination of nature and social conditions. As he says elsewhere, "Tell me what you possess and I will tell you what you think." Literature is the history of manners, and the writer is not a creator but a secretary to society. But Balzac allows some room for the self-direction of individuals, and is not so strict a determinist as he sometimes seems to claim. Taine made an equally elaborate and more dogmatic effort to represent man as a convergence of forces rather than a self-mover. In his *History of English Literature* he studies literature as a "transcript" of contemporary manners. Rejecting the picture of the artist as isolated and godlike, arbitrarily composing autonomous works, Taine finds the writer to be shaped by three factors. These are his race, with its inherited characteristics; the milieu in which he lives; and the moment of history when he appears. Influences such as climate, geographical position, political situation, and social conditions are among the operative forces which oblige an artist to write in his distinctive way. Taine's metaphors are often mechanical: the race is an inner mainspring, the milieu is pressure from without, the moment is the impulsion already acquired. Behind the work of art lies the man, and behind the visible man is the invisible man, whose traits in turn are the product of the three forces which stand behind him. Flaubert, though not altogether hostile to this reduction of individual authority, resisted Taine's theory as a deprivation of the last vestiges of freedom which the imagination could claim. He thought the theory could explain only a writer's general characteristics, never the special features which constituted his individuality.

The form of determinism that appears in some of Tolstoy's writings is closer to Taine than to Balzac. For Tolstoy men are instruments of history, sums of tendencies that emerge in them inexorably. Napoleon, who prided himself on being the master of events, was as much their plaything as his lowliest soldier. But whereas Taine thinks the causes of each human action can be minutely ascertained, Tolstoy explicitly denies this possibility. History moves too mountainously, he thinks, for this to be possible. Tolstoy implies that the surrender of the egoistic will, and the submission to the larger will of humanity (or, it may be, of God) as embodied in historical forces, is the restricted form of our possible freedom. The heroes of his fiction are those who surmise their almost involuntary places in this great scheme.[2]

A second school of realists also acknowledges the force of determinism, but of a naturalistic rather than historical kind.[3] Man is nature's creature. In his youth Theodore Dreiser came painfully to the belief that man could only be

[2] In connection with this historical determination in literary theory, see Hegel's philosophy of history in Section 4.

[3] Compare the selections from Darwin and Schopenhauer, and from Henry Adams and Marinetti, in Section 3.

regarded as a function of nature, manipulated without consideration. The human image, as it appears in naturalistic fiction, is often that of the helpless victim. This image can be represented most sharply in "the lower depths" of society, where helplessness is magnified by economic stress. An early pronouncement of the naturalists, the preface by the brothers Goncourt to *Germinie Lacerteux*, sees the novel as a clinic specializing in the diseased conditions of the lower classes, and conducted in the hope that sympathy may be aroused for curing those conditions.

This theory is carried to its outward bound in Zola. Developing the Goncourts' clinical metaphor, with some appeals to Balzac's theories, Zola proposes to apply to the human animal the experimental method of the natural sciences, and especially that of medicine.[4] He scoffs at the notion that there may be reaches of the mind not subject to such investigation or somehow undetermined. The mind is now seen to be a part of the body: "Metaphysical man has given way to physiological man." He wishes to reveal the mechanism which sways animate beings as well as inanimate things. Zola rebuffs the charge that he advocates photographic realism. It is true that the experimental method begins with what has been observed and may require a special investigation of a particular set of circumstances. But it proceeds then to modify or vary phenomena so as to study them more perfectly; having done so, it directs the phenomena to their necessary conclusion on the basis of probability and of nature's "fixed laws." A fictional situation is such an experiment, and the novel a laboratory (the naturalists' counterpart to the symbolists' labyrinth).

Zola agrees with the Goncourts that the ultimate object of naturalism is to know phenomena and to make ourselves masters of them. The novelist establishes his experimental results as guideposts to enable society to avoid aberrations signaled by them. While he grants that a novelist should possess genius, a word he prefers to imagination, Zola considers that this works more splendidly in naturalistic than in romantic fiction, because the former is more directly responsive to natural laws. The style of a novel is secondary; the best writing is not the most lyrical, but the most scientifically straightforward. The artist and the scientist are professional colleagues.

Not all novelists in this school share Zola's enthusiasm for literature as physiological experimentation; they generally take pride, however, in probing further than other writers do. For Strindberg the virtue of naturalism is its rejection of simple explanations, its willingness to examine the complex motivations of every action. Individuals are largely determined, he thinks, by heredity, by the situations in which they find themselves, by health or disease, by their unwilled proclivities. These act upon them in varying degrees. Individuals are not personifications of fixed traits; they alter their composi-

4 Zola's conception of experimental method, depending on the idea of fixed natural laws, is strikingly different from the more recent notions expounded by Werner Heisenberg in Section 3.

tion as the forces brought to bear upon them shift their weight. Consequently Strindberg prefers to represent his characters as somewhat characterless. He also discards many of the formal aspects of drama, such as traditional sets and lighting, because they are not suited to the unheroic, almost will-less, personages of his plays.

Some of the naturalists have themselves rebelled against the absolute determinism of nature. The Goncourts thought they might "dematerialize" naturalism by allowing into it dreams, symbols, moral ideas, and romantic feelings which puristic theory had outlawed. Flaubert, who was sometimes considered the leader of the school although in many ways he was closer to the symbolists, complained that Zola had elevated a method into a program.

According to Zola, determinism could be distinguished from fatalism by the fact that it considered the human condition to be alterable and improvable. This aspiration is to be found also in the Goncourts, and it becomes the dominant theme in what can be called melioristic realism. If naturalism moves toward science, this form of realism moves toward ethics. Its eye is always on what life should be. While the naturalists emphasize a book's honesty and accuracy, these realists attach more weight to its sincerity and loftiness of purpose. In "What Is Art?" Tolstoy, a chief exponent of this form of realism in his later life, finds art to be the ethical communication of feelings, binding men together in the brotherhood that comes from the shared sympathy of writer and readers. The value of art is therefore measurable in terms of infectiousness. Tolstoy says nothing here of the historical determinism so prominent in *War and Peace,* but he is again concerned with a supra-personal force, identified now more specifically with the divine and manifested in brotherhood. Here individual life finds its genuine expression. Art is the creation of a community of feeling to unite men everywhere, and in all times, with each other and with God.

The consequence of his theory is that Tolstoy depreciates beauty, which most symbolists have exalted as the sole end of art, and celebrates goodness instead. He declares that the two often run in opposite directions, because beauty is linked to the passions, while goodness is bound to man's religious perceptions. By this standard Tolstoy condemns most of the art of his time as decadent, including many of his own works. He particularly objects to the idea that art can be written for an elite; to do so is to deny the first principle of art, since society is thereby split instead of being joined. The decadent artist confirms his own isolation and that of his readers.

Dostoevsky's emphasis is furiously prophetic, a quality which seems to impugn his realism for some readers. Against this objection, which he knew, he defended his writing as based upon the only kind of realism that is genuine. For there is no purpose in describing the commonplace; a writer in search of radical truth must be prepared to make use of the most outlandish situations and characters. Dostoevsky distinguishes between the ordinary and the typical; the typical is the unforeseen embodiment of movements that the artist recognizes to be occurring in society. So he defends his invention in *The*

Idiot of Prince Myshkin, a Christlike figure who at first sight might appear fantastic, because, on the basis of all Dostoevsky has seen and felt, such a man *must* exist. For Dostoevsky, true realism is permeated by a sense of life as a battlefield between the extremes of Christian hope and unchristian chaos, and the situations and personages must reflect this violent conflict in its most flagrant forms. He is more peremptory than Tolstoy in fusing his sense of what should and should not be into what is.[5]

Other versions of melioristic realism make their appearance in writings of George Sand and, later, of H. G. Wells. George Sand remonstrated with Flaubert for creating a religion of art, detached from moral concerns and natural sympathies. She accused him of treating reality as if it were inert and unimprovable. His dispassionateness was merely self-isolation, and necessarily emerged as pessimism. He sought learning, not wisdom. In short, she said, he had sold his soul to false gods of aestheticism, when the true religion was that of humanity. Only here could one embrace the good and the true as well as the beautiful, value life more highly than the form in which it was put, acknowledge virtue as well as vice and folly, and devote oneself to the improvement of man's lot. Flaubert's reply was courteous but unyielding. He declined to commit his art to the current fine phrases, knowing that they conflicted with both historical and psychological evidence. He wished to go beyond timely notions of good and evil, of heroism and villainy, to the truth, the essence of things. His object was indeed beauty, but to write well is to think well, and so to eschew with severity every opinion that had only a humanitarian claim upon him.

A later stage of this controversy is to be found in the debate of H. G. Wells and Henry James. In defense of his own theory, Wells argued that the novel was a help to conduct because it aided people in their adjustments to their environment and to each other. Moreover, the novel is life, and so must reflect something of the unschematic, disorganized way in which relationships compose life. The novel is not a monumental addendum to reality; in fact, its claim to be art is minor and incidental. To this Henry James replied that a novel cannot be merely saturation in circumstances; its subject does not matter, but whatever it is about, it must be achieved by deliberately cultivated form.[6]

The principal heir of the realistic school of Tolstoy is socialist realism. This derives not only from sympathy with the proletariat, but from the particular kind of historical determinism propounded by Marx and Engels. According to them, as feudalism gives way to capitalism, and the middle-class triumphs, moral obligations between the classes disappears, and only a cash nexus is left.[7] But under capitalism productive forces are developed to such an extent that the proletariat comes into being, gathers strength, and event-

[5] Related selections from Dostoevsky appear in Sections 7 and 9.
[6] For the premises from which James and Flaubert are arguing, see "The Autonomy of Art" in Section 1. A related selection from James appears in Section 7.
[7] See Marx on "alienation" in Section 7.

ually will overthrow the middle class. Since there is then no other class to be exploited, the inhuman relationship of money will fade, and the free development of each and all will be at last possible. Marx and Engels emphasize that economic production molds the institutions and ideologies at a given time; life is not determined by consciousness, but consciousness by material life.[8] As the economic basis of society has shifted, so has the whole "superstructure" of ideas, sentiments, modes of thought, views of life, and artistic works. In the new era, art will necessarily be proletarian and serve the new society as a moral instrument.

Later writers have elaborated upon this foundation. The best Marxist criticism is of course far from the simple-minded, nationalistic realism which Soviet officials sometimes call for in public. Leon Trotsky explains that the new art of communist society will not necessarily deal only with workers, but will keep the struggles of the proletariat at the center of its attention. Against the formalists, who claim for art an independent, homeless status, Trotsky asserts that artistic creation turns old forms inside out under the influence of new stimuli which originate outside of art. So the deed antedates the word; changes in living conditions give rise to new ways of feeling which find expression in art as in other activities.

Georg Lukács applies himself specifically to the form socialist realism may take. He is sure it will supplant earlier forms of fictional presentation because it can do more than they. Naturalism failed to achieve the objectivity for which it strove because it dealt with the lifeless average; and subjectivity, seeking to elicit the truth of individual life, created nuance-ridden individuals with no firm footing in material existence. The inner life of man can only be portrayed, Lukács thinks, when organically connected with social and historical realism. He finds a model in Balzac, who in spite of his monarchical sympathies had a keen sense of this connection. What is required above all in the writer is accuracy of response to historical conditions.

In the writings of Alain Robbe-Grillet a new form of realism is put forward. Like Lukács, he objects to naturalism, but on quite other grounds. He maintains that we have forced nature into complicity with man by our habit of pathetic fallacy, the conferral, in metaphor, of human qualities upon nature. This confusion must now end; nature is not man, and Robbe-Grillet calls upon the two worlds to keep their distance from each other. All our assumptions of relationship, and of pre-established orders, have to be abrogated if we are to reach the truth of man and of being. Robbe-Grillet differs from most realists in emphasizing the discontinuity of man and nature. He focuses upon the situation of men shorn of their illusions of harmony with nature or even with society.[9]

[8] See the opposite contention of Hegel, whose determinism Marx built upon after turning it upside down (Section 4).
[9] Though Robbe-Grillet rightly distinguishes himself from the existentialists as well as the romantics and the old-fashioned realists, he has obviously been influenced by existentialism (see Section 8).

GEORGE ELIOT

A Realism of Love

"This Rector of Broxton is little better than a pagan!" I hear one of my readers exclaim. "How much more edifying it would have been if you had made him give Arthur some truly spiritual advice. You might have put into his mouth the most beautiful things—quite as good as reading a sermon."

Certainly I could, if I held it the highest vocation of the novelist to represent things as they never have been and never will be. Then, of course, I might re-fashion life and character entirely after my own liking; I might select the most unexceptionable type of clergyman, and put my own admirable opinions into his mouth on all occasions. But it happens, on the contrary, that my strongest effort is to avoid any such arbitrary picture, and to give a faithful account of men and things as they have mirrored themselves in my mind. The mirror is doubtless de-fective; the outlines will sometimes be disturbed, the reflection faint or confused; but I feel as much bound to tell you as precisely as I can what that reflection is, as if I were in the witness-box narrating my experience on oath.

Sixty years ago—it is a long time, so no wonder things have changed—all clergy-men were not zealous; indeed there is reason to believe that the number of zealous clergymen was small, and it is probable that if one among the small minority had owned the livings of Broxton and Hayslope in the year 1799, you would have liked him no better than you like Mr. Irwine. Ten to one, you would have thought him a tasteless, indiscreet, methodistical man. It is so very rarely that facts hit that nice medium required by our own enlightened opinions and refined taste! Perhaps you will say, "Do improve the facts a little, then; make them more ac-cordant with those correct views which it is our privilege to possess. The world is not just what we like; do touch it up with a tasteful pencil, and make believe it is not quite such a mixed entangled affair. Let all people who hold unexception-able opinions act unexceptionably. Let your most faulty characters always be on the wrong side, and your virtuous ones on the right. Then we shall see at a glance whom we are to condemn, and whom we are to approve. Then we shall be able to admire, without the slightest disturbance of our prepossessions: we shall hate and despise with that true ruminant relish which belongs to undoubting con-fidence."

But, my good friend, what will you do then with your fellow-parishioner who opposes your husband in the vestry?—with your newly-appointed vicar, whose style of preaching you find painfully below that of his regretted predecessor?—

From *Adam Bede* [1864], Book II, Ch. XVII, "In Which the Story Pauses a Little."

with the honest servant who worries your soul with her one failing?—with your neighbour, Mrs. Green, who was really kind to you in your last illness, but has said several ill-natured things about you since your convalescence?—nay, with your excellent husband himself, who has other irritating habits besides that of not wiping his shoes? These fellow-mortals, every one, must be accepted as they are: you can neither straighten their noses, nor brighten their wit, nor rectify their dispositions; and it is these people—amongst whom your life is passed—that it is needful you should tolerate, pity, and love: it is these more or less ugly, stupid, inconsistent people, whose movements of goodness you should be able to admire—for whom you should cherish all possible hopes, all possible patience. And I would not, even if I had the choice, be the clever novelist who could create a world so much better than this, in which we get up in the morning to do our daily work, that you would be likely to turn a harder, colder eye on the dusty streets and the common green fields—on the real breathing men and women, who can be chilled by your indifference or injured by your prejudice; who can be cheered and helped onward by your fellow-feeling, your forbearance, your out-spoken, brave justice.

So I am content to tell my simple story, without trying to make things seem better than they were; dreading nothing, indeed, but falsity, which, in spite of one's best efforts, there is reason to dread. Falsehood is so easy, truth so difficult. The pencil is conscious of a delightful facility in drawing a griffin—the longer the claws, and the larger the wings, the better; but that marvellous facility which we mistook for genius is apt to forsake us when we want to draw a real unexaggerated lion. Examine your words well, and you will find that even when you have no motive to be false, it is a very hard thing to say the exact truth, even about your own immediate feelings—much harder than to say something fine about them which is *not* the exact truth.

It is for this rare, precious quality of truthfulness that I delight in many Dutch paintings, which lofty-minded people despise. I find a source of delicious sympathy in these faithful pictures of a monotonous homely existence, which has been the fate of so many more among my fellow-mortals than a life of pomp or of absolute indigence, of tragic suffering or of world-stirring actions. I turn, without shrinking, from cloud-borne angels, from prophets, sibyls, and heroic warriors, to an old woman bending over her flower-pot, or eating her solitary dinner, while the noonday light, softened perhaps by a screen of leaves, falls on her mob-cap, and just touches the rim of her spinning-wheel, and her stone jug, and all those cheap common things which are the precious necessaries of life to her;—or I turn to that village wedding, kept between four brown walls, where an awkward bridegroom opens the dance with a high-shouldered, broad-faced bride, while elderly and middle-aged friends look on, with very irregular noses and lips and probably with quart-pots in their hands, but with an expression of unmistakeable contentment and goodwill. "Foh!" says my idealistic friend, "what vulgar details! What good is there in taking all these pains to give an exact like-ness of old women and clowns? What a low phase of life!—what clumsy, ugly people!"

But bless us, things may be lovable that are not altogether handsome, I hope? I am not at all sure that the majority of the human race have not been ugly, and even among those "lords of their kind," the British, squat figures, ill-shapen nostrils, and dingy complexions are not startling exceptions. Yet there is a great deal of family love amongst us. I have a friend or two whose class of features is such that the Apollo curl on the summit of their brows would be decidedly trying; yet to my certain knowledge tender hearts have beaten for them, and their miniatures—flattering, but still not lovely—are kissed in secret by motherly lips. I have seen many an excellent matron, who could never in her best days have been handsome, and yet she had a packet of yellow love-letters in a private drawer, and sweet children showered kisses on her sallow cheeks. And I believe there have been plenty of young heroes, of middle stature and feeble beards, who have felt quite sure they could never love anything more insignificant than a Diana, and yet have found themselves in middle life happily settled with a wife who waddles. Yes! thank God; human feeling is like the mighty rivers that bless the earth: it does not wait for beauty—it flows with resistless force and brings beauty with it.

All honour and reverence to the divine beauty of form! Let us cultivate it to the utmost in men, women, and children—in our gardens and in our houses. But let us love that other beauty too, which lies in no secret of proportion, but in the secret of deep human sympathy. Paint us an angel, if you can, with a floating violet robe, and a face paled by the celestial light; paint us yet oftener a Madonna, turning her mild face upward and opening her arms to welcome the divine glory; but do not impose on us any aesthetic rules which shall banish from the region of Art those old women scraping carrots with their work-worn hands, those heavy clowns taking holiday in a dingy pot-house, those rounded backs and stupid weather-beaten faces that have bent over the spade and done the rough work of the world—those homes with their tin pans, their brown pitchers, their rough curs, and their clusters of onions. In this world there are so many of these common coarse people, who have no picturesque sentimental wretchedness! It is so needful we should remember their existence, else we may happen to leave them quite out of our religion and philosophy, and frame lofty theories which only fit a world of extremes. Therefore let Art always remind us of them; therefore let us always have men ready to give the loving pains of a life to the faithful representing of commonplace things—men who see beauty in these commonplace things, and delight in showing how kindly the light of heaven falls on them. There are few prophets in the world; few sublimely beautiful women; few heroes. I can't afford to give all my love and reverence to such rarities: I want a great deal of those feelings for my everyday fellow-men, especially for the few in the foreground of the great multitude, whose faces I know, whose hands I touch, for whom I have to make way with kindly courtesy. Neither are picturesque lazzaroni or romantic criminals half so frequent as your common labourer, who gets his own bread, and eats it vulgarly but creditably with his own pocket-knife. It is more needful that I should have a fibre of sympathy connecting me with that vulgar citizen who weighs out my sugar in a vilely-assorted cravat and waistcoat, than with the handsomest rascal in red scarf and green feathers;—more needful that my heart should swell with loving admiration at some trait of gentle goodness in the faulty people who sit at the same hearth with me, or in the clergyman of my own parish, who is perhaps rather too corpulent, and in other respects is not an Oberlin or a Tillotson, than at the deeds of heroes whom I shall never know except by hearsay, or at the sublimest abstract of all clerical graces that was ever conceived by an able novelist.

False Ideals Exposed

We have seen that as Man grows through the ages, he finds himself bolder by the growth of his courage: that is, of his spirit (for so the common people name it), and dares more and more to love and trust instead of to fear and fight. But his courage has other effects; he also raises himself from mere consciousness to knowledge by daring more and more to face facts and tell himself the truth. For in his infancy of helplessness and terror he could not face the inexorable; and facts being of all things the most inexorable, he masked all the threatening ones as fast as he discovered them; so that now every mask requires a hero to tear it off. The king of terrors, Death, was the Arch-Inexorable: Man could not bear the dread of that. He must persuade himself tht Death can be propitiated, circumvented, abolished. How he fixed the mask of personal immortality on the face of Death for this purpose we all know. And he did the like with all disagreeables as long as they remained inevitable. Otherwise he must have gone mad with terror of the grim shapes around him, headed by the skeleton with the scythe and hourglass. The masks were his ideals, as he called them; and what, he would ask, would life be without ideals? Thus he became an idealist, and remained so until he dared to begin pulling the masks off and looking the spectres in the face— dared, that is, to be more and more a realist. But all men are not equally brave; and the greatest terror prevailed whenever some realist bolder than the rest laid hands on a mask which they did not yet dare to do without.

We have plenty of these masks around us still: some of them more fantastic than any of the Sandwich islanders' masks in the British Museum. In our novels and romances especially we see the most beautiful of all the masks: those devised to disguise the brutalities of the sexual instinct in the earlier stages of its development, and to soften the rigorous aspect of the iron laws by which Society regulates its gratification. When the social organism becomes bent on civilization, it has to force marriage and family life on the individual, because it can perpetuate itself in no other way whilst love is still known only by fitful glimpses, the basis of sexual relationship being in the main mere physical appetite. Under these circumstances men try to graft pleasure on necessity by desperately pretending that the institution forced upon them is a congenial one, making it a point of public decency to assume always that men spontaneously love their kindred better than their chance acquaintances, and that the woman once desired is always desired: also that the family is woman's proper sphere, and that no really womanly woman ever forms an attachment, or even knows what it means, until she is requested to do so by a man. Now if anyone's childhood has been embittered by the dislike of his mother and the ill-temper of his father; if his wife has ceased to care for him and he is heartily tired of his wife; if his brother is going to law with him over the division of the family property, and his son acting in studied defiance of his plans and wishes, it is hard for him to persuade himself that passion is eternal and that blood is thicker than water. Yet if he tells himself the truth, all his life seems a waste and a failure by the light of it. It comes then to this, that his neighbors

From "Ideals and Idealists" [1890], *The Quintessence of Ibsenism*, London, 1922 (3rd edition), pp. 28-35; reprinted by permission of the Society of Authors.

must either agree with him that the whole system is a mistake, and discard it for a new one, which cannot possibly happen until social organization so far outgrows the institution that Society can perpetuate itself without it; or else they must keep him in countenance by resolutely making believe that all the illusions with which it has been marked are realities.

For the sake of precision, let us imagine a community of a thousand persons, organized for the perpetuation of the species on the basis of the British family as we know it at present. Seven hundred of them, we will suppose, find the British family arrangement quite good enough for them. Two hundred and ninety-nine find it a failure, but must put up with it since they are in a minority. The remaining person occupies a position to be explained presently. The 299 failures will not have the courage to face the fact that they are irremediable failures, since they cannot prevent the 700 satisfied ones from coercing them into conformity with the marriage law. They will accordingly try to persuade themselves that, whatever their own particular domestic arrangements may be, the family is a beautiful and holy natural institution. For the fox not only declares that the grapes he cannot get are sour: he also insists that the sloes he *can* get are sweet. Now observe what has happened. The family as it really is is a conventional arrangement, legally enforced, which the majority, because it happens to suit them, think good enough for the minority, whom it happens not to suit at all. The family as a beautiful and holy natural institution is only a fancy picture of what every family would have to be if everybody was to be suited, invented by the minority as a mask for the reality, which in its nakedness is intolerable to them. We call this sort of fancy picture an Ideal; and the policy of forcing individuals to act on the assumption that all ideals are real, and to recognize and accept such action as standard moral conduct, absolutely valid under all circumstances, contrary conduct or any advocacy of it being discountenanced and punished as immoral, may therefore be described as the policy of Idealism. Our 299 domestic failures are therefore become idealists as to marriage; and in proclaiming the ideal in fiction, poetry, pulpit and platform oratory, and serious private conversations, they will far outdo the 700 who comfortably accept marriage as a matter of course, never dreaming of calling it an "institution," much less a holy and beautiful one, and being pretty plainly of opinion that Idealism is a crackbrained fuss about nothing. The idealists, hurt by this, will retort by calling them Philistines. We then have our society classified as 700 Philistines and 299 idealists, leaving one man unclassified: the man strong enough to face the truth the idealists are shirking.

Such a man says of marriage, "This thing is a failure for many of us. It is insufferable that two human beings, having entered into relations which only warm affection can render tolerable, should be forced to maintain them after such affections have ceased to exist, or in spite of the fact that they have never arisen. The alleged natural attractions and repulsions upon which the family ideal is based do not exist; and it is historically false that the family was founded for the purpose of satisfying them. Let us provide otherwise for the social ends which the family subserves, and then abolish its compulsory character altogether." What will be the attitude of the rest to this outspoken man? The Philistines will simply think him mad. But the idealists will be terrified beyond measure at the proclamation of their hidden thought—at the presence of the traitor among the conspirators of silence—at the rending of the beautiful veil they and their poets have woven to hide the unbearable face of the truth. They will crucify him, burn him, violate their own ideals of family affection by taking his children away from him, ostracize him, brand him as immoral, profligate, filthy, and appeal against him to the despised Philistines, specially idealized for the occasion as Society. How far they will proceed against him depends on how far his courage exceeds theirs. At his worst, they call him cynic and paradoxer: at his best they do their utmost to ruin him if not to take his life. Thus, purblindly courageous moralists like Mandeville and Larochefoucauld, who merely state unpleasant facts without denying the validity of current ideals, and who indeed depend on those ideals to make their statements piquant, get off with nothing worse than this name of cynic, the free use of which is a familiar mark of the zealous idealist. But take the case of the man who has already served as an example: Shelley. The idealists did not call Shelley a cynic: they called him a fiend until they invented a new illusion to enable them to enjoy the beauty of his lyrics, this illusion being nothing less than the pretence that since he was at bottom an idealist himself, his ideals must be identical with those of Tennyson and Longfellow, neither of whom ever wrote a line in which some highly respectable ideal was not implicit.[1]

Here the admission that Shelley, the realist, was an idealist too, seems to spoil the whole argument. And it certainly spoils its verbal consistency. For we unfortunately use this word ideal indifferently to denote both the institution which the ideal masks and the mask itself, thereby producing desperate confusion of thought, since the institution may be an effete and poisonous one, whilst the mask may be, and indeed generally is, an image of what we would fain have in its place. If the existing facts, with their masks on, are to be called ideals, and the future possibilities which the masks depict are also to be called ideals—if, again, the man who is defending existing institutions by maintaining their identity with their masks is to be confounded under one name with the man who is striving to realize the future possibilities by tearing the mask and the thing masked asunder, then the position cannot be intelligibly described by mortal pen: you and I, reader, will be at cross purposes at every sentence unless you allow me to distinguish pioneers like Shelley and Ibsen as realists from the idealists of my imaginary community of one thousand. If you ask why I have not allotted the terms the other way, and called Shelley and Ibsen idealists and the conventionalists realists, I reply that Ibsen himself, though he has not formally made the distinction, has so repeatedly harped on conventions and conventionalists as ideals and idealists that if I were now perversely to call them realities and realists, I should confuse

---

[1] The following are examples of the two stages of Shelley criticism: "We feel as if one of the darkest of the fiends had been clothed with a human body to enable him to gratify his enmity against the human race, and as if the supernatural atrocity of his hate were only heightened by his power to do injury. So strongly has this impression dwelt upon our minds that we absolutely asked a friend, who had seen this individual, to describe him to us—as if a cloven hoof, or horn, or flames from the mouth, must have marked the external appearance of so bitter an enemy of mankind." (*Literary Gazette*, 19th May 1821.)

"A beautiful and ineffectual angel, beating in the void his luminous wings in vain." (MATTHEW ARNOLD, in the preface to his selection of poems by Byron, dated 1881.)

The 1881 opinion is much sillier than the 1821 opinion. Further samples will be found in the articles of Henry Salt, one of the few writers on Shelley who understand his true position as a social pioneer.

readers of The Wild Duck and Rosmersholm more than I should help them. Doubtless I shall be reproached for puzzling people by thus limiting the meaning of the term ideal. But what, I ask, is that inevitable passing perplexity compared to the inextricable tangle I must produce if I follow the custom, and use the word indiscriminately in its two violently incompatible senses? If the term realist is objected to on account of some of its modern associations, I can only recommend you, if you must associate it with something else than my own description of its meaning (I do not deal in definitions), to associate it, not with Zola and Maupassant, but with Plato.

Now let us return to our community of 700 Philistines, 299 idealists, and 1 realist. The mere verbal ambiguity against which I have just provided is as nothing beside that which comes of any attempt to express the relations of these three sections, simple as they are, in terms of the ordinary system of reason and duty. The idealist, higher in the ascent of evolution than the Philistine, yet hates the highest and strikes at him with a dread and rancor of which the easy-going Philistine is guiltless. The man who has risen above the danger and the fear that his acquisitiveness will lead him to theft, his temper to murder, and his affections to debauchery: this is he who is denounced as an arch-scoundrel and libertine, and thus confounded with the lowest because he is the highest. And it is not the ignorant and stupid who maintain this error, but the literate and the cultured. When the true prophet speaks, he is proved to be both rascal and idiot, not by those who have never read of how foolishly such learned demonstrations have come off in the past, but by those who have themselves written volumes on the crucifixions, the burnings, the stonings, the headings and hangings, the Siberia transportations, the calumny and ostracism which have been the lot of the pioneer as well as of the camp follower. It is from men of established literary reputation that we learn that William Blake was mad, that Shelley was spoiled by living in a low set, that Robert Owen was a man who did not know the world, that Ruskin was incapable of comprehending political economy, that Zola was a mere blackguard, and that Ibsen was "a Zola with a wooden leg." The great musician, accepted by the unskilled listener, is vilified by his fellow-musicians: it was the musical culture of Europe that pronounced Wagner the inferior of Mendelssohn and Meyerbeer. The great artist finds his foes among the painters, and not among the men in the street: it was the Royal Academy which placed forgotten nobodies above Burne Jones. It is not rational that it should be so; but it is so, for all that.

The realist at last loses patience with ideals altogether, and sees in them only something to blind us, something to numb us, something to murder self in us, something whereby, instead of resisting death, we can disarm it by committing suicide. The idealist, who has taken refuge with the ideals because he hates himself and is ashamed of himself, thinks that all this is so much the better. The realist, who has come to have a deep respect for himself and faith in the validity of his own will, thinks it so much the worse. To the one, human nature, naturally corrupt, is held back from ruinous excesses only by self-denying conformity to the ideals. To the other these ideals are only swaddling clothes which man has outgrown, and which insufferably impede his movements. No wonder the two cannot agree. The idealist says, "Realism means egotism; and egotism means depravity." The realist declares that when a man abnegates the will to live and be free in a world of the living and free, seeking only to conform to ideals for the sake of being, not himself, but "a good man," then he is morally dead and rotten, and must be left unheeded to abide his resurrection, if that by good luck arrive before his bodily death.[2] Unfortunately, this is the sort of speech that nobody but a realist understands. It will be more amusing as well as more convincing to take an actual example of an idealist criticizing a realist.

[2] The above was written in 1890, ten years before Ibsen, in *When We Dead Awaken*, fully adopted its metaphor without, as far as I know, having any knowledge of my essay. Such an anticipation is a better proof than any mere argument that I found the right track of Ibsen's thought. (1912.)

GUSTAVE FLAUBERT

Heroic Honesty

Dear Friend,—I have just received the *Bovary*, and first of all I feel the necessity of thanking you for it (if I am coarse, I am not ungrateful); you have rendered me a service in accepting the book, such as it is, and I will not forget it.

Admit that you thought me, and that you still think me (more than ever perhaps), violently ridiculous! Some day I shall be delighted to admit that you were right; I promise you that then I will make you the humblest apologies. But you must understand, dear friend, that before all things I wanted to try an experiment, provided the apprenticeship were not too rough.

Do you really believe that this mean reality, whose reproduction disgusts you, does not make my gorge rise as much as yours? If you knew me better, you would know that I hold the everyday life in detestation. Personally I have always kept myself as far away from it as I could. But æsthetically I wanted this time, and only this time, to exhaust it thoroughly. So I took the thing in an heroic fashion, I mean a minute one, accepting everything, saying everything, depicting everything—an ambitious statement!

I explain myself badly, but sufficiently well for you to understand the real meaning of my opposition to your criticism, judicious as it was. You were by the way of writing me a different book.

You were hitting at the innermost poetry from which the type upon which it was conceived followed (as a philosopher would say). Lastly, I believed myself to be wanting in what I owed to myself and to you if I performed an act not of conviction but of deference.

Letters to Laurence Pichat [1856] and to Louis Bouilhet [1856], translated from the French, in John Charles Tarner, *Gustave Flaubert as seen in his Works and Correspondence*, London, 1895, pp. 198-9, 197-8. Reprinted by permission of Constable & Co.

Art claims for herself neither complaisance nor politeness, nothing but faith—faith always, and liberty. And on that point I cordially shake hands with you. Under the barren tree with the ever-green leaves, entirely yours.

Bovary goes on pianissimo. Be sure and tell me what kind of monstrosity to post on the slope of the Bois-Guillaume. Ought my man to have an eruption on his face, red eyes, a hump, a nose wanting? Should he be an idiot, or a bandy? I am very much puzzled. Devil take father Hugo with his cripples sitting in bowls like snails in the rain! It is most annoying.

I am going on very slowly. I give myself an accursed lot of trouble. I have just suppressed phrases at the end of five or six pages, which have cost me the work of entire days. It is impossible for me to see the effect of any one of them before it is finished, re-finished, polished. It is an insane way of working, but what can I do? I have a conviction that the things best in themselves are those that I cut out. One only succeeds in producing an effect by the negation of exuberance; and exuberance is precisely what charms me.

Do you know that my mother about six weeks ago said a splendid thing to me (a thing to make the Muse hang herself for jealousy at not having invented it). Here it is: "The mania for phrases has dried up your heart."

Try, my good fellow, and send me by next Sunday, or sooner if you can, the following morsels of medical information. They are going up the slopes, Homais is looking at the blind man with the bleeding eyes (you know the mask) and he makes him a speech; he uses scientific words, thinks that he can cure him, and gives him his address. It is, of course, necessary that Homais should make a mistake, for the poor beast is incurable. If you have not enough in your medicine-bag to supply me with the material for five or six sturdy lines, draw from Follin and send it me. I hope that in a month Mistress Bovary will have the arsenic in her stomach. Shall I bring her to you buried? I doubt it.

I. You are an excellent beast to have replied to me so quickly. The idea of "following a regular diet" is excellent, and I accept it with enthusiasm; as to an operation, that is impossible because of the club-foot, and besides, as it is Homais himself who wishes to undertake the cure, all surgery must be excluded.

II. I should like some scientific words designating the different parts of the damaged eye (or eyelids). The whole is damaged, and is a mere squash, in which nothing can be distinguished. None the less Homais employs fine words and distinguishes something to dazzle the gallery.

III. Lastly, he must speak of some pomade (of his own invention?) good for scrofulous affections, and which he intends to use upon the mendicant. I make him invite the beggar to come to visit him at Yonville in order to have my rascal in at Emma's death! There we are, old fellow. Think a little over all this, and send me something for Sunday.

I am working moderately, and without gusto, or rather with disgust. I am really tired of this work; it is a regular "impot" to me now.

We shall probably have much to correct: I have five dialogues in succession, and all say the same thing.

ANTON CHEKHOV

Dunghills as Artistic Material

Even your praise of "On the Road" has not lessened my anger as an author, and I hasten to avenge myself for what you say about "Mire." Be on your guard, and take firm hold of the back of your chair that you do not faint. Well, here goes.

It is best to meet every critical article with a silent bow, even if it is abusive and unjust—such is the literary etiquette. It is not the correct thing to answer, and all who do so are justly blamed for excessive vanity. But since your criticism is like "an evening conversation on the steps of the Babinko lodge" . . . and as, without touching on the literary aspects of the story, it raises general questions of principle, I shall not be sinning against the etiquette if I allow myself to continue our conversation.

In the first place, I, like you, do not admire literature of the kind we are discussing. As a reader and "a private citizen" I am glad to avoid it, but if you ask my honest nd sincere opinion about it, I shall say that it is still an open question whether it has a right to exist,—a question that has as yet not been settled. . . . You and I and the critics of all the world have no such firm certainty as would give us the right to disown this literature. I do not know who is right: Homer, Shakespeare, Lope de Vega, the ancients generally who did not fear to grub in the "dung-hill," but who were more stable in their moral relations than we; or the modern writers, fastidious on paper, but coldly cynical in soul and in their manner of life? I do not know who has bad taste: the Greeks, who were not ashamed to sing such love as really is in beautiful Nature, or the readers of Gaboriau, Marlitt, Per Bobo. Like the problems of non-resistance to evil, free-will, etc., this question can be settled only in the future. We can only think about it, but to solve it means to go beyond the limits of our competency. Reference to Turgeniev and Tolstoy, who avoided this "dung-hill," does not clear up the question. Their aversion does not prove anything; there were writers before them who not only regarded sordidness as "scoundrelly among scoundrels," but held the same view of descriptions of *muzhiks* and clerks and all beneath the titular rank. And a single period, no matter how brilliant, does not give us the right to draw an inference in favor of this or the other tendency. Nor does reference to the corrupting influence of a given literary tendency solve the question. Everything in this world is relative and approximate. There are people who will be corrupted even by juvenile literature, who read, with particular pleasure, the piquant passages in the Psalter and the Proverbs of Solomon, while there are those who become the purer the more they know about the evil side of life. Publicists, lawyers, physicians, initiated into all the secret human sins, are not reputed to be immoral; realistic writers are often more moral than archimandrites. And finally, no literature can in its cynicism surpass actual life; a wine-glassful will not make drunk the man who has already emptied a whole cask.

2. That the world "swarms with male and female scum" is perfectly true. Human nature is imperfect, and it would, therefore, be strange to find only righteous

Letter to M. V. Kiselev [1887], translated from the Russian by Constance Karnett in *The Personal Papers of Anton Chekhov*, ed. Matthew Josephson, New York, 1948, pp. 127-31; reprinted by permission of Crown Publishers.

people on this earth. But to think that the task of literature is to gather the pure grain from the muck heap, is to reject literature itself. Aristic literature is called so just because it depicts life as it really is. Its aim is truth,—unconditional and honest. To narrow down its functions to such a specialty as selecting the "unsullied," is as fatal to it as to have Levitan paint a tree and to forbid him to include the dirty bark and the yellow leaves. I agree with you that the "cream" is a fine thing, but a litterateur is not a confectioner, not a dealer in cosmetics, not an entertainer; he is a man bound, under compulsion, by the realization of his duty, and by his conscience; having put his hand to the plow he must not plead weakness; and no matter how painful it is to him, he is constrained to overcome his aversion, and soil his imagination with the sordidness of life. He is just like any ordinary reporter. What would you say if a newspaper reporter, because of his fastidiousness or from a wish to give pleasure to his readers, were to describe only honest mayors, high-minded ladies, and virtuous railroad contractors? To a chemist, nothing on earth is unclean. A writer must be as objective as a chemist; he must abandon the subjective line; he must know that dung-heaps play a very respectable part in a landscape, and that evil passions are as inherent in life as good ones.

3. Writers are the children of their age, and therefore, like the rest of the public, ought to surrender to the external conditions of society. Thus, they must be absolutely decent. Only this have we the right to require of the realists. For the rest, you say nothing against the form and execution of "Mire." . . . And so, I take it, I have been decent.

4. I admit that I seldom consult my conscience when I write. This is due to habit and the brief, compressed form of my work. Let us say that when I express this or that opinion about literature, I do not take myself into account.

5. You write: "If I were the editor I would have returned to you this feuilleton for your own good." Why not go further? Why not go for the editors who print such stories? Why not denounce the Administration of the Press for not suppressing immoral newspapers?

The fate of literature would be woeful (both little and great literature) if you left it to the will of individuals. That's the first thing. In the second place, there is no police which we can consider competent in literary matters. I agree that we must have curbs and whips, for knaves find their way even into literature, but, think what you will, you cannot find a better police for literature than criticism and the author's own conscience. People have been trying to discover such a police since the creation of the world, but nothing better has been found. You would wish me to suffer the loss of one hundred and fifteen roubles and be censured by the editor. Others, among them your father, are delighted with the story. Some send letters of reproach to Souvorin, reviling everything, the newspaper, me, etc. Who, then, is right? Who is the judge?

6. Further, you write: "Leave such writing to spiritless and unfortunate scribblers like Okreits, Pince-nez or Aloe."

May Allah pardon me if you wrote those lines sincerely! To be condescending toward humble people because of their humbleness does not do honor to the human heart. In literature, the lower ranks are as necessary as in the army,—so says the mind, and the heart ought to confirm this most thoroughly.

HONORÉ DE BALZAC

Society as Historical Organism

In giving the general title of "The Human Comedy" to a work begun nearly thirteen years since, it is necessary to explain its motive, to relate its origin, and briefly sketch its plan, while endeavouring to speak of these matters as though I had no personal interest in them. This is not so difficult as the public might imagine. Few works conduce to much vanity; much labour conduces to great diffidence. This observation accounts for the study of their own works made by Corneille, Molière, and other great writers; if it is impossible to equal them in their fine conceptions, we may try to imitate them in this feeling.

The idea of *The Human Comedy* was at first as a dream to me, one of those impossible projects which we caress and then let fly; a chimera that gives us a glimpse of its smiling woman's face, and forthwith spreads its wings and returns to a heavenly realm of phantasy. But this chimera, like many another, has become a reality; has its behests, its tyranny, which must be obeyed.

The idea originated in a comparison between Humanity and Animality.

It is a mistake to suppose that the great dispute which has lately made a stir, between Cuvier and Geoffroi Saint-Hilaire, arose from a scientific innovation. Unity of structure, under other names, had occupied the greatest minds during the two previous centuries. As we read the extraordinary writings of the mystics who studied the sciences in their relation to infinity, such as Swedenborg, Saint-Martin, and others, and the works of the greatest authors on Natural History—Leibnitz, Buffon, Charles Bonnet, etc., we detect in the *monads* of Leibnitz, in the *organic molecules* of Buffon, in the *vegetative force* of Needham, in the correlation of similar organs of Charles Bonnet—who in 1760 was so bold as to write, "Animals vegetate as plants do"—we detect, I say, the rudiments of the great law of Self for Self, which lies at the root of *Unity of Plan*. There is but one Animal. The Creator works on a single model for every organised being. "The Animal" is elementary, and takes its external form, or, to be accurate, the differences in its form, from the environment in which it is obliged to develop. Zoological species are the result of these differences. The announcement and defence of this system, which is indeed in harmony with our pre-conceived ideas of Divine Power, will be the eternal glory of Geoffroi Saint-Hilaire, Cuvier's victorious opponent on this

Preface [1842] to *The Human Comedy*, from *At the Sign of the Cat and Racket*, translated from the French by Clara Bell, London and New York, 1897; reprinted by permission of J. M. Dent & Sons Ltd.

point of higher science, whose triumph was hailed by Goethe in the last article he wrote.

I, for my part, convinced of this scheme of nature long before the discussion to which it has given rise, perceived that in this respect society resembled nature. For does not society modify Man, according to the conditions in which he lives and acts, into men as manifold as the species in Zoology? The differences between a soldier, an artisan, a man of business, a lawyer, an idler, a student, a statesman, a merchant, a sailor, a poet, a beggar, a priest, are as great, though not so easy to define, as those between the wolf, the lion, the ass, the crow, the shark, the seal, the sheep, etc. Thus social species have always existed, and will always exist, just as there are zoological species. If Buffon could produce a magnificent work by attempting to represent in a book the whole realm of zoology, was there not room for a work of the same kind on society? But the limits set by nature to the variations of animals have no existence in society. When Buffon describes the lion, he dismisses the lioness with a few phrases; but in society a wife is not always the female of the male. There may be two perfectly dissimilar beings in one household. The wife of a shopkeeper is sometimes worthy of a prince, and the wife of a prince is often worthless compared with the wife of an artisan. The social state has freaks which Nature does not allow herself; it is nature *plus* society. The description of social species would thus be at least double that of animal species, merely in view of the two sexes. Then, among animals the drama is limited; there is scarcely any confusion; they turn and rend each other—that is all. Men, too, rend each other; but their greater or less intelligence makes the struggle far more complicated. Though some savants do not yet admit that the animal nature flows into human nature through an immense tide of life, the grocer certainly becomes a peer, and the noble sometimes sinks to the lowest social grade. Again, Buffon found that life was extremely simple among animals. Animals have little property, and neither arts nor sciences; while man, by a law that has yet to be sought, has a tendency to express his culture, his thoughts, and his life in everything he appropriates to his use. Though Leuwenhoek, Swammerdam, Spallanzani, Réaumur, Charles Bonnet, Müller, Haller, and other patient investigators have shown us how interesting are the habits of animals, those of each kind are, at least to our eyes, always and in every age alike; whereas the dress, the manners, the speech, the dwelling of a prince, a banker, an artist, a citizen, a priest, and a pauper are absolutely unlike, and change with every phase of civilisation.

Hence the work to be written needed a threefold form—men, women, and things; that is to say, persons and the material expression of their minds; man, in short, and life.

As we read the dry and discouraging list of events called History, who can have failed to note that the writers of all periods, in Egypt, Persia, Greece, and Rome, have forgotten to give us the history of manners? The fragment of Petronius on the private life of the Romans excites rather than satisfies our curiosity. It was from observing this great void in the field of history that the Abbé Barthélemy devoted his life to a reconstruction of Greek manners in *Le Jeune Anacharsis*.

But how could such a drama, with the four or five thousand persons which a society offers, be made interesting? How, at the same time, please the poet, the philosopher, and the masses who want both poetry and philosophy under striking imagery? Though I could conceive of the importance and of the poetry of such a history of the human heart, I saw no way of writing it; for hitherto the most famous story-tellers had spent their talent in creating two or three typical actors, in depicting one aspect of life. It was with this idea that I read the works of Walter Scott. Walter Scott, the modern troubadour, or finder (*treuvère = trouveur*), had just then given an aspect of grandeur to a class of composition unjustly regarded as of the second rank. Is it not really more difficult to compete with personal and parochial interests by writing of Daphnis and Chloe, Roland, Amadis, Panurge, Don Quixote, Manon Lescaut, Clarissa, Lovelace, Robinson Crusoe, Gil Blas, Ossian, Julie d'Etanges, My Uncle Toby, Werther, Corinne, Adolphe, Paul and Virginia, Jeanie Deans, Claverhouse, Ivanhoe, Manfred, Mignon, than to set forth in order facts more or less similar in every country, to investigate the spirit of laws that have fallen into desuetude, to review the theories which mislead nations, or, like some metaphysicians, to explain what *Is?* In the first place, these actors, whose existence becomes more prolonged and more authentic than that of the generations which saw their birth, almost always live solely on condition of their being a vast reflection of the present. Conceived in the womb of their own period, the whole heart of humanity stirs within their frame, which often covers a complete system of philosophy. Thus Walter Scott raised to the dignity of the philosophy of History the literature which, from age to age, sets perennial gems in the poetic crown of every nation where letters are cultivated. He vivified it with the spirit of the past; he combined drama, dialogue, portrait, scenery, and description; he fused the marvellous with truth—the two elements of the times; and he brought poetry into close contact with the familiarity of the humblest speech. But as he had not so much devised a system as hit upon a manner in the ardour of his work, or as its logical outcome, he never thought of connecting his compositions in such a way as to form a complete history of which each chapter was a novel, and each novel the picture of a period.

It was by discerning this lack of unity, which in no way detracts from the Scottish writer's greatness, that I perceived at once the scheme which would favour the execution of my purpose, and the possibility of executing it. Though dazzled, so to speak, by Walter Scott's amazing fertility, always himself and always original, I did not despair, for I found the source of his genius in the infinite variety of human nature. Chance is the greatest romancer in the world; we have only to study it. French society would be the real author; I should only be the secretary. By drawing up an inventory of vices and virtues, by collecting the chief facts of the passions, by depicting characters, by choosing the principal incidents of social life, by composing types out of a combination of homogeneous characteristics, I might perhaps succeed in writing the history which so many historians have neglected: that of Manners. By patience and perseverance I might produce for France in the nineteenth century the book which we must all regret that Rome, Athens, Tyre, Memphis, Persia, and India have not bequeathed to us; that history of their social life which, prompted by the Abbé Barthélemy, Monteil patiently and steadily tried to write for the middle ages, but in an unattractive form.

The work, so far, was nothing. By adhering to the strict lines of a reproduction a writer might be a more or less faithful, and more or less successful painter of types of humanity, a narrator of the dramas of private life, an archaeologist of social furniture, a cataloguer of professions, a registrar of good and evil; but to deserve the praise of which every artist must be ambitious, must I not also investigate the reasons or the cause of these social effects, detect the hidden sense of this vast assembly of figures, passions, and incidents? And finally, having sought—I will not say having found—this reason, this motive power, must I not reflect on first principles, and discover in what particulars societies approach or deviate from the eternal law of truth and beauty? In spite of the wide scope of the preliminaries, which might of themselves constitute a book, the work, to be complete, would need a conclusion. Thus depicted, society ought to bear in itself the reason of its working.

The law of the writer, in virtue of which he is a writer, and which I do not hesitate to say makes him the equal, or perhaps the superior, of the statesman, is his judgment, whatever it may be, on human affairs, and his absolute devotion to certain principles. Machiavelli, Hobbes, Bossuet, Leibnitz, Kant, Montesquieu *are* the science which statesmen apply. "A writer ought to have settled opinions on morals and politics; he should regard himself as a tutor of men; for men need no masters to teach them to doubt," says Bonald. I took these noble words as my guide long ago; they are the written law of the monarchical writer. And those who would confute me by my own words will find that they have misinterpreted some ironical phrase, or that they have turned against me a speech given to one of my actors—a trick peculiar to calumniators.

As to the intimate purpose, the soul of this work, these are the principles on which it is based.

Man is neither good nor bad; he is born with instincts and capabilities; society, far from depraving him, as Rousseau asserts, improves him, makes him better; but self-interest also developes his evil tendencies. Christianity, above all, Catholicism, being—as I have pointed out in *The Country Doctor* (*Le Médecin de Campagne*)—a complete system for the repression of the depraved tendencies of man, is the most powerful element of social order.

In reading attentively the presentment of society cast, as it were, from the life, with all that is good and all that is bad in it, we learn this lesson—if thought, or if passion, which combines thought and feeling, is the vital social element, it is also its destructive element. In this respect social life is like the life of man. Nations live long only by moderating their vital energy. Teaching, or rather education, by religious bodies is the grand principle of life for nations, the only means for diminishing the sum of evil and increasing the sum of good in all society. Thought, the living principle of good and ill, can only be trained, quelled, and guided by religion. The only possible religion is Christianity (see the letter from Paris in *Louis Lambert*, in which the young mystic explains, à propos to Swedenborg's doctrines, how there has never been but one religion since the world began). Christianity created modern nationalities, and it will preserve them. Hence, no doubt, the necessity for the monarchical principle. Catholicism and Royalty are twin principles.

As to the limits within which these two principles should be confined by various institutions, so that they may not become absolute, every one will feel that a brief preface ought not to be a political treatise. I cannot, therefore, enter on religious discussions, nor on the political discussions of the day. I write under the light of two eternal truths—Religion and Monarchy; two necessities, as they are shown to be by contemporary events, towards which every writer of sound sense ought to try to guide the country back. Without being an enemy to election, which is an excellent principle as a basis of legislation, I reject election regarded as *the only social instrument*, especially so badly organized as it now is (1842); for it fails to represent imposing minorities, whose ideas and interests would occupy the attention of a monarchical government. Elective power extended to all gives us government by the masses, the only irresponsible form of government, under which tyranny is unlimited, for it calls itself law. Besides, I regard the family and not the individual as the true social unit. In this respect, at the risk of being thought retrograde, I side with Bossuet and Bonald instead of going with modern innovators. Since election has become the only social instrument, if I myself were to exercise it no contradiction between my acts and my words should be inferred. An engineer points out that a bridge is about to fall, that it is dangerous for any one to cross it; but he crosses it himself when it is the only road to the town. Napoleon adapted election to the spirit of the French nation with wonderful skill. The least important members of his Legislative Body became the most famous orators of the Chamber after the Restoration. No Chamber has ever been the equal of the *Corps Législatif*, comparing them man for man. The elective system of the Empire was, then, indisputably the best.

Some persons may, perhaps, think that this declaration is somewhat autocratic and self-assertive. They will quarrel with the novelist for wanting to be an historian, and will call him to account for writing politics. I am simply fulfilling an obligation—that is my reply. The work I have undertaken will be as long as a history; I was compelled to explain the logic of it, hitherto unrevealed, and its principles and moral purpose.

Having been obliged to withdraw the prefaces formerly published, in response to essentially ephemeral criticisms, I will retain only one remark.

Writers who have a purpose in view, were it only a reversion to principles familiar in the past because they are eternal, should always clear the ground. Now every one who, in the domain of ideas, brings his stone by pointing out an abuse, or setting a mark on some evil that it may be removed—every such man is stigmatised as immoral. The accusation of immorality, which has never failed to be cast at the courageous writer, is, after all, the last that can be brought when nothing else remains to be said to a romancer. If you are truthful in your pictures; if by dint of daily and nightly toil you succeed in writing the most difficult language in the world, the word *immoral* is flung in your teeth. Socrates was immoral; Jesus Christ was immoral; they both were persecuted in the name of the society they overset or reformed. When a man is to be killed he is taxed with immorality. These tactics, familiar in party warfare, are a disgrace to those who use them. Luther and Calvin knew well what they were about when they shielded themselves behind damaged worldly interests! And they lived all the days of their life.

When depicting all society, sketching it in the immensity of its turmoil, it happened—it could not but happen—that the picture displayed more of evil than of good; that some part of the fresco represented a guilty couple; and the critics at once raised the cry of immorality, without pointing out the morality of another portion intended to be a perfect contrast. As the critic knew nothing of the general plan I could forgive him, all the more because one can no more hinder criticism than the use of eyes, tongues, and judgment. Also the time for an impartial verdict is not yet come for me. And, after all, the author who cannot make up his mind to face the fire of criticism should no more think of writing than a traveller should start on his journey counting on a perpetually clear sky. On this point it remains to be said that the most conscientious moralists doubt greatly whether society can show as many good actions as bad ones; and in the picture I have painted of it there are more virtuous figures than reprehensible ones. Blameworthy actions, faults and crimes, from the lightest to the most atrocious, always meet with punishment, human or divine, signal or secret. I have done better than the historian, for I am free. Cromwell here on earth escaped all punishment but that inflicted by thoughtful men. And on this point there have been divided schools. Bossuet even showed some consideration for the great regicide. William of Orange, the usurper, Hugues Capet, another usurper, lived to old age with no more qualms or fears than Henri iv. or Charles i. The lives of Catherine ii. and of Frederic of Prussia would be conclusive against any kind of moral law, if they were judged by the twofold aspect of the morality which guides ordinary mortals, and that which is in use by crowned heads; for, as Napoleon said, for kings and statesmen there are the lesser and the higher morality. My scenes of political life are founded on this profound observation. It is not a law to history, as it is to romance, to make for a beautiful ideal. History is, or ought to be, what it was; while romance ought to be "the better world," as was said by Mme. Necker, one of the most distinguished thinkers of the last century.

Still, with this noble falsity, romance would be nothing if it were not true in detail. Walter Scott, obliged as he was to conform to the ideas of an essentially hypocritical nation, was false to humanity in his picture of woman, because his models were schismatics. The Protestant woman has no ideal. She may be chaste, pure, virtuous; but her unexpansive love will always be as calm and methodical as the fulfillment of a duty. It might seem as though the Virgin Mary had chilled the hearts of those sophists who have banished her from heaven with her treasures of lovingkindness. In Protestantism there is no possible future for the woman who has sinned; while, in the Catholic Church, the hope of forgiveness makes her sublime. Hence, for the Protestant writer there is but one Woman, while the Catholic writer find a new woman in each new situation. If Walter Scott had been a Catholic, if he had set himself the task of describing truly the various phases of society which have successively existed in Scotland, perhaps the painter to Effie and Alice—the two figures for which he blamed himself in his later years— might have admitted passion with its sins and punishments, and the virtues revealed by repentance. Passion is the sum-total of humanity. Without passion, religion, history, romance, art, would all be useless.

Some persons, seeing me collect such a mass of facts and paint them as they are, with passion for their motive power, have supposed, but wrongly, that I must belong to the school of Sensualism and Materialism—two aspects of the same thing—Pantheism. But their misapprehension was perhaps justified—or inevitable. I do not share the belief in indefinite progress for society as a whole; I believe in man's improvement in himself. Those who insist on reading in me the intention to consider man as a finished creation are strangely mistaken. *Séraphita*, the doctrine in action of the Christian Buddha, seems to me an ample answer to this rather heedless accusation.

In certain fragments of this long work I have tried to popularise the amazing facts, I may say the marvels of electricity, which in man is metamorphosed into an incalculable force; but in what way do the phenomena of brain and nerves, which prove the existence of an undiscovered world of psychology, modify the necessary and undoubted relations of the worlds to God? In what way can they shake the Catholic dogma? Though irrefutable facts should some day place thought in the class of fluids which are discerned only by their effects while their substance evades our senses, even when aided by so many mechanical means, the result will be the same as when Christopher Columbus detected that the earth is a sphere, and Galileo demonstrated its rotation. Our future will be unchanged. The wonders of animal magnetism, with which I have been familiar since 1820; the beautiful experiments of Gall, Lavater's successor; all the men who have studied mind as opticians have studied light—two not dissimilar things—point to a conclusion in favour of the mystics, the disciples of St. John, and of those great thinkers who have established the spiritual world—the sphere in which are revealed the relations of God and man.

A sure grasp of the purport of this work will make it clear that I attach to common, daily facts, hidden or patent to the eye, to the acts of individual lives, and to their causes and principles, the importance which historians have hitherto ascribed to the events of public national life. The unknown struggle which goes on in a valley of the Indre between Mme. de Mortsauf and her passion is perhaps as great as the most famous of battles (*Le Lys dans la Vallée*). In one the glory of the victor is at stake; in the other it is heaven. The misfortunes of the two Birotteaus, the priest and the perfumer, to me are those of mankind. La Fosseuse (*Médecin de Campagne*) and Mme. Graslin (*Curé de Village*) are almost the sum-total of woman. We all suffer thus every day. I have had to do a hundred times what Richardson did but once. Lovelace has a thousand forms, for social corruption takes the hues of the medium in which it lives. Clarissa, on the contrary, the lovely image of impassioned virtue, is drawn in lines of distracting purity. To create a variety of Virgins it needs a Raphael. In this respect, perhaps literature must yield to painting.

Still, I may be allowed to point out how many irreproachable figures—as regards their virtue—are to be found in the portions of this work already published: Pierrette Lorrain, Ursule Mirouët, Constance Birotteau, La Fosseuse, Eugénie Grandet, Marguerite Claës, Pauline de Villenoix, Madame Jules, Madame de la Chanterie, Eve Chardon, Mademoiselle d'Esgrignon, Madame Firmiani, Agathe Rouget, Renée de Maucombe; besides several figures in the middle-distance, who, though less conspicuous than these, nevertheless, offer the reader an example of domestic virtue; Joseph Lebas, Genestas, Benassis, Bonnet the curé, Minoret the doctor, Pillerault, David Séchard, the two Birotteaus, Chaperon the priest, Judge Popinot, Bourgeat, the Sauviats, the Tascherons, and many more. Do not all these solve the difficult literary problem which consists in making a virtuous person interesting?

It was no small task to depict the two or three thousand conspicuous types of a period; for this is, in fact, the number presented to us by each generation, and which the Human Comedy will require. This crowd of actors, of characters, this multitude of lives, needed a setting—if I may be pardoned the expression, a gallery. Hence the very natural division, as already known, into Scenes of Private Life, of Provincial Life, of Parisian, Political, Military, and Country Life. Under these six heads are classified all the studies of manners which form the history of society at large, of all its *faits et gestes*, as our ancestors would have said. These six classes correspond, indeed, to familiar conceptions. Each has its own sense and meaning, and answers to an epoch in the life of man. I may repeat here, but very briefly, what was written by Felix Davin—a young genius snatched from literature by an early death. After being informed of my plan, he said that the Scenes of Private Life represented childhood and youth and their errors, as the Scenes of Provincial Life represented the age of passion, scheming, self-interest, and ambition. Then the Scenes of Parisian Life give a picture of the tastes and vice and unbridled powers which conduce to the habits peculiar to great cities, where the extremes of good and evil meet. Each of these divisions has its local colour—Paris and the Provinces—a great social antithesis which held for me immense resources.

And not man alone, but the principal events of life, fall into classes by types. There are situations which occur in every life, typical phases, and this is one of the details I most sought after. I have tried to give an idea of the different districts of our fine country. My work has its geography, as it has its genealogy and its families, its places and things, its persons and their deeds; as it has its heraldry, its nobles and commonalty, its artisans and peasants, its politicians and dandies, its army—in short, a whole world of its own.

After describing social life in these three portions, I had to delineate certain exceptional lives, which comprehend the interests of many people, or of everybody, and are in a degree outside the general law. Hence we have Scenes of Political Life. This vast picture of society being finished and complete, was it not needful to display it in its most violent phase, beside itself, as it were, either in self-defence or for the sake of conquest? Hence the Scenes of Military Life, as yet the most incomplete portion of my work, but for which room will be allowed in this edition, that it may form part of it when done. Finally, the Scenes of Country Life are, in a way, the evening of this long day, if I may so call the social drama. In that part are to be found the purest natures, and the application of the great principles of order, politics, and morality.

Such is the foundation, full of actors, full of comedies and tragedies, on which are raised the Philosophical Studies—the second part of my work, in which the social instrument of all these effects is displayed, and the ravages of the mind are painted, feeling after feeling; the first of this series, *Wild Ass's Skin*, to some extent forms a link between the Philosophical Studies and Studies of Manners, by a work of almost Oriental fancy, in which life itself is shown in a mortal struggle with the very element of all passion.

Besides these, there will be a series of Analytical Studies, of which I will say nothing, for one only is published as yet—The Physiology of Marriage.

In the course of time I propose writing two more works of this class. First, the Pathology of Social Life, then an Anatomy of Educational Bodies, and a Monograph on Virtue.

In looking forward to what remains to be done, my readers will perhaps echo what my publishers say, "Please God to spare you!" I only ask to be less tormented by men and things than I have hitherto been since I began this terrific labour. I have had this in my favour, and I thank God for it, that the talents of the time, the finest characters and the truest friends, as noble in their private lives as the former are in public life, have wrung my hand and said, Courage!

And why should I not confess that this friendship, and the testimony here and

there of persons unknown to me, have unheld me in my career, both against myself and against unjust attacks; against the calumny which has often persecuted
me, against discouragement, and against the too eager hopefulness whose utterances are misinterpreted as those of overweening conceit? I had resolved to display stolid stoicism in the face of abuse and insults; but on two occasions base
slanders have necessitated a reply. Though the advocates of forgiveness of injuries
may regret that I should have displayed my skill in literary fence, there are many
Christians who are of opinion that we live in times when it is as well to show
sometimes that silence springs from generosity.

The vastness of a plan which includes both a history and a criticism of society,
an analysis of its evils, and a discussion of its principles, authorises me, I think, in
giving to my work the title under which it now appears—"THE HUMAN COMEDY."
Is this too ambitious? Is it not exact? That, when it is complete, the public must
pronounce.

HIPPOLYTE TAINE

Art as Historical Product

History, within a hundred years in Germany, and within sixty years in France,
has undergone a transformation, owing to a study of literatures.

The discovery has been made that a literary work is not a mere play of the
imagination, the isolated caprice of an excited brain, but a transcript of contemporary manners and customs and the sign of a particular state of intellect.
The conclusion derived from this is that, through literary monuments, we can
retrace the way in which men felt and thought many centuries ago. This method
has been tried and found successful.

We have meditated over these ways of feeling and thinking and have accepted
them as facts of prime significance. We have found that they were dependent on
most important events, that they explain these, and that these explain them, and
that henceforth it was necessary to give them their place in history, and one of the
highest. This place has been assigned to them, and hence all is changed in history—the aim, the method, the instrumentalities, and the conceptions of laws
and of causes. It is this change as now going on, and which must continue to go
on, that is here attempted to be set forth.

On turning over the large stiff pages of a folio volume, or the yellow leaves of a
manuscript, in short, a poem, a code of laws, a confession of faith, what is your
first comment? You say to yourself that the work before you is not of its own
creation. It is simply a mold like a fossil shell, an imprint similar to one of those
forms embedded in a stone by an animal which once lived and perished. Beneath
the shell was an animal and behind the document there was a man. Why do you

From "Introduction," *History of English Literature* [1864], translated from the French by
Henry von Laun, revised edition, New York and London, 1900, Vol. I, pp. 1-2, 5-9, 13-19,
24-7.

study the shell unless to form some idea of the animal? In the same way do you study the document in order to comprehend the man; both shell and document are dead fragments and of value only as indications of the complete living being. The aim is to reach this being; this is what you strive to reconstruct. It is a mistake to study the document as if it existed alone by itself. That is treating things merely as a pedant, and you subject yourself to the illusions of a book-worm. At bottom mythologies and languages are not existences; the only realities are human beings who have employed words and imagery adapted to their organs and to suit the original cast of their intellects. A creed is nothing in itself. Who made it? Look at this or that portrait of the sixteenth century, the stern, energetic features of an archbishop or of an English martyr. Nothing exists except through the individual; it is necessary to know the individual himself. Let the parentage of creeds be established, or the classification of poems, or the growth of constitutions, or the transformations of idioms, and we have only cleared the ground. True history begins when the historian has discerned beyond the mists of ages the living, active man, endowed with passions, furnished with habits, special in voice, feature, gesture, and costume, distinctive and complete, like anybody that you have just encountered in the street. Let us strive then, as far as possible, to get rid of this great interval of time which prevents us from observing the man with our eyes, the eyes of our own head. What revelations do we find in the calendered leaves of a modern poem? A modern poet, a man like De Musset, Victor Hugo, Lamartine, or Heine, graduated from a college and travelled, wearing a dress-coat and gloves, favored by ladies, bowing fifty times and uttering a dozen witticisms in an evening, reading daily newspapers, generally occupying an apartment on the second story, not over-cheerful on account of his nerves, and especially because, in this dense democracy in which we stifle each other, the discredit of official rank exaggerates his pretensions by raising his importance, and, owing to the delicacy of his personal sensations, leading him to regard himself as a Deity. Such is what we detect behind modern meditations and sonnets. . . .

On observing the visible man with your own eyes what do you try to find in him? The invisible man. These words which your ears catch, those gestures, those airs of the head, his attire and sensible operations of all kinds, are, for you, merely so many expressions; these express something, a soul. An inward man is hidden beneath the outward man, and the latter simply manifests the former. You have observed the house in which he lives, his furniture, his costume, in order to discover his habits and tastes, the degree of his refinement or rusticity, his extravagance or economy, his follies or his cleverness. You have listened to his conversation and noted the inflections of his voice, the attitudes he has assumed, so as to judge of his spirit, self-abandonment or gayety, his energy or his rigidity. You consider his writings, works of art, financial and political schemes, with a view to measure the reach and limits of his intelligence, his creative power and self-command, to ascertain the usual order, kind, and force of his conceptions, in what way he thinks and how he resolves. All these externals are so many avenues converging to one centre, and you follow these only to reach that centre; here is the real man, namely, that group of faculties and of sentiments which produces the rest. Behold a new world, an infinite world; for each visible action involves an infinite train of reasonings and emotions, new or old sensations which have combined to bring this into light and which, like long ledges of rock sunk deep in the earth, have cropped out above the surface and attained their level. It is this sub-terranean world which forms the second aim, the special object of the historian. If his critical education suffices, he is able to discriminate under every ornament in architecture, under every stroke of the brush in a picture, under each phrase of literary composition, the particular sentiment out of which the ornament, the stroke, and the phrase have sprung; he is a spectator of the inward drama which has developed itself in the breast of the artist or writer; the choice of words, the length or shortness of the period, the species of metaphor, the accent of a verse, the chain of reasoning—all are to him an indication; while his eyes are reading the text his mind and soul are following the steady flow and ever-changing series of emotions and conceptions from which this text has issued; he is working out its psychology. Should you desire to study this operation, regard the promoter and model of all the high culture of the epoch, Goethe, who, before composing his "Iphigenia," spent days in making drawings of the most perfect statues and who, at last, his eyes filled with the noble forms of antique scenery and his mind pene-trated by the harmonious beauty of antique life, succeeded in reproducing inter-nally, with such exactness, the habits and yearnings of Greek imagination as to provide us with an almost twin sister of the "Antigone" of Sophocles and of the goddesses of Phidias. This exact and demonstrated divination of bygone senti-ments has, in our days, given a new life to history. There was almost complete ignorance of this in the last century; men of every race and of every epoch were represented as about alike, the Greek, the barbarian, the Hindoo, the man of the Renaissance and the man of the eighteenth century, cast in the same mold and after the same pattern, and after a certain abstract conception which served for the whole human species. There was a knowledge of man but not of men. There was no penetration into the soul itself; nothing of the infinite diversity and won-derful complexity of souls had been detected; it was not known that the moral organization of a people or of an age is as special and distinct as the physical structure of a family of plants or of an order of animals.

History to-day, like zoölogy, has found its anatomy, and whatever branch of it is studied, whether philology, languages or mythologies, it is in this way that labor must be given to make it produce new fruit. Among so many writers who, since Herder, Ottfried Müller, and Goethe have steadily followed and rectified this great effort, let the reader take two historians and two works, one "The Life and Letters of Cromwell" by Carlyle, and the other the "Port Royal" of Sainte-Beuve. He will see how precisely, how clearly, and how profoundly we detect the soul of a man beneath his actions and works; how, under an old general and in place of an ambitious man vulgarly hypocritical, we find one tormented by the disordered reveries of a gloomy imagination, but practical in instinct and faculties, thor-oughly English and strange and incomprehensible to whoever has not studied the climate and the race; how, with about a hundred scattered letters and a dozen or more mutilated speeches, we follow him from his farm and his team to his gen-eral's tent and to his Protector's throne, in his transformation and in his develop-ment, in his struggles of conscience and in his statesman's resolutions, in such a way that the mechanism of his thought and action becomes visible and the ever renewed and fitful tragedy, within which racked this great gloomy soul, passes like the tragedies of Shakespeare into the souls of those who behold them. We see how, behind convent disputes and the obstinacy of nuns, we recover one of the great provinces of human psychology; how fifty or more characters, rendered invisible through the uniformity of a narration careful of the properties, come forth in full daylight, each standing out clear in its countless diversities; how, underneath theological dissertations and monotonous sermons, we discern the throbbings of ever-breathing hearts, the excitements and depressions of the religious life, the unforeseen reaction and pell-mell stir of natural feeling, the infiltrations of surrounding society, the intermittent triumphs of grace, presenting so many shades of difference that the fullest description and most flexible style can scarcely garner in the vast harvest which the critic has caused to germinate in this abandoned field. And the same elsewhere. Germany, with its genius, so pliant, so broad, so prompt in transformations, so fitted for the reproduction of the remotest and strangest states of human thought; England, with its matter-of-fact mind, so suited to the grappling with moral problems, to making them clear by figures, weights, and measures, by geography and statistics, by texts and common sense; France, at length, with its Parisian culture and drawing-room habits, with its unceasing analysis of characters and of works, with its ever ready irony at detecting weaknesses, with its skilled finesse in discriminating shades of thought—all have ploughed over the same ground, and we now begin to comprehend that no region of history exists in which this deep sub-soil should not be reached if we would secure adequate crops between the furrows.

Such is the second step, and we are now in train to follow it out. Such is the proper aim of contemporary criticism. . . . Ulterior evolution must start from this point. I have often attempted to expose what this evolution is; in my opinion, it is a new road open to history and which I shall strive to describe more in detail.

After having observed in a man and noted down one, two, three and then a multitude of sentiments, do these suffice and does your knowledge of him seem complete? Does a memorandum book constitute a psychology? It is not a psychology, and here, as elsewhere, the search for causes must follow the collection of facts. It matters not what the facts may be, whether physical or moral, they always spring from causes; there are causes for ambition, for courage, for veracity, as well as for digestion, for muscular action, and for animal heat. Vice and virtue are products like vitriol and sugar; every complex fact grows out of the simple facts with which it is affiliated and on which it depends.

We must therefore try to ascertain what simple facts underlie moral qualities the same as we ascertain those that underlie physical qualities, and, for example, let us take the first fact that comes to hand, a religious system of music, that of a Protestant church. A certain inward cause has inclined the minds of worshippers towards these grave, monotonous melodies, a cause much greater than its effect; that is to say, a general conception of the veritable outward forms of worship which man owes to God; it is this general conception which has shaped the architecture of the temple, cast out statues, dispensed with paintings, effaced ornaments, shortened ceremonies, confined the members of a congregation to high pews which cut off the view, and governed the thousand details of decoration, posture, and all other externals. This conception itself again proceeds from a more general cause, an idea of human conduct in general, inward and outward, prayers, actions, dispositions of every sort that man is bound to maintain toward the Deity; it is this which has enthroned the doctrine of grace, lessened the importance of the clergy, transformed the sacraments, suppressed observances, and changed the religion of discipline into one of morality. This conception, in its turn, depends on a third one, still more general, that of moral perfection as this is found in a perfect God, the impeccable judge, the stern overseer, who regards every soul as sinful, meriting punishment, incapable of virtue or of salvation, except through a stricken conscience which He provokes and the renewal of the heart which He brings about. Here is the master conception, consisting of duty erected into the absolute sovereign of human life, and which prostrates all other ideals at the feet of the moral ideal. Here we reach what is deepest in man; for, to explain this conception, we must consider the race he belongs to, say the German, the Northman, the formation and character of his intellect, his ways in general of thinking and feeling, that tardiness and frigidity of sensation which keeps him from rashly and easily falling under the empire of sensual enjoyments, that bluntness of taste, that irregularity and those outbursts of conception which arrest in him the birth of refined and harmonious forms and methods; that disdain of appearances, that yearning for truth, that attachment to abstract, bare ideas which develop conscience in him at the expense of everything else.

Here the search comes to an end. We have reached a certain primitive disposition, a particular trait belonging to sensations of all kinds, to every conception peculiar to an age or to a race, to characteristics inseparable from every idea and feeling that stir in the human breast. Such are the grand causes, for these are universal and permanent causes, present in every case and at every moment, everywhere and always active, indestructible, and inevitably dominant in the end, since, whatever accidents cross their path, being limited and partial, end in yielding to the obscure and incessant repetition of their energy; so that the general structure of things and all the main features of events are their work, all religions and philosophies, all poetic and industrial systems, all forms of society and of the family, all, in fine, being imprints bearing the stamp of their seal. . . .

Three different sources contribute to the production of this elementary moral state, race, environment, and epoch. What we call race consists of those innate and hereditary dispositions which man brings with him into the world and which are generally accompanied with marked differences of temperament and of bodily structure. They vary in different nations. Naturally, there are varieties of men as there are varieties of cattle and horses, some brave and intelligent, and others timid and of limited capacity; some capable of superior conceptions and creations, and others reduced to rudimentary ideas and contrivances; some specially fitted for certain works, and more richly furnished with certain instincts, as we see in the better endowed species of dogs, some for running and others for fighting, some for hunting and others for guarding houses and flocks. We have here a distinct force; so distinct that, in spite of the enormous deviations which both the other motors impress upon it, we still recognize, and which a race like the Aryan people, scattered from the Ganges to the Hebrides, established under all climates, ranged along every degree of civilization, transformed by thirty centuries of revolutions, shows nevertheless in its languages, in its religions, in its literatures, and in its philosophies, the community of blood and of intellect which still to-day binds together all its offshoots. However they may differ, their parentage is not lost; barbarism, culture and grafting, differences of atmosphere and of soil, fortunate or unfortunate occurrences, have operated in vain; the grand characteristics of the original form have lasted, and we find that the two or three leading features of the primitive imprint are again apparent under the subsequent imprints with which time has overlaid them.

There is nothing surprising in this extraordinary tenacity. Although the immensity of the distance allows us to catch only a glimpse in a dubious light of the origin of the species, the events of history throw sufficient light on events anterior to history to explain the almost unshaken solidity of primordial traits. At the moment of encountering them, fifteen, twenty, and thirty centuries before our era, in an Aryan, Egyptian, or Chinese, they represent the work of a much greater number of centuries, perhaps the work of many myriads of centuries. For, as soon as an animal is born it must adapt itself to its surroundings; it breathes in another way, it renews itself differently, it is otherwise stimulated according as the atmosphere, the food, and the temperature are different. A different climate and situation create different necessities and hence activities of a different kind; and hence, again, a system of different habits, and finally, a system of different aptitudes and instincts. Man, thus compelled to put himself in equilibrium with circumstances, contracts a corresponding temperament and character, and his character, like his temperament, are acquisitions all the more stable because of the outward impression being more deeply imprinted in him by more frequent repetitions and transmitted to his offspring by more ancient heredity. So that at each moment of time, the character of a people may be considered as a summary of all antecedent actions and sensations; that is to say, as a quantity and as a weighty mass, not infinite, since all things in nature are limited, but disproportionate to the rest and almost impossible to raise, since each minute of an almost infinite past has contributed to render it heavier, and, in order to turn the scale, it would require, on the other side, a still greater accumulation of actions and sensations. Such is the first and most abundant source of these master faculties from which historic events are derived; and we see at once that if it is powerful it is owing to its not being a mere source, but a sort of lake, and like a deep reservoir wherein other sources have poured their waters for a multitude of centuries.

When we have thus verified the internal structure of a race we must consider the environment in which it lives. For man is not alone in the world; nature envelops him and other men surround him; accidental and secondary folds come and overspread the primitive and permanent fold, while physical or social circumstances derange or complete the natural groundwork surrendered to them. At one time climate has had its effect. Although the history of Aryan nations can be only obscurely traced from their common country to their final abodes, we can nevertheless affirm that the profound difference which is apparent between the Germanic races on the one hand, and the Hellenic and Latin races on the other, proceeds in great part from the differences between the countries in which they have established themselves—the former in cold and moist countries, in the depths of gloomy forests and swamps, or on the borders of a wild ocean, confined to melancholic or rude sensations, inclined to drunkenness and gross feeding, leading a militant and carnivorous life; the latter, on the contrary, living amidst the finest scenery, alongside of a brilliant, sparkling sea inviting navigation and commerce, exempt from the grosser cravings of the stomach, disposed at the start to social habits and customs, to political organization, to the sentiments and faculties which develop the art of speaking, the capacity for enjoyment and invention in the sciences, in art, and in literature.

At another time, political events have operated, as in the two Italian civilizations: the first one tending wholly to action, to conquest, to government, and to legislation, through the primitive situation of a city of refuge, a frontier emporium, and of an armed aristocracy which, importing and enrolling foreigners and the vanquished under it, sets two hostile bodies facing each other, with no outlet for its internal troubles and rapacious instincts but systematic warfare; the second one, excluded from unity and political ambition on a grand scale by the permanency of its municipal system, by the cosmopolite situation of its pope and by the military intervention of neighboring states, and following the bent of its magnificent and harmonious genius, is wholly carried over to the worship of voluptuousness and beauty. Finally, at another time, social conditions have imposed their stamp as, eighteen centuries ago, by Christianity, and twenty-five centuries ago by Buddhism, when, around the Mediterranean as in Hindostan, the extreme effects of Aryan conquest and organization led to intolerable oppression, the crushing of the individual, utter despair, the whole world under the ban of a curse, with the development of metaphysics and visions, until man, in this dungeon of despondency, feeling his heart melt, conceived of abnegation, charity, tender love, gentleness, humility, human brotherhood, here in the idea of universal nothingness, and there under that of the fatherhood of God. Look around at the regulative instincts and faculties implanted in a race; in brief, the turn of mind according to which it thinks and acts at the present day; we shall find most frequently that its work is due to one of these prolonged situations, to these enveloping circumstances, to these persistent gigantic pressures brought to bear on a mass of men who, one by one, and all collectively, from one generation to another, have been unceasingly bent and fashioned by them, in Spain a crusade of eight centuries against the Mohammedans, prolonged yet longer even to the exhaustion of the nation through the expulsion of the Moors, through the spoliation of the Jews, through the establishment of the Inquisition, through the Catholic wars; in England, a political establishment of eight centuries which maintains man erect and respectful, independent and obedient, all accustomed to struggling together in a body under the sanction of law; in France, a Latin organization which, at first imposed on docile barbarians, then levelled to the ground under the universal demolition, forms itself anew under the latent workings of national instinct, developing under hereditary monarchs and ending in a sort of equalized, centralized, administrative republic under dynasties exposed to revolutions. Such are the most efficacious among the observable causes which mold the primitive man; they are to nations what education, pursuit, condition, and abode are to individuals, and seem to comprise all, since the external forces which fashion human matter, and by which the outward acts on the inward, are comprehended in them.

There is, nevertheless, a third order of causes, for, with the forces within and without, there is the work these have already produced together, which work itself contributes towards producing the ensuing work; beside the permanent impulsion and the given environment there is the acquired momentum. When national character and surrounding circumstances operate it is not on a *tabula rasa*, but on one already bearing imprints. According as this *tabula* is taken at one or at another moment so is the imprint different, and this suffices to render the total effect different. Consider, for example, two moments of a literature or of an art, French tragedy under Corneille and under Voltaire, and Greek drama under Aeschylus and under Euripides, Latin poetry under Lucretius and under Claudian, and Italian painting under Da Vinci and under Guido. Assuredly, there is no change of general conception at either of these two extreme points; ever the same human type must be portrayed or represented in action; the cast of the verse, the dramatic structure, the physical form have all persisted. But there is this among these differences, that one of the artists is a precursor and the other a successor, that the first one has no model and the second one has a model; that the former sees things face to face, and that the latter sees them through the intermediation of the former, that many departments of art have become more perfect, that the simplicity and grandeur of the impression have diminished, that what is pleasing and refined in form has augmented—in short, that the first work has determined the second. In this respect, it is with a people as with a plant; the same sap at the same temperature and in the same soil produces, at different stages of its successive elaborations, different developments, buds, flowers, fruits, and seeds, in such a way that the condition of the following is always that of the preceding and is born of its death.

Now, if you no longer regard a brief moment, as above, but one of those grand periods of development which embraces one or many centuries like the Middle Ages, or our last classic period, the conclusion is the same. A certain dominating conception has prevailed throughout; mankind, during two hundred years, during five hundred years, have represented to themselves a certain ideal figure of man, in mediæval times the knight and the monk, in our classic period the courtier and refined talker; this creative and universal conception has monopolized the entire field of action and thought, and, after spreading its involuntarily systematic works over the world, it languished and then died out, and now a new idea has arisen destined to a like domination and to equally multiplied creations. Note here that the latter depends in part on the former, and that it is the former, which, combining its effect with those of national genius and surrounding circumstances, will impose their bent and their direction on new-born things. It is according to this law that great historic currents are formed, meaning by this, the long rule of a form of intellect or of a master idea, like that period of spontaneous creations called the Renaissance, or that period of oratorical classifications called the Classic Age, or that series of mystic systems called the Alexandrine and Christian epoch, or that series of mythological efflorescences found at the origins of Germany, India, and Greece. Here as elsewhere, we are dealing merely with a mechanical problem: the total effect is a compound wholly determined by the grandeur and direction of the forces which produce it. The sole difference which separates these moral problems from physical problems lies in this, that in the former the directions and grandeur cannot be estimated by or stated in figures with the same precision as in the latter. If a want, a faculty, is a quantity capable of degrees, the same as pressure or weight, this quantity is not measurable like that of the pressure or weight. We cannot fix it in an exact or approximative formula; we can obtain or give of it only a literary impression; we are reduced to noting and citing the prominent facts which make it manifest and which nearly, or roughly, indicate about what grade on the scale it must be ranged at. And yet, notwithstanding the methods of notation are not the same in the moral sciences as in the physical sciences, nevertheless, as matter is the same in both, and is equally composed of forces, directions and magnitudes, we can still show that in one as in the other, the final effect takes place according to the same law. This is great or small, according as the fundamental forces are great or small and act more or less precisely in the same sense, according as the distinct effects of race, environment and epoch combine to enforce each other or combine to neutralize each other.

Thus are explained the long impotences and the brilliant successes which appear irregularly and with no apparent reason in the life of a people; the causes of these consist in internal concordances and contrarieties. There was one of these concordances when, in the seventeenth century, the social disposition and conversational spirit innate in France encountered drawing-room formalities and the moment of oratorical analysis; when, in the nineteenth century, the flexible, profound genius of Germany encountered the age of philosophic synthesis and of cosmopolite criticism. One of these contrarieties happened when, in the seventeenth century, the blunt, isolated genius of England awkwardly tried to don the new polish of urbanity, and when, in the sixteenth century, the lucid, prosaic French intellect tried to gestate a living poesy. It is this secret concordance of creative forces which produced the exquisite courtesy and noble cast of literature under Louis XIV and Bossuet, and the grandiose metaphysics and broad critical sympathy under Hegel and Goethe. It is this secret contrariety of creative forces which produced the literary incompleteness, the licentious plays, the abortive drama of Dryden and Wycherly, the poor Greek importations, the gropings, the minute beauties and fragments of Ronsard and the Pleiad. We may confidently affirm that the unknown creations toward which the current of coming ages is bearing us will spring from and be governed by these primordial forces; that, if these forces could be measured and computed we might deduce from them, as from a formula, the characters of future civilization; and that if, notwithstanding the evident rudeness of our notations, and the fundamental inexactitude of our measures, we would nowadays form some idea of our general destinies, we must base our conjectures on an examination of these forces. For, in enumerating them, we run through the full circle of active forces; and when the race, the environment, and the moment have been considered—that is to say the inner mainspring, the pressure from without, and the impulsion already acquired—we have exhausted not only all real causes but again all possible causes of movement. . . .

History has reached this point at the present day, or rather it is nearly there, on the threshold of this inquest. The question as now stated is this: Given a literature, a philosophy, a society, an art, a certain group of arts, what is the moral state of things which produces it? And what are the conditions of race, epoch, and environment the best adapted to produce this moral state? There is a distinct moral state for each of these formations and for each of their branches; there is one for art in general as well as for each particular art; for architecture, painting, sculpture, music, and poetry, each with a germ of its own in the large field of human psychology; each has its own law, and it is by virtue of this law that we see each shoot up, apparently haphazard, singly and alone, amidst the miscarriages of their neighbors, like painting in Flanders and Holland in the seventeenth century, like poetry in England in the sixteenth century, like music in Germany in the eighteenth century. At this moment, and in these countries, the conditions for one art and not for the others are fulfilled, and one branch only has bloomed out amidst the general sterility. It is these laws of human vegetation which history must now search for; it is this special psychology of each special formation which must be got at; it is the composition of a complete table of these peculiar conditions that must now be worked out.

There is nothing more delicate and nothing more difficult. Montesquieu undertook it, but in his day the interest in history was too recent for him to be successful; nobody, indeed, had any idea of the road that was to be followed, and even at the present day we scarcely begin to obtain a glimpse of it. Just as astronomy, at bottom, is a mechanical problem, and physiology, likewise, a chemical problem, so is history, at bottom, a problem of psychology. There is a particular system of inner impressions and operations which fashions the artist, the believer, the musician, the painter, the nomad, the social man; for each of these, the filiation, intensity, and interdependence of ideas and of emotions are different; each has his own moral history, and his own special organization, along with some master tendency and with some dominant trait. To explain each of these would require a chapter devoted to a profound internal analysis, and that is a work that can scarcely be called sketched out at the present day. But one man, Stendhal, through a certain turn of mind and a peculiar education, has attempted it, and even yet most of his readers find his works paradoxical and obscure. His talent and ideas were too premature. His admirable insight, his profound sayings carelessly thrown out, the astonishing precision of his notes and logic, were not understood; people were not aware that, under the appearances and talk of a man of the world, he explained the most complex of internal mechanisms; that his finger touched the great mainspring, that he brought scientific processes to bear in the history of the heart, the art of employing figures, of decomposing, of deducing; that he was the first to point out fundamental causes such as nationalities, climates, and temperaments; in short, that he treated sentiments as they should be treated, that is to say, as a naturalist and physicist, by making classifications and estimating forces. On account of all this he was pronounced dry and eccentric and allowed to live in isolation, composing novels, books of travel and taking notes, for which he counted upon, and has obtained, about a dozen or so of readers. And yet his works are those in which we of the present day may find the most satisfactory efforts that have been made to clear the road I have just striven to describe. Nobody has taught one better how to observe with one's own eyes, first, to regard humanity around us and life as it is, and next, old and authentic documents; how to read more than merely the black and white of the page; how to detect under old print and the scrawl of the text the veritable sentiment and the train of thought, the mental state in which the words were penned. In his writings, as in those of Sainte-Beuve and in those of the German critics, the reader will find how much is to be derived from a literary document; if this document is rich and we know how to interpret it, we will find in it the psychology of a particular soul, often that of an age, and sometimes that of a race. In this respect, a great poem, a good novel, the confessions of a superior man, are more instructive than a mass of historians and histories; I would give fifty volumes of charters and a hundred diplomatic files for the memoirs of Cellini, the epistles of Saint Paul, the table-talk of Luther, or the comedies of Aristophanes.

Herein lies the value of literary productions. They are instructive because they are beautiful; their usefulness increases with their perfection; and if they provide us with documents, it is because they are monuments. The more visible a book renders sentiments the more literary it is, for it is the special office of literature to take note of sentiments. The more important the sentiments noted in a book the higher its rank in literature, for it is by representing what sort of a life a nation or an epoch leads, that a writer rallies to himself the sympathies of a nation or of an epoch. Hence, among the documents which bring before our eyes the sentiments of preceding generations, a literature and especially a great literature, is incomparably the best. It resembles those admirable instruments of remarkable sensitiveness which physicists make use of to detect and measure the most profound and delicate changes that occur in a human body. There is nothing approaching this in constitutions or religions; the articles of a code or of a catechism do no more than depict mind in gross and without finesse; if there are documents which show life and spirit in politics and in creeds, they are the eloquent discourses of the pulpit and the tribune, memoirs and personal confessions, all belonging to literature, so that, outside of itself, literature embodies whatever is good elsewhere. It is mainly in studying literatures that we are able to produce moral history, and arrive at some knowledge of the psychological laws on which events depend.

I have undertaken to write a history of a literature and to ascertain the psychology of a people; in selecting this one, it is not without a motive. A people had to be taken possessing a vast and complete literature, which is rarely found. There are few nations which, throughout their existence, have thought and written well in the full sense of the word. Among the ancients, Latin literature is null at the beginning, and afterward borrowed and an imitation. Among the moderns, German literature is nearly a blank for two centuries.[1] Italian and Spanish literatures come to an end in the middle of the seventeenth century. Ancient Greece, and modern France and England, alone offer a complete series of great and expressive monuments. I have chosen the English because, as this still exists and is open to direct observation, it can be better studied than that of an extinct civilization of which fragments only remain; and because, being different, it offers better than that of France very marked characteristics in the eyes of a Frenchman. Moreover, outside of what is peculiar to English civilization, apart from a spontaneous development, it presents a forced deviation due to the latest and most effective conquest to which the country was subject; the three given conditions out of which it issues—race, climate, and the Norman conquest—are clearly and distinctly visible in its literary monuments; so that we study in this history the two most potent motors of human transformation, namely, nature and constraint, and we study them, without any break or uncertainty, in a series of authentic and complete monuments. I have tried to define these primitive motors, to show their gradual effects, and explain how their insensible operation has brought religions and literary productions into full light, and how the inward mechanism is developed by which the barbarous Saxon became the Englishman of the present day.

[1] From 1550 to 1750. TRANSLATOR'S NOTE.

GUSTAVE FLAUBERT

Shortcomings of Taine's Theory

I am glad if Taine's *English Literature* interests you. His book is excellent and solid, though I cannot accept his premises. There is something more in Art than the surroundings in which it is produced and the psychological antecedents of the artist. The type and the school are explicable on that basis, but never the individuality, the specific quality which makes one what one is. This method leads one perforce to set little store by talent. The only significance of the master-piece is as a historical document. It is the radically opposite standpoint to La Harpe's and to the old criticism. In the old days it was believed that literature was an entirely individual matter, and that books dropped like thunderbolts from the skies. Now we have come to deny all will and all absolutes. The truth, I think, lies in the middle.

Letter to Mme. Roger des Genettes [1864], *Letters*, ed. Richard Rumbold and translated from the French by J. M. Cohen, London, 1950, p. 145; reprinted by permission of George Weidenfeld and Nicolson Ltd. and Philosophical Library, New York.

LEO TOLSTOY

Man as the Creature of History

Had Napoleon not taken offense at the demand that he should withdraw beyond the Vistula, and not ordered his troops to advance, there would have been no war; but had all his sergeants objected to serving a second term then also there could have been no war. Nor could there have been a war had there been no English intrigues and no Duke of Oldenburg, and had Alexander not felt in-sulted, and had there not been an autocratic government in Russia, or a Revolu-tion in France and a subsequent dictatorship and Empire, or all the things that produced the French Revolution, and so on. Without each of these causes noth-ing could have happened. So all these causes—myriads of causes—coincided to bring it about. And so there was no one cause for that occurrence, but it had to occur because it had to. Millions of men, renouncing their human feelings and reason, had to go from west to east to slay their fellows, just as some centuries previously hordes of men had come from the east to the west, slaying their fellows.

The actions of Napoleon and Alexander, on whose words the event seemed to hang, were as little voluntary as the actions of any soldier who was drawn into the campaign by lot or by conscription. This could not be otherwise, for in order that the will of Napoleon and Alexander (on whom the event seemed to depend) should be carried out, the concurrence of innumerable circumstances

From *War and Peace* [1865-69], translated from the Russian by Aylmer Maude, London and New York, 1933, Vol. II, pp. 257-9; reprinted by permission of Oxford University Press.

was needed without any one of which the event could not have taken place. It was necessary that millions of men in whose hands lay the real power—the soldiers who fired, or transported provisions and guns—should consent to carry out the will of these weak individuals, and should have been induced to do so by an infinite number of diverse and complex causes.

We are forced to fall back on fatalism as an explanation of irrational events (that is to say, events the reasonableness of which we do not understand). The more we try to explain such events in history reasonably, the more unreasonable and incomprehensible do they become to us.

Each man lives for himself, using his freedom to attain his personal aims, and feels with his whole being that he can now do or abstain from doing this or that action; but as soon as he has done it, that action performed at a certain moment in time becomes irrevocable and belongs to history, in which it has not a free but a predestined significance.

There are two sides to the life of every man, his individual life, which is the more free the more abstract its interests, and his elemental hive life in which he inevitably obeys laws laid down for him.

Man lives consciously for himself, but is an unconscious instrument in the attainment of the historic, universal, aims of humanity. A deed done is irrevocable, and its result coinciding in time with the actions of millions of other men assumes an historic significance. The higher a man stands on the social ladder, the more people he is connected with and the more power he has over others, the more evident is the predestination and inevitability of his every action.

"The king's heart is in the hands of the Lord."

A king is history's slave.

History, that is, the unconscious, general, hive life of mankind, uses every moment of the life of kings as a tool for its own purposes.

Though Napoleon at that time, in 1812, was more convinced than ever that it depended on him, *verser* (*ou ne pas verser*) *le sang des ses peuples* [to shed (or not to shed) the blood of his peoples]—as Alexander expressed it in the last letter he wrote him—he had never been so much in the grip of inevitable laws, which compelled him, while thinking that he was acting on his own volition, to perform for the hive life—that is to say, for history—whatever had to be performed.

The people of the west moved eastwards to slay their fellow men, and by the law of coincidence thousands of minute causes fitted in and coordinated to produce that movement and war: reproaches for the nonobservance of the Continental System, the Duke of Oldenburg's wrongs, the movement of troops into Prussia [undertaken, as it seemed to Napoleon, only for the purpose of securing an armed peace], the French Emperor's love and habit of war coinciding with his people's inclinations, allurement by the grandeur of the preparations, and the expenditure on those preparations and the need of obtaining advantages to compensate for that expenditure, the intoxicating honors he received in Dresden, the diplomatic negotiations which, in the opinion of contemporaries, were carried on with a sincere desire to attain peace, but which only wounded the self-love of both sides, and millions and millions of other causes that adapted themselves to the event that was happening or coincided with it.

When an apple has ripened and falls, why does it fall? Because of its attraction to the earth, because its stalk withers, because it is dried by the sun, because it grows heavier, because the wind shakes it, or because the boy standing below wants to eat it?

Nothing is the cause. All this is only the coincidence of conditions in which all vital organic and elemental events occur. And the botanist who finds that the apple falls because the cellular tissue decays and so forth is equally right with the child who stands under the tree and says the apple fell because he wanted to eat it and prayed for it. Equally right or wrong is he who says that Napoleon went to Moscow because he wanted to, and perished because Alexander desired his destruction, and he who says that an undermined hill weighing a million tons fell because the last navvy struck it for the last time with his mattock. In historic events, the so-called great men are labels giving names to events, and like labels they have but the smallest connection with the event itself.

Every act of theirs, which appears to them an act of their own will, is in an historical sense involuntary and is related to the whole course of history and predestined from eternity.

THEODORE DREISER

Man as Natural Mechanism

At this time I had the fortune to discover Huxley and Tyndall and Herbert Spencer, whose introductory volume to his *Synthetic Philosophy* (*First Principles*) quite blew me, intellectually, to bits. Hitherto, until I had read Huxley, I had some lingering filaments of Catholicism trailing about me, faith in the existence of Christ, the soundness of his moral and sociologic deductions, the brotherhood of man. But on reading *Science and Hebrew Tradition* and *Science and Christian Tradition*, and finding both the Old and New Testaments to be not compendiums of revealed truth but mere records of religious experiences, and very erroneous ones at that, and then taking up *First Principles* and discovering that all I deemed substantial—man's place in nature, his importance in the universe, this too, too solid earth, man's very identity save as an infinitesimal speck of energy or a "suspended equation" drawn or blown here and there by larger forces in which he moved quite unconsciously as an atom—all questioned and dissolved into other and less understandable things, I was completely thrown down in my conceptions or non-conceptions of life.

Up to this time there had been in me a blazing and unchecked desire to get on and the feeling that in doing so we did get somewhere; now in its place was the definite conviction that spiritually one got nowhere, that there was no hereafter, that one lived and had his being because one had to, and that it was of no importance. Of one's ideals, struggles, deprivations, sorrows and joys, it could only be said that they were chemic compulsions, something which for some inexplicable but unimportant reason responded to and resulted from the hope of pleasure and the fear of pain. Man was a mechanism, undevised and uncreated, and a badly and carelessly driven one at that.

I fear that I cannot make you feel how these things came upon me in the course of a few weeks' reading and left me numb, my gravest fears as to the unsolvable disorder and brutality of life eternally verified. I felt as low and hopeless at times as a beggar of the streets. There was of course this other matter of necessity, internal chemical compulsion, to which I had to respond whether I would or no. I was daily facing a round of duties which now more than ever verified all that I had suspected and that these books proved. With a gloomy eye I began to watch how the chemical—and their children, the mechanical—forces operated through man and outside him, and this under my very eyes. Suicides seemed sadder since there was no care for them; failures the same. One of those periodic scandals breaking out in connection with the care of prisoners in some local or state jail, I saw how self-interest, the hope of pleasure or the fear of pain caused jailers or wardens or a sheriff to graft on prisoners, feed them rotten meat, torture them into silence and submission, and then, politics interfering (the hope of pleasure again and the fear of pain on the part of some), the whole thing hushed up, no least measure of the sickening truth breaking out in the subservient papers. Life could or would do nothing for those whom it so shamefully abused.

Again, there was a poor section, one street in the East Pittsburgh district, shut off by a railroad at one end (the latter erecting a high fence to protect itself from trespass) and by an arrogant property owner at the other end; those within were actually left without means of ingress and egress. Yet instead of denouncing either or both, the railroads being so powerful and the citizen prosperous and within his "rights," I was told to write a humorous article but not to "hurt anybody's feelings." Also before my eyes were always those regions of indescribable poverty and indescribable wealth previously mentioned, which were always carefully kept separate by the local papers, all the favors and compliments and commercial and social aids going to those who had, all the sniffs and indifferences and slights going to those who had not; and when I read Spencer I could only sigh. All I could think of was that since nature would not or could not do anything for man, he must, if he could, do something for himself; and of this I saw no prospect, he being a product of these self-same accidental, indifferent and bitterly cruel forces.

EDMOND AND JULES DE GONCOURT

Clinical Realism

We must ask pardon of the public for offering it this book, and give it due warning of what it will find therein.

The public loves fictitious novels! this is a true novel.

It loves books which make a pretence of introducing their readers to fashionable society: this book deals with the life of the street.

It loves little indecent books, memoirs of courtesans, alcove confessions, erotic obscenity, the scandal tucked away in pictures in a bookseller's shop window; that which is contained in the following pages is rigidly clean and pure. Do not expect the photograph of Pleasure *décolletée:* the following study is the clinic of Love.

Again, the public loves to read pleasant, soothing stories, adventures that end happily, imaginative works that disturb neither its digestion nor its peace of mind: this book furnishes entertainment of a melancholy, violent sort calculated to disarrange the habits and injure the health of the public.

The Preface to the first edition of *Germinie Lacerteux* [1864], translated from the French by John Chestershire, Philadelphia, 1897, pp. 5-7.

Why then have we written it? For no other purpose than to annoy the public and offend its tastes?

By no means.

Living as we do in the nineteenth century, in an age of universal suffrage, of democracy, of liberalism, we asked ourselves the question whether what are called "the lower classes" had no rights in the novel; if that world beneath a world, the common people, must needs remain subject to the literary interdict, and helpless against the contempt of authors who have hitherto said no word to imply that the common people possess a heart and soul. We asked ourselves whether, in these days of equality in which we live, there are classes unworthy the notice of the author and the reader, misfortunes too lowly, dramas too foul-mouthed, catastrophes too commonplace in the terror they inspire. We were curious to know if that conventional symbol of a forgotten literature, of a vanished Society, Tragedy, is definitely dead; if, in a country where castes no longer exist and aristocracy has no legal status, the miseries of the lowly and the poor would appeal to public interest, emotion, compassion, as forcibly as the miseries of the great and the rich; if, in a word, the tears that are shed in low life have the same power to cause tears to flow as the tears shed in high life.

These thoughts led us to venture upon the humble tale, *Sœur Philomène*, in 1861; they lead us to put forth *Germinie Lacerteux* today.

Now, let the book be spoken slightingly of; it matters little. At this day, when the sphere of the Novel is broadening and expanding, when it is beginning to be the serious, impassioned, living form of literary study and social investigation, when it is becoming, by virtue of analysis and psychological research, the true History of contemporary morals, when the novel has taken its place among the necessary elements of knowledge, it may properly demand its liberty and freedom of speech. And to encourage it in the search for Art and Truth, to authorize it to disclose misery and suffering which it is not well for the fortunate people of Paris to forget, and to show to people of fashion what the Sisters of Charity have the courage to see for themselves, what the queens of old compelled their children to touch with their eyes in the hospitals: the visible, palpitating human suffering that teaches charity; to confirm the novel in the practice of that religion which the last century called by the vast and far-reaching name, *Humanity*:—it needs no other warrant than the consciousness that that is its right.

Paris, October 1864

EMILE ZOLA

The Novel as Social Science

In my literary essays I have often spoken of the application of the experimental method to the novel and to the drama. The return to nature, the naturalistic evo-

From "The Experimental Novel" [1880], *The Experimental Novel and Other Essays*, translated from the French by Belle M. Sherman, New York, 1893, pp. 1-10, 11-18, 19-24, 25-7, 28-31, 34-9, 41-2, 43-5, 46-7, 48-54.

lution which marks the century, drives little by little all the manifestation of human intelligence into the same scientific path. Only the idea of a literature governed by science is doubtless a surprise, until explained with precision and understood. It seems to me necessary, then, to say briefly and to the point what I understand by the experimental novel.

I really only need to adapt, for the experimental method has been established with strength and marvelous clearness by Claude Bernard in his "Introduction à l'Étude de la Médecine Experimentale." This work, by a savant whose authority is unquestioned, will serve me as a solid foundation. I shall here find the whole question treated, and I shall restrict myself to irrefutable arguments and to giving the quotations which may seem necessary to me. This will then be but a compiling of texts, as I intend on all points to intrench myself behind Claude Bernard. It will often be but necessary for me to replace the word "doctor" by the word "novelist," to make my meaning clear and to give it the rigidity of a scientific truth.

What determined my choice, and made me choose "L'Introduction" as my basis, was the fact that medicine, in the eyes of a great number of people, is still an art, as is the novel. Claude Bernard all his life was searching and battling to put medicine in a scientific path. In his struggle we see the first feeble attempts of a science to disengage itself little by little from empiricism,[1] and to gain a foothold in the realm of truth, by means of the experimental method. Claude Bernard demonstrates that this method, followed in the study of inanimate bodies in chemistry and in physics, should be also used in the study of living bodies, in physiology and medicine. I am going to try and prove for my part that if the experimental method leads to the knowledge of physical life, it should also lead to the knowledge of the passionate and intellectual life. It is but a question of degree in the same path which runs from chemistry to physiology, then from physiology to anthropology and to sociology. The experimental novel is the goal.

To be more clear, I think it would be better to give a brief résumé of "L'Introduction" before I commence. The applications which I shall make of the texts will be better understood if the plan of the work and the matters treated are explained.

Claude Bernard, after having declared that medicine enters the scientific path, with physiology as its foundation, and by means of the experimental method, first explains the differences which exist between the sciences of observation and the sciences of experiment. He concludes, finally, that experiment is but provoked observation. All experimental reasoning is based on doubt, for the experimentalist should have no preconceived idea, in the face of nature, and should always retain his liberty of thought. He simply accepts the phenomena which are produced, when they are proved.

In the second part he reaches his true subject and shows that the spontaneity of living bodies is not opposed to the employment of experiment. The difference is simply that an inanimate body possesses merely the ordinary, external environment, while the essence of the higher organism is set in an internal and perfected environment endowed with constant physico-chemical properties exactly like the external environment; hence there is an absolute determinism in the existing con-

[1] Zola uses empiricism in this essay in the sense of "haphazard observation" in contrast with a scientific experiment undertaken to prove a certain truth. TRANSLATOR'S NOTE.

ditions of natural phenomena; for the living as for the inanimate bodies. He calls determinism the cause which determines the appearance of these phenomena. This nearest cause, as it is called, is nothing more than the physical and material condition of the existence or manifestation of the phenomena. The end of all experimental method, the boundary of all scientific research, is then identical for living and for inanimate bodies; it consists in finding the relations which unite a phenomenon of any kind to its nearest cause, or, in other words, in determining the conditions necessary for the manifestation of this phenomenon. Experimental science has no necessity to worry itself about the "why" of things; it simply explains the "how."

After having explained the experimental considerations common to living beings and to inanimate, Claude Bernard passes to the experimental considerations which belong specially to living beings. The great and only difference is this, that there is presented to our consideration, in the organism of living beings, a harmonious group of phenomena. He then treats of practical experiments on living beings, of vivisection, of the preparatory anatomical conditions, of the choice of animals, of the use of calculation in the study of phenomena, and lastly of the physiologist's laboratory.

Finally, in the last part of "L'Introduction," he gives some examples of physiological experimental investigations in support of the ideas which he has formulated. He then furnishes some examples of experimental criticism in physiology. In the end he indicates the philosophical obstacles which the experimental doctor encounters. He puts in the first rank the false application of physiology to medicine, the scientific ignorance as well as certain illusions of the medical mind. Further, he concludes by saying that empirical medicine and experimental medicine, not being incompatible, ought, on the contrary, to be inseparable one from the other. His last sentence is that experimental medicine adheres to no medical doctrine nor any philosophical system.

This is, very broadly, the skeleton of "L'Introduction" stripped of its flesh. I hope that this rapid *exposé* will be sufficient to fill up the gaps which my manner of proceeding is bound to produce; for, naturally, I shall cite from the work only such passages as are necessary to define and comment upon the experimental novel. I repeat that I use this treatise merely as a solid foundation on which to build, but a foundation very rich in arguments and proofs of all kinds. Experimental medicine, which but lisps as yet, can alone give us an exact idea of experimental literature, which, being still unhatched, is not even lisping.

I

The first question which presents itself is this: Is experiment possible in literature, in which up to the present time observation alone has been employed?

Claude Bernard discusses observation and experiment at great length. There exists, in the first place, a very clear line of demarcation, as follows: "The name of 'observer' is given to him who applies the simple or complex process of investigation in the study of phenomena which he does not vary, and which he gathers, consequently, as nature offers them to him; the name of 'experimentalist' is given to him who employs the simple and complex process of investigation to vary or modify, for an end of some kind, the natural phenomena, and to make them appear under circumstances and conditions in which they are not presented by nature." For instance, astronomy is a science of observation, because you cannot conceive of an astronomer acting upon the stars; while chemistry is an experimental science, as the chemist acts upon nature and modifies it. This, according to Claude Bernard, is the only true and important distinction which separates the observer from the experimentalist.

I cannot follow him in his discussion of the different definitions given up to the present time. As I have said before, he finishes by coming to the conclusion that experiment is but provoked observation. I repeat his words: "In the experimental method the search after facts, that is to say, investigation, is always accompanied by a reason, so that ordinarily the experimentalist makes an experiment to confirm and verify the value of an experimental idea. In this case you can say that experiment is an observation instigated for the purpose of verification."

To determine how much observation and experimenting there can be in the naturalistic novel, I only need to quote the following passages:

"The observer relates purely and simply the phenomena which he has under his eyes. . . . He should be the photographer of phenomena, his observation should be an exact representation of nature. . . . He listens to nature and he writes under its dictation. But once the fact is ascertained and the phenomenon observed, an idea or hypothesis comes into his mind, reason intervenes, and the experimentalist comes forward to interpret the phenomenon. The experimentalist is a man who, in pursuance of a more or less probable, but anticipated, explanation of observed phenomena, institutes an experiment in such a way that, according to all probability, it will furnish a result which will serve to confirm the hypothesis or preconceived idea. The moment that the result of the experiment manifests itself, the experimentalist finds himself face to face with a true observation which he has called forth, and which he must ascertain, as all observation, without any preconceived idea. The experimentalist should then disappear, or rather transform himself instantly into the observer, and it is not until after he has ascertained the absolute results of the experiment, like that of an ordinary observation, that his mind comes back to reasoning, comparing, and judging whether the experimental hypothesis is verified or invalidated by these same results."

The mechanism is all there. It is a little complicated, it is true, and Claude Bernard is led on to say: "When all this passes into the brain of a savant who has given himself up to the study of a science as complicated as medicine still is, then there is such an entanglement between the result of observation and what belongs to experiment that it will be impossible and, besides, useless to try to analyze, in their inextricable *mélange*, each of these terms." In one word, it might be said that observation "indicates" and that experiment "teaches."

Now, to return to the novel, we can easily see that the novelist is equally an observer and an experimentalist. The observer in him gives the facts as he has observed them, suggests the point of departure, displays the solid earth on which his characters are to tread and the phenomena to develop. Then the experimentalist appears and introduces an experiment, that is to say, sets his characters going in a certain story so as to show that the succession of facts will be such as the requirements of the determinism of the phenomena under examination call for. Here it is nearly always an experiment "*pour voir*," as Claude Bernard calls it.

The novelist starts out in search of a truth. I will take as an example the character of the *Baron Hulot*, in "Cousine Bette," by Balzac. The general fact observed by Balzac is the ravages that the amorous temperament of a man makes in his home, in his family, and in society. As soon as he has chosen his subject he starts from known facts; then he makes his experiment, and exposes *Hulot* to a series of trials, placing him amid certain surroundings in order to exhibit how the complicated machinery of his passions works. It is then evident that there is not only observation there, but that there is also experiment; as Balzac does not remain satisfied with photographing the facts collected by him, but interferes in a direct way to place his character in certain conditions, and of these he remains the master. The problem is to know what such a passion, acting in such a surrounding and under such circumstances, would produce from the point of view of an individual and of society; and an experimental novel, "Cousine Bette," for example, is simply the report of the experiment that the novelist conducts before the eyes of the public. In fact, the whole operation consists in taking facts in nature, then in studying the mechanism of these facts, acting upon them, by the modification of circumstances and surroundings, without deviating from the laws of nature. Finally, you possess knowledge of the man, scientific knowledge of him, in both his individual and social relations.

Doubtless we are still far from certainties in chemistry and even physiology. Nor do we know any more the reagents which decompose the passions, rendering them susceptible of analysis. Often, in this essay, I shall recall in similar fashion this fact, that the experimental novel is still younger than experimental medicine, and the latter is but just born. But I do not intend to exhibit the acquired results, I simply desire to clearly expose a method. If the experimental novelist is still groping in the most obscure and complex of all the sciences, this does not prevent this science from existing. It is undeniable that the naturalistic novel, such as we understand it to-day, is a real experiment that a novelist makes on man by the help of observation. . . .

But see what splendid clearness breaks forth when this conception of the application of the experimental method to the novel is adequately grasped and is carried out with all the scientific rigor which the matter permits to-day. A contemptible reproach which they heap upon us naturalistic writers is the desire to be solely photographers. We have in vain declared that we admit the necessity of an artist's possessing an individual temperament and a personal expression; they continue to reply to us with these imbecile arguments, about the impossibility of being strictly true, about the necessity of arranging facts to produce a work of art of any kind. Well, with the application of the experimental method to the novel that quarrel dies out. The idea of experiment carries with it the idea of modification. We start, indeed, from the true facts, which are our indestructible basis; but to show the mechanism of these facts it is necessary for us to produce and direct the phenomena; this is our share of invention, here is the genius in the book. Thus without having recourse to the questions of form and of style, which I shall examine later, I maintain even at this point that we must modify nature, without departing from nature, when we employ the experimental method in our novels. If we bear in mind this definition, that "observation indicates and experiment teaches," we can even now claim for our books this great lesson of experiment.

The writer's office, far from being lessened, grows singularly from this point of view. An experiment, even the most simple, is always based on an idea, itself born of an observation. As Claude Bernard says: "The experimental idea is not arbitrary, nor purely imaginary; it ought always to have a support in some observed reality, that is to say, in nature." It is on this idea and on doubt that he bases all the method. "The appearance of the experimental idea," he says further on, "is entirely spontaneous and its nature absolutely individual, depending upon the mind in which it originates; it is a particular sentiment, a *quid proprium*, which constitutes the originality, the invention, and the genius of each one." Further, he makes doubt the great scientific lever. "The doubter is the true savant; he doubts only himself and his interpretations; he believes in science; he even admits in the experimental sciences a criterion or a positive principle, the determinism of phenomena, which is absolute in living beings as in inanimate bodies." Thus, instead of confining the novelist within narrow bounds, the experimental method gives full sway to his intelligence as a thinker, and to his genius as a creator. He must see, understand, and invent. Some observed fact makes the idea start up of trying an experiment, of writing a novel, in order to attain to a complete knowledge of the truth. Then when, after careful consideration, he has decided upon the plan of his experiment, he will judge the results at each step with the freedom of mind of a man who accepts only facts conformable to the determinism of phenomena. He set out from doubt to reach positive knowledge; and he will not cease to doubt until the mechanism of the passion, taken to pieces and set up again by him, acts according to the fixed laws of nature. There is no greater, no more magnificent work for the human mind. We shall see, further on, the miseries of the scholastics, of the makers of systems, and those theorizing about the ideal, compared with the triumph of the experimentalists.

I sum up this part by repeating that the naturalistic novelists observe and experiment, and that all their work is the offspring of the doubt which seizes them in the presence of truths little known and phenomena unexplained, until an experimental idea rudely awakens their genius some day, and urges them to make an experiment, to analyze facts, and to master them.

II

Such, then, is the experimental method. But for a long time it has been held that this method cannot be applied to living beings. This is the important point in the question that I am going to examine with Claude Bernard. The reasoning subsequently will be of the simplest; if the experimental method can be carried from chemistry and physics into physiology and medicine, it can be also carried from physiology into the naturalistic novel.

Cuvier—to cite the name of only one scientific man—pretended that experiment as applied to inanimate bodies could not be used with living beings; physiology, according to his way of thinking, should be purely a science of observation and of anatomical deduction. The vitalists even admit a vital force in unceasing battle with the physical and chemical forces neutralizing their action. Claude Bernard, on the contrary, denies all presence of a mysterious force, and affirms that experiment is applicable everywhere. "I propose," he says, "to establish the fact that the science of the phenomena of life can have no other basis than the science of the phenomena of inanimate bodies, and that there are, in this connection, no differences between the principles of biological science and those of physics and chemistry. In fact, the end the experimental method proposes is the same everywhere; it consists in connecting, by experiment, the natural phenomena to their conditions of existence or to their nearest causes."

It seems to me useless to enter into the complicated explanations and reasonings of Claude Bernard. I have already said that he insists upon the existence of an interior condition in living beings. "In experimenting on inanimate bodies," he says, "there is only one condition to be considered, that is, the exterior earthly condition; while among the higher living organisms there are at least two conditions to consider: the exterior condition or extra-organic, and the interior or inter-organic. The complexity due to the existence of an interior organic condition is the only reason for the great difficulties which we encounter in the experimental determination of living phenomena, and in the application of the means capable of modifying them." And he starts out from this fact to establish the principle that there are fixed laws governing the physiological elements plunged into an interior condition, as there are fixed laws for governing the chemical elements which are steeped in an exterior condition. Hence, you can experiment on a living being as well as on an inanimate one; it is only a question of putting yourself in the desired conditions.

I insist upon this, because, I repeat once more, the important point of the question is there. Claude Bernard, in speaking of the vitalists, writes thus: "They consider life as a mysterious and supernatural agent, which acts arbitrarily, free from all determinism, and they condemn as materialists all those who endeavor to trace vital phenomena to definite organic and physico-chemical conditions. These are false ideas, which it is not easy to root out once they have become domiciled in the mind; only the progress of science can dissipate them." And he lays down this axiom: "With living beings as well as inanimate, the conditions of the existence of each phenomenon are determined in an absolute manner."

I restrain myself for fear of complicating the argument to too great an extent.

Thus you see the progress which science has made. In the last century a more exact application of the experimental method creates physics and chemistry, which then are freed from the irrational and supernatural. Men discover that there are fixed laws, thanks to analysis, and make themselves masters of phenomena. Then a new point is gained. Living beings, in which the vitalists still admitted a mysterious influence, are in their turn brought under and reduced to the general mechanism of matter. Science proves that the existing conditions of all phenomena are the same in living beings as in inanimate; and from that time on physiology assumes little by little the certainty of chemistry and medicine. But are we going to stop there? Evidently not. When it has been proved that the body of man is a machine, whose machinery can be taken apart and put together again at the will of the experimenter, then we can pass to the passionate and intellectual acts of man. Then we shall enter into the domain which up to the present has belonged to physiology and literature; it will be the decisive conquest by science of the hypotheses of philosophers and writers. We have experimental chemistry and medicine; we shall have an experimental physiology, and later on an experimental novel. It is an inevitable evolution, the goal of which it is easy to see to-day. All things hang together; it is necessary to start from the determin-ism of inanimate bodies in order to arrive at the determinism of living beings; and since savants like Claude Bernard demonstrate how that fixed laws govern the human body, we can easily proclaim, without fear of being mistaken, the hour in which the laws of thought and passion will be formulated in their turn. A like determinism will govern the stones of the roadway and the brain of man.

This opinion is to be found in "L'Introduction." I cannot repeat too often that I take all my arguments from Claude Bernard's work. After having explained that any completely special phenomena may be the result of the more and more complex combination and co-operation of the organized elements, he writes the following: "I am persuaded that the obstacles which surround the experimental study of psychological phenomena are in great measure due to difficulties of this order; for notwithstanding the marvelous nature and the delicacy of their mani-festations, it is impossible, so it seems to me, not to bring cerebral phenomena, like all the phenomena of living bodies, under the laws of a scientific determin-ism." This is clear. Later, without doubt, science will find this determinism for all the cerebral and sensory manifestations of man.

Now, science enters into the domain of us novelists, who are to-day the ana-lyzers of man, in his individual and social relations. We are continuing, by our observations and experiments, the work of the physiologist, who has continued that of the physicist and the chemist. We are making use, in a certain way, of scientific psychology to complete scientific physiology; and to finish the series we have only to bring into our studies of nature and man the decisive tool of the experimental method. In one word, we should operate on the characters, the pas sions, on the human and social data, in the same way that the chemist and the physicist operate on inanimate beings, and as the physiologist operates on living beings. Determinism dominates everything. It is scientific investigation, it is ex-perimental reasoning, which combats one by one the hypotheses of the idealists, and which replaces purely imaginary novels by novels of observation and ex-periment.

I certainly do not intend at this point to formulate laws. In the actual condi-tion of the science of man the obscurity and confusion are still too great to risk the slightest synthesis. All that can be said is that there is an absolute determin-ism for all human phenomena. From that on investigation is a duty. We have the method; we should go forward, even if a whole lifetime of effort ends but in the conquest of a small particle of the truth. . . . We are lisping yet, we are the last comers, but that should be only one incentive the more to push us forward to more exact studies; now that we possess the tool, the experimental method, our goal is very plain—to know the determinism of phenomena and to make our-selves master of these phenomena.

Without daring, as I say, to formulate laws, I consider that the question of heredity has a great influence in the intellectual and passionate manifestations of man. I also attach considerable importance to the surroundings. I ought to touch upon Darwin's theories; but this is only a general study of the experimental method as applied to the novel, and I should lose myself were I to enter into de-tails. I will only say a word on the subject of surroundings. We have just seen the great importance given by Claude Bernard to the study of those inter-organic conditions which must be taken into account if we wish to find the determinism of phenomena in living beings. Well, then! in the study of a family, of a group of living beings, I think that the social condition is of equal importance. Some day the physiologist will explain to us the mechanism of the thoughts and the passions; we shall know how the individual machinery of each man works; how he thinks, how he loves, how he goes from reason to passion and folly; but these phenomena, resulting as they do from the mechanism of the organs, acting under the influence of an interior condition, are not produced in isolation or in the bare void. Man is not alone; he lives in society, in a social condition; and consequently, for us novelists, this social condition unceasingly modifies the phenomena. Indeed our great study is just there, in the reciprocal effect of society on the individual and the individual on society. For the physiologist, the exterior and interior conditions are purely chemical and physical, and this aids him in finding the laws which govern them easily. We are not yet able to prove that the social condition is also physical and chemical. It is that certainly, or rather it is the variable product of a group of living beings, who themselves are absolutely submissive to the physical and chemical laws which govern alike living beings and inanimate. From this we shall see that we can act upon the social conditions, in acting upon the phenomena of which we have made ourselves master in man. And this is what constitutes the experimental novel: to possess a knowledge of the mechanism of the phenomena inherent in man, to show the machinery of his intellectual and sensory manifestations, under the influences of heredity and environment, such as physiology shall give them to us, and then finally to exhibit man living in social conditions produced by himself, which he modifies daily, and in the heart of which he himself experiences a continual transformation. Thus, then, we lean on physiology; we take man from the hands of the physiologist solely, in order to continue the solution of the problem, and to solve scientifically the question of how men behave when they are in society.

These general ideas will be sufficient to guide us to-day. Later on, when science is farther advanced, when the experimental novel has brought forth decisive results, some critic will explain more precisely what I have but indicated to-day.

Elsewhere Claude Bernard confesses how difficult it is to apply the experimental method to living beings. "The living body," he says, "especially among the higher animals, never falls into chemical or physical indifference with the exterior conditions; it possesses an incessant movement, an organic evolution apparently spontaneous and constant; and notwithstanding the fact that this evolution has need of exterior circumstances to manifest itself, it is, however, independent in its course and movement." And he concludes as I have: "In short, it is only in the physical and chemical conditions of the interior that we shall find the principle that governs the exterior phenomena of life." But whatever complexities may present themselves, and even when extraordinary phenomena are produced, the application of the experimental method is imperative. If the phenomena of life have a complexity and an apparent difference from those of inanimate bodies, they do not offer this difference, except by reason of determined or determinable conditions which belong to them. Therefore, even should the sciences dealing with life differ from the others in their application and in their special laws, they are not to be distinguished by their scientific method."

I must say one word as to the limits which Claude Bernard assigns to science. According to him we shall always be ignorant of the "why" of things; we can only know the "how." It is this that he expresses in the following terms: "The nature of our minds urges us to seek the essence or the 'why' of things. In this we see further than the goal it has been given us to attain to; for experiment soon teaches us that we must not go beyond the 'how'; that is to say, beyond the nearest cause or the condition of the existence of any phenomenon." Further on he gives this example: "If we can discover 'why' opium and its alkaloids produce sleep, we shall know the mechanism of such slumber, and know 'how' opium or its essence produces sleep; for slumber only takes place because the active substance is about to put itself in contact with certain organic elements which it modifies." The practical conclusion of all this is the following: "Science has precisely the privilege of teaching us what we are ignorant of, through its substitution of reason and experiment for sentiment, and by showing us clearly the limit of our actual knowledge. But, by a marvelous compensation, in proportion as science humbles our pride, it strengthens our power." All these considerations are strictly applicable to the experimental novel. In order not to lose itself in philosophical speculations, in order to replace idealistic hypothesis by a slow conquest of the unknown, it must continue the search after the "how" of things. This is its exact rôle, and it is from this that it must draw, as we are going to see, its reasons for being and its moral.

I have reached this point: the experimental novel is a consequence of the scientific evolution of the century; it continues and completes physiology, which itself leans for support on chemistry and medicine; it substitutes for the study of the abstract and the metaphysical man the study of the natural man, governed by physical and chemical laws, and modified by the influences of his surroundings; it is in one word the literature of our scientific age, as the classical and romantic literature corresponded to a scholastic and theological age. Now I will pass to the great question of the application of all this, and of its justification.

III

The object of the experimental method in physiology and in medicine is to study phenomena in order to become their master. Claude Bernard in each page of "L'Introduction" comes back to this idea. He declares: "All natural philosophy is summed up in this: To know the laws which govern phenomena. The experimental problem reduces itself to this: To foresee and direct phenomena." . . .

This, then, is the end, this is the purpose in physiology and in experimental medicine: to make one's self master of life in order to be able to direct it. Let us suppose that science advances and that the conquest of the unknown is finally completed; the scientific age which Claude Bernard saw in his dreams will then be realized. When that time comes the doctor will be the master of maladies; he will cure without fail; his influence upon the human body will conduce to the welfare and strength of the species. We shall enter upon a century in which man, grown more powerful, will make use of nature and will utilize its laws to produce upon the earth the greatest possible amount of justice and freedom. There is no nobler, higher, nor grander end. Here is our rôle as intelligent beings: to penetrate to the wherefore of things, to become superior to these things, and to reduce them to a condition of subservient machinery.

Well, this dream of the physiologist and the experimental doctor is also that of the novelist, who employs the experimental method in his study of man as a simple individual and as a social animal. Their object is ours; we also desire to master certain phenomena of an intellectual and personal order, to be able to direct them. We are, in a word, experimental moralists, showing by experiment in what way a passion acts in a certain social condition. The day in which we gain control of the mechanism of this passion we can treat it and reduce it, or at least make it as inoffensive as possible. And in this consists the practical utility and high morality of our naturalistic works, which experiment on man, and which dissect piece by piece this human machinery in order to set it going through the influence of the environment. When things have advanced further, when we are in possession of the different laws, it will only be necessary to work upon the individuals and the surroundings if we wish to find the best social condition. In this way we shall construct a practical sociology, and our work will be a help to political and economical sciences. I do not know, I repeat, of a more noble work, nor of a grander application. To be the master of good and evil, to regulate life, to regulate society, to solve in time all the problems of socialism, above all, to give justice a solid foundation by solving through experiment the questions of criminality—is not this being the most useful and the most moral workers in the human workshop?

Let us compare, for one instant, the work of the idealistic novelists to ours; and here this word idealistic refers to writers who cast aside observation and experiment, and base their works on the supernatural and the irrational, who admit, in a word, the power of mysterious forces outside of the determinism of the phenomena. Claude Bernard shall reply to this for me: "What distinguishes experimental reasoning from scholastic is the fecundity of the one and the sterility of the other. It is precisely the scholastic, who believes he has absolute certitude, who attains to no results. This is easily understood, since by his belief in an absolute principle he puts himself outside of nature, in which everything is relative. It is, on the contrary, the experimenter, who is always in doubt, who does not think he possesses absolute certainty about anything, who succeeds in mastering the phenomena which surround him, and in increasing his power over nature." By and by I shall return to this question of the ideal, which is in truth but the question of indeterminism. Claude Bernard says truly: "The intellectual conquest of man consists in diminishing and driving back indeterminism, and so, gradually, by the aid of the experimental method, gaining ground for determinism." We experimental novelists have the same task; our work is to go from the known to the unknown, to make ourselves masters of nature; while the idealistic novelists deliberately remain in the unknown, through all sorts of religious and philosophical prejudices, under the astounding pretense that the unknown is nobler and more beautiful than the known. If our work, often cruel, if our terrible pictures needed justification, I should find, indeed, with Claude Bernard this argument conclusive: "You will never reach really fruitful and luminous generalizations on the phenomena of life until you have experimented yourself and stirred up in the hospital, the amphitheater, and the laboratory the fetid or palpitating sources of life. If it were necessary for me to give a comparison which would explain my sentiments on the science of life, I should say that it is a superb salon, flooded with light, which you can only reach by passing through a long and nauseating kitchen." . . .

In our novels, when we experiment on a dangerous wound which poisons society, we proceed in the same way as the experimentalist doctor; we try to find the simple initial cause in order to reach the complex causes of which the action is the result. Go back once more to the example of *Baron Hulot* in "Cousine Bette." See the final result, the dénouement of the novel: an entire family is destroyed, all sorts of secondary dramas are produced, under the action of *Hulot's* amorous temperament. It is there, in this temperament, that the initial cause is found. One member, *Hulot*, becomes rotten, and immediately all around him are tainted, the social circulus is interrupted, the health of that society is compromised. What emphasis Balzac lays on the character of *Baron Hulot*; with what scrupulous care he analyzes him! The experiment deals with him chiefly, because its object is to master the symptoms of this passion in order to govern it. Suppose that *Hulot* is cured, or at least restrained and rendered inoffensive, immediately the drama ceases to have any longer any *raison d'être*; the equilibrium, or more truly the health, of the social body is again established. Thus the naturalistic novelists are really experimental moralists.

And I reach thus the great reproach with which they think to crush the naturalistic novelists, by treating them as fatalists. How many times have they wished to prove to us that as soon as we did not accept free will, that as soon as man was no more to us than a living machine, acting under the influence of heredity and surroundings, we should fall into gross fatalism, we should debase humanity to the rank of a troop marching under the baton of destiny. It is necessary to define our terms: we are not fatalists, we are determinists, which is not at all the same thing. Claude Bernard explains the two terms very plainly: "We have given the name of determinism to the nearest or determining cause of phenomena. We never act upon the essence of phenomena in nature, but only for their determinism, and by this very fact, that we act upon it, determinism differs from fatalism, upon which we could not act at all. Fatalism assumes that the appearance of any phenomenon is necessary apart from its conditions, while determinism is just the condition essential for the appearance of any phenomenon, and such appearance is never forced. Once the search for the determinism of phenomena is placed as a fundamental principle of the experimental method, there is no longer either materialism, or spiritualism, or inanimate matter, or living matter; there remain but phenomena of which it is necessary to determine the conditions, that is to say, the circumstances which play, by their proximity to these phenomena, the rôle of nearest cause." This is decisive. All we do is to apply this method in our novels, and we are the determinists who experimentally try to determine the condition of the phenomena, without departing in our investigations from the laws of nature. As Claude Bernard very truly says, the moment that we can act, and that we do act, on the determining cause of phenomena—by modifying their surroundings, for example—we cease to be fatalists.

Here you have, then, the moral purpose of the experimental novelist clearly defined. I have often said that we do not have to draw a conclusion from our works; and this means that our works carry their conclusion with them. An experimentalist has no need to conclude, because, in truth, experiment concludes for him. A hundred times, if necessary, he will repeat the experiment before the public; he will explain it; but he need neither become indignant nor approve of it personally; such is the truth, such is the way phenomena work; it is for society to produce or not to produce these phenomena, according as the result is useful or dangerous. You cannot imagine, as I have said elsewhere, a savant being provoked with azote because azote is dangerous to life; he suppresses azote when it is harmful, and not otherwise. As our power is not the same as that of a savant, as we are experimentalists without being practitioners, we ought to content ourselves with searching out the determinism of social phenomena, and leaving to legislators and to men of affairs the care of controlling sooner or later these phenomena in such a way as to develop the good and reject the bad, from the point of view of their utility to man.

In our rôle as experimental moralists we show the mechanism of the useful and the useless, we disengage the determinism of the human and social phenomena so that, in their turn, the legislators can one day dominate and control these phenomena. In a word, we are working with the whole country toward that great object, the conquest of nature and the increase of man's power a hundredfold. Compare with ours the work of the idealistic writers, who rely upon the irrational and the supernatural, and whose every flight upward is followed by a deeper fall into metaphysical chaos. We are the ones who possess strength and morality.

IV

I have said before that I chose "L'Introduction" because medicine is still looked upon by many as an art. Claude Bernard proves that it ought to be a science, and in his book we see the birth of a science, a very instructive spectacle in itself, and which shows us that the scientific domain is extending and conquering all the manifestations of human intelligence. Since medicine, which was an art, is becoming a science, why should not literature also become a science by means of the experimental method? . . .

Since feeling is the starting point of the experimental method, since reason subsequently intervenes to end in experiment, and to be controlled by it, the genius of the experimentalist dominates everything, and this is what has made the experimental method, so inert in other hands, such a powerful tool in the hands of Claude Bernard. I have said the word: method is but the tool; it is the workman, it is the idea, which he brings, which makes the *chef-d'œuvre*. I have already quoted these lines: "It is a particular feeling, a *quid proprium*, which constitutes the originality, the invention, or the genius of each one." This, then, is the part taken by genius in the experimental novel. As Claude Bernard says again: "The idea is the seed; the method is the soil which furnishes the conditions for developing and prospering it, and bringing forth its best fruits, according to nature." Thus everything is reduced to a question of method. If you are content to remain in the *a priori* idea, and enjoy your own feelings without finding any basis for it in reason or any verification in experiment, you are a poet; you venture upon hypotheses which you cannot prove; you are struggling vainly in a painful indeterminism, and in a way that is often injurious. Listen to these lines of "L'Introduction": "Man is naturally a metaphysician and proud; he believes that the idealistic creations of his brain, which coincide with his feelings, represent the reality. Thus it follows that the experimental method is not innate and natural to man, for it is only after having wandered for a long time among theological and scholastical discussions that he ends by recognizing the sterility of his efforts in this path. Man then perceives that he cannot dictate laws to nature, because he does not possess in himself the knowledge and the criterion of exterior things; he realizes that in order to arrive at the truth he must, on the contrary, study the natural laws and submit his ideas, if not his reason, to experiment, that is to say, to the criterion of facts." What becomes of the genius of the experimental novelist? The genius, the idea *a priori*, remains, only it is controlled by experiment. The experiment naturally cannot destroy his genius; on the contrary, it confirms it. To take the case of a poet, for example: To show he has genius is it necessary that his feeling, his idea, *a priori*, should be false? Evidently not, for the genius of a man will be so much the greater when experiment has proved the truth of his personal idea. Our age of lyricism, our romantic disease, was alone capable of measuring a man's genius by the quantity of nonsense and folly which he put in circulation. I conclude by saying that in our scientific century experiment must prove genius.

This is the drift of our quarrel with the idealistic writers. They always start out from an irrational source of some kind, such as a revelation, a tradition, or conventional authority. As Claude Bernard declares: "We must admit nothing occult; there are but phenomena and the conditions of phenomena." We naturalistic novelists submit each fact to the test of observation and experiment, while the idealistic writers admit mysterious elements which escape analysis, and therefore remain in the unknown, outside of the influence of the laws governing nature. This question of the ideal, from the scientific point of view, reduces itself to a question of indeterminate or determinate. All that we do not know, all that escapes us still, that is truly the ideal, and the aim of our human efforts is each day to reduce the ideal, to conquer truth from the unknown. We are all idealists, if we mean by this that we busy ourselves with the ideal. But I dub those idealists who take refuge in the unknown for the pleasure of being there, who have a taste but for the most risky hypotheses, who disdain to submit them to the test of experiment under the pretext that the truth is in themselves and not in the things. These writers, I repeat, accomplish a vain and harmful task, while the observer and the experimentalist are the only ones who work for the strength and happiness of man, making him more and more the master of nature. There is neither nobility, nor dignity, nor beauty, nor morality in not knowing, in lying, in pretending that you are greater according as you advance in error and confusion. The only great and moral works are those of truth.

What we alone must accept is what I will call the stimulus of the ideal. Certainly our science is very limited as yet, beside the enormous mass of things of which we are ignorant. This great unknown which surrounds us ought to inspire us with the desire to pierce it, to explain it by means of scientific methods. And this does not refer only to scientific men; all the manifestations of human intelligence are connected together, all our efforts have their birth in the need we feel of making ourselves masters of the truth. Claude Bernard explains this very clearly when he writes: "The sciences each possess, if not a special method, at least special processes, and, moreover, they reciprocally serve as tools for one another. Mathematics serves as a tool to physics, to chemistry, and to biology in very different measure; physics and chemistry serve as powerful tools to physiology and medicine. In this mutual help which the sciences are to each other, you must distinguish clearly the savant who advances each science and he who makes use of it. The physician and the chemist are not mathematicians because they employ calculation; the physiologist is not a chemist or a physician because he uses chemical reactions or medical instruments, any more than the chemist and the physician are physiologists because they study the compositions or the properties of certain liquids and certain animal or vegetable tissues." This is the reply which Claude Bernard can be said to make for us naturalists to the critics who taunt us with making pretensions to science. We are neither chemists nor physicians nor physiologists; we are simply novelists who depend upon the sciences for support. We certainly do not pretend to have made discoveries in physiology which we do not practice; only, being obliged to make a study of man, we feel we cannot deny the efficacy of the new physiological truths. And I will add that the novelists are certainly the workers who rely at once upon the greatest number of sciences, for they treat of them all and must know them all, as the novel has become a general inquiry on nature and on man. This is why we have been led to apply to our work the experimental method as soon as this method had become the most powerful tool of investigation. We sum up investigation, we throw ourselves anew into the conquest of the ideal, employing all forms of knowledge.

Let it be well understood that I am speaking of the "how" of things and not of the "why." For an experimental savant, the ideal which he is endeavoring to reduce, the indeterminate, is always restricted to the "how." He leaves to philosophers the other ideal, that of the "why," which he despairs of determining. I think that the experimental novelists equally ought not to occupy themselves with this unknown quality, unless they wish to lose themselves in the follies of the poets and the philosophers. It is surely an object large enough to try to know the entire mechanism of nature, without troubling one's self for the time being with the origin of the mechanism. If we some day succeed in knowing it, we shall doubtless owe our knowledge to method, and it is better then to begin at the beginning with the study of phenomena, instead of hoping that a sudden revelation will reveal to us the secret of the world. We are the workmen; we will leave to the metaphysicians this great unknown of the "why" they have struggled with so vainly for centuries, in order to confine our efforts to that other unknown of the "how," which is cleared away more and more every day by our investigation. The only ideal which ought to exist for us, the naturalistic novelists, should be one which we can conquer. . . .

Though I have frequently written the same words and given the same advice, I will repeat them here: "The experimental method alone can bring the novel out of the atmosphere of lies and errors in which it is plunged. All my literary life has been controlled by this conviction. I am deaf to the voices of the critics who demand that I shall formulate the laws of heredity and the influence of surroundings in my characters; those who make these discouraging objections and denials but speak from slothfulness of mind, from an infatuation for tradition, from an attachment more or less conscious to philosophical and religious beliefs. The experimental direction which the novel is taking to-day is a definite one. And it is no longer the ephemeral influence of a personal system of any kind, it is the result of the scientific evolution, of the study of man himself. My convictions in this respect are so strong that I endeavor to impress them clearly upon the minds of the young writers who read my works; for I think it necessary, above all things else, to inspire them with the scientific spirit, and to initiate them into the ideas and the tendencies of modern science."

V

. . . I have already repeated twenty times that naturalism is not a personal fantasy, but that it is the intellectual movement of the century. Perhaps they will believe Claude Bernard, who speaks with greater authority on this subject than I can lay claim to; he declares that: "The revolution which the experimental method has caused in science consists mainly in the substitution of a scientific criterion for a personal authority. It is the characteristic of the experimental method to depend only on itself, as it carries within itself its criterion, which is experiment. It recognizes no authority but that of facts, and it frees itself from personal authority." Consequently, it no longer admits the authority of any theory either. "The idea should always remain independent; it must be enchained neither by scientific, nor philosophical, nor religious beliefs. Man must be strong and free in the manifestation of his ideas, must follow his instinct, and not dwell upon the puerile fears of the contradiction of any theories; . . . he must modify theory by adapting it to nature, and not nature by adapting it to theory." From this there results an incomparable breadth. "The experimental method is the scientific method which proclaims the liberty of thought. It not only throws off the philosophical and theological yoke, but it no longer admits scientific personal authority. This is not said from pride or boastfulness. The experimentalist, on the contrary, shows his humility in denying personal authority, for he doubts his own knowledge, and he submits the authority of men to that of experiment and the laws which govern nature."

This is why I have said so many times that naturalism is not a school, as it is not embodied in the genius of one man, nor in the ravings of a group of men, as was romanticism; that it consists simply in the application of the experimental method to the study of nature and of man. Hence it is nothing but a vast movement, a march forward in which everyone is a workman, according to his genius. All theories are admitted, and the theory which carries the most weight is the one which explains the most. There does not appear to me to be a literary or scientific path larger or more direct. Everyone, the great and the small, moves freely, working and investigating together, each one in his own specialty, and recognizing no other authority than that of facts proved by experiment. Therefore in naturalism there could be neither innovators nor leaders; there are simply workmen, some more skillful than others. . . .

I have said that in the experimental novel it is best for us to hold to the strictly scientific point of view if we wish to base our studies on solid ground; not to go out from the "how," not to attach ourselves to the "why." However, it is very certain that we cannot always escape this need of our intelligence, this restless curiosity which makes us desire to know the essence of things. I think that it is best for us to accept the philosophical system, which adapts itself the best to the actual condition of the sciences, but simply from a speculative point of view. . . . Behind a science, behind a manifestation of any kind of the human intelligence, there always lies more or less clearly what Claude Bernard calls a philosophical system. To this system it is not well to attach one's self devotedly, but to hold tenaciously to the facts, free to modify the system if the facts call for it. But the system exists none the less, and it exists so much the more as science is less advanced and less firm. For us naturalistic novelists, who are still in the lisping stage, hypothesis is fatal. By and by I will take up the rôle of hypothesis in literature.

Nevertheless, if in practice Claude Bernard thrusts aside philosophical system, he recognizes the necessity of philosophy. "From a scientific point of view, philosophy represents the eternal desire of the human reason after knowledge of the unknown. Hence philosophers always confine themselves to questions that are in dispute, and to those lofty regions that lie beyond the boundaries of science. In this way they communicate to science a certain inspiration which animates and ennobles it. They strengthen the mind—developing it by an intellectual gymnastics—at the same time that they ever carry it toward the never-completed solution of great problems. Thus they keep up a cult of the unknown, and quicken the sacred fire of investigation, which ought never to be extinguished in the heart of a savant." This passage is very fine, but the philosophers have never been told in better terms that their hypotheses are pure poetry. Claude Bernard evidently looks upon the philosophers, among whom he believes he has a great many friends, as musicians often gifted with genius, whose music encourages the savants while they work and inspires the sacred fire of their great discoveries. But the philosophers, left to themselves, will sing forever and never discover a single truth.

I have neglected until now the question of form in the naturalistic novel, because it is precisely there that individuality shows in literature. Not only is a writer's genius to be found in the feeling and in the idea *a priori* but also in the form and style. . . . If you wish my true opinion upon this subject, it is this: that to-day an exaggerated importance is given to form. I have a great deal to say on this subject, but it would carry me beyond the limits of this essay. In reality, I think that the form of expression depends upon the methods; that language is only one kind of logic, and its construction natural and scientific. He who writes the best will not be the one who gallops madly among hypotheses, but the one who walks straight ahead in the midst of truths. We are actually rotten with lyricism; we are very much mistaken when we think that the characteristic of a good style is a sublime confusion with just a dash of madness added; in reality, the excellence of a style depends upon its logic and clearness.

Claude Bernard considers that philosophers are really musicians who play a sort of Marseillaise made up of hypotheses, and swell the hearts of the savants as they rush to attack the unknown; and he has much the same idea of artists and writers. I have remarked that a great many of the most intelligent savants, jealous of the scientific certainty which they enjoy, would very willingly confine literature to the ideal. They themselves seem to feel the need of taking little recreations in the world of lies after the fatigue of their exact labors, and they are fond of amusing themselves with the most daring hypotheses, and with fictions which they know perfectly well to be false and ridiculous. Claude Bernard was right when he said: "Literary and artistic productions will never grow old in the sense that they are the expressions of sentiments as unchangeable as human nature." In fact, form is sufficient to immortalize a work; the spectacle of a powerful individuality reproducing nature in superb language will interest all ages; only the works of a savant, from this same point of view, will be read always, for the reason that the thought of a great savant who knows how to write is much more interesting than that of a poet. However far astray the savant may be in his hypothesis, he still remains the equal of the poet, who is certain to have been equally mistaken. The point to be emphasized is this, that our domain is not limited to the expression of sentiments as unchangeable as human nature because it is essential also to exhibit the working of these sentiments.

We have not exhausted our matter when we have depicted anger, avarice, and love; all nature and all of man belong to us, not only in their phenomena, but in the causes of these phenomena. I well know that this is an immense field, the entrance to which they would willingly have refused us; but we have broken down the barriers and have entered it in triumph. This is why I do not accept the following words of Claude Bernard: "In art and letters personality dominates everything. There one is dealing with a spontaneous creation of the mind that has nothing in common with the verification of natural phenomena, in which our minds can create nothing." I have here detected one of our most illustrious savants sharing in the attempt to refuse to letters the *entrée* to the scientific field. I do not know what letters he refers to in this definition of a literary work: "A spontaneous creation of the mind that has nothing in common with the verification of natural phenomena." Doubtless he has lyrical poetry in his mind, for he never could have written that phrase had he understood the experimental novel as shown in the works of Balzac and Stendhal. I can only repeat what I have said before, that apart from the matter of form and style, the experimental novelist is only one special kind of savant, who makes use of the tools of all other savants, observation and analysis. Our field is the same as the physiologist's, only that it is greater. We operate, like him, on man; and Claude Bernard recognizes this fact himself, that the cerebral phenomena can be determined the same as other phenomena. It is true that Claude Bernard can tell us that we are lost in hypotheses; but to conclude from this that we shall never arrive at the truth sits very badly on him, as he has struggled all his life to make a science of medicine, which the great majority of his contemporaries look upon as an art.

Let us clearly define now what is meant by an experimental novelist. Claude Bernard gives the following definition of an artist: "What is an artist? He is a man who realizes in a work of art an idea or a sentiment which is personal to him." I absolutely reject this definition. On this basis if I represented a man as walking on his head, I should have made a work of art, if such happened to be my personal sentiments. But in that case I should be a fool and nothing else. So one must add that the personal feeling of the artist is always subject to the higher law of truth and nature. We now come to the question of hypothesis. The artist starts out from the same point as the savant; he places himself before nature, has an idea *a priori*, and works according to this idea. Here alone he separates himself from the savant, if he carries out his idea to the end without verifying its truth by the means of observation and experiment. Those who make use of experiment might well be called experimental artists; but then people will tell us that they are no longer artists, since such people regard art as the burden of personal error which the artist has put into his study of nature. I contend that the personality of the writer should only appear in the idea *a priori* and in the form, not in the infatuation for the false. I see no objection, besides, to its showing in the hy-

pothesis, but it is necessary to clearly understand what you mean by these words.
It has often been said that writers ought to open the way for savants. This is true, for we have seen in "L'Introduction" that hypothesis and empiricism precede and prepare for the scientific state which is established finally by the experimental method. Man commenced by venturing certain explanations of phenomena, the poets gave expression to their emotions, and the savants ended by mastering hypotheses and fixing the truth. Claude Bernard always assigns the rôle of pioneers to the philosophers. It is a very noble rôle, and to-day it is the writers who should assume it and who should endeavor to fill it worthily. Only let it be well understood that each time that a truth is established by the savants the writers should immediately abandon their hypothesis to adopt this truth; otherwise they will remain deliberately in error without benefiting anyone. It is thus that science, as it advances, furnishes to us writers a solid ground upon which we should lean for support, to better enable us to shoot into new hypotheses. In a word, every phenomenon, once clearly determined, destroys the hypothesis which it replaces, and it is then necessary to transport your hypothesis one step further into the new unknown which arises. I will take a very simple example in order to make myself better understood: it has been proved that the earth revolves around the sun; what would you think of a poet who should adopt the old belief that the sun revolves around the earth? Evidently the poet, if he wishes to risk a personal explanation of any fact, should choose a fact whose cause is not already known. This, then, illustrates the position hypothesis should occupy for experimental novelists; we must accept determined facts, and not attempt to risk about them our personal sentiments, which would be ridiculous, building throughout on the territory that science has conquered; then before the unknown, but only then, exercising our intuition and suggesting the way to science, free to make mistakes, happy if we produce any data toward the solution of the problem. Here I stand at Claude Bernard's practical programme, who is forced to accept empiricism as a necessary forerunner. In our experimental novel we can easily risk a few hypotheses on the questions of heredity and surroundings, after having respected all that science knows to-day about the matter. We can prepare the ways, we can furnish the results of observation, human data which may prove very useful. A great lyrical poet has written lately that our century is a century of prophets. Yes, if you wish it; only let it be well understood that these prophets rely neither upon the irrational nor the supernatural. If the prophets thought best to bring up again the most elementary notions, to serve up nature with a strange religious and philosophical sauce, to hold fast to the metaphysical man, to confound and obscure everything, the prophets, notwithstanding their genius in the matter of style, would never be anything but great gooses ignorant whether they would get wet if they jumped into the water. In our scientific age it is a very delicate thing to be a prophet, as we no longer believe in the truths of revelation, and in order to be able to foresee the unknown we must begin by studying the known.

The conclusion to which I wish to come is this: If I were to define the experimental novel I should not say, as Claude Bernard says, that a literary work lies entirely in the personal feeling, for the reason that in my opinion the personal feeling is but the first impulse. Later nature, being there, makes itself felt, or at least that part of nature of which science has given us the secret, and about which we have no longer any right to romance. The experimental novelist is therefore the

one who accepts proven facts, who points out in man and in society the mechanism of the phenomena over which science is mistress, and who does not interpose his personal sentiments, except in the phenomena whose determinism is not
yet settled, and who tries to test, as much as he can, this personal sentiment, this
idea *a priori*, by observation and experiment.

I cannot understand how our naturalistic literature can mean anything else. I
have only spoken of the experimental novel, but I am fairly convinced that the
same method, after having triumphed in history and in criticism, will triumph
everywhere, on the stage and in poetry even. It is an inevitable evolution. Literature, in spite of all that can be said, does not depend merely upon the author; it
is influenced by the nature it depicts and by the man whom it studies. Now if the
savants change their ideas of nature, if they find the true mechanism of life, they
force us to follow them, to precede them even, so as to play our rôle in the new
hypotheses. The metaphysical man is dead; our whole territory is transformed by
the advent of the physiological man. No doubt "Achilles' Anger," "Dido's Love,"
will last forever on account of their beauty; but to-day we feel the necessity of
analyzing anger and love, of discovering exactly how such passions work in the
human being. This view of the matter is a new one; we have become experimentalists instead of philosophers. In short, everything is summed up in this great
fact: the experimental method in letters, as in the sciences, is in the way to explain the natural phenomena, both individual and social, of which metaphysics,
until now, has given only irrational and supernatural explanations.

AUGUST STRINDBERG

A Naturalistic Manifesto

Theatre has long seemed to me—in common with much other art—a *Biblia Pau-
perum*, a Bible in pictures for those who cannot read what is written or printed;
and I see the playwright as a lay preacher peddling the ideas of his time in popular form, popular enough for the middle-classes, mainstay of theatre audiences,
to grasp the gist of the matter without troubling their brains too much. For this
reason theatre has always been an elementary school for the young, the semi-
educated, and for women who still have a primitive capacity for deceiving themselves and letting themselves be deceived—who, that is to say, are susceptible to
illusion and to suggestion from the author. I have therefore thought it not unlikely that in these days, when that rudimentary and immature thought-process
operating through fantasy appears to be developing into reflection, research and
analysis, that theatre, like religion, might be discarded as an outworn form for
whose appreciation we lack the necessary conditions. This opinion is confirmed
by the major crisis still prevailing in the theatres of Europe, and still more by the

Preface to *Miss Julie* [1888], from *Plays*, translated from the Swedish by Elizabeth Sprigge,
Chicago, 1955, pp. 94-8. Copyright 1955 by Elizabeth Sprigge; reprinted by permission of
Willis Kingsley Wing and Constable & Co.

fact that in those countries of culture, producing the greatest thinkers of the age, namely England and Germany, drama—like other fine arts—is dead.

Some countries, it is true, have attempted to create a new drama by using the old forms with up-to-date contents, but not only has there been insufficient time for these new ideas to be popularized, so that the audience can grasp them, but also people have been so wrought up by the taking of sides that pure, disinterested appreciation has become impossible. One's deepest impressions are upset when an applauding or a hissing majority dominates as forcefully and openly as it can in the theatre. Moreover, as no new form has been devised for these new contents, the new wine has burst the old bottles.

In this play I have not tried to do anything new, for this cannot be done, but only to modernize the form to meet the demands which may, I think, be made on this art today. To this end I chose—or surrendered myself to—a theme which claims to be outside the controversial issues of today, since questions of social climbing or falling, of higher or lower, better or worse, of man and woman, are, have been, and will be of lasting interest. When I took this theme from a true story told me some years ago, which made a deep impression, I saw it as a subject for tragedy, for as yet it is tragic to see one favored by fortune go under, and still more to see a family heritage die out, although a time may come when we have grown so developed and enlightened that we shall view with indifference life's spectacle, now seeming so brutal, cynical, and heartless. Then we shall have dispensed with those inferior, unreliable instruments of thought called feelings, which become harmful and superfluous as reasoning develops.

The fact that my heroine rouses pity is solely due to weakness; we cannot resist fear of the same fate overtaking us. The hyper-sensitive spectator may, it is true, go beyond this kind of pity, while the man with belief in the future may actually demand some suggestion for remedying the evil—in other words some kind of policy. But, to begin with, there is no such thing as absolute evil; the downfall of one family is the good fortune of another, which thereby gets a chance to rise, and, fortune being only comparative, the alternation of rising and falling is one of life's principal charms. Also, to the man of policy, who wants to remedy the painful fact that the bird of prey devours the dove, and lice the bird of prey, I should like to put the question: why should it be remedied? Life is not so mathematically idiotic as only to permit the big to eat the small; it happens just as often that the bee kills the lion or at least drives it mad.

That my tragedy depresses many people is their own fault. When we have grown strong as the pioneers of the French revolution, we shall be happy and relieved to see the national parks cleared of ancient rotting trees which have stood too long in the way of others equally entitled to a period of growth—as relieved as we are when an incurable invalid dies.

My tragedy "The Father" was recently criticized for being too sad—as if one wants cheerful tragedies! Everybody is clamoring for this supposed "joy of life," and theatre managers demand farces, as if the joy of life consisted in being ridiculous and portraying all human beings as suffering from St. Vitus's dance or total idiocy. I myself find the joy of life in its strong and cruel struggles, and my pleasure in learning, in adding to my knowledge. For this reason I have chosen for this play an unusual situation, but an instructive one—an exception, that is to say, but a great exception, one proving the rule, which will no doubt annoy all lovers of the commonplace. What will offend simple minds is that my plot is not simple, nor its point of view single. In real life an action—this, by the way, is a somewhat new discovery—is generally caused by a whole series of motives, more or less fundamental, but as a rule the spectator chooses just one of these—the one which his mind can most easily grasp or that does most credit to his intelligence. A suicide is committed. Business troubles, says the man of affairs. Unrequited love, say the women. Sickness, says the invalid. Despair, says the down-and-out. But it is possible that the motive lay in all or none of these directions, or that the dead man concealed his actual motive by revealing quite another, likely to reflect more to his glory.

I see Miss Julie's tragic fate to be the result of many circumstances: the mother's character, the father's mistaken upbringing of the girl, her own nature, and the influence of her fiancé on a weak, degenerate mind. Also, more directly, the festive mood of Midsummer Eve, her father's absence, her monthly indisposition, her pre-occupation with animals, the excitement of dancing, the magic of dusk, the strongly aphrodisiac influence of flowers, and finally the chance that drives the couple into a room alone—to which must be added the urgency of the excited man.

My treatment of the theme, moreover, is neither exclusively physiological nor psychological. I have not put the blame wholly on the inheritance from her mother, nor on her physical condition at the time, nor on immorality. I have not even preached a moral sermon; in the absence of a priest I leave this to the cook.

I congratulate myself on this multiplicity of motives as being up-to-date, and if others have done the same thing before me, then I congratulate myself on not being alone in my "paradoxes," as all innovations are called.

In regard to the drawing of the characters, I have made my people somewhat "characterless" for the following reasons. In the course of time the word character has assumed manifold meanings. It must have originally signified the dominating trait of the soul-complex, and this was confused with temperament. Later it became the middle-class term for the automaton, one whose nature had become fixed or who had adapted himself to a particular rôle in life. In fact a person who had ceased to grow was called a character, while one continuing to develop—the skilful navigator of life's river, sailing not with sheets set fast, but veering before the wind to luff again—was called characterless, in a derogatory sense, of course, because he was so hard to catch, classify, and keep track of. This middle-class conception of the immobility of the soul was transferred to the stage where the middle-class has always ruled. A character came to signify a man fixed and finished: one who invariably appeared either drunk or jocular or melancholy, and characterization required nothing more than a physical defect such as a club-foot, a wooden leg, a red nose; or the fellow might be made to repeat some such phrase as: "That's capital!" or: "Barkis is willin'!" This simple way of regarding human beings still survives in the great Molière. Harpagon is nothing but a miser, although Harpagon might have been not only a miser, but also a first-rate financier, an excellent father, and a good citizen. Worse still, his "failing" is a distinct advantage to his son-in-law and his daughter, who are his heirs, and who therefore cannot criticize him, even if they have to wait a while to get to bed. I do not believe, therefore, in simple stage characters; and the summary judgments of authors—this man is stupid, that one brutal, this jealous, that stingy, and so forth

—should be challenged by the Naturalists who know the richness of the soul-complex and realize that vice has a reverse side very much like virtue.

Because they are modern characters, living in a period of transition more fever-ishly hysterical than its predecessor at least, I have drawn my figures vacillating, disintegrated, a blend of old and new. Nor does it seem to me unlikely that, through newspapers and conversations, modern ideas may have filtered down to the level of the domestic servant.

My souls (characters) are conglomerations of past and present stages of civilization, bits from books and newspapers, scraps of humanity, rags and tatters of fine clothing, patched together as is the human soul. And I have added a little evolutionary history by making the weaker steal and repeat the words of the stronger, and by making the characters borrow ideas or "suggestions" from one another.

Miss Julie is a modern character, not that the half-woman, the man-hater, has not existed always, but because now that she has been discovered she has stepped to the front and begun to make a noise. The half-woman is a type who thrusts herself forward, selling herself nowadays for power, decorations, distinctions, diplomas, as formerly for money. The type implies degeneration; it is not a good type and it does not endure; but it can unfortunately transmit its misery, and degenerate men seem instinctively to choose their mates from among such women, and so they breed, producing offspring of indeterminate sex to whom life is torture. But fortunately they perish, either because they cannot come to terms with reality, or because their repressed instincts break out uncontrollably, or again because their hopes of catching up with men are shattered. The type is tragic, revealing a desperate fight against nature, tragic too in its Romantic inheritance now dissipated by Naturalism, which wants nothing but happiness—and for happiness strong and sound species are required.

But Miss Julie is also a relic of the old warrior nobility now giving way to the new nobility of nerve and brain. She is a victim of the discord which a mother's "crime" has produced in a family, a victim too of the day's complaisance, of circumstances, of her own defective constitution, all of which are equivalent to the Fate or Universal Law of former days. The Naturalist has abolished guilt with God, but the consequences of the action—punishment, imprisonment or the fear of it—he cannot abolish, for the simple reason that they remain whether he is acquitted or not. An injured fellow-being is not so complacent as outsiders, who have not been injured, can afford to be. Even if the father had felt impelled to take no vengeance, the daughter would have taken vengeance on herself, as she does here, from that innate or acquired sense of honor which the upper-classes inherit—whether from Barbarism or Aryan forebears, or from the chivalry of the Middle Ages, who knows? It is a very beautiful thing, but it has become a danger nowadays to the preservation of the race. It is the nobleman's *hara-kiri*, the Japanese law of inner conscience which compels him to cut his own stomach open at the insult of another, and which survives in modified form in the duel, a privilege of the nobility. And so the valet Jean lives on, but Miss Julie cannot live without honor. This is the thrall's advantage over the nobleman, that he lacks this fatal preoccupation with honor. And in all of us Aryans there is something of the nobleman, or the Don Quixote, which makes us sympathize with the man who commits suicide because he has done something ignoble and lost his honor.

And we are noblemen enough to suffer at the sight of fallen greatness littering the earth like a corpse—yes, even if the fallen rise again and make restitution by honorable deeds. Jean, the valet, is a race-builder, a man of marked characteristics. He was a laborer's son who has educated himself towards becoming a gentleman. He has learnt easily, through his well-developed senses (smell, taste, vision)—and he also has a sense of beauty. He has already bettered himself, and is thick-skinned enough to have no scruples about using other people's services. He is already foreign to his associates, despising them as part of the life he has turned his back on, yet also fearing and fleeing from them because they know his secrets, pry into his plans, watch his rise with envy, and look forward with pleasure to his fall. Hence his dual, indeterminate character, vacillating between love of the heights and hatred of those who have already achieved them. He is, he says himself, an aristocrat; he has learned the secrets of good society. He is polished, but vulgar within; he already wears his tails with taste, but there is no guarantee of his personal cleanliness.

He has some respect for his young lady, but he is frightened of Kristin, who knows his dangerous secrets, and he is sufficiently callous not to allow the night's events to wreck his plans for the future. Having both the slave's brutality and the master's lack of squeamishness, he can see blood without fainting and take disaster by the horns. Consequently he emerges from the battle unscathed, and probably ends his days as a hotel-keeper. And even if *he* does not become a Rumanian Count, his son will doubtless go to the university and perhaps become a county attorney.

The light which Jean sheds on a lower-class conception of life, life seen from below, is on the whole illuminating—when he speaks the truth, which is not often, for he says what is favorable to himself rather than what is true. When Miss Julie suggests that the lower-classes must be oppressed by the attitude of their superiors, Jean naturally agrees, as his object is to gain her sympathy; but when he perceives the advantage of separating himself from the common herd, he at once takes back his words.

It is not because Jean is now rising that he has the upper hand of Miss Julie, but because he is a man. Sexually he is the aristocrat because of his virility, his keener senses, and his capacity for taking the initiative. His inferiority is mainly due to the social environment in which he lives, and he can probably shed it with his valet's livery.

The slave mentality expresses itself in his worship of the Count (the boots), and his religious superstition; but he worships the Count chiefly because he holds that higher position for which Jean himself is striving. And this worship remains even when he has won the daughter of the house and seen how empty is that lovely shell.

I do not believe that a love relationship in the "higher" sense could exist between two individuals of such different quality, but I have made Miss Julie imagine that she is in love, so as to lessen her sense of guilt, and I let Jean suppose that if his social position were altered he would truly love her. I think love is like the hyacinth which has to strike roots in darkness *before* it can produce a vigorous flower. In this case it shoots up quickly, blossoms and goes to seed all at the same time, which is why the plant dies so soon.

As for Kristin, she is a female slave, full of servility and sluggishness acquired in front of the kitchen fire, and stuffed full of morality and religion, which are her cloak and scape-goat. She goes to church as a quick and easy way of unloading her household thefts on to Jesus and taking on a fresh cargo of guiltlessness. For the rest she is a minor character, and I have therefore sketched her in the same manner as the Pastor and the Doctor in "The Father," where I wanted ordinary human beings, as are most country pastors and provincial doctors. If these minor characters seem abstract to some people this is due to the fact that ordinary people are to a certain extent abstract in pursuit of their work; that is to say, they are without individuality, showing, while working, only one side of themselves. And as long as the spectator does not feel a need to see them from other sides, there is nothing wrong with my abstract presentation.

In regard to the dialogue, I have departed somewhat from tradition by not making my characters catechists who ask stupid questions in order to elicit a smart reply. I have avoided the symmetrical, mathematical construction of French dialogue, and let people's minds work irregularly, as they do in real life where, during a conversation, no topic is drained to the dregs, and one mind finds in another a chance cog to engage in. So too the dialogue wanders, gathering in the opening scenes material which is lated picked up, worked over, repeated, expounded and developed like the theme in a musical composition.

The plot speaks for itself, and as it really only concerns two people, I have concentrated on these, introducing only one minor character, the cook, and keeping the unhappy spirit of the father above and behind the action. I have done this because it seems to me that the psychological process is what interests people most today. Our inquisitive souls are no longer satisfied with seeing a thing happen; we must also know how it happens. We want to see the wires themselves, to watch the machinery, to examine the box with the false bottom, to take hold of the magic ring in order to find the join, and look at the cards to see how they are marked.

In this connection I have had in view the documentary novels of the Goncourt brothers, which appeal to me more than any other modern literature.

As far as the technical side of the work is concerned I have made the experiment of abolishing the division into acts. This is because I have come to the conclusion that our capacity for illusion is disturbed by the intervals, during which the audience has time to reflect and escape from the suggestive influence of the author-hypnotist. My play will probably take an hour and a half, and as one can listen to a lecture, a sermon, or a parliamentary debate for as long as that or longer, I do not think a theatrical performance will be fatiguing in the same length of time. As early as 1872, in one of my first dramatic attempts, "The Outlaw," I tried this concentrated form, although with scant success. The play was written in five acts, and only when finished did I become aware of the restless, disjointed effect that it produced. The script was burnt and from the ashes rose a single well-knit act—fifty pages of print, playable in one hour. The form of the present play is, therefore, not new, but it appears to be my own, and changing tastes may make it timely. My hope is one day to have an audience educated enough to sit through a whole evening's entertainment in one act, but one would have to try this out to see. Meanwhile, in order to provide respite for the audience and the players, without allowing the audience to escape from the illusion, I have introduced three art forms: monologue, mime, and ballet. These are all part of drama, having their origins in classic tragedy, monody having become monologue and the chorus, ballet.

Monologue is now condemned by our realists as unnatural, but if one provides motives for it one makes it natural, and then can use it to advantage. It is, surely, natural for a public speaker to walk up and down the room practicing his speech, natural for an actor to read his part aloud, for a servant girl to talk to her cat, a mother to prattle to her child, an old maid to chatter to her parrot, and a sleeper to talk in his sleep. And in order that the actor may have a chance, for once, of working independently, free from the author's direction, it is better that the monologue should not be written, but only indicated. For since it is of small importance what is said in one's sleep or to the parrot or to the cat—none of it influences the action—a talented actor, identifying himself with the atmosphere and the situation, may improvise better than the author, who cannot calculate ahead how much may be said or how long taken without waking the audience from the illusion.

Some Italian theatres have, as we know, returned to improvisation, thereby producing actors who are creative, although within the bounds set by the author. This may well be a step forward, or even the beginning of a new art-form worthy to be called *productive*.

In places where monologue would be unnatural I have used mime, leaving here an even wider scope for the actor's imagination, and more chance for him to win independent laurels. But so as not to try the audience beyond endurance, I have introduced music—fully justified by the Midsummer Eve dance—to exercise its powers of persuasion during the dumb show. But I beg the musical director to consider carefully his choice of compositions, so that conflicting moods are not induced by selections from the current operetta or dance show, or by folk-tunes of too local a character.

The ballet I have introduced cannot be replaced by the usual kind of "crowd-scene," for such scenes are too badly played—a lot of grinning idiots seizing the opportunity to show off and thus destroying the illusion. And as peasants cannot improvise their taunts, but use ready-made phrases with a double meaning. I have not composed their lampoon, but taken a little-known song and dance which I myself noted down in the Stockholm district. The words are not quite to the point, but this too is intentional, for the cunning, i.e. weakness, of the slave prevents him from direct attack. Nor can there be clowning in a serious action, or coarse joking in a situation which nails the lid on a family coffin.

As regards the scenery, I have borrowed from impressionist painting its asymmetry and its economy; thus, I think, strengthening the illusion. For the fact that one does not see the whole room and all the furniture leaves scope for conjecture—that is to say imagination is roused and complements what is seen. I have succeeded too in getting rid of those tiresome exits through doors, since scenery doors are made of canvas, and rock at the slightest touch. They cannot even express the wrath of an irate head of the family who, after a bad dinner, goes out slamming the door behind him, "so that the whole house shakes." On the stage it rocks. I have also kept to a single set, both in order to let the characters develop in their métier and to break away from over-decoration. When one has only one set, one may expect it to be realistic; but as a matter of fact nothing is harder than to get a stage room that looks something like a room, however easily the scene painter can produce flaming volcanoes and water-falls. Presumably the walls must be of canvas; but it seems about time to dispense with painted shelves and cooking utensils. We are asked to accept so many stage conventions that we might at least be spared the pain of painted pots and pans.

I have set the back wall and the table diagonally so that the actors may play full-face and in half-profile when they are sitting opposite one another at the table. In the opera Aïda I saw a diagonal background, which led the eye to unfamiliar perspectives and did not look like mere reaction against boring straight lines.

Another much needed innovation is the abolition of foot-lights. This lighting from below is said to have the purpose of making the actors' faces fatter. But why, I ask, should all actors have fat faces? Does not this under-lighting flatten out all the subtlety of the lower part of the face, specially the jaw, falsify the shape of the nose and throw shadows up over the eyes? Even if this were not so, one thing is certain: that the lights hurt the performers' eyes, so that the full play of their expression is lost. The foot-lights strike part of the retina usually protected—except in sailors who have to watch sunlight on water—and therefore one seldom sees anything other than a crude rolling of the eyes, either sideways or up towards the gallery, showing their whites. Perhaps this too causes that tiresome blinking of the eyelashes, especially by actresses. And when anyone on the stage wants to speak with his eyes, the only thing he can do is to look straight at the audience, with whom he or she then gets into direct communication, outside the framework of the set—a habit called, rightly or wrongly, "greeting one's friends."

Would not sufficiently strong side-lighting, with some kind of reflectors, add to the actor's powers of expression by allowing him to use the face's greatest asset:—the play of the eyes?

I have few illusions about getting the actors to play to the audience instead of with it, although this is what I want. That I shall see an actor's back throughout a critical scene is beyond my dreams, but I do wish crucial scenes could be played, not in front of the prompter's box, like duets expecting applause, but in the place required by the action. So, no revolutions, but just some small modifications, for to make the stage into a real room with the fourth wall missing would be too upsetting altogether.

I dare not hope that the actresses will listen to what I have to say about make-up, for they would rather be beautiful than life-like, but the actor might consider whether it is to his advantage to create an abstract character with grease-paints, and cover his face with it like a mask. Take the case of a man who draws a choleric charcoal line between his eyes and then, in this fixed state of wrath, has to smile at some repartee. What a frightful grimace the result is! And equally, how is that false forehead, smooth as a billiard ball, to wrinkle when the old man loses his temper?

In a modern psychological drama, where the subtlest reactions of a character need to be mirrored in the face rather than expressed by sound and gesture, it would be worth while experimenting with powerful side-lighting on a small stage and a cast without make-up, or at least with the minimum.

If, in addition, we could abolish the visible orchestra, with its distracting lamps and its faces turned toward the audience; if we could have the stalls raised so that the spectators' eyes were higher than the players' knees; if we could get rid of the boxes (the center of my target), with their tittering diners and supper-parties, and have total darkness in the auditorium during the performance; and if, first and foremost, we could have a *small* stage and a *small* house, then perhaps a new dramatic art might arise, and theatre once more become a place of entertainment for educated people. While waiting for such a theatre we may as well go on writing so as to stock that repertory of the future.

I have made an attempt! If it has failed, there is time enough to try again!

EDMOND AND JULES DE GONCOURT
The Fad of Naturalism

After reading Edgar Allan Poe. Something the critics have not noticed: a new literary world, pointing to the literature of the twentieth century. Scientific miracles, fables on the pattern A + B; a clear-sighted, sickly literature. No more poetry, but analytic fantasy. Something monomaniacal. Things playing a more important part than people; love giving way to deductions and other sources of ideas, style, subject, and interest; the basis of the novel transferred from the heart to the head, from the passion to the idea, from the drama to the denouement.

There is now only one consuming interest left in our life, the passion for the study of living reality. Apart from that there is nothing but boredom and emptiness. Admittedly we have galvanized history into reality, and done so with a truer truthfulness than other historians. But now the truth that is dead no longer holds any interest for us. We are like a man accustomed to drawing from a wax dummy who has suddenly been presented with a living model, or rather life itself with its entrails warm and active, its guts palpitating.

In the novel as we understand it, the material description of things and places is not description for the sake of description. It is a means of installing the reader in a certain setting favourable to the moral emotion which should arise from those things and places.

This evening Flaubert, while paying tribute to his colleague's genius, attacked the prefaces, the doctrines, the naturalist professions of faith, in a word all the

From *Pages from the Goncourt Journal*, translated from the French by Robert Baldick, New York and London, 1962, pp. 19-20, 106-107, 229, 232, 289, 365; reprinted by permission of the copyright holders and Oxford University Press.

rather flamboyant humbug with which Zola helps along the sale of his books. Zola replied roughly to this effect: "You, you had private means which allowed you to remain independent of a good many things. But I had to earn my living with nothing but my pen; I had to go through the mill of journalism and write all sorts of shameful stuff; and it has left me with—how shall I put it?—a certain taste for charlatanism. . . . I consider the word *Naturalism* as ridiculous as you do, but I shall go on repeating it over and over again, because you have to give things new names for the public to think that they are new. . . . You know, I divide what I write into two parts. On the one hand there are my novels, on which I shall be judged and on which I wish to be judged; and on the other hand there are my articles for the *Bien public*, for Russia and for Marseilles, which are just so much charlatanism to puff my books. . . . First of all I took a nail and with a blow of the hammer I drove it one inch into the public's brain; then with a second blow I drove it two inches in. . . . Well, that hammer of mine is the journalism I write myself around my novels."

Yesterday, at the dinner given on the occasion of Turgenev's departure for Russia, we talked about love, about the love that is depicted in books.

I said that so far love had not been studied scientifically in the novel and that we had presented only its poetic aspects. Zola, who had brought the conversation round to this subject, in order to pick our brains for his new book, asserted that love was not a special feeling, that it did not affect people as overwhelmingly as it was said to, that the phenomena you found in it were also to be found in friendship, patriotism and so on, and that the greater intensity of love was due simply to the prospect of copulation.

Turgenev replied that this was not true, that love was a feeling with a special *colour* of its own, and that Zola was on the wrong tack if he would not recognize this colour, this difference of quality. He said that love had an effect on a man that no other feeling produced, and that a person who was really in love felt as if he had been born again. He spoke of a heaviness of the heart which had nothing human about it. He spoke of the eyes of the first woman he had ever loved as of something quite intangible and entirely divorced from materiality. . . .

There is one unfortunate thing about all this, and that is that neither Flaubert, for all his bragging about such matters, nor Zola, nor I have ever been seriously in love and that we are all incapable of describing love. Only Turgenev could do it, but he lacks precisely that critical judgement that we could bring to the task if we had been in love as he has.

Zola came to see me today. He looks and behaves like a wholesale dealer in copy. He kept grumbling that the lines in the *Gil Blas* contained four letters more than the lines in all the other papers. That is why he has sold the novel to Dumont for 20,000 francs, because with those four letters his copy would have come to only 18,000 lines. Now he does not care how many cuts the paper makes . . . it will still have to pay him 20,000 francs.

He is worried about the novel he has to do next, *Les Paysans*. He wants to spend a month on a farm in Beauce, with a letter of recommendation from a rich landlord to his farmer, a letter announcing the arrival, with her husband, of a sick woman in need of country air. "You see," he said, "all we need is a couple of beds in a whitewashed room. . . . And of course our meals at the farmer's table. . . . Otherwise I shouldn't learn anything. . . ."

As for *Les Chemins de fer*, his novel about the noise and bustle of a railway station and a man living in all that noise and bustle, with some sort of dramatic plot, he does not see his way to writing that yet. . . .

He would rather make a start on something about a strike in a mining district, beginning with a bourgeois having his throat slit on the first page. . . . Then the sentence, with some of the men condemned to death and others sent to prison. . . . The trial serving as a pretext for a serious, thoroughgoing study of the social question.

In my interview with Huret, I could have said: "I gave the complete formula of naturalism in *Germinie Lacerteux*, and *L'Assommoir* was written from beginning to end on the lines laid down in that book. Later I was the first to abandon naturalism—not, like Zola, for a sordid reason, inspired by the success of *L'Abbé Constantin* which made him write *Le Rêve*—but because I considered that the genre, in its original form, was worn out. . . . Yes, I was the first to abandon naturalism for what the young writers are now using to fill its place—dreams, symbolism, satanism, etc., etc.—when I wrote *Les Frères Zemganno* and *La Faustin*, for in those books I, the inventor of naturalism, tried to dematerialize it long before anyone else thought of doing so."

LEO TOLSTOY

Art as Ethical Communication

What is art if we put aside the conception of beauty, which confuses the whole matter? The latest and most comprehensible definitions of art, apart from the conception of beauty, are the following:—(1) *a*, Art is an activity arising even in the animal kingdom, and springing from sexual desire and the propensity to play (Schiller, Darwin, Spencer), and *b*, accompanied by a pleasurable excitement of the nervous system (Grant Allen). This is the physiological-evolutionary definition. (2) Art is the external manifestation, by means of lines, colours, movements, sounds, or words, of emotions felt by man (Véron). This is the experimental definition. According to the very latest definition (Sully), (3) Art is "the production of some permanent object or passing action which is fitted not only to supply an active enjoyment to the producer, but to convey a pleasurable impression to a number of spectators or listeners, quite apart from any personal advantage to be derived from it."

Notwithstanding the superiority of these definitions to the metaphysical definitions which depended on the conception of beauty, they are yet far from exact. The first, the physiological-evolutionary definition (1) *a*, is inexact, because instead of speaking about the artistic activity itself, which is the real matter in hand, it treats of the derivation of art. The modification of it, *b*, based on the physiological effects on the human organism, is inexact because within the limits of such definition many other human activities can be included, as has occurred in the neo-æsthetic theories which reckon as art the preparation of handsome clothes, pleasant scents, and even of victuals.

The experimental definition, (2), which makes art consist in the expression of emotions, is inexact because a man may express his emotions by means of lines, colours, sounds, or words and yet may not act on others by such expression—and then the manifestation of his emotions is not art.

The third definition (that of Sully) is inexact because in the production of objects or actions affording pleasure to the producer and a pleasant emotion to the spectators or hearers apart from personal advantage, may be included the showing of conjuring tricks or gymnastic exercises, and other activities which are not art. And further, many things the production of which does not afford pleasure to the

From "What Is Art?" [1898], *What Is Art? and Other Essays*, translated from the Russian by Aylmer Maude, London and New York, 1930, pp. 119-26, 141-2, 175-80, 228-30, 238-42; reprinted by permission of Oxford University Press.

producer and the sensation received from which is unpleasant, such as gloomy, heart-rending scenes in a poetic description or a play, may nevertheless be undoubted works of art.

The inaccuracy of all these definitions arises from the fact that in them all (as also in the metaphysical definitions) the object considered is the pleasure art may give, and not the purpose it may serve in the life of man and of humanity.

In order to define art correctly it is necessary first of all to cease to consider it as a means to pleasure, and to consider it as one of the conditions of human life. Viewing it in this way we cannot fail to observe that art is one of the means of intercourse between man and man.

Every work of art causes the receiver to enter into a certain kind of relationship both with him who produced or is producing the art, and with all those who, simultaneously, previously, or subsequently, receive the same artistic impression.

Speech transmitting the thoughts and experiences of men serves as a means of union among them, and art serves a similar purpose. The peculiarity of this latter means of intercourse, distinguishing it from intercourse by means of words, consists in this, that whereas by words a man transmits his thoughts to another, by art he transmits his feelings. . . .

The feelings with which the artist infects others may be most various—very strong or very weak, very important or very insignificant, very bad or very good: feelings of love of one's country, self-devotion and submission to fate or to God expressed in a drama, raptures of lovers described in a novel, feelings of voluptuousness expressed in a picture, courage expressed in a triumphal march, merriment evoked by a dance, humour evoked by a funny story, the feeling of quietness transmitted by an evening landscape or by a lullaby, or the feeling of admiration evoked by a beautiful arabesque—it is all art.

If only the spectators or auditors are infected by the feelings which the author has felt, it is art.

To evoke in oneself a feeling one has once experienced and having evoked it in oneself then by means of movements, lines, colours, sounds, or forms expressed in words, so to transmit that feeling that others experience the same feeling—this is the activity of art.

Art is a human activity consisting in this, that one man consciously by means of certain external signs, hands on to others feelings he has lived through, and that others are infected by these feelings and also experience them.

Art is not, as the metaphysicians say, the manifestation of some mysterious Idea of beauty or God; it is not, as the æsthetic physiologists say, a game in which man lets off his excess of stored-up energy; it is not the expression of man's emotions by external signs; it is not the production of pleasing objects; and, above all, it is not pleasure; but it is a means of union among men joining them together in the same feelings, and indispensable for the life and progress towards well-being of individuals and of humanity.

As every man, thanks to man's capacity to express thoughts by words, may know all that has been done for him in the realms of thought by all humanity before his day, and can in the present, thanks to this capacity to understand the thoughts of others, become a sharer in their activity and also himself hand on to his contemporaries and descendants the thoughts he has assimilated from others as well as those that have arisen in himself; so, thanks to man's capacity to be infected with the feelings of others by means of art, all that is being lived through by his contemporaries is accessible to him, as well as the feelings experienced by men thousands of years ago, and he has also the possibility of transmitting his own feelings to others.

If people lacked the capacity to receive the thoughts conceived by men who preceded them and to pass on to others their own thoughts, men would be like wild beasts, or like Kasper Hauser.

And if men lacked this other capacity of being infected by art, people might be almost more savage still, and above all more separated from, and more hostile to, one another.

And therefore the activity of art is a most important one, as important as the activity of speech itself and as generally diffused.

As speech does not act on us only in sermons, orations, or books, but in all those remarks by which we interchange thoughts and experiences with one another, so also art in the wide sense of the word permeates our whole life, but it is only to some of its manifestations that we apply the term in the limited sense of the word.

We are accustomed to understand art to be only what we hear and see in theatres, concerts, and exhibitions; together with buildings, statues, poems, and novels. . . . But all this is but the smallest part of the art by which we communicate with one another in life. All human life is filled with works of art of every kind—from cradle-song, jest, mimicry, the ornamentation of houses, dress, and utensils, to church services, buildings, monuments, and triumphal processions. It is all artistic activity. So that by art, in the limited sense of the word, we do not mean all human activity transmitting feelings but only that part which we for some reason select from it and to which we attach special importance.

This special importance has always been given by men to that part of this activity which transmits feelings flowing from their religious perception, and this small part they have specifically called art, attaching to it the full meaning of the word.

That was how men of old—Socrates, Plato, and Aristotle—looked on art. Thus did the Hebrew prophets and the ancient Christians regard art. Thus it was, and still is, understood by the Mohammedans, and thus it still is understood by religious folk among our own peasantry.

Some teachers of mankind—such as Plato in his *Republic*, and people like the primitive Christians, the strict Mohammedans, and the Buddhists—have gone so far as to repudiate all art.

People viewing art in this way (in contradiction to the prevalent view of to-day which regards any art as good if only it affords pleasure) held and hold that art (as contrasted with speech, which need not be listened to) is so highly dangerous in its power to infect people against their wills, that mankind will lose far less by banishing all art than by tolerating each and every art.

Evidently such people were wrong in repudiating all art, for they denied what cannot be denied—one of the indispensable means of communication without which mankind could not exist. But not less wrong are the people of civilized European society of our class and day in favouring any art if it but serves beauty, that is, gives people pleasure.

Formerly people feared lest among works of art there might chance to be some causing corruption, and they prohibited art altogether. Now they only fear lest they should be deprived of any enjoyment art can afford, and they patronize any art. And I think the last error is much grosser than the first and that its consequences are far more harmful. . . .

"We only need escape for a moment from the habit of considering this trinity of Goodness, Beauty, and Truth presented to us by Baumgarten, to be as true as the Trinity of religion, and need only ask ourselves what we all have always understood by the words which form this triad, to be convinced of the utterly fantastic nature of the union into one, of three absolutely different words and conceptions, which are not even commensurable in meaning.

"Goodness, Beauty, and Truth are put on one level, and all three conceptions are treated as though they were fundamental and metaphysical: whereas in reality such is not at all the case.

"Goodness is the eternal, the highest, aim of our life. However we may understand goodness our life is nothing but a striving towards the good, that is, towards God.

"Goodness is really the fundamental metaphysical perception which forms the essence of our consciousness: a perception not defined by reason.

"Goodness is that which cannot be defined by anything else but which defines everything else.

"But Beauty—if we do not want mere words, but speak of what we understand —beauty is nothing but what pleases us. The notion of beauty not only does not coincide with goodness, but rather is contrary to it; for the good most often coincides with victory over the passions while beauty is at the root of our passions.

"The more utterly we surrender ourselves to beauty the farther we depart from goodness. I know that to this people always reply that there is a moral and spiritual beauty, but this is merely playing with words, for by spiritual and moral beauty nothing else is understood but goodness. For the most part, beauty of soul, or goodness, not only does not coincide with what is ordinarily understood as beauty but is opposed to it.

"As to truth—still less can we attribute to this member of the trinity identity with goodness, or even any independent existence at all.

"By truth we merely mean the correspondence of an expression or of the definition of an object, with reality, or with an understanding of the object common to every one, and therefore it is a means of arriving at the good. But what is there in common between the conceptions of beauty and truth on the one hand, and of goodness on the other? Truth spoken expressly to cause annoyance certainly does not harmonize with goodness.

"Not only are beauty and truth not conceptions equivalent to goodness, and not only do they not form one entity with goodness, but they do not even coincide with it. For instance, Socrates and Pascal as well as many others, considered that learning the truth about unnecessary things does not accord with goodness. With beauty, truth has not even anything in common, but for the most part is in contradiction with it, for truth generally exposes the deception and destroys the illusion which is a chief condition of beauty.

"And lo and behold! the arbitrary conjunction into one, of these three conceptions which are not commensurable but foreign to one another, has served as the basis for that amazing theory according to which the difference between good art transmitting good feeling, and bad art transmitting bad feeling, is completely obliterated, and one of the lowest manifestations of art, art merely for enjoyment —that art against which all the teachers of humanity have warned mankind—has come to be considered the highest art." . . .

I have no right and no authority to condemn the new art on the ground that I (a man educated in the first half of the nineteenth century) do not understand it; I can only say that it is incomprehensible to me. The only advantage the art I acknowledge has over the Decadent art lies in the fact that the art I recognize is comprehensible to a somewhat larger number of people than present-day art.

The fact that I am accustomed to a certain exclusive art and can understand it, but am unable to understand another still more exclusive art, does not give me a right to conclude that my art is the real, true art, and that the other one, which I do not understand, is an unreal, a bad, art. I can only conclude that art, becoming ever more and more exclusive, has become more and more incomprehensible to an ever-increasing number of people, and that in this, its progress towards greater and greater incomprehensibility (on one level of which I am standing with the art familiar to me), it has reached a point where it is understood by a very small number of the elect, and the number of these chosen people is becoming ever smaller and smaller.

As soon as ever the art of the upper classes separated itself from universal art a conviction arose that art may be art and yet be incomprehensible to the masses. And as soon as this position was admitted it had inevitably to be admitted also that art may be intelligible only to the very smallest number of the elect and eventually to two, or to one, of our nearest friends, or to oneself alone—which is practically what is being said by modern artists:—"I create and understand myself, and if any one does not understand me so much the worse for him."

The assertion that art may be good art and at the same time incomprehensible to a great number of people, is extremely unjust, and its consequences are ruinous to art itself; but at the same time it is so common and has so eaten into our conceptions, that it is impossible to make sufficiently clear its whole absurdity.

Nothing is more common than to hear it said of reputed works of art that they are very good but very difficult to understand. We are quite used to such assertions, and yet to say that a work of art is good but incomprehensible to the majority of men, is the same as saying of some kind of food that it is very good but most people can't eat it. The majority of men may not like rotten cheese or putrefying grouse, dishes esteemed by people with perverted tastes; but bread and fruit are only good when they are such as please the majority of men. And it is the same with art. Perverted art may not please the majority of men, but good art always pleases every one. . . .

Moreover it cannot be said that the majority of people lack the taste to esteem the highest works of art. The majority always have understood and still understand what we also recognize as being the very best art: the epic of Genesis, the Gospel parables, folk-legends, fairy-tales, and folk-songs, are understood by all. How can it be that the majority has suddenly lost its capacity to understand what is high in our art? . . .

Art is differentiated from activity of the understanding, which demands preparation and a certain sequence of knowledge (so that one cannot learn trigonometry before knowing geometry), by the fact that it acts on people independently of their state of development and education, that the charm of a picture, of sounds, or of forms, infects any man whatever his plane of development.

The business of art lies just in this: to make that understood and felt which in the form of an argument might be incomprehensible and inaccessible. Usually it seems to the recipient of a truly artistic impression that he knew the thing before, but had been unable to express it.

And such has always been the nature of good, supreme art; the *Iliad*, the *Odyssey*; the stories of Isaac, Jacob, and Joseph; the Hebrew prophets, the psalms, the Gospel parables; the story of Sakya Muni and the hymns of the Vedas, all transmit very exalted feelings and are nevertheless quite comprehensible now to us, educated or uneducated, just as they were comprehensible to the men of those times, long ago, who were even less educated than our labourers. People talk about incomprehensibility; but if art is the transmission of feelings flowing from man's religious perception, how can a feeling be incomprehensible which is founded on religion, that is, on man's relation to God? Such art should be, and has actually always been, comprehensible to everybody, because every man's relation to God is one and the same. This is why the churches and the images in them were always comprehensible to every one. The hindrance to an understanding of the best and highest feelings (as is said in the Gospel) lies not at all in deficiency of development or learning, but on the contrary in false development and false learning. A good and lofty work of art may be incomprehensible, but not to simple, unperverted, peasant labourers (what is highest is understood by them)—it may be and often is unintelligible to erudite, perverted people destitute of religion. And this continually occurs in our society in which the highest feelings are simply not understood. For instance, I know people who consider themselves most refined, and who say that they do not understand the poetry of love of one's neighbour, of self-sacrifice, or of chastity. . . .

Art cannot be incomprehensible to the great masses only because it is very good—as artists of our day are fond of telling us. Rather we are bound to conclude that this art in unintelligible to the great masses only because it is very bad art, or even is not art at all. So that the favourite argument (naïvely accepted by the cultured crowd), that in order to feel art one has first to understand it (which really only means habituate oneself to it), is the truest indication that what we are asked to understand by such a method is either very bad, exclusive art, or is not art at all.

People say that works of art do not please the people because they are incapable of understanding them. But if the aim of works of art is to infect people with the emotion the artist has experienced, how can one talk about not understanding? . . .

Mark this above all: if only it be admitted that art may be unintelligible to any one of sound mind and yet be art, there is no reason why any circle of perverted people should not compose works tickling their own perverted feelings and comprehensible to no one but themselves, and call it "art," as is actually being done by the so-called Decadents.

The direction art has taken may be compared to placing on a large circle other circles, smaller and smaller, until a cone is formed, the apex of which is no longer a circle at all. That is what has happened to the art of our times. . . .

Art in our society has become so perverted that not only has bad art come to be considered good, but even the very perception of what art really is has been lost. In order to be able to speak about the art of our society it is, therefore, first of all necessary to distinguish art from counterfeit art.

There is one indubitable sign distinguishing real art from its counterfeit—namely, the infectiousness of art. If a man without exercising effort and without altering his standpoint, on reading, hearing, or seeing another man's work experiences a mental condition which unites him with that man and with others who are also affected by that work, then the object evoking that condition is a work of art. And however poetic, realistic, striking, or interesting, a work may be, it is not a work of art if it does not evoke that feeling (quite distinct from all other feelings) of joy and of spiritual union with another (the author) and with others (those who are also infected by it). . . .

The chief peculiarity of this feeling is that the recipient of a truly artistic impression is so united to the artist that he feels as if the work were his own and not some one else's—as if what it expresses were just what he had long been wishing to express. A real work of art destroys in the consciousness of the recipient the separation between himself and the artist, and not that alone, but also between himself and all whose minds receive this work of art. In this freeing of our personality from its separation and isolation, in this uniting of it with others, lies the chief characteristic and the great attractive force of art.

If a man is infected by the author's condition of soul, if he feels this emotion and this union with others, then the object which has effected this is art; but if there be no such infection, if there be not this union with the author and with others who are moved by the same work—then it is not art. And not only is infection a sure sign of art, but the degree of infectiousness is also the sole measure of excellence in art.

The stronger the infection the better is the art, as art, speaking of it now apart from its subject-matter—that is, not considering the value of the feelings it transmits.

And the degree of the infectiousness of art depends on three conditions:—

(1) On the greater or lesser individuality of the feeling transmitted; (2) on the greater or lesser clearness with which the feeling is transmitted; (3) on the sincerity of the artist, that is, on the greater or lesser force with which the artist himself feels the emotion he transmits.

The more individual the feeling transmitted the more strongly does it act on the recipient; the more individual the state of soul into which he is transferred the more pleasure does the recipient obtain and therefore the more readily and strongly does he join in it.

Clearness of expression assists infection because the recipient who mingles in consciousness with the author is the better satisfied the more clearly that feeling is transmitted which, as it seems to him, he has long known and felt and for which he has only now found expression.

But most of all is the degree of infectiousness of art increased by the degree of sincerity in the artist. As soon as the spectator, hearer, or reader, feels that the artist is infected by his own production and writes, sings, or plays, for himself, and not merely to act on others, this mental condition of the artist infects the recipient; and, on the contrary, as soon as the spectator, reader, or hearer, feels that the author is not writing, singing, or playing, for his own satisfaction—does not himself feel what he wishes to express, but is doing it for him, the recipient—resistance immediately springs up, and the most individual and the newest feelings and the cleverest technique not only fail to produce any infection but actually repel.

I have mentioned three conditions of contagion in art, but they may all be summed up into one, the last, sincerity; that is, that the artist should be impelled by an inner need to express his feeling. That condition includes the first; for if the artist is sincere he will express the feeling as he experienced it. And as each man is different from every one else, his feeling will be individual for every one else; and the more individual it is—the more the artist has drawn it from the depths of his nature—the more sympathetic and sincere will it be. And this same sincerity will impel the artist to find clear expression for the feeling which he wishes to transmit.

Therefore this third condition—sincerity—is the most important of the three. It is always complied with in peasant art, and this explains why such art always acts so powerfully; but it is a condition almost entirely absent from our upper-class art, which is continually produced by artists actuated by personal aims of covetousness or vanity.

Such are the three conditions which divide art from its counterfeits, and which also decide the quality of every work of art considered apart from its subject-matter. . . .

The essence of the Christian perception consists in the recognition by every man of his sonship to God and of the consequent union of men with God and with one another, as is said in the Gospel (John xvii. 21). Therefore the subject-matter of Christian art is of a kind that feeling can unite men with God and with one another.

The expression *unite men with God and with one another* may seem obscure to people accustomed to the misuse of these words that is so customary, but the words have a perfectly clear meaning nevertheless. They indicate that the Christian union of man (in contradiction to the partial, exclusive, union of only certain men) is that which unites all without exception.

Art, all art, has this characteristic, that it unites people. Every art causes those to whom the artist's feeling is transmitted to unite in soul with the artist and also with all who receive the same impression. But non-Christian art while uniting some people, makes that very union a cause of separation between these united people and others; so that union of this kind is often a source not merely of division but even of enmity towards others. Such is all patriotic art, with its anthems, poems, and monuments; such is all Church art, that is, the art of certain cults, with their images, statues, processions, and other local ceremonies. Such art is belated and non-Christian, uniting the people of one cult only to separate them yet more sharply from the members of other cults, and even to place them in relations of hostility to one another. Christian art is such only as tends to unite all without exception, either by evoking in them the perception that each man and all men stand in a like relation towards God and towards their neighbour, or by evoking in them identical feelings, which may even be the very simplest, provided that they are not repugnant to Christianity and are natural to every one without exception.

Good Christian art of our time may be unintelligible to people because of im-perfections in its form or because men are inattentive to it, but it must be such that all men can experience the feelings it transmits. It must be the art not of some one group of people, or of one class, or of one nationality, or of one religious cult; that is, it must not transmit feelings accessible only to a man educated in a certain way, or only to an aristocrat, or a merchant, or only to a Russian, or a native of Japan, or a Roman Catholic, or a Buddhist, and so on, but it must trans-mit feelings accessible to every one. Only art of this kind can in our time be acknowledged to be good art, worthy of being chosen out from all the rest of art and encouraged.

Christian art, that is, the art of our time, should be catholic in the original meaning of the word, that is, universal, and therefore it should unite all men. And only two kinds of feeling unite all men: first, feelings flowing from a per-ception of our sonship to God and of the brotherhood of man; and next, the simple feelings of common life accessible to every one without exception—such as feelings of merriment, of pity, of cheerfulness, of tranquillity, and so forth. Only these two kinds of feelings can now supply material for art good in its subject-matter.

And the action of these two kinds of art apparently so dissimilar, is one and the same. The feelings flowing from the perception of our sonship to God and the brotherhood of man—such as a feeling of sureness in truth, devotion to the will of God, self-sacrifice, respect for and love of man—evoked by Christian religious perception; and the simplest feelings, such as a softened or a merry mood caused by a song or an amusing jest intelligible to every one, or by a touching story, or a drawing, or a little doll: both alike produce one and the same effect—the loving union of man with man. Sometimes people who are together, if not hostile to one another, are at least estranged in mood and feeling, till perhaps a story, a per-formance, a picture, or even a building, but oftenest of all music, unites them all as by an electric flash, and in place of their former isolation or even enmity they are conscious of union and mutual love. Each is glad that another feels what he feels; glad of the communion established not only between him and all present, but also with all now living who will yet share the same impression; and, more than that, he feels the mysterious gladness of a communion which, reaching be-yond the grave, unites us with all men of the past who have been moved by the same feelings and with all men of the future who will yet be touched by them. And this effect is produced both by religious art which transmits feelings of love of God and one's neighbour, and by universal art transmitting the very simplest feelings common to all men.

The art of our time should be appraised differently from former art chiefly in this, that the art of our time, that is, Christian art (basing itself on a religious perception which demands the union of man), excludes from the domain of art good in its subject-matter, everything transmitting exclusive feelings which do not unite men but divide them. It relegates such work to the category of art that is bad in its subject-matter; while on the other hand it includes in the category of art that is good in subject-matter a section not formerly admitted as deserving of selection and respect, namely, universal art transmitting even the most trifling and simple feelings if only they are accessible to all men without exception, and there-fore unite them. Such art cannot but be esteemed good in our time, for it attains the end which Christianity, the religious perception of our time, sets before humanity.

Christian art either evokes in men feelings which through love of God and of one's neighbour draw them to closer and ever closer union and make them ready for, and capable of, such union; or evokes in them feelings which show them that they are already united in the joys and sorrows of life. And therefore the Christian art of our time can be and is of two kinds: first, art transmitting feelings flowing from a religious perception of man's position in the world in relation to God and to his neighbour—religious art in the limited meaning of the term; and secondly, art transmitting the simplest feelings of common life, but such always as are accessible to all men in the whole world—the art of common life—the art of the people—universal art. Only these two kinds of art can be considered good art in our time.

The first, religious art—transmitting both positive feelings of love of God and one's neighbour, and negative feelings of indignation and horror at the violation of love—manifests itself chiefly in the form of words, and to some extent also in painting and sculpture: the second kind, universal art, transmitting feelings accessible to all, manifests itself in words, in painting, in sculpture, in dances, in architecture, and most of all in music.

F. M. DOSTOEVSKY

Prophetic Realism

Three weeks ago (December 18 by the Style here) I attacked another novel, and am now working day and night. The idea of the book is the old one which I always have so greatly liked; but it is so difficult that hitherto I never have had the courage to carry it out; and if I'm setting to work at it now, it's only because I'm in a desperate plight. The basic idea is the representation of a truly perfect and noble man. And this is more difficult than anything else in the world, particularly nowadays. All writers, not ours alone but foreigners also, who have sought to represent Absolute Beauty, were unequal to the task, for it is an infinitely difficult one. The beautiful is the ideal; but ideals, with us as in civilized Europe, have long been wavering. There is in the world only one figure of absolute beauty: Christ. That infinitely lovely figure is, as a matter of course, an infinite marvel (the whole Gospel of St. John is full of this thought: John sees the wonder of the Incarnation, the visible apparition of the Beautiful). I have gone too far in my explanation. I will only say further that of all the noble figures in Christian literature, I reckon Don Quixote as the most perfect. But Don Quixote is noble only by being at the same time comic. And Dickens's Pickwickians (they were certainly much weaker than Don Quixote, but still it's a powerful

From letters to his niece [1868], and to Strachen [1869], *Letters of Dostoevsky*, translated from the Russian by E. C. Mayne, New York, 1917, pp. 135-6, 150-51, 158-9; reprinted by permission of The Macmillan Company and Chatto & Windus Ltd.

work) are comic, and this it is which gives them their great value. The reader feels sympathy and compassion with the Beautiful, derided and unconscious of its own worth. The secret of humour consists precisely in this art of wakening the reader's sympathy. Jean Valjean is likewise a remarkable attempt, but he awakens sympathy only by his terrible fate and the injustice of society towards him. I have not yet found anything similar to that, anything so *positive*, and therefore I fear that the book may be a "positive" failure. Single details will perhaps come out not badly. But I fear that the novel may be tiresome. It is to be very extensive. The first part I wrote in twenty-three days, and have lately sent off. This first part has no action at all. It is confessedly only a prologue. It is right that it should not compromise the whole work in any way, but it illuminates nothing, and poses no problem. My sole aim is to awake at least such interest in the reader as will make him read the second part. That second part I am beginning to-day, and shall finish in a month. (I have always worked as quickly as that.) I believe that it will be stronger and more significant than the first part. Well, dear, wish me luck! The novel is called "The Idiot."

I have my own idea about art, and it is this: What most people regard as fantastic and lacking in universality, I hold to be the inmost essence of truth. Arid observation of everyday trivialities I have long ceased to regard as realism—it is quite the reverse. In any newspaper one takes up, one comes across reports of wholly authentic facts, which nevertheless strike one as extraordinary. Our writers regard them as fantastic, and take no account of them; and yet they are the truth, for they are facts. But who troubles to observe, record, describe, them? They happen every day and every moment, therefore they are not "exceptional." . . .

The Russians are often unjustly reproached with beginning all sorts of things, making great plans—but never carrying out even the most trivial of them. This view is obsolete and shallow, and false besides. It is a slander on the Russian national character; and even in Bielinsky's time it was prevalent. How paltry and petty is such a way of driving home actualities! Always the same old story! In this way, we shall let all true actuality slip through our fingers. And who will really delineate the facts, will steep himself in them? Of Turgenev's novel I don't wish even to speak; the devil knows what it may mean! But is not my fantastic "Idiot" the very dailiest truth? Precisely such characters *must* exist in those strata of our society which have divorced themselves from the soil—which actually are becoming fantastic. But I'll talk of it no more! In my book much was written in haste, much is too drawn-out, much has miscarried; but much, too, is extremely good. I am not defending the novel, but the idea. Do tell me your view of it; and, of course, quite frankly. The more you find fault with me, the higher shall I rate your honesty.

Now here's what I propose:

1. A long novel entitled "Atheism" (but for God's sake, let this be entirely between ourselves); before I attack it, I shall have to read a whole library of

atheistic works by Catholic and Orthodox-Greek writers. Even in the most favourable circumstances it can't be ready for two years. I have my principal figure ready
in my mind. A Russian of our class, getting on in years, not particularly cultured,
though not uncultured either, and of a certain degree of social importance, loses
quite suddenly, in ripe age, his belief in God. His whole life long he has been
wholly taken up by his work, has never dreamed of escaping from the rut, and up
to his forty-fifth year, has distinguished himself in no wise. (The working-out will
be pure psychology: profound in feeling, human, and thoroughly Russian.) The
loss of faith has a colossal effect on him (the treatment of the story, and the
environment, are both largely conceived). He tries to attach himself to the
younger generation—the atheists, Slavs, Occidentalists, the Russian Sectarians and
Anchorites, the mystics: amongst others he comes across a Polish Jesuit; thence
he descends to the abysses of the Chlysty-sect;[1] and finds at last salvation in Russian soil, the Russian Saviour, and the Russian God. (For heaven's sake, don't
speak of this to anyone; when I have written this last novel, I shall be ready to
die, for I shall have uttered therein my whole heart's burden.) My dear friend,
I have a totally different conception of truth and realism from that of our "realists" and critics. My God! If one could but tell categorically all that we Russians
have gone through during the last ten years in the way of spiritual development,
all the realists would shriek that it was pure fantasy! And yet it would be pure
realism! It *is* the one true, deep realism; theirs is altogether too superficial. Is not
the figure of Lyubim Torzov, for instance, at bottom hideously unmeaning? Yet
it's the boldest thing they've produced. And they call *that* profound realism!
With such realism, one couldn't show so much as the hundredth part of the true
facts. But our idealists have actually *predicted* many of the actual facts—really,
that has been done. My dear fellow, don't laugh at my conceit; for I'm like Paul:
"Nobody praises me, so I'll praise myself."

[1] A flagellant sect still widely spread over Russia. TRANSLATOR'S NOTE.

GEORGE SAND AND GUSTAVE FLAUBERT

The Counter-Religions of Humanity and Art

Nahant, 8 December 1874

Poor dear friend,

I love you all the more because you are growing more unhappy. How you torment
yourself, and how you disturb yourself about life! for all of which you complain,
is life; it has never been better for anyone or in any time. One feels it more or

From letters of George Sand to Gustave Flaubert [1874, 1876], *Letters of George Sand
and Gustave Flaubert*, translated from the French by Aimée L. McKenzie, New York, 1921,
pp. 330-31, 350-56; reprinted by permission of Duckworth & Co. Ltd.
Letter of Gustave Flaubert to George Sand [1875], *Selected Letters*, translated from the
French by Francis Steegmuller, London, 1954, pp. 249-51. Copyright 1953 by Francis Steegmuller; reprinted by permission of Farrar, Straus & Co. and Hamish Hamilton Ltd.

less, one understands it more or less, one suffers with it more or less, and the more one is in advance of the age one lives in, the more one suffers. We pass like shadows on a background of clouds which the sun seldom pierces, and we cry ceaselessly for the sun which can do no more for us. It is for us to clear away our clouds.

You love literature too much; it will destroy you and you will not destroy the imbecility of the human race. Poor dear imbecility, that, for my part, I do not hate, that I regard with maternal eyes: for it is a childhood and all childhood is sacred. What hatred you have devoted to it! what warfare you wage on it!

You have too much knowledge and intelligence, you forget that there is something above art: namely, wisdom, of which art at its apogee is only the expression. Wisdom comprehends all: beauty, truth, goodness, enthusiasm, in consequence. It teaches us to see outside of ourselves, something more elevated than is in ourselves, and to assimilate it little by little, through contemplation and admiration.

But I shall not succeed in changing you. I shall not even succeed in making you understand how I envisage and how I lay hold upon *happiness*, that is to say, the acceptation of life whatever it may be! There is one person who could change you and save you, that is father Hugo; for he has one side on which he is a great philosopher, while at the same time he is the great artist that you require and that I am not. You must see him often. I believe that he will quiet you: I have not enough tempest in me now for you to understand me. As for him, I think that he has kept his thunderbolts and that he has all the same acquired the gentleness and the compassion of age.

See him, see him often and tell him your troubles, which are great, I see that, and which turn too much to *spleen*. You think too much of the dead, you think that they have too soon reached their rest. They have not. They are like us, they are searching. They labor in the search.

Every one is well, and embraces you. As for me, I do not get well, but I have hopes, well or not, to keep on still so as to bring up my grandchildren, and to love you as long as I have a breath left.   G. SAND

Nahant, 12 January 1776

My cherished Cruchard,

I want to write to you every day; time is lacking absolutely. At last here is a free moment; we are buried under the snow; it is the sort of weather that I adore: this whiteness is like general purification, and the amusements of the house seem more intimate and sweeter. Can anyone hate the winter in the country? The snow is one of the most beautiful sights of the year!

It appears that I am not clear in my sermons; I have that much in common with the orthodox, but I am not of them; neither in my idea of equality, nor of authority, have I any fixed plan. You seem to think that I want to convert you to a doctrine. Not at all, I don't think of such a thing. Everyone sets off from a point of view, the free choice of which I respect. In a few words, I can give a résumé of mine: not to place oneself behind an opaque glass through which one can see only the reflection of one's own nose. To see as far as possible the good, the bad, about, around, yonder, everywhere; to perceive the continual gravitation of all tangible and intangible things towards the necessity of the decent, the good, the true, the beautiful.

I don't say that humanity is on the way to the heights. I believe it in spite of everything; but I do not argue about it, it is useless because each one judges according to his own personal vision, and the general aspect is for the moment poor and ugly. Besides, I do not need to be sure of the safety of the planet and its inhabitants in order to believe in the necessity of the good and the beautiful; if the planet departs from that law it will perish; if the inhabitants discard it they will be destroyed. Other stars, other souls will pass over their bodies, so much the worse! But, as for me, I want to gravitate up to my last breath, not with the certitude nor the need for finding elsewhere a *good place*, but because my sole joy is in keeping myself with my family on an upward road.

In other words, I am fleeing the sewer, and I am seeking the dry and the clean, certain that it is the law of my existence. Being a man amounts to little; we are still near the monkey from which they say we proceed. Very well! a further reason for separating ourselves still more from it and for being at least at the height of the relative truth that our race has been admitted to comprehend; a very poor truth, very limited, very humble! well, let us possess it as much as we can and not permit anyone to take it from us.

We are, I think, quite agreed; but I practice this simple religion and you do not practice it, since you let yourself become discouraged; your heart has not been penetrated with it, since you curse life and desire death like a Catholic who yearns for compensation, were it only the rest eternal. You are no surer than another of this compensation. Life is perhaps eternal, and therefore work is eternal. If this is so, let us do our day's work bravely. If it is otherwise, if the MOI perishes entirely, let us have the honor of having done our stated task, it is our duty; for we have evident duties only toward ourselves and our equals. What we destroy in ourselves, we destroy in them. Our abasement lowers them, our falls drag them down; we owe it to them to remain erect so that they shall not fall. The desire for an early death, as that for a long life, is therefore a weakness, and I do not want you to admit any longer that it is a right. I thought that I had it once; I believed, however, what I believe today; but I lacked strength, and like you I said: "I cannot help it." I lied to myself. One can help everything. One has the strength that one thinks one has not, when one desires ardently to *gravitate*, to mount a step each day, to say to oneself: "The Flaubert of tomorrow must be superior to the one of yesterday, and the one of day after tomorrow more steady and more lucid still."

When you feel you are on the ladder, you will mount very quickly. You are about to enter gradually upon the happiest and most favorable time of life: old age. It is then that art reveals itself in its sweetness; as long as one is young, it manifests itself with anguish. You prefer a well-turned phrase to all metaphysics. I also, I love to see condensed into a few words what elsewhere fills volumes; but these volumes, one must have understood them completely (either to admit them or to reject them) in order to find the sublime résumé which becomes literary art in its fullest expression; that is why one should not scorn the efforts of the human mind to arrive at the truth.

I tell you that, because you have excessive prejudices *as to words*. In truth, you read, you dig, you work much more than I and a crowd of others do. You have richer than all of us; you are a rich man, and you complain like a poor man. Be acquired learning that I shall never attain. Therefore you are a hundred times charitable to a beggar who has his mattress full of gold, but who wants to be nourished only on well-turned phrases and choice words. But brute, ransack your own mattress and eat your gold. Nourish yourself with the ideas and feelings accumulated in your head and your heart; the words and the phrases, *the form* to which you attach so much importance, will issue by itself from your digestion. You consider it as an end, it is only an effect. Happy manifestations proceed only from an emotion, and an emotion proceeds only from a conviction. One is not moved at all by the things that one does not believe with all one's heart.

I do not say that you do not believe: on the contrary, all your life of affection, of protection, and of charming and simple goodness, proves that you are the most convinced individual in the world. But, as soon as you handle literature, you want, I don't know why, to be another man, one who should disappear, one who destroys himself, who does not exist! What an absurd mania! what a false rule of *good taste!* Our work is worth only what we are worth.

Who is talking about putting yourself on the stage? That, in truth, is of no use, unless it is done frankly by way of a chronicle. But to withdraw one's soul from what one does, what is that unhealthy fancy? To hide one's own opinion about the characters that one puts on the stage, to leave the reader therefore uncertain about the opinion that he should have of them, that is to desire not to be understood, and from that moment, the reader leaves you; for if he wants to understand the story that you are telling him, it is on the condition that you should show him plainly that this one is a strong character and that one weak.

L'Education sentimentale has been a misunderstood book, as I have told you repeatedly, but you have not listened to me. There should have been a short preface, or, at a good opportunity, an expression of blame, even if only a happy epithet to condemn the evil, to characterize the defect, to signalize the effort. All the characters in that book are feeble and come to nothing, except those with bad instincts; that is what you are reproached with, because people did not understand that you wanted precisely to depict a deplorable state of society that encourages these bad instincts and ruins noble efforts; when people do not understand us it is always our fault. What the reader wants, first of all, is to penetrate into our thought, and that is what you deny him, arrogantly. He thinks that you scorn him and that you want to ridicule him. For my part, I understood you, for I knew you. If anyone had brought me your book without its being signed, I should have thought it beautiful, but strange, and I should have asked myself if you were immoral, skeptical, indifferent or heartbroken. You say that it ought to be like that, and that M. Flaubert will violate the rules of good taste if he shows his thought and the aim of his literary enterprise. It is false in the highest degree. When M. Flaubert writes well and seriously, one attaches oneself to his personality. One wants to sink or swim with him. If he leaves you in doubt, you lose interest in his work, you neglect it, or you give it up.

I have already combated your favorite heresy, which is that one writes for twenty intelligent people and does not care a fig for the rest. It is not true, since the lack of success irritates you and troubles you. Besides, there have not been twenty critics favorable to this book which was so well written and so important.

So one must not write for twenty persons any more than for three, or for a hundred thousand.

One must write for all those who have a thirst to read and who can profit by good reading. Then one must go straight to the most elevated morality within oneself, and not make a mystery of the moral and profitable meaning of one's book. People found that with *Madame Bovary*. If one part of the public cried scandal, the healthiest and the broadest part saw in it a severe and striking lesson given to a woman without conscience and without faith, to vanity, to ambition, to irrationality. They pitied her; art required that, but the lesson was clear, and it would have been more so, it would have been so for *everybody*, if you had wished it, if you had shown more clearly the opinion that you had, and that the public ought to have had, about the heroine, her husband, and her lovers.

That desire to depict things as they are, the adventures of life as they present themselves to the eye, is not well thought out, in my opinion. Depict inert things as a realist, as a poet, it's all the same to me, but, when one touches on the emotions of the human heart, it is another thing. You cannot abstract yourself from this contemplation; for man, that is yourself, and men, that is the reader. Whatever you do, your tale is a conversation between you and the reader. If you show him the evil coldly, without ever showing him the good, he is angry. He wonders if it is he that is bad, or if it is you. You work, however, to rouse him and to interest him; you will never succeed if you are not roused yourself, or if you hide it so well that he thinks you indifferent. He is right: supreme impartiality is an anti-human thing, and a novel ought to be human above everything. If it is not, the public is not pleased in its being well written, well composed and conscientious in every detail. The essential quality is not there: interest. The reader breaks away likewise from a book where all the characters are good without distinctions and without weaknesses; he sees clearly that that is not human either. I believe that art, this special art of narration, is only worth while through the opposition of characters; but, in their struggle, I prefer to see the right prevail. Let events overwhelm the honest man, I agree to that, but let him not be soiled or belittled by them, and let him go to the stake feeling that he is happier than his executioners.

15 January 1876

It is three days since I wrote this letter, and every day I have been on the point of throwing it into the fire; for it is long and diffuse and probably useless. Natures opposed on certain points understand each other with difficulty, and I am afraid that you will not understand me any better today than formerly. However, I am sending you this scrawl so that you can see that I am occupied with you almost as much as with myself.

You must have success after that bad luck which has troubled you deeply. I tell you wherein lie the certain conditions for your success. Keep your cult for form; but pay more attention to the substance. Do not take true virtue for a commonplace in literature. Give it its representative, make honest and strong men pass among the fools and the imbeciles that you love to ridicule. Show what is solid at the bottom of these intellectual abortions; in short, abandon the convention of the realist and return to the true reality, which is a mingling of the beautiful and the ugly, the dull and the brilliant, but in which the desire of good finds its place and its occupation all the same.

I embrace you for all of us.

G. SAND

TO GEORGE SAND

I have given a great deal of thought to your good letter of the 18th, so affectionate and motherly. I have read it at least ten times, and confess that I am not sure I understand it. Just what do you think I should do? Be more specific.

I constantly do all that I can to broaden my mind, and I write according to the dictates of my heart. The rest is beyond my control.

I assure you that I do not paint the world in "desolate colors" for my own pleasure; after all, I cannot change my eyes. As for my "lack of convictions," alas! I am only too full of convictions. I burst with suppressed anger and indignation. But my ideal of Art demands that the artist show none of this, and that he appear in his work no more than God in nature. The man is nothing, the work is everything! This discipline, which may be based on a false premise, is not easy to observe. And for me, at least, it is a kind of perpetual sacrifice that I burn on the altar of good taste. It would be very agreeable for me to say what I think, and relieve M. Gustave Flaubert's feelings by means of such utterances; but of what importance is the aforesaid gentleman?

I think as you do, *mon maître,* that Art is not merely criticism and satire; that is why I have never deliberately tried to write either one or the other. I have always endeavored to penetrate into the essence of things and to emphasize the most general truths; and I have purposely avoided the accidental and the dramatic. No monsters, no heroes!

You say: "I have no literary advice to give you, I do not pass judgment on writers, your friends, etc." But why not? I want your advice; I long to hear your opinions. Who should give advice and opinions if not you?

Speaking of my friends, you call them my "school." But I am wrecking my health trying *not* to have a school. A *priori,* I reject all schools. Those writers whom I often see and whom you mention admire everything that I despise and worry but little about the things that torment me. Technical detail, factual data, historical truth, and accuracy of portrayal I look upon as very secondary. I aim at *beauty* above all else, whereas my companions give themselves little trouble about it. Where I am devastated by admiration or horror, they are unmoved; sentences that make me swoon seem very ordinary to them. Goncourt is very happy when he has picked up in the street some word that he can stick into a book; I am very satisfied when I have written a page without assonances or repetitions. I would willingly exchange all Gavarni's captions for a few such marvels as Victor Hugo's "*l'ombre était nuptiale, auguste et solennelle,*" or Montesquieu's "*Les vices d'Alexandre étaient extrêmes comme ses vertus. Il était terrible dans sa colère. Elle le rendait cruel.*"

I try to think well in order to write well. But my aim is to write well—I have never said it was anything else.

You say that I lack any "well-defined and comprehensive perspective on life." You will not lighten my darkness—mine or anyone else's—with metaphysics. The words "religion" or "Catholicism" on the one hand, "progress," "brotherhood," "democracy" on the other, no longer satisfy the spiritual demands of our time. The brand-new dogma of equality, preached by radicalism, is given the lie by experimental psychology and by history. I do not see how it is possible today to establish a new principle, or to respect the old ones. Hence I keep seeking—without ever finding—that idea which is supposed to be the foundation of everything.

Meanwhile I repeat to myself what Littré once said to me: "Ah, my friend, man is an unstable compound, and the earth a very inferior planet." Nothing comforts me more than the hope that I shall soon be leaving it and shall not be moving to another, which might be worse. "I should prefer not to die," Marat said. Ah, no! Enough of toil and trouble!

I am now writing a little something of no consequence which will be eminently suitable for young girls. The whole thing will run to only thirty pages. It will take me another two months. Such is my lightning pace. I will send it to you as soon as it appears—not the pace, the story. GUSTAVE FLAUBERT

H. G. WELLS AND HENRY JAMES
The Counter-Claims of Content and Form

[HENRY JAMES]

We bracket together Mr. Wells and Mr. Bennett for the particular reason that with the sharpest differences of character and range they yet come together under our so convenient measure of value by saturation. Each is ideally immersed in his own body of reference, in a closer notation, a sharper specification of the signs of life and consciousness in the human scene and the human subject than the three or four generations before them had at all been moved to insist on. They had insisted, these generations, on almost nothing whatever; what was to come to them had come, an enormous affluence and freshness at its best, and to our continued appreciation as well as to the honour of their sweet susceptibility, because again and again the great miracle of genius took place, while they gaped, in their social and sentimental sky. For our own time that miracle has not been

Henry James, "The Younger Generation," *Times Literary Supplement*, March 19 and April 2, 1914, pp. 133-4 and 137-8; reprinted by permission of Paul R. Reynolds Inc.

H. G. Wells, "Digression about Novels," *Experiment in Autobiography*, London and New York, 1934, pp. 410-15; reprinted by permission of the Executors of the Estate of H. G. Wells and A. P. Watt and Son.

H. G. Wells, "Of Art, of Literature, of Mr. Henry James," *Boon*, London, 1915, pp. 102-10; reprinted by permission of A. P. Watt and Son and the Executors of the Estate of H. G. Wells.

Letter of Henry James to H. G. Wells [1915], *The Letters of Henry James*, edited and with an introduction by Percy Lubbock, New York and London, 1920, Vol. II, pp. 488-90. Copyright 1920 by Charles Scribner's Sons; copyright renewal 1948 William James and Mrs. Margaret James Porter; reprinted by permission of Charles Scribner's Sons and Paul R. Reynolds Inc.

These selections have been reprinted in *Henry James and H. G. Wells*, ed. Leon Edel and Gordon N. Ray, Urbana, Illinois, 1958, pp. 180-92, 216-21, 244-8, 265-7.

markedly renewed, but we have learned a little to insist, and we thus get back on one hand something of what we have lost on the other. To this nearer view of commoner things the authors we have named, taking one with another, strike us as having gathered themselves up in a spirit never yet apparent on our literary scene, and with an instinctive divination, we make out, of what had most kept their predecessors clear of it.

What had this lion in the path been, we see them after a fashion ask themselves, but the fond superstition that the key of the situation, of each and every one that could turn up for the novelist, was the sentimental key, which might fit into no single lock of the great chamber of closeness and freshness at all? Was it not for all the world as if even the brightest practitioners of the past, those we now distinguish as saved for glory in spite of themselves, had been as sentimental as they could, or, to give the trick another name, as romantic and thereby as shamelessly "dodgy"?—just in order not to *be* close and fresh, not to be authentic, as that takes time and trouble, takes talent, and you can be sentimental, you can be romantic, you can be dodgy, alas! not a bit less on the footing of genius than on the footing of mediocrity or even of imbecility? The sentimental habit and the spirit of romance stood out to sea as far as possible, through all the Victorian age, the moment the shore appeared to offer the least difficulty to hugging; and that age bristled with examples of this showy retreat caught in the very act. All revolutions have been prepared in spite of their so often striking us as sudden; and so it was doubtless that, when scarce longer ago than the other day, Mr. Arnold Bennett had the fortune to lay his hand on a general scene and a cluster of agents deficient to a peculiar degree in properties that might interfere with the desirable density of illustration—deficient, that is, in such connexions as might carry the imagination off to some sport on its own account—we recognized at once a set of conditions auspicious to the newer kind of appeal. The state of inordinate possession on the chronicler's part, the mere state as such and as an energy directly exhibited, became the whole interest, neither more nor less, became the sense and the meaning and the picture and the drama, and seemed at first all so sufficiently to constitute them that it scarce mattered what they were in themselves. What we recognize the author as doing is simply recording his possession or, to repeat our more emphatic term, his saturation; and to see him as virtually shut up to that process is a note of all the more moment that we see our selected cluster of interesting juniors, and whether by his direct action on their collective impulse or not, embroiled, as we venture to call it, in the same predicament. They squeeze out to the utmost the plump and more or less juicy orange of a particular acquainted state and let this affirmation of energy, however directed or undirected, constitute for them the "treatment" of the theme.

Nothing is further from us, of course, than to undervalue the particular acquainted state, that of saturation and possession, however it may have been brought about; for it represents on behalf of the novelist, as on that of any painter of things seen, felt or imagined, just one-half of his authority, the other half being represented, naturally by the application he is inspired to make of that advantage. Therefore this fine secured half is so much gained at the start; and the fact of its brightly being there may really by itself project upon the course colour and form enough to make us at times, under the genial force, almost not miss the answer to the question of application. When the author of "Clayhanger" has put down upon the table, in dense unconfused array, every fact required to make the life of the Five Towns press upon us and to make our sense of it, so full fed, content us, we may very well go on for the time in the captive condition, the beguiled and bemused condition, the acknowledgment of which is in general our highest tribute to the temporary master of our sensibility. Nothing at such moments—or rather at the end of them, when the end begins to threaten—may be of a more curious strain than the dawning unrest that suggests to us fairly our first critical comment: "Yes, yes; but is this *all?* These are the circumstances of the interest—we see, we see; but where is the interest itself, where and what is its centre and how are we to measure it in relation to *that?*"

There are people to tell us in plenty of course that to "measure" an interest is none of our affair; that we have but to take it on the cheapest and easiest terms and be thankful; and that if by our very confession we have been led the imaginative dance the music has done for us all that it pretends to. Which words, however, have only to happen to be for us the most unintelligent conceivable not in the least to arrest our wonderment as to where our bedrenched consciousness may still not awkwardly leave us for the pleasure of appreciation. The more appreciation plays up in us, the more we recognise and are able to number the sources of our enjoyment, the greater is the provision for security in that attitude, which corresponds, by the same stroke, with the reduced danger of waste in the undertaking to amuse us. It all comes back to our amusement, and to the noblest surely, on the whole, that we know; and it is in the very nature of clinging appreciation not to sacrifice consentingly a single shade of the art that makes for this blessing. From our solicitudes spring our questions, and not least the one to which we give ourselves for the moment here—this moment of our being regaled as never yet with the fruits of the movement (if the name be not of too pompous an application where the flush and the heat of accident too seem so candidly to look forth), in favour of the "expression of life" in terms as loose as may pretend to an effect of expression at all. The relegation of terms to the limbo of delusions outlived so far as ever really cultivated becomes of necessity, it will be plain, the great mark of the faith that for the novelist to show he "knows all about" a certain congeries of aspects, the more numerous within their mixed circle the better, is thereby to set in motion with due intensity the pretension to interest. The state of knowing all about whatever it may be has thus only to become consistently and abundantly active to pass for his supreme function; and to its so becoming active few difficulties appear to be described, so great may on occasion become the mere excitement and exhilaration of activity.

We should have only to remount the current with a certain energy to come straight up against Tolstoy as the great illustrative master-hand on all this ground of disconnexion of method from matter—and so prompt in us the remark that of all great painters of the social picture it was given that epic genius most to serve admirably as a rash adventurer and a "caution," and execrably, pestilentially, as a model. In this strange union of relations he stands alone: from no other great projector of the human image and the human idea is so much truth to be extracted under an equal leakage of its value, that is an equal failure to exhibit, to present the value. All the proportions in him are so much the largest that the drop of attention to our cases nearer at hand might by its violence leave little of the principle alive; which fact need not disguise from us none the less that as we take Mr. H. G. Wells and Mr. Arnold Bennett to derive, by multiplied if diluted transmissions, from the great Russian, so, observing the distances, we may profitably detect an unexhausted influence in our minor, our still considerably less rounded vessels. Highly attaching the game, as might be, or inquiring as to the centre of the interest or the sense of the whole in "The Passionate Friends" or in "The Old Wives' Tale," after having sought those luxuries in vain through the general length and breadth of "War and Peace"; this as preparing us to address a like friendly challenge to Mr. Cannan's "Round the Corner," say, or to Mr. Lawrence's "Sons and Lovers"—should we wish to be very friendly to Mr. Lawrence— or to Mr. Hugh Walpole's "Duchess of Wrexe," or even to Mr. Compton Mackenzie's "Sinister Street" and "Carnival"; discernibly, we hasten to add, though certain betrayals of a controlling and a pointed intention do comparatively gleam out of the two fictions last named. "The Old Wives' Tale" is the history of two sisters, daughters of a prosperous draper in a Staffordshire town, who, separating early in life, through the flight of one of them to Paris with an ill-chosen husband and the confirmed and prolonged local pitch of the career of the other, are reunited, conclusively, by the return of the fugitive after much Parisian experience and by her gradually pacified acceptance of the conditions of her birthplace. The divided current flows together again, and the chronicle closes with the simple drying up determined by the death of the sisters. That is all; the canvas is covered, ever so closely and vividly covered, by the exhibition of innumerable small facts and aspects, at which we assist with the most comfortable sense of their substantial truth. The sisters, and more particularly the less adventurous, are at home in their author's mind; they sit and move at their ease in the square chamber of his attention to a degree beyond which the production of that ideal harmony between creature and creator could scarcely go, and all by an art of demonstration so familiar and so "quiet" that the truth and the poetry, to use Goethe's distinction, melt utterly together, and we see no difference between the subject of the show and the showman's "feeling," let alone the showman's manner, about it.

This felt identity of the elements—because we at least consciously feel—becomes in the novel we refer to, and not less in "Clayhanger," which our words equally describe, a source for us of abject confidence, confidence truly so abject in the solidity of every appearance that it may be said to represent our whole relation to the work and completely to exhaust our reaction upon it. "Clayhanger"—of the two fictions even the more densely packed with all the evidence in what we should call the case presented did we but learn meanwhile for what case, or for a case of what, to take it—inscribes the annals, the private more particularly, of a provincial printer in a considerable way of business, beginning with his early boyhood and going on to the complications of his maturity. This most monumental of Mr. Bennett's recitals, taking it with the supplement of "Hilda Lessways," already before us, and with more of the catalogue to follow, is so describable through its being a monument exactly not to an idea, a pursued and captured meaning, or, in short, to anything whatever but just simply of the quarried and gathered material it happens to contain, the stones and bricks and rubble and cement and promiscuous constituents of every sort that have been heaped in it and thanks to which it quite massively piles itself up. Our perusal and our enjoyment are our watching of the growth of the pile and of the capacity, industry, energy, with which the operation is directed. While we watch and wait we are amused—were it not for that, truly, we should wonder still more; but we may ask ourselves, as has already been noted, why on such ambiguous terms we should consent to be, and why the practice doesn't at a given moment break down. Our answer then brings us back to that many-fingered grasp of the orange that the author squeezes. This particular orange is of the largest and most rotund, and his trust in the consequent flow of its nature communicative. Such is the case always, and most naturally, with that air of a person who has something, who at the very least has much, to tell us: we *like* to be affected by it, we meet it half-way and lend ourselves, sinking in it up to the chin. Up to the chin only, indeed, beyond doubt; we even then feel our head emerge, for judgment and articulate question; and it is from that position that we remind ourselves how the real reward of our patience is still to come—the reward attending not at all the immediate sense of immersion, but reserved for the after-sense, which is a very different matter, whether in the form of a glow or of a chill.

If Mr. Bennett's tight rotundity, then, is of the handsomest size and his manipulation of it so firm, what are we to say of Mr. Wells's, who, a novelist very much as Lord Bacon was a philosopher, affects us as taking all knowledge for his province and as inspiring in us to the very highest degree the confidence enjoyed by himself?—enjoyed, we feel, with a breadth with which it has been given no one of his fellow-craftsmen to enjoy anything. If confidence alone could lead utterly captive we should all be huddled in a bunch at Mr. Wells's heels, which is indeed where we *are* abjectly gathered, so far as that force does operate. It is literally Mr. Wells's own mind, and the experience of his own mind, incessant and extraordinarily various, extraordinarily reflective, even with all sorts of conditions made, of whatever he may expose it to, that forms the reservoir tapped by him, that suffices for his exhibition of grounds of interest. The more he knows and knows, or at any rate learns and learns—the more, in other words, he establishes his saturation—the greater is our impression of his holding it good enough for us, such as we are, that he shall but turn out his mind and its contents upon us by any free familiar gesture and as from a high window forever open (Mr. Wells having as many windows as an agent who has bought up the lot of the most eligible to retail for a great procession).

Such things as "The New Machiavelli," "Marriage," "The Passionate Friends," are so very much more attestations of the presence of material than of an interest in the use of it that we ask ourselves again and again why so fondly neglected a state of leakage comes not to be fatal to *any* provision of quantity, or even to stores more specially selected for the ordeal than Mr. Wells's always strike us as being. Is not the witnessed pang of waste, in fact, great just in proportion as we are touched by our author's fine offhandedness as to the value of the stores, about which he can for the time make us believe what he will? So that, to take an example susceptible of brief statement, we wince at a certain quite peculiarly gratuitous sacrifice to the casual in "Marriage" very much as at seeing some fine and indispensable little part of a mechanism slip through profane fingers and lose itself. Who does not remember what ensues after a little upon the aviational descent of the hero of that fiction into the garden occupied, in company with her parents, by the young lady with whom he is to fall in love?—and this even though the whole opening scene so constituted, with all the comedy hares its function appears to be to start, remains with its back squarely turned, aesthetically speaking, to the quarter in which the picture develops. The point for our mortification is that by one of the first steps in this development, the first impression on him having been made, the hero accidentally meets the heroine, of a summer eventide, in a leafy lane which supplies them with the happiest occasion to pursue their acquaintance—or in other words supplies the author with the liveliest consciousness (as we feel it should be) that just so the relation between the pair, its seed already sown, and the fact of that bringing about all that is still to come, pushes aside whatever veil and steps forth into life. To show it step forth and affirm itself as a relation, what is this but the interesting function of the whole passage, on the performance of which what follows is to hang?—and yet who can say that when the ostensible sequence *is* presented, and our young lady, encountered again by her stirred swain, under cover of night, in a favouring wood, is at once encompassed by his arms and pressed to his lips and heart (for celebration thus of their third meeting), we do not assist at a well-nigh heartbreaking miscarriage of "effect"? We see effect, invoked in vain, simply stand off unconcerned; effect not having been at all consulted in advance, she is not to be secured on such terms. And her presence would so have redounded—perfectly punctual creature that she is on a made appointment and a clear understanding—to the advantage of all concerned. The bearing of the young man's act is all in our having begun to conceive it as possible, begun even to desire it, in the light of what has preceded; therefore if the participants have *not* been shown us as on the way to it, nor the question of it made beautifully to tremble for us in the air, its happiest connexions fail and we but stare at it mystified. The instance is undoubtedly trifling, but in the infinite complex of such things resides for a work of art the shy virtue, shy at least till wooed forth, of the whole susceptibility.

The case of Mr. Wells might take us much further—such remarks as there would be to make, say, in such a connexion as a due understanding, on the part of "The Passionate Friends" (not as associated persons but as a composed picture), of what that composition is specifically about and where, for treatment of this interest, it undertakes to find its centre; all of which, we are willing, however, to grant, falls away before the large assurance and incorrigible levity with which this adventurer carries his lapses, for more of an adventurer as he is than any other of the company. The composition, as we have called it, heaven save the mark! is simply at any and every moment "about" Mr. Wells's own most general adventure; which is quite enough while it preserves, as we trust it will long continue to do, its present robust pitch.

[H. G. WELLS]

I set out to write novels, as distinguished from those pseudo-scientific stories in which imaginative experience rather than personal conduct was the matter in hand, on the assumption that problems of adjustment were the essential matter for novel-writing. *Love and Mr. Lewisham* was entirely a story about a dislocation and an adjustment.

But across the track of that train of thought came another in which the novel presented itself not as an ethical enquiry but as the rendering of a system of impressions. In this distended and irregularly interesting folder, which I find so hard to reduce to straightforward explicitness, I find myself worrying round various talks and discussions I had with Henry James a third of a century ago. He was a very important figure in the literary world of that time and a shrewd and penetrating critic of the technique by which he lived. He liked me and he found my work respectable enough to be greatly distressed about it. I bothered him and he bothered me. We were at cross purposes based as I shall show later on very fundamental differences, not only of temperament but training. He had no idea of the possible use of the novel as a help to conduct. His mind has turned away from any such idea. From his point of view there were not so much "novels" as The Novel, and it was a very high and important achievement. He thought of it as an Art Form and of novelists as artists of a very special and exalted type. He was concerned about their greatness and repute. He saw us all as Masters or would-be Masters, little Masters and great Masters, and he was plainly sorry that "Cher Maître" was not an English expression. One could not be in a room with him for ten minutes without realizing the importance he attached to the dignity of this art of his. I was by nature and education unsympathetic with this mental disposition. But I was disposed to regard a novel as about as much an art form as a market place or a boulevard. It had not even necessarily to get anywhere. You went by it on your various occasions.

That was entirely out of key with James's assumptions. I recall a talk I had with him soon after the publication of *Marriage*. With tact and circumlocution, James broke it to me, that he found a remarkable deficiency in that story. It was a deficiency that he had also observed in a vast proportion of contemporary fiction, it had exercised him very fruitfully, and his illuminating comments spread out from that starting point to a far-reaching tentacular discussion of what a novel should do and be.

The point he was stressing was this: *Marriage* is the story of a young man of science, Trafford, who, apparently without much previous experience, pilots a friend's aeroplane (in 1912!) and crashes, he and the friend together, into a croquet party and the Pope family and the life of Marjorie Pope. Thereupon there is bandaging, ambulance work and much coming and going and Marjorie, who is already engaged to a Mr. Magnet, falls deeply in love with Trafford. She drives to the village in a donkey cart to do some shopping and meets the lamed Trafford, also driving a donkey cart and their wheels interlock and they fall talking. All that—except for the writing of it—was tolerable according to James. But then, in order to avoid the traffic in the high road the two young people take their respective donkey carts into a side lane and remain there talking for three hours. And this is where James's objection came in. Of the three hours of intercourse in the lane the novel tells nothing, except that the young people emerged in open and declared love with each other. This, said James, wasn't playing the game. I had cut out an essential, after a feast of irrelevant particulars. Gently but firmly he insisted that I did not myself know what had happened and what was said in that lane; that there was even a touch of improbability about their staying there so long and that this lack of information and probability at a crucial point was due to the fact that I had not thought out the individualities concerned with sufficient care and thoroughness. I had not cared enough about these individualities. Moreover in the conversations between the two principals, the man in particular supplied information about himself and his position in life in such a way as to talk at the reader instead of to the girl. The talk was in fact more for the benefit of the former. Trafford had to supply this information because I had been too inept or hasty to convey it in any other way. Or because there was too much to convey in any other way. Henry James was quite right in saying that I had not thought out these two people to the pitch of saturation and that they did not behave unconsciously and naturally. But my defence is that that did not matter, or at least that for the purposes of the book it did not matter very much.

Now I do not exactly remember the several other points he made in that elaborate critical excursion, nor did I attempt any reprisals upon his own work, but his gist was plain. If the Novel was properly a presentation of real people as real people, in absolutely natural reaction in a story, then my characters were not simply sketchy, they were eked out by wires and pads of non-living matter and they stood condemned. His discourse, which had evidently been maturing against my visit, covered not only my work but that of several of my contemporaries whom he had also read with interest and distaste. And the only point upon which I might have argued but which I did not then argue, was this, that the Novel was not necessarily, as he assumed, this real through and through and absolutely true treatment of people more living than life. It might be more and less than that and still be a novel. . . .

Tried by Henry James's standards I doubt if any of my novels can be taken in any other fashion. There are flashes and veins of character duly "treated" and living individuals in many of them, but none that satisfy his requirements fully. A lot of *Kipps* may pass, some of *Tono-Bungay, Mr. Britling Sees it Through* and *Joan and Peter* and let me add, I have a weakness for Lady Harman and for Theodore Bulpington and——. But I will not run on. These are pleas in extenuation. The main indictment is sound, that I sketch out scenes and individuals, often quite crudely, and resort even to conventional types and symbols, in order to get on to a discussion of relationships. The important point which I tried to argue with Henry James was that the novel of completely consistent characterization arranged beautifully in a story and painted deep and round and solid, no more exhausts the possibilities of the novel, than the art of Velazquez exhausts the possibilities of the painted picture.

The issue exercised my mind considerably. I had a queer feeling that we were both incompatibly right. I wrote one or two lectures and critical papers on the scope of the novel, and I argued with myself and others, that realism and exhaustive presentation were not its only objectives. I think I might have gone further and maintained that they were not even its proper objectives but at best only graces by the way, but at the time I was not clear enough to say that. I might have made a good case by asserting that fiction was necessarily fictitious through and through, and that the real analogy to Velazquez who painted straight from dwarfs and kings, would be biography, character drawn straight from life and not an invented story. James was very much against the idea that there was a biographical element in any good novel, and he and his brother William were very severe upon Vernon Lee when she produced a character in a short story (*Lady Tal*, 1892) markedly like Henry. But it is beyond the power of man to "create" individuals absolutely. If we do not write from models then we compile and fabricate. Every "living" character in a novel is drawn, frankly or furtively, from life—is filched from biography whole or in scraps, a portrait or a patch-up, and its actions are a reflection upon moral conduct. At whatever number of "removes" from facts we may be, we are still imputing motives to somebody. That is the conclusion I am coming to now, but I did not have it ready at that time. I allowed it to be taken for granted that there was such a thing as The Novel, a great and stately addendum to reality, a sort of super-reality with "created" persons in it, and by implication I admitted that my so-called novels were artless self-revelatory stuff, falling far away from a stately ideal by which they had to be judged.

But now I ask when and where has that great ideal been realized—or can it ever be realized?

[H. G. WELLS]

"He makes literature include philosophy?"

"Everything. It's all the central things. It's the larger Bible to him, a thing about which all the conscious direction of life revolves. It's alive with passion and will. Or if it isn't, then it ought to be. . . . And then as the antagonist comes this artist, this man who seems to regard the whole seething brew of life as a vat from which you skim, with slow, dignified gestures, works of art. . . . Works of art whose only claim is their art. . . . Hallery is going to be very impatient about art."

"Ought there to be such a thing as a literary artist?" some one said.

"Ought there, in fact, to be Henry James?" said Dodd.

"I don't think so. Hallery won't think so. You see, the discussion will be very fundamental. There's contributory art, of course, and a way of doing things better or worse. Just as there is in war, or cooking. But the way of doing isn't the end. First the end must be judged—and then if you like talk of how it is done. Get there as splendidly as possible. But get there. James and George Moore, neither of them take it like that. They leave out getting there, or the thing they get to is so trivial as to amount to scarcely more than an omission. . . ."

Boon reflected. "In early life both these men poisoned their minds in studios. Thought about pictures even might be less studio-ridden than it is. But James has never discovered that a novel isn't a picture. . . . That life isn't a studio. . . .

"He wants a novel to be simply and completely *done*. He wants it to have a unity, he demands homogeneity. . . . Why *should* a book have that? For a picture it's reasonable, because you have to see it all at once. But there's no need to see a book all at once. It's like wanting to have a whole county done in one style and period of architecture. It's like insisting that a walking tour must stick to one valley. . . .

"But James *begins* by taking it for granted that a novel is a work of art that must be judged by its oneness. Judged first by its oneness. Some one gave him that idea in the beginning of things and he has never found it out. He doesn't find things out. He doesn't even seem to want to find things out. You can see that in him; he is eager to accept things—elaborately. You can see from his books that he accepts etiquettes, precedences, associations, claims. That is his peculiarity. He accepts very readily and then—elaborates. He has, I am convinced, one of the strongest, most abundant minds alive in the whole world, and he has the smallest penetration. Indeed, he has no penetration. He is the culmination of the Superficial type. Or else he would have gone into philosophy and been greater even than his wonderful brother. . . . But here he is, spinning about, like the most tremendous of water-boatmen—you know those insects?—kept up by surface tension. As if, when once he pierced the surface, he would drown. It's incredible. A water-boatman as big as an elephant. I was reading him only yesterday—'The Golden Bowl'; it's dazzling how never for a moment does he go through."

"Recently he's been explaining himself," said Dodd.

"His 'Notes on Novelists.' It's one sustained demand for the picture effect. Which is the denial of the sweet complexity of life, of the pointing this way and that, of the spider on the throne. Philosophy aims at a unity and never gets there. . . . That true unity which we all suspect, and which no one attains, if it is to be got at all it is to be got by penetrating, penetrating down and through. The picture, on the other hand, is forced to a unity because it can see only one aspect at a time. I am doubtful even about that. Think of Hogarth or Carpaccio. But if the novel is to follow life it must be various and discursive. Life is diversity and entertainment, not completeness and satisfaction. All actions are half-hearted, shot delightfully with wandering thoughts—about something else. All true stories are a felt of irrelevances. But James sets out to make his novels with the presupposition that they can be made continuously relevant. And perceiving the discordant things, he tries to get rid of them. He sets himself to pick the straws out of the hair of Life before he paints her. But without the straws she is no longer the mad woman we love. He talks of 'selection,' and of making all of a novel definitely *about* a theme. He objects to a 'saturation' that isn't oriented. And he objects, if you go into it, for no clear reason at all. Following up his conception of selection, see what in his own practice he omits. In practice James's selection becomes just omission and nothing more. He omits everything that demands digressive treatment or collateral statement. For example, he omits opinions. In all his novels you will find no people with defined political opinions, no people with religious opinions, none with clear partisanships or with lusts or whims, none definitely up to any specific impersonal thing. There are no poor people dominated by the imperatives of Saturday night and Monday morning, no dreaming types—and don't we all more or less live dreaming? And none are ever decently forgetful. All that much of humanity he clears out before he begins his story. It's like cleaning rabbits for the table.

"But you see how relentlessly it follows from the supposition that the novel is a work of art aiming at pictorial unities!

"All art too acutely self-centered comes to this sort of thing. James's denatured people are only the equivalent in fiction of those egg-faced, black-haired ladies, who sit and sit, in the Japanese colour-prints, the unresisting stuff for an arrangement of blacks. . . .

"Then with the eviscerated people he has invented he begins to make up stories. What stories they are! Concentrated on suspicion, on a gift, on possessing a 'piece' of old furniture, on what a little girl may or may not have noted in an emotional situation. These people cleared for artistic treatment never make a lusty love, never go to angry war, never shout at an election or perspire at poker; never in any way *date*. . . . And upon the petty residuum of human interest left to them they focus minds of a Jamesian calibre. . . .

"The only living human motives left in the novels of Henry James are a certain avidity and an entirely superficial curiosity. Even when relations are irregular or when sins are hinted at, you feel that these are merely attitudes taken up, gambits before the game of attainment and over-perception begins. . . . His people nose out suspicions, hint by hint, link by link. Have you ever known living human beings do that? The thing his novel is *about* is always there. It is like a church lit but without a congregation to distract you, with every light and line focused on the high altar. And on the altar, very reverently placed, intensely there, is a dead kitten, an egg-shell, a bit of string. . . . Like his 'Altar of the Dead,' with nothing to the dead at all. . . . For if there was they couldn't all be candles and the effect would vanish. . . . And the elaborate, copious emptiness of the whole Henry James exploit is only redeemed and made endurable by the elaborate, copious wit. Upon the desert his selection has made Henry James erects palatial metaphors. . . . The chief fun, the only exercise, in reading Henry James is this clambering over vast metaphors. . . .

"Having first made sure that he has scarcely anything left to express, he then sets to work to express it, with an industry, a wealth of intellectual stuff that dwarfs Newton. He spares no resource in the telling of his dead inventions. He brings up every device of language to state and define. Bare verbs he rarely tolerates. He splits his infinitives and fills them up with adverbial stuffing. He presses the passing colloquialism into his service. His vast paragraphs sweat and struggle; they could not sweat and elbow and struggle more if God Himself was the processional meaning to which they sought to come. And all for tales of nothingness. . . . It is leviathan retrieving pebbles. It is a magnificent but painful hippopotamus resolved at any cost, even at the cost of its dignity, upon picking up a pea which has got into a corner of its den. Most things, it insists, are beyond it, but it can, at any rate, modestly, and with an artistic singleness of mind, pick up that pea. . . ."

[HENRY JAMES]

My dear Wells.

I am bound to tell you that I don't think your letter makes out any sort of case for the bad manners of *Boon*, so far as your indulgence in them at the expense of your poor old H. J. is concerned—I say "your" simply because he has *been* yours, in the most liberal, continual, sacrificial, the most admiring and abounding critical way, ever since he began to know your writings: as to which you have had copious testimony. Your comparison of the book to a waste-basket strikes me as the reverse of felicitous, for what one throws into that receptacle is exactly what one *doesn't* commit to publicity and make the affirmation of one's estimate of one's contemporaries by. I should liken it much rather to the preservative portfolio or drawer in which what is withheld from the basket is savingly laid away. Nor do I feel it anywhere evident that my "view of life and literature," or what you impute to me as such, is carrying everything before it and becoming a public menace—so unaware do I seem, on the contrary, that my products constitute an example in any measurable degree followed or a cause in any degree successfully pleaded: I can't but think that if this were the case I should find it somewhat attested in their circulation—which, alas, I have reached a very advanced age in the entirely defeated hope of. But I *have* no view of life and literature, I maintain, other than that our form of the latter in especial is admirable exactly by its range and variety, its plasticity and liberality, its fairly living on the sincere and shifting experience of the individual practitioner. That is why I have always so admired your so free and strong application of it, the particular rich receptacle of intelligences and impressions emptied out with an energy of its own, that your genius constitutes; and *that* is in particular why, in my letter of two or three days since, I pronounced it curious and interesting that you should find the case I constitute myself only ridiculous and vacuous to the extent of your having to proclaim your sense of it. The curiosity and the interest, however, in this latter connection are of course for my mind those of the break of perception (perception of the vivacity of *my* variety) on the part of a talent so generally inquiring and apprehensive as yours. Of course for myself I live, live intensely and am fed by life, and my value, whatever it be, is in my own kind of expression of that. Therefore I am pulled up to wonder by the fact that for you my kind (my sort of sense of expression and sort of sense of life alike) doesn't exist; and that wonder is, I admit, a disconcerting comment on my idea of the various appreciability of our addiction to the novel and of all the personal and intellectual history, sympathy and curiosity, behind the given example of it. It is when that history and curiosity have been determined in the way most different from my own that I myself want to get at them—precisely *for* the extension of life, which is the novel's best gift. But that is another matter. Meanwhile I absolutely dissent from the claim that there are any differences whatever in the amenability to art of forms of literature aesthetically determined, and hold your distinction between a form that is (like) painting and a form that is (like) architecture for wholly null and void. There is no sense in which architecture is aesthetically "for use" that doesn't leave any other art whatever exactly as much so; and so far from that of literature being irrelevant to the literary report upon life, and to its being made as interesting as possible, I regard it as relevant in a degree that leaves everything else behind. It is art that *makes* life, makes interest, makes importance, for our consideration and application of these things, and I know of no substitute whatever for the force and beauty of its process. If I were Boon I should say that any pretence of such a substitute is helpless and hopeless humburg; but I wouldn't be Boon for the world, and am only yours faithfully   HENRY JAMES

KARL MARX AND FRIEDRICH ENGELS

Social Reality as Class Struggle

The history of all hitherto existing society is the history of class struggles.

Freeman and slave, patrician and plebeian, lord and serf, guild-master and journeyman, in a word, oppressor and oppressed, stood in constant opposition to one another, carried on uninterrupted, now hidden, now open fight, a fight that each time ended, either in a revolutionary reconstitution of society at large, or in the common ruin of the contending classes.

In the earlier epochs of history we find almost everywhere a complicated arrangement of society into various orders, a manifold gradation of social rank. In ancient Rome we have patricians, knights, plebians, slaves; in the middle ages, feudal lords, vassals, guild-masters, journeymen, apprentices, serfs; in almost all of these classes, again, subordinate gradations.

The modern bourgeois society that has sprouted from the ruins of feudal society has not done away with class antagonisms. It has but established new classes, new conditions of oppression, new forms of struggle in place of the old ones.

Our epoch, the epoch of the bourgeoisie, possesses, however, this distinctive feature; it has simplified the class antagonisms. Society as a whole is more and more splitting up into two great hostile camps, into two great classes directly facing each other: Bourgeoisie and Proletariat.

From the serfs of the Middle Ages sprang the chartered burghers of the earliest towns. From these burgesses the first elements of the bourgeoisie were developed.

The discovery of America, the rounding of the Cape, opened up fresh ground for the rising bourgeoisie. The East Indian and Chinese markets, the colonization of America, trade with the colonies, the increase in the means of exchange and in commodities generally, gave to commerce, to navigation, to industry, an impulse never before known, and thereby, to the revolutionary element in the tottering feudal society, a rapid development.

The feudal system of industry, under which industrial production was monopolized by close guilds, now no longer sufficed for the growing wants of the new market. The manufacturing system took its place. The guild-masters were pushed on one side by the manufacturing middle class; division of labor between the different corporate guilds vanished in the face of division of labor in each single workshop.

From *The Communist Manifesto* [1848], translated from the German by Samuel Moore, *Essentials of Marx,* ed. Algernon Lee, New York, 1926, pp. 31-44, 52, 53.

Meantime the markets kept ever growing, the demand ever rising. Even manufacture no longer sufficed. Thereupon, steam and machinery revolutionized industrial production. The place of manufacture was taken by the giant Modern Industry, the place of the industrial middle-class, by industrial millionaires, the leaders of whole industrial armies, the modern bourgeois.

Modern industry has established the world-market, for which the discovery of America paved the way. This market has given an immense development to commerce, to navigation, to communication by land. This development has, in its turn, reacted on the extension of industry; and in proportion as industry, commerce, navigation, railways extended, in the same proportion the bourgeoisie developed, increased its capital, and pushed into the background every class handed down from the Middle Ages.

We see, therefore, how the modern bourgeoisie is itself the product of a long course of development, of a series of revolutions in the modes of production and of exchange.

Each step in the development of the bourgeoisie was accompanied by a corresponding political advance of that class. An oppressed class under the sway of the feudal nobility; an armed and self-governing association in the medieval commune, (here independent urban republic, as in Italy and Germany, there taxable "third estate" of the monarchy, as in France); afterwards, in the period of manufacture proper, serving either the semi-feudal or the absolute monarchy as a counterpoise against the nobility, and in fact corner stone of the great monarchies in general—the bourgeoisie has at last, since the establishment of modern industry and of the world-market, conquered for itself, in the modern representative state, exclusive political sway. The executive of the modern state is but a committee for managing the common affairs of the whole bourgeoisie.

The bourgeoisie, historically, has played a most revolutionary part.

The bourgeoisie, wherever it has got the upper hand, has put an end to all feudal, patriarchal, idylic relations. It has pitilessly torn asunder the motley feudal ties that bound man to his "natural superiors," and has left no other nexus between man and man than naked self-interest, than callous "cash payment." It has drowned the most heavenly ecstasies of religious fervor, of chivalrous enthusiams, of philistine sentimentalism, in the icy water of egotistical calculation. It has resolved personal worth into exchange value, and in place of the numberless indefeasible chartered freedoms, has set up that single, unconscionable freedom—Free Trade. In one word, for exploitation, veiled by religious and political illusions, it has substituted naked, shameless, direct, brutal exploitation.

The bourgeoisie has stripped of its halo every occupation hitherto honored and looked up to with reverent awe. It has converted the physician, the lawyer, the priest, the poet, the man of science, into its paid wage laborers.

The bourgeoisie has torn away from the family its sentimental veil, and has reduced the family relation to a mere money relation.

The bourgeoisie has disclosed how it came to pass that the brutal display of vigor in the Middle Ages, which reactionists so much admire, found its fitting complement in the most slothful indolence. It has been the first to show what man's activity can bring about. It has accomplished wonders far surpassing Egyptian pyramids, Roman aqueducts, and Gothic cathedrals; it has conducted expeditions that put in the shade all former exoduses of nations and crusades.

The bourgeoisie cannot exist without constantly revolutionizing the instruments of production, and thereby the relations of production, and with them the whole relations of society. Conservation of the old modes of production in unaltered form was, on the contrary, the first condition of existence for all earlier industrial classes. Constant revolutionizing of production, uninterrupted disturbance of all social conditions, everlasting uncertainty and agitation distinguish the bourgeois epoch from all earlier ones. All fixed, fast-frozen relations, with their train of ancient and venerable prejudices and opinions, are swept away, all new-formed ones become antiquated before they can ossify. All that is solid melts into the air, all that is holy is profaned, and man is at last compelled to face with sober senses, his real conditions of life, and his relations with his kind.

The need of a constantly expanding market for its products drives the bourgeoisie over the whole surface of the globe. It must elbow-in everywhere, settle everywhere, establish connections everywhere.

The bourgeoisie has through its exploitation of the world-market given a cosmopolitan character to production and consumption in every country. To the great chagrin of reactionists, it has drawn from under the feet of industry the national ground on which it stood. All old-established national industries have been destroyed or are daily being destroyed. They are dislodged by new industries, whose introduction becomes a life and death question for all civilized nations, by industries that no longer work up indigenous raw material, but raw material drawn from the remotest zones; industries whose products are consumed, not only at home, but in every quarter of the globe. In place of the old wants, satisfied by the productions of the country, we find new wants, requiring for their satisfaction the products of distant lands and climes. In place of the old local and national seclusion and self sufficiency, we have intercourse in every direction, universal interdependence of nations. And as in material, so also in intellectual production. The intellectual creations of individual nations become common property. National onesidedness and narrowmindedness become more and more impossible, and from the numerous national and local literatures there arises a world-literature.

The bourgeoisie, by the rapid improvement of all instruments of production, by the immensely facilitated means of communication, draws all, even the most barbarian nations, into civilization. The cheap prices of its commodities are the heavy artillery with which it batters down all Chinese walls, with which it forces the barbarians' intensely obstinate hatred of foreigners to capitulate. It compels all nations, on pain of extinction, to adopt the bourgeois mode of production; it compels them to introduce what it calls civilization into their midst, *i.e.*, to become bourgeois themselves. In a word, it creates a world after its own image.

The bourgeoisie has subjected the country to the rule of the towns. It has created enormous cities, has greatly increased the urban population as compared with the rural, and has thus rescued a considerable part of the population from the idiocy of rural life. Just as it has made the country dependent on the towns, so it has made barbarian and semi-barbarian countries dependent on civilized ones, nations of peasants on nations of bourgeois, the East on the West.

The bourgeoisie keeps more and more doing away with the scattered state of the population, of the means of production, and of property. It has agglomerated population, centralized means of production, and has concentrated property in a few hands. The necessary consequence of this was political centralization. Independent, or but loosely connected provinces, with separate interests, laws, governments, and systems of taxation, became lumped together in one nation, with one government, one code of laws, one national class-interest, one frontier and one customs' tariff.

The bourgeoisie, during its rule of scarce one hundred years, has created more massive and more colossal productive forces than have all preceding generations together. Subjection of nature's forces to man, machinery, application of chemistry to industry and agriculture, steam-navigation, railways, electric telegraphs, clearing of whole continents for cultivation, canalization of rivers, whole populations conjured out of the ground—what earlier century had even a presentiment that such productive forces slumbered in the lap of social labor?

We see then, the means of production and of exchange on whose foundation the bourgeoisie built itself up, were generated in feudal society. At a certain stage in the development of these means of production and of exchange, the conditions under which feudal society produced and exchanged, the feudal organization of agriculture and manufacturing industry—in one word, the feudal relations of property—became no longer compatible with the already developed productive forces; they became so many fetters. They had to burst asunder; they were burst asunder.

Into their places stepped free competition, accompanied by a social and political constitution adapted to it, and by the economical and political sway of the bourgeois class.

A similar movement is going on before our own eyes. Modern bourgeois society with its relations of production, of exchange, and of property, a society that has conjured up such gigantic means of production and of exchange, is like the sorcerer, who is no longer able to control the powers of the nether world whom he has called up by his spells. For many a decade past, the history of industry and commerce is but the history of the revolt of modern productive forces against modern conditions of production, against the property relations that are the conditions for the existence of the bourgeoisie and of its rule. It is enough to mention the commercial crises that by their periodical return put on its trial, each time more threateningly, the existence of the entire bourgeois society. In these crises a great part not only of the existing products, but also of the previously created productive forces, are periodically destroyed. In these crises there breaks out an epidemic that, in all earlier epochs, would have seemed an absurdity—the epidemic of over-production. Society suddenly finds itself put back into a state of momentary barbarism; it appears as if a famine, a universal war of devastation, had cut off the supply of every means of subsistence; industry and commerce seem to be destroyed; and why? Because there is too much civilization, too much means of subsistence, too much industry, too much commerce. The productive forces at the disposal of society no longer tend to further the development of the conditions of bourgeois property; on the contrary, they have become too powerful for these conditions by which they are confined, and as soon as they overcome these limitations they bring disorder into the whole of bourgeois society, endanger the existence of bourgeois property. The conditions of bourgeois society are too narrow to comprise the wealth created by them. And how does the bourgeoisie get over these crises? On the one hand by enforced destruction of a mass of productive forces; on the other, by the conquest of new markets, and by the more thorough exploitation of the old ones. That is to say, by paving the way for more extensive and more destructive crises, and by diminishing the means whereby crises are prevented.

The weapons with which the bourgeoisie felled feudalism to the ground are now turned against the bourgeoisie itself.

But not only has the bourgeoisie forged the weapons that bring death to itself; it has also called into existence the men who are to wield those weapons—the modern working class—the proletarians.

In proportion as the bourgeoisie,—that is, as capital, is developed, in the same proportion is the proletariat, the modern working class, developed, a class of laborers who live only so long as they find work, and who find work only so long as their labor increases capital. These laborers, who must sell themselves piece-meal, are a commodity, like every other article of commerce, and are consequently exposed to all the vicissitudes of competition, to all the fluctuations of the market.

Owing to the extensive use of machinery and to division of labor, the work of the proletarians has lost all individual character, and, consequently, all charm for the workman. He becomes an appendage of the machine, and it is only the most simple, most monotonous, and most easily acquired knack that is required of him. Hence, the cost of production of a workman is restricted almost entirely to the means of subsistence that he requires for his maintenance, and for the propagation of his race. But the price of a commodity, and also of labor, is equal to its cost of production. In proportion, therefore, as the repulsiveness of the work increases the wage decreases. Nay more, in proportion as the use of machinery and division of labor increase, in the same proportion the burden of toil increases, whether by prolongation of the working hours, by increase of the work enacted in a given time, or by increased speed of the machinery, and so forth.

Modern industry has converted the little workshop of the patriarchal master into the great factory of the industrial capitalist. Masses of laborers, crowded into factories, are organized like soldiers. As privates of the industrial army they are placed under the command of a perfect hierarchy of officers and sergeants. Not only are they the slaves of the bourgeois class and of the bourgeois state, they are daily and hourly enslaved by the machine, by the foreman, and, above all, by the individual bourgeois manufacturer himself. The more openly this despotism pro-claims gain to be its end and aim, the more petty, the more hateful and the more embittering it is.

The less the skill and exertion or strength implied in manual labor, in other words, the more modern industry becomes developed, the more is the labor of men superseded by that of women. Differences of age and sex have no longer any distinctive social validity for the working class. All are instruments of labor, more or less expensive to use, according to their age and sex.

No sooner is the exploitation of the laborer by the manufacturer so far at an end that he receives his wages in cash, than he is set upon by the other portions of the bourgeoisie, the landlord, the shopkeeper, the pawnbroker, and so forth.

The lower strata of the middle class—the small trades-people, shopkeepers and retired tradesmen generally, the handicraftsmen and peasants—all these sink gradually into the proletariat, partly because their diminutive capital does not suffice for the scale on which modern industry is carried on, and is swamped in the competition with the large capitalists, partly because their specialized skill is rendered worthless by new methods of production. Thus the proletariat is recruited from all classes of the population.

The proletariat goes through various stages of development. With its birth begins its struggle with the bourgeoisie. At first the contest is carried on by individual laborers, then by the workpeople of a factory, then by the operatives of one trade, in one locality, against the individual bourgeois who directly exploits them. They direct their attacks not against the bourgeois conditions of production, but against the instruments of production themselves; they destroy imported wares that compete with their labor, they smash machinery, they set factories ablaze, they seek to restore by force the vanished status of the workman of the Middle Ages.

At this stage the laborers still form an incoherent mass scattered over the whole country, and broken up by their mutual competition. If anywhere they unite to form more compact bodies, this is not yet the consequence of their own active union, but of the union of the bourgeoisie, which class, in order to attain its own political ends, is compelled to set the whole proletariat in motion, and is moreover, for a time, still able to do so. At this stage, therefore, the proletarians do not fight their enemies, but the enemies of their enemies, the remnants of absolute monarchy, the landowners, the non-industrial bourgeois, the petty bourgeoisie. Thus the whole historical movement is concentrated in the hands of the bourgeoisie, every victory so obtained is a victory for the bourgeoisie.

But with the development of industry the proletariat not only increases in number; it becomes concentrated in greater masses, its strength grows and it feels that strength more. The various interests and conditions of life within the ranks of the proletariat are more and more equalized, in proportion as machinery obliterates all distinctions of labor, and nearly everywhere reduces wages to the same low level. The growing competition among the bourgeois, and the resulting commercial crises, make the wages of the workers ever more fluctuating; the unceasing improvement of machinery, ever more rapidly developing, makes their livelihood more and more precarious; the collisions between individual workmen and individual bourgeois take more and more the character of collisions between two classes. Thereupon the workers begin to form combinations (trade unions) against the bourgeois; they club together in order to keep up the rate of wages; they found permanent associations in order to make provision beforehand for these occasional revolts. Here and there the contest breaks out into riots.

Now and then the workers are victorious, but only for a time. The real fruit of their battle lies not in the immediate result, but in the ever expanding union of workers. This union is helped on by the improved means of communication that are created by modern industry, and that places the workers of different localities in contact with one another. It was just this contact that was needed to centralize the numerous local struggles, all of the same character, into one national struggle between classes. But every class struggle is a political struggle. And that union, to attain which the burghers of the Middle Ages with their miserable highways, required centuries, the modern proletarians, thanks to railways, achieve in a few years.

This organization of the proletarians into a class, and consequently into a political party, is continually being upset again by the competition between the workers themselves. But it ever rises up again, stronger, firmer, mightier. It compels legislative recognition of particular interests of the workers by taking advantage of the divisions among the bourgeoisie itself. Thus the Ten-Hours-Bill in England was carried.

Altogether collisions between the classes of the old society further, in many ways, the development of the proletariat. The bourgeoisie finds itself involved in a constant battle—at first with the aristocracy; later on, with those portions of the bourgeoisie itself whose interests have become antagonistic to the progress of industry; at all times, with the bourgeoisie of foreign countries. In all these battles it sees itself compelled to appeal to the proletariat, to ask for its help, and thus to drag it into the political arena. The bourgeoisie itself, therefore, supplies the proletariat with its own elements of political and general education; in other words, it furnishes the proletariat with weapons for fighting the bourgeoisie.

Further, as we have already seen, entire sections of the ruling classes are, by the advance of industry, precipitated into the proletariat, or are at least threatened in their conditions of existence. These also supply the proletariat with fresh elements of enlightenment and progress.

Finally, in times when the class-struggle nears the decisive hour, the process of dissolution going on within the ruling class, in fact within the whole range of an old society, assumes such a violent, glaring character that a small section of the ruling class cuts itself adrift and joins the revolutionary class, the class that holds the future in its hands. Just as, therefore, at an earlier period, a section of the nobility went over to the bourgeoisie, so now a portion of the bourgeoisie goes over to the proletariat, and in particular, a portion of the bourgeois ideologists, who have raised themselves to the level of comprehending theoretically the historical movements as a whole.

Of all the classes that stand face to face with the bourgeoisie today the proletariat alone is a really revolutionary class. The other classes decay and finally disappear in the face of modern industry; the proletariat is its special and essential product.

The lower middle-class, the small manufacturer, the shopkeeper, the artisan, the peasant, all these fight against the bourgeoisie, to save from extinction their existence as fractions of the middle class. They are therefore not revolutionary, but conservative. Nay, more; they are reactionary, for they try to roll back the wheel of history. If by chance they are revolutionary, they are so only in view of their impending transfer into the proletariat; they thus defend not their present, but their future interests; they desert their own standpoint to place themselves at that of the proletariat.

The "dangerous class," the social scum, that passively rotting mass thrown off by the lowest layers of the old society, may here and there be swept into the movement by a proletarian revolution; its conditions of life, however, prepare it far more for the part of a bribed tool of reactionary intrigue.

In the conditions of the proletariat, those of old society at large are already virtually swamped. The proletarian is without property; his relation to his wife and children has no longer anything in common with the bourgeois family relations; modern industrial labor, modern subjection to capital, the same in England as in France, in America as in Germany, has stripped him of every trace of national character. Law, morality, religion, are to him so many bourgeois prejudices, behind which lurk in ambush just as many bourgeois interests.

All the preceding classes that got the upper hand sought to fortify their already acquired status by subjecting society at large to their conditions of appropriation. The proletarians cannot become masters of the productive forces of society, except by abolishing their own previous mode of appropriation, and thereby also every other previous mode of appropriation. They have nothing of their own to secure and to fortify; their mission is to destroy all previous securities for and insurances of individual property.

All previous historical movements were movements of minorities, or in the interest of minorities. The proletarian movement is the self-conscious, independent movement of the immense majority. The proletariat, the lowest stratum of our present society, cannot stir, cannot raise itself up without the whole superincumbent strata of official society being sprung into the air.

Though not in substance, yet in form, the struggle of the proletariat with the bourgeoisie is at first a national struggle. The proletariat of each country must, of course, first of all settle matters with its own bourgeoisie.

In depicting the most general phases of the development of the proletariat, we have traced the more or less veiled civil war, raging within existing society, up to the point where that war breaks out into open revolution, and where the violent overthrow of the bourgeoisie, lays the foundation for the sway of the proletariat.

Hitherto every form of society has been based, as we have already seen, on the antagonism of oppressing and oppressed classes. But in order to oppress a class, certain conditions must be assured to it under which it can at least continue its slavish existence. The serf, in the period of serfdom, raised himself to membership in the commune, just as the petty bourgeois, under the yoke of feudal absolutism, managed to develop into a bourgeois. The modern laborer, on the contrary, instead of rising with the progress of industry, sinks deeper and deeper below the conditions of existence of his own class. He becomes a pauper, and pauperism develops more rapidly than population and wealth. And here it becomes evident that the bourgeoisie is unfit any longer to be the ruling class in society, and to impose its conditions of existence upon society as an over-riding law. It is unfit to rule, because it is incompetent to assure an existence to its slave within his slavery, because it cannot help letting him sink into such a state that it has to feed him, instead of being fed by him. Society can no longer live under this bourgeoisie; in other words, its existence is no longer compatible with society.

The essential condition for the existence, and for the sway of the bourgeois class, is the formation and augmentation of capital; the condition for capital is wage-labor. Wage-labor rests exclusively on competition between the laborers. The advance of industry, whose involuntary promoter is the bourgeoisie, replaces the isolation of the laborers, due to competition, by their revolutionary combination, due to association. The development of modern industry, therefore, cuts from under its feet the very foundation on which the bourgeoisie produces and appropriates products. What the bourgeoisie therefore produces, above all, are its own grave-diggers. Its fall and the victory of the proletariat are equally inevitable. . . .

We have seen above that the first step in the revolution by the working class is to raise the proletariat to the position of ruling class, to win the battle of democracy.

The proletariat will use its political supremacy to wrest, by degrees, all capital from the bourgeoisie, to centralize all instruments of production in the hands of the state,—that is, of the proletariat organized as a ruling class; and to increase the total productive forces as rapidly as possible.

Of course, in the beginning, this cannot be effected except by means of despotic inroads on the rights of property, and on the conditions of bourgeois production; by means of measures, therefore, which appear economically insufficient and untenable, but which in the course of movement outstrip themselves, necessitate further inroads upon the old social order, and are unavoidable as a means of entirely revolutionizing the mode of production. . . .

When, in the course of development, class distinctions have disappeared, and all production has been concentrated in the hands of a vast association of the whole nation, the public power will lose its political character. Political power, properly so called, is merely the organization power of one class for oppressing another. If the proletariat during its contest with the bourgeoisie is compelled, by the force of circumstances, to organize itself as a class, if, by means of a revolution, it makes itself the ruling class, and, as such, sweeps away by force the old conditions of production, then it will, along with these conditions, have swept away the conditions for the existence of class antagonisms, and of classes generally, and will thereby have abolished its own supremacy as a class.

In place of the old bourgeois society, with its classes and class antagonisms, we shall have an association in which the free development of each is the condition for the free development of all.

KARL MARX AND FRIEDRICH ENGELS

The Economic Sources of Consciousness

In direct contrast to German philosophy, which descends from heaven to earth, here we ascend from earth to heaven. That is to say, we do not set out from what men say, imagine, conceive, nor from men as narrated, thought of, imagined, conceived, in order to arrive at men in the flesh. We set out from real, active men, and on the basis of their real life process we demonstrate the development of the ideological reflexes and echoes of this life process. The phantoms formed in the human brain are also, necessarily, sublimates of their material life process, which is empirically verifiable and bound to material premises. Morality, religion, metaphysics, all the rest of ideology and their corresponding forms of consciousness, thus no longer retain the semblance of independence. They have no history, no development; but men, developing their material production and their material

From *The German Ideology* [completed 1846], ed. R. Pascal and translated from the German by W. Lough and C. P. Magill, London, 1938, pp. 14-15, 28-32; reprinted by permission of International Publishers Co., Inc. and Lawrence and Wishart.

intercourse, alter, along with this, their real existence, their thinking, and the products of their thinking. Life is not determined by consciousness, but consciousness by life. In the first method of approach the starting point is consciousness taken as the living individual; in the second it is the real, living individuals themselves, as they are in actual life, and consciousness is considered solely as *their* consciousness.

This method of approach is not devoid of premises. It starts out from the real premises, and does not abandon them for a moment. . . .

Our conception of history depends on our ability to expound the real process of production, starting out from the simple material production of life, and to comprehend the form of intercourse connected with this and created by this (i.e., civil society in its various stages), as the basis of all history; further, to show it in its action as state, and so, from this starting point, to explain the whole mass of different theoretical products and forms of consciousness, religion, philosophy, ethics, etc., and trace their origins and growth, by which means, of course, the whole thing can be shown in its totality (and therefore, too, the reciprocal action of these various sides on one another). It has not, like the idealistic view of history, in every period to look for a category, but remains constantly on the real ground of history; it does not explain practice from the idea, but explains the formation of ideas from material practice, and accordingly it comes to the conclusion that all forms and products of consciousness cannot be dissolved by mental criticism, by resolution into "self-consciousness" or transformation into "apparitions," "specters," "fancies," etc., but only by the practical overthrow of the actual social relations which gave rise to this idealistic humbug; that not criticism but revolution is the driving force of history, also of religion, of philosophy, and all other types of theory. It shows that history does not end by being resolved into "self-consciousness" as "spirit of the spirit" but that in it at each stage there is found a material result: a sum of productive forces, a historically created relation of individuals to nature and to one another, which is handed down to each generation from its predecessor; a mass of productive forces, different forms of capital, and conditions, which, indeed, is modified by the new generation on the one hand, but also on the other prescribes for it its conditions of life and gives it a definite development, a special character. It shows that circumstances make men just as much as men make circumstances.

This sum of productive forces, forms of capital, and social forms of intercourse, which every individual and generation finds in existence as something given, is the real basis of what the philosophers have conceived as "substance" and "essence of man," and what they have deified and attacked: a real basis which is not in the least disturbed, in its effect and influence on the development of men, by the fact that these philosophers revolt against it as "self-consciousness" and "the unique." These conditions of life, which different generations find in existence, decide also whether or not the periodically recurring revolutionary convulsion will be strong enough to overthrow the basis of all existing forms. And if these material elements of a complete revolution are not present (namely, on the one hand the existence of productive forces, on the other the formation of a revolutionary mass, which revolts not only against separate conditions of society up till then, but against the very "production of life" till then, the "total activity" on which it was based), then, as far as practical development is concerned, it is absolutely immaterial whether the "idea" of this revolution has been expressed a hundred times already, as the history of communism proves.

In the whole conception of history up to the present this real basis of history has been either totally neglected or else considered as a minor matter, quite irrelevant to the course of history. History must therefore always be written according to an extraneous standard; the real production of life seems to be beyond history, while the truly historical appears to be separated from ordinary life, something extra-superterrestrial. With this the relation of man to nature is excluded from history, and hence the antithesis of nature and history is created. The exponents of this conception of history have consequently been able to see in history only the political actions of princes and states, religious and all sorts of theoretical struggles, and in particular in each historical epoch have had to share the *illusion of that epoch*. For instance, if an epoch imagines itself to be actuated by purely "political" or "religious" motives, although "religion" and "politics" are only forms of its true motives, the historian accepts this opinion. The "idea," the "conception" of these conditioned men about their real practice is transformed into the sole determining, active force, which controls and determines their practice. When the crude form in which the division of labor appears with the Indians and Egyptians calls forth the caste system in their state and religion, the historian believes that the caste system is the power which has produced this crude social form. While the French and the English at least hold by the political illusion, which is moderately close to reality, the Germans move in the realm of the "pure spirit" and make religious illusion the driving force of history.

The Hegelian philosophy of history is the last consequence, reduced to its "finest expression," of all this German historiography, for which it is not a question of real, or even of political, interests, but of pure thoughts, which inevitably appear, even to St. Bruno, as a series of "thoughts" that devour one another and are finally swallowed up in "self-consciousness." And equally inevitably, and more logically, the course of history appears to the blessed Max Stirner, who knows not a thing about real history, as a mere tale of "knights," robbers, and ghosts, from whose visions he can, of course, save himself only by "unholiness." This conception is truly religious: it postulates religious man as the primitive man, and in its imagination puts the religious production of fancies in the place of the real production of the means of subsistence and of life itself. This whole conception of history, together with its dissolution and the scruples and qualms resulting from it, is a purely *national* affair of the Germans and has only *local* interest for the Germans, as for instance the important question treated several times of late: how really we "pass from the realm of God to the realm of man"—as if this "realm of God" has ever existed anywhere save in the imagination, and the learned gentlemen, without being aware of it, were not constantly living in the "realm of man," to which they are now seeking the way; and as if the learned pastime (for it is nothing more) of explaining the mystery of this theoretical bubble-blowing did not, on the contrary, lie in demonstrating its origin in actual earthly conditions.

Always, for these Germans, it is simply a matter of resolving the nonsense of earlier writers into some other freak, i.e., of presupposing that all this nonsense has a special meaning which can be discovered; while really it is only a question of explaining this theoretical talk from the actual existing conditions. The real, prac

tical dissolution of these phrases, the removal of these notions from the consciousness of men, will, as we have already said, be effected by altered circumstances,
not by theoretical deductions. For the mass of men, i.e., the proletariat, these
theoretical notions do not exist, and hence do not require to be dissolved, and if
this mass ever had any theoretical notions, e.g., religion, etc., these have now long
been dissolved by circumstances.

LEON TROTSKY
The Limitations of Formalism

The quarrels about "pure art" and about art with a tendency took place between
the liberals and the "populists." They do not become us. Materialistic dialectics
are above this; from the point of view of an objective historical process, art is
always a social servant and historically utilitarian. It finds the necessary rhythm of
words for dark and vague moods, it brings thought and feeling closer or contrasts
them with one another, it enriches the spiritual experience of the individual and
of the community, it refines feeling, makes it more flexible, more responsive, it
enlarges the volume of thought in advance and not through the personal method
of accumulated experience, it educates the individual, the social group, the class
and the nation. And this it does quite independently of whether it appears in a
given case under the flag of a "pure" or of a frankly tendencious art. In our Russian social development tendenciousness was the banner of the intelligentsia
which sought contact with the people. The helpless intelligentsia, crushed by
Tsarism and deprived of a cultural environment, sought support in the lower strata
of society and tried to prove to the "people" that it was thinking only of them,
living only for them and that it loved them "terribly." And just as the "populists"
who went to the people were ready to do without clean linen and without a comb
and without a toothbrush, so the intelligentsia was ready to sacrifice the "subtleties" of form in its art, in order to give the most direct and spontaneous expression
to the sufferings and hopes of the oppressed. On the other hand, "pure" art was
the banner of the rising bourgeoisie, which could not openly declare its bourgeois
character, and which at the same time tried to keep the intelligentsia in its service. The Marxist point of view is far removed from these tendencies, which were
historically necessary, but which have become historically *passé*. Keeping on the
plane of scientific investigation, Marxism seeks with the same assurance the social
roots of the "pure" as well as of the tendencious art. It does not at all "incrim-
inate" a poet with the thoughts and feelings which he expresses, but raises questions of a much more profound significance, namely, to which order of feelings
does a given artistic work correspond in all its peculiarities? What are the social
conditions of these thoughts and feelings? What place do they occupy in the

From "The Formalist School," and "Revolution and Social Art," *Literature and Revolution*
[1924], translated from the Russian by Rose Strunsky, New York, 1925, pp. 168-83, 234-6;
reprinted by permission of International Publishers Co., Inc.

historic development of a society and of a class? And, further, what literary heritage has entered into the elaboration of the new form? Under the influence of what historic impulse have the new complexes of feelings and thoughts broken through the shell which divides them from the sphere of poetic consciousness? The investigation may become complicated, detailed or individualized, but its fundamental idea will be that of the subsidiary rôle which art plays in the social process.

Each class has its own policy in art, that is, a system of presenting demands on art, which changes with time; for instance, the Maecenas-like protection of court and grand seigneur, the automatic relationship of supply and demand which is supplemented by complex methods of influencing the individual, and so forth, and so on. The social and even the personal dependence of art was not concealed, but was openly announced as long as art retained its court character. The wider, more popular, anonymous character of the rising bourgeoisie led, on the whole, to the theory of "pure art," though there were many deviations from this theory. As indicated above, the tendencious literature of the "populist" intelligentsia was imbued with a class interest; the intelligentsia could not strengthen itself and could not conquer for itself a right to play a part in history without the support of the people. But in the revolutionary struggle, the class egotism of the intelligentsia was turned inside out, and in its left wing, it assumed the form of highest self-sacrifice. That is why the intelligentsia not only did not conceal art with a tendency, but proclaimed it, thus sacrificing art, just as it sacrificed many other things.

Our Marxist conception of the objective social dependence and social utility of art, when translated into the language of politics, does not at all mean a desire to dominate art by means of decrees and orders. It is not true that we regard only that art as new and revolutionary which speaks of the worker, and it is nonsense to say that we demand that the poets should describe inevitably a factory chimney, or the uprising against capital! Of course the new art cannot but place the struggle of the proletariat in the center of its attention. But the plough of the new art is not limited to numbered strips. On the contrary, it must plow the entire field in all directions. Personal lyrics of the very smallest scope have an absolute right to exist within the new art. Moreover, the new man cannot be formed without a new lyric poetry. But to create it, the poet himself must feel the world in a new way. If Christ alone or Sabaoth himself bends over the poet's embraces (as in the case of Akhmatova, Tsvetaeva, Shkapskaya and others), then this only goes to prove how much behind the times his lyrics are and how socially and æsthetically inadequate they are for the new man. Even where such terminology is not a survival of experience so much as of words, it shows psychologic inertia and therefore stands in contradiction to the consciousness of the new man. No one is going to prescribe themes to the poet or intends to prescribe them. Please write about anything you can think of! But allow the new class which considers itself, and with reason, called upon to build a new world, to say to you in any given case: It does not make new poets of you to translate the philosophy of life of the Seventeenth Century into the language of the Acméists. The form of art is, to a certain and very large degree, independent, but the artist who creates this form, and the spectator who is enjoying it, are not empty machines, one for creating form and the other for appreciating it. They are living people, with a crystallized psychology representing a certain unity, even if not entirely harmonious. This psychology is the result of social conditions. The creation and perception of art forms is one of the functions of this psychology. And no matter how wise the Formalists try to be, their whole conception is simply based upon the fact that they ignore the psychological unity of the social man, who creates and who consumes what has been created.

The proletariat has to have in art the expression of the new spiritual point of view which is just beginning to be formulated within him, and to which art must help him give form. This is not a state order, but an historic demand. Its strength lies in the objectivity of historic necessity. You cannot pass this by, nor escape its force.

The Formalist school seems to try to be objective. It is disgusted, and not without reason, with the literary and critical arbitrariness which operates only with tastes and moods. It seeks precise criteria for classification and valuation. But owing to its narrow outlook and superficial methods, it is constantly falling into superstitions, such as graphology and phrenology. These two "schools" have also the task of establishing purely objective tests for determining human character; such as the number of the flourishes of one's pen and their roundness, and the peculiarities of the bumps on the back of one's head. One may assume that pen-flourishes and bumps do have some relation to character; but this relation is not direct, and human character is not at all exhausted by them. An apparent objectivism based on accidental, secondary and inadequate characteristics leads inevitably to the worst subjectivism. In the case of the Formalist school it leads to the superstition of the word. Having counted the adjectives, and weighed the lines, and measured the rhythms, a Formalist either stops silent with the expression of a man who does not know what to do with himself, or throws out an unexpected generalization which contains five per cent of Formalism and ninety-five per cent of the most uncritical intuition.

In fact, the Formalists do not carry their idea of art to its logical conclusion. If one is to regard the process of poetic creation only as a combination of sounds or words, and to seek along these lines the solution of all the problems of poetry, then the only perfect formula of "poetics" will be this: Arm yourself with a dictionary and create by means of algebraic combinations and permutations of words, all the poetic works of the world which have been created and which have not yet been created. Reasoning "formally" one may produce "Eugene Onegin" in two ways: either by subordinating the selection of words to a preconceived artistic idea (as Pushkin himself did), or by solving the problem algebraically. From the "Formal" point of view, the second method is more correct, because it does not depend upon mood, inspiration, or other unsteady things, and has besides the advantage that while leading to "Eugene Onegin" it may bring one to an incalculable number of other great works. All that one needs is infinity in time, called eternity. But as neither mankind nor the individual poet have eternity at their disposal, the fundamental source of poetic words will remain, as before, the preconceived artistic idea understood in the broadest sense, as an accurate thought and as a clearly expressed personal or social feeling and as a vague mood. In its striving towards artistic materialization, this subjective idea will be stimulated and jolted by form and may be sometimes pushed on to a path which was entirely unforeseen. This simply means that verbal form is not a passive reflection of a preconceived artistic idea, but an active element which influences the idea itself. But such an active mutual relationship—in which form influences and at times entirely transforms content—is known to us in all fields of social and even biologic life. This is no reason at all for rejecting Darwinism and Marxism and for the creation of a Formalist school either in biology or sociology.

Victor Shklovsky, who flits lightly from verbal Formalism to the most subjective valuations, assumes a very uncompromising attitude towards the historico-materialistic theory of art. In a booklet which he published in Berlin, under the title of "The March of the Horse," he formulates in the course of three small pages—brevity is a fundamental and, at any rate, an undoubted merit of Shklovsky —five (not four and not six, but five) exhaustive arguments against the materialist conception of art. Let us examine these arguments, because it won't harm us to take a look and see what kind of chaff is handed out as the last word in scientific thought (with the greatest variety of scientific references on these same three microscopic pages).

"If the environment and the relations of production," says Shklovsky, "influenced art, then would not the themes of art be tied to the places which would correspond to these relations? But themes are homeless." Well, and how about butterflies? According to Darwin, they also "correspond" to definite relations, and yet they flit from place to place, just like an unweighted litterateur.

It is not easy to understand why Marxism should be supposed to condemn themes to a condition of serfdom. The fact that different peoples and different classes of the same people make use of the same themes, merely shows how limited the human imagination is, and how man tries to maintain an economy of energy in every kind of creation, even in the artistic. Every class tries to utilize, to the greatest possible degree, the material and spiritual heritage of another class. Shklovsky's argument could be easily transferred into the field of productive technique. From ancient times on, the wagon has been based on one and the same theme, namely, axles, wheels, and a shaft. However, the chariot of the Roman patrician was just as well adapted to his tastes and needs as was the carriage of Count Orlov, fitted out with inner comforts, to the tastes of this favorite of Catherine the Great. The wagon of the Russian peasant is adapted to the needs of his household, to the strength of his little horse, and to the peculiarities of the country road. The automobile, which is undoubtedly a product of the new technique, shows, nevertheless, the same "theme," namely, four wheels on two axles. Yet every time a peasant's horse shies in terror before the blinding lights of an automobile on the Russian road at night, a conflict of two cultures is reflected in the episode.

"If environment expressed itself in novels," so runs the second argument, "European science would not be breaking its head over the question of where the stories of 'A Thousand and One Nights' were made, whether in Egypt, India, or Persia." To say that man's environment, including the artist's, that is, the conditions of his education and life, find expression in his art also, does not mean to say that such expression has a precise geographic, ethnographic and statistical character. It is not at all surprising that it is difficult to decide whether certain novels were made in Egypt, India or Persia, because the social conditions of these countries have much in common. But the very fact that European science is "breaking its head" trying to solve this question from these novels themselves, shows that these novels reflect an environment, even though unevenly. No one can jump beyond himself. Even the ravings of an insane person contain nothing that the sick man had not received before from the outside world. But it would be an insanity of another order to regard his ravings as the accurate reflection of an external world. Only an experienced and thoughtful psychiatrist, who knows the past of the patient, will be able to find the reflected and distorted bits of reality in the contents of his ravings. Artistic creation, of course, is not a raving, though it is also a deflection, a changing and a transformation of reality, in accordance with the peculiar laws of art. However fantastic art may be, it cannot have at its disposal any other material except that which is given to it by the world of three dimensions and by the narrower world of class society. Even when the artist creates heaven and hell, he merely transforms the experience of his own life into his phantasmagorias, almost to the point of his landlady's unpaid bill.

"If the features of class and caste are deposited in art," continues Shklovsky, "then how does it come that the various tales of the Great Russians about their nobleman are the same as their fairy tales about their priest?"

In essence, this is merely a paraphrase of the first argument. Why cannot the fairy tales about the nobleman and about the priest be the same, and how does this contradict Marxism? The proclamations which are written by well-known Marxists not infrequently speak of landlords, capitalists, priests, generals and other exploiters. The landlord undoubtedly differs from the capitalist, but there are cases when they are considered under one head. Why, then, cannot folk-art in certain cases treat the nobleman and the priest together, as the representatives of the classes which stand above the people and which plunder them? In the cartoons of Moor and of Deni, the priest often stands side by side with the landlord, without any damage to Marxism.

"If ethnographic traits were reflected in art," Shklovsky goes on, "the folk-lore about the peoples beyond the border would not be interchangeable and could not be told by any one folk about another."

As you see, there is no letting up here. Marxism does not maintain at all that ethnographic traits have an independent character. On the contrary, it emphasizes the all-determining significance of natural and economic conditions in the formation of folk-lore. The similarity of conditions in the development of the herding and agricultural and primarily peasant peoples, and the similarity in the character of their mutual influence upon one another, cannot but lead to the creation of a similar folk-lore. And from the point of view of the question that interests us here, it makes absolutely no difference whether these homogeneous themes arose independently among different peoples, as the reflection of a life-experience which was homogeneous in its fundamental traits and which was reflected through the homogeneous prism of a peasant imagination, or whether the seeds of these fairy tales were carried by a favorable wind from place to place, striking root wherever the ground turned out to be favorable. It is very likely that, in reality, these methods were combined.

And finally, as a separate argument—"The reason (i.e., Marxism) is incorrect in the fifth place"—Shklovsky points to the theme of abduction which goes through Greek comedy and reaches Ostrovsky. In other words, our critic repeats, in a special form, his very first argument (as we see, even in so far as formal logic is concerned, all is not well with our Formalist). Yes, themes migrate from people to people, from class to class, and even from author to author. This means only that the human imagination is economical. A new class does not begin to create all of culture from the beginning, but enters into possession of the past, assorts it, touches it up, rearranges it, and builds on it further. If there were no such utilization of the "second-hand" wardrobe of the ages, historic processes would have no progress at all. If the theme of Ostrovsky's drama came to him through the Egyptians and through Greece, then the paper on which Ostrovsky developed his theme came to him as a development of the Egyptian papyrus through the Greek parchment. Let us take another and closer analogy: the fact that the critical methods of the Greek Sophists, who were the pure Formalists of their day, have penetrated the theoretic consciousness of Shklovsky, does not in the least change the fact that Shklovsky himself is a very picturesque product of a definite social environment and of a definite age.

Shklovsky's destruction of Marxism in five points reminds us very much of those articles which were published against Darwinism in the magazine "The Orthodox Review" in the good old days. If the doctrine of the origin of man from the monkey were true, wrote the learned Bishop Nikanor of Odessa thirty or forty years ago, then our grandfathers would have had distinct signs of a tail, or would have noticed such a characteristic in their grandfathers and grandmothers. Second, as everybody knows, monkeys can only give birth to monkeys. . . . Fifth, Darwinism is incorrect, because it contradicts Formalism—I beg your pardon, I meant to say the formal decisions of the universal church conferences. The advantage of the learned monk consisted, however, in the fact that he was a frank *passéist* and took his cue from the Apostle Paul and not from physics, chemistry or mathematics, as the Futurist, Shklovsky, does.

It is unquestionably true that the need for art is not created by economic conditions. But neither is the need for food created by economics. On the contrary, the need for food and warmth creates economics. It is very true that one cannot always go by the principles of Marxism in deciding whether to reject or to accept a work of art. A work of art should, in the first place, be judged by its own law, that is, by the law of art. But Marxism alone can explain why and how a given tendency in art has originated in a given period of history; in other words, who it was who made a demand for such an artistic form and not for another, and why.

It would be childish to think that every class can entirely and fully create its own art from within itself, and, particularly, that the proletariat is capable of creating a new art by means of closed art guilds or circles, or by the Organization for Proletarian Culture, etc. Generally speaking, the artistic work of man is continuous. Each new rising class places itself on the shoulders of its preceding one. But this continuity is dialectic, that is, it finds itself by means of internal repulsions and breaks. New artistic needs or demands for new literary and artistic points of view are stimulated by economics, through the development of a new class, and minor stimuli are supplied by changes in the position of the class, under the influence of the growth of its wealth and cultural power. Artistic creation is always a complicated turning inside out of old forms, under the influence of new stimuli which originate outside of art. In this large sense of the word, art is a handmaiden. It is not a disembodied element feeding on itself, but a function of social man indissolubly tied to his life and environment. And how characteristic it is—if one were to reduce every social superstition to its absurdity—that Shklov-

sky has come to the idea of art's absolute independence from the social environment at a period of Russian history when art has revealed with such utter frankness its spiritual, environmental and material dependence upon definite social
classes, subclasses and groups!

Materialism does not deny the significance of the element of form, either in
logic, jurisprudence, or art. Just as a system of jurisprudence can and must be
judged by its internal logic and consistency, so art can and must be judged from
the point of view of its achievements in form, because there can be no art without them. However, a juridical theory which attempted to establish the independence of law from social conditions would be defective at its very base. Its
moving force lies in economics—in class contradictions. The law gives only a
formal and an internally harmonized expression of these phenomena, not of their
individual peculiarities, but of their general character, that is, of the elements that
are repetitive and permanent in them. We can see now with a clarity which is
rare in history how new law is made. It is not done by logical deduction, but by
empirical measurement and by adjustment to the economic needs of the new
ruling class. Literature, whose methods and processes have their roots far back
in the most distant past and represent the accumulated experience of verbal
craftsmanship, expresses the thoughts, feelings, moods, points of view and hopes
of the new epoch and of its new class. One cannot jump beyond this. And there
is no need of making the jump, at least, for those who are not serving an epoch
already past nor a class which has already outlived itself.

The methods of formal analysis are necessary, but insufficient. You may count
up the alliterations in popular proverbs, classify metaphors, count up the number
of vowels and consonants in a wedding song. It will undoubtedly enrich our
knowledge of folk art, in one way or another; but if you don't know the peasant
system of sowing, and the life that is based on it, if you don't know the part the
scythe plays, and if you have not mastered the meaning of the church calendar
to the peasant, of the time when the peasant marries, or when the peasant women
give birth, you will have only understood the outer shell of folk art, but the kernel
will not have been reached. The architectural scheme of the Cologne cathedral
can be established by measuring the base and the height of its arches, by determining the three dimensions of its naves, the dimensions and the placement of
the columns, etc. But without knowing what a mediæval city was like, what a
guild was, or what was the Catholic Church of the Middle Ages, the Cologne
cathedral will never be understood. The effort to set art free from life, to declare
it a craft self-sufficient unto itself, devitalizes and kills art. The very need of such
an operation is an unmistakable symptom of intellectual decline.

The analogy with the theological arguments against Darwinism which was
made above may appear to the reader external and anecdotal. That may be true,
to some extent. But a much deeper connection exists. The Formalist theory inevitably reminds a Marxist who has done any reading at all of the familiar tunes
of a very old philosophic melody. The jurists and the moralists (to recall at random the German Stammler, and our own subjectivist Mikhailovsky) tried to
prove that morality and law could not be determined by economics, because economic life was unthinkable outside of juridical and ethical norms. True, the formalists of law and morals did not go so far as to assert the complete independence
of law and ethics from economics. They recognized a certain complex mutual

relationship of "factors," and these "factors," while influencing one another, retained the qualities of independent substances, coming no one knew whence. The assertion of complete independence of the æsthetic "factor" from the influence of social conditions, as is made by Shklovsky, is an instance of specific hyperbole whose roots, by the way, lie in social conditions too; it is the megalomania of æsthetics turning our hard reality on its head. Apart from this peculiarity, the constructions of the Formalists have the same kind of defective methodology that every other kind of idealism has. To a materialist, religion, law, morals and art represent separate aspects of one and the same process of social development. Though they differentiate themselves from their industrial basis, become complex, strengthen and develop their special characteristics in detail, politics, religion, law, ethics and æsthetics remain, none the less, functions of social man and obey the laws of his social organization. The idealist, on the other hand, does not see a unified process of historic development which evolves the necessary organs and functions from within itself, but a crossing or combining and interacting of certain independent principles—the religious, political, juridical, æsthetic and ethical substances, which find their origin and explanation in themselves. The (dialectic) idealism of Hegel arranges these substances (which are the eternal categories) in some sequence by reducing them to a genetic unity. Regardless of the fact that this unity with Hegel is the absolute spirit, which divides itself in the process of its dialectic manifestation into various "factors," Hegel's system, because of its dialectic character, not because of its idealism, gives an idea of historic reality which is just as good as the idea of a man's hand that a glove gives when turned inside out. But the Formalists (and their greatest genius was Kant) do not look at the dynamics of development, but at a cross-section of it, on the day and at the hour of their own philosophic revelation. At the crossing of the line they reveal the complexity and multiplicity of the object (not of the process, because they do not think of processes). This complexity they analyze and classify. They give names to the elements, which are at once transformed into essences, into sub-absolutes, without father or mother; to wit, religion, politics, morals, law, art. Here we no longer have a glove of history turned inside out, but the skin torn from the separate fingers, dried out to a degree of complete abstraction, and this hand of history turns out to be the product of the "interaction" of the thumb, the index, the middle finger, and all the other "factors." The æsthetic "factor" is the little finger, the smallest, but not the least beloved.

In biology, vitalism is a variation of the same fetish of presenting the separate aspects of the world-process, without understanding its inner relation. A creator is all that is lacking for a super-social, absolute morality or æsthetics, or for a super-physical absolute "vital force." The multiplicity of independent factors, "factors" without beginning or end, is nothing but a masked polytheism. Just as Kantian idealism represents historically a translation of Christianity into the language of rationalistic philosophy, so all the varieties of idealistic formalization, either openly or secretly, lead to a God, as the Cause of all causes. In comparison with the oligarchy of a dozen sub-absolutes of the idealistic philosophy, a single personal Creator is already an element of order. Herein lies the deeper connection between the Formalist refutations of Marxism and the theological refutations of Darwinism.

The Formalist school represents an abortive idealism applied to the questions of art. The Formalists show a fast ripening religiousness. They are followers of St. John. They believe that "In the beginning was the Word." But we believe that in the beginning was the deed. The word followed, as its phonetic shadow. . . .

This explains the dualism of every literary tendency; on the one hand, it adds something to the technique of art, heightening (or lowering) the general level of craftsmanship; on the other hand, in its concrete historic form, it expresses definite demands which, in the final analysis, have a class character. We say class, but this also means individual, because a class speaks through an individual. It also means national, because the spirit of a nation is determined by the class which rules it and which subjects literature to itself.

Let us take up Symbolism. What is it understood to mean: is it the art of transforming reality symbolically, a method of artistic creation in form? Or is it that particular symbolic tendency which was represented by Blok, Sologub, and others? Russian Symbolism did not invent symbols. It only grafted them more closely to the organism of the modernized Russian language. In this sense, the future art, no matter what lines it will follow, will not wish to reject the Symbolist heritage in form. But the actual Russian Symbolism of certain definite years made use of the symbol for a precise social purpose. What was its purpose? The Decadent school, which preceded Symbolism, sought the solution of all artistic problems in the personal experiences of sex, death, and the rest, or rather of none but sex and death. It could not but exhaust itself in a very short time. From this— not from social impulses—followed the need to find a higher sanction for one's demands and feelings and moods, and so to enrich and elevate them. Symbolism, which made of the symbol not only a method of art, but a symbol of faith, seemed to the intelligentsia the artistic bridge to Mysticism. In this concretely sociologic sense, and not in any abstract formal sense, Symbolism was not merely a method of artistic technique, but the intelligentsia's escape from reality, its way of constructing another world, its artistic bringing up in self-sufficient day-dreaming, contemplation and passivity. In Blok we find Zhukovsky modernized! And the old Marxian symposiums and pamphlets (of 1908 and after) on the subject of the "literary decline," no matter how crude and one-sided some of their generalizations may have been, and no matter how they tended to mere scribbling, gave an incomparably more significant and correct social literary diagnosis and prognosis that Chuzhak did, for instance. He gave thought to the problem of form sooner and more attentively than many other Marxists, but because of the influence of the current schools of art, he saw in them the growing stages of a proletarian culture, and not the stages of the intelligentsia's growing estrangement from the masses.

What are we to understand under the term realism? At various periods, and by various methods, realism gave expression to the feelings and needs of different social groups. Each one of these realistic schools is subject to a separate and social literary definition, and a separate formal and literary estimation. What have they in common? A definite and important feeling for the world. It consists in a feeling for life as it is, in an artistic acceptance of reality, and not in a shrinking from it, in an active interest in the concrete stability and mobility of life. It is a striving either to picture life as it is or to idealize it, either to justify or to condemn it, either to photograph it or generalize and symbolize it. But it is always a preoccupation with our life of three dimensions as a sufficient and invaluable theme for art. In this large philosophic sense, and not in the narrow sense of a literary school, one may say with certainty that the new art will be realistic. The Revolution cannot live together with mysticism. Nor can the Revolution live together with romanticism, if that which Pilnyak, the Imagists and others call romanticism is, as it may be feared, mysticism shyly trying to establish itself under a new name. This is not being doctrinaire, this is an insuperable psychological fact. Our age cannot have a shy and portable mysticism, something like a pet dog that is carried along "with the rest." Our age wields an axe. Our life, cruel, violent and disturbed to its very bottom, says: "I must have an artist of a single love. Whatever way you take hold of me, whatever tools and instruments created by the development of art you choose, I leave to you, to your temperament and to your genius. But you must understand me as I am, you must take me as I will become, and there must be no one else besides me."

This means a realistic monism, in the sense of a philosophy of life, and not a "realism" in the sense of the traditional arsenal of literary schools. On the contrary, the new artist will need all the methods and processes evolved in the past, as well as a few supplementary ones, in order to grasp the new life. And this is not going to be artistic eclecticism, because the unity of art is created by an active world-attitude and active life-attitude.

GEORG LUKÁCS

Historical Truth in Fiction

Marxism is not a Baedeker of history, but a signpost pointing the direction in which history moves forward. The final certainty it affords consist in the assurance that the development of mankind does not and cannot finally lead to nothing and nowhere.

Of course, such generalizations do not do full justice to the guidance given by Marxism, a guidance extending to every topical problem of life. Marxism combines a consistent following of an unchanging direction with incessant theoretical and practical allowances for the deviousness of the path of evolution. Its well-defined philosophy of history is based on a flexible and adaptable acceptance and analysis of historical development. This apparent duality—which is in reality the dialectic unity of the materialist world-view—is also the guiding principle of Marxist aesthetics and literary theory.

Those who do not know Marxism at all or know it only superficially or at second-hand, may be surprised by the respect for the classical heritage of mankind which one finds in the really great representatives of this doctrine and by

From *Studies in European Realism* [1948], translated from the Hungarian by Edith Bone, pp. 4-19. Copyright © 1964 by Grosset & Dunlap; reprinted by permission of Grosset & Dunlap and C. Abramsky.

their incessant references to that classical heritage. Without wishing to enter into too much detail, we mention as an instance, in philosophy, the heritage of Hegelian dialectics, as opposed to the various trends in the latest philosophies. "But all this is long out of date," the modernists cry. "All this is the undesirable, outworn legacy of the nineteenth century," say those who—intentionally or unintentionally, consciously or unconsciously—support the Fascist ideology and its pseudo-revolutionary rejection of the past, which is in reality a rejection of culture and humanism. Let us look without prejudice at the bankruptcy of the very latest philosophies; let us consider how most philosophers of our day are compelled to pick up the broken and scattered fragments of dialectic (falsified and distorted in this decomposition) whenever they want to say something even remotely touching its essence about present-day life; let us look at the modern attempts at a philosophical synthesis and we shall find them miserable, pitiful caricatures of the old genuine dialectic, now consigned to oblivion.

It is not by chance that the great Marxists were jealous guardians of our classical heritage in their aesthetics as well as in other spheres. But they do not regard this classical heritage as a reversion to the past; it is a necessary outcome of their philosophy of history that they should regard the past as irretrievably gone and not susceptible of renewal. Respect for the classical heritage of humanity in aesthetics means that the great Marxists look for the true highroad of history, the true direction of its development, the true course of the historical curve, the formula of which they know; and because they know the formula they do not fly off at a tangent at every hump in the graph, as modern thinkers often do because of their theoretical rejection of the idea that there is any such thing as an unchanged general line of development.

For the sphere of aesthetics this classical heritage consists in the great arts which depict man as a whole in the whole of society. Again it is the general philosophy (here: proletarian humanism), which determines the central problems posed in aesthetics. The Marxist philosophy of history analyses man as a whole, and contemplates the history of human evolution as a whole, together with the partial achievement, or non-achievement of completeness in its various periods of development. It strives to unearth the hidden laws governing all human relationships. Thus the object of proletarian humanism is to reconstruct the complete human personality and free it from the distortion and dismemberment to which it has been subjected in class society. These theoretical and practical perspectives determine the criteria by means of which Marxist aesthetics establish a bridge back to the classics and at the same time discover new classics in the thick of the literary struggles of our own time. The ancient Greeks, Dante, Shakespeare, Goethe, Balzac, Tolstoy all give adequate pictures of great periods of human development and at the same time serve as signposts in the ideological battle fought for the restoration of the unbroken human personality.

Such viewpoints enable us to see the cultural and literary evolution of the nineteenth century in its proper light. They show us that the true heirs of the French novel, so gloriously begun early in the last century, were not Flaubert and especially not Zola, but the Russian and Scandinavian writers of the second half of the century. The present volume contains my studies of French and Russian realist writers seen in this perspective.

If we translate into the language of pure aesthetics the conflict (conceived in the sense of the philosophy of history) between Balzac and the later French novel, we arrive at the conflict between realism and naturalism. Talking of a conflict here may sound a paradox to the ears of most writers and readers of our day. For most present-day writers and readers are used to literary fashions swinging to and fro between the pseudo-objectivism of the naturalist school and the mirage-subjectivism of the psychologist or abstract-formalist school. And inasmuch as they see any worth in realism at all, they regard their own false extreme as a new kind of near-realism or realism. Realism however is not some sort of middle way between false objectivity and false subjectivity, but on the contrary the true, solution-bringing third way, opposed to all the pseudo-dilemmas engendered by the wrongly posed questions of those who wander without a chart in the labyrinth of our time. Realism is the recognition of the fact that a work of literature can rest neither on a lifeless average, as the naturalists suppose, nor on an individual principle which dissolves its own self into nothingness. The central category and criterion of realist literature is the type, a peculiar synthesis which organically binds together the general and the particular both in characters and situations. What makes a type a type is not its average quality, not its mere individual being, however profoundly conceived; what makes it a type is that in it all the humanly and socially essential determinants are present on their highest level of development, in the ultimate unfolding of the possibilities latent in them, in extreme presentation of their extremes, rendering concrete the peaks and limits of men and epochs.

True great realism thus depicts man and society as complete entities, instead of showing merely one or the other of their aspects. Measured by this criterion, artistic trends determined by either exclusive introspection or exclusive extraversion equally impoverish and distort reality. Thus realism means a three-dimensionality, an all-roundness, that endows with independent life characters and human relationships. It by no means involves a rejection of the emotional and intellectual dynamism which necessarily develops together with the modern world. All it opposes is the destruction of the completeness of the human personality and of the objective typicality of men and situations through an excessive cult of the momentary mood. The struggle against such tendencies acquired a decisive importance in the realist literature of the nineteenth century. Long before such tendencies appeared in the practice of literature, Balzac had already prophetically foreseen and outlined the entire problem in his tragi-comic story *Le Chef d'Oeuvre Inconnu*. Here experiment on the part of a painter to create a new classic three-dimensionality by means of an ecstasy of emotion and colour quite in the spirit of modern impressionism, leads to complete chaos. Fraunhofer, the tragic hero, paints a picture which is a tangled chaos of colours out of which a perfectly modelled female leg and foot protrude as an almost fortuitous fragment. Today a considerable section of modern artists has given up the Fraunhofer-like struggle and is content with finding, by means of new aesthetic theories, a justification for the emotional chaos of their works.

The central aesthetic problem of realism is the adequate presentation of the complete human personality. But as in every profound philosophy of art, here, too, the consistent following-up to the end of the aesthetic viewpoint leads us beyond pure aesthetics: for art, precisely if taken in its most perfect purity, is saturated with social and moral humanistic problems. The demand for a realistic creation of types is in opposition both to the trends in which the biological being of man, the physiological aspects of self-preservation and procreation are dominant (Zola and his disciples) and to the trends which sublimate man into purely mental, psychological processes. But such an attitude, if it remained within the sphere of formal aesthetic judgments, would doubtless be quite arbitrary, for there is no reason why, regarded merely from the point of view of good writing, erotic conflict with its attendant moral and social conflicts should be rated higher than the elemental spontaneity of pure sex. Only if we accept the concept of the complete human personality as the social and historical task humanity has to solve; only if we regard it as the vocation of art to depict the most important turning-points of this process with all the wealth of the factors affecting it; only if aesthetics assign to art the role of explorer and guide, can the content of life be systematically divided up into spheres of greater and lesser importance; into spheres that throw light on types and paths and spheres that remain in darkness. Only then does it become evident that any description of mere biological processes—be these the sexual act or pain and sufferings, however detailed and from the literary point of view perfect it may be—results in a levelling-down of the social, historical and moral being of men and is not a means but an obstacle to such essential artistic expression as illuminating human conflicts in all their complexity and completeness. It is for this reason that the new contents and new media of expression contributed by naturalism have led not to an enrichment but to an impoverishment and narrowing-down of literature.

Apparently similar trains of thought were already put forward in early polemics directed against Zola and his school. But the psychologists, although they were more than once right in their concrete condemnation of Zola and the Zola school, opposed another no less false extreme to the false extreme of naturalism. For the inner life of man, its essential traits and essential conflicts can be truly portrayed only in organic connection with social and historical factors. Separated from the latter and developing merely its own immanent dialectic, the psychologist trend is no less abstract, and distorts and impoverishes the portrayal of the complete human personality no less than does the naturalist biologism which it opposes.

It is true that, especially regarded from the viewpoint of modern literary fashions, the position in respect of the psychologist school is at the first glance less obvious than in the case of naturalism. Everyone will immediately see that a description in the Zola manner of, say, an act of copulation between Dido and Aeneas or Romeo and Juliet would resemble each other very much more closely than the erotic conflicts depicted by Virgil and Shakespeare, which acquaint us with an inexhaustible wealth of culture and human facts and types. Pure introspection is apparently the diametrical opposite of naturalist levelling-down, for what it describes are quite individual, non-recurring traits. But such extremely individual traits are also extremely abstract, for this very reason of non-recurrence. Here, too, Chesterton's witty paradox holds good, that the inner light is the worst kind of lighting. It is obvious to everyone that the coarse biologism of the naturalists and the rough outlines drawn by propagandist writers deform the true picture of the complete human personality. Much fewer are those who realize that the psychologists' punctilious probing into the human soul and their transformation of human beings into a chaotic flow of ideas destroy no less surely every possibility of a literary presentation of the complete human personality. A Joyce-like shoreless torrent of associations can create living human beings just as little as Upton Sinclair's coldly calculated all-good and all-bad stereotypes.

Owing to lack of space this problem cannot be developed here in all its breadth. Only one important and at present often neglected point is to be stressed here because it demonstrates that the live portrayal of the complete human personality is possible only if the writer attempts to create types. The point in question is the organic, indissoluble connection between man as a private individual and man as a social being, as a member of a community. We know that this is the most difficult question of modern literature today and has been so ever since modern *bourgeois* society came into being. On the surface the two seem to be sharply divided and the appearance of the autonomous, independent existence of the individual is all the more pronounced, the more completely modern *bourgeois* society is developed. It seems as if the inner life, genuine "private" life, were proceeding according to its own autonomous laws and as if its fulfilments and tragedies were growing ever more independent of the surrounding social environment. And correspondingly, on the other side, it seems as if the connection with the community could manifest itself only in high-sounding abstractions, the adequate expression for which would be either rhetoric or satire.

An unbiassed investigation of life and the setting aside of these false traditions of modern literature leads easily enough to the uncovering of the true circumstances, to the discovery which had long been made by the great realists of the beginning and middle of the nineteenth century and which Gottfried Keller expressed thus: "Everything is politics." The great Swiss writer did not intend this to mean that everything was immediately tied up with politics; on the contrary, in his view—as in Balzac's and Tolstoy's—every action, thought and emotion of human beings is inseparably bound up with the life and struggles of the community, i.e., with politics; whether the humans themselves are conscious of this, unconscious of it or even trying to escape from it, objectively their actions, thoughts and emotions nevertheless spring from and run into politics.

The true great realists not only realized and depicted this situation—they did more than that, they set it up as a demand to be made on men. They knew that this distortion of objective reality (although, of course, due to social causes), this division of the complete human personality into a public and a private sector was a mutilation of the essence of man. Hence they protested not only as painters of reality, but also as humanists, against this fiction of capitalist society however unavoidable this spontaneously formed superficial appearance. If as writers, they delved deeper in order to uncover the true types of man, they had inevitably to unearth and expose to the eyes of modern society the great tragedy of the complete human personality.

In the works of such great realists as Balzac we can again find a third solution opposed to both false extremes of modern literature, exposing as an abstraction, as a vitiation of the true poesy of life, both the feeble commonplaces of the well-intentioned and honest propagandist novels and the spurious richness of a preoccupation with the details of private life.

This brings us face to face with the question of the topicality today of the great realist writers. Every great historical period is a period of transition, a contradictory unity of crisis and renewal, of destruction and rebirth; a new social order and a new type of man always come into being in the course of a unified though contradictory process. In such critical, transitional periods the tasks and responsibility of literature are exceptionally great. But only truly great realism can cope with such responsibilities; the accustomed, the fashionable media of expression, tend more and more to hamper literature in fulfilling the tasks imposed by history. It should surprise no one if from this point of view we turn against the individualistic, psychologist trends in literature. It might more legitimately surprise many that these studies express a sharp opposition to Zola and Zolaism.

Such surprise may be due in the main to the fact that Zola was a writer of the left and his literary methods were dominant chiefly, though by no means exclusively, in left-wing literature. It might appear, therefore, that we are involving ourselves in a serious contradiction, demanding on the one hand the politization of literature and on the other hand attacking insidiously the most vigorous and militant section of left-wing literature. But this contradiction is merely apparent. It is, however, well suited to throw light on the true connection between literature and *Weltanschauung*.

The problem was first raised (apart from the Russian democratic literary critics) by Engels, when he drew a comparison between Balzac and Zola. Engels showed that Balzac, although his political creed was legitimist royalism, nevertheless inexorably exposed the vices and weakness of royalist feudal France and described its death agony with magnificent poetic vigour. This phenomenon, references to which the reader will find more than once in these pages, may at the first glance again—and mistakenly—appear contradictory. It might appear that the *Weltanschauung* and political attitude of serious great realists are a matter of no consequence. To a certain extent this is true. For from the point of view of the self-recognition of the present and from the point of view of history and posterity, what matters is the picture conveyed by the work; the question to what extent this picture conforms to the views of the authors is a secondary consideration.

This, of course, brings us to a serious problem of aesthetics. Engels, in writing about Balzac, called it "the triumph of realism"; it is a problem that goes down to the very roots of realist artistic creation. It touches the essence of true realism: the great writer's thirst for truth, his fanatic striving for reality—or expressed in terms of ethics: the writer's sincerity and probity. A great realist such as Balzac, if the intrinsic artistic development of situations and characters he has created comes into conflict with his most cherished prejudices or even his most sacred convictions, will, without an instant's hesitation, set aside these his own prejudices and convictions and describe what he really sees, not what he would prefer to see. This ruthlessness towards their own subjective world-picture is the hallmark of all great realists, in sharp contrast to the second-raters, who nearly always succeed in bringing their own *Weltanschauung* into "harmony" with reality, that is forcing a falsified or distorted picture of reality into the shape of their own world-view. This difference in the ethical attitude of the greater and lesser writers is closely linked with the difference between genuine and spurious creation. The characters created by the great realists, once conceived in the vision of their creator, live an independent life of their own: their comings and goings, their development, their destiny is dictated by the inner dialectic of their social and individual existence. No writer is a true realist—or even a truly good writer, if he can direct the evolution of his own characters at will.

All this is however merely a description of the phenomenon. It answers the question as to the ethics of the writer: what will he do if he sees reality in such and such a light? But this does not enlighten us at all regarding the other question: what does the writer see and how does he see it? And yet it is here that the most important problems of the social determinants of artistic creation arise. In the course of these studies we shall point out in detail the basic differences which arise in the creative methods of writers according to the degree to which they are bound up with the life of the community, take part in the struggles going on around them or are merely passive observers of events. Such differences determine creative processes which may be diametrical opposites; even the experience which gives rise to the work will be structurally different, and in accordance with this the process of shaping the work will be different. The question whether a writer lives within the community or is a mere observer of it, is determined not by psychological, not even by typological factors; it is the evolution of society that determines (not automatically, not fatalistically, of course), the line the evolution of an author will take. Many a writer of a basically contemplative type has been driven to an intense participation in the life of the community by the social conditions of his time; Zola, on the contrary, was by nature a man of action, but his epoch turned him into a mere observer and when at last he answered the call of life, it came too late to influence his development as a writer.

But even this is as yet only the formal aspect of this problem, although no longer the abstractly formal. The question grows essential and decisive only when we examine concretely the position taken up by a writer. What does he love and what does he hate? It is thus that we arrive at a deeper interpretation of the writer's true *Weltanschauung*, at the problem of the artistic value and fertility of the writer's world-view. The conflict which previously stood before us as the conflict between the writer's world-view and the faithful portrayal of the world he sees, is now clarified as a problem within the *Weltanschauung* itself, as a conflict between a deeper and a more superficial level of the writer's own *Weltanschauung*.

Realists such as Balzac or Tolstoy in their final posing of questions always take the most important, burning problems of the community for their starting-point; their pathos as writers is always stimulated by those sufferings of the people which are the most acute at the time; it is these sufferings that determine the objects and direction of their love and hate and through these emotions determine also what they see in their poetic visions and how they see it. If, therefore, in the process of creation their conscious world-view comes into conflict with the world seen in their vision, what really emerges is that their true conception of the world is only superficially formulated in the consciously held world-view and the real depth of their *Weltanschauung*, their deep ties with the great issues of their time, their sympathy with the sufferings of the people can find adequate expression only in the being and fate of their characters.

No one experienced more deeply than Balzac the torments which the transition to the capitalist system of production inflicted on every section of the people, the profound moral and spiritual degradation which necessarily accompanied this transformation on every level of society. At the same time Balzac was also deeply aware of the fact that this transformation was not only socially inevitable, but at the same time progressive. This contradiction in his experience Balzac attempted to force into a system based on a Catholic legitimism and tricked out with

Utopian conceptions of English Toryism. But this system was contradicted all the time by the social realities of his day and the Balzacian vision which mirrored them. This contradiction itself clearly expressed, however, the real truth: Balzac's profound comprehension of the contradictorily progressive character of capitalist development.

It is thus that great realism and popular humanism are merged into an organic unity. For if we regard the classics of the social development that determined the essence of our age, from Goethe and Walter Scott to Gorki and Thomas Mann, we find *mutatis mutandis* the same structure of the basic problem. Of course every great realist found a different solution for the basic problem in accordance with his time and his own artistic personality. But they all have in common that they penetrate deeply into the great universal problems of their time and inexorably depict the true essense of reality as they see it. From the French revolution onwards the development of society moved in a direction which rendered inevitable a conflict between such aspirations of men of letters and the literature and public of their time. In this whole age a writer could achieve greatness only in the struggle against the current of everyday life. And since Balzac the resistance of daily life to the deeper tendencies of literature, culture and art has grown ceaselessly stronger. Nevertheless there were always writers who in their life-work, despite all the resistance of the day, fulfilled the demand formulated by Hamlet: "to hold the mirror up to nature," and by means of such a reflected image aided the development of mankind and the triumph of humanist principles in a society so contradictory in its nature that it on the one hand gave birth to the ideal of the complete human personality and on the other hand destroyed it in practice.

The great realists of France found worthy heirs only in Russia. All the problems mentioned here in connection with Balzac apply in an even greater measure to Russian literary development and notably to its central figure Leo Tolstoy. It is not by chance that Lenin (without having read Engels' remarks about Balzac) formulated the Marxist view of the principles of true realism in connection with Tolstoy. Hence there is no need for us to refer to these problems again here. There is all the more need, however, to call attention to the erroneous conceptions current in respect of the historical and social foundations of Russian realism, errors which in many cases are due to deliberate distortion or concealment of facts. In Britain, as everywhere else in Europe, the newer Russian literature is well known and popular among the intelligent reading public. But as everywhere else, the reactionaries have done all they could to prevent this literature from becoming popular; they felt instinctively that Russian realism, even if each single work may not have a definite social tendency, is an antidote to all reactionary infection.

But however widespread familiarity with Russian literature may have been in the West, the picture formed in the minds of readers was nevertheless incomplete and largely false. It was incomplete because the great champions of Russian revolutionary democracy, Herzen and Bielinski, Chernyshevski and Dobrolyubov were not translated and even their names were known to very few outside the reach of the Russian language. And it is only now that the name of Saltykov-Shchedrin is getting to be known, although in him the newer Russian literature had produced a satirist unrivalled anywhere in the world since the days of Jonathan Swift.

What is more, the conception of Russian literature was not only incomplete, it was also distorted. The great Russian realist Tolstoy was claimed by reactionary ideologies for their own and the attempt was made to turn him into a mystic gazing into the past; into an "aristocrat of the spirit" far removed from the struggles of the present. This falsification of the image of Tolstoy served a second purpose as well; it helped to give a false impression of the tendencies predominant in the life of the Russian people. The result was the myth of a "holy Russia" and Russian mysticism. Later, when the Russian people in 1917 fought and won the battle for liberation, a considerable section of the *intelligentsia* saw a contradiction between the new free Russia and the older Russian literature. One of the weapons of counter-revolutionary propaganda was the untrue allegation that the new Russia had effected a complete volte-face in every sphere of culture and had rejected, in fact was persecuting, older Russian literature.

These counter-revolutionary allegations have long been refuted by the facts. The literature of the White Russian émigrés, which claimed to be the continuation of the allegedly mystical Russian literature, quickly showed its own sterility and futility, once it was cut off from the Russian soil and the real Russian problems. On the other hand, it was impossible to conceal from the intelligent reading public that in the Soviet Union the vigorous treatment of the fresh issues thrown up by the rejuvenated life of the nation was developing a rich and interesting new literature and the discerning readers of this literature could see for themselves how deeply rooted were the connections between it and Russian classical realism. (It will suffice to refer here to Sholokhov, the heir to Tolstoy's realism.)

The reactionary campaign of misrepresentation directed against the Soviet Union reached its culminating point before and during the late war, and then collapsed in the course of the same war, when the liberated peoples of the Soviet Union in their struggle against German Nazi imperialism demonstrated to the world such strength and such achievements in the sphere of moral and material culture that the old-style slanders and misrepresentations ceased to be effective. On the contrary a very large number of people began to ask: what was the source of the mighty popular forces, the manifestations of which were witnessed by the whole world during the war. Such dangerous thoughts required counter-measures and now we see a fresh wave of slander and misrepresentation breaking against the rock of Soviet civilization. Nevertheless the history of the internal and external evolution of the Russian people still remains an exciting and interesting problem for the reading public of every country.

In examining the history of the liberation of the Russian people and of the consolidation of its achievements, we must not overlook the important part played by literature in these historical events,—a part greater than the usual influence exercised by literature on the rising or falling fortunes of any civilized nation. On the one hand no other literature is as public-spirited as the Russian and on the other hand there has scarcely been any society in which literary works excited so much attention and provoked such crises as in Russian society in the classical realist period of Russian literature. Hence, although a very wide public is acquainted with Russian literature, it may not be superfluous to present this freshly arising problem in a new light. The new problems imperatively demand that our analysis penetrate, both from the social and the aesthetic viewpoint, to the true roots of Russian social development.

It is for this reason that our first study attempts to fill one of the greatest gaps in our knowledge of Russian literature by giving a characterization of the little-known great Russian revolutionary-democratic critics Bielinski, Chernyshevski and Dobrolyubov. Closely linked with this question is a revaluation of the well-known classical realists, or rather a characterization and appreciation which is somewhat more in accordance with historical truth. In the past, western critics and readers in their approach to Tolstoy and others took for their guide the views on society, philosophy, religion, art, and so on, which these great men had themselves expressed in articles, letters, diaries, and the like. They thought to find a key to the understanding of the often unfamiliar great works of literature in these conscious opinions. In other words reactionary criticism interpreted the works of Tolstoy and Dostoyevski by deriving the alleged spiritual and artistic content of these works from certain reactionary views of the authors.

The method employed in the present studies is the exact opposite of this. It is a very simple method: it consists in first of all examining carefully the real social foundations on which say Tolstoy's existence rested and the real social forces under the influence of which the human and the literary personality of this author developed. Secondly, in close connection with the first approach, the question is asked: what do Tolstoy's works represent, what is their real spiritual and intellectual content and how does the writer build up his aesthetic forms in the struggle for the adequate expression of such contents? Only if, after an unbiassed examination, we have uncovered and understood these objective relationships, are we in a position to provide a correct interpretation of the conscious views expressed by the author and correctly evaluate his influence on literature.

The reader will see later that in applying this method a quite new picture of Tolstoy will emerge. This revaluation will be new only to the non-Russian reading public. In Russian literature itself the method of appreciation outlined in the preceding has an old tradition behind it: Bielinski and Herzen were the precursors of the method, the culminating points of which are marked by the names of Lenin and Stalin. It is this method that the author of the present book is attempting to apply to an analysis of the works of Tolstoy. That Tolstoy is followed by Gorki in this book will surprise no one; the essay on Gorki is also a polemic against reactionary literary trends, is also to some extent a revaluation; and its main theme is the close link between Gorki the great innovator and his precursors in Russian literature and an examination of the question to what extent Gorki continued and developed classical Russian realism. The uncovering of these connections is at the same time the answer to the question: where is the bridge between old and new culture, between the old and the new Russian literature?

Finally the last paper gives a short outline of Tolstoy's influence on Western literature, discusses how Tolstoy came to be a figure of international stature and attempts to define the social and artistic significance of his influence on world literature. This paper, too, is an attack on the reactionary conception of Russian realism, but an attack which also marshals allies: it shows how the finest German, French, English and American writers opposed such reactionary distortions, and fought for a correct understanding of Tolstoy and of Russian literature. The reader will see from this that the opinions put forward are not idle speculations of a solitary and isolated writer but a world-wide trend of thought constantly gaining in strength.

In the remarks about method the social tendencies underlying the essays have been strongly stressed and their significance could scarcely be exaggerated. Nevertheless the main emphasis in these papers is on the aesthetic, not the social, analysis; investigation of the social foundations is only a means to the complete grasp of the aesthetic character of Russian classical realism. This point of view is not an invention of the author. Russian literature owed its influence not only to its new social and human content but chiefly to the fact of being a really great literature. For this reason it is not enough to eradicate the old firmly-rooted false notions regarding its historical and social foundations; it is also necessary to draw the literary and aesthetic conclusions from the correct evaluation of those social and historical foundations. Only then can it be understood why great Russian realism has played a leading part in world literature for three quarters of a century and has been a beacon of progress and an effective weapon in the struggle against open and covert literary reaction and against the decadence masquerading as innovation.

Only if we have a correct aesthetic conception of the essence of Russian classical realism can we see clearly the social and even political importance of its past and future fructifying influence on literature. With the collapse and eradication of Fascism a new life has begun for every liberated people. Literature has a great part to play in solving the new tasks imposed by the new life in every country. If literature is really to fulfil this role, a role dictated by history, there must be as a natural prerequisite, a philosophical and political rebirth of the writers who produce it. But although this is an indispensable prerequisite, it is not enough. It is not only the opinions that must change, but the whole emotional world of men; and the most effective propagandists of the new, liberating, democratic feeling are the men of letters. The great lesson to be learnt from the Russian development is precisely the extent to which a great realist literature can fructifyingly educate the people and transform public opinion. But such results can be achieved only by a truly great, profound and all-embracing realism. Hence, if literature is to be a potent factor of national rebirth, it must itself be reborn in its purely literary, formal, aesthetic aspects as well. It must break with reactionary, conservative traditions which hamper it and resist the seeping-in of decadent influences which lead into a blind alley.

In these respects the Russian writers' attitude to life and literature is exemplary, and for this, if for no other, reason it is most important to destroy the generally accepted reactionary evalution of Tolstoy, and, together with the elimination of such false ideas, to understand the human roots of his literary greatness. And what is most important of all; to show how such greatness comes from the human and artistic identification of the writer with some broad popular movement. It matters little in this connection what popular movement it is in which the writer finds this link between himself and the masses; that Tolstoy sinks his roots into the mass of the Russian peasantry, and Gorki of the industrial workers and landless peasants. For both of them were to the bottom of their souls bound up with the movements seeking the liberation of the people and struggling for it. The result of such a close link in the cultural and literary sphere was then and is to-day that the writer can overcome his isolation, his relegation to the role of a mere observer, to which he would otherwise be driven by the present state of capitalist society. He thus becomes able to take up a free, unbiassed, critical attitude towards those tendencies of present-day culture which are unfavourable to art and literature. To fight against such tendencies by purely artistic methods, by the mere formal use of new forms, is a hopeless undertaking, as the tragic fate of the great writers of the West in the course of the last century clearly shows. A close link with a mass movement struggling for the emancipation of the common people does, on the other hand, provide the writer with the broader viewpoint, with the fructifying subject-matter from which a true artist can develop the effective artistic forms which are commensurate with the requirements of the age, even if they go against the superficial artistic fashions of the day.

These very sketchy remarks were required before we could express our final conclusion. Never in all its history did mankind so urgently require a realist literature as it does to-day. And perhaps never before have the traditions of great realism been so deeply buried under a rubble of social and artistic prejudice. It is for this reason that we consider a revaluation of Tolstoy and Balzac so important. Not as if we wished to set them up as models to be imitated by the writers of our day. To set an example means only: to help in correctly formulating the task and studying the conditions of a successful solution. It was thus that Goethe aided Walter Scott, and Walter Scott aided Balzac. But Walter Scott was no more an imitator of Goethe than Balzac was of Scott. The practical road to a solution for the writer lies in an ardent love of the people, a deep hatred of the people's enemies and the people's own errors, the inexorable uncovering of truth and reality, together with an unshakable faith in the march of mankind and their own people towards a better future.

There is to-day in the world a general desire for a literature which could penetrate with its beam deep into the tangled jungle of our time. A great realist literature could play the leading part, hitherto always denied to it, in the democratic rebirth of nations. If in this connection we evoke Balzac in opposition to Zola and his school, we believe that we are helping to combat the sociological and aesthetic prejudices which have prevented many gifted authors from giving their best to mankind. We know the potent social forces which have held back the development of both writers and literature: a quarter-century of reactionary obscurantism which finally twisted itself into the diabolical grimace of the Fascist abomination.

Political and social liberation from these forces is already an accomplished fact, but the thinking of the great masses is still bedevilled by the fog of reactionary ideas which prevents them from seeing clearly. This difficult and dangerous situation puts a heavy responsibility on the men of letters. But it is not enough for a writer to see clearly in matters political and social. To see clearly in matters of literature is no less indispensable and it is to the solution of these problems that this book hopes to bring its contribution.

Budapest, December, 1948

ALAIN ROBBE-GRILLET

Dehumanizing Nature

> The novel passes for a minor art only because of its obstinate attachment to
> exhausted techniques.   NATHALIE SARRAUTE

It is scarcely reasonable, at first glance, to think that a *new* literature may one
day—now, for example—be possible. The many attempts which have been made
for more than fifty years to pull the art of narrative out of its rut have resulted, at
best, in merely a few isolated works. None of these, whatever its interest, has
attracted a public comparable to that enjoyed by the bourgeois novel. The only
conception of the novel in effect today remains, in fact, that of Balzac.

Or one might go further and say, that of Madame de la Fayette. Already sacrosanct in her age, psychological analysis constituted the basis of all prose; presided
at the conception of the book, at the description of its characters, at the development of its plot. A *good* novel, ever since, has remained the study of a passion
—or a conflict of passions, or the absence of passion—in a given milieu. Most
contemporary novelists of the traditional sort—those, that is, who actually win
the approval of their readers—could insert long passages from *La Princesse de
Clèves* or from *Père Goriot* into their own books without awakening the least
suspicion in the vast public which devours whatever they turn out. They would
scarcely need to change more than a phrase here and there, modify certain constructions, give a glimpse of their own "manner" by means of a word, a "daring"
image, the rhythm of a sentence. . . . But all of them admit, without seeing
anything peculiar about it, that their preoccupations as writers date back several
centuries.

What is there to be surprised at in this? The raw material—the French language—has undergone only very slight modifications for three hundred years; and,
while society has transformed itself little by little, while industrial techniques
have made considerable progress, our intellectual civilization has remained precisely the same. We live according to essentially the same habits and prohibitions
—moral, alimentary, religious, sexual, hygienic, familial, etc. And of course there
is always the human "heart," which, as everyone knows, is eternal. There's nothing new under the sun, it's all been said before, we've come on the stage too
late, etc.

"A Fresh Start for Fiction," translated from the French by Richard Howard, *Evergreen
Review*, I, No. 3, 1957, pp. 99-104; "Three Reflected Visions," translated from the French
by Bruce Morrisette, ibid., 105-7; "Old 'Values' and the New Novel," translated from the
French by Bruce Morrisette, *Evergreen Review*, III, No. 9, 1959, pp. 100-118.
Reprinted by permission of Grove Press, Georges Borchardt, and John Calder Ltd.

The risk of encountering such objections is merely increased if one dares claim that this new literature is not only possible in the future, but is already being written, and that it is going to represent—in its fulfillment—a revolution more total than those from which such movements as romanticism and naturalism were born.

Such promises as "Now things are going to change!" will invariably meet with ridicule. How will they go about changing? In what direction? And—especially —why now?

The art of the novel, however, has achieved such a degree of stagnation—a lassitude noted and remarked on by almost the whole of criticism—that it is scarcely imaginable that it can survive for long without radical changes. To minds of many, the solution is simple indeed: no change is possible, the art of the novel is in the process of dying. We have no such guarantees. History will reveal, in a few decades, whether the various fits and starts which have been noted are signs of a death agony or a rebirth.

In any case, one must not deceive oneself as to the difficulties such a revolution will encounter. They are considerable. The whole caste system of our literary life (from publisher to the most modest reader, including bookseller and critic) has no choice but to fight against the unknown form which is attempting to establish itself. The minds best disposed toward the idea of a necessary transformation, those most willing to countenance and even recognize the values of experiment, remain, in spite of everything, the heirs of a tradition. A new form always seems to be more or less an absence of any form at all, since it is unconsciously judged by reference to consecrated forms. In one of our most celebrated encyclopedic dictionaries, we can read, in an article on Schoenberg: ". . . author of audacious works, written without regard for any rules whatever"! This brief judgment is found under the heading *Music*, evidently written by a specialist.

The stammering, newborn work will always be regarded as a monster, even by those who find the experiment fascinating. There will be some curiosity, of course, some gestures of interest, always some provision for the future. And some praise; though what is sincere will always be addressed to the vestiges of what is already familiar, to all those bonds from which the new work has not yet broken and which desperately seek to imprison it in the past.

For if the norms of the past serve to measure the present, they also can be used to construct it. The writer himself, despite his will to be independent, is situated in an intellectual civilization and a literature—that is, what *has been* written, a literature of the past. It is impossible for him to escape altogether from this tradition of which he is the product. Sometimes even the elements he has tried the hardest to uproot seem, on the contrary, to bloom more vigorously than ever in the very work by which he had hoped to destroy them; and he will be congratulated, of course, with relief, for having cultivated them so reverently.

Thus it will undoubtedly be those who specialize in the novel (novelists, critics, fanatic readers) who will have the most difficulty pulling themselves out of its rut.

Even the least "conditioned" observer is unable to look at the world which surrounds him with entirely unprejudiced eyes. There is no question of reviving that naïve concern for objectivity at which the analyst of the soul (subjective) finds it so easy to smile. Objectivity in the general sense of the term—total impersonality of observation—is all too evidently an illusion. But *freedom* of observation *should* be possible, and yet, unfortunately, it is not. At every instant, a continuous fringe of culture (psychology, ethics, metaphysics, etc.) is being added to things, disguising their real strangeness, making them more comprehensible, more reassuring. Sometimes the camouflage is complete: a gesture slips from our mind, supplanted by the emotions which supposedly produced it, and we remember a landscape as *austere* or *calm* without being able to evoke a single outline, a single determining element. Even if we immediately think, "That's literary," we don't try to react against it. We accept the fact that what is *literary* (the word has become pejorative) functions as a screen set with bits of variously colored glass that fracture our field of vision into tiny assimilable facets.

And if something resists this systematic appropriation of the visual, if an element of the world breaks in on us without finding any place in the interpretive screen, we can always make use of our convenient category of the "absurd" to absorb this awkward residue.

But the world is neither significant nor absurd. It *is*, quite simply. That, in any case, is the most remarkable thing about it. And suddenly this evidence strikes us with irresistible force. All at once the whole beautiful construction collapses: opening our eyes to the unexpected, we have experienced once too often the shock of this stubborn reality we were pretending to have mastered. Around us, defying the mob of our animistic or protective adjectives, the things *are there*. Their surfaces are clear and smooth, *intact*, neither dubiously glittering, nor transparent. All our literature has not yet succeeded in penetrating their smallest corner, in softening their slightest curve.

The innumerable filmed novels encumbering our screen provide us an occasion for reliving this curious experience as often as we like. The cinema, another heir of the psychological and naturalist tradition, more often than not has as its sole purpose the transposition of a story into images: it aims exclusively at imposing on the spectator, through the intermediary of some well-chosen scenes, the same meaning that the sentences had for the reader. But at any given moment the filmed story can draw us out of our interior comfort toward this proffered world with a violence that one would seek in vain in the corresponding text, whether novel or scenario.

One can readily perceive the nature of the transformation. In the original novel, the objects and gestures forming the very tissue of the plot disappeared completely, leaving behind only their *significations*: the empty chair became only absence or expectation, the hand placed on a shoulder became a sign of friendliness, the bars on the window became only the impossibility of leaving. . . . But in the cinema, one *sees* the chair *too*, the movement of the hand, the shape of the bars. What they signify remains obvious, but, instead of monopolizing our attention, it becomes something added, even something in excess, because what touches us, what persists in our memory, what appears as essential and irreducible to vague intellectual concepts, are the gestures themselves, the objects, the movements, and the contours, to which the image has suddenly (and unintentionally) restored their *reality*.

It may seem arbitrary that such fragments of crude reality in the film narrative, which the camera cannot help presenting, strike us so vividly, whereas identical scenes in real life do not suffice to free us of our blindness. Actually, it is as if the very conventions of the photographic medium (the two dimensions, the black-and-white images, the frame of the screen, the difference of scale between scenes) help to free us from our own conventions. The slightly "unaccustomed" aspect of this reproduced world reveals at the same time the unaccustomed character of the world that surrounds us: unaccustomed, too, to the degree that it refuses to conform to our habits of apprehension and to our demands.

Instead of this universe of "signification" (psychological, social, functional) we must try to construct a world both more solid and more immediate. Let it be first of all by their *presence* that objects and gestures impose themselves, and let this presence continue to make itself felt beyond all explanatory theory that might try to enclose it in some system of reference, whether sentimental, sociological, Freudian, or metaphysical.

In this future universe of the novel, gestures and objects will be "there" before being "something"; and they will still be there afterwards, hard, unalterable, eternally present, mocking their own meaning, which tries in vain to reduce them to the role of precarious tools between a formless past and an indeterminate future.

Thus objects will little by little lose their inconsistency and their secrets; will renounce their false mystery, that suspect interiority which Roland Barthes has called the "romantic 'heart' of things." No longer will objects be merely the vague reflection of the hero's vague soul, the image of his torments, the mainstay of his desires. Or rather, if objects must still accept this tyranny, it will be only in appearance, only to show all the more clearly to what extent they remain independent and alien.

As for the novel's characters, they may in themselves be rich with multiple interpretations; they may, according to the preoccupations of each author, give rise to all kinds of commentaries—psychological, psychiatric, religious, or political, yet their indifference to these supposed riches will quickly be apparent. Whereas the traditional hero is constantly incited, cornered, and destroyed by these "interpretations" proposed by the author, and endlessly rejected into an immaterial and unstable *elsewhere*, always more remote and blurred, the future hero of the novel will remain, on the contrary, "there." It is the commentaries which will seek "elsewhere"; in the face of his irrefutable presence, they will appear useless, superfluous, even dishonest.

All this might seem very theoretical, very illusory, if something were not actually changing—changing totally, definitively—in our relationships with the universe. Which is why we glimpse an answer to the old ironic question, "Why now?" There is today, in fact, a new element that separates us—this time radically —from Balzac, as from Gide or Madame de la Fayette: it is the dismissal of the old myth of "depth."

We know that the whole literature of the novel was based on this myth, and on it alone. The traditional role of the writer consisted in excavating Nature, in burrowing deeper and deeper to reach some ever more intimate strata, in finally bringing to light some fragment of a disconcerting secret. Having descended into the abyss of human passions, he would send to the seemingly tranquil world (the one on the surface) triumphant messages describing the mysteries he had actually touched with his own hands. And the sacred dizziness that then seized the reader, far from causing him anguish or nausea, reassured him as to his power of domination over the world. There were chasms, certainly, but thanks to such valiant speleologists, their depths could be sounded.

It is not surprising, given these conditions, that the literary phenomenon par excellence has resided in this one word, so all-inclusive and unique, which attempts to summon up all the inner qualities, the hidden *soul* of things. *Profundity* has functioned like a trap in which the writer captured the universe in order to hand it over to society.

The revolution which has taken place is in proportion to the power of the old order. Not only do we no longer consider the world as our very own, our private property, designed according to our needs and readily domesticated, but we no longer believe in its "depth."

While essentialist conceptions of man were facing their destruction, the notion of "condition" replaced that of "nature," the *surface* of things ceased being the mask that concealed their "heart" (a door opening on the worst "beyonds" of metaphysics).

It is therefore the whole literary language that has to change, that is changing already. We witness from day to day the growing repugnance that people of greater awareness feel for words of a visceral, analogical, incantatory character. On the other hand, the visual or descriptive adjective—the word that contents itself with measuring, locating, limiting, defining—indicates a difficult but most likely direction for the novel of the future.

THE DRESSMAKER'S DUMMY

The coffee pot is on the table.

It is a round table with four legs, covered with an oilcloth checkered red and gray on a neutral background—a yellowish-white that was once ivory, perhaps, or just white. In the middle of the table is a porcelain tile instead of the usual table mat: the design on the tile is completely covered, or at least made unrecognizable, by the coffee pot that is standing on it.

The coffee pot is made of brown earthenware. It is in the form of a sphere surmounted by a cylindrical percolator and a mushroom-shaped lid. The spout is an S with flattened sides, slightly more rounded at the base. The handle has more or less the shape of an ear, or rather of the outer rim of an ear. Even so, it would be a deformed ear—too round and without enough lobe: more or less an ear shaped like a pot handle. The spout, the handle, and the mushroom-shaped lid are cream color. The rest of the pot is a bright, shiny, even shade of brown.

There is nothing else on the table except the oilcloth, the tile and the coffee pot.

To the right, in front of the window, stands the dressmaker's dummy.

Behind the table, on the mantlepiece, is a large rectangular mirror in which can be seen half the french window (the right half), and, to the left (that is, to the left of the window), the reflection of the mirrored wardrobe. In the mirror of the wardrobe the window can be seen again, all of it this time, and the right way around (that is, the right half on the right, the left half on the left).

Thus, above the mantlepiece there are actually three halves of the window that can be successively distinguished without a break in continuity—they are, respectively (from left to right), the left half seen the right way around, the right half, also seen the right way around, and the right half seen in reverse. Since the wardrobe is standing exactly in the corner of the room, extending as far as the edge of the window, the two right halves of the window appear to be separated only by a narrow upright of the wardrobe, which could also be part of the window frame (the right upright of the left half exactly overlaps the left upright of the right half). The three halves make it possible to see, on the other side of the window screen, the leafless trees of the garden.

In this way, the window occupies the entire surface of the mirror except for the upper portion, in which can be seen a strip of the ceiling and the top of the mirrored wardrobe.

Also in the mirror on the mantlepiece can be seen two other dummies, one in front of the first, narrowest section of the window, all the way to the left; and the other in front of the third half (the one farthest to the right). The dummies are neither facing toward nor away from one another; the one on the right is turned so that its right side is facing toward the one on the left, which is slightly smaller and standing with its left side turned to face the one on the right. But this is hard to discern at first glance, for the two reflections are actually facing the same way and both therefore seem to be showing the same side—probably the left one.

The three dummies are standing in a row. The one in the middle, placed on the right side of the mirror, and about as much larger than the one on its right as it is smaller than the other one on its left, is facing in exactly the same direction on the table.

On the spherical part of the coffee pot there is a distorted reflection of the window, a more or less quadrilateral figure with its sides composed of circular arcs. The line formed by the wooden uprights between the two halves of the window suddenly spreads out at the bottom of this reflection into a rather shapeless blotch. This is certainly the shadow of the dummy.

The room is very bright, for the window is exceptionally large, although it has only two sections.

A good smell of hot coffee is coming out of the coffee pot on the table.

The dummy is not where it belongs: usually it is kept in the angle of the window, on the side opposite the mirrored wardrobe. The wardrobe has been put where it is to make fittings more convenient.

The design on the tile is an owl with two huge, almost frightening eyes. But, for the moment, nothing can be seen because of the coffee pot.

————

Is there not, first of all, something faintly fraudulent about this term "humanity" that is constantly being thrown up to us? If the word is not entirely devoid of meaning, just what does it signify?

Apparently those who use it constantly, who employ it as their single criterion for praise or blame, confuse (voluntarily, perhaps) the precise and strict consideration of man in his situation in the world—the phenomena of man's existence—with a certain anthropocentric atmosphere, vague yet all-encompassing, that confers on everything its so-called "meaning," that is, that sends out through the interior of everything a more or less crafty network of feelings and thoughts. By simplifying the position of these new inquisitors, we may summarize it in two sentences. If I say, "The world is mankind," I shall always obtain absolution; but if I say, "Things are things, and man is only man," I shall be immediately judged guilty of a crime against humanity.

The crime is to state that something exists in the world which is not mankind, which makes no signs to man, which has nothing in common with him. From their viewpoint, the crime lies especially in recognizing this separation, this distance, without making any effort to transcend or to sublimate it.

Let us try another approach. How can a work of art be "inhuman," or "anti-human"? How can they, in particular, accuse a novel of turning against or away from man when it follows from page to page each of his steps, describing only what he does, what he sees, or what he imagines? And let it be made clear at once that it is not the character in the novel who is under attack from the critics. In so far as he is a "character," an individual moved by torments and passions, no one will ever accuse *him* of being inhuman, even if he should be a sadistic psychopath and a criminal—rather the contrary, many would say.

But in the novel the eye of this man comes to rest on things with a hard insistence: he sees them, but refuses to make them part of himself, refuses to enter into any conniving or doubtful relationship with them, refuses to ask anything of them or to feel towards them any agreement or disagreement whatsoever. He may even, by chance, make them a support for his passion, for the line of sight that he directs at the world. But his glance limits itself to taking precise measurements; and his passion, likewise, stops at the surface of objects, without trying to penetrate them, since there is nothing inside, and without pretending to address to them the least emotional appeal, since they would not answer.

To condemn in the name of "humanity" a novel that presents such a character is to adopt the viewpoint of Humanism, which decrees that it is not enough to depict man as *there*, where he is, but commands us to proclaim that man is everywhere. Under the pretext that man can have only a subjective knowledge of the world, Humanism chooses man as the justification of everything. Like a "soul bridge" erected between man and things, the vision of Humanism is, above all, a pledge of solidarity.

In the realm of literature this solidarity is expressed mainly through the systematic search for analogies, or for analogical relationships.

Metaphor, in fact, is never an innocent figure of speech. To say that time is "capricious" or a mountain "majestic," to speak of the "heart" of the forest, of a "pitiless" sun, of a village "crouching" in the hollow of a valley is, to some extent, to furnish information about the things themselves: forms, dimensions, situations, etc. But the choice of an analogical vocabulary, however simple, always goes beyond giving an account of purely physical data; and what is added cannot be attributed to literary concerns only. The height of the mountain takes on, regardless of the writer's intention, a moral value; the heat of the sun becomes the result of an implied volition. In almost all contemporary literature these anthropomorphic analogies are reiterated too insistently, too coherently, not to be regarded as clues to a whole metaphysical system.

One must conclude that the writers who use such terminology are more or less consciously setting up a constant *rapport* between the universe and the human being who inhabits it. Thus the feelings of man are made to appear to originate one by one from his contacts with the world, and to find in the world their natural correspondences, if not their fulfillment.

Metaphor, which is supposed to express only comparison without concealed meaning, always introduces in fact a subterranean communication, a movement of sympathy—or of antipathy—which is its true *raison d'être*. As far as comparison is concerned, metaphor is nearly always useless, adding nothing new to the description. What loss would the village suffer if it were merely "situated" in the hollow of the valley? The word "crouching" gives no additional information. It does, on the other hand, transport the reader (guided by the author) into the hypothetical soul of the village. If I accept the word "crouching" I am no longer merely a spectator; I become myself the village (for the duration of the phrase), and the hollow of the valley functions as a sort of pit in which I seek refuge.

Taking these adhesive possibilities of the metaphor as their stronghold, the defenders of metaphor will reply that it thus possesses the advantage of bringing out an element not previously felt. Becoming the village—they say—the reader will project himself into the situation of the village, and therefore understand it better. Similarly for the mountain: I will depict it better, they claim, by stating that it is majestic than by measuring the angle at which my sight must be lifted to judge its height. . . . And this is sometimes true; but such procedure always implies a more serious counterpart. It is precisely this participation that is dangerous, because it leads directly to the idea of a hidden unity.

In truth, one must add, this additional benefit in descriptive value is only an excuse: the true practitioners of the metaphor aim only at the idea of a nondescriptive communication. If they lacked the verb "crouch" they would not even mention the position of the village. The height of the mountain would mean nothing to them if it did not offer the moral spectacle of "majesty."

For them such a spectacle never remains entirely exterior. It always implies, to one extent or another, a gift received by man. The things around us are like the fairies in fairy tales, each bringing to the new-born babe some future characteristic as a present. Thus the mountain may bring me for the first time the feeling of majesty; or so it is implied. This feeling would then develop within me and, proliferating, engender others: magnificence, prestige, heroism, nobility, pride. In turn I would apply these feelings to other objects, even of small size (I would speak of a proud oak tree, of a vase with noble lines . . .), and the world would become the depository of all my aspirations towards greatness, would become at once the image and the justification of these aspirations, for all eternity.

It would be the same for each emotion, and in these ceaseless interchanges, multiplied to infinity, I would never again be able to find the true origin of anything. Was majesty first inside me, or outside of me? The very question would lose all meaning. Nothing would be left between myself and the world but a sublime community of feelings.

Having acquired the habit, I would easily progress further. Once I accepted the principle of this communion, I would speak of the sadness of a landscape, of the indifference of a stone, of the fatuousness of a coal bucket. These new metaphors furnish no appreciable additional information concerning the objects subjected to my scrutiny, but the world of things will now have been so thoroughly contaminated by my emotions that it will be ready henceforth to express any and all feelings and traits of character. I will forget that it is I, and I alone, who feel sadness or solitude. These affective elements will come to be regarded as the profound reality of the material universe, the only reality, supposedly, worthy of my attention.

The problem transcends that of merely describing human consciousness, using objects as materials, as one might construct a cabin from logs. To confuse my own sadness with the sadness that I attribute to a landscape, to view this relationship as something more than superficial, is to admit, by the same token, that my present life is to a degree predestined; for this landscape existed *before* I came: if it is really sad, it was already sad prior to my arrival, and this *rapport* that I feel today between its form and my emotional state must have awaited me since before my birth—this particular sadness was therefore always destined for me. . . .

So it becomes clear to what a tremendous extent the idea of human "nature" is bound up with the vocabulary of analogy. This nature, common to all men, eternal and inalienable, no longer even needs God to support it. It is sufficient to know that Mont Blanc has been waiting for me in the "heart" of the Alps since prehistoric times, and with it all my ideas of greatness and purity. . . .

Such a nature, moreover, does not belong to man alone, since it constitutes the bond between his spirit and things: it is, then, a common essence for all "creation" that we are invited to accept. The universe and I have but a single soul, a single secret.

Belief in this kind of nature turns out thus to be the very basis of Humanism, as generally conceived. So it is not by chance that Nature itself—mineral, vegetable, animal—should be the original recipient of an anthropomorphic vocabulary. Nature—mountain, sea, forest, desert, valley—is at once our model and our heart. She is, at one and the same time, within us and outside of us. She is neither temporary nor accidental. She paralyzes us, judges us, and assures our salvation.

To refuse this alleged "nature" and the vocabulary which perpetuates its myth, to consider objects as having only exteriors and surfaces, is not—as has been claimed—to deny man; but it does require that we reject the "pananthropic" idea contained in traditional (if not any other) Humanism. For such a refusal is, in the last analysis, nothing else than the logical consequence of asserting personal freedom.

In this cleansing operation, nothing must be overlooked. On closer scrutiny, we perceive that it is not only anthropocentric (mental or visceral) analogies that must be attacked. *All* analogies are equally dangerous. Perhaps the most dangerous of all are those crafty ones in which man is not even mentioned.

Let us cite some random examples. To find among the clouds the form of a horse may still be considered, perhaps, simple description entailing no evil consequences. But to speak of the "gallop" of a cloud, or of its "wind-blown mane," is no longer an innocent process. For if a cloud (or a wave, or a hill) is endowed with a mane, if in another passage the mane of a stallion "shoots forth arrows," if these arrows . . . etc. The reader confronted with such images will emerge from the universe of forms to find himself immersed anew in a universe of meanings. Between the wave and the horse, he will be urged to sense a unified field of deeper meaning: wildness, pride, power, untamed fury. . . . The idea of any kind of "nature" leads inevitably to that of a nature common to all things, that is, a superior nature. Interiorness always leads to transcendence.

The stain widens—from the bow to the horse, from the horse to the wave, and from the wave to love. A common nature, to repeat, can and must be only an eternal answer to the single question forever asked by our Greco-Christian civilization. The Sphinx stands before me, questions me, and I do not even have to seek to understand the terms of the riddle. There is only one possible answer, one answer to everything: man.

Well! To this I say, No.

There are questions, there are answers—both in the plural. The only singularity is that man, from his own point of view, must be the single witness.

Man looks out at the world, and the world does not return his glance. Man beholds things and he sees, in our time, that he can in reality escape from the metaphysical pact that others have signed for him, long ago, and that he can at the same time escape from enslavement and fear. That he can . . . that he *will be able*, at least, some day.

Yet these considerations do not lead him to refuse all contact with the world; on the contrary, he makes use of the world for material ends. A utensil, as utensil, never has hidden depths; a utensil is wholly form and matter—and use.

Man takes up his hammer (or a stone that he has chosen) and he strikes the end of a post that he wishes to drive into the ground. While he is using it, the hammer (or the stone) is only form and matter: it has weight, a striking surface, an extremity which allows a grip. Man then sets down the tool; if he no longer needs it, the hammer is now nothing more than an object among objects. Outside of its use, it has no meaning.

And modern (or future) man no longer feels this absence of meaning as a lack, or as an emotional distress. Faced with this emptiness, he succumbs henceforth to no dizziness. His heart no longer requires a hollow place in which to take refuge.

For, by refusing communion, he also refuses tragedy.

We may define tragedy as an attempt to salvage, to "recuperate" the separation between man and things, and to make of that distance a new value. Tragedy is a sort of contest then in which victory arises from defeat. It appears thus as the latest invention of Humanism struggling to allow nothing to escape from its domain. Since the pact between man and things has finally been denounced, Humanism saves its empire by declaring immediately a new form of solidarity, in which the divorce between man and objects becomes itself the main road to salvation.

It is still, as it were, a kind of communion, but a painful one, forever on the point of achievement and yet always postponed, and whose efficacy is proportional to its inaccessibility. It is a procedure of reversal, a trap—and a lie.

Surely it is obvious to what extent this kind of union is a perverted one: instead of seeking the good, it now blesses evil. Misery, failure, solitude, guilt, madness: such are the accidents of our existence that we are now expected to welcome as the best tokens of our salvation. Welcome, not merely accept; for we are supposed to nourish them at our own expense while continuing to struggle against them. Tragedy wishes neither a true acceptance nor an outright refusal. It sublimates the state of disparity.

Let us analyze, for example, how "solitude" functions. I call out. No one answers me. Instead of concluding that there is no one there—which would be an observation pure and simple, dated and localized in space and time—I decide to act as if someone were there, but a someone who, for one reason or another, refuses to answer. The silence that follows my outcry is hence no longer a true silence; it is now enhanced with content, with depth of meaning, with a soul—which sends me back at once to my own soul. The distance between my call, heard in my own ears, and the mute (or even deaf . . .) interlocutor to whom it is addressed, becomes an anguish; my hope and my anguish then confer meaning on my life. Nothing henceforth counts for me except this false emptiness and the problems it creates for me. Should I cry out longer? Louder? Should I try other words? Again I try. . . . Quickly I understand that no one will answer; but the invisible presence that I continue to evoke by my calls forces me to utter forever into the silence my cry of misery. Soon the sound I emit begins to benumb me. As if bewitched, I call out again and again. My solitude, exacerbated, is transformed at last by my failing mind into a higher necessity, into a promise of redemption. And I must, to achieve this, cry out obstinately until death—and all for nothing.

Following the normal processes of habit, my solitude then ceases to appear as merely an accidental or momentary fact of my existence. It becomes part of me, of the whole world: it is our nature (again!). It has become, it is now, an eternal solitude.

Wherever we find distance, separation, duality, or cleavage, we also find the possibility of experiencing these as suffering, with the subsequent elevation of such suffering to the status of a sublime necessity. Such pseudo-necessity is both a path towards a metaphysical "beyond" and a door closed against any realistic future. If tragedy consoles us today, it also forbids all more solid conquests for tomorrow. Under the guise of perpetual movement, it actually paralyzes the world in a state of monotonously whirring accursedness. There is no longer any question of seeking a remedy for our misfortunes, once tragedy sets its sights upon making us love our ills.

Contemporary Humanism thus directs at us an oblique attack, and one which threatens to deceive us utterly. Because the salvage operation is no longer directed at things themselves, we might at first glance be inclined to believe that a rupture between objects and man had at least been achieved. We soon discover that this is not true: whether the pact is made with things, or with their removal from man, it all comes down to the same thing. The "soul bridge" is still left between things and ourselves; indeed, it is even reinforced as a result.

This is why tragic philosophy never aims at eliminating separations, but rather seeks to multiply them. Distance between man and other men, between man and himself, between man and the world, between the world and itself: nothing is left untouched. All is torn apart, fissured, split, thrown out of joint. Inside the most homogenous objects, as within the least ambiguous situations, appears a sort of secret distance. In reality it is only an *inner* distance, a false distance, which is actually an open road, leading (once more!) to reconciliation.

Everything is contaminated. Above all the novel, which is the primary domain in our days of the tragic spirit. From women in love who become nuns to policemen who become gangsters, including along the way tormented criminals, prostitutes with pure souls, righteous men constrained by their conscience to commit injustices, sadists motivated by love, lunatics led by logic, the typical "character" of the novel must be, above all else, a *double* being. The plot will be "human" to the degree that it is equivocally dual, and the whole novel will be regarded as "true" in so far as it contains contradictions.

It is easy to laugh at this; it is less easy to free oneself from the conditioning effects imposed by tragedy on our mental patterns. One can go so far as to state that rejecting the ideas of "nature" and predestination leads *directly* to tragedy. There is no significant piece of contemporary literature that does not express at the same time the affirmation of our freedom and the "tragic" principle of its abandonment.

At least two great novels, in recent decades, have presented us with two new forms of this fatal complicity, under the names of *absurdity* and *nausea*.

Albert Camus, everyone knows, has designated as *absurdity* the impassable abyss that stands between man and the world, between the aspirations of the human spirit and the incapacity of the world to satisfy them. The "absurd" is therefore, for him, neither in man nor in things, but in the impossibility of establishing between the two any *rapport* other than "strangeness."

Readers must have noticed, however, that the hero of *L'Étranger* (*The Stranger*) carries on with the world an obscure kind of connivance, composed of bitterness and fascination. The relationships between this man and the objects around him are in no way innocent: "absurdity" constantly leads to disappointment, withdrawal, revolt. It would hardly be an exaggeration to argue that it is actually *things* that finally draw the protagonist into his criminal act: the sun, the sea, the dazzling sand, the glistening knife, the spring gushing from the rocks, the revolver. . . . And, as to be expected, the principal role, among these things, is played by Nature.

Nor is the novel written in as *neutral* or "cleansed" style as the first pages might lead us to believe. Instead, only objects already burdened with a flagrantly obvious human significance are neutralized, carefully, and for moral reasons (thus the mother's coffin, described minutely with respect to the form and depth of penetration of its screws). Together with this we discover, more and more as the moment of the murder approaches, the most revealing classical metaphors, referring directly to man, or implying his omnipresence. The countryside is "gorged with sunlight," the evening is "like a melancholy truce," the holes in the roadway reveal the "shining flesh" of the tar, the earth is "blood colored," the sunlight is a "dazzling rain," its reflection on a shell is a "sword of light," the day has "cast anchor in an ocean of boiling metal." . . . Without counting the "breathing" of the "lazy" waves, the "sleeping" promontory, the "panting" sea and the "cymbals" of the sun. . . .

The central scene of the novel is the perfect image of a painful solidarity. The implacable sun is always "the same," its reflection on the knife blade held by the Arab "touches" the hero's forehead and "grinds into" his eyes. His hand clenches the revolver; he wishes to "shake" the sun; he fires repeatedly, four times. "And it was like four sharp knocks that I had struck upon the door of misfortune."

Thus "absurdity" turns out to be a form of tragic Humanism. It is not a recognition of the separation between man and objects. It is a lovers' quarrel between them, which leads to a crime of passion. The world is accused of complicity in murder.

When Sartre writes (in his *Explication de L'Étranger*) that the Stranger "refuses anthropomorphism," he gives us, as proved by the above citations, an incomplete view of the work. Sartre has certainly noticed these passages, but prefers to think that Camus, "unfaithful to his principles, is creating poetry." Could one not say, rather, that these metaphors are the real "explication" of the novel? Camus does not refuse anthropomorphism, but uses it with great economy and subtlety, in order to give it greater weight.

All of which fits into the pattern, since the real object is, as Sartre admits, to show us (in Pascal's words) "the natural misery of our condition."

What does Sartre's own novel *La Nausée* (*Nausea*) offer us? Ostensibly the author wishes to present strictly visceral relationships with the world, avoiding all efforts at description (allegedly vain) in order to arrive at a shady intimacy, depicted as illusory and yet as something to which the narrator cannot imagine refusing to yield: in fact, his primary object seems to be to yield to it as much as possible, in order to reach complete self-awareness.

Significantly, the first three perceptions registered near the start of the novel all enter through the sense of touch, not through sight. The three objects which engender the narrator's "revelation" are, in order, the beach pebble, the door handle, and the Autodidact's hand. Each time, it is the physical contact with the narrator's hand that produces the shock that he feels. Touch does provide in daily life, of course, a more intimate sensation than sight: no one fears contracting a contagious disease merely by looking at an afflicted person. Smell is already more suspect: it implies a penetration into the body by the foreign thing. The domain of sight, moreover, includes many degrees of perception: form, for example, generally appears more certain than color, which changes with the lighting, with the background, with the subject who beholds it.

We are not surprised to find therefore that Roquentin's eyes, in this novel, are more drawn to colors—especially to the more uncertain shades—than to lines; if it is not touch, it is almost always the sight of an uncertain color that upsets him and brings on the "nausea." Witness the importance acquired, at the beginning of the novel, by Cousin Adolph's suspenders, scarcely standing out against the blue of his shirt. They are "mauve . . . hiding in the blue, but with a false humility . . . as if, starting out to be violet, they had stopped short without giving up their pretensions. You feel like saying to them, 'Go ahead, *turn* violet and let's get it over.' But no, they stay suspended, stubborn in their unsuccessful effort. Sometimes the blue surrounding them slides over and covers them completely; for a moment I cannot see them. But it is only a wave; soon the blue pales here and there and I see the little spots of hesitant mauve reappear, spread out, blend together, and turn again into the suspenders." But the reader is still left ignorant of their form.

Farther on, in the public gardens, the famous chestnut-tree root concentrates within itself all its absurdity and hypocrisy, in its *black* color. "Black? I felt the word collapsing like a deflated balloon, emptying itself of all meaning with extraordinary rapidity. Black? The root *was not* black; it was not the color black that covered this piece of wood . . . but rather a confused effort to imagine black made by someone who had never seen black, and who, unable to stop imagining, had thought up some ambiguous thing, beyond all colors." And Roquentin adds the commentary: "Colors, tastes, odors, were never true, never really themselves and nothing else."

Colors produce in him, that is, sensations analogous to those of touch: they constitute an appeal, followed by a withdrawal, then a new outcry, etc. This "suspicious" contact is accompanied by nameless impressions, demanding and yet refusing acceptance. Color has the same effect on the eyes as physical contact on the palm of the hand: it manifests an indiscreet "personality" (double, of course) on the part of the object, a sort of shameful insistence which combines a moan, a defiance, and a denial. "If . . . objects touch me, it is unendurable. I fear entering into contact with them as if they were living creatures." Color changes, therefore it is alive. This is Roquentin's discovery: things, like himself, are alive.

Sounds appear to him as similarly adulterated (except for melodies, which do not *exist*). There remains the visual perception of lines; we feel that Roquentin avoids dealing with them. Yet he takes exception to this last refuge of coincidence with the self: the only lines which exactly coincide are the lines of geometry, the circle, for instance—"but then the circle does not exist either."

We find ourselves once more in a wholly "tragi-fied" universe, marked by fascination with disparity, by solidarity with things *because* they bear within themselves their own negation, by redemption (here, accession to self-awareness) through the very impossibility of reaching a true agreement. We find, that is, the ultimate salvaging of all separations, failures, solitudes and contradictions.

Therefore analogy turns out to be the only descriptive mode which Roquentin is willing seriously to consider. Looking at the cardboard box containing his ink bottle, he decides that geometry is powerless to describe it: to say that it is a parallelepiped is to say nothing whatever about "it." On the contrary, Sartre speaks to us of the "true" sea that "grovels" beneath a thin green film designed to "deceive" us, he compares the "cold" light of the sun to a "strict judgment," he notes the "happy death-rattle" of a fountain, the leather-covered bench of a tram becomes for him a "dead ass" floating adrift, its shaggy red plush has "thousands of little legs," the Autodidact's hand is a "fat white worm," etc. We would have to cite each object in the book, for they are all deliberately presented in this fashion. The most highly figured is, of course, the chestnut-tree root, which becomes in turn a "black fingernail," "boiled leather," "mildew," a "dead snake," a "vulture's claw," an "obese foot," "seal skin," and so on *ad nauseam*. . . .

Without wishing to limit consideration to this particular, but important point of view, we may say that "existence" is characterized in Sartre's novel by the presence of interior distances, and that his "nausea" is a painful visceral penchant felt by man for these distances. The "conniving smile of things" ends in a grimace: "All the objects surrounding me are made of the same matter as myself, a sort of rotten suffering."

And yet are we not asked to elevate to the status of a higher necessity Roquentin's sad celibacy, his lost love, his "botched life," the Autodidact's sad and ridiculous fate—all these maledictions of earthly life? Where, then, is our freedom? Those who would have no part in this malediction are threatened openly with the supreme moral condemnation of being *salauds*, real dirty dogs of mankind. It is all as if Sartre—who can scarcely be accused of *essentialism*—had, in this novel at least, glorified to the utmost the ideas of nature and tragedy. The struggle against these ideas has led, once more, to a position that endows them with new strength.

Drowned in their depths, man ends by no longer seeing *things*; his role is soon restricted to feeling, in their name, entirely *humanized* impressions and desires. "In brief, it is less a matter of observing the pebble than of moving into its heart and seeing the world with its eyes. . . ."—it is in his study of Francis Ponge that Sartre writes these words. Roquentin in *La Nausée* had already said, "I *was* the chestnut-tree root." The two positions are close: the aim is ostensibly, in both cases, to think "with" things and not *about* them.

Ponge himself pays little attention to "description." He doubtless realizes perfectly that his texts would be of little use to a future archeologist in reconstructing, from our vanished civilization, a cigarette or a candle. Without our daily familiarity with these objects, Ponge's texts based on them would be only beautiful hermetic poems.

Instead of descriptions, we get such statements as these: the *cageot* or wicker hamper is "dumbfounded to find itself in an awkward position," the trees in spring "take credit for being dupes" and release a "vomit of greenness," and the butterfly "takes revenge for its long amorphous humiliation as a caterpillar."

Is this really "taking sides" with things (Ponge calls his poems *Le Parti-pris des choses*), representing them "from their own point of view"? Obviously Ponge cannot delude himself on this point. The flagrant psychological and moral anthropomorphism that he constantly practices can only have as its aim the setting up of a human order, general and absolute. To claim that he speaks *for* things, *with* them, from their *heart*, amounts under such conditions to a denial of their reality, of their opaque presence: in this universe peopled by things, things become nothing more than mirrors endlessly reflecting man's own image. Peaceful and domesticated, objects look back at man with his own glance.

Such *reflection*, in the case of Ponge, is of course far from gratuitous. The give-and-take between man and his natural doubles comes from an active intelligence, anxious to understand itself and to mend its ways. Throughout his subtle pages the most insignificant pebble, the least stick of wood, endlessly teaches him lessons, expresses his being and judges it, points in the direction of progress to be made. Contemplation of the world becomes for man a permanent apprenticeship to life, happiness, wisdom and death.

What Ponge offers us, in sum, is a definitive and smiling reconciliation. It is the same old affirmation of Humanism: the world is man. But at what a cost! For if we abandon the moral viewpoint of perfectionism, "taking sides with things" (*Le Parti-pris des choses*) is of no further avail to us. If above all, we prefer freedom to wisdom, we are forced to smash all these mirrors so artfully set up before us by Francis Ponge, in order to discover, once more, the hard dry objects that exist behind them, unpenetrated, and as foreign to ourselves as ever.

François Mauriac, who states that he first read Ponge's poem *Le Cageot* (*The Wicker Hamper*) on the recommendation of Jean Paulhan, must have remembered little of that text when he termed *Technique du cageot* the description of objects advocated in my own writings (see *Le Figaro littéraire* of July 28, 1956). Or else I must have expressed myself very badly indeed.

To describe things, in point of fact, requires that we place ourselves deliberately outside, in front of, them. We must neither appropriate them to ourselves, nor transfer anything to them. Admitted at the outset as *not* being man, they remain always out of reach and are not, in the end, to be either accepted in a natural alliance or redeemed by suffering. To limit oneself to description is obviously to challenge all other modes of approach to objects. It entails calling sympathy antirealistic, deeming tragedy productive of madness, and relegating understanding to the exclusive realm of science.

This last viewpoint is certainly not one to be scorned. Science is the only honest means available to man for deriving advantage from the world around him. But this advantage is only material; however disinterested science may be, it is only justified by the eventual development of utilitarian techniques. Literature has other aims. Only science, however, can claim to know the *inside* of things. The "insideness" of the pebble, the tree, or the snail that Francis Ponge gives us, of course, laughs at science (and much more so than Sartre seems to think); it represents in no way what is really *in* these things, but only what man can project into them of himself. Having observed with a certain amount of rigor the behavior of certain objects, Ponge goes on to construct human analogies, speaking of man, always of man, while now and then leaning a negligent hand on things. Little does Ponge care that the snail does not really "eat" earth, or that the function of chlorophyll involves the absorption and not the "exhalation" of carbon dioxide. His eye is as careless as his memory of natural science, and his only criterion is the truth of the feelings expressed by images of this type—human feelings, of course, and human nature, a "nature" common to everything!

The sciences of mineralogy, botany, zoology, on the other hand, pursue the knowledge of textures (internal as well as external), their organization, their function, and their origin. Yet outside their own domains, these disciplines have no further use, except for the abstract enrichment of our intelligence. The world around us reverts to a smooth surface, without meaning, without soul, without values, on which we have no hold. Like the workman who lays down the hammer that he no longer needs, we find ourselves once more face to face with objects.

To describe this surface, then, comes down to this: to construct its exteriority and independence. I probably have no more to say "about" the carton of my ink bottle than I would have to say "with" it; if I write that it is a parallelepiped, I do not claim to extract from it any essence, and I claim even less to deliver it over to a reader whose imagination will then seize upon it and adorn it with multiple colorings—for this is precisely what I would prevent.

The most common complaints addressed against such geometric information, that "it says nothing to the spirit," that "a photograph or a dimensioned sketch would give a better account of the form," etc., are strange objections indeed. Can anyone imagine that I had not thought of all that from the outset? Something entirely different is at issue. The photograph or the sketch aims only at reproducing the object: they are successful in proportion as they give rise to as many interpretations (and the same errors) as the model. Formal verbal description, on the other hand, is above all a limitation: when it says "parallelepiped," it knows that it penetrates into absolutely no *beyond*, but rather cuts short any possibility of seeking one.

To record the separation between an object and myself, the distances pertaining to the object itself (its *exterior* distances, that is, its measurements), and the distances between objects; to insist, further, on the fact that these are *only distances* (and not heartrending separations)—all this amounts to taking for granted that things are "there" and that they are only things, each limited to itself. It is no longer a question of choosing between a happy agreement and an unhappy solidarity. Henceforth we refuse *all* complicity with objects.

But we must refuse first of all the vocabulary of analogy and of traditional Humanism, as well as the idea of tragedy and all other ideas that lead to a belief in a deeper, or higher, nature of man, of things, or of both together. We must refuse, that is, any idea of pre-established order.

In such a perspective the privileged sense is obviously that of sight, particularly sight directed at the outlines of forms (rather than at colors, flashes of light, or transparencies). Optical description is best equipped to render distances, without interferences; the human glance, in its simplest state, allows things to remain in their respective places.

But there are risks. Falling unawares upon some detail, one's glance isolates it, tries to bring it forward; and, sensing failure in this attempt, redoubles its efforts, without succeeding either in seizing upon the object entirely or in putting it back in its place. . . . This is close to the "absurd" relationship. Or else contemplation may become so heavily insistent that everything starts to waver, to give way, to melt together . . . and "fascination" begins, leading to "nausea."

Yet these are lesser risks, and Sartre himself recognizes the *cleansing* power of the visual sense. Disturbed by contact with something, by some suspect tactile impression, Roquentin lowers his eyes to his hand: "The pebble was flat, dry on one side, wet and muddy on the other. I held it by the edges, my fingers spread apart, to avoid getting dirty." And he no longer understands why he had been so upset. Likewise, later, as he enters his room: "I stopped short, because in my hand I felt a cold object which held my attention as with some sort of personality. I opened my hand, and looked: I was merely holding the handle to the door." Afterwards Roquentin takes issue with colors, for which the eye is powerless to exercise its cleansing function: "The black tree stump *refused to go away*, it remained there in my eyes, like a piece of something caught in one's throat. I could neither accept nor reject it." And previously there was the incident of the "mauve" color of the suspenders and the "dishonest transparency" of the glass of beer.

We must use the means we have at our disposal. Vision remains despite every-thing our best weapon, especially when it is restricted to contours. As for its "sub-jectivity"—the principal reproach made by the opposition—how does that limit its value? Quite obviously there can never be anything except the world as seen from *my point of view* (or that of any man); I shall never know any other. The relative subjectivity of my viewpoint serves, indeed, to define my situation in the world. I merely refrain from attempting, in my turn, to convert this situation into a form of servitude.

So despite Roquentin's claim that "Sight is an abstract invention, a cleansed and simplified idea, a human idea," it nevertheless remains the most efficient working process between myself and the world.

For efficiency is the real issue. To measure distances, without vain regrets, with-out hatred, without despair, between separated things, should permit us to iden-tify what is not separated, what is *one*—since it is false to assert that everything is double. False, or at least questionable. Questionable as far as man is concerned, we hope. Already proven false as far as things are concerned: for once scraped clean, things relate only to themselves, with no chinks or crevices for us to slip into, and without causing us the least dizziness.

One question remains: is it possible to escape from tragedy?

Today the rule of tragedy encompasses all my feelings and thoughts, it con-ditions me utterly. My body may be satisfied, my heart happy, but my conscience remains anxious. I claim that this anxiety, this misery, is *situated* in space and time, like all unhappiness, like everything in the world. I claim that man, some day, will free himself of it. But I have no proof of the future. For me also, it is a *bet*.[1] "Man is a sick animal," wrote Unamuno in *The Tragic Sense of Life*. The bet consists in holding that he can be cured, and that if this is true it would be folly to shut him up forever in his present sickness and unhappiness. I have noth-ing to lose. The bet, all things considered, is the only reasonable one.

I say I have no proof. I can detect, however, that the systematic *tragi-fication* of the world in which I live is frequently the result of a deliberate intention. This is sufficient, for me, to cast doubt upon any proposition tending to set up tragedy as natural and definitive. When doubt arises, I cannot do otherwise than seek further for a solution.

Such a struggle—I will be told—is indeed the supreme tragic illusion. To try to combat the idea of tragedy is already to succumb to it. And it is so "natural" to take refuge in objects. . . . Perhaps. But perhaps *not*. And, if *that* is true. . . .

[1] The author here refers to the famous *pari de Pascal* in which Pascal "bets" on the prob-ability of Christian immortality.   TRANSLATOR'S NOTE.

3
NATURE

Struggle

CHARLES DARWIN: The Struggle for Existence and Natural Selection
ARTHUR SCHOPENHAUER: The Will in Nature

Organicism

A. N. WHITEHEAD: Nature as Organism
RAINER MARIA RILKE: Nature, Man, and Art
MARCEL PROUST: The Life of the Hawthorn
ANDRÉ GIDE: Natural Joy
D. H. LAWRENCE: The Death of Pan

Mechanical Force

HENRY ADAMS: The New Multiverse
F. T. MARINETTI: The Joy of Mechanical Force
D. H. LAWRENCE: The Physics of Human Character

Indeterminacy

WILLIAM JAMES: Pluralism, Pragmatism, and Instrumental Truth
JOHN DEWEY: Thought as a Natural Event
WERNER HEISENBERG: Non-Objective Science and Uncertainty

Introduction

The realist is predominantly a social man, and the symbolist a solitary mind, but the public world of the one and the imaginative world of the other are closely engaged with the natural world that surrounds them. Even though immediate contact with nature has become a relatively small part of modern experience, ideas of nature still bulk large in the modern consciousness. We apprehend it as both biological and physical, and in both of these dimensions it has more than one aspect. It is a principle of biological struggle, of battle for survival, yet it is also a principle of organic harmony, vital unison in things. It is automatic material energy, a complex of mechanical physical forces that menace human existence; but in still another perspective it may be seen as the very source and sanction of human inventiveness, or even as a construction of human intelligence, created by scientists in the course of physical experiment.

Darwin depicts a biological nature wherein species of living things arise in fantastic profuseness, to disappear or persist depending upon their adaptability to the conditions of life. All living creatures are engaged in an endless struggle with their physical environment, including other creatures; and it is the total economy of nature, not some intrinsic value in the individual or the species, that determines the outcome of their battle to survive.[1] Though this theory of "natural selection" may seem to destroy the traditional stability of nature and many moral values traditionally associated with the natural world, it does not appall Darwin. He finds a reassuring symmetry and basic wholeness in the world he pictures. He conceives of nature as a generative principle that he can still compare, in the traditional way, to a woman—or to a great tree whose branches, whether they grow or fall, do so according to an ultimately creative and harmonious urge. The complicated forms of life as known today need not conceal the essential simplicity of nature, for all these forms are related and ramify either from one simple ancestral form or at least from a very small number of primordial forms.[2]

In Schopenhauer's more metaphysical conception, both organic and inor-

[1] Compare the literary naturalism illustrated in Section 2.
[2] A related selection from Darwin appears in Section 4.

ganic nature are manifestations of the Will, the reality behind all the phenomenal objects of which we have "ideas." The metaphysical Will, eternally at "variance with itself," is grand but purposeless. It is a "will to live," and as such it is reflected in the multiple forms of natural life; but its "living" is no more than a drive to remain in existence, a sheer activity or energy that is notably reflected in the blind forces of inorganic matter.[3] If for Darwin life is a flourishing tree, Schopenhauer characteristically calls attention to the way a tree is smothered by a vine, much as one gravitational pull overcomes another. His nature is a vista of frantic crowding and clutching by things affirming themselves. Yet the Will, as Schopenhauer conceives it, is one and eternal, and the natural world, though all particular things are transitory, is its eternal mirror. While Darwin's theory is more affirmative and sanguine and can lead to the concept of evolutionary "progress," Schopenhauer's pessimism is not without consolation. The individuals that are born, struggle, and die constitute an immortal process, though an aimless one. The forms of nature, its conflicting Ideas, are perennial (Schopenhauer does not contemplate the disappearance of species), even though the individual thinker and his ideas, as well as the particular objects he knows, are doomed to vanish.[4]

Whitehead is preoccupied with organisms in relation to their environment, and at the same time he is seeking to interpret the world of physics, the science of inorganic energy. But he is quite different from both Darwin and Schopenhauer in his central concern—the structure of nature and the way we come to know it. He regards the official philosophy of early twentieth-century science, which he traces back to the seventeenth century, as misleading because of its mechanistic assumptions: it makes objects falsely self-sufficient and isolates them from the minds that apprehend them. Whitehead would establish instead a recognition that he finds first expressed in the romantic poets: we do not perceive particular elements in nature as discrete entities, to the exclusion of other elements or to the exclusion of ourselves.[5] Things and the perception of things are *events*, modes of interaction with other events in space and time. Parts of nature assume individuality by drawing the surrounding world into themselves and delimiting it; but these individual unities must also be seen in terms of larger unities of which they are functions. As in a plant, the whole dominates each part, and as in organic growth every partial whole virtually contains the whole that transcends it.[6]

The romantic poets cited by Whitehead often associate this organic structure of nature with a vital spirit—"one life within us and abroad"—that ren-

[3] In human beings, Schopenhauer's "will" is one form of the Unconscious (see Section 5).
[4] For related selections from Schopenhauer, see Sections 5 and 7.
[5] See the selection from Wordsworth in Section 1.
[6] As Whitehead's allusion to romantic poetry suggests, his organistic philosophy of nature has something in common with the post-Kantian idealism of which Coleridge (see Section 1) is typical. Compare also the mythical nature described by Cassirer (Section 6). With Whitehead's attack on Cartesian dualism, compare the selection from Maritain in Section 9.

ders nature everywhere alive and urgent. Romantic vitalism has persisted into later literature. Rilke desires to touch the mysterious life in a landscape and to reconcile, in a moment of art, the individual with the All, the human with the non-human but somehow animate world of nature. Proust is similarly convinced of a kind of *mana* or divinity (though he avoids all such general terms) inhabiting the hawthorn; and Gide, enraptured by fruits of the earth, finds in them example and sanction for human freedom. Yet for these writers the life of nature is as elusive as it is fascinating. Rilke and Proust record a sense of exclusion from the vital spirit that attracts them. Their reward comes only in rare moments, or endlessly escapes, and even Gide has an air of asserting a greater revelation than he has actually experienced. For Lawrence, Pan is a potentiality no longer actual in most of the human world, though always ready to live again if men can find him. Once rooted downward and reaching upward like a tree, Pan has been killed by the machine.[7]

For others, real nature is mechanical—the inhumanity and the uncontrollability of natural force are its distinctive (and may even be its most humanly valuable) characteristics. Henry Adams finds that the old, benign natural order has become inconceivable to the mind of this century. We are situated in a chaotic multiverse, subjected to an "insanity of force."[8] Instead of the image of the mother, Aphrodite or the Madonna, the symbol of our attempt to achieve equilibrium with nature must be the dynamo, which tries to humanize and rationalize an essentially impersonal and irrational power. Adams deplores this new world, in which machines are the most important inhabitants, though at times it greatly excites him. The world of force delights Marinetti, whose Futurism celebrates a mechanized humanity. Marinetti extols machines for their amorality, their speed, their mad strength, and wants men to imitate them.[9] At times D. H. Lawrence, who is usually opposed to mechanism, responds to this same fascination of non-human force: he proposes to treat people as inorganic solids and energies rather than sickeningly personal "minds."

With the indeterminists (William James, Dewey, and Heisenberg are various examples), "nature" is one of the few large words that may still be used with any confidence. Like Whitehead, these writers are concerned with the implications of scientific method; but whereas Whitehead introduces an organic structure into the universe of classical physics, they propose a purely experimental world where everything, whether a "fact" or a "theory," is tentative. In some ways their results are the same. For James and Dewey, as for

[7] The symbolist doctrine represented in Section 1 sometimes approaches vitalism. Even closer are the passages headed "Self-Realization" in Section 7 and some versions of the Unconscious (Section 5). See also related selections from Gide and Lawrence in Section 9. In direct contrast is the outlook of most of the existentialists (Section 8) and of a writer like T. E. Hulme (Section 9).

[8] Compare the nature envisaged by Dreiser in Section 2.

[9] Two movements historically related to Futurism—Dadaism and Surrealism—are represented in Section 5.

Whitehead, the distinction between subjective and objective realms and between idealism and materialism becomes irrelevant. Both an "object" and the "concept" of the "object" are natural, and they are events or occurrences in nature, not static entities. But James and Dewey emphasize the openness of nature, the way in which "truth" grows and changes in the experimental process of the world. Theories are instrumental expedients, temporary bridges between aspects of the natural experience they describe and of which they are part.[10] Within the sphere of physical science, Heisenberg confirms this principle of indeterminacy, which James and Dewey apply on a larger scale to all human knowledge and activity. For the physicist, the content of "nature" has become largely relative to the instruments through which it is apprehended. The mere observation of minute particles is now known to affect their behavior. In many cases, natural "laws" must be viewed as statistical formulas rather than eternal sequences of cause and effect. All three of these writers envisage a world without fixed and universal attributes—incomplete, emergent, and even contradictory.[11]

[10] A related selection from William James appears in Section 7.
[11] There is some analogy between these philosophies of natural experiment and the linguistic experimentalism of the symbolist (see Section 1). Compare also Croce's view that all knowledge, including science, is "historical knowledge" (Section 4).

CHARLES DARWIN

The Struggle for Existence and Natural Selection

How have all those exquisite adaptations of one part of the organisation to an-other part, and to the conditions of life, and of one organic being to another being, been perfected? We see these beautiful co-adaptations most plainly in the woodpecker and the mistletoe; and only a little less plainly in the humblest para-site which clings to the hairs of a quadruped or feathers of a bird; in the structure of the beetle which dives through the water: in the plumed seed which is wafted by the gentlest breeze; in short, we see beautiful adaptations everywhere and in every part of the organic world.

Again, it may be asked, how is it that varieties, which I have called incipient species, become ultimately converted into good and distinct species, which in most cases obviously differ from each other far more than do the varieties of the same species? How do those groups of species, which constitute what are called distinct genera, and which differ from each other more than do the species of the same genus, arise? All these results . . . follow from the struggle for life. Owing to this struggle, variations, however slight and from whatever cause proceeding, if they be in any degree profitable to the individuals of a species, in their infinitely complex relations to other organic beings and to their physical conditions of life, will tend to the preservation of such individuals, and will generally be inherited by the offspring. The offspring, also, will thus have a better chance of surviving, for, of the many individuals of any species which are periodically born, but a small number can survive. I have called this principle, by which each slight variation, if useful, is preserved, by the term Natural Selection, in order to mark its rela-tion to man's power of selection. But the expression often used by Mr. Herbert Spencer of the Survival of the Fittest is more accurate, and is sometimes equally convenient. We have seen that man by selection can certainly produce great re-sults, and can adapt organic beings to his own uses, through the accumulation of slight but useful variations, given to him by the hand of Nature. But Natural Selection, as we shall hereafter see, is a power incessantly ready for action, and is as immeasurably superior to man's feeble efforts, as the works of Nature are to those of Art. . . .

Nothing is easier than to admit in words the truth of the universal struggle for life, or more difficult—at least I have found it so—than constantly to bear this

From *On the Origin of Species by means of Natural Selection* [1859; 6th edition 1872], Lon-don, 1911, pp. 75-7, 77-8, 99-103, 662-3, 668-70.

conclusion in mind. Yet unless it be thoroughly engrained in the mind, the whole economy of nature, with every fact on distribution, rarity, abundance, extinction, and variation, will be dimly seen or quite misunderstood. We behold the face of nature bright with gladness, we often see superabundance of food; we do not see or we forget, that the birds which are idly singing round us mostly live on insects or seeds, and are thus constantly destroying life; or we forget how largely these songsters, or their eggs, or their nestlings, are destroyed by birds and beasts of prey; we do not always bear in mind, that, though food may be now superabundant, it is not so at all seasons of each recurring year. . . .

I should premise that I use this term [Struggle for Existence] in a large and metaphorical sense including dependence of one being on another, and including (which is more important) not only the life of the individual, but success in leaving progeny. Two canine animals, in a time of dearth, may be truly said to struggle with each other which shall get food and live. But a plant on the edge of a desert is said to struggle for life against the drought, though more properly it should be said to be dependent on the moisture. A plant which annually produces a thousand seeds, of which only one of an average comes to maturity, may be more truly said to struggle with the plants of the same and other kinds which already clothe the ground. The mistletoe is dependent on the apple and a few other trees, but can only in a far-fetched sense be said to struggle with these trees, for, if too many of these parasites grow on the same tree, it languishes and dies. But several seedling mistletoes, growing close together on the same branch, may more truly be said to struggle with each other. As the mistletoe is disseminated by birds, its existence depends on them; and it may metaphorically be said to struggle with other fruit-bearing plants, in tempting the birds to devour and thus disseminate its seeds. In these several senses, which pass into each other, I use for convenience' sake the general term of Struggle for Existence. . . .

Several writers have misapprehended or objected to the term Natural Selection. Some have even imagined that natural selection induces variability, whereas it implies only the preservation of such variations as arise and are beneficial to the being under its conditions of life. No one objects to agriculturists speaking of the potent effects of man's selection; and in this case the individual differences given by nature, which man for some object selects, must of necessity first occur. Others have objected that the term selection implies conscious choice in the animals which become modified; and it has even been urged that, as plants have no volition, natural selection is not applicable to them! In the literal sense of the word, no doubt, natural selection is a false term; but who ever objected to chemists speaking of the elective affinities of the various elements?—and yet an acid cannot strictly be said to elect the base with which it in preference combines. It has been said that I speak of natural selection as an active power or Deity; but who objects to an author speaking of the attraction of gravity as ruling the movements of the planets? Every one knows what is meant and is implied by such metaphorical expressions; and they are almost necessary for brevity. So again it is difficult to avoid personifying the word Nature; but I mean by Nature, only the aggregate action and product of many natural laws, and by laws the sequence of events as ascertained by us. With a little familiarity such superficial objections will be forgotten.

We shall best understand the probable course of natural selection by taking the case of a country undergoing some slight physical change, for instance, of climate. The proportional numbers of its inhabitants will almost immediately undergo a change, and some species will probably become extinct. We may conclude, from what we have seen of the intimate and complex manner in which the inhabitants of each country are bound together, that any change in the numerical proportions of the inhabitants, independently of the change of climate itself, would seriously affect the others. If the country were open on its borders, new forms would certainly immigrate, and this would likewise seriously disturb the relations of some of the former inhabitants. Let it be remembered how powerful the influence of a single introduced tree or mammal has been shown to be. But in the case of an island, or of a country partly surrounded by barriers, into which new and better adapted forms could not freely enter, we should then have places in the economy of nature which would assuredly be better filled up, if some of the original inhabitants were in some manner modified; for, had the area been open to immigration, these same places would have been seized on by intruders. In such cases, slight modifications, which in any way favoured the individuals of any species, by better adapting them to their altered conditions, would tend to be preserved; and natural selection would have free scope for the work of improvement.

We have good reason to believe, as shown in the first chapter, that changes in the conditions of life give a tendency to increased variability; and in the foregoing cases the conditions have changed, and this would manifestly be favourable to natural selection, by affording a better chance of the occurrence of profitable variations. Unless such occur, natural selection can do nothing. Under the term of "variations," it must never be forgotten that mere individual differences are included. As man can produce a great result with his domestic animals and plants by adding up in any given direction individual differences, so could natural selection, but far more easily from having incomparably longer time for action. Nor do I believe that any great physical change, as of climate, or any unusual degree of isolation to check immigration, is necessary in order that new and unoccupied places should be left, for natural selection to fill up by improving some of the varying inhabitants. For as all the inhabitants of each country are struggling together with nicely balanced forces, extremely slight modifications in the structure or habits of one species would often give it an advantage over others; and still further modifications of the same kind would often still further increase the advantage, as long as the species continued under the same conditions of life and profited by similar means of subsistence and defence. No country can be named in which all the native inhabitants are now so perfectly adapted to each other and to the physical conditions under which they live, that none of them could be still better adapted or improved; for in all countries, the natives have been so far conquered by naturalised productions, that they have allowed some foreigners to take firm possession of the land. And as foreigners have thus in every country beaten some of the natives, we may safely conclude that the natives might have been modified with advantage, so as to have better resisted the intruders.

As man can produce, and certainly has produced, a great result by his methodical and unconscious means of selection, what may not natural selection effect? Man can act only on external and visible characters: Nature, if I may be allowed to personify the natural preservation or survival of the fittest, cares nothing for appearances, except in so far as they are useful to any being. She can act on every internal organ, on every shade of constitutional difference, on the whole machinery of life. Man selects only for his own good: Nature only for that of the being which she tends. Every selected character is fully exercised by her, as is implied by the fact of their selection. Man keeps the natives of many climates in the same country; he seldom exercises each selected character in some peculiar and fitting manner; he feeds a long and a short beaked pigeon on the same food; he does not exercise a long-backed or long-legged quadruped in any peculiar manner; he exposes sheep with long and short wool to the same climate. He does not allow the most vigorous males to struggle for the females. He does not rigidly destroy all inferior animals, but protects during each varying season, as far as lies in his power, all his productions. He often begins his selection by some half-monstrous form; or at least by some modification prominent enough to catch the eye or to be plainly useful to him. Under nature, the slightest differences of structure or constitution may well turn the nicely-balanced scale in the struggle for life, and so be preserved. How fleeting are the wishes and efforts of man! how short his time! and consequently how poor will be his results, compared with those accumulated by Nature during whole geological periods! Can we wonder, then, that Nature's productions should be far "truer" in character than man's productions; that they should be infinitely better adapted to the most complex conditions of life, and should plainly bear the stamp of far higher workmanship?

It may metaphorically be said that natural selection is daily and hourly scrutinising, throughout the world, the slightest variations; rejecting those that are bad, preserving and adding up all that are good; silently and insensibly working, *whenever and wherever opportunity offers*, at the improvement of each organic being in relation to its organic and inorganic conditions of life. We see nothing of these slow changes in progress, until the hand of time has marked the lapse of ages, and then so imperfect is our view into long-past geological ages, that we see only that the forms of life are now different from what they formerly were. . . .

The affinities of all the beings of the same class have sometimes been represented by a great tree. I believe this simile largely speaks the truth. The green and budding twigs may represent existing species; and those produced during former years may represent the long succession of extinct species. At each period of growth all the growing twigs have tried to branch out on all sides, and to overtop and kill the surrounding twigs and branches, in the same manner as species and groups of species have at all times overmastered other species in the great battle for life. The limbs divided into great branches, and these into lesser and lesser branches, were themselves once, when the tree was young, budding twigs; and this connection of the former and present buds by ramifying branches may well represent the classification of all extinct and living species in groups subordinate to groups. Of the many twigs which flourished when the tree was a mere bush, only two or three, now grown into great branches, yet survive and bear the other branches; so with the species which lived during long-past geological periods, very few have left living and modified descendants. From the first growth of the tree, many a limb and branch has decayed and dropped off; and these fallen branches of various sizes may represent those whole orders, families, and genera which have now no living representatives, and which are known to us only in a fossil state.

As we here and there see a thin straggling branch springing from a fork low down in a tree, and which by some chance has been favoured and is still alive on its summit, so we occasionally see an animal like the Ornithorhynchus or Lepidosiren, which in some small degree connects by its affinities two large branches of life, and which has apparently been saved from fatal competition by having inhabited a protected station. As buds give rise by growth to fresh buds, and these, if vigorous, branch out and overtop on all sides many a feebler branch, so by generation I believe it has been with the great Tree of Life, which fills with its dead and broken branches the crust of the earth, and covers the surface with its ever-branching and beautiful ramifications. . . .

It may be asked how far I extend the doctrine of the modification of species. The question is difficult to answer, because the more distinct the forms are which we consider, by so much the arguments in favour of community of descent become fewer in number and less in force. But some arguments of the greatest weight extend very far. All the members of whole classes are connected together by a chain of affinities, and all can be classed on the same principle, in groups subordinate to groups. Fossil remains sometimes tend to fill up very wide intervals between existing orders.

Organs in a rudimentary condition plainly show that an early progenitor had the organ in a fully developed condition; and this in some cases implies an enormous amount of modification in the descendants. Throughout whole classes various structures are formed on the same pattern, and at a very early age the embryos closely resemble each other. Therefore I cannot doubt that the theory of descent with modification embraces all the members of the same great class or kingdom. I believe that animals are descended from at most only four or five progenitors, and plants from an equal or lesser number.

Analogy would lead me one step farther, namely, to the belief that all animals and plants are descended from some one prototype. But analogy may be a deceitful guide. Nevertheless all living things have much in common, in their chemical composition, their cellular structure, their laws of growth, and their liability to injurious influences. We see this even in so trifling a fact as that the same poison often similarly affects plants and animals; or that the poison secreted by the gall-fly produces monstrous growths on the wild rose or oak-tree. With all organic beings, excepting perhaps some of the very lowest, sexual reproduction seems to be essentially similar. With all, as far as is at present known, the germinal vesicle is the same; so that all organisms start from a common origin. If we look even to the two main divisions—namely, to the animal and vegetable kingdoms—certain low forms are so far intermediate in character that naturalists have disputed to which kingdom they should be referred. As Professor Asa Gray has remarked, "the spores and other reproductive bodies of many of the lower algæ may claim to have first a characteristically animal, and then an unequivocally vegetable existence." Therefore, on the principle of natural selection with divergence of character, it does not seem incredible that, from some such low and intermediate form, both animals and plants may have been developed; and, if we admit this, we must likewise admit that all the organic beings which have ever lived on this earth may be descended from some one primordial form. . . .

Authors of the highest eminence seem to be fully satisfied with the view that each species has been independently created. To my mind it accords better with what we know of the laws impressed on matter by the Creator, that the production and extinction of the past and present inhabitants of the world should have been due to secondary causes, like those determining the birth and death of the individual. When I view all beings not as special creations, but as the lineal descendants of some few beings which lived long before the first bed of the Cambrian system was deposited, they seem to me to become ennobled. Judging from the past, we may safely infer that not one living species will transmit its unaltered likeness to a distant futurity. And of the species now living very few will transmit progeny of any kind to a far distant futurity; for the manner in which all organic beings are grouped, shows that the greater number of species in each genus, and all the species in many genera, have left no descendants, but have become utterly extinct. We can so far take a prophetic glance into futurity as to foretell that it will be the common and widely-spread species, belonging to the larger and dominant groups within each class, which will ultimately prevail and procreate new and dominant species. As all the living forms of life are the lineal descendants of those which lived long before the Cambrian epoch, we may feel certain that the ordinary succession by generation has never once been broken, and that no cataclysm has desolated the whole world. Hence we may look with some confidence to a secure future of great length. And as natural selection works solely by and for the good of each being, all corporeal and mental endowments will tend to progress towards perfection.

It is interesting to contemplate a tangled bank, clothed with many plants of many kinds, with birds singing on the bushes, with various insects flitting about, and with worms crawling through the damp earth, and to reflect that these elaborately constructed forms, so different from each other, and dependent upon each other in so complex a manner, have all been produced by laws acting around us. These laws, taken in the largest sense, being Growth with Reproduction; Inheritance which is almost implied by reproduction; Variability from the indirect and direct action of the conditions of life, and from use and disuse: a Ratio of Increase so high as to lead to a Struggle for Life, and as a consequence to Natural Selection, entailing Divergence of Character and the Extinction of less-improved forms. Thus, from the war of nature, from famine and death, the most exalted object which we are capable of conceiving, namely, the production of the higher animals, directly follows. There is grandeur in this view of life, with its several powers, having been originally breathed by the Creator into a few forms or into one; and that, whilst this planet has gone cycling on according to the fixed law of gravity, from so simple a beginning endless forms most beautiful and most wonderful have been, and are being evolved.

The Will in Nature

We are not satisfied with knowing that we have ideas, that they are such and such, and that they are connected according to certain laws. . . . We wish to know the significance of these ideas; we ask whether this world is merely idea; in which case it would pass by us like an empty dream or a baseless vision, not worth our notice; or whether it is also something else, something more than idea, and if so, what. Thus much is certain, that this something we seek for must be completely and in its whole nature different from the idea; that the forms and laws of the idea must therefore be completely foreign to it; further, that we cannot arrive at it from the idea under the guidance of the laws which merely combine objects, ideas, among themselves. . . .

Thus we see already that we can never arrive at the real nature of things from without. However much we investigate, we can never reach anything but images and names. We are like a man who goes round a castle seeking in vain for an entrance, and sometimes sketching the façades. And yet this is the method that has been followed by all philosophers before me.

In fact, the meaning for which we seek of that world which is present to us only as our idea, or the transition from the world as mere idea of the knowing subject to whatever it may be besides this, would never be found if the investigator himself were nothing more than the pure knowing subject (a winged cherub without a body). But he is himself rooted in that world; he finds himself in it as an *individual*, that is to say, his knowledge, which is the necessary supporter of the whole world as idea, is yet always given through the medium of a body. . . . His body is, for the pure knowing subject, an idea like every other idea, an object among objects. Its movements and actions are so far known to him in precisely the same way as the changes of all other perceived objects, and would be just as strange and incomprehensible to him if their meaning were not explained for him in an entirely different way. . . . The answer is *will*. This and this alone gives him the key to his own existence, reveals to him the significance, shows him the inner mechanism of his being, of his action, of his movements. The body is given in two entirely different ways to the subject of knowledge, who becomes an individual only through his identity with it. It is given as an idea in intelligent perception, as an object among objects and subject to the laws of objects. And it is also given in quite a different way as that which is immediately known to every one, and is signified by the word *will*. Every true act of his will is also at once and without exception a movement of his body. The act of will and the movement of the body are not two different things objectively known, which the bond of causality unites; they do not stand in the relation of cause and effect; they are one and the same, but they are given in entirely different ways,—immediately, and again in perception for the understanding. . . . It is only in reflection that to will and to act are different; in reality they are one. Every true, genuine, immediate act of will is also, at once and immediately, a visible act of the body. And,

From *The World as Will and Idea* [1818], translated from the German by R. B. Haldane and J. Kemp, London, 1883, Vol. I, pp. 128-31, 136, 142-3, 169-70, 190-93, 358-9; reprinted by permission of Routledge & Kegan Paul Ltd.

corresponding to this, every impression upon the body is also, on the other hand, at once and immediately an impression upon the will. As such it is called pain when it is opposed to the will; gratification or pleasure when it is in accordance with it. The degrees of both are widely different. It is quite wrong, however, to call pain and pleasure ideas, for they are by no means ideas, but immediate affections of the will in its manifestation, the body; compulsory, instantaneous willing or not-willing of the impression which the body sustains. . . .

The double knowledge which each of us has of the nature and activity of his own body, and which is given in two completely different ways, has now been clearly brought out. We shall accordingly make further use of it as a key to the nature of every phenomenon in nature, and shall judge of all objects which are not our own bodies, and are consequently not given to our consciousness in a double way but only as ideas, according to the analogy of our own bodies, and shall therefore assume that as in one aspect they are idea, just like our bodies and in this respect are analogous to them, so in another aspect, what remains of objects when we set aside their existence as idea . . . must in its inner nature be the same as that in us which we call *will*. For what other kind of existence or reality should we attribute to the rest of the material world? Whence should we take the elements out of which we construct such a world? Besides will and idea nothing is known to us or thinkable. If we wish to attribute the greatest known reality to the material world which exists immediately only in our idea, we give it the reality which our own body has for each of us; for that is the most real thing for every one. . . .

Whoever . . . has with me gained this conviction will find that of itself it affords him the key to the knowledge of the inmost being of the whole of nature; for he now transfers it to all those phenomena which are not given to him, like his own phenomenal existence, both in direct and indirect knowledge, but only in the latter, thus merely one-sidedly as *idea* alone. He will recognise this will of which we are speaking not only in those phenomenal existences which exactly resemble his own, in men and animals as their inmost nature, but the course of reflection will lead him to recognise the force which germinates and vegetates in the plant, and indeed the force through which the crystal is formed, that by which the magnet turns to the north pole, the force whose shock he experiences from the contact of two different kinds of metals, the force which appears in the elective affinities of matter as repulsion and attraction, decomposition and combination, and, lastly, even gravitation, which acts so powerfully throughout matter, draws the stone to the earth and the earth to the sun,—all these, I say, he will recognise as different only in their phenomenal existence, but in their inner nature as identical, as that which is directly known to him so intimately and so much better than anything else, and which in its most distinct manifestation is called *will*. . . . Phenomenal existence is idea and nothing more. All idea, of whatever kind it may be, all *object*, is *phenomenal* existence, but the *will* alone is a *thing in itself*. As such, it is throughout not idea, but *toto genere* different from it; it is that of which all idea, all object, is the phenomenal appearance, the visibility, the objectification. It is the inmost nature, the kernel, of every particular thing, and also of the whole. It appears in every blind force of nature and also in the preconsidered action of man; and the great difference between these two is merely in the degree of the manifestation, not in the nature of what manifests itself. . . .

The lowest grades of the objectification of will are to be found in those most universal forces of nature which partly appear in all matter without exception, as gravity and impenetrability, and partly have shared the given matter among them, so that certain of them reign in one species of matter and others in another species, constituting its specific difference, as rigidity, fluidity, elasticity, electricity, magnetism, chemical properties and qualities of every kind. They are in themselves immediate manifestations of will, just as much as human action; and as such they are groundless, like human character. . . . They themselves . . . can never be called either effect or cause, but are the prior and presupposed conditions of all causes and effects through which their real nature unfolds and reveals itself. It is therefore senseless to demand a cause of gravity or electricity, for they are original forces. Their expressions, indeed, take place in accordance with the law of cause and effect, so that every one of their particular manifestations has a cause, which is itself again just a similar particular manifestation which determines that this force must express itself here, must appear in space and time; but the force itself is by no means the effect of a cause, nor the cause of an effect. It is therefore a mistake to say "gravity is the cause of a stone falling;" for the cause in this case is rather the nearness of the earth, because it attracts the stone. Take the earth away and the stone will not fall, although gravity remains. The force itself lies quite outside the chain of causes and effects, which presupposes time, because it only has meaning in relation to it; but the force lies outside time. . . .

In the higher grades of the objectivity of will we see individuality occupy a prominent position, especially in the case of man, where it appears as the great difference of individual characters, i.e., as complete personality, outwardly expressed in strongly marked individual physiognomy, which influences the whole bodily form. None of the brutes have this individuality in anything like so high a degree, though the highest species of them have a trace of it; but the character of the species completely predominates over it, and therefore they have little individual physiognomy. The farther down we go, the more completely is every trace of the individual character lost in the common character of the species, and the physiognomy of the species alone remains. . . .

The one will . . . always seeks the highest possible objectification, and has therefore in this case given up the lower grades of its manifestation after a conflict, in order to appear in a higher grade, and one so much the more powerful. No victory without conflict: since the higher Idea or objectification of will can only appear through the conquest of the lower, it endures the opposition of these lower Ideas, which, although brought into subjection, still constantly strive to obtain an independent and complete expression of their being. The magnet that has attracted a piece of iron carries on a perpetual conflict with gravitation, which, as the lower objectification of will, has a prior right to the matter of the iron; and in this constant battle the magnet indeed grows stronger, for the opposition excites it, as it were, to greater effort. In the same way every manifestation of the will, including that which expresses itself in the human organism, wages a constant war against the many physical and chemical forces which, as lower Ideas, have a prior right to that matter. Thus the arm falls which for a while, overcoming gravity, we have held stretched out; thus the pleasing sensation of health, which proclaims the victory of the Idea of the self-conscious organism over the physical and chemical laws, which originally governed the humours of the body, is so often interrupted, and is indeed always accompanied by greater or less discomfort, which arises from the resistance of these forces, and on account of which the vegetative part of our life is constantly attended by slight pain. Thus also digestion weakens all the animal functions, because it requires the whole vital force to overcome the chemical forces of nature by assimilation. Hence also in general the burden of physical life, the necessity of sleep, and, finally, of death; for at last these subdued forces of nature, assisted by circumstances, win back from the organism, wearied even by the constant victory, the matter it took from them, and attain to an unimpeded expression of their being. . . .

Thus everywhere in nature we see strife, conflict, and alternation of victory, and in it we shall come to recognise more distinctly that variance with itself which is essential to the will. Every grade of the objectification of will fights for the matter, the space, and the time of the others. The permanent matter must constantly change its form; for under the guidance of causality, mechanical, physical, chemical, and organic phenomena, eagerly striving to appear, wrest the matter from each other, for each desires to reveal its own Idea. This strife may be followed through the whole of nature; indeed nature exists only through it. Yet this strife itself is only the revelation of that variance with itself which is essential to the will. This universal conflict becomes most distinctly visible in the animal kingdom. For animals have the whole of the vegetable kingdom for their food, and even within the animal kingdom every beast is the prey and the food of another; that is, the matter in which its Idea expresses itself must yield itself to the expression of another Idea, for each animal can only maintain its existence by the constant destruction of some other. Thus the will to live everywhere preys upon itself, and in different forms is its own nourishment, till finally the human race, because it subdues all the others, regards nature as a manufactory for its use. Yet even the human race . . . reveals in itself with most terrible distinctness this conflict, this variance with itself of the will. Meanwhile we can recognise this strife, this subjugation, just as well in the lower grades of the objectification of will. Many insects (especially ichneumon-flies) lay their eggs on the skin, and even in the body of the larvæ of other insects, whose slow destruction is the first work of the newly hatched brood. The young hydra, which grows like a bud out of the old one, and afterwards separates itself from it, fights while it is still joined to the old one for the prey that offers itself, so that the one snatches it out of the mouth of the other. But the bulldog-ant of Australia affords us the most extraordinary example of this kind; for if it is cut in two, a battle begins between the head and the tail. The head seizes the tail with its teeth, and the tail defends itself bravely by stinging the head: the battle may last for half an hour, until they die or are dragged away by other ants. This contest takes place every time the experiment is tried. On the banks of the Missouri one sometimes sees a mighty oak the stem and branches of which are so encircled, fettered, and interlaced by a gigantic wild vine, that it withers as if choked. The same thing shows itself in the lowest grades; for example, when water and carbon are changed into vegetable sap, or vegetables or bread into blood by organic assimilation; and so also in every case in which animal secretion takes place, along with the restriction of chemical forces to a subordinate mode of activity. This also occurs in unorganised nature, when, for example, crystals in process of formation meet, cross, and mutually disturb each other to such an extent that they are unable to assume the pure crystalline form, so that almost every cluster of crystals is an image of such a conflict of will at this low grade of its objectification; or again, when a magnet forces its magnetism upon iron, in order to express its Idea in it; or when galvanism overcomes chemical affinity, decomposes the closest combinations, and so entirely suspends the laws of chemistry that the acid of a decomposed salt at the negative pole must pass to the positive pole without combining with the alkalies through which it goes on its way, or turning red the litmus paper that touches it. On a large scale it shows itself in the relation between the central body and the planet, for although the planet is in absolute dependence, yet it always resists, just like the chemical forces in the organism; hence arises the constant tension between centripetal and centrifugal force, which keeps the globe in motion, and is itself an example of that universal essential conflict of the manifestation of will which we are considering. . . .

Will is the thing-in-itself, the inner content, the essence of the world. Life, the visible world, the phenomenon, is only the mirror of the will. Therefore life accompanies the will as inseparably as the shadow accompanies the body; and if will exists, so will life, the world, exist. Life is, therefore, assured to the will to live; and so long as we are filled with the will to live we need have no fear for our existence, even in the presence of death. It is true we see the individual come into being and pass away; but the individual is only phenomenal, exists only for the knowledge which is bound to . . . the principle of individuation. Certainly, for this kind of knowledge, the individual receives his life as a gift, rises out of nothing, then suffers the loss of this gift through death, and returns again to nothing. But we desire to consider life philosophically . . . and in this sphere we shall find that neither the will, the thing-in-itself in all phenomena, nor the subject of knowing, that which perceives all phenomena, is affected at all by birth or by death. Birth and death belong merely to the phenomenon of will, thus to life; and it is essential to this to exhibit itself in individuals which come into being and pass away, as fleeting phenomena appearing in the form of time—phenomena of that which in itself knows no time, but must exhibit itself precisely in the way we have said, in order to objectify its peculiar nature. Birth and death belong in like manner to life, and hold the balance as reciprocal conditions of each other, or, if one likes the expression, as poles of the whole phenomenon of life. The wisest of all mythologies, the Indian, expresses this by giving to the very god that symbolises destruction, death (as Brahma, the most sinful and the lowest god of the Trimurti, symbolises generation, coming into being, and Vishnu maintaining or preserving), by giving, I say, to Siva as an attribute not only the necklace of skulls, but also the lingam, the symbol of generation, which appears here as the counterpart of death, thus signifying that generation and death are essentially correlatives, which reciprocally neutralise and annul each other. It was precisely the same sentiment that led the Greeks and Romans to adorn their costly sarcophagi, just as we see them now, with feasts, dances, marriages, the chase, fights of wild beasts, bacchanalians, &c.; thus with representations of the full ardour of life, which they place before us not only in such revels and sports, but also in sensual groups, and even go so far as to represent the sexual intercourse of satyrs and goats. Clearly the aim was to point in the most impressive manner away from the death of the mourned individual to the immortal life of nature, and thus to indicate, though without abstract knowledge, that the whole of nature is the phenomenon and also the fulfilment of the will to live. The form of this phenomenon is time, space, and causality, and by means of these individuation, which carries with it that the individual must come into being and pass away. But this no more affects the will to live, of whose manifestation the individual is, as it were, only a particular example or specimen, than the death of an individual injures the whole of nature. For it is not the individual, but only the species that Nature cares for, and for the preservation of which she so earnestly strives, providing for it with the utmost prodigality through the vast surplus of the seed and the great strength of the fructifying impulse. The individual, on the contrary, neither has nor can have any value for Nature, for her kingdom is infinite time and infinite space, and in these infinite multiplicity of possible individuals. Therefore she is always ready to let the individual fall, and hence it is not only exposed to destruction in a thousand ways by the most insignificant accident, but originally destined for it, and conducted towards it by Nature herself from the moment it has served its end of maintaining the species. . . .

That generation and death are to be regarded as something belonging to life, and essential to this phenomenon of the will, arises also from the fact that they both exhibit themselves merely as higher powers of the expression of that in which all the rest of life consists. This is through and through nothing else than the constant change of matter in the fixed permanence of form; and this is what constitutes the transitoriness of the individual and the permanence of the species. Constant nourishment and renewal differ from generation only in degree, and constant excretion differs only in degree from death. The first shows itself most simply and distinctly in the plant. The plant is throughout a constant recurrence of the same impulse of its simplest fibre, which groups itself into leaf and branch. It is a systematic aggregate of similar plants supporting each other, whose constant reproduction is its single impulse. It ascends to the full satisfaction of this tendency through the grades of its metamorphosis, finally to the blossom and fruit, that compendium of its existence and effort in which it now attains, by a short way, to that which is its single aim, and at a stroke produces a thousand-fold what, up till then, it effected only in the particular case—the repetition of itself. Its earlier growth and development stands in the same relation to its fruit as writing stands to printing. With the animal it is clearly quite the same. The process of nourishing is a constant reproduction; the process of reproduction is a higher power of nourishing. The pleasure which accompanies the act of procreation is a higher power of the agreeableness of the sense of life. On the other hand, excretion, the constant exhalation and throwing off of matter, is the same as that which, at a higher power, death, is the contrary of generation. And if here we are always content to retain the form without lamenting the discarded matter, we ought to bear ourselves in the same way if in death the same thing happens, in a higher degree and to the whole, as takes place daily and hourly in a partial manner in excretion: if we are indifferent to the one, we ought not to shrink from the other. Therefore, from this point of view, it appears just as perverse to desire the continuance of an individuality which will be replaced by other individuals as to desire the permanence of matter which will be replaced by other matter. It appears just as foolish to embalm the body as it would be carefully to preserve its excrement. As to the individual consciousness which is bound to the individual body, it is absolutely interrupted every day by sleep. Deep sleep is, while it lasts, in no way different from death, into which, in fact, it often passes continuously, as in the case of freezing to death. It differs only with regard to the future, the awaking. Death is a sleep in which individuality is forgotten; everything else wakes again, or rather never slept. . . .

Dogmas change and our knowledge is deceptive; but Nature never errs, her procedure is sure, and she never conceals it. Everything is entirely in Nature, and Nature is entire in everything. She has her centre in every brute. It has surely found its way into existence, and it will surely find its way out of it. In the meantime it lives, fearless and without care, in the presence of annihilation, supported by the consciousness that it is Nature herself, and imperishable as she is. Man alone carries about with him, in abstract conceptions, the certainty of his death; yet this can only trouble him very rarely, when for a single moment some occasion calls it up to his imagination. Against the mighty voice of Nature reflection can do little. In man, as in the brute which does not think, the certainty that springs from his inmost consciousnes that he himself is Nature, the world, predominates as a lasting frame of mind; and on account of this no man is observably disturbed by the thought of certain and never-distant death, but lives as if he would live for ever.

A. N. WHITEHEAD

Nature as Organism

When you are criticising the philosophy of an epoch, do not chiefly direct your attention to those intellectual positions which its exponents feel it necessary explicitly to defend. There will be some fundamental assumptions which adherents of all the variant systems within the epoch unconsciously presuppose. Such assumptions appear so obvious that people do not know what they are assuming because no other way of putting things has ever occurred to them. With these assumptions a certain limited number of types of philosophic systems are possible, and this group of systems constitutes the philosophy of the epoch.

One such assumption underlies the whole philosophy of nature during the modern period. It is embodied in the conception which is supposed to express the most concrete aspect of nature. The Ionian philosophers asked, What is nature made of? The answer is couched in terms of stuff, or matter, or material—the particular name chosen is indifferent—which has the property of simple location in space and time, or, if you adopt the more modern ideas, in space-time. What I mean by matter, or material, is anything which has this property of *simple location*. By simple location I mean one major characteristic which refers equally both to space and to time, and other minor characteristics which are diverse as between space and time.

The characteristic common both to space and time is that material can be said to be *here* in space and *here* in time, or *here* in space-time, in a perfectly definite sense which does not require for its explanation any reference to other regions of space-time. Curiously enough this character of simple location holds whether we look on a region of space-time as determined absolutely or relatively. For if a region is merely a way of indicating a certain set of relations to other entities, then this characteristic, which I call simple location, is that material can be said to have just these relations of position to the other entities without requiring for its explanation any reference to other regions constituted by analogous relations of position to the same entities. In fact, as soon as you have settled, however you do settle, what you mean by a definite place in space-time, you can adequately state the relation of a particular material body to space-time by saying that it is

From *Science and the Modern World*, New York, 1926, pp. 71-2, 73-5, 76-7, 79-81, 81-2, 83-4, 93-5, 101-2, 104-7, 115-16, 120-26, 127, 133-4, 135-7. Copyright 1925 by the Macmillan Company, renewed 1953 by Evelyn Whitehead; reprinted by permission of the Macmillan Company and Cambridge University Press.

just there, in that place; and, so far as simple location is concerned, there is nothing more to be said on the subject.

The answer, therefore, which the seventeenth century gave to the ancient question of the Ionian thinkers, "What is the world made of?" was that the world is a succession of instantaneous configurations of matter—or of material, if you wish to include stuff more subtle than ordinary matter, the ether for example.

We cannot wonder that science rested content with this assumption as to the fundamental elements of nature. The great forces of nature, such as gravitation, were entirely determined by the configurations of masses. Thus the configurations determined their own changes, so that the circle of scientific thought was completely closed. This is the famous mechanistic theory of nature, which has reigned supreme ever since the seventeenth century. It is the orthodox creed of physical science. Furthermore, the creed justified itself by the pragmatic test. It worked. Physicists took no more interest in philosophy. They emphasised the anti-rationalism of the Historical Revolt. But the difficulties of this theory of materialistic mechanism very soon became apparent. The history of thought in the eighteenth and nineteenth centuries is governed by the fact that the world had got hold of a general idea which it could neither live with nor live without.

This simple location of instantaneous material configurations is what Bergson has protested against, so far as it concerns time and so far as it is taken to be the fundamental fact of concrete nature. He calls it a distortion of nature due to the intellectual "spatialisation" of things. I agree with Bergson in his protest: but I do not agree that such distortion is a vice necessary to the intellectual apprehension of nature. I shall in subsequent lectures endeavour to show that this spatialisation is the expression of more concrete facts under the guise of very abstract logical constructions. There is an error; but it is merely the accidental error of mistaking the abstract for the concrete. It is an example of what I will call the "Fallacy of Misplaced Concreteness." This fallacy is the occasion of great confusion in philosophy. It is not necessary for the intellect to fall into the trap, though in this example there has been a very general tendency to do so. . . .

There is another presupposition of thought which must be put beside the theory of simple location. I mean the two correlative categories of Substance and Quality. . . . Of course, substance and quality, as well as simple location, are the most natural ideas for the human mind. It is the way in which we think of things, and without these ways of thinking we could not get our ideas straight for daily use. There is no doubt about this. The only question is, How concretely are we thinking when we consider nature under these conceptions? My point will be, that we are presenting ourselves with simplified editions of immediate matters of fact. When we examine the primary elements of these simplified editions, we shall find that they are in truth only to be justified as being elaborate logical constructions of a high degree of abstraction. . . .

Let us consider how the notions of substance and quality arise. We observe an object as an entity with certain characteristics. Furthermore, each individual entity is apprehended through its characteristics. For example, we observe a body; there is something about it which we note. Perhaps, it is hard, and blue, and round, and noisy. We observe something which possesses these qualities: apart from these qualities we do not observe anything at all. Accordingly, the entity is a substratum, or substance, of which we predicate qualities. Some of the qualities are essential, so that apart from them the entity would not be itself; while other qualities are accidental and changeable.

In respect to material bodies, the qualities of having a quantitative mass, and of simple location somewhere, were held by John Locke at the close of the seventeenth century to be . . . essential qualities of substances whose spatio-temporal relationships constitute nature. The orderliness of these relationships constitutes the order of nature. The occurrences of nature are in some way apprehended by minds, which are associated with living bodies. Primarily, the mental apprehension is aroused by the occurrences in certain parts of the correlated body, the occurrences in the brain, for instance. But the mind in apprehending also experiences sensations which, properly speaking, are qualities of the mind alone. These sensations are projected by the mind so as to clothe appropriate bodies in external nature. Thus the bodies are perceived as with qualities which in reality do not belong to them, qualities which in fact are purely the offspring of the mind. Thus nature gets credit which should in truth be reserved for ourselves; the rose for its scent: the nightingale for his song: and the sun for his radiance. The poets are entirely mistaken. They should address their lyrics to themselves, and should turn them into odes of self-congratulation on the excellency of the human mind. Nature is a dull affair, soundless, scentless, colourless; merely the hurrying of material, endlessly, meaninglessly.

However you disguise it, this is the practical outcome of the characteristic scientific philosophy which closed the seventeenth century.

In the first place, we must note its astounding efficiency as a system of concepts for the organisation of scientific research. In this respect, it is fully worthy of the genius of the century which produced it. It has held its own as the guiding principle of scientific studies ever since. It is still reigning. Every university in the world organises itself in accordance with it. No alternative system of organising the pursuit of scientific truth has been suggested. It is not only reigning, but it is without a rival.

And yet—it is quite unbelievable. This conception of the universe is surely framed in terms of high abstractions, and the paradox only arises because we have mistaken our abstraction for concrete realities. . . . The enormous success of the scientific abstractions, yielding on the one hand *matter* with its *simple location* in space and time, on the other hand *mind*, perceiving, suffering, reasoning, but not interfering, has foisted onto philosophy the task of accepting them as the most concrete rendering of fact.

Thereby, modern philosophy has been ruined. It has oscillated in a complex manner between three extremes. There are the dualists, who accept matter and mind as on an equal basis, and the two varieties of monists, those who put mind inside matter, and those who put matter inside mind. But this juggling with abstractions can never overcome the inherent confusion introduced by the ascription of *misplaced concreteness* to the scientific scheme of the seventeenth century. . . . It involves a fundamental duality, with *material* on the one hand, and on the other hand *mind*. In between there lie the concepts of life, organism, function, instantaneous reality, interaction, order of nature, which collectively form the Achilles heel of the whole system. . . .

In outline, my procedure is to start from the analysis of the status of space and of time, or in modern phraseology, the status of space-time. There are two characters of either. Things are separated by space, and are separated by time: but they are also together in space, and together in time, even if they be not contemporaneous. I will call these characters the *separative* and the *prehensive* characters of space-time. There is yet a third character of space-time. Everything which is in space receives a definite limitation of some sort, so that in a sense it has just that shape which it does have and no other, also in some sense it is just in this place and no other. Analogously for time, a thing endures during a certain period, and through no other period. I will call this the *modal* character of space-time. It is evident that the modal character taken by itself gives rise to the idea of simple location. But it must be conjoined with the separative and prehensive characters.

For simplicity of thought, I will first speak of space only, and will afterwards extend the same treatment to time.

The volume is the most concrete element of space. But the separative character of space, analyses a volume into sub-volumes, and so on indefinitely. Accordingly, taking the separative character in isolation, we should infer that a volume is a mere multiplicity of non-voluminous elements, of points in fact. But it is the unity of volume which is the ultimate fact of experience, for example, the voluminous space of this hall. This hall as a mere multiplicity of points is a construction of the logical imagination.

Accordingly, the prime fact is the prehensive unity of volume, and this unity is mitigated or limited by the separated unities of the innumerable contained parts. We have a prehensive unity, which is yet held apart as an aggregate of contained parts. But the prehensive unity of the volume is not the unity of a mere logical aggregate of parts. The parts form an ordered aggregate, in the sense that each part is something from the standpoint of every other part, and also from the same standpoint every other part is something in relation to it. . . . Exactly analogous considerations hold with respect to durations in time. An instant of time, without duration, is an imaginative logical construction. Also each duration of time mirrors in itself all temporal durations. . . .

We can substitute the concept, that the realisation is a gathering of things into the unity of a prehension; and that what is thereby realised is the prehension, and not the things. This unity of a prehension defines itself as a *here* and a *now*, and the things so gathered into the grasped unity have essential reference to other places and other times. . . . Note that the idea of simple location has gone. The things which are grasped into a realised unity, here and now, are not the castle, the cloud, and the planet simply in themselves; but they are the castle, the cloud, and the planet from the standpoint, in space and time, of the prehensive unification. In other words, it is the perspective of the castle over there from the standpoint of the unification here. It is, therefore, aspects of the castle, the cloud, and the planet which are grasped into unity here. . . . Perception is simply the cognition of prehensive unification; or more shortly, perception is cognition of prehension. The actual world is a manifold of prehensions; and a "prehension" is a "prehensive occasion"; and a prehensive occasion is the most concrete finite entity, conceived as what it is in itself and for itself and not as from its aspect in the essence of another such occasion. . . .

Nature is conceived as a complex of prehensive unifications. Space and time exhibit the general scheme of interlocked relations of these prehensions. You cannot tear any one of them out of its context. Yet each one of them within its context has all the reality that attaches to the whole complex. Conversely, the totality has the same reality as each prehension; for each prehension unifies the modalities to be ascribed, from its standpoint, to every part of the whole. A prehension is a process of unifying. Accordingly, nature is a process of expansive development, necessarily transitional from prehension to prehension. What is achieved is thereby passed beyond, but it is also retained as having aspects of itself present to prehensions which lie beyond it.

Thus nature is a structure of evolving processes. The reality is the process. It is nonsense to ask if the colour red is real. The colour red is ingredient in the process of realisation. The realities of nature are the prehensions in nature, that is to say, the events in nature.

Now that we have cleared space and time from the taint of simple location, we may partially abandon the awkward term prehension. This term was introduced to signify the essential unity of an event, namely, the event as one entity, and not as a mere assemblage of parts or of ingredients. It is necessary to understand that space-time is nothing else than a system of pulling together of assemblages into unities. But the word *event* just means one of these spatio-temporal unities. Accordingly, it may be used instead of the term "prehension" as meaning the thing prehended.

An event has contemporaries. This means that an event mirrors within itself the modes of its contemporaries as a display of immediate achievement. An event has a past. This means that an event mirrors within itself the modes of its predecessors, as memories which are fused into its own content. An event has a future. This means that an event mirrors within itself such aspects as the future throws back on to the present, or, in other words, as the present has determined concerning the future. Thus an event has anticipation:

> The prophetic soul
> Of the wide world dreaming on things to come.

These conclusions are essential for any form of realism. For there is in the world for our cognisance, memory of the past, immediacy of realisation, and indication of things to come. . . .

The doctrine which I am maintaining is that the whole concept of materialism only applies to very abstract entities, the products of logical discernment. The concrete enduring entities are organisms, so that the plan of the *whole* influences the very characters of the various subordinate organisms which enter into it. In the case of an animal, the mental states enter into the plan of the total organism and thus modify the plans of the successive subordinate organisms until the ultimate smallest organisms, such as electrons, are reached. Thus an electron within a living body is different from an electron outside it, by reason of the plan of the body. The electron blindly runs either within or without the body; but it runs within the body in accordance with its character within the body; that is to say, in accordance with the general plan of the body, and this plan includes the mental state. But the principle of modification is perfectly general throughout nature, and represents no property peculiar to living bodies. . . .

So far as concerns English literature we find, as might be anticipated, the most interesting criticism of the thoughts of science among the leaders of the romantic reaction which accompanied and succeeded the epoch of the French Revolution. In English literature, the deepest thinkers of this school were Coleridge, Wordsworth, and Shelley. Keats is an example of literature untouched by science. We may neglect Coleridge's attempt at an explicit philosophical formulation. It was influential in his own generation; but in these lectures it is my object only to mention those elements of the thought of the past which stand for all time. Even with this limitation, only a selection is possible. For our purposes Coleridge is only important by his influence on Wordsworth. Thus Wordsworth and Shelley remain.

Wordsworth was passionately absorbed in nature. It has been said of Spinoza, that he was drunk with God. It is equally true that Wordsworth was drunk with nature. But he was a thoughtful, well-read man, with philosophical interests, and sane even to the point of prosiness. In addition, he was a genius. He weakens his evidence by his dislike of science. We all remember his scorn of the poor man whom he somewhat hastily accuses of peeping and botanising on his mother's grave. Passage after passage could be quoted from him, expressing this repulsion. In this respect, his characteristic thought can be summed up in his phrase, "We murder to dissect."

In this latter passage, he discloses the intellectual basis of his criticism of science. He alleges against science its absorption in abstractions. His consistent theme is that the important facts of nature elude the scientific method. It is important therefore to ask, what Wordsworth found in nature that failed to receive expression in science. I ask this question in the interest of science itself; for one main position in these lectures is a protest against the idea that the abstractions of science are irreformable and unalterable. Now it is emphatically not the case that Wordsworth hands over inorganic matter to the mercy of science, and concentrates on the faith that in the living organism there is some element that sciences cannot analyse. Of course he recognises, what no one doubts, that in some sense living things are different from lifeless things. But that is not his main point. It is the brooding presence of the hills which haunts him. His theme is nature *in solido*, that is to say, he dwells on that mysterious presence of surrounding things, which imposes itself on any separate element that we set up as an individual for its own sake. He always grasps the whole of nature as involved in the tonality of the particular instance. That is why he laughs with the daffodils, and finds in the primrose thoughts "too deep for tears."

Wordsworth's greatest poem is, by far, the first book of *The Prelude*. It is pervaded by this sense of the haunting presences of nature. A series of magnificent passages, too long for quotation, express this idea. Of course, Wordsworth is a poet writing a poem, and is not concerned with dry philosophical statements. But it would hardly be possible to express more clearly a feeling for nature, as exhibiting entwined prehensive unities, each suffused with modal presences of others:

> Ye Presences of Nature in the sky
> And on the earth! Ye Visions of the hills!
> And Souls of lonely places! can I think
> A vulgar hope was yours when ye employed
> Such ministry, when ye through many a year
> Haunting me thus among my boyish sports,

> On caves and trees, upon the woods and hills,
> Impressed upon all forms the characters
> Of danger or desire; and thus did make
> The surface of the universal earth,
> With triumph and delight, with hope and fear,
> Work like a sea? . . .

In thus citing Wordsworth, the point which I wish to make is that we forget how strained and paradoxical is the view of nature which modern science imposes on our thoughts. Wordsworth, to the height of genius, expresses the concrete facts of our apprehension, facts which are distorted in the scientific analysis. Is it not possible that the standardised concepts of science are only valid within narrow limitations, perhaps too narrow for science itself?

Shelley's attitude to science was at the opposite pole to that of Wordsworth. He loved it, and is never tired of expressing in poetry the thoughts which it suggests. It symbolises to him joy, and peace, and illumination. What the hills were to the youth of Wordsworth, a chemical laboratory was to Shelley. It is unfortunate that Shelley's literary critics have, in this respect, so little of Shelley in their own mentality. They tend to treat as a casual oddity of Shelley's nature what was, in fact, part of the main structure of his mind, permeating his poetry through and through. If Shelley had been born a hundred years later, the twentieth century would have seen a Newton among chemists.

For the sake of estimating the value of Shelley's evidence it is important to realise this absorption of his mind in scientific ideas. It can be illustrated by lyric after lyric. I will choose one poem only, the fourth act of his *Prometheus Unbound*. The Earth and the Moon converse together in the language of accurate science. Physical experiments guide his imagery. For example, the Earth's exclamation,

> The vaporous exultation not to be confined!

is the poetic transcript of "the expansive force of gases," as it is termed in books on science. Again, take the Earth's stanza,

> I spin beneath my pyramid of night,
> Which points into the heavens,—dreaming delight,
> Murmuring victorious joy in my enchanted sleep;
> As a youth lulled in love-dreams faintly sighing,
> Under the shadow of his beauty lying,
> Which round his rest a watch of light and warmth doth keep.

This stanza could only have been written by someone with a definite geometrical diagram before his inward eye—a diagram which it has often been my business to demonstrate to mathematical classes. As evidence, note especially the last line which gives poetical imagery to the light surrounding night's pyramid. This idea could not occur to anyone without the diagram. But the whole poem and other poems are permeated with touches of this kind.

Now the poet, so sympathetic with science, so absorbed in its ideas, can simply make nothing of the doctrine of secondary qualities which is fundamental to its concepts. For Shelley nature retains its beauty and its colour. Shelley's nature is in its essence a nature of organisms, functioning with the full content of our perceptual experience. We are so used to ignoring the implication of orthodox scientific doctrine, that it is difficult to make evident the criticism upon it which is thereby implied. If anybody could have treated it seriously, Shelley would have done so.

Furthermore Shelley is entirely at one with Wordsworth as to the interfusing of the Presence in nature. Here is the opening stanza of his poem entitled *Mont Blanc*:

> The everlasting universe of Things
> Flows through the Mind, and rolls its rapid waves,
> Now dark—now glittering—now reflecting gloom—
> Now lending splendour, where from secret springs
> The source of human thought its tribute brings
> Of waters,—with a sound but half its own,
> Such as a feeble brook will oft assume
> In the wild woods, among the Mountains lone,
> Where waterfalls around it leap for ever,
> Where woods and winds contend, and a vast river
> Over its rocks ceaselessly bursts and raves.

Shelley has writen these lines with explicit reference to some form of idealism, Kantian or Berkeleyan or Platonic. But however you construe him, he is here an emphatic witness to a prehensive unification as constituting the very being of nature.

Berkeley, Wordsworth, Shelley are representative of the intuitive refusal seriously to accept the abstract materialism of science.

There is an interesting difference in the treatment of nature by Wordsworth and by Shelley, which brings forward the exact questions we have got to think about. Shelley thinks of nature as changing, dissolving, transforming as it were at a fairy's touch. The leaves fly before the West Wind

> Like ghosts from an enchanter fleeing.

In his poem *The Cloud* it is the transformations of water which excite his imagination. The subject of the poem is the endless, eternal, elusive change of things:

> I change but I cannot die.

This is one aspect of nature, its elusive change: a change not merely to be expressed by locomotion, but a change of inward character. This is where Shelley places his emphasis, on the change of what cannot die.

Wordsworth was born among hills; hills mostly barren of trees, and thus showing the minimum of change with the seasons. He was haunted by the enormous permanences of nature. For him change is an incident which shoots across a background of endurance,

> Breaking the silence of the seas
> Among the farthest Hebrides.

Every scheme for the analysis of nature has to face these two facts, *change* and *endurance*. There is yet a third fact to be placed by it, *eternality*, I will call it.

The mountain endures. But when after ages it has been worn away, it has gone. If a replica arises, it is yet a new mountain. A colour is eternal. It haunts time like a spirit. It comes and it goes. But where it comes, it is the same colour. It neither survives nor does it live. It appears when it is wanted. The mountain has to time and space a different relation from that which colour has. In the previous lecture, I was chiefly considering the relation to space-time of things which, in my sense of the term, are eternal. It was necessary to do so before we can pass to the consideration of the things which endure. . . .

The literature of the nineteenth century, especially its English poetic literature, is a witness to the discord between the aesthetic intuitions of mankind and the mechanism of science. Shelley brings vividly before us the elusiveness of the eternal objects of sense as they haunt the change which infects underlying organisms. Wordsworth is the poet of nature as being the field of enduring permanences carrying within themselves a message of tremendous significance. The eternal objects are also there for him,

> The light that never was, on sea or land.

Both Shelley and Wordsworth emphatically bear witness that nature cannot be divorced from its aesthetic values, and that these values arise from the cumulation, in some sense, of the brooding presence of the whole on to its various parts. Thus we gain from the poets the doctrine that a philosophy of nature must concern itself at least with these six notions: change, value, eternal objects, endurance, organism, interfusion. . . . In a certain sense, everything is everywhere at all times. For every location involves an aspect of itself in every other location. Thus every spatio-temporal standpoint mirrors the world.

If you try to imagine this doctrine in terms of our conventional views of space and time, which presuppose simple location, it is a great paradox. But if you think of it in terms of our naïve experience, it is a mere transcript of the obvious facts. You are in a certain place perceiving things. Your perception takes place where you are, and is entirely dependent on how your body is functioning. But this functioning of the body in one place, exhibits for your cognisance an aspect of the distant environment, fading away into the general knowledge that there are things beyond. If this cognisance conveys knowledge of a transcendent world, it must be because the event which is the bodily life unifies in itself aspects of the universe.

This is a doctrine extremely consonant with the vivid expression of personal experience which we find in the nature-poetry of imaginative writers such as Wordsworth or Shelley. The brooding, immediate presences of things are an obsession to Wordsworth. What the theory does do is to edge cognitive mentality away from being the necessary substratum of the unity of experience. That unity is now placed in the unity of an event. Accompanying this unity, there may or there may not be cognition. . . .

One all-pervasive fact, inherent in the very character of what is real is the transition of things, the passage one to another. This passage is not a mere linear procession of discrete entities. However we fix a determinate entity, there is always a narrower determination of something which is presupposed in our first choice. Also there is always a wider determination into which our first choice fades by transition beyond itself. The general aspect of nature is that of evolutionary expansiveness. These unities, which I call events, are the emergence into actuality of something. How are we to characterise the something which thus emerges? The name *"event"* given to such a unity, draws attention to the inherent transitoriness, combined with the actual unity. But this abstract word cannot be sufficient to characterise what the fact of the reality of an event is in itself. A moment's thought shows us that no one idea can in itself be sufficient. For every idea which finds its significance in each event must represent something which contributes to what realisation is in itself. Thus no one word can be adequate. But conversely, nothing must be left out. Remembering the poetic rendering of our concrete experience, we see at once that the element of value, of being valuable, of having value, of being an end in itself, of being something which is for its own sake, must not be omitted in any account of an event as the most concrete actual something. "Value" is the word I use for the intrinsic reality of an event. Value is an element which permeates through and through the poetic view of nature. We have only to transfer to the very texture of realisation in itself that value which we recognise so readily in terms of human life. This is the secret of Wordsworth's worship of nature. Realisation therefore is in itself the attainment of value. But there is no such thing as mere value. Value is the outcome of limitation. The definite finite entity is the selected mode which is the shaping of attainment; apart from such shaping into individual matter of fact there is no attainment. The mere fusion of all that there is would be the nonentity of indefiniteness. The salvation of reality is its obstinate, irreducible, matter-of-fact entities, which are limited to be no other than themselves. Neither science, nor art, nor creative action can tear itself away from obstinate, irreducible, limited facts. The endurance of things has its significance in the self-retention of that which imposes itself as a definite attainment for its own sake. That which endures is limited, obstructive, intolerant, infecting its environment with its own aspects. But it is not self-sufficient. The aspects of all things enter into its very nature. It is only itself as drawing together into its own limitation the larger whole in which it finds itself. Conversely it is only itself by lending its aspects to this same environment in which it finds itself. The problem of evolution is the development of enduring harmonies of enduring shapes of value, which merge into higher attainments of things beyond themselves. Aesthetic attainment is interwoven in the texture of realisation. The endurance of an entity represents the attainment of a limited aesthetic success, though if we look beyond it to its external effects, it may represent an aesthetic failure. Even within itself, it may represent the conflict between a lower success and a higher failure. The conflict is the presage of disruption.

Nature, Man, and Art

Let it be confessed: landscape is foreign to us, and we are fearfully alone amongst trees which blossom and by streams which flow. Alone with the dead one is not nearly so defenceless as when alone with Trees. For, however mysterious death may be, life that is not our life is far more mysterious, life that is not concerned with us, and which, without seeing us, celebrates its festivals, as it were, at which we look on with a certain embarrassment, like chance guests who speak another language.

It is true, many people would cite our connexion with Nature, in whom we have our origin and in whom we are the final fruits of a great ascending genealogical tree. He who does that cannot, however, deny that, when we trace this genealogical tree downwards from ourselves, shoot by shoot, branch by branch, it is very soon lost in darkness; in a darkness inhabited by extinct mammoths, by monsters full of hatred and hostility, and that we come, the further back we go, to increasingly strange and horrible beings, so that we are forced to assume that, ultimately, we shall find Nature as the most horrible and strangest of all. The fact that we have had intercourse with Nature for thousands of years is of little significance here; for this intercourse has been very one-sided. It always seems that Nature does not know at all that we cultivate her and timidly put a small part of her forces to our own use. In many places we increase her fertility and in others we choke, with the pavement of our cities, wonderful springs ready to rise from the soil. We divert the rivers to our factories, but they are oblivious of the machines which they drive. We play with obscure forces, which we cannot lay hold of, by the names we give them, as children play with fire, and it seems for a moment as if all the energy had lain unused in things until we came to apply it to our transitory life and its needs. But repeatedly throughout the millenaries these forces shake off their names and rise like an oppressed class against their little lords, no, not even *against*—they simply rise, and civilizations fall from the shoulders of the earth, which becomes large and spacious once again and alone with its seas, its stars, and its trees.

It makes little difference that we change the uppermost surface of the earth, that we regulate its forests and meadows and get coal and metals from its crust, that we receive the fruits of the trees as though they were destined for us, when we remember at the same time one single hour in which Nature acted irrespective of us, our hopes, our life, with that sublime loftiness and indifference which fill all her movements. She knows nothing of us. And whatever men may have achieved, no man has been great enough to cause her to sympathize with his pain, to share in his rejoicing. Sometimes she has accompanied great and immortal hours of history with her mighty, tumultuous music, or has seemed, at a moment of decision, to stand silent, windless, holding her breath, or to surround a moment of harmless social gaiety with fluttering blossom, hovering butterflies, and dancing winds—but only at the next moment to turn aside and leave

From "Worpswede" [1903], *Selected Works*, translated from the German by G. Craig Houston, London, 1954, Vol. I, pp. 7-10. Copyright 1954 by G. Craig Houston. All rights reserved. Reprinted by permission of New Directions and The Hogarth Press.

in the lurch those with whom she seemed just now to have shared everything.

The ordinary man, who lives with men, and sees Nature only in as far as she has reference to himself, is seldom aware of this problematic and uncanny relationship. He sees the surface of the things, which he and his like have created through the centuries, and likes to believe that the whole earth is concerned with him because a field can be cultivated, a forest thinned, and a river made navigable. His eye, focused almost entirely on men, sees Nature also, but incidentally, as something obvious and actual that must be exploited as much as possible. Children see Nature differently; solitary children in particular, who grow up amongst adults, foregather with her by a kind of like-mindedness and live within her, like the smaller animals, entirely at one with the happenings of forest and sky and in innocent, obvious harmony with them. But just because of this, there comes later for youth and maiden that lonely period filled with deep, trembling melancholy, when they feel unutterably forlorn, just at the time of their physical maturing; when they feel that the things and events in Nature have *no longer*, and their fellow-men have *not yet*, any sympathy for them. Spring comes, even when they are sad, the roses bloom, and the nights are full of nightingales, even though they would like to die; and when at last they would smile once more, the autumn days are there, the heavy days of November, which seem to fall without cessation, and on which a long sunless winter follows. And, on the other hand, they see people, equally strange to them and unconcerned, with their business, their cares, their successes and joys, and they do not understand it. And finally, some of them make up their minds and join these people in order to share their work and their fate, to be useful, to be helpful, to serve the enlargement of life somehow, whilst the others, unwilling to leave the Nature they have lost, go in pursuit of her and try now, consciously and by the use of their concentrated will, to come as near to her again as they were in their childhood without knowing it. It will be understood that the latter are artists: poets or painters, composers or architects, fundamentally lonely spirits, who, in turning to Nature, put the eternal above the transitory, that which is most profoundly based on law above that which is fundamentally ephemeral, and who, since they cannot persuade Nature to concern herself with them, see their task to be the understanding of Nature, so that they make take their place somewhere in her great design. And the whole of humanity comes nearer to Nature in these isolated and lonely ones. It is not the least and is, perhaps, the peculiar value of art, that it is the medium in which man and landscape, form and world, meet and find one another. In actuality they live beside one another, scarcely knowing aught of one another, and in the picture, the piece of architecture, the symphony, in a word, in art, they seem to come together in a higher, prophetic truth, to rely upon one another, and it is as if, by completing one another, they became that perfect unity, which is the very essence of a work of art.

From this point of view the theme and purpose of all art would seem to lie in the reconciliation of the Individual and the All, and the moment of exaltation, the artistically important Moment, would seem to be that in which the two scales of the balance counterpoise one another. And, indeed, it would be very tempting to show this relationship in various works of art; to show how a symphony mingles the voices of a stormy day with the tumult of our blood, how a building owes its character half to us and half to the forest.

The Life of the Hawthorn

It was in these "Month of Mary" services that I can remember having first fallen in love with hawthorn-blossom. The hawthorn was not merely in the church, for there, holy ground as it was, we had all of us a right of entry; but, arranged upon the altar itself, inseparable from the mysteries in whose celebration it was playing a part, it thrust in among the tapers and the sacred vessels its rows of branches, tied to one another horizontally in a stiff, festal scheme of decoration; and they were made more lovely still by the scalloped outline of the dark leaves, over which were scattered in profusion, as over a bridal train, little clusters of buds of a dazzling whiteness. Though I dared not look at them save through my fingers, I could feel that the formal scheme was composed of living things, and that it was Nature herself who, by trimming the shape of the foliage, and by adding the crowning ornament of those snowy buds, had made the decorations worthy of what was at once a public rejoicing and a solemn mystery. Higher up on the altar, a flower had opened here and there with a careless grace, holding so unconcernedly, like a final, almost vaporous bedizening, its bunch of stamens, slender as gossamer, which clouded the flower itself in a white mist, that in following these with my eyes, in trying to imitate, somewhere inside myself, the action of their blossoming, I imagined it as a swift and thoughtless movement of the head with an enticing glance from her contracted pupils, by a young girl in white, careless and alive. . . .

When, before turning to leave the church, I made a genuflection before the altar, I felt suddenly, as I rose again, a bitter-sweet fragrance of almonds steal towards me from the hawthorn-blossom, and I then noticed that on the flowers themselves were little spots of a creamier colour, in which I imagined that this fragrance must lie concealed, as the taste of an almond cake lay in the burned parts, or the sweetness of Mlle. Vinteuil's cheeks beneath their freckles. Despite the heavy, motionless silence of the hawthorns, these gusts of fragrance came to me like the murmuring of an intense vitality, with which the whole altar was quivering like a roadside hedge explored by living antennae, of which I was reminded by seeing some stamens, almost red in colour, which seemed to have kept the springtime virulence, the irritant power of stinging insects now transmuted into flowers. . . .

I found the whole path throbbing with the fragrance of hawthorn-blossom. The hedge resembled a series of chapels, whose walls were no longer visible under the mountains of flowers that were heaped upon their altars; while underneath, the sun cast a square of light upon the ground, as though it had shone in upon them through a window; the scent that swept out over me from them was as rich, and as circumscribed in its range, as though I had been standing before the Lady-altar, and the flowers, themselves adorned also, held out each its little bunch of glittering stamens with an air of inattention, fine, radiating "nerves" in the flamboyant style of architecture, like those which, in church, framed the stair to the rood-loft

From *Swann's Way* [1919], *Remembrance of Things Past*, translated from the French by C. K. Scott Moncrieff, New York, 1932-34, Vol. I, pp. 85-7, 106-8. Copyright 1928 and renewed 1956 by The Modern Library, Inc. Reprinted from Volume I of *Remembrance of Things Past* by permission of Random House, Inc., and Chatto & Windus Ltd.

or closed the perpendicular tracery of the windows, but here spread out into pools of fleshy white, like strawberry-beds in spring. How simple and rustic, in comparison with these, would seem the dog-roses which, in a few weeks' time, would be climbing the same hillside path in the heat of the sun, dressed in the smooth silk of their blushing pink bodices, which would be undone and scattered by the first breath of wind.

But it was in vain that I lingered before the hawthorns, to breathe in, to marshall before my mind (which knew not what to make of it), to lose in order to rediscover their invisible and unchanging odour, to absorb myself in the rhythm which disposed their flowers here and there with the light-heartedness of youth, and at intervals as unexpected as certain intervals of music; they offered me an indefinite continuation of the same charm, in an inexhaustible profusion, but without letting me delve into it any more deeply, like those melodies which one can play over a hundred times in succession without coming any nearer to their secret. I turned away from them for a moment so as to be able to return to them with renewed strength. My eyes followed up the slope which, outside the hedge, rose steeply to the fields, a poppy that had strayed and been lost by its fellows, or a few cornflowers that had fallen lazily behind, and decorated the ground here and there with their flowers like the border of a tapestry, in which may be seen at intervals hints of the rustic theme which appears triumphant in the panel itself; infrequent still, spaced apart as the scattered houses which warn us that we are approaching a village, they betokened to me the vast expanse of waving corn beneath the fleecy clouds, and the sight of a single poppy hoisting upon its slender rigging and holding against the breeze its scarlet ensign, over the buoy of rich black earth from which it sprang, made my heart beat as does a wayfarer's when he perceives, upon some low-lying ground, an old and broken boat which is being caulked and made seaworthy, and cries out, although he has not yet caught sight of it, "The Sea!"

And then I returned to my hawthorns, and stood before them as one stands before those masterpieces of painting which, one imagines, one will be better able to "take in" which one has looked away, for a moment, at something else; but in vain did I shape my fingers into a frame, so as to have nothing but the hawthorns before my eyes; the sentiment which they aroused in me remained obscure and vague, struggling and failing to free itself, to float across and become one with the flowers. They themselves offered me no enlightenment, and I could not call upon any other flowers to satisfy this mysterious longing. And then, inspiring me with that rapture which we feel on seeing a work by our favourite painter quite different from any of those that we already know, or, better still, when some one has taken us and set us down in front of a picture of which we have hitherto seen no more than a pencilled sketch, or when a piece of music which we have heard played over on the piano bursts out again in our ears with all the splendour and fullness of an orchestra, my grandfather called me to him, and, pointing to the hedge of Tansonville, said: "You are fond of hawthorns; just look at this pink one; isn't it pretty?"

And it was indeed a hawthorn, but one whose flowers were pink, and lovelier even than the white. It, too, was in holiday attire, for one of those days which are the only true holidays, the holy days of religion, because they are not appointed by any capricious accident, as secular holidays are appointed, upon days which are not specially ordained for such observances, which have nothing about them that is essentially festal—but it was attired even more richly than the rest, for the flowers which clung to its branches, one above another, so thickly as to leave no part of the tree undecorated, like the tassels wreathed about the crook of a rococo shepherdess, were every one of them "in colour," and consequently of a superior quality, by the aesthetic standards of Combray, to the "plain," if one was to judge by the scale of prices at the "stores" in the Square, or at Camus's, where the most expensive biscuits were those whose sugar was pink. And for my own part I set a higher value on cream cheese when it was pink, when I had been allowed to tinge it with crushed strawberries. And these flowers had chosen precisely the colour of some edible and delicious thing, or of some exquisite addition to one's costume for a great festival, which colours, inasmuch as they make plain the reason for their superiority, are those whose beauty is most evident to the eyes of children, and for that reason must always seem more vivid and more natural than any other tints, even after the child's mind has realised that they offer no gratification to the appetite, and have not been selected by the dressmaker. And, indeed, I had felt at once, as I had felt before the white blossom, but now still more marvelling, that it was in no artificial manner, by no device of human construction, that the festal intention of these flowers was revealed, but that it was Nature herself who had spontaneously expressed it (with the simplicity of a woman from a village shop, labouring at the decoration of a street altar for some procession) by burying the bush in these little rosettes, almost too ravishing in colour, this rustic "pompadour." High up on the branches, like so many of those tiny rose-trees, their pots concealed in jackets of paper lace, whose slender stems rise in a forest from the altar on the greater festivals, a thousand buds were swelling and opening, paler in colour, but each disclosing as it burst, as at the bottom of a cup of pink marble, its blood-red stain, and suggesting even more strongly than the full-blown flowers the special, irresistible quality of the hawthorn-tree, which, wherever it budded, wherever it was about to blossom, could bud and blossom in pink flowers alone. Taking its place in the hedge, but as different from the rest as a young girl in holiday attire among a crowd of dowdy women in everyday clothes, who are staying at home, equipped and ready for the "Month of Mary," of which it seemed already to form a part, it shone and smiled in its cool, rosy garments, a Catholic bush indeed, and altogether delightful.

ANDRÉ GIDE

Natural Joy

That man is born for happiness,
Is what all nature teaches.

An all-pervading joy suffuses the earth and the earth exudes it at the sun's call. It is joy that thrills the atmosphere in which the elements come to life and, still

From *Later Fruits of the Earth* [1935], in *Fruits of the Earth*, translated from the French by Dorothy Bussy, New York, 1949, pp. 187, 190, 203, 213, 247-8, 258, 287-9. Copyright 1949 by Alfred A. Knopf, Inc.; reprinted by permission of Alfred A. Knopf, Inc. and Martin Secker & Warburg Ltd.

submissive, make their escape from the primal rigour. . . . Lovely complexities are born from the interweaving of the laws of nature—the seasons, the movement of the tides, the vapours that are drawn up and showered down again in streams, the tranquil alternation of the days, the periodic recurrence of the winds—everything, as it comes into being, sways to and fro in a harmonious rhythm. Everything is prepared for the organisation of joy, and soon joy is born; it flutters unwittingly in the leaf, it takes name and diversity, becomes fragrance in the flower, flavour in the fruit, a conscious voice in the bird. So that the return, the informing and then the disappearance of life imitate the circuitous passage of water which evaporates in the sunshine and then regathers again to fall in the shower.

Each animal is nothing but a parcel of joy.

Everything is glad to be and every being rejoices. You call it fruit when joy becomes succulence, bird when it is turned into song.

All nature indeed teaches that man is born for happiness. It is the effort after pleasure that makes the plant germinate, fills the hive with honey, and the human heart with love.

No more delay! No more delay! O obstructed road! I push on. It is my turn. The sunbeam has signed to me; my desire is the surest of guides and this morning I am in love with the whole world.

A thousand luminous threads cross and intertwine on my heart. Out of thousands of fragile perceptions I weave a miraculous garment. Through it the god laughs and I smile back to the god. Who was it said that great Pan was dead? I saw him through the mist of my breath. My lips are stretched towards him. Was it not he who whispered in my ear this morning, "What are you waiting for?"

With mind and hand I brush aside all intercepting veils, so that there shall be nothing before me but what is brilliant and bare.

I am in bondage to my past. Not a gesture to-day but was determined by what I was yesterday. But I who am at this moment, I, instantaneous, fleeting, irreplaceable, I escape. . . .

Oh! to be able to escape from myself! I would overleap the barriers behind which self-respect has confined me. My nostril dilates to the wind. Oh! to weigh anchor, bound for the wildest adventure . . . And that it should be without consequence for the future.

My mind boggles at the word—consequence. Consequence of our acts. Consequence with ourselves. Am I to expect nothing from myself but a sequel? Consequence—compromise—a road traced beforehand. I want now not to walk but to leap. With the spring of my muscles to push off, to reject my past; to have no more promises to keep; I have made too many! Future, how I should love you, if you could be unfaithful!

What wind from sea or mountain will carry you, my soaring thoughts? Blue bird, fluttering and beating your wings on the sheer extremity of that rock, you advance as far as the present can carry you, and already, your straining eyes take flight, you escape into the future.

O new anxieties! Questions that have never yet been put! . . . I am weary with yesterday's struggle; I have more than exhausted its bitterness; I have ceased to believe in it; I lean over the future's gulf without giddiness. Winds of the abyss, bear me away!

I do not find in the letter of the Gospels any actual prohibitions. But the important thing is that we should contemplate God with the clearest possible eyes, and I feel that every object on this earth that I covet becomes opaque by very reason of my coveting it, and that the whole world then loses its transparence, or else my eyes lose their clearness, so that God ceases to be perceptible to my soul, and by abandoning the Creator for the creature, my soul ceases to live in eternity and loses possession of the kingdom of God.

It is towards pleasure that all nature's efforts tend. It is pleasure that makes the blade of grass grow, the bud develop, and the flower bloom. It is pleasure that opens the corolla to the sunbeam's kisses, invites every living thing to espousals, sends the obtuse larva to its nymphosis and from the prison of its chrysalis makes the butterfly escape. With pleasure for a guide, all things aspire to greater thriving, to increased consciousness, to progress. . . . And this is why I have found more instruction in pleasure than in books; why I have found in books more obfuscation than light.

There was no deliberation nor method about it. It was unreflectively that I plunged into this ocean of delights, astonished to find myself swimming in it, not to feel myself sinking. It is in pleasure that we become wholly conscious of ourselves.

All this took place of no set purpose; it was quite naturally that I let myself go. I had of course heard it said that human nature was bad, but I wanted to put it to the proof. I felt indeed less curious about myself than about others—or rather, the secret workings of carnal desire drove me out of myself towards an enchanting confusion.

To seek a system of morals did not seem to me very wise, nor even possible, as long as I did not know who and what I was. When I stopped looking for myself it was in love that I found myself again.

For some time I had to consent to the abandonment of all moral considerations and cease resisting my desires. They alone were capable of instructing me. I yielded to them.

What evolutionist would ever suppose the slightest connection between the caterpillar and the butterfly—if it were not known that they are in fact the same creature? Filiation appears impossible—and there is identity. If I had been a naturalist, I think it is upon this enigma that I should have concentrated all the energies and enquiries of my mind.

Had it been given to only a very few of us to witness this metamorphosis, it would perhaps seem more astonishing. But we cease to be surprised at a constant miracle.

And not only does the shape change, but the habits, the appetites. . . .

Know thyself. A maxim as pernicious as it is ugly. To observe oneself is to arrest one's development. The caterpillar that tried "to know itself" would never become a butterfly.

If then I call nature God, it is for simplicity's sake and because it irritates the theologians. For you may have noticed that such people shut their eyes to nature, or if they happen to glance at it, they are incapable of observing it.

Instead of trying to get instruction from men, let your teaching come from God. Man has grown crooked. His history is simply that of his false pretences and his sham excuses. "A market-gardener's cart," I once wrote, "carries with it more truths than Cicero's finest periods." There is man's history and the history so rightly called *natural*. In *Natural History* you must listen to the voice of God. And don't be satisfied with listening to it vaguely; put definite questions to God and insist on his answering you definitely. Don't be satisfied with gazing—observe.

You will notice then that everything that is young is tender. In how many sheathes is not every bud wrapped round! But all that at first protected the tender germ, when once germination is accomplished, hinders it; and no growth is possible unless it bursts the sheathes in which at first it was swaddled.

Mankind clings to its swaddling-clothes, but it will never grow unless it succeeds in getting rid of them. The child that has been weaned is not ungrateful if it pushes away its mother's breast. It is no longer milk that it needs. Comrade, you must refuse henceforth to seek your nourishment in the milk of tradition, man-distilled and man-filtered. You have teeth now with which to bite and chew and you must find your food in what is real. Stand up erect, naked and valiant; burst your wrappings, push aside your props; to grow straight you need nothing now but the urge of your sap and the sun's call.

You will notice that every plant casts its seeds to a distance; either the seeds have a delicious covering that tempts the bird's appetite, so that they are carried to places they could not otherwise reach; or else, equipped with spirals or feathers, they trust themselves to the wandering breezes. For, if it nourishes the same kind of plant too long, the soil becomes impoverished and poisonous, and the new generation cannot find its food in the same place as the preceding one. Do not try to eat again what your fathers before you have already digested. Look at the winged seeds of the plane or the sycamore flying off as if they understood that the paternal shade can offer them nothing but a dwindling and atrophied existence.

And you will notice too that the rush of the sap goes preferably to swell the buds at the extreme tips of the branches, those that are furthest from the trunk.

Understand this rightly and put the longest possible distance between you and the past.

Understand rightly the Greek fable. It teaches us that Achilles was invulnerable except in that spot of his body which had been made soft by the remembrance of his mother's touch.

D. H. LAWRENCE

The Death of Pan

At the beginning of the Christian era, voices were heard off the coasts of Greece, out to sea, on the Mediterranean, wailing: "Pan is dead! Great Pan is dead!"

The father of fauns and nymphs, satyrs and dryads and naiads was dead, with only the voices in the air to lament him. Humanity hardly noticed.

But who was he, really? Down the long lanes and overgrown ridings of history we catch odd glimpses of a lurking rustic god with a goat's white lightning in his eyes. A sort of fugitive, hidden among leaves, and laughing with the uncanny derision of one who feels himself defeated by something lesser than himself.

An outlaw, even in the early days of the gods. A sort of Ishmael among the bushes.

Yet always his lingering title: The Great God Pan. As if he was, or had been, the greatest.

Lurking among the leafy recesses, he was almost more demon than god. To be feared, not loved or approached. A man who should see Pan by daylight fell dead, as if blasted by lightning.

Yet you might dimly see him in the night, a dark body within the darkness. And then, it was a vision filling the limbs and the trunk of a man with power, as with new, strong-mounting sap. The Pan-power! You went on your way in the darkness secretly and subtly elated with blind energy, and you could cast a spell, by your mere presence, on women and on men. But particularly on women.

In the woods and the remote places ran the children of Pan, all the nymphs and fauns of the forest and the spring and the river and the rocks. These, too, it was dangerous to see by day. The man who looked up to see the white arms of a nymph flash as she darted behind the thick wild laurels away from him followed helplessly. He was a nympholept. Fascinated by the swift limbs and the wild, fresh sides of the nymph, he followed for ever, for ever, in the endless monotony of his desire. Unless came some wise being who could absolve him from the spell.

But the nymphs, running among the trees and curling to sleep under the bushes, made the myrtles blossom more gaily, and the spring bubble up with greater urge, and the birds splash with a strength of life. And the lithe flanks of the faun gave life to the oak-groves, the vast trees hummed with energy. And the

"Pan in America" [1926], *Phoenix*, New York, 1936, pp. 22-31; reprinted by permission of The Viking Press Inc., Lawrence Pollinger Ltd. and the Estate of the late Mrs. Frieda Lawrence.

wheat sprouted like green rain returning out of the ground, in the little fields, and the vine hung its black drops in abundance, urging a secret.

Gradually men moved into cities. And they loved the display of people better than the display of a tree. They liked the glory they got of overpowering one another in war. And, above all, they loved the vainglory of their own words, the pomp of argument and the vanity of ideas.

So Pan became old and grey-bearded and goat-legged, and his passion was degraded with the lust of senility. His power to blast and to brighten dwindled. His nymphs became coarse and vulgar.

Till at last the old Pan died, and was turned into the devil of the Christians. The old god Pan became the Christian devil, with the cloven hoofs and the horns, the tail, and the laugh of derision. Old Nick, the Old Gentleman who is responsible for all our wickednesses, but especially our sensual excesses—this is all that is left of the Great God Pan.

It is strange. It is a most strange ending for a god with such a name. Pan! All! That which is everything has goat's feet and a tail! With a black face!

This really is curious.

Yet this was all that remained of Pan, except that he acquired brimstone and hell-fire, for many, many centuries. The nymphs turned into the nasty-smelling witches of a Walpurgis night, and the fauns that danced became sorcerers riding the air, or fairies no bigger than your thumb.

But Pan keeps on being reborn, in all kinds of strange shapes. There he was, at the Renaissance. And in the eighteenth century he had quite a vogue. He gave rise to an "ism," and there were many pantheists, Wordsworth one of the first. They worshipped Nature in her sweet-and-pure aspect, her Lucy Gray aspect.

"Oft have I heard of Lucy Gray," the school-child began to recite, on examination-day.

"So have I," interrupted the bored inspector.

Lucy Gray, alas, was the form that William Wordsworth thought fit to give to the Great God Pan.

And then he crossed over to the young United States: I mean Pan did. Suddenly he gets a new name. He becomes the Oversoul, the Allness of everything. To this new Lucifer Gray of a Pan Whitman sings the famous *Song of Myself*: "I am All, and All is Me." That is: "I am Pan, and Pan is me."

The old goat-legged gentleman from Greece thoughtfully strokes his beard, and answers: "All A is B, but all B is not A." Aristotle did not live for nothing. All Walt is Pan, but all Pan is not Walt.

This, even to Whitman, is incontrovertible. So the new American pantheism collapses.

Then the poets dress up a few fauns and nymphs, to let them run riskily—oh, would there were any risk—in their private "grounds." But, alas, these tame guinea-pigs soon became boring. Change the game.

We still *pretend* to believe that there is One mysterious Something-or-other back of Everything, ordaining all things for the ultimate good of humanity. It wasn't back of the Germans in 1914, of course, and whether it's back of the bolshevists is still a grave question. But still, it's back of *us*, so that's all right.

Alas, poor Pan! Is this what you've come to? Legless, hornless, faceless, even smileless, you are less than everything or anything, except a lie.

And yet here, in America, the oldest of all, old Pan is still alive. When Pan was greatest, he was not even Pan. He was nameless and unconceived, mentally. Just as a small baby new from the womb may say Mama! Dada! whereas in the womb it said nothing; so humanity, in the womb of Pan, said nought. But when humanity was born into a separate idea of itself, it said *Pan*.

In the days before man got too much separated off from the universe, he *was* Pan, along with all the rest.

As a tree still is. A strong-willed, powerful thing-in-itself, reaching up and reaching down. With a powerful will of its own it thrusts green hands and huge limbs at the light above, and sends huge legs and gripping toes down, down between the earth and rocks, to the earth's middle.

Here, on this little ranch under the Rocky Mountains, a big pine tree rises like a guardian spirit in front of the cabin where we live. Long, long ago the Indians blazed it. And the lightning, or the storm, has cut off its crest. Yet its column is always there, alive and changeless, alive and changing. The tree has its own aura of life. And in winter the snow slips off it, and in June it sprinkles down its little catkin-like pollen-tips, and it hisses in the wind, and it makes a silence within a silence. It is a great tree, under which the house is built. And the tree is within the allness of Pan. At night, when the lamplight shines out of the window, the great trunk dimly shows, in the near darkness, like an Egyptian column, supporting some powerful mystery in the over-branching darkness. By day, it is just a tree.

It is just a tree. The chipmunks skelter a little way up it, the little black-and-white birds, tree-creepers, walk quick as mice on its rough perpendicular, tapping; the bluejays throng on its branches, high up, at dawn, and in the afternoon you hear the faintest rustle of many little wild doves alighting in its upper remoteness. It is a tree, which is still Pan.

And we live beneath it, without noticing. Yet sometimes, when one suddenly looks far up and sees those wild doves there, or when one glances quickly at the inhuman-human hammering of a woodpecker, one realizes that the tree is asserting itself as much as I am. It gives out life, as I give out life. Our two lives meet and cross one another, unknowingly: the tree's life penetrates my life, and my life the tree's. We cannot live near one another, as we do, without affecting one another.

The tree gathers up earth-power from the dark bowels of the earth, and a roaming sky-glitter from above. And all unto itself, which is a tree, woody, enormous, slow but unyielding with life, bristling with acquisitive energy, obscurely radiating some of its great strength.

It vibrates its presence into my soul, and I am with Pan. I think no man could live near a pine tree and remain quite suave and supple and compliant. Something fierce and bristling is communicated. The piny sweetness is rousing and defiant, like turpentine, the noise of the needles is keen with æons of sharpness. In the volleys of wind from the western desert, the tree hisses and resists. It does not lean eastward at all. It resists with a vast force of resistance, from within itself, and its column is a ribbed, magnificent assertion.

I have become conscious of the tree, and of its interpenetration into my life. Long ago, the Indians must have been even more acutely conscious of it, when they blazed it to leave their mark on it.

I am conscious that it helps to change me, vitally. I am even conscious that shivers of energy cross my living plasm, from the tree, and I become a degree more like unto the tree, more bristling and turpentiney, in Pan. And the tree gets a certain shade and alertness of my life, within itself.

Of course, if I like to cut myself off, and say it is all bunk, a tree is merely so much lumber not yet sawn, then in a great measure I shall *be* cut off. So much depends on one's attitude. One can shut many, many doors of receptivity in oneself; or one can open many doors that are shut.

I prefer to open my doors to the coming of the tree. Its raw earth-power and its raw sky-power; its resinous erectness and resistance, its sharpness of hissing needles and relentlessness of roots, all that goes to the primitive savageness of a pine tree, goes also to the strength of man.

Give me of your power, then, oh tree! And I will give you of mine.

And this is what men must have said, more naïvely, less sophisticatedly, in the days when all was Pan. It is what, in a way, the aboriginal Indians still say, and still *mean*, intensely: especially when they dance the sacred dance, with the tree; or with the spruce twigs tied above their elbows.

Give me your power, oh tree, to help me in my life. And I will give you my power: even symbolized in a rag torn from my clothing.

This is the oldest Pan.

Or again, I say: "Oh you, you big tree, standing so strong and swallowing juice from the earth's inner body, warmth from the sky, beware of me. Beware of me, because I am strongest. I am going to cut you down and take your life and make you into beams for my house, and into a fire. Prepare to deliver up your life to me."

Is this any less true then when the lumberman glances at a pine tree, sees if it will cut good lumber, dabs a mark or a number upon it, and goes his way absolutely without further thought or feeling? Is he truer to life? Is it truer to life to insulate oneself entirely from the influence of the tree's life, and to walk about in an inanimate forest of standing lumber, marketable in St. Louis, Mo.? Or is it truer to life to know, with a pantheistic sensuality, that the tree has its own life, its own assertive existence, its own living relatedness to me: that my life is added to, or militated against, by the tree's life?

Which is really truer?

Which is truer, to live among the living, or to run on wheels?

And who can sit with the Indians around a big camp-fire of logs, in the mountains at night, when a man rises and turns his breast and his curiously-smiling bronze face away from the blaze, and stands voluptuously warming his thighs and buttocks and loins, his back to the fire, faintly smiling the inscrutable Pan-smile into the dark trees surrounding, without hearing him say, in the Pan-voice: "Aha! Tree! Aha! Tree! Who has triumphed now? I drank the heat of your blood into my face and breast, and now I am drinking it into my loins and buttocks and legs, oh tree! I am drinking your heat right through me, oh tree! Fire is life, and I take your life for mine. I am drinking it up, oh tree, even into my buttocks. Aha! Tree! I am warm! I am strong! I am happy, tree, in this cold night in the mountains!"

And the old man, glancing up and seeing the flames flapping in flamy rags at the dark smoke, in the upper fire-hurry towards the stars and the dark spaces between the stars, sits stonily and inscrutably: yet one knows that he is saying: "Go back, oh fire! Go back like honey! Go back, honey of life, to where you came from, before you were hidden in the tree. The trees climb into the sky and steal the honey of the sun, like bears stealing from a hollow tree-trunk. But when the tree falls and is put on to the fire, the honey flames and goes straight back to where it came from. And the smell of burning pine is as the smell of honey."

So the old man says, with his lightless Indian eyes. But he is careful never to utter one word of the mystery. Speech is the death of Pan, who can but laugh and sound the reed-flute.

Is it better, I ask you, to cross the room and turn on the heat at the radiator, glancing at the thermometer and saying: "We're just a bit below the level, in here"? Then to go back to the newspaper!

What can a man do with his life but live it? And what does life consist in, save a vivid relatedness between the man and the living universe that surrounds him? Yet man insulates himself more and more into mechanism, and repudiates everything but the machine and the contrivance of which he himself is master, god in the machine.

Morning comes, and white ash lies in the fire-hollow, and the old man looks at it broodingly.

"The fire is gone," he says in the Pan silence, that is so full of unutterable things. "Look! there is no more tree. We drank his warmth, and he is gone. He is way, way off in the sky, his smoke is in the blueness, with the sweet smell of a pine-wood fire, and his yellow flame is in the sun. It is morning, with the ashes of night. There is no more tree. Tree is gone. But perhaps there is fire among the ashes. I shall blow it, and it will be alive. There is always fire, between the tree that goes and the tree that stays. One day I shall go—"

So they cook their meat, and rise, and go in silence.

There is a big rock towering up above the trees, a cliff. And silently a man glances at it. You hear him say, without speech:

"Oh, you big rock! If a man fall down from you, he dies. Don't let me fall down from you. Oh, you big pale rock, you are so still, you know lots of things. You know a lot. Help me, then, with your stillness. I go to find deer. Help me find deer."

And the man slips aside, and secretly lays a twig, or a pebble, some little object in a niche of the rock, as a pact between him and the rock. The rock will give him some of its radiant-cold stillness and enduring presence, and he makes a symbolic return, of gratitude.

Is it foolish? Would it have been better to invent a gun, to shoot his game from a great distance, so that he need not approach it with any of that living stealth and preparedness with which one live thing approaches another? Is it better to have a machine in one's hands, and so avoid the life-contact: the trouble! the pains! Is it better to see the rock as a mere nothing, not worth noticing because it has no value, and you can't eat it as you can a deer?

But the old hunter steals on, in the stillness of the eternal Pan, which is so full of soundless sounds. And in his soul he is saying: "Deer! Oh, you thin-legged deer! I am coming! Where are you, with your feet like little stones bounding down a hill? I know you. Yes, I know you. But you don't know me. You don't know where I am, and you don't know me, anyhow. But I know you. I am thinking of you. I shall get you. I've got to get you. I got to; so it will be.—I shall get you, and shoot an arrow right in you."

In this state of abstraction, and subtle, hunter's communion with the quarry—a weird psychic connexion between hunter and hunted—the man creeps into the mountains.

And even a white man who is a born hunter must fall into this state. Gun or no gun! He projects his deepest, most primitive hunter's consciousness abroad, and finds his game, not by accident, nor even chiefly by looking for signs, but primarily by a psychic attraction, a sort of telepathy: the hunter's telepathy. Then when he finds his quarry, he aims with a pure, spellbound volition. If there is no flaw in his abstracted huntsman's *will*, he cannot miss. Arrow or bullet, it flies like a movement of pure will, straight to the spot. And the deer, once she has let her quivering alertness be overmastered or stilled by the hunter's subtle, hynotic, *following* spell, she cannot escape.

This is Pan, the Pan-mystery, the Pan-power. What can men who sit at home in their studies, and drink hot milk and have lamb's-wool slippers on their feet, and write anthropology, what *can* they possibly know about men, the men of Pan?

Among the creatures of Pan there is an eternal struggle for life, between lives. Man, defenceless, rapacious man, has needed the qualities of every living thing, at one time or other. The hard, silent abidingness of rock, the surging resistance of a tree, the still evasion of a puma, the dogged earth-knowledge of the bear, the light alertness of the deer, the sky-prowling vision of the eagle: turn by turn man has needed the power of every living thing. Tree, stone, or hill, river, or little stream, or waterfall, or salmon in the fall—man can be master and complete in himself, only by assuming the living powers of each of them, as the occasion requires.

He used to make himself master by a great effort of will, and sensitive, intuitive cunning, and immense labour of body.

Then he discovered the "idea." He found that all things were related by certain *laws*. The moment man learned to abstract, he began to make engines that would do the work of his body. So, instead of concentrating upon his quarry, or upon the living things which made his universe, he concentrated upon the engines or instruments which should intervene between him and the living universe, and give him mastery.

This was the death of the great Pan. The idea and the engine came between man and all things, like a death. The old connexion, the old Allness, was severed, and can never be ideally restored. Great Pan is dead.

Yet what do we live for, except to live? Man has lived to conquer the phenomenal universe. To a great extent he has succeeded. With all the mechanism of the human world, man is to a great extent master of all life, and of most phenomena.

And what then? Once you have conquered a thing, you have lost it. Its real relation to you collapses.

A conquered world is no good to man. He sits stupefied with boredom upon his conquest.

We need the universe to live again, so that we can live with it. A conquered universe, a dead Pan, leaves us nothing to live with.

You have to abandon the conquest, before Pan will live again. You have to live to live, not to conquer. What's the good of conquering even the North Pole, if after the conquest you've nothing left but an inert fact? Better leave it a mystery.

It was better to be a hunter in the woods of Pan, than it is to be a clerk in a city store. The hunter hungered, laboured, suffered tortures of fatigue. But at least he lived in a ceaseless living relation to his surrounding universe.

At evening, when the deer was killed, he went home to the tents, and threw down the deer-meat on the swept place before the tent of his women. And the women came out to greet him softly, with a sort of reverence, as he stood before the meat, the life-stuff. He came back spent, yet full of power, bringing the life-stuff. And the children looked with black eyes at the meat, and at that wonder-being, the man, the bringer of meat.

Perhaps the children of the store-clerk look at their father with a *tiny* bit of the same mystery. And perhaps the clerk feels a fragment of the old glorification, when he hands his wife the paper dollars.

But about the tents the women move silently. Then when the cooking-fire dies low, the man crouches in silence and toasts meat on a stick, while the dogs lurk round like shadows and the children watch avidly. The man eats as the sun goes down. And as the glitter departs, he says: "Lo, the sun is going, and I stay. All goes, but still I stay. Power of deer-meat is in my belly, power of sun is in my body. I am tired, but it is with power. There the small moon gives her first sharp sign. So! So! I watch her. I will give her something; she is very sharp and bright, and I do not know her power. Lo! I will give the woman something for this moon, which troubles me above the sunset, and has power. Lo! how very curved and sharp she is! Lo! how she troubles me!"

Thus, always aware, always watchful, subtly poising himself in the world of Pan, among the powers of the living universe, he sustains his life and is sustained. There is no boredom, because *everything* is alive and active, and danger is inherent in all movement. The contact between all things is keen and wary: for wariness is also a sort of reverence, or respect. And nothing, in the world of Pan, may be taken for granted.

So when the fire is extinguished, and the moon sinks, the man says to the woman: "Oh, woman, be very soft, be very soft and deep towards me, with the deep silence. Oh, woman, do not speak and stir and wound me with the sharp horns of yourself. Let me come into the deep, soft places, the dark, soft places deep as between the stars. Oh, let me lose there the weariness of the day: let me come in the power of the night. Oh, do not speak to me, nor break the deep night of my silence and my power. Be softer than dust, and darker than any flower. Oh, woman, wonderful is the craft of your softness, the distance of your dark depths. Oh, open silently the deep that has no end, and do not turn the horns of the moon against me."

This is the might of Pan, and the power of Pan.

And still, in America, among the Indians, the oldest Pan is alive. But here, also, dying fast.

It is useless to glorify the savage. For he will kill Pan with his own hands, for the sake of a motor-car. And a bored savage, for whom Pan is dead, is the stupefied image of all boredom.

And we cannot return to the primitive life, to live in tepees and hunt with bows and arrows.

Yet live we must. And once life has been conquered, it is pretty difficult to live.

What are we going to do, with a conquered universe? The Pan relationship, which the world of man once had with all the world, was better than anything man has now. The savage, today, if you give him the chance, will become more mechanical and unliving than any civilized man. But civilized man, having conquered the universe, may as well leave off bossing it. Because when all is said and done, life itself consists in a live relatedness between man and his universe: sun, moon, stars, earth, trees, flowers, birds, animals, men, everything—and not in a "conquest" of anything by anything. Even the conquest of the air makes the world smaller, tighter, and more airless.

And whether we are a store-clerk or a bus-conductor, we can still choose between the living universe of Pan, and the mechanical conquered universe of modern humanity. The machine has no windows. But even the most mechanized human being has only got his windows nailed up, or bricked in.

HENRY ADAMS
The New Multiverse

He had been some weeks in London when he received a telegram from his brother-in-law at the Bagni di Lucca telling him that his sister had been thrown from a cab and injured, and that he had better come on. He started that night, and reached the Bagni di Lucca on the second day. Tetanus had already set in.

The last lesson—the sum and term of education—began then. He had passed through thirty years of rather varied experience without having once felt the shell of custom broken. He had never seen Nature—only her surface—the sugar-coating that she shows to youth. Flung suddenly in his face, with the harsh brutality of chance, the terror of the blow stayed by him thenceforth for life, until repetition made it more than the will could struggle with; more than he could call on himself to bear. He found his sister, a woman of forty, as gay and brilliant in the terrors of lockjaw as she had been in the careless fun of 1859, lying in bed in consequence of a miserable cab-accident that had bruised her foot. Hour by hour the muscles grew rigid, while the mind remained bright, until after ten days of fiendish torture she died in convulsions.

One has heard and read a great deal about death, and even seen a little of it, and knew by heart the thousand commonplaces of religion and poetry which seemed to deaden one's senses and veil the horror. Society being immortal, could put on immortality at will. Adams being mortal, felt only the mortality. Death took features altogether new to him, in these rich and sensuous surroundings. Nature enjoyed it, played with it, the horror added to her charm, she liked the torture, and smothered her victim with caresses. Never had one seen her so winning. The hot Italian summer brooded outside, over the market-place and the picturesque peasants, and, in the singular color of the Tuscan atmosphere, the hills and vineyards of the Apennines seemed bursting with mid-summer blood. The sick-room itself glowed with the Italian joy of life; friends filled it; no harsh northern lights pierced the soft shadows; even the dying woman shared the sense of the Italian summer, the soft, velvet air, the humor, the courage, the sensual fulness of Nature and man. She faced death, as women mostly do, bravely and even gaily, racked slowly to unconsciousness, but yielding only to violence, as a soldier sabred in battle. For many thousands of years, on these hills and plains, Nature had gone on sabring men and women with the same air of sensual pleasure.

From *The Education of Henry Adams*, Boston and New York, 1918, pp. 287-9, 379-82, 421-2, 457-61, 496-500; reprinted by permission of Houghton Mifflin Co. and Constable and Co.

Impressions like these are not reasoned or catalogued in the mind; they are felt as part of violent emotion; and the mind that feels them is a different one from that which reasons; it is thought of a different power and a different person. The first serious consciousness of Nature's gesture—her attitude towards life—took form then as a phantasm, a nightmare, an insanity of force. For the first time, the stage-scenery of the senses collapsed; the human mind felt itself stripped naked, vibrating in a void of shapeless energies, with resistless mass, colliding, crushing, wasting, and destroying what these same energies had created and labored from eternity to perfect. Society became fantastic, a vision of pantomime with a mechanical motion; and its so-called thought merged in the mere sense of life, and pleasure in the sense. The usual anodynes of social medicine became evident artifice. Stoicism was perhaps the best; religion was the most human; but the idea that any personal deity could find pleasure or profit in torturing a poor woman, by accident, with a fiendish cruelty known to man only in perverted and insane temperaments, could not be held for a moment. For pure blasphemy, it made pure atheism a comfort. God might be, as the Church said, a Substance, but He could not be a Person.

With nerves strained for the first time beyond their power of tension, he slowly travelled northwards with his friends, and stopped for a few days at Ouchy to recover his balance in a new world; for the fantastic mystery of coincidences had made the world, which he thought real, mimic and reproduce the distorted nightmare of his personal horror. He did not yet know it, and he was twenty years in finding it out; but he had need of all the beauty of the Lake below and of the Alps above, to restore the finite to its place. For the first time in his life, Mont Blanc for a moment looked to him what it was—a chaos of anarchic and purposeless forces—and he needed days of repose to see it clothe itself again with the illusions of his senses, the white purity of its snows, the splendor of its light, and the infinity of its heavenly peace.

Until the Great Exposition of 1900 closed its doors in November, Adams haunted it, aching to absorb knowledge, and helpless to find it. He would have liked to know how much of it could have been grasped by the best-informed man in the world. While he was thus meditating chaos, Langley came by, and showed it to him. At Langley's behest, the Exhibition dropped its superfluous rags and stripped itself to the skin, for Langley knew what to study, and why, and how; while Adams might as well have stood outside in the night, staring at the Milky Way. Yet Langley said nothing new, and taught nothing that one might not have learned from Lord Bacon, three hundred years before; but though one should have known the "Advancement of Science" as well as one knew the "Comedy of Errors," the literary knowledge counted for nothing until some teacher should show how to apply it. Bacon took a vast deal of trouble in teaching King James I and his subjects, American or other, towards the year 1620, that true science was the development or economy of forces; yet an elderly American in 1900 knew neither the formula nor the forces; or even so much as to say to himself that his historical business in the Exposition concerned only the economies or developments of force since 1893, when he began the study at Chicago.

Nothing in education is so astonishing as the amount of ignorance it accumulates in the form of inert facts. Adams had looked at most of the accumulations of art in the storehouses called Art Museums; yet he did not know how to look at the art exhibits of 1900. He had studied Karl Marx and his doctrines of history with profound attention, yet he could not apply them at Paris. Langley, with the ease of a great master of experiment, threw out of the field every exhibit that did not reveal a new application of force, and naturally threw out, to begin with, almost the whole art exhibit. Equally, he ignored almost the whole industrial exhibit. He led his pupil directly to the forces. His chief interest was in new motors to make his airship feasible, and he taught Adams the astonishing complexities of the new Daimler motor, and of the automobile, which, since 1893, had become a nightmare at a hundred kilometres an hour, almost as destructive as the electric tram which was only ten years older; and threatening to become as terrible as the locomotive steam-engine itself, which was almost exactly Adams's own age.

Then he showed his scholar the great hall of dynamos, and explained how little he knew about electricity or force of any kind, even of his own special sun, which spouted heat in inconceivable volume, but which, as far as he knew, might spout less or more, at any time, for all the certainty he felt in it. To him, the dynamo itself was but an ingenious channel for conveying somewhere the heat latent in a few tons of poor coal hidden in a dirty engine-house carefully kept out of sight; but to Adams the dynamo became a symbol of infinity. As he grew accustomed to the great gallery of machines, he began to feel the forty-foot dynamos as a moral force, much as the early Christians felt the Cross. The planet itself seemed less impressive, in its old-fashioned, deliberate, annual or daily revolution, than this huge wheel, revolving within arm's-length at some vertiginous speed, and barely murmuring—scarcely humming an audible warning to stand a hair's-breadth further for respect of power—while it would not wake the baby lying close against its frame. Before the end, one began to pray to it; inherited instinct taught the natural expression of man before silent and infinite force. Among the thousand symbols of ultimate energy, the dynamo was not so human as some, but it was the most expressive.

Yet the dynamo, next to the steam-engine, was the most familiar of exhibits. For Adams's objects its value lay chiefly in its occult mechanism. Between the dynamo in the gallery of machines and the engine-house outside, the break of continuity amounted to abysmal fracture for a historian's objects. No more relation could he discover between the steam and the electric current than between the Cross and the cathedral. The forces were interchangeable if not reversible, but he could see only an absolute *fiat* in electricity as in faith. Langley could not help him. Indeed, Langley seemed to be worried by the same trouble, for he constantly repeated that the new forces were anarchical, and specially that he was not responsible for the new rays, that were little short of parricidal in their wicked spirit towards science. His own rays, with which he had doubled the solar spectrum, were altogether harmless and beneficent; but Radium denied its God—or, what was to Langley the same thing, denied the truths of his Science. The force was wholly new.

A historian who asked only to learn enough to be as futile as Langley or Kelvin, made rapid progress under this teaching, and mixed himself up in the tangle of ideas until he achieved a sort of Paradise of ignorance vastly consoling to his fatigued senses. He wrapped himself in vibrations and rays which were new, and he would have hugged Marconi and Branly had he met them, as he hugged the dynamo; while he lost his arithmetic in trying to figure out the equation between the discoveries and the economies of force. The economies, like the discoveries, were absolute, supersensual, occult; incapable of expression in horse-power. What mathematical equivalent could he suggest as the value of a Branly coherer? Frozen air, or the electric furnace, had some scale of measurement, no doubt, if somebody could invent a thermometer adequate to the purpose; but X-rays had played no part whatever in man's consciousness, and the atom itself had figured only as a fiction of thought. In these seven years man had translated himself into a new universe which had no common scale of measurement with the old. He had entered a supersensual world, in which he could measure nothing except by chance collisions of movements imperceptible to his senses, perhaps even imperceptible to his instruments, but perceptible to each other, and so to some known ray at the end of the scale. Langley seemed prepared for anything, even for an indeterminable number of universes interfused—physics stark mad in metaphysics.

The work of domestic progress is done by masses of mechanical power—steam, electric, furnace, or other—which have to be controlled by a score or two of individuals who have shown capacity to manage it. The work of internal government has become the task of controlling these men, who are socially as remote as heathen gods, alone worth knowing, but never known, and who could tell nothing of political value if one skinned them alive. Most of them have nothing to tell, but are forces as dumb as their dynamos, absorbed in the development or economy of power. They are trustees for the public, and whenever society assumes the property, it must confer on them that title; but the power will remain as before, whoever manages it, and will then control society without appeal, as it controls its stokers and pit-men. Modern politics is, at bottom, a struggle not of men but of forces. The men become every year more and more creatures of force, massed about central power-houses. The conflict is no longer between the men, but between the motors that drive the men, and the men tend to succumb to their own motive forces.

The child born in 1900 would, then, be born into a new world which would not be a unity but a multiple. Adams tried to imagine it, and an education that would fit it. He found himself in a land where no one had ever penetrated before; where order was an accidental relation obnoxious to nature; artificial compulsion imposed on motion; against which every free energy of the universe revolted; and which, being merely occasional, resolved itself back into anarchy at last. He could not deny that the law of the new multiverse explained much that had been most obscure, especially the persistently fiendish treatment of man by man; the perpetual effort of society to establish law, and the perpetual revolt of society against the law it had established; the perpetual building up of authority by force, and the perpetual appeal to force to overthrow it; the perpetual symbolism of a higher law, and the perpetual relapse to a lower one; the perpetual victory of the principles of freedom, and their perpetual conversion into principles of power; but the staggering problem was the outlook ahead into the despotism of artificial order which nature abhorred. The physicists had a phrase for it, unintelligible to the vulgar: "All that we win is a battle—lost in advance—with the irreversible phenomena in the background of nature."

All that a historian won was a vehement wish to escape. He saw his education complete, and was sorry he ever began it. As a matter of taste, he greatly preferred his eighteenth-century education when God was a father and nature a mother, and all was for the best in a scientific universe. He repudiated all share in the world as it was to be, and yet he could not detect the point where his responsibility began or ended.

As history unveiled itself in the new order, man's mind had behaved like a young pearl oyster, secreting its universe to suit its conditions until it had built up a shell of *nacre* that embodied all its notions of the perfect. Man knew it was true because he made it, and he loved it for the same reason. He sacrificed millions of lives to acquire his unity, but he achieved it, and justly thought it a work of art. The woman especially did great things, creating her deities on a higher level than the male, and, in the end, compelling the man to accept the Virgin as guardian of the man's God. The man's part in his Universe was secondary, but the woman was at home there, and sacrificed herself without limit to make it habitable, when man permitted it, as sometimes happened for brief intervals of war and famine; but she could not provide protection against forces of nature. She did not think of her universe as a raft to which the limpets stuck for life in the surge of a supersensual chaos; she conceived herself and her family as the centre and flower of an ordered universe which she knew to be unity because she had made it after the image of her own fecundity; and this creation of hers was surrounded by beauties and perfections which she knew to be real because she herself had imagined them.

Even the masculine philosopher admired and loved and celebrated her triumph, and the greatest of them sang it in the noblest of his verses:—

> Alma Venus, coeli subter labentia signa
> Quae mare navigerum, quae terras frugiferenteis
> Concelebras . . . .
> Quae quoniam rerum naturam sola gubernas,
> Nec sine te quidquam dias in luminis oras
> Exoritur, neque fit laetum neque amabile quidquam;
> Te sociam studeo!

Neither man nor woman ever wanted to quit this Eden of their own invention, and could no more have done it of their own accord than the pearl oyster could quit its shell; but although the oyster might perhaps assimilate or embalm a grain of sand forced into its aperture, it could only perish in face of the cyclonic hurricane or the volcanic upheaval of its bed. Her supersensual chaos killed her.

Such seemed the theory of history to be imposed by science on the generation born after 1900. For this theory, Adams felt himself in no way responsible. Even as historian he had made it his duty always to speak with respect of everything that had ever been thought respectable—except an occasional statesman; but he had submitted to force all his life, and he meant to accept it for the future as for the past. All his efforts had been turned only to the search for its channel. He never invented his facts; they were furnished him by the only authorities he could find. As for himself, according to Helmholz, Ernst Mach, and Arthur Balfour, he was henceforth to be a conscious ball of vibrating motions, traversed in every direction by infinite lines of rotation or vibration, rolling at the feet of the Virgin at Chartres or of M. Poincaré in an attic at Paris, a centre of supersensual chaos. The discovery did not distress him. A solitary man of sixty-five years or more, alone in a Gothic cathedral or a Paris apartment, need fret himself little about a few illusions more or less. He should have learned his lesson fifty years earlier; the times had long passed when a student could stop before chaos or order; he had no choice but to march with his world.

Nevertheless, he could not pretend that his mind felt flattered by this scientific outlook. Every fabulist has told how the human mind has always struggled like a frightened bird to escape the chaos which caged it; how—appearing suddenly and inexplicably out of some unknown and unimaginable void; passing half its known life in the mental chaos of sleep; victim even when awake to its own ill-adjustment, to disease, to age, to external suggestion, to nature's compulsion; doubting its sensations, and, in the last resort, trusting only to instruments and averages—after sixty or seventy years of growing astonishment, the mind wakes to find itself looking blankly into the void of death. That it should profess itself pleased by this performance was all that the highest rules of good breeding could ask; but that it should actually be satisfied would prove that it existed only as idiocy. Satisfied, the future generation could scarcely think itself, for even when the mind existed in a universe of its own creation, it had never been quite at ease. As far as one ventured to interpret actual science, the mind had thus far adjusted itself by an infinite series of infinitely delicate adjustments forced on it by the infinite motion of an infinite chaos of motion; dragged at one moment into the unknowable and unthinkable, then trying to scramble back within its senses and to bar the chaos out, but always assimilating bits of it, until at last, in 1900, a new avalanche of unknown forces had fallen on it, which required new mental powers to control. If this view was correct, the mind could gain nothing by flight or by fight; it must merge in its supersensual multiverse, or succumb to it.

The new American—the child of incalculable coal-power, chemical power, electric power, and radiating energy, as well as of new forces yet undetermined—must be a sort of God compared with any former creation of nature. At the rate of progress since 1800, every American who lived into the year 2000 would know how to control unlimited power. He would think in complexities unimaginable to an earlier mind. He would deal with problems altogether beyond the range of earlier society. To him the nineteenth century would stand on the same plane with the fourth—equally childlike—and he would only wonder how both of them, knowing so little, and so weak in force, should have done so much. Perhaps even he might go back, in 1964, to sit with Gibbon on the steps of Ara Cœli.

Meanwhile he was getting education. With that, a teacher who had failed to educate even the generation of 1870, dared not interfere. The new forces would educate. History saw few lessons in the past that would be useful in the future; but one, at least, it did see. The attempt of the American of 1800 to educate the American of 1900 had not often been surpassed for folly; and since 1800 the forces and their complications had increased a thousand times or more. The attempt of the American of 1900 to educate the American of 2000, must be even blinder than that of the Congressman of 1800, except so far as he had learned his ignorance. During a million or two of years, every generation in turn had toiled with endless agony to attain and apply power, all the while betraying the deepest alarm and horror at the power they created. The teacher of 1900, if foolhardy, might stimulate; if foolish, might resist; if intelligent, might balance, as wise and foolish have often tried to do from the beginning; but the forces would continue to educate, and the mind would continue to react. All the teacher could hope was to teach it reaction.

Even there his difficulty was extreme. The most elementary books of science betrayed the inadequacy of old implements of thought. Chapter after chapter closed with phrases such as one never met in older literature: "The cause of this phenomenon is not understood"; "science no longer ventures to explain causes"; "the first step towards a causal explanation still remains to be taken"; "opinions are very much divided"; "in spite of the contradictions involved"; "science gets on only by adopting different theories, sometimes contradictory." Evidently the new American would need to think in contradictions, and instead of Kant's famous four antinomies, the new universe would know no law that could not be proved by its anti-law.

To educate—one's self to begin with—had been the effort of one's life for sixty years; and the difficulties of education had gone on doubling with the coal-output, until the prospect of waiting another ten years, in order to face a seventh doubling of complexities, allured one's imagination but slightly. The law of acceleration was definite, and did not require ten years more study except to show whether it held good. No scheme could be suggested to the new American, and no fault needed to be found, or complaint made; but the next great influx of new forces seemed near at hand, and its style of education promised to be violently coercive. The movement from unity into multiplicity, between 1200 and 1900, was unbroken in sequence, and rapid in acceleration. Prolonged one generation longer, it would require a new social mind. As though thought were common salt in indefinite solution it must enter a new phase subject to new laws. Thus far, since five or ten thousand years, the mind had successfully reacted, and nothing yet proved that it would fail to react—but it would need to jump.

Nearly forty years had passed since the ex-private secretary landed at New York with the ex-Ministers Adams and Motley, when they saw American society as a long caravan stretching out towards the plains. As he came up the bay again, November 5, 1904, an older man than either his father or Motley in 1868, he found the approach more striking than ever—wonderful—unlike anything man had ever seen—and like nothing he had ever much cared to see. The outline of the city became frantic in its effort to explain something that defied meaning. Power seemed to have outgrown its servitude and to have asserted its freedom. The cylinder had exploded, and thrown great masses of stone and steam against the sky. The city had the air and movement of hysteria, and the citizens were crying, in every accent of anger and alarm, that the new forces must at any cost be brought under control. Prosperity never before imagined, power never yet wielded by man, speed never reached by anything but a meteor, had made the world irritable, nervous, querulous, unreasonable and afraid. All New York was demanding new men, and all the new forces, condensed into corporations, were demanding a new type of man—a man with ten times the endurance, energy, will and mind of the old type—for whom they were ready to pay millions at sight. As one jolted over the pavements or read the last week's newspapers, the new man seemed close at hand, for the old one had plainly reached the end of his strength, and his failure had become catastrophic. Every one saw it, and every municipal election shrieked chaos. A traveller in the highways of history looked out of the club window on the turmoil of Fifth Avenue, and felt himself in Rome, under Diocletian, witnessing the anarchy, conscious of the compulsion, eager for the solution, but unable to conceive whence the next impulse was to come or how it was to act. The two-thousand-years failure of Christianity roared upward from Broadway, and no Constantine the Great was in sight.

F. T. MARINETTI

The Joy of Mechanical Force

We have been up all night, my friends and I, beneath mosque lamps whose copper domes, as open-worked as our souls, yet had electric hearts. And, while we trod our native sloth into opulent Persian carpets, we carried our discussion to the farthest limits of logic and covered sheets of paper with insane scrawls.

A vast pride swelled in our breasts, to feel ourselves standing alone, like light-houses or advanced guards, facing the army of enemy stars that camp in heavenly bivouacs. Alone with the greasers in the infernal engine-rooms of great ships, alone with the dark phantoms that rummage in the red bellies of bewitched loco-motives, alone with the drunks fluttering, battering their wings against the walls!

And unexpectedly, like festive villages that the Po in flood suddenly unsettles and uproots to sweep them off, over the falls and eddies of a deluge, to the sea, we were disturbed by the rumbling of enormous double-decker trams, passing in fits and starts, streaked with lights.

"The Foundation of Futurism" ["Manifesto of Futurism," 1909], translated from the French by Eugen Weber; reprinted by permission of Dodd, Mead and Company from *Paths to the Present* by Eugen Weber. Copyright © 1960 by Dodd, Mead and Company, Inc.

Then the silence got worse. As we listened to the exhausted prayer of the old canal and heard the grating bones of palaces moribund in their greenery whiskers, all of a sudden hungry cars roared beneath our windows.

"Come," I said, "my friends! Let us go! At last Mythology and the mystic Ideal have been surpassed. We shall witness the birth of the Centaur and, soon, we'll see the first Angels fly! We must shake the gates of life to test the hinges and the locks! . . . Let us go! This is truly the first sun that dawns above the earth! Nothing equals the splendor of our red sword battling for the first time in the millennial gloom."

We approached the three snuffling machines to stroke their breasts. I stretched out on mine like a corpse in my coffin, but suddenly awoke beneath the steering wheel—blade of a guillotine—that threatened my stomach.

The great broom of folly tore us from ourselves and swept us through the streets, precipitous and profound like dry torrent beds. Here and there, unhappy lamps in windows taught us to despise our mathematical eyes.

"The scent," I cried, "the scent suffices for wild beasts!"

And we pursued, alike to young lions, Death of the dark fur spotted with pale crosses, that slipped ahead of us in the vast mauve sky, palpable and alive.

And yet we had no ideal Mistress high as the clouds, no cruel Queen to whom to offer our corpses twisted into Byzantine rings! Nothing to die for besides the desire to rid ourselves of our too weighty courage!

We went on, crushing the watchdogs on the thresholds of houses, leaving them flattened under our tires like a collar under the iron. Cajoling Death preceded me on every curve, offering her pretty paw and, by turns, lying flat with a jarring clamp of jaws to throw me velvety looks from the depths of puddles.

"Let us abandon Wisdom like a hideous vein-stone and enter like pride-spiced fruit into the vast maw of the wind! Let us give ourselves to the Unknown to eat, not for despair, but simply to enrich the unplumbable wells of Absurdity!"

As I spoke these words, I veered suddenly upon myself with the drunken folly of poodles chasing their own tail and there, at once, were two disapproving cyclists, reeling before me like two persuasive and yet contradictory arguments. Their inane undulations scanned over my ground. . . . What a bore! Phooey! . . . I cup off sharply and, in disgust, I pitched—bang!—into a ditch. . . .

Ah! motherly ditch, half full of muddy water! Factory ditch! I tasted by mouthfuls your bracing slime that recalls the saintly black breast of my Sudanese nurse!

As I rose, a shiny, stinking gadabout, I felt the red-hot iron of joy deliciously pierce my heart.

A crowd of fishermen and gouty naturalists had gathered in terror around the prodigy. Patient and meddlesome, they raised high above great iron casting nets to fish out my car that lay like a great mired shark. It emerged slowly, leaving behind in the ditch like scales, its heavy body of common sense, and its padding of comfort.

They thought my good shark dead, but I awoke it with a single caress on its all-powerful rump and there it was, revived, running full speech ahead upon its fins.

Then, face hidden by the good factory slime, covered by metal dross, by useless sweat and heavenly soot, carrying out crushed arms in a sling, amid the plaints of prudent fishermen and distressed naturalists, we dictated our first wills to all the *living* men on earth:

FUTURISTIC MANIFESTO

1. We want to sing the love of danger, the habit of danger and of temerity.

2. The essential elements of our poetry will be courage, daring, and revolt.

3. Literature having up to now magnified thoughtful immobility, ecstasy, and sleep, we want to exalt the aggressive gesture, the feverish insomnia, the athletic step, the perilous leap, the box on the ear, and the fisticuff.

4. We declare that the world's wonder has been enriched by a fresh beauty: the beauty of speed. A racing car with its trunk adorned by great exhaust pipes like snakes with an explosive breath . . . a roaring car that seems to be driving under shrapnel, is more beautiful than the *Victory of Samothrace*.

5. We want to sing the man who holds the steering wheel, whose ideal stem pierces the Earth, itself launched on the circuit of its orbit.

6. The poet must expend himself with warmth, refulgence, and prodigality, to increase the enthusiastic fervor of the primordial elements.

7. There is no more beauty except in struggle. No masterpiece without an aggressive character. Poetry must be a violent attack against the unknown forces, summoning them to lie down before man.

8. We stand on the far promontory of centuries! . . . What is the use of looking behind us, since our task is to smash the mysterious portals of the impossible? Time and Space died yesterday. We live already in the absolute, since we have already created the eternal omnipresent speed.

9. We want to glorify war—the only hygiene of the world—militarism, patriotism, the anarchist's destructive gesture, the fine Ideas that kill, and the scorn of woman.

10. We want to demolish museums, libraries, fight against moralism, feminism, and all opportunistic and utilitarian cowardices.

11. We shall sing the great crowds tossed about by work, by pleasure, or revolt; the many-colored and polyphonic surf of revolutions in modern capitals; the nocturnal vibration of the arsenals and the yards under their violent electrical moons; the gluttonous railway stations swallowing smoky serpents; the factories hung from the clouds by the ribbons of their smoke; the bridges leaping like athletes hurled over the diabolical cutlery of sunny rivers; the adventurous steamers that sniff the horizon; the broad-chested locomotives, prancing on the rails like great steel horses curbed by long pipes, and the gliding flight of airplanes whose propellers snap like a flag in the wind, like the applause of an enthusiastic crowd.

It is in Italy that we launch this manifesto of tumbling and incendiary violence, this manifesto through which today we set up *Futurism*, because we want to deliver Italy from its gangrene of professors, of archaeologists, of guides, and of antiquarians.

Italy has been too long a great secondhand brokers' market. We want to rid it of the innumerable museums that cover it with innumerable cemeteries.

Museums, cemeteries! . . . Truly identical in the sinister jostling of bodies that do not know each other. Great public dormitories where one sleeps forever side by side with beings hated or unknown. Reciprocal ferocity of painters and of sculptors killing each other with line and color in the same gallery.

They can be visited once a year as the dead are visited once a year. . . . We can accept that much! We can even conceive that flowers may once a year be left for *la Gioconda!* . . . But we cannot admit that our sorrows, our fragile courage, our anxiety may be taken through there every day! . . . Do you want to be poisoned? Do you want to rot?

What can one find in an old painting beside the embarrassing contortions of the artist trying to break the barriers that are impassable to his desire to wholly express his dream?

To admire an old painting is to pour our sensitiveness into a funeral urn, instead of throwing it forward by violent casts of creation and action. Do you mean thus to waste the best of you in a useless admiration of the past that must necessarily leave you exhausted, lessened, trampled?

As a matter of fact the daily frequentation of museums, of libraries and of academies (those cemeteries of wasted efforts, those calvaries of crucified dreams, those catalogues of broken impulses! . . .) is for the artist what the prolonged tutelage of parents is for intelligent young men, drunk with their talent and their ambitious will.

For the dying, the invalid, the prisoner, it will do. Since the future is forbidden them, there may be a salve for their wounds in the wonderful past. . . . But we want nothing of it—we the young, the strong, the living *Futurists!*

Let the good incendiaries come with their carbonized fingers! . . . Here they are! Here they are! . . . Set the library stacks on fire! Turn the canals in their course to flood the museum vaults! . . . There go the glorious canvases, floating adrift! Take up the picks and the hammers! Undermine the foundations of the venerable cities!

The oldest among us are not yet thirty; this means that we have at least ten years to carry out our task. When we are forty, let those younger and more valiant than we kindly throw us into the waste basket like useless manuscripts! . . . They will come after us from afar, from everywhere, prancing on the light rhythm of their first poems, clawing the air with their crooked fingers, sniffing at academy gates the good scent of our rotting intellects already intended for the catacombs of libraries.

But we shall not be there. They will find us at last, on some winter night, out in the country, under a sad hangar on which the monotonous rain strums, crouching by our trembling planes, warming our hands over the miserable fire of our books of today gaily blazing under the scintillating flight of their images.

They will gather in a mob around us, panting with anguish and spite, and all exasperated by our untiring courage will bound forward to kill us with the more hatred for the love and admiration in their hearts. And Injustice, strong and wholesome, will glitter radiantly in their eyes. For art can be nothing but violence, cruelty and injustice.

The oldest among us are not yet thirty and yet we have already squandered great treasures, treasures of energy, of love, of courage and eager will, hastily, deliriously, countlessly, breathlessly, with both hands.

Look at us! We are not out of breath. . . . Our heart is not in the least tired! For it feeds on fire, on hatred, on speed! . . . You find it surprising? That is because you do not even remember having lived!—Up on the crest of the world, once more we hurl our challenge to the stars!

Your objections? Enough! Enough! I know them! Fair enough! We know well enough what our fine, false intelligence asserts.—We are only, it says, the summary and the extension of our forebears.—Perhaps! Let it be so! . . . What does it matter? . . . But we don't want to listen! Beware of repeating these infamous words! Rather, look up!

Up on the crest of the world, once more we hurl our challenge to the stars!

D. H. LAWRENCE

The Physics of Human Character

I don't agree with you about *The Wedding Ring*. You will find that in a while you will like the book as a whole. I don't think the psychology is wrong: it is only that I have a different attitude to my characters, and that necessitates a different attitude in you, which you are not prepared to give. As for its being my *cleverness* which would pull the thing through—that sounds odd to me, for I don't think I am so very clever, in that way. I think the book is a bit futuristic— quite unconsciously so. But when I read Marinetti—"the profound intuitions of life added one to the other, word by word, according to their illogical conception, will give us the general lines of an intuitive physiology of matter"—I see something of what I am after. I translate him clumsily, and his Italian is obfuscated— and I don't care about physiology of matter—but somehow—that which is physic— non-human, in humanity, is more interesting to me than the old-fashioned human element—which causes one to conceive a character in a certain moral scheme and make him consistent. The certain moral scheme is what I object to. In Turgenev, and in Tolstoi, and in Dostoievsky, the moral scheme into which all the characters fit—and it is nearly the same scheme—is, whatever the extraordinariness of the characters themselves, dull, old, dead. When Marinetti writes: "It is the solidity of a blade of steel that is interesting by itself, that is, the incomprehending and inhuman alliance of its molecules in resistance to, let us say, a bullet. The heat of a piece of wood or iron is in fact more passionate, for us, than the laughter or tears of a woman"—then I know what he means. He is stupid, as an artist, for contrasting the heat of the iron and the laugh of the woman. Because what is interesting in the laugh of the woman is the same as the binding of the molecules of steel or their action in heat; it is the inhuman will, call it physiology, or like Marinetti—physiology of matter, that fascinates me. I don't so much care about what the woman *feels*—in the ordinary usage of the word. That

Letter to Edward Garnett [June 5, 1914], *Collected Letters of D. H. Lawrence*, ed. by Harry T. Moore, New York, 1962, Vol. I, pp. 281-2; reprinted by permission of The Viking Press Inc., Lawrence Pollinger Ltd., and the Estate of the late Mrs. Frieda Lawrence.

presumes an *ego* to feel with. I only care about what the woman *is*—what she *is*—inhumanly, physiologically, materially—according to the use of the word: but for me, what she *is* as a phenomenon (or as representing some greater, inhuman will), instead of what she feels according to the human conception. That is where the futurists are stupid. Instead of looking for the new human phenomenon, they will only look for the phenomena of the science of physics to be found in human beings. They are crassly stupid. But if anyone would give them eyes, they would pull the right apples off the tree, for their stomachs are true in appetite. You mustn't look in my novel for the old stable *ego*—of the character. There is another *ego*, according to whose action the individual is unrecognisable, and passes through, as it were, allotropic states which it needs a deeper sense than any we've been used to exercise, to discover are states of the same single radically unchanged element. (Like as diamond and coal are the same pure single element of carbon. The ordinary novel would trace the history of the diamond—but I say, "Diamond, what! This is carbon." And my diamond might be coal or soot, and my theme is carbon.) You must not say my novel is shaky—it is not perfect, because I am not expert in what I want to do. But it is the real thing, say what you like. And I shall get my reception, if not now, then before long. Again I say, don't look for the development of the novel to follow the lines of certain characters: the characters fall into the form of some other rhythmic form, as when one draws a fiddle-bow across a fine tray delicately sanded, the sand takes lines unknown.

WILLIAM JAMES

Pluralism, Pragmatism, and Instrumental Truth

What at bottom is meant by calling the universe many or by calling it one?

Pragmatically interpreted, pluralism or the doctrine that it is many means only that the sundry parts of reality *may be externally related*. Everything you can think of, however vast or inclusive, has on the pluralistic view a genuinely "external" environment of some sort or amount. Things are "with" one another in many ways, but nothing includes everything, or dominates over everything. The word "and" trails along after every sentence. Something always escapes. "Ever not quite" has to be said of the best attempts made anywhere in the universe at attaining all-inclusiveness. The pluralistic world is thus more like a federal republic than like an empire or a kingdom. However much may be collected, however much may report itself as present at any effective centre of consciousness or action, something else is self-governed and absent and unreduced to unity.

Monism, on the other hand, insists that when you come down to reality as such, to the reality of realities, everything is present to *everything* else in one vast instantaneous co-implicated completeness—nothing can in *any* sense, functional or substantial, be really absent from anything else, all things interpenetrate and telescope together in the great total conflux.

For pluralism, all that we are required to admit as the constitution of reality is what we ourselves find empirically realized in every minimum of finite life. Briefly it is this, that nothing real is absolutely simple, that every smallest bit of experience is a *multum in parvo* plurally related, that each relation is one aspect, character, or function, way of its being taken, or way of its taking something else; and that a bit of reality when actively engaged in one of these relations is not *by that very fact* engaged in all the other relations simultaneously. The relations are not *all* what the French call *solidaires* with one another. Without losing its identity a thing can either take up or drop another thing, like the log I spoke of, which by taking up new carriers and dropping old ones can travel anywhere with a light escort.

For monism, on the contrary, everything, whether we realize it or not, drags the whole universe along with itself and drops nothing. The log starts and arrives with all its carriers supporting it. If a thing were once disconnected, it could

From *A Pluralistic Universe*, New York, 1909, pp. 321-4, and *Pragmatism: A New Name for Some Old Ways of Thinking* [1907], New York, 1909, pp. 52-61; reprinted by permission of Longmans, Green & Co., Ltd. and Paul R. Reynolds Inc.

never be connected again, according to monism. The pragmatic difference between the two systems is thus a definite one. It is just thus, that if *a* is once out of sight of *b* or out of touch with it, or, more briefly, "out" of it at all, then, according to monism, it must always remain so, they can never get together; whereas pluralism admits that on another occasion they may work together, or in some way be connected again. Monism allows for no such things as "other occasions" in reality—in *real* or absolute reality, that is.

———————

Metaphysics has usually followed a very primitive kind of quest. You know how men have always hankered after unlawful magic, and you know what a great part in magic *words* have always played. If you have his name, or the formula of incantation that binds him, you can control the spirit, genie, afrite, or whatever the power may be. Solomon knew the names of all the spirits, and having their names, he held them subject to his will. So the universe has always appeared to the natural mind as a kind of enigma, of which the key must be sought in the shape of some illuminating or power-bringing word or name. That word names the universe's *principle*, and to possess it is after a fashion to possess the universe itself. "God," "Matter," "Reason," "the Absolute," "Energy," are so many solving names. You can rest when you have them. You are at the end of your metaphysical quest.

But if you follow the pragmatic method, you cannot look on any such word as closing your quest. You must bring out of each word its practical cash-value, set it at work within the stream of your experience. It appears less as a solution, then, than as a program for more work, and more particularly as an indication of the ways in which existing realities may be *changed*.

Theories thus become instruments, not answers to enigmas, in which we can rest. We don't lie back upon them, we move forward, and, on occasion, make nature over again by their aid. Pragmatism unstiffens all our theories, limbers them up and sets each one at work. Being nothing essentially new, it harmonizes with many ancient philosophic tendencies. It agrees with nominalism for instance, in always appealing to particulars; with utilitarianism in emphasizing practical aspects; with positivism in its disdain for verbal solutions, useless questions and metaphysical abstractions.

All these, you see, are *anti-intellectualist* tendencies. Against rationalism as a pretension and a method pragmatism is fully armed and militant. But, at the outset, at least, it stands for no particular results. It has no dogmas, and no doctrines save its method. . . . [But] the word pragmatism has come to be used in a still wider sense, as meaning also a certain *theory of truth*. . . .

One of the most successfully cultivated branches of philosophy in our time is what is called inductive logic, the study of the conditions under which our sciences have evolved. Writers on this subject have begun to show a singular unanimity as to what the laws of nature and elements of fact mean, when formulated by mathematicians, physicists and chemists. When the first mathematical, logical, and natural uniformities, the first *laws*, were discovered, men were so carried away by the clearness, beauty and simplification that resulted, that they believed themselves to have deciphered authentically the eternal thoughts of the Almighty. His mind also thundered and reverberated in syllogisms. He also thought in conic sections, squares and roots and ratios, and geometrized like Euclid. He made Kepler's laws for the planets to follow; he made velocity increase proportionally to the time in falling bodies; he made the law of the sines for light to obey when refracted; he established the classes, orders, families and genera of plants and animals, and fixed the distances between them. He thought the archetypes of all things, and devised their variations; and when we rediscover any one of these his wondrous institutions, we seize his mind in its very literal intention.

But as the sciences have developed farther, the notion has gained ground that most, perhaps all, of our laws are only approximations. The laws themselves, moreover, have grown so numerous that there is no counting them; and so many rival formulations are proposed in all the branches of science that investigators have become accustomed to the notion that no theory is absolutely a transcript of reality, but that any one of them may from some point of view be useful. Their great use is to summarize old facts and to lead to new ones. They are only a man-made language, a conceptual shorthand, as some one calls them, in which we write our reports of nature; and languages, as is well known, tolerate much choice of expression and many dialects.

Thus human arbitrariness has driven divine necessity from scientific logic. If I mention the names of Sigwart, Mach, Ostwald, Pearson, Milhaud, Poincaré, Duhem, Ruyssen, those of you who are students will easily identify the tendency I speak of, and will think of additional names.

Riding now on the front of this wave of scientific logic Messrs. Schiller and Dewey appear with their pragmatistic account of what truth everywhere signifies. Everywhere, these teachers say, "truth" in our ideas and beliefs means the same thing that it means in science. It means, they say, nothing but this, *that ideas (which themselves are but parts of our experience) become true just in so far as they help us to get into satisfactory relation with other parts of our experience*, to summarize them and get about among them by conceptual short-cuts instead of following the interminable succession of particular phenomena. Any idea upon which we can ride, so to speak; any idea that will carry us prosperously from any one part of our experience to any other part, linking things satisfactorily, working securely, simplifying, saving labor; is true for just so much, true in so far forth, true *instrumentally*. This is the "instrumental" view of truth taught so successfully at Chicago, the view that truth in our ideas means their power to "work," promulgated so brilliantly at Oxford.

Messrs. Dewey, Schiller and their allies, in reaching this general conception of all truth, have only followed the example of geologists, biologists and philologists. In the establishment of these other sciences, the successful stroke was always to take some simple process actually observable in operation—as denudation by weather, say, or variation from parental type, or change of dialect by incorporation of new words and pronunciations—and then to generalize it, making it apply to all times, and produce great results by summating its effects through the ages.

The observable process which Schiller and Dewey particularly singled out for generalization is the familiar one by which any individual settles into *new opinions*. The process here is always the same. The individual has a stock of old opinions already, but he meets a new experience that puts them to a strain. Somebody contradicts them; or in a reflective moment he discovers that they contradict each other; or he hears of facts with which they are incompatible; or desires arise in him which they cease to satisfy. The result is an inward trouble to which his mind till then had been a stranger, and from which he seeks to escape by modifying his previous mass of opinions. He saves as much of it as he can, for in this matter of belief we are all extreme conservatives. So he tries to change first this opinion, and then that (for they resist change very variously), until at last some new idea comes up which he can graft upon the ancient stock with a minimum of disturbance of the latter, some idea that mediates between the stock and the new experience and runs them into one another most felicitously and expediently.

This new idea is then adopted as the true one. It preserves the older stock of truths with a minimum of modification, stretching them just enough to make them admit the novelty, but conceiving that in ways as familiar as the case leaves possible. An *outrée* explanation, violating all our preconceptions, would never pass for a true account of a novelty. We should scratch round industriously till we found something less eccentric. The most violent revolutions in an individual's beliefs leave most of his old order standing. Time and space, cause and effect, nature and history, and one's own biography remain untouched. New truth is always a go-between, a smoother-over of transitions.

JOHN DEWEY

Thought as a Natural Event

The occurrence of reflection is crucial for dualistic metaphysics as well as for idealistic ontologies. Reflection occurs only in situations qualified by uncertainty, alternatives, questioning, search, hypotheses, tentative trials or experiments which test the worth of thinking. A naturalistic metaphysics is bound to consider reflection as itself a natural event occurring *within* nature because of traits of the latter. It is bound to inference from the empirical traits of thinking in precisely the same way as the sciences make inferences from the happening of suns, radioactivity, thunder-storms or any other natural event. Traits of reflection are as truly indicative or evidential of the traits of *other* things as are the traits of these events. A theory of the nature of the occurrence and career of a sun reached by denial of the obvious traits of the sun, or by denial that these traits are so connected with the traits of other natural events that they can be used as evidence concerning the nature of these other things, would hardly possess scientific standing. Yet philosophers, and strangely enough philosophers who call themselves realists, have constantly held that the traits which are characteristic of thinking, namely, uncertainty, ambiguity, alternatives, inquiring, search, selection, experimental reshaping of external conditions, do not possess the same existential character as do the objects of valid knowledge. They have denied that these traits are

From *Experience and Nature*, Chicago and London, 1925, pp. 68-77; reprinted by permission of Open Court Publishing Company.

evidential of the character of the world within which thinking occurs. They have not, as realists, asserted that these traits are mere appearances; but they have often asserted and implied that such things are only personal or psychological in contrast with a world of objective nature. But the interests of empirical and denotative method and of naturalistic metaphysics wholly coincide. The world must actually be such as to generate ignorance and inquiry; doubt and hypothesis, trial and temporal conclusions; the latter being such that they develop out of existences which while wholly "real" are not as satisfactory, as good, or as significant, as those into which they are eventually re-organized. The ultimate evidence of genuine hazard, contingency, irregularity and indeterminateness in nature is thus found in the occurrence of thinking. The traits of natural existence which generate the fears and adorations of superstitious barbarians generate the scientific procedures of disciplined civilization. The superiority of the latter does not consist in the fact that they are based on "real" existence, while the former depend wholly upon a human nature different from nature in general. It consists in the fact that scientific inquiries reach *objects* which are better, because reached by method which controls them and which adds greater control to life itself, method which mitigates accident, turns contingency to account, and releases thought and other forms of endeavor.

The conjunction of problematic and determinate characters in nature renders every existence, as well as every idea and human act, an experiment in fact, even though not in design. To be intelligently experimental is but to be conscious of this intersection of natural conditions so as to profit by it instead of being at its mercy. The Christian idea of this world and this life as a probation is a kind of distorted recognition of the situation; distorted because it applied wholesale to one stretch of existence in contrast with another, regarded as original and final. But in truth anything which can exist at any place and at any time occurs subject to tests imposed upon it by surroundings, which are only in part compatible and reinforcing. These surroundings test its strength and measure its endurance. As we can discourse of change only in terms of velocity and acceleration which involves relations to other things, so assertion of the permanent and enduring is comparative. The stablest thing we can speak of is not free from conditions set to it by other things. That even the solid earth mountains, the emblems of constancy, appear and disappear like the clouds is an old theme of moralists and poets. The fixed and unchanged being of the Democritean atom is now reported by inquirers to possess some of the traits of his non-being, and to embody a temporary equilibrium in the economy of nature's compromises and adjustment. A thing may endure *secula seculorum* and yet not be everlasting; it will crumble before the gnawing tooth of time, as it exceeds a certain measure. Every existence is an event.

This fact is nothing at which to repine and nothing to gloat over. It is something to be noted and used. If it is discomfiting when applied to good things, to our friends, possessions and precious selves, it is consoling also to know that no evil endures forever; that the longest lane turns sometime, and that the memory of loss of nearest and dearest grows dim in time. The eventful character of all existences is no reason for consigning them to the realm of mere appearance any more than it is a reason for idealizing flux into a deity. The important thing is measure, relation, ratio, knowledge of the comparative tempos of change. In mathematics some variables are constants in some problems; so it is in nature and life. The rate of change of some things is so slow, or is so rhythmic, that these changes have all the advantages of stability in dealing with more transitory and irregular happenings—if we know enough. Indeed, if any one thing that concerns us is subject to change, it is fortunate that all other things change. A thing "absolutely" stable and unchangeable would be out of the range of the principle of action and reaction, of resistance and leverage as well as of friction. Here it would have no applicability, no potentiality of use as measure and control of other events. To designate the slower and the regular rhythmic events structure, and more rapid and irregular ones process, is sound practical sense. It expresses the function of one in respect to the other.

But spiritualistic idealism and materialism alike treat this relational and functional distinction as something fixed and absolute. One doctrine finds structure in a framework of ideal forms, the other finds it in matter. They agree in supposing that structure has some superlative reality. This supposition is another form taken by preference for the stable over the precarious and uncompleted. The fact is that all structure is structure *of* something; anything defined as structure is a character of *events*, not something intrinsic and *per se*. A set of traits is called structure, because of its limiting function in relation to other traits of events. A house has a structure; in comparison with the disintegration and collapse that would occur without its presence, this structure is fixed. Yet it is not something external to which the changes involved in building and using the house have to submit. It is rather an arrangement of changing events such that properties which change slowly, limit and direct a series of quick changes and give them an order which they do not otherwise possess. Structure is constancy of means, of things used for consequences, not of things taken by themselves or absolutely. Structure is what makes construction possible and cannot be discovered or defined except in some realized construction, construction being, of course, an evident order of changes. The isolation of structure from the changes whose stable ordering it is, renders it mysterious—something that is metaphysical in the popular sense of the word, a kind of ghostly queerness.

The "matter" of materialists and the "spirit" of idealists is a creature similar to the constitution of the United States in the minds of unimaginative persons. Obviously the real constitution is certain basic relationships among the activities of the citizens of the country; it is a property or phase of these processes, so connected with them as to influence their rate and direction of change. But by literalists it is often conceived of as something external to them; in itself fixed, a rigid framework to which *all* changes must accommodate themselves. Similarly what we call matter is that character of natural events which is so tied up with changes that are sufficiently rapid to be perceptible as to give the latter a characteristic rhythmic order, the causal sequence. It is no cause or source of events or processes; no absolute monarch; no principle of explanation; no substance behind or underlying changes—save in that sense of substance in which a man well fortified with this world's goods, and hence able to maintain himself through vicissitudes of surroundings, is a man of substance. The name designates a character in operation, not an entity.

That structure, whether of the kind called material or of the kind summed up in the word mental, is stable or permanent relationally and in its office, may be shown in another way. There is no action without reaction; there is no exclusively one-way exercise of conditioning power, no mode of regulation that operates wholly from above to below or from within outwards or from without inwards. Whatever influences the changes of other things is itself changed. The idea of an activity proceeding only in one direction, of an unmoved mover, is a survival of Greek physics. It has been banished from science, but remains to haunt philosophy. The vague and mysterious properties assigned to mind and matter, the very conceptions of mind and matter in traditional thought, are ghosts walking underground. The notion of matter actually found in the practice of science has nothing in common with the matter of materialists—and almost everybody is still a materialist as to matter, to which he merely adds a second rigid structure which he calls mind. The matter of science is a character of natural events and changes as they change; their character of regular and stable order.

Natural events are so complex and varied that there is nothing surprising in their possession of different characterizations, characters so different that they can be easily treated as opposites.

Nothing but unfamiliarity stands in the way of thinking of both mind and matter as different characters of natural events, in which matter expresses their sequential order, and mind the order of their meanings in their logical connections and dependencies. Processes may be eventful for functions which taken in abstract separation are at opposite poles, just as physiological processes eventuate in both anabolic and katabolic functions. The idea that matter and mind are two sides or "aspects" of the same things, like the convex and the concave in a curve, is literally unthinkable.

A curve is an intelligible object and concave and convex are defined in terms of this object; they are indeed but names for properties involved in its meaning. We do not start with convexity and concavity as two independent things and then set up an unknown *tertium quid* to unite two disparate things. In spite of the literal absurdity of the comparison, it may be understood however in a way which conveys an inkling of the truth. That to which both mind and matter belong is the complex of events that constitute nature. This becomes a mysterious *tertium quid*, incapable of designation, only when mind and matter are taken to be static structures instead of functional characters. It is a plausible prediction that if there were an interdict placed for a generation upon the use of mind, matter, consciousness as nouns, and we were obliged to employ adjectives and adverbs, conscious and consciously, mental and mentally, material and physically, we should find many of our problems much simplified.

We have selected only a few of the variety of the illustrations that might be used in support of the idea that the significant problems and issues of life and philosophy concern the rate and mode of the conjunction of the precarious and the assured, the incomplete and the finished, the repetitious and the varying, the safe and sane and the hazardous. If we trust to the evidence of experienced things, these traits, and the modes and tempos of their interaction with each other, are fundamental features of natural existence. The experience of their various consequences, according as they are relatively isolated, unhappily or happily combined, is evidence that wisdom, and hence that love of wisdom which is philosophy, is concerned with choice and administration of their proportioned union. Structure and process, substance and accident, matter and energy, permanence and flux, one and many, continuity and discreteness, order and progress, law and liberty, uniformity and growth, tradition and innovation, rational will and impelling desires, proof and discovery, the actual and the possible, are names given to various phases of their conjunction, and the issue of living depends upon the art with which these things are adjusted to each other.

While metaphysics may stop short with noting and registering these traits, man is not contemplatively detached from them. They involve him in his perplexities and troubles, and are the source of his joys and achievements. The situation is not indifferent to man, because it forms man as a desiring, striving, thinking, feeling creature. It is not egotism that leads man from contemplative registration of these traits to interest in managing them, to intelligence and purposive art. Interest, thinking, planning, striving, consummation and frustration are a drama enacted by these forces and conditions. A particular choice may be arbitrary; this is only to say that it does not approve itself to reflection. But choice is not arbitrary, not in a universe like this one, a world which is not finished and which has not consistently made up its mind where it is going and what it is going to do. Or, if we call it arbitrary, the arbitrariness is not ours but that of existence itself. And to call existence arbitrary or by any moral name, whether disparaging or honorific, is to patronize nature. To assume an attitude of condescension toward existence is perhaps a natural human compensation for the straits of life. But it is an ultimate source of the covert, uncandid and cheap in philosophy. This compensatory disposition it is which forgets that reflection exists to guide choice and effort. Hence its love of wisdom is but an unlaborious transformation of existence by dialectic, instead of an opening and enlarging of the ways of nature in man. A true wisdom, devoted to the latter task, discovers in thoughtful observation and experiment the method of administering the unfinished processes of existence so that frail goods shall be substantiated, secure goods be extended, and the precarious promises of good that haunt experienced things be more liberally fulfilled.

WERNER HEISENBERG

Non-Objective Science and Uncertainty

In the nineteenth century nature still appeared as a set of laws in space and time in which man and man's intervention in nature could be ignored in principle, if not in practice.

Matter was thought of in terms of its mass, which remained constant through all changes, and which required forces to move it. Because, from the eighteenth century onwards, chemical experiments could be classified and explained by the

From The Physicist's Conception of Nature [1955] by Werner Heisenberg, translated by Arnold J. Pomerans, New York, 1958, pp. 12-16, 28-9, 33-41. © 1955 by Rowohlt Taschenbuch Verlag, GmbH; © 1958 by Hutchinson & Co. Ltd. Reprinted by permission of Harcourt, Brace & World, Inc. and Hutchinson & Company, Ltd.

atomic hypothesis of ancient times, it appeared reasonable to take over the view of ancient philosophy that atoms were the real substance, the immutable building-stones of matter. Just as in the philosophy of Democritus, the differences in material qualities were considered to be merely apparent; smell or colour, temperature or viscosity, were not actual qualities of matter but resulted from the interaction of matter and our senses, and had to be explained by the arrangements and movements of atoms, and by the effect of these arrangements on our minds. It is thus that there arose the over-simplified world-view of nineteenth-century materialism: atoms move in space and time as the real and immutable substances, and it is their arrangement and motion that create the colourful phenomena of the world of our senses. . . .

The first, but not yet very dangerous, incursion into this world-view took place in the second half of the last century with the development of the theory of electricity, in which not matter but fields of force were considered to be the real explanation. Interactions between fields of force without any matter to propagate the force were very much more difficult to understand than the materialist picture of atomic physics, and introduced an element of abstraction and a lack of clarity into what appeared otherwise to be so reasonable a world-view. Attempts were not lacking to return once more to the simpler concepts of materialist philosophy by way of the ether, which was supposed to be an elastic medium transmitting these fields of force; yet no such attempt had any real success. Even so, one could take comfort from the fact that changes in the fields of force could still be considered as processes in space and time, and that they could be described objectively, *i.e.*, without any reference to the manner in which they were observed, and thus in accordance with the generally held idealized view of laws of space and time. Furthermore, fields of force, *i.e.*, forces which can only be observed by their effect on atoms, could be considered as produced by atoms, and so as explaining atomic movements in some way. Thus atoms still remained as the actual essence, and between them there was empty space, real only inasmuch as it was a transmitter of fields of force.

In this world-view it did not matter overmuch that after the discovery of radioactivity at the end of the last century, the atoms of chemistry could no longer be considered as the ultimate indivisible building-stones of matter. These were now thought to consist of three kinds of basic units—the protons, neutrons and electrons of today. The practical consequences of this new knowledge have been the transmutation of elements and the rise of atomic physics, and they have thus become extremely important. Basically, however, nothing has been changed in principle by our acceptance of protons, neutrons and electrons as the smallest building-stones of matter, if we interpret these as the real essence. What is important for the materialistic world-view is simply the possibility that such small building-stones of elementary particles exist and that they may be considered the ultimate objective reality. Thus, the well-constructed world-view of the nineteenth and early twentieth centuries was preserved, and thanks to its simplicity it managed to retain its full power of conviction for a number of decades.

But in our century it is just in this sphere that fundamental changes have taken place in the basis of atomic physics which have made us abandon the world-view of ancient atomic philosophy. It has become clear that the desired objective reality of the elementary particles is too crude an over-simplification of what really happens, and that it must give way to very much more abstract conceptions. For if we wish to form a picture of the nature of these elementary particles, we can no longer ignore the physical processes through which we obtain our knowledge of them. While, in observing everyday objects, the physical process involved in making the observation plays a subsidiary role only, in the case of the smallest building particles of matter, every process of observation produces a large disturbance. We can no longer speak of the behaviour of the particle independently of the process of observation. As a final consequence, the natural laws formulated mathematically in quantum theory no longer deal with the elementary particles themselves but with our knowledge of them. Nor is it any longer possible to ask whether or not these particles exist in space and time objectively, since the only processes we can refer to as taking place are those which represent the interplay of particles with some other physical system, *e.g.*, a measuring instrument.

Thus, the objective reality of the elementary particles has been strangely dispersed, not into the fog of some new ill-defined or still unexplained conception of reality, but into the transparent clarity of a mathematics that no longer describes the behaviour of the elementary particles but only our knowledge of this behaviour. The atomic physicist has had to resign himself to the fact that his science is but a link in the infinite chain of man's argument with nature, *and that it cannot simply speak of nature "in itself."* Science always presupposes the existence of man and, as Bohr has said, we must become conscious of the fact that we are not merely observers but also actors on the stage of life. . . .

When we speak of the picture of nature in the exact science of our age, we do not mean a picture of nature so much as a *picture of our relationships with nature.* The old division of the world into objective processes in space and time and the mind in which these processes are mirrored—in other words, the Cartesian difference between *res cogitans* and *res extensa*—is no longer a suitable starting point for our understanding of modern science. Science, we find, is now focused on the network of relationships between man and nature, on the framework which makes us as living beings dependent parts of nature, and which we as human beings have simultaneously made the object of our thoughts and actions. Science no longer confronts nature as an objective observer, but sees itself as an actor in this interplay between man and nature. The scientific method of analysing, explaining and classifying has become conscious of its limitations, which arise out of the fact that by its intervention science alters and refashions the object of investigation. In other words, method and object can no longer be separated. *The scientific world-view has ceased to be a scientific view in the true sense of the word.* . . .

The use of the concept of causality for describing the law of cause and effect is of relatively recent origin. In previous philosophies the word *causa* had a very much more general significance than it has today. Thus scholasticism, following Aristotle, spoke of four kinds of "causes": the *causa formalis* which might be considered as the form or the spiritual essence of a thing, the *causa materialis* which referred to the matter of which the thing consisted, the *cause finalis* or the purpose for which the thing was created, and finally, the *causa efficiens*. Only the *causa efficiens* corresponds to what is meant by the word "cause" today.

The transformation of *causa* into the modern concept of cause have taken place in the course of centuries, in close connection with the changes in man's conception of reality and with the creation of science at the beginning of the modern age. As material processes became more prominent in man's conception of reality, the word *causa* was used increasingly to refer to the particular material event which preceded, and had in some way caused, the event to be explained. Thus even Kant, who frequently did what at root amounted to drawing philosophic consequences from the developments in science since Newton's time, already used the word "causality" in a nineteenth-century sense. When we experience an event we always assume that there was another event preceding it from which the second has followed according to some law. Thus the concept of causality became narrowed down, finally, to refer to our belief that events in nature are uniquely determined, or, in other words, that an exact knowledge of nature or some part of it would suffice, at least in principle, to determine the future. Newton's physics was so constructed that the future motion of a system could be calculated from its particular state at a given time. The idea that nature really was like this was perhaps enunciated most generally and most lucidly by Laplace when he spoke of a demon, who at a given time, by knowing the position and motion of every atom, would be capable of predicting the entire future of the world. When the word "causality" is interpreted in this very narrow sense, we speak of "determinism," by which we mean that there are immutable natural laws that uniquely determine the future state of any system from its present state. . . .

From its very beginnings atomic physics evolved concepts which do not really fit this picture. True, they do not contradict it basically, but the approach of atomic physics was by its very character different from that of determinism. Even in the ancient atomic theory of Democritus and Leucippus it was assumed that large-scale processes were the results of many irregular processes on a small scale. That this is basically the case is illustrated by innumerable examples in everyday life. Thus, a farmer need only know that a cloud has condensed and watered his fields. He does not bother about the path of each individual drop of rain. To give another example, we know precisely what is meant by the word "granite," even when we are ignorant of the form, colour, and chemical composition of each small constituent crystal. Thus we always use concepts which describe behaviour on the large scale without in the least bothering about the individual processes that take place on the small scale.

This notion of the statistical combination of many small individual events was already used in ancient atomic theory as the basis for an explanation of the world, and was generalized in the concept that all the sensory qualities of matter were indirectly caused by the position and movements of the atoms. Thus Democritus wrote that things only *appeared* to be sweet or bitter, and only appeared to have colour, for in reality there existed only atoms and empty space. Now, if the processes which we can observe with our senses are thought to arise out of the interactions of many small individual processes, we must needs conclude that all natural laws may be considered to be only statistical laws. True, even statistical law can lead to statements with so high a degree of probability that they are almost certain, but there can always be exceptions in principle. The concept of statistical law is frequently thought to be contradictory. Thus it is contended that while it is possible to look upon natural processes either as determined by laws, or else as running their course without any order whatever, we cannot form any picture of processes obeying statistical laws.

Yet we must remind the reader that in everyday life all of us encounter statistical laws with every step we take, and make these laws the basis of our practical actions. Thus, when an engineer is constructing a dam he always bases his calculations on the average yearly rainfall, although he cannot have the faintest idea when it will rain and how much of it at a time. When speaking of statistical laws we generally mean that a particular physical system is known incompletely. The most common example is the throw of dice. Since no one side of a die is heavier than any other, and since it is thus impossible to predict which side will turn up, we can assume that in a large number of throws precisely one in six will turn up with five dots.

From the very beginning of modern times attempts have been made to explain both qualitatively and also quantitatively the behaviour of matter through the statistical behaviour of atoms. Robert Boyle demonstrated that we could understand the relations between the pressure and the volume of a gas if we looked upon pressure as the many thrusts of the individual atoms on the walls of the vessel. Similarly thermodynamical phenomena have been explained by the assumption that atoms move more violently in a hot body than in a cold one. This statement could be given a quantitative mathematical formulation and in this way the laws of heat could be understood.

This application of the concept of statistical laws was finally formulated in the second half of the last century as the so-called *statistical mechanics*. In this theory, which is based on Newton's mechanics, the consequences that spring from an incomplete knowledge of a complicated mechanical system are investigated. Thus in principle it is not a renunciation of determinism. While it is held that the details of events are fully determined according to the laws of Newton's mechanics, the condition is added that the mechanical properties of the *system* are not fully known.

Gibbs and Boltzmann managed to formulate this kind of incomplete knowledge mathematically, and Gibbs was able to demonstrate that, in particular, our conception of temperature is closely related to the incompleteness of our knowledge. When we know the temperature of a particular system, it means that the system must be considered to be only one out of a whole set of systems. This set of systems can be described accurately by mathematics, but not the particular system with which we are concerned. With this Gibbs had half-unconsciously taken a step which later on was to have the most important consequences. Gibbs was the first to introduce a physical concept which can only be applied to an object when our knowledge of the object is incomplete. If for instance the motion and position of each molecule in a gas were known, then it would be pointless to continue speaking of the temperature of the gas. The concept of temperature can only be used meaningfully when the system is not fully known and we wish to derive statistical conclusions from our incomplete knowledge. . . .

Although the discoveries of Gibbs and Boltzmann made an incomplete knowledge of a system part of the formulation of physical laws, nevertheless determinism was still present in principle until Max Planck's famous discovery ushered in quantum theory. Planck, in his work on the theory of radiation, had originally encountered an element of uncertainty in radiation phenomena. He had shown that a radiating atom does not deliver up its energy continuously, but discretely in bundles. This assumption of a discontinuous and pulse-like transfer of energy, like every other notion of atomic theory, leads us once more to the idea that the emission of radiation is a statistical phenomenon. However, it took two and a half decades before it became clear *that quantum theory actually forces us to formulate these laws precisely as statistical laws* and to depart radically from determinism. Since the work of Einstein, Bohr and Sommerfeld, Planck's theory has proved to be the key with which the door to the entire sphere of atomic physics could be opened. Chemical processes could be explained by means of the Rutherford-Bohr atomic model, and since then, chemistry, physics and astrophysics have been fused into unity. With the mathematical formulation of quantum-theoretical laws pure determinism had to be abandoned.

Since I cannot speak of the mathematical methods here, I should merely like to mention some aspects of the strange situation confronting the physicist in atomic physics.

We can express the departure from previous forms of physics by means of the so-called uncertainty relations. It was discovered that it was impossible to describe simultaneously both the position and the velocity of an atomic particle with any prescribed degree of accuracy. We can either measure the position very accurately —when the action of the instrument used for the observation obscures our knowledge of the velocity, or we can make accurate measurements of the velocity and forego knowledge of the position. The product of the two uncertainties can never be less than Planck's constant. This formulation makes it quite clear that we cannot make much headway with the concepts of Newtonian mechanics, since in the calculation of a mechanical process it is essential to know simultaneously the position and velocity at a particular moment, and this is precisely what quantum theory considers to be impossible.

Another formulation is that of Niels Bohr, who introduced the *concept of complementarity*. By this he means that the different intuitive pictures which we use to describe atomic systems, although fully adequate for given experiments, are nevertheless mutually exclusive. Thus, for instance, the Bohr atom can be described as a small-scale planetary system, having a central atomic nucleus about which the external electrons revolve. For other experiments, however, it might be more convenient to imagine that the atomic nucleus is surrounded by a system of stationary waves whose frequency is characteristic of the radiation emanating from the atom. Finally, we can consider the atom chemically. We can calculate its heat of reaction when it becomes fused with other atoms, but in that case we cannot simultaneously describe the motion of the electrons. Each picture is legitimate when used in the right place, but the different pictures are contradictory and therefore we call them mutually complementary. The uncertainty that is attached to each of them is expressed by the uncertainty relation, which is sufficient for avoiding logical contradiction between the different pictures.

Even without entering into the mathematics of quantum theory these brief comments might have helped us to realize *that the incomplete knowledge of a system must be an essential part of every formulation in quantum theory.* Quantum theoretical laws must be of a statistical kind. To give an example: we know that the radium atom emits alpha-radiation. Quantum theory can give us an indication of the probability that the alpha-particle will leave the nucleus in unit time, but it cannot predict at what precise point in time the emission will occur, for this is uncertain in principle. We cannot even assume that new laws still to be discovered will allow us to determine this precise point in time; were this possible the alpha-particle could not also be considered to behave as a wave leaving the atomic nucleus, a fact which we can prove experimentally. The various experiments proving both the wave nature and also the particle nature of atomic matter create a paradox which forces us to devise a formulation of statistical laws.

4

CULTURAL HISTORY

Idealism

Patterns of Repetition

History and Imagination

Religion and History

Primitive Survivals

4

Introduction

The traditional assumption that permanence is better than change, Being superior to Becoming, eternity more real than time, is often set aside, questioned, or even reversed in modern thought. In the indeterminate world pictured by James and Dewey, as well as Whitehead's world of events and Heisenberg's world of physical experiment, time is of central importance and in effect nature is historicized. These writers deal with processes of becoming rather than states of being, and with processes in which developing human action or feeling is intimately involved.[1] Historicism in a more usual sense of the term is evident in the protest of literary realists against the symbolist worship of inclusive and definitive form. The realist holds that if anything is "real" it is neither the static order created by an individual artist nor the hypothetical total order of the cosmos but the cumulative temporal experience of mankind. Here a specifically human truth, a historical reality, is affirmed.[2]

Hegel, the greatest modern historicist, postulates a universal Spirit that is manifest in both space and time, nature and history, but most significantly unfolds itself on the world-historical stage. The essence of this Spirit is "freedom"; its goal is the complete realization of freedom; its field is the temporal sequence of concrete events, actions, and historical epochs. Freedom is equivalent to "self-consciousness"—the capacity, peculiar to Spirit, of at once knowing and being what it knows.[3] In every human culture the substance of Spirit comes to partial knowledge of itself; and every culture is destined to be superseded as the Spirit moves onward, reflexively knowing what it has been and approaching its goal of total self-possession. There is no room for accident here, no element of chance; the ruins of time record the progress of historical reality. On the other hand, Hegel's system has no place for individual human creativity, since every innovator, even the greatest, works at the behest of historical necessity.[4]

[1] See Section 3.
[2] See Section 2, especially "Socialist Realism." For the temporal emphasis in psychology, see William James and Bergson in Section 7.
[3] Compare the selection from Hegel in Section 7.
[4] Compare the historical determinism of the literary realists (especially Tolstoy) and of Marx and Engels in Section 2.

453

History is freedom for Croce also, but his conception is much less transcendental: Crocean history is not the work of universal Spirit but the creative activity of the human spirit and of individual human minds. Croce maintains that in seeking to know things we are always trying to grasp situations in which we must act. Any given situation is a kind of "past," which we need to comprehend as the premise for our future. Therefore all knowledge, even that of natural science, is historical knowledge. In one sense, history enables us to escape from the past, in which we would otherwise be enclosed and trapped. In another sense, it is our way of claiming the past, which would be incomprehensible to us if we ourselves, as human beings, did not virtually contain the human heritage. Considered as the process and product of solving human problems, history has no *a priori* logic, no necessary sequence of causes and effects, and no predictability. It is truly "history as the story of liberty," essentially indeterminate.[5]

In contrast to Hegel, for whom history moves toward the completion of Spirit, and Croce, for whom history is freely constructed by men, Vico, Nietzsche, and Spengler concentrate on rhythmic repetitions in human experience. They stabilize time (especially Vico and Nietzsche) by asserting that there are no real novelties in it, and Vico and Spengler discover a meaningful pattern by marking off the phases in which everything recurs.[6]

Vico's world, like Croce's, is knowable because it is made by men, but for Vico the human possibilities latent in any single human mind are continuously being acted out in historical cycles. These constitute an ideal, eternal history ordained by Providence, which men re-create in the actual history of all nations.[7] A cycle is a sequence of three ages: religious, heroic, and human. Though details may vary from one cycle to another, the essential characteristics of each age are repeated in every cycle, and every cycle ends only to begin, as James Joyce (an ardent Viconian) writes in *Finnegans Wake*, "the same anew."[8]

Nietzsche's "eternal return" is not periodic like Vico's but perennial. The whole range of human existence at any moment, from the most squalid depths to the heights of self-mastery, has recurred and will recur endlessly through infinite time. The moment is "eternal," but not as a point of contact between history and some super-historical source of meaning: it is wholly immanent, the supreme expression of a man-centered world. The highest achievement of the heroic personality is to affirm the entire content of the

[5] Compare "indeterminism" in the philosophy of nature (Section 3).
[6] Another attempt to picture permanence within the realm of time—though not on the plane of public history—is Bergson's "duration" (see Section 7).
[7] Compare Blake's visionary history (Section 6).
[8] Since the "religious" phase to which Vico's cycles always return is an age of "hieroglyphic language" and "divine poetry," and since Vico's scheme of cycles, according to him, is itself an esoteric tradition, he is closely related to some of the exponents of myth represented in Section 6.

454

eternal moment—not merely to submit to it as an external fate but to "will" it in "joy."[9]

Spengler's system is cyclical, much in the manner of Vico, yet he, like Nietzsche, has no faith in a transcendent Providence. He offers a philosophy of history to account for the historical phase in the midst of which he writes —an era of decline in every aspect of human endeavor. This is the one great opportunity of the modern epoch—to understand the pattern that underlies the inevitable decay of all great cultures. We alone are in a position to see what a culture is—a dense complex of inner "analogies"—and to perceive that cultures are born, flourish, and die like biological organisms.[10] Each is unique, but the life-phases through which it must pass are morphologically the same as those of other cultures widely dispersed in space and time. In every case, the culture moves toward "civilization," when vitality diminishes, artificiality sets in, and rationalism is substituted for creativity. The classical world moved from culture to civilization in the fourth century, the modern world in the nineteenth.[11] By study of the morphology of culture we may predict our own future, and for Spengler this power in itself is apparently sufficient compensation for the somber prospect that opens before him.

Yeats incorporated many different attitudes toward history into the historical section of A Vision, his schematic world-picture. He is especially close to Spengler, but Yeats gives a new emphasis to Spengler's notion of cultural "symbology." He conceives of human existence—past, present, and future— as totally symbolic, a visionary yet substantial pageant. Events and works of art, persons and mythical types, passions and ideas and their embodiments are all made of the same imaginative stuff, like words in a living poem that has been constantly rewritten through time. The whole is governed by Yeats's scheme of interpenetrating cones or "gyres." In contrast to Spengler's biological categories, Yeats propounds a geometrical scheme to represent his view of life as a scheduled interplay of opposites (the subjective and the objective, the personal and the abstract, the spiritual and the secular). If history for him is a poem, it is an ironic poem, a structure of complex counterpoint.[12]

Malraux is more concerned with distinguishing the creative history of art from the deterministic history that surrounds it. As Yeats himself says elsewhere, "works of art beget works of art": an original imagination remakes the artistic world that has been constituted by previous artists. What is char-

[9] For related selections from Nietzsche, see Sections 1, 5, 7, 8, 9.
[10] In this emphasis on death as the inherent direction of all organisms, Spengler is in striking contrast to the vitalists represented in Section 3. In his conception of a style or symbolic form in culture he is close to symbolist ideas of poetic form (see Section 1).
[11] Compare Nietzsche's picture of "Alexandrian" culture in Section 7. Spengler's sense of a modern decline, though not his explanation of it, is comparable to that of Henry Adams (Section 3).
[12] For related selections from Yeats, see Sections 1 and 7.

acteristic of our time, however, is an awareness that the entire history of art is our heritage. In our "museum without walls," all styles become wholly present and simultaneous. Therefore we rejoice not so much in a new style as in the triumph of the man-made world of style, the whole of art, over the world of "fate." Our imaginary museum, existing in a timeless moment, is an emblem of man's conquest of the human situation—of the gods, nature, time, and death. It signifies a human self-redemption.[13]

In strong reaction against all forms of modern historicism, Berdyaev reasserts the dependence of human history on a meaning that enters it from above. Only because of Christ's redemption of man from bondage to subhuman nature is there such a thing as human freedom, and without a sense of freedom there is no such thing as a sense of history. All human efforts are doomed to failure; history is the record of human imperfection. But historical failure still has meaning in terms of a super-historical purpose, while it can only lead to despair if we aim at an end within history itself.[14]

Another critique of historicism, though in a very different vein, is suggested by Darwin and Frazer. They point out that the subhuman and the prehistoric persist in the body, social institutions, and mental habits of the most advanced historical man. In the perspective of zoology and anthropology, recorded history is suddenly diminished to a tiny portion of earthly time. Yet both Darwin and Frazer are complacently confident of the superiority of modern man, whatever volcanoes may lie beneath his surface.[15] It is a more profound shock to discover, as did Henry Miller at Mycenae, that on occasion men may have risen out of the primeval darkness only to live in love and terror of it and finally to lapse back into it. Mycenae is a mystery that defies all notions of historical order and development—inexplicable on idealist or cyclical or Christian or evolutionary grounds.

[13] A related selection from Malraux appears in Section 1. In their different ways, both Malraux and Yeats, like Spengler, have extended symbolist aesthetics (Section 1) into a theory of artistic and cultural history. Therefore all three have an affinity with the world of myth, which is at once aesthetic, cultural, and historical (see Section 6).
[14] A related selection from Berdyaev appears in Section 6. His attack on historicism is part of the neo-orthodoxy illustrated in Section 9.
[15] See a related selection from Darwin in Section 3 and from Frazer in Section 6. Compare the Freudian account of the origins of culture (Section 5).

G. W. F. HEGEL

History as the Self-Realization of Spirit

The only Thought which Philosophy brings with it to the contemplation of History, is the simple conception of *Reason;* that Reason is the Sovereign of the World; that the history of the world, therefore, presents us with a rational process. This conviction and intuition is a hypothesis in the domain of history as such. In that of Philosophy it is no hypothesis. It is there proved by speculative cognition, that Reason—and this term may here suffice us, without investigating the relation sustained by the Universe to the Divine Being,—is *Substance,* as well as *Infinite Power;* its own *Infinite Material* underlying all the natural and spiritual life which it originates, as also the *Infinite Form*—that which sets this Material in motion. On the one hand, Reason is the *substance* of the Universe; viz. that by which and in which all reality has its being and subsistence. On the other hand, it is the *Infinite Energy* of the Universe; since Reason is not so powerless as to be incapable of producing anything but a mere ideal, a mere intention— having its place outside reality, nobody knows where; something separate and abstract, in the heads of certain human beings. It is *the infinite complex of things,* their entire Essence and Truth. It is its own material which it commits to its own Active Energy to work up; not needing, as finite action does, the conditions of an external material of given means from which it may obtain its support, and the objects of its activity. It supplies its own nourishment, and is the object of its own operations. While it is exclusively its own basis of existence, and absolute final aim, it is also the energising power realising this aim; developing it not only in the phenomena of the Natural, but also of the Spiritual Universe—the History of the World. That this "Idea" or "Reason" is the *True,* the *Eternal,* the absolutely *powerful* essence; that it reveals itself in the World, and that in that World nothing else is revealed but this and its honour and glory—is the thesis which, as we have said, has been proved in Philosophy, and is here regarded as demonstrated. . . .

The nature of Spirit may be understood by a glance at its direct opposite— *Matter.* As the essence of Matter is Gravity, so, on the other hand, we may affirm that the substance, the essence of Spirit is Freedom. All will readily assent to the doctrine that Spirit, among other properties, is also endowed with Freedom; but philosophy teaches that all the qualities of Spirit exist only through Freedom;

From *Introduction to the Philosophy of History* [1832], translated from the German by J. Sibree, New York, 1899, pp. 9-10, 17-20, 71-9.

that all are but means for attaining Freedom; that all seek and produce this and this alone. It is a result of speculative Philosophy, that Freedom is the sole truth of Spirit. Matter possesses gravity in virtue of its tendency towards a central point. It is essentially composite; consisting of parts that *exclude* each other. It seeks its Unity; and therefore exhibits itself as self-destructive, as verging towards its opposite [an indivisible point]. If it could attain this, it would be Matter no longer, it would have perished. It strives after the realisation of its Idea; for in Unity it exists *ideally*. Spirit, on the contrary, may be defined as that which has its centre in itself. It has not a unity outside itself, but has already found it; it exists *in* and *with itself*. Matter has its essence out of itself; Spirit is *self-contained existence* (Bei-sich-selbst-seyn). Now this is Freedom, exactly. For if I am dependent, my being is referred to something else which I am not; I cannot exist independently of something external. I am free, on the contrary, when my existence depends upon myself. This self-contained existence of Spirit is none other than self-consciousness—consciousness of one's own being. Two things must be distinguished in consciousness; first, the fact *that I know*; secondly, *what I know*. In *self* consciousness these are merged in one; for Spirit *knows itself*. It involves an appreciation of its own nature, as also an energy enabling it to realise itself; to make itself *actually* that which it is *potentially*. According to this abstract definition it may be said of Universal History, that it is the exhibition of Spirit in the process of working out the knowledge of that which it is potentially. And as the germ bears in itself the whole nature of the tree, and the taste and form of its fruits, so do the first traces of Spirit virtually contain the whole of that History. The Orientals have not attained the knowledge that Spirit—Man *as such* —is free; and because they do not know this they are not free. They only know that *one is free*. But on this very account, the freedom of that one is only caprice; ferocity—brutal recklessness or passion, or a mildness and tameness of the desires, which is itself only an accident of Nature—mere caprice like the former.—That *one* is therefore only a Despot; not a *free man*. The consciousness of Freedom first arose among the Greeks, and therefore they were free; but they, and the Romans likewise, knew only that *some* are free,—not man as such. Even Plato and Aristotle did not know this. The Greeks, therefore, had slaves; and their whole life and the maintenance of their splendid liberty, was implicated with the institution of slavery: a fact moreover, which made that liberty on the one hand only an accidental, transient and limited growth; on the other hand, constituted it a rigorous thraldom of our common nature—of the Human. The German nations, under the influence of Christianity, were the first to attain the consciousness, that man, as man, is free: that it is the *freedom* of Spirit which constitutes its essence. This consciousness arose first in religion, the inmost region of Spirit; but to introduce the principle into the various relations of the actual world, involves a more extensive problem than its simple implantation; a problem whose solution and application require a severe and lengthened process of culture. In proof of this, we may note that slavery did not cease immediately on the reception of Christianity. Still less did liberty predominate in States; or Governments and Constitutions adopt a rational organization, or recognise freedom as their basis. That application of the principle to political relations; the thorough moulding and interpenetration of the constitution of society by it, is a process identical with history itself. I have already directed attention to the distinction here involved, between a principle as such, and its *application; i.e.* its introduction and carrying out in the actual phenomena of Spirit and Life. This is a point of fundamental importance in our science, and one which must be constantly respected as essential. And in the same way as this distinction has attracted attention in view of the *Christian* principle of self-consciousness—Freedom; it also shews itself as an essential one, in view of the principle of Freedom *generally.* The History of the world is none other than the progress of the consciousness of Freedom; a progress whose development according to the necessity of its nature, it is our business to investigate.

The general statement given above, of the various grades in the consciousness of Freedom—and which we applied in the first instance to the fact that the Eastern nations knew only that *one* is free; the Greek and Roman world only that *some* are free; whilst *we* know that all men absolutely (man *as* man) are free —supplies us with the natural division of Universal History, and suggests the mode of its discussion. This is remarked, however, only incidentally and anticipatively; some other ideas must be first explained.

The destiny of the spiritual World, and—since this is the *substantial* World, while the physical remains subordinate to it, or, in the language of speculation, has no truth *as against* the spiritual—the *final cause of the World at large*, we allege to be the *consciousness* of its own freedom on the part of Spirit, and *ipso facto*, the *reality* of that freedom. But that this term "Freedom," without further qualification, is an indefinite, and incalculable ambiguous term; and that while that which it represents is the *ne plus ultra* of attainment, it is liable to an infinity of misunderstandings, confusions and errors, and to become the occasion for all imaginable excesses,—has never been more clearly known and felt than in modern times. Yet, for the present, we must content ourselves with the term itself without farther definition. Attention was also directed to the importance of the infinite difference between a principle in the abstract, and its realisation in the concrete. In the process before us, the essential nature of freedom—which involves in it absolute necessity—is to be displayed as coming to a consciousness of itself (for it is in its very nature, self-consciousness) and thereby realising its existence. Itself is its own object of attainment, and the sole aim of Spirit. This result it is, at which the process of the World's History has been continually aiming; and to which the sacrifices that have ever and anon been laid on the vast altar of the earth, through the long lapses of ages, have been offered. This is the only aim that sees itself realised and fulfilled; the only pole of repose amid the ceaseless change of events and conditions, and the sole efficient principle that pervades them. This final aim is God's purpose with the world; but God is the absolutely perfect Being, and can, therefore, will nothing other than himself—his own Will. The Nature of His Will—that is, His Nature itself—is what we here call the Idea of Freedom; translating the language of Religion into that of Thought. . . .

It is the concrete spirit of a people which we have distinctly to recognise, and since it is Spirit it can only be comprehended spiritually, that is, by thought. It is this alone which takes the lead in all the deeds and tendencies of that people, and which is occupied in realising itself—in satisfying its ideal and becoming self-conscious,—for its great business is self-production. But for spirit, the highest attainment is self-knowledge; an advance not only to the *intuition*, but to the *thought*—the clear conception of itself. This it must and is also destined to accomplish; but the accomplishment is at the same time its dissolution, and the rise of another spirit, another world-historical people, another epoch of Universal History. This transition and connection leads us to the connection of the whole —the idea of the World's History as such—which we have now to consider more closely, and of which we have to give a representation.

History in general is therefore the development of Spirit in *Time*, as Nature is the development of the Idea in *Space*.

If then we cast a glance over the World's History generally, we see a vast picture of changes and transactions; of infinitely manifold forms of peoples, states, individuals, in unresting succession. Everything that can enter into and interest the soul of man—all our sensibility to *goodness, beauty and greatness*—is called into play. On every hand aims are adopted and pursued, which we recognise, whose accomplishment we desire—we hope and fear for them. In all these occurrences and changes we behold human action and suffering predominant; everywhere something akin to ourselves, and therefore everywhere something that excites our interest for or against. Sometimes it attracts us by beauty, freedom, and rich variety, sometimes by energy such as enables even vice to make itself interesting. Sometimes we see the more comprehensive mass of some general interest advancing with comparative slowness, and subsequently sacrificed to an infinite complication of trifling circumstances, and so dissipated into atoms. Then, again, with a vast expenditure of power a trivial result is produced; while from what appears unimportant a tremendous issue proceeds. On every hand there is the motliest throng of events drawing us within the circle of its interest, and when one combination vanishes another immediately appears in its place.

The general thought—the category which first presents itself in this restless mutation of individuals and peoples, existing for a time and then vanishing—is that of *change* at large. The sight of the ruins of some ancient sovereignty directly leads us to contemplate this thought of change in its negative aspect. What traveller among the ruins of Carthage, of Palmyra, Persepolis, or Rome, has not been stimulated by reflections on the transiency of kingdoms and men, and to sadness at the thought of a vigorous and rich life now departed—a sadness which does not expend itself on personal losses and the uncertainty of one's own undertakings, but is a disinterested sorrow at the decay of a splendid and highly cultured national life! But the next consideration which allies itself with that of change, is, that change while it imports dissolution, involves at the same time the rise of *a new life*—that while death is the issue of life, life is also the issue of death. This is a grand conception; one which the Oriental thinkers attained, and which is perhaps the highest in their metaphysics. In the Idea of *Metempsychosis* we find it evolved in its relation to individual existence; but a myth more generally known, is that of the *Phoenix* as a type of the Life of *Nature*; eternally preparing for itself its funeral pile, and consuming itself upon it; but so that from its ashes is produced the new, renovated, fresh life. But this image is only Asiatic; oriental not occidental. Spirit—consuming the envelope of its existence—does not merely pass into another envelope, nor rise rejuvenescent from the ashes of its previous form; it comes forth exalted, glorified, a purer spirit. It certainly makes war upon itself—consumes its own existence; but in this very destruction it works up with existence into a new form, and each successive phase becomes in its turn a material, working on which it exalts itself to a new grade.

If we consider Spirit in this aspect—regarding its changes not merely as rejuvenescent transitions, *i.e.*, returns to the same form, but rather as manipulations of itself, by which it multiplies the material for future endeavours—we see it exerting itself in a variety of modes and directions; developing its powers and gratifying its desires in a variety which is inexhaustible; because every one of its creations, in which it has already found gratification, meets it anew as material, and is a new stimulus to plastic activity. The abstract conception of mere change gives place to the thought of Spirit manifesting, developing, and perfecting its powers in every direction which its manifold nature can follow. What powers it inherently possesses we learn from the variety of products and formations which it originates. In this pleasurable activity, it has to do only with itself. As involved with the conditions of mere nature—internal and external—it will indeed meet in these not only opposition and hindrance, but will often see its endeavours thereby fail; often sink under the complications in which it is entangled either by Nature or by itself. But in such case it perishes in fulfilling its own destiny and proper function, and even thus exhibits the spectacle of self-demonstration as spiritual activity.

The very essence of Spirit is activity; it realises its potentiality—makes itself its own deed, its own work—and thus it becomes an object to itself; contemplates itself as an objective existence. Thus is it with the Spirit of a people: it is a Spirit having strictly defined characteristics, which erects itself into an objective world, that exists and persists in a particular religious form of worship, customs, constitution and political laws—in the whole complex of its institutions—in the events and transactions that make up its history. That is its work—that is what this particular Nation *is*. Nations are what their deeds are. Every Englishman will say: We are the men who navigate the ocean, and have the commerce of the world; to whom the East Indies belong and their riches; who have a parliament, juries, &c.—The relation of the individual to that Spirit is that he appropriates to himself this substantial existence; that it becomes his character and capability, enabling him to have a definite place in the world—to be *something*. For he finds the being of the people to which he belongs an already established, firm world—objectively present to him—with which he has to incorporate himself. In this its work, therefore—its world—the Spirit of the people enjoys its existence and finds its satisfaction.—A Nation is moral—virtuous—vigorous—while it is engaged in realising its grand objects, and defends its work against external violence during the process of giving to its purposes an objective existence. The contradiction between its potential, subjective being—its inner aim and life—and its *actual* being is removed; it has attained full reality, has itself objectively present to it. But this having been attained, the activity displayed by the Spirit of the people in question is no longer needed; it has its desire. The Nation can still accomplish much in war and peace at home and abroad; but the living substantial soul itself may be said to have ceased its activity. The essential, supreme interest has consequently vanished from its life, for interest is present only where there is opposition. The nation lives the same kind of life as the individual when passing from maturity to old age—in the enjoyment of itself—in the satisfaction of being exactly what is desired and was able to attain. Although its imagination might have transcended that limit, it nevertheless abandoned any such aspirations as objects of *actual endeavour*, if the real world was less than favourable to their attainment—and restricted its aim by the conditions thus imposed. This mere *customary life* (the watch wound up and going on of itself) is that which brings on natural death. Custom is activity without opposition, for which there remains only a formal duration; in which the fulness and zest that originally characterised the aim of life is out of the question,— a merely external sensuous existence which has ceased to throw itself enthusiastically into its object. Thus perish individuals, thus perish peoples by a natural death; and though the latter may continue in being, it is an existence without intellect or vitality; having no need of its institutions, because the need for them is satisfied,—a political nullity and tedium. In order that a truly universal interest may arise, the Spirit of a People must advance to the adoption of some new purpose: but whence can this new purpose originate? It would be a higher, more comprehensive conception of itself—a transcending of its principle—but this very act would involve a principle of a new order, a new National Spirit.

Such a new principle does in fact enter into the Spirit of a people that has arrived at full development and self-realisation; it dies not a simply natural death, —for it is not a mere single individual, but a spiritual, generic life; in its case natural death appears to imply destruction through its own agency. The reason of this difference from the single natural individual, is that the Spirit of a people exists as a *genus*, and consequently carries within it its own negation, in the very generality which characterises it. A people can only die a violent death when it has become naturally dead in itself, as *e.g.*, the German Imperial Cities, the German Imperial Constitution.

It is not of the nature of the all-pervading Spirit to die this merely natural death; it does not simply sink into the senile life of mere custom, but—as being a National Spirit belonging to Universal History—attains to the consciousness of what its work is; it attains to a conception of itself. In fact it is world-historical only in so far as a *universal principle* has lain in its fundamental element—in its grand aim: only so far is the work which such a spirit produces, a moral, political organization. If it be mere desires that impel nations to activity, such deeds pass over without leaving a trace; or their traces are only ruin and destruction. Thus, it was first Chronos—Time—that ruled; the Golden Age, without moral products; and what was produced—the offspring of that Chronos—was devoured by it. It was Jupiter—from whose head Minerva sprang, and to whose circle of divinities belong Apollo and the Muses—that first put a constraint upon Time, and set a bound to its principle of decadence. He is the Political god, who produced a moral work—the State.

In the very element of an achievement the quality of generality, of thought, is contained; without thought it has no objectivity; that is its basis. The highest point in the development of a people is this,—to have gained a conception of its life and condition,—to have reduced its laws, its ideas of justice and morality to a science; for in this unity [of the objective and subjective] lies the most intimate unity that Spirit can attain to in and with itself. In its work it is employed in rendering itself an object of its own contemplation; but it cannot develop itself objectively in its essential nature, except in *thinking* itself.

At this point, then, Spirit is acquainted with its principles—the general character of its acts. But at the same time, in virtue of its very generality, this work of thought is different in point of form from the actual achievements of the national genius, and from the vital agency by which those achievements have been performed. We have then before us a *real* and an *ideal* existence of the Spirit of the

Nation. If we wish to gain the general idea and conception of what the Greeks were, we find it in Sophocles and Aristophanes, in Thucydides and Plato. In these individuals the Greek spirit conceived and thought itself. This is the profounder kind of satisfaction which the Spirit of a people attains; but it is "ideal," and distinct from its "real" activity.

At such a time, therefore, we are sure to see a people finding satisfaction in the *idea* of virtue; putting *talk* about virtue partly side by side with actual virtue, but partly in the place of it. On the other hand pure, universal thought, since its nature is universality, is apt to bring the Special and Spontaneous—Belief, Trust, Customary Morality—to reflect upon itself, and its primitive simplicity; to shew up the limitation with which it is fettered,—partly suggesting reasons for renouncing duties, partly itself *demanding reasons*, and the connection of such requirements with Universal Thought; and not finding that connection, seeking to impeach the authority of duty generally, as destitute of a sound foundation.

At the same time the isolation of individuals from each other and from the Whole makes its appearance; their aggressive selfishness and vanity; their seeking personal advantage and consulting this at the expense of the State at large. That inward principle in transcending its outward manifestations is subjective also in *form*—viz., selfishness and corruption in the unbound passions and egotistic interests of men.

Zeus, therefore, who is represented as having put a limit to the devouring agency of Time, and stayed this transiency by having established something inherently and independently durable—Zeus and his race are themselves swallowed up, and that by the very power that produced them—the principle of thought, perception, reasoning, insight derived from rational grounds, and the requirement of such grounds.

Time is the negative element in the sensuous world. Thought is the same negativity, but it is the deepest, the infinite form of it, in which therefore all existence generally is dissolved; first *finite* existence,—*determinate*, limited form: but existence *generally*, in its objective character, is limited; it appears therefore as a mere datum—something immediate—authority;—and is either intrinsically finite and limited, or presents itself as a limit for the thinking subject, and its infinite reflection on itself [unlimited abstraction].

But first we must observe how the life which proceeds from death, is itself, on the other hand, only individual life; so that, regarding the species as the real and substantial in this vicissitude, the perishing of the individual is a regress of the species into individuality. The perpetuation of the race is, therefore, none other than the monotonous repetition of the same kind of existence. Further, we must remark how perception,—the comprehension of being by thought,—is the source and birthplace of a new, and in fact higher form, in a principle which while it preserves, dignifies its material. For Thought is that *Universal*—that *Species* which is immortal, which preserves identity with itself. The particular form of Spirit not merely passes away in the world by natural causes in Time, but is annulled in the automatic self-mirroring activity of consciousness. Because this annulling is an activity of Thought, it is at the same time conservative and elevating in its operation. While then, on the one side, Spirit annuls the reality, the permanence of that which it *is*, it gains on the other side, the essence, the Thought, the Universal element of that which *it only was* [its transient conditions]. Its principle is no longer that immediate import and aim which it was previously, but the *essence* of that import and aim.

The result of this process is then that Spirit, in rendering itself objective and making this its being an object of thought, on the one hand destroys the determinate form of its being, on the other hand gains a comprehension of the universal element which it involves, and thereby gives a new form to its inherent principle. In virtue of this, the substantial character of the National Spirit has been altered,—that is, its principle has risen into another, and in fact a higher principle.

It is of the highest importance in apprehending and comprehending History to have and to understand the thought involved in this transition. The individual traverses as a unity various grades of development, and remains the same individual; in like manner also does a people, till the Spirit which it embodies reaches the grade of universality. In this point lies the fundamental, the Ideal necessity of transition. This is the soul—the essential consideration—of the philosophical comprehension of History.

Spirit is essentially the result of its own activity; its activity is the transcending of immediate, simple, unreflected existence,—the negation of that existence, and the returning into itself. We may compare it with the seed; for with this the plant begins, yet it is also the result of the plant's entire life. But the weak side of life is exhibited in the fact that the commencement and the result are disjoined from each other. Thus also is it in the life of individuals and peoples. The life of a people ripens a certain fruit; its activity aims at the complete manifestation of the principle which it embodies. But this fruit does not fall back into the bosom of the people that produced and matured it; on the contrary, it becomes a poison-draught to it. That poison-draught it cannot let alone, for it has an insatiable thirst for it: the taste of the draught is its annihilation, though at the same time the rise of a new principle.

We have already discussed the final aim of progression. The principles of the successive phases of Spirit that animate the Nations in a necessitated gradation, are themselves only steps in the development of the one universal Spirit, which through them elevates and completes itself to a self-comprehending *totality*.

While we are thus concerned exclusively with the Idea of Spirit, and in the History of the World regard everything as only its manifestation, we have, in traversing the past,—however extensive its periods,—only to do with what is *present*; for philosophy, as occupying itself with the True, has to do with the *eternally present*. Nothing in the past is lost for it, for the Idea is ever present; Spirit is immortal; with it there is no past, no future, but an essential *now*. This necessarily implies that the present form of Spirit comprehends within it all earlier steps. These have indeed unfolded themselves in succession independently; but what Spirit is it has always been essentially; distinctions are only the development of this essential nature. The life of the ever present Spirit is a circle of progressive embodiments, which looked at in one respect still exist beside each other, and only as looked at from another point of view appear as past. The grades which Spirit seems to have left behind it, it still possesses in the depths of its present.

History as Human Self-Knowledge

What constitutes history may be thus described: it is the act of comprehending and understanding induced by the requirements of practical life. These require-ments cannot be satisfied by recourse to action unless first of all the phantoms and doubts and shadows by which one is beset have been dispelled through the statement and resolution of a problem—that is to say—by an act of thought. In the seriousness of some requirement of practical life lies the necessary condition for this effort. It may be a moral requirement, the requirement of understanding one's situation in order that inspiration and action and the good life may follow upon this. It may be a merely economic requirement, that of discernment of one's advantage. It may be an aesthetic requirement, like that of getting clear the mean-ing of a word, or an allusion, or a state of mind, in order fully to grasp and enjoy a poem; or again an intellectual requirement like that of solving a scientific question by correcting and amplifying information about its terms through lack of which one had been perplexed and doubtful. Such knowledge of "the actual situation," as it is called, refers to the course of real life as it has gone on up to that point, and in so far as it does so, it is historical knowledge. Historical works of all times and of all peoples have come to birth in this manner and always will be born like this, out of fresh requirements which arise, and out of the perplexities involved in these. We shall not understand the history of men and of other times unless we ourselves are alive to the requirements which that history satisfied, nor will our successors understand the history of our time unless they fulfil these conditions. It often happens that the historical sense of a book is lifeless to us, and becomes mere literary form or a learned book of reference or an exciting pastime until suddenly it springs to life through new experience gained out of the course of events and through new requirements born in us which have their counterpart in, and bear a more or less intimate resemblance to those of former times; rather like certain images of Christ and the Virgin which are said suddenly to shed scarlet blood when they are hurt by some sinner or blasphemer. Historical science and culture in all its detailed elaboration exists for the purpose of maintaining and' develop-ing the active and civilized life of human society. If that impulse is barely present, historical culture is at its lowest ebb, as, for example, among Oriental peoples. When there is a sudden break or suspension in the process of civilized life, as there was in Europe in the early Middle Ages, then the writing of his-tory almost ceases and relapses into barbarism, together with the society to which it belongs. . . .

The practical requirements which underlie every historical judgment give to all history the character of "contemporary history" because, however remote in time events there recounted may seem to be, the history in reality refers to present needs and present situations wherein those events vibrate. Suppose that I have to choose between accomplishing or evading an act of expiation and turn my thoughts towards understanding what "expiation" is, what forms and transfor-

From *History as the Story of Liberty* [1938], translated from the Italian by Sylvia Sprigge, New York and London, 1941, pp. 17-20, 28-30, 32-6, 40-41, 43-4, 59; reprinted by permis-sion of George Allen and Unwin Ltd.

mations it has gone through—this institute or sentiment—before attaining a purely moral significance. Even the scapegoat of the Hebrews and all the many magical rites of primitive peoples form a part of the drama in my mind at such a time, and as I run over their history in my mind I compose the history of the situation in which I myself am.

Similarly the present state of my mind constitutes the material, and consequently the documentation for an historical judgment, the living documentation which I carry within myself. That which is usually called in an historical sense, documentation, whether written, sculptured or portrayed or imprisoned in gramophone records, or maybe existing in natural objects, skeletons or fossils, these things are not in fact documentation unless they stimulate and hold fast in me the memory of states of mind which are mine. For all other purposes they remain coloured tints, paper, stone, metal or shellac discs and the like, with no psychic efficacy whatever. If I have no feelings (however quiescent) of Christian love, of salvation by faith, of gentlemanly honour, of Jacobin radicalism or of reverence for ancient tradition, I shall vainly scan the pages of the Gospels or the Pauline epistles or the Carolingian epics, or the speeches made in the National Convention, or the lyrics, dramas and romances in which the nineteenth century recorded its nostalgia for the Middle Ages. Man is a microcosm, not in the natural sense, but in the historical sense, a compendium of universal history. The documents specifically known as such by research workers will loom very small in the total mass of documents if we bear in mind all those other documents upon which we continually rely, such as the language we speak, the customs which are familiar to us, the intuition and reasoning we use almost by instinct, the experiences which we carry as it were in our body. Without these other documents some of our historical recollections would be difficult, nay altogether impossible as is observed in certain diseased conditions from which one emerges with loss of memory and identity, as though wholly new and strange in the world to which one previously belonged. It may be noticed, by the way, that the hint of this truth that history does not come to us from without but lives within us, was one of the motives which led the philosophers of the romantic age (Fichte and others) astray into their theory of a history to be constructed a priori from pure and abstract logic and free of all documentation. . . .

Historical necessity within the logical meaning which we have determined, which is thought aware of the gravity of its task and not to be diverted from its course, must be carefully distinguished from erroneous interpretations of the same phrase. One is that history is necessary because preceding events determine those which follow in a chain of cause and effect. The following simple and fundamental truth can never be sufficiently insisted on; many minds lost in the shadows of naturalism and positivism find it hard to grasp: that "cause" (though it may seem superfluous we must here too insist that we mean the concept and not the word "cause" which belongs to ordinary conversation) the concept of cause must and should remain outside history because it was born in the realm of natural science and its place is there. . . . No one has yet succeeded in practice in relating a fragment of history by matching certain causes with their effects; though some have succeeded in adding to a narrative constructed by a different method (the spontaneous method proper to history), an improper causal terminology by way of "scientific" embellishment. Or they may as a sentimental consequence of the deterministic concept, have set out to relate history in the pessimistic and sceptical vein common to man when history, instead of seeming to have been enacted by him and to be preceding by his own initiative, falls upon him like a heap of stones which roll down from a high mountain to the bottom and pin him down there.

The other false notion of necessity is speciously presented as follows: There is a logic in history; there must be, for if there is logic in man there is also logic in history, and if the human mind thinks history it obviously thinks it logically. But the word "logic" in the above sentence means something very different from the "logicalness" of a design or programme in accordance with which history begins, develops and ends, and which it is the duty of the historian to unravel, so that he may find behind the apparent events a hidden mould giving a true and ultimate interpretation. Philosophers have frequently reasoned on this basis, deducing their design from the concept of an idea or of the Spirit or even of Matter; although Idea, Spirit, Matter were only different disguises for a transcendental God, who could think and impose his thought upon men and have it carried out. This is the naked and bare form to which the design must be reduced, and in that form contemplated: a form which Thomas Campanella in his sonnets with no satirical or burlesque intention describes as a "book of words of the comedy of jesting" or as "a scenario" such as the theatrical managers of his day used to outline the action of the comedy, and to give each actor his part during the rehearsal. Abbé Galiani found another simile for it in the vantage of card-cheats, who play with loaded or marked dice. However that may be, no one has yet written such a history; and the embarrassment of its partisans and adherents has already been shown in their method, by their very request, both contradictory and superfluous, that historical research should reveal a design beyond the range of evidence and documents, and therefore unattainable by those means. They made histories and christened them as such by using evidence sometimes as a symbol, sometimes as a superfluous ornament to decorate the display they made of their beliefs, tendencies, hopes and fears, in politics, religion or philosophy. On a par with causality, the transcendental God is a stranger to human history, which would not exist if that God did exist; for History is its own mystic Dionysus, its own suffering Christ, redeemer of sins.

Another false concept disappears from history together with this doubly false idea of necessity, from which it is derived; the concept of historical foresight. If the last act only in the divine programme was generally revealed (for example the coming of the Anti-Christ, the end of the world and the universal judgment day), yet the rest of the programme from the present backwards, was also—on that view—written in the book of Providence, and one small section might through grace be revealed to some pious man. Similarly with the causal concept the Chain of Cause and Effect proceeded and by calculation future links in it could be foreseen. In practice, however, it became confessedly impossible to predict anything, in the first case because of the inscrutability of the divine will, in the second because of the enormous complexity of the various causes concerned, so that the faithful naturalist behaved like the naturalistic author of the story of the Rougon Macquart family; Zola in that novel worked out their family tree from the trunk to the branches and twiglets, submitting them to the cause of heredity, but then over the niche prepared for a child about to be born had nothing to ask but the ironic question left unanswered: "Quel sera-t-il?" . . .

It is not enough to say that history is historical judgment, it is necessary to add that every judgment is an historical judgment or, quite simply, history. If judgment is a relation between a subject and a predicate, then the subject or the event, whatever it is that is being judged, is always an historical fact, a becoming, a process under way, for there are no immobile facts nor can such things be envisaged in the world of reality. Historical judgment is embodied even in the merest perception of the judging mind (if it did not judge there would not even be perception but merely blind and dumb sensation): for example the perception that the object in front of me is a stone, and that it will not fly away of its own accord like a bird at the sound of my approach makes it expedient that I should dislodge it with my stick or with my foot. The stone is really a process under way, struggling against the forces of disintegration and yielding only bit by bit, and my judgment refers to one aspect of its history.

But we may not rest here either, nor renounce further consequences: historical judgment is not a variety of knowldege, but it is knowledge itself; it is the form which completely fills and exhausts the field of knowing, leaving no room for anything else.

In point of fact all concrete knowledge whatever is on a par with historical judgment, bound to life, that is to action, of which it marks a pause or an anticipation having for its function to break down (as we have said) any obstacles barring a clear view of the situation from which it must specifically and with determination emerge. Knowledge for the sake of knowledge, so far from having anything aristocratic or sublime about it (as some believe), would be an idiotic pastime for idiots, or for the idiotic moments which we all have in us; in reality there is no such thing, it is intrinsically impossible and the stimulus ceases with the failure of the material itself and of the end of knowledge. Those intellectuals who see salvation in the withdrawal of the artist or the thinker from the world around him, in his deliberate non-participation in vulgar practical contrasts—vulgar in so far as they are practical—do without knowing it compass the death of the intellect. In a paradisal state without work or struggle in which there were no obstacles to overcome, there could be no thought, because every motive for thought would have disappeared; neither any real contemplation, because active and poetic contemplation contains in itself a world of practical struggles and of affections. . . .

Natural science, therefore, is not seriously at variance or in opposition to the theory that all genuine knowledge is historical knowledge; like history it deals with the actual and humble world. It is not so with philosophy, or, if you like, with the traditional idea of a philosophy which has its eyes fixed on heaven, and expects supreme truth from that quarter. This division of heaven and earth, this dualist conception of a reality which transcends reality, of metaphysics over physics, this contemplation of the concept without or outside judgment, for ever imprints the same character, whatever denomination the transcendental reality may bear: God or Matter, Idea or Will; it makes no difference, while beneath or against each of them there is presumed to subsist some inferior or merely phenomenal reality.

But historical thought has played a nasty trick on this respectable transcendental philosophy, as upon its twin, transcendental religion, of which the former is the reasoned or theological form; the trick of turning it into history, by interpreting all its concepts, doctrines, disputes, and even its disconsolate sceptical renunciations, as historical facts and affirmations, which arose out of certain requirements, that were thus partly satisfied and partly unsatisfied. In this way historical thought did due justice to the age-long domination of transcendental philosophy (a domination which was also a service to human society) and marked its end with a decent obituary. It can be said that once transcendental philosophy was subjected to historical criticism, philosophy itself ceased to enjoy an autonomous existence because its claim to autonomy was founded upon its metaphysical character. That which has taken its place is no longer philosophy, but history, or, which amounts to the same thing, philosophy in so far as it is history and history in so far as it is philosophy: "History-Philosophy," of which the principle is the identity of the universal and the individual, of the intellect and the intuition, and which regards as arbitrary and illegitimate any separation of those two elements, they being in reality a single element. It is a curious fate that history should for a long time have been considered and treated as the most humble form of knowledge, while philosophy was considered as the highest, and that now it not only is superior to philosophy but annihilates it. This so-called history which had been relegated to a back seat was not in truth history, but chronicles and research, superficially considered and based on hearsay: the other kind of history which has now asserted itself is historical thought, sole and integral form of knowledge. When the old metaphysical philosophy tried to lend a helping hand to history in order to draw it out of the depths, it was not to history but to the chronicle that the hand was given, and as this could not be raised to the rank of history by reason of its metaphysical character, a "philosophy of history" was superimposed upon it, a process of excogitation and guess-work, to which we have referred above, a sort of divine programme which history carries out like someone who tries to make a more or less careful copy of a model. The "philosophy of history" was a consequence of mental impotence, or, as Vico said of myths, of bankruptcy of the mind.

Among the various didactic forms of literature there certainly are works which may be classed as philosophy and not as history because they seem to treat of abstract concepts, purged of any intuitive elements. But if these treatises are not mere circlings in the void, if they contain full and concrete judgments, then the intuitive element is always there, even if it is latent to the vulgar eye, which is only on the look out for it when it appears as an incrustation of chronicle writing or of erudition. The intuitive element is there, in the very fact that the philosophical arguments formulated in it answer the need for light on particular historical conditions: the knowledge of these conditions explains the argument just as these conditions are themselves explained by the arguments. I was going to say, to take a living example, that even the methodological elucidations which I am giving here are not really intelligible unless with an explicit mental reference (normally made by me simply in an implicit way) to the political, moral and intellectual conditions of our times, which they help to describe and judge. . . .

The conclusions of all modern philosophy, from Descartes and Vico and Kant and Hegel down to contemporary thinkers, are that thought is as active as action, that it is neither a copy nor a recipient for a reality, nor therefore does it provide knowledge of reality by serving such purposes; on the contrary, its work consists in setting and solving problems, and not merely in passively receiving fragments of reality; finally, thought does not stand outside life but is its vital function. But the sophism to which we have referred above maintains that thought cannot be distinguished from will, that each of these is equally active, and it pretends that the distinction of which we have just spoken is identical with that which is erroneously made between the activity of will and the passivity of thought. This argument is a sophistry and therefore invalid; and the ancient distinction between knowledge and will, thought and action, stands intact.

Yes, it is unaltered in its substance although greatly modified and deepened by reference to the way in which it was previously conceived as a juxtaposition or parallelism or a divergence of two faculties of the soul, and also as touching the precedence of knowledge over will and practical action, or inversely of the latter over the former. For if knowledge is necessary to practice, practice as we have demonstrated above is necessary to knowledge, and cannot arise without it. There is a circle of the spirit which, when recognized, does away with all need of a primary absolute and a secondary dependent, by continually making the first the second and the second the first. This circle is the true unity and identity of the spirit with itself, of a spirit which feeds on itself and goes beyond itself. Every other unity is static and dead, mechanical and not organic, mathematical and not speculative or dialectic.

If the attempt to cancel the distinction between these two elements of the spirit were not puerile and ingenious, its effect would be to destroy the life of the spirit in a simultaneous destruction of thought and action. Once identified with the will, and with the aims of the will, thought would cease to be the creator of life, and by becoming tendencious it would decay into untruth. Will and action being no longer illumined by truth, would then be debased to passionate and pathological fury and spasm. Nothing of this kind happens because it would be against the nature of things that it should, and against the life of the spirit, which continually resists the seductions whereby practical interests try to interrupt or mislead the logic of truth, and labours ceaselessly to transform blind passion into enlightened will and action: so that there is no need to fear that the order of things will collapse or that the world will come to an end. . . .

We are products of the past and we live immersed in the past, which encompasses us. How can we move towards the new life, how create new activities without getting out of the past and without placing ourselves above it? And how can we place ourselves above the past if we are in it and it is in us? There is no other way out except through thought, which does not break off relations with the past but rises ideally above it and converts it into knowledge. The past must be faced or, not to speak in metaphors, it must be reduced to a mental problem which can find its solution in a proposition of truth, the ideal premise for our new activity and our new life. This is how we daily behave, when, instead of being prostrated by the vexations which beset us, and of bewailing and being shamed by errors we have committed, we examine what has happened, analyse its origin, follow its history, and, with an informed conscience and under an intimate inspiration, we outline what ought and should be undertaken and willingly and brightly get ready to undertake it. Humanity always behaves in the same way when faced with its great and varied past. The writing of histories—as

Goethe once noted—is one way of getting rid of the weight of the past. Historical thought transforms it into its own material and transfigures it into its object, and the writing of history liberates us from history. . . .

Hegel's famous statement that history is the history of liberty was repeated without being altogether understood and then spread throughout Europe by Cousin, Michelet and other French writers. But Hegel and his disciples used it with the significance which we have criticized above, of a history of the first birth of liberty, of its growth, of its maturity and of its stable permanence in the definite era in which it is incapable of further development. (The formula was: Orient, Classic World, Germanic World = one free, some free, all free.) The statement is adduced in this place with a different intention and content, not in order to assign to history the task of creating a liberty which did not exist in the past but will exist in the future, but to maintain that liberty is the eternal creator of history and itself the subject of every history. As such it is on the one hand the explanatory principle of the course of history, and on the other the moral ideal of humanity.

GIAMBATTISTA VICO
The Three Ages

Human choice, by its nature most uncertain, is made certain and determined by the common sense of men with respect to human needs or utilities, which are the two sources of the natural law of the gentes.

Common sense is judgment without reflection, shared by an entire class, an entire people, an entire nation, or the entire human race. This axiom, with the following definition, will provide a new art of criticism concerning the founders of nations, who must have preceded by more than a thousand years the writers with whom criticism has so far been occupied.

Uniform ideas originating among entire peoples unknown to each other must have a common ground of truth. This axiom is a great principle which establishes the common sense of the human race as the criterion taught to the nations by divine providence to define what is certain in the natural law of the gentes. And the nations reach this certainty by recognizing the underlying agreements which, despite variations of detail, obtain among them all in respect of this law. Thence issues the mental dictionary for assigning origins to all the divers articulated languages. It is by means of this dictionary that the ideal eternal history is conceived. . . .

Two great remnants of Egyptian antiquity have come down to us. One of them is that the Egyptians reduced all preceding world time to three ages; namely, the age of gods, the age of heroes, and the age of men. The other is that during these three ages three languages had been spoken, corresponding in order to the three aforesaid ages; namely, the hieroglyphic or sacred language, the symbolic or figurative (which is the heroic) language, and the epistolary or vulgar language of men employing conventional signs for communicating the common needs of their life. . . .

Men first feel necessity, then look for utility, next attend to comfort, still later amuse themselves with pleasure, thence grow dissolute in luxury, and finally go mad and waste their substance.

From *The New Science* [3rd edition, 1744], translated from the Italian by T. G. Bergin and M. H. Fisch, Ithaca, 1948, pp. 57, 62, 70-71, 93, 301-10, 377-82. Copyright 1948 by Cornell University; reprinted by permission of Cornell University Press.

The nature of peoples is first crude, then severe, then benign, then delicate, finally dissolute.

In the human race first appear the huge and grotesque, like the cyclopes; then the proud and magnanimous, like Achilles; then the valorous and just, like Aristides and Scipio Africanus; nearer to us, imposing figures with great semblances of virtue accompanied by great vices, who among the vulgar win a name for true glory, like Alexander and Caesar; still later, the melancholy and reflective, like Tiberius; finally the dissolute and shameless madmen, like Caligula, Nero, and Domitian. This axiom shows that the first sort were necessary in order to make one man obey another in the family-state and prepare him to be law-abiding in the city-state that was to come; the second sort who naturally did not yield to their peers, were necessary to establish the aristocratic commonwealths on the basis of the families; the third sort, to open the way for popular liberty; the fourth, to bring in the monarchies; the fifth, to establish them; the sixth, to overthrow them. This, with the preceding axioms gives a part of the principles of the ideal eternal history traversed in time by every nation in its rise, development, maturity, decline, and fall. . . .

We make bold to affirm that he who meditates this Science narrates to himself this ideal eternal history so far as he himself makes it for himself by that proof "it had, has, and will have to be." For the first indubitable principle posited above is that this world of nations has certainly been made by men, and its guise must therefore be found within the modifications of our own human mind. . . . And history cannot be more certain than when he who creates the things also narrates them. Now, as geometry, when it constructs the world of quantity out of its elements, or contemplates that world, is creating it for itself, just so does our Science [create for itself the world of nations], but with a reality greater by just so much as the institutions having to do with human affairs are more real than points, lines, surfaces, and figures are. And this very fact is an argument, O reader, that these proofs are of a kind divine and should give thee a divine pleasure, since in God knowledge and creation are one and the same thing. . . .

We shall now, by the aid of this philosophical and philological illumination, and relying on the axioms concerning the ideal eternal history, discuss . . . the course the nations run, proceeding in all their various and diverse customs with constant uniformity upon the division of the three ages which the Egyptians said had elapsed before them in their world, namely, the successive ages of gods, heroes, and men. For the nations will be seen to develop in conformity with this division, by a constant and uninterrupted order of causes and effects present in every nation, through three kinds of natures. From these natures arise three kinds of customs, and in virtue of these customs three kinds of natural laws of the gentes are observed; and in consequence of these laws three kinds of civil states or commonwealths are instituted. And to the end that men who have come to human society may on the one hand communicate to each other the three kinds of all the aforesaid major institutions, three kinds of languages and as many of characters are formed; and to the end that they may on the other hand justify them, three kinds of jurisprudence assisted by three kinds of author-

ity and three kinds of reason in as many of judgments. The three kinds of jurisprudence prevail in three sects of times, which the nations profess in the course
of their lives. These [eleven] triadic special unities, with many others that derive
from them and will also be enumerated, . . . are all embraced by one general
unity. This is the unity of the religion of a provident divinity, which is the unity
of spirit that informs and gives life to this world of nations. Having discussed
these institutions above in widely separate passages, we shall here exhibit the order
of their development.

The first nature, by a powerful deceit of imagination, which is most robust in
the weakest at reasoning, was a poetic or creative nature which we may be allowed to call divine, as it ascribed to physical things the being of substances animated by gods, assigning the gods to them according to its idea of each. This
nature was that of the theological poets, who were the earliest wise men in all the
gentile nations, when all the gentile nations were founded on the belief which
each of them had in certain gods of its own. Furthermore it was a nature all
fierce and cruel; but, through that same error of their imagination, men had a
terrible fear of the gods whom they themselves had created, From this there remained these two eternal properties: one, that religion is the only means powerful
enough to restrain the fierceness of peoples; and the other, that religions flourish
when they are inwardly revered by those who preside over them.

The second was heroic nature, believed by the heroes themselves to be of
divine origin; for, since they believed that the gods made and did everything,
they held themselves to be sons of Jove, as having been generated under his
auspices. Being thus of the human [not a bestial] species, they justly regarded
their heroism as including the natural nobility in virtue of which they were the
princes of the human race. And this natural nobility they made their boast over
those who had fled from the infamous and bestial promiscuity to save themselves
from the strife it entailed, and had taken refuge in their asylums; for, since they
had come thither without gods, the heroes regarded them as beasts. . . .

The third was human nature, intelligent and hence modest, benign, and reasonable, recognizing for laws conscience, reason, and duty.

The first customs were all tinged with religion and piety, like those of Deu-
calion and Pyrrha, fresh from the flood. The second were choleric and punctilious, like those related of Achilles. The third are dutiful, taught to everyone by
his own sense of civil duty.

The first law was divine, for men believed themselves and all their institutions to
depend on the gods, since they thought everything was a god or was made or done
by a god.

The second was heroic law, the law of force, but controlled by religion, which
alone can keep force within bounds where there are no human laws or none strong
enough to curb it. Hence providence ordained that the first peoples, ferocious by
nature, should be persuaded by this their religion to acquiesce naturally in force,
and that, being as yet incapable of reason, they should measure right by fortune,
with a view to which they took counsel by auspicial divination. This law of force is
the law of Achilles, who referred every right to the tip of his spear.

The third is the human law dictated by fully developed human reason.

The first was divine, or, as the Greeks would say, theocratic, in which men believed that everything was commanded by the gods. This was the age of oracles, which are the earliest institution we read of in history.

The second were heroic or aristocratic governments, which is as much as to say governments of the optimates in the sense of the most powerful. In Greek they were called governments of Heraclids (men sprung from the race of Hercules), in the sense of nobles; these were scattered throughout early Greece, and survived at Sparta. They were also called governments of Curetes, which the Greeks found scattered in Saturnia (ancient Italy), Crete, and Asia; and hence governments of Quirites among the Romans, that is, of armed priests in public assembly. In governments of this kind, in virtue of the distinction of a nobler nature ascribed to divine origin, as we have noted above, all civil rights were confined to the ruling orders of the heroes themselves, and the plebeians, being considered of bestial origin, were only permitted to enjoy life and natural liberty.

The third are human governments, in which, in virtue of the equality of the intelligent nature which is the proper nature of man, all are accounted equal under the laws, inasmuch as all are born free in their cities. This is the case in the free popular cities in which all or the majority make up the just forces of the city, in virtue of which they are the lords of popular liberty. It is also the case in monarchies, in which the monarchs make all their subjects equal under their laws, and, having all the force of arms in their own hands, are themselves the only bearers of any distinction in civil nature.

Three kinds of languages:

The first of these was a divine mental language by mute religious acts or divine ceremonies, from which there survived in Roman civil law the *actus legitimi* which accompanied all their civil transactions. This language belongs to religions by the eternal property that it concerns them more to be reverenced than to be reasoned, and it was necessary in the earliest times when men did not yet possess articulate speech.

The second was by heroic blazonings, with which arms are made to speak; this kind of speech survived in military discipline.

The third is by articulate speech, which is used by all nations today.

Three kinds of characters:

The first were divine, properly called hieroglyphics, used, as we have shown above, by all nations in their beginnings. And they were certain imaginative universals, dictated naturally by the human mind's innate property of delighting in the uniform. Since they could not achieve this by logical abstraction, they did it by imaginative representation. To these poetic universals they reduced all the particular species belonging to each genus, as to Jove everything concerning the auspices, to Juno everything touching marriage, and so on.

The second were heroic characters, which were also imaginative universals to which they reduced the various species of heroic things, as to Achilles all the deeds of valiant fighters and to Ulysses all the devices of clever men. These imaginative genera, as the human mind later learned to abstract forms and properties from subjects, passed over into intelligible genera, which prepared the way for the philosophers, from whom the authors of the New Comedy, which came in the most human times of Greece, took the intelligible genera of human customs and portrayed them in their comedies.

Finally, there were invented the vulgar characters which went along with the vulgar languages. The latter are composed of words, which are genera, as it were, of the particulars previously employed by the heroic languages; as, to repeat an example cited above, out of the heroic phrase "The blood boils in my heart" they made the word "I am angry." In like fashion, of a hundred and twenty thousand hieroglyphic characters (the number still used, for example, by the Chinese) they made a few letters, to which, as to genera, they reduced the hundred and twenty thousand words (of which the Chinese vulgar spoken language is composed). This invention certainly is the work of a mind more than human. . . . It is easy to understand how the common sense of marvel led the nations to believe that these letters had been invented for them by men eminent in divinity, as by St. Jerome in the case of the Illyrians, St. Cyril in that of the Slavs. . . . But such an opinion can be convicted of manifest falsity if we pose the simple question: Why did they not teach letters of their own creation? Cadmus, for example, brought letters from Phoenicia to the Greeks, yet the latter afterward used letters of very different forms from the Phoenician.

Such languages and letters were under the sovereignty of the vulgar of the various peoples, whence both are called vulgar. In virtue of this sovereignty over languages and letters, the free peoples must also be masters of their laws, for they impose on the laws the senses in which they constrain the powerful to observe them, even against their will, as we noted in the Axioms. It is naturally not in the power of monarchs to deprive the people of this sovereignty, but, in virtue of this very inalienable nature of human civil affairs, such sovereignty, inseparable from the people, contributes largely to the power of the monarchs, for they may issue their royal laws, which the nobles must accept, according to the senses that their peoples give to them. This sovereignty over vulgar letters and languages implies that, in the order of civil nature, the free popular commonwealths preceded the monarchies.

Three kinds of jurisprudence, or [legal] wisdom.

The first was a divine wisdom called mystic theology, which means the science of divine speech or the understanding of the divine mysteries of divination. This science of auspicial divinity was the vulgar wisdom whose sages were the theological poets, who were the first sages of the gentile world. From this mystic theology they were called *mystai*, or mystics, which the well-informed Horace translates as interpreters of the gods. To this first jurisprudence therefore belonged the first and proper interpreting, called *interpretari* for *interpatrari*; that is, "to enter into the fathers," as the gods were at first called. Dante would call it *indiarsi*, to enter into the mind of God. This sort of jurisprudence measured justice only by the solemnity of the divine ceremonies; whence the Romans preserved such a superstitious regard for the *actus legitimi*, and they retained in their laws the phrases *iustae nuptiae, iustum testamentum*, for solemnized nuptials and testaments.

The second was the heroic jurisprudence, taking precautions by the use of certain proper words. Such is the wisdom of Ulysses, who speaks so adroitly in Homer that he obtains the advantages he seeks while always observing the propriety of his words. Hence all the reputation of the ancient Roman jurisconsults rested in their *cavere*, their taking care or making sure; and their *de iure respondere* was nothing but cautioning clients who had to present their cases in court to set forth the facts to the praetor with such circumstances that the formulae for action would be satisfied and the praetor would be unable to withhold them. Similarly in the returned barbarian times all the reputation of the doctors rested on finding safeguards for contracts and wills and on knowing how to draw pleadings and articles; which correspond exactly to the *cavere* and the *de iure respondere* of the Roman jurisconsults.

The third is human jurisprudence, which looks to the truth of the facts themselves and benignly bends the rule of law to all the requirements of the equity of the causes. This kind of jurisprudence is observed in the free popular commonwealths and even more under the monarchies, which are both human governments.

––––––––––

Let us now conclude this work with Plato, who conceives a fourth kind of commonwealth, in which good honest men would be supreme lords. This would be the true natural aristocracy. This commonwealth conceived by Plato was brought into being by providence from the first beginnings of the nations. For it ordained that men of gigantic stature, stronger than the rest, who were to wander on the mountain heights as do the beasts of stronger natures, should, at the first thunderclaps after the universal flood, take refuge in the caves of the mountains, subject themselves to a higher power which they imagined as Jove, and, all amazement as they were all pride and cruelty, humble themselves before a divinity. For in this order of human institutions we cannot conceive how divine providence could have employed any other counsel to halt them in their bestial wandering through the great forest of the earth, to the end of introducing among them the order of human civil institutions.

Here was formed a state so to speak of monastic commonwealths or of solitary sovereigns under the government of a Greatest and Best whom they themselves created for their faith out of the flash of the thunderbolts, in which this true light of God shone forth for them: that he governs mankind. Hence they came to imagine that all the human benefits supplied to them and all the aids provided for their human needs were so many gods, and feared and revered them as such. Then, between the powerful restraints of frightful superstition and the goading stimuli of bestial lust (which must both have been extremely violent in such men), as they felt the aspect of the heavens to be terrible to them and hence to inhibit their use of venery, they must have learned to hold in check the impulse of the bodily motion of lust. Thus they began to use human liberty, which consists in controlling the motions of concupiscence and giving them another direction; for since this liberty does not come from the body, whence comes concupiscence, it must come from the mind and is therefore properly human. The new direction took the form of forcibly seizing their women, who were naturally shy and unruly, dragging them into their caves, and, in order to have intercourse with them, keeping them there as perpetual lifelong companions. Thus, with the first human, which is to say chaste and religious, couplings, they gave a beginning to matrimony. Thereby they became certain fathers of certain children by certain women.

Thus they founded the families and governed them with a cyclopean family sovereignty over their children and their wives, such as was proper to such proud and savage natures, so that later as cities arose men might be found disposed to stand in awe of the civil sovereignty. Thus providence ordained certain household commonwealths of monarchic form under fathers (in that state princes) best in sex, age, and virtue. These fathers, in the state we must call that of nature (which was identical with the state of the families), must have formed the first natural orders, as being those who were pious, chaste, and strong. Since they were settled on their lands and could no longer escape by flight (as they had previously done in their bestial wanderings), in order to defend themselves and their families they had to kill the wild beasts that attacked them. And in order to provide sustenance for themselves and their families, as they had ceased foraging, they had to tame the earth and sow grain. All this for the salvation of the nascent human race.

Meanwhile, scattered through the plains and valleys and preserving the infamous promiscuity of things and of women, there remained a great number of the impious, the unchaste, and the nefarious—impious in having no fear of gods, unchaste in their use of shameless bestial venery, and nefarious in their frequent intercourse with their own mothers and daughters. After a long time, driven by the ills occasioned by their bestial society, weak, astray, and solitary, relentlessly pursued by the robust and violent because of quarrels engendered by their infamous promiscuity, they came at last to seek refuge in the asylums of the fathers. The latter, taking them under their protection, proceeded to extend their family kingdoms to include these *famuli* through the clienteles. Thus they developed commonwealths on the basis of orders naturally superior by reason of virtues certainly heroic. First, piety, for they adored divinity, though because of their little light they multiplied and divided it into many gods formed according to their various apprehensions. . . . And in virtue of their piety they were also endowed with prudence, taking counsel from the auspices of the gods; with temperance, each coupling chastely with the one woman whom he had taken under the divine auspices as perpetual companion for life; with strength for slaying beasts and taming the earth; and with magnanimity in giving succor to the weak and aid to those in danger. Such was the nature of the Herculean commonwealths, in which the pious, wise, chaste, strong, and magnanimous cast down the proud and defended the weak, which is the mark of excellence in civil governments.

But finally the family fathers, having become great by the religion and virtue of their ancestors and through the labors of their clients, began to abuse the laws of protection and to govern the clients harshly. When they had thus departed from the natural order, which is that of justice, their clients rose in mutiny against them. But since without order (which is to say without God) human society cannot stand for a moment, providence led the family fathers naturally to unite themselves with their kindred in orders against their clients. To pacify the latter, they conceded to them, in the world's first agrarian law, the bonitary ownership of the fields, retaining for themselves the optimal or sovereign family ownership. Thus the first cities arose upon reigning orders of nobles. And as the natural order declined which had been based, in accordance with the then state of nature, on [superiority of] kind, sex, age, and virtue, providence called the civil order into being along with the cities. And first of all [civil orders], that which approximated most closely to nature: that in virtue of nobility of humankind (for in that state of affairs nobility could be based only on generating in human fashion with wives taken under divine auspices) and thus in virtue of a heroism, the nobles should rule over the plebeians (who did not contract marriage with such solemnities), and now that divine rules had ceased (under which the families had been governed by divine auspices) and the heroes had to rule in virtue of the form of the heroic governments themselves, that the basic institutions of these commonwealths should be religion safeguarded within the heroic orders, and that through this religion all civil laws and institutions should belong to the heroes alone. But since nobility had now become a gift of fortune, providence caused to arise among the nobles the order of the family fathers themselves, as being naturally more worthy because of age. And among the fathers it caused the most spirited and robust to arise as kings whose duty it should be to lead the others and gird them in orders to resist and overawe the clients who rebelled against them.

But with the passage of the years and the far greater development of human minds, the plebs of the peoples finally became suspicious of the pretensions of such heroism and understood themselves to be of equal human nature with the nobles, and therefore insisted that they too should enter into the civil institutions of the cities. Since in due time the peoples were to become sovereign, providence permitted a long antecedent struggle of plebs with nobility over piety and religion in the heroic contests for the extension of the auspices by the nobles to the plebeians, with a view to securing thereby the extension of all public and private civil institutions regarded as dependent on the auspices. Thus the very care for piety and attachment to religion brought the people to civil sovereignty. In this respect the Roman people went beyond all others in the world, and for that reason it became the master people of the world. In this way, as the natural order merged more and more with the civil orders, the popular commonwealths were born. In these everything had to be reduced to lot or balance, and providence therefore, in order that neither chance nor fate should rule, ordained that the census should be the measure of fitness for office. Thereby the industrious and not the lazy, the frugal and not the prodigal, the provident and not the idle, the magnanimous and not the fainthearted—in a word, the rich with some virtue or semblance thereof, and not the poor with their many shameless vices—were considered the best for governing. In such commonwealths the entire peoples, who have in common the desire for justice, command laws that are just because they are good for all. Such a law Aristotle divinely defines as will without passions, which would be the will of a hero who has command of his passions. These commonwealths gave birth to philosophy. By their very form they inspired it to form the hero, and for that purpose to interest itself in truth. All this was ordained by providence to the end that, since virtuous actions were no longer prompted by religious sentiments as formerly, philosophy should make the virtues understood in their idea, and by dint of reflection thereon, if men were without virtue they should at least be ashamed of their vices. Only so can people prone to ill-doing be held to their duty. And from the philosophies providence permitted eloquence to arise and, from the very form of these popular commonwealths in which good laws are commanded, to become impassioned for justice, and from these ideas of virtue to inflame the peoples to command good laws. Such eloquence, we resolutely affirm, flourished in Rome in the time of Scipio Africanus, when civil wisdom and military valor, which happily united in establishing at Rome on the ruins of Carthage the empire of the world, must necessarily have brought in their train a robust and most prudent eloquence.

But as the popular states became corrupt, so also did the philosophies. They descended to skepticism. Learned fools fell to calumniating the truth. Thence arose a false eloquence, ready to uphold either of the opposed sides of a case indifferently. Thus it came about that, by abuse of eloquence like that of the tribunes of the plebs at Rome, when the citizens were no longer content with making wealth the basis of rank, they strove to make it an instrument of power. And as furious south winds whip up the sea, so these citizens provoked civil wars in their commonwealths and drove them to total disorder. Thus they caused the commonwealths to fall from a perfect liberty into the perfect tyranny of anarchy or the unchecked liberty of the free peoples, which is the worst of all tyrannies.

To this great disease of cities providence applies one of these three great remedies in the following order of human civil institutions.

It first ordains that there be found among these peoples a man like Augustus to arise and establish himself as a monarch and, by force of arms, take in hand all the institutions and all the laws, which, though sprung from liberty, no longer avail to regulate and hold it within bounds. On the other hand providence ordains that the very form of the monarchic state shall confine the will of the monarchs, in spite of their unlimited sovereignty, within the natural order of keeping the peoples content and satisfied with both their religion and their natural liberty. For without this universal satisfaction and content of the peoples, monarchic states are neither lasting nor secure.

Then, if providence does not find such a remedy within, it seeks it outside. And since peoples so far corrupted had already become naturally slaves of their unrestrained passions—of luxury, effeminacy, avarice, envy, pride, and vanity—and in pursuit of the pleasures of their dissolute life were falling back into all the vices characteristic of the most abject slaves (having become liars, tricksters, calumniators, thieves, cowards, and pretenders), providence decrees that they become slaves by the natural law of the gentes which springs from this nature of nations, and that they become subject to better nations, which, having conquered them by arms, preserve them as subject provinces. Herein two great lights of natural order shine forth. First, that he who cannot govern himself must let himself be governed by another who can. Second, that the world is always governed by those who are naturally fittest.

But if the peoples are rotting in that ultimate civil disease and cannot agree on a monarch from within, and are not conquered and preserved by better nations from without, then providence for their extreme ill has its extreme remedy at hand. For such peoples, like so many beasts, have fallen into the custom of each man thinking only of his own private interests and have reached the extreme of delicacy, or better of pride, in which like wild animals they bristle and lash out at the slightest displeasure. Thus no matter how great the throng and press of their bodies, they live like wild beasts in a deep solitude of spirit and will, scarcely any two being able to agree since each follows his own pleasure or caprice. By reason of all this, providence decrees that, through obstinate factions and desperate civil wars, they shall turn their cities into forests and the forests into dens and lairs of men. In this way, through long centuries of barbarism, rust will consume the misbegotten subtleties of malicious wits that have turned them into beasts made more inhuman by the barbarism of reflection than the first men had been made by the barbarism of sense. For the latter displayed a generous savagery, against which one could defend oneself or take flight or be on one's guard: but the former, with a base savagery, under soft words and embraces, plots against the life and fortune of friends and intimates. Hence peoples who have reached this point of premeditated malice, when they receive this last remedy of providence and are thereby stunned and brutalized, are sensible no longer of comforts, delicacies, pleasures, and pomp, but only of the sheer necessities of life. And the few survivors in the midst of an abundance of the things necessary for life naturally become sociable and, returning to the primitive simplicity of the first world of peoples, are again religious, truthful, and faithful. Thus providence brings back among them the piety, faith, and truth which are the natural foundations of justice as well as the graces and beauties of the eternal order of God.

The clear and simple observation we have made on the institutions of the entire human race, if we had been told nothing more by the philosophers, historians, grammarians, and jurisconsults, would lead us to say certainly that this is the great city of the nations that was founded and is governed by God. Lycurgus, Solon, the decemvirs, and the like have been eternally praised to the skies as wise legislators, because it has hitherto been believed that by their good institutions and good laws they had founded Sparta, Athens, and Rome, the three cities that outshone all others in the fairest and greatest civil virtues. Yet they were all of short duration and even of small extent as compared with the universe of peoples, which was ordered by such institutions and secured by such laws that even in its decay it assumes those forms of states by which alone it may everywhere be preserved and perpetually endure. And must we not then say that this is a counsel of a superhuman wisdom? For without the force of laws (whose force, according to Dio, is like that of a tyrant), but making use of the very customs of men (in the practice of which they are as free of all force as in the expression of their own nature, whence the same Dio said that customs were like kings in commanding by pleasure), it divinely rules and conducts [the aforesaid city].

It is true that men have themselves made this world of nations (and we took this as the first incontestable principle of our Science, since we despaired of finding it from the philosophers and philologists, but this world without doubt has issued from a mind often diverse, at times quite contrary, and always superior to the particular ends that men had proposed to themselves; which narrow ends, made means to serve wider ends, it has always employed to preserve the human race upon this earth. Men mean to gratify their bestial lust and abandon their offspring, and they inaugurate the chastity of marriage from which the families arise. The fathers mean to exercise without restraint their paternal power over their clients, and they subject them to the civil powers from which the cities arise. The reigning orders of nobles mean to abuse their lordly freedom over the plebeians, and they are obliged to submit to the laws which establish popular liberty. The free peoples mean to shake off the yoke of their laws, and they become subject to monarchs. The monarchs mean to strengthen their own positions by debasing their subjects with all the vices of dissoluteness, and they dispose them to endure slavery at the hands of stronger nations. The nations mean to dissolve themselves, and their remnants flee for safety to the wilderness, whence, like the phoenix, they rise again. That which did all this was mind, for men did it with intelligence; it was not fate, for they did it by choice; not chance, for the results of their always so acting are perpetually the same.

Eternal Recurrence

"Stop, dwarf!" I said. "I! Or you! But I am the stronger of us two—you do not know my abysmal thought! That thought—you could not endure!"

Then something occurred which lightened me: for the dwarf jumped from my shoulder, the inquisitive dwarf! And he squatted down upon a stone in front of me. But a gateway stood just where we had halted.

"Behold this gateway, dwarf!" I went on: "it has two aspects. Two paths come together here: no one has ever reached their end.

"This long lane behind us: it goes on for an eternity. And that long lane ahead of us—that is another eternity.

"They are in opposition to one another, these paths; they abut on one another: and it is here at this gateway that they come together. The name of the gateway is written above it: 'Moment.'

"But if one were to follow them further and ever further and further: do you think, dwarf, that these paths would be in eternal opposition?" . . .

"Behold this moment!" I went on. "From this gateway Moment a long, eternal lane runs *back*: an eternity lies behind us.

"Must not all things that *can* run have already run along this lane? Must not all things that *can* happen *have* already happened, been done, run past?

"And if all things have been here before: what do you think of this moment, dwarf? Must not this gateway, too, have been here—before?

"And are not all things bound fast together in such a way that this moment draws after it all future things? *Therefore*—draws itself too?

"For all things that *can* run *must* also run once again forward along this long lane.

"And this slow spider that creeps along in the moonlight, and this moonlight itself, and I and you at this gateway whispering together, whispering of eternal things—must we not all have been here before?

"—and must we not return and run down that other lane out before us, down that long, terrible lane—must we not return eternally?"

"O Zarathustra," said the animals then, "all things themselves dance for such as think as we: they come and offer their hand and laugh and flee—and return.

"Everything goes, everything returns; the wheel of existence rolls for ever. Everything dies, everything blossoms anew; the year of existence runs on for ever.

"Everything breaks, everything is joined anew; the same house of existence builds itself for ever. Everything departs, everything meets again; the ring of existence is true to itself for ever.

From *Thus Spoke Zarathustra* [1883], translated from the German by R. J. Hollingdale, 1961, pp. 178-9, 234, 236-8, 331-3; reprinted by permission of Penguin Books Inc.

"Existence begins in every instant; the ball There rolls around every Here. The middle is everywhere. The path of eternity is crooked."

" 'Alas, man recurs eternally! The little man recurs eternally!'

"I had seen them both naked, the greatest man and the smallest man: all too similar to one another, even the greatest all too human!

"The greatest all too small!—that was my disgust at man! And eternal recurrence even for the smallest! that was my disgust at all existence!

"Ah, disgust! Disgust! Disgust!" Thus spoke Zarathustra and sighed and shuddered; for he remembered his sickness. But his animals would not let him speak further.

"Speak no further, convalescent!"—thus his animals answered him, "but go out to where the world awaits you like a garden.

"Go out to the roses and bees and flocks of doves! But go out especially to the song-birds, so that you may learn *singing* from them!

"For convalescents should sing; let the healthy talk. And when the healthy man, too, desires song, he desires other songs than the convalescent."

"O you buffoons and barrel-organs, do be quiet!" answered Zarathustra and smiled at his animals. "How well you know what comfort I devised for myself in seven days!

"That I have to sing again—*that* comfort and *this* convalescence did I devise for myself: do you want to make another hurdy-gurdy song out of that, too?"

"Speak no further," his animals answered once more; "rather first prepare yourself a lyre, convalescent, a new lyre!

"For behold, O Zarathustra! New lyres are needed for your new songs.

"Sing and bubble over, O Zarathustra, heal your soul with new songs, so that you may bear your great destiny, that was never yet the destiny of any man!

"For your animals well know, O Zarathustra, who you are and must become: behold, *you are the teacher of the eternal recurrence,* that is now *your* destiny!

"That you have to be the first to teach this doctrine—how should this great destiny not also be your greatest danger and sickness!

"Behold, we know what you teach: that all things recur eternally and we ourselves with them, and that we have already existed an infinite number of times before and all things with us.

"You teach that there is a great year of becoming, a colossus of a year: this year must, like an hour-glass, turn itself over again and again, so that it may run down and run out anew:

"So that all these years resemble one another, in the greatest things and in the smallest, so that we ourselves resemble ourselves in each great year, in the greatest things and in the smallest.

"And if you should die now, O Zarathustra: behold, we know too what you would then say to yourself—but your animals ask you not to die yet!

"You would say—and without trembling, but rather gasping for happiness: for a great weight and oppression would have been lifted from you, most patient of men!

" 'Now I die and decay,' you would say, 'and in an instant I shall be nothingness. Souls are as mortal as bodies.

" 'But the complex of causes in which I am entangled will recur—it will create me again! I myself am part of these causes of the eternal recurrence.

" 'I shall return, with this sun, with this earth, with this eagle, with this serpent —*not* to a new life or a better life or a similar life:

" 'I shall return eternally to this identical and self-same life, in the greatest things and in the smallest, to teach once more the eternal recurrence of all things,

" 'To speak once more the teaching of the great noontide of earth and man, to tell man of the Superman once more.

" 'I spoke my teaching, I broke upon my teaching: thus my eternal fate will have it—as prophet do I perish!

" 'Now the hour has come when he who is going down shall bless himself. Thus —*ends* Zarathustra's down-going.' "

You grape-vine! Why do you praise me? For I cut you! I am cruel, you bleed: what means your praise of my intoxicated cruelty?

"What has become perfect, everything ripe—wants to die!" thus you speak. Blessed, blessed be the vine-knife! But everything unripe wants to live: alas!

Woe says: "Fade! Be gone, woe!" But everything that suffers wants to live, that it may grow ripe and merry and passionate,

passionate for remoter, higher, brighter things. "I want heirs," thus speaks everything that suffers, "I want children, I do not want *myself*."

Joy, however, does not want heirs or children, joy wants itself, wants eternity, wants recurrence, wants everything eternally the same.

Woe says: "Break, bleed, heart! Walk, legs! Wings, fly! Upward! Upward, pain!" Very well! Come on! my old heart: *Woe says: Fade! Go!*

What do you think, you Higher Men? Am I a prophet? A dreamer? A drunkard? An interpreter of dreams? A midnight bell?

A drop of dew? An odour and scent of eternity? Do you not hear it? Do you not smell it? My world has just become perfect, midnight is also noonday,

pain is also joy, a curse is also a blessing, the night is also a sun—be gone, or you will learn: a wise man is also a fool.

Did you ever say Yes to one joy? O my friends, then you said Yes to *all* woe as well. All things are chained and entwined together, all things are in love;

if ever you wanted one moment twice, if ever you said: "You please me, happiness, instant, moment!" then you wanted *everything* to return!

you wanted everything anew, everything eternal, everything chained, entwined together, everything in love, O that is how you *loved* the world,

you everlasting men, loved it eternally and for all time: and you say even to woe: "Go, but return!" *For all joy wants—eternity!*

All joy wants the eternity of all things, wants honey, wants dregs, wants intoxicated midnight, wants graves, wants the consolation of graveside tears, wants gilded sunsets, *what* does joy not want! it is thirstier, warmer, hungrier, more fearful, more secret than all woe, it wants *itself*; it bites into *itself*, the will of the ring wrestles within it,

it wants love, it wants hatred, it is superabundant, it gives, throws away, begs for someone to take it, thanks him who takes, it would like to be hated;

so rich is joy that it thirsts for woe, for Hell, for hatred, for shame, for the lame, for the *world*—for it knows, oh it knows this world!

You Higher Men, joy longs for you, joy the intractable, blissful—for your woe, you ill-constituted! All eternal joy longs for the ill-constituted.

For all joys wants itself, therefore it also wants heart's agony! O happiness! O pain! Oh break, heart! You Higher Men, learn this, learn that joy wants eternity,

joy wants the eternity of all things, *wants deep, deep, deep eternity!*

Have you now learned my song? Have you divined what it means? Very well! Come on! You Higher Men, now sing my roundelay!

Now sing yourselves the song whose name is "Once more," whose meaning is "To all eternity!"—sing, you Higher Men, Zarathustra's roundelay!

> O Man! Attend!
> What does deep midnight's voice contend?
> "I slept my sleep,
> "And now awake at dreaming's end:
> "The world is deep,
> "Deeper than day can comprehend.
> "Deep is its woe,
> "Joy—deeper than heart's agony:
> "Woe says: Fade! Go!
> "But all joy wants eternity,
> "Wants deep, deep, deep eternity!"

OSWALD SPENGLER

The Organic Logic of History

In this book is attempted for the first time the venture of predetermining history, of following the still untravelled stages in the destiny of a Culture, and specifically of the only Culture of our time and on our planet which is actually in the phase of fulfilment—the West-European-American.

Hitherto the possibility of solving a problem so far-reaching has evidently never been envisaged, and even if it had been so, the means of dealing with it were either altogether unsuspected or, at best, inadequately used.

From *The Decline of the West* [1918], translated from the German by Charles F. Atkinson, New York and London, 1926-28, Vol. I, pp. 3-9, 15, 21, 105-7, 31-7, 40-45; reprinted by permission of George Allen & Unwin Ltd.

Is there a logic of history? Is there, beyond all the casual and incalculable elements of the separate events, something that we may call a metaphysical structure of historic humanity, something that is essentially independent of the outward forms—social, spiritual and political—which we see so clearly? Are not these actualities indeed secondary or derived from that something? Does world-history present to the seeing eye certain grand traits, again and again, with sufficient constancy to justify certain conclusions? And if so, what are the limits to which reasoning from such premisses may be pushed?

Is it possible to find in life itself—for human history is the sum of mighty life-courses which already have had to be endowed with ego and personality, in customary thought and expression, by predicating entities of a higher order like "the Classical" or "the Chinese Culture," "Modern Civilization"—a series of stages which must be traversed, and traversed moreover in an ordered and obligatory sequence? For everything organic the notions of birth, death, youth, age, lifetime are fundamentals—may not these notions, in this sphere also, possess a rigorous meaning which no one has as yet extracted? In short, is all history founded upon general biographic archetypes?

The decline of the West, which at first sight may appear, like the corresponding decline of the Classical Culture, a phenomenon limited in time and space, we now perceive to be a philosophical problem that, when comprehended in all its gravity, includes within itself every great question of Being.

If therefore we are to discover in what form the destiny of the Western Culture will be accomplished, we must first be clear as to what culture *is*, what its relations are to visible history, to life, to soul, to nature, to intellect, what the forms of its manifestation are and how far these forms—peoples, tongues and epochs, battles and ideas, states and gods, arts and craft-works, sciences, laws, economic types and world-ideas, great men and great events—may be accepted and pointed to as symbols.

The means whereby to identify dead forms is Mathematical Law. The means whereby to understand living forms is Analogy. By these means we are enabled to distinguish polarity and periodicity in the world.

It is, and has always been, a matter of knowledge that the expression-forms of world-history are limited in number, and that eras, epochs, situations, persons are ever repeating themselves true to type. Napoleon has hardly ever been discussed without a side-glance at Caesar and Alexander—analogies of which, as we shall see, the first is morphologically quite inacceptable and the second is correct—while Napoleon himself conceived of his situation as akin to Charlemagne's. The French Revolutionary Convention spoke of Carthage when it meant England, and the Jacobins styled themselves Romans. Other such comparisons, of all degrees of soundness and unsoundness, are those of Florence with Athens, Buddha with Christ, primitive Christianity with modern Socialism, the Roman financial magnate of Caesar's time with the Yankee. Petrarch, the first passionate archaeologist (and is not archæology itself an expression of the sense that history is repetition?) related himself mentally to Cicero, and but lately Cecil Rhodes, the organizer of British South Africa, who had in his library specially prepared translations of the classical lives of the Caesars, felt himself akin to the Emperor Hadrian. The fated Charles XII of Sweden used to carry Quintus Curtius's life of Alexander in his pocket, and to copy that conqueror was his deliberate purpose. . . .

Analogies, in so far as they laid bare the organic structure of history, might be a blessing to historical thought. Their technique, developing under the influence of a comprehensive idea, would surely eventuate in inevitable conclusions and logical mastery. . . . Thus our theme, which originally comprised only the limited problem of present-day civilization, broadens itself into a new philosophy— *the* philosophy of the future, so far as the metaphysically-exhausted soil of the West can bear such, and in any case the only philosophy which is within the *possibilities* of the West-European mind in its next stages. It expands into the conception of a *morphology of world history*, of the world-as-history in contrast to the morphology of the world-as-nature that hitherto has been almost the only theme of philosophy. And it reviews once again the forms and movements of the world in their depths and final significance, but this time according to an entirely different ordering which groups them, not in an ensemble picture inclusive of everything known, but in a picture of *life*, and presents them not as things-become, but as things-becoming.

The *world-as-history*, conceived, viewed and given form from out of its opposite the *world-as-nature*—here is a new aspect of human existence on this earth. As yet, in spite of its immense significance, both practical and theoretical, this aspect has not been realized, still less presented. Some obscure inkling of it there may have been, a distant momentary glimpse there has often been, but no one has deliberately faced it and taken it in with all its implications. We have before us two possible ways in which man may inwardly possess and experience the world around him. With all rigour I distinguish (as to form, not substance) the organic from the mechanical world-impression, the content of images from that of laws, the picture and symbol from the formula and the system, the instantly actual from the constantly possible, the intents and purposes of imagination ordering according to plan from the intents and purposes of experience dissecting according to scheme; and—to mention even thus early an opposition that has never yet been noted, in spite of its significance—the domain of *chronological* from that of *mathematical number*.

Consequently, in a research such as that lying before us, there can be no question of taking spiritual-political events, as they become visible day by day on the surface, at their face value, and arranging them on a scheme of "causes" or "effects" and following them up in the obvious and intellectually easy directions. Such a "pragmatic" handling of history would be nothing but a piece of "natural science" in disguise, and for their part, the supporters of the materialistic idea of history make no secret about it—it is their adversaries who largely fail to see the similarity of the two methods. What concerns us is not what the historical facts which appear at this or that time *are*, per se, but what they signify, what they point to, *by appearing*. Present-day historians think they are doing a work of supererogation in bringing in religious and social, or still more art-history, details to "illustrate" the political sense of an epoch. But the decisive factor—decisive, that is, in so far as visible history is the expression, sign and embodiment of soul—they forget. I have not hitherto found one who has carefully considered the *mor-*

phological relationship that inwardly binds together the expression-forms of all branches of a Culture, who has gone beyond politics to grasp the ultimate and fundamental ideas of Greeks, Arabians, Indians and Westerners in mathematics, the meaning of their early ornamentation, the basic forms of their architecture, philosophies, dramas and lyrics, their choice and development of great arts, the detail of their craftsmanship and choice of materials—let alone appreciated the decisive importance of these matters for the form-problems of history. Who amongst them realizes that between the Differential Calculus and the dynastic principle of politics in the age of Louis XIV, between the Classical city-state and the Euclidean geometry, between the space-perspective of Western oil-painting, and the conquest of space by railroad, telephone and long-range weapon, between contrapuntal music and credit economies, there are deep uniformities? Yet, viewed from this morphological standpoint, even the humdrum facts of politics assume a symbolic and even a metaphysical character, and—what has perhaps been impossible hitherto—things such as the Egyptian administrative system, the Classical coinage, analytical geometry, the cheque, the Suez Canal, the book-printing of the Chinese, the Prussian Army, and the Roman road-engineering can, as symbols, be made *uniformly* understandable and appreciable.

But at once the fact presents itself that as yet there exists no theory-enlightened art of historical treatment. What passes as such draws its methods almost exclusively from the domain of that science which alone has completely disciplined the methods of cognition, viz., physics, and thus we imagine ourselves to be carrying on historical research when we are really following out objective connexions of cause and effect. It is a remarkable fact that the old-fashioned philosophy never imagined even the possibility of there being any other relation than this between the conscious human understanding and the world outside. Kant, who in his main work established the formal rules of cognition, took *nature* only as the object of reason's activity, and neither he himself, nor anyone after him, noted the reservation. Knowledge, for Kant, is mathematical knowledge. He deals with innate intuition-forms and categories of the reason, but he never thinks of the wholly different mechanism by which historical impressions are apprehended. And Schopenhauer, who, significantly enough, retains but one of the Kantian categories, viz., causality, speaks contemptuously of history. That there is, besides a necessity of cause and effect—which I may call the *logic of space*—another necessity, an organic necessity in life, that of Destiny—the *logic of time*—is a fact of the deepest inward certainty, a fact which suffuses the whole of mythological religions and artistic thought and constitutes the essence and kernel of all history (in contradistinction to nature) but is unapproachable through the cognition-forms which the "Critique of Pure Reason" investigates. This fact still awaits its theoretical formulation. As Galileo says in a famous passage of his *Saggiatore*, philosophy, as Nature's great book, is written "in mathematical language." We await, today, the philosopher who will tell us in what language history is written and how it is to be read.

Mathematics and the principle of Causality lead to a naturalistic Chronology, and the idea of Destiny to a historical ordering of the phenomenal world. Both orderings, each on its own account, cover the *whole* world. The difference is only in the eyes by which and through which this world is realized.

If we are to enquire into the sense of all history we must begin by solving a question which has never yet been put, viz., *for whom* is there History? The question is seemingly paradoxical, for history is obviously for everyone to this extent, that every man, with his whole existence and consciousness, is a part of history. But it makes a great difference whether anyone lives under the constant impression that his life is an element in a far wider life-course that goes on for hundreds and thousands of years, or conceives of himself as something rounded off and self-contained. For the latter type of consciousness there is certainly no world-history, no *world-as-history*. But how if the self-consciousness of a whole nation, how if a whole Culture rests on this ahistoric spirit? How must actuality appear to it? The world? Life? Consider the Classical Culture. In the world-consciousness of the Hellenes all experience, not merely the personal but the common past, was immediately transmuted into a timeless, immobile, mythically-fashioned background for the particular momentary present; thus the history of Alexander the Great began even before his death to be merged by Classical sentiment in the Dionysus legend, and to Caesar there seemed at the least nothing preposterous in claiming descent from Venus. . . .

This pure Present, whose greatest symbol is the Doric column, in itself predicates the *negation of time* (of direction). For Herodotus and Sophocles, as for Themistocles or a Roman consul, the past is subtilized instantly into an impression that is timeless and changeless, *polar and not periodic* in structure—in the last analysis, of such stuff as myths are made of—whereas for our world-sense and our inner eye the past is a definitely periodic and purposeful organism of centuries or millennia. . . .

This, then, is our task. We men of the Western Culture are, with our historical sense, an exception and not a rule. World-history is *our* world picture and not all mankind's. Indian and Classical man formed no image of a world in progress, and perhaps when in due course the civilization of the West is extinguished, there will never again be a Culture and a human type in which "world-history" is so potent a form of the waking consciousness.

"Mankind" . . . has no aim, no idea, no plan, any more than the family of butterflies or orchids. "Mankind" is a zoological expression, or an empty word. But conjure away the phantom, break the magic circle, and at once there emerges an astonishing wealth of *actual* forms—the Living with all its immense fullness, depth and movement—hitherto veiled by a catchword, a dryasdust scheme, and a set of personal "ideals." I see, in place of that empty figment of *one* linear history which can only be kept up by shutting one's eyes to the overwhelming multitude of the facts, the drama of *a number* of mighty Cultures, each springing with primitive strength from the soil of a mother-region to which it remains firmly bound throughout its whole life-cycle; each stamping its material, its mankind, in *its own* image; each having *its own* idea, *its own* passions, *its own* life, will and feeling, *its own* death. Here indeed are colours, lights, movements, that no intellectual eye has yet discovered. Here the Cultures, peoples, languages, truths, gods, landscapes bloom and age as the oaks and the stone-pines, the blossoms, twigs and leaves—but there is no ageing "Mankind." Each Culture has its own new possibilities of self-expression which arise, ripen, decay, and never return. There is not *one* sculpture, *one* painting, *one* mathematics, *one* physics, but many, each in its deepest essence different from the others, each limited in duration and self-contained, just as each species of plant has its peculiar blossom or fruit, its special type of growth and decline. These cultures, sublimated life-essences, grow with the same superb aimlessness as the flowers of the field. They belong, like the plants and the animals, to the living Nature of Goethe, and not to the dead Nature of Newton. I see world-history as a picture of endless formations and transformations, of the marvellous waxing and waning of organic forms. . . .

A boundless mass of human Being, flowing in a stream without banks; up-stream, a dark past wherein our time-sense loses all powers of definition and restless or uneasy fancy conjures up geological periods to hide away an eternally-unsolvable riddle; down-stream, a future even so dark and timeless—such is the groundwork of the Faustian picture of human history.

Over the expanse of the water passes the endless uniform wave-train of the generations. Here and there bright shafts of light broaden out, everywhere dancing flashes confuse and disturb the clear mirror, changing, sparkling, vanishing. These are what we call the clans, tribes, peoples, races which unify a series of generations within this or that limited area of the historical surface. As widely as these differ in creative power, so widely do the images that they create vary in duration and plasticity, and when the creative power dies out, the physiognomic, linguistic and spiritual identification-marks vanish also and the phenomenon subsides again into the ruck of the generations. Aryans, Mongols, Germans, Kelts, Parthians, Franks, Carthaginians, Berbers, Bantus are names by which we specify some very heterogeneous images of this order.

But over this surface, too, the great Cultures accomplish their majestic wave-cycles. They appear suddenly, swell in splendid lines, flatten again and vanish, and the face of the waters is once more a sleeping waste.

A Culture is born in the moment when a great soul awakens out of the proto-spirituality (*dem urseelenhaften Zustande*) of ever-childish humanity, and detaches itself, a form from the formless, a bounded and mortal thing from the boundless and enduring. It blooms on the soil of an exactly-definable landscape, to which plant-wise it remains bound. It dies when this soul has actualized the full sum of its possibilities in the shape of peoples, languages, dogmas, arts, states, sciences, and reverts into the proto-soul. But its living existence, that sequence of great epochs which define and display the stages of fulfilment, is an inner passionate struggle to maintain the Idea against the powers of Chaos without and the unconscious muttering deep-down within. It is not only the artist who struggles against the resistance of the material and the stifling of the idea within him. Every Culture stands in a deeply-symbolical, almost in a mystical, relation to the Extended, the space, in which and through which it strives to actualize itself. The aim once attained—the idea, the entire content of inner possibilities, fulfilled and made externally actual—the Culture suddenly hardens, it mortifies, its blood congeals, its force breaks down, and it becomes *Civilization*, the thing which we feel and understand in the words Egypticism, Byzantinism, Mandarinism. As such they may, like a worn-out giant of the primeval forest, thrust their decaying branches towards the sky for hundreds or thousands of years, as we see in China, in India, in the Islamic world. It was thus that the Classical Civilization rose gigantic, in the Imperial age, with a false semblance of youth and strength and fullness, and robbed the young Arabian Culture of the East of light and air.

This—the inward and outward fulfilment, the finality, that awaits every living Culture—is the purport of all the historic "declines," amongst them that decline of the Classical which we know so well and fully, and another decline, entirely comparable to it in course and duration, which will occupy the first centuries of the coming millennium but is heralded already and sensible in and around us to-day—the decline of the West. Every Culture passes through the age-phases of the individual man. Each has its childhood, youth, manhood and old age. It is a young and trembling soul, heavy with misgivings, that reveals itself in the morning of Romanesque and Gothic. It fills the Faustian landscape from the Provence of the troubadours to the Hildesheim cathedral of Bishop Bernward. The spring wind blows over it. "In the works of the old-German architecture," says Goethe, "one sees the blossoming of an extraordinary state. Anyone immediately confronted with such a blossoming can do no more than wonder; but one who can see into the secret inner life of the plant and its rain of forces, who can observe how the bud expands, little by little, sees the thing with quite other eyes and knows what he is seeing." Childhood speaks to us also—and in the same tones —out of early-Homeric Doric, out of early-Christian (which is really early-Arabian) art and out of the works of the Old Kingdom in Egypt that began with the Fourth Dynasty. There a mythic world-consciousness is fighting like a harassed debtor against all the dark and daemonic in itself and in Nature, while slowly ripening itself for the pure, day-bright expression of the existence that it will at last achieve and know. The more nearly a Culture approaches the noon culmination of its being, the more virile, austere, controlled, intense the form-language it has secured for itself, the more assured its sense of its own power, the clearer its lineaments. In the spring all this had still been dim and confused, tentative, filled with childish yearning and fears—witness the ornament of Romanesque-Gothic church porches of Saxony and southern France, the early-Christian catacombs, the Dipylon vases. But there is now the full consciousness of ripened creative power that we see in the time of the early Middle Kingdom of Egypt, in the Athens of the Pisistratidae, in the age of Justinian, in that of the Counter-Reformation, and we find every individual trait of expression deliberate, strict, measured, marvellous in its ease and self-confidence. And we find, too, that everywhere, at moments, the coming fulfilment suggested itself; in such moments were created the head of Amenemhet III (the so-called "Hyksos Sphinx" of Tanis), the domes of Hagia Sophia, the paintings of Titian. Still later, tender to the point of fragility, fragrant with the sweetness of late October days, come the Cnidian Aphrodite and the Hall of the Maidens in the Erechtheum, the arabesques on Saracen horseshoe-arches, the Zwinger of Dresden, Watteau, Mozart. At last, in the grey dawn of Civilization, the fire in the Soul dies down. The dwindling powers rise to one more, half-successful, effort of creation, and produce the Classicism that is common to all dying Cultures. The soul thinks once again, and in Romanticism looks back piteously to its childhood; then finally, weary, reluctant, cold, it loses its desire to be, and, as in Imperial Rome, wishes itself out of the overlong daylight and back in the darkness of protomysticism, in the womb of the mother, in the grave. The spell of a "second religiousness" comes upon it, and Late-Classical man turns to the practice of the cults of Mithras, of Isis, of the Sun—those very cults into which a soul just born in the East has been pouring a new wine of dreams and fears and loneliness.

For every Culture has *its own* Civilization. In this work, for the first time the two words, hitherto used to express an indefinite, more or less ethical, distinction, are used in a *periodic* sense, to express a strict and necessary *organic succession*. The Civilization is the inevitable *destiny* of the Culture, and in this principle we obtain the viewpoint from which the deepest and gravest problems of historical morphology become capable of solution. Civilizations are the most external and artificial states of which a species of developed humanity is capable. They are a conclusion, the thing-become succeeding the thing-becoming, death following life, rigidity following expansion, intellectual age and the stone-built, petrifying world-city following mother-earth and the spiritual childhood of Doric and Gothic. They are an end, irrevocable, yet by inward necessity reached again and again.

So, for the first time, we are enabled to understand the Romans as the *successors* of the Greeks, and light is projected into the deepest secrets of the late-Classical period. What, but this, can be the meaning of the fact—which can only be disputed by vain phrases—that the Romans were barbarians who did not *precede* but *closed* a great development? Unspiritual, unphilosophical, devoid of art, clannish to the point of brutality, aiming relentlessly at tangible successes, they stand between the Hellenic Culture and nothingness. An imagination directed purely to practical objects—they had religious laws governing godward relations as they had other laws governing human relations, but there was no specifically Roman saga of gods—was something which is not found at all in Athens. In a word, Greek *soul*—Roman *intellect*; and this antithesis is the differentia between Culture and Civilization. Nor is it only to the Classical that it applies. Again and again there appears this type of strong-minded, completely non-metaphysical man, and in the hands of this type lies the intellectual and material destiny of each and every "late" period. Such are the men who carried through the Babylonian, the Egyptian, the Indian, the Chinese, the Roman Civilizations, and in such periods do Buddhism, Stoicism, Socialism ripen into definitive world-conceptions which enable a moribund humanity to be attacked and re-formed in its intimate structure. *Pure* Civilization, as a historical process, consists in a progressive *taking-down* of forms that have become inorganic or dead.

The transition from Culture to Civilization was accomplished for the Classical world in the 4th, for the Western in the 19th Century. From these periods onward the great intellectual decisions take place, not as in the days of the Orpheus-movement or the Reformation in the "whole world" where not a hamlet is too small to be unimportant, but in three or four world-cities that have absorbed into themselves the whole content of History, while the old wide landscape of the Culture, become merely provincial, serves only to feed the cities with what remains of its higher mankind.

World-city and province—the two basic ideas of every civilization—bring up a wholly new form-problem of History, the very problem that we are living through to-day with hardly the remotest conception of its immensity. In place of a world, there is a *city*, *a point*, in which the whole life of broad regions is collecting while the rest dries up. In place of a type-true people, born of and grown on the soil, there is a new sort of nomad, cohering unstably in fluid masses, the parasitical city dweller, traditionless, utterly matter-of-fact, religionless, clever, unfruitful, deeply contemptuous of the countryman and especially that highest form of countryman, the country gentleman. This is a very great stride towards the inorganic, towards the end—what does it signify? France and England have already taken the step and Germany is beginning to do so. After Syracuse, Athens, and Alexandria comes Rome. After Madrid, Paris, London come Berlin and New York. It is the destiny of whole regions that lie outside the radiation-circle of one of these cities—of old Crete and Macedon and to-day the Scandinavian North—to become "provinces." . . .

The world-city means cosmopolitanism in place of "home," cold matter-of-fact in place of reverence for tradition and age, scientific irreligion as a fossil representative of the older religion of the heart, "society" in place of the state, natural instead of hard-earned rights. It was in the conception of *money* as an inorganic and abstract magnitude, entirely disconnected from the notion of the fruitful earth and the primitive values, that the Romans had the advantage of the Greeks. Thenceforward any high ideal of life becomes largely a question of money. Unlike the Greek stoicism of Chrysippus, the Roman stoicism of Cato and Seneca presupposes a private income; and, unlike that of the 18th Century, the social-ethical sentiment of the 20th, if it is to be realized at a higher level than that of professional (and lucrative) agitation, is a matter for millionaires. To the world-city belongs not a folk but a mass. Its uncomprehending hostility to all the traditions representative of the Culture (nobility, church, privileges, dynasties, convention in art and limits of knowledge in science), the keen and cold intelligence that confounds the wisdom of the peasant, the new-fashioned naturalism that in relation to all matters of sex and society goes back far beyond Rousseau and Socrates to quite primitive instincts and conditions, the reappearance of the *panem et circenses* in the form of wage-disputes and football-grounds—all these things betoken the definite closing-down of the Culture and the opening of a quite new phase of human existence—anti-provincial, late, futureless, but quite inevitable.

This is what has to be *viewed*, and viewed not with the eyes of the partisan, the ideologue, the up-to-date novelist, not from this or that "standpoint," but in a high, time-free perspective embracing whole millenniums of historical world-forms, if we are really to comprehend the great crisis of the present.

To me it is a symbol of the first importance that in the Rome of Crassus—triumvir and all-powerful building-site speculator—the Roman people with its proud inscriptions, the people before whom Gauls, Greeks, Parthians, Syrians afar trembled, lived in appalling misery in the many-storied lodging-houses of dark suburbs, accepting with indifference or even with a sort of sporting interest the consequences of the military expansion: that many famous old-noble families, descendants of the men who defeated the Celts and the Samnites, lost their ancestral homes through standing apart from the wild rush of speculation and were reduced to renting wretched apartments; that, while along the Appian Way there arose the splendid and still wonderful tombs of the financial magnates, the corpses of the people were thrown along with animal carcases and town refuse into a monstrous common grave—till in Augustus's time it was banked over for the avoidance of pestilence and so became the site of Maecenas's renowned park; that in depopulated Athens, which lived on visitors and on the bounty of rich foreigners, the mob of parvenu tourists from Rome gaped at the works of the Periclean age with as little understanding as the American globetrotter in the Sistine Chapel at those of Michelangelo, every removable art-piece having ere this been taken away or bought at fancy prices to be replaced by the Roman buildings which grew up, colossal and arrogant, by the side of the low and modest structures of the old time. In such things—which it is the historian's business not to praise or to blame but to consider morphologically—there lies, plain and immediate enough for one who has learnt to see, an *idea*.

For it will become manifest that, from this moment on, all great conflicts of world-outlook, of politics, of art, of science, of feeling will be under the influence of this one opposition. What is the hall-mark of a politic of Civilization to-day, in contrast to a politic of Culture yesterday? It is, for the Classical rhetoric, and for the Western journalism, both serving that abstract which represents the power of Civilization—*money*. It is the money-spirit which penetrates unremarked the historical forms of the people's existence, often without destroying or even in the least disturbing these forms—the form of the Roman state, for instance, underwent very much less alteration between the elder Scipio and Augustus than is usually imagined. Though forms subsist, the great political parties nevertheless cease to be more than reputed centres of decision. The decisions in fact lie elsewhere. A small number of superior heads, whose names are very likely not the best-known, settle everything. . . .

Here, then, I lay it down that *Imperialism*, of which petrifacts such as the Egyptian empire, the Roman, the Chinese, the Indian may continue to exist for hundreds or thousands of years—dead bodies, amorphous and dispirited masses of men, scrap-material from a great history—is to be taken as the typical symbol of the passing away. Imperialism is Civilization unadulterated. In this phenomenal form the destiny of the West is now irrevocably set. The energy of culture-man is directed inwards, that of civilization-man outwards. And thus I see in Cecil Rhodes the first man of a new age. He stands for the political style of a far-ranging, Western, Teutonic and especially German future, and his phrase "expansion is everything" is the Napoleonic reassertion of the indwelling tendency of *every* Civilization that has fully ripened—Roman, Arab or Chinese. It is not a matter of choice—it is not the conscious will of individuals, or even that of whole classes of peoples that decides. The expansive tendency is a doom, something daemonic and immense, which grips, forces into service, and uses up the late mankind of the world-city stage, willy-nilly, aware or unaware. Life is the process of effecting possibilities, and for the brain-man there are *only extensive* possibilities.

———

To birth belongs death, to youth age, to life generally its form and its allotted span. The present is a civilized, emphatically not a cultured time, and *ipso facto* a great number of life-capacities fall out as impossible. This may be deplorable, and may be and will be deplored in pessimist philosophy and poetry, but it is not in our power to make otherwise. It will not be—already it is not—permissible to defy clear historical experience and to expect, merely because we hope, that this will spring or that will flourish.

It will no doubt be objected that such a world-outlook, which in giving this certainly as to the outlines and tendency of the future cuts off all far-reaching hopes, would be unhealthy for all and fatal for many, once it ceased to be a mere theory and was adopted as a practical scheme of life by the group of personalities effectively moulding the future.

Such is not my opinion. We are civilized, not Gothic or Rococo, people; we have to reckon with the hard cold facts of a *late* life, to which the parallel is to be found not in Pericles's Athens but in Caesar's Rome. Of great painting or great music there can no longer be, for Western people, any question. Their architectural possibilities have been exhausted these hundred years. Only *extensive* possibilities are left to them. Yet, for a sound and vigorous generation that is filled with unlimited hopes, I fail to see that it is any disadvantage to discover betimes that some of these hopes must come to nothing. And if the hopes thus doomed should be those most dear, well, a man who is worth anything will not be dismayed. It is true that the issue may be a tragic one for some individuals who in their decisive years are overpowered by the conviction that in the spheres of architecture, drama, painting, there is nothing left for *them* to conquer. What matter if they do go under! It has been the convention hitherto to admit no limits of any sort in these matters, and to believe that each period had its own task to do in each sphere. Tasks therefore were found by hook or by crook, leaving it to be settled posthumously whether or not the artist's faith was justified and his life-work necessary. Now, nobody but a pure romantic would take this way out. Such a pride is not the pride of a Roman. What are we to think of the individual who, standing before an exhausted quarry, would rather be told that a new vein will be struck to-morrow—the bait offered by the radically false and mannerized art of the moment—than be shown a rich and virgin clay-bed near by? The lesson, I think, would be of benefit to the coming generations, as showing them what is possible—and therefore necessary—and what is excluded from the inward potentialities of their time. Hitherto an incredible total of intellect and power has been squandered in false directions. The West-European, however historically he may think and feel, is at a certain stage of life invariably uncertain of his own direction; he gropes and feels his way and, if unlucky in environment, he loses it. But now at last the work of centuries enables him to view the disposition of his own life in relation to the general culture-scheme and to test his own powers and purposes. And I can only hope that men of the new generation may be moved by this book to devote themselves to technics instead of lyrics, the sea instead of the paint-brush, and politics instead of epistemology. Better they could not do. . . .

Systematic philosophy, then, lies immensely far behind us, and ethical has been wound up. *But a third possibility, corresponding to the Classical Scepticism, still remains to the soul-world* of the present-day West, and it can be brought to light by the hitherto unknown methods of historical morphology. That which is a possibility is a necessity. The Classical scepticism is ahistoric, it doubts by denying outright. But that of the West, if it is an inward necessity, a symbol of the autumn of our spirituality, is obliged to be historical through and through. Its solutions are got by treating everything as relative, as a historical phenomenon, and its procedure is psychological. Whereas the Sceptic philosophy arose within Hellenism as the negation of philosophy—declaring philosophy to be purposeless —we, on the contrary, regard the *history of philosophy* as, in the last resort, philosophy's gravest theme. This *is* "skepsis," in the true sense, for whereas the Greek is led to renounce absolute standpoints by contempt for the intellectual past, we are led to do so by comprehension of that past as an organism.

In this work it will be our task to sketch out this unphilosophical philosophy— the last that West Europe will know. Scepticism is the expression of a pure Civilization; and it dissipates the world-picture of the Culture that has gone before. For us, its success will lie in resolving all the older problems into one, the genetic. The conviction that what *is* also *has become*, that the natural and cognizable is rooted in the historic, that the World as the actual is founded on an Ego as the potential actualized, that the "when" and the "how long" hold as deep a secret as the "what," leads directly to the fact that everything, whatever else it may be, must at any rate be *the expression of something living*. Cognitions and judgments too are acts of living men. The thinkers of the past conceived external actuality as produced by cognition and motiving ethical judgments, but to the thought of the future they are above all *expressions and symbols. The Morphology of world-history becomes inevitably a universal symbolism.*

With that, the claim of higher thought to possess general and eternal truths falls to the ground. Truths are truths only in relation to a particular mankind. Thus, my own philosophy is able to express and reflect *only* the Western (as distinct from the Classical, Indian, or other) soul, and that soul *only* in its present civilized phase by which its conception of the world, its practical range and its sphere of effect are specified.

W. B. YEATS

History as Symbolic Reality

THE HISTORICAL CONES

One must bear in mind that the Christian Era, like the two thousand years, let us say, that went before it, is an entire wheel, and each half of it an entire wheel, that each half when it comes to its 28th Phase reaches the 15th Phase or the 1st Phase of the entire era. It follows therefore that the 15th Phase of each millennium, to keep the symbolic measure of time, is Phase 8 or Phase 22 of the entire era, that Aphrodite rises from a stormy sea, that Helen could not be Helen but for beleaguered Troy. The era itself is but half of a greater era and its Phase 15 comes also at a period of war or trouble. The greater number is always more

[In A Vision, Yeats presents an elaborate symbolic pattern which he applies not only to history, as in the following selection, but also to individual lives. His basic symbol is a pair of interpenetrating cones or "gyres" (signifying the world of change) that move within a sphere (emblematic of eternity). The gyres, with their points at the bases of each other, represent the oppositions and reciprocities of human existence; one expands as the other diminishes. These symbols of sphere and gyres are equivalent to another set of symbols, in which a circle or "wheel" is marked off into "phases" that correspond to the waxing and waning of the moon. There are twenty-eight such phases, with varying degrees of moonlight and darkness. They can also be pictured as planes cutting across the interlocking cones at various points. Whether expressed in terms of gyres or phases of the moon, Yeats's opposing principles are called the "primary" and the "antithetical." Roughly speaking, we can say that the primary (denoted by the moon's degree of darkness) is a principle of relative passivity, of objectivity, rationalism, materialism, external morality, democratic equalitarianism—while the antithetical (denoted by the moon's degree of light) is a principle of activity, of subjectiveness, imagination, idealism, personal will, aristocratic distinction. The result of the mixture of these principles at any one phase must be measured in terms of four "faculties," which usually are at odds with one another: "Will" and "Mask" (approximately, imaginative power and the image of what we seek to become) and "Creative Mind" and "Body of Fate" (approximately, the intellect and the environment). Every man goes through all the phases—with the exception of the first and fifteenth, which do not appear in human life. Moreover, every man belongs in general to a phase of human nature, which may or may not be the phase of his particular historical era. History, in turn, proceeds through the sequence of all the phases, infinitely repeating a cycle or "great year" of two thousand years; but repeated with each cycle there are two complete lesser cycles, and the great year itself is a repetition of a larger cycle superimposed upon it.]

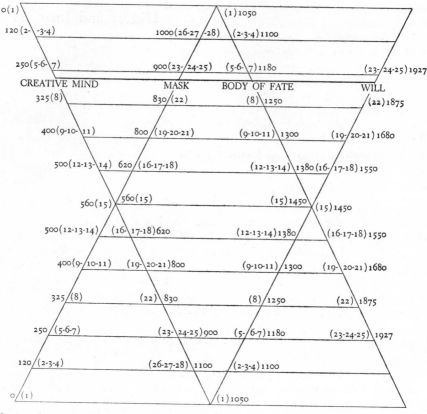

The numbers in brackets refer to phases, and the other numbers to dates A.D. The line cutting the cones a little below 250, 900, 1180 and 1927 shows four historical *Faculties* related to the present moment, May 1925.

primary than the lesser and precisely because it contains it. A millennium is the symbolic measure of a being that attains its flexible maturity and then sinks into rigid age.

A civilisation is a struggle to keep self-control, and in this it is like some great tragic person, some Niobe who must display an almost superhuman will or the cry will not touch our sympathy. The loss of control over thought comes towards the end; first a sinking in upon the moral being, then the last surrender, the irrational cry, revelation—the scream of Juno's peacock.

2000 B.C. TO A.D. 1

I imagine the annunciation that founded Greece as made to Leda, remembering that they showed in a Spartan temple, strung up to the roof as a holy relic, an unhatched egg of hers; and that from one of her eggs came Love and from the other War. But all things are from antithesis, and when in my ignorance I try to imagine what older civilisation that annunciation rejected I can but see bird and woman blotting out some corner of the Babylonian mathematical starlight.

Was it because the older civilisation like the Jewish thought a long life a proof of Heavenly favour that the Greek races thought those whom the Gods love must die young, hurling upon some age of crowded comedy their tragic sense? Certainly their tribes, after a first multitudinous revelation—dominated each by its *Daimon* and oracle-driven—broke up a great Empire and established in its stead an intellectual anarchy. At some 1000 years before Christ I imagine their religious system complete and they themselves grown barbaric and Asiatic. Then came Homer, civil life, a desire for civil order dependent doubtless on some oracle, and then (Phase 10 of the new millennium) for independent civil life and thought. At, let me say, the sixth century B.C. (Phase 12) personality begins, but there is as yet no intellectual solitude. A man may rule his tribe or town but he cannot separate himself from the general mass. With the first discovery of solitude (Phases 13 and 14) comes, as I think, the visible art that interests us most today, for Phidian art, like the art of Raphael, has for the moment exhausted our attention. I recall a Nike at the Ashmolean Museum with a natural unsystematised beauty like that before Raphael, and above all certain pots with strange half-supernatural horses dark on a light ground. Self-realisation attained will bring desire of power—systematisation for its instrument—but as yet clarity, meaning, elegance, all things separated from one another in luminous space, seem to exceed all other virtues. One compares this art with the thought of Greek philosophers before Anaxagoras, where one discovers the same phases, always more concerned with the truth than with its moral or political effects. One longs for the lost dramatists, the plays that were enacted before Aeschylus and Sophocles arose, both Phidian men.

But one must consider not the movement only from the beginning to the end of the ascending cone, but the gyres that touch its sides, the horizontal dance.

> Hands gripped in hands, toes close together,
> Hair spread on the wind they made;
> That lady and that golden king
> Could like a brace of blackbirds sing.

Side by side with Ionic elegance there comes after the Persian wars a Doric vigour, and the light-limbed dandy of the potters, the Parisian-looking young woman of the sculptors, her hair elaborately curled, give place to the athlete. One suspects a deliberate turning away from all that is Eastern, or a moral propaganda like that which turned the poets out of Plato's Republic, and yet it may be that the preparation for the final systematisation had for its apparent cause the destruction, let us say, of Ionic studios by the Persian invaders, and that all came from the resistance of the *Body of Fate* to the growing solitude of the soul. Then in Phidias Ionic and Doric influence unite—one remembers Titian—and all is transformed by the full moon, and all abounds and flows. With Callimachus pure Ionic revives again, as Furtwängler has proved, and upon the only example of his work known to us, a marble chair, a Persian is represented, and may one not discover a Persian symbol in that bronze lamp, shaped like a palm, known to us by a description in Pausanias? But he was an archaistic workman, and those who set him to work brought back public life to an older form. One may see in masters and man a momentary dip into ebbing Asia.

Each age unwinds the thread another age had wound, and it amuses one to remember that before Phidias, and his westward-moving art, Persia fell, and that when full moon came round again, amid eastward-moving thought, and brought Byzantine glory, Rome fell; and that at the outset of our westward-moving Renaissance Byzantium fell; all things dying each other's life, living each other's death.

After Phidias the life of Greece, which being *antithetical* had moved slowly and richly through the *antithetical* phases, comes rapidly to an end. Some Greek or Roman writer whose name I forget will soon speak of the declining comeliness of the people, and in the arts all is systematised more and more, and the antagonist recedes. Aristophanes' passion-clouded eye falls before what one must believe, from Roman stage copies, an idler glance. (Phases 19, 20, 21.) Aristotle and Plato end creative system—to die into the truth is still to die—and formula begins. Yet even the truth into which Plato dies is a form of death, for when he separates the Eternal Ideas from Nature and shows them self-sustained he prepares the Christian desert and the Stoic suicide.

I identify the conquest of Alexander and the break-up of his kingdom, when Greek civilisation, formalised and codified, loses itself in Asia, with the beginning and end of the 22nd Phase, and his intention recorded by some historian to turn his arms westward shows that he is but a part of the impulse that creates Hellenised Rome and Asia. There are everywhere statues where every muscle has been measured; every position debated, and these statues represent man with nothing more to achieve, physical man finished and complacent, the women slightly tinted, but the men, it may be, who exercise naked in the open air, the colour of mahogany. Every discovery after the epoch of victory and defeat (Phase 22) which substitutes mechanics for power is an elimination of intellect by delight in technical skill (Phase 23), by a sense of the past (Phase 24), by some dominant belief (Phase 25). After Plato and Aristotle, the mind is as exhausted as were the armies of Alexander at his death, but the Stoics can discover morals and turn philosophy into a rule of life. Among them doubtless—the first beneficiaries of Plato's hatred of imitation—we may discover the first benefactors of our modern individuality, sincerity of the trivial face, the mask torn away. Then, a Greece that Rome has conquered, and a Rome conquered by Greece, must, in the last three phases of the wheel, adore, desire being dead, physical or spiritual force.

This adoration which begins in the second century before Chirst creates a world-wide religious movement as the world was then known, which, being swallowed up in what came after, has left no adequate record. One knows not into how great extravagance Asia, accustomed to abase itself, may have carried what soon sent Greeks and Romans to stand naked in a Mithraic pit, moving their bodies as under a shower-bath that those bodies might receive the blood of the bull even to the last drop. The adored image took everywhere the only form possible as the *antithetical* age died into its last violence—a human or animal form. Even before Plato that collective image of man dear to Stoic and Epicurean alike, the moral double of bronze or marble athlete, had been invoked by Anaxagoras when he declared that thought and not the warring opposites created the world. At that sentence the heroic life, passionate fragmentary man, all that had been imagined by great poets and sculptors began to pass away, and instead of seeking noble antagonists, imagination moved towards divine man and the ridiculous devil. Now must sages lure men away from the arms of women because in those arms man becomes a fragment; and all is ready for revelation.

When revelation comes athlete and sage are merged; the earliest sculptured image of Christ is copied from that of the Apotheosis of Alexander the Great; the tradition is founded which declares even to our own day that Christ alone was exactly six feet high, perfect physical man. Yet as perfect physical man He must die, for only so can *primary* power reach *antithetical* mankind shut within the circle of its senses, touching outward things alone in that which seems most personal and physical. When I think of the moment before revelation I think of Salome—she, too, delicately tinted or maybe mahogany dark—dancing before Herod and receiving the Prophet's head in her indifferent hands, and wonder if what seems to us decadence was not in reality the exaltation of the muscular flesh and of civilisation perfectly achieved. Seeking images, I see her anoint her bare limbs according to a medical prescription of that time, with lion's fat, for lack of the sun's ray, that she may gain the favour of a king, and remember that the same impulse will create the Galilean revelation and deify Roman Emperors whose sculptured heads will be surrounded by the solar disk. Upon the throne and upon the cross alike the myth becomes a biography.

A.D. 1 TO A.D. 1050

God is now conceived of as something outside man and man's handiwork, and it follows that it must be idolatry to worship that which Phidias and Scopas made, and seeing that He is a Father in Heaven, that Heaven will be found presently in the Thebaid, where the world is changed into a featureless dust and can be run through the fingers; and these things are testified to from books that are outside human genius, being miraculous, and by a miraculous Church, and this Church, as the gyre sweeps wider, will make man also featureless as clay or dust. Night will fall upon man's wisdom now that man has been taught that he is nothing. He had discovered, or half-discovered, that the world is round and one of many like it, but now he must believe that the sky is but a tent spread above a level floor, and that he may be stirred into a frenzy of anxiety and so to moral transformation, blot out the knowledge or half-knowledge that he has lived many times, and think that all eternity depends upon a moment's decision. Heaven itself, transformation finished, must appear so vague and motionless that it seems but a concession to human weakness. It is even essential to this faith to declare that God's messengers, those beings who show His will in dreams or announce it in visionary speech, were never men. The Greeks thought them great men of the past, but now that concession to mankind is forbidden. All must be narrowed into the sun's image cast out of a burning-glass and man be ignorant of all but the image.

The mind that brought the change, if considered as man only, is a climax of whatever Greek and Roman thought was most a contradiction to its age; but considered as more than man He controlled what Neo-Pythagorean and Stoic could not—irrational force. He could announce the new age, all that had not been thought of, or touched, or seen, because He could substitute for reason, miracle.

We say of Him because His sacrifice was voluntary that He was love itself, and yet that part of Him which made Christendom was not love but pity, and not pity for intellectual despair, though the man in Him, being *antithetical* like His age, knew it in the Garden, but *primary* pity, that for the common lot, man's death, seeing that He raised Lazarus, sickness, seeing that He healed many, sin, seeing that He died.

Love is created and preserved by intellectual analysis, for we love only that which is unique, and it belongs to contemplation, not to action, for we would not change that which we love. A lover will admit a greater beauty than that of his mistress but not its like, and surrenders his days to a delighted laborious study of all her ways and looks, and he pities only if something threatens that which has never been before and can never be again. Fragment delights in fragment and seeks possession, not service; whereas the Good Samaritan discovers himself in the likeness of another, covered with sores and abandoned by thieves upon the roadside, and in that other serves himself. The opposites are gone; he does not need his Lazarus; they do not each die the other's life, live the other's death.

It is impossible to do more than select an arbitrary general date for the beginning of Roman decay (Phases 2 to 7, A.D. 1 to A.D. 250). Roman sculpture—sculpture made under Roman influence whatever the sculptor's blood—did not, for instance, reach its full vigour, if we consider what it had of Roman as distinct from Greek, until the Christian Era. It even made a discovery which affected all sculpture to come. The Greeks painted the eyes of marble statues and made out of enamel or glass or precious stones those of their bronze statues, but the Roman was the first to drill a round hole to represent the pupil, and because, as I think, of a preoccupation with the glance characteristic of a civilisation in its final phase. The colours must have already faded from the marbles of the great period, and a shadow and a spot of light, especially where there is much sunlight, are more vivid than paint, enamel, coloured glass or precious stone. They could now express in stone a perfect composure. The administrative mind, alert attention had driven out rhythm, exaltation of the body, uncommitted energy. May it not have been precisely a talent for this alert attention that had enabled Rome and not Greece to express those final *primary* phases? One sees on the pediments troops of marble Senators, officials serene and watchful as befits men who know that all the power of the world moves before their eyes, and needs, that it may not dash itself to pieces, their unhurried, unanxious, never-ceasing care. Those riders upon the Parthenon had all the world's power in their moving bodies, and in a movement that seemed, so were the hearts of man and beast set upon it, that of a dance; but presently all would change and measurement succeed to pleasure, the dancing-master outlive the dance. What need had those young lads for careful eyes? But in Rome of the first and second centuries, when the dancing-master himself has died, the delineation of character as shown in face and head, as with us of recent years, is all in all, and sculptors, seeking the custom of occupied officials, stock in their workshops toga'd marble bodies upon which can be screwed with the least possible delay heads modelled from the sitters with the most scrupulous realism. When I think of Rome I see always those heads with their world-considering eyes, and those bodies as conventional as the metaphors in a leading article, and compare in my imagination vague Grecian eyes gazing at nothing, Byzantine eyes of drilled ivory staring upon a vision, and those eyelids of China and of India, those veiled or half-veiled eyes weary of world and vision alike.

Meanwhile the irrational force that would create confusion and uproar as with the cry "The Babe, the Babe is born"—the women speaking unknown tongues, the barbers and weavers expounding Divine revelation with all the vulgarity of their servitude, the tables that move or resound with raps—but creates a negligible sect.

All about it is an *antithetical* aristocratic civilisation in its completed form, every detail of life hierarchical, every great man's door crowded at dawn by petitioners, great wealth everywhere in few men's hands, all dependent upon a few, up to the Emperor himself who is a God dependent upon a greater God, and everywhere in court, in the family, an inequality made law, and floating over all the Romanised Gods of Greece in their physical superiority. All is rigid and stationary, men fight for centuries with the same sword and spear, and though in naval warfare there is some change of tactics to avoid those single combats of ship with ship that needed the seamanship of a more skilful age, the speed of a sailing ship remains unchanged from the time of Pericles to that of Constantine. Though sculpture grows more and more realistic and so renews its vigour, this realism is without curiosity. The athlete becomes the boxer that he may show lips and nose beaten out of shape, the individual hairs show at the navel of the bronze centaur, but the theme has not changed. Philosophy alone, where in contact with irrational force—holding to Egyptian thaumaturgy and the Judean miracle but at arm's length—can startle and create. Yet Plotinus is as *primary*, as much a contradiction of all that created Roman civilisation, as St. Peter, and his thought has its roots almost as deep among the *primary* masses. The founder of his school was Ammonius Sacca, an Alexandrine porter. His thought and that of Origen, which I skimmed in my youth, seem to me to express the abstract synthesis of a quality like that of race, and so to display a character which must always precede Phase 8. Origen, because the Judean miracle has a stronger hold upon the masses than Alexandrian thaumaturgy, triumphs when Constantine (Phase 8) puts the Cross upon the shields of his soldiers and makes the bit of his war-horse from a nail of the True Cross, an act equivalent to man's cry for strength amid the animal chaos at the close of the first lunar quarter. Seeing that Constantine was not converted till upon his deathbed, I see him as half statesman, half thaumaturgist, accepting in blind obedience to a dream the new fashionable talisman, two sticks nailed together. The Christians were but six millions of the sixty or seventy of the Roman Empire, but, spending nothing upon pleasure, exceedingly rich like some Nonconformist sect of the eighteenth century. The world became Christian, "that fabulous formless darkness" as it seemed to a philosopher of the fourth century, blotted out "every beautiful thing," not through the conversion of crowds or general change of opinion, or through any pressure from below, for civilisation was *antithetical* still, but by an act of power.

I have not the knowledge (it may be that no man has the knowledge) to trace the rise of the Byzantine State through Phases 9, 10 and 11. My diagram tells me that a hundred and sixty years brought that State to its 15th Phase, but I that know nothing but the arts and of these little, cannot revise the series of dates "approximately correct" but given, it may be, for suggestion only. With a desire for simplicity of statement I would have preferred to find in the middle, not at the end, of the fifth century Phase 12, for that was, so far as the known evidence carries us, the moment when Byzantium became Byzantine and substituted for formal Roman magnificence, with its glorification of physical power, an architecture that suggests the Sacred City in the Apocalypse of St. John. I think if I could be given a month of Antiquity and leave to spend it where I chose, I would spend it in Byzantium a little before Justinian opened St. Sophia and closed the Academy of Plato. I think I could find in some little wine-shop some philosophical worker in mosaic who could answer all my questions, the supernatural descending nearer to him than to Plotinus even, for the pride of his delicate skill would make what was an instrument of power to princes and clerics, a murderous madness in the mob, show as a lovely flexible presence like that of a perfect human body.

I think that in early Byzantium, maybe never before or since in recorded history, religious, aesthetic and practical life were one, that architect and artificers—though not, it may be, poets, for language had been the instrument of controversy and must have grown abstract—spoke to the multitude and the few alike. The painter, the mosaic worker, the worker in gold and silver, the illuminator of sacred books, were almost impersonal, almost perhaps without the consciousness of individual design, absorbed in their subject-matter and that the vision of a whole people. They could copy out of old Gospel books those pictures that seemed as sacred as the text, and yet weave all into a vast design, the work of many that seemed the work of one, that made building, picture, pattern, metal-work of rail and lamp, seem but a single image; and this vision, this proclamation of their invisible master, had the Greek nobility, Satan always the still half-divine Serpent, never the horned scarecrow of the didactic Middle Ages.

The ascetic, called in Alexandria "God's Athlete," has taken the place of those Greek athletes whose statues have been melted or broken up or stand deserted in the midst of cornfields, but all about him is an incredible splendour like that which we see pass under our closed eyelids as we lie between sleep and waking, no representation of a living world but the dream of a somnambulist. Even the drilled pupil of the eye, when the drill is in the hand of some Byzantine worker in ivory, undergoes a somnambulistic change, for its deep shadow among the faint lines of the tablet, its mechanical circle, where all else is rhythmical and flowing, give to Saint or Angel a look of some great bird staring at miracle. Could any visionary of those days, passing through the Church named with so un-theological a grace "The Holy Wisdom," can even a visionary of today wandering among the mosaics at Ravenna or in Sicily, fail to recognise some one image seen under his closed eyelids? To me it seems that He, who among the first Christian communities was little but a ghostly exorcist, had in His ascent to a full Divinity made possible this sinking-in upon a supernatural splendour, these walls with their little glimmering cubes of blue and green and gold.

I think that I might discover an oscillation, a revolution of the horizontal gyre like that between Doric and Ionic art, between the two principal characters of Byzantine art. Recent criticism distinguishes between Greco-Roman figures, their stern faces suggesting Greek wall-painting at Palmyra, Greco-Egyptian painting upon the cases of mummies, where character delineations are exaggerated as in much work of our time, and that decoration which seems to undermine our self-control, and is, it seems, of Persian origin, and has for its appropriate symbol a vine whose tendrils climb everywhere and display among their leaves all those strange images of bird and beast, those forms that represent no creature eye has ever seen, yet are begotten one upon the other as if they were themselves living creatures. May I consider the domination of the first *antithetical* and that of the second *primary*, and see in their alternation the work of the horizontal gyre? Strzygowski thinks that the church decorations where there are visible representations of holy persons were especially dear to those who believed in Christ's double nature, and that wherever Christ is represented by a bare Cross and all the rest is bird and beast and tree, we may discover an Asiatic art dear to those who thought Christ contained nothing human.

If I were left to myself I would make Phase 15 coincide with Justinian's reign, that great age of building in which one may conclude Byzantine art was perfected; but the meaning of the diagram may be that a building like St. Sophia, where all, to judge by the contemporary description, pictured ecstasy, must unlike the declamatory St. Peter's precede the moment of climax. Of the moment of climax itself I can say nothing, and of what followed from Phase 17 to Phase 21 almost nothing, for I have no knowledge of the time; and no analogy from the age after Phidias, or after our own Renaissance, can help. We and the Greeks moved towards intellect, but Byzantium and the Western Europe of that day moved from it. If Strzygowski is right we may see in the destruction of images but a destruction of what was Greek in decoration accompanied perhaps by a renewed splendour in all that came down from the ancient Persian Paradise, an episode in some attempt to make theology more ascetic, spiritual and abstract. Destruction was apparently suggested to the first iconoclastic Emperor by followers of a Monophysite Bishop, Xenaias, who had his see in that part of the Empire where Persian influence had been strongest. The return of the images may, as I see things, have been the failure of synthesis (Phase 22) and the first sinking-in and dying-down of Christendom into the heterogeneous loam. Did Europe grow animal and literal? Did the strength of the victorious party come from zealots as ready as their opponents to destroy an image if permitted to grind it into powder, mix it with some liquid and swallow it as a medicine? Did mankind for a season do, not what it would, or should, but what it could, accept the past and the current belief because they prevented thought? In Western Europe I think I may see in Johannes Scotus Erigena the last intellectual synthesis before the death of philosophy, but I know little of him except that he is founded upon a Greek book of the sixth century, put into circulation by a last iconoclastic Emperor, though its Angelic Orders gave a theme to the image-makers. I notice too that my diagram makes Phase 22 coincide with the break-up of Charlemagne's Empire and so clearly likens him to Alexander, but I do not want to concern myself, except where I must, with political events.

Then follows, as always must in the last quarter, heterogeneous art; hesitation amid architectural forms, some book tells me; an interest in Greek and Roman literature; much copying out and gathering together; yet outside a few courts and monasteries another book tells me an Asiatic and anarchic Europe. The intellectual cone has so narrowed that secular intellect has gone, and the strong man rules with the aid of local custom; everywhere the supernatural is sudden, violent, and as dark to the intellect as a stroke or St. Vitus' dance. Men under the Caesars, my own documents tell me, were physically one but intellectually many, but that is now reversed, for there is one common thought or doctrine, town is shut off from town, village from village, clan from clan. The spiritual life is alone overflowing, its cone expanded, and yet this life—secular intellect extinguished—has little effect upon men's conduct, is perhaps a dream which passes beyond the reach of conscious mind but for some rare miracle or vision. I think of it as like that profound reverie of the somnambulist which may be accompanied by a sensuous dream—a Romanesque stream perhaps of bird and beast images—and yet neither affect the dream nor be affected by it.

It is indeed precisely because this double mind is created at full moon that the *antithetical* phases are but, at the best, phases of a momentary illumination like that of a lightning flash. But the full moon that now concerns us is not only Phase 15 of its greater era, but the final phase, Phase 28, of its millennium, and in its physical form, human life grown once more automatic. I knew a man once who, seeking for an image of the Absolute, saw one persistent image, a slug, as though it were suggested to him that Being which is beyond human comprehension is mirrored in the least organised forms of life. Intellectual creation has ceased, but men have come to terms with the supernatural and are agreed that, if you make the usual offerings, it will remember to live and let live; even Saint or Angel does not seem very different from themselves: a man thinks his guardian Angel jealous of his mistress; a King, dragging a Saint's body to a new church, meets some difficulty upon the road, assumes a miracle, and denounces the Saint as a churl. Three Roman courtesans who have one after another got their favourite lovers chosen Pope have, it pleases one's mockery to think, confessed their sins, with full belief in the supernatural efficacy of the act, to ears that have heard their cries of love, or received the Body of God from hands that have played with their own bodies. Interest has narrowed to what is near and personal and, seeing that all abstract secular thought has faded, those interests have taken the most physical forms. In monasteries and in hermit cells men freed from the intellect at last can seek their God upon all fours like beasts or children. Ecclesiastical Law, in so far as that law is concerned not with government, Church or State, but with the individual soul, is complete; all that is necessary to salvation is known, yet there is apathy everywhere. Man awaits death and judgment with nothing to occupy the worldly faculties and helpless before the world's disorder, drags out of the subconscious the conviction that the world is about to end. Hidden, except at rare moments of excitement or revelation, even then shown but in symbol, the stream set in motion by the Galilean Symbol has filled its basin, and seems motionless for an instant before it falls over the rim. In the midst of the basin stands, in motionless contemplation, blood that is not His blood upon His Hands and Feet, One that feels but for the common lot, and mourns over the length of years and the inadequacy of man's fate to man. Two thousand years before, His predecessor, careful of heroic men alone, had so stood and mourned over the shortness of time, and man's inadequacy to his fate.

Full moon over, that last Embodiment shall grow more like ourselves, putting off that stern majesty, borrowed, it may be, from the Phidian Zeus—if we can trust Cefalù and Monreale; and His Mother—putting off her harsh Byzantine image—stand at His side.

A.D. 1050 TO THE PRESENT DAY

When the tide changed and faith no longer sufficed, something must have happened in the courts and castles of which history has perhaps no record, for with the first vague dawn of the ultimate *antithetical* revelation man, under the eyes of the Virgin, or upon the breast of his mistress, became but a fragment. Instead of that old alternation, brute or ascetic, came something obscure or uncertain that could not find its full explanation for a thousand years. A certain Byzantine Bishop had said upon seeing a singer of Antioch, "I looked long upon her beauty, knowing that I would behold it upon the day of judgment, and I wept to remember that I had taken less care of my soul than she of her body," but when in the *Arabian Nights* Harun Al-Rashid looked at the singer Heart's Miracle, and on the instant loved her, he covered her head with a little silk veil to show that her beauty "had already retreated into the mystery of our faith." The Bishop saw a beauty that would be sanctified, but the Caliph that which was its own sanctity, and it was this latter sanctity, come back from the first Crusade or up from Arabian Spain or half Asiatic Provence and Sicily, that created romance. What forgotten reverie, what initiation, it may be, separated wisdom from the monastery and, creating Merlin, joined it to passion? When Merlin in Chrestien de Troyes loved Ninian he showed her a cavern adorned with gold mosaics and made by a prince for his beloved, and told her that those lovers died upon the same day and were laid "in the chamber where they found delight." He thereupon lifted a slab of red marble that his art alone could lift and showed them wrapped in winding-sheets of white samite. The tomb remained opened, for Ninian asked that she and Merlin might return to the cavern and spend their night near those dead lovers, but before night came Merlin grew sad and fell asleep, and she and her attendants took him "by head and foot" and laid him "in the tomb and replaced the stone," for Merlin had taught her the magic words, and "from that hour none beheld Merlin dead or alive." Throughout the German *Parsifal* there is no ceremony of the Church, neither Marriage nor Mass nor Baptism, but instead we discover that strangest creation of romance or of life, "the love trance." Parsifal in such a trance, seeing nothing before his eyes but the image of his absent love, overcame knight after knight, and awakening at last looked amazed upon his dinted sword and shield; and it is to his lady and not to God or the Virgin that Parsifal prayed upon the day of battle, and it was his lady's soul, separated from her entranced or sleeping body, that went beside him and gave him victory.

The period from 1005 to 1180 is attributed in the diagram to the first two gyres of our millennium, and what interests me in this period, which corresponds to the Homeric period some two thousand years before, is the creation of the Arthurian Tales and Romanesque architecture. I see in Romanesque the first movement to a secular Europe, but a movement so instinctive that as yet there is no antagonism to the old condition. Every architect, every man who lifts a chisel, may be a cleric of some kind, yet in the overflowing ornament where the human form has all but disappeared and where no bird or beast is copied from nature, where all is more Asiatic than Byzantium itself, one discovers the same impulse that created Merlin and his jugglery.

I do not see in Gothic architecture, which is a character of the next gyre, that of Phases 5, 6 and 7, as did the nineteenth-century historians, ever looking for the image of their own age, the creation of a new communal freedom, but a creation of authority, a suppression of that freedom though with its consent, and certainly St. Bernard when he denounced the extravagance of Romanesque saw it in that

light. I think of that curious sketchbook of Villars de Honecourt with its insistence upon mathematical form, and I see that form in Mont St. Michel—Church,
Abbey, Fort and town, all that dark geometry that makes Byzantium seem a sun-
lit cloud—and it seems to me that the Church grows secular that it may fight a
new-born secular world. Its avowed appeal is to religion alone: nobles and great
ladies join the crowds that drag the Cathedral stones, not out of love for beauty
but because the stones as they are trundled down the road cure the halt and the
blind; yet the stones once set up traffic with the enemy. The mosaic pictures
grown transparent fill the windows, quarrel one with the other like pretty women,
and draw all eyes, and upon the faces of the statues flits once more the smile that
disappeared with archaic Greece. That smile is physical, *primary* joy, the escape
from supernatural terror, a moment of irresponsible common life before *antithetical* sadness begins. It is as though the pretty worshippers, while the Domini-
can was preaching with a new and perhaps incredible sternness, let their imaginations stray, as though the observant sculptor, or worker in ivory, in modelling his
holy women has remembered their smiling lips.

Are not the cathedrals and the philosophy of St. Thomas the product of the
abstraction that comes before Phase 8 as before Phase 22, and of the moral synthesis that at the end of the first quarter seeks to control the general anarchy?
That anarchy must have been exceedingly great, or man must have found a
hitherto unknown sensitiveness, for it was the shock that created modern civilization. The diagram makes the period from 1250 to 1300 correspond to Phase 8,
certainly because in or near that period, chivalry and Christendom having proved
insufficient, the King mastered the one, the Church the other, reversing the
achievement of Constantine, for it was now the mitre and the crown that protected the Cross. I prefer, however, to find my example of the first victory of
personality where I have more knowledge. Dante in the *Convito* mourns for solitude, lost through poverty, and writes the first sentence of modern autobiography,
and in the *Divina Commedia* imposes his own personality upon a system and a
phantasmagoria hitherto impersonal; the King everywhere has found his kingdom.

The period from 1300 to 1380 is attributed to the fourth gyre, that of Phases
9, 10 and 11, which finds its character in painting from Giotto to Fra Angelico,
in the Chronicles of Froissart and in the elaborate canopy upon the stained glass
of the windows. Every old tale is alive, Christendom still unbroken; painter and
poet alike find new ornament for the tale, they feel the charm of everything but
the more poignantly because that charm is archaistic; they smell a pot of dried
roses. The practical men, face to face with rebellion and heresy, are violent as
they have not been for generations, but the artists separated from life by the
tradition of Byzantium can even exaggerate their gentleness, and gentleness and
violence alike express the gyre's hesitation. The public certainty that sufficed for
Dante and St. Thomas has disappeared, and there is yet no private certainty. Is it
that the human mind now longs for solitude, for escape from all that hereditary
splendour, and does not know what ails it; or is it that the Image itself encouraged
by the new technical method, the flexible brush-stroke instead of the unchanging
cube of glass, and wearied of its part in a crowded ghostly dance, longs for a solitary human body? That body comes in the period from 1380 to 1450 and is discovered by Masaccio, and by Chaucer who is partly of the old gyre, and by Villon
who is wholly of the new.

Masaccio, a precocious and abundant man, dying like Aubrey Beardsley in his six-and-twentieth year, cannot move us, as he did his immediate successors, for he discovered a naturalism that begins to weary us a little; making the naked young man awaiting baptism shiver with the cold, St. Peter grow red with the exertion of dragging the money out of the miraculous fish's mouth, while Adam and Eve, flying before the sword of the Angel, show faces disfigured by their suffering. It is very likely because I am a poet and not a painter that I feel so much more keenly that suffering of Villon—of the 13th Phase as man, and of it or near it in epoch—in whom the human soul for the first time stands alone before a death ever present to imagination, without help from a Church that is fading away; or is it that I remember Aubrey Beardsley, a man of like phase though so different epoch, and so read into Villon's suffering our modern conscience which gathers intensity as we approach the close of an era? Intensity that has seemed to me pitiless self-judgment may have been but heroic gaiety. With the approach of solitude bringing with it an ever-increasing struggle with that which opposes solitude—sensuality, greed, ambition, physical curiosity in all its species—philosophy has returned driving dogma out. Even amongst the most pious the worshipper is preoccupied with himself, and when I look for the drilled eyeball, which reveals so much, I notice that its edge is no longer so mechanically perfect, nor, if I can judge by casts at the Victoria and Albert Museum, is the hollow so deep. Angel and Florentine noble must look upward with an eye that seems dim and abashed as though to recognise duties to Heaven, an example to be set before men, and finding both difficult seem a little giddy. There are no miracles to stare at, for man descends the hill he once climbed with so great toil, and all grows but natural again.

As we approach the 15th Phase, as the general movement grows more and more westward in character, we notice the oscillation of the horizontal gyres, as though what no Unity of Being, yet possible, can completely fuse displays itself in triumph.

Donatello, as later Michael Angelo, reflects the hardness and astringency of Myron, and foretells what must follow the Renaissance; while Jacopo della Guercia and most of the painters seem by contrast, as Raphael later on, Ionic and Asiatic. The period from 1450 to 1550 is allotted to the gyre of Phase 15, and these dates are no doubt intended to mark somewhat vaguely a period that begins in one country earlier and in another later. I do not myself find it possible to make more than the first half coincide with the central moment, Phase 15 of the Italian Renaissance—Phase 22 of the cone of the entire era—the breaking of the Christian synthesis as the corresponding period before Christ, the age of Phidias, was the breaking of Greek traditional faith. The first half covers the principal activity of the Academy of Florence which formulated the reconciliation of Paganism and Christianity. This reconciliation, which to Pope Julius meant that Greek and Roman Antiquity were as sacred as that of Judea, and like it "a vestibule of Christianity," meant to the mind of Dürer—a visitor to Venice during the movement of the gyre—that the human norm, discovered from the measurement of ancient statues, was God's first handiwork, that "perfectly proportioned human body" which had seemed to Dante Unity of Being symbolised. The ascetic, who had a thousand years before attained his transfiguration upon the golden ground of Byzantine mosaic, had turned not into an athlete but into that unlabouring form the athlete dreamed of: the second Adam had become the first.

Because the 15th Phase can never find direct human expression, being a supernatural incarnation, it impressed upon work and thought an element of strain and artifice, a desire to combine elements which may be incompatible, or which suggest by their combination something supernatural. Had some Florentine Platonist read to Botticelli Porphyry upon the Cave of the Nymphs? for I seem to recognise it in that curious cave, with a thatched roof over the nearer entrance to make it resemble the conventional manger, in his "Nativity" in the National Gallery. Certainly the glimpse of forest trees, dim in the evening light, through the far entrance, and the deliberate strangeness everywhere, gives one an emotion of mystery which is new to painting.

Botticelli, Crivelli, Mantegna, Da Vinci, who fall within the period, make Masaccio and his school seem heavy and common by something we may call intellectual beauty or compare perhaps to that kind of bodily beauty which Castiglione called "the spoil or monument of the victory of the soul." Intellect and emotion, *primary* curiosity and the *antithetical* dream, are for the moment one. Since the rebirth of the secular intellect in the eleventh century, faculty has been separating from faculty, poetry from music, the worshipper from the worshipped, but all have remained within a common fading circle—Christendom—and so within the human soul. Image has been separated from image but always as an exploration of the soul itself; forms have been displayed in an always clear light, have been perfected by separation from one another till their link with one another and with common associations has been broken; but, Phase 15 past, these forms begin to jostle and fall into confusion, there is as it were a sudden rush and storm. In the mind of the artist a desire for power succeeds to that for knowledge, and this desire is communicated to the forms and to the onlooker.

The eighth gyre, which corresponds to Phases 16, 17 and 18 and completes itself say between 1550 and 1650, begins with Raphael, Michael Angelo and Titian, and the forms, as in Titian, awaken sexual desire—we had not desired to touch the forms of Botticelli or even of Da Vinci—or they threaten us like those of Michael Angelo, and the painter himself handles his brush with a conscious facility or exultation. The subject-matter may arise out of some propaganda as when Raphael in the Camera della Segnatura, and Michael Angelo in the Sistine Chapel, put, by direction of the Pope, Greek Sages and Doctors of the Church, Roman Sibyls and Hebrew Prophets, opposite one another in apparent equality. From this on, all is changed, and where the Mother of God sat enthroned, now that the Soul's unity has been found and lost, Nature seats herself, and the painter can paint only what he desires in the flesh, and soon, asking less and less for himself, will make it a matter of pride to paint what he does not at all desire. I think Raphael almost of the earlier gyre—perhaps a transitional figure—but Michael Angelo, Rabelais, Aretino, Shakespeare, Titian—Titian is so markedly of the 14th Phase as a man that he seems less characteristic—I associate with the mythopoeic and ungovernable beginning of the eighth gyre. I see in Shakespeare a man in whom human personality, hitherto restrained by its dependence upon Christendom or by its own need for self-control, burst like a shell. Perhaps secular intellect, setting itself free after five hundred years of struggle, has made him the greatest of dramatists, and yet because an *antithetical* age alone could confer upon an art like his the unity of a painting or of a temple pediment, we might, had the total works of Sophocles survived—they too born of a like struggle though with a different enemy—not think him greatest. Do we not feel an unrest like that of travel itself when we watch those personages, more living than ourselves, amid so much that is irrelevant and heterogeneous, amid so much *primary* curiosity, when we are carried from Rome to Venice, from Egypt to Saxon England, or in the one play from Roman to Christian mythology?

Were he not himself of a later phase, were he of the 16th Phase like his age and so drunk with his own wine, he had not written plays at all, but as it is he finds his opportunity among a crowd of men and women who are still shaken by thought that passes from man to man in psychological contagion. I see in Milton, who is characteristic of the moment when the first violence of the gyre has begun to sink, an attempted return to the synthesis of the Camera della Segnatura and the Sistine Chapel. It is this attempt made too late that, amid all the music and magnificence of the still violent gyre, gives him his unreality and his cold rhetoric. The two elements have fallen apart in the hymn "On the Morning of Christ's Nativity," the one is sacred, the other profane; his classical mythology is an artificial ornament; whereas no great Italian artist from 1450 to the sack of Rome saw any difference between them, and when difference came, as it did with Titian, it was God and the Angels that seemed artificial.

The gyre ebbs out in order and reason, the Jacobean poets succeed the Elizabethan, Cowley and Dryden the Jacobean as belief dies out. Elsewhere Christendom keeps a kind of spectral unity for a while, now with one, now with the other element of the synthesis dominant; a declamatory holiness defaces old churches, innumerable Tritons and Neptunes pour water from their mouths. What had been a beauty like the burning sun fades out in Vandyke's noble ineffectual faces, and the Low Countries, which have reached the new gyre long before the rest of Europe, convert the world to a still limited curiosity, to certain recognised forms of the picturesque constantly repeated, chance travellers at an inn door, men about a fire, men skating, the same pose or grouping, where the subject is different, passing from picture to picture. The world begins to long for the arbitrary and accidental, for the grotesque, the repulsive and the terrible, that it may be cured of desire. The moment has come for the ninth gyre, Phases 19, 20 and 21, for the period that begins for the greater part of Europe with 1650 and lasts, it may be, to 1875.

The beginning of the gyre like that of its forerunner is violent, a breaking of the soul and world into fragments, and has for a chief character the materialistic movement at the end of the seventeenth century, all that comes out of Bacon perhaps, the foundation of our modern inductive reasoning, the declamatory religious sects and controversies that first in England and then in France destroy the sense of form, all that has its very image and idol in Bernini's big Altar in St. Peter's with its figures contorted and convulsed by religion as though by the devil. Men change rapidly from deduction to deduction, opinion to opinion, have but one impression at a time and utter it always, no matter how often they change, with the same emphasis. Then the gyre develops a new coherence in the external scene; and violent men, each master of some generalisation, arise one after another: Napoleon, a man of the 20th Phase in the historical 21st—personality in its hard final generalisation—typical of all. The artistic life, where most characteristic of the general movement, shows the effect of the closing of the *tinctures*. It is external, sentimental and logical—the poetry of Pope and Gray, the philosophy of Johnson and of Rousseau—equally simple in emotion or in thought, the old oscillation in a new form. Personality is everywhere spreading out its fingers in vain, or grasping with an always more convulsive grasp a world where the predominance of physical science, of finance and economics in all their forms, of democratic politics, of vast populations, of architecture where styles jostle one another, of newspapers where all is heterogeneous, show that mechanical force will in a moment become supreme.

That art discovered by Dante of marshalling into a vast *antithetical* structure *antithetical* material became through Milton Latinised and artificial—the Shades, as Sir Thomas Browne said, "steal or contrive a body"—and now it changes that it may marshal into a still *antithetical* structure *primary* material, and the modern novel is created, but even before the gyre is drawn to its end the happy ending, the admired hero, the preoccupation with desirable things, all that is undisguisedly *antithetical* disappears.

All the art of the gyre that is not derived from the external scene is a Renaissance echo growing always more conventional or more shadowy, but since the Renaissance—Phase 22 of the cone of the era—the "Emotion of Sanctity," that first relation to the *spiritual primary*, has been possible in those things that are most intimate and personal, though not until Phase 22 of the millennium cone will general thought be ready for its expression. A mysterious contact is perceptible first in painting and then in poetry and last in prose. In painting it comes where the influence of the Low Countries and that of Italy mingle, but always rarely and faintly. I do not find it in Watteau, but there is a preparation for it, a sense of exhaustion of old interests—"they do not believe even in their own happiness," Verlaine said—and then suddenly it is present in the faces of Gainsborough's women as it has been in no face since the Egyptian sculptor buried in a tomb that image of a princess carved in wood. Reynolds had nothing of it, an ostentatious fashionable man fresh from Rome, he stayed content with fading Renaissance emotion and modern curiosity. In frail women's faces the soul awakes —all its prepossessions, the accumulated learning of centuries swept away—and looks out upon us wise and foolish like the dawn. Then it is everywhere, it finds the village Providence of the eighteenth century and turns him into Goethe, who for all that comes to no conclusion, his Faust after his hundred years but reclaiming land like some Sir Charles Grandison or Voltaire in his old age. It makes the heroines of Jane Austen seek, not as their grandfathers and grandmothers would have done, theological or political truth, but simply good breeding, as though to increase it were more than any practical accomplishment. In poetry alone it finds its full expression, for it is a quality of the emotional nature (*Celestial Body* acting through *Mask*); and creates all that is most beautiful in modern English poetry from Blake to Arnold, all that is not a fading echo. One discovers it in those symbolist writers who like Verhaeren substitute an entirely personal wisdom for the physical beauty or passionate emotion of the fifteenth and sixteenth centuries. In painting it shows most often where the aim has been archaistic, as though it were an accompaniment of what the popular writers call decadence, as though old emotions had first to be exhausted. I think of the French portrait-painter Ricard, to whom it was more a vision of the mind than a research, for he would say to his sitter, "You are so fortunate as to resemble your picture," and of Charles Ricketts, my education in so many things. How often his imagination moves stiffly as though in fancy dress, and then there is something—Sphinx, Danaides—that makes me remember Callimachus' return to Ionic elaboration and shudder as though I stared into an abyss full of eagles. Everywhere this vision, or rather this contact, is faint or intermittent and it is always fragile; Dickens was able with a single book, *Pickwick*, to substitute for Jane Austen's privileged and perilous research the camaraderie of the inn parlour, qualities that every man might hope to possess, and it did not return till Henry James began to write.

Certain men have sought to express the new emotion through the *Creative Mind*, though fit instruments of expression do not yet exist, and so to establish, in the midst of our ever more abundant *primary* information, *antithetical* wisdom; but such men, Blake, Coventry Patmore at moments, Nietzsche, are full of morbid excitement and few in number, unlike those who, from Richardson to Tolstoi, from Hobbes down to Spencer, have grown in number and serenity. They were begotten in the Sistine Chapel and still dream that all can be transformed if they be but emphatic; yet Nietzsche, when the doctrine of the Eternal Recurrence drifts before his eyes, knows for an instant that nothing can be so transformed and is almost of the next gyre.

The period from 1875 to 1927 (Phase 22—in some countries and in some forms of thought the phase runs from 1815 to 1927) is like that from 1250 to 1300 (Phase 8) a period of abstraction, and like it also in that it is preceded and followed by abstraction. Phase 8 was preceded by the Schoolmen and followed by legalists and inquisitors, and Phase 22 was preceded by the great popularisers of physical science and economic science, and will be followed by social movements and applied science. Abstraction which began at Phase 19 will end at Phase 25, for these movements and this science will have for their object or result the elimination of intellect Our generation has witnessed a first weariness, has stood at the climax, at what in *The Trembling of the Veil* I call *Hodos Chameliontos*, and when the climax passes will recognise that there common secular thought began to break and disperse. Tolstoi in *War and Peace* had still preference, could argue about this thing or that other, had a belief in Providence and a disbelief in Napoleon, but Flaubert in his *St. Anthony* had neither belief nor preference, and so it is that, even before the general surrender of the will, there came synthesis for its own sake, organisation where there is no masterful director, books where the author has disappeared, painting where some accomplished brush paints with an equal pleasure, or with a bored impartiality, the human form or an old bottle, dirty weather and clean sunshine. I too think of famous works where synthesis has been carried to the utmost limit possible, where there are elements of inconsequence or discovery of hitherto ignored ugliness, and I notice that when the limit is approached or past, when the moment of surrender is reached, when the new gyre begins to stir, I am filled with excitement. I think of recent mathematical research; even the ignorant can compare it with that of Newton—so plainly of the 19th Phase—with its objective world intelligible to intellect; I can recognise that the limit itself has become a new dimension, that this ever-hidden thing which makes us fold our hands has begun to press down upon multitudes. Having bruised their hands upon that limit, men, for the first time since the seventeenth century, see the world as an object of contemplation, not as something to be remade, and some few, meeting the limit in their special study, even doubt if there is any common experience, doubt the possibility of science.

WRITTEN AT CAPRI, FEBRUARY 1925

ANDRÉ MALRAUX

The Triumph of Art over History

A Romanesque crucifix was not regarded by its contemporaries as a work of sculpture; nor Cimabue's *Madonna* as a picture. Even Pheidias' *Pallas Athene* was not, primarily, a statue.

So vital is the part played by the art museum in our approach to works of art to-day that we find it difficult to realize that no museums exist, none has ever existed, in lands where the civilization of modern Europe is, or was, unknown; and that, even amongst us, they have existed for barely two hundred years. They bulked so large in the nineteenth century and are so much part of our lives today that we forget they have imposed on the spectator a wholly new attitude towards the work of art. For they have tended to estrange the works they bring together from their original functions and to transform even portraits into "pictures." Though Caesar's bust and the equestrian *Charles* V remain for us Caesar and the Emperor Charles, *Count-Duke Olivares* has become pure Velazquez. What do we care who the *Man with the Helmet* or the *Man with the Glove* may have been in real life? For us their names are Rembrandt and Titian. The men who sat for these portraits have lapsed into nonentity. Until the nineteenth century a work of art was essentially a representation of something real or imaginary, which conditioned its existence *qua* work of art. Only in the artist's eyes was painting specifically painting, and often, even for him, it also meant a "poetic" rendering of his subject. The effect of the museum was to suppress the model in almost every portrait (even that of a dream-figure) and to divest works of art of their functions. It did away with the significance of Palladium, of Saint and Saviour; ruled out associations of sanctity, qualities of adornment and possession, of likeness or imagination. Each exhibit is a representation of something, differing from the thing itself, this specific difference being its *raison d'être*.

In the past a Gothic statue was a component part of the Cathedral; similarly a classical picture was tied up with the setting of its period, and not expected to consort with works of different mood and outlook. Rather, it was kept apart from them, so as to be the more appreciated by the spectator. True, there were picture collections and *cabinets d'antiques* in the seventeenth century, but they did not modify that attitude towards art of which Versailles is the symbol. Whereas the modern art-gallery not only isolates the work of art from its context but makes it foregather with rival or even hostile works. It is a confrontation of metamorphoses.

The reason why the art museum made its appearance in Asia so belatedly (and, even then, only under European influence and patronage) is that for an Asiatic, and especially the man of the Far East, artistic contemplation and the picture gallery are incompatible. In China the full enjoyment of works of art necessarily involved ownership, except where religious art was concerned; above all it demanded their isolation. A painting was not exhibited, but unfurled before an art-lover in a fitting state of grace; its function was to deepen and enhance his communion with the universe. The practice of pitting works of art against each

From *The Voices of Silence* [1951], translated from the French by Stuart Gilbert, New York, 1953, pp. 13-16, 68-9, 310-11, 334, 461, 626-35, 639; reprinted by permission of Doubleday & Co., Inc. and Martin Secker & Warburg Ltd.

other, an intellectual activity, is at the opposite pole from the mood of relaxation which alone makes contemplation possible. To the Asiatic's thinking an art collection (except for educational purposes) is as preposterous as would be a concert in which one listened to a programme of ill-assorted pieces following in unbroken succession.

For over a century our approach to art has been growing more and more intellectualized. The art museum invites criticism of each of the expressions of the world it brings together; and a query as to what they have in common. To the "delight of the eye" there has been added—owing to the sequence of conflicting styles and seemingly antagonistic schools—an awareness of art's impassioned quest, its age-old struggle to remould the scheme of things. Indeed an art gallery is one of the places which show man at his noblest. But our knowledge covers a wider field than our museums. The visitor to the Louvre knows that he will not find the great English artists significantly represented there; nor Goya, nor Michelangelo (as painter), nor Piero della Francesca, nor Grünewald—and that he will see but little of Vermeer. Inevitably in a place where the work of art has no longer any function other than that of being a work of art, and at a time when the artistic exploration of the world is in active progress, the assemblage of so many masterpieces—from which, nevertheless, so many are missing—conjures up in the mind's eye *all* the world's masterpieces. How indeed could this mutilated possible fail to evoke the whole gamut of the possible?

Of what is it necessarily deprived? Of all that forms an integral part of a whole (stained glass, frescoes); of all that cannot be moved; of all that is difficult to display (sets of tapestries); of all that the collection is unable to acquire. Even when the greatest zeal has gone to its making, a museum owes much to opportunities that chance has thrown in its way. All Napoleon's victories did not enable him to bring the Sistine to the Louvre, and no art patron, however wealthy, will take to the Metropolitan Museum the Royal Portal of Chartres or the Arezzo frescoes. From the eighteenth to the twentieth century what migrated was the portable; far more pictures by Rembrandt than Giotto frescoes have found their way to sales. Thus the Art Museum, born when the easel-picture was the one living form of art, came to be a pageant not of color but of pictures; not of sculpture but of statues.

The Grand Tour rounded it off in the nineteenth century. Yet in those days a man who had seen the totality of European masterpieces was a very rare exception. Gautier saw Italy (but not Rome) only when he was thirty-nine; Edmond de Goncourt when he was thirty-three; Hugo as a child; Baudelaire and Verlaine, never. The same holds good for Spain; for Holland rather less, as Flanders was relatively well known. The eager crowds that thronged the Salons—composed largely of real connoisseurs—owed their art education to the Louvre. Baudelaire never set eyes on the masterpieces of El Greco, Michelangelo, Masaccio, Piero della Francesca or Grünewald; or of Titian, or of Hals or Goya—the Galerie d'Orléans notwithstanding.

What had he seen? What (until 1900) had been seen by all those writers whose views on art still impress us as revealing and important; whom we take to be speaking of the same works as those we know, and referring to the same *data* as those available to us? They had visited two or three galleries, and seen reproductions (photographs, prints or copies) of a handful of the masterpieces of

European art; most of their readers had seen even less. In the art knowledge of those days there was a pale of ambiguity, a sort of no man's land—due to the fact that the comparison of a picture in the Louvre with another in Madrid was that of a present picture with a memory. Visual memory is far from being infallible, and often weeks had intervened between the inspections of the two canvases. From the seventeenth to the nineteenth century, pictures, interpreted by engraving, had *become* engravings; they had kept their drawing but lost their colors, which were replaced by "interpretation," their expression in black-and-white; also, while losing their dimensions, they acquired margins. The nineteenth-century photograph was merely a more faithful print, and the art-lover of the time "knew" pictures in the same manner as we now "know" stained-glass windows.

Nowadays an art student can examine color reproductions of most of the world's great paintings, can make acquaintance with a host of second-rank pictures, archaic arts, Indian, Chinese and Pre-Columbian sculpture of the best periods, Romanesque frescoes, Negro and "folk" art, a fair quantity of Byzantine art. How many statues could be seen in reproduction in 1850? Whereas the modern art-book has been pre-eminently successful with sculpture (which lends itself better than pictures to reproduction in black-and-white). Hitherto the connoisseur duly visited the Louvre and some subsidiary galleries, and memorized what he saw, as best he could. We, however, have far more great works available to refresh our memories than those which even the greatest of museums could bring together. For a "Museum without Walls" is coming into being, and (now that the plastic arts have invented their own printing-press) it will carry infinitely farther that revelation of the world of art, limited perforce, which the "real" museums offer us within their walls.

It is not research-work that has led to the understanding of El Greco; it is modern art. Each genius that breaks with the past deflects, as it were, the whole range of earlier forms. Who was it reopened the eyes of the statues of classical antiquity— the excavators or the great masters of the Renaissance? Who, if not Raphael, forced an eclipse on Gothic art? The destiny of Pheidias lay in the hands of Michelangelo (who had never seen his statues); Cézanne's austere genius has magnified for us the Venetians (who were his despair); it is in the light of those pathetic candles which Van Gogh, already mad, fixed round his straw hat so as to paint the Café d'Arles by night, that Grünewald has come into his own. In 1910 it was assumed that the Winged Victory, when restored, would regain her ancient gold, her arms, her trumpet. Instead, she has regained her prow and, like a herald of the dawn, crowns the high stairway of the Louvre; it is not towards Alexandria that we have set her flight, but towards the Acropolis. Metamorphosis is not a matter of chance; it is a law governing the life of every work of art. We have learned that, if death cannot still the voice of genius, the reason is that genius triumphs over death not by reiterating its original language, but by constraining us to listen to a language constantly modified, sometimes forgotten—as it were an echo answering each passing century with its own voice—and what the masterpiece keeps up is not a monologue, however authoritative, but a *dialogue* indefeasible by Time. . . .

I name that man an artist who *creates* forms, be he an ambassador like Rubens, an image-maker like Gislebert of Autun, an *ignotus* like the Master of Chartres, an illuminator like Limbourg, a king's friend and court official like Velazquez, a *rentier* like Cézanne, a man possessed like Van Gogh or a vagabond like Gauguin; and I call that man an artisan who *reproduces* forms, however great may be the charm or sophistication of his craftsmanship. How many arts have been discovered since we have learnt to isolate them from the productions of the handicrafts that grew up around them! The indistinguishable herd of Gallo-Romans are not to be confused with that unknown man who carved the Poitiers capital, or the band of craftsmen responsible for the Palmyra tombs with that one unknown artist who foreshadowed Byzantium, or the artisans who carved the blue Gandhara schist with the masters of the great Buddhist figures and the prophets of the Wei period, or the servile followers of the Byzantine canon with him who made the mosaics of St. Luke's in Phocis. It would be as inept as likening to Poussin Raphael's imitators or the seventeenth-century decorators. The fact that our conception of the artist was something quite unknown in the Middle Ages (and for many thousand years before) and that a genius like Van Eyck was commissioned to design set pieces and to paint coffers, does not affect the fact that painters and sculptors, when possessed of genius, transfigured the art they had inherited, and the creative joy of the man who *invented* the Moissac *Christ*, the Chartres *Kings* and the *Uta* was different in kind from the satisfaction felt by the cabinet maker who had just completed a perfect chest. Though a serf, a serf-artist is none the less an artist. And when even the least sophisticated sculptor of the High Middle Ages (like the contemporary painter haunted by art's long history) invented a system of forms, he did not accomplish this by freeing his art from subservience to nature or to his personal emotions, but as a result of his conflict with a previous type of art. Thus at Chartres as in Egypt, at Florence as in Babylon, art was begotten of life upon an art preceding it. . . .

Every great style of the past impresses us as being a special interpretation of the world, but this collective conquest is obviously a sum total of the individual conquests that have gone to its making. Always these are victories over forms, achieved by means of forms, they are not the allegorical expression of some ideology. *The Last Judgment* was the outcome of a meditation on figures, and not a declaration of faith. Once we realize how all-important is the significance of styles, we understand why every artist of genius—whether like Gauguin and Cézanne he makes himself a recluse, or like Van Gogh a missionary, or like young Tintoretto exhibits his canvases in a booth on the Rialto—becomes a transformer of the meaning of the world, which he masters by reducing it to forms he has selected or invented, just as the philosopher reduces it to concepts and the physicist to laws. And he attains this mastery not through his visual experience of the world itself, but by a victory over one of the forms of an immediate predecessor that he has taken over and transmuted in the crucible of genius. . . .

It is as a creative act that the great work appeals to us, and a great artist is not autonomous because he is original, but *vice versa*; hence his august solitude. But we now have learnt in what constellation these solitary stars have their appointed place; great artists are not transcribers of the scheme of things, they are its *rivals*.

That thrill of creation which we experience when we see a masterpiece is not unlike the feeling of the artist who created it; such a work is a fragment of the world which he has annexed and which belongs to him alone. The conflict of his early days (which gave rise to his genius) is over and he has lost his feeling of subjection. And for us, too, this work of art is a fragment of the world of which Man has taken charge. The artist has not only expelled his masters from the canvas, but reality as well—not necessarily the outer aspects of reality, but reality at its deepest level—the "scheme of things"—and replaced it by his own. A great portrait is primarily a picture and only secondarily the likeness (or analysis) of a face. The masterpiece is not wholly identical with truth, as the artist often thinks. It is something that was not and now *is*: not an achievement but a birth—life confronting life on its own ground and animated by the ever-rolling stream of Time, man's Time, by which it is nourished and which it transforms. And this holds good whether the masterpiece be a Toltec mask or a *Fête galante*; whether its maker be a Gislebert d'Autun, a Grünewald or a Leonardo.

The most drastic metamorphosis of our age is the change that has come over our attitude to art. We no longer apply the term "art" to any particular form it may have assumed in any given place or period, but give it a wider application, covering more than all the forms so far accepted. Gazing at the horses of the Acropolis and those of the Lascaux caves, we do not have the same emotion as was Plato's gazing at the former; nor that of Suger when gazing at the St. Denis statues. Our emotional responses are such as neither Plato nor Suger could experience, for implicit in them is our visual experience of all the glorious debris we have salvaged from the past. On this plane the *Koré of Euthydikos* is a sister to the most poignant Christ Crucified; *The Thinker*, a Pre-Columbian figure, even *The Beggar Woman, The Three Crosses* and the best Buddhist paintings share in the glory of the Panathenaic frieze, in the cosmic frenzies of Rubens' *Kermesse*, the brooding horror of *The Shootings of May Third*—and perhaps in that purity of heart which Cézanne and Van Gogh brought to painting. All the same we do not share the feelings of Plato contemplating the Acropolis in its perfection, or those of Suger contemplating his basilica. We are coming to understand (our modern churches make this all too plain) that a sacred edifice is not a decorated house but *something else*, and that the world of art is no more an emotionalized world than a glorified world, but *another* world, the same as that of music and architecture. The solemn plainsong of the interiors of Santa Sophia and the Egyptian hypogea, of the Imperial Mosque of Ispahan and of the aisles of Bourges Cathedral gives their full meaning to the colonnades of Karnak and the Parthenon, to the epic towers of Laon, to the Capitolium—to the statues accompanying them and to the whole Museum without Walls. How remote they seem now: both the Romantic conception of beauty under a dual aspect and the long-drawn conflict between pagan and Christian art in Europe! The avenues of shadow which throughout their infinite recession impose the stamp of the human on that which seems least human—on the void—seem a symbol of what the art of the past is coming to mean to us: one of man's very rare *creations*, inventive though man is. The feeling of being in the presence of something with a life of its own that we experience when confronted by the masterpiece, is conveyed to us, though less vividly, by that never-ending process of transmutation running parallel to history which enabled the Egyptians to body forth a People of the Dead, the Negro races simulacra of their spirits, and so many others men-like-gods. Thus, too, Grüne-wald was enabled to build up from the plague victims of Alsace the *Christ Cruci-fied* of Issenheim, Michelangelo to ennoble with the imprint of his indomitable style a dying slave, Rubens and Goya to transmute a country fair and a corpse respectively into the cosmic visions of the *Kermesse* and *Nada*, Chardin and Cézanne to conjure up with a pitcher or a dish of apples a whole secret kingdom. "Humanization" this process might be called in the deepest, certainly the most enigmatic, sense of the word. The art resuscitated by our metamorphosis is a realm as vast and varied as was life itself in ages previous to ours. We subject that art to a passionate enquiry, akin to that questioning of the scheme of things inherent in our present-day art and culture. Just as the crucial historical event of the nineteenth century was the birth of a new consciousness of history, so the crucial expression of the metamorphosis of this century is our consciousness of it. Thus today art means to us that underlying continuity due to a latent kinship between the works of art of all ages which is an historical continuity, since never does an art destroy *all* that it has inherited; El Greco broke with Titian, but not by painting pictures like Cézanne's. But art also involves a constant metamorphosis of forms due both to the nature of the creative act and to the ineluctable march of Time. For Time includes all the forms of the past in the evolutionary change it imposes on the whole world of human experience; indeed our awareness of this process coincides with our awareness of duration itself. With us this awareness is no longer like the feeling of the traveler who himself remains unchanged in the changing scenes of Space and Time; it is more like the feeling symbolized by the seed which grows into the tree. Every art of the living gives a leading place to Man in its vast metamorphosis of the art of the dead; our resuscitations of so-called retrograde arts, the welcome we give to the arts of savages and the metamorphosis our century has brought to works of the Greek archaics, the Wei Masters, to Grünewald, Leonardo, Michelangelo, Rubens, Chardin and Goya, stem all alike from the fact that these manifestations of the creative spirit reveal a latent power they all possessed, though unawares: that mysterious power, peculiar to great artists, of revealing Man upon his highest level. Each manifestation of this power has come to mean to us, beyond and above what it purported to be, an incarnation of that which sponsors their underlying unity—and perhaps other, as yet unknown, powers. Thus now, behind this immemorial pageant in which the gods march side by side with creative man in a fraternity at last accepted, we are beginning to glimpse that which the gods sometimes embodied, sometimes fought against, and sometimes bowed to: the Might of Destiny. . . .

In that world of chaos and catastrophe which the spectator of *Œdipus* was invited to explore, what fascinated him more than the vengeful satisfaction which the sight of kings rolled in the dust gave the Greek populace was its simultaneous revelation of human servitude and man's indomitable faculty of transcending his estate, making his very subjection testify to his greatness. For when the tragedy was over, the Athenian spectator decided to see the play again, not to put out his eyes; when he saw the Eumenides massed on the tawny rocks of the orchestra (like the man who sees a statue of the Crucified, or a pictured face, or a landscape), he had a feeling that Man was holding his own amongst those blind forces of which he had once been the vassal and escaping from a destiny-ridden world into a world controlled by human minds.

We know only too well what that word "destiny" implies: the mortal element in all that is doomed to die. There is a "fault" (as a geologist might call it), sometimes plain to see and sometimes imperceptible, in the human personality, from which no god can always guard us; the saints call it a "dryness of the soul," and, for Christendom, that cry "Why hast Thou forsaken me?" is the most human of all cries. Time flows—perhaps towards eternity; assuredly towards death. But destiny is not death; it consists of all that forces on us the awareness of our human predicament, and even the happiness of such a man as Rubens is not immune from it, for destiny means something lying deeper than misfortune. This is why, seeking escape, man has so often made love his refuge; and it is why religions defend man against destiny (even when they do not defend him against death) by linking him up with God or with the cosmos. That part of man's nature which yearns for transcendence and for immortality is familiar to us. We know, too, that a man's consciousness of himself functions through channels other than those of his awareness of the outside world; every man's self is a tissue of fantastic dreams. I have written elsewhere of the man who fails to recognize his own voice on the gramophone, because he is hearing it for the first time through his ears and not through his throat; and because our throat alone transmits to us our inner voice, I called this book *La Condition Humaine* (Man's Fate). The function of those other voices which are art's is but to ensure the transmission of this inner voice. Our Museum without Walls teaches us that the rule of destiny is threatened whenever a world of Man, whatever be the nature of that world, emerges from the world *tout court*. For every masterpiece, implicitly or openly, tells of a human victory over the blind force of destiny. The artist's voice owes its power to the fact that it arises from a pregnant solitude that conjures up the universe so as to impose on it a human accent; and what survives for us in the great arts of the past is the indefeasible inner voice of civilizations that have passed away. But this surviving, yet not immortal, voice soaring towards the gods has for its accompaniment the tireless orchestra of death. Our awareness of destiny, as profound as that of the Oriental, but covering a far wider field of reference, stands in the same relation to the various "fates" of the past as does our Museum without Walls to the Collections of Antiquities of our forefathers; indifferent to those wraithlike marble forms, it is the obsession of the twentieth century and it is to counter this that there is tentatively taking form, for the first time in history, the concept of a world-wide humanism.

In the same way as Goya defied syphilis by recapturing the nightmare visions of primeval man, and Watteau fought consumption with melodious dreams of beauty, so some civilizations seem to combat destiny by allying themselves with the cosmic rhythms, and others by obliterating them. Nevertheless, in our eyes, the art of all has this in common, that it expresses a *defense* against fatality; for a non-Christian the company of statues in the cathedrals expresses not so much Christ as the defense, by means of Christ, of Christians against destiny. Any art that takes no part in this age-old dialogue is a mere art of delectation, and as such, dead to our thinking. Earlier civilizations when they retrieved the past read into it "messages" apt to solve contemporary problems; whereas our art culture makes no attempt to search the past for precedents, but transforms the entire past into a sequence of provisional responses to a problem that remains intact.

Over-simplified as is this summary, it suggests why the cultures of civilizations that have died out strike us not so much as being radically different, but as being cultures of different parts of the same plant. All the same, their sequence cannot be syncretized into a sort of cultural theosophy, for the good reason that mankind proceeds in terms of metamorphoses of a deep-seated order, it is not a matter of mere accretions or even of a continuous growth; Athens was not the childhood of Rome—still less was Sumer. We can affiliate the knowledge of the Fathers of the Church to that of the great Indian thinkers, but not the Christian experience of the former to the Hinduist experience of the latter; that is to say we can affiliate everything except essentials.

Thus our culture is not built up of earlier cultures reconciled with each other, but of irreconcilable fragments of the past. We know that it is not an inventory, but a heritage involving a metamorphosis; that the past is something to be conquered and annexed; also that it is within us and through us that the dialogue of Shades (that favorite art-form of the rhetorician) comes to life. If Aristotle and the Prophets of Israel met on the banks of the Styx, what would they exchange but insults? Montaigne had to be born before the dialogue between Christ and Plato could arise. Our resuscitations are not conditioned by any preconceived humanism; like Montaigne, they point the way to a humanism unconceived as yet.

When we survey the charnel-house of dead values, we realize that values live and die in conjunction with the vicissitudes of man. Like the individuals who express the highest values, they are man's form of defense; each hero, saint or sage stands for a victory over the human situation. All the same the Buddhist saints could no more resemble St. Peter and St. Augustine than Leonidas resembled Bayard, or Socrates resembled Gandhi. The succession of values, changing with each civilization—the ethic of Taoism, Hindu submission to the scheme of things, the Greek spirit of enquiry, the medieval communion of men, the cult of Reason and then that of history—all show still more clearly how values decline once they lose their power of rescuing man from his human bondage.

Similarly the values which are incarnated or created by artistic genius (genius and not the mere portrayal of an epoch) decline in the eyes of the human groups to which they make their appeal (whether a Christian community or a sect), once they cease to defend those groups, and reappear when they seem to be defending others. We do not seek to find in any of them an anticipation of our present-day values; we are the heirs not so much of this or that value in particular (or of each and all) as of something that runs deeper: that undercurrent of the stream of human consciousness which brought them into being. We have at last become aware of their true nature, in the same manner as Hegelianism became aware not of forgotten values but of history; it is art as an organic whole, liberated by our modern art, that our culture for the first time is arraying against destiny. The men of the Renaissance did not prefer the few great Greek works they had set eyes upon to the Alexandrine statues, and would not have preferred the *Koré of Euthydikos* to the *Laocoön*. It is we, the men of today, who are bringing to light the treasures of the ages, now that creation itself has become for our artists a supreme value; we who are wresting from the dead past the living past of the museum. Thus our characteristic response to the mutilated statue, the bronze dug up from the earth, is revealing. It is not that we prefer time-worn bas-reliefs, or rusted statuettes as such, nor is it the vestiges of death that grip us in them, but those of life. Mutilation is the scar left by the struggle with Time, and a reminder of it—Time which is as much a part of ancient works of art as the material they are made of, and thrusts up through the fissures, from a dark underworld where all is at once chaos and determinism. Hercules' mutilated torso is the symbol of all the world's museums. . . .

When we welcome amongst us all these antagonistic elements, is it not obvious that our eclecticism, defying history, merges them in a past whose whole conception is other than that of the real past, and which acts as a defense, in depth, of our own culture? Under the beaten gold of the Mycenean masks where once men saw only the dust of a dead beauty, there throbbed a secret power whose rumor, echoing down the ages, at last we can hear again. And issuing from the darkness of ancient empires, the voices of the statues that sang at sunrise murmur an answer to Klee's gossamer brushstrokes and the blue of Braque's grapes. Though always tied up with history, the creative act has never changed its nature from the far-off days of Sumer to those of the School of Paris, but has vouched throughout the ages for a conquest as old as man. Though a Byzantine mosaic, a Rubens, a work by Rembrandt and one by Cézanne display a mastery distinct in kind, each imbued in its own manner with that which has been mastered, all unite with the paintings of the Magdalenian epoch in speaking the immemorial language of Man the conqueror, though the territory conquered was not the same. The lesson of the Nara Buddha and of the Sivaic Death Dancers is not a lesson of Buddhism or Hinduism, and our Museum without Walls opens up a field of infinite possibilities bequeathed us by the past, revealing long-forgotten vestiges of that unflagging creative drive which affirms man's victorious presence. Each of the masterpieces is a purification of the world, but their common message is that of their existence, and the victory of each individual artist over his servitude, spreading like ripples on the sea of time, implements art's eternal victory over the human situation.

All art is a revolt against man's fate.

NICOLAS BERDYAEV
The Historical Meaning of Christianity

The exclusively historical character and dynamism of Christianity are the result of the Coming of Christ, which constitutes the central fact of Christian history. This fact is unique and non-recurring,—the essential quality of everything historical. And it focuses the whole of world history. . . .

The exceptionally dynamic and historical character of Christianity is the result of the fact that it conclusively revealed for the first time the existence of the principle of freedom, which was ignored by both the ancient and the Hebrew worlds. Christian freedom postulates the fulfilment of history through the agency of a free subject and spirit. And such a fulfilment constitutes the essential nature of both Christianity and history, because the structure of the latter is impossible without the postulate of a freely-acting subject determining the historical destinies of mankind. The Greeks affirmed the reason and necessity of good. To them it was the necessary result of the victory of reason. Socrates was the exponent of this Hellenic conception, which regarded good as based upon law and principles considered to be irrefutable by reason. The principles which contradict this were considered to be accidental and irrational. Thus the Greek conception of good took no account of freedom; and Greek philosophy, even at its height, never produced an authentic theory of good.

Christianity, on the other hand, affirmed the freedom of good. It affirmed that good is the product of the free spirit and that only such good can possess a true value and reality. It denied the compulsory and reasonable necessity of good. And this constitutes the essential feature of the Christian conception. Christianity affirmed that freedom is the highest achievement of the higher divine reason and that it determines the destiny of both man and the world, and thus makes history. Christian Providence is synonymous with freedom and not fatality. Unlike the ancient world, Christianity is not content to submit to fate. Such submissiveness as the highest wisdom attainable by man had been expressed in both Greek tragedy and philosophy. But the Christian spirit is based upon a principle that rebels against such submission. The freedom to choose and affirm the good, rooted in the will and not in reason, presupposes in its turn that freedom of the creative and active subject without which a true dynamism of history is impossible. The

From *The Meaning of History* [1923], translated from the Russian by George Reavey, New York and London, 1936, pp. 108, 110-15, 197-201; reprinted by permission of Geoffrey Bles Ltd.

completely unhistorical or anti-historical nature of the ancient cultures of both India and China is due to the fact that the freedom of the creative subject was not revealed therein. Neither was it revealed in the philosophy of the Vedantas, one of the greatest philosophical systems, nor, again, in those philosophies which have a certain conception of freedom as an absolute blend and union of the human and divine spirits. India, too, ignored the idea of human freedom. And this accounts for the fact that this otherwise original culture lacks an historical character. Thus Christianity was the first to reveal conclusively the freedom of the creative subject which had been ignored by the pre-Christian world. And this discovery of the inner dynamic principles of history determining the fulfilment of the historical destinies of man, peoples and mankind, eventually produced that eventful world history which coincides with the Christian era.

What is the main theme of universal history? In my opinion it is that of man's destiny seen in the light of the interaction between the human spirit and nature, which constitutes the foundation and motivating principle of the "historical." We can observe in the history of mankind various stages of interaction between the human spirit and nature which fall into historical epochs. The initial stage, which was the direct result of the celestial-historical drama of man's alienation from God, of the Fall as a drama of freedom, had plunged man and the human spirit into the uttermost depths of natural necessity. The fall into these depths was accompanied by man's servitude to the natural elements which had held the human spirit and will spellbound. In the primal stages of history the human spirit is immersed in elemental nature; this is the state of the savage and barbarous peoples, the ancient cultures and the early history of the ancient world. The human spirit would seem to have lost its original freedom and have ceased to be even conscious of it. Immersed in the depths of necessity, man does not in his philosophy attain to the consciousness of freedom or of himself as a creative spiritual subject. The fact that the spellbound human spirit had lost its freedom as a result of its original alienation from the spirit of God explains why the true principle of freedom was not revealed in the ancient world. Freedom had been transformed into necessity, and the spirit was incapable of attaining either to a religious revelation or a philosophical apprehension of freedom.

The theme of man's worldly destiny is the liberation of the creative human spirit from the depths of natural necessity and its enslavement by the lowest elements. It was a theme that preoccupied the ancient world. The immersion of the human spirit in elemental nature is associated with man's bitter dependence on and torturing fear of the natural demons. The fallen human spirit, though rooted in and dominated by nature, was nevertheless in profound harmony with it. Man sensed natural life as a living organism, inspired and peopled with demons who were in perpetual contact with him; and its spiritual life was thus more familiar to him than in the subsequent stages of his history. Ancient myths speak of man's association with these natural spirits. The fallen human spirit had ceased to dominate nature and had of its own free will become the slave and indivisible part of nature in a prehistorical world. Man's dependence on nature was synonymous with his union with it. The pagan world was peopled with demons and man was powerless to dominate either them or the natural cycle. Man's image therefore corresponded not with the highest divine but the baser nature peopled with elemental spirits. Man adapted himself to the forms of this base nature, which had enslaved him and whose chains he could not break of his own free will.

The greatest contribution of Christianity, although it is not fully recognized by the Christian world, consisted in that it liberated man from the power of the baser elemental nature and demons. It did so through the agency of Christ and the mystery of Redemption. It rescued man forcibly from his immersion in elemental nature and revived his spirituality. It distinguished him from baser nature and set him up as an independent spiritual being, freeing him from submission to the natural world and exalting him to the heavens. Christianity alone restored the spiritual freedom of which man had been deprived by the power of the demons, the natural spirits and elemental forces in the pre-Christian world. The essential contribution of Christianity therefore lay in that it liberated man and offered a free solution for human destiny. And this is the high significance of man's Redemption from his outer and inner slavery, from those evil elements active in his own nature. His enslavement by the natural demons was, indeed, synonymous with his enslavement by his own baser self, from which he was unable to free himself because his freedom had become transformed into necessity. And this had come about through his own fault. But the Christian Redemption wrought by the coming of the Divine Man, the God-Man, the Man as the Second Hypostasis of the Divine Trinity, restituted the power of freedom and the image of his high divine origin to man, thus erasing the imprint of his slavery and animal origin. Only the coming of the Divine Man, His assumption of all the consequences of man's actions in the world, His sufferings and expiatory blood, and the mystery of the Redemption, could liberate man from the subjection of the baser elements and invest him once again with his lost Divine Sonship.

Ancient religions and mysteries had also aspired towards Redemption. The mysteries of Osiris, Adonis and Dionysos, were the obscure presentiments and passionate thirst for a true mystery of Redemption. In these mysteries man thirsted passionately to free himself from the slavery of nature and to achieve immortality; but the ancient mysteries never succeeded in achieving man's final liberation because they were involved in the cycle of baser elemental nature. They were immanent natural mysteries in which man experienced the joy of Redemption from his bitter state of subjection in the inmost depths of the natural cycle. Thus the mysteries of Dionysos were celebrated in the order of the natural cycles themselves, those of death and birth, winter and spring. But they failed either to exalt man above elemental nature or to achieve a real Redemption. The ancient world in celebrating these mysteries expressed a passionate thirst for deliverance; and, on the eve of its fall, it was more than ever gripped by the fear and terror of the natural demons. This terror reached its climax and became really unbearable in the last days of this world when the mystical cults extended their influence and power. The life of those who thirsted for Redemption became really tragic. Christianity alone saved man from this cycle of elemental natural life and re-established his dignity by restoring the freedom of the human spirit; and it thus inaugurated a new era in his destiny. The latter is now determined and solved by the agency of a free active subject, and man once again becomes conscious of his freedom.

History is in truth the path to another world. It is in this sense that its content is religious. But the perfect state is impossible within history itself; it can only be realized outside its framework. This is the fundamental conclusion of the meta-physics of history and the secret of historical process itself. In its perpetual transition from one epoch to another, mankind struggles in vain to resolve its destiny within history. Disappointed in its expectations, feeling itself imprisoned within the circle of history, it realizes that its problem cannot be solved within the process of history itself, but only on a transcendental plane. The problem of history is determined by the nature of time. To solve it requires an inversion of the entire historical perspective, a transfer of attention to extra-historical considerations, to the urge of history towards super-history. We must admit within the hermetic circle of history the super-historical energy, the irruption within the relations of terrestrial phenomena of the celestial noumenon—the future Coming of Christ. This concept of the ineluctable end of history is at once the final conclusion and fundamental premiss of the metaphysics of history.

So long as we consider the solution of the historical process as immanent within the problem itself, as a product of the time torrent, we cannot fail to arrive at the most hopelessly pessimistic conclusions. Such an approach cannot possibly yield a general solution valid for all the problems of all the periods of history. Man's historical experience has been one of steady failure and there are no grounds for supposing that it will ever be anything else. Not one single project elaborated within the historical process has ever proved successful. None of the problems of any given historical epoch whatsoever has been solved, no aims attained, no hopes realized. This radical failure of the historical process, when we regard it as a whole, can only be interpreted as the failure to realize the Kingdom of God. To situate the Kingdom of God as a solution of human destiny within the historical process itself is tantamount to excluding its realization and even its preparation.

Examining specific periods of history and their respective problems, we feel them to be consumed with an inner disease and impotent to arrive at a solution. To consider only modern history, its profound failure is amazing. The Revolutionary ideal did not succeed, if we are to judge by the extreme disparity between its achievement and its intention. . . . The fact is that no single revolution has ever succeeded in breaking the bonds of history. One may speak of revolutions as capital events in the destiny of mankind, as phenomena of inner and inexorable determination subserved by all that went before, but the fact remains that they have never solved the problems with which they were confronted. This has always been and always will be the case. It is only the experience of historical failure itself that has proved fruitful, in the sense that the consciousness of humanity has thereby been increased. What go by the name of achievements have always belied the plans and hopes of their artificers. Revolution ends in reaction, whose function is to define the experience. And the reaction itself is more often than not reactionary in the worst sense, causing human society to regress. Thus the spiritual reaction at the beginning of the nineteenth century proved one of the most positive effects of the French Revolution. The spiritual revival to which it gave rise conferred tremendous importance on this period, but an importance that did not consist with the revolutionary purpose. The same might even be said of the great central key event of universal history, of that Christianity which inaugurated an era and determined the course of all that was to follow. For Christianity also was a complete and utter failure. The enemies of Christianity take a malicious pleasure in indicating this very fact as the capital objection against Christianity. They repudiate Christianity because it did not succeed on earth. This is a criticism capable of quite a different import and interpretation. It is true that Christianity shared the collapse of every other historical process. Two thousand years have not sufficed to realize the ideals of Christian faith and consciousness. They will never be realized within the framework of human time and history. They can only be realized by a victory over time, by the transition from time to eternity, by the triumphant passage from the historical to the super-historical process. But the failure of Christianity can no more be used as an argument against its higher truth than the failure of history can be taken to imply the aimlessness and emptiness of history.

The failure of history does not mean that history is devoid of necessity or relevance. Similarly the failure of Christianity does not mean that Christianity is not the highest truth. Historical success and achievement do not constitute a valid criterion of the true. The nature of history and all that it contains is such that nothing perfect can be realized in time. The profound significance of historical destiny and experience does not depend on any realization. It exists beyond the limits of history. The failure, so painfully clear within the framework of historical time and terrestrial reality, does not imply limitation and failure outside that framework. It rather goes to prove that the destiny of man reserves a higher realization for his potentialities than any to be achieved in his purely historical experience.

CHARLES DARWIN

The Pre-Human in the Human

We thus learn that man is descended from a hairy, tailed quadruped, probably arboreal in its habits, and an inhabitant of the Old World. This creature, if its whole structure had been examined by a naturalist, would have been classed amongst the Quadrumana, as surely as the still more ancient progenitor of the Old and New World monkeys. The Quadrumana and all the higher mammals are probably derived from an ancient marsupial animal, and this through a long series of diversified forms, from some amphibian-like creature, and this again from some fish-like animal. In the dim obscurity of the past we can see that the early progenitor of all the Vertebrata must have been an aquatic animal provided with branchiæ, with the two sexes united in the same individual, and with the most important organs of the body (such as the brain and heart) imperfectly or not at all developed. This animal seems to have been more like the larvæ of the existing marine Ascidians than any other known form. . . .

The main conclusion arrived at in this work, namely, that man is descended from some lowly organised form, will, I regret to think, be highly distasteful to many. But there can hardly be a doubt that we are descended from barbarians. The astonishment which I felt on first seeing a party of Fuegians on a wild and broken shore will never be forgotten by me, for the reflection at once rushed into my mind—such were our ancestors. These men were absolutely naked and be-daubed with paint, their long hair was tangled, their mouths frothed with excitement, and their expression was wild, startled, and distrustful. They possessed hardly any arts, and like wild animals lived on what they could catch; they had no government, and were merciless to every one not of their own small tribe. He who has seen a savage in his native land will not feel much shame, if forced to acknowledge that the blood of some more humble creature flows in his veins. For my own part I would as soon be descended from that heroic little monkey, who braved his dreaded enemy in order to save the life of his keeper, or from that old baboon, who descending from the mountains, carried away in triumph his young comrade from a crowd of astonished dogs—as from a savage who delights to torture his enemies, offers up bloody sacrifices, practises infanticide without remorse, treats his wives like slaves, knows no decency, and is haunted by the grossest superstitions.

Man may be excused for feeling some pride at having risen, though not through

From *The Descent of Man*, New York and London, 1871, Vol. II, pp. 372, 386-7.

his own exertions, to the very summit of the organic scale; and the fact of his having thus risen, instead of having been aboriginally placed there, may give him hope for a still higher destiny in the distant future. But we are not here concerned with hopes or fears, only with the truth as far as our reason permits us to discover it; and I have given the evidence to the best of my ability. We must, however, acknowledge, as it seems to me, that man with all his noble qualities, with sympathy which feels for the most debased, with benevolence which extends not only to other men but to the humblest living creature, with his god-like intellect which has penetrated into the movements and constitutions of the solar system—with all these exalted powers—Man still bears in his bodily frame the indelible stamp of his lowly origin.

SIR JAMES G. FRAZER

The Savage in the Human

[MENTAL ANTHROPOLOGY]

On the physical side human anatomy had been studied for centuries, and was, I take it, firmly established on its main lines long before the appearance of Darwin; the new idea imported into the science was that the human body, like the bodies of all animals, is not a finished product, a fixed type, struck out by Nature or created by God at a blow, but that it is rather a merely temporary effect, the result of a long process of what resembles growth rather than construction or creation, a growth which we have no reason to suppose has been arrested, but is probably still going on and may cause our descendants to differ as far from us as we now differ from our remotest ancestors in the scale of animated being. It is only the slowness of the process that hides the movement from our eyes and suggests the conclusion, so flattering to human vanity, that Nature has reached her consummation in us and can no farther go. An immediate result of the promulgation of the evolution theory was thus to give an immense impulse to comparative anatomy; for it was now recognized that man's bodily frame is not an isolated structure, but that it is closely related to that of many of the other animals, and that the one structure cannot be fully understood without the other. Not the least important branch of what we may call the new anatomy was the science of embryology, which by a comparison of the human and animal embryos was able to demonstrate their close resemblance for a considerable period of their development, and thus to supply a powerful argument in favour of the conclusion that man and what he calls the lower animals have had a common origin, and that for an incalculable time they probably pursued nearly parallel lines of evolution. In fact, embryology shows that the very process of evolution, which we postulate for

From "The Scope and Method of Mental Anthropology" [1921], *Garnered Sheaves*, London, 1931, pp. 236-7, and from "The Scope of Social Anthropology," *Psyche's Task*, London, 1913, pp. 162-3, 170-73; reprinted by permission of Trinity College, Cambridge, and Macmillan & Co. Ltd.

the past history of our race, is summarily reproduced in the life-history of every man and woman who is born into the world.

Turning now from the physical to the mental side of man's nature, we may say that the evolution theory has in like manner opened up a new province of inquiry which has been left unoccupied by the older philosophy. Whenever in former days a philosopher set himself to inquire into the principles of the human mind, it was his own particular mind, or at most the minds of his civilized contemporaries, that he proceeded to investigate. When Descartes turned his eyes inwards and reflected on the operations of his own mind, he believed himself to be probing to the very deepest foundations accessible to human intelligence. It never occurred to him, I imagine, to apply for information to the mind of a Zulu or a Hottentot, still less of a baboon or a chimpanzee. Yet the doctrine of evolution has rendered it highly probable that the mind of the philosopher is indissolubly linked to the minds of these barbarous peoples and strange animals, and that, if we would fully understand it, we must not disdain to investigate the intelligence of these our humble relations.

[SOCIAL ANTHROPOLOGY]

The study might . . . be described as the embryology of human thought and institutions, or, to be more precise, as that enquiry which seeks to ascertain, first, the beliefs and customs of savages, and, second, the relics of these beliefs and customs which have survived like fossils among peoples of higher culture. In this description of the sphere of Social Anthropology it is implied that the ancestors of the civilized nations were once savages, and that they have transmitted, or may have transmitted, to their more cultured descendants ideas and institutions which, however incongruous with their later surroundings, were perfectly in keeping with the modes of thought and action of the ruder society in which they originated. In short, the definition assumes that civilization has always and everywhere been evolved out of savagery. The mass of evidence on which this assumption rests is in my opinion so great as to render the induction incontrovertible. At least, if any one disputes it I do not think it worth while to argue with him. There are still, I believe, in civilized society people who hold that the earth is flat and that the sun goes round it; but no sensible man will waste time in the vain attempt to convince such persons of their error, even though these flatteners of the earth and circulators of the sun appeal with perfect justice to the evidence of their senses in support of their hallucination, which is more than the opponents of man's primitive savagery are able to do.

Thus the study of savage life is a very important part of Social Anthropology. For by comparison with civilized man the savage represents an arrested or rather retarded stage of social development, and an examination of his customs and beliefs accordingly supplies the same sort of evidence of the evolution of the human mind that an examination of the embryo supplies of the evolution of the human body. To put it otherwise, a savage is to a civilized man as a child is to an adult; and just as the gradual growth of intelligence in a child corresponds to, and in a sense recapitulates, the gradual growth of intelligence in the species, so a study of savage society at various stages of evolution enables us to follow approximately, though of course not exactly, the road by which the ancestors of the higher races must have travelled in their progress upward through barbarism to civilization. In short, savagery is the primitive condition of mankind, and if we would understand what primitive man was we must know what the savage now is.

But here it is necessary to guard against a common misapprehension. The savages of to-day are primitive only in a relative, not in an absolute sense. They are primitive by comparison with us; but they are not primitive by comparison with truly primaeval man, that is, with man as he was when he first emerged from the purely bestial stage of existence. Indeed, compared with man in his absolutely pristine state even the lowest savage of today is doubtless a highly developed and cultured being, since all evidence and all probability are in favour of the view that every existing race of men, the rudest as well as the most civilized, has reached its present level of culture, whether it be high or low, only after a slow and painful progress upwards, which must have extended over many thousands, perhaps millions, of years. Therefore when we speak of any known savages as primitive, which the usage of the English language permits us to do, it should always be remembered that we apply the term primitive to them in a relative, not in an absolute sense. . . .

Systematic enquiries carried on among the less educated classes, and especially among the peasantry, of Europe have revealed the astonishing, nay, alarming truth that a mass, if not the majority, of people in every civilized country is still living in a state of intellectual savagery, that, in fact, the smooth surface of cultured society is sapped and mined by superstition. Only those whose studies have led them to investigate the subject are aware of the depth to which the ground beneath our feet is thus, as it were, honeycombed by unseen forces. We appear to be standing on a volcano which may at any moment break out in smoke and fire to spread ruin and devastation among the gardens and palaces of ancient culture wrought so laboriously by the hands of many generations. After looking on the ruined Greek temples of Paestum and contrasting them with the squalor and savagery of the Italian peasantry, Renan said, "I trembled for civilization, seeing it so limited, built on so weak a foundation, resting on so few individuals even in the country where it is dominant."

If we examine the superstitious beliefs which are tacitly but firmly held by many of our fellow-countrymen, we shall find, perhaps to our surprise, that it is precisely the oldest and crudest superstitions which are most tenacious of life, while views which, though also erroneous, are more modern and refined, soon fade from the popular memory. For example, the high gods of Egypt and Babylon, of Greece and Rome, have for ages been totally forgotten by the people and survive only in the books of the learned; yet the peasants, who never even heard of Isis and Osiris, of Apollo and Artemis, of Jupiter and Juno, retain to this day a firm belief in witches and fairies, in ghosts and hobgoblins, those lesser creatures of mythical fancy in which their fathers believed long before the great deities of the ancient world were ever thought of, and in which, to all appearance, their descendants will continue to believe long after the great deities of the present day shall have gone the way of all their predecessors. The reason why the higher forms of superstition or religion (for the religion of one generation is apt to become the superstition of the next) are less permanent than the lower is simply that the higher beliefs, being a creation of superior intelligence, have little hold on the minds of the vulgar, who nominally profess them for a time in conformity with the will of their betters, but readily shed and forget them as soon as these beliefs have gone out of fashion with the educated classes. But while they dismiss without a pang or an effort articles of faith which were only superficially imprinted on their minds by the weight of cultured opinion, the ignorant and foolish multitude cling with a sullen determination to far grosser beliefs which really answer to the coarser texture of their undeveloped intellect. Thus while the avowed creed of the enlightened minority is constantly changing under the influence of reflection and enquiry, the real, though unavowed, creed of the mass of mankind appears to be almost stationary, and the reason why it alters so little is that in the majority of men, whether they are savages or outwardly civilized beings, intellectual progress is so slow as to be hardly perceptible. The surface of society, like that of the sea, is in perpetual motion; its depths, like those of the ocean, remain almost unmoved. . . .

The savage is not a different sort of being from his civilized brother: he has the same capacities, mental and moral, but they are less fully developed: his evolution has been arrested, or rather retarded, at a lower level. And as savage races are not all on the same plane, but have stopped or tarried at different points of the upward path, we can to a certain extent, by comparing them with each other, construct a scale of social progression and mark out roughly some of the stages on the long road that leads from savagery to civilization. In the kingdom of mind such a scale of mental evolution answers to the scale of morphological evolution in the animal kingdom.

From what I have said I hope you have formed some idea of the extreme importance which the study of savage life possesses for a proper understanding of the early history of mankind. The savage is a human document, a record of man's efforts to raise himself above the level of the beast. It is only of late years that the full value of the document has been appreciated; indeed, many people are probably still of Dr. Johnson's opinion, who, pointing to the three large volumes of *Voyages to the South Seas* which had just come out, said: "Who will read them through? A man had better work his way before the mast than read them through; they will be eaten by rats and mice before they are read through. There can be little entertainment in such books; one set of savages is like another." But the world has learned a good deal since Dr. Johnson's day; and the records of savage life, which the sage of Bolt Court consigned without scruple to the rats and mice, have now their place among the most precious archives of humanity. Their fate has been like that of the Sibylline Books. They were neglected and despised when they might have been obtained complete; and now wise men would give more than a king's ransom for their miserably mutilated and imperfect remains.

An Archaic Mystery

If Epidaurus spells peace Mycenae, which is outwardly as calm and hushed, awakens wholly different thoughts and emotions. At Tiryns the day before I was introduced to the Cyclopean world. We entered the ruins of the once impregnable citadel through a womb-like aperture made, if not by supermen, certainly by giants. The walls of the womb were as smooth as alabaster; they had been polished by thick coats of fleece, for here during the long period of night which settled over this region the shepherds brought their flocks for shelter. Tiryns is prehistoric in character. Little remains of this once formidable pioneer settlement save a few colossal ramparts. Why it should be so I don't know, but to me it seems to antedate, at least in spirit, the cave shelters of the Dordogne region. One feels that the terrain has undergone profound alterations. Supposedly Tiryns was settled by an off-shoot from Crete during the Minoan period; if so, the spirit underwent profound transformations, like the land itself. Tiryns is no more like Knossus, for example, than New York is like Rome or Paris. Tiryns represents a relapse, just as America represents Europe in its most degenerate aspects. Crete of the Minoan epochs stands for a culture based upon peace: Tiryns smells of cruelty, barbarism, suspicion, isolation. It is like an H. G. Wells setting for a prehistoric drama, for a thousand years' war between one-eyed giants and blunderfooted dinosaurs.

Mycenae, which follows Tiryns in point of time, is quite another scene. The stillness of it to-day resembles the exhaustion of a cruel and intelligent monster which has been bled to death. Mycenae, and again I give only my impressions and intuitions, seems to have experienced a vast cycle of development and degeneration. It seems to stand outside time, in any historical sense. In some mysterious fashion the same Aegean race which brought the seeds of culture from Crete to Tiryns here evolved to a godlike grandeur, threw out a quick spawn of heroes, Titans, demi-gods, and then, as if exhausted and dazzled by the unprecedented and divine-like flowering, relapsed into a dark and bloody intestinal conflict which lasted for centuries, ending at a point so far back as to appear mythological to their successors. At Mycenae the gods once walked the earth, of that there can be no question. And at Mycenae the progeny of these same gods produced a type of man who was artistic to the core and at the same time monstrous in his passions. The architecture was Cyclopean, the ornaments of a delicacy and grace unrivalled in any period of art. Gold was abundant and used unstintingly. Everything about the place is contradictory. It is one of the navels of the human spirit, the place of attachment to the past and of complete severance too. It wears an impenetrable air: it is grim, lovely, seductive and repellent. What happened here is beyond all conjecture. The historians and the archaeologists have woven a slim and altogether unsatisfying fabric to cover the mystery. They piece together fragmentary items which are linked in the customary manner to suit their necessitous logic. Nobody has yet penetrated the secret of this hoary scene. It defies the feeble

533

processes of the intellectual mind. We must await the return of the gods, the restoration of faculties which now lie dormant.

It was a Sunday morning when Katsimbalis and I left Nauplia for Mycenae. It was hardly eight o'clock when we arrived at the little station bearing this legendary name. Passing through Argos the magic of this world suddenly penetrated my bowels. Things long forgotten came back with frightening clarity. I was not sure whether I was recalling things I had read as a child or whether I was tapping the universal memory of the race. The fact that these places still existed, still bore their ancient names, seemed incredible. It was like a resurrection and the day we had chosen for the journey was more like Easter than Thanksgiving Day. From the station to the ruins was a walk of several kilometers. As at Epidaurus there was a sublime stillness all about. We walked leisurely towards the encircling hills which rise up from the gleaming Argive plain. A few birds were wheeling overhead in the unbroken vault of blue. Suddenly we came upon a little boy crying as if his heart would break. He was standing in the field beside the road. His weeping had absolutely no relation to the hushed and tranquil world in which he stood; it was as if he had been set down in the green field by a spirit from the outside world. What could a little boy be crying about at such an hour in such a wondrous world? Katsimbalis went over and spoke to him. He was crying because his sister had stolen his money. How much money? Three drachmas. Money, money. . . . Even here there was such a thing as money. The word money never sounded so preposterous to me before. How could one think such a word in this world of terror and beauty and magic? If he had lost a donkey or a parrot I could have understood. But three drachmas—I just couldn't visualize the meaning of three drachmas. I couldn't believe he was weeping. It was an hallucination. Let him stand there and weep—the spirit would come and fetch him again; he didn't belong, he was an anomaly.

After you pass the little hostelry run by Agamemnon and his wife, which faces a field of Irish green, you become immediately aware that the earth is sown with the bodies and the relics of legendary figures. Even before Katsimbalis opened his mouth I knew they were lying all about us—the earth tells you so. The approach to the place of horror is fantastically inviting. There are smooth green mounds, hummocks, hillocks, tumuli everywhere, and beneath them, not very deep either, lie the warriors, the heroes, the fabulous innovators who without machinery erected the most formidable fortifications. The sleep of the dead is so deep that the earth and all who walk it dream; even the huge carrion birds who wheel above seem drugged and hypnotized. As one rises slowly with the rising terrain the blood thickens, the heart slows down, the mind comes to rest obsessively on the shuddering image of an endless chain of assassinations. There are two distinct worlds impinging on one another—the heroic world of daylight and the claustral world of dagger and poison. Mycenae, like Epidaurus, swims in light. But Epidaurus is all open, exposed, irrevocably devoted to the spirit. Mycenae folds in upon itself, like a fresh-cut navel, dragging its glory down into the bowels of the earth where the bats and the lizards feed upon it gloatingly. Epidaurus is a bowl from which to drink the pure spirit: the blue of the sky is in it and the stars and the winged creatures who fly between, scattering song and melody. Mycenae, after one turns the last bend, suddenly folds up into a menacing crouch, grim, defiant, impenetrable. Mycenae is closed in, huddled up, writhing with muscular contortions like a wrestler. Even the light, which falls on it with merciless clarity, gets sucked in, shunted off, grayed, beribboned. There were never two worlds so closely juxtaposed and yet so antagonistic. It is Greenwich here with respect to everything that concerns the soul of man. Move a hair's breadth either way and you are in a totally different world. This is the great shining bulge of horror, the high slope whence man, having attained his zenith, slipped back and fell into the bottomless pit.

It was still early morning when we slipped through the lion's gate. No sign of a guardian about. Not a soul in sight. The sun is steadily rising and everything is clearly exposed to view. And yet we proceed timidly, cautiously, fearing we know not what. Here and there are open pits looking ominously smooth and slimy. We walk between the huge slabs of stone that form the circular enclosure. My book knowledge is nil. I can look on this mass of rubble with the eyes of a savage. I am amazed at the diminutive proportions of the palace chambers, of the dwelling places up above. What colossal walls to protect a mere handful of people! Was each and every inhabitant a giant? What dread darkness fell upon them in their evil days to make them burrow into the earth, to hide their treasures from the light, to murder incestuously in the deep bowels of the earth? We of the New World, with millions of acres lying waste and millions unfed, unwashed, unsheltered, we who dig into the earth, who work, eat, sleep, love, walk, ride, fight, buy, sell and murder there below ground, are we going the same way? I am a native of New York, the grandest and the emptiest city in the world; I am standing now at Mycenae, trying to understand what happened here over a period of centuries. I feel like a cockroach crawling about amidst dismantled splendors. It is hard to believe that somewhere back in the leaves and branches of the great genealogical tree of life my progenitors knew this spot, asked the same questions, fell back senseless into the void, were swallowed up and left no trace of thought save these ruins, the scattered relics in museums, a sword, an axle, a helmet, a death mask of beaten gold, a bee-hive tomb, an heraldic lion carved in stone, an exquisite drinking vase. I stand at the summit of the walled citadel and in the early morning I feel the approach of the cold breath from the shaggy gray mountain towering above us. Below, from the great Argive plain the mist is rising. It might be Pueblo, Colorado, so dislocated is it from time and boundary. Down there, in that steaming plain where the automotrice crawls like a caterpillar, is it not possible there once stood wigwams? Can I be sure there never were any Indians here? Everything connected with Argos, shimmering now in the distance as in the romantic illustrations for text-books, smacks of the American Indian. I must be crazy to think thus, but I am honest enough to admit the thought. Argos gleams resplendent, a point of light shooting arrows of gold into the blue. Argos belongs to myth and fable: her heroes never took on flesh. But Mycenae, like Tiryns, is peopled with the ghosts of antediluvial men, Cyclopean monsters washed up from the sunken ridges of Atlantis. Mycenae was first heavy-footed, slow, sluggish, ponderous, thought embodied in dinosaurian frames, war reared in anthropophagous luxury, reptilian, ataraxic, stunning and stunned. Mycenae swung full circle, from limbo to limbo. The monsters devoured one another, like crocodiles. The rhinoceros man gored the hippopotamic man. The walls fell on them, crushed them, flattened them into the primeval ooze. A brief night. Lurid lightning flashes, thunder cannonading between the fierce shoulders of the hills. The eagles fly out, the plain is scavengered, the grass shoots forth. (This is a Brooklyn lad talking. Not a word of truth in it, until the gods bring forth the evidence.) The eagles, the hawks, the snot-knobbed vultures, gray with greed like the parched and barren mountain-sides. The air is alive with winged scavengers. Silence—century upon century of silence, during which the earth puts on a coat of soft green. A mysterious race out of nowhere swoops down upon the country of Argolis. Mysterious only because men have forgotten the sight of the gods. The gods are returning, in full panoply, man-like, making use of the horse, the buckler, the javelin, carving precious jewels, smelting ores, blowing fresh vivid images of war and love on bright dagger blades. The gods stride forth over the sun-lit swards, full-statured, fearless, the gaze frighteningly candid and open. A world of light is born. Man looks at man with new eyes. He is awed, smitten by his own gleaming image reflected everywhere. It goes on thus, century upon century swallowed like cough-drops, a poem, an heraldic poem, as my friend Durrell would say. While the magic is on the lesser men, the initiates, the Druids of the Peloponnesus, prepare the tombs of the gods, hide them away in the soft flanks of the hillocks and hummocks. The gods will depart one day, as mysteriously as they came, leaving behind the human-like shell which deceives the unbelieving, the poor in spirit, the timid souls who have turned the earth into a furnace and a factory.

We have just come up from the slippery staircase, Katsimbalis and I. We have not descended it, only peered down with lighted matches. The heavy roof is buckling with the weight of time. To breathe too heavily is enough to pull the world down over our ears. Katsimbalis was for crawling down on all fours, on his belly if needs be. He has been in many a tight spot before; he has played the mole on the Balkan front, has wormed his way through mud and blood, has danced like a madman from fear and frenzy, killed all in sight including his own men, has been blown skyward clinging to a tree, has had his brain concussed, his rear blunderbussed, his arms hanging in shreds, his face blackened with powder, his bones and sinews wrenched and unsocketed. He is telling me it all over again as we stand midway to earth and sky, the lintel sagging more and more, the matches giving out. "We don't want to miss this," he pleads. But I refuse to go back down into that slimy well of horrors. Not if there were a pot of gold to be filched would I make the descent. I want to see the sky, the big birds, the short grass, the waves of blinding light, the swamp mist rising over the plain.

5

THE UNCONSCIOUS

Unreason and Reason

The Freudian Unconscious

Liberation of the Unconscious

Introduction

As behind recorded history we encounter primitive man in his natural habitat,[1] so beneath the public man we eventually come to something equally primitive: the unconscious mind. The Unconscious is nature-in-man, the basic stuff behind human consciousness, as prehistoric man stands behind the history of culture. If modern historicism exemplifies a shift of emphasis from the world of Being to the world of Becoming, the modern conception of the Unconscious implies an even more drastic shift of perspective. The traditional primacy of ideas over feeling, purpose over instinct, reason over energy, is hereby questioned and often repudiated.

Goethe in his autobiography describes a primal, undifferentiated force that he calls the Demoniac. This is an energy not reducible to rational and moral categories but cutting across them as the warp the woof. It seems to lie at a point where inorganic matter, organic nature, and the human mind come together. Knowable only as the mutual contradiction of all the principles we ordinarily assume, the Demoniac is both seductive and terrifying. Goethe at once recognized and drew back from it, he says, by depicting it in his art. William Blake's response to a similar discovery is less cautious. He takes the fact of irrational energy to mean the collapse of old and false rational distinctions between body and soul, physical evil and spiritual good. For Blake active energy is the essence of the undivided body-soul, and the famous faculty of reason, instead of being its opposite and master, is merely the outward bound of energy; indeed, reason or "the Devourer" exists only in terms of the "Prolific" energy it measures.[2]

In Schopenhauer's world of will and idea, the irrational "will to live," ceaselessly striving and suffering, is the primary reality of human experience.[3] Schopenhauer argues that we have attributed too much significance to "ideas": thought and knowledge are secondary functions of man. Unable to alter the drive of the will, reason can only modify the particular forms in

[1] See "Primitive Survivals" in Section 4.
[2] For related selections from Blake, see Sections 1, 6, and 9.
[3] For Schopenhauer's concept of the will in nature, see Section 3. See also Schopenhauer's ethics in Section 7.

which desire is expressed. To Schopenhauer the scene of the will's activity is always bleak, for when it is strugggling to sustain itself, it is in pain; and when it is without an object for which to struggle, it suffers from ennui. Pain and boredom are the two poles between which man oscillates, whether he be civilized or uncivilized.

Nietzsche's dialectic of Apollo and Dionysus, though derived from Schopenhauer's scheme of idea and will, is cast on a different plane and presented in a somewhat different spirit. These are two "art-gods,"[4] and there is joyful affirmation in both—in the visions of Apollo and the rhapsodies of Dionysus —as well as in the interplay of the Apollonian and Dionysian principles. Apollo is the god of shapely appearances, of individuality, and of ethical measure. His world is associated with Olympus, with mountaintops, with sunlight, with stability, with idealistic dreams, while the world of Dionysus is pictured in terms of lower, chthonic powers, forests, darkness, dynamic excess, drunkenness. The personal nobility for which Apollo strives has for counterpart the self-forgetfulness that Dionysus offers; the former culminates in the rapturous illusion of transcendence, the latter in the agonized ecstasy of death. The two appear in Greek history with now one, now the other, triumphant. In Greek tragedy, Nietzsche thinks, they conjoin in a moment of supreme artistic achievement. But his headiest praise goes to Dionysus, the "genius of the heart," the god of dynamic existence, who reconciles man with nature, who is strong, evil, profound, and beautiful.[5]

Although Freud's conception of the unconscious was developed without any direct dependence on such forerunners as Goethe, Blake, Schopenhauer, and Nietzsche, he spoke in an era that had long been preparing for the revelation he brought. In one sense, it is true, Freud is a strong exponent of reason and of the practical values of the daylight world of consciousness. He holds to a faith that objective science can describe the irrational depths of man and to some extent re-orient the blind mechanisms of instinct. But in another sense Freud confirms and extends the irrationalistic bent of his predecessors, for the mind he describes has almost none of the features traditionally associated with human thought. Perception and consciousness, whereby we are in contact with external reality, occupy only a tiny territory on the outskirts of the psyche, which is largely either "preconscious" or unconscious. The unconscious realm, in turn, is largely made up of what Freud calls the Id, a sea of amoral, instinctual energy. The Ego, which reaches up from the unconscious into the preconscious, was originally a part of the Id, a cortical layer, but has gradually attained a little independence from it and even

[4] At a number of points Nietzsche's emphasis on aesthetics in *The Birth of Tragedy* brings him close to the symbolist tradition represented in Section 1.

[5] For related selections from Nietzsche, see Sections 1, 4, 7, 8, and 9. The dialectic of unreason and reason, which runs through all Freud's predecessors and reappears within his own system, is somewhat analogous to the dialectic of imagination and thought in symbolist literary theory (Section 1), the interplay of existence and essence in existentialism (Section 8), and the interrelation of intuition and intellect in Bergson's philosophy (Section 7).

some imperfect control over it. A third subconscious area is that of the Super-Ego, which is a prolongation of parental influence and a defender of moral sanctions. The Ego must perilously mediate between the perceptual world without and the Id and Super-Ego within; it must try to extend its own juris-diction by adjustments with the Super-Ego and by extending itself as it can through the Id. "Where Id was," says Freud in a modern proverb, "there shall Ego be."

Within the mind as a whole two instincts are in constant struggle. One is the love (and life) instinct which Freud calls Eros but to which he often refers by the name of its specific kind of energy, "libido." Against this is ranged the destructive death-wish, the desire of the living thing to revert to an inorganic state or to turn aggressively against others. The first is an im-pulse to establish ever greater unities and to preserve them, while the second would undo all. Freud suggests that they are not unlike the old forces of attraction and repulsion. In dreams the instincts, both libidinal and destructive, meet directly with the repressive operation of the Ego and Super-Ego; here we have the clearest instance of a confrontation that is always going on in us, the same that gives rise to neurotic disorders of per-sonality. The dream fulfills instinctual wishes by compromise; it deflects, dilutes, or realigns the conflict within the latent dream-thoughts. The most fundamental instinctual pattern, according to Freud, is the Oedipus com-plex, wherein both of the prime instincts are equally at work. In men, the libido is turned toward the mother, the destructive urge toward the father; in women, the reverse is true. The guilt-feelings bound up with this com-plex, Freud suggests, may be the original basis and the sustaining force of human society.[6]

Thomas Mann pays tribute to Freud as prophet of a modern humanism that is no less humane for being disillusioned.[7] He achieves this pre-eminence by devotion to psychological truth, by articulating the uncomfortable notion that disease is an all-important clue to human nature, and by demolishing the old view of man as a distinctively rational being. In pointed contrast is D. H. Lawrence's denunciation of the Freudian outlook.[8] Lawrence dismisses the Freudian unconscious as a grotesque figment of the conscious mind, and he substitutes his own unscientific, intuitive account of the deeper psyche. If the unconscious is not distorted by abstract ideas, it is seen to have a complex balance and creative function. It is not an inescapable tragic burden but an in-exhaustible source of human good.[9]

In Tzara's Dadaist pronouncements, the attack on consciousness is part of

[6] Freud's belief that civilized social behavior grows out of ancient patterns still alive in the Unconscious goes far beyond Darwin's and Frazer's attitude toward primitive survivals (see Sections 4 and 6).
[7] Another portion of Mann's essay on Freud appears in Section 6.
[8] Freud's leading rival as interpreter of the Unconscious, Carl Jung, is represented in Sec-tion 6.
[9] For related selections from Lawrence, see Sections 3, 7, and 9.

a large-scale assault on all forms of established order. Knowledge is merely the sound "boom," and everyone is entitled to his own "boomboom"; the nub of life is subjectivity, which is not so much chaos, though Tzara admiringly calls it that, as a joyful spontaneity. We should express ourselves in a disconnected series of acts and words like lyrical cries out of the "inexhaustible and uncontrollable" unconscious. Dadaism verges over into the more elaborate program of Surrealism. As Breton explains, the surrealist breaks through the "provoking insanities of 'realism' "—conventional forms and presuppositions—into subjective truth. He systematically liberates his thought from the control of reason inside the mind and society outside. Breton's program calls for social as well as artistic revolution, though the emphasis is artistic. By whatever means—chiefly by automatic writing and imitation of dreams—the individual must strive to achieve surreality, the absolute of the unconscious.[10]

[10] Futurism, which in some ways overlaps Dadaism and Surrealism, is represented in Section 3.

JOHANN WOLFGANG VON GOETHE

The Demoniac

He thought he could detect in nature—both animate and inanimate, with soul or without soul—something which manifests itself only in contradictions, and which, therefore, could not be comprehended under any idea, still less under one word. It was not godlike, for it seemed unreasonable; not human, for it had no understanding; nor devilish, for it was beneficent; nor angelic, for it often betrayed a malicious pleasure. It resembled chance, for it evolved no consequences: it was like Providence, for it hinted at connection. All that limits us it seemed to penetrate; it seemed to sport at will with the necessary elements of our existence; it contracted time and expanded space. In the impossible alone did it appear to find pleasure, while it rejected the possible with contempt.

To this principle, which seemed to come in between all other principles to separate them, and yet to link them together, I gave the name of Demoniac, after the example of the ancients, and of those who, at any rate, had perceptions of the same kind. I tried to screen myself from this fearful principle, by taking refuge, according to my usual habits, in an imaginary creation. . . .

Although this demoniacal element can manifest itself in all corporeal and incorporeal things, and even expresses itself most distinctly in animals, yet with man especially has it a most wonderful connection, forming in him a power, which, if it be not opposed to the moral order of the world, nevertheless does often so cross it that one may be regarded as the warp and the other as the woof.

For the phenomena which it gives rise to, there are innumerable names; for all philosophies and religions have tried in prose and poetry to solve this enigma, and to read once for all the riddle, an employment which they are welcome to continue.

But the most fearful manifestation of the demoniacal is when it is seen predominating in some individual character. During my life I have observed several instances of this, either more closely or remotely. Such persons are not always the most eminent men, either morally or intellectually; and it is seldom that they recommend themselves to our affections by goodness of heart: a tremendous energy seems to be seated in them; and they exercise a wonderful power over all creatures, and even over the elements; and, indeed, who shall say how much farther such influence may extend? All the moral powers combined are of no

From *Truth and Fiction Relating to My Life* [1811-22], translated from the German by J. Oxenford, Boston, 1882, Vol. I, pp. 321-3.

543

avail against them: in vain does the more enlightened portion of mankind attempt to throw suspicion upon them as deceived if not deceivers,—the mass is still drawn on by them. Seldom if ever do the great men of an age find their equals among their contemporaries, and they are to be overcome by nothing but by the universe itself; and it is from observation of this fact, that the strange but most striking proverb must have risen, *Nemo contra Deum nisi Deus ipse.*

WILLIAM BLAKE

Energy and Reason

All Bibles or sacred codes have been the causes of the following Errors:

  1. That Man has two real existing principles: Viz: a Body & a Soul.

  2. That Energy, call'd Evil, is alone from the Body; & that Reason, call'd Good, is alone from the Soul.

  3. That God will torment Man in Eternity for following his Energies.

But the following Contraries to these are True:

  1. Man has no Body distinct from his Soul; for that call'd Body is a portion of Soul discern'd by the five Senses, the chief inlets of Soul in this age.

  2. Energy is the only life, and is from the Body; and Reason is the bound or outward circumference of Energy.

  3. Energy is Eternal Delight.

The Giants who formed this world into its sensual existence, and now seem to live in it in chains, are in truth the causes of its life & the sources of all activity; but the chains are the cunning of weak and tame minds which have power to resist energy; according to the proverbs, the weak in courage is strong in cunning.

Thus one portion of being is the Prolific, the other the Devouring: to the Devourer it seems as if the producer was in his chains; but it is not so, he only takes portions of existence and fancies that the whole.

But the Prolific would cease to be Prolific unless the Devourer, as a sea, received the excess of his delights.

Some will say: "Is not God alone the Prolific?" I answer: "God only Acts & Is, in existing beings or Men."

These two classes of men are always upon earth, & they should be enemies: whoever tries to reconcile them seeks to destroy existence.

Religion is an endeavour to reconcile the two.

From "The Marriage of Heaven and Hell" [1793], *Complete Writings*, ed. Geoffrey Keynes, London, 1957, p. 149; reprinted by permission of the Nonesuch Press.

ARTHUR SCHOPENHAUER

Will and Knowledge

The assertion of an empirical freedom of the will, a freedom of indifference, agrees precisely with the doctrine that places the inner nature of man in a *soul*, which is originally a *knowing*, and indeed really an abstract *thinking* nature, and only in consequence of this a *willing* nature—a doctrine which thus regards the will as of a secondary or derivative nature, instead of knowledge which is really so. The will indeed came to be regarded as an act of thought, and to be identified with the judgment, especially by Descartes and Spinoza. According to this doctrine every man must become what he is only through his knowledge; he must enter the world as a moral cipher come to know the things in it, and thereupon determine to be this or that, to act thus or thus, and may also through new knowledge achieve a new course of action, that is to say, become another person. Further, he must first know a thing to be *good*, and in consequence of this will it, instead of first *willing* it, and in consequence of this calling it *good*. According to my fundamental point of view, all this is a reversal of the true relation. Will is first and original; knowledge is merely added to it as an instrument belonging to the phenomenon of will. Therefore every man is what he is through his will, and his character is original, for willing is the basis of his nature. Through the knowledge which is added to it he comes to know in the course of experience *what he is, i. e.,* he learns his character. Thus he *knows* himself in consequence of and in accordance with the nature of his will, instead of *willing* in consequence of and in accordance with his knowing. According to the latter view, he would only require to consider how he would like best to be, and he would be it; that is its doctrine of the freedom of the will. Thus it consists really in this, that a man is his own work guided by the light of knowledge. I, on the contrary, say that he is his own work before all knowledge, and knowledge is merely added to it to enlighten it. Therefore he cannot resolve to be this or that, nor can he become other than he is; but he *is* once for all, and he knows in the course of experience *what* he is. According to one doctrine he *wills* what he knows, and according to the other he *knows* what he wills.

The motives which determine the manifestation of the character or conduct influence it through the medium of knowledge. But knowledge is changeable, and often vacillates between truth and error, yet, as a rule, is rectified more and more in the course of life, though certainly in very different degrees. Therefore the conduct of a man may be observably altered without justifying us in concluding that his character has been changed. What the man really and in general wills, the striving of his inmost nature, and the end he pursues in accordance with it, this we can never change by influence upon him from without by instruction, otherwise we could transform him. From without the will can only be affected by motives. But these can never change the will itself; for they have power over it only under the presupposition that it is precisely such as it is. All that they can do is thus to alter the direction of its effort, i.e., bring it about that it shall seek

From *The World as Will and Idea* [1818], translated from the German by R. B. Haldane and J. Kemp, London, 1883-86, Vol. I, pp. 377-80, 401-3; reprinted by permission of Routledge & Kegan Paul Ltd.

in another way than it has hitherto done that which it invariably seeks. Therefore instruction, improved knowledge, in other words, influence from without, may indeed teach the will that it erred in the means it employed, and can therefore bring it about that the end after which it strives once for all according to its inner nature shall be pursued on an entirely different path and in an entirely different object from what has hitherto been the case. But it can never bring about that the will shall will something actually different from what it has hitherto willed; this remains unchangeable, for the will is simply this willing itself, which would have to be abolished. The former, however, the possible modification of knowledge, and through knowledge of conduct, extends so far that the will seeks to attain its unalterable end, for example, Mohammed's paradise, at one time in the real world, at another time in a world of imagination, adapting the means to each, and thus in the first case applying prudence, might, and fraud, and in the second case, abstinence, justice, alms, and pilgrimages to Mecca. But its effort itself has not therefore changed, still less the will itself. Thus, although its action certainly shows itself very different at different times, its willing has yet remained precisely the same. . . .

At every grade that is enlightened by knowledge, the will appears as an individual. The human individual finds himself as finite in infinite space and time, and consequently as a vanishing quantity compared with them. He is projected into them, and, on account of their unlimited nature, he has always a merely relative, never absolute *when* and *where* of his existence; for his place and duration are finite parts of what is infinite and boundless. His real existence is only in the present, whose unchecked flight into the past is a constant transition into death, a constant dying. For his past life, apart from its possible consequences for the present, and the testimony regarding the will that is expressed in it, is now entirely done with, dead, and no longer anything; and, therefore, it must be, as a matter of reason, indifferent to him whether the content of that past was pain or pleasure. But the present is always passing through his hands into the past; the future is quite uncertain and always short. Thus his existence, even when we consider only its formal side, is a constant hurrying of the present into the dead past, a constant dying. But if we look at it from the physical side; it is clear that, as our walking is admittedly merely a constantly prevented falling, the life of our body is only a constantly prevented dying, an ever-postponed death: finally, in the same way, the activity of our mind is a constantly deferred ennui. Every breath we draw wards off the death that is constantly intruding upon us. In this way we fight with it every moment, and again, at longer intervals, through every meal we eat, every sleep we take, every time we warm ourselves, etc. In the end, death must conquer, for we became subject to him through birth, and he only plays for a little while with his prey before he swallows it up. We pursue our life, however, with great interest and much solicitude as long as possible, as we blow out a soap-bubble as long and as large as possible, although we know perfectly well that it will burst.

We saw that the inner being of unconscious nature is a constant striving without end and without rest. And this appears to us much more distinctly when we consider the nature of brutes and man. Willing and striving is its whole being, which may be very well compared to an unquenchable thirst. But the basis of all willing is need, deficiency, and thus pain. Consequently, the nature of brutes and man is subject to pain originally and through its very being. If, on the other hand, it lacks objects of desire, because it is at once deprived of them by a too easy satisfaction, a terrible void and ennui comes over it, i.e., its being and existence itself becomes an unbearable burden to it. Thus its life swings like a pendulum backwards and forwards between pain and ennui. This has also had to express itself very oddly in this way; after man had transferred all pain and torments to hell, there then remained nothing over for heaven but ennui.

But the constant striving which constitutes the inner nature of every manifestation of will obtains its primary and most general foundation at the higher grades of objectification, from the fact that here the will manifests itself as a living body, with the iron command to nourish it; and what gives strength to this command is just that this body is nothing but the objectified will to live itself. Man, as the most complete objectification of that will, is in like measure also the most necessitous of all beings: he is through and through concrete willing and needing; he is a concretion of a thousand necessities. With these he stands upon the earth, left to himself, uncertain about everything except his own need and misery. Consequently the care for the maintenance of that existence under exacting demands, which are renewed every day, occupies, as a rule, the whole of human life. To this is directly related the second claim, that of the propagation of the species. At the same time he is threatened from all sides by the most different kinds of dangers, from which it requires constant watchfulness to escape. With cautious steps and casting anxious glances round him he pursues his path, for a thousand accidents and a thousand enemies lie in wait for him. Thus he went while yet a savage, thus he goes in civilised life; there is no security for him. The life of the great majority is only a constant struggle for this existence itself, with the certainty of losing it at last. But what enables them to endure this wearisome battle is not so much the love of life as the fear of death, which yet stands in the background as inevitable, and may come upon them at any moment. Life itself is a sea, full of rocks and whirlpools, which man avoids with the greatest care and solicitude, although he knows that even if he succeeds in getting through with all his efforts and skill, he yet by doing so comes nearer at every step to the greatest, the total, inevitable, and irremediable shipwreck, death; nay, even steers right upon it: this is the final goal of the laborious voyage, and worse for him than all the rocks from which he has escaped.

Dionysos and Apollo

I

Much will have been gained for esthetics once we have succeeded in apprehending directly—rather than merely *ascertaining*—that art owes its continuous evolution to the Apollonian-Dionysiac duality, even as the propagation of the species depends on the duality of the sexes, their constant conflicts and periodic acts of reconciliation. I have borrowed my adjectives from the Greeks, who developed their mystical doctrines of art through plausible *embodiments*, not through purely conceptual means. It is by those two art-sponsoring deities, Apollo and Dionysos, that we are made to recognize the tremendous split, as regards both origins and objectives, between the plastic, Apollonian arts and the non-visual art of music inspired by Dionysos. The two creative tendencies developed alongside one another, usually in fierce opposition, each by its taunts forcing the other to more energetic production, both perpetuating in a discordant concord that agon which the term *art* but feebly denominates: until at last, by the thaumaturgy of an Hellenic act of will, the pair accepted the yoke of marriage and, in this condition, begot Attic tragedy, which exhibits the salient features of both parents.

To reach a closer understanding of both these tendencies, let us begin by viewing them as the separate art realms of *dream* and *intoxication*, two physiological phenomena standing toward one another in much the same relationship as the Apollonian and Dionysiac. It was in a dream, according to Lucretius, that the marvelous gods and goddesses first presented themselves to the minds of men. That great sculptor, Phidias, beheld in a dream the entrancing bodies of more-than-human beings, and likewise, if anyone had asked the Greek poets about the mystery of poetic creation, they too would have referred him to dreams and instructed him much as Hans Sachs instructs us in *Die Meistersinger*:

> My friend, it is the poet's work
> Dreams to interpret and to mark.
> Believe me that man's true conceit
> In a dream becomes complete:
> All poetry we ever read
> Is but true dreams interpreted.

The fair illusion of the dream sphere, in the production of which every man proves himself an accomplished artist, is a precondition not only of all plastic art, but even, as we shall see presently, of a wide range of poetry. Here we enjoy an immediate apprehension of form, all shapes speak to us directly, nothing seems indifferent or redundant. Despite the high intensity with which these dream realities exist for us, we still have a residual sensation that they are illusions; at least such has been my experience—and the frequency, not to say normality, of the experience is borne out in many passages of the poets. Men of philosophical disposition are known for their constant premonition that our everyday reality, too, is an illusion, hiding another, totally different kind of reality. It was Schopenhauer who considered the ability to view at certain times all men and things as mere phantoms or dream images to be the true mark of philosophic talent. The person who is responsive to the stimuli of art behaves toward the reality of dream much the way the philosopher behaves toward the reality of existence: he observes exactly and enjoys his observations, for it is by these images that he interprets life, by these processes that he rehearses it. Nor is it by pleasant images only that such plausible connections are made: the whole divine comedy of life, including its somber aspects, its sudden balkings, impish accidents, anxious expectations, moves past him, not quite like a shadow play—for it is he himself, after all, who lives and suffers through these scenes—yet never without giving a fleeting sense of illusion; and I imagine that many persons have reassured themselves amidst the perils of dream by calling out, "It is a dream! I want it to go on." I have even heard of people spinning out the causality of one and the same dream over three or more successive nights. All these facts clearly bear witness that our innermost being, the common substratum of humanity, experiences dreams with deep delight and a sense of real necessity. This deep and happy sense of the necessity of dream experiences was expressed by the Greeks in the image of Apollo. Apollo is at once the god of all plastic powers and the soothsaying god. He who is etymologically the "lucent" one, the god of light, reigns also over the fair illusion of our inner world of fantasy. The perfection of these conditions in contrast to our imperfectly understood waking reality, as well as our profound awareness of nature's healing powers during the interval of sleep and dream, furnishes a symbolic analogue to the soothsaying faculty and quite generally to the arts, which make life possible and worth living. But the image of Apollo must incorporate that thin line which the dream image may not cross, under penalty of becoming pathological, of imposing itself on us as crass reality: a discreet limitation, a freedom from all extravagant urges, the sapient tranquillity of the plastic god. His eye must be sunlike, in keeping with his origin. Even at those moments when he is angry and ill-tempered there lies upon him the consecration of fair illusion. In an eccentric way one might say of Apollo what Schopenhauer says, in the first part of *The World as Will and Idea*, of man caught in the veil of Maya: "Even as on an immense, raging sea, assailed by huge wave crests, a man sits in a little rowboat trusting his frail craft, so, amidst the furious torments of this world, the individual sits tranquilly, supported by the *principium individuationis* and relying on it." One might say that the unshakable confidence in that principle has received its most magnificent expression in Apollo, and that Apollo himself may be regarded as the marvelous divine image of the *principium individuationis*, whose looks and gestures radiate the full delight, wisdom, and beauty of "illusion."

In the same context Schopenhauer has described for us the tremendous awe which seizes man when he suddenly begins to doubt the cognitive modes of experience, in other words, when in a given instance the law of causation seems to suspend itself. If we add to this awe the glorious transport which arises in man, even from the very depths of nature, at the shattering of the *principium individuationis,* then we are in a position to apprehend the essence of Dionysiac rapture, whose closest analogy is furnished by physical intoxication. Dionysiac stirrings arise either through the influence of those narcotic potions of which all primitive races speak in their hymns, or through the powerful approach of spring, which penetrates with joy the whole frame of nature. So stirred, the individual forgets himself completely. It is the same Dionysiac power which in medieval Germany drove ever increasing crowds of people singing and dancing from place to place; we recognize in these St. John's and St. Vitus' dancers the bacchic choruses of the Greeks, who had their precursors in Asia Minor and as far back as Babylon and the orgiastic Sacaea. There are people who, either from lack of experience or out of sheer stupidity, turn away from such phenomena, and, strong in the sense of their own sanity, label them either mockingly or pityingly "endemic diseases." These benighted souls have no idea how cadaverous and ghostly their "sanity" appears as the intense throng of Dionysiac revelers sweeps past them.

Not only does the bond between man and man come to be forged once more by the magic of the Dionysiac rite, but nature itself, long alienated or subjugated, rises again to celebrate the reconciliation with her prodigal son, man. The earth offers its gifts voluntarily, and the savage beasts of mountain and desert approach in peace. The chariot of Dionysos is bedecked with flowers and garlands; panthers and tigers stride beneath his yoke. If one were to convert Beethoven's "Paean to Joy" into a painting, and refuse to curb the imagination when that multitude prostrates itself reverently in the dust, one might form some apprehension of Dionysiac ritual. Now the slave emerges as a freeman; all the rigid, hostile walls which either necessity or despotism has erected between men are shattered. Now that the gospel of universal harmony is sounded, each individual becomes not only reconciled to his fellow but actually at one with him—as though the veil of Maya had been torn apart and there remained only shreds floating before the vision of mystical Oneness. Man now expresses himself through song and dance as the member of a higher community; he has forgotten how to walk, how to speak, and is on the brink of taking wing as he dances. Each of his gestures betokens enchantment; through him sounds a supernatural power, the same power which makes the animals speak and the earth render up milk and honey. He feels himself to be godlike and strides with the same elation and ecstasy as the gods he has seen in his dreams. No longer the *artist,* he has himself become a *work of art:* the productive power of the whole universe is now manifest in his transport, to the glorious satisfaction of the primordial One. The finest clay, the most precious marble—man—is here kneaded and hewn, and the chisel blows of the Dionysiac world artist are accompanied by the cry of the Eleusinian mystagogues: "Do you fall on your knees, multitudes, do you divine your creator?"

II

So far we have examined the Apollonian and Dionysiac states as the product of formative forces arising directly from nature without the mediation of the human artist. At this stage artistic urges are satisfied directly, on the one hand through the imagery of dreams, whose perfection is quite independent of the intellectual rank, the artistic development of the individual; on the other hand, through an ecstatic reality which once again takes no account of the individual and may even destroy him, or else redeem him through a mystical experience of the collective. In relation to these immediate creative conditions of nature every artist must appear as "imitator," either as the Apollonian dream artist or the Dionysiac ecstatic artist, or, finally (as in Greek tragedy, for example) as dream and ecstatic artist in one. We might picture to ourselves how the last of these, in a state of Dionysiac intoxication and mystical self-abrogation, wandering apart from the reveling throng, sinks upon the ground, and how there is then revealed to him his own condition—complete oneness with the essence of the universe—in a dream similitude.

Having set down these general premises and distinctions, we now turn to the Greeks in order to realize to what degree the formative forces of nature were developed in them. Such an inquiry will enable us to assess properly the relation of the Greek artist to his prototypes or, to use Aristotle's expression, his "imitation of nature." Of the dreams the Greeks dreamed it is not possible to speak with any certainty, despite the extant dream literature and the large number of dream anecdotes. But considering the incredible accuracy of their eyes, their keen and unabashed delight in colors, one can hardly be wrong in assuming that their dreams too showed a strict consequence of lines and contours, hues and groupings, a progression of scenes similar to their best bas-reliefs. The perfection of these dream scenes might almost tempt us to consider the dreaming Greek as a Homer and Homer as a dreaming Greek; which would be as though the modern man were to compare himself in his dreaming to Shakespeare.

Yet there is another point about which we do not have to conjecture at all: I mean the profound gap separating the Dionysiac Greeks from the Dionysiac barbarians. Throughout the range of ancient civilization (leaving the newer civilizations out of account for the moment) we find evidence of Dionysiac celebrations which stand to the Greek type in much the same relation as the bearded satyr, whose name and attributes are derived from the he-goat, stands to the god Dionysos. The central concern of such celebrations was, almost universally, a complete sexual promiscuity overriding every form of established tribal law; all the savage urges of the mind were unleashed on those occasions until they reached that paroxysm of lust and cruelty which has always struck me as the "witches' cauldron" *par excellence*. It would appear that the Greeks were for a while quite immune from these feverish excesses which must have reached them by every known land or sea route. What kept Greece safe was the proud, imposing image of Apollo, who in holding up the head of the Gorgon to those brutal and grotesque Dionysiac forces subdued them. Doric art has immortalized Apollo's majestic rejection of all license. But resistance became difficult, even impossible, as soon as similar urges began to break forth from the deep substratum of Hellenism itself. Soon the function of the Delphic god developed into something quite different and much more limited: all he could hope to accomplish now was to wrest the destructive weapon, by a timely gesture of pacification, from his opponent's hand. That act of pacification represents the most important event in the history of Greek ritual; every department of life now shows symptoms of a revolutionary change. The two great antagonists have been reconciled. Each feels obliged henceforth to keep to his bounds, each will honor the other by the bestowal of periodic gifts, while the cleavage remains fundamentally the same. And yet, if we examine what happened to the Dionysiac powers under the pressure of that treaty we notice a great difference: in the place of the Babylonian Sacaea, with their throwback of men to the condition of apes and tigers, we now see entirely new rites celebrated: rites of universal redemption, of glorious transfiguration. Only now has it become possible to speak of nature's celebrating an *esthetic* triumph; only now has the abrogation of the *principium individuationis* become an esthetic event. That terrible witches' brew concocted of lust and cruelty has lost all power under the new conditions. Yet the peculiar blending of emotions in the heart of the Dionysiac reveler—his ambiguity if you will—seems still to hark back (as the medicinal drug harks back to the deadly poison) to the days when the infliction of pain was experienced as joy while a sense of supreme triumph elicited cries of anguish from the heart. For now in every exuberant joy there is heard an undertone of terror, or else a wistful lament over an irrecoverable loss. It is as though in these Greek festivals a sentimental trait of nature were coming to the fore, as though nature were bemoaning the fact of her fragmentation, her decomposition into separate individuals. The chants and gestures of these revelers, so ambiguous in their motivation, represented an absolute *novum* in the world of the Homeric Greeks; their Dionysiac music, in especial, spread abroad terror and a deep shudder. It is true: music had long been familiar to the Greeks as an Apollonian art, as a regular beat like that of waves lapping the shore, a plastic rhythm expressly developed for the portrayal of Apollonian conditions. Apollo's music was a Doric architecture of sound—of barely hinted sounds such as are proper to the cithara. Those very elements which characterize Dionysiac music and, after it, music quite generally: the heart-shaking power of tone, the uniform stream of melody, the incomparable resources of harmony—all those elements had been carefully kept at a distance as being inconsonant with the Apollonian norm. In the Dionysiac dithyramb man is incited to strain his symbolic faculties to the utmost; something quite unheard of is now clamoring to be heard: the desire to tear asunder the veil of Maya, to sink back into the original oneness of nature; the desire to express the very essence of nature symbolically. Thus an entirely new set of symbols springs into being. First, all the symbols pertaining to physical features: mouth, face, the spoken word, the dance movement which coordinates the limbs and bends them to its rhythm. Then suddenly all the rest of the symbolic forces—music and rhythm as such, dynamics, harmony—assert themselves with great energy. In order to comprehend this total emancipation of all the symbolic powers one must have reached the same measure of inner freedom those powers themselves were making manifest; which is to say that the votary of Dionysos could not be understood except by his own kind. It is not difficult to imagine the awed surprise with which the Apollonian Greek must have looked on him. And that surprise would be further increased as the latter realized, with a shudder, that all this was not so alien to him after all, that his Apollonian consciousness was but a thin veil hiding from him the whole Dionysiac realm.

III

In order to comprehend this we must take down the elaborate edifice of Apollonian culture stone by stone until we discover its foundations. At first the eye is struck by the marvelous shapes of the Olympian gods who stand upon its pediments, and whose exploits, in shining bas-relief, adorn its friezes. The fact that among them we find Apollo as one god among many, making no claim to a privileged position, should not mislead us. The same drive that found its most complete representation in Apollo generated the whole Olympian world, and in this sense we may consider Apollo the father of that world. But what was the radical need out of which that illustrious society of Olympian beings sprang?

Whoever approaches the Olympians with a different religion in his heart, seeking moral elevation, sanctity, spirituality, loving-kindness, will presently be forced to turn away from them in ill-humored disappointment. Nothing in these deities reminds us of asceticism, high intellect, or duty: we are confronted by luxuriant, triumphant *existence*, which deifies the good and the bad indifferently. And the beholder may find himself dismayed in the presence of such overflowing life and ask himself what potion these heady people must have drunk in order to behold, in whatever direction they looked, Helen laughing back at them, the beguiling image of their own existence. But we shall call out to this beholder, who has already turned his back: Don't go! Listen first to what the Greeks themselves have to say of this life, which spreads itself before you with such a puzzling serenity. An old legend has it that King Midas hunted a long time in the woods for the wise Silenus, companion of Dionysos, without being able to catch him. When he had finally caught him the king asked him what he considered man's greatest good. The daemon remained sullen and uncommunicative until finally, forced by the king, he broke into a shrill laugh and spoke: "Ephemeral wretch, begotten by accident and toil, why do you force me to tell you what it would be your greatest boon not to hear? What would be best for you is quite beyond your reach: not to have been born, not to *be*, to be *nothing*. But the second best is to die soon."

What is the relation of the Olympian gods to this popular wisdom? It is that of the entranced vision of the martyr to his torment.

Now the Olympian magic mountain opens itself before us, showing us its very roots. The Greeks were keenly aware of the terrors and horrors of existence; in order to be able to live at all they had to place before them the shining fantasy of the Olympians. Their tremendous distrust of the titanic forces of nature: *Moira*, mercilessly enthroned beyond the knowable world; the vulture which fed upon the great philanthropist Prometheus; the terrible lot drawn by wise Oedipus; the curse on the house of Atreus which brought Orestes to the murder of his mother: that whole Panic philosophy, in short, with its mythic examples, by which the gloomy Etruscans perished, the Greeks conquered—or at least hid from view—again and again by means of this artificial Olympus. In order to live at all the Greeks had to construct these deities. The Apollonian need for beauty had to develop the Olympian hierarchy of joy by slow degrees from the original titanic hierarchy of terror, as roses are seen to break from a thorny thicket. How else could life have been borne by a race so hypersensitive, so emotionally intense, so equipped for suffering? The same drive which called art into being as a completion and consummation of existence, and as a guarantee of further existence, gave rise also to that Olympian realm which acted as a transfiguring mirror to the Hellenic will. The gods justified human life by living it themselves—the only satisfactory theodicy ever invented. To exist in the clear sunlight of such deities was now felt to be the highest good, and the only real grief suffered by Homeric man was inspired by the thought of leaving that sunlight, especially when the departure seemed imminent. Now it became possible to stand the wisdom of Silenus on its head and proclaim that it was the worst evil for man to die soon, and second worst for him to die at all. Such laments as arise now arise over short-lived Achilles. over the generations ephemeral as leaves, the decline of the heroic age. It is not unbecoming to even the greatest hero to yearn for an afterlife, though it be as a day laborer. So impetuously, during the Apollonian phase, does man's will desire to remain on earth, so identified does he become with existence, that even his lament turns to a song of praise.

It should have become apparent by now that the harmony with nature which we late-comers regard with such nostalgia, and for which Schiller has coined the cant term *naïve*, is by no means a simple and inevitable condition to be found at the gateway to every culture, a kind of paradise. Such a belief could have been endorsed only by a period for which Rousseau's Emile was an artist and Homer just such an artist nurtured in the bosom of nature. Whenever we encounter "naïveté" in art, we are face to face with the ripest fruit of Apollonian culture— which must always triumph first over titans, kill monsters, and overcome the somber contemplation of actuality, the intense susceptibility to suffering, by means of illusions strenuously and zestfully entertained. But how rare are the instances of true naïveté, of that complete identification with the beauty of appearance! It is this achievement which makes Homer so magnificent—Homer, who, as a single individual, stood to Apollonian popular culture in the same relation as the individual dream artist to the oneiric capacity of a race and of nature generally. The naïveté of Homer must be viewed as a complete victory of Apollonian illusion. Nature often uses illusions of this sort in order to accomplish its secret purposes. The true goal is covered over by a phantasm. We stretch out our hands to the latter, while nature, aided by our deception, attains the former. In the case of the Greeks it was the will wishing to behold itself in the work of art, in the transcendence of genius; but in order so to behold itself its creatures had first to view themselves as glorious, to transpose themselves to a higher sphere, without having that sphere of pure contemplation either challenge them or upbraid them with insufficiency. It was in that sphere of beauty that the Greeks saw the Olympians as their mirror images; it was by means of that esthetic mirror that the Greek will opposed suffering and the somber wisdom of suffering which always accompanies artistic talent. As a monument to its victory stands Homer, the naïve artist.

IV

We can learn something about that naïve artist through the analogy of dream. We can imagine the dreamer as he calls out to himself, still caught in the illusion of his dream and without disturbing it, "This is a dream, and I want to go on dreaming," and we can infer, on the one hand, that he takes deep delight in the contemplation of his dream, and, on the other, that he must have forgotten the day, with its horrible importunity, so to enjoy his dream. Apollo, the interpreter of dreams, will furnish the clue to what is happening here. Although of the two halves of life—the waking and the dreaming—the former is generally considered not only the more important but the only one which is truly lived, I would, at the risk of sounding paradoxical, propose the opposite view. The more I have come to realize in nature those omnipotent formative tendencies and, with them, an intense longing for illusion, the more I feel inclined to the hypothesis that the original Oneness, the ground of Being, ever-suffering and contradictory, time and again has need of rapt vision and delightful illusion to redeem itself. Since we ourselves are the very stuff of such illusions, we must view ourselves as the truly non-existent, that is to say, as a perpetual unfolding in time, space, and causality —what we label "empiric reality." But if, for the moment, we abstract from our own reality, viewing our empiric existence, as well as the existence of the world at large, as the *idea* of the original Oneness, produced anew each instant, then our dreams will appear to us as illusions of illusions, hence as a still higher form of satisfaction of the original desire for illusion. It is for this reason that the very core of nature takes such a deep delight in the naïve artist and the naïve work of art, which likewise is merely the illusion of an illusion. Raphael, himself one of those immortal "naïve" artists, in a symbolic canvas has illustrated that reduction of illusion to further illusion which is the original act of the naïve artist and at the same time of all Apollonian culture. In the lower half of his "Transfigura- tion," through the figures of the possessed boy, the despairing bearers, the help- less, terrified disciples, we see a reflection of original pain, the sole ground of being: "illusion" here is a reflection of eternal contradiction, begetter of all things. From this illusion there rises, like the fragrance of ambrosia, a new illusory world, invisible to those enmeshed in the first: a radiant vision of pure delight, a rapt seeing through wide-open eyes. Here we have, in a great symbol of art, both the fair world of Apollo and its substratum, the terrible wisdom of Silenus, and we can comprehend intuitively how they mutually require one another. But Apollo appears to us once again as the apotheosis of the *principium individuationis*, in whom the eternal goal of the original Oneness, namely its redemption through illusion, accomplishes itself. With august gesture the god shows us how there is need for a whole world of torment in order for the individual to produce the re- demptive vision and to sit quietly in his rocking rowboat in mid-sea, absorbed in contemplation.

If this apotheosis of individuation is to be read in normative terms, we may infer that there is one norm only: the individual—or, more precisely, the observ- ance of the limits of the individual: *sophrosyne*. As a moral deity Apollo demands self-control from his people and, in order to observe such self-control, a knowledge of self. And so we find that the esthetic necessity of beauty is accompanied by the imperatives, "Know thyself," and "Nothing too much." Conversely, excess and *hubris* come to be regarded as the hostile spirits of the non-Apollonian sphere, hence as properties of the pre-Apollonian era—the age of Titans—and the extra-Apollonian world, that is to say the world of the barbarians. It was because of his Titanic love of man that Prometheus had to be devoured by vultures; it was because of his extravagant wisdom which succeeded in solving the riddle of the Sphinx that Oedipus had to be cast into a whirlpool of crime: in this fashion does the Delphic god interpret the Greek past.

The effects of the Dionysiac spirit struck the Apollonian Greeks as titanic and barbaric; yet they could not disguise from themselves the fact that they were es- sentially akin to those deposed Titans and heroes. They felt more than that: their whole existence, with its temperate beauty, rested upon a base of suffering and *knowledge* which had been hidden from them until the reinstatement of Diony-sos uncovered it once more. And lo and behold! Apollo found it impossible to live without Dionysos. The elements of titanism and barbarism turned out to be quite as fundamental as the Apollonian element. And now let us imagine how the ecstatic sounds of the Dionysiac rites penetrated ever more enticingly into that artificially restrained and discreet world of illusion, how this clamor expressed the whole outrageous gamut of nature—delight, grief, knowledge—even to the most piercing cry; and then let us imagine how the Apollonian artist with his thin, monotonous harp music must have sounded beside the demoniac chant of the multitude! The muses presiding over the illusory arts paled before an art which enthusiastically told the truth, and the wisdom of Silenus cried "Woe!" against the serene Olympians. The individual, with his limits and moderations, forgot himself in the Dionysiac vortex and became oblivious to the laws of Apollo. Indis-creet extravagance revealed itself as truth, and contradiction, a delight born of pain, spoke out of the bosom of nature. Wherever the Dionysiac voice was heard, the Apollonian norm seemed suspended or destroyed. Yet it is equally true that, in those places where the first assault was withstood, the prestige and majesty of the Delphic god appeared more rigid and threatening than before. The only way I am able to view Doric art and the Doric state is as a perpetual military encamp-ment of the Apollonian forces. An art so defiantly austere, so ringed about with fortifications—an education so military and exacting—a polity so ruthlessly cruel—could endure only in a continual state of resistance against the titanic and bar-baric menace of Dionysos.

Up to this point I have developed at some length a theme which was sounded at the beginning of this essay: how the Dionysiac and Apollonian elements, in a continuous chain of creations, each enhancing the other, dominated the Hellenic mind; how from the Iron Age, with its battles of Titans and its austere popular philosophy, there developed under the aegis of Apollo the Homeric world of beauty; how this "naïve" splendor was then absorbed once more by the Dionysiac torrent, and how, face to face with this new power, the Apollonian code rigidified into the majesty of Doric art and contemplation. If the earlier phase of Greek history may justly be broken down into four major artistic epochs dramatizing the battle between the two hostile principles, then we must inquire further (lest Doric art appear to us as the acme and final goal of all these striving tendencies) what was the true end toward which that evolution moved. And our eyes will come to rest on the sublime and much lauded achievement of the dramatic dith-yramb and Attic tragedy, as the common goal of both urges; whose mysterious marriage, after long discord, ennobled itself with such a child, at once Antigone and Cassandra.

Genius of the heart: as it is possessed by that great Hidden One, the Tempter-God and born Rat-Catcher of the Conscience, whose voice can climb into the underworld of any psyche, who never speaks a word or looks a look in which there is not some hind-sight, some complexity of allure, whose craftsmanship includes knowing how to be an illusion—not an illusion of what he is, but of what consti-tutes one more compulsion upon his followers to follow him ever more intimately and thoroughly—*genius of the heart* which renders dumb all that is loud and complaisant, teaching it how to listen, which smooths rough souls and creates a taste in them for a new desire: to lie still like a mirror so that the deep sky might be reflected in them—*genius of the heart* which teaches the bungling and precipitous hand to hesitate and handle things delicately, which guesses the hidden and forgotten treasure, the drop of goodness and sweet intelligence beneath layers of murky, thick ice; which is a divining rod for every speck of gold that lies buried in its dungeon of deep muck and sand—*genius of the heart,* upon whose touch everyone departs richer, not full of grace, not surprised, not enriched and oppressed as though by strange goods, but richer in himself, newer than before, cracked wide open, blown upon and drawn out by a spring wind, more uncertain now perhaps, more delicate, fragile, and broken, but full of hopes that have no names as yet, full of new will and flow, full of new ill will and counterflow—but what am I doing, my friends? Of whom am I speaking? Did I forget myself so far as not to tell you his name? Unless you yourselves have guessed who this questionable spirit and God is; who it is that demands such praise! For, as happens to everyone who from his early years has been a wanderer and an exile, many a strange and precarious spirit has run across my path. Foremost of all of them, and again and again, the one I was telling you about, no less a one than the God *Dionysos,* that great Ambivalent One and Tempter-God, the one to whom I once, as you know, in all secrecy and all reverence, sacrificed my first-born (having been the last, it seems to me, to sacrifice anything to him, for I found no one who understood what I was doing at that time). Meanwhile I learned much, all too much, about this God's philosophy by word of mouth, as I have said—I, the last disciple and initiate of the God Dionysos. It is really time, therefore, to give you, my friends, a small taste of this philosophy, insofar as I am permitted. *Sotto voce,* as is proper, for it is a matter of many things that are mysterious, new, exotic, strange, uncanny. Even that Dionysos is a philosopher and hence that gods philosophize seems to me a piece of precarious news, designed to create suspicion among philosophers. Among you, my friends, it is probably safer to tell it—unless it is told too late or at the wrong time—for you no longer like to believe in God or any gods nowadays, as you tell me. Furthermore, I may have to be more frank in my tale than the stern habits of your ears will like. In any event, the God in question always went further, a great deal further, when *he* held such discourses; he was always many steps ahead of me. . . . If it were allowed, I should accord him, as is the human custom, many beautiful solemn titles of pomp and virtue, much extolling of his explorer's and discoverer's courage, of his daring candor, his truthfulness, his love for wisdom. But a God such as he does not know what to do with such respectable clap-trap and pomp. "Keep it," he would say, "keep it for yourself and whoever is like you, whoever else needs such stuff! I have no reason to cover my nakedness!" One may easily guess that this type of divinity and philosopher lacks modesty. Once, for example, he said "I love mankind under certain conditions" (alluding to Ariadne who was there at the time), "man seems to me to be a pleasant, courageous, inventive animal who has not his likes on earth; he can find his way around any labyrinth. I wish him well; I often contemplate how I might advance him, how I might make him stronger, more evil, and deeper than he is." "Stronger, more evil, and deeper?" I asked, shocked. "Yes," he said once more, "stronger, more evil, deeper, and also—more beautiful!"—and saying this he smiled his halcyon smile, this Tempter-God, as though he had de-livered himself of an enchanting courtesy. One sees at once that it is not only modesty which this divinity lacks. . . . There are good reasons, in fact, for sup-posing that all the gods could learn from us men in several respects. We men are more—humane. . . .

SIGMUND FREUD
The Structure of the Unconscious

[CONSCIOUS, UNCONSCIOUS, PRECONSCIOUS]

The starting point for this investigation is provided by a fact without parallel, which defies all explanation or description—the fact of consciousness. Nevertheless, if anyone speaks of consciousness, we know immediately and from our own most personal experience what is meant by it. Many people, both inside and outside the science of psychology, are satisfied with the assumption that consciousness alone is mental, and nothing then remains for psychology but to discriminate in the phenomenology of the mind between perceptions, feelings, intellective processes and volitions. It is generally agreed, however, that these conscious processes do not form unbroken series which are complete in themselves; so that there is no alternative to assuming that there are physical or somatic processes which accompany the mental ones and which must admittedly be more complete than the mental series, since some of them have conscious processes parallel to them but others have not. It thus seems natural to lay the stress in psychology upon these somatic processes, to see in *them* the true essence of what is mental and to try to arrive at some other assessment of the conscious processes. The majority of philosophers, however, as well as many other people, dispute this position and declare that the notion of a mental thing being unconscious is self-contradictory.

But it is precisely this that psychoanalysis is obliged to assert, and this is its second fundamental hypothesis. It explains the supposed somatic accessory processes as being what is essentially mental and disregards for the moment the quality of consciousness. . . .

We are soon led to make an important division in this unconscious. Some processes become conscious easily; they may then cease to be conscious, but can become conscious once more without any trouble: as people say, they can be reproduced or remembered. This reminds us that consciousness is in general a very highly fugitive condition. What is conscious is conscious only for a moment. If

From *An Outline of Psychoanalysis* [1940], translated from the German by James Strachey, London and New York, 1949, pp. 34-5, 37-9. Copyright 1949 by W. W. Norton & Co., Inc.; reprinted by permission of W. W. Norton & Co., and The Hogarth Press Ltd.
From *New Introductory Lectures on Psychoanalysis* [1933], translated from the German by W. J. H. Sprott, New York, 1933, pp. 104-5, 105-7, 108-12. Copyright 1933 by Sigmund Freud; copyright renewed © 1961 by W. J. H. Sprott; reprinted by permission of W. W. Norton & Co., Inc.

our perceptions do not confirm this, the contradiction is merely an apparent one. It is explained by the fact that the stimuli of perception can persist for some time, so that in the course of it the perception of them can be repeated. The whole position can be clearly seen from the conscious perception of our intellective processes; it is true that these may persist, but they may just as easily pass in a flash. Everything unconscious that behaves in this way, that can easily exchange the unconscious condition for the conscious one, is therefore better described as "capable of entering consciousness," or as *preconscious*. Experience has taught us that there are hardly any mental processes, even of the most complicated kind, which cannot on occasion remain preconscious, although as a rule they press forward, as we say, into consciousness. There are other mental processes or mental material which have no such easy access to consciousness, but which must be inferred, discovered, and translated into conscious form in the manner that has been described. It is for such material that we reserve the name of the unconscious proper.

Thus we have attributed three qualities to mental processes: they are either conscious, preconscious, or unconscious. The division between the three classes of material which have these qualities is neither absolute nor permanent. What is preconscious becomes conscious, as we have seen, without any activity on our part; what is unconscious can, as a result of our efforts, be made conscious, though in the process we may have an impression that we are overcoming what are often very strong resistances. When we make an attempt of this kind upon someone else, we ought not to forget that the conscious filling up of the breaks in his perceptions—the construction which we are offering him—does not so far mean that we have made conscious in him the unconscious material in question. All that is so far true is that the material is present in his mind in two versions, first in the conscious reconstruction that he has just received and secondly in its original unconscious condition.

[ID, EGO, SUPER-EGO]

[The id is] . . . a chaos, a cauldron of seething excitement. We suppose that it is somewhere in direct contact with somatic processes, and takes over from them instinctual needs and gives them mental expression, but we cannot say in what substratum this contact is made. These instincts fill it with energy, but it has no organisation and no unified will, only an impulsion to obtain satisfaction for the instinctual needs, in accordance with the pleasure-principle. The laws of logic—above all, the law of contradiction—do not hold for processes in the id. Contradictory impulses exist side by side without neutralising each other or drawing apart; at most they combine in compromise formations under the overpowering economic pressure towards discharging their energy. There is nothing in the id which can be compared to negation, and we are astonished to find in it an exception to the philosophers' assertion that space and time are necessary forms of our mental acts. In the id there is nothing corresponding to the idea of time, no recognition of the passage of time, and (a thing which is very remarkable and awaits adequate attention in philosophic thought) no alteration of mental processes by the passage of time. Conative impulses which have never got beyond the id, and even impressions which have been pushed down into the id by repression, are virtually immortal and are preserved for whole decades as though they had only recently occurred. They can only be recognised as belonging to the past, deprived of their significance, and robbed of their charge of energy, after they have been made conscious by the work of analysis, and no small part of the therapeutic effect of analytic treatment rests upon this fact.

It is constantly being borne in upon me that we have made far too little use of our theory of the indubitable fact that the repressed remains unaltered by the passage of time. This seems to offers us the possibility of an approach to some really profound truths. But I myself have made no further progress here.

Naturally, the id knows no values, no good and evil, no morality. The economic, or, if you prefer, the quantitative factor, which is so closely bound up with the pleasure-principle, dominates all its processes. Instinctual cathexes seeking discharge,—that, in our view, is all that the id contains. It seems, indeed, as if the energy of these instinctual impulses is in a different condition from that in which it is found in the other regions of the mind. It must be far more fluid and more capable of being discharged, for otherwise we should not have those displacements and condensations, which are so characteristic of the id and which are so completely independent of the qualities of what is cathected. . . .

As regards a characterization of the ego, in so far as it is to be distinguished from the id and the super-ego, we shall get on better if we turn our attention to the relation between it and the most superficial portion of the mental apparatus; which we call the Pcpt-cs (perceptual-conscious) system. This system is directed on to the external world, it mediates perceptions of it, and in it is generated, while it is functioning, the phenomenon of consciousness. It is the sense-organ of the whole apparatus, receptive, moreover, not only of excitations from without but also of such as proceed from the interior of the mind. One can hardly go wrong in regarding the ego as that part of the id which has been modified by its proximity to the external world and the influence that the latter has had on it, and which serves the purpose of receiving stimuli and protecting the organism from them, like the cortical layer with which a particle of living substance surrounds itself. This relation to the external world is decisive for the ego. The ego has taken over the task of representing the external world for the id, and so of saving it; for the id, blindly striving to gratify its instincts in complete disregard of the superior strength of outside forces, could not otherwise escape annihilation. In the fulfilment of this function, the ego has to observe the external world and preserve a true picture of it in the memory traces left by its perceptions, and, by means of the reality-test, it has to eliminate any element in this picture of the external world which is a contribution from internal sources of excitation. On behalf of the id, the ego controls the path of access to motility, but it interpolates between desire and action the procrastinating factor of thought, during which it makes use of the residues of experience stored up in memory. In this way it dethrones the pleasure-principle, which exerts undisputed sway over the processes in the id, and substitutes for it the reality-principle, which promises greater security and greater success.

The relation to time, too, which is so hard to describe, is communicated to the ego by the perceptual system; indeed it can hardly be doubted that the mode in which this system works is the source of the idea of time. What, however, especially marks the ego out in contradistinction to the id, is a tendency to synthesise its contents, to bring together and unify its mental processes which is entirely absent from the id. When we come to deal presently with the instincts in mental life, I hope we shall succeed in tracing this fundamental characteristic of the ego to its source. It is this alone that produces that high degree of organisation which the ego needs for its highest achievements. The ego advances from the function of perceiving instincts to that of controlling them, but the latter is only achieved through the mental representative of the instinct becoming subordinated to a larger organisation, and finding its place in a coherent unity. In popular language, we may say that the ego stands for reason and circumspection, while the id stands for the untamed passions. . . .

The proverb tells us that one cannot serve two masters at once. The poor ego has a still harder time of it; it has to serve three harsh masters, and has to do its best to reconcile the claims and demands of all three. These demands are always divergent and often seem quite incompatible; no wonder that the ego so frequently gives way under its task. The three tyrants are the external world, the super-ego and the id. When one watches the efforts of the ego to satisfy them all, or rather, to obey them all simultaneously, one cannot regret having personified the ego, and established it as a separate being. It feels itself hemmed in on three sides and threatened by three kinds of danger, towards which it reacts by developing anxiety when it is too hard pressed. Having originated in the experiences of the perceptual system, it is designed to represent the demands of the external world, but it also wishes to be a loyal servant of the id, to remain upon good terms with the id, to recommend itself to the id as an object, and to draw the id's libido on to itself. In its attempt to mediate between the id and reality, it is often forced to clothe the Ucs. commands of the id with its own Pcs. rationalisations, to gloss over the conflicts between the id and reality, and with diplomatic dishonesty to display a pretended regard for reality, even when the id persists in being stubborn and uncompromising. On the other hand, its every movement is watched by the severe super-ego, which holds up certain norms of behaviour, without regard to any difficulties coming from the id and the external world; and if these norms are not acted up to, it punishes the ego with the feelings of tension which manifest themselves as a sense of inferiority and guilt. In this way, goaded on by the id, hemmed in by the super-ego, and rebuffed by reality, the ego struggles to cope with its economic task of reducing the forces and influences which work in it and upon it to some kind of harmony; and we may well understand how it is that we so often cannot repress the cry: "Life is not easy." When the ego is forced to acknowledge its weakness, it breaks out into anxiety: reality anxiety in face of the external world, normal anxiety in face of the super-ego, and neurotic anxiety in face of the strength of the passions in the id.

I have represented the structural relations within the mental personality, as I have explained them to you, in a simple diagram, which I here reproduce.

You will observe how the super-ego goes down into the id; as the heir to the Oedipus complex it has, after all, intimate connections with the id. It lies further from the perceptual system than the ego. The id only deals with the external world through the medium of the ego, at least in this diagram. It is certainly still too early to say how far the drawing is correct; in one respect I know it is not. The space taken up by the unconscious id ought to be incomparably greater than that given to the ego or to the preconscious. You must, if you please, correct that in your imagination.

And now, in concluding this certainly rather exhausting and perhaps not very illuminating account, I must add a warning. When you think of this dividing up of the personality into ego, super-ego and id, you must not imagine sharp dividing lines such as are artificially drawn in the field of political geography. We cannot do justice to the characteristics of the mind by means of linear contours, such as occur in a drawing or in a primitive painting, but we need rather the areas of colour shading off into one another that are to be found in modern pictures. After we have made our separations, we must allow what we have separated to merge again. Do not judge too harshly of a first attempt at picturing a thing so elusive as the human mind. It is very probable that the extent of these differentiations varies very greatly from person to person; it is possible that their function itself may vary, and that they may at times undergo a process of involution. This seems to be particularly true of the most insecure and, from the phylogenetic point of view, the most recent of them, the differentiation between the ego and the super-ego. It is also incontestable that the same thing can come about as a result of

mental disease. It can easily be imagined, too, that certain practices of mystics may succeed in upsetting the normal relations between the different regions of the mind, so that, for example, the perceptual system becomes able to grasp relations in the deeper layers of the ego and in the id which would otherwise be inaccessible to it. Whether such a procedure can put one in possession of ultimate truths, from which all good will flow, may be safely doubted. All the same, we must admit that the therapeutic efforts of psycho-analysis have chosen much the same method of approach. For their object is to strengthen the ego, to make it more independent of the super-ego, to widen its field of vision, and so to extend its organisation that it can take over new portions of the id. Where id was, there shall ego be.

It is reclamation work, like the draining of the Zuyder Zee.

SIGMUND FREUD

The Instincts

[LIBIDO AND THE DEATH INSTINCT]

The power of the id expresses the true purpose of the individual organism's life. This consists in the satisfaction of its innate needs. No such purpose as that of keeping itself alive or of protecting itself from dangers by means of anxiety can be attributed to the id. That is the business of the ego, which is also concerned with discovering the most favorable and least perilous method of obtaining satisfaction, taking the external world into account. The superego may bring fresh needs to the fore, but its chief function remains the *limitation* of satisfactions.

The forces which we assume to exist behind the tensions caused by the needs of the id are called instincts. They represent the somatic demands upon mental life. Though they are the ultimate cause of all activity, they are by nature conservative; the state, whatever it may be, which a living thing has reached, gives rise to a tendency to re-establish that state so soon as it has been abandoned. It is possible to distinguish an indeterminate number of instincts and in common practice this in in fact done. For us, however, the important question arises whether we may not be able to derive all of these various instincts from a few fundamental ones. We have found that instincts can change their aim (by displacement) and also that they can replace one another—the energy of one instinct passing over to another. This latter process is still insufficiently understood. After long doubts and vacillations we have decided to assume the existence of only two basic instincts, *Eros* and *the destructive instinct*. (The contrast between the instincts of self-preservation and of the preservation of the species, as well as the contrast between ego-love and object-love, fall within the bounds of Eros.) The aim of the first of these basic instincts is to establish ever greater unities and to preserve them thus—in short, to bind together; the aim of the second, on the contrary, is to undo connections and so to destroy things. We may suppose that the final aim of the destructive instinct is to reduce living things to an inorganic state. For this reason we also call it the *death instinct*. If we suppose that living things appeared later than inanimate ones and arose out of them, then the death instinct agrees with the formula that we have stated, to the effect that instincts tend toward a return to an earlier state. We are unable to apply the formula to Eros (the love instinct). That would be to imply that living substance had once been a unity but had subsequently been torn apart and was now tending toward re-union.[1]

In biological functions the two basic instincts work against each other or combine with each other. Thus, the act of eating is a destruction of the object with the final aim of incorporating it, and the sexual act is an act of aggression having as its purpose the most intimate union. This interaction of the two basic instincts with and against each other gives rise to the whole variegation of the phenomena of life. The analogy of our two basic instincts extends from the region of animate things to the pair of opposing forces—attraction and repulsion—which rule in the inorganic world.[2]

Modifications in the proportions of the fusion between the instincts have the most noticeable results. A surplus of sexual aggressiveness will change a lover into a sexual murderer, while a sharp diminution in the aggressive factor will lead to shyness or impotence.

There can be no question of restricting one or the other of the basic instincts to a single region of the mind. They are necessarily present everywhere. We may picture an initial state of things by supposing that the whole available energy of Eros, to which we shall henceforward give the name of *libido*, is present in the as yet undifferentiated ego-id and serves to neutralize the destructive impulses which are simultaneously present. (There is no term analogous to "libido" for describing the energy of the destructive instinct.) It becomes relatively easy for us to follow the later vicissitudes of the libido; but this is more difficult with the destructive instinct.

So long as that instinct operates internally, as a death instinct, it remains silent; we only come across it after it has become diverted outward as an instinct of destruction. That that diversion should occur seems essential for the preservation of the individual; the musculature is employed for the purpose. When the superego begins to be formed, considerable amounts of the aggressive instinct become fixated within the ego and operate there in a self-destructive fashion. This is one of the dangers to health to which mankind become subject on the path to cultural development. The holding back of aggressiveness is in general unhealthy and leads to illness. A person in a fit of rage often demonstrates how the transition from restrained aggressiveness to self-destructiveness is effected, by turning his aggressiveness against himself: he tears his hair or beats his face with his fists—treatment which he would evidently have preferred to apply to someone else. Some portion of self-destructiveness remains permanently within, until it at length succeeds in doing the individual to death, not, perhaps, until his libido has been used up or has become fixated in some disadvantageous way. Thus it may in general be suspected that the *individual* dies of his internal conflicts but that the *species* dies of its unsuccessful struggle against the external world, when the latter undergoes changes of a kind that cannot be dealt with by the adaptations which the species has acquired.

It is difficult to say anything of the behavior of the libido in the id and in the

---

[1] Something of the sort has been imagined by poets, but nothing like it is known to us from the actual history of living substance. AUTHOR'S NOTE.

[2] This picture of the basic forces or instincts, which still arouses much opposition among analysts, was already a familiar one to the philosopher Empedocles of Acragas. AUTHOR'S NOTE.

superego. Everything that we know about it relates to the ego, in which the whole available amount of libido is at first stored up. We call this state of things absolute, primary *narcissism*. It continues until the ego begins to cathect[3] the presentation of objects with libido—to change narcissistic libido into *object libido*. Throughout life the ego remains the great reservoir from which libidinal cathexes are sent out on to objects and into which they are also once more withdrawn, like the pseudopodia of a body of protoplasm. It is only when someone is completely in love that the main quantity of libido is transferred on to the object and the object to some extent takes the place of the ego. A characteristic of libido which is important in life is its *mobility*, the ease with which it passes from one object to another. This must be contrasted with the *fixation* of libido to particular objects, which often persists through life.

There can be no question that the libido has somatic sources, that it streams into the ego from various organs and parts of the body. This is most clearly seen in the case of the portion of the libido which, from its instinctual aim, is known as sexual excitation. The most prominent of the parts of the body from which this libido arises are described by the name of *erotogenic zones*, though strictly speaking the whole body is an erotogenic zone. The greater part of what we know about Eros—that is, about its exponent, the libido—has been gained from the study of the sexual function, which, indeed, in the popular view, if not in our theory, coincides with Eros. We have been able to form a picture of the way in which the sexual impulse, which is destined to exercise a decisive influence on our life, gradually develops out of successive contributions from a number of component instincts, which represent particular erotogenic zones.

[LIBIDO]

Libido is an expression taken from the theory of the emotions. We call by that name the energy, regarded as a quantitative magnitude (though not at present actually measurable), of those instincts which have to do with all that may be comprised under the word "love." The nucleus of what we mean by love naturally consists (and this is what is commonly called love, and what the poets sing of) in sexual love with sexual union as its aim. But we do not separate from this—what in any case has a share in the name "love"—on the one hand, self-love, and on the other, love for parents and children, friendship and love for humanity in general, and also devotion to concrete objects and to abstract ideas. Our justification lies in the fact that psycho-analytic research has taught us that all these tendencies are an expression of the same instinctual impulses; in relations between the sexes these impulses force their way towards sexual union, but in other circumstances they are diverted from this aim or are prevented from reaching it, though always preserving enough of their original nature to keep their identity recognizable (as in such features as the longing for proximity, and self-sacrifice).

We are of opinion, then, that language has carried out an entirely justifiable

---

[3] The words "cathexis" and "to cathect" are used as renderings of the German "*Besetzung*" and "*besetzen*." These are the terms with which Freud expresses the idea of psychical energy being lodged in or attaching itself to mental structures or processes, somewhat on the analogy of an electric charge. TRANSLATOR'S NOTE.

piece of unification in creating the word "love" with its numerous uses, and that we cannot do better than take it as the basis of our scientific discussions and ex- positions as well. By coming to this decision, psycho-analysis has let loose a storm of indignation, as though it had been guilty of an act of outrageous innovation. Yet it has done nothing original in taking love in this "wider" sense. In its origin, function, and relation to sexual love, the "Eros" of the philosopher Plato coin- cides exactly with the love-force, the libido of psycho-analysis, as has been shown in detail by Nachmansohn (1915) and Pfister (1921); and when the apostle Paul, in his famous epistle to the Corinthians, praises love above all else, he certainly understands it in the same "wider" sense. But this only shows that men do not always take their great thinkers seriously, even when they profess most to admire them.

Psycho-analysis, then, gives these love instincts the name of sexual instincts, *a potiori* and by reason of their origin. The majority of "educated" people have regarded this nomenclature as an insult, and have taken their revenge by retorting upon psycho-analysis with the reproach of "pan-sexualism." Anyone who con- siders sex as something mortifying and humiliating to human nature is at liberty to make use of the more genteel expressions "Eros" and "erotic." I might have done so myself from the first and thus have spared myself much opposition. But I did not want to, for I like to avoid concessions to faintheartedness. One can never tell where that road may lead one; one gives way first in words, and then little by little in substance too. I cannot see any merit in being ashamed of sex; the Greek word "Eros," which is to soften the affront, is in the end nothing more than a translation of our German word *Liebe* [love]; and finally, he who knows how to wait need make no concessions.

[THE CONSERVATIVE NATURE OF INSTINCT]

At this point we cannot escape a suspicion that we may have come upon the track of a universal attribute of instincts and perhaps of organic life in general which has not hitherto been clearly recognized or at least not explicitly stressed. *It seems, then, that an instinct is an urge inherent in organic life to restore an earlier state of things* which the living entity has been obliged to abandon under the pressure of external disturbing forces; that is, it is a kind of organic elasticity, or, to put it another way, the expression of the inertia inherent in organic life.

This view of instincts strikes us as strange because we have become used to see in them a factor impelling towards change and development, whereas we are now asked to recognize in them the precise contrary—an expression of the *conservative* nature of living substance. On the other hand we soon call to mind examples from animal life which seem to confirm the view that instincts are historically deter- mined. Certain fishes, for instance, undertake laborious migrations at spawning- time in order to deposit their spawn in particular waters far removed from their customary haunts. In the opinion of many biologists what they are doing is merely to seek out the localities in which their species formerly resided but which in the course of time they have exchanged for others. The same explanation is believed to apply to the migratory flights of birds of passage—but we are quickly relieved of the necessity for seeking for further examples by the reflection that the most impressive proofs of there being an organic compulsion to repeat lie in the phenomena of heredity and the facts of embryology. We see how the germ of a living animal is obliged in the course of its development to recapitulate (even if only in a transient and abbreviated fashion) the structures of all the forms from which it is sprung, instead of proceeding quickly by the shortest path to its final shape. This behaviour is only to a very slight degree attributable to mechanical causes, and the historical explanation cannot accordingly be neglected. So too the power of regenerating a lost organ by growing afresh a precisely similar one extends far up into the animal kingdom.

We shall be met by the plausible objection that it may very well be that, in addition to the conservative instincts which impel towards repetition, there may be others which push forward towards progress and the production of new forms. This argument must certainly not be overlooked, and it will be taken into account at a later stage. But for the moment it is tempting to pursue to its logical conclusion the hypothesis that all instincts tend towards the restoration of an earlier state of things. The outcome may give an impression of mysticism or of sham profundity; but we can feel quite innocent of having had any such purpose in view. We seek only for the sober results of research or of reflection based on it; and we have no wish to find in those results any quality other than certainty.[4]

Let us suppose, then, that all the organic instincts are conservative, are acquired historically and tend towards the restoration of an earlier state of things. It follows that the phenomena of organic development must be attributed to external disturbing and diverting influences. The elementary living entity would from its very beginning have had no wish to change; if conditions remained the same, it would do no more than constantly repeat the same course of life. In the last resort, what has left its mark on the development of organisms must be the history of the earth we live in and of its relation to the sun. Every modification which is thus imposed upon the course of the organism's life is accepted by the conservative organic instincts and stored up for further repetition. Those instincts are therefore bound to give a deceptive appearance of being forces tending towards change and progress, whilst in fact they are merely seeking to reach an ancient goal by paths alike old and new. Moreover it is possible to specify this final goal of all organic striving. It would be in contradiction to the conservative nature of the instincts if the goal of life were a state of things which had never yet been attained. On the contrary, it must be an *old* state of things, an initial state from which the living entity has at one time or other departed and to which it is striving to return by the circuitous paths along which its development leads. If we are to take it as a truth that knows no exception that everything living dies for *internal* reasons—becomes inorganic once again—then we shall be compelled to say that "*the aim of all life is death*" and, looking backwards, that "*inanimate things existed before living ones.*"

The attributes of life were at some time evoked in inanimate matter by the action of a force of whose nature we can form no conception. It may perhaps have been a process similar in type to that which later caused the development of consciousness in a particular stratum of living matter. The tension which then arose

[4] The reader should not overlook the fact that what follows is the development of an extreme line of thought. Later on, when account is taken of the sexual instincts, it will be found that the necessary limitations and corrections are applied to it. AUTHOR'S NOTE.

in what had hitherto been an inanimate substance endeavoured to cancel itself out. In this way the first instinct came into being: the instinct to return to the inanimate state. It was still an easy matter at that time for a living substance to die; the course of its life was probably only a brief one, whose direction was determined by the chemical structure of the young life. For a long time, perhaps, living substance was thus being constantly created afresh and easily dying, till decisive external influences altered in such a way as to oblige the still surviving substance to diverge ever more widely from its original course of life and to make ever more complicated *détours* before reaching its aim of death. These circuitous paths to death, faithfully kept to by the conservative instincts, would thus present us today with the picture of the phenomena of life. If we firmly maintain the exclusively conservative nature of instincts, we cannot arrive at any other notions as to the origin and aim of life.

The implications in regard to the great groups of instincts which, as we believe, lie behind the phenomena of life in organisms must appear no less bewildering. The hypothesis of self-preservative instincts, such as we attribute to all living beings, stands in marked opposition to the idea that instinctual life as a whole serves to bring about death. Seen in this light, the theoretical importance of the instincts of self-preservation, of self-assertion and of mastery greatly diminishes. They are component instincts whose function it is to assure that the organism shall follow its own path to death, and to ward off any possible ways of returning to inorganic existence other than those which are immanent in the organism itself. We have no longer to reckon with the organism's puzzling determination (so hard to fit into any context) to maintain its own existence in the face of every obstacle. What we are left with is the fact that the organism wishes to die only in its own fashion. Thus these guardians of life, too, were originally the myrmidons of death. Hence arises the paradoxical situation that the living organism struggles most energetically against events (dangers, in fact) which might help it to attain its life's aim rapidly—by a kind of short-circuit. Such behaviour is, however, precisely what characterizes purely instinctual as contrasted with intelligent efforts.

But let us pause for a moment and reflect. It cannot be so. The sexual instincts, to which the theory of the neuroses gives a quite special place, appear under a very different aspect.

The external pressure which provokes a constantly increasing extent of development has not imposed itself upon *every* organism. Many have succeeded in remaining up to the present time at their lowly level. Many, though not all, such creatures, which must resemble the earliest stages of the higher animals and plants, are, indeed, living today. In the same way, the whole path of development to natural death is not trodden by *all* the elementary entities which compose the complicated body of one of the higher organisms. Some of them, the germ-cells, probably retain the original structure of living matter and, after a certain time, with their full complement of inherited and freshly acquired instinctual dispositions, separate themselves from the organism as a whole. These two characteristics may be precisely what enables them to have an independent existence. Under favourable conditions, they begin to develop—that is, to repeat the performance to which they owe their existence; and in the end once again one portion of their substance pursues its development to a finish, while another portion harks back once again as a fresh residual germ to the beginning of the process of development. These germ-cells, therefore, work against the death of the living substance and succeed in winning for it what we can only regard as potential immortality, though that may mean no more than a lengthening of the road to death. We must regard as in the highest degree significant the fact that this function of the germ-cell is reinforced, or only made possible, if it coalesces with another cell similar to itself and yet differing from it.

The instincts which watch over the destinies of these elementary organisms that survive the whole individual, which provide them with a safe shelter while they are defenceless against the stimuli of the external world, which bring about their meeting with other germ-cells, and so on—these constitute the group of the sexual instincts. They are conservative in the same sense as the other instincts in that they bring back earlier states of living substance; but they are conservative to a higher degree in that they are peculiarly resistant to external influences; and they are conservative too in another sense in that they preserve life itself for a comparatively long period. They are the true life instincts. They operate against the purpose of the other instincts, which leads, by reason of their function, to death; and this fact indicates that there is an opposition between them and the other instincts, an opposition whose importance was long ago recognized by the theory of the neuroses. It is as though the life of the organism moved with a vacillating rhythm. One group of instincts rushes forward so as to reach the final aim of life as swiftly as possible; but when a particular stage in the advance has been reached, the other group jerks back to a certain point to make a fresh start and so prolong the journey. And even though it is certain that sexuality and the distinction between the sexes did not exist when life began, the possibility remains that the instincts which were later to be described as sexual may have been in operation from the very first, and it may not be true that it was only at a later time that they started upon their work of opposing the activities of the "ego instincts."

Let us now hark back for a moment ourselves and consider whether there is any basis at all for these speculations. Is it really the case that, *apart from the sexual instincts*, there are no instincts that do not seek to restore an earlier state of things? that there are none that aim at a state of things which has never yet been attained? I know of no certain example from the organic world that would contradict the characterization I have thus proposed. There is unquestionably no universal instinct towards higher development observable in the animal or plant world, even though it is undeniable that development does in fact occur in that direction. But on the one hand it is often merely a matter of opinion when we declare that one stage of development is higher than another, and on the other hand biology teaches us that higher development in one respect is very frequently balanced or outweighed by involution in another. Moreover there are plenty of animal forms from whose early stages we can infer that their development has, on the contrary, assumed a retrograde character. Both higher development and involution might well be the consequences of adaptation to the pressure of external forces; and in both cases the part played by instincts might be limited to the retention (in the form of an internal source of pleasure) of an obligatory modification.

It may be difficult, too, for many of us, to abandon the belief that there is an instinct towards perfection at work in human beings, which has brought them to their present high level of intellectual achievement and ethical sublimation and which may be expected to watch over their development into supermen. I have no faith, however, in the existence of any such internal instinct and I cannot see how this benevolent illusion is to be preserved. The present development of human beings requires, as it seems to me, no different explanation from that of animals. What appears in a minority of human individuals as an untiring impulsion towards further perfection can easily be understood as a result of the instinctual repression upon which is based all that is most precious in human civilization. The repressed instinct never ceases to strive for complete satisfaction, which would consist in the repetition of a primary experience of satisfaction. No substitutive or reactive formations and no sublimations will suffice to remove the repressed instinct's persisting tension; and it is the difference in amount between the pleasure of satisfaction which is *demanded* and that which is actually *achieved* that provides the driving factor which will permit of no halting at any position attained, but, in the poet's words, "*ungebändigt immer vorwärts dringt.*" The backward path that leads to complete satisfaction is as a rule obstructed by the resistances which maintain the repressions. So there is no alternative but to advance in the direction in which growth is still free—though with no prospect of bringing the process to a conclusion or of being able to reach the goal.

SIGMUND FREUD

The Theory of Dreams

The condition of repose without stimuli, which the state of sleep attempts to bring about, is threatened from three sides: in a chance fashion by external stimuli during sleep, by interests of the day before which have not yet abated and, in an unavoidable manner, by the unsatisfied repressed impulses, which are ready to seize on any opportunity for expression. On account of the nightly reduction of the repressive forces, the risk is run that the repose of sleep will be broken every time the outer and inner disturbances manage to link up with one of the unconscious sources of energy. The dream-process allows the result of such a combination to discharge itself through the channel of a harmless hallucinatory experience, and thus insures the continuity of sleep. There is no contradiction of this function in the fact that the dream sometimes wakes the sleeper in a state of anxiety; it is rather a sign that the watcher regards the situation as being too dangerous and no longer thinks he can cope with it. Quite often, indeed, while we are still asleep, we are aware of the comforting thought, which is there to prevent our waking up: "after all, it is only a dream." . . .

From *New Introductory Lectures on Psychoanalysis* [1933], translated from the German by W. J. H. Sprott, New York, 1933, pp. 28-9, 29-35, 43-5. Copyright 1933 by Sigmund Freud; copyright renewed © 1961 by W. J. H. Sprott; reprinted by permission of W. W. Norton & Co., Inc.

The process of dream-work is something quite new and strange, the like of which has never before been known. It has given us our first glimpse into those processes which go on in our unconscious mental system, and shows us that they are quite different from what we know about our conscious thought, and that to this latter they must necessarily appear faulty and preposterous. The importance of this discovery is increased when we realise that the same mechanisms—we hardly dare call them "thought processes"—are at work in the formation of neurotic symptoms as have turned the latent dream-thoughts into the manifest dream.

In what follows I cannot avoid making my exposition a schematic one. Supposing we have before us in a given instance all the latent thoughts, more or less affectively toned, which have taken the place of the manifest dream after a complete interpretation. We shall then notice a distinction among them, and this distinction will take us a long way. Almost all these dream-thoughts will be recognised or acknowledged by the dreamer; he will admit that he thought thus at one time or another, or that he might very well have done so. But he may resist the acceptation of one single thought, it is foreign to him, perhaps even repellent; it may be that he will passionately repudiate it. Now it becomes clear to us that the other thoughts are bits of his conscious, or, more correctly, of his pre-conscious thought; they might very well have been thought during waking life, and have probably formed themselves during the day. This one rejected thought, or, better, this one impulse, is a child of the night; it belongs to the unconscious of the dreamer, and is therefore disowned and repudiated by him. It had to await the nightly relaxation of repression in order to achieve any sort of expression. In any case the expression that it obtains is enfeebled, distorted and disguised; without the work of interpretation we should never have discovered it. It is thanks to its connection with the other unobjectionable dream-thoughts that this unconscious impulse has had the opportunity of slipping past the barrier of the censorship in an unostentatious disguise; on the other hand, the pre-conscious dream-thoughts owe to the same connection their power of occupying the mental life, even during sleep. We can, indeed, have no doubt about this: the unconscious impulse is the real creator of the dream, it provides the psychic energy required for its formation. Just like any other instinctual impulse it can do no other than seek its own satisfaction, and our experience in dream-interpretation shows us, moreover, that this is the meaning of all dreaming. In every dream an instinctual wish is displayed as fulfilled. The nightly cutting-off of mental life from reality, and the regression to primitive mechanisms which it makes possible, enable this desired instinctual satisfaction to be experienced in a hallucinatory fashion as actually happening. On account of the same process of regression ideas are turned into visual pictures in the dream; the latent dream-thoughts are, that is to say, dramatized and illustrated.

From this piece of dream-work we obtain information about some of the most striking and peculiar characteristics of the dream. Let me repeat the stages of dream-formation. The introduction: the wish to sleep, the voluntary withdrawal from the outside world. Two things follow from this: firstly, the possibility for older and more primitive modes of activity to manifest themselves, i.e. regression; and secondly, the decrease of the repression-resistance which weighs on the unconscious. As a result of this latter feature an opportunity for dream-formation presents itself, which is seized upon by the factors which are the occasion of the dream; that is to say, the internal and external stimuli which are in activity. The dream which thus eventuates is already a compromise-formation; it has a double function: it is on the one hand in conformity with the ego ("ego-syntonic"), since it subserves the wish to sleep by draining off the stimuli which would otherwise disturb it, while on the other hand it allows to a repressed impulse the satisfaction which is possible in these circumstances in the form of an hallucinatory wish-fulfilment. The whole process of dream-formation, which is permitted by the sleeping ego, is, however, under the control of the censorship, a control which is exercised by what is left of the forces of repression. I cannot explain the process more simply; it is not in itself simpler than that. But now I can proceed with the description of the dream-work.

Let us go back once more to the latent dream-thoughts. Their dominating element is the repressed impulse, which has obtained some kind of expression, toned down and disguised though it may be, by associating itself with stimuli which happen to be there and by tacking itself on the residue of the day before. Just like any other impulse this one presses forward toward satisfaction in action, but the path to motor discharge is closed to it on account of the physiological characteristics of the state of sleep, and so it is forced to travel in the retrograde direction to perception, and content itself with an hallucinatory satisfaction. The latent dream-thoughts are therefore turned into a collection of sensory images and visual scenes. As they are travelling in this direction something happens to them which seems to us new and bewildering. All the verbal apparatus by means of which the more subtle thought-relations are expressed, the conjunctions and prepositions, the variations of declension and conjugation, are lacking, because the means of portraying them are absent: just as in primitive, grammarless speech, only the raw material of thought can be expressed, and the abstract is merged again in the concrete from which it sprang. What is left over may very well seem to lack coherence. It is as much the result of the archaic regression in the mental apparatus as of the demands of the censorship that so much use is made of the representation of certain objects and processes by means of symbols which have become strange to conscious thought. But of more far-reaching import are the other alterations to which the elements comprising the dream-thoughts are subjected. Such of them as have any point of contact are *condensed* into new unities. When the thoughts are translated into pictures those forms are indubitably preferred which allow of this kind of telescoping, or condensation; it is as though a force were at work which subjected the material to a process of pressure or squeezing together. As a result of condensation one element in a manifest dream may correspond to a number of elements of the dream-thoughts; but conversely one of the elements from among the dream-thoughts may be represented by a number of pictures in the dream.

Even more remarkable is the other process of *displacement* or transference of accent, which in conscious thinking figures only as an error in thought or as a method employed in jokes. For the individual ideas which make up the dream-thoughts are not all of equal value; they have various degrees of affective-tone attached to them, and corresponding to these, they are judged as more or less important, and more or less worthy of attention. In the dream-work these ideas are separated from their affects; the affects are treated separately. They may be transferred to something else, they may remain where they were, they may undergo transformation, or they may disappear from the dream entirely. The importance of the ideas which have been shorn of their affect, reappears in the dream in the form of the sensuous vividness of the dream-pictures; but we notice that this accent, which should lie on important elements, has been transferred to unimportant ones, so that what seems to be pushed to the forefront in the dream, as the most important element in it, only plays a subsidiary role in the dream-thoughts, and conversely, what is important among the dream-thoughts obtains only incidental and rather indistinct representation in the dream. No other factor in the dream-work plays such an important part in rendering the dream strange and unintelligible to the dreamer. Displacement is the chief method employed in the process of *dream-distortion*, which the dream-thoughts have to undergo under the influence of the censorship.

After these operations on the dream-thoughts the dream is almost ready. There is still, however, a more or less non-constant factor, the so-called secondary elaboration, that makes its appearance after the dream has come into consciousness as an object of perception. When the dream has come into consciousness, we treat it in exactly the same way that we treat any content of perception; we try to fill in the gaps, we add connecting links, and often enough we let ourselves in for serious misunderstandings. But this, as it were, rationalizing activity, which at its best provides the dream with a smooth façade, such as cannot correspond to its real content, may be altogether absent in some cases, or only operate in a very feeble way, in which case the dream displays to view all its gaps and inconsistencies. On the other hand, one must not forget that the dream-work too does not always function with equal force; quite often it limits its activity to certain parts of the dream-thoughts, while others are allowed to come into the dream unaltered. In this event one has the impression that one has carried out the most complicated and subtle intellectual operations during the dream, that one has made brilliant speculations or jokes, or that one has come to decisions or solved problems; really, however, all this is the result of our normal mental activity, and may just as well have happened during the day before the dream as during the night. It has nothing to do with the dream-work, nor does it display any feature which is characteristic of dreams. It is perhaps not superfluous once more to emphasise the distinction which subsists among the dream-thoughts themselves, between the unconscious impulse and the residues of the preceding day. While the latter exhibit the whole variety of our mental activity, the former, which is the real motive force of the dream, always finds its outlet in a wish-fulfilment. . . .

Only two serious difficulties face the wish-fulfilment theory of dreams, the examination of which leads us far afield and for which we have found no completely satisfactory solution. The first difficulty is presented by the fact that people who have had severe shocks or who have gone through serious psychic traumas (such as were frequent during the war, and are also found to lie at the back of traumatic hysteria) are continually being put back into the traumatic situation in dreams. According to our acceptation of the function of dreams, this ought not to be the case. What conative impulse could possibly be satisfied by this reinstatement of a most painful traumatic experience? It is indeed hard to guess. We meet with the second fact almost daily in our analytical work; it does not involve such a serious objection as the other. You know that it is one of the tasks of psycho-analysis to lift the veil of amnesia which shrouds the earliest years of childhood and to bring the expressions of infantile sexual life which are hidden behind it into conscious memory. Now these first sexual experiences of the child are bound up with painful impressions of anxiety, prohibition, disappointment and punishment. One can understand why they have been repressed; but, if so, it is difficult to see why they should have such easy access to dream-life, why they should provide the pattern for so many dream-phantasies, and why dreams are full of reproductions of these infantile scenes and allusions to them. The pain that attaches to them, and the wish-fulfilling tendency of the dream-work would seem to be incompatible. But perhaps in this case we exaggerate the difficulty. All the imperishable and unrealisable desires which provide the energy for the formation of dreams throughout one's whole life are bound up with these same childish experiences, and one can well trust to their ability with their powerful upward thrust to force even material of a painful nature to the surface. And, on the other hand, in the manner in which this material is reproduced the efforts of the dream-work are unmistakable; it disowns pain by means of distortion and turns disappointment into fulfilment. In the case of the traumatic neuroses it is quite different; here the dream habitually ends in anxiety. In my opinion we ought not to shirk the admission that in such cases the function of the dream fails. I will not have recourse to the saying that the exception proves the rule; the validity of this phrase seems to me very dubious. But at any rate the exception does not do away with the rule. If for the purposes of investigation one isolates from every other mental process a single psychic activity like the dream, one is enabled to discover the laws which govern it; if one then puts it back into its place, one must be prepared to find that one's discoveries are obscured and interfered with when they come into contact with other forces. We assert that the dream is a wish-fulfilment; in order to take these last objections into account, you may say that the dream is an *attempted* wish-fulfilment. But for those who have an understanding for the dynamics of the mind you will not be saying anything different. Under certain conditions the dream can only achieve its end in a very incomplete way, or has to abandon it entirely; an unconscious fixation to the trauma seems to head the list of these obstacles to the dream-function. The sleeper has to dream, because the nightly relaxation of repression allows the upward thrust of the traumatic fixation to become active; but sometimes his dream-work, which endeavours to change the memory traces of the traumatic event into a wish-fulfilment, fails to operate.

SIGMUND FREUD

The Oedipus Complex

We speak of "love" when we lay the accent upon the mental side of the sexual impulses and disregard, or wish to forget for a moment, the demands of the fundamental physical or "sensual" side of the impulses. At about the time when the mother becomes the love-object, the mental operation of repression has already begun in the child and has withdrawn from him the knowledge of some part of his sexual aims. Now with this choice of the mother as love-object is connected all that which, under the name of *"the Oedipus complex,"* has become of such great importance in the psycho-analytic explanation of the neuroses, and which has had a perhaps equally important share in causing the opposition against psycho-analysis. . . .

You all know the Greek myth of King Oedipus, whose destiny it was to slay his father and to wed his mother, who did all in his power to avoid the fate prophesied by the oracle, and who in self-punishment blinded himself when he discovered that in ignorance he had committed both these crimes. I trust that many of you have yourselves experienced the profound effect of the tragic drama fashioned by Sophocles from this story. The Attic poet's work portrays the gradual discovery of the deed of Oedipus, long since accomplished, and brings it slowly to light by skilfully prolonged enquiry, constantly fed by new evidence; it has thus a certain resemblance to the course of a psycho-analysis. In the dialogue the deluded mother-wife, Jocasta, resists the continuation of the enquiry; she points out that many people in their dreams have mated with their mothers, but that dreams are of no account. To us dreams are of much account, especially typical dreams which occur in many people; we have no doubt that the dream Jocasta speaks of is intimately related to the shocking and terrible story of the myth.

It is surprising that Sophocles' tragedy does not call forth indignant remonstrance in its audience. . . . For at bottom it is an immoral play; it sets aside the individual's responsibility to social law, and displays divine forces ordaining the crime and rendering powerless the moral instincts of the human being which would guard him against the crime. It would be easy to believe that an accusation against destiny and the gods was intended in the story of the myth; in the hands of the critical Euripides, at variance with the gods, it would probably have become such an accusation. But with the reverent Sophocles there is no question of such an intention; the pious subtlety which declares it the highest morality to bow to the will of the gods, even when they ordain a crime, helps him out of the difficulty. I do not believe that this moral is one of the virtues of the drama, but neither does it detract from its effect; it leaves the hearer indifferent; he does not react to this, but to the secret meaning and content of the myth itself. He reacts as though by self-analysis he had detected the Oedipus complex in himself, and had recognized the will of the gods and the oracle as glorified disguises of his own unconscious; as though he remembered in himself the wish to do away with his

From *General Introduction to Psychoanalysis* [1916], translated from the German by Joan Riviere, New York, 1924, pp. 289, 290-96. Copyright © 1963 by Joan Riviere. Reprinted by permission of Liveright Publishers, New York, and George Allen & Unwin Ltd.

father and in his place to wed his mother, and must abhor the thought. The poet's words seem to him to mean: "In vain do you deny that you are accountable, in vain do you proclaim how you have striven against these evil designs. You are guilty, nevertheless; for you could not stifle them; they still survive unconsciously in you." And psychological truth is contained in this; even though man has repressed his evil desires into his Unconscious and would then gladly say to himself that he is no longer answerable for them, he is yet compelled to feel his responsibility in the form of a sense of guilt for which he can discern no foundation.

There is no possible doubt that one of the most important sources of the sense of guilt which so often torments neurotic people is to be found in the Oedipus complex. More than this: in 1913, under the title of *Totem und Tabu*, I published a study of the earliest forms of religion and morality in which I expressed a suspicion that perhaps the sense of guilt of mankind as a whole, which is the ultimate source of religion and morality, was acquired in the beginnings of history through the Oedipus complex. I should much like to tell you more of this, but I had better not; it is difficult to leave this subject when once one begins upon it, and we must return to individual psychology.

Now what does direct observation of children, at the period of object-choice before the latency period, show us in regard to the Oedipus complex? Well, it is easy to see that the little man wants his mother all to himself, finds his father in the way, becomes restive when the latter takes upon himself to caress her, and shows his satisfaction when the father goes away or is absent. He often expresses his feelings directly in words and promises his mother to marry her; this may not seem much in comparison with the deeds of Oedipus, but it is enough in fact; the kernel of each is the same. Observation is often rendered puzzling by the circumstance that the same child on other occasions at this period will display great affection for the father; but such contrasting—or, better, *ambivalent*—states of feeling, which in adults would lead to conflicts, can be tolerated alongside one another in the child for a long time, just as later on they dwell together permanently in the unconscious. One might try to object that the little boy's behaviour is due to egoistic motives and does not justify the conception of an erotic complex; the mother looks after all the child's needs and consequently it is to the child's interest that she should trouble herself about no one else. This too is quite correct; but it is soon clear that in this, as in similar dependent situations, egoistic interests only provide the occasion on which the erotic impulses seize. When the little boy shows the most open sexual curiosity about his mother, wants to sleep with her at night, insists on being in the room while she is dressing, or even attempts physical acts of seduction, as the mother so often observes and laughingly relates, the erotic nature of this attachment to her is established without a doubt. Moreover, it should not be forgotten that a mother looks after a little daughter's needs in the same way without producing this effect; and that often enough a father eagerly vies with her in trouble for the boy without succeeding in winning the same importance in his eyes as the mother. In short, the factor of sex preference is not to be eliminated from the situation by any criticisms. From the point of view of the boy's egoistic interests it would merely be foolish if he did not tolerate two people in his service rather than only one of them.

As you see, I have only described the relationship of a boy to his father and mother; things proceed in just the same way, with the necessary reversal, in little girls. The loving devotion to the father, the need to do away with the superfluous mother and to take her place, the early display of coquetry and the arts of later womanhood, make up a particularly charming picture in a little girl, and may cause us to forget its seriousness and the grave consequences which may later result from this situation. Let us not fail to add that frequently the parents themselves exert a decisive influence upon the awakening of the Oedipus complex in a child, by themselves following the sex attraction where there is more than one child; the father in an unmistakable manner prefers his little daughter with marks of tenderness, and the mother, the son: but even this factor does not seriously impugn the spontaneous nature of the infantile Oedipus complex. When other children appear, the Oedipus complex expands and becomes a family complex. Reinforced anew by the injury resulting the egoistic interests, it actuates a feeling of aversion towards these new arrivals and an unhesitating wish to get rid of them again. These feelings of hatred are as a rule much more often openly expressed than those connected with the parental complex. If such a wish is fulfilled and after a short time death removes the unwanted addition to the family, later analysis can show what a significant event this death is for the child, although it does not necessarily remain in memory. Forced into the second place by the birth of another child and for the first time almost entirely parted from the mother, the child finds it very hard to forgive her for this exclusion of him; feelings which in adults we should describe as profound embitterment are roused in him, and often become the ground-work of a lasting estrangement. That sexual curiosity and all its consequences is usually connected with these experiences has already been mentioned. As these new brothers and sisters grow up the child's attitude to them undergoes the most important transformations. A boy may take his sister as love-object in place of his faithless mother; where there are several brothers to win the favour of a little sister hostile rivalry, of great importance in after life, shows itself already in the nursery. A little girl takes an older brother as a substitute for the father who no longer treats her with the same tenderness as in her earliest years; or she takes a little sister as a substitute for the child that she vainly wished for from her father.

So much and a great deal more of a similar kind is shown by direct observation of children, and by consideration of clear memories of childhood, uninfluenced by any analysis. Among other things you will infer from this that a child's position in the sequence of brothers and sisters is of very great significance for the course of his later life, a factor to be considered in every biography. What is even more important, however, is that in the face of these enlightening considerations, so easily to be obtained, you will hardly recall without smiling the scientific theories accounting for the prohibition of incest. What has not been invented for this purpose! We are told that sexual attraction is diverted from the members of the opposite sex in one family owing to their living together from early childhood; or that a biological tendency against in-breeding has a mental equivalent in the horror of incest! Whereby it is entirely overlooked that no such rigorous prohibitions in law and custom would be required if any trustworthy natural barriers against the temptation to incest existed. The opposite is the truth. The first choice of object in mankind is regularly an incestuous one, directed to the mother and sister of men, and the most stringent prohibitions are required to prevent this sustained infantile tendency from being carried into effect. In the savage and primitive peoples surviving today the incest prohibitions are a great deal stricter than with us; Theodor Reik has recently shown in a brilliant work that the meaning of the savage rites of puberty which represent re-birth is the loosening of the boy's incestuous attachment to the mother and his reconciliation with the father.

Mythology will show you that incest, ostensibly so much abhorred by men, is permitted to their gods without a thought; and from ancient history you may learn that incestuous marriage with a sister was prescribed as a sacred duty for kings (the Pharaohs of Egypt and the Incas of Peru); it was therefore in the nature of a privilege denied to the common herd.

Incest with the mother is one of the crimes of Oedipus and parricide the other. Incidentally, these are the two great offences condemned by totemism, the first social-religious institution of mankind. Now let us turn from the direct observation of children to the analytic investigation of adults who have become neurotic; what does analysis yield in further knowledge of the Oedipus complex? Well, this is soon told. The complex is revealed just as the myth relates it; it will be seen that every one of these neurotics was himself an Oedipus or, what amounts to the same thing, has become a Hamlet in his reaction to the complex. To be sure, the analytic picture of the Oedipus complex is an enlarged and accentuated edition of the infantile sketch; the hatred of the father and the death-wishes against him are no longer vague hints, the affection for the mother declares itself with the aim of possessing her as a woman. Are we really to accredit such grossness and intensity of the feelings to the tender age of childhood; or does the analysis deceive us by introducing another factor? It is not difficult to find one. Every time anyone describes anything past, even if he be a historian, we have to take into account all that he unintentionally imports into that past period from present and intermediate times, thereby falsifying it. With the neurotic it is even doubtful whether this retroversion is altogether unintentional; we shall hear later on that there are motives for it and we must explore the whole subject of the "retrogressive phantasy-making" which goes back to the remote past. We soon discover, too, that the hatred against the father has been strengthened by a number of motives arising in later periods and other relationships in life, and that the sexual desires towards the mother have been moulded into forms which would have been as yet foreign to the child. But it would be a vain attempt if we endeavoured to explain the whole of the Oedipus complex by "retrogressive phantasy-making," and by motives originating in later periods of life. The infantile nucleus, with more or less of the accretions to it, remains intact, as is confirmed by direct observation of children.

The clinical fact which confronts us behind the form of the Oedipus complex as established by analysis now becomes of the greatest practical importance. We learn that at the time of puberty, when the sexual instinct first asserts its demands in full strength, the old familiar incestuous objects are taken up again and again invested by the libido. The infantile object-choice was but a feeble venture in play, as it were, but it laid down the direction for the object-choice of puberty. At this time a very intense flow of feeling towards the Oedipus complex or in reaction to it comes into force; since their mental antecedents have become intolerable, however, these feelings must remain for the most part outside consciousness. From the time of puberty onward the human individual must devote himself to the great task of *freeing himself from the parents*; and only after this detachment is accomplished can he cease to be a child and so become a member of the social community. For a son, the task consists in releasing his libidinal desires from his mother, in order to employ them in the quest of an external love-object in reality; and in reconciling himself with his father if he has remained antagonistic to him, or in freeing himself from his domination if, in the reaction to the infantile revolt, he has lapsed into subservience to him. These tasks are laid down for every man; it is noteworthy how seldom they are carried through ideally, that is, how seldom they are solved in a manner psychologically as well as socially satisfactory. In neurotics, however, this detachment from the parents is not accomplished at all; the son remains all his life in subjection to his father, and incapable of transferring his libido to a new sexual object. In the reversed relationship the daughter's fate may be the same. In this sense the Oedipus complex is justifiably regarded as the kernel of the neuroses.

You will imagine how incompletely I am sketching a large number of the connections bound up with the Oedipus complex which practically and theoretically are of great importance. I shall not go into the variations and possible inversions of it at all. Of its less immediate effects I should like to allude to one only, which proves it to have influenced literary production in a far-reaching manner. Otto Rank has shown in a very valuable work that dramatists throughout the ages have drawn their material principally from the Oedipus and incest complex and its variations and masked forms. It should also be remarked that long before the time of psycho-analysis the two criminal offences of Oedipus were recognized as the true expressions of unbridled instinct. Among the works of the Encyclopædist Diderot you will find the famous dialogue, *Le Neveu de Rameau*, which was translated into German by no less a person than Goethe. There you may read these remarkable words: *Si le petit sauvage était abandonné à lui-même, qu'il conserva toute son imbecillité et qu'il réunit au peu de raison de l'enfant au berceau la violence des passions de l'homme de trente ans, il tordrait le cou à son père et coucherait avec sa mère.*

There is yet one thing more which I cannot pass over. The mother-wife of Oedipus must not remind us of dreams in vain. Do you still remember the results of our dream-analyses, how so often the dream-forming wishes proved perverse and incestuous in their nature, or betrayed an unsuspected enmity to near and beloved relatives? We then left the source of these evil strivings of feeling unexplained. Now you can answer this question yourselves. They are dispositions of the libido, and investments of objects by libido, belonging to early infancy and long since given up in conscious life, but which at night prove to be still present and in a certain sense capable of activity. But, since all men and not only neurotic persons have perverse, incestuous, and murderous dreams of this kind, we may infer that those who are normal to-day have also made the passage through the perversions and the object-investments of the Oedipus complex; and that this is the path of normal development; only that neurotics show in a magnified and exaggerated form what we also find revealed in the dream-analyses of normal people.

The Origins of Culture

The development of civilization appears to us as a peculiar process which mankind undergoes, and in which several things strike us as familiar. We may characterize this process with reference to the changes which it brings about in the familiar instinctual dispositions of human beings, to satisfy which is, after all, the economic task of our lives. A few of these instincts are used up in such a manner that something appears in their place which, in an individual, we describe as a character-trait. The most remarkable example of such a process is found in the anal erotism of young human beings. Their original interest in the excretory function, its organs and products, is changed in the course of their growth into a group of traits which are familiar to us as parsimony, a sense of order and cleanliness—qualities which, though valuable and welcome in themselves, may be intensified till they become markedly dominant and produce what is called the anal character. How this happens we do not know, but there is no doubt about the correctness of the finding. Now we have seen that order and cleanliness are important requirements of civilization, although their vital necessity is not very apparent, any more than their suitability as sources of enjoyment. At this point we cannot fail to be struck by the similarity between the process of civilization and the libidinal development of the individual. Other instincts [besides anal erotism] are induced to displace the conditions for their satisfaction, to lead them into other paths. In most cases this process coincides with that of the *sublimation* (of instinctual aims) with which we are familiar, but in some it can be differentiated from it. Sublimation of instinct is an especially conspicuous feature of cultural development; it is what makes it possible for higher psychical activities, scientific, artistic or ideological, to play such an important part in civilized life. If one were to yield to a first impression, one would say that sublimation is a vicissitude which has been forced upon the instincts entirely by civilization. But it would be wiser to reflect upon this a little longer. . . . It is impossible to overlook the extent to which civilization is built up upon a renunciation of instinct, how much it presupposes precisely the non-satisfaction (by suppression, repression or some other means?) of powerful instincts. This "cultural frustration" dominates the large field of social relationships between human beings. As we already know, it is the cause of the hostility against which all civilizations have to struggle. It will also make severe demands on our scientific work, and we shall have much to explain here. . . .

The task seems an immense one, and it is natural to feel diffidence in the face of it. But here are such conjectures as I have been able to make.

After primal man had discovered that it lay in his own hands, literally, to improve his lot on earth by working, it cannot have been a matter of indifference to him whether another man worked with or against him. The other man ac-

From *Civilization and Its Discontents* [1930], translated from the German by James Strachey, in *The Standard Edition of the Complete Psychological Works of Sigmund Freud*, London, 1961, Vol. XXI, pp. 96-7, 99-101, 122, 123-4, 127-8, 131-3, 134. © 1961 by James Strachey, first American edition 1962. Reprinted by permission of the Hogarth Press Ltd. and W. W. Norton & Co., Inc.

quired the value for him of a fellow-worker, with whom it was useful to live together. Even earlier, in his ape-like prehistory, man had adopted the habit of
forming families, and the members of his family were probably his first helpers.
One may suppose that the founding of families was connected with the fact that
a moment came when the need for genital satisfaction no longer made its appearance like a guest who drops in suddenly, and, after his departure, is heard
of no more for a long time, but instead took up its quarters as a permanent
lodger. When this happened, the male acquired a motive for keeping the female,
or, speaking more generally, his sexual objects, near him; while the female, who
did not want to be separated from her helpless young, was obliged, in their interests, to remain with the stronger male. In this primitive family one essential
feature of civilization is still lacking. The arbitrary will of its head, the father, was
unrestricted. In *Totem and Taboo* [1912–13] I have tried to show how the way
led from this family to the succeeding stage of communal life in the form of
bands of brothers. In overpowering their father, the sons had made the discovery
that a combination can be stronger than a single individual. The totemic culture
is based on the restrictions which the sons had to impose on one another in order
to keep this new state of affairs in being. The taboo-observances were the first
"right" or "law." The communal life of human beings had, therefore, a two-fold
foundation: the compulsion to work, which was created by external necessity, and
the power of love, which made the man unwilling to be deprived of his sexual
object—the woman—and made the woman unwilling to be deprived of the part of
herself which had been separated off from her—her child. Eros and Ananke [Love
and Necessity] have become the parents of human civilization too. The first result
of civilization was that even a fairly large number of people were now able to
live together in a community. And since these two great powers were co-operating
in this, one might expect that the further development of civilization would proceed smoothly towards an even better control over the external world and towards
a further extension of the number of people included in the community. Nor is
it easy to understand how this civilization could act upon its participants otherwise than to make them happy. . . .

In all that follows I adopt the standpoint . . . that the inclination to aggression is an original, self-subsisting instinctual disposition in man, and . . .
that it constitutes the greatest impediment to civilization. At one point in the
course of this enquiry I was led to the idea that civilization was a special process
which mankind undergoes, and I am still under the influence of that idea. I may
now add that civilization is a process in the service of Eros, whose purpose is to
combine single human individuals, and after that families, then races, peoples
and nations, into one great unity, the unity of mankind. Why this has to happen,
we do not know; the work of Eros is precisely this. These collections of men are
to be libidinally bound to one another. Necessity alone, the advantages of work
in common, will not hold them together. But man's natural aggressive instinct,
the hostility of each against all and of all against each, opposes this programme of
civilization. This aggressive instinct is the derivative and the main representative
of the death instinct which we have found alongside of Eros and which shares
world-dominion with it. And now, I think, the meaning of the evolution of
civilization is no longer obscure to us. It must present the struggle between Eros
and Death, between the instinct of life and the instinct of destruction, as it

works itself out in the human species. This struggle is what all life essentially consists of, and the evolution of civilization may therefore be simply described as the struggle for life of the human species. And it is this battle of the giants that our nurse-maids try to appease with their lullaby about Heaven. . . .

What means does civilization employ in order to inhibit the aggressiveness which opposes it, to make it harmless, to get rid of it, perhaps? We have already become acquainted with a few of these methods, but not yet with the one that appears to be the most important. This we can study in the history of the development of the individual. What happens in him to render his desire for aggression innocuous? Something very remarkable, which we should never have guessed and which is nevertheless quite obvious. His aggressiveness is introjected, internalized; it is, in point of fact, sent back to where it came from—that is, it is directed towards his own ego. There it is taken over by a portion of the ego, which sets itself over against the rest of the ego as super-ego, and which now, in the form of "conscience," is ready to put into action against the ego the same harsh aggressiveness that the ego would have liked to satisfy upon other, extraneous individuals. The tension between the harsh super-ego and the ego that is subjected to it, is called by us the sense of guilt; it expresses itself as a need for punishment. Civilization, therefore, obtains mastery over the individual's dangerous desire for aggression by weakening and disarming it and by setting up an agency within him to watch over it, like a garrison in a conquered city. . . .

Thus we know of two origins of the sense of guilt: one arising from fear of an authority, and the other, later on, arising from fear of the super-ego. The first insists upon a renunciation of instinctual satisfactions; the second, as well as doing this, presses for punishment, since the continuance of the forbidden wishes cannot be concealed from the super-ego. We have also learned how the severity of the super-ego—the demands of conscience—is to be understood. It is simply a continuation of the severity of the external authority, to which it has succeeded and which it has in part replaced. We now see in what relationship the renunciation of instinct stands to the sense of guilt. Originally, renunciation of instinct was the result of fear of an external authority: one renounced one's satisfactions in order not to lose its love. If one has carried out this renunciation, one is, as it were, quits with the authority and no sense of guilt should remain. But with fear of the super-ego the case is different. Here, instinctual renunciation is not enough, for the wish persists and cannot be concealed from the super-ego. Thus, in spite of the renunciation that has been made, a sense of guilt comes about. This constitutes a great economic disadvantage in the erection of a super-ego, or, as we may put it, in the formation of a conscience. Instinctual renunciation now no longer has a completely liberating effect; virtuous continence is no longer rewarded with the assurance of love. A threatened external unhappiness—loss of love and punishment on the part of the external authority—has been exchanged for a permanent internal unhappiness, for the tension of the sense of guilt. . . .

We cannot get away from the assumption that man's sense of guilt springs from the Oedipus complex and was acquired at the killing of the father by the brothers banded together. On that occasion an act of aggression was not suppressed but carried out; but it was the same act of aggression whose suppression in the child is supposed to be the source of his sense of guilt. At that point I should not be surprised if the reader were to exclaim angrily: "So it makes no difference whether one kills one's father or not—one gets a feeling of guilt in either case! We may take leave to raise a few doubts here. Either it is not true that the sense of guilt comes from suppressed aggressiveness, or else the whole story of the killing of the father is a fiction and the children of primaeval man did not kill their fathers any more often than children do nowadays. Besides, if it is not fiction but a plausible piece of history, it would be a case of something happening which everyone expects to happen—namely, of a person feeling guilty because he really has done something which cannot be justified. And of this event, which is after all an everyday occurrence, psycho-analysis has not yet given any explanation."

That is true, and we must make good the omission. Nor is there any great secret about the matter. When one has a sense of guilt after having committed a misdeed, and because of it, the feeling should more properly be called *remorse*. It relates only to a deed that has been done, and, of course, it presupposes that a *conscience*—the readiness to feel guilty—was already in existence before the deed took place. Remorse of this sort can, therefore, never help us to discover the origin of conscience and of the sense of guilt in general. What happens in these everyday cases is usually this: an instinctual need acquires the strength to achieve satisfaction in spite of the conscience, which is, after all, limited in its strength; and with the natural weakening of the need owing to its having been satisfied, the former balance of power is restored. Psycho-analysis is thus justified in excluding from the present discussion the case of a sense of guilt due to remorse, however frequently such cases occur and however great their practical importance.

But if the human sense of guilt goes back to the killing of the primal father, that was after all a case of "remorse." Are we to assume that [at that time] a conscience and a sense of guilt were not, as we have presupposed, in existence before the deed? If not, where, in this case, did the remorse come from? There is no doubt that this case should explain the secret of the sense of guilt to us and put an end to our difficulties. And I believe it does. This remorse was the result of the primordial ambivalence of feeling towards the father. His sons hated him, but they loved him, too. After their hatred had been satisfied by their act of aggression, their love came to the fore in their remorse for the deed. It set up the super-ego by identification with the father; it gave that agency the father's power, as though as a punishment for the deed of aggression they had carried out against him, and it created the restrictions which were intended to prevent a repetition of the deed. And since the inclination to aggressiveness against the father was re-peated in the following generations, the sense of guilt, too, persisted, and it was reinforced once more by every piece of aggressiveness that was suppressed and carried over to the super-ego. Now, I think, we can at last grasp two things per-fectly clearly: the part played by love in the origin of conscience and the fatal inevitability of the sense of guilt. Whether one has killed one's father or has abstained from doing so is not really the decisive thing. One is bound to feel guilty in either case, for the sense of guilt is an expression of the conflict due to ambivalence, of the eternal struggle between Eros and the instinct of destruction or death. This conflict is set going as soon as men are faced with the task of living together. So long as the community assumes no other form than that of the family, the conflict is bound to express itself in the Oedipus complex, to establish the conscience and to create the first sense of guilt. When an attempt is made to widen the community, the same conflict is continued in forms which are dependent on the past; and it is strengthened and results in a further intensification of the sense of guilt. Since civilization obeys an internal erotic impulsion which causes human beings to unite in a closely-knit group, it can only achieve this aim through an ever-increasing reinforcement of the sense of guilt. What began in relation to the father is completed in relation to the group. If civilization is a necessary course of development from the family to humanity as a whole, then—as a result of the inborn conflict arising from ambivalence, of the eternal struggle between the trends of love and death—there is inextricably bound up with it an increase of the sense of guilt, which will perhaps reach heights that the individual finds hard to tolerate. . . . The price we pay for our advance in civilization is a loss of happiness through the heightening of the sense of guilt.

THOMAS MANN

The Significance of Freud

We are gathered here to do honour to a great scientist. And the question may very properly be raised: what justifies a man of letters in assuming the role of spokesman on such an occasion? . . . The choice of an artist as the encomiast of a great scientist is a comment upon both. In the first place, one deduces from it a connection between the man of genius we now honour and the world of creative literature; in the second place, it displays the peculiar relations between the writer and the field of science whose declared and acknowledged master and creator the other is. Now, the unique and remarkable thing about this mutual close relation is that it remained for so long unconscious—that is, in that region of the soul which we have learned to call the unconscious, a realm whose discovery and investigation, whose conquest for humanity, are precisely the task and mission of the wise genius whose fame we celebrate. The close relation between literature and psychoanalysis has been known for a long time to both sides. But the solemn significance of this hour lies, at least in my eyes and as a matter of personal feeling, in that on this evening there is taking place the first official meeting between the two spheres, in the acknowledgment and demonstration of their relationship.

I repeat that the profound sympathy between the two spheres had existed for a long time unperceived. Actually we know that Sigmund Freud, that mighty spirit in whose honour we are gathered together, founder of psychoanalysis as a general method of research and as a therapeutic technique, trod the steep path alone and independently, as physician and natural scientist, without knowing that

From "Freud and the Future" [1936], *Essays of Three Decades*, translated from the German by H. T. Lowe-Porter, New York, 1947, pp. 303-11, 323-4. Copyright 1947 by Alfred A. Knopf, Inc.; reprinted by permission of Random House, Alfred A. Knopf, Inc. and Martin Secker & Warburg Ltd.

reinforcement and encouragement lay to his hand in literature. He did not know Nietzsche, scattered throughout whose pages one finds premonitory flashes of truly Freudian insight; he did not know Novalis, whose romantic-biologic fantasies so often approach astonishingly close to analytic conceptions; he did not know Kierkegaard, whom he must have found profoundly sympathetic and encouraging for the Christian zeal which urged him on to psychological extremes; and, finally, he did not know Schopenhauer, the melancholy symphonist of a philosophy of the instinct, groping for change and redemption. Probably it must be so. By his unaided effort, without knowledge of any previous intuitive achievement, he had methodically to follow out the line of his own researches; the driving force of his activity was probably increased by this very freedom from special advantage. And we think of him as solitary—the attitude is inseparable from our earliest picture of the man. Solitary in the sense of the word used by Nietzsche in that ravishing essay "What Is the Meaning of Ascetic Ideals?" when he characterizes Schopenhauer as "a genuine philosopher, a self-poised mind, a man and gallant knight, stern-eyed, with the courage of his own strength, who knows how to stand alone and not wait on the beck and nod of superior officers." In this guise of man and gallant knight, a knight between Death and the Devil, I have been used to picture to myself our psychologist of the unconscious, ever since his figure first swam into my mental ken.

That happened late—much later than one might have expected, considering the connection between this science and the poetic and creative impulse in general and mine in particular. The connection, the bond between them, is twofold: it consists first in a love of truth, in a sense of truth, a sensitiveness and receptivity for truth's sweet and bitter, which largely expresses itself in a psychological excitation, a clarity of vision, to such an extent that the conception of truth actually almost coincides with that of psychological perception and recognition. And secondly it consists in an understanding of disease, a certain affinity with it, ouweighed by fundamental health, and an understanding of its productive significance.

As for the love of truth: the suffering, morally conditioned love of truth *as psychology*—that has its origin in Nietzsche's lofty school, where in fact the coincidence of "truth" and "psychological truth," of the knower with the psychologist, is striking indeed. His proud truthfulness, his very conception of intellectual honesty, his conscious and melancholy fearlessness in its service, his self-knowledge, self-crucifixion—all this has psychological intention and bearing. Never shall I forget the deepening, strengthening, formative effect upon my own powers produced by my acquaintance with Nietzsche's psychological agony. In *Tonio Kröger* the artist speaks of being "sick of knowledge." That is true Nietzsche language; and the youth's melancholy has reference to the Hamlet-like in Nietzsche's nature, in which his own mirrored itself: a nature called to knowledge without being genuinely born to it. These are the pangs and anguishes of youth, destined to be lightened and tranquillized as years flowed by and brought ripeness with them. But there has remained with me the desire for a psychological interpretation of knowledge and truth; I still equate them with psychology and feel the psychological will to truth as a desire for truth in general; still interpret psychology as truth in the most actual and courageous sense of the word. One would call the tendency a naturalistic one, I suppose, and ascribe it to a training in literary naturalism; it forms a precondition of receptivity for the natural science of the psyche—in other words, for what is known as psychoanalysis.

I spoke of a second bond between that science and the creative impulse: the understanding of disease, or, more precisely, of disease as an instrument of knowledge. That, too, one may derive from Nietzsche. He well knew what he owed to his morbid state, and on every page he seems to instruct us that there is no deeper knowledge without experience of disease, and that all heightened healthiness must be achieved by the route of illness. This attitude too may be referred to his experience; but it is bound up with the nature of the intellectual man in general, of the creative artist in particular, yes, with the nature of humanity and the human being, of which last of course the creative artist is an extreme expression. "*L'humanité*," says Victor Hugo, "*s'affirme par l'infirmité*." A saying which frankly and profoundly admits the delicate constitution of all higher humanity and culture and their connoisseurship in the realm of disease. Man has been called "*das kranke Tier*" because of the burden of strain and explicit difficulties laid upon him by his position between nature and spirit, between angel and brute. What wonder, then, that by the approach through abnormality we have succeeded in penetrating most deeply into the darkness of human nature; that the study of disease—that is to say, neurosis—has revealed itself as a first-class technique of anthropological research?

The literary artist should be the last person to be surprised at the fact. Sooner might he be surprised that he, considering his strong general and individual tendency, should have so late become aware of the close sympathetic relations which connected his own existence with psychoanalytic research and the life-work of Sigmund Freud. I realized this connection only at a time when his achievement was no longer thought of as merely a therapeutic method, whether recognized or disputed; when it had long since outgrown his purely medical implications and become a world movement which penetrated into every field of science and every domain of the intellect: literature, the history of art, religion and prehistory; mythology, folklore, pedagogy, and what not—thanks to the practical and constructive zeal of experts who erected a structure of more general investigation round the psychiatric and medical core. Indeed, it would be too much to say that I came to psychoanalysis. It came to me. Through the friendly interest that some young workers in the field had shown in my work, from *Little Herr Friedemann* to *Death in Venice, The Magic Mountain*, and the *Joseph* novels, it gave me to understand that in my way I "belonged"; it made me aware, as probably behoved it, of my own latent, preconscious sympathies; and when I began to occupy myself with the literature of psychoanalysis I recognized, arrayed in the ideas and the language of scientific exactitude, much that had long been familiar to me through my youthful mental experiences.

Perhaps you will kindly permit me to continue for a while in this autobiographical strain, and not take it amiss if instead of speaking of Freud I speak of myself. And indeed I scarcely trust myself to speak *about* him. What new thing could I hope to say? But I shall also, quite explicitly, be speaking in his honour in speaking of myself, in telling you how profoundly and peculiarly certain experiences decisive for my development prepared me for the Freudian experience. More than once, and in many places, I have confessed to the profound, even shattering impression made upon me as a young man by contact with the philosophy of Arthur Schopenhauer, to which then a monument was erected in the pages of *Buddenbrooks*. Here first, in the pessimism of a metaphysics already very strongly equipped on the natural-science side, I encountered the dauntless zeal for truth that stands for the moral aspect of the psychology of the unconscious. This metaphysics, in obscure revolt against centuries-old beliefs, preached the primacy of the instinct over mind and reason; it recognized the will as the core and the essential foundation of the world, in man as in all other created beings; and the intellect as secondary and accidental, servant of the will and its pale illuminant. This it preached not in malice, not in the anti-human spirit of the mind-hostile doctrines of today, but in the stern love of truth characteristic of the century which combated idealism out of love for the ideal. It was so sincere, that nine-teenth century, that—through the mouth of Ibsen—it pronounced the lie, the lies of life, to be indispensable. Clearly there is a vast difference whether one assents to a lie out of sheer hatred of truth and the spirit or for the sake of that spirit, in bitter irony and anguished pessimism! Yet the distinction is not clear to every-body today.

Now, Freud, the psychologist of the unconscious, is a true son of the century of Schopenhauer and Ibsen—he was born in the middle of it. How closely related is his revolution to Schopenhauer's, not only in its content, but also in its moral attitude! His discovery of the great role played by the unconscious, the id, in the soul-life of man challenged and challenges classical psychology, to which the con-sciousness and the psyche are one and the same, as offensively as once Schopen-hauer's doctrine of the will challenged philosophical belief in reason and the intellect. Certainly the early devotee of *The World as Will and Idea* is at home in the admirable essay that is included in Freud's *New Introductory Essays in Psychoanalysis* under the title "The Anatomy of the Mental Personality." It de-scribes the soul-world of the unconscious, the id, in language as strong, and at the same time in as coolly intellectual, objective, and professional a tone, as Schopenhauer might have used to describe his sinister kingdom of the will. "The domain of the id," he says, "is the dark, inaccessible part of our personality; the little that we know of it we have learned through the study of dreams and of the formation of neurotic symptoms." He depicts it as a chaos, a melting-pot of seething excitations. The id, he thinks, is, so to speak, open towards the somatic, and receives thence into itself compulsions which there find psychic expression—in what substratum is unknown. From these impulses it receives its energy; but it is not organized, produces no collective will, merely the striving to achieve satis-faction for the impulsive needs operating under the pleasure principle. In it no laws of thought are valid, and certainly not the law of opposites. "Contradictory stimuli exist alongside each other without cancelling each other out or even de-tracting from each other; at most they unite in compromise forms under the compulsion of the controlling economy for the release of energy." You perceive that this is a situation which, in the historical experience of our own day, can take the upper hand with the ego, with a whole mass-ego, thanks to a moral devasta-tion which is produced by worship of the unconscious, the glorification of its dynamic as the only life-promoting force, the systematic glorification of the primi-tive and irrational. For the unconscious, the id, is primitive and irrational, is pure dynamic. It knows no values, no good or evil, no morality. It even knows no time, no temporal flow, nor any effect of time upon its psychic process. "Wish stimuli," says Freud, "which have never overpassed the id, and impressions which have been repressed into its depths, are virtually indestructible, they survive decade after decade as though they had just happened. They can only be recognized as belonging to the past, devalued and robbed of their charge of energy, by becoming conscious through the analytic procedure." And he adds that therein lies preeminently the healing effect of analytic treatment. We perceive accordingly how antipathetic deep analysis must be to an ego that is intoxicated by a worship of the unconscious to the point of being in a condition of subterranean dynamic. It is only too clear and understandable that such an ego is deaf to analysis and that the name of Freud must not be mentioned in its hearing.

As for the ego itself, its situation is pathetic, well-nigh alarming. It is an alert, prominent, and enlightened little part of the id—much as Europe is a small and lively province of the greater Asia. The ego is that part of the id which became modified by contact with the outer world; equipped for the reception and preservation of stimuli; comparable to the integument with which any piece of living matter surrounds itself. A very perspicuous biological picture. Freud writes indeed a very perspicuous prose, he is an artist of thought, like Schopenhauer, and like him a writer of European rank. The relation with the outer world is, he says, decisive for the ego, it is the ego's task to represent the world to the id—for its good! For without regard for the superior power of the outer world the id, in its blind striving towards the satisfaction of its instincts, would not escape destruction. The ego takes cognizance of the outer world, it is mindful, it honourably tries to distinguish the objectively real from whatever is an accretion from its inward sources of stimulation. It is entrusted by the id with the lever of action; but between the impulse and the action it has interposed the delay of the thought-process, during which it summons experience to its aid and thus possesses a certain regulative superiority over the pleasure principle which rules supreme in the unconscious, correcting it by means of the principle of reality. But even so, how feeble it is! Hemmed in between the unconscious, the outer world, and what Freud calls the super-ego, it leads a pretty nervous and anguished existence. Its own dynamic is rather weak. It derives its energy from the id and in general has to carry out the latter's behests. It is fain to regard itself as the rider and the unconscious as the horse. But many a time it is ridden by the unconscious; and I take leave to add what Freud's rational morality prevents him from saying, that under some circumstances it makes more progress by this illegitimate means. . . .

And now this word "future": I have used it in the title of my address, because it is this idea, the idea of the future, that I involuntarily like best to connect with the name of Freud. . . . I hold that we shall one day recognize in Freud's life-work the cornerstone for the building of a new anthropology and therewith of a new structure, to which many stones are being brought up today, which shall be the future dwelling of a wiser and freer humanity. This physicianly psychologist will, I make no doubt at all, be honoured as the path-finder towards a humanism of the future, which we dimly divine and which will have experienced much that the earlier humanism knew not of. It will be a humanism standing in a different relation to the powers of the lower world, the unconscious, the id: a relation bolder, freer, blither, productive of a riper art than any possible in our neurotic, fear-ridden, hate-ridden world. Freud is of the opinion that the significance of psychoanalysis as a science of the unconscious will in the future far outrank its value as a therapeutic method. But even as a science of the unconscious it is a therapeutic method, in the grand style, a method overarching the individual case. Call this, if you choose, a poet's utopia; but the thought is after all not unthinkable that the resolution of our great fear and our great hate, their conversion into a different relation to the unconscious which shall be more the artist's, more ironic and yet not necessarily irreverent, may one day be due to the healing effect of this very science.

The analytic revelation is a revolutionary force. With it a blithe scepticism has come into the world, a mistrust that unmasks all the schemes and subterfuges of our own souls. Once roused and on the alert, it cannot be put to sleep again. It infiltrates life, undermines its raw naïveté, takes from it the strain of its own ignorance, de-emotionalizes it, as it were, inculcates the taste for understatement, as the English call it—for the deflated rather than for the inflated words, for the cult which exerts its influence by moderation, by modesty. Modesty—what a beautiful word! In the German (*Bescheidenheit*) it originally had to do with knowing and only later got its present meaning; while the Latin word from which the English comes means a way of doing—in short, both together give us almost the sense of the French *savoir faire*—to know how to do. May we hope that this may be the fundamental temper of that more blithely objective and peaceful world which the science of the unconscious may be called to usher in?

Its mingling of the pioneer with the physicianly spirit justifies such a hope. Freud once called his theory of dreams "a bit of scientific new-found land won from superstition and mysticism." The word "won" expresses the colonizing spirit and significance of his work. "Where id was, shall be ego," he epigrammatically says. And he calls analysis a cultural labour comparable to the draining of the Zuider Zee. Almost in the end the traits of the venerable man merge into the lineaments of the grey-haired Faust, whose spirit urges him

> to shut the imperious sea from the shore away,
> Set narrower bounds to the broad water's waste.
>
> Then open I to many millions space
> Where they may live, not safe-secure, but free
> And active. And such a busy swarming I would see
> Standing amid free folk on a free soil.

The free folk are the people of a future freed from fear and hate, and ripe for peace.

D. H. LAWRENCE

A Non-Freudian Unconscious

One thing . . . psychoanalysis all along the line fails to determine, and that is the nature of the pristine unconscious in man. The incest-craving is or is not inherent in the pristine psyche. When Adam and Eve became aware of sex in themselves, they became aware of that which was pristine in them, and which preceded all knowing. But when the analyst discovers the incest motive in the unconscious, surely he is only discovering a term of humanity's repressed *idea* of sex. It is not even *suppressed* sex-consciousness, but *repressed*. That is, it is nothing pristine and anterior to mentality. It is in itself the mind's ulterior motive. That is, the incest-craving is propagated in the pristine unconscious by the mind itself, even though unconsciously. The mind acts as incubus and procreator of its own horrors, *deliberately unconsciously*. And the incest motive is in its origin not a pristine impulse, but a logical extension of the existent idea of sex and love. The mind, that is, transfers the idea of incest into the affective-passional psyche, and keeps it there as a repressed motive.

This is as yet a mere assertion. It cannot be made good until we determine the nature of the true, pristine unconscious, in which all our genuine impulse arises—a very different affair from that sack of horrors which psychoanalysts would have us believe is source of motivity. The Freudian unconscious is the cellar in which the mind keeps its own bastard spawn. The true unconscious is the well-head, the fountain of real motivity. The sex of which Adam and Eve became conscious derived from the very God who bade them be not conscious of it— it was not spawn produced by secondary propagation from the mental consciousness itself. . . .

This motivizing of the passional sphere from the ideal is the final peril of human consciousness. It is the death of all spontaneous, creative life, and the substituting of the mechanical principle.

It is obvious that the ideal becomes a mechanical principle, if it be applied to the affective soul as a fixed motive. An ideal established in control of the passional soul is no more and no less than a supreme machine-principle. And a machine, as we know, is the active unit of the material world. Thus we see how it is that in the end pure idealism is identical with pure materialism, and the

From *Psychoanalysis and the Unconscious*, New York, 1921, pp. 23-5, 30-36, 39-41, 66-8, 70-72, 77-8, 83-5, 99-101; reprinted by permission of Lawrence Pollinger Ltd. and the Estate of the late Mrs. Frieda Lawrence.

most ideal peoples are the most completely material. Ideal and material are identical. The ideal is but the god in the machine—the little, fixed, machine principle which works the human psyche automatically.

We are now in the last stages of idealism. And psychoanalysis alone has the courage necessary to conduct us through these last stages. The identity of love with sex, the single necessity for fulfilment through love, these are our fixed ideals. We must fulfil these ideals in their extremity. And this brings us finally to incest, even incest-worship. We have no option, whilst our ideals stand.

Why? Because incest is the logical conclusion of our ideals, when these ideals have to be carried into passional effect. And idealism has no escape from logic. And once he has built himself in the shape of any ideal, man will go to any logical length rather than abandon his ideal corpus. Nay, some great cataclysm has to throw him down and destroy the whole fabric of his life before the motor-principle of his dominant ideal is destroyed. Hence psychoanalysis as the advance-guard of science, the evangel of the last *ideal* liberty. For of course there is a great fascination in a completely effected idealism. Man is then undisputed master of his own fate, and captain of his own soul. But better say engine-driver, for in truth he is no more than the little god in the machine, this master of fate. He has invented his own automatic principles, and he works himself according to them, like any little mechanic inside the works.

But ideal or not, we are all of us between the pit and the pendulum, or the walls of red-hot metal, as may be. If we refuse the Freudian *pis-aller* as a means of escape, we have still to find some way out. For there we are, all of us, trapped in a corner where we cannot, and simply do not know how to fulfil our own natures, passionally. We don't know in which way fulfilment lies. If psychoanalysis discovers incest, small blame to it.

Yet we do know this much: that the pushing of the ideal to any further lengths will not avail us anything. We have actually to go back to our own unconscious. But not to the unconscious which is the inverted reflection of our ideal consciousness. We must discover, if we can, the true unconscious, where our life bubbles up in us, prior to any mentality. The first bubbling life in us, which is innocent of any mental alteration, this is the unconscious. It is pristine, not in any way ideal. It is the spontaneous origin from which it behooves us to live.

What then is the true unconscious? It is not a shadow cast from the mind. It is the spontaneous life-motive in every organism. Where does it begin? It begins where life begins. But that is too vague. It is no use talking about life and the unconscious in bulk. You can talk about electricity, because electricity is a homogeneous force, conceivable apart from any incorporation. But life is inconceivable as a general thing. It exists only in living creatures. So that life begins, now as always, in an individual living creature. In the beginning of the individual living creatures is the beginning of life, every time and always, and life has no beginning apart from this. Any attempt at a further generalization takes us merely beyond the consideration of life into the region of mechanical homogeneous force. This is shown in the cosmologies of eastern religions.

The beginning of life is in the beginning of the first individual creature. You may call the naked, unicellular bit of plasm the first individual, if you like. Mentally, as far as thinkable simplicity goes, it is the first. So that we may say that life begins in the first naked unicellular organism. And where life begins the unconscious also begins. But mark, the first naked unicellular organism is an *individual*. It is a specific individual, not a mathematical unit, like a unit of force.

Where the individual begins, life begins. The two are inseparable, life and individuality. And also, where the individual begins, the unconscious, which is the specific life-motive, also begins. We are trying to trace the unconscious to its source. And we find that this source, in all the higher organisms, is the first ovule cell from which an individual organism arises. At the moment of conception, when a procreative male nucleus fuses with the nucleus of the female germ, at that moment does a new unit of life, of consciousness, arise in the universe. . . .

Having established so much, we can really approach the unconscious. By the unconscious we wish to indicate that essential unique nature of every individual creature, which is, by its very nature, unanalysable, undefinable, inconceivable. It cannot be conceived, it can only be experienced, in every single instance. And being inconceivable, we will call it the unconscious. As a matter of fact, *soul* would be a better word. By the unconscious we do mean the soul. But the word *soul* has been vitiated by the idealistic use, until nowadays it means only that which a man conceives himself to be. And that which a man conceives himself to be is something far different from his true unconscious. So we must relinquish the ideal word soul.

If, however, the unconscious is inconceivable, how do we know it at all? We know it by direct experience. All the best part of knowledge is inconceivable. We know the sun. But we cannot conceive the sun, unless we are willing to accept some theory of burning gases, some cause-and-effect nonsense. And even if we do have a mental conception of the sun as a sphere of blazing gas—which it certainly isn't—we are just as far from knowing what *blaze* is. Knowledge is always a matter of whole experience, what St. Paul calls knowing in full, and never a matter of mental conception merely. This is indeed the point of all full knowledge: that it is contained mainly within the unconscious, its mental or conscious reference being only a sort of extract or shadow.

———————

At the solar plexus the new psyche acts in a mode of attractive vitalism, drawing its objective unto itself as by vital magnetism. Here it drinks in, as it were, the contiguous universe, as during the womb-period it drank from the living continuum of the mother. It is darkly self-centred, exultant and positive in its own existence. It is all-in-all to itself, its own great subject. It knows no objective. It only knows its own vital potency, which potency draws the external object unto itself, subjectively, as the blood-stream was drawn into the fœtus, by subjective attraction. Here the psyche is to itself the *All*. Blindly self-positive.

This is the first mode of consciousness for every living thing—fascinating in all young things. The second half of the same mode commences as soon as direct activity sets up in the lumbar ganglion. Then the psyche recoils upon itself, in its first reaction against continuity with the outer universe. It recoils even against its own mode of assimilatory unison. Even it must break off, interrupt the great psychic-assimilation process which goes on at the sympathetic centre. It must recoil clean upon itself, break loose from any attachment whatsoever. And then it must try its *power*, often playfully.

This reaction is still subjective. When a child stiffens and draws away, when it screams with pure temper, it takes no note of that from which it recoils. It has no objective consciousness of that from which it reacts, the mother principally. It is like a swimmer endlessly kicking the water away behind him, with strong legs vividly active from the spinal ganglia. Like a man in a boat pushing off from the shore, it merely thrusts away, in order to ride free, ever more free. It is a purely subjective motion, in the negative direction. . . .

As yet we see the unconscious active on one plane only and entirely dependent on *two* individuals. But immediately following the establishment of the circuit of the powerful, subjective, abdominal plane comes the quivering of the whole system into a new degree of consciousness. And two great upper centres are awake.

The diaphragm really divides the human body, psychically as well as organically. The two centres beneath the diaphragm are centres of dark subjectivity, centripetal, assimilative. Once these are established, in the thorax the two first centres of objective consciousness become active, with ever-increasing intensity. The great thoracic sympathetic plexus rouses like a sun in the breast, the thoracic ganglion fills the shoulders with strength. There are now two planes of primary consciousness—the first, the lower, the subjective unconscious, active beneath the diaphragm, and the second upper, objective plane, active above the diaphragm, in the breast. . . .

The great sympathetic plexus of the breast is the heart's mind. This thoracic plexus corresponds directly in the upper man to the solar plexus in the lower. But it is a correspondence in creative opposition. From the sympathetic centre of the breast as from a window the unconscious goes forth seeking its object, to dwell upon it. When a child leans its breast against its mother it becomes filled with a primal awareness of *her*—not of itself desiring her or partaking of her—but of her as she is in herself. This is the first great acquisition of primal objective knowledge, the objective content of the unconscious. Such knowledge we call the treasure of the heart. When the ancients located the first seat of consciousness in the heart, they were neither misguided nor playing with metaphor. For by consciousness they meant, as usual, objective consciousness only. And from the cardiac plexus goes forth that strange effluence of the self which seeks and dwells upon the beloved, lovingly roving like the fingers of an infant or a blind man over the face of the treasured object, gathering her mould into itself and transferring her mould for ever into its own deep unconscious psyche. This is the first acquiring of objective knowledge, sightless, unspeakably direct. It is a dwelling of the child's unconscious within the form of the mother, the gathering of a pure, eternal impression. . . .

Consciousness develops on successive planes. On each plane there is the dual polarity, positive and negative, of the sympathetic and voluntary nerve centres. The first plane is established between the poles of the sympathetic solar plexus and the voluntary lumbar ganglion. This is the active first plane of the subjective unconscious, from which the whole of consciousness arises.

Immediately succeeding the first plane of subjective dynamic consciousness arises the corresponding first plane of objective consciousness, the objective unconscious, polarized in the cardiac plexus and the thoracic ganglion, in the breast. There is a perfect correspondence in difference between the first abdominal and the first thoracic planes. These two planes polarize each other in a fourfold polarity, which makes the first great field of individual, self-dependent consciousness.

Each pole of the active unconscious manifests a specific activity and gives rise
to a specific kind of dynamic or creative consciousness. On each plane, the negative voluntary pole *complements* the positive sympathetic pole, and yet the consciousness originating from the complementary poles is not merely negative versus positive, it is categorically different, opposite. Each is pure and perfect in
itself.

But the moment we enter the two planes of corresponding consciousness, lower
and upper, we find a whole new range of complements. The upper, dynamic-
objective plane is complementary to the lower, dynamic-subjective. The mystery
of creative opposition exists all the time between the two planes, and this unison
in opposition between the two planes forms the first whole field of consciousness.
Within the individual the polarity is fourfold. In a relation between two individuals the polarity is already eightfold. . . .

A soul cannot come into its own through that love alone which is unison. If
it stress the one mode, the sympathetic mode, beyond a certain point, it breaks
its own integrity, and corruption sets in, in the living organism. On both planes
of love, upper and lower, the two modes must act complementary to one another, the sympathetic and the separatist. It is the absolute failure to see this,
that has torn the modern world into two halves, the one half warring for the
voluntary, objective, separatist control, the other for the pure sympathetic. The
individual psyche divided against itself divides the world against itself, and an
unthinkable progress of calamity ensues unless there be a reconciliation.

The goal of life is the coming to perfection of each single individual. This cannot take place without the tremendous interchange of love from all the four
great poles of the first, basic field of consciousness. There must be the twofold
passionate flux of sympathetic love, subjective-abdominal and objective-devotional, both. And there must be the twofold passional circuit of separatist realization, the lower, vital *self-realization*, and the upper, intense realization of the
other, a realization which includes a recognition of abysmal *otherness*. To stress
any one mode, any one interchange, is to hinder all, and to cause corruption in
the end. The human psyche must have strength and pride to accept the whole
fourfold nature of its own creative activity.

TRISTAN TZARA

Dadaism

There is a literature that does not reach the voracious mass. It is the work of
creators, issued from a real necessity in the author, produced for himself. It ex
presses the knowledge of a supreme egoism, in which laws wither away. Every

From "Dada Manifesto" [1918] and "Lecture on Dada" [1922], translated from the
French by Robert Motherwell, *Dada Painters and Poets*, by Robert Motherwell, New York,
1951, pp. 78-9, 81, 246-51; reprinted by permission of George Wittenborn, Inc., Publishers,
1018 Madison Avenue, New York 21, N.Y.

page must explode, either by profound heavy seriousness, the whirlwind, poetic frenzy, the new, the eternal, the crushing joke, enthusiasm for principles, or by the way in which it is printed. On the one hand a tottering world in flight, betrothed to the glockenspiel of hell, on the other hand: new men. Rough, bouncing, riding on hiccups. Behind them a crippled world and literary quacks with a mania for improvement.

I say unto you: *there is no beginning and we do not tremble, we are not sentimental. We are a furious wind, tearing the dirty linen of clouds and prayers, preparing the great spectacle of disaster, fire, decomposition.* We will put an end to mourning and replace tears by sirens screeching from one continent to another. Pavilions of intense joy and widowers with the sadness of poison. Dada is the signboard of abstraction; advertising and business are also elements of poetry.

I destroy the drawers of the brain and of social organization: spread demoralization wherever I go and cast my hand from heaven to hell, my eyes from hell to heaven, restore the fecund wheel of a universal circus to objective forces and the imagination of every individual.

Philosophy is the question: from which side shall we look at life, God, the idea or other phenomena. Everything one looks at is false. I do not consider the relative result more important than the choice between cake and cherries after dinner. The system of quickly looking at the other side of a thing in order to impose your opinion indirectly is called dialectics, in other words, haggling over the spirit of fried potatoes while dancing method around it.

If I cry out:

> Ideal, ideal, ideal,
> Knowledge, knowledge, knowledge,
> Boomboom, boomboom, boomboom,

I have given a pretty faithful version of progress, law, morality and all other fine qualities that various highly intelligent men have discussed in so many books, only to conclude that after all everyone dances to his own personal boomboom, and that the writer is entitled to his boomboom: the satisfaction of pathological curiosity; a private bell for inexplicable needs; a bath; pecuniary difficulties; a stomach with repercussions in life; the authority of the mystic wand formulated as the bouquet of a phantom orchestra made up of silent fiddle bows greased with philtres made of chicken manure. With the blue eye-glasses of an angel they have excavated the inner life for a dime's worth of unanimous gratitude. If all of them are right and if all pills are Pink Pills, let us try for once not to be right. Some people think they can explain rationally, by thought, what they think. But that is extremely relative. Psychoanalysis is a dangerous disease, it puts to sleep the anti-objective impulses of man and systematizes the bourgeoisie. There is no ultimate Truth. The dialectic is an amusing mechanism which guides us / in a banal kind of way / to the opinions we had in the first place. Does anyone think that, by a minute refinement of logic, he has demonstrated the truth and established the correctness of these opinions? Logic imprisoned by the senses is an organic disease. To this element philosophers always like to add: the power of observation. But actually this magnificent quality of the mind is the proof of its impotence. We observe, we regard from one or more points of view, we choose them among the millions that exist. Experience is also a product of chance and individual faculties. Science disgusts me as soon as it becomes a speculative system, loses its character of utility—that is so useless but is at least individual. I detest greasy objectivity, and harmony, the science that finds everything in order. Carry on, my children, humanity . . . Science says we are the servants of nature: everything is in order, make love and bash your brains in. Carry on, my children, humanity, kind bourgeois and journalist virgins . . . I am against systems, the most acceptable system is on principle to have none. To complete oneself, to perfect oneself in one's own littleness, to fill the vessel with one's individuality, to have the courage to fight for and against thought, the mystery of bread, the sudden burst of an infernal propeller into economic lilies. . . .

Every product of disgust capable of becoming a negation of the family is Dada; a protest with the fists of its whole being engaged in destructive action: *Dada; knowledge of all the means rejected up until now by the shamefaced sex of comfortable compromise and good manners: Dada; abolition of logic, which is the dance of those impotent to create: Dada; of every social hierarchy and equation set up for the sake of values by our valets: Dada; every object, all objects, sentiments, obscurities, apparitions and the precise clash of parallel lines are weapons for the fight: Dada; abolition of memory: Dada; abolition of archaeology: Dada; abolition of prophets: Dada; abolition of the future: Dada; absolute and unquestionable faith in every god that is the immediate product of spontaneity: Dada;* elegant and unprejudiced leap from a harmony to the other sphere; trajectory of a word tossed like a screeching phonograph record; to respect all individuals in their folly of the moment: whether it be serious, fearful, timid, ardent, vigorous, determined, enthusiastic; to divest one's church of every useless cumbersome accessory; to spit out disagreeable or amorous ideas like a luminous waterfall, or coddle them —with the extreme satisfaction that it doesn't matter in the least—with the same intensity in the thicket of one's soul—pure of insects for blood well-born, and gilded with bodies of archangels. Freedom: Dada Dada Dada, a roaring of tense colors, and interlacing of opposites and of all contradictions, grotesques, inconsistencies: LIFE

Ladies and Gentlemen:

I don't have to tell you that for the general public and for you, the refined public, a Dadaist is the equivalent of a leper. But that is only a manner of speaking. When these same people get close to us, they treat us with that remnant of elegance that comes from their old habit of belief in progress. At ten yards distance, hatred begins again. If you ask me why, I won't be able to tell you.

Another characteristic of Dada is the continuous breaking off of our friends. They are always breaking off and resigning. The first to tender his resignation from the Dada movement *was myself*. Everybody knows that Dada is nothing. I broke away from Dada and from myself as soon as I understood the implications of *nothing*.

If I continue to do something, it is because it amuses me, or rather because I have a need for activity which I use up and satisfy wherever I can. Basically, the true Dadas have always been separate from Dada. Those who acted as if Dada were important enough to resign from with a big noise have been motivated by a desire for personal publicity, proving that counterfeiters have always wriggled like unclean worms in and out of the purest and most radiant religions.

I know that you have come here today to hear explanations. Well, don't expect to hear any explanations about Dada. You explain to me why you exist. You haven't the faintest idea. You will say: I exist to make my children happy. But in your hearts you know that isn't so. You will say: I exist to guard my country against barbarian invasions. That's a fine reason. You will say: I exist because God wills. That's a fairy tale for children. You will never be able to tell me why you exist but you will always be ready to maintain a serious attitude about life. You will never understand that life is a pun, for you will never be alone enough to reject hatred, judgments, all these things that require such an effort, in favor of a calm level state of mind that makes everything equal and without importance.

Dada is not at all modern. It is more in the nature of a return to an almost Buddhist religion of indifference. Dada covers things with an artificial gentleness, a snow of butterflies released from the head of a prestidigitator. Dada is immobility and does not comprehend the passions. You will call this a paradox, since Dada is manifested only in violent acts. Yes, the reactions of individuals contaminated by *destruction* are rather violent, but when these reactions are exhausted, annihilated by the Satanic insistence of a continuous and progressive "What for?" what remains, what dominates is *indifference*. But with the same note of conviction I might maintain the contrary.

I admit that my friends do not approve this point of view. But the *Nothing* can be uttered only as the reflection of an individual. And that is why it will be valid for everyone, since everyone is important only for the individual who is expressing himself.—I am speaking of myself. Even that is too much for me. How can I be expected to speak of all men at once, and satisfy them too?

Nothing is more delightful than to confuse and upset people. People one doesn't like. What's the use of giving them explanations that are merely food for curiosity? The truth is that people love nothing but themselves and their little possessions, their income, their dog. This state of affairs derives from a false conception of property. If one is poor in spirit, one possesses a sure and indomitable intelligence, a savage logic, a point of view that can not be shaken. Try to be empty and fill your brain cells with a petty happiness. Always destroy what you have in you. On random walks. Then you will be able to understand many things. You are not more intelligent than we, and we are not more intelligent than you.

Intelligence is an organization like any other, the organization of society, the organization of a bank, the organization of chit-chat. At a society tea. It serves to create order and clarity where there is none. It serves to create a state hierarchy. To set up classifications for rational work. To separate questions of a material order from those of a cerebral order, but to take the former very seriously. Intelligence is the triumph of sound education and pragmatism. Fortunately life is something else and its pleasures are innumerable. They are not paid for in the coin of liquid intelligence.

These observations of everyday conditions have led us to a realization which constitutes our minimum basis of agreement, aside from the sympathy which binds us and which is inexplicable. It would not have been possible for us to found our agreement on principles. For everything is relative. What are the Beautiful, the Good, Art, Freedom? Words that have a different meaning for every individual. Words with the pretension of creating agreement among all, and that is why they are written with capital letters. Words which have not the moral value and objective force that people have grown accustomed to finding in them. Their meaning changes from one individual, one epoch, one country to the next. Men are different. It is diversity that makes life interesting. There is no common basis in men's minds. The unconscious is inexhaustible and uncontrollable. Its force surpasses us. It is as mysterious as the last particle of a brain cell. Even if we knew it, we could not reconstruct it.

What good did the theories of the philosophers do us? Did they help us to take a single step forward or backward? What is forward, what is backward? Did they alter our forms of contentment? We are. We argue, we dispute, we get excited. The rest is sauce. Sometimes pleasant, sometimes mixed with a limitless boredom, a swamp dotted with tufts of dying shrubs.

We have had enough of the intelligent movements that have stretched beyond measure our credulity in the benefits of science. What we want now is spontaneity. Not because it is better or more beautiful than anything else. But because everything that issues freely from ourselves, without the intervention of speculative ideas, represents us. We must intensify this quantity of life that readily spends itself in every quarter. Art is not the most precious manifestation of life. Art has not the celestial and universal value that people like to attribute to it. Life is far more interesting. Dada knows the correct measure that should be given to art: with subtle, perfidious methods, Dada introduces it into daily life. And vice versa. In art, Dada reduces everything to an initial simplicity, growing always more relative. It mingles its caprices with the chaotic wind of creation and the barbaric dances of savage tribes. It wants logic reduced to a personal minimum, while literature in its view should be primarily intended for the individual who makes it. Words have a weight of their own and lend themselves to abstract construction. The absurd has no terrors for me, for from a more exalted point of view everything in life seems absurd to me. Only the elasticity of our conventions creates a bond between disparate acts. The Beautiful and the True in art do not exist; what interests me is the intensity of a personality transposed directly, clearly into the work; the man and his vitality; the angle from which he regards the elements and in what manner he knows how to gather sensation, emotion, into a lacework of words and sentiments.

Dada tries to find out what words mean before using them, from the point of view not of grammar but of representation. Objects and colors pass through the same filter. It is not the new technique that interests us, but the spirit. Why do you want us to be preoccupied with a pictorial, moral, poetic, literary, political or social renewal? We are well aware that these renewals of means are merely the successive cloaks of the various epochs of history, uninteresting questions of fashion and facade. We are well aware that people in the costumes of the Renaissance were pretty much the same as the people of today, and that Chouang-Dsi was just as Dada as we are. You are mistaken if you take Dada for a modern school, or even for a reaction against the schools of today. Several of my statements have struck you as old and natural, what better proof that you were Dadaist without knowing it, perhaps even before the birth of Dada.

You will often hear that Dada is a state of mind. You may be gay, sad, afflicted, joyous, melancholy or Dada. Without being literary, you can be romantic, you can be dreamy, weary, eccentric, a businessman, skinny, transfigured, vain, amiable or Dada. This will happen later on in the course of history when Dada has become a precise, habitual word, when popular repetition has given it the character of a word organic with its necessary content. Today no one thinks of the literature of the Romantic school in representing a lake, a landscape, a character. Slowly but surely, a Dada character is forming.

Dada is here, there and a little everywhere, such as it is, with its faults, with its personal differences and distinctions which it accepts and views with indifference.

We are often told that we are incoherent, but into this word people try to put an insult that it is rather hard for me to fathom. Everything is incoherent. The gentleman who decides to take a bath but goes to the movies instead. The one who wants to be quiet but says things that haven't even entered his head. Another who has a precise idea on some subject but succeeds only in expressing the opposite in words which for him are a poor translation. There is no logic. Only relative necessities discovered *a posteriori*, valid not in any exact sense but only as explanations.

The acts of life have no beginning or end. Everything happens in a completely idiotic way. That is why everything is alike. Simplicity is called Dada.

Any attempt to conciliate an inexplicable momentary state with logic strikes me as a boring kind of game. The convention of the spoken language is ample and adequate for us, but for our solitude, for our intimate games and our literature we no longer need it.

The beginnings of Dada were not the beginnings of an art, but of a disgust. Disgust with the magnificence of philosophers who for 3000 years have been explaining everything to us (what for?), disgust with the pretensions of these artists-God's-representatives-on-earth, disgust with passion and with real pathological wickedness where it was not worth the bother; disgust with a false form of domination and restriction *en masse*, that accentuates rather than appeases man's instinct of domination, disgust with all the catalogued categories, with the false prophets who are nothing but a front for the interests of money, pride, disease, disgust with the lieutenants of a mercantile art made to order according to a few infantile laws, disgust with the divorce of good and evil, the beautiful and the ugly (for why is it more estimable to be red rather than green, to the left rather than the right, to be large or small?). Disgust finally with the Jesuitical dialectic which can explain everything and fill people's minds with oblique and obtuse ideas without any physiological basis or ethnic roots, all this by means of blinding artifice and ignoble charlatan's promises.

As Dada marches it continuously destroys, not in extension but in itself. From all these disgusts, may I add, it draws no conclusion, no pride, no benefit. It has even stopped combating anything, in the realization that it's no use, that all this doesn't matter. What interests a Dadaist is his own mode of life. But here we approach the great secret.

Dada is a state of mind. That is why it transforms itself according to races and events. Dada applies itself to everything, and yet it is nothing, it is the point where the yes and the no and all the opposites meet, not solemnly in the castles of human philosophies, but very simply at street corners, like dogs and grasshoppers.

Like everything in life, Dada is useless.

Dada is without pretension, as life should be.

Perhaps you will understand me better when I tell you that Dada is a virgin microbe that penetrates with the insistence of air into all the spaces that reason has not been able to fill with words or conventions.

ANDRÉ BRETON

Surrealism

In an article, "Enter the Mediums," published in *Littérature*, 1922, reprinted in *Les Pas Perdus*, 1924, and subsequently in the *Surrealist Manifesto*, I explained the circumstance that had originally put us, my friends and myself, on the track of the surrealist activity we still follow and for which we are hopeful of gaining ever more numerous new adherents in order to extend it further than we have so far succeeded in doing. It reads:

"It was in 1919, in complete solitude and at the approach of sleep, that my attention was arrested by sentences more or less complete, which became perceptible to my mind without my being able to discover (even by very meticulous analysis) any possible previous volitional effort. One evening in particular, as I was about to fall asleep, I became aware of a sentence articulated clearly to a point excluding all possibility of alteration and stripped of all quality of vocal sound; a curious sort of sentence which came to me bearing—in sober truth—not a trace of any relation whatever to any incidents I may at that time have been involved in; an insistent sentence, it seemed to me, a sentence I might say, that *knocked at the window*. I was prepared to pay no further attention to it when the organic character of the sentence detained me. I was really bewildered. Unfortunately, I am unable to remember the exact sentence at this distance, but it ran approximately like this: 'A man is cut in half by the window.' What made it plainer was the fact that it was accompanied by a feeble visual representation of a man in the process of walking, but cloven, at half his height, by a window perpendicular to the axis of his body. Definitely, there was the form, re-erected against space, of a man leaning out of a window. But the window following the man's locomotion, I understood that I was dealing with an image of great rarity. Instantly the idea came to me to use it as material for poetic construction. I had no sooner invested it with that quality, than it had given place to a succession of all but intermittent sentences which left me no less astonished, but in a state, I would say, of extreme detachment.

"Preoccupied as I still was at that time with Freud, and familiar with his methods of investigation, which I had practised occasionally upon the sick during the War, I resolved to obtain from myself what one seeks to obtain from patients, namely a monologue poured out as rapidly as possible, over which the subject's critical faculty has no control—the subject himself throwing reticence to the winds

From *What Is Surrealism?* [1934], translated from the French by David Gascoigne, London, 1936; reprinted by permission of Faber & Faber Ltd.

—and which as much as possible represents *spoken thought*. It seemed and still seems to me that the speed of thought is no greater than that of words, and hence does not exceed the flow of either tongue or pen. It was in such circumstances that, together with Philippe Soupault, whom I had told about my first ideas on the subject, I began to cover sheets of paper with writing, feeling a praiseworthy contempt for whatever the literary result might be. Ease of achievement brought about the rest. By the end of the first day of the experiment we were able to read to one another about fifty pages obtained in this manner and to compare the results we had achieved. The likeness was on the whole striking. There were similar faults of construction, the same hesitant manner, and also, in both cases, an illusion of extraordinary verve, much emotion, a considerable assortment of images of a quality such as we should never have been able to obtain in the normal way of writing, a very special sense of the picturesque, and, here and there, a few pieces of out and out buffoonery. The only differences which our two texts presented appeared to me to be due essentially to our respective temperaments, Soupault's being less static than mine, and, if he will allow me to make this slight criticism, to his having scattered about at the top of certain pages—doubtlessly in a spirit of mystification—various words under the guise of titles. I must give him credit, on the other hand, for having always forcibly opposed the least correction of any passage that did not seem to me to be quite the thing. In that he was most certainly right.

"It is of course difficult in these cases to appreciate at their just value the various elements in the result obtained; one may even say that it is entirely impossible to appreciate them at a first reading. To you who may be writing them, these elements are, in appearance, *as strange as to anyone else*, and you are yourself naturally distrustful of them. Poetically speaking, they are distinguished chiefly by a very high degree of *immediate absurdity*, the peculiar quality of that absurdity being, on close examination, their yielding to whatever is most admissible and legitimate in the world: divulgation of a given number of facts and properties on the whole not less objectionable than the others."

The word "surrealism" having thereupon become descriptive of the *generalizable* undertaking to which we had devoted ourselves, I thought it indispensable, in 1924, to define this word once and for all:

"SURREALISM, *n*. Pure psychic automatism, by which it is intended to express, verbally, in writing, or by other means, the real process of thought. Thought's dictation, in the absence of all control exercised by the reason and outside all aesthetic or moral preoccupations.

"ENCYCL. *Philos.* Surrealism rests in the belief in the superior reality of certain forms of association neglected heretofore; in the omnipotence of the dream and in the disinterested play of thought. It tends definitely to do away with all other psychic mechanisms and to substitute itself for them in the solution of the principal problems of life. Have professed *absolute surrealism*: Messrs. Aragon, Baron, Boiffard, Breton, Carrive, Crevel, Delteil, Desnos, Eluard, Gérard, Limbour, Malkine, Morise, Naville, Noll, Péret, Picon, Soupault, Vitrac.

"These till now appear to be the only ones, and there would not have been any doubt on that score were it not for the strange case of Isidore Ducasse, of whose extra-literary career I lack all data. Were one to consider their output only superficially, a goodly number of poets might well have passed for surrealists, beginning with Dante and Shakespeare at his best. *In the course of many attempts I have made towards an analysis of what, under false pretences, is called genius, I have found nothing that could in the end be attributed to any other process than this."*

There followed an enumeration that will gain, I think, by being clearly set out thus:

"Young's *Night Thoughts* are surrealist from cover to cover. It was unfortunately a priest who spoke; a bad priest, to be sure, yet a priest.

"Heraclitus is surrealist in dialectic.

"Lulle is surrealist in definition.

"Flamel is surrealist in the night of gold.

"Swift is surrealist in malice.

"Sade is surrealist in sadism.

"Carrière is surrealist in drowning.

"Monk Lewis is surrealist in the beauty of evil.

"Achim d'Arnim is surrealist absolutely, in space and time.

"Rabbe is surrealist in death.

"Baudelaire is surrealist in morals.

"Rimbaud is surrealist in life and elsewhere.

"Hervey Saint-Denys is surrealist in the directed dream.

"Carroll is surrealist in nonsense.

"Huysmans is surrealist in pessimism.

"Seurat is surrealist in design.

"Picasso is surrealist in cubism.

"Vaché is surrealist in myself.

"Roussel is surrealist in anecdote. Etc.

"They were not always surrealists—on this I insist—in the sense that one can disentangle in each of them a number of preconceived notions to which—very naively!—they clung. And they clung to them so because they had not heard the *surrealist voice*, the voice that exhorts on the eve of death and in the roaring storm, and because they were unwilling to dedicate themselves to the task of no more than orchestrating the score replete with marvellous things. They were proud instruments; hence the sounds they produced were not always harmonious sounds.

"We, on the contrary, who have not given ourselves to processes of filtering, who through the medium of our work have been content to be silent receptacles of so many echoes, modest *registering machines* that are not hypnotized by the pattern that they trace, we are perhaps serving a yet much nobler cause. So we honestly give back the talent lent to us. You may talk of the 'talent' of this yard of platinum, of this mirror, of this door and of this sky, if you wish.

"We have no talent. . . ."

The *Manifesto* also contained a certain number of practical recipes, entitled: "Secrets of the Magic Surrealist Art," such as the following:

"*Written Surrealist Composition or First and Last Draft.*

"Having settled down in some spot most conducive to the mind's concentration upon itself, order writing material to be brought to you. Let your state of mind be as passive and receptive as possible. Forget your genius, talents, as well as the genius and talents of others. Repeat to yourself that literature is pretty well the sorriest road that leads to everywhere. Write quickly without any previously chosen subject, quickly enough not to dwell on, and not to be tempted to read over, what you have written. The first sentence will come of itself; and this is self-evidently true, because there is never a moment but some sentence alien to our conscious thought clamours for outward expression. It is rather difficult to speak of the sentence to follow, since it doubtless comes in for a share of our conscious activity and so do the other sentences, if it is conceded that the writing of the first sentence must have involved even a minimum of consciousness. But that should in the long run matter little, because therein precisely lies the greatest interest in the surrealist exercise. Punctuation of course necessarily hinders the stream of absolute continuity which preoccupies us. But you should particularly distrust the prompting whisper. If through a fault ever so trifling there is a forewarning of silence to come, a fault, let us say, of inattention, break off unhesitatingly the line that has become too lucid. After the word whose origin seems suspect you should place a letter, any letter, l for example, always the letter l, and restore the arbitrary flux by making that letter the initial of the word to follow."

I shall pass over the more or less correlated considerations which the Manifesto discussed in their bearing on the possibilities of plastic expression in surrealism. These considerations did not assume with me a relatively dogmatic turn until later (Surrealism and Painting, 1928).

I believe that the real interest of that book—there was no lack of people who were good enough to concede interest, for which no particular credit is due to me because I have no more than given expression to sentiments shared with friends, present and former—rests only subordinately on the formula above given. It is rather confirmatory of a turn of thought which, for good or ill, is peculiarly distinctive of our time. The defence originally attempted of that turn of thought still seems valid to me in what follows:

"We still live under the reign of logic, but the methods of logic are applied nowadays only to the resolution of problems of secondary interest. The absolute rationalism which is still the fashion does not permit consideration of any facts but those strictly relevant to our experience. Logical ends, on the other hand, escape us. Needless to say that even experience has had limits assigned to it. It revolves in a cage from which it becomes more and more difficult to release it. Even experience is dependent on immediate utility, and common sense is its keeper. Under colour of civilization, under pretext of progress, all that rightly or wrongly may be regarded as fantasy or superstition has been banished from the mind, all uncustomary searching after truth has been proscribed. It is only by what must seem sheer luck that there has recently been brought to light an aspect of mental life—to my belief by far the most important—with which it was supposed that we no longer had any concern. All credit for these discoveries must go to Freud. Based on these discoveries a current of opinion is forming that will enable the explorer of the human mind to continue his investigations, justified as he will be in taking into account more than mere summary realities. The imagination is perhaps on the point of reclaiming its rights. If the depths of our minds harbour strange forces capable of increasing those on the surface, or of successfully contending with them, then it is all in our interest to canalize them, to canalize them first in order to submit them later, if necessary, to the control of the reason. The analysts themselves have nothing to lose by such a proceeding.

But it should be observed that there are no means designed *a priori* for the bringing about of such an enterprise, that until the coming of the new order it might just as well be considered the affair of poets and scientists, and that its success will not depend on the more or less capricious means that will be employed. . . .

"I am resolved to render powerless that *hatred of the marvellous* which is so rampant among certain people, that ridicule to which they are so eager to expose it. Briefly: The marvellous is always beautiful, anything that is marvellous is beautiful; indeed, nothing but the marvellous is beautiful. . . .

"The admirable thing about the fantastic is that it is no longer fantastic: there is only the real. . . .

"Interesting in a different way from the future of surrealist *technics* (theatrical, philosophical, scientific, critical) appears to me the application of surrealism to action. Whatever reservations I might be inclined to make with regard to responsibility in general, I should quite particularly like to know how the first misdemeanours whose surrealist character is indubitable will be *judged*. When surrealist methods extend from writing to action, there will certainly arise the need of a new morality to take the place of the current one, the cause of all our woes."

The *Manifesto of Surrealism* has improved on the Rimbaud principle that the poet must turn *seer*. Man in general is going to be summoned to manifest through life those *new sentiments* which the gift of vision will so suddenly have placed within his reach:

"Surrealism, as I envisage it, displays our complete *nonconformity* so clearly that there can be no question of claiming it as witness when the real world comes up for trial. On the contrary, it can but testify to the complete state of distraction to which we hope to attain here below. Kant distracted by women, Pasteur distracted by 'grapes,' Curie distracted by traffic, are profoundly symptomatic in this respect. The world is only very relatively proportionate to thought, and incidents of this kind are only the most striking episodes of a war of independence in which I glory in taking part. Surrealism is the 'invisible ray' that shall enable us one day to triumph over our enemies. 'You tremble no more, carcase.' This summer the roses are blue; the wood is made of glass. The earth wrapped in its foliage makes as little effect on me as a ghost. Living and ceasing to live are imaginary solutions. Existence is elsewhere."

Surrealism then was securing expression in all its purity and force. The freedom it possesses is a perfect freedom in the sense that it recognizes no limitations exterior to itself. As it was said on the cover of the first issue of *La Révolution Surréaliste*, "it will be necessary to draw up a new declaration of the Rights of Man." The concept of surreality, concerning which quarrels have been sought with us repeatedly and which it was attempted to turn into a metaphysical or mystic rope to be placed afterwards round our necks, lends itself no longer to misconstruction, nowhere does it declare itself opposed to the need of transforming the world which henceforth will more and more definitely yield to it.

As I said in the *Manifesto*:

"I believe in the future transmutation of those two seemingly contradictory states, dream and reality, into a sort of absolute reality, of surreality, so to speak. I am looking forward to its consummation, certain that I shall never share in it, but death would matter little to me could I but taste the joy it will yield ultimately."

Aragon expressed himself in very much the same way in *Une Vague de Rêves* (1924):

"It should be understood that the real is a relation like any other; the essence of things is by no means linked to their reality, there are other relations beside reality, which the mind is capable of grasping, and which also are primary like chance, illusion, the fantastic, the dream. These various groups are united and brought into harmony in one single order, surreality. . . . This surreality—a relation in which all notions are merged together—is the common horizon of religions, magics, poetry, intoxications, and of all life that is lowly—that trembling honeysuckle you deem sufficient to populate the sky with for us."

And René Crevel, in *L'Esprit contre la Raison:*

"The poet does not put the wild animals to sleep in order to play the tamer, but, the cages wide open, the keys thrown to the winds, he journeys forth, a traveller who thinks not of himself, but of the voyage, of dream-beaches, forests of hands, soul-endowed animals, all undeniable surreality."

I was to sum up the idea in these terms in *Surrealism and Painting* (1928):

"All that I love, all that I think and feel inclines me towards a particular philosophy of immanence according to which surreality will reside in reality itself, will be neither superior nor exterior to it. And conversely, because the container shall be also the contained. One might almost say that it will be a communicating vessel placed between the container and the contained. That is to say, I resist with all my strength temptations which, in painting and literature, might have the immediate tendency to withdraw thought from life as well as place life under the aegis of thought."

After years of endeavour and perplexities, when a variety of opinions had disputed amongst themselves the direction of the craft in which a number of persons of unequal ability and varying powers of resistance had originally embarked together, the surrealist idea recovered in the *Second Manifesto* all the brilliancy of which events had vainly conspired to despoil it. It should be emphasized that the *First Manifesto* of 1924 did no more than sum up the conclusions we had drawn during what one may call the *heroic epoch* of surrealism, which stretches from 1919 to 1923. The concerted elaboration of the first automatic texts and our excited reading of them, the first results obtained by Max Ernst in the domain of "collage" and of painting, the practice of surrealist "speaking" during the hypnotic experiments introduced among us by René Crevel and repeated every evening for over a year, uncontrovertibly mark the decisive stages of surrealist exploration during this first phase. After that, up till the taking into account of the social aspect of the problem round about 1925 (though not formally sanctioned until 1930), surrealism began to find itself a prey to characteristic wranglings. These wranglings account very clearly for the expulsion-orders and tickets-of-leave which, as we went along, we had to deal out to certain of our companions of the first and second hour. Some people have quite gratuitously concluded from this that we are apt to overestimate *personal questions.* During the last ten years, surrealism has almost unceasingly been obliged to defend itself against deviations to the right and to the left. On the one hand we have had to struggle against the will of those who would maintain surrealism on a purely speculative level and treasonably transfer it on to an artistic and literary plane (Artaud, Desnos, Ribemont-Dessaignes, Vitrac) at the cost of all the hope for subversion we have placed in it; on the other, against the will of those who would place it on a purely practical basis, available at any moment to be sacrificed to an ill-conceived political militancy (Naville, Aragon)—at the cost, this time, of what constitutes the originality and reality of its researches, at the cost of the autonomous risk that it has to run. Agitated though it was, the epoch that separates the two *Manifestoes* was none the less a rich one, since it saw the publication of so many works in which the vital principles of surrealism were amply accounted for. It suffices to recall particularly *Le Paysan de Paris* and *Traité du Style* by Aragon, *L'Esprit contre la Raison* and *Etes-vous Fous* by René Crevel, *Deuil pour Deuil* by Desnos, *Capitale de la Douleur* and *L'Amour la Poésie* by Eluard, *La Femme 100 Têtes* by Ernst, *La Révolution et les Intellectuels* by Naville, *Le Grand Jeu* by Péret, and my own *Nadja*. The poetic activity of Tzara, although claiming until 1930 no connection with surrealism, is in perfect accord with ours.

We were forced to agree with Pierre Naville when he wrote:

"Surrealism is at the crossroads of several thought-movements. We assume that it affirms the possibility of a certain steady downward readjustment of the mind's rational (and not simply conscious) activity towards more absolutely *coherent* thought, irrespective of whatever direction that thought may take; that is to say, that it proposes or would at least like to propose a new solution of all problems, but chiefly moral. It is, indeed, in that sense that it is epoch-making. That is why one may express the essential characteristic of surrealism by saying that it seeks to calculate the quotient of the unconscious by the conscious."

It should be pointed out that in a number of declarations in *La Révolution et les Intellectuels. Que peuvent faire les surréalistes?* (1926), this same author demonstrated the utter vanity of intellectual bickerings in the face of the human exploitation which results from the wage-earning system. These declarations gave rise amongst us to considerable anxiety and, attempting for the first time to justify surrealism's social implications, I desired to put an end to it in *Légitime Defense*. This pamphlet set out to demonstrate that there is no fundamental antinomy in the basis of surrealist thought. In reality, we are faced with two problems, one of which is the problem raised, at the beginning of the twentieth century, by the discovery of the relations between the conscious and the unconscious. That was how the problem chose to present itself to us. We were the first to apply to its resolution a particular method, which we have not ceased to consider both the most suitable and the most likely to be brought to perfection; there is no reason why we should renounce it. The other problem we are faced with is that of the social action we should pursue. We consider that this action has its own method in dialectical materialism, and we can all the less afford to ignore this action since, I repeat, we hold the liberation of man to be the *sine qua non* condition of the *liberation of the mind*, and we can expect this liberation of man to result only from the proletarian Revolution. These two problems are essentially distinct and we deplore their becoming confused by not remaining so. There is good reason, then, to take up a stand against all attempts to weld them together and, more especially, against the urge to abandon all such researches as ours in order to devote ourselves to the poetry and art of propaganda. Surrealism, which has been the object of brutal and repeated summonses in this respect, now feels the need of making some kind of counter-attack. Let me recall the fact that its very definition holds that it must escape, in its written manifestations, or any others, from all *control* exercised by the reason. Apart from the puerility of wishing to bring a supposedly Marxist control to bear on the immediate aspect of such manifestations, this control cannot be envisaged in *principle*. And how ill-boding does this distrust seem, coming as it does from men who declare themselves Marxists, that is to say possessed not only of a strict line in revolutionary matters, but also of a marvellously open mind and an insatiable curiosity!

This brings us to the eve of the *Second Manifesto*. These objections had to be put an end to, and for that purpose it was indispensable that we should proceed to liquidate certain individualist elements amongst us, more or less openly hostile to one another, whose intentions did not, in the final analysis, appear as irreproachable, nor their motives as disinterested, as might have been desired. An important part of the work was devoted to a statement of the reasons which moved surrealism to dispense for the future with certain collaborators. It was attempted, on the same occasion, to complete the specific method of creation proposed six years earlier, and thoroughly to tidy up surrealist ideas.

"Whatever may have been the controversial issues raised by former or present followers of surrealism, all will admit that the drift of surrealism has always and chiefly been towards a general and emphatic *crisis in consciousness* and that it is only when this is in being or is shown to be impossible that the success or historic eclipse of the movement will be decided.

"Intellectually it was and still is a question of exposing by every available means, and to learn at all costs to identify, the factitious character of the conflicts hypocritically calculated to hinder the setting on foot of any unusual agitation to give mankind were it only a faint understanding of its latent possibilities and to inspire it to free itself from its fetters by all the means available. The horror of death, the pantomime of the beyond, the total breakdown of the most beautiful intellect in dream, the towers of Babel, the mirror of inconstancies, the insuperable silver-splashed wall of the brain, all these startling images of human catastrophes are perhaps nothing but images after all. There is a hint in all this of a belief that there exists a certain spiritual plane on which life and death, the real and the imaginary, the past and the future, the communicable and the incommunicable, the high and the low, are not conceived of as opposites. It would therefore be vain to attribute to surrealism any other motive than the hope to determine that plane, as it would be absurd to ascribe to it a purely destructive or constructive character: the point at issue being precisely this, that construction and destruction should no longer be flaunted against one another. It becomes clear also that surrealism is not at all interested in taking into account what passes alongside it under the guise of art and is in fact anti-art, philosophy or anti-philosophy, all, in a word, that has not for its ultimate end the conversion of the being into a jewel, internal and unseeing, with a soul that is neither of ice nor of fire. What, indeed, do they expect of surrealism, who are still anxious about the position they may occupy *in the world?* On that mental plane from which one may for oneself alone embark on the perilous, but, we think, supreme exploit, on that plane the footfalls of those who come or go are no longer of any importance, because their echo will be repeated in a land in which, by delimitation, surrealism possesses no listening ear. It is not desirable that surrealism should be dependent on the whim of this or that person. If it declares itself capable of ransoming thought from a serfdom more and more task-driven, to bring it back to the path of complete understanding, to restore to it its pristine purity, it is indeed no more than right that it should be judged only by what it has done and by what it has still to accomplish in the fulfilment of its promise. . . .

"While surrealism undertakes particularly the critical investigation of the notions of reality and unreality, of reason and unreason, of reflection and impulse, of knowing and 'fatal' ignorance, of utility and uselessness, there is nevertheless between it and Historical Materialism this similarity in tendency, that it sets out from the 'colossal abortion' of the Hegelian system. I do not see how limits, those for instance of the economic framework, can be assigned to the exercise of a thought which is definitely adapted to negation and the negation of negation. How allow that the dialectical method is only to be applied validly to solving social problems? It is the whole of surrealism's ambition to supply it with nowise conflicting possibilities of application in the most immediate conscious domain. I really cannot see, *pace* a few muddle-headed revolutionaries, why we should abstain from taking up the problems of love, of dreaming, of madness, of art and of religion, so long as we consider these problems from the same angle as they, and we too, consider Revolution. And I have no hesitation in saying that nothing systematic had been done in this direction before surrealism, and for us also at the point where we found it, 'the dialectical method in its Hegelian form could not be put into application.' For us also it was imperative to have done with idealism proper, and our coining of the word 'surrealism' is enough to show that this was so, as it is to show the need for us—to use Engels's example—of going beyond the childish development: 'The rose is a rose. The rose is not a rose. And yet the rose is a rose.' Nevertheless—if I may say so parenthetically—we had to set 'the rose' in a profitable movement of less innocuous contradictions, a movement in which the rose is successively the rose out of the garden, the rose which holds a singular place in a dream, the rose which it is impossible to extract from 'the optical bouquet,' the rose which may change its properties completely by passing into automatic writing, the rose which retains only what the painter has allowed it to retain of a rose in a surrealist painting, and finally the rose, quite different from itself, which goes back into the garden. That is a long way from any idealist standpoint, and we should not disclaim an idealist view if we were not continuing to suffer the attacks of an elementary materialism. These attacks emanate from those who, out of low conservatism, oppose the investigation of the relation of thought to matter, and those who, through ill-digested revolutionary sectarianism, and while ignoring the whole of what is being asked of them, confuse this materialism with the materialism which Engels distinguished as essentially different from it and defined as being primarily an *intuition of the world* which had to put itself to the test and be realized. '*In the course of the development of philosophy idealism became untenable and was contradicted by modern materialism. The latter is the negation of negation and is not simply the old materialism restored: to the enduring foundations of this old materialism it adds the whole of what has been thought in philosophy and natural science throughout an evolution of two thousand years, and adds too the product of this long history itself.*' It is also essential to the proper appreciation of our starting-point to understand that we regard philosophy as *outclassed*. In this we are, I believe, at one with all those for whom reality has more than a theoretical importance, for whom it is a question of life and death to appeal passionately, as Feuerbach insisted, to this reality: *we* so appeal by committing ourselves *entirely*, without reservation, to the principle of historical materialism; *he* so appealed by casting in the face of the astounded intellectual world the idea that 'man is what he eats' and that there would be better prospects of success for a future revolution if the people were better fed, specifically if they were given peas instead of potatoes. . . .

"It was to be expected that surrealism should make its appearance in the midst of, and perhaps thanks to, an uninterrupted succession of falterings, zigzags and defections, which constantly exact the rediscussion of its original data, i.e. it is called back to the initial principle of its activity and at the same time is subject to the interrogation of the *chancy morrow* when the heart's feelings may have waxed or waned. I have to admit that everything has not been done to bring this undertaking off, if only that we have not taken full advantage of the means which have been defined for our group nor fully tested the ways of investigation recommended when the movement was born. The problem of social action is—as I have already said and as I insist—only one form of a more general problem which surrealism finds it its duty to raise, and this problem is *the problem of human expression in all its forms*. Whoever says 'expression' says, to begin with, 'language.' It is not therefore surprising that in the beginning surrealism should have confined itself almost entirely to the plane of language, nor that it should, after some incursion or other, return to that plane as if for the pleasure of behaving there in a conquered land. Nothing, indeed, can prevent the land from being to a great extent conquered. The hordes of words which were literally unleashed and to which Dada and surrealism deliberately opened their doors, are not, whatever anyone thinks, words which withdraw vainly. They will penetrate, at leisure, but certainly, the idiotic little towns of that literature which is still taught and, easily failing to distinguish between low and lofty quarterings, they will capture a fine number of turrets. In the belief that poetry alone so far is all that has been seriously shaken by us, the inhabitants are not really on their guard: they are building here and there a few unimportant ramparts. There is a pretence that it has not been noticed how much the logical mechanism of the sentence is proving more and more impotent by itself to give man the emotive shock which really gives some value to his life. On the other hand, the productions of that spontaneous or *more* spontaneous, direct or *more* direct, activity, such as surrealism is providing in ever greater numbers, in the form of books, pictures and films—these which man first looked upon with amazement, he is now placing about the home, and it is to them that, more or less timorously, he is committing the task of revolutionizing his ways of feeling. No doubt when I say 'man,' that man is not Everyman, and he must be allowed 'time' to become Everyman. But note how admirably and perversely insinuating a small number of quite modern works have already proved, those precisely about which the least that can be said is that they are pervaded by an especially unhealthy atmosphere: Baudelaire, Rimbaud (despite the reservations I have made), Huysmans, and Lautréamont—to mention only poetry. Do not let us be afraid of making a law unto ourselves of this unhealthiness. We want it to be impossible to say that we have not done everything to annihilate that foolish illusion of happiness and *good understanding* which it will be the glory of the nineteenth century to have exposed. Truly we have not ceased to be fanatically attracted by these rays of sunshine full of miasma. But at this moment, when the public authorities in France are preparing a grotesque celebration of the centenary of Romanticism, we for our part say that this Romanticism—of which we are quite ready to appear historically today as the tail, though in that case *an excessively prehensile tail*—this Romanticism is, we say, in its very essence in 1930 the negation of these authorities and this celebration; we say that for Romanticism to be a hundred years old is for it to be young, and that what has wrongly been called its heroic period can no longer pass for anything but the pulings of a being who is now only beginning to make known its wants through us; and finally we say that if it should be held that all that was thought before this infant—all that was thought 'classically'—was good, then incontestably he is out for *the whole of evil.*"

These considerations preface the critical examination of the changes and alterations which the most typical forms of surrealist expression have undergone in the course of time. This has been, as it happens, nothing less than *a rallying back to principles:*

"It is, as I was beginning to say above, regrettable that more systematic and sustained efforts, such as surrealism has constantly called for, have not been suplied in the way of automatic writing and of accounts of dreams. In spite of the way in which we have insistently included material of this sort in surrealist publications, and the remarkable place they occupy in certain works, it has to be admitted that sometimes their interest in such a context has been slight, or that they rather give the effect of being 'bravura pieces.' The presence in these items of an evident pattern has also greatly hampered the species of conversion we had hoped to bring about through them. The excessive negligence of which most of their authors were guilty is to blame: generally these authors were content to let their pens run over paper without observing in the least what was at the time going on inside themselves—this duplication being nevertheless easier to seize and more interesting to consider than that of reflective writing—or else they put together more or less arbitrary dream-elements intended to set forth their picturesqueness rather than to make visible usefully how they had come about. Such distortion of course nullifies any benefit that might be obtained from this sort of operation. Indeed, the great value of these operations for surrealism lies in the possibility they have of yielding to the reader particular logical planes, precisely those in which the logical faculty which is exercised in everything and for everything in consciousness, does not act. What am I saying! Not only do these logical planes remain unexplored, but further, we remain as little informed as ever regarding the origin of the *voice* which it is open to each one of us to hear, and which in the most singular fashion talks to us of something different from what we believe we are thinking, sometimes becoming solemn when we are most lighthearted, or talking nonsense when we are wretched.

"Nobody expressing himself does more than take advantage of a very obscure possibility of conciliation between what he knew he had to say and what on the same subject he didn't know he had to say and yet has said. The most rigorous line of thought is unable to forgo this assistance, undesirable though it yet is from the point of view of rigour. Truly, the idea gets torpedoed in the heart of the sentence enunciating it, even when this sentence escapes having any charming liberty taken with its meaning. Dadaism aimed especially at calling attention to the torpedoing. By appealing to automatism, as is well known, surrealism sets out to prevent the torpedoing of some vessel or other: something like a phantomship (some people have tried to make use of this image against me, but hardworn as it may be, I find it good, and I use it again).

"There is no need to indulge in subtleties: inspiration is familiar enough. And there can be no mistake: it is inspiration which has supplied the supreme need of expression in all times and in all places. A common remark is that inspiration either *is* or is not, and when it is not, nothing summoned to replace it by the human skill which interest obliterates, by the discursive intelligence, or by the talent acquired with labour, can make up in us for the lack of it. We recognize it easily by the way it completely takes possession of the mind, so that for long periods when any problem is set we are momentarily prevented from being the playthings of one rational solution rather than another; and by that kind of short-circuit which it sets up between a given idea and what answers to it (in writing, for example). Just as in the physical world, the short-circuit occurs when the two 'poles' of the machine are linked by a conductor having little or no resistance. In poetry and in painting, surrealism has done everything it could to increase the number of the short-circuits. Its dearest aim now and in the future must be the artificial reproduction of that ideal moment in which a man who is a prey to a particular emotion, is suddenly caught up by 'the stronger than himself,' and thrust, despite his bodily inertia, into immortality. If he were then lucid and awake, he would issue from that predicament in terror. The great thing is that he should not be free to come out, that he should go on talking all the time the mysterious ringing is going on: indeed, it is thanks to that whereby he ceases to belong to himself that he belongs to us. Provided the products of psychic activity which dreaming and automatic writing are, are as much as possible distracted from the will to express, as much as possible lightened of ideas of responsibility ever ready to act as brakes, and as much as possible kept independent of all that is not *the passive life of the intelligence,* these products have the following advantages: that they alone furnish the material for appreciating the grand style to the body of critics who in the artistic domain are strangely disabled; that they allow of a general reclassification of lyrical values; and that they offer a key to go on opening indefinitely that box of never-ending drawers which is called man, and so dissuade him from making an about-turn for reasons of self-preservation on those occasions in the dark when he runs into the externally closed doors of the 'beyond,' of reality, of reason, of genius, and of love. The day will be when these palpable evidences of an existence other than the one we believe ourselves to be leading will no longer be treated as cavalierly as now. It will then seem surprising that, having been so close to *truth* as we are, we in general should have taken care to provide ourselves with some literary alibi or other instead of plunging into the water though ignorant of swimming, and going into the fire though not believing in the phoenix, in order to attain this truth."

Some of you may be perhaps astonished, by the way, to find me dealing thus with automatic texts and accounts of dreams:

"If I feel I must insist so much on the value of the two operations, it is not

because they seem to me to constitute in themselves alone the intellectual panacea, but because for the trained observer they lend themselves less than any others
to confusion or trickery, and that further they are the best that have been found
to invest man with a valid sense of his resources. It goes without saying that the
conditions imposed on us by life make it impossible for such an apparently un-
motivated exercise of thought to go on uninterruptedly. Those who have yielded
themselves up to it unreservedly, however low some of them may later have fallen,
will one day turn out not to have been quite vainly projected into such a complete *internal faerie*. In comparison with this faerie, a return to any premeditated
activity of mind, however it may appeal to the majority of their contemporaries,
will in their eyes provide but a poor spectacle.

"These very direct means, means which are, let us say it again, open to all,
means which we persist in putting forward as soon as the question is no longer
essentially to produce works of art, but to light up the unrevealed and yet re-
vealable part of our being in which all the beauty, all the love and all the virtue
with which we scarcely credit ourselves are shining intensely—these immediate
means are not the only ones. Notably, it seems that now there is much to be
expected of certain methods of pure deception, the application of which to art
and life would have the effect of fixing attention neither on the real nor on the
imaginary, but on the, so to speak, *hither side of the real*. It is easy to imagine
novels which cannot end as there are problems which remain unsolved. When,
however, shall we have the novel in which the characters, having been abundantly
defined with a minimum of particularities, will act in an altogether foreseeable
way in view of an unforeseen result; and, inversely, the novel in which psychology
will not scamp its great but futile duties at the expense of the characters and
events, but will really hold up (as a microscopic slide is held up) between two
blades a fraction of a second, and in this will be surprised the germs of incidents;
this other novel, in which the verisimilitude of the scenery will for the first time
fail to hide from us the strange symbolical life which even the most definite and
most common objects lead in dreams; again, the novel in which the construction
will be quite simple, but in which, however, an elopement will be described with
the words for fatigue, a storm described with precision, but *gaily*, etc.? Whoever
believes with us that it is time to have done with the provoking insanities of
'realism' will have no difficulty in adding to these proposals for himself."

6
MYTH

Myth in Primitive Thought

SIR JAMES G. FRAZER: The King of the Wood

BRONISLAW MALINOWSKI: The Social Psychology of Myth

ERNST CASSIRER: The Validity and Form of Mythical Thought

The Collective Unconscious

C. G. JUNG: The Collective Unconscious and Archetypes

C. G. JUNG: The Psychological Function of Archetypes

C. G. JUNG: The Principal Archetypes

Myth and Literature

FRIEDRICH SCHLEGEL: Modern Mythology

VICTOR HUGO: Imaginative Types

RICHARD WAGNER: The Folk and the Myth

WILLIAM BLAKE: Visionary History

NICOLAS BERDYAEV: Myth as Memory

THOMAS MANN: Psychoanalysis, the Lived Myth, and Fiction

T. S. ELIOT: Myth and Literary Classicism

Introduction

In various ways, the idea of myth points toward the realms of nature, of cultural history, and of unconscious thought.[1] The modern return to mythical forms is in part an attempt to reconstitute the value-laden natural environment that physical science has tended to discredit. At the same time, it is a repossession of a cultural heritage. Though history itself has produced the increasingly rational, disinherited mind of modern man, history may also be invoked as a non-rational, mythical memory, a man-made record of men's intuitive conceptions of themselves. These mythical forms are still available because in another sense they are outside of history, residing in a timeless world below the threshold of consciousness. Myths are public and communicable, but they express subliminal mental patterns that come close to the compulsive drives of the unconscious.

The most influential name associated with the study of myth early in this century is that of Sir James G. Frazer, who begins *The Golden Bough* by conjuring up an extraordinary scene that took place for many years in ancient times at Nemi, south of Rome. There, circling about a sacred tree, was an armed priest ever on the alert to ward off his successor, who could take office only by murdering him. Nothing could be more absurd to the reason than this behavior, but the sanctioned succession of murders and vigils swayed the minds of generations of men. Frazer explains that the weird custom originated in a vegetation myth, and he demonstrates that comparable myths have existed not only in antiquity but also among contemporary savage tribes. Yet Frazer is essentially a rationalist. Though he recognizes and fully illustrates the workings of myth in human culture, myth for him is a primitive habit of mind that we have largely outgrown; it is an addiction to magic. He grants that religion is not so far removed from it, but he hopes that science will succeed religion in the same way that religion has succeeded the magical habit of mind.[2]

Malinowski, while he is respectful to Frazer, is not so much disposed to insist on the distinction between primitive and civilized societies. He assumes

[1] See Sections 3, 4, and 5.
[2] For a related selection from Frazer, see Section 4.

that the myth-making function is universal, though seen most clearly among savage peoples. This function, according to him, is neither quasi-scientific nor quasi-historical, as other interpreters have maintained: myth is not a fanciful way of describing natural phenomena or a disguised chronicle of actual persons and events. Rather, mythical stories serve as a practical cultural force, completely shaping and motivating the moral and social life of a group. The "primitive" does not feel his myth as a fiction referring to something other than itself, but as an articulation of cultural values. Sanctified by its archaic origin, the living form of myth gives warranty to every individual act, thought, and ritualistic performance.

Cassirer takes this interpretation a step further: he considers myth to be one of the basic forms of all human thought, co-ordinate with science, art, and language.[3] To indicate the character of mythical thought, he contrasts it with "discursive" or theoretical thinking. Facts offer themselves to the theoretical mind to be co-ordinated with other facts within a large scheme and so to lose their isolation and immediacy. But intuitions present themselves to the mythical mind directly; the momentary apprehension subordinates everything else to itself. Even the thinker is blotted out by the intensity of his thought. The resultant concentration of meaning is so great that the sacred object is felt to be identical with the whole of reality. It has "mana," it is embedded in a "field of force," and its relation with other objects is not logical, but one of metaphorical identity.

Once we accept mythical thought as having a validity of its own, we are prepared to find that something very much like myth is still at work beneath the surface of the rational or "civilized" mind. Freud often touches on this affinity between myth and the unconscious, notably in his account of the Oedipus complex; but Freud primarily confines himself to analysis of the individual unconscious, and he conceives of the universal patterns of the unconscious mainly on the analogy of organic functions of the body rather than poetic forms.[4] For Jung the idea of myth is more important—indeed, all-important. He postulates a "collective unconscious" beneath the individual unconscious, and he maintains that it is "an ocean of images and figures." These "archetypes" are instinctual, primordial; they are the radical elements of all myth and of all the fantasies and dreams of men. Strictly speaking, they are inaccessible to consciousness—mere predispositions of the psyche, unfilled outlines, formal laws. We know of them only by means of the overt myths, fantasies, and actual behavior that give them specific content in individual instances and that are the conscious embodiment of the unconscious archetypes.

[3] Cassirer's theory of myth is part of a philosophy of symbolic forms that derives from Kantian premises (compare the selection from Kant in Section 1). The form and function of myth, as Cassirer pictures them, often coincide with central symbolist ideas about the form and function of poetry (Section 1).
[4] See Section 5.

It may be asked what attitude consciousness should take toward the unconscious myth-making forces and toward the universal archetypes that subsume even the individual unconscious. Jung replies, somewhat like Freud, that consciousness has grown out of the unconscious as a very late development in nature, but nevertheless it can claim to be a necessary condition for any truly human life. It is a method of direction and control of archetypal compulsions.[5] Yet Jung is as much concerned with asserting the inherent value of the archetypes, and hence of the myths in which they are revealed, as he is with supporting the uneasy rule of conscious thought. Though baleful and destructive in many of their manifestations, the archetypes are the essence of man; in them the whole nature of man strives to realize itself. If they are reflected in psychic disturbances, one of the functions of spontaneous art is to relieve these disorders by expressing the mysterious inner forces of the psyche.

Jung denominates the most disturbing of the archetypes as the *shadow*, the *anima*, the *animus*, and the *mother*. The shadow is the archetypal dark self, obsessively driven toward evil; the anima is the male's archetype of the female, the animus is the female's archetype of the male. The mother archetype, one of the most important, has a multitude of mythical dimensions, both positive and negative, good and evil. Such pre-existent forms assume various contents as they emerge into the individual experience of life and are projected outward by the psyche. Since they often have disastrous effects upon the individual's apprehension of the world, Jung's therapy aims at making the patient aware that his world consists of projected forms. In this way he is saved from damaging illusions and at the same time regains a precious part of himself, his portion of the racial unconscious.

If myth-making is as fundamental a human function as Jung asserts, the persistence of myth in all literatures is readily explained. Even without falling back on Jungian psychology, however, we may be tempted to identify myth with art in general and particularly with the art of poetry. Friedrich Schlegel was one of the first to perceive that such a premise would give a new strength and purpose to the creation of poetry. He proposes that poets of his time should conceive themselves in the role of myth-makers engaged in a communal enterprise. The spontaneous mythologies of ancient or primitive peoples would then find their correlative in an artfully constructed modern mythos. (Yeats developed *A Vision* on a similar theory.) The ideal and the real, which tend to fall apart and oppose each other in modern literature, would be co-ordinate dimensions of the created myth.[6] Victor Hugo does not call for a return to the mythical ground of poetry but proclaims that this has never been lost. Poetic creation is a constant reshaping of the mask of man

[5] Compare the dialectic of reason and unreason in Section 5.
[6] In effect, Schlegel proposes a communal effort of the same sort as Mallarmé and other symbolists prescribe on an individual basis (Section 1). Like Cassirer long after him, Schlegel is building upon the Kantian ideas briefly illustrated in Section 1. For Yeats, see Section 4.

619

into human types, an evocation of the infinite latent forms of mankind. The great figures of literature are substantial phantoms, "the ideal realized." Neither Schlegel nor Hugo is interested in the revival of archaic or classical materials; both affirm that myth is not a particular content but a persistent way of thinking. Wagner approaches the union of art and myth in a different way. For him, the spontaneous myths of folk culture, which are communal and artless expressions of a shared life, are the source of all higher aesthetic value. These folk creations dictate the form and meaning of the most sophisticated art of later eras. The individual artist is not the maker or discoverer of the myth, but its completer, eliciting the order already implicit in his materials and compressing them into a compact, plastic whole.[7]

The view that myth is art is not sufficient for Blake, who declares that myth is the inner structure of all human history. The artist, who dwells in Eden, apprehends history as a visionary pattern that was written out before time began. Blake denies any truth to the scientific analysis of history in terms of causes and consequences; historical actions can be understood only by the mythic imagination of the artist and in terms of their inherent mythical meaning. On quite similar grounds Berdyaev denies that the real stuff of history consists of objective empirical data. Such history has some limited validity, but true history is a mythical reality, an ideal world created and perpetuated by popular memory. Berdyaev sees each man as a microcosm in which all the great historical epochs co-exist and are accessible. By turning to this inner memory men can apprehend the inner flow of history, which is essentially the drama of God's love for the world, "celestial history," a great concrete myth.[8]

The role of myth in modern literature is associated by Thomas Mann with the psychological revolution announced by Schopenhauer and Nietzsche, formulated by Freud, and carried on by Jung.[9] All these writers, as Mann reads them, share the concept of a specifically human world of freedom and determinism, a psychological cosmos. The Freudian psyche, though it seems in one way wholly predetermined, is nevertheless a human arena where man makes his own conditions—as is even more apparent in the collective unconscious of Jung. Myths claim the same kind of psychological reality. Known or unknown, they lie within us; we fancy ourselves original, but are really imitating or performing, for life is a steady mythical identification, a procession in the footsteps of others, a sacred repetition. Yet this world of man is reborn through us; we remake it at every turn. It is at once passively experienced and actively created, at once historic and prophetic, timely and timeless. Sustained by his faith in "lived myth," a faith that in itself is quite

[7] Compare Nietzsche's account of the origin of Greek tragedy (Section 5). A related selection from Wagner appears in Section 1.
[8] In various ways, the historical theories of Vico, Spengler, and Yeats (Section 4) are comparable to the theory of mythical history in Blake and Berdyaev. See related selections from Blake in Sections 1, 5, and 9; from Berdyaev, in Section 4.
[9] Another portion of Mann's essay appears in Section 5.

primitive yet validated by the most modern of sciences, Mann gains the subject and the method of his *Joseph* novels.[10]

Mann espouses myth as neither a traditionalist nor a modernist but a humanist. T. S. Eliot's commendation of Joyce's *Ulysses*, on the other hand, is explicitly based on the tenets of a modern "classicism." He treats Joyce's use of the *Odyssey* as an effort to find an external order and a source of meaning that will lend form and value to the confusion of modern life. In point of fact, Joyce's book is probably closer in spirit to Mann than to Eliot; but Eliot's posture in this essay is characteristic of his own approach to mythical materials. The "classicist" in myth would avail himself of the depths of meaning within the forms of ancient story, but he wants the form more than the meaning, the discipline of orthodoxy more than the fullness of tradition.[11] And the element of myth in his art is not so much a creative method, a resumption of the role of mythic poet, as it is an intellectual strategy, a device for gaining perspective on himself and on his myth-forsaken time.

[10] Compare the Yeatsian vision of history (Section 4). The Bergsonian and Proustian sense of endurance is analogous on the plane of personal life.
[11] Eliot's basic position is similar to that of T. E. Hulme (see Section 9).

SIR JAMES G. FRAZER
The King of the Wood

1. *Diana and Virbius.*—Who does not know Turner's picture of the Golden Bough? The scene, suffused with the golden glow of imagination in which the divine mind of Turner steeped and transfigured even the fairest natural landscape, is a dream-like vision of the little woodland lake of Nemi—"Diana's Mirror," as it was called by the ancients. No one who has seen that calm water, lapped in a green hollow of the Alban hills, can ever forget it. The two characteristic Italian villages which slumber on its banks, and the equally Italian palace whose terraced gardens descend steeply to the lake, hardly break the stillness and even the solitariness of the scene. Diana herself might still linger by this lonely shore, still haunt these woodlands wild.

In antiquity this sylvan landscape was the scene of a strange and recurring tragedy. On the northern shore of the lake, right under the precipitous cliffs on which the modern village of Nemi is perched, stood the sacred grove and sanctuary of Diana Nemorensis, or Diana of the Wood. The lake and the grove were sometimes known as the lake and grove of Aricia. But the town of Aricia (the modern La Riccia) was situated about three miles off, at the foot of the Alban Mount, and separated by a steep descent from the lake, which lies in a small crater-like hollow on the mountain side. In this sacred grove there grew a certain tree round which at any time of the day, and probably far into the night, a grim figure might be seen to prowl. In his hand he carried a drawn sword, and he kept peering warily about him as if at every instant he expected to be set upon by an enemy. He was a priest and a murderer; and the man for whom he looked was sooner or later to murder him and hold the priesthood in his stead. Such was the rule of the sanctuary. A candidate for the priesthood could only succeed to office by slaying the priest, and having slain him, he retained office till he was himself slain by a stronger or a craftier.

The post which he held by this precarious tenure carried with it the title of king; but surely no crowned head ever lay uneasier, or was visited by more evil dreams, than his. For year in, year out, in summer and winter, in fair weather and in foul, he had to keep his lonely watch, and whenever he snatched a troubled slumber it was at the peril of his life. The least relaxation of his vigilance, the smallest abatement of his strength of limb or skill of fence, put him in jeopardy; grey hairs might seal his death-warrant. To gentle and pious pilgrims at the shrine the sight of him might well seem to darken the fair landscape, as when a cloud suddenly blots the sun on a bright day. The dreamy blue of Italian skies, the dappled shade of summer woods, and the sparkle of waves in the sun, can have accorded but ill with that stern and sinister figure. Rather we picture to ourselves the scene as it may have been witnessed by a belated wayfarer on one of those wild autumn nights when the dead leaves are falling thick, and the winds seem to sing the dirge of the dying year. It is a sombre picture, set to melancholy music —the background of forest showing black and jagged against a lowering and stormy sky, the sighing of the wind in the branches, the rustle of the withered leaves under foot, the lapping of the cold water on the shore, and in the foreground, pacing to and fro, now in twilight and now in gloom, a dark figure with a glitter of steel at the shoulder whenever the pale moon, riding clear of the cloud-rack, peers down at him through the matted boughs.

The strange rule of this priesthood has no parallel in classical antiquity, and cannot be explained from it. To find an explanation we must go farther afield. No one will probably deny that such a custom savours of a barbarous age, and, surviving into imperial times, stands out in striking isolation from the polished Italian society of the day, like a primaeval rock rising from a smooth-shaven lawn. It is the very rudeness and barbarity of the custom which allow us a hope of explaining it. For recent researches into the early history of man have revealed the essential similarity with which, under many superficial differences, the human mind has elaborated its first crude philosophy of life. Accordingly, if we can show that a barbarous custom, like that of the priesthood of Nemi, has existed elsewhere; if we can detect the motives which led to its institution; if we can prove that these motives have operated widely, perhaps universally, in human society, producing in varied circumstances a variety of institutions specifically different but generically alike; if we can show, lastly, that these very motives, with some of their derivative institutions, were actually at work in classical antiquity; then we may fairly infer that at a remoter age the same motives gave birth to the priesthood of Nemi. Such an inference, in default of direct evidence as to how the priesthood did actually arise, can never amount to demonstration. But it will be more or less probable according to the degree of completeness with which it fulfils the conditions I have indicated. The object of this book is, by meeting these conditions, to offer a fairly probable explanation of the priesthood of Nemi.

I begin by setting forth the few facts and legends which have come down to us on the subject. According to one story the worship of Diana at Nemi was instituted by Orestes, who, after killing Thoas, King of the Tauric Chersonese (the Crimea), fled with his sister to Italy, bringing with him the image of the Tauric Diana hidden in a faggot of sticks. After his death his bones were transported from Aricia to Rome and buried in front of the temple of Saturn, on the Capitoline slope, beside the temple of Concord. The bloody ritual which legend ascribed to the Tauric Diana is familiar to classical readers; it is said that every stranger who landed on the shore was sacrificed on her altar. But transported to Italy, the rite assumed a milder form. Within the sanctuary at Nemi grew a certain tree of which no branch might be broken. Only a runaway slave was allowed to break off, if he could, one of its boughs. Success in the attempt entitled him to fight the priest in single combat, and if he slew him he reigned in his stead with the title of King of the Wood (*Rex Nemorensis*). According to the public opinion of the ancients the fateful branch was that Golden Bough which, at the Sibyl's bidding, Aeneas plucked before he essayed the perilous journey to the world of the dead. The flight of the slave represented, it was said, the flight of Orestes; his combat with the priest was a reminiscence of the human sacrifices once offered to the Tauric Diana. This rule of succession by the sword was observed down to imperial times; for amongst his other freaks Caligula, thinking that the priest of Nemi had held office too long, hired a more stalwart ruffian to slay him; and a Greek traveller, who visited Italy in the age of the Antonines, remarks that down to his time the priesthood was still the prize of victory in a single combat.

Of the worship of Diana at Nemi some leading features can still be made out. From the votive offerings which have been found on the site, it appears that she was conceived of especially as a huntress, and further as blessing men and women with offspring, and granting expectant mothers an easy delivery. Again, fire seems to have played a foremost part in her ritual. For during her annual festival, held on the thirteenth of August, at the hottest time of the year, her grove shone with a multitude of torches, whose ruddy glare was reflected by the lake; and throughout the length and breadth of Italy the day was kept with holy rites at every domestic hearth. Bronze statuettes found in her precinct represent the goddess herself holding a torch in her raised right hand; and women whose prayers had been heard by her came crowned with wreaths and bearing lighted torches to the sanctuary in fulfilment of their vows. Some one unknown dedicated a perpetually burning lamp in a little shrine at Nemi for the safety of the Emperor Claudius and his family. The terra-cotta lamps which have been discovered in the grove may perhaps have served a like purpose for humbler persons. If so, the analogy of the custom to the Catholic practice of dedicating holy candles in churches would be obvious. Further, the title of Vesta borne by Diana at Nemi points clearly to the maintenance of a perpetual holy fire in her sanctuary. A large circular basement at the north-east corner of the temple, raised on three steps and bearing traces of a mosaic pavement, probably supported a round temple of Diana in her character of Vesta, like the round temple of Vesta in the Roman Forum. Here the sacred fire would seem to have been tended by Vestal Virgins, for the head of a Vestal in terra-cotta was found on the spot, and the worship of a perpetual fire, cared for by holy maidens, appears to have been common in Latium from the earliest to the latest times. Further, at the annual festival of the goddess, hunting dogs were crowned and wild beasts were not molested; young people went through a purificatory ceremony in her honour; wine was brought forth, and the feast consisted of a kid, cakes served piping hot on plates of leaves, and apples still hanging in clusters on the boughs.

But Diana did not reign alone in her grove at Nemi. Two lesser divinities shared her forest sanctuary. One was Egeria, the nymph of the clear water which, bubbling from the basaltic rocks, used to fall in graceful cascades into the lake at the place called Le Mole, because here were established the mills of the modern village of Nemi. The purling of the stream as it ran over the pebbles is mentioned by Ovid, who tells us that he had often drunk of its water. Women with child used to sacrifice to Egeria, because she was believed, like Diana, to be able to grant them an easy delivery. Tradition ran that the nymph had been the wife or mistress of the wise king Numa, that he had consorted with her in the secrecy of the sacred grove, and that the laws which he gave the Romans had been inspired by communion with her divinity. Plutarch compares the legend with other tales of the loves of goddesses for mortal men, such as the love of Cybele and the Moon for the fair youths Attis and Endymion. According to some, the trysting-place of the lovers was not in the woods of Nemi but in a grove outside the dripping Porta Capena at Rome, where another sacred spring of Egeria gushed from a dark cavern. Every day the Roman Vestals fetched water from this spring to wash the temple of Vesta, carrying it in earthenware pitchers on their heads. In Juvenal's time the natural rock had been encased in marble, and the hallowed spot was profaned by gangs of poor Jews, who were suffered to squat, like gypsies, in the grove. We may suppose that the spring which fell into the lake of Nemi was the true original Egeria, and that when the first settlers moved down from the Alban hills to the banks of the Tiber they brought the nymph with them and found a new home for her in a grove outside the gates. The remains of baths which have been discovered within the sacred precinct, together with many terra-cotta models of various parts of the human body, suggest that the waters of Egeria were used to heal the sick, who may have signified their hopes or testified their gratitude by dedicating likenesses of the diseased members to the goddess, in accordance with a custom which is still observed in many parts of Europe. To this day it would seem that the spring retains medicinal virtues.

The other of the minor deities at Nemi was Virbius. Legend had it that Virbius was the young Greek hero Hippolytus, chaste and fair, who learned the art of venery from the centaur Chiron, and spent all his days in the greenwood chasing wild beasts with the virgin huntress Artemis (the Greek counterpart of Diana) for his only comrade. Proud of her divine society, he spurned the love of women, and this proved his bane. For Aphrodite, stung by his scorn, inspired his stepmother Phaedra with love of him; and when he disdained her wicked advances she falsely accused him to his father Theseus. The slander was believed, and Theseus prayed to his sire Poseidon to avenge the imagined wrong. So while Hippolytus drove in a chariot by the shore of the Saronic Gulf, the sea-god sent a fierce bull forth from the waves. The terrified horses bolted, threw Hippolytus from the chariot, and dragged him at their hoofs to death. But Diana, for the love she bore Hippolytus, persuaded the leech Aesculapius to bring her fair young hunter back to life by his simples. Jupiter, indignant that a mortal man should return from the gates of death, thrust down the meddling leech himself to Hades. But Diana hid her favourite from the angry god in a thick cloud, disguised his features by adding years to his life, and then bore him far away to the dells of Nemi, where she entrusted him to the nymph Egeria, to live there, unknown and solitary, under the name of Virbius, in the depths of the Italian forest. There he reigned a king, and there he dedicated a precinct to Diana. He had a comely son, Virbius, who, undaunted by his father's fate, drove a team of fiery steeds to join the Latins in the war against Aeneas and the Trojans. Virbius was worshipped as a god not only at Nemi but elsewhere; for in Campania we hear of a special priest devoted to his service. Horses were excluded from the Arician grove and santuary because horses had killed Hippolytus. It was unlawful to touch his image. Some thought that he was the sun. "But the truth is," says Servius, "that he is a deity associated with Diana, as Attis is associated with the Mother of the Gods, and Erichthonius with Minerva, and Adonis with Venus." What the nature of that association was we shall enquire presently. Here it is worth observing that in his long and chequered career this mythical personage has displayed a remarkable tenacity of life. For we can hardly doubt that the Saint Hippolytus of the Roman calendar, who was dragged by horses to death on the thirteenth of August, Diana's own day, is no other than the Greek hero of the same name, who, after dying twice over as a heathen sinner, has been happily resuscitated as a Christian saint.

It needs no elaborate demonstration to convince us that the stories told to account for Diana's worship at Nemi are unhistorical. Clearly they belong to that large class of myths which are made up to explain the origin of a religious ritual and have no other foundation than the resemblance, real or imaginary, which may be traced between it and some foreign ritual. The incongruity of these Nemi myths is indeed transparent, since the foundation of the worship is traced now to Orestes and now to Hippolytus, according as this or that feature of the ritual has to be accounted for. The real value of such tales is that they serve to illustrate the nature of the worship by providing a standard with which to compare it; and further, that they bear witness indirectly to its venerable age by showing that the true origin was lost in the mists of a fabulous antiquity. In the latter respect these Nemi legends are probably more to be trusted than the apparently historical tradition, vouched for by Cato the Elder, that the sacred grove was dedicated to Diana by a certain Egerius Baebius or Laevius of Tusculum, a Latin dictator, on behalf of the peoples of Tusculum, Aricia, Lanuvium, Laurentum, Cora, Tibur, Pometia, and Ardea. This tradition indeed speaks for the great age of the sanctuary, since it seems to date its foundation sometime before 495 B.C., the year in which Pometia was sacked by the Romans and disappears from history. But we cannot suppose that so barbarous a rule as that of the Arician priesthood was deliberately instituted by a league of civilised communities, such as the Latin cities undoubtedly were. It must have been handed down from a time beyond the memory of man, when Italy was still in a far ruder state than any known to us in the historical period. The credit of the tradition is rather shaken than confirmed by another story which ascribes the foundation of the sanctuary to a certain Manius Egerius, who gave rise to the saying, "There are many Manii at Aricia." This proverb some explained by alleging that Manius Egerius was the ancestor of a long and distinguished line, whereas others thought it meant that there were many ugly and deformed people at Aricia, and they derived the name Manius from *Mania,* a bogey or bugbear to frighten children. A Roman satirist uses the name Manius as typical of the beggars who lay in wait for pilgrims on the Arician slopes. These differences of opinion, together with the discrepancy between Manius Egerius of Aricia and Egerius Laevius of Tusculum, as well as the resemblance of both names to the mythical Egeria, excite our suspicion. Yet the tradition recorded by Cato seems too circumstantial, and its sponsor too respectable, to allow us to dismiss it as an idle fiction. Rather we may suppose that it refers to some ancient restoration or reconstruction of the sanctuary, which was actually carried out by the confederate states. At any rate it testifies to a belief that the grove had been from early times a common place of worship for many of the oldest cities of the country, if not for the whole Latin confederacy.

2. *Artemis and Hippolytus.*—I have said that the Arician legends of Orestes and Hippolytus, though worthless as history, have a certain value in so far as they may help us to understand the worship at Nemi better by comparing it with the ritual and myths of other sanctuaries. We must ask ourselves, Why did the author of these legends pitch upon Orestes and Hippolytus in order to explain Virbius and the King of the Wood? In regard to Orestes, the answer is obvious. He and the image of the Tauric Diana, which could only be appeased with human blood, were dragged in to render intelligible the murderous rule of succession to the Arician priesthood. In regard to Hippolytus the case is not so plain. The manner of his death suggests readily enough a reason for the exclusion of horses from the grove; but this by itself seems hardly enough to account for the identification. We must try to probe deeper by examining the worship as well as the legend or myth of Hippolytus.

He had a famous sanctuary at his ancestral home of Troezen, situated on that beautiful, almost landlocked bay, where groves of oranges and lemons, with tall cypresses soaring like dark spires above the garden of Hesperides, now clothe the strip of fertile shore at the foot of the rugged mountains. Across the blue water of the tranquil bay, which it shelters from the open sea, rises Poseidon's sacred island, its peaks veiled in the sombre green of the pines. On this fair coast Hippolytus was worshipped. Within his sanctuary stood a temple with an ancient image. His service was performed by a priest who held office for life; every year a sacrificial festival was held in his honour; and his untimely fate was yearly mourned, with weeping and doleful chants, by unwedded maids. Youths and maidens dedicated locks of their hair in his temple before marriage. His grave existed at Troezen, though the people would not show it. It has been suggested, with great plausibility, that in the handsome Hippolytus, beloved of Artemis, cut off in his youthful prime, and yearly mourned by damsels, we have one of those mortal lovers of a goddess who appear so often in ancient religion, and of whom Adonis is the most familiar type. The rivalry of Artemis and Phaedra for the affection of Hippolytus reproduces, it is said, under different names, the rivalry of Aphrodite and Proserpine for the love of Adonis, for Phaedra is merely a double of Aphrodite. The theory probably does no injustice either to Hippolytus or to Artemis. For Artemis was originally a great goddess of fertility, and, on the principles of early religion, she who fertilises nature must herself be fertile, and to be that she must necessarily have a male consort. On this view, Hippolytus was the consort of Artemis at Troezen, and the shorn tresses offered to him by the Troezenian youths and maidens before marriage were designed to strengthen his union with the goddess, and so to promote the fruitfulness of the earth, of cattle, and of mankind. It is some confirmation of this view that within the precinct of Hippolytus at Troezen there were worshipped two female powers named Damia and Auxesia, whose connexion with the fertility of the ground is unquestionable. When Epidaurus suffered from a dearth, the people, in obedience to an oracle, carved images of Damia and Auxesia out of sacred olive wood, and no sooner had they done so and set them up than the earth bore fruit again. Moreover, at Troezen itself, and apparently within the precinct of Hippolytus, a curious festival of stone-throwing was held in honour of these maidens, as the Troezenians called them; and it is easy to show that similar customs have been practised in many lands for the express purpose of ensuring good crops. In the story of the tragic death of the youthful Hippolytus we may discern an analogy with similar tales of other fair but mortal youths who paid with their lives for the brief rapture of the love of an immortal goddess. These hapless lovers were probably not always mere myths, and the legends which traced their spilt blood in the purple bloom of the violet, the scarlet stain of the anemone, or the crimson flush of the rose were no idle poetic emblems of youth and beauty fleeting as the summer flowers. Such fables contain a deeper philosophy of the relation of the life of man to the life of nature—a sad philosophy which gave birth to a tragic practice. What that philosophy and that practice were, we shall learn later on.

3. *Recapitulation.*—We can now perhaps understand why the ancients identified Hippolytus, the consort of Artemis, with Virbius, who, according to Servius, stood to Diana as Adonis to Venus, or Attis to the Mother of the Gods. For Diana, like Artemis, was a goddess of fertility in general, and of childbirth in particular. As such she, like her Greek counterpart, needed a male partner. That partner, if Servius is right, was Virbius. In his character of the founder of the sacred grove and first king of Nemi, Virbius is clearly the mythical predecessor or archetype of the line of priests who served Diana under the title of Kings of the Wood, and who came, like him, one after the other, to a violent end. It is natural, therefore, to conjecture that they stood to the goddess of the grove in the same relation in which Virbius stood to her; in short, that the mortal King of the Wood had for his queen the woodland Diana herself. If the sacred tree which he guarded with his life was supposed, as seems probable, to be her special embodiment, her priest may not only have worshipped it as his goddess but embraced it as his wife. There is at least nothing absurd in the supposition, since even in the time of Pliny a noble Roman used thus to treat a beautiful beech-tree in another sacred grove of Diana on the Alban hills. He embraced it, he kissed it, he lay under its shadow, he poured wine on its trunk. Apparently he took the tree for the goddess. The custom of physically marrying men and women to trees is still practised in India and other parts of the East. Why should it not have obtained in ancient Latium?

Reviewing the evidence as a whole, we may conclude that the worship of Diana in her sacred grove at Nemi was of great importance and immemorial antiquity; that she was revered as the goddess of woodlands and of wild creatures, probably also of domestic cattle and of the fruits of the earth; that she was believed to bless men and women with offspring and to aid mothers in childbed; that her holy fire, tended by chaste virgins, burned perpetually in a round temple within the precinct; that associated with her was a water-nymph Egeria who discharged one of Diana's own functions by succouring women in travail, and who was popularly supposed to have mated with an old Roman king in the sacred grove; further, that Diana of the Wood herself had a male companion Virbius by name, who was to her what Adonis was to Venus, or Attis to Cybele; and, lastly, that this mythical Virbius was represented in historical times by a line of priests known as Kings of the Wood, who regularly perished by the swords of their successors, and whose lives were in a manner bound up with a certain tree in the grove, because so long as that tree was uninjured they were safe from attack.

Clearly these conclusions do not of themselves suffice to explain the peculiar rule of succession to the priesthood. But perhaps the survey of a wider field may lead us to think that they contain in germ the solution of the problem. To that wider survey we must now address ourselves. It will be long and laborious, but may possess something of the interest and charm of a voyage of discovery, in which we shall visit many strange foreign lands, with strange foreign peoples, and still stranger customs. The wind is in the shrouds: we shake out our sails to it, and leave the coast of Italy behind us for a time.

We may illustrate the course which thought has hitherto run by likening it to a web woven of three different threads—the black thread of magic, the red thread of religion, and the white thread of science, if under science we may include those simple truths, drawn from observation of nature, of which men in all ages have possessed a store. Could we then survey the web of thought from the beginning, we should probably perceive it to be at first a chequer of black and white, a patchwork of true and false notions, hardly tinged as yet by the red thread of religion. But carry your eye farther along the fabric and you will remark that, while the black and white chequer still runs through it, there rests on the middle portion of the web, where religion has entered most deeply into its texture, a dark crimson stain, which shades off insensibly into a lighter tint as the white thread of science is woven more and more into the tissue. To a web thus chequered and stained, thus shot with threads of diverse hues, but gradually changing colour the farther it is unrolled, the state of modern thought, with all its divergent aims and conflicting tendencies, may be compared. Will the great movement which for centuries has been slowly altering the complexion of thought be continued in the near future? or will a reaction set in which may arrest progress and even undo much that has been done? To keep up our parable, what will be the colour of the web which the Fates are now weaving on the humming loom of time? will it be white or red? We cannot tell. A faint glimmering light illumines the backward portion of the web. Clouds and thick darkness hide the other end.

Our long voyage of discovery is over and our bark has drooped her weary sails in port at last. Once more we take the road to Nemi. It is evening, and as we climb the long slope of the Appian Way up to the Alban Hills, we look back and see the sky aflame with sunset, its golden glory resting like the aureole of a dying saint over Rome and touching with a crest of fire the dome of St. Peter's. The sight once seen can never be forgotten, but we turn from it and pursue our way darkling along the mountain side, till we come to Nemi and look down on the lake in its deep hollow, now fast disappearing in the evening shadows. The place has changed but little since Diana received the homage of her worshippers in the sacred grove. The temple of the sylvan goddess, indeed, has vanished and the King of the Wood no longer stands sentinel over the Golden Bough. But Nemi's woods are still green, and as the sunset fades above them in the west, there comes to us, borne on the swell of the wind, the sound of the church bells of Aricia ringing the Angelus. *Ave Maria!* Sweet and solemn they chime out from the distant town and die lingeringly away across the wide Campagnan marshes. *Le roi est mort, vive le roi! Ave Maria!*

BRONISLAW MALINOWSKI
The Social Psychology of Myth

By the examination of a typical Melanesian culture and by a survey of the opinions, traditions, and behaviour of these natives, I propose to show how deeply the sacred tradition, the myth, enters into their pursuits, and how strongly it controls their moral and social behaviour. In other words, the thesis of the present work is that an intimate connection exists between the word, the mythos, the sacred tales of a tribe on the one hand, and their ritual acts, their moral deeds, their social organization, and even their practical activities on the other.

In order to gain a background for our description of the Melanesian facts, I shall briefly summarize the present state of the science of mythology. Even a superficial survey of the literature would reveal that there is no monotony to complain of as regards the variety of opinions or the acrimony of polemics. To take only the recent up-to-date theories advanced in explanation of the nature of myth, legend, and fairytale, we should have to head the list, at least as regards output and self-assertion, by the so-called school of Nature-mythology which flourishes mainly in Germany. The writers of the school maintain that primitive man is highly interested in natural phenomena, and that his interest is predominantly of a theoretical, contemplative, and poetical character. In trying to express and interpret the phases of the moon, or the regular and yet changing path of the sun across the skies, primitive man constructs symbolic personified rhapsodies. To writers of this school every myth possesses as its kernel or ultimate reality some natural phenomenon or other, elaborately woven into a tale to an extent which sometimes almost masks and obliterates it. There is not much agreement among these students as to what type of natural phenomenon lies at the bottom of most mythological productions. There are extreme lunar mythologists so completely moonstruck with their idea that they will not admit that any other phenomenon could lend itself to a savage rhapsodic interpretation except that of earth's nocturnal satellite. The Society for the Comparative Study of Myth, founded in Berlin in 1906, and counting among its supporters such famous scholars as Ehrenreich, Siecke, Winckler, and many others, carried on their business under the sign of the moon. Others, like Frobenius for instance, regard the sun as the only subject around which primitive man has spun his symbolic tales. Then there is the school of meteorological interpreters who regard wind, weather, and colours of the skies as the essence of myth. To this belonged such well-known writers of the older generation as Max Müller and Kuhn. Some of these departmental mythologists fight fiercely for their heavenly body or principle; others have a more catholic taste, and prepare to agree that primeval man has made his mythological brew from all the heavenly bodies taken together.

I have tried to state fairly and plausibly this naturalistic interpretation of myths, but as a matter of fact this theory seems to me to be one of the most extravagant views ever advanced by an anthropologist or humanist—and that means a great deal. It has received an absolutely destructive criticism from the great psychologist Wundt, and appears absolutely untenable in the light of any of Sir James Frazer's writings. From my own study of living myths among savages, I should say that primitive man has to a very limited extent the purely artistic or scientific interest in nature; there is but little room for symbolism in his ideas and tales; and myth, in fact, is not an idle rhapsody, not an aimless outpouring of vain imaginings, but a hard-working, extremely important cultural force. Besides ignoring the cultural function of myth, this theory imputes to primitive man a number of imaginary interests, and it confuses several clearly distinguishable types of story, the fairy tale, the legend, the saga, and the sacred tale or myth.

In strong contrast to this theory which makes myth naturalistic, symbolic, and imaginary, stands the theory which regards a sacred tale as a true historical record of the past. This view, recently supported by the so-called Historical School in Germany and America, and represented in England by Dr. Rivers, covers but part of the truth. There is no denying that history, as well as natural environment, must have left a profound imprint on all cultural achievements, hence also on myths. But to take all mythology as mere chronicle is as incorrect as to regard it as the primitive naturalist's musings. It also endows primitive man with a sort of scientific impulse and desire for knowledge. Although the savage has something of the antiquarian as well as of the naturalist in his composition, he is, above all, actively engaged in a number of practical pursuits, and has to struggle with various difficulties; all his interests are tuned up to this general pragmatic outlook. Mythology, the sacred lore of the tribe, is, as we shall see, a powerful means of assisting primitive man, of allowing him to make the two ends of his cultural patrimony meet. We shall see, moreover, that the immense services to primitive culture performed by myth are done in connection with religious ritual, moral influence, and sociological principle. Now religion and morals draw only to a very limited extent upon an interest in science or in past history, and myth is thus based upon an entirely different mental attitude.

The close connection between religion and myth which has been overlooked by many students has been recognized by others. Psychologists like Durkheim, Hubert, and Mauss, anthropologists like Crawley, classical scholars like Miss Jane Harrison have all understood the intimate association between myth and ritual, between sacred tradition and the norms of social structure. All of these writers have been to a greater or lesser extent influenced by the work of Sir James Frazer. In spite of the fact that the great British anthropologist, as well as most of his followers, have a clear vision of the sociological and ritual importance of myth, the facts which I shall present will allow us to clarify and formulate more precisely the main principles of a sociological theory of myth.

I might present an even more extensive survey of the opinions, divisions, and controversies of learned mythologists. The science of mythology has been the meeting-point of various scholarships: the classical humanist must decide for himself whether Zeus is the moon, or the sun, or a strictly historical personality; and whether his ox-eyed spouse is the morning star, or a cow, or a personification of the wind—the loquacity of wives being proverbial. Then all these questions have to be re-discussed upon the stage of mythology by the various tribes of archæologists, Chaldean and Egyptian, Indian and Chinese, Peruvian and Mayan. The historian and the sociologist, the student of literature, the grammarian, the Germanist and the Romanist, the Celtic scholar and the Slavist discuss, each little crowd among themselves. Nor is mythology quite safe from logicians and psychologists, from the metaphysician and the epistemologist—to say nothing of such visitors as the theosophist, the modern astrologist, and the Christian Scientist. Finally, we have the psycho-analyst who has come at last to teach us that the myth is a day-dream of the race, and that we can only explain it by turning our back upon nature, history, and culture, and diving deep into the dark pools of the sub-conscious, where at the bottom there lie the usual paraphernalia and symbols of psychoanalytic exegesis. So that when at last the poor anthropologist and student of folk-lore come to the feast, there are hardly any crumbs left for them!

If I have conveyed an impression of chaos and confusion, if I have inspired a sinking feeling towards the incredible mythological controversy with all the dust and din which it raises, I have achieved exactly what I wanted. For I shall invite my readers to step outside the closed study of the theorist into the open air of the anthropological field, and to follow me in my mental flight back to the years which I spent among a Melanesian tribe of New Guinea. There, paddling on the lagoon, watching the natives under the blazing sun at their garden-work, following them through the patches of jungle, and on the winding beaches and reefs, we shall learn about their life. And again, observing their ceremonies in the cool of the afternoon or in the shadows of the evening, sharing their meals round their fires, we shall be able to listen to their stories.

For the anthropologist—one and only among the many participants in the mythological contest—has the unique advantage of being able to step back behind the savage whenever he feels that his theories become involved and the flow of his argumentative eloquence runs dry. The anthropologist is not bound to the scanty remnants of culture, broken tablets, tarnished texts, or fragmentary inscriptions. He need not fill out immense gaps with voluminous, but conjectural, comments. The anthropologist has the myth-maker at his elbow. Not only can he take down as full a text as exists, with all its variations, and control it over and over; he has also a host of authentic commentators to draw upon; still more he has the fulness of life itself from which the myth has been born. And as we shall see, in this live context there is as much to be learned about the myth as in the narrative itself.

Myth as it exists in a savage community, that is, in its living primitive form, is not merely a story told but a reality lived. It is not of the nature of fiction, such as we read to-day in a novel, but it is a living reality, believed to have once happened in primeval times, and continuing ever since to influence the world and human destinies. This myth is to the savage what, to a fully believing Christian, is the Biblical story of Creation, of the Fall, of the Redemption by Christ's Sacrifice on the Cross. As our sacred story lives in our ritual, in our morality, as it governs our faith and controls our conduct, even so does his myth for the savage.

The limitation of the study of myth to the mere examination of texts has been fatal to a proper understanding of its nature. The forms of myth which come to us from classical antiquity and from the ancient sacred books of the East and other similar sources have come down to us without the context of living faith, without the possibility of obtaining comments from true believers, without the concomitant knowledge of their social organization, their practised morals, and their popular customs—at least without the full information which the modern field-worker can easily obtain. Moreover, there is no doubt that in their present literary form these tales have suffered a very considerable transformation at the hands of scribes, commentators, learned priests, and theologians. It is necessary to go back to primitive mythology in order to learn the secret of its life in the study of a myth which is still alive—before, mummified in priestly wisdom, it has been enshrined in the indestructible but lifeless repository of dead religions.

Studied alive, myth, as we shall see, is not symbolic, but a direct expression of its subject-matter; it is not an explanation in satisfaction of a scientific interest, but a narrative resurrection of a primeval reality, told in satisfaction of deep religious wants, moral cravings, social submissions, assertions, even practical requirements. Myth fulfils in primitive culture an indispensable function: it expresses, enhances, and codifies belief; it safeguards and enforces morality; it vouches for the efficiency of ritual and contains practical rules for the guidance of man. Myth is thus a vital ingredient of human civilization; it is not an idle tale, but a hard-worked active force; it is not an intellectual explanation or an artistic imagery, but a pragmatic charter of primitive faith and moral wisdom.

I shall try to prove all these contentions by the study of various myths; but to make our analysis conclusive it will first be necessary to give an account not merely of myth, but also of fairy tale, legend, and historical record. . . .

The *folk-tale*, as we know, is a seasonal performance and an act of sociability. The *legend*, provoked by contact with unusual reality, opens up past historical vistas. The *myth* comes into play when rite, ceremony, or a social or moral rule demands justification, warrant of antiquity, reality, and sanctity.

In the subsequent chapters of this book we will examine a number of myths in detail, but for the moment let us glance at the subjects of some typical myths. Take, for instance, the annual feast of the return of the dead. Elaborate arrangements are made for it, especially an enormous display of food. When this feast approaches, tales are told of how death began to chastise man, and how the power of eternal rejuvenation was lost. It is told why the spirits have to leave the village and do not remain at the fireside, finally why they return once in a year. Again, at certain seasons in preparation for an overseas expedition, canoes are overhauled and new ones built to the accompaniment of a special magic. In this there are mythological allusions in the spells, and even the sacred acts contain elements which are only comprehensible when the story of the flying canoe, its ritual and its magic are told. In connection with ceremonial trading, the rules, the magic, even the geographical routes are associated with corresponding mythology. There is no important magic, no ceremony, no ritual without belief; and the belief is spun out into accounts of concrete precedent. The union is very intimate, for myth is not only looked upon as a commentary of additional information, but it is a warrant, a charter, and often even a practical guide to the activities with which it is connected. On the other hand the rituals, ceremonies, customs, and social organizations contain at times direct references to myth, and they are regarded as the results of mythical event. The cultural fact is a monument in which the myth is embodied; while the myth is believed to be the real cause which has brought about the moral rule, the social grouping, the rite, or the custom. Thus these stories form an integral part of culture. Their existence and influence not merely transcend the act of telling the narrative, not only do they draw their substance from life and its interests—they govern and control many cultural features, they form the dogmatic backbone of primitive civilization.

This is perhaps the most important point of the thesis which I am urging: I maintain that there exists a special class of stories, regarded as sacred, embodied in ritual, morals, and social organization, and which form an integral and active part of primitive culture. These stories live not by idle interest, not as fictitious or even as true narratives; but are to the natives a statement of a primeval, greater, and more relevant reality, by which the present life, fates, and activities of mankind are determined, the knowledge of which supplies man with the motive for ritual and moral actions, as well as with indications as to how to perform them.

In order to make the point at issue quite clear, let us once more compare our conclusions with the current views of modern anthropology, not in order idly to criticize other opinions, but so that we may link our results to the present state of knowledge, give due acknowledgment for what we have received, and state where we have to differ clearly and precisely.

It will be best to quote a condensed and authoritative statement, and I shall choose for this purpose the definition and analysis given in *Notes and Queries on Anthropology*, by the late Miss C. S. Burne and Professor J. L. Myres. Under the heading "Stories, Sayings, and Songs," we are informed that "this section includes many *intellectual* efforts of peoples. . . ." which "represent the earliest attempts to exercise reason, imagination, and memory." With some apprehension we ask where is left the emotion, the interest, and ambition, the social role of all the stories, and the deep connection with cultural values of the more serious ones? After a brief classification of stories in the usual manner we read about the sacred tales: "*Myths* are stories which, however marvellous and improbable to us, are nevertheless related in all good faith, because they are intended, or believed by the teller, to explain by means of something concrete and intelligible an abstract idea or such vague and difficult conceptions as Creation, Death, distinctions of race or animal species, the different occupations of men and women; the origins of rites and customs, or striking natural objects or prehistoric monuments; the meaning of the names of persons or places. Such stories are sometimes described as *ætiological*, because their purpose is to explain why something exists or happens."

Here we have in a nutshell all that modern science at its best has to say upon the subject. Would our Melanesians agree, however, with this opinion? Certainly not. They do not want to "explain," to make "intelligible" anything which happens in their myths—above all not an abstract idea. Of that there can be found to my knowledge no instance either in Melanesia or in any other savage community. The few abstract ideas which the natives possess carry their concrete commentary in the very word which expresses them. When being is described by verbs to lie, to sit, to stand, when cause and effect are expressed by words signifying foundation and the past standing upon it, when various concrete nouns tend towards the meaning of space, the word and the relation to concrete reality make the abstract idea sufficiently "intelligible." Nor would a Trobriander or any other native agree with the view that "Creation, Death, distinctions of race or animal species, the different occupations of men and women" are "vague and difficult conceptions." Nothing is more familiar to the native than the different occupations of the male and female sex; there is nothing to be *explained* about it. But though familiar, such differences are at times irksome, unpleasant, or at least limiting, and there is the need to justify them, to vouch for their antiquity and reality, in short to buttress their validity. Death, alas, is not vague, or abstract, or difficult to grasp for any human being. It is only too hauntingly real, too concrete, too easy to comprehend for anyone who has had an experience affecting his near relatives or a personal foreboding. If it were vague or unreal, man would have no desire so much as to mention it; but the idea of death is fraught with horror, with a desire to remove its threat, with the vague hope that it may be, not explained, but rather explained away, made unreal, and actually denied. Myth, warranting the belief in immortality, in eternal youth, in a life beyond the grave, is not an intellectual reaction upon a puzzle, but an explicit act of faith born from the innermost instinctive and emotional reaction to the most formidable and haunting idea. Nor are the stories about "the origins of rites and customs" told in mere explanation of them. They never explain in any sense of the word; they always state a precedent which constitutes an ideal and a warrant for its continuance, and sometimes practical directions for the procedure.

ERNST CASSIRER

The Validity and Form of Mythical Thought

"Mythology is inevitable, it is natural, it is an inherent necessity of language, if we recognize in language the outward form and manifestation of thought; it is in fact the dark shadow which language throws upon thought, and which can never disappear till language becomes entirely commensurate with thought, which it never will. Mythology, no doubt, breaks out more fiercely during the early periods of the history of human thought, but it never disappears altogether. Depend upon it, there is mythology now as there was in the time of Homer, only we do not perceive it, because we ourselves live in the very shadow of it, and because we all shrink from the full meridian light of truth. . . . Mythology, in the highest sense, is the power exercised by language on thought in every possible sphere of mental activity."[1]

It might seem an idle pursuit to hark back to such points of view, which have long been abandoned by the etymology and comparative mythological research of today, were it not for the fact that this standpoint represents a typical attitude which is ever recurrent in all related fields, in mythology as in linguistic studies, in theory of art as well as in theory of knowledge. For Max Müller the mythical world is essentially a world of illusion—but an illusion that finds its explanation whenever the original, necessary self-deception of the mind, from which the error arises, is discovered. This self-deception is rooted in language, which is forever making game of the human mind, ever ensnaring it in that iridescent play of

[1] Max Müller, "The Philosophy of Mythology," appended to *The Science of Religion* (London, 1873), pp. 353-5. AUTHOR'S NOTE.

From *Language and Myth* [1925], translated from the German by Susanne K. Langer, New York and London, 1946, pp. 5-10, 32-3, 62-4, 71-2, 91-3. Copyright 1946 by Susanne K. Langer; reprinted with her permission.

meanings that is its own heritage. And this notion that myth does not rest upon a positive *power* of formulation and creation, but rather upon a mental *defect*—that we find in it a "pathological" influence of speech—this notion has its proponents even in modern ethnological literature.

But when we reduce it to its philosophical lowest terms, this attitude turns out to be simply the logical result of that naïve realism which regards the reality of objects as something directly and unequivocally given, literally something tangible—ἀπρὶξ ταῖν χεροῖν, as Plato says. If reality is conceived in this manner, then of course everything which has not this solid sort of reality dissolves into mere fraud and illusion. This illusion may be ever so finely wrought, and flit about us in the gayest and loveliest colors; the fact remains that this image has no independent content, no intrinsic meaning. It does indeed reflect a reality—but a reality to which it can never measure up, and which it can never adequately portray. From this point of view all artistic creation becomes a mere imitation, which must always fall short of the original. Not only simple imitation of a sensibly presented model, but also what is known as idealization, manner, or style, must finally succumb to this verdict; for measured by the naked "truth" of the object to be depicted, idealization itself is nothing but subjective misconception and falsification. And it seems that all other processes of mental gestation involve the same sort of outrageous distortion, the same departure from objective reality and the immediate data of experience. For all mental processes fail to grasp reality itself, and in order to represent it, to hold it at all, they are driven to the use of symbols. But all symbolism harbors the curse of mediacy; it is bound to obscure what it seeks to reveal. Thus the sound of *speech* strives to "express" subjective and objective happening, the "inner" and the "outer" world; but what of this it can retain is not the life and individual fullness of existence, but only a dead abbreviation of it. All that "denotation" to which the spoken word lays claim is really nothing more than mere suggestion; a "suggestion" which, in face of the concrete variegation and totality of actual experience, must always appear a poor and empty shell. That is true of the external as well as the inner world: "When *speaks* the soul, alas, the *soul* no longer speaks!"

From this point it is but a single step to the conclusion which the modern skeptical critics of language have drawn: the complete dissolution of any alleged truth content of language, and the realization that this content is nothing but a sort of phantasmagoria of the spirit. Moreover, from this standpoint, not only myth, art, and language, but even theoretical knowledge itself becomes a phantasmagoria; for even knowledge can never reproduce the true nature of things as they are, but must frame their essence in "concepts." But what are concepts save formulations and creations of thought, which, instead of giving us the true forms of objects, show us rather the forms of thought itself? Consequently all schemata which science evolves in order to classify, organize, and summarize the phenomena of the real world turn out to be nothing but arbitrary schemes—airy fabrics of the mind, which express not the nature of things, but the nature of mind. So knowledge, as well as myth, language, and art, has been reduced to a kind of fiction—to a fiction that recommends itself by its usefulness, but must not be measured by any strict standard of truth, if it is not to melt away into nothingness.

Against this self-dissolution of the spirit there is only one remedy: to accept in all seriousness what Kant calls his "Copernican revolution." Instead of measuring the content, meaning, and truth of intellectual forms by something extraneous which is supposed to be reproduced in them, we must find in these forms themselves the measure and criterion for their truth and intrinsic meaning. Instead of taking them as mere copies of something else, we must see in each of these spiritual forms a spontaneous law of generation; an original way and tendency of expression which is more than a mere record of something initially given in fixed categories of real existence. From this point of view, myth, art, language and science appear as symbols; not in the sense of mere figures which refer to some given reality by means of suggestion and allegorical renderings, but in the sense of forces each of which produces and posits a world of its own. In these realms the spirit exhibits itself in that inwardly determined dialectic by virtue of which alone there is any reality, any organized and definite Being at all. Thus the special symbolic forms are not imitations, but *organs* of reality, since it is solely by their agency that anything real becomes an object for intellectual apprehension, and as such is made visible to us. The question as to what reality is apart from these forms, and what are its independent attributes becomes irrelevant here. For the mind, only that can be visible which has some definite form; but every form of existence has its source in some peculiar way of seeing, some intellectual formulation and intuition of meaning. . . .

This holds, perhaps, even more for the basic mythical conceptions of mankind than for language. Such conceptions are not culled from a ready-made world of Being, they are not mere products of fantasy which vapor off from fixed, empirical, realistic existence, to float above the actual world like a bright mist; to primitive consciousness they present the *totality* of Being. The mythical form of conception is not something super-added to certain definite *elements* of empirical existence; instead, the primary "experience" itself is steeped in the imagery of myth and saturated with its atmosphere. Man lives with *objects* only in so far as he lives with these *forms*; he reveals reality to himself, and himself to reality, in that he lets himself and the environment enter into this plastic medium, in which the two do not merely make contact, but fuse with each other. . . .

The aim of theoretical thinking . . . is primarily to deliver the contents of sensory or intuitive experience from the isolation in which they originally occur. It causes these contents to transcend their narrow limits, combines them with others, compares them, and concatenates them in a definite order, in all-inclusive context. It proceeds "discursively," in that it treats the immediate content only as a point of departure, from which it can run the whole gamut of impressions in various directions, until these impressions are fitted together into one unified conception, one closed system. In this system there are no more isolated points; all its members are reciprocally related, refer to one another, illumine and explain each other. Thus every separate event is ensnared, as it were, by invisible threads of thought, that bind it to the whole. The theoretical significance which it receives lies in the fact that it is stamped with the character of this totality.

Mythical thinking, when viewed in its most elementary forms, bears no such stamp; in fact, the character of intellectual unity is directly hostile to its spirit. For in this mode, thought does not dispose freely over the data of intuition, in order to relate and compare them to each other, but is captivated and enthralled by the intuition which suddenly confronts it. It comes to rest in the immediate experience; the sensible present is so great that everything else dwindles before it. For a person whose apprehension is under the spell of this mythico-religious attitude, it is as though the whole world were simply annihilated; the immediate content, whatever it be, that commands his religious interest so completely fills his consciousness that nothing else can exist beside and apart from it. The ego is spending all its energy on this single object, lives in it, loses itself in it. Instead of a widening of intuitive experience, we find here its extreme limitation; instead of expansion that would lead through greater and greater spheres of being, we have here an impulse toward concentration; instead of extensive distribution, intensive compression. This focusing of all forces on a single point is the prerequisite for all mythical thinking and mythical formulation. When, on the one hand, the entire self is given up to a single impression, is "possessed" by it and, on the other hand, there is the utmost tension between the subject and its object, the outer world; when external reality is not merely viewed and contemplated, but overcomes a man in sheer immediacy, with emotions of fear or hope, terror or wish fulfillment: then the spark jumps somehow across, the tension finds release, as the subjective excitement becomes objectified, and confronts the mind as a god or a daemon.

Here we have the mythico-religious protophenomenon which Usener has sought to fix with the term "momentary god." "In absolute immediacy," he says, "the individual phenomenon is deified, without the intervention of even the most rudimentary class concept; that *one* thing which you see before you, that and nothing else is the god." . . .

But it appears that the new findings which ethnology and comparative religion have put at our disposal during the three decades since the publication of Usener's work enables us to go back one step further yet. A few years before Usener's book there appeared a work by the English missionary Codrington: *The Melanesians: Studies in their Anthropology and Folk-Lore* (1891), which enriched the discipline of religious history by a very important concept. Codrington shows the root of all Melanesian religion to be the concept of a "supernatural power," which permeates all things and events, and may be present now in objects, now in persons, yet is never bound exclusively to any single and individual subject or object as its host, but may be transmitted from place to place, from thing to thing, from person to person. In this light, the whole existence of things and the activity of mankind seem to be embedded, so to speak, in a mythical "field of force," an atmosphere of potency which permeates everything, and which may appear in concentrated form in certain extraordinary objects, removed from the realm of everyday affairs, or in specially endowed persons, such as distinguished warriors, priests, or magicians. The core of this world view, however, of the "mana" concept which Codrington found among the Melanesians, is not so much the idea of such particular embodiments, as the notion of a "power" in general, able to appear now in this form, now in that, to enter into one object and then into another; a power that is venerated for its "holiness" as well as feared for the dangers it contains. For that power which is conceived in a positive sense as "mana" has also a negative aspect of the power of "taboo." Every manifestation of the divine potency, be it vested in persons or things, animate or inanimate, falls outside the realm of the "profane," and belongs to a special sphere of being which has to be separated from the ordinary and mundane by set lines of division, and by all sorts of protective measures.

Since Codrington's early discoveries, the science of ethnology has proceeded to trace the diffusion of these concepts all over the earth. Certain terms that correspond exactly to the meaning of mana may be found not only among the South Sea Islanders, but also among a great many American Indian tribes, as well as in Australia and in Africa. Precisely the same notion of a universal, essentially undifferentiated Power may be found in the Algonquin "manitu," the "wakanda" of the Sioux, the "orenda" of the Iroquois, and in various African religions. On the basis of such observations, students of ethnology and comparative religion have largely come to regard this conception not merely as a universal *phenomenon*, but as nothing less than a special *category* of mythic consciousness. The "Taboo-Mana Formula" has been regarded as the "minimum definition of religion," i.e., as the expression of a distinction which constitutes one of the essential, indispensable conditions of religious life as such, and represents the lowest level of it that we know. . . .

At this point one can see how far prior the level of consciousness which begets these verbal forms is even to that on which the "momentary gods" are produced. For the momentary god, despite his transiency, is nevertheless always an individual, personal form, whereas here the holy, the divine, that which besets a man with sudden terror or wonder, still has an entirely impersonal, one might say "anonymous," character. But this nameless Presence forms the background against which definite daemonic or divine images can take shape. If the "momentary god" is the first *actual* form originated by the creative, mythico-religious consciousness, this actuality is grounded, none the less, in the general potency of mythico-religious feeling. The division of the realm of the "holy" from that of the "profane" is the prerequisite for any *definite* divinities whatsoever. The Self feels steeped, as it were; in a mythico-religious atmosphere, which ever enfolds it, and in which it now lives and moves; it takes only a spark, a touch, to create the god or daemon out of this charged atmosphere. . . .

Two logical concepts, subsumed under the next-higher category, as their *genus proximum*, retain their distinctive characters despite the relationship into which they have been brought. In mythico-linguistic thought, however, exactly the opposite tendency prevails. Here we find in operation a law which might actually be called the law of the leveling and extinction of specific differences. Every part of a whole is the whole itself; every specimen is equivalent to the entire species. The part does not merely represent the whole, or the specimen its class; they are identical with the totality to which they belong; not merely as mediating aids to reflective thought, but as genuine presences which actually contain the power, significance and efficacy of the whole. Here one is reminded forcefully of the principle which might be called the basic principle of verbal as well as mythic "metaphor"— the principle of *pars pro toto*. It is a familiar fact that all mythic thinking is governed and permeated by this principle. Whoever has brought any part of a whole into his power has thereby acquired power, in the magical sense, over the whole itself. What significance the part in question may have in the structure and coherence of the whole, what function it fulfills, is relatively unimportant— the mere fact that it is or has been a part, that it has been connected with the whole, no matter how casually, is enough to lend it the full significance and power of that greater unity. For instance, to hold magical dominion over another person's body one need only attain possession of his pared nails or cut-off hair, his spittle or his excrement; even his shadow, his reflection or his footprints serve the same purpose. The Pythagoreans still observed the injunction to smooth the bed soon after arising so that the imprint of the body, left upon the mattress, could not be used to the owner's detriment. Most of what is known as "magic of analogy" springs from the same fundamental attitude; and the very nature of this magic shows that the concept in question is not one of mere analogy, but of a real identification. If, for instance, a rain-making ceremony consists of sprinkling water on the ground to attract the rain, or rain-stopping magic is made by pouring water on red hot stones where it is consumed amid hissing noise, both ceremonies owe their true magical sense to the fact that the rain is not just represented, but is felt to be really present in each drop of water. The rain as a mythic "power," the "daemon" of the rain is actually there, whole and undivided, in the sprinkled or evaporated water, and is thus amenable to magical control.

This mystic relationship which obtains between a whole and its parts holds also between genus and species, and between the species and its several instances. Here, too, each form is entirely merged with the other; the genus or species is not only represented by an individual member of it, but lives and acts in it. If, under the totemistic conception of the world, a group or clan is organized by totems, and if its individual members take their names from the totem animal or plant, this is never a mere arbitrary division by means of conventional verbal or mythical "insignia," but a matter of genuine community of essence. . . .

C. G. JUNG
The Collective Unconscious and Archetypes

If it were permissible to personify the unconscious, we might call it a collective human being combining the characteristics of both sexes, transcending youth and age, birth and death, and, from having at his command a human experience of one or two million years, almost immortal. If such a being existed, he would be exalted above all temporal change; the present would mean neither more nor less to him than any year in the one hundredth century before Christ; he would be a dreamer of age-old dreams and, owing to his immeasurable experience, he would be an incomparable prognosticator. He would have lived countless times over the life of the individual, of the family, tribe and people, and he would possess the living sense of the rhythm of growth, flowering and decay.

Unfortunately—or rather let us say, fortunately—this being dreams. At least it seems to us as if the collective unconscious, which appears to us in dreams, had no consciousness of its own contents—though of course we cannot be sure of this, any more than we are in the case of insects. The collective unconscious, moreover, seems not to be a person, but something like an unceasing stream or perhaps an ocean of images and figures which drift into consciousness in our dreams or in abnormal states of mind.

It would be positively grotesque for us to call this immense system of experience of the unconscious psyche an illusion, for our visible and tangible body itself is just such a system. It still carries within it the discernible traces of primeval evolution, and it is certainly a whole that functions purposively—for otherwise we could not live. It would never occur to anyone to look upon comparative anatomy or physiology as nonsense. And so we cannot dismiss the collective unconscious as illusion, or refuse to recognize and study it as a valuable source of knowledge.

From "The Basic Postulates of Analytical Psychology" (1931), *Modern Man in Search of a Soul*, translated from the German by W. S. Dell and C. F. Baynes, New York and London, 1933, pp. 215-16; reprinted by permission of Harcourt, Brace & World, Inc. and Routledge & Kegan Paul Ltd.
From "Archetypes of the Collective Unconscious" [1934, 1954], "The Psychology of the Child Archetype" [1951], and "Psychological Aspects of the Mother Archetype" [1954], *The Collected Works of C. G. Jung*, translated from the German by R. F. C. Hull, New York, 1959, Vol. IX, part 1, pp. 3-7, 152-7, 332; reprinted by permission of the Bollingen Foundation and Routledge & Kegan Paul Ltd.

The hypothesis of a collective unconscious belongs to the class of ideas that people at first find strange but soon come to possess and use as familiar conceptions. This has been the case with the concept of the unconscious in general. After the philosophical idea of the unconscious, in the form presented chiefly by Carus and von Hartmann, had gone down under the overwhelming wave of materialism and empiricism, leaving hardly a ripple behind it, it gradually reappeared in the scientific domain of medical psychology.

At first the concept of the unconscious was limited to denoting the state of repressed or forgotten contents. Even with Freud, who makes the unconscious—at least metaphorically—take the stage as the acting subject, it is really nothing but the gathering place of forgotten and repressed contents, and has a functional significance thanks only to these. For Freud, accordingly, the unconscious is of an exclusively personal nature,[1] although he was aware of its archaic and mythological thought-forms.

A more or less superficial layer of the unconscious is undoubtedly personal. I call it the *personal unconscious*. But this personal unconscious rests upon a deeper layer, which does not derive from personal experience and is not a personal acquisition but is inborn. This deeper layer I call the *collective unconscious*. I have chosen the term "collective" because this part of the unconscious is not individual but universal; in contrast to the personal psyche, it has contents and modes of behaviour that are more or less the same everywhere and in all individuals. It is, in other words, identical in all men and thus constitutes a common psyche substrate of a suprapersonal nature which is present in every one of us.

Psychic existence can be recognized only by the presence of contents that are *capable of consciousness*. We can therefore speak of an unconscious only in so far as we are able to demonstrate its contents. The contents of the personal unconscious are chiefly the *feeling-toned complexes*, as they are called; they constitute the personal and private side of psychic life. The contents of the collective unconscious, on the other hand, are known as *archetypes*.

The term "archetype" occurs as early as Philo Judaeus,[2] with reference to the *Imago Dei* (God-image) in man. It can also be found in Irenaeus, who says: "The creator of the world did not fashion these things directly from himself but copied them from archetypes outside himself."[3] In the *Corpus Hermeticum*,[4] God is called τὸ ἀρχέτυπον φῶς (archetypal light). The term occurs several times in Dionysius the Areopagite, as for instance in *De caelesti hierarchia*, II, 4: "immaterial Archetypes,"[5] and in *De divinis nominibus*, I, 6: "Archetypal stone."[6] The term "archetype" is not found in St. Augustine, but the idea of it is. Thus in

[1] In his later works Freud differentiated the basic view mentioned here. He called the instinctual psyche the "id," and his "super-ego" denotes the collective consciousness, of which the individual is partly conscious and partly unconscious (because it is repressed). AUTHOR'S NOTE, as are all the following.
[2] *De opificio mundi*, I, 69. Cf. Colson/Whitaker trans., I, p. 55.
[3] *Adversus haereses* II, 7, 5: "Mundi fabricator non a semetipso fecit haec, sed de alienis archetypis transtulit." (Cf. Roberts/Rambaut trans., I, p. 139.)
[4] Scott, *Hermetica*, I, p. 140.
[5] In Migne, P.G., vol. 3, col. 144.
[6] Ibid., col. 595. Cf. *The Divine Names* (trans. by Rolt), pp. 62, 72.

De diversis quaestionibus LXXXIII he speaks of "*ideae principales,* 'which are themselves not formed . . . but are contained in the divine understanding.' "[7] "Archetype" is an explanatory paraphrase of the Platonic εἶδος. For our purposes this term is apposite and helpful, because it tells us that so far as the collective unconscious contents are concerned we are dealing with archaic or—I would say—primordial types, that is, with universal images that have existed since the remotest times. The term "représentations collectives," used by Lévy-Bruhl to denote the symbolic figures in the primitive view of the world, could easily be applied to unconscious contents as well, since it means practically the same thing. Primitive tribal lore is concerned with archetypes that have been modified in a special way. They are no longer contents of the unconscious, but have already been changed into conscious formulae taught according to tradition, generally in the form of esoteric teaching. This last is a typical means of expression for the transmission of collective contents originally derived from the unconscious.

Another well-known expression of the archetypes is myth and fairytale. But here too we are dealing with forms that have received a specific stamp and have been handed down through long periods of time. The term "archetype" thus applies only indirectly to the "représentations collectives," since it designates only those psychic contents which have not yet been submitted to conscious elaboration and are therefore an immediate datum of psychic experience. In this sense there is a considerable difference between the archetype and the historical formula that has evolved. Especially on the higher levels of esoteric teaching the archetypes appear in a form that reveals quite unmistakably the critical and evaluating influence of conscious elaboration. Their immediate manifestation, as we encounter it in dreams and visions, is much more individual, less understandable, and more naïve than in myths, for example. The archetype is essentially an unconscious content that is altered by becoming conscious and by being perceived, and it takes its colour from the individual consciousness in which it happens to appear.[8]

What the word "archetype" means in the nominal sense is clear enough, then, from its relations with myth, esoteric teaching, and fairytale. But if we try to establish what an archetype is *psychologically,* the matter becomes more complicated. So far mythologists have always helped themselves out with solar, lunar, meteorological, vegetal, and other ideas of the kind. The fact that myths are first and foremost psychic phenomena that reveal the nature of the soul is something they have absolutely refused to see until now. Primitive man is not much interested in objective explanations of the obvious, but he has an imperative need—or rather, his unconscious psyche has an irresistible urge—to assimilate all outer sense

---

[7] Migne, *P.L.,* vol. 40, col. 30. "Archetype" is used in the same way by the alchemists, as in the "Tractatus aureus" of Hermes Trismegistus (*Theatrum chemicum,* IV, 1613, p. 718): "As God [contains] all the treasure of his godhead . . . hidden in himself as in an archetype [*in se tanquam archetypo absconditum*] . . . in like manner Saturn carries the similitudes of metallic bodies hiddenly in himself." In the "Tractatus de igne et sale" of Vigenerus (*Theatr. chem.,* VI, 1661, p. 3), the world is "ad archetypi sui similitudinem factus" (made after the likeness of its archetype) and is therefore called the "magnus homo" (the "homo maximus" of Swedenborg).

[8] One must, for the sake of accuracy, distinguish between "archetype" and "archetypal ideas." The archetype as such is a hypothetical and irrepresentable model, something like the "pattern of behaviour" in biology.

experiences to inner, psychic events. It is not enough for the primitive to see the sun rise and set; this external observation must at the same time be a psychic happening: the sun in its course must represent the fate of a god or hero who, in the last analysis, dwells nowhere except in the soul of man. All the mythologized processes of nature, such as summer and winter, the phases of the moon, the rainy seasons, and so forth, are in no sense allegories[9] of these objective occurrences; rather they are symbolic expressions of the inner, unconscious drama of the psyche which becomes accessible to man's consciousness by way of projection—that is, mirrored in the events of nature. . . .

Primitive man impresses us so strongly with his subjectivity that we should really have guessed long ago that myths refer to something psychic. His knowledge of nature is essentially the language and outer dress of an unconscious psychic process. But the very fact that this process is unconscious gives us the reason why man has thought of everything except the psyche in his attempts to explain myths. He simply didn't know that the psyche contains all the images that have ever given rise to myths, and that our unconscious is an acting and suffering subject with an inner drama which primitive man rediscovers, by means of analogy, in the processes of nature both great and small.

It became clear from many separate investigations that the psychopathology of the neuroses and of many psychoses cannot dispense with the hypothesis of a dark side of the psyche, i.e., the unconscious. It is the same with the psychology of dreams, which is really the *terra intermedia* between normal and pathological psychology. In the dream, as in the products of psychoses, there are numberless interconnections to which one can find parallels only in mythological associations of ideas (or perhaps in certain poetic creations which are often characterized by a borrowing, not always conscious, from myths). Had thorough investigation shown that in the majority of such cases it was simply a matter of forgotten knowledge, the physician would not have gone to the trouble of making extensive researches into individual and collective parallels. But, in point of fact, typical mythologems were observed among individuals to whom all knowledge of this kind was absolutely out of the question, and where indirect derivation from religious ideas that might have been known to them, or from popular figures of speech, was impossible. Such conclusions forced us to assume that we must be dealing with "autochthonous" revivals independent of all tradition, and, consequently, that "myth-forming" structural elements must be present in the unconscious psyche.

These products are never (or at least very seldom) myths with a definite form, but rather mythological components which, because of their typical nature, we can call "motifs," "primordial images," types or—as I have named them—*archetypes*. The child archetype is an excellent example. Today we can hazard the formula that the archetypes appear in myths and fairytales just as they do in dreams and in the products of psychotic fantasy. The medium in which they are em-

[9] An allegory is a paraphrase of a conscious content, whereas a symbol is the best possible expression for an unconscious content whose nature can only be guessed, because it is still unknown.

bedded is, in the former case, an ordered and for the most part immediately understandable context, but in the latter case a generally unintelligible, irrational, not to say delirious sequence of images which nonetheless does not lack a certain hidden coherence. In the individual, the archetypes appear as involuntary manifestations of unconscious processes whose existence and meaning can only be inferred, whereas the myth deals with traditional forms of incalculable age. They hark back to a prehistoric world whose spiritual preconceptions and general conditions we can still observe today among existing primitives. Myths on this level are as a rule tribal history handed down from generation to generation by word of mouth. Primitive mentality differs from the civilized chiefly in that the conscious mind is far less developed in scope and intensity. Functions such as thinking, willing, etc. are not yet differentiated; they are pre-conscious, and in the case of thinking, for instance, this shows itself in the circumstance that the primitive does not think *consciously*, but that thoughts *appear*. The primitive cannot assert that he thinks; it is rather that "something thinks in him." The spontaneity of the act of thinking does not lie, causally, in his conscious mind, but in his unconscious. Moreover, he is incapable of any conscious effort of will; he must put himself beforehand into the "mood of willing," or let himself be put—hence his *rites d'entrée et de sortie*. His consciousness is menaced by an almighty unconscious: hence his fear of magical influences which may cross his path at any moment; and for this reason, too, he is surrounded by unknown forces and must adjust himself to them as best he can. Owing to the chronic twilight state of his consciousness, it is often next to impossible to find out whether he merely dreamed something or whether he really experienced it. The spontaneous manifestation of the unconscious and its archetypes intrudes everywhere into his conscious mind, and the mythical world of his ancestors—for instance, the *alchera* or *bugari* of the Australian aborigines—is a reality equal if not superior to the material world. It is not the world as we know it that speaks out of his unconscious, but the unknown world of the psyche, of which we know that it mirrors our empirical world only in part, and that, for the other part, it moulds this empirical world in accordance with its own psychic assumptions. The archetype does not proceed from physical facts, but describes how the psyche experiences the physical fact, and in so doing the psyche often behaves so autocratically that it denies tangible reality or makes statements that fly in the face of it.

The primitive mentality does not *invent* myths, it *experiences* them. Myths are original revelations of the preconscious psyche, involuntary statements about unconscious psychic happenings, and anything but allegories of physical processes. Such allegories would be an idle amusement for an unscientific intellect. Myths, on the contrary, have a vital meaning. Not merely do they represent, they *are* the psychic life of the primitive tribe, which immediately falls to pieces and decays when it loses its mythological heritage, like a man who has lost his soul. A tribe's mythology is its living religion, whose loss is always and everywhere, even among the civilized, a moral catastrophe. But religion is a vital link with psychic processes independent of and beyond consciousness, in the dark hinterland of the psyche. Many of these unconscious processes may be indirectly occasioned by consciousness, but never by conscious choice. Others appear to arise spontaneously, that is to say, from no discernible or demonstrable conscious cause.

Modern psychology treats the products of unconscious fantasy-activity as self-portraits of what is going on in the unconscious, or as statements of the unconscious psyche about itself. They fall into two categories. First, fantasies (including dreams) of a personal character, which go back unquestionably to personal experiences, things forgotten or repressed, and can thus be completely explained by individual anamnesis. Second, fantasies (including dreams) of an impersonal character, which cannot be reduced to experiences in the individual's past, and thus cannot be explained as something individually acquired. These fantasy-images undoubtedly have their closest analogues in mythological types. We must therefore assume that they correspond to certain *collective* (and not personal) structural elements of the human psyche in general, and, like the morphological elements of the human body, are *inherited*. Although tradition and transmission by migration certainly play a part, there are, as we have said, very many cases that cannot be accounted for in this way and drive us to the hypothesis of "autochthonous revival." These cases are so numerous that we are obliged to assume the existence of a collective psychic substratum. I have called this the *collective unconscious*.

The products of this second category resemble the types of structures to be met with in myth and fairytale so much that we must regard them as related. It is therefore wholly within the realm of possibility that both, the mythological types as well as the individual types, arise under quite similar conditions. As already mentioned, the fantasy-products of the second category (as also those of the first) arise in a state of reduced intensity of consciousness (in dreams, delirium, reveries, visions, etc.). In all these states the check put upon unconscious contents by the concentration of the conscious mind ceases, so that the hitherto unconscious material streams, as though from opened side-sluices, into the field of consciousness. This mode of origination is the general rule.

Reduced intensity of consciousness and absence of concentration and attention, Janet's *abaissement du niveau mental*, correspond pretty exactly to the primitive state of consciousness in which, we must suppose, myths were originally formed. It is therefore exceedingly probable that the mythological archetypes, too, made their appearance in much the same manner as the manifestations of archetypal structures among individuals today.

The methodological principle in accordance with which psychology treats the products of the unconscious is this: Contents of an archetypal character are manifestations of processes in the collective unconscious. Hence they do not refer to anything that is or has been conscious, but to something essentially unconscious. In the last analysis, therefore, it is impossible to say what they refer to. Every interpretation necessarily remains an "as-if." The ultimate core of meaning may be circumscribed, but not described. Even so, the bare circumscription denotes an essential step forward in our knowledge of the pre-conscious structure of the psyche, which was already in existence when there was as yet no unity of personality (even today the primitive is not securely possessed of it) and no consciousness at all. We can also observe this pre-conscious state in early childhood, and as a matter of fact it is the dreams of this early period that not infrequently bring extremely remarkable archetypal contents to light.

If, then, we proceed in accordance with the above principle, there is no longer any question whether a myth refers to the sun or the moon, the father or the mother, sexuality or fire or water; all it does is to circumscribe and give an approximate description of an *unconscious core of meaning*. The ultimate meaning of this nucleus was never conscious and never will be. It was, and still is, only interpreted, and every interpretation that comes anywhere near the hidden sense (or, from the point of view of scientific intellect, nonsense, which comes to the same thing) has always, right from the beginning, laid claim not only to absolute truth and validity but to instant reverence and religious devotion. Archetypes were, and still are, living psychic forces that demand to be taken seriously, and they have a strange way of making sure of their effect. Always they were the bringers of protection and salvation, and their violation has as its consequence the "perils of the soul" known to us from the psychology of primitives. Moreover, they are the unfailing causes of neurotic and even psychotic disorders, behaving exactly like neglected or maltreated physical organs or organic functional systems.

An archetypal content expresses itself, first and foremost, in metaphors. If such a content should speak of the sun and identify with it the lion, the king, the hoard of gold guarded by the dragon, or the power that makes for the life and health of man, it is neither the one thing nor the other, but the unknown third thing that finds more or less adequate expression in all these similes, yet—to the perpetual vexation of the intellect—remains unknown and not to be fitted into a formula. For this reason the scientific intellect is always inclined to put on airs of enlightenment in the hope of banishing the spectre once and for all. Whether its endeavours were called euhemerism, or Christian apologetics, or Enlightenment in the narrow sense, or Positivism, there was always a myth hiding behind it, in new and disconcerting garb, which then, following the ancient and venerable pattern, gave itself out as ultimate truth. In reality we can never legitimately cut loose from our archetypal foundations unless we are prepared to pay the price of a neurosis, any more than we can rid ourselves of our body and its organs without committing suicide. If we cannot deny the archetypes or otherwise neutralize them, we are confronted, at every new stage in the differentiation of consciousness to which civilization attains, with the task of finding a new *interpretation* appropriate to this stage, in order to connect the life of the past that still exists in us with the life of the present, which threatens to slip away from it. If this link-up does not take place, a kind of rootless consciousness comes into being no longer oriented to the past, a consciousness which succumbs helplessly to all manner of suggestions and, in practice, is susceptible to psychic epidemics.

Again and again I encounter the mistaken notion that an archetype is determined in regard to its content, in other words that it is a kind of unconscious idea (if such an expression be admissible). It is necessary to point out once more that archetypes are not determined as regards their content, but only as regards their form, and then only to a very limited degree. A primordial image is determined as to its content only when it has become conscious and is therefore filled out with the material of conscious experience. Its form, however, as I have explained elsewhere, might perhaps be compared to the axial system of a crystal, which, as it were, preforms the crystalline structure in the mother liquid, without having any material existence of its own. This first appears according to the specific way in which the ions and molecules aggregate. The archetype in itself is empty and purely formal, nothing but a *facultas praeformandi*, a possibility of representation which is given a priori. The representations themselves are not inherited, only the forms, and in that respect they correspond in every way to the instincts, which are also determined in form only. The existence of the instincts can no more be proved than the existence of the archetypes, so long as they do not manifest themselves concretely. With regard to the definiteness of the form, our comparison with the crystal is illuminating inasmuch as the axial system determines only the stereometric structure but not the concrete form of the individual crystal. This may be either large or small, and it may vary endlessly by reason of the different size of its planes or by the growing together of two crystals. The only thing that remains constant is the axial system, or rather, the invariable geometric proportions underlying it. The same is true of the archetype. In principle, it can be named and has an invariable nucleus of meaning—but always only in principle, never as regards its concrete manifestation.

C. G. JUNG

The Psychological Function of Archetypes

I have already mentioned that Freud established the existence of archaic vestiges and primitive modes of functioning in the unconscious. Subsequent investigations have confirmed this result and brought together a wealth of observational material. In view of the structure of the body it would be astonishing if the psyche were the only biological phenomenon not to show clear traces of its evolutionary history, and it is altogether probable that these marks are closely connected with the instinctual base. Instinct and the archaic mode meet in the biological conception of the "pattern of behavior." There are in fact no amorphous instincts, as every instinct bears in itself the pattern of its situation. Always it fulfills an image, and the image has fixed qualities. The instinct of the leaf-cutting ant fulfills the image of ant, tree, leaf, cutting, transport, and the little ant garden of fungi. If any of these conditions is lacking, the instinct does not function, because it cannot exist without its total pattern, without its image. Such an image is an a priori type. It is inborn in the ant prior to any activity, for there can be no activity at all unless an instinct of corresponding pattern initiates and makes it possible. This schema holds true of all instincts and is found in identical form in all individuals of the same species. The same is true also of man: he has in him these a priori instinct types which provide the occasion and the pattern for his activities, in so far as he functions instinctively. As a biological being he has no choice but to act in a specifically human way and fulfill his pattern of behavior.

From "On the Nature of the Psyche" [1954], *The Collected Works of C. G. Jung*, translated from the German by R. F. C. Hull, New York, 1960, Vol. VIII, pp. 200-206, 209-11, 212, 213; reprinted by permission of the Bollingen Foundation and Routledge & Kegan Paul Ltd.

This sets narrow limits to his possible range of volition, the more narrow the more primitive he is, and the more his consciousness is dependent upon the instinctual sphere. Although from one point of view it is quite correct to speak of the pattern of behavior as a still existing archaic vestige, as Nietzsche did in respect of the function of dreams, such an attitude does scant justice to the biological and psychological meaning of these types. They are not just relics or vestiges of earlier modes of functioning; they are the ever-present and biologically necessary regulators of the instinctual sphere, whose range of action covers the whole realm of the psyche and only loses its absoluteness when limited by the relative freedom of the will. We may say that the image represents the *meaning* of the instinct.

Although the existence of an instinctual pattern in human biology is probable, it seems very difficult to prove the existence of distinct types empirically. For the organ with which we might apprehend them—consciousness—is not only itself a transformation of the original instinctual image, but also its transformer. It is therefore not surprising that the human mind finds it impossible to classify man into precise types similar to those we know in the animal kingdom. I must confess that I can see no direct way to solve this problem. And yet I have succeeded, or so I believe, in finding at least an indirect way of approach to the instinctual image.

In what follows I would like to give a brief description of how this discovery took place. I had often observed patients whose dreams pointed to a rich store of fantasy material. Equally, from the patients themselves, I got the impression that they were stuffed full of fantasies, without their being able to tell me just where the inner pressure lay. I therefore took up a dream image or an association of the patient's, and, with this as a point of departure, set him the task of elaborating or developing his theme by giving free rein to his fantasy. This, according to individual taste and talent, could be done in any number of ways, dramatic, dialectic, visual, acoustic, or in the form of dancing, painting, drawing, or modeling. The result of this technique was a vast number of complicated designs whose diversity puzzled me for years, until I was able to recognize that in this method I was witnessing the spontaneous manifestation of an unconscious process which was merely assisted by the technical ability of the patient, and to which I later gave the name "individuation process." But long before this recognition dawned upon me I had made the discovery that this method often diminished, to a considerable degree, the frequency and intensity of the dreams, thus reducing the inexplicable pressure exerted by the unconscious. In many cases this brought a large measure of therapeutic success, which encouraged both myself and the patient to press forward despite the baffling nature of the results. I felt bound to insist that they were baffling, if only to stop myself from framing, on the basis of certain theoretical assumptions, interpretations which I felt were not only inadequate but liable to prejudice the ingenuous productions of the patient. The more I suspected these configurations of harboring a certain purposefulness, the less inclined I was to risk any theories about them. This reticence was not made easy for me, since in many cases I was dealing with patients who needed an intellectual *point d'appui* if they were not to get totally lost in the darkness. I had to try to give provisional interpretations at least, so far as I was able, interspersing them with innumerable "perhapses" and "ifs" and "buts" and never stepping beyond the bounds of the picture lying before me. I always took good care to let the interpretation of each image tail off into a question whose answer was left to the free fantasy activity of the patient.

The chaotic assortment of images that at first confronted me reduced itself in the course of the work to certain well-defined themes and formal elements which repeated themselves in identical or analogous form with the most varied individuals. I mention, as the most salient characteristics, chaotic multiplicity and order; duality; the opposition of light and dark, upper and lower, right and left; the union of opposites in a third, the quaternity (square, cross), rotation (circle, sphere), and finally the centering process and a radial arrangement that usually followed some quaternary system. Triadic formations, apart from the *complexio oppositorum* in a third, were relatively rare and formed notable exceptions which could be explained by special conditions. The centering process is, in my experience, the never-to-be-surpassed climax of the whole development, and is characterized as such by the fact that it brings with it the greatest possible therapeutic effect. The typical features listed above go to the limits of abstraction, yet at the same time they are the simplest expressions of the formative principles here at work. In actual reality the patterns are infinitely more variegated and far more concrete than this would suggest. Their variety defies description. I can only say that there is probably no motif in any known mythology that does not at some time appear in these configurations. If there was any conscious knowledge of mythological motifs worth mentioning in my patients, it is left far behind by the ingenuities of creative fantasy.

These facts show in an unmistakable manner how fantasies guided by unconscious regulators coincide with the records of man's mental activity as known to us from tradition and ethnological research. All the abstract features I have mentioned are in a certain sense conscious: everyone can count up to four and knows what a circle is and a square; but, as formative principles, these are unconscious and by the same token their psychological meaning is not conscious either. My most fundamental views and ideas derive from these experiences. First I made the observations, and only then did I hammer out my views. And so it is with the hand that guides the crayon or brush, the foot that executes the dance step, with the eye and the ear, with the word and the thought: a dark impulse is the ultimate arbiter of the pattern, an unconscious a priori precipitates itself into plastic form, and one has no inkling that another person's consciousness is being guided by these same principles at the very point where one feels utterly exposed to the boundless subjective vagaries of chance. Over the whole procedure there seems to reign a dim foreknowledge not only of the pattern, but of its meaning. Image and meaning are identical; and as the first takes shape, so the latter becomes clear.

These experiences and reflections lead me to believe that there are certain collective unconscious conditions which act as regulators and stimulators of creative fantasy activity and call forth corresponding formations by availing themselves of the existing conscious material. They behave exactly like the motive forces of dreams, for which reason active imagination, as I have called this method, to some extent takes the place of dreams. The existence of these unconscious regulators— I sometimes refer to them as "dominants" because of their mode of functioning— seemed to me so important that I based upon it my hypothesis of an impersonal collective unconscious. The most remarkable thing about this method, I felt, was that it did not involve a *reductio in primam figuram*, but rather a synthesis—supported by an attitude voluntarily adopted, though for the rest wholly natural—of passive conscious material and unconscious influences, hence a kind of spontaneous amplification of the archetypes. The images are not to be thought of as a reduction of conscious contents to their simplest denominator, as this would be the direct road to the primordial images which I said previously was unimaginable; they only make their appearance in the course of amplification.

On this natural amplification process I also based my method of eliciting the meaning of dreams, for dreams behave in exactly the same way as active imagination, only the support of conscious contents is lacking. To the extent that the archetypes intervene in the shaping of conscious contents by regulating, modifying, and motivating them, they act like the instincts. It is therefore very natural to suppose that these factors are connected with the instincts and to inquire whether the typical situational patterns which these collective form-principles apparently represent are not in the end identical with the instinctual patterns, namely, with the patterns of behavior. I must admit that up to the present I have not got hold of any argument that would finally refute this possibility.

Before I pursue my reflections further, I must stress one aspect of the archetypes which will be obvious to anybody who has practical experience in these matters. That is, the archetypes have, when they appear, a distinctly numinous character which can only be described as "spiritual," if "magical" is too strong a word. Consequently this phenomenon is of the utmost significance for the psychology of religion. In its effects it is anything but unambiguous. It can be healing or destructive, but never indifferent, provided of course that it has attained a certain degree of clarity. This aspect deserves the epithet "spiritual" above all else. It not infrequently happens that the archetype appears in the form of a *spirit* in dreams or fantasy products, or even comports itself like a ghost. There is a mystical aura about its numinosity, and it has a corresponding effect upon the emotions. It mobilizes philosophical and religious convictions in the very people who deemed themselves miles above any such fits of weakness. Often it drives with unexampled passion and remorseless logic towards its goal and draws the subject under its spell, from which despite the most desperate resistance he is unable, and finally no longer even willing, to break free, because the experience brings with it a depth and fullness of meaning that was unthinkable before. . . .

I would like to make the way in which the archetype functions clear from this simple example: While sojourning in equatorial East Africa, on the southern slopes of Mount Elgon, I found that the natives used to step out of their huts at sunrise, hold their hands before their mouths, and spit or blow into them vigorously. Then they lifted their arms and held their hands with the palms toward the sun. I asked them the meaning of what they did, but nobody could give me an explanation. They had always done it like that, they said, and had learnt it from their parents. The medicine man, he would know what it meant. So I asked the medicine man. He knew as little as the others, but assured me that his grandfather had still known. It was just what people did at every sunrise, and at the first phase of the new moon. For these people, as I was able to show, the moment when the sun or the new moon appeared was "*mungu*," which corresponds to the Melanesian words "*mana*" or "*mulungu*" and is translated by the missionaries as "God." Actually the word "*athista*" in Elgonyi means sun as well as God, although they deny that the sun is God. Only the moment when it rises is *mungu* or *athista*. Spittle and breath mean soul-substance. Hence they offer their soul to God, but do not know what they are doing and never have known. They do it, motivated by the same preconscious archetype which the ancient Egyptians, on their monuments, also ascribed to the sun-worshiping dog-headed baboon, albeit in full knowledge that this ritual gesture was in honor of God. The behavior of the Elgonyi certainly strikes us as exceedingly primitive, but we forget that the educated Westerner behaves no differently. What the meaning of the Christmas tree might be our forefathers knew even less than ourselves, and it is only quite recently that we have bothered to find out at all.

The archetype is pure, unvitiated nature,[1] and it is nature that causes man to utter words and perform actions whose meaning is unconscious to him, so unconscious that he no longer gives it a thought. A later, more conscious humanity, faced with such meaningful things whose meaning none could declare, hit upon the idea that these must be the last vestiges of a Golden Age, when there were men who knew all things and taught wisdom to the nations. In the degenerate days that followed, these teachings were forgotten and were now only repeated as mindless mechanical gestures. In view of the findings of modern psychology it cannot be doubted that there are preconscious archetypes which were never conscious and can be established only indirectly through their effects upon the conscious contents. There is in my opinion no tenable argument against the hypothesis that all the psychic functions which today seem conscious to us were once unconscious and yet worked as if they *were* conscious. We could also say that all the psychic phenomena to be found in man were already present in the natural unconscious state. To this it might be objected that it would then be far from clear why there is such a thing as consciousness at all. I would, however, remind the reader that, as we have already seen, all unconscious functioning has the automatic character of an instinct, and that the instincts are always coming into collision or, because of their compulsiveness, pursuing their courses unaltered by any influence even under conditions that may positively endanger the life of the individual. As against this, consciousness enables him to adapt in an orderly way and to check the instincts, and consequently cannot be dispensed with. Man's capacity for consciousness alone makes him man.

The achievement of a synthesis of conscious and unconscious contents, and the conscious realization of the archetype's effects upon the conscious contents, represents the climax of a concentrated spiritual and psychic effort, in so far as this is undertaken consciously and of set purpose. That is to say, the synthesis can also be prepared in advance and brought to a certain point—William James's "bursting point"—unconsciously, whereupon it irrupts into consciousness of its own volition and confronts the latter with the formidable task of assimilating the contents that have burst in upon it, yet without damaging the viability of the two systems, i.e., of ego consciousness on the one hand and the irrupted complex on the other. . . .

Absorption into the instinctual sphere, therefore, does not and cannot lead to conscious realization and assimilation of instinct, because consciousness struggles in a regular panic against being swallowed up in the primitivity and unconsciousness of sheer instinctuality. This fear is the eternal burden of the hero myth and

---

[1] "Nature" here means simply that which is, and always was, given. AUTHOR'S NOTE.

the theme of countless taboos. The closer one comes to the instinct world, the more violent is the urge to shy away from it and to rescue the light of consciousness from the murks of the sultry abyss. Psychologically, however, the archetype as an image of instinct is a spiritual goal toward which the whole nature of man strives; it is the sea to which all rivers wend their way, the prize which the hero wrests from the fight with the dragon. . . .

The archetypal representations (images and ideas) mediated to us by the unconscious should not be confused with the archetype as such. They are very varied structures which all point back to one essentially "irrepresentable" basic form. The latter is characterized by certain formal elements and by certain fundamental meanings, although these can be grasped only approximately. The archetype as such is a psychoid factor that belongs, as it were, to the invisible, ultraviolet end of the psychic spectrum. It does not appear, in itself, to be capable of reaching consciousness.

C. G. JUNG
The Principal Archetypes

The archetypes most clearly characterized from the empirical point of view are those which have the most frequent and the most disturbing influence on the ego. These are the *shadow*, the *anima*, and the *animus*. The most accessible of these, and the easiest to experience, is the shadow, for its nature can in large measure be inferred from the contents of the personal unconscious. The only exceptions to this rule are those rather rare cases where the positive qualities of the personality are repressed, and the ego in consequence plays an essentially negative or unfavorable role.

The shadow is a moral problem that challenges the whole ego personality, for no one can become conscious of the shadow without considerable moral effort. To become conscious of it involves recognizing the dark aspects of the personality as present and real. This act is an essential condition for any kind of self-knowledge, and it therefore, as a rule, meets with considerable resistance. Indeed, self-knowledge as a psychotherapeutic measure frequently requires much painstaking work extending over a long period.

Closer examination of the dark characteristics—that is, the inferiorities constituting the shadow—reveals that they have an *emotional* nature, a kind of *autonomy*, and accordingly an *obsessive* or, better, *possessive* quality. Emotion, incidentally, is not an activity of the individual but something that happens to him. Affects occur usually where adaptation is weakest, and at the same time they

From "Aion: Contributions to the Symbolism of the Self" [1951] and "Psychological Aspects of the Mother Archetype" [1954], *The Collected Works of C. G. Jung*, translated from the German by R. F. C. Hull, New York, 1959, Vol. IX, part 2, pp. 8-9, 10-13, 13-14, 16, 19-20; part 1, pp. 80-84. Reprinted by permission of the Bollingen Foundation and Routledge & Kegan Paul Ltd.

reveal the reason for its weakness, namely, a certain degree of inferiority and the existence of a lower level of personality. On this lower level with its uncontrolled or scarcely controlled emotions one behaves more or less like a primitive, who is not only the passive victim of his affects but also singularly incapable of moral judgment.

Although, with insight and good will, the shadow can to some extent be assimilated into the conscious personality, experience shows that there are certain features which offer the most obstinate resistance to moral control and prove almost impossible to influence. These resistances are usually bound up with *projections*, which are not recognized as such, and their recognition is a moral achievement beyond the ordinary. While some traits peculiar to the shadow can be recognized without too much difficulty as one's own personal qualities, in this case both insight and good will are unavailing because the cause of the emotion appears to lie, beyond all possibility of doubt, in the *other person*. No matter how obvious it may be to the neutral observer that it is a matter of projections, there is little hope that the subject will perceive this himself. He must be convinced that he throws a very long shadow before he is willing to withdraw his emotionally toned projections from their object. . . .

One might assume that projections like these, which are so very difficult if not impossible to dissolve, would belong to the realm of the shadow—that is, to the negative side of the personality. This assumption however becomes untenable after a certain point, because the symbols that then appear no longer refer to the same but to the opposite sex, in a man's case to a woman and vice versa. The source of projections is no longer the shadow—which is always of the same sex as the subject—but a contrasexual figure. Here we meet the *animus* of a woman and the *anima* of a man, two corresponding archetypes whose autonomy and unconsciousness explain the stubbornness of their projections. Though the shadow is a motif as well known to mythology as anima and animus, it represents first and foremost the personal unconscious, and its content can therefore be made conscious without too much difficulty. In this it differs from anima and animus, for whereas the shadow can be seen through and recognized fairly easily, the anima and animus are much further away from consciousness and in normal circumstances are seldom if ever realized. With a little self-criticism one can see through the shadow—so far as its nature is personal. But when it appears as an archetype, one encounters the same difficulties as with anima and animus. In other words, it is quite within the bounds of possibility for a man to recognize the relative evil of his nature, but it is a rare and shattering experience for him to gaze into the face of absolute evil. . . .

What, then, is this projection-making factor? The East calls it the "Spinning Woman"—Maya, who creates illusion by her dancing. Had we not long since known it from the symbolism of dreams, this hint from the Orient would put us on the right track: the enveloping, embracing, and devouring element points unmistakably to the mother,[1] that is, to the son's relation to the real mother, to her imago, and to the woman who is to become a mother for him. His Eros is passive

---

[1] Here and in what follows, the word "mother" is not meant in the literal sense but as a symbol of everything that functions as a mother. AUTHOR'S NOTE.

like a child's; he hopes to be caught, sucked in, enveloped, and devoured. He seeks, as it were, the protecting, nourishing, charmed circle of the mother, the condition of the infant released from every care, in which the outside world bends over him and even forces happiness upon him. No wonder the real world vanishes from sight!

If this situation is dramatized, as the unconscious usually dramatizes it, then there appears before you on the psychological stage a man living regressively, seeking his childhood and his mother, fleeing from a cold cruel world which denies him understanding. Not infrequently a mother appears beside him who apparently shows not the slightest concern that her little son should become a man, but who, with tireless and self-immolating effort, neglects nothing that might hinder him from growing up and marrying. You behold the secret conspiracy between mother and son, and how each helps the other to betray life.

Where does the guilt lie? With the mother, or with the son? Probably with both. The unsatisfied longing of the son for life and the world ought to be taken seriously. There is in him a desire to touch reality, to embrace the earth and fructify the field of the world. But he makes no more than a series of impatient beginnings, for his initiative as well as his staying power are crippled by the secret memory that the world and happiness may be had as a gift—from the mother. It makes demands on the masculinity of a man, on his ardor, above all on his courage and resolution, when it comes to throwing his whole being into the scales. For this he would need a faithless Eros, one capable of forgetting the mother and of hurting himself by deserting the first love of his life. The mother, foreseeing this danger, has carefully inculcated into him the virtues of faithfulness, devotion, loyalty, so as to protect him from the moral disruption which is the risk of every life adventure. He has learned these lessons only too well, and remains true to his mother, perhaps causing her the deepest anxiety (when, in her honor, he turns out to be a homosexual, for example) and at the same time affords her an unconscious satisfaction of a mythological nature, for in the relationship now reigning between them, there is consummated the immemorial and most sacred archetype of the marriage of mother and son.

At this level of the myth, which probably illustrates the nature of the collective unconscious better than any other, the mother is both old and young, Demeter and Persephone, and the son is spouse and sleeping infant all in one. The imperfections of real life, with its laborious adaptations and manifold disappointments, naturally cannot compete with such a state of indescribable fulfillment.

In the case of the son, the projection-making factor is identical with the *mother imago*, and this is consequently taken to be the real mother. The projection can only be dissolved when he comes to realize that in the realm of his psyche there exists an image of the mother and not only of the mother, but also of the daughter, the sister, the beloved, the heavenly goddess, and the earth spirit Baubo. Every mother and every beloved is forced to become the carrier and embodiment of this omnipresent and ageless image which corresponds to the deepest reality in a man. It is his own, this perilous image of Woman; she stands for the loyalty which in the interests of life he cannot always maintain; she is the vital compensation for the risks, struggles, sacrifices which all end in disappointment; she is the solace for all the bitterness of life. Simultaneously, she is the great illusionist, the seductress who draws him into life—not only into its reasonable and useful aspects but into its frightful paradoxes and ambivalences where good and evil, success and ruin, hope and despair counterbalance one another. . . .

The projection-making factor is the anima, or rather the unconscious as represented by the anima. Whenever she appears, in dreams, visions, and fantasies, she takes on personified forms, thus demonstrating that the factor she embodies possesses all the outstanding characteristics of a feminine being. She is not an invention of the conscious mind, but a spontaneous production of the unconscious. Nor is she a substitute figure for the mother. On the contrary, there is every likelihood that the numinous qualities which make the mother imago so dangerously powerful stem from the collective archetype of the anima, which is incarnated anew in every male child.

Since the anima is an archetype that is manifest in men, it is reasonable to suppose that an equivalent archetype must be present in women; for just as the man is compensated by a feminine element, so woman is compensated by a masculine one. . . . Just as the mother seems to be the first carrier of the projection-making factor for the son, so is the father for the daughter. . . . Woman is compensated by a masculine element and therefore her unconscious has, so to speak, a masculine imprint. This results in a considerable psychological difference between men and women, and accordingly I have called the projection-making factor in women the animus, which means reason or spirit. The animus corresponds to the paternal Logos just as the anima corresponds to the maternal Eros. It is far from my intention to give these two intuitive concepts too specific a definition. I use Eros and Logos merely as conceptual aids to describe the fact that woman's consciousness is characterized more by the connective quality of Eros than by the discrimination and cognition associated with Logos. In men, Eros, the function of relationship, is usually less developed than Logos. In women, on the other hand, Eros is an expression of their true nature, while their Logos is often only a regrettable accident. . . .

Like the anima, the animus too has a positive aspect. Through the figure of the father he expresses not only conventional opinion but—equally—what we call "spirit," philosophical or religious ideas in particular, or rather the attitude resulting from them. Thus the animus is a psychopomp, a mediator between the conscious and the unconscious and a personification of the latter. Just as the anima becomes, through integration, the Eros of consciousness, so the animus becomes a Logos; and in the same way that the anima gives relationship and relatedness to a man's consciousness, the animus gives woman's consciousness a capacity for reflection, deliberation, and self-knowledge. . . .

Not all the contents of the anima and animus are projected, however. Many of them appear spontaneously in dreams and so on, and many more can be made conscious through active imagination. In this way we find that thoughts, feelings, and affects are alive in us which we would never have believed possible in the figures of anima and animus. They personify those of its contents which, when withdrawn from projection, can be integrated into consciousness. To this extent, both figures represent *functions* which filter the contents of the collective unconscious through to the conscious mind. They appear or behave as such, however, only so long as the tendencies of the conscious and unconscious do not diverge too greatly. Should any tension arise, these functions, harmless till then, confront the conscious mind in personified form and behave rather like systems split off from the personality, or like part souls. This comparison is inadequate insofar as nothing previously belonging to the ego personality has split off from it; on the contrary, the two figures represent a disturbing accretion. The reason for their behaving in this way is that though the *contents* of anima and animus can be integrated, they themselves cannot, since they are archetypes. As such they are the foundation stones of the psychic structure, which in its totality exceeds the limits of consciousness and therefore can never become the object of direct cognition. The effects of anima and animus can indeed be made conscious, but they themselves are factors transcending consciousness and beyond the reach of perception and volition.

Like any other archetype, the mother archetype appears under an almost infinite variety of aspects. I mention here only some of the more characteristic. First in importance are the personal mother and grandmother, stepmother and mother-in-law; then any woman with whom a relationship exists, for example, a nurse or governess or perhaps a remote ancestress. Then there are what might be termed mothers in a figurative sense. To this category belongs the goddess, and especially the Mother of God, the Virgin, and Sophia. Mythology offers many variations of the mother archetype, as for instance the mother who reappears as the maiden in the myth of Demeter and Kore; or the mother who is also the beloved, as in the Cybele-Attis myth. Other symbols of the mother in a figurative sense appear in things representing the goal of our longing for redemption, such as Paradise, the Kingdom of God, the Heavenly Jerusalem. Many things arousing devotion or feelings of awe, as for instance the Church, university, city or country, Heaven, Earth, the woods, the sea or any still waters, matter even, the underworld and the moon, can be mother-symbols. The archetype is often associated with things and places standing for fertility and fruitfulness: the cornucopia, a plowed field, a garden. It can be attached to a rock, a cave, a tree, a spring, a deep well, or to various vessels such as the baptismal font, or to vessel-shaped flowers like the rose or the lotus. Because of the protection it implies, the magic circle or mandala can be a form of mother archetype. Hollow objects such as ovens and cooking vessels are associated with the mother archetype, and, of course, the uterus, *yoni*, and anything of a like shape. Added to this list there are many animals, such as the cow, hare, and helpful animals in general.

All these symbols can have a positive, favorable meaning or a negative, evil meaning. An ambivalent aspect is seen in the goddess of fate (Moira, Graeae, Norns). Evil symbols are the witch, the dragon (or any devouring and entwining animal, such as a large fish or a serpent), the grave, the sarcophagus, deep water, death, nightmares and bogies (Empusa, Lilith, etc.). This list is not, of course, complete; it presents only the most important features of the mother archetype.

The qualities associated with it are maternal solicitude and sympathy; the magic authority of the female; the wisdom and spiritual exaltation that transcend reason; any helpful instinct or impulse; all that is benign, all that cherishes and sustains, that fosters growth and fertility. The place of magic transformation and rebirth, together with the underworld and its inhabitants, are presided over by the mother. On the negative side the mother archetype may connote anything secret, hidden, dark; the abyss, the world of the dead, anything that devours, seduces, and poisons, that is terrifying and inescapable like fate. All these attributes of the mother archetype have been fully described and documented in my book *Symbols of Transformation*. There I formulated the ambivalence of these attributes as "the loving and the terrible mother." Perhaps the historical example of the dual nature of the mother most familiar to us is the Virgin Mary, who is not only the Lord's mother, but also, according to the medieval allegories, his cross. In India, "the loving and terrible mother" is the paradoxical Kali. Sankhya philosophy has elaborated the mother archetype into the concept of *prakrti* (matter) and assigned to it the three *gunas* or fundamental attributes: *sattva, rajas, tamas*: goodness, passion, and darkness. These are three essential aspects of the mother: her cherishing and nourishing goodness, her orgiastic emotionality, and her Stygian depths. The special feature of the philosophical myth, which shows Prakrti dancing before Purusha in order to remind him of "discriminating knowledge," does not belong to the mother archetype but to the archetype of the anima, which in a man's psychology invariably appears, at first, mingled with the mother-image.

Although the figure of the mother as it appears in folklore is more or less universal, this image changes markedly when it appears in the individual psyche. In treating patients one is at first impressed, and indeed arrested, by the apparent significance of the personal mother. This figure of the personal mother looms so large in all personalistic psychologies that, as we know, they never got beyond it, even in theory, to other important etiological factors. My own view differs from that of other medico-psychological theories principally in that I attribute to the personal mother only a limited etiological significance. That is to say, all those influences which the literature describes as being exerted on the children do not come from the mother herself, but rather from the archetype projected upon her, which gives her a mythological background and invests her with authority and numinosity.[2] The etiological and traumatic effects produced by the mother must be divided into two groups: (1) those corresponding to traits of character or attitudes actually present in the mother, and (2) those referring to traits which the mother only seems to possess, the reality being composed of more or less fantastic (i.e., archetypal) projections on the part of the child. Freud himself had already seen that the real etiology of neuroses does not lie in traumatic effects, as he at first suspected, but in a peculiar development of infantile fantasy. This is not to deny that such a development can be traced back to disturbing influences emanating from the mother. I myself make it a rule to look first for the cause of infantile neuroses in the mother, as I know from experience that a child is much more likely to develop normally than neurotically, and that in the great majority of cases definite causes of disturbances can be found in the parents, especially in the mother. The contents of the child's abnormal fantasies can be referred to the personal mother only in part, since they often contain clear and unmistakable allusions which could not possibly have reference to human beings. This is especially true where definitely mythological products are concerned, as is frequently the case in infantile phobias where the mother may appear as a wild beast, a witch, a specter, an ogre, a hermaphrodite, and so on. It must be borne in mind,

---

[2] American psychology can supply us with any amount of examples. A blistering but instructive lampoon on this subject is Philip Wylie's *Generation of Vipers* (New York 1942). AUTHOR'S NOTE.

however, that such fantasies are not always of unmistakably mythological origin, and, even if they are, they may not always be rooted in the unconscious archetype but may have been occasioned by fairy tales or accidental remarks. A thorough investigation is therefore indicated in each case. For practical reasons, such an investigation cannot be made so readily with children as with adults, who almost invariably transfer their fantasies to the physician during treatment—or, to be more precise, the fantasies transfer themselves to him automatically.

When that happens, nothing is gained by brushing them aside as ridiculous, for archetypes are among the inalienable assets of every psyche. They form the "treasure in the realm of shadowy thoughts" of which Kant spoke, and of which we have ample evidence in the countless treasure motifs of mythology. An archetype as such is in no sense just an annoying prejudice; it becomes so only when it is in the wrong place. In themselves, archetypal images are among the highest values of the human psyche; they have peopled the heavens of all races from time immemorial. To discard them as valueless would be a distinct loss. Our task is not, therefore, to deny the archetype, but to dissolve the projections, in order to restore their contents to the individual who has involuntarily lost them by projecting them outside himself.

FRIEDRICH SCHLEGEL

Modern Mythology

In view of the seriousness with which you honour art, my friends, I wish to summon you to ask yourselves this question: Is the power of inspiration to become increasingly fragmented even in poetry, and, having exhausted itself in its struggle against a hostile world, is it to rest in lonely silence? Is the highest and holiest thing we know to remain forever without name or form, abandoned in darkness to chance? Is Love truly uncapturable, and can there be said to be an art worthy of the name if it does not possess the power of casting its spell over the spirit of Love, so that Love does its bidding and is brought to inform art's beautiful creations as art dictates and chooses?

You above all must know what I mean. You are poets yourselves, and in your poetry you must often have felt that you lacked a firm basis for your activity, a maternal soil, a sky, a vital atmosphere.

To work outwards from within—this is what the modern poet must do, and many have done it magnificently, but hitherto only each one for himself, each work like an original creation *ex nihilo*.

I will go straight to my goal. It is my contention that our poetry lacks a center, such as mythology was for the ancients, and the essential shortcomings of modern poetry in relation to that of antiquity may be summed up in these words: we have no mythology. But let me add that we are close to acquiring one, or rather it is time that we seriously collaborate in producing one.

For it will come to us in a quite opposite way from the original mythology, which was everywhere the first blossoming of youthful imagination, clinging directly to—and rooting itself in—what was most immediate and alive in the sensuous world. The new mythology must, on the contrary, be fashioned out of the profoundest depths of the spirit; it must be the most artificial of all works of art, for it is to encompass all others, it is to be a new course or a vessel for the ancient, eternal fountainhead of poetry and itself the everlasting Poem which contains within itself the seeds of all other poems.

You may well smile at this mystical Poem and the disorder which might be conceived to arise from such a thronging abundance of poetic works. But the highest beauty, indeed the highest order, is, after all, only that of chaos, chaos of a kind that merely awaits the touch of Love in order to unfold into a harmonious

From "Dialogue on Poetry" [1800], translated from the German by Irving Wohlfarth and the editors.

world, such as ancient mythology and poetry indeed were. For mythology and poetry are both one and indivisible. All the poems of antiquity link together till out of ever greater limbs and members a whole is formed; all fuses, everywhere there lives one and the same spirit in different expressions. And thus it is truly no empty figure to say that ancient poetry is a single, indivisible, completed poem. Why should what has already been not emerge anew? In a different manner, of course. And why not in a finer, greater manner?

I ask you only not to give way to complete disbelief in the possibility of a new mythology. But I will welcome doubts from all sides and pointing in all directions, in order that the investigation may gain in freedom and richness. And now lend an attentive ear to my speculations! In view of the circumstances I am unwilling to venture more than speculations. But I hope these speculations will through you become truths. For they are, to some extent, if you care to make them such, suggestions to be tried out.

If a new mythology can work its way out of the innermost depths of the spirit only by its own force, then we find in the great phenomenon of the age—in idealism!—a very significant hint and a notable manifestation of what we are seeking. Idealism has arisen, as if out of nothingness, in just this way, and in the world of the spirit a fixed point is now constituted whence man's faculties can expand on all sides in steady development, sure of never losing themselves and their way back. The great revolution will seize all the sciences and the arts. Already you see its effect in physics, where idealism had actually burst forth at an earlier stage before the science was even touched by the magic wand of philosophy. And this great and miraculous fact can at the same time serve you as a hint of the secret coherence and inner unity of the age. Idealism—which from a practical standpoint is nothing other than the spirit of that revolution whose great maxims we must practise and propagate in strength and freedom—is, theoretically speaking, however great it may also prove to be in this respect, merely a part, a branch, a mode of expression for the phenomenon of all phenomena: namely, that mankind is struggling with all its might to find its center. Mankind must, as matters stand, go under or rejuvenate itself. Which is the more probable, and what may not be hoped of such an age of rejuvenation?—Grey antiquity will come alive once more, and the most distant future of civilization will be presaged. Yet this is not what initially concerns me here: for I wish to overleap nothing, but to lead you step by step to the certainty of the holiest mysteries.

Just as it is of the essence of the spirit to be self-determining and, in eternal alternation, to go out of itself and return to itself, just as every thought is nothing but the result of such an activity, so the same process is in general visible in every form of idealism, which is itself merely the recognition of spiritual self-determination and a new life redoubled by this act of recognition. The new life most gloriously manifests its secret powers by an unlimited abundance of new inventions, by a general communicability, and by a vital efficacy. Naturally the phenomenon takes on a new form in every individual; therefore the outcome must often fall short of our expectation. But insofar as necessary laws permit us to anticipate a large-scale development, our expectation cannot be disappointed. Idealism in every form must, in one way or another, go out of itself in order to be able to return to itself and thereby retain its essential qualities. Hence there must and will come forth from its womb a new and equally limitless realism, and thus idealism will not merely be an example for the new mythology in its mode of genesis but also, indirectly, its source. Already traces of a similar trend can be discerned almost everywhere; especially in physics, which appears to be deficient only in lacking a mythological conception of nature.

I too have long carried within me the ideal of such a realism, and if hitherto it did not come to the point of formulation, this was simply because I am still seeking the proper organ for it. Yet I know that I can find it only in poetry, for realism will never be able to re-emerge in the form of philosophy or indeed of any system. And even according to a universal tradition there is reason to expect that this new realism, being necessarily of idealist origin and resting, as it were, on idealist foundations, will appear as poetry, for poetry is said, after all, to be based on the harmony of the real and the ideal. . . .

And what is every beautiful mythology but a hieroglyphic expression of surrounding nature in a transfiguration of imagination and love?

Mythology has a great advantage. What at other times perpetually flees from consciousness is nevertheless to be seen here and held fast in spiritual sensuality, just as the soul in the surrounding body, though it shimmers before our eyes, speaks to our ears.

This is the essential point—that in our quest for what is highest we should not rely solely on our feelings. To be sure, nothing will ever flow from dry feelings; this is a well-known truth against which I am least disposed to rebel. But everywhere we should cling to the world of forms and should develop, kindle, sustain, in a word *fashion* even the highest subjects through contact with equivalents or analogies or, with equal propriety, opposites. But if the highest things actually cannot be deliberately molded, then let us immediately relinquish all claims to any free art of ideas, which would in that event be an empty name.

Mythology is such a poem of nature. In its fabric the supreme values are actually shaped by art; all is connection and transformation, related and translated, and this relation and translation constitute its peculiar procedure, its inner life, its method, if I may so express myself.

Therein I find a great resemblance with that large inventiveness of Romantic poetry, which manifests itself not in individual insights but in the construction of the whole, and which our friend has so often expounded to us in the works of Cervantes and Shakespeare. Indeed, this artfully ordered confusion, this charming symmetry of contradictions, this miraculous, perpetual alternation of enthusiasm and irony, which extends even to the tiniest aspects of the whole—these seem to me already to constitute an indirect mythology. The organization is the same, and assuredly the arabesque is the oldest and most fundamental form of the human imagination. Neither such invention nor any mythology can exist without an original, inimitable, and frankly inexplicable element, which, after all the transformations, still makes it possible for the old nature and power to shine through, and with naive profundity allows a glimpse of the perverse, the crazy, or the silly. For that is the beginning of all poetry, to suspend the course and laws of logically reasoning thought and to transport us back to the fine confusion of the imagination, the original chaos of human nature, for which I have till now found no finer symbol than the colorful throng of the old gods. . . .

But the other mythologies, too, must be revived, in the measure of their depth, their beauty, and their articulation, in order to hasten on the emergence of the new mythology. If only the treasures of the Orient were as accessible to us as those of antiquity! What a new source of poetry might flow to us from India if German artists with the universality and depth of mind and genius for translation that is peculiar to them had the opportunity which an increasingly insensitive and brutal nation knows little how to exploit! In the Orient we must seek the supreme Romantic elements, and once we have access to the source then perhaps the semblance of southern fire we now find so attractive in Spanish poetry will look merely occidental and meagre. . . .

And so let us in the name of life hesitate no longer, but let each according to his lights hasten on the great enterprise to which we are called. Be worthy of the greatness of the epoch, and the mist will clear before your eyes; before you there will be light. All thought is divination, but man is only just beginning to become aware of his powers of divination. What immeasurable expansions will men yet experience, and even at this very time! In my estimation, whoever understands the epoch, which is to say the great process of general rejuvenation and the principles of perpetual revolution, should be able to grasp both poles of humanity, to understand the deeds of the earliest men and to know the character of the golden age that is yet to come. Then idle chatter would cease and man would come to the realization of what he is, and would understand the earth and the sun.

This is what I mean by the new mythology.

VICTOR HUGO

Imaginative Types

Thus each great poet tries on in his turn this immense human mask. And such is the strength of the soul which shines through the mysterious aperture of the eyes, that this look changes the mask, and from terrible makes it comic, then pensive, then grieved, then young and smiling, then decrepit, then sensual and gluttonous, then religious, then outrageous; and it is Cain, Job, Atreus, Ajax, Priam, Hecuba, Niobe, Clytemnestra, Nausicaa, Pistoclerus, Grumio, Davus, Pasicompsa, Chimène, Don Arias, Don Diego, Mudarra, Richard III, Lady Macbeth, Desdemona, Juliet, Romeo, Lear, Sancho Panza, Pantagruel, Panurge, Arnolphe, Dandin, Sganarelle, Agnes, Rosine, Victorine, Basile, Almaviva, Cherubin, Manfred.

From the direct divine creation proceeds Adam, the prototype. From the indirect divine creation—that is to say, from the human creation—proceed other Adams, the types.

A type does not reproduce any man in particular; it cannot be exactly superposed upon any individual; it sums up and concentrates under one human form a whole family of characters and minds. A type is no abridgment: it is a condensation. It is not one, it is all. Alcibiades is but Alcibiades, Petronius is but Petronius, Bassompierre is but Bassompierre, Buckingham is but Buckingham, Fronsac is but Fronsac, Lauzun is but Lauzun; but take Lauzun, Fronsac, Buckingham, Bassom-

From William Shakespeare [1864], translated from the French by M. B. Anderson, London, 1899, pp. 173-6.

pierre, Petronius, and Alcibiades, and bray them in the mortar of the dream, and there issues from it a phantom more real than them all,—Don Juan. Take usurers individually, and no one of them is that fierce merchant of Venice, crying: "Go, Tubal, fee me an officer, bespeak him a fortnight before; I will have the heart of him if he forfeit." Take all the usurers together, from the crowd of them is evolved a total,—Shylock. Sum up usury, you have Shylock. The metaphor of the people, who are never mistaken, confirms unawares the invention of the poet; and while Shakespeare makes Shylock, the popular tongue creates the bloodsucker. Shylock is the embodiment of Jewishness; he is also Judaism,—that is to say, his whole nation, the high as well as the low, faith as well as fraud; and it is because he sums up a whole race, such as oppression has made it, that Shylock is great. The Jews are, however, right in saying that none of them—not even the mediaeval Jew—is Shylock. Men of pleasure may with reason say that no one of them is Don Juan. No leaf of the orange-tree when chewed gives the flavour of the orange; yet there is a deep affinity, an identity of roots, a sap rising from the same source, a sharing of the same subterranean shadow before life. The fruit contains the mystery of the tree, and the type contains the mystery of the man. Hence the strange vitality of the type.

For—and this is the marvel—the type lives. Were it but an abstraction, men would not recognize it, and would allow this shadow to go its way. The tragedy termed "classic" makes phantoms; the drama creates living types. A lesson which is a man; a myth with a human face so plastic that it looks at you and that its look is a mirror; a parable which nudges you; a symbol which cries out "Beware!"; an idea which is nerve, muscle, and flesh,—which has a heart to love, bowels to suffer, eyes to weep, and teeth to devour or to laugh; a psychical conception with the relief of actual fact, which, if it be pricked, bleeds red,—such is the type. O power of all poetry! These types are beings. They breathe, they palpitate, their steps are heard on the floor, they exist. They exist with an existence more intense than that of any creature thinking himself alive there in the street. These phantoms are more substantial than man. In their essence is that eternal element which belongs to masterworks, which makes Trimalchio live, while M. Romieu is dead.

Types are cases foreseen of God; genius realizes them. It seems that God prefers to teach man a lesson through man, in order to inspire confidence. The poet walks the street with living men; he has their ear. Hence the efficacy of types. Man is a premise, the type the conclusion; God creates the phenomenon, genius gives it a name; God creates the miser only, genius forms Harpagon; God creates the traitor only, genius makes Iago; God creates the coquette, genius makes Célimène; God creates the citizen only, genius makes Chrysale; God creates the king only, genius makes Grandgousier. Sometimes, at a given moment, the type issues full-grown from some unknown collaboration of the mass of the people with a great natural actor, an involuntary and powerful realizer; the crowd is a midwife; in an epoch which bears at one extreme Talleyrand, and at another Chodruc-Duclos, there springs up suddenly, in a flash of lightning, under the mysterious incubation of the theatre, that spectre Robert Macaire.

Types go and come on a common level in Art and in Nature; they are the ideal realized. The good and the evil of man are in these figures. From each of them springs, in the eyes of the thinker, a humanity.

As we have said before, as many types, as many Adams. The man of Homer, Achilles, is an Adam: from him comes the species of the slayers; the man of

Aeschylus, Prometheus, is an Adam: from him comes the race of the wrestlers; the man of Shakespeare, Hamlet, is an Adam: to him belongs the family of the dreamers. Other Adams, created by poets, incarnate,—this one, passion; another, duty; another, reason; another, conscience; another, the fall; another, the ascension.

Prudence, drifting into trepidation, passes from the old man Nestor to the old old man Géronte. Love, drifting into appetite, passes from Daphne to Lovelace. Beauty, entwined with the serpent, passes from Eve to Melusina. The types begin in Genesis, and a link of their chain passes through Restif de la Bretonne and Vadé. The lyric suits them,—Billingsgate does not misbecome them. They speak a country dialect by the mouth of Gros-René, and in Homer they say to Minerva, who takes them by the hair: "What wouldst thou with me, Goddess?"

A surprising exception has been conceded to Dante. The man of Dante is Dante. Dante has, so to speak, recreated himself in his poem: he is his own type; his Adam is himself. For the action of his poem he has sought out no one. He has taken Virgil only as a supernumerary. Moreover, he made himself epic at once, without even giving himself the trouble to change his name. What he had to do was in fact simple,—to descend into hell, and remount to heaven. What use was it to trouble himself for so little? He knocks gravely at the door of the Infinite and says: "Open! I am Dante."

RICHARD WAGNER

The Folk and the Myth

Who is then the Folk?—It is absolutely necessary that, before proceeding further, we should agree upon the answer to this weightiest of questions.

"The Folk" was from of old the inclusive term for *all the units* which made up the total of a *commonality*. In the beginning, it was the family and the tribe; next, the tribes united by like speech into a nation. Practically, by the Roman world-dominion which engulfed the nations, and theoretically, by the Christian religion which admitted of naught but men, *i.e.* no racial, but only *Christian* men —the idea of "the People" has so far broadened out, or even evaporated, that we may either include in it mankind in general, or, upon the arbitrary political hypothesis, a certain, and generally the propertyless portion of the Commonwealth. But beyond a frivolous meaning, this term has also acquired an ineradicable *moral* one; and because of it, in times of stir and trouble all men are eager to number themselves among the People; each one gives out that he is careful for the People's weal, and no one will permit himself to be excluded from it. Therefore in these latter days the question has also been frequently broached, in the most diverse of senses: Who then is the People? In the sum total of the body politic, can a separate

From "The Art-Work of the Future" [1849], *Prose Works*, translated from the German by W. A. Ellis, London, 1893, Vol. I, pp. 74-5.
From "Opera and Drama" [1875], *Art, Life and Theories*, translated from the German by E. L. Burlingame, New York, 1889, pp. 153-6. Translations revised by the editors.

party, a particular fraction of the said body claim this name for itself alone? Rather, are we not all alike "the People," from the beggar to the prince?

This question must therefore be answered according to the conclusive and world-historical sense that now lies at its root, as follows:—

The "Folk" is the epitome of all those men *who feel a common and collective Want*. To it belong, then, all of those who recognise their individual want as a collective want, or find it based thereon; ergo, all those who can hope for the stilling of their want in nothing but the stilling of a common want, and therefore spend their whole life's strength upon the stilling of their thus acknowledged common want. For only that want which urges to the uttermost, is genuine want; but this want alone is the force of true need (*"Bedürfniss"*); but a common and collective need is the only true need; only he who feels within him a true need, has a right to its assuagement; but only the assuagement of a genuine need is necessity; and it is *the Folk alone that acts according to necessity's behests*, and therefore irresistibly, victoriously, and rightly as none besides.

In the *Mythos* the poetic faculty common to all People still perceives things exactly as the eye sees them, and no farther; and not as, in themselves, they really are. The vast multiplicity of surrounding phenomena, and the relations between them which man is still unable to perceive, first produce upon him an effect of unrest; in order to subdue this feeling, he seeks for something calculated to link these manifestations together—which he may be able to regard as their Primary Cause. But discovery of the real conection is open only to an intelligence conceiving of these manifestations according to their reality.

As for the connection which is merely conjured up by the kind of man who is incapable of viewing these manifestations otherwise than in the light of the immediate impression they make upon him—that is simply the effect of fancy; and the Cause arrived at in this way a mere product of a poetical power of imagination.

God and gods are the first creations of the human poetic faculty: in them man represents to himself the essence of natural manifestations as derived from a Cause; but his spontaneous notion of this Cause is none other than that of his own humanity, on which his poetic Primary Cause is exclusively based.

Should his impulse, seeking to still the inward unrest due to the multiplicity of manifestations, proceed to represent this imagined cause as plainly as possible (since he can only regain rest through the senses which have caused the disturbance), he must present his God not only in a shape most suitable to be apprehended by his purely human intuition but also outwardly the most intelligible.

All understanding comes to us from Love; and the natural impulse of man is toward the being of his own species. Just as the human form is to him the most intelligible, so also will the qualities of natural manifestations—which he does not yet know in their reality—be rendered most intelligible to him by being reduced to human shape.

The entire intuition of the People in favour of shape shows itself, in Mythos, by conveying the widest association of the most various manifestations to the senses in the most succinct form. At first a mere image formed by fancy, this form now assumes a more or less human demeanour, the plainer it is to become.

Yet, in spite of this, its content is really both superhuman and supernatural: and is, in point of fact, the same co-operative, collective and comprehensive force and faculty which can only be admitted to be human and natural when generally associated with the action of human and natural forces; but which appear super-human and supernatural by the very fact that they are ascribed to *one* imagined individual, represented in the shape of man.

In the Mythos, therefore, the People exercises its fancy in reducing the greatest range of conceivable reality and actuality to the smallest, most succinct and most plastic shape; and it therefore becomes the real creator of art; for these shapes must necessarily win artistic form and content, if, as is their peculiarity, they really spring from man's longing that the representation of manifestations should be thoroughly intelligible; and that they should therefore correspond to man's yearning not merely to include recognition of himself (and of his own peculiar—nay, divinely creative, nature) in the object represented, but to regard that recognition as of first importance.

Art, by the very meaning of the term, is nothing else than fulfilment of the desire to recognise oneself in an admired or beloved object, to find oneself again in the manifestations of the outer world, as controlled by their representation. In the object he has represented, the Artist says to himself: "So, too, art thou; so dost thou feel and think; and so wouldst thou act, if, freed from all the arbitrary compulsion of outward events of life, thou could act according to thy choice." Thus did the People in Mythos form its idea of *God*; thus its *Hero*; and also, finally, its *Man*.

Greek tragedy is the artistic realisation of the contents and spirit of Greek Mythos. As in this Mythos, the widest-ranging manifestations were ultimately compressed into a more and more compact shape, and the Drama took this shape and represented it in the most compressed and compact of forms.

The common intention as to the nature of manifestations, which in the Mythos, had condensed itself from a view of nature to one of human morality, here appeals in its distinctest, most pregnant form to the receptive power of men generally; as an art-work, originating in fancy and proceeding to reality. As in drama the shapes that had been in Mythos merely shapes of thought, came to be represented by men in person; the action, now presented in a state of reality, now compressed itself, in thorough keeping with the nature of Mythos, into a compact plastic whole.

If we admit that a man's disposition can only be convincingly revealed to us by his actions, and that the character of a man always depends upon perfect agreement between his disposition and his action; then this action, and there-fore the underlying disposition—entirely in the sense of the Mythos—gains sig-nificance, and becomes consistent with comprehensive contents as it displays it-self with the utmost conciseness. An action which consists of many parts is either extravagant, redundant and unintelligible—when all these parts are of equally suggestive, or decisive importance; or else it is petty, arbitrary and mean-ingless—when these parts are nothing but odds and ends of action.

The content of an action is the disposition which underlies it. Should this dis-position be one which is great and comprehensive, or one which, in some given direction, makes exhaustive demands upon human nature, then it also ordains an action which shall be decisive, one and indivisible; for only in such an action can a great conception be brought home to our minds.

Now, by its nature, the contents of Greek Mythos were of this comprehensive but compact order; and in their tragedy, their expression proved itself with the utmost certainty to be the one necessary and decisive action. The problem for the tragic poet was to cause this action in its fullest meaning to proceed from the disposition exhibited by the performers, and to do this in a manner fully vindicated; to bring to understanding the necessity of the action, by and in the demonstrated truth of the disposition.

The unity of the tragic poet's art-work, in respect of form, was indicated beforehand, however, in the contours of the Mythos; so that he had only to carry it out as a living structure; and by no means, in favour of any spontaneously imagined structure, to break it up and piece it together again. The tragic poet merely imparted the content and nature of the myth in the most conclusive and intelligible manner.

Thus Greek tragedy is nothing but the artistic fulfillment of the Myth itself; just as the Myth had been the poetic expression of that life-view common to all.

WILLIAM BLAKE

Visionary History

The Britons (say historians) were naked civilized men, learned, studious, abstruse in thought and contemplation; naked, simple, plain in their acts and manners; wiser than after-ages. They were overwhelmed by brutal arms, all but a small remnant; Strength, Beauty, and Ugliness escaped the wreck, and remain for ever unsubdued, age after age.

The British Antiquities are now in the Artist's hands; all his visionary contemplations, relating to his own country and its ancient glory, when it was, as it again shall be, the source of learning and inspiration. Arthur was a name for the constellation Arcturus, or Boötes, the keeper of the North Pole. And all the fables of Arthur and his round table; of the warlike naked Britons; of Merlin; of Arthur's conquest of the whole world; of his death, or sleep, and promise to return again; of the Druid monuments or temples; of the pavement of Watling-street; of London stone; of the caverns in Cornwall, Wales, Derbyshire, and Scotland; of the Giants of Ireland and Britain; of the elemental beings called by us by the general name of Fairies; and of these three who escaped, namely Beauty, Strength, and Ugliness. Mr. B. has in his hands poems of the highest antiquity. Adam was a Druid, and Noah; also Abraham was called to succeed the Druidical age, which began to turn allegoric and mental signification into corporeal command, whereby human sacrifice would have depopulated the earth.

From "A Descriptive Catalogue of Pictures" [1809], *Complete Writings*, ed. Geoffrey Keynes, London, 1957, pp. 577-8; reprinted by permission of Nonesuch Press.

All these things are written in Eden. The artist is an inhabitant of that happy country; and if every thing goes on as it has begun, the world of vegetation and generation may expect to be opened again to Heaven, through Eden, as it was in the beginning.

The Strong Man represents the human sublime. The Beautiful Man represents the human pathetic, which was in the wars of Eden divided into male and female. The Ugly Man represents the human reason. They were originally one man, who was fourfold; he was self-divided, and his real humanity slain on the stems of generation, and the form of the fourth was like the Son of God. How he became divided is a subject of great sublimity and pathos. The Artist has written it under inspiration, and will, if God please, publish it; it is voluminous, and contains the ancient history of Britain, and the world of Satan and of Adam.

In the mean time he has painted this Picture, which supposes that in the reign of that British Prince, who lived in the fifth century, there were remains of those naked Heroes in the Welch Mountains; they are there now, Gray saw them in the person of his bard on Snowdon; there they dwell in naked simplicity; happy is he who can see and converse with them above the shadows of generation and death. The giant Albion, was Patriarch of the Atlantic; he is the Atlas of the Greeks, one of those the Greeks called Titans. The stories of Arthur are the acts of Albion, applied to a Prince of the fifth century, who conquered Europe, and held the Empire of the world in the dark age, which the Romans never again recovered. In this Picture, believing with Milton the ancient British History, Mr. B. has done as all the ancients did, and as all the moderns who are worthy of fame, given the historical fact in its poetical vigour so as it always happens, and not in that dull way that some Historians pretend, who, being weakly organized themselves, cannot see either miracle or prodigy; all is to them a dull round of probabilities and possibilities; but the history of all times and places is nothing else but improbabilities and impossibilities; what we should say was impossible if we did not see it always before our eyes.

The antiquities of every Nation under Heaven, is no less sacred than that of the Jews. They are the same thing, as Jacob Bryant and all antiquaries have proved. How other antiquities came to be neglected and disbelieved, while those of the Jews are collected and arranged, is an enquiry worthy both of the Antiquarian and the Divine. All had originally one language, and one religion: this was the religion of Jesus, the everlasting Gospel. Antiquity preaches the Gospel of Jesus. The reasoning historian, turner and twister of causes and consequences, such as Hume, Gibbon, and Voltaire, cannot with all their artifice turn or twist one fact or disarrange self evident action and reality. Reasons and opinions concerning acts are not history. Acts themselves alone are history, and these are neither the exclusive property of Hume, Gibbon, nor Voltaire, Echard, Rapin, Plutarch, nor Herodotus. Tell me the Acts, O historian, and leave me to reason upon them as I please; away with your reasoning and your rubbish! All that is not action is not worth reading. Tell me the What; I do not want you to tell me the Why, and the How; I can find that out myself, as well as you can, and I will not be fooled by you into opinions, that you please to impose, to disbelieve what you think improbable or impossible. His opinions, who does not see spiritual agency, is not worth any man's reading; he who rejects a fact because it is improbable, must reject all History and retain doubts only.

NICOLAS BERDYAEV
Myth as Memory

History is not an objective empirical datum; it is a myth. Myth is no fiction, but a reality; it is, however, one of a different order from that of the so-called objective empirical fact. Myth is the story preserved in popular memory of a past event and transcends the limits of the external objective world, revealing an ideal world, a subject-object world of facts. According to Schelling, mythology is the primordial history of mankind. But myths are not peculiar to the remote past; various more recent epochs have been rich in the elements of myth-creation.

All great historical epochs, even those of modern history with their tendency to discredit mythology, give rise to myths. Thus the age of the great French Revolution, although ushered in by the rationalistic enlightenment, teems with myths. In the first place there is the myth of the Revolution itself, which was fostered by historians for a long enough period of time; it was only much later that they began to discredit it, as Taine had done in his *History of the Revolution*. Similar myths were current concerning the age of the Renaissance and the Reformation, the Middle Ages, not to speak of remoter periods of history when thought had not as yet been illuminated by the bright light of reason. . . .

Each man represents by virtue of his inner nature a sort of microcosm in which the whole world of reality and all the great historical epochs combine and coexist. He is not merely a minute fragment of the universe, but rather a world in his own right, a world revealed or hidden according as consciousness is more or less penetrating and extensive. In this development of self-consciousness the whole history of the world is apprehended, together with all the great epochs which historical science investigates, by submitting them to the critical test of historical monuments, scriptures and archaeological data. But assuming an external stimulus for every profound act of remembrance, it should be possible for man to apprehend history within himself; he should be able, for example, to discover within himself the profoundest strata of the Hellenic world and thus grasp the essentials of Greek history. Similarly, the historian must discover within himself the deep strata of Jewish history before he can grasp its essential nature.

Thus this microcosm would seem to contain in itself all the historical epochs of the past which have not been entirely covered over by the subsequent strata of time and of more recent historical life; these past epochs may appear to be buried in the depths, but they can never be completely obliterated. The inner clarification and elaboration of man's consciousness ought therefore to help him to burst through the outer strata and penetrate into the depths of time, a penetration that is really into the depths of his own nature. Only deep down in his own self can man really discover the secrets of time; for these, far from being something superficial and alien, something imposed and forced upon him from without, represent on the contrary the deepest and most mysterious strata implicit in himself. A narrow consciousness would either disregard these strata or relegate them to a secondary plane.

Historical myths have a profound significance for the act of remembrance. A

From *The Meaning of History* [1923], translated from the Russian by George Reavey, New York and London, 1936, pp. 21-5, 52; reprinted by permission of Geoffrey Bles Ltd.

myth contains the story that is preserved in popular memory and that helps to bring to life some deep stratum buried in the depths of the human spirit. The divorce of the subject from object as the result of enlightened criticism may provide material for historical knowledge; but in so far as it destroys the myth and dissociates the depths of time from those of man, it only serves to divorce man from history. It also leads us to reconsider the significance of the part played by tradition in the inner comprehension of history. For the historical tradition which criticism had thought to discredit makes possible a great and occult act of remembrance. It represents, indeed, no external impulse or externally imposed fact alien to man, but one that is a manifestation of the inner mysterious life, in which he can attain to the knowledge of himself and feel himself to be an inalienable participant.

I do not mean to imply that tradition should be exempt from historical criticism or accepted at its own valuation or taken for granted without question. I believe that historical criticism has done a great deal of objective and scientific work in this sphere, and that there exists no justification for re-establishing a merely traditional history. My argument is rather that tradition possesses an inner value. This latter, however, must not be made to depend upon fables such as that, for example, of the foundation of Rome, which was discredited by Niebuhr and the more recent historians. The tradition of a people is valuable in so far as it symbolizes the historical destiny of that people. This symbolism is of primary importance for the elaboration of a philosophy of history and for the apprehension of its inner significance. Tradition is synonymous with the knowledge of historical life; for its symbolism reveals the inner life and the profound organic union of historical reality with that which man discovers through his own spiritual self-knowledge. This tie between tradition and the revelations of self-knowledge is in the highest degree precious. The external facts of history have a tremendous importance. But the inner current of mysterious life, whose flow even external reality cannot intercept, is much more important for the building up of a philosophy of history. It proves that history is to be apprehended only from within and that this apprehension depends more and more on the inner state of our consciousness, on its breadth and depth. . . .

I am therefore inclined to believe that the mysteries of the divine as well as of the human and world life, with all their complexity of historical destiny, admit of solution only through concrete mythology. The knowledge of the divine life is not attainable by means of abstract philosophical thought based upon the principles of formalist or rationalistic logic, but only by means of a concrete myth which conceives the divine life as a passionate destiny of concrete and active persons, the divine Hypostases.

This is, therefore, not a philosophy, but a mythology. The Gnostics had such a mythology. And that explains their success in apprehending, in spite of certain deficiencies and confusions in their thought, the divine mysteries as those of an historical destiny better than the abstract philosophers, who were content to remain within the framework of their philosophies. Such a mythology makes possible the apprehension of the essence of celestial history, of the stages, the aeons or ages of the divine life. The very conception of the divine aeons is bound up with concrete destiny and is essentially illusive and inapprehensible to any abstract philosophical system. Only a mythology, which conceives the divine

celestial life as celestial history and as a drama of love and freedom unfolding itself between God and His other self, which He loves and for whose reciprocal
love He thirsts, and only an admission of God's longing for His other self, can
provide a solution of celestial history and, through it, of the destinies of both
man and the world.

THOMAS MANN

Psychoanalysis, the Lived Myth, and Fiction

But Freud's description of the id and the ego—is it not to a hair Schopenhauer's
description of the Will and the Intellect, a translation of the latter's metaphysics
into psychology? So he who had been initiated into the metaphysics of Schopenhauer and in Nietzsche tasted the painful pleasure of psychology—he must needs
have been filled with a sense of recognition and familiarity when first, encouraged
thereto by its denizens, he entered the realms of psychoanalysis and looked
about him.

He found too that his new knowledge had a strange and strong retroactive
effect upon the old. After a sojourn in the world of Freud, how differently, in the
light of one's new knowledge, does one reread the reflections of Schopenhauer,
for instance his great essay "Transcendent Speculations on Apparent Design in
the Fate of the Individual"! And here I am about to touch upon the most profound and mysterious point of contact between Freud's natural-scientific world
and Schopenhauer's philosophic one. For the essay I have named, a marvel of
profundity and penetration, constitutes this point of contact. The pregnant and
mysterious idea there developed by Schopenhauer is briefly this: that precisely as
in a dream it is our own will that unconsciously appears as inexorable objective
destiny, everything in it proceeding out of ourselves and each of us being the
secret theatre-manager of our own dreams, so also in reality the great dream
that a single essence, the will itself, dreams with us all, our fate, may be the
product of our inmost selves, of our wills, and we are actually ourselves bringing
about what seems to be happening to us. I have only briefly indicated here the
content of the essay, for these representations are winged with the strongest and
most sweeping powers of suggestion. But not only does the dream psychology
which Schopenhauer calls to his aid bear an explicitly psychoanalytic character,
even to the presence of the sexual argument and paradigm; but the whole com-
plexus of thought is a philosophical anticipation of analytical conceptions, to a
quite astonishing extent. For, to repeat what I said in the beginning, I see in the
mystery of the unity of the ego and the world, of being and happening, in the
perception of the apparently objective and accidental as a matter of the soul's
own contriving, the innermost core of psychoanalytic theory.

And here there occurs to me a phrase from the pen of C. G. Jung, an able but somewhat ungrateful scion of the Freudian school, in his significant introduction to the Tibetan *Book of the Dead*. "It is so much more direct, striking, impressive, and thus convincing," he says, "to see how it happens to me than to see how I do it." A bold, even an extravagant statement, plainly betraying the calmness with which in a certain school of psychology certain things are regarded which even Schopenhauer considered prodigiously daring speculation. Would this unmasking of the "happening" as in reality "doing" be conceivable without Freud? Never! It owes him everything. It is weighted down with assumptions, it could not be understood, it could never have been written, without all that analysis has brought to light about slips of tongue and pen, the whole field of human error, the retreat into illness, the psychology of accidents, the self-punishment compulsion—in short, all the wizardry of the unconscious. Just as little, moreover, would that close-packed sentence of Jung's, including its psychological premises, have been possible without Schopenhauer's adventurous pioneering speculation. Perhaps this is the moment, my friends, to indulge on this festive occasion in a little polemic against Freud himself. He does not esteem philosophy very highly. His scientific exactitude does not permit him to regard it as a science. He reproaches it with imagining that it can present a continuous and consistent picture of the world; with overestimating the objective value of logical operations; with believing in intuitions as a source of knowledge and with indulging in positively animistic tendencies, in that it believes in the magic of words and the influence of thought upon reality. But would philosophy really be thinking too highly of itself on these assumptions? Has the world ever been changed by anything save by thought and its magic vehicle the Word? I believe that in actual fact philosophy ranks before and above the natural sciences and that all method and exactness serve its intuitions and its intellectual and historical will. In the last analysis it is always a matter of the *quod erat demonstrandum*. Scientific freedom from assumptions is or should be a moral fact. But intellectually it is, as Freud points out, probably an illusion. One might strain the point and say that science has never made a discovery without being authorized and encouraged thereto by philosophy.

All this by the way. But it is in line with my general intention to pause a little longer at the sentence that I quoted from Jung. In this essay and also as a general method which he uses by preference, Jung applies analytical evidence to form a bridge between Occidental thought and Oriental esoteric. Nobody has focused so sharply as he the Schopenhauer-Freud perception that "the giver of all given conditions resides in ourselves—a truth which despite all evidence in the greatest as well as in the smallest things *never* becomes conscious, though it is only too often necessary, even indispensable, that it should be." A great and costly change, he thinks, is needed before we understand how the world is "given" by the nature of the soul; for man's animal nature strives against seeing himself as the maker of his own conditions. It is true that the East has always shown itself stronger than the West in the conquest of our animal nature, and we need not be surprised to hear that in its wisdom it conceives even the gods among the "given conditions" originating from the soul and one with her, light and reflection of the human soul. This knowledge, which, according to the *Book of the Dead*, one gives to the deceased to accompany him on his way, is a paradox to the Occidental mind, conflicting with its sense of logic, which distinguishes between subject and object and refuses to have them coincide or make one proceed from the other. True, European mysticism has been aware of such attitudes, and Angelus Silesius said:

> I know that without me God cannot live a moment;
> If I am destroyed He must give up the ghost.

But on the whole a psychological conception of God, an idea of the godhead which is not pure condition, absolute reality, but one with the soul and bound up with it, must be intolerable to Occidental religious sense—it would be equivalent to abandoning the idea of God.

Yet religion—perhaps even etymologically—essentially implies a bond. In Genesis we have talk of the bond (covenant) between God and man, the psychological basis of which I have attempted to give in the mythological novel *Joseph and His Brothers*. Perhaps my hearers will be indulgent if I speak a little about my own work; there may be some justification for introducing it here in this hour of formal encounter between creative literature and the psychoanalytic. It is strange—and perhaps strange not only to me—that in this work there obtains precisely that psychological theology which the scholar ascribes to Oriental esoteric. This Abram is in a sense the father of God. He perceived and brought Him forth; His mighty qualities, ascribed to Him by Abram, were probably His original possession, Abram was not their inventor, yet in a sense he was, by virtue of his recognizing them and therewith, by taking thought, making them real. God's mighty qualities—and thus God Himself—are indeed something objective, exterior to Abram; but at the same time they are in him and of him as well; the power of his own soul is at moments scarcely to be distinguished from them, it consciously interpenetrates and fuses with them—and such is the origin of the bond which then the Lord strikes with Abram, as the explicit confirmation of an inward fact. The bond, it is stated, is made in the interest of both, to the end of their common sanctification. Need human and need divine here entwine until it is hard to say whether it was the human or the divine that took the initiative. In any case the arrangement shows that the holiness of man and the holiness of God constituted a twofold process, one part being most intimately bound up with the other. Wherefore else, one asks, should there be a bond at all?

The soul as "giver of the given"—yes, my friends, I am well aware that in the novel this conception reaches an ironic pitch which is not authorized either in Oriental wisdom or in psychological perception. But there is something thrilling about the unconscious and only later discovered harmony. Shall I call it the power of suggestion? But sympathy would be a better word: a kind of intellectual affinity, of which naturally psychoanalysis was earlier aware than was I, and which proceeded out of those literary appreciations which I owed to it at an earlier stage. The latest of these was an offprint of an article that appeared in *Imago*, written by a Viennese scholar of the Freudian school, under the title "On the Psychology of the Older School of Biography." The rather dry title gives no indication of the remarkable contents. The writer shows how the older and simpler type of biography and in particular the written lives of artists, nourished and conditioned by popular legend and tradition, assimilate, as it were, the life of the subject to the conventionalized stock-in-trade of biography in general, thus imparting a sort of sanction to their own performance and establishing its genuineness; making it authentic in the sense of "as it always was" and "as it has been written." For man sets store by recognition, he likes to find the old in the new, the typical in the individual. From that recognition he draws a sense of the familiar in life, whereas if it painted itself as entirely new, singular in time and space, without any possibility of resting upon the known, it could only bewilder and alarm. The question, then, which is raised by the essay, is this: can any line be sharply and unequivocally drawn between the formal stock-in-trade of legendary biography and the characteristics of the single personality—in other words, between the typical and the individual? A question negatived by its very statement. For the truth is that life is a mingling of the individual elements and the formal stock-in-trade; a mingling in which the individual, as it were, only lifts his head above the formal and impersonal elements. Much that is extra-personal, much unconscious identification, much that is conventional and schematic, is none the less decisive for the experience not only of the artist but of the human being in general. "Many of us," says the writer of the article, " 'live' today a biographical type, the destiny of a class or rank or calling. The freedom in the shaping of the human being's life is obviously connected with that bond which we term 'lived *vita.*' " And then, to my delight, but scarcely to my surprise, he begins to cite from *Joseph*, the fundamental motif of which he says is precisely this idea of the "lived life," life as succession, as a moving in others' steps, as identification—such as Joseph's teacher, Eliezer, practises with droll solemnity. For in him time is cancelled and all the Eliezers of the past gather to shape the Eliezer of the present, so that he speaks in the first person of that Eliezer who was Abram's servant, though he was far from being the same man.

I must admit that I find the train of thought extraordinarily convincing. The essay indicates the precise point at which the psychological interest passes over into the mythical. It makes it clear that the typical is actually the mythical, and that one may as well say "lived myth" as "lived life." But the mythus as lived is the epic idea embodied in my novel; and it is plain to me that when as a novelist I took the step in my subject-matter from the bourgeois and individual to the mythical and typical my personal connection with the analytic field passed into its acute stage. The mythical interest is as native to psychoanalysis as the psychological interest is to all creative writing. Its penetration into the childhood of the individual soul is at the same time a penetration into the childhood of mankind, into the primitive and mythical. Freud has told us that for him all natural science, medicine, and psychotherapy were a lifelong journey round and back to the early passion of his youth for the history of mankind, for the origins of religion and morality—an interest which at the height of his career broke out to such magnificent effect in *Totem and Taboo*. The word *Tiefenpsychologie* ("deep" psychology) has a temporal significance; the primitive foundations of the human soul are likewise primitive time, they are those profound time-sources where the myth has its home and shapes the primeval norms and forms of life. For the myth is the foundation of life; it is the timeless schema, the pious formula into which life flows when it reproduces its traits out of the unconscious. Certainly when a writer has acquired the habit of regarding life as mythical and typical there comes a curious heightening of his artist temper, a new refreshment to his perceiving and shaping powers, which otherwise occurs much later in life; for while in the life of the human race the mythical is an early and primitive stage, in the life of the individual it is a late and mature one. What is gained is an insight into the higher truth depicted in the actual; a smiling knowledge of the eternal, the ever-being and authentic; a knowledge of the schema in which and according to which the supposed individual lives, unaware, in his naïve belief in himself as unique in space and time, of the extent to which his life is but formula and repetition and his path marked out for him by those who trod it before him. His character is a mythical role which the actor just emerged from the depths to the light plays in the illusion that it is his own and unique, that he, as it were, has invented it all himself, with a dignity and security of which his supposed unique individuality in time and space is not the source, but rather which he creates out of his deeper consciousness in order that something which was once founded and legitimized shall again be represented and once more for good or ill, whether nobly or basely, in any case after its own kind conduct itself according to pattern. Actually, if his existence consisted merely in the unique and the present, he would not know how to conduct himself at all; he would be confused, helpless, unstable in his own self-regard, would not know which foot to put foremost or what sort of face to put on. His dignity and security lie all unconsciously in the fact that with him something timeless has once more emerged into the light and become present; it is a mythical value added to the otherwise poor and valueless single character; it is native worth, because its origin lies in the unconscious.

Such is the gaze which the mythically oriented artist bends upon the phenomena about him—an ironic and superior gaze, as you can see, for the mythical knowledge resides in the gazer and not in that at which he gazes. But let us suppose that the mythical point of view could become subjective; that it could pass over into the active ego and become conscious there, proudly and darkly yet joyously, of its recurrence and its typicality, could celebrate its role and realize its own value exclusively in the knowledge that it was a fresh incarnation of the traditional upon earth. One might say that such a phenomenon alone could be the "lived myth"; nor should we think that it is anything novel or unknown. The life in the myth, life as a sacred repetition, is a historical form of life, for the man of ancient times lived thus. An instance is the figure of the Egyptian Cleopatra, which is Ishtar, Astarte, Aphrodite in person. Bachofen, in his description of the cult of Bacchus, the Dionysiac religion, regards the Egyptian queen as the consummate picture of a Dionysiac *stimula*; and according to Plutarch it was far more her erotic intellectual culture than her physical charms that entitled her to represent the female as developed into the earthly embodiment of Aphrodite. But her Aphrodite nature, her role of Hathor-Isis, is not only objective, not only a treatment of her by Plutarch or Bachofen; it was the content of her subjective existence as well, she lived the part. This we can see by the manner of her death: she is supposed to have killed herself by laying an asp upon her bosom. But the snake was the familiar of Ishtar, the Egyptian Isis, who is represented clad in a garment of scales; also there exists a statuette of Ishtar holding a snake to her bosom. So that if Cleopatra's death was as the legend represents, the manner of it was a manifestation of her mythical ego. Moreover, did she not adopt the falcon hood of the goddess Isis and adorn herself with the insignia of Hathor, the cow's horns with the crescent moon between? And name her two children by Mark Anthony Helios and Selene? No doubt she was a very significant figure indeed—significant in the antique sense, that she was well aware who she was and in whose footsteps she trod!

The ego of antiquity and its consciousness of itself were different from our own, less exclusive, less sharply defined. It was, as it were, open behind; it received much from the past and by repeating it gave it presentness again. The Spanish scholar Ortega y Gasset puts it that the man of antiquity, before he did anything, took a step backwards, like the bull-fighter who leaps back to deliver the mortal thrust. He searched the past for a pattern into which he might slip as into a diving-bell, and being thus at once disguised and protected might rush upon his present problem. Thus his life was in a sense a reanimation, an archaizing attitude. But it is just this life as reanimation that is the life as myth. Alexander walked in the footsteps of Miltiades; the ancient biographers of Cæsar were convinced, rightly or wrongly, that he took Alexander as his prototype. But such "imitation" meant far more than we mean by the word today. It was a mythical identification, peculiarly familiar to antiquity; but it is operative far into modern times, and at all times is psychically possible. How often have we not been told that the figure of Napoleon was cast in the antique mould! He regretted that the mentality of the time forbade him to give himself out for the son of Jupiter Ammon, in imitation of Alexander. But we need not doubt that—at least at the period of his Eastern exploits—he mythically confounded himself with Alexander; while after he turned his face westwards he is said to have declared: "I am Charlemagne." Note that: not "I am like Charlemagne" or "My situation is like Charlemagne's," but quite simply: "I am he." That is the formulation of the myth. Life, then—at any rate, significant life—was in ancient times the reconstitution of the myth in flesh and blood; it referred to and appealed to the myth; only through it, through reference to the past, could it approve itself as genuine and significant. The myth is the legitimization of life; only through and in it does life find self-awareness, sanction, consecration. Cleopatra fulfilled her Aphrodite character even unto death—and can one live and die more significantly or worthily than in the celebration of the myth? We have only to think of Jesus and His life, which was lived in order that that which was written might be fulfilled. It is not easy to distinguish between His own consciousness and the conventionalizations of the Evangelists. But His word on the Cross, about the ninth hour, that "*Eli, Eli, lama sabachthani?*" was evidently not in the least an outburst of despair and disillusionment; but on the contrary a lofty messianic sense of self. For the phrase is not original, not a spontaneous outcry. It stands at the beginning of the Twenty-second Psalm, which from one end to the other is an announcement of the Messiah. Jesus was quoting, and the quotation meant: "Yes, it is I!" Precisely thus did Cleopatra quote when she took the asp to her breast to die; and again the quotation meant: "Yes, it is I!"

Let us consider for a moment the word "celebration" which I used in this connection. It is a pardonable, even a proper usage. For life in the myth, life, so to speak, in quotation, is a kind of celebration, in that it is a making present of the past, it becomes a religious act, the performance by a celebrant of a prescribed procedure; it becomes a feast. For a feast is an anniversary, a renewal of the past in the present. Every Christmas the world-saving Babe is born again on earth, to suffer, to die, and to arise. The feast is the abrogation of time, an event, a solemn narrative being played out conformably to an immemorial pattern; the events in it take place not for the first time, but ceremonially according to the prototype. It achieves presentness as feasts do, recurring in time with their phases and hours following on each other in time as they did in the original occurrence. In antiquity each feast was essentially a dramatic performance, a mask; it was the scenic reproduction, with priests as actors, of stories about the gods—as for instance the life and sufferings of Osiris. The Christian Middle Ages had their mystery play, with heaven, earth, and the torments of hell—just as we have it later in Goethe's *Faust*; they had their carnival farce, their folk-mime. The artist eye has a mythical slant upon life, which makes it look like a farce, like a theatrical performance of a prescribed feast, like a Punch and Judy epic, wherein mythical character puppets reel off a plot abiding from past time and now again present in a jest. It only lacks that this mythical slant pass over and become subjective in the performers themselves, become a festival and mythical consciousness of part and play, for an epic to be produced such as that in the first volume of the *Joseph and His Brothers* series, particularly in the chapter "The Great Hoaxing." There a mythical recurrent farce is tragicomically played by personages all of whom well know in whose steps they tread: Isaac, Esau, and Jacob; and who act out the cruel and grotesque tale of how Esau the Red is led by the nose and cheated of his birthright to the huge delight of all the bystanders. Joseph too is another such celebrant of life; with charming mythological hocus-pocus he enacts in his own person the Tammuz-Osiris myth, "bringing to pass" anew the story of the mangled, buried, and arisen god, playing his festival game with that which mysteriously and secretly shapes life out of its own depths—the unconscious. The mystery of the metaphysician and psychologist, that the soul is the giver of all given conditions, becomes in Joseph easy, playful, blithe—like a consummately artistic performance by a fencer or juggler. It reveals his *infantile* nature—and the word I have used betrays how closely, though seeming to wander so far afield, we have kept to the subject of our evening's homage.

Infantilism—in other words, regression to childhood—what a role this genuinely psychoanalytic element plays in all our lives! What a large share it has in shaping the life of a human being; operating, indeed, in just the way I have described: as mythical identification, as survival, as a treading in footprints already made! The bond with the father, the imitation of the father, the game of being the father, and the transference to father-substitute pictures of a higher and more developed type—how these infantile traits work upon the life of the individual to mark and shape it! I use the word "shape," for to me in all seriousness the happiest, most pleasurable element of what we call education (*Bildung*), the shaping of the human being, is just this powerful influence of admiration and love, this childish identification with a father-image elected out of profound affinity. The artist in particular, a passionately childlike and play-possessed being, can tell us of the mysterious yet after all obvious effect of such infantile imitation upon his own life, his productive conduct of a career which after all is often nothing but a reanimation of the hero under very different temporal and personal conditions and with very different, shall we say childish means. The *imitatio* Goethe, with its Werther and Wilhelm Meister stages, its old-age period of *Faust* and *Diwan*, can still shape and mythically mould the life of an artist—rising out of his unconscious, yet playing over—as is the artist way—into a smiling, childlike, and profound awareness.

The Joseph of the novel is an artist, playing with his *imitatio dei* upon the unconscious string; and I know not how to express the feelings which possess me—something like a joyful sense of divination of the future—when I indulge in this encouragement of the unconscious to play, to make itself fruitful in a serious product, in a narrational meeting of psychology and myth, which is at the same time a celebration of the meeting between poetry and analysis.

T. S. ELIOT

Myth and Literary Classicism

[ULYSSES]

Mr. Joyce's book has been out long enough for no more general expression of praise, or expostulation with its detractors, to be necessary; and it has not been out long enough for any attempt at a complete measurement of its place and significance to be possible. All that one can usefully do at this time, and it is a great deal to do, for such a book, is to elucidate any aspect of the book—and the number of aspects is indefinite—which has not yet been fixed. I hold this book to be the most important expression which the present age has found; it is a book to which we are all indebted, and from which none of us can escape. These are postulates for anything that I have to say about it, and I have no wish to waste the reader's time by elaborating my eulogies; it has given me all the surprise, delight, and terror that I can require, and I will leave it at that.

Amongst all the criticisms I have seen of the book, I have seen nothing—unless we except, in its way, M. Valery Larbaud's valuable paper which is rather an Introduction than a criticism—which seemed to me to appreciate the significance of the method employed—the parallel to the *Odyssey*, and the use of appropriate styles and symbols to each division. Yet one might expect this to be the first peculiarity to attract attention; but it has been treated as an amusing dodge, or scaffolding erected by the author for the purpose of disposing his realistic tale, of no interest in the completed structure. The criticism which Mr. Aldington directed upon *Ulysses* several years ago seems to me to fail by this oversight—but, as Mr. Aldington wrote before the complete work had appeared, fails more honorably than the attempts of those who had the whole book before them. Mr. Aldington treated Mr. Joyce as a prophet of chaos; and wailed at the flood of Dadaism which his prescient eye saw bursting forth at the tap of the magician's rod. Of course, the influence which Mr. Joyce's book may have is from my point of view an irrelevance. A very great book may have a very bad influence indeed; and a mediocre book may be in the event most salutary. The next generation is responsible for its own soul; a man of genius is responsible to his peers, not to a studio full of uneducated and undisciplined coxcombs. Still, Mr. Aldington's

"Ulysses, Order, and Myth," *The Dial*, LXXV, 1923, pp. 480-83. Reprinted by permission of the author. A new note by Mr. Eliot, commenting on this essay, appears at the end of the selection.

pathetic solicitude for the half-witted seems to me to carry certain implications about the nature of the book itself to which I cannot assent; and this is the important issue. He finds the book, if I understand him, to be an invitation to chaos, and an expression of feelings which are perverse, partial, and a distortion of reality. But unless I quote Mr. Aldington's words I am likely to falsify. "I say, moreover," he says, "that when Mr. Joyce, with his marvellous gifts, uses them to disgust us with mankind, he is doing something which is false and a libel on humanity." It is somewhat similar to the opinion of the urbane Thackeray upon Swift. "As for the moral, I think it horrible, shameful, unmanly, blasphemous: and giant and great as this Dean is, I say we should hoot him." (This, of the conclusion of the Voyage to the Houyhnhnms—which seems to me one of the greatest triumphs that the human soul has ever achieved. It is true that Thackeray later pays Swift one of the finest tributes that a man has ever given or received: "So great a man he seems to me that thinking of him is like thinking of an empire falling." And Mr. Aldington, in his time, is almost equally generous.)

Whether it is possible to libel humanity (in distinction to libel in the usual sense, which is libeling an individual or a group in contrast with the rest of humanity) is a question for philosophical societies to discuss; but of course if *Ulysses* were a "libel" it would simply be a forged document, a powerless fraud, which would never have extracted from Mr. Aldington a moment's attention. I do not wish to linger over this point: the interesting question is that begged by Mr. Aldington when he refers to Mr. Joyce's "great *undisciplined* talent."

I think that Mr. Aldington and I are more or less agreed as to what we want in principle, and agreed to call it classicism. It is because of this agreement that I have chosen Mr. Aldington to attack on the present issue. We are agreed as to what we want, but not as to how to get it, or as to what contemporary writing exhibits a tendency in that direction. We agree, I hope, that "classicism" is not an alternative to "romanticism," as of political parties, Conservative and Liberal, Republican and Democrat, on a "turn-the-rascals-out" platform. It is a goal toward which all good literature strives, so far as it is good, according to the possibilities of its place and time. One can be "classical," in a sense, by turning away from nine tenths of the material which lies at hand, and selecting only mummified stuff from a museum—like some contemporary writers, about whom one could say some nasty things in this connection, if it were worth while (Mr. Aldington is not one of them). Or one can be classical in tendency by doing the best one can with the material at hand.

The confusion springs from the fact that the term is applied to literature and to the whole complex of interests and modes of behavior and society of which literature is a part; and it has not the same bearing in both applications. It is much easier to be a classicist in literary criticism than in creative art—because in criticism you are responsible only for what you want, and in creation you are responsible for what you can do with material which you must simply accept. And in this material I include the emotions and feelings of the writer himself, which, for that writer, are simply material which he must accept—not virtues to be enlarged or vices to be diminished. The question, then, about Mr. Joyce, is: how much living material does he deal with, and how does he deal with it: deal with, not as a legislator or exhorter, but as an artist?

It is here that Mr. Joyce's parallel use of the *Odyssey* has a great importance. It has the importance of a scientific discovery. No one else has built a novel upon such a foundation before: it has never before been necessary. I am not begging the question in calling *Ulysses* a "novel"; and if you call it an epic it will not matter. If it is not a novel, that is simply because the novel is a form which will no longer serve; it is because the novel, instead of being a form, was simply the expression of an age which had not sufficiently lost all form to feel the need of something stricter. Mr. Joyce has written one novel—the *Portrait*; Mr. Wyndham Lewis has written one novel—*Tarr*. I do not suppose that either of them will ever write another "novel." The novel ended with Flaubert and with James. It is, I think, because Mr. Joyce and Mr. Lewis, being "in advance" of their time, felt a conscious or probably unconscious dissatisfaction with the form, that their novels are more formless than those of a dozen clever writers who are unaware of its obsolescence.

In using the myth, in manipulating a continuous parallel between contemporaneity and antiquity, Mr. Joyce is pursuing a method which others must pursue after him. They will not be imitators, any more than the scientist who uses the discoveries of an Einstein in pursuing his own, independent, further investigations. It is simply a way of controlling, of ordering, of giving a shape and a significance to the immense panorama of futility and anarchy which is contemporary history. It is a method already adumbrated by Mr. Yeats, and of the need for which I believe Mr. Yeats to have been the first contemporary to be conscious. It is a method for which the horoscope is auspicious. Psychology (such as it is, and whether our reaction to it be comic or serious), ethnology, and *The Golden Bough* have concurred to make possible what was impossible even a few years ago. Instead of narrative method, we may now use the mythical method. It is, I seriously believe, a step toward making the modern world possible for art, toward that order and form which Mr. Aldington so earnestly desires. And only those who have won their own discipline in secret and without aid, in a world which offers very little assistance to that end, can be of any use in furthering this advance.

In re-reading, for the first time after many years, this expression of my critical opinion, I am unfavourably impressed by the overconfidence in my own views and the intemperance with which I expressed them. The sentence beginning *"The next generation is responsible for its own soul"* strikes me as both pompous and silly. And Wyndham Lewis, before he died, wrote two books, *The Revenge for Love* and *Self-Condemned*, which are not only far superior to *Tarr* but which are definitely "novels." To say that the novel ended with Flaubert and James was possibly an echo of Ezra Pound and is certainly absurd. To say that other writers must follow the procedure of *Ulysses* is equally absurd. But I disagree as much now as I did then with the words quoted from Mr. Aldington writing in the *English Review* in 1921.

January 1964   T.S.E.

7

SELF-CONSCIOUSNESS

Self-Realization

JEAN-JACQUES ROUSSEAU: An Experiment in Self-Revelation
ANDRÉ GIDE: The Value of Inconsistency
D. H. LAWRENCE: The Living Self
RAINER MARIA RILKE: The Self and Reality
WASSILY KANDINSKY: An Expressionist Credo

The Field of Consciousness

HENRY JAMES: Centers of Consciousness
WILLIAM JAMES: The Stream of Consciousness
HENRI BERGSON: Duration
MARCEL PROUST: The Recapturing of Time

The Divided Self

FRIEDRICH SCHLEGEL: The Ironic Consciousness
G. W. F. HEGEL: The Contrite Consciousness
KARL MARX: Alienation
SØREN KIERKEGAARD: Indirect Communication
FRIEDRICH NIETZSCHE: The Masks of Truth
W. B. YEATS: The Anti-Self

Freedom

ARTHUR SCHOPENHAUER: Sympathy and Asceticism
FRIEDRICH NIETZSCHE: Self-Overcoming
F. M. DOSTOEVSKY: The Perverse Self

Introduction

Modern exploration of the unconscious mind and of the heritage of myth has been part of a larger concern with the distinctive qualities and value of subjective life. But if the Unconscious is primarily a personal subjective world for Freud, it is primarily super-personal for Jung; and if the forms of myth are closely related to the private visions of symbolist poets, they are also public, communal, and historical.[1] Subjective life at its most intense is personal and private, wholly individual, and the value of subjective reality in this sense is a modern article of faith. The individual person has turned round upon himself, seeking to know all that he is and to unify all that he knows himself to be. The totality of the self has become the object of an inner quest. This cultivation of self-consciousness—uneasy, ardent introspection—often amounts to an almost religious enterprise.

A first principle of self-consciousness is that nothing, however inglorious or unpleasant, should be ignored. Jean-Jacques Rousseau's *Confessions* is the prototype of many later examples of the elevation of candor into a prime virtue. Rousseau premised his book upon his capacity to be wholly honest with himself and the reader. "Every human heart, no matter how pure," he insists, "conceals some odious vice." But he displays his vices primarily as evidence of his personal uniqueness and his ability to overcome any desire for concealment. Though he passes judgment on his misdeeds and calls attention to his virtues, he professes to be more interested in the truth about his own nature than in moral self-evaluation. What he would reveal is the astonishing, idiosyncratic phenomenon of himself, and what he would claim as his superiority over other men is his self-knowledge and his openness.

Rousseau conceives his past life as a sequence of feelings, all of which live on within him and are readily remembered. But he has little notion of inner growth. He appears to regard his self as an entity with fixed and pre-ordained traits that are manifested in a series of biographical events. Other writers emphasize rather that the self is an unending process. André Gide, and such varied authors as Lawrence, Rilke, and Kandinsky, picture a long struggle for self-definition. They regard true selfhood as something to be achieved

[1] See Sections 5 and 6.

and re-achieved because they are constantly betrayed into falsehood by inner and outer deceptions.[2] Gide discovers that a factitious self has been proffered him, like some inherited office, by his well-meaning parents and teachers. To repudiate social sanctions, formal and informal, is his first arduous step toward self-affirmation. The second is to free himself from his own self-rationalizations, to liberate the extreme possibilities, however inconsistent, that reside within him. Gide seeks his distinctive self by self-multiplication. He cultivates an inner heterogeneity in the face of all single-minded virtues or patterns that claim authority in him. Similarly, Lawrence sees a deprivation of natural energy and impulse as the great peril of our time. The self, changing and full of incongruous parts, is besieged by the parson, the philosopher, and the scientist, all of whom conspire against life by their neat formulations of it. Against their Procrustean molds Lawrence offers the living ambiguity of a successful fictional character as an exemplar of vital freedom in human beings—for a novel is successful, according to him, precisely insofar as it eludes any single, reductive formula.

Rilke is more intent upon the self's confrontation of ultimate realities like God and Death. He asks whether these vast abstractions, alien and terrifying to us, are not actually states of ourselves that we have externalized in order to simplify our existence. If so, then by reassuming them as part of ourselves we can at once nullify the terror of the unknown and come into our birthright. For Rilke, art is the incorporation of such seemingly distant and external realities into the act of self-knowledge. For Kandinsky, a valid work of art presupposes the inner wholeness and substantiality of its maker. The artist's personal integrity and spiritual wealth are won by a constant vigilance against the demoralizing climate of the time. Art is the expression of this inner truth in defiance of external canons of correctness or of objective representation.

The idea of a *field* of consciousness is assumed by Henry James when he argues for a fictional technique that would place the center of a novel in the mind of an observant character.[3] This intense perceiver is not only self-aware, so that the story becomes the adventure of his feelings and thoughts, but also an instrument whereby the "values" of the objective situation surrounding him may be recorded. To some extent, the distinction between external and internal disappears: all that matters is the world as possessed and defined by the central figure. William James undertakes a psychological description of the unfolding field of individual consciousness. In opposition to the static self and atomic sensations of traditional psychology, he pictures experience

2 Compare the symbolist idea of artistic heroism (Section 1). In contrast, Rousseau has more of an affinity with the heroic honesty of the realist (Section 2). For related selections from Gide, see Sections 1, 3, and 9; from Lawrence, Sections 3, 5, and 9; from Rilke, Sections 1 and 3.
3 For a related selection from Henry James, see Section 2. The concept of a field of consciousness is related to the symbolistic form of idealism illustrated in Section 1. Compare also Whitehead's organicism (Section 3).

as a continuous and perpetually altering "stream." The resting places in the stream, the ideas and objects to which we cling as reference points, are no more important than the "feelings of tendency," the "transitive" relations, that suffuse them.

William James's metaphor of the "stream of consciousness," which converts the self from an entity into a movement or activity, is obviously analogous to Bergson's "bottomless, bankless river."[4] Bergson uses this figure to propound his metaphysical concept of duration, in terms of which the self is essentially temporal, always opening out into the future but incorporating its entire past. Bergson holds that we create ourselves continually; consciousness cannot go through the same state twice; we move toward a future that cannot be predicted. Nevertheless, the self endures out of the past into the present; there is a continuity of personality like a thread on a ball or like the distinctive palette of a particular artist. Paradoxically past, present, and future—changing yet continuous—multiple yet one—the self can never be wholly grasped by intellectual concepts. But it can be "intuited." Intuition of the enduring self is the great subject of Proust, who knew Bergson's work well. The Proustian memory, activated by a concrete sensation, rediscovers a concrete past that the abstract intellect has simplified and partially lost. By recapturing past time, Proust re-enters the fluid world of endurance and thereby repossesses himself.[5]

The very term "self-consciousness," however, implies an inner division between the self that is conscious and the self of which it is conscious. Friedrich Schlegel even contends that all thought is an internal dialogue. Like Gide long after, he views consciousness as ironic in the sense that it cannot properly exist without a play of voices within itself.[6] Hegel interprets the intrinsic duality of self-consciousness as a conflict between a "changing" or individual aspect of the self and a "changeless" or universal aspect. These parts pursue and undermine each other and produce a "negative" state of self-alienation; yet they are really parts of one undivided soul, and their war comes to an end when consciousness attains the recognition of its own unity in the synthesis of Spirit.[7] Karl Marx applies the same general conception to human experience under modern economic conditions. According to Marx, the individual modern man is estranged from himself because, having no personal interest in the objective product of his labor, he has no personal relation to his own act of production. This self-estrangement of the individual is

[4] There is a certain parallel between this temporalization of consciousness and the more general temporalization of reality by philosophers of history (Section 4). A related selection from William James appears in Section 3.
[5] For a related selection from Proust, see Section 3. The quest for "concreteness" in William James, Bergson, and Proust is comparable to Whitehead's insistence on "concrete fact" (Section 3) and to the existentialist demand for subjective concreteness (Section 8). The Bergsonian and Proustian idea of duration has some affinity to the concept of myth, especially as the latter is expounded by Mann (Section 6).
[6] A related selection from Schlegel appears in Section 6.
[7] For a related selection from Hegel, see Section 4.

actually estrangement from universal man, the human species, in which he no longer participates as a productive being. Marx envisages a new society in which work and worker, the worker and himself, himself and humanity, will be reunited, and the alienated consciousness will be healed, at one with itself.[8]

Kierkegaard contends that the state of self-division, "ironic" or "negative," is part of the very definition of personal existence. We cannot escape from it, he thinks, by an easy Hegelian or Marxist synthesis, for a paradoxical tension of individual and universal must remain if the universal is to be apprehended at all. Truth is given only to the "subjective" thinker, who becomes more and more isolated as he "inwardly" assimilates the universal truth, and becomes more and more capable of genuine knowledge as he affirms his finite and changeable human nature. Universal truth being knowable only by existing individuals, valid communication cannot be the "direct" statement of an objective universal. The mode of rendering is all-important for Kierkegaard; it must be "indirect," artistic, even deceptive, if it is to convey a subjective truth and not a worthless objective substitute. Like Schlegel, Kierkegaard discovers his model in Socratic irony. The audience must be deceived out of its "positive" illusions into "negative" truth by the theatrical devices of an indirect author. As an example from his own experience, Kierkegaard relates how he posed as an idler in order to mislead the world as to his real thoughts and make it more unsuspectingly amenable to the "aesthetic" rendering of ethical and religious insights in his works.[9]

The masks of Nietzsche and Yeats are other forms of indirection. Nietzsche wears a mask because personal truth is either too delicate to be displayed without protection or too complex and terrible to be apprehended directly. The mask is as natural to the great man as the face to a lesser one. Yeats deliberately makes a mask in order to quarrel with himself, to subject himself to his other self, and thereby to attain real personality. Art becomes a self-discipline, a redemption of his everyday nature by possibilities dimly felt or envisaged.[10]

Back of the Yeatsian aesthetic lies the morality of Schopenhauer and Nietzsche, both of whom would transcend the human condition by ascetic self-discipline of the individual will. But Schopenhauer looks toward the traditional virtue of selfless love, participation in the universal suffering, and toward a deliberate self-mortification.[11] Nietzschean asceticism decisively rejects the "Slave-Morality" of sympathetic communion, finding in it only a shameful retreat from natural life and a propagation of mediocrity and weakness. To see life as tragedy, to accept suffering without self-abasement, to assert oneself with pride, is the vocation of the free individual. The self-

[8] For a related selection from Marx and Engels, see Section 2.

[9] Further selections from Kierkegaard appear in Section 8. Compare the symbolist problem of imagination and thought (Section 1).

[10] Compare the selections from Nietzsche and Yeats in Section 1, as well as the general idea of depersonalization illustrated in that section.

[11] For related selections from Schopenhauer, see Sections 3 and 5.

mastery of the Nietzschean superman does not eradicate the will to live but expresses the will to power, of which the highest form is power over himself.[12]

This power is precisely what Dostoevsky's Underground Man denies that he possesses. His self-consciousness is an incurable disease; his knowledge serves only to make him aware of his own unanswerable questions, his virtue to disgust him with his loathesome vices, his candor to reveal his trickiness, his persistence to demonstrate his utter volatility. He offers a disquieting counterstatement to Rousseau's program of self-revelation. And yet he really is knowing, candid, and persistent—even virtuous in his peculiar way. If he cannot achieve the freedom of love or of self-denial or of self-mastery, at least he can proclaim that he is far more alive than his audience. In all his individual ambiguity and torment, he *exists,* as they do not in their complacent social identities. Even though he can express his freedom only by perversity, he clings to it with some joy and pride; for in that minimal form he still touches upon the value of selfhood that others have asserted more confidently and perhaps with less right to make the claim.[13]

[12] See related selections from Nietzsche in Sections 1, 4, 5, 8, and 9.
[13] See related selections from Dostoevsky in Sections 2 and 9. The Underground Man is one of the main sources of Camus's idea of "absurdity" (Section 8).

JEAN-JACQUES ROUSSEAU

An Experiment in Self-Revelation

I have resolved on an enterprise which has no precedent, and which, once complete, will have no imitator. My purpose is to display to my kind a portrait in every way true to nature, and the man I shall portray will be myself.

Simply myself. I know my own heart and understand my fellow man. But I am made unlike any one I have ever met; I will even venture to say that I am like no one in the whole world. I may be no better, but at least I am different. Whether Nature did well or ill in breaking the mould in which she formed me, is a question which can only be resolved after the reading of my book.

Let the last trump sound when it will, I shall come forward with this work in my hand, to present myself before my Sovereign Judge, and proclaim aloud: "Here is what I have done, and if by chance I have used some immaterial embellishment it has been only to fill a void due to a defect of memory. I may have taken for fact what was no more than probability, but I have never put down as true what I knew to be false. I have displayed myself as I was, as vile and despicable when my behaviour was such, as good, generous, and noble when I was so. I have bared my secret soul as Thou thyself hast seen it, Eternal Being! So let the numberless legion of my fellow men gather round me, and hear my confessions. Let them groan at my depravities, and blush for my misdeeds. But let each one of them reveal his heart at the foot of Thy throne with equal sincerity, and may any man who dares, say "I was a better man than he.' "

My passions are extremely strong, and while I am under their sway nothing can equal my impetuosity. I am amenable to no restraint, respect, fear, or decorum. I am cynical, bold, violent, and daring. No shame can stop me, no fear of danger alarm me. Except for the one object in my mind the universe for me is non-existent. But all this lasts only a moment; and the next moment plunges me into complete annihilation. Catch me in a calm mood, I am all indolence and timidity. Everything alarms me, everything discourages me. I am frightened by a buzzing fly. I am too lazy to speak a word or make a gesture. So much am I a slave to fears

From *Confessions* [1718], translated from the French by J. M. Cohen, 1958, pp. 17, 44, 65, 86-9, 113-15, 169-70, 261-3, 372-3, 478-9, 605-6; reprinted by permission of Penguin Books Inc.

and shames that I long to vanish from mortal sight. If action is necessary I do not know what to do; if I must speak I do not know what to say; if anyone looks at me I drop my eyes. When roused by passion, I can sometimes find the right words to say, but in ordinary conversation I can find none, none at all. I find conversation unbearable owing to the very fact that I am obliged to speak.

Before I go further I must present my reader with an apology, or rather a justification, for the petty details I have just been entering into, and for those I shall enter into later, none of which may appear interesting in his eyes. Since I have undertaken to reveal myself absolutely to the public, nothing about me must remain hidden or obscure. I must remain incessantly beneath his gaze, so that he may follow me in all the extravagances of my heart and into every least corner of my life. Indeed, he must never lose sight of me for a single instant, for if he finds the slightest gap in my story, the smallest hiatus, he may wonder what I was doing at that moment and accuse me of refusing to tell the whole truth. I am laying myself sufficiently open to human malice by telling my story, without rendering myself more vulnerable by any silence.

But, alas, I have not said all that I have to say about my time at Mme de Vercellis's. For though my condition was apparently unchanged I did not leave her house as I had entered it. I took away with me lasting memories of a crime and the unbearable weight of a remorse which, even after forty years, still burdens my conscience. In fact the bitter memory of it, far from fading, grows more painful with the years. Who would suppose that a child's wickedness could have such cruel results? It is for these only too probable consequences that I can find no consolation. I may have ruined a nice, honest, and decent girl, who was certainly worth a great deal more than I, and doomed her to disgrace and misery.

It is almost inevitable that the breaking up of an establishment should cause some confusion in the house, and that various things should be mislaid. But so honest were the servants and so vigilant were M. and Mme Lorenzi that nothing was found missing when the inventory was taken. Only Mlle Pontal lost a little pink and silver ribbon, which was quite old. Plenty of better things were within my reach, but this ribbon alone tempted me. I stole it, and as I hardly troubled to conceal it it was soon found. They inquired how I had got hold of it. I grew confused, stammered, and finally said with a blush that it was Marion who had given it to me. Marion was a young girl from the Maurienne whom Mme de Vercellis had taken as her cook when she had ceased to give dinners and had discharged her chef, since she had no more need of good soup than of fine stews. Marion was not only pretty. She had that fresh complexion that one never finds except in the mountains, and such a sweet and modest air that one had only to see her to love her. What is more she was a good girl, sensible and absolutely trustworthy. They were extremely surprised when I mentioned her name. But they had no less confidence in me than in her, and decided that it was important to find which of us was a thief. She was sent for, to face a considerable number of people, including the Comte de la Roque himself. When she came she was shown the ribbon. I boldly accused her. She was confused, did not utter a word, and threw me a glance that would have disarmed the devil, but my cruel heart resisted. In the end she firmly denied the theft. But she did not get indignant. She merely turned to me, and begged me to remember myself and not disgrace an innocent girl who had never done me any harm. But, with infernal impudence, I repeated my accusation, and declared to her face that she had given me the ribbon. The poor girl started to cry, but all she said to me was, "Oh, Rousseau, I thought you were a good fellow. You make me very sad, but I should not like to be in your place." That is all. She continued to defend herself with equal firmness and sincerity, but never allowed herself any reproaches against me. This moderation, contrasted with my decided tone, prejudiced her case. It did not seem natural to suppose such diabolical audacity on one side and such angelic sweetness on the other. They seemed unable to come to a definite decision, but they were prepossessed in my favour. In the confusion of the moment they had not time to get to the bottom of the business; and the Comte de la Roque, in dismissing us both, contented himself with saying that the guilty one's conscience would amply avenge the innocent. His prediction was not wide of the mark. Not a day passes on which it is not fulfilled.

I do not know what happened to the victim of my calumny, but she cannot possibly have found it easy to get a good situation after that. The imputation against her honour was cruel in every respect. The theft was only a trifle, but after all, it was a theft and, what is worse, had been committed in order to lead a boy astray. Theft, lying, and obstinacy—what hope was there for a girl in whom so many vices were combined? I do not even consider misery and friendlessness the worst dangers to which she was exposed. Who can tell to what extremes the depressed feeling of injured innocence might have carried her at her age? And if my remorse at having perhaps made her unhappy is unbearable, what can be said of my grief at perhaps having made her worse than myself?

This cruel memory troubles me at times and so disturbs me that in my sleepless hours I see this poor girl coming to reproach me for my crime, as if I had committed it only yesterday. So long as I have lived in peace it has tortured me less, but in the midst of a stormy life it deprives me of that sweet consolation which the innocent feel under persecution. It brings home to me indeed what I think I have written in one of my books, that remorse sleeps while fate is kind but grows sharp in adversity. Nevertheless I have never been able to bring myself to relieve my heart by revealing this in private to a friend. Not with the most intimate friend, not even with Mme de Warens, has this been possible. The most that I could do was to confess that I had a terrible deed on my conscience, but I have never said in what it consisted. The burden, therefore, has rested till this day on my conscience without any relief; and I can affirm that the desire to some extent to rid myself of it has greatly contributed to my resolution of writing these *Confessions*.

I have been absolutely frank in the account I have just given, and no one will accuse me, I am certain, of palliating the heinousness of my offence. But I should not fulfil the aim of this book if I did not at the same time reveal my inner feelings and hesitated to put up such excuses for myself as I honestly could. Never was deliberate wickedness further from my intention than at that cruel moment.

When I accused that poor girl, it is strange but true that my friendship for her was the cause. She was present in my thoughts, and I threw the blame on the first person who occurred to me. I accused her of having done what I intended to do myself. I said that she had given the ribbon to me because I meant to give it to her. When afterwards I saw her in the flesh my heart was torn. But the presence of all those people prevailed over my repentance. I was not much afraid of punishment, I was only afraid of disgrace. But that I feared more than death, more than crime, more than anything in the world. I should have rejoiced if the earth had swallowed me up and stifled me in the abyss. But my invincible sense of shame prevailed over everything. It was my shame that made me impudent, and the more wickedly I behaved the bolder my fear of confession made me. I saw nothing but the horror of being found out, of being publicly proclaimed, to my face, as a thief, a liar, and a slanderer. Utter confusion robbed me of all other feeling. If I had been allowed time to come to my senses, I should most certainly have admitted everything. If M. de la Roque had taken me aside and said: "Do not ruin that poor girl. If you are guilty tell me so," I should immediately have thrown myself at his feet, I am perfectly sure. But all they did was to frighten me, when what I needed was encouragement. My age also should be taken into account. I was scarcely more than a child. Indeed I still was one. In youth real crimes are even more reprehensible than in riper years; but what is no more than weakness is much less blameworthy, and really my crime amounted to no more than weakness. So the memory tortures me less on account of the crime itself than because of its possible evil consequences. But I have derived some benefit from the terrible impression left with me by the sole offence I have committed. For it has secured me for the rest of my life against any act that might prove criminal in its results. I think also that my loathing of untruth derives to a large extent from my having told that one wicked lie. If this is a crime that can be expiated, as I venture to believe, it must have been atoned for by all the misfortunes that have crowded the end of my life, by forty years of honest and upright behaviour under difficult circumstances. Poor Marion finds so many avengers in this world that, however great my offence against her may have been, I have little fear of carrying the sin on my conscience at death. That is all I have to say on the subject. May I never have to speak of it again.

In me are united two almost irreconcilable characteristics, though in what way I cannot imagine. I have a passionate temperament and lively and headstrong emotions. Yet my thoughts arise slowly and confusedly, and are never ready till too late. It is as if my heart and my brain did not belong to the same person. Feelings come quicker than lightning and fill my soul, but they bring me no illumination; they burn me and dazzle me. I feel everything and I see nothing; I am excited but stupid; if I want to think I must be cool. The astonishing thing is, though, that I have considerable tact, some understanding, and a certain skill with people so long as they will wait for me. I can make excellent replies impromptu, if I have a moment to think, but on the spur of the moment I can never say or do anything right. I could conduct a most delightful conversation by post, as they say the Spaniards play chess. When I read the story of that Duke of Savoy who turned round on his homeward journey to cry, "Mind out, my fine Paris merchant!" I recognize myself.

But I do not suffer from this combination of quick emotion and slow thoughts only in company. I know it too when I am alone and when I am working. Ideas take shape in my head with the most incredible difficulty. They go round in dull circles and ferment, agitating me and overheating me till my heart palpitates. During this stir of emotion I can see nothing clearly, and cannot write a word; I have to wait. Insensibly all this tumult grows quiet, the chaos subsides, and everything falls into place, but slowly, and after long and confused perturbations. Have you ever been to the opera in Italy? During changes of scenery wild and prolonged disorder reigns in their great theatres. The furniture is higgledy-piggledy; on all sides things are being shifted and everything seems upside down; it is as if they were bent on universal destruction; but little by little everything falls into place, nothing is missing, and, to one's surprise, all the long tumult is succeeded by a delightful spectacle. That is almost exactly the process that takes place in my brain when I want to write. If I had known in the past how to wait and then put down in all their beauty the scenes that painted themselves in my imagination, few authors would have surpassed me.

This is the explanation of the extreme difficulty I have in writing. My blotted, scratched, confused, illegible manuscripts attest to the pain they have cost me. There is not one that I have not had to rewrite four or five times before sending it to the printer. I have never been able to do anything with my pen in my hand, and my desk and paper before me; it is on my walks, among the rocks and trees, it is at night in my bed when I lie awake, that I compose in my head; and you can imagine how slowly, for I am completely without verbal memory and have never been able to memorize half a dozen verses in my life. Some of my paragraphs I have shaped and reshaped mentally for five or six nights before they were fit to be put down on paper. It is for that reason that I am more successful in works that demand labour than in things which need a light touch. I have never caught the knack of letter-writing, for instance; it is a real torture to me. I never write a letter on the most trivial subject that does not cost me hours of weariness. For if I try to put down immediately what comes to me, I do not know how to begin or end; my letter is a long, muddled rigmarole, and scarcely understandable when it is read.

But not only do I find ideas difficult to express, I find them equally difficult to take in. I have studied men, and I think I am a fairly good observer. But all the same I do not know how to see what is before my eyes; I can only see clearly in retrospect, it is only in my memories that my mind can work. I have neither feeling nor understanding for anything that is said or done or that happens before my eyes. All that strikes me is the external manifestation. But afterwards it all comes back to me, I remember the place and the time, the tone of voice and look, the gesture and situation; nothing escapes me. Then from what a man has done or said I can read his thoughts, and I am rarely mistaken.

Seeing that I am so little master of myself when I am alone, imagine what I am like in conversation, when in order to speak to the point one must think promptly of a dozen things at a time. The mere thought of all the conventions, of which I am sure to forget at least one, is enough to frighten me. I cannot understand how a man can have the confidence to speak in company. For not a word should be uttered without taking everyone present into account, without knowing their characters and their histories, in order to be certain of not offending anyone. In that respect men who live in society are at a great advantage. Knowing better what not to say, they are more certain of what they say. But even then they often make blunders. Consider then the predicament of a man who has come in out of the blue; it is almost impossible for him to talk for a moment without blundering.

In private conversation there is another difficulty, which I consider worse, the necessity of always talking. You have to reply each time you are spoken to, and if the conversation fails, to set it going again. This unbearable constraint would be enough in itself to disgust me with society. I can think of no greater torture than to be obliged to talk continually and without a moment for reflection. I do not know whether this is just an aspect of my mortal aversion to any sort of compulsion, but I have only to be absolutely required to speak and I infallibly say something stupid. But what is even more fatal is that, instead of keeping quiet when I have nothing to say, it is at just those times that I have a furious desire to chatter. In my anxiety to fulfil my obligations as quickly as possible I hastily gabble a few ill-considered words, and am only too glad if they mean nothing at all. So anxious am I to conquer or hide my ineptitude that I rarely fail to make it apparent. Among countless examples which I could cite I will relate one, which does not belong to my youth but to a time when I had lived for some while in society. By then I should have acquired a social manner and ease if that had been possible. One evening I was with two fine ladies and one gentleman whom I can name; it was the Duke de Gontaut. There was no one else in the room, and I compelled myself to contribute a few words—goodness knows what—to a four-cornered conversation, in which the other three had certainly no need of my help. The mistress of the house sent for a laudanum draught which she took twice a day for her digestion. The other lady, seeing her make a wry face, asked with a laugh, "Is that from Doctor Tronchin's prescription?" "I don't think so," answered the first lady in the same light tone. "That's about as good as she deserves," put in the gallant Rousseau in his witty way. Everyone was speechless; there was not a word, there was not a smile, and the next moment the conversation took another turn. Addressed to anyone else this blunder might have been only silly, but said to a lady too charming not to have some stories attached to her name, a lady whom I had certainly no wish to offend, it was dreadful; and I think the two witnesses of my discomfiture had all they could do not to burst out laughing. That is the kind of witticism I produce when I feel I must speak, but have nothing to say. It will be a long time before I forget that occasion. For not only is it very vivid in itself, but it had consequences that remain in my head to remind me of it only too often.

I think that I have sufficiently explained why, though I am not a fool, I am very often taken for one, even by people in a good position to judge.

These long details of my early youth may well seem extremely childish, and I am sorry for it. Although in certain respects I have been a man since birth, I was for a long time, and still am, a child in many others. I never promised to present the public with a great personage. I promised to depict myself as I am; and to know me in my latter years it is necessary to have known me well in my youth. As objects generally make less impression on me than does the memory of them, and as all my ideas take pictorial form, the first features to engrave themselves on my mind have remained there, and such as have subsequently imprinted themselves have combined with these rather than obliterated them. There is a certain sequence of impressions and ideas which modify those that follow them, and it is necessary to know the original set before passing any judgements. I endeavour in all cases to explain the prime causes, in order to convey the interrelation of results. I should like in some way to make my soul transparent to the reader's eye, and for that purpose I am trying to present it from all points of view, to show it in all lights, and to contrive that none of its movements shall escape his notice, so that he may judge for himself of the principle which has produced them.

If I made myself responsible for the result and said to him, "Such is my character," he might suppose, if not that I am deceiving him, at least that I am deceiving myself. But by relating to him in simple detail all that has happened to me, all that I have done, all that I have felt, I cannot lead him into error, unless wilfully; and even if I wish to, I shall not easily succeed by this method. His task is to assemble these elements and to assess the being who is made up of them. The summing-up must be his, and if he comes to wrong conclusions, the fault will be of his own making. But, with this in view, it is not enough for my story to be truthful, it must be detailed as well. It is not for me to judge of the relative importance of events; I must relate them all, and leave the selection to him. That is the task to which I have devoted myself up to this point with all my courage, and I shall not relax in the sequel. But memories of middle age are always less sharp than those of early youth. So I have begun by making the best possible use of the former. If the latter come back to me in the same strength, impatient readers will perhaps be bored, but I shall not be displeased with my labours. I have only one thing to fear in this enterprise; not that I may say too much or tell untruths, but that I may not tell everything and may conceal the truth.

After two years of patient silence, in spite of my resolutions I take up the pen once more. Suspend your judgement, reader, as to the reasons that force me to it. You cannot judge them till you have read me to the end.

You have seen my peaceful youth flow by in a uniform and pleasant enough way, without great set-backs or remarkable spells of prosperity. This middling state of things was largely the result of my ardent but feeble nature, which was more easily discouraged than roused to activity, which quitted its repose when rudely shocked but soon relapsed into it again out of lassitude and natural inclination, and which, whilst keeping me far from the great virtues and even farther from the great vices, always brought me back to the quiet and idle life for which I felt I had been born, never allowing me to achieve anything of importance, either good or bad.

What a different picture I shall soon have to fill in! After favouring my wishes for thirty years, for the next thirty fate opposed them; and from this continual opposition between my situation and my desires will be seen to arise great mistakes, incredible misfortunes, and every virtue that can do credit to adversity except strength of character. . . .

I have only one faithful guide on which I can count; the succession of feelings which have marked the development of my being, and thereby recall the events that have acted upon it as cause or effect. I easily forget my misfortunes, but I cannot forget my faults, and still less my genuine feelings. The memory of them is too dear ever to be effaced from my heart. I may omit or transpose facts, or make mistakes in dates; but I cannot go wrong about what I have felt, or about what my feelings have led me to do; and these are the chief subjects of my story. The true object of my confessions is to reveal my inner thoughts exactly in all the situations of my life. It is the history of my soul that I have promised to recount, and to write it faithfully I have need of no other memories; it is enough if I enter again into my inner self, as I have done till now. . . .

I wrote the first part with pleasure at Wootton or in the Château of Trye; and every memory I had to recall was such a fresh delight. I returned to them again and again with renewed pleasure, and I was able to revise my descriptions at my ease until I was satisfied with them. Today my enfeebled brain and memory make me almost incapable of work, and I am only undertaking this task under compulsion, with a heart oppressed by grief. It can offer me nothing but misfortunes, treasons, perfidies, and sad, heart-rending recollections; and I would give everything in the world if I could enshroud what I have to say in the darkness of time. Being forced to speak in spite of myself, I am also obliged to conceal myself, to be cunning, to try to deceive, and to abase myself to conduct that is not in my nature. The ceiling under which I live has eyes, the walls that enclose me have ears. Uneasy and distracted, surrounded by spies and by vigilant and malevolent watchers, I hurriedly put on paper a few disjointed sentences that I have hardly time to re-read, let alone to correct. I know that despite the huge barriers which are ceaselessly erected all round me, they are always afraid that the truth will escape through some crack. How am I to set about piercing those barriers? I am attempting to do so, but with little hope of success. Judge whether this is stuff out of which pretty pictures can be made, or such as can colour them with attractive colours. I warn those who intend to begin this book, therefore, that nothing will save them from progressive boredom except the desire to complete their knowledge of a man, and a genuine love of truth and justice.

I am well aware that should these memoirs eventually see the light of day I shall myself be perpetuating the memory of an incident of which I intended to suppress all trace. But there are others that I am handing down with equal reluctance. The great object of my undertaking, always present to my eyes, and my indispensable duty to fulfil it in its entirety, will not allow me to be deterred by weak considerations which might deflect me from my goal. In my strange, indeed unique, situation I owe too much to truth to owe anything more to any person. If I am to be known I must be known in all situations, good and bad. My *Confessions* are necessarily linked with the tales of many others; and in everything bearing on myself I record the truth about myself and others with equal frankness, in the belief that I owe no more consideration to other people than I show towards myself, although I should like to show them much more. I want always to be fair and truthful, to say as much good as I can of others, and only to speak evil when it concerns myself and in so far as I am compelled to do so. Who has the right to demand more of me, in the situation I am in? My *Confessions* are not intended to appear in my lifetime, or in the lifetime of the persons concerned. If I were master of my own destiny and that of my book's, it would not see the light till long after my death and theirs. But the attempts made by my powerful oppressors, who dread the truth, to destroy every trace of it, compel me to make every effort consonant with the strictest justice and the most scrupulous fairness, in order to preserve them. If my memory were to be eclipsed with me, rather than compromise anyone I would uncomplainingly endure an unjust and transitory obloquy. But since my name is fated to live, I must endeavour to transmit with it the memory of that unfortunate man who bore it, as he actually was and not as his unjust enemies unremittingly endeavour to paint him.

As my ultimate plan, if I could entirely dispense with copying, was to go far away from Paris, where the constant stream of visitors made living costly and robbed me of the time I should have spent in providing for it, in order to guard myself in my retirement against the boredom that is said to overtake authors when they lay down the pen, I kept an occupation in reserve which would fill up the void in my solitary life, yet not tempt me to publish anything more so long as I lived. I do not know what whim had prompted him, but Rey had been urging me for some time now to write my memoirs. Although up to that point my life had not been particularly interesting so far as incidents were concerned, I felt that with the frank treatment I was capable of giving it it might become so. For I decided to make it a work unique and unparalleled in its truthfulness, so that for once at least the world might behold a man as he was within. I had always been amused at Montaigne's false ingenuousness, and at his pretence of confessing his faults while taking good care only to admit to likeable ones; whereas I, who believe, and always have believed, that I am on the whole the best of men, felt that there is no human heart, however pure, that does not conceal some odious vice. I knew that I was represented in the world under features so unlike my own and at times so distorted, that notwithstanding my faults, none of which I intended to pass over, I could not help gaining by showing myself as I was. Besides, this could not be done without also showing other people as they were, and consequently the work could only appear after my death and that of many others; which further emboldened me to write my *Confessions,* for which I should never have to blush before anyone. I resolved therefore to devote my leisure to the execution of this undertaking, and I set about collecting the letters and papers which might guide or assist my memory, with deep regrets for all that I had already torn up, burnt or lost.

I added what follows on the occasion of reading these *Confessions* to the Count and Countess d'Egmont, Prince Pignatelli, the Marchioness de Mesmes, and the Marquis de Juigné.

I have told the truth. If anyone knows anything contrary to what I have here recorded, though he prove it a thousand times, his knowledge is a lie and an imposture; and if he refuses to investigate and inquire into it during my lifetime he is no lover of justice or of truth. For my part, I publicly and fearlessly declare that anyone, even if he has not read my writings, who will examine my nature, my character, my morals, my likings, my pleasures, and my habits with his own eyes and can still believe me a dishonourable man, is a man who deserves to be stifled.

Thus I concluded my reading, and everyone was silent. Mme d'Egmont was the only person who seemed moved. She trembled visibly but quickly controlled herself, and remained quiet, as did the rest of the company. Such was the advantage I derived from my reading and my declaration.

ANDRÉ GIDE

The Value of Inconsistency

Yes, I feel throughout my diversity a constancy; I feel that what is diverse in me is still *myself*. But for the very reason that I know and feel the existence of this constancy, why should I strive to obtain it? All through my life I have never sought to know myself; that is to say I have never sought myself. It seemed to me that such seeking, or rather, the success of such seeking brought with it a limitation and impoverishment of self, and that only rather poor and limited personalities succeeded in finding and understanding themselves; or, more truly, that this self-knowledge limited the self and its development; for such as one found oneself, so one remained, anxious henceforth to resemble oneself; and that it was better to persevere in safeguarding future possibilities—the perpetual and elusive process of becoming. I dislike inconsistency less than a kind of persistent consistency, less than the determination to be true to oneself, and than the fear of giving oneself away. I think moreover that such inconsequence is only apparent and that it responds to some more secret continuity. I think too that here, as always, we are deceived by words, for language imposes on us more logic than often exists in life; and that the most precious part of ourselves is that which remains unformulated.

I

"Have you noted," said Édouard, "the sort of moral anchylosis produced in M. by his assumption of never being in the wrong? It is an assumption that many

From *Later Fruits of the Earth* [1935], in *Fruits of the Earth*, translated from the French by Dorothy Bussy, New York, 1949, p. 231. Copyright 1949 by Alfred A. Knopf, Inc.; reprinted by permission of Random House, Alfred A. Knopf, Inc. and Martin Secker & Warburg Ltd.
From Journal of 1923, *Journals*, translated from the French by Justin O'Brien, New York, 1947-51, Vol. II, pp. 341-5. Copyright 1947, 1948, 1949, 1951, 1956 by Alfred A. Knopf, Inc.; reprinted by permission of Random House, Alfred A. Knopf, Inc. and Martin Secker & Warburg Ltd.

people make; I made it too in my youth, and if now I am so sensitive to it in others, it is because I myself had the greatest difficulty getting rid of it. My parents had accustomed me to act, not according to my inner urge, but according to an ethical rule outside of me, which they considered applicable to all men, so that, in the same circumstances, any creature whatever, no matter how different from me, would have seen the same moral postulate rise up before him, which he could not escape without flinching and without incurring the blame of others (which would still be bearable), but also some self-reprobation or other that my upbringing in fact had striven to make unbearable to me. Not to have acted, in whatever combination of circumstances, precisely as I was expected to act seemed to me abominable to such a point that all inner peace was immediately compromised, that peace without which I believed that I could not live—while on the contrary . . . but at that time could I admit, could I suspect even, that whatever is newest in each creature and most peculiar to him is perhaps not the most detestable?"

A great error is revealed here: minds accustomed to live according to the rule cease to recognize, as soon as someone escapes the rule, any other domination than that of one's own sweet will; a person seems to them a slave as soon as he is a slave to his passions, and, as he escapes the passions when he lives according to duty, he ceases to seem to them a slave and it seems to them that he is free the moment the slavery to which he submits is a moral, banal, and commonly accepted slavery. They cry out: "O Lord, deliver us from ourselves," and their way of delivering themselves is to bend their thought, their will, their whole being until they desire nothing to which their moral being cannot give complete assent, so that they have an illusion of acting freely while already their choice has ceased to be free, and that constraint to which they submit and the very difficulty they experience in submitting to it are at once a pledge of the error into which their nature hurled them and of the truth of that rule which forces and counterfeits their most sincere impulses.

But the rigorous puritan upbringing by which my parents had fashioned my childhood, but the habit and need of a discipline, allowed me to glimpse, once escaped from the common rule, something quite different from a mere surrender; and this allowed me to shrug my shoulders when I heard myself accused of listening henceforth only to the invitation of pleasure. To rediscover, underneath the factitious creature, the unspoiled self was not, or so it seemed to me, so easy a task; and that new rule of life which was becoming mine: to act according to the greatest sincerity, implied a resolution, a perspicacity, an effort that strained my whole will, so that I never seemed more moral to myself than at the time when I had decided to cease being moral; I mean: to be moral henceforth only in my own way. And I came to understand that perfect sincerity, the kind that, in my opinion, leads to the most valor and greatest dignity, sincerity not only of the act itself but of the motive, can be achieved only through the most constant, but also the least bitter, effort, only with the clearest vision (I mean: the least suspect of self-satisfaction), and the most irony.

It soon became apparent to me that I had gained almost nothing; that I was still acting only according to the best motive, so long as I made my acts measure up to that approbation which implied, before acting, a sort of deliberation and weighing in imagination, whence the action was delayed and blocked. The promptest, the most sudden action henceforth seemed to me preferable; it seemed to me that my act was all the more sincere since I had swept away before it all those preambles by which I used to attempt to justify it to myself. Henceforth, acting in any way whatever and not giving myself time to reflect, my least acts seemed to me more significant since they were no longer reasoned out. At the same time I delivered myself from anxiety, perplexity, and remorse. And perhaps that intimate gymnastic to which I had first submitted had not been altogether useless and helped me to achieve that state of joy which made me recognize my act to be good solely from the pleasure I took in doing it.

The Greeks, who, not only in the multitude of their statues but also in themselves, left us such a beautiful image of humanity, recognized as many gods as there are instincts, and the problem for them was to keep the inner Olympus in equilibrium, not to subjugate and subdue any of the gods.

It is not so much by his acts that a lover of humanity makes himself useful as by his example. I mean: by his very figure, by the image he offers and leaves behind, and by the happiness and serenity it radiates.

II

T. explains:

. . . There is a certain indulgence by which every sentiment we experience is exaggerated; and often one does not suffer so much as one imagines oneself to be suffering.

I have never been able to renounce anything; and protecting in me both the best and the worst, I have lived as a man torn asunder. But how can it be explained that this cohabitation of extremes in me led not so much to restlessness and suffering as to a pathetic intensification of the sentiment of existence, of life? The most opposite tendencies never succeeded in making me a tormented person; but rather perplexed—for torment accompanies a state one longs to get away from, and I did not long to escape what brought into operation all the potentialities of my being. That *state of dialogue* which, for so many others, is almost intolerable became necessary to me. This is also because, for those others, it can only be injurious to action, whereas for me, far from leading to sterility, it invited me to the work of art and immediately preceded creation, led to equilibrium and harmony.

It must, however, be recognized that, for a number of souls, which I consider among the best tempered, happiness lies not in comfort and quietude, but in ardor. A sort of magnificent using up is all the more desirable to them since they are constantly being renewed by it and do not so much suffer from the wearing away as they rejoice in their perpetual re-creation. As for me, I can tell you that I have never so keenly felt myself growing old as in that very quietude to which your rule of conduct invites one, but which you are less likely to achieve the more earnestly and nostalgically you strive to attain it. Your belief in the survival of souls is nourished by the need of that quietude and your *lack of hope* of enjoying it in life.

Shall I tell you what keeps me from believing in eternal life? It is that almost perfect satisfaction I enjoy in effort itself and in the immediate realization of happiness and harmony.

III

I was like the prodigal son who goes squandering his possessions. And that imponderable treasure which the slow virtue of my fathers, from generation to generation, had patiently accumulated on my head, no, I was not unaware of its value; but the unknown I could hope for by renouncing it seemed to me even more precious. The words of Christ rose up luminously before me like the column of fire that guided the chosen people in the night, and in the heavy darkness in which I decided to adventure I kept repeating to myself: "Sell all your goods and give them to the poor." My heart was filled with apprehension and joy, or more exactly: with the apprehension of my joy. For, thought I, it is not a question of interpreting the divine words to attain complete happiness; it is a question of accepting them without reservations, of understanding them "in spirit and in truth;" and then at last, and then above all, to put them into practice, for, as it is said in the Gospel, "every one that heareth these sayings of mine and doeth them not . . ."

I began then to seek out which, among the thoughts, opinions, and tendencies of my soul and mind that were most familiar to me, were the ones that I most certainly derived from my ancestors, from my upbringing and puritan formation, which at first had constituted my strength, from that sort of mortal atmosphere in which I was beginning to stifle. And doubtless, pushing that relinquishment to the extreme, to the absurd, I should have ended up in complete impoverishment—for "what have you that you have not received?"—but yet it was complete impoverishment that I coveted as the truest possession. Resolved to give up in this manner every personal possession and convinced that I could not hope to dispose of everything except on condition that I possessed nothing in my own right, I repudiated every personal opinion, every habit, every modesty, my very virtue, as one throws off a tunic in order to offer an unveiled body to the contact of the wave, to the passing winds, to the sun. Strengthened by these abnegations, I soon felt my soul only as a loving will (yes, this is the way I defined it to myself), palpitating, open to all comers, like unto everything, impersonal, a naïve confusion of appetites, greeds, desires. And if perhaps I had been frightened by the disorder into which their anarchy led me, was I not able to reassure myself at once by recalling these words of Christ: "Why should you be troubled?" I surrendered then to this provisional disorder, trusting in a more sincere and natural order that would organize itself, I thought, and believing moreover that the disorder itself was less dangerous for my soul than an arbitrary and necessarily artificial order, since I had not invented it. Divine ray! I exclaimed, isn't what is opposed to you above all that false wisdom of men, made up of fear, lack of confidence, and presumption? I resign everything to you. I surrender myself. Drive out all shadow from me. Inspire me.

Considering later on that nothing separates one more from God than pride and that nothing made me prouder than my virtue, I began to detest that very virtue and everything on which I could pride myself, everything that allowed me to say: I am not like you, common run of men! And I am well aware that this excess of renunciation, this repudiation of virtue through the love of virtue itself, would appear, as merely an abominable sophistry to the pious soul who reads me.

Paradox or sophistry that thenceforth bent my life, whether or not the devil prompted it I shall examine later on. It is enough for me to say for the moment that I advanced boldly on this path that was so new. What am I saying: path? Every step I took forward was a venture into the unknown.

D. H. LAWRENCE

The Living Self

We have curious ideas of ourselves. We think of ourselves as a body with a spirit in it, or a body with a soul in it, or a body with a mind in it. *Mens sana in corpore sano.* The years drink up the wine, and at last throw the bottle away, the body, of course, being the bottle.

It is a funny sort of superstition. Why should I look at my hand, as it so cleverly writes these words, and decide that it is a mere nothing compared to the mind that directs it? Is there really any huge difference between my hand and my brain? Or my mind? My hand is alive, it flickers with a life of its own. It meets all the strange universe in touch, and learns a vast number of things, and knows a vast number of things. My hand, as it writes these words, slips gaily along, jumps like a grasshopper to dot an *i*, feels the table rather cold, gets a little bored if I write too long, has its own rudiments of thought, and is just as much *me* as is my brain, my mind, or my soul. Why should I imagine that there is a *me* which is more *me* than my hand is? Since my hand is absolutely alive, me alive.

Whereas, of course, as far as I am concerned, my pen isn't alive at all. My pen *isn't me* alive. Me alive ends at my finger-tips.

Whatever is me alive is me. Every tiny bit of my hands is alive, every little freckle and hair and fold of skin. And whatever is me alive is me. Only my finger-nails, those ten little weapons between me and an inanimate universe, they cross the mysterious Rubicon between me alive and things like my pen, which are not alive, in my own sense.

So, seeing my hand is all alive, and me alive, wherein is it just a bottle, or a jug, or a tin can, or a vessel of clay, or any of the rest of that nonsense? True, if I cut it it will bleed, like a can of cherries. But then the skin that is cut, and the veins that bleed, and the bones that should never be seen, they are all just as alive as the blood that flows. So the tin can business, or vessel of clay, is just bunk.

And that's what you learn, when you're a novelist. And that's what you are very liable *not* to know, if you're a parson, or a philosopher, or a scientist, or a stupid person. If you're a parson, you talk about souls in heaven. If you're a novelist, you know that paradise is in the palm of your hand, and on the end of your nose, because both are alive; and alive, and man alive, which is more than you can say, for certain, of paradise. Paradise is after life, and I for one am not keen on any-

From "Why the Novel Matters," *Phoenix*, New York, 1936, pp. 533-8; reprinted by permission of The Viking Press Inc., Lawrence Pollinger Ltd, and the Estate of the late Mrs. Frieda Lawrence.

thing that is *after* life. If you are a philosopher, you talk about infinity, and the pure spirit which knows all things. But if you pick up a novel, you realize immediately that infinity is just a handle to this self-same jug of a body of mine; while as for knowing, if I find my finger in the fire, I know that fire burns, with a knowledge so emphatic and vital, it leaves Nirvana merely a conjecture. Oh, yes, my body, me alive, *knows,* and knows intensely. And as for the sum of all knowledge, it can't be anything more than an accumulation of all the things I know in the body, and you, dear reader, know in the body.

These damned philosophers, they talk as if they suddenly went off in steam, and were then much more important than they are when they're in their shirts. It is nonsense. Every man, philosopher included, ends in his own finger-tips. That's the end of his man alive. As for the words and thoughts and sighs and aspirations that fly from him, they are so many tremulations in the ether, and not alive at all. But if the tremulations reach another man alive, he may receive them into his life, and his life may take on a new colour, like a chameleon creeping from a brown rock on to a green leaf. All very well and good. It still doesn't alter the fact that the so-called spirit, the message or teaching of the philosopher or the saint, isn't alive at all, but just a tremulation upon the ether, like a radio message. All this spirit stuff is just tremulations upon the ether. If you, as man alive, quiver from the tremulation of the ether into new life, that is because you are man alive, and you take sustenance and stimulation into your alive man in a myriad ways. But to say that the message, or the spirit which is communicated to you, is more important than your living body, is nonsense. You might as well say that the potato at dinner was more important.

Nothing is important but life. And for myself, I can absolutely see life nowhere but in the living. Life with a capital L is only man alive. Even a cabbage in the rain is cabbage alive. All things that are alive are amazing. And all things that are dead are subsidiary to the living. Better a live dog than a dead lion. But better a live lion than a live dog. *C'est la vie!*

It seems impossible to get a saint, or a philosopher, or a scientist, to stick to this simple truth. They are all, in a sense, renegades. The saint wishes to offer himself up as spiritual food for the multitude. Even Francis of Assisi turns himself into a sort of angel-cake, of which anyone may take a slice. But an angel-cake is rather less than man alive. And poor St. Francis might well apologize to his body, when he is dying: "Oh, pardon me, my body, the wrong I did you through the years!" It was no wafer, for others to eat.

The philosopher, on the other hand, because he can think, decides that nothing but thoughts matter. It is as if a rabbit, because he can make little pills, should decide that nothing but little pills matter. As for the scientist, he has absolutely no use for me so long as I am man alive. To the scientist, I am dead. He puts under the microscope a bit of dead me, and calls it me. He takes me to pieces, and says first one piece, and then another piece, is me. My heart, my liver, my stomach have all been scientifically me, according to the scientist; and nowadays I am either a brain, or nerves, or glands, or something more up-to-date in the tissue line.

Now I absolutely flatly deny that I am a soul, or a body, or a mind, or an intelligence, or a brain, or a nervous system, or a bunch of glands, or any of the rest of these bits of me. The whole is greater than the part. And therefore, I, who am man alive, am greater than my soul, or spirit, or body, or mind, or consciousness, or anything else that is merely a part of me. I am a man, and alive. I am man alive, and as long as I can, I intend to go on being man alive.

For this reason I am a novelist. And being a novelist, I consider myself superior to the saint, the scientist, the philosopher, and the poet, who are all great masters of different bits of man alive, but never get the whole hog.

The novel is the one bright book of life. Books are not life. They are only tremulations on the ether. But the novel as a tremulation can make the whole man alive tremble. Which is more than poetry, philosophy, science, or any other book-tremulation can do.

The novel is the book of life. In this sense, the Bible is a great confused novel. You may say, it is about God. But it is really about man alive. Adam, Eve, Sarai, Abraham, Isaac, Jacob, Samuel, David, Bath-Sheba, Ruth, Esther, Solomon, Job, Isaiah, Jesus, Mark, Judas, Paul, Peter: what is it but man alive, from start to finish? Man alive, not mere bits. Even the Lord is another man alive, in a burning bush, throwing the tablets of stone at Moses's head.

I do hope you begin to get my idea, why the novel is supremely important, as a tremulation on the ether. Plato makes the perfect ideal being tremble in me. But that's only a bit of me. Perfection is only a bit, in the strange make-up of man alive. The Sermon on the Mount makes the selfless spirit of me quiver. But that, too, is only a bit of me. The Ten Commandments set the old Adam shivering in me, warning me that I am a thief and a murderer, unless I watch it. But even the old Adam is only a bit of me.

I very much like all these bits of me to be set trembling with life and the wisdom of life. But I do ask that the whole of me shall tremble in its wholeness, some time or other.

And this, of course, must happen in me, living.

But as far as it can happen from a communication, it can only happen when a whole novel communicates itself to me. The Bible—but *all* the Bible—and Homer, and Shakespeare: these are the supreme old novels. These are all things to all men. Which means that in their wholeness they affect the whole man alive, which is the man himself, beyond any part of him. They set the whole tree trembling with a new access of life, they do not just stimulate growth in one direction.

I don't want to grow in any one direction any more. And, if I can help it, I don't want to stimulate anybody else into some particular direction. A particular direction ends in a *cul-de-sac*. We're in a *cul-de-sac* at present.

I don't believe in any dazzling revelation, or in any supreme Word. "The grass withereth, the flower fadeth, but the Word of the Lord shall stand for ever." That's the kind of stuff we've drugged ourselves with. As a matter of fact, the grass withereth, but comes up all the greener for that reason, after the rains. The flower fadeth, and therefore the bud opens. But the Word of the Lord, being man-uttered and a mere vibration on the ether, becomes staler and staler, more and more boring, till at last we turn a deaf ear and it ceases to exist, far more finally than any withered grass. It is grass that renews its young like the eagle, not any Word.

We should ask for no absolutes, or absolute. Once and for all and for ever, let us have done with the ugly imperialism of any absolute. There is no absolute good, there is nothing absolutely right. All things flow and change, and even change is not absolute. The whole is a strange assembly of apparently incongruous parts, slipping past one another.

Me, man alive, I am a very curious assembly of incongruous parts. My yea! of today is oddly different from my yea! of yesterday. My tears of tomorrow will have nothing to do with my tears of a year ago. If the one I love remains unchanged and unchanging, I shall cease to love her. It is only because she changes and startles me into change and defies my inertia, and is herself staggered in her inertia by my changing, that I can continue to love her. If she stayed put, I might as well love the pepper-pot.

In all this change, I maintain a certain integrity. But woe betide me if I try to put my finger on it. If I say of myself, I am this, I am that!—then, if I stick to it, I turn into a stupid fixed thing like a lamp-post. I shall never know wherein lies my integrity, my individuality, my me. I *can* never know it. It is useless to talk about my ego. That only means that I have made up an *idea* of myself, and that I am trying to cut myself out to pattern. Which is no good. You can cut your cloth to fit your coat, but you can't clip bits off your living body, to trim it down to your idea. True, you can put yourself into ideal corsets. But even in ideal corsets, fashions change.

Let us learn from the novel. In the novel, the characters can do nothing but *live*. If they keep on being good, according to pattern, or bad, according to pattern, or even volatile, according to pattern, they cease to live, and the novel falls dead. A character in a novel has got to live, or it is nothing.

We, likewise, in life have got to live, or we are nothing.

What we mean by living is, of course, just as indescribable as what we mean by *being*. Men get ideas into their heads, of what they mean by Life, and they proceed to cut life out to pattern. Sometimes they go into the desert to seek God, sometimes they go into the desert to seek cash, sometimes it is wine, woman, and song, and again it is water, political reform, and votes. You never know what it will be next: from killing your neighbour with hideous bombs and gas that tears the lungs, to supporting a Foundlings Home and preaching infinite Love, and being co-respondent in a divorce.

In all this wild welter, we need some sort of guide. It's no good inventing Thou Shalt Nots!

What then? Turn truly, honourably to the novel, and see wherein you are man alive, and wherein you are dead man in life. You may love a woman as man alive, and you may be making love to a woman as sheer dead man in life. You may eat your dinner as man alive, or as a mere masticating corpse. As man alive you may have a shot at your enemy. But as a ghastly simulacrum of life you may be firing bombs into men who are neither your enemies nor your friends, but just things you are dead to. Which is criminal, when the things happen to be alive.

To be alive, to be man alive, to be whole man alive: that is the point. And at its best, the novel, and the novel supremely, can help you. It can help you not to be dead man in life. So much of a man walks about dead and a carcass in the street and house, today: so much of women is merely dead. Like a pianoforte with half the notes mute.

But in the novel you can see, plainly, when the man goes dead, the woman goes inert. You can develop an instinct for life, if you will, instead of a theory of right and wrong, good and bad.

In life, there is right and wrong, good and bad, all the time. But what is right in one case is wrong in another. And in the novel you see one man becoming a corpse, because of his so-called goodness, another going dead because of his so-called wickedness. Right and wrong is an instinct: but an instinct of the whole consciousness in a man, bodily, mental, spiritual at once. And only in the novel are *all* things given full play, or at least, they may be given full play, when we realize that life itself, and not inert safety, is the reason for living. For out of the full play of all things emerges the only thing that is anything, the wholeness of a man, the wholeness of a woman, man alive, and live woman.

RAINER MARIA RILKE

The Self and Reality

Villa Alberti, 11 Keferstrasse
Munich, November 8, 1915

Your letter, L.H., may be taken up from so many angles, almost every sentence calls for ten letters—not that one need answer everything in it that is question (and what in it is not question?), no, but of course these are all the questions that have always been covered up again with more questions or (at best) showed more transparent under the influence of other self-illuminating questions—; they are the great question-dynasties—who then has ever answered?

What is expressed in the suffering that is written into Malte Laurids Brigge (forgive me if I mention this book again when we have just discussed it) is really only *this*, with every means and always anew and by every manifestation this, *This*: how is it possible to live when after all the elements of this life are utterly incomprehensible to us? If we are continually inadequate in love, uncertain in decision and impotent in the face of death, how is it possible to exist? In this book, achieved under the deepest obligation, I did not manage to express all of my astonishment over the fact that men have had for thousands of years to deal with life (not to mention God), and yet towards these first most immediate problems—strictly speaking, these only problems (for what else have we to do, to-day still and for how long to come?)—they remain such helpless novices, so between fright and subterfuge, so miserable. Isn't that incomprehensible? My astonishment over this fact, whenever I yield to it, drives me first into the greatest dismay and then into a sort of horror, but behind the horror again there is something else and again something else, something so intensive that I cannot tell by the feeling whether it is white-hot or icy. I tried once before, years ago, to write about Malte, to someone who had been frightened by the book, that I myself sometimes thought of it as a hollow form, a negative mold, all the grooves

Letter to L. H. [November 8, 1915], *Letters*, translated from the German by Jane Bannard Greene and M. D. Herter Norton, New York, 1945-48, Vol. II, pp. 146-9. Copyright 1947 and 1948 by W. W. Norton & Co., Inc.; reprinted by permission of W. W. Norton & Co.

and indentations of which are agony, disconsolations and most painful insights, but the casting from which, were it possible to make one (as with a bronze the positive figure one would get out of it), would perhaps be happiness, assent,— most perfect and most certain bliss. Who knows, I ask myself, whether we do not always approach the gods so to speak from behind, separated from their sublimely radiant face through nothing but themselves, quite near to the expression we yearn for, only just standing behind it—but what does that mean save that our countenance and the divine face are looking out in the same direction, are at one; and this being so, how are we to approach the god from the space that lies in front of him?

Does it perplex you, my saying God and gods and for the sake of completeness haunting you with these dogmatic terms (as with a ghost), thinking that they must immediately mean something to you? But assume the metaphysical. Let us agree that since his earliest beginnings man has shaped gods in whom here and there were contained only the dead and threatening and destructive and frightful, violence, anger, superpersonal stupor, tied up as it were into a tight knot of malice: the alien, if you like, but, already to some extent implied in this alien, the admission that one was aware of it, endured it, yes, acknowledged it for the sake of a sure, secret relationship and connection: [for] *we were these too*, only that so far we have not known what to do with this side of our experience; they were too big, too dangerous, too many-sided, they grew beyond us to an exaggerated significance; it was not possible, in addition to the many demands of existence, set up for use and performance, always to treat with these unmanageable and un-graspable states; and so one agreed to put them outside now and then.—But since they were excess—the strongest, indeed the *too* strong, the powerful, indeed the violent, the incomprehensible, often the monstrous—how should they not, brought together in one place, exercise influence, effect, force, superiority? And, remember, from the outside now. Could one not treat the history of God as a part, never before broached, of the human mind, a part always postponed, saved up, and at last let slip, for which there was once a time of decision and calm, and which—there where it had been pushed aside—gradually grew into a tension against which the impulse of the individual, ever again scattered and pettily wounded of heart, hardly counts any more.

And so you see, it was the same with death. Experienced, and yet in its reality not to be experienced, knowing better than we all the time and yet never rightly admitted by us, hurting and from the start outstripping the meaning of life; it too, so that it should not continually interrupt us in the search for this meaning, was dismissed, pushed out; death, which is probably so near us that we cannot at all determine the distance between it and the life-center within us without its becom-ing something external, daily held further from us, lurking somewhere in the void in order to attack this one and that according to its evil choice—; more and more death became suspected of being the contradiction, the opponent, the in-visible antagonism in the air, that which shrivels up our joys, the dangerous glass of our happiness, out of which we may be spilled at any instant.

God and death were now outside, were the *other*, the *one* being our life that now, at the cost of this elimination, seemed to become human, friendly, possible, achievable, in a firm sense ours. But since in this life-course for beginners, as it were, this preparatory class in life, the things to be classified and understood were still innumerable, and really strict distinctions could not be made between problems solved and problems only temporarily passed over, there resulted, even in this restricted form, no straight and reliable progress; instead one just lived along, as it came, on real profits and wrong additions, and in the total result there was bound in the end to reappear as fundamental error that very condition upon the assumption of which this whole experiment in existence was set up; that is, while from every accepted meaning God and death seemed to have been subtracted (as something not here-and-now, but later, elsewhere and different), the smaller cycle of the merely here-and-now revolved faster and faster, the so-called progress happened in a world self-preoccupied and forgetful that, however it might exert itself, it was beaten from the start by death and God. Now this might still have made a kind of sense had we been able to keep God and death at a distance, as mere ideas in the realm of mind; but Nature knew nothing of this removal we had somehow accomplished—if a tree blossoms, death blossoms in it as well as life, and the field is full of death, which from its reclining face sends out a rich expression of life, and the beasts go patiently from one [to the] other—and everywhere about us death is still at home and he watches us out of the cracks in things, and a rusty nail, sticking up somewhere out of a plank, does nothing day and night but rejoice over death.

And love too, which mixes the ciphers between people to introduce a game of near and far in which we always line up only to a certain distance, as though the universe were full and space nowhere save in us;—love too takes no heed of our divisions, but sweeps us, trembling as we are, into an endless consciousness of the whole. Lovers do not live out of the detached here-and-now; as though no division had ever been undertaken, they enter into the enormous possessions of their heart, of them one may say that God becomes real to them and that death does not harm them: *for being full of life, they are full of death.*

But of the experiencing of life we need not speak here; it is a secret, not one that locks itself away, not one that demands to be hidden; it is the secret that is sure of itself, that stands open like a temple, whose entrances glory in being entrances, singing between gigantic pillars that they are the portals.

WASSILY KANDINSKY

An Expressionist Credo

A work of art is born of the artist in a mysterious and secret way. Detached from him it acquires autonomous life, becomes an entity. Nor is its existence casual and inconsequent; it has a definite and purposeful strength, alike in its material and spiritual life. It exists and has power to create spiritual atmosphere; and from this internal standpoint alone can one judge whether it is a good work of art or bad. If its form is "poor," it is too weak to call forth spiritual vibration. Likewise

From *Concerning the Spiritual in Art* [1912], translated from the German by F. Golffing, M. Harrison, and F. Ostertag, New York, 1947, pp. 74-5; reprinted by permission of George Wittenborn, Inc., Publishers, 1018 Madison Avenue, New York 21, N.Y.

a picture is not necessarily "well painted" if it possesses the "values" of which the French so constantly speak. It is only well painted if its spiritual value is completed and satisfying. "Good drawing" is drawing that cannot be altered without destruction of this inner value, quite irrespective of its correctness as anatomy, botany or any other science. This is not a question of a violation of natural form, but of the need of the artist for such a form. Similarly, colors are not used because they are true to nature but because they are necessary to the particular picture. The artist is not only justified in using, but is under a moral obligation to use, only those forms which fulfill his *own* need. Absolute freedom from anatomy or anything else of the kind must be given to the artist in his choice of means. Such spiritual freedom is as necessary in art as it is in life.

But blind following of scientific precept is less blameworthy than its blind and purposeless rejection. At least the former produces an imitation of material objects which may have some use. The latter is an artistic fraud, bringing confusion in its train. The former leaves the spiritual atmosphere empty; the latter poisons it.

Painting is an art; and art is not vague production, transitory and isolated, but a power which must be directed to the development and refinement of the human soul. . . .

If art rejects this work, a pit remains unbridged; no other power can take the place of art in this activity. And sometimes when the human soul is gaining greater strength, art also grows in power, for the two are inextricably connected and complementary. Conversely, at those times when the soul tends to be choked by materialist lack of belief, art becomes purposeless, and it is said that art exists for art's sake alone. The relation between art and the soul is, as it were, doped into unconsciousness. The artist and the public drift apart, until at last the public turns its back, or regards the artist as a juggler whose skill and dexterity alone are worthy of applause. It is important for the artist to gauge his position correctly, to realize that he has a duty to his art and to himself, that he is not a king but a servant of a noble end. He must search his soul deeply, develop it and guard it, so that his art may have something on which to rest and does not remain flesh without bones.

The artist must have something to communicate, since mastery over form is not the end but, instead, the adapting of form to internal significance.

The artist's life is not one of pleasure. He must not live irresponsibly; he has a difficult work to perform, one which often proves a crown of thorns. He must realize that his acts, feelings and thoughts are the imponderable but sound material from which his work is to rise; he is free in art, but not in life.

Compared with non-artists the artist has a triple responsibility: (1) he must return the talent which he has; (2) his actions, feelings and thoughts, like those of every man, create a spiritual atmosphere which is either pure or infected; (3) his actions and thoughts are the material for his creations, which in turn influence the spiritual atmosphere. The artist is a king, as Peladan says, not only because he has great powers, but also because he has great obligations.

If the artist be guardian of beauty, beauty can be measured only by the yardstick of internal greatness and necessity.

That is beautiful which is produced by internal necessity, which springs from the soul.

HENRY JAMES
Centers of Consciousness

This in fact I have ever found rather terribly the point—that the figures in any picture, the agents in any drama, are interesting only in proportion as they feel their respective situations; since the consciousness, on their part, of the complication exhibited forms for us their link of connexion with it. But there are degrees of feeling—the muffled, the faint, the just sufficient, the barely intelligent, as we may say; and the acute, the intense, the complete, in a word—the power to be finely aware and richly responsible. It is those moved in this latter fashion who "get most" out of all that happens to them and who in so doing enable us, as readers of their record, as participators by a fond attention, also to get most. Their being finely aware—as Hamlet and Lear, say, are finely aware—*makes* absolutely the intensity of their adventure, gives the maximum of sense to what befalls them. We care, our curiosity and our sympathy care, comparatively little for what happens to the stupid, the coarse and the blind; care for it, and for the effects of it, at the most as helping to precipitate what happens to the more deeply wondering, to the really sentient. Hamlet and Lear are surrounded, amid their complications, by the stupid and the blind, who minister in all sorts of ways to their recorded fate. Persons of markedly limited sense would, on such a principle as that, play a part in the career of my tormented youth [the hero of *The Princess Casamassima*]; but he wouldn't be of markedly limited sense himself— he would note as many things and vibrate to as many occasions as I might venture to make him.

There wouldn't moreover simply be the question of his suffering—of which we might soon get enough; there would be the question of what, all beset and all perceptive, he should thus adventurously do, thus dream and hazard and attempt. The interest of the attitude and the act would be the actor's imagination and vision of them, together with the nature and degree of their felt return upon him. So the intelligent creature would be required and so some picture of his intelligence involved. The picture of an intelligence appears for the most part, it is true, a dead weight for the reader of the English novel to carry, this reader having so often the wondrous property of caring for the displayed tangle of human relations

Extract from the Preface [1908] to *The Princess Casamassima*, copyright 1908 Charles Scribner's Sons; renewal copyright 1936 Henry James, from *The Art of the Novel*, Critical Prefaces by Henry James, with an Introduction by Richard P. Blackmur, New York and London, 1934, pp. 62-3, 66-71. Reprinted by permission of Charles Scribner's Sons.

without caring for its intelligibility. The teller of a story is primarily, none the less, the listener to it, the reader of it, too; and, having needed thus to make it out, distinctly, on the crabbed page of life, to disengage it from the rude human character and the more or less Gothic text in which it has been packed away, the very essence of his affair has been the *imputing* of intelligence. The basis of his attention has been that such and such an imbroglio has got started—on the page of life —because of something that some one has felt and more or less understood.

I recognise at the same time, and in planning "The Princess Casamassima" felt it highly important to recognise, the danger of filling too full any supposed and above all any obviously limited vessel of consciousness. If persons either tragically or comically embroiled with life allow us the comic or tragic value of their embroilment in proportion as their struggle is a measured and directed one, it is strangely true, none the less, that beyond a certain point they are spoiled for us by this carrying of a due light. . . .

The whole thing comes to depend thus on the *quality* of bewilderment characteristic of one's creature, the quality involved in the given case or supplied by one's data. There are doubtless many such qualities, ranging from vague and crepuscular to sharpest and most critical; and we have but to imagine one of these latter to see how easily—from the moment it gets its head at all—it may insist on playing a part. There we have then at once a case of feeling, of ever so many possible feelings, stretched across the scene like an attached thread on which the pearls of interest are strung. There are threads shorter and less tense, and I am far from implying that the minor, the coarser and less fruitful forms and degrees of moral reaction, as we may conveniently call it, may not yield lively results. They have their subordinate, comparative, illustrative human value—that appeal of the witness which is often so penetrating. Verily even, I think, no "story" is possible without its fools—as most of the fine painters of life, Shakespeare, Cervantes and Balzac, Fielding, Scott, Thackeray, Dickens, George Meredith, George Eliot, Jane Austen, have abundantly felt. At the same time I confess I never see the *leading* interest of any human hazard but in a consciousness (on the part of the moved and moving creature) subject to fine intensification and wide enlargement. It is as mirrored in that consciousness that the gross fools, the headlong fools, the fatal fools play their part for us—they have much less to show us in themselves. The troubled life mostly at the centre of our subject—whatever our subject, for the artistic hour, happens to be—embraces them and deals with them for its amusement and its anguish: they are apt largely indeed, on a near view, to be all the cause of its trouble. This means, exactly, that the person capable of feeling in the given case more than another of what is to be felt for it, and so serving in the highest degree to *record* it dramatically and objectively, is the only sort of person on whom we can count not to betray, to cheapen or, as we say, give away, the value and beauty of the thing. By so much as the affair matters *for* some such individual, by so much do we get the best there is of it, and by so much as it falls within the scope of a denser and duller, a more vulgar and more shallow capacity, do we get a picture dim and meagre.

The great chroniclers have clearly always been aware of this; they have at least always either placed a mind of some sort—in the sense of a reflecting and colouring medium—in possession of the general adventure (when the latter has not been purely epic, as with Scott, say, as with old Dumas and with Zola); or else paid signally, as to the interest created, for their failure to do so. We may note more-over in passing that this failure is in almost no case intentional or part of a plan, but has sprung from their limited curiosity, their short conception of the particular sensibility projected. Edgar of Ravenswood for instance, visited by the tragic tempest of "The Bride of Lammermoor," has a black cloak and hat and feathers more than he has a mind; just as Hamlet, while equally sabled and draped and plumed, while at least equally romantic, has yet a mind still more than he has a costume. The situation represented is that Ravenswood loves Lucy Ashton through dire difficulty and danger, and that she in the same way loves him; but the relation so created between them is by this neglect of the "feeling" question never shown us as primarily taking place. It is shown only in its secondary, its con-fused and disfigured aspects—where, however, luckily, it is presented with great romantic good faith. The thing has nevertheless paid for its deviation, as I say, by a sacrifice of intensity; the centre of the subject is empty and the development pushed off, all round, toward the frame—which is, so to speak, beautifully rich and curious. But I mention that relation to each other of the appearances in a par-ticular work only as a striking negative case; there are in the connexion I have glanced at plenty of striking positive ones. It is very true that Fielding's hero in "Tom Jones" is but as "finely," that is but as intimately, bewildered as a young man of great health and spirits may be when he hasn't a grain of imagination: the point to be made is, at all events, that his sense of bewilderment obtains alto-gether on the comic, never on the tragic plane. He has so much "life" that it amounts, for the effect of comedy and application of satire, almost to his having a mind, that is to his having reactions and a full consciousness; besides which his author—he handsomely possessed of a mind—has such an amplitude of reflexion for him and round him that we see him through the mellow air of Fielding's fine old moralism, fine old humour and fine old style, which somehow really enlarge, make every one and every thing important.

All of which furthers my remarking how much I have been interested, on read-ing "The Princess Casamassima" over, to recognize my sense, sharp from far back, that clearness and concreteness constantly depend, for any pictorial whole, on some *concentrated* individual notation of them. That notation goes forward here in the mind of little Hyacinth, immensely quickened by the fact of its so matter-ing to his very life what he does make of things: which passion of intelligence is, as I have already hinted, precisely his highest value for our curiosity and our sym-pathy. Yet if his highest it is not at all his only one, since the truth for "a young man in a book" by no means entirely resides in his being either exquisitely sensi-tive or shiningly clever. It resides in some such measure of these things as may consort with the fine measure of other things too—with that of the other faces of his situation and character. If he's too sensitive and too clever for *them*, if he knows more than is likely or natural—for *him*—it's as if he weren't at all, as if he were false and impossible. Extreme and attaching always the difficulty of fixing at a hundred points the place where one's impelled *bonhomme* may feel enough and "know" enough—or be in the way of learning enough—for his maximum dramatic value without feeling and knowing too much for his minimum verisimilitude, his proper fusion with the fable. This is the charming, the tormenting, the eternal little matter *to be made right*, in all the weaving of silver threads and tapping on golden nails; and I should take perhaps too fantastic a comfort—I mean were not the comforts of the artist just of the raw essence of fantasy—in any glimpse of such achieved rightnesses, whether in my own work or that of others. In no work whatever, doubtless, are they the felicities the most frequent; but they have so inherent a price that even the traceable attempt at them, wherever met, sheds, I think, a fine influence about.

I have for example a weakness of sympathy with that constant effort of George Eliot's which plays through Adam Bede and Felix Holt and Tito Melema, through Daniel Deronda and through Lydgate in "Middlemarch," through Maggie Tulliver, through Romola, through Dorothea Brooke and Gwendolen Harleth; the effort to show their adventures and their history—the author's subject-matter all—as determined by their feelings and the nature of their minds. Their emotions, their stirred intelligence, their moral consciousness, become thus, by sufficiently charmed perusal, our own very adventure. The creator of Deronda and of Romola is charged, I know, with having on occasion—as in dealing with those very celebrities themselves—left the figure, the concrete man and woman, too abstract by reason of the quantity of soul employed; but such mischances, where imagination and humour still keep them company, often have an interest that is wanting to agitations of the mere surface or to those that may be only taken for granted. I should even like to give myself the pleasure of retracing from one of my own productions to another the play of a like instinctive disposition, of catching in the fact, at one point after another, from "Roderick Hudson" to "The Golden Bowl," that provision for interest which consists in placing advantageously, placing right in the middle of the light, the most polished of possible mirrors of the subject. Rowland Mallet, in "Roderick Hudson," is exactly such a mirror, not a bit autobiographic or formally "first person" though he be, and I might exemplify the case through a long list, through the nature of such a "mind" even as the all-objective Newman in "The American," through the thickly-peopled imagination of Isabel Archer in "The Portrait of a Lady" (her imagination positively the deepest depth of her imbroglio) down to such unmistakeable examples as that of Merton Densher in "The Wings of the Dove," that of Lambert Strether in "The Ambassadors" (*he* a mirror verily of miraculous silver and quite pre-eminent, I think, for the connexion) and that of the Prince in the first half and that of the Princess in the second half of "The Golden Bowl." I should note the extent to which these persons are, so far as their other passions permit, intense *perceivers*, all, of their respective predicaments, and I should go on from them to fifty other examples; even to the divided Vanderbank of "The Awkward Age," the extreme pinch of whose romance is the vivacity in him, to his positive sorrow and loss, of the state of being aware; even to scanted Fleda Vetch in "The Spoils of Poynton," through whose own delicate vision of everything so little of the human value of her situation is wasted for us; even to the small recording governess confronted with the horrors of "The Turn of the Screw" and to the innocent child patching together all ineffectually those of "What Maisie Knew"; even in short, since I may name so few cases, to the disaffected guardian of an overgrown legend in "The Birthplace," to the luckless fine artist of "The Next Time," trying to despoil himself, for a "hit" and bread and butter, of his fatal fineness, to blunt the tips of his intellectual fingers, and to the hapless butler Brooksmith, ruined by good talk, disqualified for common domestic service by the beautiful growth of his habit of quiet attention, his faculty of appreciation.

The Stream of Consciousness

Most books start with sensations, as the simplest mental facts, and proceed synthetically, constructing each higher stage from those below it. But this is abandoning the empirical method of investigation. No one ever had a simple sensation by itself. Consciousness, from our natal day, is of a teeming multiplicity of objects and relations, and what we call simple sensations are results of discriminative attention, pushed often to a very high degree. It is astonishing what havoc is wrought in psychology by admitting at the outset apparently innocent suppositions, that nevertheless contain a flow. The bad consequences develop themselves later on, and are irremediable, being woven through the whole texture of the work. The notion that sensations, being the simplest things, are the first things to take up in psychology is one of these suppositions. The only thing which psychology has a right to postulate at the outset is the fact of thinking itself, and that must first be taken up and analyzed. If sensations then prove to be amongst the elements of the thinking, we shall be no worse off as respects them than if we had taken them for granted at the start.

The first fact for us, then, as psychologists, is that thinking of some sort goes on. I use the word thinking . . . for every form of consciousness indiscriminately. If we could say in English "it thinks," as we say "it rains" or "it blows," we should be stating the fact most simply and with the minimum of assumption. As we cannot, we must simply say that *thought goes on.* . . .

It is obvious and palpable that our state of mind is never precisely the same. Every thought we have of a given fact is, strictly speaking, unique, and only bears a resemblance of kind with our other thoughts of the same fact. When the identical fact recurs, we *must* think of it in a fresh manner, see it under a somewhat different angle, apprehend it in different relations from those in which it last appeared. And the thought by which we cognize it is the thought of it-in-those-relations, a though suffused with the consciousness of all that dim context. Often we are ourselves struck at the strange differences in our successive views of the same thing. We wonder how we ever could have opined as we did last month about a certain matter. We have outgrown the possibility of that state of mind, we know not how. From one year to another we see things in new lights. What was unreal has grown real, and what was exciting is insipid. . . .

No doubt it is often *convenient* to formulate the mental facts in an atomistic sort of way, and to treat the higher states of consciousness as if they were all built out of unchanging simple ideas. It is convenient often to treat curves as if they were composed of small straight lines, and electricity and nerve-force as if they were fluids. But in the one case as in the other we must never forget that we are talking symbolically, and that there is nothing in nature to answer to our words. *A permanently existing "idea" or "Vorstellung" which makes its appearance before the footlights of consciousness at periodical intervals, is as mythological an entity as the Jack of Spades.*

What makes it convenient to use the mythological formulas is the whole or-

From *The Principles of Psychology*, New York, 1890, pp. 224-5, 233, 235-42, 243-6, 249-55.

ganization of speech, which, as was remarked a while ago, was not made by psychologists, but by men who were as a rule only interested in the facts their mental states revealed. They only spoke of their states as *ideas of this or of that thing*. What wonder, then, that the thought is most easily conceived under the law of the thing whose name it bears! If the thing is composed of parts, then we suppose that the thought of the thing must be composed of the thoughts of the parts. If one part of the thing have appeared in the same thing or in other things on former occasions, why then we must be having even now the very same "idea" of that part which was there on those occasions. If the thing is simple, its thought is simple. If it is multitudinous, it must require a multitude of thoughts to think it. If a succession, only a succession of thoughts can know it. If permanent, its thought is permanent. And so on *ad libitum*. What after all is so natural as to assume that one object, called by one name, should be known by one affection of the mind? But, if language must thus influence us, the agglutinative languages, and even Greek and Latin with their declensions, would be the better guides. Names did not appear in them inalterable, but changed their shape to suit the context in which they lay. It must have been easier then than now to conceive of the same object as being thought of at different times in non-identical conscious states. . . .

A necessary consequence of the belief in permanent self-identical psychic facts that absent themselves and recur periodically is the Humian doctrine that our thought is composed of separate independent parts and is not a sensibly continuous stream. That this doctrine entirely misrepresents the natural appearances is what I next shall try to show. . . .

I can only define "continuous" as that which is without breach, crack, or division. I have already said that the breach from one mind to another is perhaps the greatest breach in nature. The only breaches that can well be conceived to occur within the limits of a single mind would either be *interruptions, time-gaps* during which the consciousness went out altogether to come into existence again at a later moment; or they would be breaks in the *quality*, or content, of the thought, so abrupt that the segment that followed had no connection whatever with the one that went before. The proposition that within each personal consciousness thought feels continuous, means two things:

1. That even where there is a time-gap the consciousness after it feels as if it belonged together with the consciousness before it, as another part of the same self;

2. That the changes from one moment to another in the quality of the consciousness are never absolutely abrupt.

The case of the time-gaps, as the simplest, shall be taken first. And first of all a word about time-gaps of which the consciousness may not be itself aware. . . . If the consciousness is not aware of them, it cannot feel them as interruptions. In the unconsciousness produced by nitrous oxide and other anæsthetics, in that of epilepsy and fainting, the broken edges of the sentient life may meet and merge over the gap, much as the feelings of space of the opposite margins of the "blind spot" meet and merge over that objective interruption to the sensitiveness of the eye. Such consciousness as this, whatever it be for the onlooking psychologist, is for itself unbroken. It *feels* unbroken; a waking day of it is sensibly a unit as long as that day lasts, in the sense in which the hours themselves are units, as having all their parts next each other, with no intrusive alien substance between. To expect the consciousness to feel the interruptions of its objective continuity as gaps, would be like expecting the eye to feel a gap of silence because it does not hear, or the ear to feel a gap of darkness because it does not see. So much for the gaps that are unfelt.

With the felt gaps the case is different. On waking from sleep, we usually know that we have been unconscious, and we often have an accurate judgment of how long. The judgment here is certainly an inference from sensible signs, and its ease is due to long practice in the particular field. The result of it, however, is that the consciousness is, *for itself*, not what it was in the former case, but interrupted and discontinuous, in the mere sense of the words. But in the other sense of continuity, the sense of the parts being inwardly connected and belonging together because they are parts of a common whole, the consciousness remains sensibly continuous and one. What now is the common whole? The natural name for it is *myself*, *I*, or *me*.

When Paul and Peter wake up in the same bed, and recognize that they have been asleep, each one of them mentally reaches back and makes connection with but *one* of the two streams of thought which were broken by the sleeping hours. As the current of an electrode buried in the ground unerringly finds its way to its own similarly buried mate, across no matter how much intervening earth; so Peter's present instantly finds out Peter's past, and never by mistake knits itself on to that of Paul. Paul's thought in turn is as little liable to go astray. The past thought of Peter is appropriated by the present Peter alone. He may have a *knowledge*, and a correct one too, of what Paul's last drowsy states of mind were as he sank into sleep, but it is an entirely different sort of knowledge from that which he has of his own last states. He *remembers* his own states, whilst he only *conceives* Paul's. Remembrance is like direct feeling; its object is suffused with a warmth and intimacy to which no object of mere conception ever attains. This quality of warmth and intimacy and immediacy is what Peter's *present* thought also possesses for itself. So sure as this present is me, is mine, it says, so sure is anything else that comes with the same warmth and intimacy and immediacy, me and mine. What the qualities called warmth and intimacy may in themselves be will have to be matter for future consideration. But whatever past feelings appear with those qualities must be admitted to receive the greeting of the present mental state, to be owned by it, and accepted as belonging together with it in a common self. This community of self is what the time-gap cannot break in twain, and is why a present thought, although not ignorant of the time-gap, can still regard itself as continuous with certain chosen portions of the past.

Consciousness, then, does not appear to itself chopped up in bits. Such words as "chain" or "train" do not describe it fitly as it presents itself in the first instance. It is nothing jointed; it flows. A "river" or a "stream" are the metaphors by which it is most naturally described. *In talking of it hereafter, let us call it the stream of thought, of consciousness, or of subjective life.*

But now there appears, even within the limits of the same self, and between thoughts all of which alike have this same sense of belonging together, a kind of jointing and separateness among the parts, of which this statement seems to take no account. I refer to the breaks that are produced by sudden *contrasts in the quality* of the successive segments of the stream of thought. If the words "chain" and "train" had no natural fitness in them, how came such words to be used at all? Does not a loud explosion rend the consciousness upon which it abruptly breaks, in twain? Does not every sudden shock, appearance of a new object, or change in a sensation, create a real interruption, sensibly felt as such, which cuts the conscious stream across at the moment at which it appears? Do not such interruptions smite us every hour of our lives, and have we the right, in their presence, still to call our consciousness a continuous stream?

This objection is based partly on a confusion and partly on a superficial introspective view.

The confusion is between the thoughts themselves, taken as subjective facts, and the things of which they are aware. It is natural to make this confusion, but easy to avoid it when once put on one's guard. The things are discrete and discontinuous; they do pass before us in a train or chain, making often explosive appearances and rending each other in twain. But their comings and goings and contrasts no more break the flow of the thought that thinks them than they break the time and the space in which they lie. A silence may be broken by a thunderclap, and we may be so stunned and confused for a moment by the shock as to give no instant account to ourselves of what has happened. But that very confusion is a mental state, and a state that passes us straight over from the silence to the sound. The transition between the thought of one object and the thought of another is no more a break in the *thought* than a joint in a bamboo is a break in the wood. It is a part of the *consciousness* as much as the joint is a part of the *bamboo.*

The superficial introspective view is the overlooking, even when the things are contrasted with each other most violently, of the large amount of affinity that may still remain between the thoughts by whose means they are cognized. Into the awareness of the thunder itself the awareness of the previous silence creeps and continues; for what we hear when the thunder crashes is not thunder *pure,* but thunder-breaking-upon-silence-and-contrasting-with-it. Our feeling of the same objective thunder, coming in this way, is quite different from what it would be were the thunder a continuation of previous thunder. The thunder itself we believe to abolish and exclude the silence; but the *feeling* of the thunder is also a feeling of the silence as just gone; and it would be difficult to find in the actual concrete consciousness of man a feeling so limited to the present as not to have an inkling of anything that went before. Here, again, language works against our perception of the truth. We name our thoughts simply, each after its thing, as if each knew its own thing and nothing else. What each really knows is clearly the thing it is named for, with dimly perhaps a thousand other things. It ought to be named after all of them, but it never is. Some of them are always things known a moment ago more clearly; others are things to be known more clearly a moment hence. Our own bodily position, attitude, condition, is one of the things of which *some* awareness, however inattentive, invariably accompanies the knowledge of whatever else we know. We think; and as we think we feel our bodily selves as the seat of the thinking. If the thinking be *our* thinking, it must be suffused through all its parts with that peculiar warmth and intimacy that makes it come as ours. . . . *Whatever* the content of the ego may be, it is habitually felt *with* everything else by us humans, and must form a *liaison* between all the things of which we become successively aware. . . .

As we take . . . a general view of the wonderful stream of our consciousness, what strikes us first is . . . [the] different pace of its parts. Like a bird's life, it seems to be made of an alternation of flights and perchings. The rhythm of language expresses this, where every thought is expressed in a sentence, and every sentence closed by a period. The resting-places are usually occupied by sensorial imaginations of some sort, whose peculiarity is that they can be held before the mind for an indefinite time, and contemplated without changing; the places of flight are filled with thoughts of relations, static or dynamic, that for the most part obtain between the matters contemplated in the periods of comparative rest.

Let us call the resting-places the "substantive parts," and the places of flight the "transitive parts," of the stream of thought. It then appears that the main end of our thinking is at all times the attainment of some other substantive part than the one from which we have just been dislodged. And we may say that the main use of the transitive parts is to lead us from one substantive conclusion to another.

Now it is very difficult, introspectively, to see the transitive parts for what they really are. If they are but flights to a conclusion, stopping them to look at them before the conclusion is reached is really annihilating them. Whilst if we wait till the conclusion *be* reached, it so exceeds them in vigor and stability that it quite eclipses and swallows them up in its glare. Let anyone try to cut a thought across in the middle and get a look at its section, and he will see how difficult the introspective observation of the transitive tracts is. The rush of the thought is so headlong that it almost always brings us up at the conclusion before we can arrest it. Or if our purpose is nimble enough and we do arrest it, it ceases forthwith to be itself. As a snowflake crystal caught in the warm hand is no longer a crystal but a drop, so, instead of catching the feeling of relation moving to its term, we find we have caught some substantive thing, usually the last word we were pronouncing, statically taken, and with its function, tendency, and particular meaning in the sentence quite evaporated. The attempt at introspective analysis in these cases is in fact like seizing a spinning top to catch its motion, or trying to turn up the gas quickly enough to see how the darkness looks. And the challenge to *produce* these psychoses, which is sure to be thrown by doubting psychologists at anyone who contends for their existence, is as unfair as Zeno's treatment of the advocates of motion, when, asking them to point out in what place an arrow *is* when it moves, he argues the falsity of their thesis from their inability to make to so preposterous a question an immediate reply. . . .

If there be such things as feelings at all, *then so surely as relations between objects exist in rerum naturâ, so surely, and more surely, do feelings exist to which these relations are known.* There is not a conjunction or a preposition, and hardly an adverbial phrase, syntactic form, or inflection of voice, in human speech, that does not express some shading or other of relation which we at some moment actually feel to exist between the larger objects of our thought. If we speak objectively, it is the real relations that appear revealed; if we speak subjectively, it is the stream of consciousness that matches each of them by an inward coloring of its own. In either case the relations are numberless, and no existing language is capable of doing justice to all their shades.

We ought to say a feeling of *and*, a feeling of *if*, a feeling of *but*, and a feeling of *by*, quite as readily as we say a feeling of *blue* or a feeling of *cold*. Yet we do not: so inveterate has our habit become of recognizing the existence of the substantive parts alone, that language almost refuses to lend itself to any other use. The Empiricists have always dwelt on its influence in making us suppose that where we have a separate name, a separate thing must needs be there to correspond with it; and they have rightly denied the existence of the mob of abstract entities, principles, and forces, in whose favor no other evidence than this could be brought up. But they have said nothing of that obverse error . . . of supposing that where there is *no* name no entity can exist. All *dumb* or anonymous psychic states have, owing to this error, been coolly suppressed; or, if recognized at all, have been named after the substantive perception they led to, as thoughts "about" this object or "about" that, the stolid word *about* engulfing all their delicate idiosyncrasies in its monotonous sound. Thus the greater and greater accentuation and isolation of the substantive parts have continually gone on. . . .

So much for the transitive states. But there are other unnamed states or qualities of states that are just as important and just as cognitive as they, and just as much unrecognized by the traditional sensationalist and intellectualist philosophies of mind. The first fails to find them at all, the second finds their *cognitive function,* but denies that anything in the way of *feeling* has a share in bringing it about. Examples will make clear what these inarticulate psychoses, due to waxing and waning excitements of the brain, are like.

Suppose three successive persons say to us: "Wait!" "Hark!" "Look!" Our consciousness is thrown into three quite different attitudes of expectancy, although no definite object is before it in any one of the three cases. Leaving out different actual bodily attitudes, and leaving out the reverberating images of the three words, which are of course diverse, probably no one will deny the existence of a residual conscious affection, a sense of the direction from which an impression is about to come, although no positive impression is yet there. Meanwhile we have no names for the psychoses in question but the names hark, look, and wait.

Suppose we try to recall a forgotten name. The state of our consciousness is peculiar. There is a gap therein; but no mere gap. It is a gap that is intensely active. A sort of wraith of the name is in it, beckoning us in a given direction, making us at moments tingle with the sense of our closeness, and then letting us sink back without the longed-for term. If wrong names are proposed to us, this singularly definite gap acts immediately so as to negate them. They do not fit into its mould. And the gap of one word does not feel like the gap of another, all empty of content as both might seem necessarily to be when described as gaps. When I vainly try to recall the name of Spalding, my consciousness is far removed from what it is when I vainly try to recall the name of Bowles. Here some ingenious persons will say: "How *can* the two consciousnesses be different when the terms which might make them different are not there? All that is there, so long as the effort to recall is vain, is the bare effort itself. How should that differ in the two cases? You are making it seem to differ by prematurely filling it out with the different names, although these, by the hypothesis, have not yet come. Stick to the two efforts as they are, without naming them after facts not yet existent, and you'll be quite unable to designate any point in which they differ." Designate, truly enough. We can only designate the difference by borrowing the names of objects not yet in the mind. Which is to say that our psychological vocabulary is wholly inadequate to name the differences that exist, even such strong differences as these. But namelessness is compatible with existence. There are innumerable consciousnesses of emptiness, no one of which taken in itself has a name, but all different from each other. The ordinary way is to assume that they are all emptinesses of consciousness, and so the same state. But the feeling of an absence is *toto cœlo* other than the absence of a feeling. It is an intense feeling. The rhythm of a lost word may be there without a sound to clothe it; or the evanescent sense of something which is the initial vowel or consonant may mock us fitfully, without growing more distinct. Every one must know the tantalizing effect of the blank rhythm of some forgotten verse, restlessly dancing in one's mind, striving to be filled out with words.

Again, what is the strange difference between an experience tasted for the first time and the same experience recognized as familiar, as having been enjoyed before, though we cannot name it or say where or when? A tune, an odor, a flavor sometimes carry this inarticulate feeling of their familiarity so deep into our consciousness that we are fairly shaken by its mysterious emotional power. But strong and characteristic as this psychosis is—it probably is due to the submaximal excitement of wide-spreading associational brain-tracts—the only name we have for all its shadings is "sense of familiarity."

When we read such phrases as "naught but," "either one or the other," "*a* is *b*, but," "although it is, nevertheless," "it is an excluded middle, there is no *tertium quid*," and a host of other verbal skeletons of logical relation, is it true that there is nothing more in our minds than the words themselves as they pass? What then is the meaning of the words which we think we understand as we read? What makes that meaning different in one phrase from what it is in the other? "Who?" "When?" "Where?" Is the difference of felt meaning in these interrogatives nothing more than their difference of sound? And is it not (just like the difference of sound itself) known and understood in an affection of consciousness correlative to it, though so impalpable to direct examination? Is not the same true of such negatives as "no," "never," "not yet"?

The truth is that large tracts of human speech are nothing but *signs of direction* in thought, of which direction we nevertheless have an acutely discriminative sense, though no definite sensorial image plays any part in it whatsoever. Sensorial images are stable psychic facts; we can hold them still and look at them as long as we like. These bare images of logical movement, on the contrary, are psychic transitions, always on the wing, so to speak, and not to be glimpsed except in flight. Their function is to lead from one set of images to another. As they pass, we feel both the waxing and the waning images in a way altogether peculiar and a way quite different from the way of their full presence. If we try to hold fast the feeling of direction, the full presence comes and the feeling of direction is lost. The blank verbal scheme of the logical movement gives us the fleeting sense of the movement as we read it, quite as well as does a rational sentence awakening definite imaginations by its words.

What is that first instantaneous glimpse of some one's meaning which we have, when in vulgar phrase we say we "twig" it? Surely an altogether specific affection of our mind. And has the reader never asked himself what kind of a mental fact is his *intention of saying a thing* before he has said it? It is an entirely definite intention, distinct from all other intentions, an absolutely distinct state of consciousness, therefore; and yet how much of it consists of definite sensorial images, either of words or of things? Hardly anything! Linger, and the words and things come into the mind; the anticipatory intention, the divination is there no more. But as the words that replace it arrive, it welcomes them successively and calls them right if they agree with it, it rejects them and calls them wrong if they do not. It has therefore a nature of its own of the most positive sort, and yet what can we say about it without using words that belong to the later mental facts that replace it? The intention *to-say-so-and-so* is the only name it can receive. One may admit that a good third of our psychic life consists in these rapid premonitory perspective views of schemes of thought not yet articulate. How comes it about that a man reading something aloud for the first time is able immediately to emphasize all his words aright, unless from the very first he have a sense of at least the form of the sentence yet to come, which sense is fused with his consciousness of the present word, and modifies its emphasis in his mind so as to make him give it the proper accent as he utters it? Emphasis of this kind is almost altogether a matter of grammatical construction. If we read "no more" we expect presently to come upon a "than;" if we read "however" at the outset of a sentence it is a "yet," a "still," or a "nevertheless," that we expect. A noun in a certain position demands a verb in a certain mood and number, in another position it expects a relative pronoun. Adjectives call for nouns, verbs for adverbs, etc. etc. And this foreboding of the coming grammatical scheme combined with each successive uttered word is so practically accurate that a reader incapable of understanding four ideas of the book he is reading aloud, can nevertheless read it with the most delicately modulated expression of intelligence.

Some will interpret these facts by calling them all cases in which certain images, by laws of association, awaken others so very rapidly that we think afterwards we felt the very *tendencies* of the nascent images to arise, before they were actually there. For this school the only possible materials of consciousness are images of a perfectly definite nature. Tendencies exist, but they are facts for the outside psychologist rather than for the subject of the observation. The tendency is thus a *psychical* zero; only its *results* are felt.

Now what I contend for, and accumulate examples to show, is that "tendencies" are not only descriptions from without, but that they are among the *objects* of the stream, which is thus aware of them from within, and must be described as in very large measure constituted of *feelings* of *tendency*, often so vague that we are unable to name them at all. It is, in short, the re-instatement of the vague to its proper place in our mental life which I am so anxious to press on the attention. Mr. Galton and Prof. Huxley have . . . made one step in advance in exploding the ridiculous theory of Hume and Berkeley that we can have no images but of perfectly definite things. Another is made in the overthrow of the equally ridiculous notion that, whilst simple objective qualities are revealed to our knowledge in subjective feelings, relations are not. But these reforms are not half sweeping and radical enough. What must be admitted is that the definite images of traditional psychology form but the very smallest part of our minds as they actually live. The traditional psychology talks like one who should say a river consists of nothing but pailsful, spoonsful, quartpotsful, barrelsful, and other moulded forms of water. Even were the pails and the pots all actually standing in the stream, still between them the free water would continue to flow. It is just this free water of consciousness that psychologists resolutely overlook. Every definite image in the mind is steeped and dyed in the free water that flows round it. With it goes the sense of its relations, near and remote, the dying echo of whence it came to us, the dawning sense of whither it is to lead. The significance, the value, of the image is all in this halo or penumbra that surrounds and escorts it,—or rather that is fused into one with it and has become bone of its bone and flesh of its flesh; leaving it, it is true, an image of the same *thing* it was before, but making it an image of that thing newly taken and freshly understood.

HENRI BERGSON

Duration

The existence of which we are most assured and which we know best is unquestionably our own, for of every other object we have notions which may be considered external and superficial, whereas, of ourselves, our perception is internal and profound. What, then, do we find? In this privileged case, what is the precise meaning of the word "exist"? . . .

I find, first of all, that I pass from state to state. I am warm or cold, I am merry or sad, I work or I do nothing, I look at what is around me or I think of something else. Sensations, feelings, volitions, ideas—such are the changes into which my existence is divided and which color it in turns. I change, then, without ceasing. But this is not saying enough. Change is far more radical than we are at first inclined to suppose.

For I speak of each of my states as if it formed a block and were a separate whole. I say indeed that I change, but the change seems to me to reside in the passage from one state to the next: of each state, taken separately, I am apt to think that it remains the same during all the time that it prevails. Nevertheless, a slight effort of attention would reveal to me that there is no feeling, no idea, no volition which is not undergoing change every moment: if a mental state ceased to vary, its duration would cease to flow. Let us take the most stable of internal states, the visual perception of a motionless external object. The object may remain the same, I may look at it from the same side, at the same angle, in the same light; nevertheless the vision I now have of it differs from that which I have just had, even if only because the one is an instant older than the other. My memory is there, which conveys something of the past into the present. My mental state, as it advances on the road of time, is continually swelling with the duration which it accumulates: it goes on increasing—rolling upon itself, as a snowball on the snow. Still more is this the case with states more deeply internal, such as sensa-

From *Creative Evolution* [1907], translated from the French by Arthur Mitchell, New York, 1911, pp. 1-7. Copyright 1911; copyright renewed 1939 by Holt, Rinehart, and Winston, Inc. Reprinted by permission of Holt, Rinehart, and Winston, and Macmillan & Co. Ltd.
From *An Introduction to Metaphysics* [1903], translated from the French by T. E. Hulme, New York, 1912, pp. 9-15, 38-9, 59-64. Reprinted by permission of G. P. Putnam's Sons.

tions, feelings, desires, etc., which do not correspond, like a simple visual perception, to an unvarying external object. But it is expedient to disregard this uninterrupted change, and to notice it only when it becomes sufficient to impress a new attitude on the body, a new direction on the attention. Then, and then only, we find that our state has changed. The truth is that we change without ceasing, and that the state itself is nothing but change.

This amounts to saying that there is no essential difference between passing from one state to another and persisting in the same state. If the state which "remains the same" is more varied than we think, on the other hand the passing from one state to another resembles, more than we imagine, a single state being prolonged; the transition is continuous. But, just because we close our eyes to the unceasing variation of every psychical state, we are obliged, when the change has become so considerable as to force itself on our attention, to speak as if a new state were placed alongside the previous one. Of this new state we assume that it remains unvarying in its turn, and so on endlessly. The apparent discontinuity of the psychical life is then due to our attention being fixed on it by a series of separate acts: actually there is only a gentle slope; but in following the broken line of our acts of attention, we think we perceive separate steps. True, our psychic life is full of the unforeseen. A thousand incidents arise, which seem to be cut off from those which precede them, and to be disconnected from those which follow. Discontinuous though they appear, however, in point of fact they stand out against the continuity of a background on which they are designed, and to which indeed they owe the intervals that separate them; they are the beats of the drum which break forth here and there in the symphony. Our attention fixes on them because they interest it more, but each of them is borne by the fluid mass of our whole psychical existence. Each is only the best illuminated point of a moving zone which comprises all that we feel or think or will—all, in short, that we are at any given moment. It is this entire zone which in reality makes up our state. Now, states thus defined cannot be regarded as distinct elements. They continue each other in an endless flow.

But, as our attention has distinguished and separated them artificially, it is obliged next to reunite them by an artificial bond. It imagines, therefore, a formless *ego*, indifferent and unchangeable, on which it threads the psychic states which it has set up as independent entities. Instead of a flux of fleeting shades merging into each other, it perceives distinct and, so to speak, *solid* colors, set side by side like the beads of a necklace; it must perforce then suppose a thread, also itself solid, to hold the beads together. But if this colorless substratum is perpetually colored by that which covers it, it is for us, in its indeterminateness, as if it did not exist, since we only perceive what is colored, or, in other words, psychic states. As a matter of fact, this substratum has no reality; it is merely a symbol intended to recall unceasingly to our consciousness the artificial character of the process by which the attention places clean-cut states side by side, where actually there is a continuity which unfolds. If our existence were composed of separate states with an impassive ego to unite them, for us there would be no duration. For an ego which does not change does not *endure*, and a psychic state which remains the same so long as it is not replaced by the following state does not *endure* either. Vain, therefore, is the attempt to range such states beside each other on the ego supposed to sustain them: never can these solids strung upon a solid make up that duration which flows. What we actually obtain in this way is an artificial imitation of the internal life, a static equivalent which will lend itself better to the requirements of logic and language, just because we have eliminated from it the element of real time. But, as regards the psychical life unfolding beneath the symbols which conceal it, we readily perceive that time is just the stuff it is made of.

There is, moreover, no stuff more resistant nor more substantial. For our duration is not merely one instant replacing another; if it were, there would never be anything but the present—no prolonging of the past into the actual, no evolution, no concrete duration. Duration is the continuous progress of the past which gnaws into the future and which swells as it advances. And as the past grows without ceasing, so also there is no limit to its preservation. Memory . . . is not a faculty of putting away recollections in a drawer, or of inscribing them in a register. There is no register, no drawer; there is not even, properly speaking, a faculty, for a faculty works intermittently, when it will or when it can, whilst the piling up of the past upon the past goes on without relaxation. In reality, the past is preserved by itself, automatically. In its entirety, probably, it follows us at every instant; all that we have felt, thought and willed from our earliest infancy is there, leaning over the present which is about to join it, pressing against the portals of consciousness that would fain leave it outside. The cerebral mechanism is arranged just so as to drive back into the unconscious almost the whole of this past, and to admit beyond the threshold only that which can cast light on the present situation or further the action now being prepared—in short, only that which can give *useful* work. At the most, a few superfluous recollections may succeed in smuggling themselves through the half-open door. These memories, messengers from the unconscious, remind us of what we are dragging behind us unawares. But, even though we may have no distinct idea of it, we feel vaguely that our past remains present to us. What are we, in fact, what is our *character*, if not the condensation of the history that we have lived from our birth—nay, even before our birth, since we bring with us prenatal dispositions? Doubtless we think with only a small part of our past, but it is with our entire past, including the original bent of our soul, that we desire, will and act. Our past, then, as a whole, is made manifest to us in its impulse; it is felt in the form of tendency, although a small part of it only is known in the form of idea.

From this survival of the past it follows that consciousness cannot go through the same state twice. The circumstances may still be the same, but they will act no longer on the same person, since they find him at a new moment of his history. Our personality, which is being built up each instant with its accumulated experience, changes without ceasing. By changing, it prevents any state, although superficially identical with another, from ever repeating it in its very depth. That is why our duration is irreversible. We could not live over again a single moment, for we should have to begin by effacing the memory of all that had followed. Even could we erase this memory from our intellect, we could not from our will.

Thus our personality shoots, grows and ripens without ceasing. Each of its moments is something new added to what was before. We may go further: it is not only something new, but something unforeseeable. Doubtless, my present state is explained by what was in me and by what was acting on me a moment ago. In analyzing it I should find no other elements. But even a superhuman intelligence would not have been able to foresee the simple indivisible form which gives to these purely abstract elements their concrete organization. For to foresee consists of projecting into the future what has been perceived in the past, or of imagaining for a later time a new grouping, in a new order, of elements already perceived. But that which has never been perceived, and which is at the same time simple, is necessarily unforeseeable. Now such is the case with each of our states, regarded as a moment in a history that is gradually unfolding: it is simple, and it cannot have been already perceived, since it concentrates in its indivisibility all that has been perceived and what the present is adding to it besides. It is an original moment of a no less original history.

The finished portrait is explained by the features of the model, by the nature of the artist, by the colors spread out on the palette; but, even with the knowledge of what explains it, no one, not even the artist, could have foreseen exactly what the portrait would be, for to predict it would have been to produce it before it was produced—an absurd hypothesis which is its own refutation. Even so with regard to the moments of our life, of which we are the artisans. Each of them is a kind of creation. And just as the talent of the painter is formed or deformed—in any case, is modified—under the very influence of the works he produces, so each of our states, at the moment of its issue, modifies our personality, being indeed the new form that we are just assuming. It is then right to say that what we do depends on what we are; but it is necessary to add also that we are, to a certain extent, what we do, and that we are creating ourselves continually. This creation of self by self is the more complete, the more one reasons on what one does. For reason does not proceed in such matters as in geometry, where impersonal premisses are given once for all, and an impersonal conclusion must perforce be drawn. Here, on the contrary, the same reasons may dictate to different persons, or to the same person at different moments, acts profoundly different, although equally reasonable. The truth is that they are not quite the same reasons, since they are not those of the same person, nor of the same moment. That is why we cannot deal with them in the abstract, from outside, as in geometry, nor solve for another the problems by which he is faced in life. Each must solve them from within, on his own account. But we need not go more deeply into this. We are seeking only the precise meaning that our consciousness gives to this word "exist," and we find that, for a conscious being, to exist is to change, to change is to mature, to mature is to go on creating oneself endlessly.

When I direct my attention inward to contemplate my own self (supposed for the moment to be inactive), I perceive at first, as a crust solidified on the surface, all the perceptions which come to it from the material world. These perceptions are clear, distinct, juxtaposed or juxtaposable one with another; they tend to group themselves into objects. Next, I notice the memories which more or less adhere to these perceptions and which serve to interpret them. These memories have been detached, as it were, from the depth of my personality, drawn to the surface by the perceptions which resemble them; they rest on the surface of my mind without being absolutely myself. Lastly, I feel the stir of tendencies and motor habits—a crowd of virtual actions, more or less firmly bound to these perceptions and memories. All these clearly defined elements appear more distinct from me, the more distinct they are from each other. Radiating, as they do, from within outwards, they form, collectively, the surface of a sphere which tends to grow larger and lose itself in the exterior world. But if I draw myself in from the periphery towards the center, if I search in the depth of my being that which is most uniformly, most constantly, and most enduringly myself, I find an altogether different thing.

There is, beneath these sharply cut crystals and this frozen surface, a continuous flux which is not comparable to any flux I have ever seen. There is a succession of states, each of which announces that which follows and contains that which precedes it. They can, properly speaking, only be said to form multiple states when I have already passed them and turn back to observe their tracks. Whilst I was experiencing them they were so solidly organized, so profoundly animated with a common life, that I could not have said where any one of them finished or where another commenced. In reality no one of them begins or ends, but all extend into each other.

This inner life may be compared to the unrolling of a coil, for there is no living being who does not feel himself coming gradually to the end of his role; and to live is to grow old. But it may just as well be compared to a continual rolling up, like that of a thread on a ball, for our past follows us, it swells incessantly with the present that it picks up on its way; and consciousness means memory.

But actually it is neither an unrolling nor a rolling up, for these two similes evoke the idea of lines and surfaces whose parts are homogeneous and superposable on one another. Now, there are no two identical moments in the life of the same conscious being. Take the simplest sensation, suppose it constant, absorb in it the entire personality: the consciousness which will accompany this sensation cannot remain identical with itself for two consecutive moments, because the second moment always contains, over and above the first, the memory that the first has bequeathed to it. A consciousness which could experience two identical moments would be a consciousness without memory. It would die and be born again continually. In what other way could one represent unconsciousness?

It would be better, then, to use as a comparison the myriad-tinted spectrum, with its insensible gradations leading from one shade to another. A current of feeling which passed along the spectrum, assuming in turn the tint of each of its shades, would experience a series of gradual changes, each of which would announce the one to follow and would sum up those which preceded it. Yet even here the successive shades of the spectrum always remain external one to another. They are juxtaposed; they occupy space. But pure duration, on the contrary, excludes all idea of juxtaposition, reciprocal externality, and extension.

Let us, then, rather, imagine an infinitely small elastic body, contracted, if it were possible, to a mathematical point. Let this be drawn out gradually in such a manner that from the point comes a constantly lengthening line. Let us fix our attention not on the line as a line, but on the action by which it is traced. Let us bear in mind that this action, in spite of its duration, is indivisible if accomplished without stopping, that if a stopping-point is inserted, we have two actions instead of one, that each of these separate actions is then the indivisible operation of which we speak, and that it is not the moving action itself which is divisible, but, rather, the stationary line it leaves behind it as its track in space. Finally, let us free ourselves from the space which underlies the movement in order to consider only the movement itself, the act of tension or extension; in short, pure mobility. We shall have this time a more faithful image of the development of our self in duration.

However, even this image is incomplete, and, indeed, every comparison will be insufficient, because the unrolling of our duration resembles in some of its aspects the unity of an advancing movement and in others the multiplicity of expanding states; and, clearly, no metaphor can express one of these two aspects without sacrificing the other. If I use the comparison of the spectrum with its thousand shades, I have before me a thing already made, whilst duration is continually in the making. If I think of an elastic which is being stretched, or of a spring which is extended or relaxed, I forget the richness of color, characteristic of duration that is lived, to see only the simple movement by which consciousness passes from one shade to another. The inner life is all this at once: variety of qualities, continuity of progress, and unity of direction. It cannot be represented by images.

But it is even less possible to represent it by *concepts*, that is by abstract, general, or simple ideas. . . .

That personality has unity cannot be denied; but such an affirmation teaches one nothing about the extraordinary nature of the particular unity presented by personality. That our self is multiple I also agree, but then it must be understood that it is a multiplicity which has nothing in common with any other multiplicity. What is really important for philosophy is to know exactly what unity, what multiplicity, and what reality superior both to abstract unity and multiplicity the multiple unity of the self actually is. Now philosophy will know this only when it recovers possession of the simple intuition of the self by the self. Then, according to the direction it chooses for its descent from this summit, it will arrive at unity or multiplicity, or at any one of the concepts by which we try to define the moving life of the self. But no mingling of these concepts would give anything which at all resembles the self that endures.

If we are shown a solid cone, we see without any difficulty how it narrows towards the summit and tends to be lost in a mathematical point, and also how it enlarges in the direction of the base into an indefinitely increasing circle. But neither the point nor the circle, nor the juxtaposition of the two on a plane, would give us the least idea of a cone. The same thing holds true of the unity and multiplicity of mental life, and of the zero and the infinite towards which empiricism and rationalism conduct personality. . . .

Let us express the same idea with more precision. If I consider duration as a multiplicity of moments bound to each other by a unity which goes through them like a thread, then, however short the chosen duration may be, these moments are unlimited in number. I can suppose them as close together as I please; there will always be between these mathematical points other mathematical points, and so on to infinity. Looked at from the point of view of multiplicity, then, duration disintegrates into a powder of moments, none of which endures, each being an instantaneity. If, on the other hand, I consider the unity which binds the moment together, this cannot endure either, since by hypothesis everything that is changing, and everything that is really durable in the duration, has been put to the account of the multiplicity of moments. As I probe more deeply into its essence, this unity will appear to me as some immobile substratum of that which is moving, as some intemporal essence of time; it is this that I shall call eternity; an eternity of death, since it is nothing else than the movement emptied of the mobility which made its life. Closely examined, the opinions of the opposing schools on the subject of duration would be seen to differ solely in this, that they attribute a capital importance to one or the other of these two concepts. Some adhere to the point of view of the multiple; they set up as concrete reality the distinct moments of a time which they have reduced to powder; the unity which enables us to call the grains a powder they hold to be much more artificial. Others, on the contrary, set up the unity of duration as concrete reality. They place themselves in the eternal. But as their eternity remains, notwithstanding, abstract, since it is empty, being the eternity of a concept which, by hypothesis, excludes from itself the opposing concept, one does not see how this eternity would permit of an indefinite number of moments coexisting in it. In the first hypothesis we have a world resting on nothing, which must end and begin again of its own accord at each instant. In the second we have an infinity of abstract eternity, about which also it is just as difficult to understand why it does not remain enveloped in itself and how it allows things to coexist with it. But in both cases, and whichever of the two metaphysics it be that one is switched into, time appears, from the psychological point of view, as a mixture of two abstractions, which admit of neither degrees nor shades. In one system as in the other, there is only one unique duration, which carries everything with it—a bottomless, bankless river, which flows without assignable force in a direction which could not be defined. Even then we can call it only a river, and the river only flows, because reality obtains from the two doctrines this concession, profiting by a moment of perplexity in their logic. As soon as they recover from this perplexity, they freeze this flux either into an immense solid sheet, or into an infinity of crystallized needles, always into a *thing* which necessarily partakes of the immobility of a *point of view*.

It is quite otherwise if we place ourselves from the first, by an effort of intuition, in the concrete flow of duration. Certainly, we shall then find no logical reason for positing multiple and diverse durations. Strictly, there might well be no other duration than our own, as, for example, there might be no other color in the world but orange. But just as a consciousness based on color, which sympathized internally with orange instead of perceiving it externally, would feel itself held between red and yellow, would even perhaps suspect beyond this last color a complete spectrum into which the continuity from red to yellow might expand naturally, so the intuition of our duration, far from leaving us suspended in the void as pure analysis would do, brings us into contact with a whole continuity of durations which we must try to follow, whether downwards or upwards; in both cases we can extend ourselves indefinitely by an increasingly violent effort, in both cases we transcend ourselves. In the first we advance towards a more and more attenuated duration, the pulsations of which, being rapider than ours, and dividing our simple sensation, dilute its quality into quantity; at the limit would be pure homogeneity, that pure *repetition* by which we define materiality. Advancing in the other direction, we approach a duration which *strains*, contracts, and intensifies itself more and more; at the limit would be eternity. No longer conceptual eternity, which is an eternity of death, but an eternity of life. A living, and therefore still moving eternity in which our own particular duration would be included as the vibrations are in light; an eternity which would be the concentration of all duration, as materiality is its dispersion. Between these two extreme limits intuition moves, and this movement is the very essence of metaphysics.

MARCEL PROUST

The Recapturing of Time

I feel that there is much to be said for the Celtic belief that the souls of those whom we have lost are held captive in some inferior being, in an animal, in a plant, in some inanimate object, and so effectively lost to us until the day (which to many never comes) when we happen to pass by the tree or to obtain possession of the object which forms their prison. Then they start and tremble, they call us by our name, and as soon as we have recognised their voice the spell is broken. We have delivered them: they have overcome death and return to share our life.

And so it is with our own past. It is a labour in vain to attempt to recapture it: all the efforts of our intellect must prove futile. The past is hidden somewhere outside the realm, beyond the reach of intellect, in some material object (in the sensation which that material object will give us) which we do not suspect. And as for that object, it depends on chance whether we come upon it or not before we ourselves must die.

Many years had elapsed during which nothing of Combray, save what was comprised in the theatre and the drama of my going to bed there, had any existence for me, when one day in winter, as I came home, my mother, seeing that I was cold, offered me some tea, a thing I did not ordinarily take. I declined at first, and then, for no particular reason, changed my mind. She sent out for one of those short, plump little cakes called "petites madeleines," which look as though they had been moulded in the fluted scallop of a pilgrim's shell. And soon, mechanically, weary after a dull day with the prospect of a depressing morrow, I raised to my lips a spoonful of the tea in which I had soaked a morsel of the cake. No sooner had the warm liquid, and the crumbs with it, touched my palate than a shudder ran through my whole body, and I stopped, intent upon the extraordinary changes that were taking place. An exquisite pleasure had invaded my senses, but individual, detached, with no suggestion of its origin. And at once the vicissitudes of life had become indifferent to me, its disasters innocuous, its brevity illusory—this new sensation having had on me the effect which love has of filling me with a precious essence; or rather this essence was not in me, it was myself. I had ceased now to feel mediocre, accidental, mortal. Whence could it have come to me, this all-powerful joy? I was conscious that it was connected with the taste of tea and cake, but that it infinitely transcended those savours, could not, indeed, be of the same nature as theirs. Whence did it come? What did it signify? How could I seize upon and define it?

I drink a second mouthful, in which I find nothing more than in the first, a third, which gives me rather less than the second. It is time to stop; the potion is losing its magic. It is plain that the object of my quest, the truth, lies not in the cup but in myself. The tea has called up in me, but does not itself understand, and can only repeat indefinitely with a gradual loss of strength, the same testimony; which I, too, cannot interpret, though I hope at least to be able to call upon the tea for it again and to find it there presently, intact and at my disposal, for my final enlightenment. I put down my cup and examine my own mind. It is for it to discover the truth. But how? What an abyss of uncertainty whenever the mind feels that some part of it has strayed beyond its own borders; when it, the seeker, is at once the dark region through which it must go seeking, where all its equipment will avail it nothing. Seek? More than that: create. It is face to face with something which does not so far exist, to which it alone can give reality and substance, which it alone can bring into the light of day.

And I begin again to ask myself what it could have been, this unremembered state which brought with it no logical proof of its existence, but only the sense that it was a happy, that it was a real state in whose presence other states of consciousness melted and vanished. I decide to attempt to make it reappear. I retrace my thoughts to the moment at which I drank the first spoonful of tea. I find again the same state, illumined by no fresh light. I compel my mind to make one further effort, to follow and recapture once again the fleeting sensation. And that nothing may interrupt it in its course I shut out every obstacle, every extraneous idea, I stop my ears and inhibit all attention to the sounds which come from the next room. And then, feeling that my mind is growing fatigued without having any success to report, I compel it for a change to enjoy that distraction which I have just denied it, to think of other things, to rest and refresh itself before the supreme attempt. And then for the second time I clear an empty space in front of it. I place in position before my mind's eye the still recent taste of that first mouthful, and I feel something start within me, something that leaves its resting-place and attempts to rise, something that has been embedded like an anchor at a great depth; I do not know yet what it is, but I can feel it mounting slowly; I can measure the resistance, I can hear the echo of great spaces traversed.

Undoubtedly what is thus palpitating in the depths of my being must be the image, the visual memory which, being linked to that taste, has tried to follow it into my conscious mind. But its struggles are too far off, too much confused; scarcely can I perceive the colourless reflection in which are blended the uncapturable whirling medley of radiant hues, and I cannot distinguish its form, cannot invite it, as the one possible interpreter, to translate to me the evidence of its contemporary, its inseparable paramour, the taste of cake soaked in tea; cannot ask it to inform me what special circumstance is in question, of what period in my past life.

Will it ultimately reach the clear surface of my consciousness, this memory, this old, dead moment which the magnetism of an identical moment has travelled so far to importune, to disturb, to raise up out of the very depths of my being? I cannot tell. Now that I feel nothing, it has stopped, has perhaps gone down again into its darkness, from which who can say whether it will ever rise? Ten times over I must essay the task, must lean down over the abyss. And each time the natural laziness which deters us from every difficult enterprise, every work of importance, has urged me to leave the thing alone, to drink my tea and to think merely of the worries of to-day and of my hopes for to-morrow, which let themselves be pondered over without effort or distress of mind.

And suddenly the memory returns. The taste was that of the little crumb of madeleine which on Sunday mornings at Combray (because on those mornings I did not go out before church-time), when I went to say good day to her in her bedroom, my aunt Léonie used to give me, dipping it first in her own cup of real or of lime-flower tea. The sight of the little madeleine had recalled nothing to my mind before I tasted it; perhaps because I had so often seen such things in the interval, without tasting them, on the trays in pastry-cooks' windows, that their image had dissociated itself from those Combray days to take its place among others more recent; perhaps because of those memories, so long abandoned and put out of mind, nothing now survived, everything was scattered; the forms of things, including that of the little scallop-shell of pastry, so richly sensual under its severe, religious folds, were either obliterated or had been so long dormant as to have lost the power of expansion which would have allowed them to resume their place in my consciousness. But when from a long-distant past nothing subsists, after the people are dead, after the things are broken and scattered, still, alone, more fragile, but with more vitality, more unsubstantial, more persistent, more faithful, the smell and taste of things remain poised a long time, like souls, ready to remind us, waiting and hoping for their moment, amid the ruins of all the rest; and bear unfaltering, in the tiny and almost impalpable drop of their essence, the vast structure of recollection.

And once I had recognized the taste of the crumb of madeleine soaked in her decoction of lime-flowers which my aunt used to give me (although I did not yet know and must long postpone the discovery of why this memory made me so happy) immediately the old grey house upon the street, where her room was, rose up like the scenery of a theatre to attach itself to the little pavilion, opening on to the garden, which had been built out behind it for my parents (the isolated panel which until that moment had been all that I could see); and with the house the town, from morning to night and in all weathers, the Square where I was sent before luncheon, the streets along which I used to run errands, the country roads we took when it was fine. And just as the Japanese amuse themselves by filling a porcelain bowl with water and steeping in it little crumbs of paper which until then are without character or form, but, the moment they become wet, stretch themselves and bend, take on colour and distinctive shape, become flowers or houses or people, permanent and recognisable, so in that moment all the flowers in our garden and in M. Swann's park, and the water-lilies on the Vivonne and the good folk of the village and their little dwellings and the parish church and the whole of Combray and of its surroundings, taking their proper shapes and growing solid, sprang into being, towns and gardens alike, from my cup of tea.

———————

Engrossed in . . . unhappy meditations . . . I had entered the court of the Guermantes residence and, in my absorption, failed to notice an automobile that was coming in; at the chauffeur's cry I had barely time to get out of the way and, in stepping back, struck my foot against some unevenly cut flagstones leading to a carriage house. In recovering my balance, I put my foot on a stone that was a little lower than the one next to it; immediately all my discouragement vanished before a feeling of happiness which I had experienced at different moments of my life, at the sight of trees I thought I recognised when driving around Balbec, or the church spires of Martinville, or the savour of a *madeleine* dipped in herb tea, or from many other sensations I have mentioned, which had seemed to me to be synthesised in the last works of Vinteuil. Just as when I tasted the *madeleine*, all anxiety as to the future, all intellectual doubt was dispelled. The misgivings that had been harassing me a moment before concerning the reality of my literary gifts, and even of literature itself, were suddenly banished as if by magic. But this time I made a firm resolve that I would not be satisfied to leave the question unanswered (as I did the day I tasted of a *madeleine* dipped in herb tea) as to why, without my having worked out any new line of reasoning or found any decisive argument, the difficulties that had seemed insoluble a short time before had now lost all their importance. The feeling of happiness which had just come over me was, indeed, exactly the same as I had experienced while eating the *madeleine*, but at that time I put off seeking the deep-lying causes for it. There was a purely material difference in the mental images evoked. A deep azure blue intoxicated my sight, impressions of coolness and dazzling light hovered near me and, in my eagerness to seize them, not daring to move—just as when I tasted the flavour of the *madeleine* and tried to bring back to my mind what it suggested to me—I stood there, swaying back and forth, as I had done a moment before, one foot on the higher stone and the other on the lower, indifferent to the possible amusement of the large crowd of chauffeurs. Each time that I merely repeated the action physically, the effort was in vain; but if I forgot the Guermantes reception and succeeded in recapturing the sensation I had felt the instant I placed my feet in that position, again the dazzling, elusive vision brushed me with its wings, as if to say, "Seize me in my flight, if you have the power, and try to solve the riddle of happiness I propound to you." And almost immediately I recognised it; it was Venice, about which my efforts at description and the supposed "snapshots" taken by my memory had never yielded me anything, but which was brought back to me by the sensation I had once felt as I stood on two uneven flagstones in the baptistry of Saint Mark's, and with that sensation came all the others connected with it that day, which had been waiting in their proper place in the series of forgotten days, until a sudden happening had imperiously commanded them to come forth. It was in the same way that the taste of the little *madeleine* had recalled Combray to my mind. But why had the mental images of Combray and Venice at their respective moments given me a joy like a sense of certainty, sufficient, without other proofs, to make me indifferent to death? While I was still putting this question to myself, determined this time to find the answer to it, I entered the Guermantes mansion—for we always put ahead of the subjective task we have to perform the outward role we are playing, and mine that day was that of an invited guest. But, when I reached the second story, a butler asked me to step for a moment into a small library adjoining the buffet, until the selection they were playing was finished, the Princess having forbidden that the doors be opened while it was being played. At that very moment a second signal came to reinforce the one I had received from the two uneven flagstones, and urged me to persevere in my task. What happened was that a servant, trying in vain to make no noise, struck a spoon against a plate. The same kind of felicity as I had received from the uneven paving stones now came over me; the sensations were again those of great heat, but entirely different, mingled with the odour of smoke, tempered by the cool fragrance of a forest setting, and I recognized that what seemed to me so delightful was the very row of trees which I had found it wearisome to study and describe and which, in a sort of hallucination, I thought now stood before me as I uncorked the bottle of beer I had with me in the railway carriage, the sound of the spoon striking the plate having given me—until I came to myself again—the illusion of the very similar noise of the hammer of a workman who had made some repairs to a wheel while our train stopped before that little clump of trees. Then one would have said that the signs which were to lift me out of my discouragement that day and restore my faith in literature had determined to come thick and fast, for when a butler who had been for a long time in the service of the Prince de Guermantes recognised me and, in order to save my going to the buffet, brought to me in the library a small plate of *petits fours* and a glass of orangeade, I wiped my mouth with the napkin he had given me; but immediately, like the character in *The Arabian Nights* who unwittingly performs precisely the rite that calls up before him, visible to his eyes alone, a docile genie, ready to transport him far away, a fresh vision of azure blue passed before my eyes; but this time it was pure and saline and it rounded upward like bluish breasts. The impression was so vivid that the moment I was re-living fused with the real present and, more dazed than on that day when I wondered whether I was really going to be received by the Princess de Guermantes or was everything going to crash about my head, I thought the servant had just opened the window toward the beach and everything called me to go down and stroll along the embankment at high tide; the napkin which I had taken to wipe my mouth had precisely the same sort of starchy stiffness as the towel with which I had had so much trouble drying myself before the window the first day of my stay at Balbec, and now, in this library of the Guermantes mansion, it spread out in its various folds and creases, like a peacock's tail, the plumage of a green and blue ocean. And I drew enjoyment, not only from those colours, but from a whole moment of my life which had brought them into being and had no doubt been an aspiration toward them, but which perhaps some feeling of fatigue or sadness had prevented me from enjoying at Balbec and which now, pure and disembodied, freed from all the imperfections of objective perception, filled me with joy. The piece they were playing was likely to finish at any moment and I be obliged to enter the salon. Therefore I made an effort to try as quickly as possible to see clearly into the nature of the identical pleasures I had just felt three separate times within a few minutes, and then to draw from them the lesson they had to give. The great difference there is between the actual impression we received from something and the artificial impression we create for ourselves when we endeavour by an effort of the will to bring the object before us again, I did not pause to consider; remembering only too well the comparative indifference with which Swann used to be able to speak of the period in his life when he was loved (because this expression suggested something so different to him) and the sudden pain caused him by Vinteuil's little phrase, which brought to mind those days themselves just as he had felt them, I understood too clearly that the sensation of the uneven flagstones, the stiffness of the napkin and the savour of the *madeleine* had awakened in me something that had no relation to what I used to endeavour to recall to mind about Venice, Balbec, Combray with the aid of a colourless, undistinguishing memory. And I understood how one can come to judge life to be mediocre, when at certain times it seems so beautiful, because this judgment and this disparaging conclusion are based on something entirely different from life itself, on mental images which have retained no trace of life. At the most, I noted incidentally that the difference between each of these real impressions and the corresponding artificial one—differences which explain why an even-toned painting of life cannot be a true likeness—was probably due to this cause, namely, that the slightest word we have spoken or the most insignificant gesture we have made at a certain moment in our life was surrounded and illumined by things that logically had no relation to it and were separated from it by our intelligence, which had no need of them for reasoning purposes; and yet, in the midst of these irrelevant objects—here, the rosy glow of eventide on the flower-covered wall of a rustic restaurant, the feeling of hunger, the yearning for women, the pleasant sensation of luxury; there, blue volutes of the morning sea, wrapped in spirals around strains of music which only partly emerge, like mermaids' shoulders—the most insignificant gesture, the simplest act remain enclosed, as it were, in a thousand sealed jars, each filled with things of an absolutely different colour, odour and temperature. Furthermore, these jars, ranged along the topmost levels of our bygone years—years during which we have been constantly changing, if only in our dreams and thoughts—stand at very different altitudes and give us the impression of strangely varied atmospheres. It is true that we have gone through these changes imperceptibly, but between our present state and the memory that suddenly comes back to us, just as between two recollections of different years, places or hours, there is such a wide difference that that fact alone, regardless even of any specific individuality, would suffice to make comparison between them impossible. Yes, if, thanks to our ability to forget, a past recollection has been able to avoid any tie, any link with the present moment, if it has remained in its own place and time, if it has kept its distance, its isolation in the depths of a valley or on the tip of a mountain peak, it suddenly brings us a breath of fresh air—refreshing just because we have breathed it once before—of that purer air which the poets have vainly tried to establish in Paradise, whereas it could not convey that profound sensation of renewal if it had not already been breathed, for the only true paradise is always the paradise we have lost. And, in passing, I noted that the work of art which I already felt myself prepared to undertake, but without my having made any conscious resolution to that effect, would present great difficulties. For I would be obliged to execute the different parts of it in somewhat different mediums. The medium suitable for recalling mornings by the sea would be very different from that required to describe afternoons in Venice, a medium distinct and new, of a very special transparence and sonority, compact, refreshing and rosy-hued. And then, different again would be the medium, if I essayed to depict the evenings at Rivebelle in the dining-room opening on the garden, when the heat seemed to disintegrate, to condense and settle to the ground, while the falling twilight still tinted the roses on the wall of the restaurant and the sky still glowed with the pastel tints of dying day. But I passed quickly over all that, under the more imperious urge which I felt to seek the reason for this feeling of happiness and the air of certainty with which it came over me, a search I had hitherto postponed. I caught an inkling of this reason when I compared these various happy impressions with one another and found that they had this in common, namely, that I felt them as if they were occurring simultaneously in the present moment and in some distant past, which the sound of the spoon against the plate, or the unevenness of the flagstones, or the peculiar savour of the *madeleine* even went so far as to make coincide with the present, leaving me uncertain in which period I was. In truth, the person within me who was at that moment enjoying this impression enjoyed in it the qualities it possessed which were common to both an earlier day and the present moment, qualities which were independent of all considerations of time; and this person came into play only when, by this process of identifying the past with the present, he could find himself in the only environment in which he could live and enjoy the essence of things, that is to say, entirely outside of time. That explained why my apprehensiveness of death vanished the moment I instinctively recognised the savour of the little *madeleine*, because at that moment the person within me was a timeless person, consequently unconcerned with the vicissitudes of the future. That person had never come to me, never manifested himself, except independently of all immediate activity, all immediate enjoyment, whenever the miracle of a resemblance with things past enabled me to escape out of the present. He alone had the power to make me recapture bygone days, times past, which had always balked the efforts of my memory and my intelligence.

And perhaps a moment ago, when I considered that Bergotte had been mistaken in speaking of the satisfactions of the intellectual life, this was because at that time I applied the term "intellectual life" to logical processes of reasoning which had no connection with it or with what was then taking place within me—just as the reason I found society and even life tiresome was because I appraised them on the basis of false impressions of the past, whereas in reality I had now such an eager desire to live that an actual moment from the past had just been revived within me on three distinct occasions.

Merely a moment from the past? Much more than that, perhaps; something which, common to both past and present, is far more essential than either.

How many times in the course of my life had I been disappointed by reality because, at the time I was observing it, my imagination, the only organ with which I could enjoy beauty, was not able to function, by virtue of the inexorable law which decrees that only that which is absent can be imagined. And now suddenly the operation of this harsh law was neutralised, suspended, by a miraculous expedient of nature by which a sensation—the sound of the spoon and that of the hammer, a similar unevenness in two paving stones—was reflected both in the past (which made it possible for my imagination to take pleasure in it) and in the present, the physical stimulus of the sound or the contact with the stones adding to the dreams of the imagination that which they usually lack, the idea of existence—and this subterfuge made it possible for the being within me to seize, isolate, immobilise for the duration of a lightning flash what it never apprehends, namely, a fragment of time in its pure state. The being that was called to life again in me when, with such a thrill of joy, I heard the sound that characterises both a spoon touching a plate and a hammer striking a car wheel, or when I felt under foot the unevenness of the pavement in the court of the Guermantes residence, similar to that in the baptistry of Saint Mark's, draws its sustenance only

from the essence of things, in that alone does it find its nourishment and its delight. It languishes in the contemplation of the present, where the senses cannot
furnish this essential substance, or in the study of the past, rendered barren for
it by the intelligence, or while awaiting a future which the will constructs out of
fragments of the past and the present from which it has withdrawn still more of
their reality, retaining only that part of them which is suited to the utilitarian,
narrowly human purpose for which it designs them. But let a sound already heard
or an odour caught in bygone years be sensed anew, simultaneously in the present
and the past, real without being of the present moment, ideal but not abstract,
and immediately the permanent essence of things, usually concealed, is set free
and our true self, which had long seemed dead but was not dead in other ways,
awakes, takes on fresh life as it receives the celestial nourishment brought to it. A
single minute released from the chronological order of time has re-created in us
the human being similarly released, in order that he may sense that minute. And
one comprehends readily how such a one can be confident in his joy; even though
the mere taste of a *madeleine* does not seem to contain logical justification for
this joy, it is easy to understand that the word "death" should have no meaning
for him; situated outside the scope of time, what could he fear from the future? . . .

There came over me a feeling of profound fatigue at the realisation that all this
long stretch of time not only had been uninterruptedly lived, thought, secreted
by me, that it was my life, my very self, but also that I must, every minute of my
life, keep it closely by me, that it upheld me, that I was perched on its dizzying
summit, that I could not move without carrying it about with me.

The date when I heard the sound—so distant and yet so deep within me—of
the little bell in the garden at Combray was a landmark I did not know I had
available in this enormous dimension of Time. My head swam to see so many
years below me, and yet within me, as if I were thousands of leagues in height.

I now understood why it was that the Duc de Guermantes, whom, as I looked
at him sitting in a chair, I marvelled to find shewing his age so little, although he
had so many more years than I beneath him, as soon as he rose and tried to stand
erect, had tottered on trembling limbs (like those of aged archbishops who have
nothing solid on them except their metallic cross, with the young divinity students flocking assiduously about them) and had wavered as he made his way along
the difficult summit of his eighty-three years, as if men were perched on giant
stilts, sometimes taller than church spires, constantly growing and finally rendering their progress so difficult and perilous that they suddenly fall. I was alarmed
that mine were already so tall beneath my feet; it did not seem as if I should have
the strength to carry much longer attached to me that past which already extended so far down and which I was bearing so painfully within me! If, at least,
there were granted me time enough to complete my work, I would not fail to
stamp it with the seal of that Time the understanding of which was this day so
forcibly impressing itself upon me, and I would therein describe men—even should
that give them the semblance of monstrous creatures—as occupying in Time a
place far more considerable than the so restricted one allotted them in space, a
place, on the contrary, extending boundlessly since, giant-like, reaching far back
into the years, they touch simultaneously epochs of their lives—with countless
intervening days between—so widely separated from one another in Time.

FRIEDRICH SCHLEGEL

The Ironic Consciousness

So profound, moreover, and lasting is this our intrinsic dualism and duplicity—(and I use the term here, not in its usual moral sense, but in a higher significa-tion, which is purely psychological and metaphysical)—so deeply is this dualism rooted in our consciousness, that even when we are, or at least think ourselves alone, we still think as two, and are constrained as it were to recognise our inmost profoundest being as essentially dramatic. This colloquy with self, or generally, this internal dialogue, is so perfectly the natural form of human thinking, that even the saintly solitaries of bygone centuries, who in the Egyptian deserts or the Alpine hermitages devoted a half-life to meditation on divine things and mys-teries, were often not able otherwise to indicate the result of such meditations, to invest it in another dress, to bring it into any other form of exposition than that of a dialogue of the soul with God. And in all religions, what properly is true prayer but a kind of dialogue, a confidential opening of the heart to the universal Father, or a filial solicitation of His benevolence?

But to pass over at once to the directly opposite aspect of the matter: even in the classical works of cultivated antiquity, at a time when these depths of a loveful feeling were not yet so widely developed, nor so completely revealed and un-veiled, we meet with this same phenomenon in another form, and one indeed of the highest intellectual clearness and brilliancy—in the graceful ornament, viz., of a truly exquisite diction. I am alluding to the characteristic distinction of the dis-courses and teaching of Socrates—that peculiar irony, such as it is found in the Platonic dialogues, and of which only a very slight trace is to be found in the works of some of the earliest poets. For what else is this scientific irony of the in-quiring thought and of the highest cognition, than a consciousness which, while it clearly perceives the secret contradictions which beset the mind, even in its most earnest pursuit of the highest aim of life, has attained nevertheless to perfect harmony with itself.

I must not, however, omit to remind you that this term in modern phraseology has fallen very far below its primary meaning, and is often so taken as to designate nothing more than a mere playful mockery. In its original Socratic sense, however, such as it is found in the whole series of the thought and the internal structure

From *The Philosophy of Language* [1829] in *The Philosophy of Life and the Philosophy of Language*, translated from the German by A. J. Morrison, London, 1847, pp. 389-90, and from *Lyceum of the Fine Arts* [1797], Fragment 108, translated by the editors.

of Plato's dialogues, where it is developed to its fullest measure and proportion, irony signifies nothing else than this amazement of the thinking spirit at itself, which so often dissolves in a light, gentle laugh. And this light laugh again oftentimes beneath its cheerful surface conceals and involves a deeper and profounder sense, another and a higher significance, even the most exalted seriousness. In the thoroughly dramatic development and exposition of thought which we meet with in the works of Plato, the dialogue form is essentially predominant. Even if all the superscriptions of names and persons, all forms of address and reply, and, in short, the whole conversational garb, were taken away from it, and we were merely to follow the inner threads of the thought according to their connexion and course, the whole would nevertheless remain a dialogue, where each answer calls forth a new question, and the eddying stream of speech and counter-speech, or rather, of thought and counter-thought, moves lively onwards. And unquestionably this form of inner dialogue is, if not in every case equally applicable and absolutely necessary, still it is all but essential, and at least highly natural and very appropriate to every form of living thought and its vivid enunciation.

Socratic irony is the only completely involuntary form of disguise—and, for that very reason, the only completely deliberate one. It is equally impossible for anyone to conceal or to reveal it. To one who does not already possess it, this irony remains a riddle even when it has been frankly admitted. . . . Socratic irony makes everything at once a joke and a serious matter, at once ingenuously open and deeply dissembled. It arises from a union of the art of life with the spirit of knowledge, from the encounter of a perfected philosophy of nature with a perfected philosophy of art. It comprises and evokes a sense of insoluble opposition between the absolute and the relative, between the impossibility and the simultaneous necessity of total communication. It is the freest kind of poetic license, for by this means one becomes superior to oneself; and yet it is also the strictest, since it is an unconditional necessity.

G. W. F. HEGEL

The Contrite Consciousness

The Contrite Consciousness is this awareness of the Self as the Divided Nature, wherein is only conflict.

This Contrite and Broken Consciousness, just because the conflict of its Nature is known as belonging to one person, must forever, in each of its two forms, have the other also present to it. Whenever, in either form, it seems to have come to

From *The Phenomenology of Mind* [1807], translated from the German by J. B. Baillie, London and New York, 1931, pp. 77-8; reprinted by permission of George Allen & Unwin Ltd.

victory and unity, it finds no rest there, but is forthwith driven over to the other. Its true home-coming, its true reconciliation with itself, will, however, display to us the law of the Spirit, as he will appear when, having come to life, he has entered the world of his manifestation. For it already belongs to the Contrite Consciousness to be one undivided soul in the midst of its doubleness. It is in fact the very gazing of one Self into another; it is both these selves; it has no nature save in so far as it unites the two. But thus far it knows not yet this its own real essence; it has not entered into possession of this unity.

For the first then, the Contrite Consciousness is but the unwon unity of the two selves. To its view the two are not one, but are at war together. And accordingly it regards one of them, viz., the simple, the Changeless Consciousness, as the True Self. The other, the multiform and fickle, it regards as the False Self. The Contrite Consciousness finds these two as mutually estranged. For its own part, because it is the awareness of this contradiction, it takes sides with the Changeless Consciousness, and calls itself the False Self. But since it is aware of the Changeless, i.e. of the True Self, its task must be one of self-deliverance, that is, the task of delivering itself from the unreality. For on the one hand it knows itself only as the fickle; and the changeless is far remote from it. And yet the Contrite Consciousness is in its genuine selfhood one with the simple and Changeless Consciousness; for therein lies its own true Self. But yet again it knows that it is not in possession of this true self. So long as the Contrite Consciousness assigns to the two selves this position, they cannot remain indifferent to each other; or, in other words, the Contrite Consciousness cannot itself be indifferent to the Changeless. For the Contrite Consciousness is, as a fact, of both kinds, and knows the relation of the changeless to the fickle as a relation of truth to falsehood. The falsehood must be turned to naught; but since the Contrite Consciousness finds both the false and the true alike necessary to it, and contradictory, there remains to it only the contradictory movement, wherein neither of the opposed elements can find repose in going over to its opponent but must create itself anew in the opponent's very bosom.

To win, then, in this strife against the adversary, is rather to be vanquished. To attain one goal, is rather to lose it in its opposite. The whole life, whatever it be, whatever it do, is aware only of the pain of this being and doing. For this Consciousness has no object besides its opposite, the true Self, and its own nothingness. In aspiration it strives hence towards the Changeless. But this aspiration is itself the Contrite Consciousness, and contains forthwith the knowledge of the opposite, namely of its own individuality. The Changeless, when it enters consciousness, is sicklied o'er with individuality, is present therewith; instead of being lost in the consciousness of Changeless, individuality arises ever afresh therein.

But one thing the Contrite Consciousness thus learns, namely that individuality is made manifest in the Changeless, and that the Changeless is made manifest in individuality. It finds that in general individuality belongs to the changeless true Self, and that in fact its own individuality also belongs thereto. For the outcome of this process is precisely the unity of this twofold consciousness. This unity, then, comes to light, but for the first only as an unity wherein the diversity of the two aspects plays the chief part. For the Contrite consciousness there thus result three ways in which individuality and the Changeless are linked. First, it rediscovers itself as again banished into its opposition to the Changeless Self; and it is cast back to the beginning of the strife, which latter still remains the element of the entire relationship. In the second place, the Contrite Consciousness learns that individuality belongs to the very essence of the Changeless, is the incarnation of the Changeless; and the latter hereupon assumes the burden of this whole range of phenomena. In the third place, the Contrite Consciousness discovers itself to be the individual who dwells in the Changeless. In the first stage the Changeless appears to consciousness only as the remote Self, that condemns individuality. In passing through the second stage, consciousness learns that the Changeless is as much an incarnate individual as it is itself; and thus, in the third stage, consciousness reaches the grade of the Spirit, rejoices to find itself in the Spirit, and becomes aware that its individuality is reconciled with the Universal.

KARL MARX

Alienation

Till now we have been considering the estrangement, the alienation of the worker only in one of its aspects, i.e., the worker's *relationship to the products of his labour*. But the estrangement is manifested not only in the result but in the *act of production*—within the *producing activity*, itself. How could the worker come to face the product of his activity as a stranger, were it not that in the very act of production he was estranging himself from himself? The product is after all but the summary of the activity, of production. If then the product of labour is alienation, production itself must be active alienation, the alienation of activity, the activity of alienation. In the estrangement of the object of labour is merely summarised the estrangement, the alienation, in the activity of labour itself.

What, then, constitutes the alienation of labour?

First, the fact that labour is *external* to the worker, i.e., it does not belong to his essential being; that in his work, therefore, he does not affirm himself but denies himself, does not feel content but unhappy, does not develop freely his physical and mental energy but mortifies his body and ruins his mind. The worker therefore only feels himself outside his work, and in his work feels outside himself. He is at home when he is not working, and when he is working he is not at home. His labour is therefore not voluntary, but coerced; it is *forced labour*. It is therefore not the satisfaction of a need; it is merely a *means* to satisfy needs external to it. Its alien character emerges clearly in the fact that as soon as no physical or other compulsion exists, labour is shunned like the plague. External labour, labour in which man alienates himself, is a labour of self-sacrifice, of mortification. Lastly, the external character of labour for the worker appears in the fact that it is not his own, but someone else's, that it does not belong to him, that in it he belongs, not to himself, but to another. Just as in religion the spontaneous activity of the human imagination, of the human brain and the human heart, operates inde-

From *The Economic and Philosophic Manuscripts of 1844*, translated from the German by Martin Milligan, edited and with an introduction by Dirk J. Struik, New York, 1964, pp. 110-14, reprinted by permission of International Publishers Co., Inc., New York and Lawrence and Wishart, London [London edition, 1961, pp. 72-7].

pendently of the individual—that is, operates on him as an alien, divine or diabolical activity—so is the worker's activity not his spontaneous activity. It belongs
to another; it is the loss of his self.

As a result, therefore, man (the worker) only feels himself freely active in his
animal functions—eating, drinking, procreating, or at most in his dwelling and in
dressing-up, etc.; and in his human functions he no longer feels himself to be
anything but an animal. What is animal becomes human and what is human
becomes animal.

Certainly eating, drinking, procreating, etc., are also genuinely human functions. But abstractly taken, separated from the sphere of all other human activity
and turned into sole and ultimate ends, they are animal functions.

We have considered the act of estranging practical human activity, labour, in
two of its aspects. (1) The relation of the worker to the *product of labour* as an
alien object exercising power over him. This relation is at the same time the relation to the sensuous external world, to the objects of nature, as an alien world
inimically opposed to him. (2) The relation of labour to the *act of production* within the *labour* process. This relation is the relation of the worker to his
own activity as an alien activity not belonging to him; it is activity as suffering,
strength as weakness, begetting as emasculating, the worker's *own* physical and
mental energy, his personal life—indeed, what is life but activity?—as an activity
which is turned against him, independent of him and not belonging to him. Here
we have *self-estrangement*, as previously we had the estrangement of the *thing*.

We have still a third aspect of *estranged labour* to deduce from the two already
considered.

Man is a species being, not only because in practice and in theory he adopts
the species as his object (his own as well as those of other things), but—and this
is only another way of expressing it—also because he treats himself as the
actual, living species; because he treats himself as a *universal* and therefore a free
being.

The life of the species, both in man and in animals, consists physically in the
fact that man (like the animal) lives on inorganic nature; and the more universal
man is compared with an animal, the more universal is the sphere of inorganic
nature on which he lives. Just as plants, animals, stones, the air, light, etc., constitute theoretically a part of human consciousness, partly as objects of natural
science, partly as objects of art—his spiritual inorganic nature, spiritual nourishment which he must first prepare to make palatable and digestible—so also
in the realm of practice they constitute a part of human life and human activity.
Physically man lives only on these products of nature, whether they appear in
the form of food, heating, clothes, a dwelling, etc. The universality of man
appears in practice precisely in the universality which makes all nature his
inorganic body—both inasmuch as nature is (1) his direct means of life, and (2)
the material, the object, and the instrument of his life-activity. Nature is man's
inorganic body—nature, that is, in so far as it is not itself the human body. Man
lives on nature—means that nature is his *body*, with which he must remain in
continuous interchange if he is not to die. That man's physical and spiritual life
is linked to nature means simply that nature is linked to itself, for man is a part
of nature.

In estranging from man (1) nature, and (2) himself, his own active functions, his life-activity, estranged labour estranges the *species* from man. It changes for him the *life of the species* into a means of individual life. First it estranges the life of the species and individual life, and secondly it makes individual life in its abstract form the purpose of the life of the species, likewise in its abstract and estranged form.

Indeed, labour, *life-activity, productive life* itself, appears in the first place merely as a *means* of satisfying a need—the need to maintain physical existence. Yet the productive life is the life of the species. It is life-engendering life. The whole character of a species—its species character—is contained in the character of its life-activity; and free, conscious activity is man's species character. Life itself appears only as a *means to life*.

The animal is immediately identical with its life activity. It does not distinguish itself from it. It is *its life activity*. Man makes his life activity itself the object of his will and of his consciousness. He has conscious life activity. It is not a determination with which he directly merges. Conscious life activity distinguishes man immediately from animal life activity. It is just because of this that he is a species being. Or rather, it is only because he is a species being that he is a Conscious Being, i.e., that his own life is an object for him. Only because of that is his activity free activity. Estranged labour reverses this relationship, so that it is just because man is a conscious being that he makes his life activity, his *essential* being, a mere means to his *existence*.

In creating a *world of objects* by his practical activity, in *his work upon* inorganic nature, man proves himself a conscious species being, i.e., as a being that treats the species as its own essential being, or that treats itself as a species being. Admittedly animals also produce. They build themselves nests, dwellings, like the bees, beavers, ants, etc. But an animal only produces what it immediately needs for itself or its young. It produces one-sidedly, whilst man produces universally. It produces only under the dominion of immediate physical need, whilst man produces even when he is free from physical need and only truly produces in freedom therefrom. An animal produces only itself, whilst man reproduces the whole of nature. An animal's product belongs immediately to its physical body, whilst man freely confronts his product. An animal forms things in accordance with the standard and the need of the species to which it belongs, whilst man knows how to produce in accordance with the standard of every species, and knows how to apply everywhere the inherent standard to the object. Man therefore also forms things in accordance with the laws of beauty.

It is just in his work upon the objective world, therefore, that man first really proves himself to be a *species being*. This production is his active species life. Through and because of this production, nature appears as *his* work and his reality. The object of labour is, therefore, the *objectification of man's species life*: for he duplicates himself not only, as in consciousness, intellectually, but also actively, in reality, and therefore he contemplates himself in a world that he has created. In tearing away from man the object of his production, therefore, estranged labour tears from him his *species life*, his real objectivity as a member of the species and transforms his advantage over animals into the disadvantage that his inorganic body, nature, is taken away from him.

Similarly, in degrading spontaneous, free activity, to a means, estranged labour makes man's species life a means to his physical existence.

The consciousness which man has of his species is thus transformed by estrangement in such a way that the species life becomes for him a means.

Estranged labour turns thus:

(3) *Man's species being*, both nature and his spiritual species property, into a being *alien* to him, into a *means* to his *individual existence*. It estranges man from his own body, as well as external nature and his spiritual essence, his *human* being.

(4) An immediate consequence of the fact that man is estranged from the product of his labour, from his life activity, from his species being is the *estrangement of man* from *man*. When man confronts himself, he confronts the *other* man. What applies to a man's relation to his work, to the product of his labour and to himself, also holds of a man's relation to the other man, and to the other man's labour and object of labour.

In fact, the proposition that man's species nature is estranged from him means that one man is estranged from the other, as each of them is from man's essential nature.

SØREN KIERKEGAARD

Indirect Communication

While objective thought is indifferent to the thinking subject and his existence, the subjective thinker is as an existing individual essentially interested in his own thinking, existing as he does in his thought. His thinking has therefore a different type of reflection, namely the reflection of inwardness, of possession, by virtue of which it belongs to the thinking subject and to no one else. While objective thought translates everything into results, and helps all mankind to cheat, by copying these off and reciting them by rote, subjective thought puts everything in process and omits the result; partly because this belongs to him who has the way, and partly because as an existing individual he is constantly in process of coming to be, which holds true of every human being who has not permitted himself to be deceived into becoming objective, inhumanly identifying himself with speculative philosophy in the abstract.

The reflection of inwardness gives to the subjective thinker a double reflection. In thinking, he thinks the universal; but as existing in his thought and as assimilating it in his inwardness, he becomes more and more subjectively isolated.

The difference between subjective and objective thinking must express itself also in the form of communication suitable to each. That is to say, the subjective

From *Concluding Unscientific Postscript* [1846], translated from the Danish by Dorothy Swenson and Walter Lowrie, Princeton, 1941, pp. 67-9, 73-9, 81-3, 246-8. Copyright 1941 by Princeton University Press; reprinted by permission of Princeton University Press.
From *The Point of View for My Work as an Author* [1859], translated from the Danish by Walter Lowrie, New York, 1962, pp. 22, 25-6, 39-40, 45-6, 49-51, 51-3; reprinted by permission of Harper & Row, Publishers.

thinker will from the beginning have his attention called to the requirement that this form should embody artistically as much of reflection as he himself has when existing in his thought. In an artistic manner, please note; for the secret does not lie in a direct assertion of the double reflection; such a direct expression of it is precisely a contradiction.

Ordinary communication between man and man is wholly immediate, because men in general exist immediately. When one man sets forth something and another acknowledges the same, word for word, it is taken for granted that they are in agreement, and that they have understood one another. Precisely because the speaker has not noticed the reduplication requisite to a thinking mode of existence, he also remains unaware of the double reflection involved in the process of communication. Hence he does not suspect that an agreement of this nature may be the grossest kind of misunderstanding. Nor does he suspect that, just as the subjective existing thinker has made himself free through the reduplication given his reflection, so the secret of all communication consists precisely in emancipating the recipient, and that for this reason he must not communicate himself directly; aye, that it is even irreligious to do so. This last holds true the more the subjective is of the essence of the matter, and hence applies first and foremost in the religious sphere; unless indeed the author of the communication is God himself, or dares appeal to the miraculous authority of an apostle, but is merely a human being, and at the same time in favor of having a meaning in what he says and does. . . .

Wherever the subjective is of importance in knowledge, and where appropriation thus constitutes the crux of the matter, the process of communication is a work of art, and doubly reflected. Its very first form is precisely the subtle principle that the personalities must be held devoutly apart from one another, and not permitted to fuse or coagulate into objectivity. It is at this point that objectivity and subjectivity part from one another.

Ordinary communication, like objective thinking in general, has no secrets; only a doubly reflected subjective thinking has them. That is to say, the entire essential content of subjective thought is essentially secret, because it cannot be directly communicated. This is the meaning of the secrecy. The fact that the knowledge in question does not lend itself to direct utterance, because its essential feature consists of the appropriation, makes it a secret for everyone who is not in the same way doubly reflected within himself. And the fact that this is the essential form of such truth, makes it impossible to express it in any other manner. Hence when anyone proposes to communicate such truth directly, he proves his stupidity; and if anyone else demands this of him, he too shows that he is stupid. Over against such an elusive and artistic communication of truth, the customary human stupidity will always raise the cry that it is egoism. And when stupidity at length prevails, and the communication becomes direct, stupidity will have gained so much, that the author of the communication will have become equally stupid with the pretended recipient.

A distinction may be drawn between a secret which is essentially a secret, and one which is so only accidentally. For example, what was said at a secret meeting of the ministry is an accidental secret as long as it is not made public; for it is in itself such as to be directly understandable as soon as it is revealed. It is an accidental secret, because no one yet knows it, or what will happen a year from now;

but when it has happened, it will be capable of being directly understood. On the other hand, when Socrates isolated himself from every external relationship by making an appeal to his *daemon*, and assumed, as I suppose, that everyone must do the same, such a view of life is essentially a secret, or constitutes an essential secret, because it cannot be communicated directly. The most that Socrates could do was to help another negatively, by a maieutic artistry, to achieve the same view. Everything subjective, which through its dialectical inwardness eludes a direct form of expression, is an essential secret. . . .

In these times much is heard about the negative, and about negative thinkers. In this connection we are often enough compelled to listen to the preachments of the positive, and to the public thanks they offer up to God and Hegel that they are not like these negative ones, but have become positive. The positive in the sphere of thought comes under the head of certainty in sense-perception, in historical knowledge, and in speculative results. But all this positiveness is sheer falsity. . . .

Negative thinkers therefore always have one advantage, in that they have something positive, being aware of the negative element in existence; the positive have nothing at all, since they are deceived. Precisely because the negative is present in existence, and present everywhere (for existence is a constant process of becoming), it is necessary to become aware of its presence continuously, as the only safeguard against it. In relying upon a positive security the subject is merely deceived.

The negativity that pervades existence, or rather, the negativity of the existing subject, which should be essentially reflected in this thinking in an adequate form, has its ground in the subject's synthesis: that he is an existing infinite spirit. The infinite and eternal is the only certainty, but as being in the subject it is in existence; and the first expression for this, is its elusiveness, and this tremendous contradiction, that the eternal becomes, that it comes into being.

Hence it is necessary for the thinking of the existing subject to have a form in which this can be reflected. If the subject says this in direct utterance, he says something untrue; for in direct utterance the elusiveness is omitted. This makes the form of the communication confusing, as when the tongue of an epileptic pronounces the wrong word, though the speaker who gives a direct utterance to the negativity of existence may not notice the contradiction as clearly as the epileptic. Let us take an example. The existing subject is eternal, but *qua* existing temporal. The elusiveness of the infinite now expresses itself through the possibility of death at any moment. All positive security is thus rendered suspect. If I am not aware of this in every moment, my positive confidence in life becomes mere childishness, in spite of its having become speculative, strutting superior in the systematic buskins. But if I do become conscious of it, this infinite thought is so infinite as to threaten to transform my existence into a vanishing nothing. Now how does the existing subject reflect this characteristic of his thinking existence? . . .

In connection with such negative principles, an elusive form of communication is the only adequate one; because a direct form of communication is based upon the security of social continuity, while the elusiveness of existence isolates me whenever I apprehend it. Everyone who is conscious of this and is content to be human, everyone who has the strength and imperturbability to refuse to become a dupe, in order to be allowed to prate about universal history, admired by the like-minded but mocked by existence, will avoid a direct form of statement. We all know that Socrates was an idler, who concerned himself neither with world-history nor with astronomy. Diogenes tells us how he gave up the study of the latter science; and when he later sometimes stood still and gazed into space, I cannot assume, though not otherwise attempting to decide what he was doing, that he was engaged in star-gazing. But he had plenty of time and the needful singularity to devote himself to the simply human, which concern is strangely enough regarded as singular in human beings; while it is not at all deemed singular to occupy oneself with world-history. From an excellent article in *Fyenske Tidsskrift* I learn that Socrates is supposed to have been somewhat ironical. It was really high time that this was said; and now that the disclosure has been made, I am in a position to appeal to this article for confirmation when I myself assume something similar. The irony of Socrates makes use, and that precisely when he wishes to bring out the infinite, makes use, among others things, of a form of speech which sounds in the first instance like the speech of a madman. Just as existence is treacherous, so also is the speech of Socrates, perhaps (I say perhaps, for I am not so wise a man as the positive author in *Fyenske Tidsskrift*) in order to prevent getting on his hands a moved and believing listener, who would proceed to appropriate positively the proposition that existence is negative. This is something that no one can understand who is able to speak only in a direct form; and it is also something it cannot help saying once for all, since its secret is that it must be present everywhere in the thought and in its reflection, just as it is present everywhere in existence. In so far, it is quite in order not to be understood, for in that manner one is at least secure against misunderstanding. Thus when Socrates says somewhere that it is a strange mode of behavior on the part of the skipper who has just safely transported you from Greece to Italy, calmly to walk back and forth on the beach after his arrival, accepting his pay as if he had done a good deed, although it is impossible for him to know whether he has rendered his passengers a genuine service, or whether it might not have been better for them to have lost their lives at sea—he speaks quite like a madman. . . .

Among so-called negative thinkers, there are some who after having had a glimpse of the negative have relapsed into positiveness, and now go out into the world like town criers, to advertise, prescribe and offer for sale their beatific negative wisdom—and of course, a result can quite well be announced through the town crier, just like herring from Holstein, and the like. These town criers of negativity are not much wiser than the positive thinkers, and it is inconsistent of the latter to be so wroth with them, since they are essentially positive. They are not existing thinkers; once upon a time perhaps they were, until they found their result; but from that moment they no longer existed as thinkers, but as town criers and auctioneers.

But the genuine subjective existing thinker is always as negative as he is positive, and *vice versa*. He continues to be such as long as he exists, not once for all in a chimerical mediation. His mode of communication is made to conform, lest through being too extraordinarily communicative he should succeed in transforming a learner's existence into something different from what a human existence in general has any right to be. He is conscious of the negativity of the infinite in existence, and he constantly keeps the wound of the negative open, which in the bodily realm is sometimes the condition for a cure. The others let the wound heal over and become positive; that is to say, they are deceived. In his mode of communication he expresses the same principle. He is therefore never a teacher but a learner; and since he is always just as negative as he is positive, he is always striving. . . .

An existing individual is constantly in process of becoming; the actual existing subjective thinker constantly reproduces this existential situation in his thoughts, and translates all his thinking into terms of process. It is with the subjective thinker as it is with a writer and his style; for he only has a style who never has anything finished, but "moves the waters of the language" every time he begins, so that the most common expression comes into being for him with the freshness of a new birth.

Thus constantly to be in process of becoming is the elusiveness that pertains to the infinite in existence. It is enough to bring a sensuous man to despair, for one always feels a need to have something finished and complete; but this desire does not come from the good, but needs to be renounced. The incessant becoming generates the uncertainty of the earthly life, where everything is uncertain. . . .

That the subjective existing thinker is as positive as he is negative, can also be expressed by saying that he is as sensitive to the comic as to the pathetic. As men ordinarily live, the comic and the pathetic are divided, so that one person has the one and another person has the other, one person a little more of the one, another, a little less. But for anyone who exists in a double reflection, the proportions are equal: as much of the pathetic, so much also of the comic. The equality in the relationship provides a mutual security, each guaranteeing the soundness of the other. The pathos which is not secured by the presence of the comic is illusion; the comic spirit that is not made secure by the presence of pathos is immature. Only one who himself produces this will understand it, otherwise not. What Socrates said about the voyage across the water sounds wholly like a jest, and yet it was an expression for the highest earnestness. If it were to be regarded merely in the light of a jest, many might be willing to follow; if regarded as sheer earnest, many an easily perspiring individual would doubtless be emotionally stirred. But suppose Socrates did not at all understand it in this one-sided manner. It would sound like jesting, if a prospective guest were to say on receiving the invitation: "You can count on me, I shall certainly come; but I must make an exception for the contingency that a tile happens to blow down from a roof, and kills me; for in that case I cannot come." But it might at the same time also be the highest earnestness; and the speaker, though jesting with men, might exist before God.

Suppose a young woman were expecting the arrival of her lover by the ship to which Socrates refers; suppose she ran down to the harbor and found Socrates there, and took occasion to ask him, in all the glow of her passion, for news of her lover. Suppose instead of answering her directly, the old wag said: "Aye, the skipper walks back and forth on the beach, jingling the money he has received from the passengers in his pocket; and that although he does not know for certain whether it might not have been better for the passengers to have perished in the waves:" what then? If she were a clever little damsel she would perceive that Socrates had told her, in a fashion, that her lover had arrived safely; and as soon as she was assured of this, what then? Why then she would laugh at Socrates and his queer speech. For she was not so silly as to entertain any uncertainty about how splendid it was that her lover had come. To be sure, such a little damsel is attuned in spirit only to a tryst with her lover, in erotic embrace on the safe shore; she is too undeveloped for a Socratic rendezvous with the divinity in the Idea, on the boundless ocean of uncertainty.

But now let us suppose that the clever little maid had been confirmed, what then? Why then she would have had precisely the same knowledge as Socrates— the only difference being in the manner of it. Yet Socrates had presumably shaped his entire life in accordance with this distinction, and in his seventieth year was still engaged in so disciplining himself as to understand with greater and greater inwardness what a lass of sixteen summers already knows. For he was not as one who knows Hebrew, and thus is in a position to say to the maiden: "There is something you do not know, and you must understand that it takes a long time to learn it." He was not as one who could carve in stone, which the damsel would readily understand that she could not do, and would know how to admire. No, he knew no more than she. What wonder then that he was so indifferent to the approach of death; the poor fellow had presumably come to see that his life was wasted, and that it was now too late for him to begin to learn what only the dis- tinguished know. What wonder then that he made absolutely no fuss about his death, as if the State were to lose in him something it could never replace. Alas, he has perhaps thought something like this: "Had I only been a professor of Hebrew, or a sculptor, or a solo dancer, to say nothing of being a world-historic genius bestowing beatific blessings on all minkind, then how could the State have recovered from the loss of my presence among them, and how could its citizens ever have learned to know what I could tell them! But as it is, no question will ever be raised about me; for what I know, everybody knows." What a jester this fellow Socrates was, to indulge himself in such frivolity about Hebrew, and the art of the sculptor, and the ballet, and the beatific benefits of world-history; and to be so deeply concerned, on the other hand, about the divinity, that although he had disciplined himself unremittingly through a long life (as a solo dancer dancing to the honor of God), he nevertheless looked forward with diffidence to the divine test, fearful lest he should be found wanting. What shall we call that?

The relative difference which exists for the immediate consciousness between the comic and the tragic, vanishes in the doubly reflected consciousness where the difference becomes infinite, thereby positing their identity. The comic expression for worship is therefore just as reverent, religiously, as its pathetic expression. What lies at the root of both the comic and the tragic in this connection, is the discrepancy, the contradiction, between the infinite and the finite, the eternal and that which becomes. A pathos which excludes the comic is therefore a misunder- standing, is not pathos at all. The subjective existing thinker is as bifrontal as existence itself. When viewed from a direction looking toward the Idea, the apprehension of the discrepancy is pathos; when viewed with the Idea behind one, the apprehension is comic. When the subjective existing thinker turns his face toward the Idea, his apprehension of the discrepancy is pathetic; when he turns his back to the Idea and lets this throw a light from behind over the same dis- crepancy, the apprehension is in terms of the comic. If I have not exhausted the comic to its entire depth, I do not have the pathos of the infinite; if I have the pathos of the infinite, I have at once also the comic. . . .

My conception of communication by means of books is very different from what I generally see put forward respecting it, and from what seems silently to be taken for granted. The indirect mode of communication makes communication an art in quite a different sense than when it is conceived in the usual manner: that the maker of the communication has to present something to the attention of one who knows, that he may judge it, or to the attention of one who does not know, that he may learn something. But no one bothers himself about the next consideration, that which makes communication dialectically so difficult, namely, that the recipient is an existing individual, and that this is essential. To stop a man on the street and stand still while talking to him, is not so difficult as to say something to a passer-by in passing, without standing still and without delaying the other, without attempting to persuade him to go the same way, but giving him instead an impulse to go precisely his own way. Such is the relation between one existing individual and another, when the communication concerns the truth as existential inwardness.

Relative to this, my dissentient opinion regarding communication, it has sometimes occurred to me whether this about indirect communication might not be communicable directly. Thus I see that Socrates, who otherwise holds so strictly to the method of question and answer (which is an indirect method), because the long speech, the dogmatizing lecture, the recitation by role, only causes confusion, sometimes himself speaks more at length, and cites as a reason for this that his interlocutor needs some items of information before the conversation can get going. This he does for example in the Gorgias. But this procedure seems to me to be an inconsistency, an impatience that fears it will take too long before a mutual understanding can be reached. The indirect method would reach the same goal, only more slowly. But speed is of no value whatever in connection with a form of understanding in which the inwardness is the understanding. To me it seems better to reach a true mutual understanding in inwardness separately, though this might take place slowly. Indeed, even if this never happened, because the time passed and the author was forgotten without anyone having understood him, to me it seems more consistent not to have made the slightest accommodation in order to get anyone to understand him, first and last so tending to his own self as not to make himself important in relation to others, which is so far from being inwardness that it is noisy externality. If he acts in this manner he will have the solace in the day of judgment, when God is the judge, that he has indulged himself in nothing for the sake of winning someone, but with the utmost exertion has labored in vain, leaving it to God to determine whether it was to have any significance or not. And this will doubtless please God better than to have a busy man say to Him: "I have won ten thousand adherents for you; some of them I won by weeping over the world's wretchedness and prophesying its early destruction, some by envisaging bright and smiling prospects for those who accepted my doctrine, others in other ways, here subtracting a little, here adding a little. They all became adherents of the truth, that is to say, moderately loyal adherents. If while I lived, you had stepped down on earth to inspect, I would have enchanted your eyes with the sight of the many adherents, just as Potemkin enchanted Catherine" . . . aye, precisely as Potemkin enchanted Catherine, namely, by means of stage properties; and the ten thousand adherents to the truth were also only a theatrical diversion.

Every one with some capacity for observation, who seriously considers what is called Christendom, or the conditions in a so-called Christian country, must surely be assailed by profound misgivings. What does it mean that all these thousands and thousands call themselves Christians as a matter of course? These many, many men, of whom the greater part, so far as one can judge, live in categories quite foreign to Christianity! . . . If then, according to our assumption, the greater number of people in Christendom only imagine themselves to be Christians, in what categories do they live? They live in aesthetic, or, at the most, in aesthetic-ethical categories.

Supposing then that a religious writer has become profoundly attentive to this illusion, Christendom, and has resolved to attack it with all the might at his disposal (with God's aid, be it noted)—what then is he to do? First and foremost, no impatience. If he becomes impatient, he will rush headlong against it and accomplish nothing. A direct attack only strengthens a person in his illusion, and at the same time embitters him. There is nothing that requires such gentle handling as an illusion, if one wishes to dispel it. If anything prompts the prospective captive to set his will in opposition, all is lost. And this is what a direct attack achieves, and it implies moreover the presumption of requiring a man to make to another person, or in his presence, an admission which he can make most profitably to himself privately. This is what is achieved by the indirect method, which, loving and serving the truth, arranges everything dialectically for the prospective captive, and then shyly withdraws (for love is always shy), so as not to witness the admission which he makes to himself alone before God—that he has lived hitherto in an illusion.

The religious writer must, therefore, first get into touch with men. That is, he must begin with aesthetic achievement. This is earnest-money. The more brilliant the achievement, the better for him. Moreover he must be sure of himself, or (and this is the one and only security) he must relate himself to God in fear and trembling, lest the event most opposite to his intentions should come to pass, and instead of setting the others in motion, the others acquire power over him, so that he ends by being bogged in the aesthetic. Therefore, he must have everything in readiness, though without impatience, with a view to bringing forward the religious promptly, as soon as he perceives that he has his readers with him, so that with the momentum gained by devotion to the aesthetic they rush headlong into contact with the religious.

It is important that religion should not be introduced either too soon or too late. If too long a time elapses, the illusion gains ground that the aesthetic writer has become older and hence religious. If it comes too soon, the effect is not violent enough. . . .

But from the point of view of my whole activity as an author, integrally conceived, the aesthetic work is a deception, and herein is to be found the deeper significance of the use of pseudonyms. A deception, however, is a rather ugly thing. To this I would make answer: One must not let oneself be deceived by the word "deception." One can deceive a person for the truth's sake, and (to recall old Socrates) one can deceive a person into the truth. Indeed, it is only by this means, i.e. by deceiving him, that it is possible to bring into the truth one who is in an illusion. Whoever rejects this opinion betrays the fact that he is not over-well versed in dialectics, and that is precisely what is especially needed when operating in this field. For there is an immense difference, a dialectical difference, between these two cases: the case of a man who is ignorant and is to have a piece of knowledge imparted to him, so that he is like an empty vessel which is to be filled or a blank sheet of paper upon which something is to be written; and the case of a man who is under an illusion and must first be delivered from that. Likewise there is a difference between writing on a blank sheet of paper and bringing to light by the application of a caustic fluid a text which is hidden under another text. Assuming then that a person is the victim of an illusion, and that in order to communicate the truth to him the first task, rightly understood, is to remove the illusion—if I do not begin by deceiving him, I must begin with direct communication. But direct communication presupposes that the receiver's ability to receive is undisturbed. But here such is not the case; an illusion stands in the way. That is to say, one must first of all use the caustic fluid. But this caustic means is negativity, and negativity understood in relation to the communication of the truth is precisely the same as deception.

What then does it mean, "to deceive?" It means that one does not begin *directly* with the matter one wants to communicate, but begins by accepting the other man's illusion as good money. . . .

I come now to the first period of my authorship and my mode of existence. Here was a religious author, but one who began as an aesthetic author; and this first stage was one of incognito and deceit. Initiated as I was very early and very thoroughly into the secret that *Mundus vult decipi*, I was not in the position of being able to wish to follow such tactics. Quite the contrary. With me it was a question of deceiving inversely on the greatest possible scale, employing every bit of knowledge I had about men and their weaknesses and their stupidities, not to profit thereby, but to annihilate myself and weaken the impression I made. The secret of the deceit which suits the world which wants to be deceived consists partly in forming a coterie and all that goes with that, in joining one or another of those societies for mutual admiration, whose members support one another with tongue and pen in the pursuit of worldly advantage; and it consists partly in hiding oneself from the human crowd, never being seen, so as to produce a fantastic effect. So I had to do exactly the opposite. I had to exist in absolute isolation and guard my solitude, but at the same time take pains to be seen every hour of the day, living as it were upon the street, in company with Tom, Dick, and Harry, and in the most fortuitous situations. This is truth's way of deceiving, the everlastingly sure way of weakening, in a worldly sense, the impression one makes. . . .

I am convinced that seldom has any author employed so much cunning, intrigue, and shrewdness to win honour and reputation in the world with a view to deceiving it, as I displayed in order to deceive it inversely in the interest of truth. On how great a scale this was carried out I shall attempt to show by one single instance, known to my friend Giødwad, the proof-reader of *Either/Or*. I was so busy when I was reading the proofs of *Either/Or* that it was impossible to spend the usual time sauntering back and forth on the street. I did not get through the work till late in the evening, and then I hastened to the theatre, where I remained literally only from five to ten minutes. And why did I do this? Because I feared the big book would create for me too great a reputation.[1] And why did I do this? Because I knew human nature, especially in Copenhagen. To be seen every night for five minutes by several hundred people sufficed to substantiate the opinion: He hasn't the least thing in the world to do; he is a mere idler.

Such was the existence I led by way of seconding my aesthetic work. Incidentally it involved a breach with all coteries. And I formed the polemical resolution to regard every eulogy as an attack, and every attack as a thing unworthy of notice. Such was my public mode of existence. I almost never made a visit, and at home the rule was strictly observed to receive no one except the poor who came to seek help. For I had no time to receive visitors at home, and any one who entered my home as a visitor might easily get a presentiment of a situation about which he should have no presentiment. Thus I existed. If Copenhagen ever has been of one opinion about anybody, I venture to say that it was of one opinion about me, that I was an idler, a dawdler, a *flâneur*, a frivolous bird, intelligent, perhaps brilliant, witty, &c.—but as for "seriousness," I lacked it utterly. I represented a worldly irony, *joie de vivre*, the subtlest form of pleasure-seeking—without a trace of "seriousness and positivity"; on the other hand, I was prodigiously witty and interesting. . . .

This is the first period: by my personal mode of existence I endeavoured to support the pseudonyms, the aesthetic work as a whole. Melancholy, incurably melancholy as I was, suffering prodigious griefs in my inmost soul, having broken in desperation from the world and all that is of the world, strictly brought up from my very childhood in the apprehension that the truth must suffer and be mocked and derided, spending a definite time every day in prayer and devout meditation, and being myself personally a penitent—in short, being what I was, I found (I do not deny it) a certain sort of satisfaction in this life, in this inverse deception, a satisfaction in observing that the deception succeeded so extraordinarily, that the public and I were on the most confidential terms, that I was quite in the fashion as the preacher of a gospel of worldliness, that though I was not in possession of the sort of distinction which can only be earned by an entirely different mode of life, yet in secret (and hence the more heartily loved) I was the darling of the public, regarded by every one as prodigiously interesting and witty. This satisfaction, which was my secret and which sometimes put me into an ecstasy, might have been a dangerous temptation. Not as though the world and such things could tempt me with their flattery and adulation. No, on that side I was safe. If I was to have been capsized, it would have to have been by this thought raised to a higher power, an obsession almost of ecstasy at the thought of how the deception was succeeding. This was an indescribable alleviation to a sense of resentment which smouldered in me from my childhood; because, long before I had

---

[1] It was for the same reason that at the moment when the whole of *Either/Or* was ready to be transcribed into a fair copy, I printed a little article in the *Fatherland* over my own signature, in which I gratuitously disclaimed that I was the author of a good many interesting articles which had appeared anonymously in various newspapers, acknowledging and admitting my idleness, and making one petition, that henceforth no one would ever regard me as the author of anything beneath which my name was not signed.

seen it with my own eyes, I had been taught that falsehood, pettiness, and injustice ruled the world.—I often had to think of these words in *Either/Or:* "If ye but knew what it is ye laugh at"—if ye but knew with whom ye have to do, who this *flâneur* is!

FRIEDRICH NIETZSCHE

The Masks of Truth

Everything deep loves masks; the deepest things have a veritable hatred of image and likeness. Might not *contrariety* be the only proper disguise to clothe the modesty of a god? A question worth asking. It would be surprising if some mystic hadn't at some time ventured upon it. There are events of such delicate nature that one would do well to bury them in gruffness and make them unrecognizable. There are deeds of love and extravagant magnanimity after which nothing is more advisable than to take a stick and beat up the eye-witness of them, to cloud his memory. There are people who know how to cloud and abuse their own memories in order to get revenge on their sole accomplice: modesty is inventive. The things of which one is most ashamed are by no means the worst things; not only cunning is found beneath a mask; there is much goodness in guile. I could imagine that a man who had something precious and vulnerable to hide might roll through life rough and round like an old green heavily hooped wine cask: the subtlety of his modesty would demand it. The destinies and delicate decisions of a man who is deeply ashamed happen to him on paths that few ever reach and of whose existence his nearest and dearest must know nothing. The danger to his life is hidden from their eyes, as is his life-security when he regains it. Such a concealed one, who instinctively uses speech for silence and withholding, and whose excuses for not communicating are inexhaustible, *wants* and encourages a mask of himself to wander about in the hearts and minds of his friends. And if he doesn't want it, one day his eyes will be opened to the fact that the mask is there anyway, and that it is good so. Every deep thinker needs a mask; even more, around every deep thinker a mask constantly grows, thanks to the continually wrong, i.e. superficial, interpretations of his every word, his every step, his every sign of life.—

Who has looked deep into the world can well understand the wisdom that lies in the fact that men are superficial. It is their instinct for self-preservation that teaches them to take things lightly, to skim over the surface, to be false. Here and there one can find a passionate and exaggerated adoration of "pure form," in philosophers and in artists. Let no one doubt that anyone who *needs* that kind of cult of surface-things has at some time or other unhappily reached *beneath* the surface. Perhaps there is an order or rank, even, in these burnt children, these born artists who can find pleasure in life only in their intention to *counterfeit* its image (to take slow revenge on life, as it were). One might deduce the degree to which they are sick of life from the degree to which they desire to see its image counterfeited, attenuated, transcendentalized, and deified. One might count the *homines religiosi* among these artists, assigning them the highest rank. It is deep, suspicious fear of incurable pessimism that forces whole millenniums to sink their teeth into a religious interpretation of life. It is that fearful instinct which intuits that man might come into possession of the truth *too soon*, before he has grown strong enough, hard enough, artist enough. Looked at in this light, piety, "living in God," would appear to be the subtlest and ultimate product of the *fear* of truth. It would appear to be the artist's adoration of and intoxication with the most consistent of all counterfeitings, the will to the reversal of truth, to untruth at any cost. Perhaps there has heretofore been no stronger medicine for beautifying man than piety. Through piety, man can become so much of a work of art, of surface, of color-play, and goodness, that one no longer suffers whenever one looks at him.

Wanderer, who are you? I see you going your way, without scorn, without love, with unfathomable eyes, damp and sad like a plummet which has returned to the light from every depth without finding satisfaction. What was it seeking down below? I see your breast which does not heave, your lips that hide their nausea, your hands which are slow to touch anything—who are you? What were you doing? Come rest here; this place is hospitable for everyman; regain your strength! Whoever you may be, what would you like? What will serve to refresh you? Just name it: I offer you all that I have. "To refresh myself? To refresh myself? Oh you inquisitive man, what are you saying? But give me . . . please give me. . . ." What? What? Tell me! "Another mask! A second mask!"—

If one listens to the footsteps of an anchorite, one can always hear something of an echo of desolation, something of the whisper and the fearful vigilance of solitude. In his strongest words, in his shriek even, there resounds a new, a more dangerous type of silence, of silent concealment. Whoever has sat alone with his soul year-in, year-out, day and night, in confidential discord and discourse, whoever became a cave-bear or a treasure seeker or a treasure guardian, a dragon, in his lair (which might be a labyrinth or a gold-mine)—in the end his very concepts will take on a unique twilight-color, an odor of depth as well as of mold, something incommunicative and repulsive that blows cold on anyone who passes by. The anchorite does not believe that any philosopher (assuming that all philosophers were once anchorites) ever expressed his essential and ultimate opinions in a book. On the contrary, one writes books in order to conceal what is concealed in one. He will doubt, in fact, that a philosopher *can* ever have an "ultimate and essential" opinion. He will suspect behind each cave a deeper cave, a more extensive, more exotic, richer world beyond the surface, a bottomless abyss beyond every bottom, beneath every "foundation." Every philosophy is a foreground-philosophy: this is an anchorite's judgment. There is something arbitrary in the fact that the philosopher stopped *here,* that he looked back and looked around, that *here* he refrained from digging deeper, that he laid aside his spade. There is, in fact, something that arouses suspicion! Each philosophy also *conceals* a philosophy; each opinion is also a hiding place; each word is also a mask.

Man, a complex, lying, artificial, and inscrutable animal, weird-looking to the other animals not so much because of his power but rather because of his guile and shrewdness, has invented the clear conscience, so that he might have the sensation, for once, that his psyche is a *simple* thing. All of morality is a continuous courageous forgery, without which an enjoyment of the sight of man's soul would be impossible. From this point of view, the concept "art" may be much more comprehensive than one commonly believes.

W. B. YEATS
The Anti-Self

I

When I come home after meeting men who are strange to me, and sometimes even after talking to women, I go over all I have said in gloom and disappointment. Perhaps I have overstated everything from a desire to vex or startle, from hostility that is but fear; or all my natural thoughts have been drowned by an undisciplined sympathy. My fellow-diners have hardly seemed of mixed humanity, and how should I keep my head among images of good and evil, crude allegories.

But when I shut my door and light the candle, I invite a Marmorean Muse, an art, where no thought or emotion has come to mind because another man has thought or felt something different, for now there must be no reaction, action only, and the world must move my heart but to the heart's discovery of itself, and I begin to dream of eyelids that do not quiver before the bayonet: all my thoughts have ease and joy, I am all virtue and confidence. When I come to put in rhyme what I have found it will be a hard toil, but for a moment I believe I have found myself and not my anti-self. It is only the shrinking from toil perhaps that convinces me that I have been no more myself than is the cat the medicinal grass it is eating in the garden.

How could I have mistaken for myself an heroic condition that from early boy-

From "Anima Hominis," *Per Amica Silentia Lunae,* London and New York, 1918, pp. 17-50. Copyright 1918 by The Macmillan Company; renewed 1946 by Gertha Georgie Yeats. Reprinted by permission of Mrs. W. B. Yeats, Macmillan and Co. Ltd., and The Macmillan Company, New York.

hood has made me superstitious? That which comes as complete, as minutely organised, as are those elaborate, brightly lighted buildings and sceneries appearing in a moment, as I lie between sleeping and waking, must come from above me and beyond me. At times I remember that place in Dante where he sees in his chamber the "Lord of Terrible Aspect," and how, seeming "to rejoice inwardly that it was a marvel to see, speaking, he said, many things among the which I could understand but few, and of these this: ego dominus tuus;" or should the conditions come, not as it were in a gesture—as the image of a man—but in some fine landscape, it is of Boehme, maybe, that I think, and of that country where we "eternally solace ourselves in the excellent beautiful flourishing of all manner of flowers and forms, both trees and plants, and all kinds of fruit."

II

When I consider the minds of my friends, among artists and emotional writers, I discover a like contrast. I have sometimes told one close friend that her only fault is a habit of harsh judgement with those who have not her sympathy, and she has written comedies where the wickedest people seem but bold children. She does not know why she has created that world where no one is ever judged, a high celebration of indulgence, but to me it seems that her ideal of beauty is the compensating dream of a nature wearied out by over-much judgement. I know a famous actress who in private life is like the captain of some buccaneer ship holding his crew to good behaviour at the mouth of a blunderbluss, and upon the stage she excels in the representation of women who stir to pity and to desire because they need our protection, and is most adorable as one of those young queens imagined by Maeterlinck who have so little will, so little self, that they are like shadows sighing at the edge of the world. When I last saw her in her own house she lived in a torrent of words and movements, she could not listen, and all about her upon the walls were women drawn by Burne-Jones in his latest period. She had invited me in the hope that I would defend those women, who were always listening, and are as necessary to her as a contemplative Buddha to a Japanese Samurai, against a French critic who would persuade her to take into her heart in their stead a Post-Impressionist picture of a fat flushed woman lying naked upon a Turkey carpet.

There are indeed certain men whose art is less an opposing virtue than a compensation for some accident of health or circumstance. During the riots over the first production of the *Playboy of the Western World* Synge was confused, without clear thought, and was soon ill—indeed the strain of that week may perhaps have hastened his death—and he was, as is usual with gentle and silent men, scrupulously accurate in all his statements. In his art he made, to delight his ear and his mind's eye, voluble dare-devils who "go romancing through a romping life time . . . to the dawning of the Judgement Day." At other moments this man, condemned to the life of a monk by bad health, takes an amused pleasure in "great queens . . . making themselves matches from the start to the end." Indeed, in all his imagination he delights in fine physical life, in life when the moon pulls up the tide. The last act of *Deirdre of the Sorrows*, where his art is at its noblest, was written upon his death-bed. He was not sure of any world to come, he was leaving his betrothed and his unwritten play—"Oh, what a waste of time," he said to me; he hated to die, and in the last speeches of Deirdre and in the middle act he accepted death and dismissed life with a gracious gesture. He gave to Deirdre the emotion that seemed to him most desirable, most difficult, most fitting, and maybe saw in those delighted seven years, now dwindling from her, the fulfilment of his own life.

III

When I think of any great poetical writer of the past (a realist is an historian and obscures the cleavage by the record of his eyes) I comprehend, if I know the lineaments of his life, that the work is the man's flight from his entire horoscope, his blind struggle in the network of the stars. William Morris, a happy, busy, most irascible man, described dim colour and pensive emotion, following, beyond any man of his time, an indolent muse; while Savage Landor topped us all in calm nobility when the pen was in his hand, as in the daily violence of his passion when he had laid it down. He had in his *Imaginary Conversations* reminded us, as it were, that the Venus de Milo is a stone, and yet he wrote when the copies did not come from the printer as soon as he expected: "I have . . . had the resolution to tear in pieces all my sketches and projects and to forswear all future undertakings. I have tried to sleep away my time and pass two-thirds of the twenty-four hours in bed. I may speak of myself as a dead man." I imagine Keats to have been born with that thirst for luxury common to many at the outsetting of the Romantic Movement, and not able, like wealthy Beckford, to slake it with beautiful and strange objects. It drove him to imaginary delights; ignorant, poor, and in poor health, and not perfectly well-bred, he knew himself driven from tangible luxury; meeting Shelley, he was resentful and suspicious because he, as Leigh Hunt recalls, "being a little too sensitive on the score of his origin, felt inclined to see in every man of birth his natural enemy."

IV

Some thirty years ago I read a prose allegory by Simeon Solomon, long out of print and unprocurable, and remember or seem to remember a sentence, "a hollow image of fulfilled desire." All happy art seems to me that hollow image, but when its lineaments express also the poverty or the exasperation that set its maker to the work, we call it tragic art. Keats but gave us his dream of luxury; but while reading Dante we never long escape the conflict, partly because the verses are at moments a mirror of his history, and yet more because that history is so clear and simple that it has the quality of art. I am no Dante scholar, and I but read him in Shadwell or in Dante Rossetti, but I am always persuaded that he celebrated the most pure lady poet ever sung and the Divine Justice, not merely because death took that lady and Florence banished her singer, but because he had to struggle in his own heart with his unjust anger and his lust; while unlike those of the great poets, who are at peace with the world and at war with themselves, he fought a double war. "Always," says Boccaccio, "both in youth and maturity he found room among his virtues for lechery;" or as Matthew Arnold preferred to change the phrase, "his conduct was exceeding irregular." Guido Cavalcanti, as Rossetti translates him, finds "too much baseness" in his friend:

> And still thy speech of me, heartfelt and kind,
> Hath made me treasure up thy poetry;
> But now I dare not, for thy abject life,
> Make manifest that I approve thy rhymes.

And when Dante meets Beatrice in Eden, does she not reproach him because, when she had taken her presence away, he followed in spite of warning dreams, false images, and now, to save him in his own despite, she has "visited . . . the Portals of the Dead," and chosen Virgil for his courier? While Gino da Pistoia complains that in his *Commedia* his "lovely heresies . . . beat the right down and let the wrong go free:"

> Therefore his vain decrees, wherein he lied,
> Must be like empty nutshells flung aside;
> Yet through the rash false witness set to grow,
> French and Italian vengeance on such pride
> May fall like Anthony on Cicero.

Dante himself sings to Giovanni Guirino "at the approach of death:"

> The King, by whose rich grave his servants be
> With plenty beyond measure set to dwell,
> Ordains that I my bitter wrath dispel,
> And lift mine eyes to the great Consistory.

V

We make out of the quarrel with others, rhetoric, but of the quarrel with ourselves, poetry. Unlike the rhetoricians, who get a confident voice from remembering the crowd they have won or may win, we sing amid our uncertainty; and, smitten even in the presence of the most high beauty by the knowledge of our solitude, our rhythm shudders. I think, too, that no fine poet, no matter how disordered his life, has ever, even in his mere life, had pleasure for his end. Johnson and Dowson, friends of my youth, were dissipated men, the one a drunkard, the other a drunkard and mad about women, and yet they had the gravity of men who had found life out and were awakening from the dream; and both, one in life and art and one in art and less in life, had a continual preoccupation with religion. Nor has any poet I have read of or heard of or met with been a sentimentalist. The other self, the anti-self or the antithetical self, as one may choose to name it, comes but to those who are no longer deceived, whose passion is reality. The sentimentalists are practical men who believe in money, in position, in a marriage bell, and whose understanding of happiness is to be so busy whether at work or at play, that all is forgotten but the momentary aim. They find their pleasure in a cup that is filled from Lethe's wharf, and for the awakening, for the vision, for the revelation of reality, tradition offers us a different word—ecstasy. An old artist wrote to me of his wanderings by the quays of New York, and how he found there a woman nursing a sick child, and drew her story from her. She spoke, too, of other children who had died: a long tragic story. "I wanted to paint her," he wrote, "if I denied myself any of the pain I could not believe in my own ecstasy." We must not make a false faith by hiding from our thoughts the causes of doubt, for faith is the highest achievement of the human intellect, the only gift man can make to God, and therefore it must be offered in sincerity. Neither must we create, by hiding ugliness, a false beauty as our offering to the world. He only can create the greatest imaginable beauty who has endured all imaginable pangs, for only when we have seen and foreseen what we dread shall we be rewarded by that dazzling unforeseen wing-footed wanderer. We could not find him if he were not in some sense of our being and yet of our being but as water with fire, a noise with silence. He is of all things not impossible the most difficult, for that only which comes easily can never be a portion of our being, "Soon got, soon gone," as the proverb says. I shall find the dark grow luminous, the void fruitful when I understand I have nothing, that the ringers in the tower have appointed for the hymen of the soul a passing bell.

The last knowledge has often come most quickly to turbulent men, and for a season brought new turbulence. When life puts away her conjuring tricks one by one, those that deceive us longest may well be the wine-cup and the sensual kiss, for our Chambers of Commerce and of Commons have not the divine architecture of the body, nor has their frenzy been ripened by the sun. The poet, because he may not stand within the sacred house but lives amid the whirlwinds that beset its threshold, may find his pardon.

VI

I think the Christian saint and hero, instead of being merely disastisfied, make deliberate sacrifice. I remember reading once an autobiography of a man who had made a daring journey in disguise to Russian exiles in Siberia, and his telling how, very timid as a child, he schooled himself by wandering at night through dangerous streets. Saint and hero cannot be content to pass at moments to that hollow image and after become their heterogeneous selves, but would always, if they could, resemble the antithetical self. There is a shadow of type on type, for in all great poetical styles there is saint or hero, but when it is all over Dante can return to his chambering and Shakespeare to his "pottle pot." They sought no impossible perfection but when they handled paper or parchment. So too will saint or hero, because he works in his own flesh and blood and not in paper or parchment, have more deliberate understanding of that other flesh and blood.

Some years ago I began to believe that our culture, with its doctrine of sincerity and self-realisation, made us gentle and passive, and that the Middle Ages and the Renaissance were right to found theirs upon the imitation of Christ or of some classic hero. St. Francis and Cæsar Borgia made themselves over-mastering, creative persons by turning from the mirror to meditation upon a mask. When I had this thought I could see nothing else in life. I could not write the play I had planned, for all became allegorical, and though I tore up hundreds of pages in my endeavour to escape from allegory, my imagination became sterile for nearly five years and I only escaped at last when I had mocked in a comedy my own thought. I was always thinking of the element of imitation in style and in life, and of the life beyond heroic imitation. I find in an old diary: "I think all happiness depends on the energy to assume the mask of some other life, on a re-birth as something not one's self, something created in a moment and perpetually renewed; in playing a game like that of a child where one loses the infinite pain of self-realisation, in a grotesque or solemn painted face put on that one may hide from the terror of judgment. . . . Perhaps all the sins and energies of the world are but the world's flight from an infinite blinding beam;" and again at an earlier date: "If we cannot imagine ourselves as different from what we are, and try to assume that second self, we cannot impose a discipline upon ourselves though we may accept one from others. Active virtue, as distinguished from the passive acceptance of a code, is therefore theatrical, consciously dramatic, the wearing of a mask. . . . Wordsworth, great poet though he be, is so often flat and heavy partly because his moral sense, being a discipline he had not created, a mere obedience, has no theatrical element. This increases his popularity with the better kind of journalists and politicians who have written books."

VII

I thought the hero found hanging upon some oak of Dodona an ancient mask, where perhaps there lingered something of Egypt, and that he changed it to his fancy, touching it a little here and there, gilding the eyebrows or putting a gilt line where the cheekbone comes; that when at last he looked out of its eyes he knew another's breath came and went within his breath upon the carven lips, and that his eyes were upon the instant fixed upon a visionary world: how else could the god have come to us in the forest? The good, unlearned books say that He who keeps the distant stars within His fold comes without intermediary, but Plutarch's precepts and the experience of old women in Soho, ministering their witchcraft to servant girls at a shilling a piece, will have it that a strange living man may win for Daemon an illustrious dead man; but now I add another thought: the Daemon comes not as like to like but seeking its own opposite, for man and Daemon feed the hunger in one another's hearts. Because the ghost is simple, the man heterogeneous and confused, they are but knit together when the man has found a mask whose lineaments permit the expression of all the man most lacks, and it may be dreads, and of that only.

The more insatiable in all desire, the more resolute to refuse deception or an easy victory, the more close will be the bond, the more violent and definite the antipathy.

VIII

I think that all religious men have believed that there is a hand not ours in the events of life, and that, as somebody says in *Wilhelm Meister*, accident is destiny; and I think it was Heraclitus who said: the Daemon is our destiny. When I think of life as a struggle with the Daemon who would ever set us to the hardest work among those not impossible, I understand why there is a deep enmity between a man and his destiny, and why a man loves nothing but his destiny. In an Anglo-Saxon poem a certain man is called, as though to call him something that summed up all heroism, 'Doom eager.' I am persuaded that the Daemon delivers and deceives us, and that he wove that netting from the stars and threw the nets from his shoulder. Then my imagination runs from Daemon to sweetheart, and I divine an analogy that evades the intellect. I remember that Greek antiquity has bid us look for the principal stars, that govern enemy and sweetheart alike, among those that are about to set, in the Seventh House as the astrologers say; and that it may be "sexual love," which is "founded upon spiritual hate," is an image of the warfare of man and Daemon; and I even wonder if there may not be some secret communion, some whispering in the dark between Daemon and sweetheart. I remember how often women when in love, grow superstitious, and believe that they can bring their lovers good luck; and I remember an old Irish story of three young men who went seeking for help in battle into the house of the gods at Slieve-na-mon. "You must first be married," some god told them, "because a man's good or evil luck comes to him through a woman."

I sometimes fence for half an hour at the day's end, and when I close my eyes upon the pillow I see a foil playing before me the button to my face. We meet always in the deep of the mind, whatever our work, wherever our reverie carries us, that other Will.

IX

The poet finds and makes his mask in disappointment, the hero in defeat. The desire that is satisfied is not a great desire, nor has the shoulder used all its might that an unbreakable gate has never strained. The saint alone is not deceived, neither thrusting with his shoulder nor holding out unsatisfied hands. He would climb without wandering to the antithetical self of the world, the Indian narrowing his thought in meditation or driving it away in contemplation, the Christian copying Christ, the antithetical self of the classical world. For a hero loves the world till it breaks him, and the poet till it has broken faith; but while the world was yet debonair, the saint has turned away, and because he renounced Experience itself, he will wear his mask as he finds it. The poet or the hero, no matter upon what bark they found their mask, so teeming their fancy, somewhat change its lineaments, but the saint, whose life is but a round of customary duty, needs nothing the whole world does not need, and day by day he scourges in his body the Roman and Christian conquerors; Alexander and Caesar are famished in his cell. His nativity is neither in disappointment nor in defeat, but in a temptation like that of Christ in the Wilderness, a contemplation in a single instant perpetually renewed of the Kingdoms of the World; all—because all renounced—continually present showing their empty thrones. Edwin Ellis, remembering that Christ also measured the sacrifice, imagined himself in a fine poem as meeting at Golgotha the phantom of "Christ the Less," the Christ who might have lived a prosperous life without the knowledge of sin, and who now wanders "companionless a weary spectre day and night."

> I saw him go and cried to him
> "Eli, thou hast forsaken me."
> The nails were burning through each limb,
> He fled to find felicity.

And yet is the saint spared—despite his martyr's crown and his vigil of desire—defeat, disappointed love, and the sorrow of parting.

> O Night, that did'st lead thus,
> O Night, more lovely than the dawn of light,

O Night, that broughtest us
Lover to lover's sight,
Lover with loved in marriage of delight!

Upon my flowery breast,
Wholly for him, and save himself for none,
There did I give sweet rest
To my beloved one;
The fanning of the cedars breathed thereon.

When the first morning air
Blew from the tower, and waved his locks aside,
His hand, with gentle care,
Did wound me in the side,
And in my body all my senses died.

All things I then forgot,
My cheek on him who for my coming came;
All ceased and I was not,
Leaving my cares and shame
Among the lilies, and forgetting them.*

X

It is not permitted to a man, who takes up pen or chisel, to seek originality, for passion is his only business, and he cannot but mould or sing after a new fashion because no disaster is like another. He is like those phantom lovers in the Japanese play who, compelled to wander side by side and never mingle, cry: "We neither wake nor sleep and passing our nights in a sorrow which is in the end a vision, what are these scenes of spring to us?" If when we have found a mask we fancy that it will not match our mood till we have touched with gold the cheek, we do it furtively, and only where the oaks of Dodona cast their deepest shadow, for could he see our handiwork the Daemon would fling himself out, being our enemy.

XI

Many years ago I saw, between sleeping and waking, a woman of incredible beauty shooting an arrow into the sky, and from the moment when I made my first guess at her meaning I have thought much of the difference between the winding movement of nature and the straight line, which is called in Balzac's *Seraphita* the "Mark of Man," but is better described as the mark of saint or sage. I think that we who are poets and artists, not being permitted to shoot beyond the tangible, must go from desire to weariness and so to desire again, and live but for the moment when vision comes to our weariness like terrible lightning, in the humility of the brutes. I do not doubt those heaving circles, those winding arcs, whether in one man's life or in that of an age, are mathematical, and that some in the world, or beyond the world, have foreknown the event and pricked upon the cal-

* Translated by Arthur Symons from *San Juan de la Cruz*. AUTHOR'S NOTE.

endar the life-span of a Christ, a Buddha, a Napoleon: that every movement, in feeling or in thought, prepares in the dark by its own increasing clarity and confidence its own executioner. We seek reality with the slow toil of our weakness and are smitten from the boundless and the unforeseen. Only when we are saint or sage, and renounce Experience itself, can we, in imagery of the Christian Caballa, leave the sudden lightning and the path of the serpent and become the bowman who aims his arrow at the centre of the sun.

XII

The doctors of medicine have discovered that certain dreams of the night, for I do not grant them all, are the day's unfulfilled desire, and that our terror of desires condemned by the conscience has distorted and disturbed our dreams. They have only studied the breaking into dreams of elements that have remained unsatisfied without purifying discouragement. We can satisfy in life a few of our passions and each passion but a little, and our characters indeed but differ because no two men bargain alike. The bargain, the compromise, is always threatened, and when it is broken we become mad or hysterical or are in some way deluded; and so when a starved or banished passion shows in a dream we, before awaking, break the logic that had given it the capacity of action and throw it into chaos again. But the passions, when we know that they cannot find fulfilment, become vision; and a vision, whether we wake or sleep, prolongs its power by rhythm and pattern, the wheel where the world is butterfly. We need no protection but it does, for if we become interested in ourselves, in our own lives, we pass out of the vision. Whether it is we or the vision that create the pattern, who set the wheel turning, it is hard to say, but certainly we have a hundred ways of keeping it near us: we select our images from past times, we turn from our own age and try to feel Chaucer nearer than the daily paper. It compels us to cover all it cannot incorporate, and would carry us when it comes in sleep to that moment when even sleep closes her eyes and dreams begin to dream; and we are taken up into a clear light and are forgetful even of our own names and actions and yet in perfect possession of ourselves murmur like Faust, "Stay, moment," and murmur in vain.

XIII

A poet, when he is growing old, will ask himself if he cannot keep his mask and his vision without new bitterness, new disappointment. Could he if he would, knowing how frail his vigour from youth up, copy Landor who lived loving and hating, ridiculous and unconquered, into extreme old age, all lost but the favour of his muses?

> The mother of the muses we are taught
> Is memory; she has left me; they remain
> And shake my shoulder urging me to sing.

Surely, he may think, now that I have found vision and mask I need not suffer any longer. He will buy perhaps some small old house where like Ariosto he can dig his garden, and think that in the return of birds and leaves, or moon and sun, and in the evening flight of the rooks he may discover rhythm and pattern like those in sleep and so never awake out of vision. Then he will remember Wordsworth withering into eighty years, honoured and empty-witted, and climb to some waste room and find, forgotten there by youth, some bitter crust.

February 25, 1917.

ARTHUR SCHOPENHAUER

Sympathy and Asceticism

We saw before that hatred and wickedness are conditioned by egoism, and egoism rests on the entanglement of knowledge in the principle of individuation. Thus we found that the penetration of that principle of individuation is the source and the nature of justice, and when it is carried further, even to its fullest extent, it is the source and nature of love and nobility of character. For this penetration alone, by abolishing the distinction between our own individuality and that of others, renders possible and explains perfect goodness of disposition, extending to disinterested love and the most generous self-sacrifice for others.

If, however, this penetration of the principle of individuation, this direct knowledge of the identity of will in all its manifestations, is present in a high degree of distinctness, it will at once show an influence upon the will which extends still further. If that veil of Mâyâ, the principle of individuation, is lifted from the eyes of a man to such an extent that he no longer makes the egotistical distinction between his person and that of others, but takes as much interest in the sufferings of other individuals as in his own, and therefore is not only benevolent in the highest degree, but even ready to sacrifice his own individuality whenever such a sacrifice will save a number of other persons, then it clearly follows that such a man, who recognises in all beings his own inmost and true self, must also regard the infinite suffering of all suffering beings as his own, and take on himself the pain of the whole world. No suffering is any longer strange to him. All the miseries of others which he sees and is so seldom able to alleviate, all the miseries he knows as possible, work upon his mind like his own. It is no longer the changing joy and sorrow of his own person that he has in view, as is the case with him who is still involved in egoism; but, since he sees through the principle of individuation, all lies equally near him. He knows the whole, comprehends its nature, and finds that it consists in a constant passing away, vain striving, inward conflict, and continual suffering. He sees where-ever he looks suffering humanity, the suffering brute creation, and a world that passes away. But all this now lies as near him as his own person lies to the egoist. Why should he now, with such knowledge of the world, assert this very life through constant acts of will, and thereby bind himself ever more closely to it, press it ever more firmly to himself? Thus he who

From *The World as Will and Idea* [1818], translated from the German by R. B. Haldane and J. Kemp, London, 1883-86, Vol. I, pp. 488-94, 505-6; reprinted by permission of Routledge and Kegan Paul Ltd.

is still involved in the principle of individuation, in egoism, only knows particular things and their relation to his own person, and these constantly become new *motives* of his volition. But, on the other hand, that knowledge of the whole, of the nature of the thing-in-itself which has been described, becomes a *quieter* of all and every volition. The will now turns away from life; it now shudders at the pleasures in which it recognises the assertion of life. Man now attains to the state of voluntary renunciation, resignation, true indifference, and perfect will-lessness. If at times, in the hard experience of our own suffering, or in the vivid recognition of that of others, the knowledge of the vanity and bitterness of life draws nigh to us also who are still wrapt in the veil of Mâyâ, and we would like to destroy the sting of the desires, close the entrance against all suffering, and purify and sanctify ourselves by complete and final renunciation; yet the illusion of the phenomenon soon entangles us again, and its motives influence the will anew; we cannot tear ourselves free. The allurement of hope, the flattery of the present, the sweetness of pleasure, the well-being which falls to our lot, amid the lamentations of a suffering world governed by chance and error, draws us back to it and rivets our bonds anew. Therefore Jesus says: "It is easier for a camel to go through the eye of a needle, than for a rich man to enter into the kingdom of God."

If we compare life to a course or path through which we must unceasingly run —a path of red-hot coals, with a few cool places here and there; then he who is entangled in delusion is consoled by the cool places, on which he now stands, or which he sees near him, and sets out to run through the course. But he who sees through the principle of individuation, and recognises the real nature of the thing-in-itself, and thus the whole, is no longer susceptible of such consolation; he sees himself in all places at once, and withdraws. His will turns round, no longer asserts its own nature, which is reflected in the phenomenon, but denies it. The phenomenon by which this change is marked, is the transition from virtue to asceticism. That is to say, it no longer suffices for such a man to love others as himself, and to do as much for them as for himself; but there arises within him a horror of the nature of which his own phenomenal existence is an expression, the will to live, the kernel and inner nature of that world which is recognised as full of misery. He therefore disowns this nature which appears in him, and is already expressed through his body, and his action gives the lie to his phenomenal existence, and appears in open contradiction to it. Essentially nothing else but a manifestation of will, he ceases to will anything, guards against attaching his will to anything, and seeks to confirm in himself the greatest indifference to everything. . . .

Asceticism then shows itself further in voluntary and intentional poverty, which not only arises *per accidens*, because the possessions are given away to mitigate the sufferings of others, but is here an end in itself, is meant to serve as a constant mortification of will, so that the satisfaction of the wishes, the sweet of life, shall not again arouse the will, against which self-knowledge has conceived a horror. He who has attained to this point, still always feels, as a living body, as concrete manifestation of will, the natural disposition for every kind of volition; but he intentionally suppresses it, for he compels himself to refrain from doing all that he would like to do, and to do all that he would like not to do, even if this has no further end than that of serving as a mortification of will. Since he himself denies the will which appears in his own person, he will not resist if another does the same, *i. e.*, inflicts wrongs upon him. Therefore every suffering coming to him from without through chance or the wickedness of others, is welcome to him, every injury, ignominy, and insult; he receives them gladly as the opportunity of learning with certainty that he no longer asserts the will, but gladly sides with every enemy of the manifestation of will which is his own person. Therefore he bears such ignominy and suffering with inexhaustible patience and meekness, returns good for evil without ostentation, and allows the fire of anger to rise within him just as little as that of the desires. And he mortifies not only the will itself, but also its visible form, its objectivity, the body. He nourishes it sparingly, lest its excessive vigour and prosperity should animate and excite more strongly the will, of which it is merely the expression and the mirror. So he practises fasting, and even resorts to chastisement and self-inflicted torture, in order that, by constant privation and suffering, he may more and more break down and destroy the will, which he recognises and abhors as the source of his own suffering existence and that of the world. If at last death comes, which puts an end to this manifestation of that will, whose existence here has long since perished through free denial of itself, with the exception of the weak residue of it which appears as the life of this body; it is most welcome, and is gladly received as a longed-for deliverance. . . .

We must not, however, suppose that when, by means of the knowledge which acts as a quieter of will, the denial of the will to live has once appeared, it never wavers or vacillates, and that we can rest upon it as on an assured possession. Rather, it must ever anew be attained by a constant battle. For since the body is the will itself only in the form of objectivity or as manifestation in the world as idea, so long as the body lives, the whole will to live exists potentially, and constantly strives to become actual, and to burn again with all its ardour. Therefore that peace and blessedness in the life of holy men which we have described is only found as the flower which proceeds from the constant victory over the will, and the ground in which it grows is the constant battle with the will to live, for no one can have lasting peace upon earth. We therefore see the histories of the inner life of saints full of spiritual conflicts, temptations, and absence of grace, *i. e.*, the kind of knowledge which makes all motives ineffectual, and as an universal quieter silences all volition, gives the deepest peace and opens the door of freedom. Therefore also we see those who have once attained to the denial of the will to live strive with all their might to keep upon this path, by enforced renunciation of every kind, by penance and severity of life, and by selecting whatever is disagreeable to them, all in order to suppress the will, which is constantly springing up anew. . . .

FRIEDRICH NIETZSCHE

Self-Overcoming

When Zarathustra arrived at the nearest of the towns lying against the forest, he found in that very place many people assembled in the market square: for it had been announced that a tight-rope walker would be appearing. And Zarathustra spoke thus to the people:

I teach you the Superman. Man is something that should be overcome. What have you done to overcome him?

All creatures hitherto have created something beyond themselves: and do you want to be the ebb of this great tide, and return to the animals rather than overcome man?

What is the ape to men? A laughing-stock or a painful embarrassment. And just so shall men be to the Superman: a laughing-stock or a painful embarrassment.

You have made your way from worm to man, and much in you is still worm. Once you were apes, and even now man is more of an ape than any ape.

But he who is the wisest among you, he also is only a discord and hybrid of plant and of ghost. But do I bid you become ghosts or plants?

Behold, I teach you the Superman.

The Superman is the meaning of the earth. Let your will say: The Superman *shall be* the meaning of the earth!

I entreat you, my brothers, *remain true to the earth*, and do not believe those who speak to you of superterrestrial hopes! They are poisoners, whether they know it or not.

They are despisers of life, atrophying and self-poisoned men, of whom the earth is weary: so let them be gone!

Once blasphemy against God was the greatest blasphemy, but God died, and thereupon these blasphemers died too. To blaspheme the earth is now the most dreadful offence, and to esteem the bowels of the Inscrutable more highly than the meaning of the earth.

Once the soul looked contemptuously upon the body: and then this contempt was the supreme good—the soul wanted the body lean, monstrous, famished. So the soul thought to escape from the body and from the earth.

Oh, this soul was itself lean, monstrous, and famished: and cruelty was the delight of this soul!

But tell me, my brothers: What does your body say about your soul? Is your soul not poverty and dirt and a miserable ease?

In truth, man is a polluted river. One must be a sea, to receive a polluted river and not be defiled.

Behold, I teach you the Superman: he is this sea, in him your great contempt can go under.

From *Thus Spoke Zarathustra* [1883], translated from the German by R. J. Hollingdale, Baltimore, 1962, pp. 41-3, 136-9; reprinted by permission of Penguin Books Inc.
From *Beyond Good and Evil* [1886], translated from the German by Marianne Cowan, Chicago, 1955, pp. 94-6, 156-60, 199-206. Copyright 1955 by Henry Regnery Company; reprinted by permission of the publisher.

What is the greatest thing you can experience? It is the hour of the great contempt. The hour in which even your happiness grows loathsome to you, and your reason and your virtue also.

The hour when you say: "What good is my happiness? It is poverty and dirt and a miserable ease. But my happiness should justify existence itself!"

The hour when you say: "What good is my reason? Does it long for knowledge as the lion for its food? It is poverty and dirt and a miserable ease!"

The hour when you say: "What good is my virtue? It has not yet driven me mad! How tired I am of my good and my evil! It is all poverty and dirt and a miserable ease!"

The hour when you say: "What good is my justice? I do not see that I am fire and hot coals. But the just man is fire and hot coals!"

The hour when you say: "What good is my pity? Is not pity the cross upon which he who loves man is nailed? But my pity is no crucifixion!"

Have you ever spoken thus? Have you ever cried thus? Ah, that I had heard you crying thus!

It is not your sin, but your moderation that cries to heaven, your very meanness in sinning cries to heaven!

Where is the lightning to lick you with its tongue? Where is the madness, with which you should be cleansed?

Behold, I teach you the Superman: he is this lightning, he is this madness!

When Zarathustra had spoken thus, one of the people cried: "Now we have heard enough of the tight-rope walker; let us see him, too!" And all the people laughed at Zarathustra. But the tight-rope walker, who thought that the words applied to him, set to work.

What urges you on and arouses your ardour, you wisest of men, do you call it "will to truth"?

Will to the conceivability of all being: that is what I call your will!

You first want to *make* all being conceivable: for, with a healthy mistrust, you doubt whether it is in fact conceivable.

But it must bend and accommodate itself to you! Thus will your will have it. It must become smooth and subject to the mind as the mind's mirror and reflection.

That is your entire will, you wisest men; it is a will to power; and that is so even when you talk of good and evil and of the assessment of values.

You want to create the world before which you can kneel: this is your ultimate hope and intoxication.

The ignorant, to be sure, the people—they are like a river down which a boat swims: and in the boat, solemn and disguised, sit the assessments of value.

You put your will and your values upon the river of becoming; what the people believe to be good and evil betrays to me an ancient will to power.

It was you, wisest men, who put such passengers in this boat and gave them splendour and proud names—you and your ruling will!

Now the river bears your boat along: it has to bear it. It is of small account if the breaking wave foams and angrily opposes its keel!

It is not the river that is your danger and the end of your good and evil, you wisest men, it is that will itself, the will to power, the unexhausted, procreating life-will.

But that you may understand my teaching about good and evil, I shall relate to you my teaching about life and about the nature of all living creatures.

I have followed the living creature, I have followed the greatest and the smallest paths, that I might understand its nature.

I caught its glance in a hundredfold mirror when its mouth was closed, that its eye might speak to me. And its eye did speak to me.

But wherever I found living creatures, there too I heard the language of obedience. All living creatures are obeying creatures.

And this is the second thing: he who cannot obey himself will be commanded. That is the nature of living creatures.

But this is the third thing I heard: that commanding is more difficult than obeying. And not only because the commander bears the burden of all who obey, and that this burden can easily crush him.

In all commanding there appeared to me to be an experiment and a risk: and the living creature always risks himself when he commands.

Yes, even when he commands himself: then also must he make amends for his commanding. He must become judge and avenger and victim of his own law.

How has this come about? thus I asked myself. What persuades the living creature to obey and to command and to practise obedience even in commanding?

Listen now to my teaching, you wisest men! Test in earnest whether I have crept into the heart of life itself and down to the roots of its heart!

Where I found a living creature, there I found will to power; and even in the will of the servant I found the will to be master.

The will of the weaker persuades it to serve the stronger; its will wants to be master over those weaker still: this delight alone it is unwilling to forgo.

And as the lesser surrenders to the greater, that it may have delight and power over the least of all, so the greatest, too, surrenders and for the sake of power stakes—life.

The devotion of the greatest is to encounter risk and danger and play dice for death.

And where sacrifice and service and loving glances are, there too is will to be master. There the weaker steals by secret paths into the castle and even into the heart of the more powerful—and steals the power.

And life itself told me this secret: "Behold," it said, "I am that *which must overcome itself again and again.*

"To be sure, you call it will to procreate or impulse towards a goal, towards the higher, more distant, more manifold: but all this is one and one secret.

"I would rather perish than renounce this one thing; and truly, where there is perishing and the falling of leaves, behold, there life sacrifices itself—for the sake of power!

"That I have to be struggle and becoming and goal and conflict of goals: ah, he who divines my will surely divines, too, along what *crooked* paths it has to go!

"Whatever I create and however much I love it—soon I have to oppose it and my love: thus will my will have it.

"And you too, enlightened man, are only a path and footstep of my will: truly, my will to power walks with the feet of your will to truth!

"He who shot the doctrine of 'will to existence' at truth certainly did not hit the truth: this will—does not exist!

"For what does not exist cannot will; but that which is in existence, how could it still want to come into existence?

"Only where life is, there is also will: not will to life, but—so I teach you—will to power!

"The living creature values many things higher than life itself; yet out of this evaluation itself speaks—the will to power!"

Thus life once taught me: and with this teaching do I solve the riddle of your hearts, you wisest men.

Truly, I say to you: Unchanging good and evil does not exist! From out of themselves they must overcome themselves again and again.

You exert power with your values and doctrines of good and evil, you assessors of values; and this is your hidden love and the glittering, trembling, and overflowing of your souls.

But a mightier power and a new overcoming grow from out your values: egg and egg-shell break against them.

And he who has to be a creator in good and evil, truly, has first to be a destroyer and break values.

Thus the greatest evil belongs with the greatest good: this, however, is the creative good.

Let us *speak* of this, you wisest men, even if it is a bad thing. To be silent is worse; all suppressed truths become poisonous.

And let everything that can break upon our truths—break! There is many a house still to build!

Thus spoke Zarathustra.

Every morality, in contrast to *laisser aller*, is a work of tyranny against "nature" and also against "reason." But this is not an objection to it—not unless one wished to decree (proceeding from some sort of morality) that all types of tyranny and irrationality are to be forbidden. What is essential and of inestimable value in each morality is that it is a long-lasting restraint. To understand Stoicism or Port-Royal or Puritanism, it is well to remember the restraints under which any language hitherto has reached its peak of power and subtlety—the restraint of metrics, the tyranny of rhyme and rhythm. How much trouble have the poets and orators of each nation always taken (not excepting several of today's prose writers) with an inexorable conscience in their ear, "for the sake of a folly" say the Utilitarian fools who think they are clever, "in deference to arbitrary laws" say the anarchists who imagine they are "free," in fact freethinkers. The strange fact, however, is that everything of freedom, subtlety, boldness, dance, and craftsmanlike certainty that one can find on earth, whether it applies to thinking, or ruling, or speaking, or persuading—in the arts as well as in codes of conduct—would never have developed save through the "tyranny of such arbitrary laws." Indeed, the probability is strong that *this* is "nature" and "natural"—and *not—laisser aller!* Every artist knows how far his most "natural" condition is from the feeling of letting oneself go, how rigorously and subtly he obeys a thousandfold law in the moment of "inspiration," in his free ordering, locating, disposing, and formgiving, how his laws mock at all formulation into concepts, precisely because they are so rigorous and well-defined (even the firmest concept, compared to them, has something teeming, manifold, and ambiguous about it). The essential thing "in heaven and on earth," it seems, is—to say it once more—that there be obedience, long continued obedience in some one direction. When this happens, something worthwhile always comes of it, something which makes living worthwhile; virtue, for example, or art or music or dance or reason or spirituality—something that transfigures us, something subtly refined, or mad, or divine. The long bondage of the spirit, the long repression in the communicability of thoughts, the discipline assumed by the thinker to think within an ecclesiastical or court-imposed system or within the framework of Aristotelian assumptions, the enduring, intellectual will to interpret all that happens according to the Christian scheme, to discover and justify the Christian God in every accident—all this violence, arbitrariness, rigor, gruesomeness and antirationality turned out to be the means for disciplining the European spirit into strength, ruthless inquisitiveness, and subtle flexibility. We must admit, of course, that much which is irreplaceable in energy and spirit was suppressed, choked out, and ruined in this same process (for here, as everywhere, "nature" shows up as that which it is, in all its wasteful and *indifferent* magnificence which outrages us but which is a mark of its distinction). That European thinkers for millenniums thought only in order to prove something (today the case is reversed and we distrust any thinker who is out to prove something), that they always knew very definitely what was *supposed* to be the result of their most rigorous thinking (think of the example of Asiatic astrology or today's harmless Christian-moral interpretation of personal events as happening "to the greater glory of God" or "for the good of the soul"!)—all this tyranny, this arbitrariness, this rigorous and grandiose stupidity has *disciplined* and *educated* the spirit. It seems that slavery, in both its coarser and its finer application, is the indispensable means for even spiritual discipline and cultivation. Lok at any morality—you will see that it is its "nature" to teach hatred of *laisser aller*, of too much freedom, and to implant the need for limited horizons, for the nearest task. It teaches the *narrowing of perspectives*, in other words stupidity in a certain sense, as a necessary condition for life and growth. "Thou shalt obey, someone or other, and for a long time; *if not*, you perish and lose your last self-respect"—this seems to me to be the moral imperative of nature. It is neither categorical, to be sure, as old Kant demanded (observe the "if not"!), nor is it directed to any individual! What does nature care about an individual! But it is directed to peoples, races, times, classes, and—above all—to the whole animal known as "man," to *mankind*.

In those late epochs which have a right to be proud of their humane sentiments, there remains so much fear, so much *superstitious* fear of the "wild cruel beast" whose conquest constitutes the pride of their humane sentiments, that even palpable truths remain unexpressed for centuries, as though by general agreement, because they look as though they might revive that wild, finally slaughtered, beast. So I am risking something perhaps, if I let one such truth out of my hands.

But let others capture it again and give it enough milk of human kindness to drink until it lies quietly and forgotten in its old corner once more.—We should relearn our lesson on cruelty and open our eyes. We should finally learn impatience with the immodest and fat errors that are virtuously and impudently making their way among us, such as the error in regard to tragedy for example, which has been force-fed by new and old philosophers alike. Practically everything that we call "superior culture" rests on the intellectualization and deepening of *cruelty*: this is my proposition. This is the wild beast that was not slaughtered at all; it lives; it flourishes; it has only been—deified. What constitutes the painful delight of tragedy is cruelty; what is pleasurable in so-called tragic pity, and basically in everything sublime right up to the highest and subtlest thrills of metaphysics, gets its sweetness from nothing other than the added ingredient of cruelty. What the Roman enjoys in the Arena, the Christian in the ecstasies of the cross, the Spaniard in the sight of the stage and the bull-fight, the modern Japanese who is drawn to tragedy, the worker in the suburbs of Paris who feels nostalgia for bloody revolutions, the female Wagnerian with will suspended who lets *Tristan und Isolde* "come over" her—what they all enjoy and seek to incorporate into themselves with a secret passionate order is the magic brew of the great Circe *Cruelty*. Naturally we must get rid of the old ridiculous psychology which knew no better than to teach that cruelty only arises at the sight of *someone else's* suffering. There is a rich, an over-rich pleasure in one's own suffering, in making oneself suffer. Wherever man is persuaded to self-negation in the religious sense, or to self-mutilation as among the Phoenicians and ascetics, or to any form of de-sensualization, decarnalization, contrition, to Puritanical repentance-paroxysms, to vivisection of the conscience, to Pascal-like *sacrifizio dell' intelletto*—there he is secretly lured and propelled by his cruelty, by the dangerous thrills of cruelty *inflicted on himself*. Ultimately, we must consider that even the man of insight—insofar as insight is paid for by the mind's opposition to its own inclinations, and often by its opposition to one's heart's desires, by its forcing one to say "no" where one would like to say "yes," to love, to adore—that such a man, too, operates as an artist and a transfigurer of cruelty. Any depth, any thoroughness is already a violation, a desire to hurt the basic will of man's mind whose trend is constantly toward illusion, toward the surface. In any desire of the mind to penetrate deeply and with understanding there is already a drop of cruelty.

––––––––––

Perhaps what I have just said about the "basic will of the mind" will not be readily understood, so that I may be permitted an elucidation.—The command-giving something which is called "mind" by the people wants to be master in itself and all around itself and to feel that it is master. It has the will to make simplicity out of multiplicity; it is a will that ties things up, tames them—a domineering and really dominant will. Its needs and capabilities are the same as those which the physiologists assign to everything that lives and grows and reproduces. The power of mind to absorb foreign elements reveals itself in its strong tendency to make the new like the old, to simplify the manifold, to overlook or reject the totally contradictory; mind also arbitrarily underlines, emphasizes, falsifies—in order to suit its own purposes—certain features and characteristics of things foreign to itself, i.e. every bit of "outside world" that comes into its ken. Its purpose is the incorporation of new "experiences," the adding of new material to old, its growth in other words, or more strictly defined, the *feeling* of its growth, the feeling of its increased power. A servant of this same will is an apparently opposite drive of the mind: a suddenly erupting decision to be ignorant, to be arbitrarily shut off, a closing of windows, an inward "no" to this or that, a refusal to be approached, a sort of defense against much that might be known, a satisfaction at being in the dark, at being enclosed within a limiting horizon, a "yes" and a benediction upon ignorance—all according to the present needs of its appropriating power, its "digestive power," metaphorically speaking. Really, the mind is more like a stomach than anything else. Furthermore we must add the occasional will of the mind to be deceived, perhaps with a reckless intuition that things are *not* this way or that, that one is simply taking them for this or that, a delight in insecurity and ambiguity, a gay self-satisfaction in the arbitrary narrowness and secrecy of a given corner, in the all-too-near, the foreground, the magnified, the minimized, the distorted, the beautified—a self-satisfaction in the arbitrary nature of all such expressions of power. And finally there is that precarious willingness of the mind to deceive other minds and to disguise itself; that constant pressure and impulsion of a creative, image-making, changable power: in this, the mind enjoys its many masks, its cunning; also the feeling of its own security, for it is best defended and concealed by its Proteus-skills. Counter to *this* will to illusion, to simplification, to the mask, to the cloak, in short this will to surfaces (for every surface is a cloak) operates that sublime impulse of the man of insight, that spirit which takes and *wants* to take things deeply, complicatedly, and thoroughly. This is the cruelty characteristic of the intellectual conscience and taste. Every courageous thinker will acknowledge it in himself, provided that he has trained and sharpened his eyes for it long enough, as is proper, and is accustomed to rigorous discipline and to rigorous words as well. He will say "There is something cruel about the tendency of my mind," regardless of the virtuous and amiable people who will try to dissuade him! Indeed, it would sound prettier if they talked about us or whispered after us or admired us in terms of "excessive candor," let us say, instead of cruelty. We free, *very* free thinkers—perhaps that will be our posthumous reputation! Meanwhile—and a long while it will be—we should be the least inclined to ornament ourselves with such moralistic word-spangles and bangles. Our entire work ruins us for that sort of taste and its cheerful lushness. They are beautiful, glittering, jingling, festive words: candor, love for truth, love for wisdom, self-sacrifice for insight, heroism of the truthful! Something about them swells one's pride. But we anchorites and marmots, we have convinced ourselves long ago, in all the secrecy of our anchorite's conscience, that this worthy word-pomp too belongs to the old lying bangles, to all the deceptive junk and gold dust of unconscious human vanity; that even beneath such flattering colors and cosmetics the frightful basic text *homo natura*, must be recognized for what it is. For to retranslate man back into nature, to master the many vain enthusiastic glosses which have been scribbled and painted over the everlasting text, *homo natura*, so that man might henceforth stand before man as he stands today before that *other* nature, hardened under the discipline of science, with unafraid Oedipus eyes and stopped up Ulysses ears, deaf to the lures of the old metaphysical bird catchers who have been fluting in at him all too long that "you are more! You are superior! You are of another origin!"—this may be a strange, mad task, but who could deny that it is a *task!* Why did we choose it, this mad task? Or, to ask it with different words, "Why insight, anyway?" Everyone will ask us this. And we, pressed for an answer, having asked the same question of ourselves hundreds of times, we have found and shall find no better answer. . . .

Every heightening of the type "man" hitherto has been the work of an aristo-cratic society—and thus it will always be; a society which believes in a long ladder of rank order and value differences in men, which needs slavery in some sense. Without the *pathos of distance* as it grows out of the deep-seated differences of caste, out of the constant view, the downward view, that the ruling caste gets of its subordinates and tools, out of its equally constant exercise in obeying and commanding, in keeping apart and keeping a distance—without this pathos of dis-tance there could not grow that other more mysterious pathos, that longing for ever greater distances within the soul itself, the evolving of ever higher, rarer, more spacious, more widely arched, more comprehensive states—in short: the heightening of the type "man," the continued "self-mastery of man," to take a moral formula in a supra-moral sense. To be sure, we must not yield to humani-tarian self-deception about the history of the origins of an aristocratic society (in other words, the pre-suppositions for the heightening of the type "man"): the truth is hard. Let us tell ourselves without indulging ourselves how every superior culture on earth got its *start!* Men whose nature was still natural, barbarians in every frightful sense of the word, men of prey, men still in possession of unbroken strength of will and power-drives—such men threw themselves upon weaker, better-behaved, more peaceable races, possibly those engaged in commerce or cattle-raising, or else upon old hollow cultures in which the last life powers were flickering away in flashing fireworks of intellect and corruption. The distinguished caste in the beginning was always the barbarian caste; their superiority lay not primarily in their physical but in their psychic power; they were more whole as human beings (which on every level also means "more whole as beasts").

Corruption is the expression of the fact that there is anarchy which threatens to spread among the instincts, and that the basic structure of the passions, called "life," has been shaken. Types of corruption are radically different from one an-other, depending on the life-structure in which they show up. When for example an aristocracy, such as that of France at the start of the Revolution, throws away its privileges with a sublime nausea, and sacrifices itself to an extravagance of its moral feelings, that is corruption. It was really only the final act of that century-long corruption in the course of which the aristocracy yielded step by step its ruling prerogatives and lowered itself until it was a *function* of royalty (and in the very end merely its ornament and crowning glory). But the essential nature of a good and healthy aristocracy is that it does *not* feel it is a function (whether of royalty or of the community) but its meaning, its highest justification. There-fore it accepts with a clear conscience the sacrifice of an enormous number of men who must *for the sake of the aristocracy* be suppressed and reduced to incomplete human beings, to slaves, to tools. It must be aristocracy's basic belief that society exists *not* for the sake of society, but only as the foundation, the skeleton structure, by means of which a select kind of creature can raise itself to a higher task, a higher level of *being*—like those sun-seeking climbing plants in Java, called *Sipo Matador*, which cling to an oak so long and so often until finally they unfold their crowns in the open air, displaying their bliss high above the oak but supported by it.

To refrain from wounding, violating, and exploiting one another, to acknowledge another's will as equal to one's own: this can become proper behavior, in a certain coarse sense, between individuals when the conditions for making it possible obtain (namely the factual similarity of the individuals as to power and standards of value, and their co-existence in one greater body). But as soon as one wants to extend this principle, to make it the *basic principle of society*, it shows itself for what it is: the will to negate life, the principle of dissolution and decay. Here one must think radically to the very roots of things and ward off all weakness of sensibility. Life itself is essential assimilation, injury, violation of the foreign and the weaker, suppression, hardness, the forcing of one's own forms upon something else, ingestion and—at least in its mildest form—exploitation. But why should we always use such words which were coined from time immemorial to reveal a calumniatory intention? Even that body to which we referred, the body within which individuals may treat each other with equality (and it is so in any healthy aristocracy)—even this body itself, if it is alive and not dying off, must do to other bodies all the things from which its members refrain; it will have to be the will to power incarnate; it will have to want to grow, to branch out, to draw others into itself, to gain supremacy. And not because it is moral or immoral in any sense but because it is *alive*, and because life simply *is* will to power. But there is no point at which the common consciousness in Europe today is less willing to lean than just here; everywhere today, and even in the guise of science, there is grandiose talk about future social conditions where there is to be no more "exploitation." To my ears that sounds as though they promised to invent a kind of life that would refrain from all the organic functions. "Exploitation" is not a part of a vicious or imperfect or primitive society: it belongs to the *nature* of living things, it is a basic organic function, a consequence of the will to power which is the will to life. Admitted that this is a novelty as a theory—as a reality it is the *basic fact* underlying all history. Let us be honest with ourselves at least this far!

Wandering through the many fine and coarse moralities which have hitherto ruled on earth, as well as those which still rule, I found certain features regularly occurring together and bound up with one another. Finally they revealed two basic types to me, and a basic difference leaped to my eye. There is *master-morality* and *slave-morality*: I add immediately that in all higher and mixed cultures there are also attempts at a mediation between these two, and even more frequently a mix-up of them and a mutual misunderstanding; at times in fact a relentless juxtaposition even within the psyche of a single individual. The moral value-differentiations arose either among a ruling type which was pleasantly conscious of its difference from the ruled—or else among the ruled, the slaves and dependents of all kinds. In the first case, when the rulers determine the concept "good," it is the elevated and proud conditions of the psyche which are felt to be what excels and determines the order of rank. The distinguished human being divorces himself from the beings in whom the opposite of such elevated and proud conditions is expressed. He despises them. One may note immediately that in the first type of morality the antithesis "good vs. bad" means "distinguished vs. despicable;" the antithesis "good vs. evil" has a different origin. What is despised is the coward, the timid man, and the petty man, he who thinks in terms of narrow utility; likewise the suspicious man with his cowed look, the one who humiliates himself, the dog-type who lets himself be mistreated, the begging flatterer, and above all the liar: it is the basic faith of all aristocrats that the common people are liars. "We truthful ones" the nobles called themselves in ancient Greece. It is obvious that the moral value-characteristics are at first applied to *people* and only later, in a transferred sense, to *acts*. This is why it is a sad mistake when moral historians begin with questions like "Why was the compassionate act praised?" The distinguished type of human being feels *himself* as value-determining; he does not need to be ratified; he judges that "which is harmful to me is harmful as such"; he knows that *he* is the something which gives honor to objects; he *creates values*. This type honors everything he knows about himself; his morality is self-glorification. In the foreground is the feeling of fullness, of power that would flow forth, the bliss of high tension, the consciousness of riches which would like to give and lavish. The distinguished man, too, helps the unhappy, but not—at least not mainly—from compassion, but more from an internal pressure that has been built up by an excess of power. The distinguished man honors himself in the mighty, including those who have power over themselves; those who know when to talk and when to keep silent; those who take delight in being rigorous and hard with themselves and who have respect for anything rigorous and hard. "Wotan placed a hard heart in my breast," says an old Scandinavian saga: this is the proper poetic expression for the soul of a proud Viking. Such a type of man is proud *not* to have been made for compassion; hence the hero of the saga adds a warning: "Whoever has not a hard heart when young will never get it at all." Distinguished and courageous men with such thoughts are at the opposite end from that morality which sees the characteristic function of morality in pity or in doing for others or *désintéressement*. Belief in oneself, pride in oneself, basic hostility and irony against "selflessness" is as sure a part of distinguished morality as an easy disdain and cautious attitude toward the fellow-feelings and the "warm heart." It is the powerful men who *understand* how to accord honor: that is their art, the domain of their invention. Profound respect for old age and for origins: their whole law stands on this twofold respect. Faith in and prepossession for one's ancestors and prejudice against the future ones is typical of the morality of the powerful. Contrariwise, when men of "modern ideas" believe almost instinctively in "progress" and in "the future" and have less and less respect for the old, that alone reveals clearly enough the undistinguished origin of their "ideas." But the point at which the morality of rulers is most foreign to current taste and most painstakingly strict in principle is this: one has duties only toward one's equals; toward beings of a lower rank, toward everything foreign to one, one may act as one sees fit, "as one's heart dictates"— in any event, "beyond good and evil." The ability and the duty to sustain enduring gratitude and enduring vengefulness—both only toward one's equals; subtlety in requital and retaliation; a subtly refined concept of friendship; a certain need to have enemies (as outlets for the passions: envy, quarrelsomeness and wantonness—basically, in order to be capable of being a good *friend*): all these are typical marks of the distinguished type of morality which, as I have indicated, is not the morality of "modern ideas" and hence is difficult today to empathize with, and equally difficult to dig out and uncover.—The situation is different with the second type of morality, the slave morality. Assuming that the violated ones, the oppressed, the suffering, the unfree, those who are uncertain and tired of themselves—assuming that they moralize: What will they have in common in their moral evaluations? Probably a pessimistic suspiciousness against the whole situation of mankind will appear; perhaps a judgment against mankind together with its position. The eye of the slave looks unfavorably upon the virtues of the powerful; he *subtly* mistrusts all the "good" that the others honor—he would like to persuade himself that even their happiness is not real. Conversely, those qualities are emphasized and illuminated which serve to make existence easier for the sufferers: here compassion, the complaisant helping hand, the warm heart, patience, diligence, humility and friendliness are honored, for these are the useful qualities and almost the only means for enduring the pressure of existence. Slave-morality is essentially a utility-morality. Here is the cornerstone for the origin of that famous Antithesis "good vs. evil." Power and dangerousness, a certain frightfulness, subtlety and strength which do not permit of despisal, are felt to belong to evil. Hence according to slave morality, the "evil" man inspires fear; according to master morality, the "good" man does and wants to, whereas the "bad" man is felt to be despicable. The antithesis reaches its sharpest point when ultimately the "good" man within a slave morality becomes the logical target of a breath of disdain—however slight and well-meaning, because he is the *undangerous* element in his morality: good natured, easily deceived, perhaps a little stupid, *un bonhomme*. Whenever slave morality preponderates, language shows a tendency to reconcile the meanings of "good" and "dumb." A final basic distinction is that the longing for *freedom*, the instinct for happiness and the subtleties of the freedom-feelings belong as necessarily to slave morality as skill and enthusiasm for reverence, for devotion, is the regular symptom of an aristocratic manner of thinking and evaluating.—This enables us to understand easily why love *as passion* (our European specialty) must be of distinguished origin; we know it was invented by the Provençal knightly poets, those magnificent inventive men of *gai saber*[1]—to whom Europe owes so much, and almost itself.

[1] Gay learning. Nietzsche used the phrase for the title of a previous work; *Die fröhliche Wissenschaft*. TRANSLATOR'S NOTE.

F. M. DOSTOEVSKY

The Perverse Self

I

I am a sick man. . . . I am a spiteful man.[1] I am an unattractive man. I believe
my liver is diseased. However, I know nothing at all about my disease, and do not
know for certain what ails me. I don't consult a doctor for it, and never have,
though I have a respect for medicine and doctors. Besides, I am extremely superstitious, sufficiently so to respect medicine, anyway (I am well-educated enough
not to be superstitious, but I am superstitious). No, I refuse to consult a doctor
from spite. That you probably will not understand. Well, I understand it, though.
Of course, I can't explain who it is precisely that I am mortifying in this case by
my spite: I am perfectly well aware that I cannot "pay out" the doctors by not
consulting them; I know better than any one that by all this I am only injuring
myself and no one else. But still, if I don't consult a doctor it is from spite. My
liver is bad, well—let it get worse!

I have been going on like that for a long time—twenty years. Now I am forty. I
used to be in the government service, but am no longer. I was a spiteful official. I
was rude and took pleasure in being so. I did not take bribes, you see, so I was
bound to find a recompense in that, at least. (A poor jest, but I will not scratch it
out. I wrote it thinking it would sound very witty; but now that I have seen myself that I only wanted to show off in a despicable way, I will not scratch it out on
purpose!)

When petitioners used to come for information to the table at which I sat, I
used to grind my teeth at them, and felt intense enjoyment when I succeeded in
making anybody unhappy. I almost always did succeed. For the most part they
were all timid people—of course, they were petitioners. But of the uppish ones
there was one officer in particular I could not endure. He simply would not be
humble, and clanked his sword in a disgusting way. I carried on a feud with him
for eighteen months over that sword. At last I got the better of him. He left off
clanking it. That happened in my youth, though.

But do you know, gentlemen, what was the chief point about my spite? Why,
the whole point, the real sting of it lay in the fact that continually, even in the
moment of the acutest spleen, I was inwardly conscious with shame that I was
not only not a spiteful but not even an embittered man, that I was simply scaring

[1] The author of the diary and the diary itself are, of course, imaginary. Nevertheless it is
clear that such persons as the writer of these notes not only may, but positively must, exist
in our society, when we consider the circumstances in the midst of which our society is
formed. I have tried to expose to the view of the public more distinctly than is commonly
done one of the characters of the recent past. He is one of the representatives of a generation still living. In this fragment, entitled "Underground," this person introduces himself and his views, and, as it were, tries to explain the causes owing to which he has
made his appearance and was bound to make his appearance in our midst. In the second
fragment there are added the actual notes of this person concerning certain events in his
life. AUTHOR'S NOTE.

From "Notes from Underground" [1864], *White Nights and Other Stories*, translated from
the Russian by Constance Garnett, New York, 1918, pp. 50-81; reprinted by permission of
William Heinemann Ltd.

sparrows at random and amusing myself by it. I might foam at the mouth, but bring me a doll to play with, give me a cup of tea with sugar in it, and maybe I should be appeased. I might even be genuinely touched, though probably I should grind my teeth at myself afterwards and lie awake at night with shame for months after. That was my way.

I was lying when I said just now that I was a spiteful official. I was lying from spite. I was simply amusing myself with the petitioners and with the officer, and in reality I never could become spiteful. I was conscious every moment in myself of many, very many elements absolutely opposite to that. I felt them positively swarming in me, these opposite elements. I knew that they had been swarming in me all my life and craving some outlet from me, but I would not let them, would not let them, purposely would not let them come out. They tormented me till I was ashamed: they drove me to convulsions and—sickened me, at last, how they sickened me! Now, are not you fancying, gentlemen, that I am expressing remorse for something now, that I am asking your forgiveness for something? I am sure you are fancying that. . . . However, I assure you I do not care if you are. . . .

It was not only that I could not become spiteful, I did not know how to become anything: neither spiteful nor kind, neither a rascal nor an honest man, neither a hero nor an insect. Now, I am living out my life in my corner, taunting myself with the spiteful and useless consolation that an intelligent man cannot become anything seriously, and it is only the fool who becomes anything. Yes, a man in the nineteenth century must and morally ought to be pre-eminently a characterless creature; a man of character, an active man, is pre-eminently a limited creature. That is my conviction of forty years. I am forty years old now, and you know forty years is a whole lifetime; you know it is extreme old age. To live longer than forty years is bad manners, is vulgar, immoral. Who does live beyond forty? Answer that, sincerely and honestly. I will tell you who do: fools and worthless fellows. I tell all old men that to their face, all these venerable old men, all these silver-haired and reverend seniors! I tell the whole world that to its face. I have a right to say so, for I shall go on living to sixty myself. To seventy! To eighty! . . . Stay, let me take breath. . . .

You imagine no doubt, gentlemen, that I want to amuse you. You are mistaken in that, too. I am by no means such a mirthful person as you imagine, or as you may imagine; however, irritated by all this babble (and I feel that you are irritated) you think fit to ask me who am I—then my answer is, I am a collegiate assessor. I was in the service that I might have something to eat (and solely for that reason), and when last year a distant relation left me six thousand roubles in his will I immediately retired from the service and settled down in my corner. I used to live in this corner before, but now I have settled down in it. My room is a wretched, horrid one in the outskirts of the town. My servant is an old country-woman, ill-natured from stupidity, and, moreover, there is always a nasty smell about her. I am told that the Petersburg climate is bad for me, and that with my small means it is very expensive to live in Petersburg. I know all that better than all these sage and experienced counsellors and monitors. . . . But I am remaining in Petersburg; I am not going away from Petersburg! I am not going away because . . . ech! Why, it is absolutely no matter whether I am going away or not going away.

But what can a decent man speak of with most pleasure?
Answer: Of himself.
Well, so I will talk about myself.

II

I want now to tell you, gentlemen, whether you care to hear it or not, why I could not even become an insect. I tell you solemnly, that I have many times tried to become an insect. But I was not equal even to that. I swear, gentlemen, that to be too conscious is an illness—a real thoroughgoing illness. For man's everyday needs, it would have been quite enough to have the ordinary human consciousness, that is, half or a quarter of the amount which falls to the lot of a cultivated man of our unhappy nineteenth century, especially one who has the fatal ill-luck to inhabit Petersburg, the most theoretical and intentional town on the whole terrestrial globe. (There are intentional and unintentional towns.) It would have been quite enough, for instance, to have the consciousness by which all so-called direct persons and men of action live. I bet you think I am writing all this from affectation, to be witty at the expense of men of action; and what is more, that from ill-bred affectation, I am clanking a sword like my officer. But, gentlemen, whoever can pride himself on his diseases and even swagger over them?

Though, after all, every one does do that; people do pride themselves on their diseases, and I do, may be, more than any one. We will not dispute it; my contention was absurd. But yet I am firmly persuaded that a great deal of consciousness, every sort of consciousness, in fact, is a disease. I stick to that. Let us leave that, too, for a minute. Tell me this: why does it happen that at the very, yes, at the very moments when I am most capable of feeling every refinement of all that is "good and beautiful," as they used to say at one time, it would, as though of design, happen to me not only to feel but to do such ugly things, such that . . . Well, in short, actions that all, perhaps, commit; but which, as though purposely, occurred to me at the very time when I was most conscious that they ought not to be committed. The more conscious I was of goodness and of all that was "good and beautiful," the more deeply I sank into my mire and the more ready I was to sink in it altogether. But the chief point was that all this was, as it were, not accidental in me, but as though it were bound to be so. It was as though it were my most normal condition, and not in the least disease or depravity, so that at last all desire in me to struggle against this depravity passed. It ended by my almost believing (perhaps actually believing) that this was perhaps my normal condition. But at first, in the beginning, what agonies I endured in that struggle! I did not believe it was the same with other people, and all my life I hid this fact about myself as a secret. I was ashamed (even now, perhaps, I am ashamed): I got to the point of feeling a sort of secret abnormal, despicable enjoyment in returning home to my corner on some disgusting Petersburg night, acutely conscious that that day I had committed a loathsome action again, that what was done could never be undone, and secretly, inwardly gnawing, gnawing at myself for it, tearing and consuming myself till at last the bitterness turned into a sort of shameful accursed sweetness, and at last—into positive real enjoyment! Yes, into enjoyment, into enjoyment! I insist upon that. I have spoken of this because I keep wanting to know for a fact whether other people feel such enjoyment. I will explain: the enjoyment was just from the too intense consciousness of one's own degradation; it was from feeling oneself that one had reached the last barrier, that it was horrible, but that it could not be otherwise; that there was no escape for you; that you never could become a different man; that even if time and faith were still left you to change into something different you would most likely not wish to change; or if you did wish to, even then you would do nothing; because perhaps in reality there was nothing for you to change into.

And the worst of it was, and the root of it all, that it was all in accord with the normal fundamental laws of over-acute consciousness, and with the inertia that was the direct result of those laws, and that consequently one was not only unable to change but could do absolutely nothing. Thus it would follow, as the result of acute consciousness, that one is not to blame in being a scoundrel; as though that were any consolation to the scoundrel once he has come to realize that he actually is a scoundrel. But enough. . . . Ech, I have talked a lot of nonsense, but what have I explained? How is enjoyment in this to be explained? But I will explain it. I will get to the bottom of it! That is why I have taken up my pen. . . .

I, for instance, have a great deal of *amour propre*. I am as suspicious and prone to take offence as a humpback or a dwarf. But upon my word I sometimes have had moments when if I had happened to be slapped in the face I should, perhaps, have been positively glad of it. I say, in earnest, that I should probably have been able to discover even in that a peculiar sort of enjoyment—the enjoyment, of course, of despair; but in despair there are the most intense enjoyments, especially when one is very acutely conscious of the hopelessness of one's position. And when one is slapped in the face—why then the consciousness of being rubbed into a pulp would positively overwhelm one. The worst of it is, look at it which way one will, it still turns out that I was always the most to blame in everything. And what is most humiliating of all, to blame for no fault of my own but, so to say, through the laws of nature. In the first place, to blame because I am cleverer than any of the people surrounding me. (I have always considered myself cleverer than any of the people surrounding me, and sometimes, would you believe it, have been positively ashamed of it. At any rate, I have all my life, as it were, turned my eyes away and never could look people straight in the face.) To blame, finally, because even if I had had magnanimity, I should only have had more suffering from the sense of its uselessness. I should certainly have never been able to do anything from being magnanimous—neither to forgive, for my assailant would perhaps have slapped me from the laws of nature, and one cannot forgive the laws of nature; nor to forget, for even if it were owing to the laws of nature, it is insulting all the same. Finally, even if I had wanted to be anything but magnanimous, had desired on the contrary to revenge myself on my assailant, I could not have revenged myself on any one for anything because I should certainly never have made up my mind to do anything, even if I had been able to. Why should I not have made up my mind? About that in particular I want to say a few words.

III

With people who know how to revenge themselves and to stand up for themselves in general, how is it done? Why, when they are possessed, let us suppose, by the feeling of revenge, then for the time there is nothing else but that feeling left in their whole being. Such a gentleman simply dashes straight for his object like an infuriated bull with its horns down, and nothing but a wall will stop him. (By the way: facing the wall, such gentlemen—that is, the "direct" persons and men of action—are genuinely nonplussed. For them a wall is not an evasion, as for us people who think and consequently do nothing; it is not an excuse for turning aside, an excuse for which we are always very glad, though we scarcely believe in it ourselves, as a rule. No, they are nonplussed in all sincerity. The wall has for them something tranquillizing, morally soothing, final—maybe even something mysterious . . . but of the wall later.)

Well, such a direct person I regard as the real normal man, as his tender mother Nature wished to see him when she graciously brought him into being on the earth. I envy such a man till I am green in the face. He is stupid. I am not disputing that, but perhaps the normal man should be stupid, how do you know? Perhaps it is very beautiful, in fact. And I am the more persuaded of that suspicion, if one can call it so, by the fact that if you take, for instance, the antithesis of the normal man, that is, the man of acute consciousness, who has come, of course, not out of the lap of Nature but out of a retort (this is almost mysticism, gentlemen, but I suspect this, too), this retort-made man is sometimes so nonplussed in the presence of his antithesis that with all his exaggerated consciousness he genuinely thinks of himself as a mouse and not a man. It may be an acutely conscious mouse, yet it is a mouse, while the other is a man, and therefore, et caetera, et caetera. And the worst of it is, he himself, his very own self, looks on himself as a mouse; no one asks him to do so; and that is an important point. Now let us look at this mouse in action. Let us suppose, for instance, that it feels insulted, too (and it almost always does feel insulted), and wants to revenge itself, too. There may even be a greater accumulation of spite in it than in *l'homme de la nature et de la vérité*. The base and nasty desire to vent that spite on its assailant rankles perhaps even more nastily in it than in *l'homme de la nature et de la vérité*. For through his innate stupidity the latter looks upon his revenge as justice pure and simple; while in consequence of his acute consciousness the mouse does not believe in the justice of it. To come at last to the deed itself, to the very act of revenge. Apart from the one fundamental nastiness the luckless mouse succeeds in creating around it so many other nastinesses in the form of doubts and questions, adds to the one question so many unsettled questions, that there inevitably works up around it a sort of fatal brew, a stinking mess, made up of its doubts, emotions, and of the contempt spat upon it by the direct men of action who stand solemnly about it as judges and arbitrators, laughing at it till their healthy sides ache. Of course the only thing left for it is to dismiss all that with a wave of its paw, and, with a smile of assumed contempt in which it does not even itself believe, creep ignominiously into its mouse-hole. There in its nasty, stinking, underground home our insulted, crushed and ridiculed mouse promptly becomes absorbed in cold, malignant and, above all, everlasting spite. For forty years together it will remember its injury down to the smallest, most ignominious details, and every time will add, of itself, details still more ignominious, spitefully teasing and tormenting itself with its own imagination. It will itself be ashamed of its imaginings, but yet it will recall it all, it will go over and over every detail, it will invent unheard-of things against itself, pretending that those things might happen, and will forgive nothing. Maybe it will begin to revenge itself, too, but, as it were, piecemeal, in trivial ways, from behind the stove, incognito, without believing either in its own right to vengeance, or in the success of its revenge, knowing that from all its efforts at revenge it will suffer a hundred times more than he on whom it revenges itself, while he, I daresay, will not even scratch himself. On its death-bed it will recall it all over again, with interest accumulated over all the years and . . .

But it is just in that cold, abominable half despair, half belief, in that conscious burying oneself alive for grief in the underworld for forty years, in that acutely recognized and yet partly doubtful hopelessness of one's position, in that hell of unsatisfied desires turned inward, in that fever of oscillations, of resolutions determined for ever and repented of again a minute later—that the savour of that strange enjoyment of which I have spoken lies. It is so subtle, so difficult of analysis, that persons who are a little limited, or even simply persons of strong nerves, will not understand a single atom of it. "Possibly," you will add on your own account with a grin, "people will not understand it either who have never received a slap in the face," and in that way you will politely hint to me that I too, perhaps, have had the experience of a slap in the face in my life, and so I speak as one who knows. I bet that you are thinking that. But set your minds at rest, gentlemen, I have not received a slap in the face, though it is absolutely a matter of indifference to me what you may think about it. Possibly, I even regret myself that I have given so few slaps in the face during my life. But enough . . . not another word on that subject of such extreme interest to you.

I will continue calmly concerning persons with strong nerves who do not understand a certain refinement of enjoyment. Though in certain circumstances these gentlemen bellow their loudest like bulls, though this, let us suppose, does them the greatest credit, yet, as I have said already, confronted with the impossible they subside at once. The impossible means the stone wall! What stone wall? Why, of course, the laws of nature, the deductions of natural science, mathematics. As soon as they prove to you, for instance, that you are descended from a monkey, then it is no use scowling, accept it for a fact. When they prove to you that in reality one drop of your own fat must be dearer to you than a hundred thousand of your fellow creatures, and that this conclusion is the final solution of all so-called virtues and duties and all such prejudices and fancies, then you have just to accept it, there is no help for it, for twice two is a law of mathematics. Just try refuting it.

"Upon my word," they will shout at you, "it is no use protesting: it is a case of twice two makes four! Nature does not ask your permission, she has nothing to do with your wishes, and whether you like her laws or dislike them, you are bound to accept her as she is, and consequently all her conclusions. A wall, you see, is a wall . . . and so on, and so on."

Merciful heavens! but what do I care for the laws of nature and arithmetic, when, for some reason, I dislike those laws and the fact that twice two makes four? Of course I cannot break through the wall by battering my head against it if I really have not the strength to knock it down, but I am not going to be reconciled to it simply because it is a stone wall and I have not the strength.

As though such a stone wall really were a consolation, and really did contain some word of conciliation, simply because it is as true as twice two makes four.

Oh, absurdity of absurdities! How much better it is to understand it all, to recognize it all, all the impossibilities and the stone wall; not to be reconciled to one of those impossibilities and stone walls if it disgusts you to be reconciled to it; by the way of the most inevitable, logical combinations to reach the most revolting conclusions on the everlasting theme, that even for the stone wall you are yourself somehow to blame, though again it is as clear as day you are not to blame in the least, and therefore grinding your teeth in silent impotence to sink into luxurious inertia, brooding on the fact that there is no one even for you to feel vindictive against, that you have not, and perhaps never will have, an object for your spite, that it is a sleight-of-hand, a bit of juggling, a card-sharper's trick, that it is simply a mess, no knowing what and no knowing who, but in spite of all these uncertainties and jugglings, still there is an ache in you, and the more you do not know, the worse the ache.

IV

"Ha, ha, ha! You will be finding enjoyment in toothache next," you cry, with a laugh.

"Well? Even in toothache there is enjoyment," I answer. I had toothache for a whole month and I know there is. In that case, of course, people are not spiteful in silence, but moan; but they are not candid moans, they are malignant moans, and the malignancy is the whole point. The enjoyment of the sufferer finds expression in those groans; if he did not feel enjoyment in them he would not moan. It is a good example, gentlemen, and I will develop it. Those moans express in the first place all the aimlessness of your pain, which is so humiliating to your consciousness; the whole legal system of Nature on which you spit disdainfully, of course, but from which you suffer all the same while she does not. They express the consciousness that you have no enemy to punish, but that you have pain; the consciousness that in spite of all possible Vagenheims you are in complete slavery to your teeth; that if some one wishes it, your teeth will leave off aching, and if he does not, they will go on aching another three months; and that finally if you are still contumacious and still protest, all that is left you for your own gratification is to thrash yourself or beat your wall with your fist as hard as you can, and absolutely nothing more. Well, these mortal insults, these jeers on the part of some one unknown, end at last in an enjoyment which sometimes reaches the highest degree of voluptuousness. I ask you, gentlemen, listen sometimes to the moans of an educated man of the nineteenth century suffering from toothache, on the second or third day of the attack, whan he is beginning to moan, not as he moaned on the first day, that is, not simply because he has toothache, not just as any coarse peasant, but as a man affected by progress and European civilization, a man who is "divorced from the soil and the national elements," as they express it nowadays. His moans become nasty, disgustingly malignant, and go on for whole days and nights. And of course he knows himself that he is doing himself no sort of good with his moans; he knows better than any one that he is only lacerating and harassing himself and others for nothing; he knows that even the audience before whom he is making his efforts, and his whole family, listen to him with loathing, do not put a ha'porth of faith in him, and inwardly understand that he might moan differently, more simply, without trills and flourishes, and that he is only amusing himself like that from ill-humour, from malignancy. Well, in all these recognitions and disgraces it is that there lies a voluptuous pleasure. As though he would say: "I am worrying you, I am lacerating your hearts, I am keeping every one in the house awake. Well, stay awake then, you, too, feel every minute that I have toothache. I am not a hero to you now, as I tried to seem before, but simply a nasty person, an impostor. Well, so be it, then! I am very glad that you see through me. It is nasty for you to hear my despicable moans: well, let it be nasty; here I will let you have a nastier flourish in a minute. . . ." You do not understand even now, gentlemen? No, it seems our development and our consciousness must go further to understand all the intricacies of this pleasure. You laugh? Delighted. My jests, gentlemen, are of course in bad taste, jerky, involved, lacking self-confidence. But of course that is because I do not respect myself. Can a man of perception respect himself at all?

V

Come, can a man who attempts to find enjoyment in the very feeling of his own degradation possibly have a spark of respect for himself? I am not saying this now from any mawkish kind of remorse. And, indeed, I could never endure saying, "Forgive me, Papa, I won't do it again," not because I am incapable of saying that—on the contrary, perhaps just because I have been too capable of it, and in what a way, too! As though of design I used to get into trouble in cases when I was not to blame in any way. That was the nastiest part of it. At the same time I was genuinely touched and penitent, I used to shed tears and, of course, deceived myself, though I was not acting in the least and there was a sick feeling in my heart at the time. . . . For that one could not blame even the laws of nature, though the laws of nature have continually all my life offended me more than anything. It is loathsome to remember it all, but it was loathsome even then. Of course, a minute or so later I would realize wrathfully that it was all a lie, a revolting lie, an affected lie, that is, all this penitence, this emotion, these vows of reform. You will ask why did I worry myself with such antics: answer, because it was very dull to sit with one's hands folded, and so one began cutting capers. That is really it. Observe yourselves more carefully, gentlemen, then you will understand that it is so. I invented adventures for myself and made up a life, so as at least to live in some way. How many times it has happened to me—well, for instance, to take offence simply on purpose, for nothing; and one knows oneself, of course, that one is offended at nothing, that one is putting it on, but yet one brings oneself, at last, to the point of being really offended. All my life I have had an impulse to play such pranks, so that in the end I could not control it in myself. Another time, twice, in fact, I tried hard to be in love. I suffered, too, gentlemen, I assure you. In the depth of my heart there was no faith in my suffering, only a faint stir of mockery, but yet I did suffer, and in the real, orthodox way; I was jealous, beside myself . . . and it was all from *ennui*, gentlemen, all from *ennui*; inertia overcame me. You know the direct, legitimate fruit of consciousness is inertia, that is, conscious sitting-with-the-hands-folded. I have referred to this already. I repeat, I repeat with emphasis: all "direct" persons and men of action are active just because they are stupid and limited. How explain that? I will tell you: in consequence of their limitation they take immediate and secondary causes for primary ones, and in that way persuade themselves more quickly and easily than other people do that they have found an infallible foundation for their activity, and their minds are at ease and you know that is the chief thing. To begin to act, you know, you must first have your mind completely at ease and no trace of doubt left in it. Why, how am I, for example, to set my mind at rest? Where are the primary causes on which I am to build? Where are my foundations? Where am I to get them from? I exercise myself in reflection, and consequently with me every primary cause at once draws after itself another still more primary, and so on to infinity. That is just the essence of every sort of consciousness and reflection. It must be a case of the laws of nature again. What is the result of it in the end? Why, just the same. Remember I spoke just now of vengeance. (I am sure you did not take it in.) I said that a man revenges himself because he sees justice in it. Therefore he has found a primary cause, that is, justice. And so he is at rest on all sides, and consequently he carries out his revenge calmly and successfully, being persuaded that he is doing a just and honest thing. But I see no justice in it, I find no sort of virtue in it either, and consequently if I attempt to revenge myself, it is only out of spite. Spite, of course, might overcome everything, all my doubts, and so might serve quite successfully in place of a primary cause, precisely because it is not a cause. But what is to be done if I have not even spite (I began with that just now, you know)? In consequence again of those accursed laws of consciousness, anger in me is subject to chemical disintegration. You look into it, the object flies off into air, your reasons evaporate, the criminal is not to be found, the wrong becomes not a wrong but a phantom, something like the toothache, for which no one is to blame, and consequently there is only the same outlet left again—that is, to beat the wall as hard as you can. So you give it up with a wave of the hand because you have not found a fundamental cause. And try letting yourself be carried away by your feelings, blindly, without reflection, without a primary cause, repelling consciousness at least for a time; hate or love, if only not to sit with your hands folded. The day after to-morrow, at the latest, you will begin despising yourself for having knowingly deceived yourself. Result: a soap-bubble and inertia. Oh, gentlemen, do you know, perhaps I consider myself an intelligent man only because all my life I have been able neither to begin nor to finish anything. Granted I am a babbler, a harmless vexatious babbler, like all of us. But what is to be done if the direct and sole vocation of every intelligent man is babble, that is, the intentional pouring of water through a sieve?

VI

Oh, if I had done nothing simply from laziness! Heavens, how I should have respected myself then. I should have respected myself because I should at least have been capable of being lazy; there would at least have been one quality, as it were, positive in me, in which I could have believed myself. Question: What is he? Answer: A sluggard; how very pleasant it would have been to hear that of oneself! It would mean that I was positively defined, it would mean that there was something to say about me. "Sluggard"—why, it is a calling and vocation, it is a career. Do not jest, it is so. I should then be a member of the best club by right, and should find my occupation in continually respecting myself. I knew a gentleman who prided himself all his life on being a connoisseur of Lafitte. He considered this as his positive virtue, and never doubted himself. He died, not simply with a tranquil, but with a triumphant, conscience, and he was quite right, too. Then I should have chosen a career for myself, I should have been a sluggard and a glutton, not a simple one, but, for instance, one with sympathies for everything good and beautiful. How do you like that? I have long had visions of it. That "good and beautiful" weighs heavily on my mind at forty. But that is at forty; then—oh, then it would have been different! I should have found for myself a form of activity in keeping with it, to be precise, drinking to the health of everything "good and beautiful." I should have snatched at every opportunity to drop a tear into my glass and then to drain it to all that is "good and beautiful." I should then have turned everything into the good and the beautiful; in the nastiest, unquestionable trash, I should have sought out the good and the beautiful. I should have exuded tears like a wet sponge. An artist, for instance, paints a picture worthy of Gay. At once I drink to the health of the artist who painted the picture worthy of Gay, because I love all that is "good and beautiful." An author has written As you will: at once I drink to the health of "any one you will" because I love all that is "good and beautiful."

I should claim respect for doing so. I should persecute any one who would not show me respect. I should live at ease, I should die with dignity, why, it is charming, perfectly charming! And what a good round belly I should have grown, what a treble chin I should have established, what a ruby nose I should have coloured for myself, so that every one would have said, looking at me: "Here is an asset! Here is something real and solid!" And, say what you like, it is very agreeable to hear such remarks about oneself in this negative age.

VII

But these are all golden dreams. Oh, tell me, who was it first announced, who was it first proclaimed, that man only does nasty things because he does not know his own interests; and that if he were enlightened, if his eyes were opened to his real normal interests, man would at once cease to do nasty things, would at once become good and noble because, being enlightened and understanding his real advantage, he would see his own advantage in the good and nothing else, and we all know that not one man can, consciously, act against his own interests, consequently, so to say, through necessity, he would begin doing good? Oh, the babe! Oh, the pure, innocent child! Why, in the first place, when in all these thousands of years has there been a time when man has acted only from his own interests? What is to be done with the millions of facts that bear witness that men, consciously, that is, fully understanding their real interests, have left them in the background and have rushed headlong on another path, to meet peril and danger, compelled to this course by nobody and by nothing, but, as it were, simply disliking the beaten track, and have obstinately, wilfully, struck out another difficult, absurd way, seeking it almost in the darkness. So, I suppose, this obstinacy and perversity were pleasanter to them than any advantage. . . . Advantage! What is advantage?

And will you take it upon yourself to define with perfect accuracy in what the advantage of man consists? And what if it so happens that a man's advantage, sometimes, not only may, but even must, consist in his desiring in certain cases what is harmful to himself and not advantageous. And if so, there can be such a case, the whole principle falls into dust. What do you think—are there such cases? You laugh; laugh away, gentlemen, but only answer me: have man's advantages been reckoned up with perfect certainty? Are there not some which not only have not been included but cannot possibly be included under any classification? You see, you gentlemen have, to the best of my knowledge, taken your whole register of human advantages from the averages of statistical figures and politico-economical formulas. Your advantages are prosperity, wealth, freedom, peace—and so on, and so on. So that the man who should, for instance, go openly and knowingly in opposition to all that list would, to your thinking, and indeed mine too, of course, be an obscurantist or an absolute madman: would not he? But, you know, this is what is surprising: why does it so happen that all these statisticians, sages and lovers of humanity, when they reckon up human advantages invariably leave out one? They don't even take it into their reckoning in the form in which it should be taken, and the whole reckoning depends upon that. It would be no great matter, they would simply have to take it, this advantage, and add it to the list. But the trouble is, that this strange advantage does not fall under any classification and is not in place in any list. I have a friend for instance . . . Ech! gentlemen, but of course he is your friend, too; and indeed there is no one, no one, to whom he is not a friend!

When he prepares for any undertaking this gentleman immediately explains to you, elegantly and clearly, exactly how he must act in accordance with the laws of reason and truth. What is more, he will talk to you with excitement and passion of the true normal interests of man; with irony he will upbraid the short-sighted fools who do not understand their own interests, nor the true significance of virtue; and, within a quarter of an hour, without any sudden outside provocation, but simply through something inside him which is stronger than all his interests, he will go off on quite a different tack—that is, act in direct opposition to what he has just been saying about himself, in opposition to the laws of reason, in opposition to his own advantage—in fact, in opposition to everything. . . . I warn you that my friend is a compound personality, and therefore it is difficult to blame him as an individual. The fact is, gentlemen, it seems there must really exist something that is dearer to almost every man than his greatest advantages, or (not to be illogical) there is a most advantageous advantage (the very one omitted of which we spoke just now) which is more important and more advantageous than all other advantages, for the sake of which a man if necessary is ready to act in opposition to all laws; that is, in opposition to reason, honour, peace, prosperity—in fact, in opposition to all those excellent and useful things if only he can attain that fundamental, most advantageous advantage which is dearer to him than all. "Yes, but it's advantage all the same" you will retort. But excuse me, I'll make the point clear, and it is not a case of playing upon words. What matters is, that this advantage is remarkable from the very fact that it breaks down all our classifications, and continually shatters every system constructed by lovers of mankind for the benefit of mankind. In fact, it upsets everything. But before I mention this advantage to you, I want to compromise myself personally, and therefore I boldly declare that all these fine systems—all these theories for explaining to mankind their real normal interests, in order that inevitably striving to pursue these interests they may at once become good and noble—are, in my opinion, so far, mere logical exercises! Yes, logical exercises.

Why, to maintain this theory of the regeneration of mankind by means of the pursuit of his own advantage is to my mind almost the same as . . . as to affirm, for instance, following Buckle, that through civilization mankind becomes softer, and consequently less bloodthirsty, and less fitted for warfare.

Logically it does seem to follow from his arguments. But man has such a predilection for systems and abstract deductions that he is ready to distort the truth intentionally, he is ready to deny the evidence of his senses only to justify his logic. I take this example because it is the most glaring instance of it. Only look about you: blood is being spilt in streams, and in the merriest way, as though it were champagne. Take the whole of the nineteenth century in which Buckle lived. Take Napoleon—the Great and also the present one. Take North America— the eternal union. Take the farce of Schleswig-Holstein. . . . And what is it that civilization softens in us? The only gain of civilization for mankind is the greater capacity for variety of sensations—and absolutely nothing more. And through the development of this many-sidedness man may come to finding enjoyment in bloodshed. In fact, this has already happened to him. Have you noticed that it is the most civilized gentlemen who have been the subtlest slaughterers, to whom the Attilas and Stenka Razins could not hold a candle, and if they are not so conspicuous as the Attilas and Stenka Razins it is simply because they are so often met with, are so ordinary and have become so familiar to us. In any case civilization has made mankind if not more blood-thirsty, at least more vilely, more loathsomely blood-thirsty. In old days he saw justice in bloodshed and with his conscience at peace exterminated those he thought proper. Now we do think bloodshed abominable and yet we engage in this abomination, and with more energy than ever. Which is worse? Decide that for yourselves.

They say that Cleopatra (excuse an instance from Roman history) was fond of sticking gold pins into her slave-girls' breasts and derived gratification from their screams and writhings. You will say that this was in the comparatively barbarous times; that these are barbarous times too, because also, comparatively speaking, pins are stuck in even now; that though man has now learned to see more clearly than in barbarous ages, he is still far from having learnt to act as reason and science would dictate. But yet you are fully convinced that he will be sure to learn when he gets rid of certain old bad habits, and when common sense and science have completely re-educated human nature and turned it in a normal direction. You are confident that then man will cease from *intentional* error and will, so to say, be compelled not to want to set his will against his normal interests. That is not all; then, you say, science itself will teach man (though to my mind it's a superfluous luxury) that he never has really had any caprice or will of his own, and that he himself is something of the nature of a piano-key or the stop of an organ, and that there are, besides, things called the laws of nature; so that everything he does is not done by his willing it, but is done of itself, by the laws of nature. Consequently we have only to discover these laws of nature, and man will no longer have to answer for his actions and life will become exceedingly easy for him. All human actions will then, of course, be tabulated according to these laws, mathematically, like tables of logarithms up to 108,000, and entered in an index; or, better still, there would be published certain edifying works of the nature of encyclopaedic lexicons, in which everything will be so clearly calculated and explained that there will be no more incidents or adventures in the world.

Then—this is all what you say—new economic relations will be established, all ready-made and worked out with mathematical exactitude, so that every possible question will vanish in the twinkling of an eye, simply because every possible answer to it will be provided. Then the "Palace of Crystal" will be built. Then . . . In fact, those will be halcyon days. Of course there is no guaranteeing (this is my comment) that it will not be, for instance, frightfully dull then (for what will one have to do when everything will be calculated and tabulated?), but on the other hand everything will be extraordinarily rational. Of course boredom may lead you to anything. It is boredom sets one sticking golden pins into people, but all that would not matter. What is bad (this is my comment again) is that I dare say people will be thankful for the gold pins then. Man is stupid, you know, phenomenally stupid; or rather he is not at all stupid, but he is so ungrateful that you could not find another like him in all creation. I, for instance, would not be in the least surprised if all of a sudden, apropos of nothing, in the midst of general prosperity a gentleman with an ignoble, or rather with a reactionary and ironical, countenance were to arise and, putting his arms akimbo, say to us all: "I say, gentlemen, hadn't we better kick over the whole show and scatter rationalism to the winds, simply to send these logarithms to the devil, and to enable us to live once more at our own sweet foolish will!" That again would not matter; but what is annoying is that he would be sure to find followers—such is the nature of man. And all that for the most foolish reason, which, one would think, was hardly worth mentioning: that is, that man everywhere and at all times, whoever he may be, has preferred to act as he chose and not in the least as his reason and advantage dictated. And one may choose what is contrary to one's own interests, and sometimes one *positively ought* (that is my idea). One's own free unfettered choice, one's own caprice—however wild it may be, one's own fancy worked up at times to frenzy—is that very "most advantageous advantage" which we have overlooked, which comes under no classification and against which all systems and theories are continually being shattered to atoms. And how do these wiseacres know that man wants a normal, a virtuous choice? What has made them conceive that man must want a rationally advantageous choice? What man wants is simply *independent* choice, whatever that independence may cost and wherever it may lead. And choice, of course, the devil only knows what choice. . . .

VIII

"Ha! ha! ha! But you know there is no such thing as choice in reality, say what you like," you will interpose with a chuckle. "Science has succeeded in so far analyzing man that we know already that choice and what is called freedom of will is nothing else than——"

Stay, gentlemen, I meant to begin with that myself. I confess, I was rather frightened. I was just going to say that the devil only knows what choice depends on, and that perhaps that was a very good thing, but I remembered the teaching of science . . . and pulled myself up. And here you have begun upon it. Indeed, if there really is some day discovered a formula for all our desires and caprices— that is, an explanation of what they depend upon, by what laws they arise, how they develop, what they are aiming at in one case and in another and so on, that is, a real mathematical formula—then, most likely, man will at once cease to feel desire, indeed, he will be certain to. For who would want to choose by rule? Besides, he will at once be transformed from a human being into an organ-stop or something of the sort; for what is a man without desires, without free will and without choice, if not a stop in an organ? What do you think? Let us reckon the chances—can such a thing happen or not?

"H'm!" you decide. "Our choice is usually mistaken from a false view of our advantage. We sometimes choose absolute nonsense because in our foolishness we see in that nonsense the easiest means for attaining a supposed advantage. But when all that is explained and worked out on paper (which is perfectly possible, for it is contemptible and senseless to suppose that some laws of nature man will never understand), then certainly so-called desires will no longer exist. For if a desire should come into conflict with reason we shall then reason and not desire, because it will be impossible retaining our reason to be *senseless* in our desires, and in that way knowingly act against reason and desire to injure ourselves. And as all choice and reasoning can be really calculated—because there will some day be discovered the laws of our so-called free will—so, joking apart, there may one day be something like a table constructed of them, so that we really shall choose in accordance with it. If, for instance, some day they calculate and prove to me that I made a long nose at some one because I could not help making a long nose at him and that I had to do it in that particular way, what *freedom* is left me, especially if I am a learned man and have taken my degree somewhere? Then I should be able to calculate my whole life for thirty years beforehand. In short, if this could be arranged there would be nothing left for us to do; anyway, we should have to understand that. And, in fact, we ought unwearyingly to repeat to ourselves that at such and such a time and in such and such circumstances Nature does not ask our leave; that we have got to take her as she is and not fashion her to suit our fancy, and if we really aspire to formulas and tables of rules, and well, even . . . to the chemical retort, there's no help for it, we must accept the retort too, or else it will be accepted without our consent. . . ."

Yes, but here I come to a stop! Gentlemen, you must excuse me for being over-philosophical; it's the result of forty years underground! Allow me to indulge my fancy. You see, gentlemen, reason is an excellent thing, there's no disputing that, but reason is nothing but reason and satisfies only the rational side of man's nature, while will is a manifestation of the whole life, that is, of the whole human life including reason and all the impulses. And although our life, in this manifestation of it, is often worthless, yet it is life and not simply extracting square roots. Here I, for instance, quite naturally want to live, in order to satisfy all my capacities for life, and not simply my capacity for reasoning, that is, not simply one-twentieth of my capacity for life. What does reason know? Reason only knows what it has succeeded in learning (some things, perhaps, it will never learn; this is a poor comfort, but why not say so frankly?) and human nature acts as a whole, with everything that is in it, consciously or unconsciously, and, even if it goes wrong, it lives. I suspect, gentlemen, that you are looking at me with compassion; you tell me again that an enlightened and developed man, such, in short, as the future man will be, cannot consciously desire anything disadvantageous to himself, that that can be proved mathematically. I thoroughly agree, it can—by mathematics.

But I repeat for the hundredth time, there is one case, one only, when man may consciously, purposely, desire what is injurious to himself, what is stupid, very stupid—simply in order to have the right to desire for himself even what is very stupid and not to be bound by an obligation to desire only what is sensible. Of course, this very stupid thing, this caprice of ours, may be in reality, gentlemen, more advantageous for us than anything else on earth, especially in certain cases. And in particular it may be more advantageous than any advantage even when it does us obvious harm, and contradicts the soundest conclusions of our reason concerning our advantage—for in any circumstances it preserves for us what is most precious and most important—that is, our personality, our individuality. Some, you see, maintain that this really is the most precious thing for mankind; choice can, of course, if it chooses, be in agreement with reason; and especially if this be not abused but kept within bounds. It is profitable and sometimes even praiseworthy. But very often, and even most often, choice is utterly and stubbornly opposed to reason . . . and . . . and . . . do you know that that, too, is profitable, sometimes even praiseworthy? Gentlemen, let us suppose that man is not stupid. (Indeed one cannot refuse to suppose that, if only from the one consideration, that, if man is stupid, then who is wise?) But if he is not stupid, he is monstrously ungrateful! Phenomenally ungrateful. In fact, I believe that the best definition of man is the ungrateful biped. But that is not all, that is not his worst defect; his worst defect is his perpetual moral obliquity, perpetual—from the days of the Flood to the Schleswig-Holstein period.

Moral obliquity and consequently lack of good sense; for it has long been accepted that lack of good sense is due to no other cause than moral obliquity. Put it to the test and cast your eyes upon the history of mankind. What will you see? Is it a grand spectacle? Grand, if you like. Take the Colossus of Rhodes, for instance, that's worth something. With good reason Mr. Anaevsky testifies of it that some say that it is the work of man's hands, while others maintain that it has been created by Nature herself. Is it many-coloured? It may be it is many-coloured, too: if one takes the dress uniforms, military and civilian, of all peoples in all ages—that alone is worth something, and if you take the undress uniforms you will never get to the end of it; no historian would be equal to the job. Is it monotonous? It may be it's monotonous too: it's fighting and fighting; they are fighting now, they fought first and they fought last—you will admit that it is almost too monotonous. In short, one may say anything about the history of the world—anything that might enter the most disordered imagination.

The only thing one can't say is that it's rational. The very word sticks in one's throat. And, indeed, this is the odd thing that is continually happening: there are continually turning up in life moral and rational persons, sages and lovers of humanity, who make it their object to live all their lives as morally and rationally as possible, to be, so to speak, a light to their neighbours simply in order to show them that it is possible to live morally and rationally in this world. And yet we all know that those very people sooner or later have been false to themselves, playing some queer trick, often a most unseemly one. Now I ask you: what can be expected of man since he is a being endowed with such strange qualities? Shower upon him every earthly blessing, drown him in a sea of happiness, so that nothing but bubbles of bliss can be seen on the surface; give him economic prosperity, such that he should have nothing else to do but sleep, eat cakes and busy himself with the continuation of his species, and even then out of sheer ingratitude. sheer spite, man would play you some nasty trick. He would even risk his cakes and would deliberately desire the most fatal rubbish, the most uneconomical absurdity, simply to introduce into all this positive good sense his fatal fantastic element. It is just his fantastic dreams, his vulgar folly, that he will desire to retain, simply in order to prove to himself—as though that were so necessary—that men still are men and not the keys of a piano, which the laws of nature threaten to control so completely that soon one will be able to desire nothing but by the calendar. And that is not all: even if man really were nothing but a piano-key, even if this were proved to him by natural science and mathematics, even then he would not become reasonable, but would purposely do something perverse out of simple ingratitude, simply to gain his point. And if he does not find means he will contrive destruction and chaos, will contrive sufferings of all sorts, only to gain his point! He will launch a curse upon the world, and as only man can curse (it is his privilege, the primary distinction between him and other animals) it may be by his curse alone he will attain his object—that is, convince himself that he is a man and not a piano-key! If you say that all this, too, can be calculated and tabulated—chaos and darkness and curses, so that the mere possibility of calculating it all beforehand would stop it all, and reason would reassert itself—then man would purposely go mad in order to be rid of reason and gain his point! I believe in it, I answer for it, for the whole work of man really seems to consist in nothing but proving to himself every minute that he is a man and not a piano-key! It may be at the cost of his skin, it may be by cannibalism! And this being so, can one help being tempted to rejoice that it has not yet come off, and that desire still depends on something we don't know?

You will scream at me (that is, if you condescend to do so) that no one is touching my free will, that all they are concerned with is that my will should of itself, of its own free will, coincide with my own normal interests, with the laws of nature and arithmetic.

Good heavens, gentlemen, what sort of free will is left when we come to tabulation and arithmetic, when it will all be a case of twice two makes four? Twice two makes four without my will. As if free will meant that!

IX

Gentlemen, I am joking, and I know myself that my jokes are not brilliant, but you know one can't take everything as a joke. I am, perhaps, jesting against the grain. Gentlemen, I am tormented by questions; answer them for me. You, for instance, want to cure men of their old habits and reform their will in accordance with science and good sense. But how do you know, not only that it is possible, but also that it is *desirable*, to reform a man in that way? And what leads you to the conclusion that man's inclinations *need* reforming? In short, how do you know that such a reformation will be a benefit to man? And to go to the root of the matter, why are you so positively convinced that not to act against his real normal interests guaranteed by the conclusions of reason and arithmetic is certainly always advantageous for man and must always be a law for mankind? So far, you know, this is only your supposition. It may be the law of logic, but not the law of humanity. You think, gentlemen, perhaps that I am mad? Allow me to defend myself. I agree that man is pre-eminently a creative animal, predestined to strive consciously for an object and to engage in engineering—that is, incessantly and eternally to make new roads, *wherever they may lead*. But the reason why he wants sometimes to go off at a tangent may just be that he is *predestined* to make the road, and perhaps, too, that however stupid the "direct" practical man may be, the thought sometimes will occur to him that the road almost always does lead *somewhere*, and that the destination it leads to is less important than the process of making it, and that the chief thing is to save the well-conducted child from despising engineering, and so giving way to the fatal idleness, which, as we all know, is the mother of all the vices. Man likes to make roads and to create, that is a fact beyond dispute. But why has he such a passionate love for destruction and chaos also? Tell me that! But on that point I want to say a couple of words myself. May it not be that he loves chaos and destruction (there can be no disputing that he does sometimes love it) because he is instinctively afraid of attaining his object and completing the edifice he is constructing? Who knows, perhaps he only loves that edifice from a distance, and is by no means in love with it at close quarters; perhaps he only loves building it and does not want to live in it, but will leave it, when completed, for the use of *les animaux domestiques*—such as the ants, the sheep, and so on. Now the ants have quite a different taste. They have a marvellous edifice of that pattern which endures for ever—the ant-heap.

With the ant-heap the respectable race of ants began and with the ant-heap they will probably end, which does the greatest credit to their perseverance and good sense. But man is a frivolous and incongruous creature, and perhaps, like a chess-player, loves the process of the game, not the end of it. And who knows (there is no saying with certainty), perhaps the only goal on earth to which mankind is striving lies in this incessant process of attaining, in other words, in life itself, and not in the thing to be attained, which must always be expressed as a formula, as positive as twice two makes four, and such positiveness is not life, gentlemen, but is the beginning of death. Anyway, man has always been afraid of this mathematical certainty, and I am afraid of it now. Granted that man does nothing but seek that mathematical certainty, he traverses oceans, sacrifices his life in the quest, but to succeed, really to find it, he dreads, I assure you. He feels that when he has found it there will be nothing for him to look for. When workmen have finished their work they do at least receive their pay, they go to the tavern, then they are taken to the police-station—and there is occupation for a week. But where can man go? Anyway, one can observe a certain awkwardness about him when he has attained such objects. He loves the process of attaining, but does not quite like to have attained, and that, of course, is very absurd. In fact, man is a comical creature; there seems to be a kind of jest in it all. But yet mathematical certainty is, after all, something insufferable. Twice two makes four seems to me simply a piece of insolence. Twice two makes four is a pert coxcomb who stands with arms akimbo barring your path and spitting. I admit that twice two makes four is an excellent thing, but if we are to give everything its due, twice two makes five is sometimes a very charming thing too.

And why are you so firmly, so triumphantly, convinced that only the normal and the positive—in other words, only what is conducive to welfare—is for the advantage of man? Is not reason in error as regards advantage? Does not man, perhaps, love something besides well-being? Perhaps he is just as fond of suffering? Perhaps suffering is just as great a benefit to him as well-being? Man is sometimes extraordinarily, passionately, in love with suffering, and that is a fact. There is no need to appeal to universal history to prove that; only ask yourself, if you are a man and have lived at all. As far as my personal opinion is concerned, to care only for well-being seems to me positively ill-bred. Whether it's good or bad, it is sometimes very pleasant, too, to smash things. I hold no brief for suffering nor for well-being either. I am standing for . . . my caprice, and for its being guaranteed to me when necessary. Suffering would be out of place in vaudevilles, for instance; I know that. In the "Palace of Crystal" it is unthinkable; suffering means doubt, negation, and what would be the good of a "palace of crystal" if there could be any doubt about it? And yet I think man will never renounce real suffering, that is, destruction and chaos. Why, suffering is the sole origin of consciousness. Though I did lay it down at the beginning that consciousness is the greatest misfortune for man, yet I know man prizes it and would not give it up for any satisfaction. Consciousness, for instance, is infinitely superior to twice two makes four. Once you have mathematical certainty there is nothing left to do or to understand. There will be nothing left but to bottle up your five senses and plunge into contemplation. While if you stick to consciousness, even though the same result is attained, you can at least flog yourself at times, and that will, at any rate, liven you up. Reactionary as it is, corporal punishment is better than nothing.

X

You believe in a palace of crystal that can never be destroyed—a palace at which one will not be able to put out one's tongue or make a long nose on the sly. And perhaps that is just why I am afraid of this edifice, that it is of crystal and can never be destroyed and that one cannot put one's tongue out at it even on the sly.

You see, if it were not a palace, but a hen-house, I might creep into it to avoid getting wet, and yet I would not call the hen-house a palace out of gratitude to it for keeping me dry. You laugh and say that in such circumstances a hen-house is as good as a mansion. Yes, I answer, if one had to live simply to keep out of the rain.

But what is to be done if I have taken it into my head that that is not the only object in life, and that if one must live one had better live in a mansion. That is my choice, my desire. You will only eradicate it when you have changed my preference. Well, do change it, allure me with something else, give me another ideal. But meanwhile I will not take a hen-house for a mansion. The palace of crystal may be an idle dream, it may be that it is inconsistent with the laws of nature and that I have invented it only through my own stupidity, through the old-fashioned irrational habits of my generation. But what does it matter to me that it is inconsistent? That makes no difference since it exists in my desires, or rather exists as long as my desires exist. Perhaps you are laughing again? Laugh away; I will put up with any mockery rather than pretend that I am satisfied when I am hungry. I know, anyway, that I will not be put off with a compromise, with a recurring zero, simply because it is consistent with the laws of nature and actually exists. I will not accept as the crown of my desires a block of buildings with tenements for the poor on a lease of a thousand years, and perhaps with a sign-board of a dentist hanging out. Destroy my desires, eradicate my ideals, show me something better, and I will follow you. You will say, perhaps, that is not worth your trouble; but in that case I can give you the same answer. We are discussing things seriously; but if you won't deign to give me your attention, I will drop your acquaintance. I can retreat into my underground hole.

But while I am alive and have desires I would rather my hand were withered off than bring one brick to such a building! Don't remind me that I have just rejected the palace of crystal for the sole reason that one cannot put out one's tongue at it. I did not say because I am so fond of putting my tongue out. Perhaps the thing I resented was, that of all your edifices there has not been one at which one could not put out one's tongue. On the contrary, I would let my tongue be cut off out of gratitude if things could be so arranged that I should lose all desire to put it out. It is not my fault that things cannot be so arranged, and that one must be satisfied with model flats. Then why am I made with such desires? Can I have been constructed simply in order to come to the conclusion that all my construction is a cheat? Can this be my whole purpose? I do not believe it.

But do you know what: I am convinced that we underground folk ought to be kept on a curb. Though we may sit forty years underground without speaking, when we do come out into the light of day and break out we talk and talk and talk. . . .

XI

The long and the short of it is, gentlemen, that it is better to do nothing! Better conscious inertia! And so hurrah for underground! Though I have said that I envy the normal man to the last drop of my bile, yet I should not care to be in his place such as he is now (though I shall not cease envying him). No, no; anyway the underground life is more advantageous. There, at any rate, one can . . . Oh, but even now I am lying! I am lying because I know myself that it is not underground that is better, but something different, quite different, for which I am thirsting, but which I cannot find! Damn underground!

I will tell you another thing that would be better, and that is, if I myself believed in anything of what I have just written. I swear to you, gentlemen, there is not one thing, not one word of what I have written, that I really believe. That is, I believe it, perhaps, but at the same time I feel and suspect that I am lying like a cobbler.

"Then why have you written all this?" you will say to me.

"I ought to put you underground for forty years without anything to do and then come to you in your cellar, to find out what stage you have reached! How can a man be left with nothing to do for forty years?

"Isn't that shameful, isn't that humiliating?" you will say, perhaps, wagging your heads contemptuously. "You thirst for life and try to settle the problems of life by a logical tangle. And how persistent, how insolent are your sallies, and at the same time what a scare you are in! You talk nonsense and are pleased with it; you say impudent things and are in continual alarm and apologizing for them. You declare that you are afraid of nothing and at the same time try to ingratiate yourself in our good opinion. You declare that you are gnashing your teeth and at the same time you try to be witty so as to amuse us. You know that your witticisms are not witty, but you are evidently well satisfied with their literary value. You may, perhaps, have really suffered, but you have no respect for your own suffering. You may have sincerity, but you have no modesty; out of the pettiest vanity you expose your sincerity to publicity and ignominy. You doubtlessly mean to say something, but hide your last word through fear, because you have not the resolution to utter it, and only have a cowardly impudence. You boast of consciousness, but you are not sure of your ground, for though your mind works, yet your heart is darkened and corrupt, and you cannot have a full, genuine consciousness without a pure heart. And how intrusive you are, how you insist and grimace! Lies, lies, lies!"

Of course I have myself made up all the things you say. That, too, is from underground. I have been for forty years listening to you through a crack under the floor. I have invented them myself, there was nothing else I could invent. It is no wonder that I have learned it by heart and it has taken a literary form. . . .

But can you really be so credulous as to think that I will print all this and give it to you to read too? And another problem: why do I call you "gentlemen," why do I address you as though you really were my readers? Such confessions as I intend to make are never printed nor given to other people to read. Anyway, I am not strong-minded enough for that, and I don't see why I should be. But you see a fancy has occurred to me and I want to realize it at all costs. Let me explain.

Every man has reminiscences which he would not tell to every one, but only to his friends. He has other matters in his mind which he would not reveal even to his friends, but only to himself, and that in secret. But there are other things which a man is afraid to tell even to himself, and every decent man has a number of such things stored away in his mind. The more decent he is, the greater the number of such things in his mind. Anyway, I have only lately determined to remember some of my early adventures. Till now I have always avoided them, even with a certain uneasiness. Now, when I am not only recalling them, but have actually decided to write an account of them, I want to try the experiment whether one can, even with oneself, be perfectly open and not take fright at the whole truth. I will observe, in parenthesis, that Heine says that a true autobiography is almost an impossibility, and that man is bound to lie about himself. He considers that Rousseau certainly told lies about himself in his confessions, and even intentionally lied, out of vanity. I am convinced that Heine is right; I quite understand how sometimes one may, out of sheer vanity, attribute regular crimes to oneself, and indeed I can very well conceive that kind of vanity. But Heine judged of people who made their confessions to the public. I write only for myself, and I wish to declare once and for all that if I write as though I were addressing readers, that is simply because it is easier for me to write in that form. It is a form, an empty form—I shall never have readers. I have made this plain already. . . .

I don't wish to be hampered by any restrictions in the compilation of my notes. I shall not attempt any system or method. I will jot things down as I remember them.

But here, perhaps, some one will catch at the word and ask me: if you really don't reckon on readers, why do you make such compacts with yourself—and on paper too—that is, that you won't attempt any system or method, that you jot things down as you remember them, and so on, and so on? Why are you explaining? Why do you apologize?

Well, there it is, I answer.

There is a whole psychology in all this, though. Perhaps it is simply that I am a coward. And perhaps that I purposely imagine an audience before me in order that I may be more dignified while I write. There are perhaps thousands of reasons. Again, what is my object precisely in writing? If it is not for the benefit of the public why should I not simply recall these incidents in my own mind without putting them on paper?

Quite so; but yet it is more imposing on paper. Theer is something more impressive in it; I shall be better able to criticize myself and improve my style. Besides, I shall perhaps obtain actual relief from writing. To-day, for instance, I am particularly oppressed by one memory of a distant past. It came back vividly to my mind a few days ago, and has remained haunting me like an annoying tune that one cannot get rid of. And yet I must get rid of it somehow. I have hundreds of such reminiscences; but at times some one stands out from the hundred and oppresses me. For some reason I believe that if I write it down I should get rid of it. Why not try?

Besides, I am bored, and I never have anything to do. Writing will be a sort of work. They say work makes man kind-hearted and honest. Well, here is a chance for me, anyway.

Snow is falling to-day, yellow and dingy. It fell yesterday, too, and a few days ago. I fancy it is the wet snow that has reminded me of that incident which I cannot shake off now. And so let it be a story apropos of the falling snow.

8

EXISTENCE

The Definition of Existence

Moments of Existence

Value in Existence

Introduction

The idea of "existence" is part of the modern conception of the self, and under this heading many of the themes of the preceding section will recur: an opposition of individual and society; an inner division of particularity and universality; temporal emergence; the struggle for authenticity; and a troubled assertion of freedom. But existentialism is a very intense and philosophically specialized form of the quest for selfhood. It has a psychological subtlety and a sense of urgency that are its own. The distinctive existentialist vocabulary—turning on such categories as being, absurdity, choice, dread, despair, commitment—is like a situational survey or map courageously drawn at a moment of supreme crisis.

Two nineteenth-century writers, Nietzsche and Kierkegaard, have been especially influential in the development of the idea of existence. The fact that one was Christian, the other not, anticipates a division that still persists among existentialists. But they set out from much the same diagnosis of the predicament of the modern individual. Both contrast the untranslatability, the subjective concreteness, the dynamic process, and the dialectical tension of individual existence with the norms of society, abstract theories, static systems, and objective knowledge.[1]

Kierkegaard denounces the conception of a person as being primarily a member of a social group, for this is to be a "specimen" in a "crowd," equivalent to what Dostoevsky calls "an ant in an antheap."[2] The crowd is destructive of true existence, for the man who belongs to it is at once relieved of individual responsibility and deprived of his freedom. To live so is to ignore the special attribute which distinguishes human life, that only one person in the world is capable of consciously being that person, undergoing his fate or attaining his salvation. The existential individual has his being in relation to himself, to another, or to God, but never in relation to a crowd. Similarly, his existence is negated by adherence to a philosophic system or to abstract religious dogmas. Like the crowd, systematic and abstract thought is "untruth,"

[1] Compare the insistence on "concreteness" in William James, Bergson, and Proust (Section 7).
[2] See the selection from Dostoevsky in Section 7.

since it pretends to have a finality that no human experience can possess. Truth resides in the individual's *striving toward* absolute truth, for in this case he acknowledges his finitude and thereby is given his portion of the infinite in the only form in which he will ever attain it in this life. Human existence, the meeting point of time and eternity, is thus analogous to the incarnation of God in Christ, the God-Man—and this religious mystery is, indeed, the very Truth toward which the individual ceaselessly strives.[3]

Nietzsche also repudiates the crowd with its leveling gregariousness and its pursuit of the "common good." Not only Christianity and its ethics of submission but also democracy and socialism, the domain of supposedly advanced "free-thinkers," are for him devices to suppress or escape from individuality. Nietzsche directs his attack against science and philosophy as well. Science is invalidated because it exalts natural phenomena and objective, rational examination of them, thereby converting the subjective being into a mere mirror of external things. Philosophy is discredited because the philosophic "will to truth" hides the crucial fact that all so-called truths are actually instruments of the individual will. Falsehoods may on occasion serve the will just as well. What matters is the philosopher himself, "the innermost desires of his nature," not the abstract validity of his philosophy. Nietzsche regards the culture of his time as vitiated by the theoretical impulse, which he calls "Alexandrian" and "Socratic," in allusion to earlier eras of intellectual analysis. Men are vaguely aware of their impasse, awaiting the new message of individual existence founded on will.[4]

Kierkegaard and Nietzsche are at one in seeking to fix upon the actuality of a person. The existentialists have carefully named and described various states of this subjective being. Camus brilliantly evokes the moment when a man discovers a lack of purpose and meaning in acts that he has performed habitually and unthinkingly, or rather, when he begins to demand that they have a meaning for him and discovers that they can provide none. Other men, nature, metaphysical reality, the very forms of logic strike him as absurd —that is, radically incommensurable with the one who appeals to them for his meaning. He can confidently assert nothing but the bare fact that he exists and that he is bound in a relation of incompatibility and hatred to things other than himself.[5] Put in a more positive way, the moment of absurdity can be described in Sartre's terms as a realization that in human life *"existence comes before essence."* Sartre declares that there is no such thing as an abstract "human nature" or essence by means of which we might define or measure our individual selves according to the usual method of reason. We must begin by recognizing the absurdity of man, his lack of any such *a priori*

---

[3] In addition to later passages in this section, related selections from Kierkegaard appear in Sections 7 and 9. Compare the selection from Tillich in Section 9. For examples of the Hegelian system, which is Kierkegaard's prime exhibit of false abstraction, see Sections 4 and 8.
[4] See related selections from Nietzsche in Sections 1, 4, 5, 7, and 9.
[5] Compare Dostoevsky's Underground Man (Section 7).

definition, and then consciously take responsibility for the particular human attributes that we individually and spontaneously will.

Most existentialists follow Kierkegaard in emphasizing that a moment comes for the individual when he must make an irrevocable choice and that such moments are our only "real" ones. For the most part, Kierkegaard says, people refuse to reach this point, taking refuge in neutrality; but by neglecting to choose they drift into a limbo of others' choices, or the obscure choices of their own unconscious, and give up all chance of becoming themselves. A living creature cannot preserve a blank personality. Nor can the choice, when made, be merely a day-to-day preference, for this is what Kierkegaard calls "aesthetic" as opposed to "ethical" choice, a choice that is actually no choice and leaves a man still submerged in the multiplicity of immediate experience. In ethical choice, everything is staked upon the decision; there is an absolute "either/or," a total exercise of individual freedom. By choosing, even by choosing wrongly, if that is done with earnestness and struggle, we become new selves that could not have existed until the choice was made. Beyond ethical choice is religious choice, the use of freedom to surrender it back to its divine giver. For Kierkegaard, this is the secret origin and goal of all freedom of choice: the individual is ultimately free only in choosing God.[6]

For Sartre, as an atheistic existentialist, precisely the opposite is true: God's non-existence is the major reason why the existing man must take responsibility for himself. Deliberately or not, the individual chooses at every instant what he is; in choosing himself he affirms a value; and thereby he makes a partial definition of man, promulgates a law of which he must assume the burden. The anguish of conscious decision in Sartre's godless world is like the agony of Kierkegaard's Abraham, the man of faith, summoned to sacrifice Isaac; but it is even more extreme since the choice must occur without any superhuman content or reward. Though an authentic choice aims at the future and is constructive, in the moment of choice a man is "forsaken"— abandoned to his own total freedom.[7]

As Sartre's allusion to Kierkegaard indicates, his use of the term "anguish" derives from the *angst* or "dread" about which Kierkegaard, and Martin Heidegger after him, have written. They use the word to describe the state of mind of a person who has begun to depart from habit and to understand his existential condition. As Heidegger describes it, dread is neither simple nervousness nor fear of something specific. Dread is about the indefinite; it is the state that Kierkegaard calls an awareness that anything is possible, that insecurity is infinite. Heidegger's dread is the presence of a negative infinity, a loss of both personal and universal being, an entry into positive Nothing-

[6] Kierkegaard's emphasis on freedom of choice and his depreciation of "aesthetic" freedom of experience is in direct contrast to vitalistic naturalism (Section 3), to the quest for self-realization (Section 7), and to Bergsonian intuition (Section 7).

[7] Sartre's conception of freedom is related to Nietzsche's doctrine of the will (Section 7) and of the death of God (Section 9).

ness. To this extent it is a roundabout approach to Being. According to Kierkegaard, the torture of dread, though it can lead to despair, can also, by destroying all trust in finite ends, prepare for the saving experience of infinite faith.

Sartre is not so much concerned with the specific qualities of anguish as with its other face—for him, the attainment of "authenticity." This is the consummation of existence and the basis for all moral judgment. Self-deception tries to bar the way, impelling a man to adopt the mask of some external role or to plead that he is driven by some overwhelming passion, or by fate, or by some other deterministic force. Such special pleading is not only erroneous but also morally culpable. Authenticity demands the wholehearted acceptance of freedom as the *sine qua non* of a man's own existence and that of mankind. Everything else is permitted, but there is one absolute moral law: that every action be taken in the name of freedom.

When the choice is made, or the absurdity of life recognized, or the dread converted, or the responsibility assumed, existence is felt as a value in itself. In their different ways the existentialists find their reason for existence in both effort and accomplishment. Camus sees a man arriving, through admission of absurdity, at an affirmation of his own worth. By emptying himself of illusion, by abandoning hope and the quest for ultimate meaning, the absurd man is enabled to realize the peculiar meaning of his very condition. For if his life is hopeless and meaningless, he is at once liberated and put in a position to exercise his freedom in a revolt against absurdity. He no longer would have it otherwise; he keeps the absurd alive as the context of his individual effort to make sense. Camus uses Sisyphus, endlessly pushing his stone up the hill only to have it roll down again, for his example of the hero who recognizes futility and scorns it. Sisyphus is the owner of his days and finds the struggle upward enough to fill his heart. Camus comes sharply to the paradox that underlies his version of existentialist thought: "One must imagine Sisyphus happy."

Sartre turns his doctrine of existential choice into a doctrine of engagement. Social action is a logical extension of individual subjective life because the individual exists only as a series of active choices. There is no individual reality except in deeds; there are no unused possibilities within a man; to live is to draw one's own portrait by all that one does. Similarly, there is no social reality except in the agreement of individuals acting in concert; it is useless to theorize about social laws dictated by abstract human nature or historical necessity.[8] Therefore personal life and social action coincide as a series of free undertakings or commitments.

Kierkegaard moved in a very different direction from both the self-sufficiency of Camus and the Sartrean social commitment. In his view, absurdity was the ground of Christian faith. First of all, faith is absurd or paradoxical

[8] Contrast the various kinds of social determinism represented in Section 2 and in Hegel's philosophy of history (Section 4).

in its form. Like aesthetic and intellectual states of mind, which are properly concerned with mere "possibilities," faith looks beyond itself; and yet, like ethical choice, which is properly concerned with a man's own individual existence, faith deals in subjective "reality." Thus the form of faith is paradoxical because it is properly concerned with *the reality of another*. But the object of faith is also paradoxical. It is the one being who is both "other" and really existent—the God-Man, whose love for and entry into the world are the ultimate paradox. In its absurdity, faith abrogates not only the aesthetic and intellectual canons but also the ethical. Abraham's willingness to obey the divine summons to sacrifice his son was truly religious because it was ethically preposterous; it was an acceptance of a wholly alien reality—in this dramatic case, a positively immoral command—as the deepest choice of his own being. Abraham is Kierkegaard's hero of faith, the model of a passionate leap from individual existence into a trans-personal religious state.

This absurd transcendence, however, is as individual a matter for Kierkegaard as Camus's absurd freedom is for him. In Jaspers's phrase, these are "philosophers of the exception:" even if they discover a world larger than the individual, it still pivots on a unique individual experience. Jaspers would emphasize "communication" and open up existence into a realm of human reason. By "reason" he does not mean an elaborate systematic construction but a common human enterprise of thought. Unique individuals, in reaching toward each other, reach toward the universal human truth that is presupposed by all attempts to communicate. Individual truth is valid only as it strives to be more than individual; a deliberate solitude, whatever its aim, leads to an impoverishment of self. Sartre concurs to the extent of maintaining that the man who realizes his own freedom is thereby confronted with a world of others whom he must conceive as equally free. Though there is no universal human nature that we can presuppose, there is a universal human condition or situation. We live in a growing community of human purposes, proposed by changing individuals but intelligible to all men.[9] Martin Buber goes further to deny that isolated existence is even possible. We exist in relation to other men, to nature, and to God. The only question is whether the relation shall be abstract and objective, an "I" to an "It," or concrete and immediate, an "I" to a "Thou." In the second relation only is there life and value. Every "Thou" tends to collapse into an "It," an inert thing, but every "It" is destined to be regenerated as a "Thou" in the eyes of art and of love.[10]

Jaspers and Buber, in contrast to Sartre, would postulate a Being that is the ground of existence—not the wholly paradoxical God of Kierkegaard but a transcendent absolute implied by all communication and every affective relation. Jaspers calls this "the Encompassing" and conceives it as a principle of open possibility, a comprehensive "horizon" that is never reached but yet

[9] Compare the similar doctrine of Croce, which he reaches on quite different grounds (Section 4).
[10] Buber approaches the kind of vitalistic communion pictured by Proust (Section 3).

807

is actually present in men's own effort to transcend every horizon. Heidegger also urges that the involvement of Being in human nature is the basic philosophic question. Metaphysics has never raised the question properly, and today especially we live in "oblivion of Being." To recover Being, not as an objective fact but as a perennial question, is to go back into the ground of metaphysics, to find the roots of our existence.

SØREN KIERKEGAARD

The Individual and the Crowd

There is a view of life which conceives that where the crowd is, there also is the truth, and that in truth itself there is need of having the crowd on its side.[1] There is another view of life which conceives that wherever there is a crowd there is untruth, so that (to consider for a moment the extreme case), even if every individual, each for himself in private, were to be in possession of the truth, yet in case they were all to get together in a crowd—a crowd to which any sort of *decisive* significance is attributed, a voting, noisy, audible crowd—untruth would at once be in evidence.[2]

For a "crowd" is the untruth. In a godly sense it is true, eternally, Christianly, as St. Paul says, that "only one attains the goal"—which is not meant in a comparative sense, for comparison takes others into account. It means that every man can be that one, God helping him therein—but only one attains the goal. And again this means that every man should be chary about having to do with "the others," and essentially should talk only with God and with himself—for only one attains the goal. And again this means that man, or to be a man, is akin to deity. —In a worldly and temporal sense, it will be said by the man of bustle, sociability, and amicableness, "How unreasonable that only one attains the goal; for it is far more likely that many, by the strength of united effort, should attain the goal; and when we are many success is more certain and it is easier for each man severally." True enough, it is far more *likely*; and it is true also with respect to all

[1] Perhaps it may be well to note here once for all a thing that goes without saying and which I never have denied, that in relation to all temporal, earthly, worldly matters the crowd may have competency, and even decisive competency as a court of last resort. But it is not of such matters I am speaking, nor have I ever concerned myself with such things. I am speaking about the ethical, about the ethico-religious, about "the truth," and I am affirming the untruth of the crowd, ethico-religiously regarded, when it is treated as a criterion for what "truth" is.

[2] Perhaps it may be well to note here, although it seems to me almost superfluous, that it naturally could not occur to me to object to the fact, for example, that preaching is done or that the truth is proclaimed, even though it were to an assemblage of hundreds of thousands. Not at all; but if there were an assemblage even of only ten—and if they should put the truth to the ballot, that is to say, if the assemblage should be regarded as the authority, if it is the crowd which turns the scale—then there *is* untruth.

From *The Point of View for My Work as an Author* [1859], translated from the Danish by Walter Lowrie, New York, 1962, pp. 110-13, 120-21; reprinted by permission of Harper & Row, Publishers.

earthly and material goods. If it is allowed to have its way, this becomes the only true point of view, for it does away with God and eternity and with man's kinship with deity. It does away with it or transforms it into a fable, and puts in its place the modern (or, we might rather say, the old pagan) notion that to be a man is to belong to a race endowed with reason, to belong to it as a specimen, so that the race or species is higher than the individual, which is to say that there are no more individuals but only specimens. . . .

A crowd—not this crowd or that, the crowd now living or the crowd long deceased, a crowd of humble people or of superior people, of rich or of poor, &c.—a crowd in its very concept[3] is the untruth, by reason of the fact that it renders the individual completely impenitent and irresponsible, or at least weakens his sense of responsibility by reducing it to a fraction. Observe that there was not one single soldier that dared lay hands upon Caius Marius—this was an instance of truth. But given merely three or four women with the consciousness or the impression that they were a crowd, and with hope of a sort in the possibility that no one could say definitely who was doing it or who began it—then they had courage for it. What a falsehood! The falsehood first of all is the notion that the crowd does what in fact only the *individual* in the crowd does, though it be every *individual*. For "crowd" is an abstraction and has no hands: but each individual has ordinarily two hands, and so when an individual lays his two hands upon Caius Marius they are the two hands of the individual, certainly not those of his neighbour, and still less those of the . . . crowd which has no hands. In the next place, the falsehood is that the crowd had the "courage" for it, for no one of the individuals was ever so cowardly as the crowd always is. For every individual who flees for refuge into the crowd, and so flees in cowardice from being an individual (who had not the courage to lay his hands upon Caius Marius, nor even to admit that he had it not), such a man contributes his share of cowardliness to the cowardliness which we know as the "crowd."—Take the highest example, think of Christ—and the whole human race, all the men that ever were born or are to be born. But let the situation be one that challenges the individual, requiring each one for himself to be alone with Him in a solitary place and as an individual to step up to Him and spit upon Him—the man never was born and never will be born with courage or insolence enough to do such a thing. This is untruth. . . .

"The individual" is the category through which, in a religious respect, this age, all history, the human race as a whole, must pass. And he who stood at Thermopylae was not so secure in his position as I who have stood in defence of this narrow defile, "the individual," with the intent at least of making people take notice of it. His duty was to prevent the hosts from pressing through the defile. If they pressed through, he was lost. My task is one which at least does not expose me to any such danger of being trampled underfoot, for my task was as a humble servant (yet, as I have said from the beginning and repeated again and again,

---

[3] The reader will also remember that here the word "crowd" is understood in a purely formal sense, not in the sense one commonly attaches to "the crowd" when it is meant as an invidious qualification, the distinction which human selfishness irreligiously erects between "the crowd" and superior persons, &c. Good God! How could a religious man hit upon such an inhuman equality! No, "crowd" stands for number, the numerical, a number of noblemen, millionaires, high dignitaries, &c.—as soon as the numerical is involved it is "crowd," "the crowd."

"without authority") to provoke, if possible, to invite, to stir up the many to press through this defile of "the individual," through which, however, no one can pass except by becoming the individual—the contrary being a categorical impossibility. And yet, if I were to desire an inscription for my tombstone, I should desire none other than "That Individual"—if that is not now understood, it surely will be.

SØREN KIERKEGAARD

Concrete Existence and Abstract System

LESSING HAS SAID THAT, IF GOD HELD ALL TRUTH IN HIS RIGHT HAND, AND IN HIS LEFT HAND HELD THE LIFELONG PURSUIT OF IT, HE WOULD CHOOSE THE LFFT HAND

Lessing's words are: "*Wenn Gott in seiner Rechten alle Wahrheit, und in seiner Linken den einzigen immer regen Trieb nach Wahrheit, obschon mit dem Zusatze mich immer und ewig zu irren, verschlossen hielte, und spräche zur mir: wähle! Ich fiele ihm mit Demuth in seine Linke und sagte: Vater, gieb! die reine Wahrheit ist ja doch nur für dich allein!*"[1] When Lessing wrote these words the System was presumably not finished; alas! and now Lessing is dead. Were he living in these times, now that the System is almost finished, or at least under construction, and will be finished by next Sunday: believe me, Lessing would have stretched out both his hands to lay hold of it. He would not have had the leisure, nor the manners, nor the exuberance, thus in jest as if to play odd and even with God, and in earnest to choose the left hand. But then, the System also has more to offer than God had in both hands; this very moment it has more, to say nothing of next Sunday, when it is quite certain to be finished.

The quoted words are found in a little essay (*Eine Duplik*, 1778) occasioned by a devout man's defence of the story of the Resurrection against the attack made upon it in the *Selections* that Lessing had had published. It will be remembered that people simply could not understand what Lessing's purpose was in publishing these fragments. Not even the high learning of *Hauptpastor* Goetze sufficed him to determine just what passage in the Apocalypse applied to Lessing, aye, was fulfilled in him. In so far Lessing has curiously enough compelled men, in their relation to him, to accept his own principle. Although even in those times there were results and finalities to spare, nobody was quite able to squeeze the life out of Lessing, and pack him away embalmed in a paragraph of universal history. A riddle he was, and a riddle he remained. If anyone were now to attempt to bring him forward again, he would get no further with him.

Here first an assurance respecting my own humble person. I shall be as willing

[1] If God held all Truth sealed up in his right hand, and in his left hand the single, always active striving after Truth, even with the proviso that I would always and forever be in error—and if he told me, "Choose!"—I would humbly seize upon his left hand and would say, "Father, grant me this! Pure Truth is surely for you alone!"

From *Concluding Unscientific Postscript* [1844], translated from the Danish by Dorothy Swenson and Walter Lowrie, Princeton, 1941, pp. 97-9, 267-8, 273. Copyright 1941 by Princeton University Press; reprinted by permission of the Princeton University Press.

as the next man to fall down in worship before the System, if only I can manage to set eyes on it. Hitherto I have had no success; and though I have young legs, I am almost weary from running back and forth between Herod and Pilate. Once or twice I have been on the verge of bending the knee. But at the last moment, when I already had my handkerchief spread on the ground, to avoid soiling my trousers, and I made a trusting appeal to one of the initiated who stood by: "Tell me now sincerely, is it entirely finished; for if so I will kneel down before it, even at the risk of ruining a pair of trousers (for on account of the heavy traffic to and fro, the road has become quite muddy),"—I always received the same answer: "No, it is not yet quite finished." And so there was another postponement—of the System, and of my homage.

System and finality are pretty much one and the same, so much so that if the system is not finished, there is no system. I have already in another place called the reader's attention to the consideration, that a system which is not quite finished is an hypothesis; while on the other hand to speak of a half-finished system is nonsense. If anyone says that this is merely a dispute about words, and that the systematic philosophers themselves say that the System is not finished, I would merely ask, why then do they call it a system? Why in general do they make use of equivocal language? When they publish their epitomes they say nothing about anything being lacking. Thus they lead their readers to suppose that everything is complete, unless they write for those better informed than they are themselves, which would doubtless seem unthinkable to systematists. But if someone makes a gesture as if to touch the structure anywhere, out comes the master builder. He is an extremely pleasant gentleman, exhibiting a courteous and friendly manner to visitors. He says: "Aye, it is true that we are still under construction, and that the System is not finished." But did he not know about this beforehand? Did he not know it when he sent out his inviting prospectus promising happiness to all mankind? If he did, why did he not say so? That is to say, why did he not refrain from calling the proffered fragment a system? For here we have it again: a fragment of a system is nonsense. A persistent striving to realize a system is on the other hand still a striving; and a striving, aye, a persistent striving, is precisely what Lessing talks about. And surely not a striving for nothing! On the contrary, Lessing speaks of a striving for truth, and he uses a remarkable phrase about it: *den einzigen immer regen Trieb*. This word *einzig* can scarcely be understood otherwise than as equivalent to infinite, in the same sense as that having one thought and one thought only is higher than having many thoughts. So it seems that these two, Lessing and the systematists, both talk about a persistent striving; only that Lessing is stupid or honest enough to call it a persistent striving, while the systematist is clever or dishonest enough to call it the System. What would be thought in other connections, about such a difference in language? When Agent Behrend had lost a silk umbrella he advertised for it, and described it in the advertisement as a cotton one; for, thought he, if I call it a silk umbrella, the finder will be more strongly tempted to keep it. So also thinks, in all probability, the systematist: "If on the title-page and in the announcements I call my production a persistent striving for the truth, alas! who will buy it or admire me? But if I call it the System, the Absolute System, everyone will surely want to buy the System"—if only the difficulty did not remain, that what the systematist sells is not the System.

Let us then proceed, but let us not try to deceive one another. I, Johannes Climacus, am a human being, neither more nor less; and I assume that anyone I may have the honor to engage in conversation with, is also a human being. If he presumes to be speculative philosophy in the abstract, pure speculative thought, I must renounce the effort to speak with him; for in that case he instantly vanishes from my sight, and from the feeble sight of every mortal. . . .

The difficulty that inheres in existence, with which the existing individual is confronted, is one that never really comes to expression in the language of abstract thought, much less receives an explanation. Because abstract thought is *sub specie aeterni* it ignores the concrete and the temporal, the existential process, *the predicament of the existing individual arising from his being a synthesis of the temporal and the eternal situated in existence.* Now if we assume that abstract thought is the highest manifestation of human activity, it follows that philosophy and the philosophers proudly desert existence, leaving the rest of us to face the worst. And something else, too, follows for the abstract thinker himself, namely, that since he is an existing individual he must in one way or another be suffering from absentmindedness.

The abstract problem of reality (if it is permissible to treat this problem abstractly, the particular and the accidental being constituents of the real, and directly opposed to abstraction) is not nearly so difficult a problem as it is to raise and to answer the question of what it means that this definite something is a reality. This definite something is just what abstract thought abstracts from. But the difficulty lies in bringing this definite something and the ideality of thought together, by penetrating the concrete particularity with thought. Abstract thought cannot even take cognizance of this contradiction, since the very process of abstraction prevents the contradiction from arising.

This questionable character of abstract thought becomes apparent especially in connection with all existential problems, where abstract thought gets rid of the difficulty by leaving it out, and then proceeds to boast of having explained everything. It explains immortality in general, and all goes quite smoothly, in that immortality is identified with eternity, with the eternity which is essentially the medium of all thought. But whether an existing individual human being is immortal, which is the difficulty, abstract thought does not trouble to inquire. It is disinterested; but the difficulty inherent in existence constitutes the interest of the existing individual, who is infinitely interested in existing. Abstract thought thus helps me with respect to my immortality by first annihilating me as a particular existing individual and then making me immortal, about as when the doctor in Holberg killed the patient with his medicine—but also expelled the fever. Such an abstract thinker, one who neglects to take into account the relationship between his abstract thought and his own existence as an individual, not careful to clarify this relationship to himself, makes a comical impression upon the mind even if he is ever so distinguished, because he is in process of ceasing to be a human being. While a genuine human being, as a synthesis of the finite and the infinite, finds his reality in holding these two factors together, infinitely interested in existing—such an abstract thinker is a duplex being: a fantastic creature who moves in the pure being of abstract thought, and on the other hand, a sometimes pitiful professorial figure which the former deposits, about as when one sets down a walking stick. . . .

All logical thinking employs the language of abstraction, and is *sub specie aeterni*. To think existence logically is thus to ignore the difficulty, the difficulty, that is, of thinking the eternal as in process of becoming. But this difficulty is unavoidable, since the thinker himself is in process of becoming. It is easier to indulge in abstract thought than it is to exist, unless we understand by this latter term what is loosely called existing, in analogy with what is loosely called being a subject. Here we have again an example of the fact that the simplest tasks are the most difficult. Existing is ordinarily regarded as no very complex matter, much less an art, since we all exist; but abstract thinking takes rank as an accomplishment. But really to exist, so as to interpenetrate one's existence with consciousness, at one and the same time eternal and as if far removed from existence, and yet also present in existence and in the process of becoming: that is truly difficult. If philosophical reflection had not in our time become something queer, highly artificial, and capable of being learned by rote, thinkers would make quite a different impression upon people, as was the case in Greece, where a thinker was an existing individual stimulated by his reflection to a passionate enthusiasm; and as was also once the case in Christendom, when a thinker was a believer who strove enthusiastically to understand himself in the existence of faith. If anything of this sort held true of the thinkers of our own age, the enterprise of pure thought would have led to one suicide after the other. For suicide is the only tolerable existential consequence of pure thought, when this type of abstraction is not conceived as something merely partial in relation to being human, willing to strike an agreement with an ethical and religious form of personal existence, but assumes to be all and highest. This is not to praise the suicide, but to respect the passion. Nowadays a thinker is a curious creature who during certain hours of the day exhibits a very remarkable ingenuity, but has otherwise nothing in common with a human being.

FRIEDRICH NIETZSCHE

The Free Thinker and the Consensus

Will they be new friends of "truth," these coming philosophers? Most probably, for all philosophers thus far have loved their truths. But surely they will not be dogmatists. It must run counter to their pride and their taste that their truth should be a truth for everyman, this having been the secret wish and ultimate motive of all dogmatic striving. "My judgment is *my* judgment, to which hardly anyone else has a right," is what the philosopher of the future will say. One must get rid of the bad taste of wishing to agree with many others. "Good" is no longer good in the mouth of my neighbor. And how could there be a "common good"! The expression contradicts itself: what can be common cannot have

From *Beyond Good and Evil* [1886], translated from the German by Marianne Cowan, Chicago, 1955, pp. 48-51. Copyright 1955 by Henry Regnery Company; reprinted by permission of the publisher.

much value. In the end it must be as it always was: great things remain for the great; abysses for the deep; delicacies and tremors for the subtle; and, all in all, all things rare for the rare!—

After all this need I say especially that they shall be free, *very* free thinkers, these philosophers of the future? It is certain, however, that they will not be merely free thinkers but something more, something superior, greater, and thoroughly different, something that does not want to be misjudged or mistaken for something else. But, as I am saying this, I feel the *obligation* (almost as much toward them as toward ourselves, who are their heralds and fore-runners, we free thinkers) to blow away from all of us an old stupid prejudice and misunderstanding which for too long a time has made the concept "free thinker" opaque, like a fog. In all the countries of Europe and in America there is something nowadays which abuses this concept. There is a very narrow, imprisoned, enchained sort of thinker who wants approximately the opposite of our intentions and instincts, not to mention that in reference to the *new* philosophers coming up this sort would have to be a closed window and a bolted door. They belong, to make it short and sad, among the *levellers*, these falsely named "free thinkers." They are glib-tongued and scribble-mad slaves of democratic taste and its "modern ideas"; all of them are men without solitude, without solitude of their own; rough and ready boys to whom we cannot deny courage or respectable conduct but of whom we must say that they are unfree and absurdly superficial, especially in their basic inclination to see the cause for *all* human misery and failure in the structure of society as it has been up to now. This about turns the truth upside down. What they would like to strive for with all their power is the universal green pasture-happiness of the herd: security, lack of danger, comfort and alleviation of life for everyone. Their most frequent repeated songs and doctrines are "equal rights" and "compassion for all that suffers." Suffering is taken by them to be something that must be *abolished*. We opposed thinkers, who have opened our eyes and our consciences to the question. "How and where has the plant 'man' flourished most strongly so far?" we imagine that it has happened every time under the opposite conditions: that the peril of man's position had to grow to enormity; that his power of invention and dissembling (his "mind") had to develop subtlety and boldness under long pressure and compulsion; that his life-will had to be stepped up to an unconditional power-will. We imagine that hardness, violence, slavery, peril in the street and in the heart, concealment, Stoicism, temptation, and devil-try of every sort, everything evil, frightful, tyrannical, brutal, and snake-like in man, serves as well for the advancement of the species "man" as their opposite. In fact we are not even saying enough when we say this much. At any rate, with our speech and our silence, we have arrived at the *other* end of all modern ideologies and herd-desires. Perhaps we are their antipodes. No wonder that we "free thinkers" are not exactly the most communicative of thinkers. No wonder that we do not want to reveal in every particular what a mind can be made free *from*, and *to* what it might feel driven. As for the dangerous formula "beyond good and evil" which at least keeps us from being mistaken for someone else, we *are* something different from "*libres-penseurs*," "*liberi pensatori*," "free-thinkers," and whatever else these good proponents of "modern ideas" like to be called. At home, or at least a guest, in many lands of the spirit; escaped many times from the stuffy pleasant corners into which preference and prejudice, youth, origin, accidental meetings with men and books, or even the weariness of our wanderings have seemed to pin us down; full of malice against the bait of dependence that lies hidden in honors or money or offices or sensuous enthusiasms; grateful even for distress and vicissitudinous disease because it always frees us from some kind of a rule and its "prejudice;" grateful to God, the devil, the sheep and the worm in us; curious to a fault; investigative to the point of cruelty; with impetuous fingers for the impalpable; with teeth and stomachs for the indigestible; ready for any trade demanding sharp-wittedness and sharp wits; ready for any venture thanks to an excess of "free will;" with fore-souls and back-souls whose ultimate intentions are not easily fathomed; with foregrounds and backgrounds that no foot can explore to the end; concealed beneath cloaks of light; conquerors, though we may look like inheritors and wastrels; arrangers and collectors from early till late; misers of our wealth and our full stuffed drawers; economical in learning and forgetting; inventive of schemes; occasionally proud of tables of categories; occasionally pedantic; occasionally night owls of work in the midst of daylight; scarecrows, even, when necessary—and today it is necessary insofar as we are the born, sworn, jealous friends of *solitude*, our own deepest midnight and mid-day solitude: this is the type of man we are, we free thinkers! And perhaps *you* too, you coming *new* philosophers, perhaps you too belong to this type.

FRIEDRICH NIETZSCHE
Subjective Will and Objective Truth

However gratefully we may meet the spirit of objectivity half-way (and who hasn't been sick to death of everything subjective and its damned *ipsissimosity!*) —in the end we must learn to be cautious even with our gratitude and to take steps against the exaggeration with which the self-stripping and depersonalization of the mind as an end in itself is currently celebrated, as a means of redemption and transfiguration. This happens particularly within the school of Pessimism which, to be sure, has good reason to accord the highest honors to "disinterested cognition." An objective man who no longer curses and scolds as the Pessimist does, the *ideal* intellectual in whom the scientific instinct after thousands of semi- and total failures for once comes to bloom and fruition, is surely one of the most precious instruments in the world. But he belongs in the hands of one who has greater power. He is only an instrument—he is a *mirror*, let us say; he is not an "end in himself." The objective man is indeed a mirror; above all he is something that wishes to be recognized and understood; he is accustomed to subordination, devoid of any pleasure other than that afforded by cognition, by "mirroring." He waits until something comes along and then spreads himself out delicately, so that even faint footprints and the slipping by of ghostly ceatures shall not be

From *Beyond Good and Evil* [1886], translated from the German by Marianne Cowan, Chicago, 1955, pp. 123-6, 1-7. Copyright 1955 by Henry Regnery Company; reprinted by permission of the publisher.
From *The Birth of Tragedy* [1872], translated from the German by Francis Golffing, New York, 1956, pp. 109-12. Copyright © 1956 by Doubleday & Co., Inc.; reprinted by permission of Doubleday & Co.

lost to his surface, to his sensitive hide. Whatever "person" is left in him seems accidental to him, often arbitrary, even more often disturbing. To such an extent he has become the passageway and reflection for other figures and events in his own estimation. Only with an effort does he recall "himself," and often he re- calls himself erroneously; he easily mixes himself up with others; he makes the wrong decision in regard to his own basic needs. In this respect alone he is un- subtle and careless. Perhaps he is plagued by his own state of health or the petti- ness and sticky atmosphere of his wife and friends, or the lack of fellowship and society. He will force himself to reflect on his tortures, but in vain. His thought instantly wanders away from himself, to a *more general* instance, and tomorrow he will know as little about what he needs as he does today. He has lost the ability and the time to take himself seriously; he is serene, not from lack of troubles, but from lack of skill in handling *his* troubles. His habit of meeting everything and every experience half way, the sunny and unembarrassed hospitality with which he accepts all comers, his type of unthinking good-naturedness, his dangerous indiffer- ence as to Yes and No: alas, there are enough instances in which he has to atone for these virtues of his; as a human being generally, he all too easily becomes the *caput mortuum* of his virtues. If one asks love or hate of him—and I mean love or hate as God, women, and animals understand them—well, he will do what he can and give what he can. But no one should be surprised when it turns out not to be much, when in this respect he shows up false, fragile, questionable, and hol- low. His love is over-intentional; his hate is artificial and really a *tour de force*, a small vanity and exaggeration. We must accept that he is only genuine insofar as he is permitted to be objective; it is only in his serene "totalism" that he is a part of nature and acts "natural." His mirroring and forever smoothing soul no longer knows how to affirm or deny; he does not command; neither does he destroy. He agrees with Leibniz: "*Je ne méprise presque rien*"—and we must not fail to hear or underrate the *presque*. He is not a model man, either; he walks neither before nor behind anyone; he places himself at too remote a point to side with either good or evil. Insofar as we have long mistaken him for a *philosopher*, for the Caesar-like disciplinarian and forcer of culture, we have honored him far too highly and have overlooked his essential nature. He is an instrument, a piece of slave—the most sublime type of slave, to be sure, but in himself: *presque rien*. The objective man is an instrument, a precious, easily injured, easily clouded instru- ment for taking measurements. As a mirror he is a work of art, to be handled carefully and honored. But he is not an aim, not a way out nor a way up, not a complementary human being through whom the *rest* of existence is justified, not a conclusion. And still less is he a beginning, an impregnation, or a first cause; he is nothing solid, nothing powerful, nothing self-reliant seeking to become master. Rather, a delicate, hollow, subtle, and mobile potter's form that must wait for some content, some substance, in order to be shaped accordingly; he is usually a man without substance or content, a "self-less" man. Hence, not a man for women, either (parenthetically remarked)—

1

The will to truth! That will which is yet to seduce us into many a venture, that famous truthfulness of which all philosophers up to this time have spoken reverently—think what questions this will to truth has posed for us! What strange, wicked, questionable questions! It has been a long story—and yet it seems hardly to have started. No wonder if just for once we become suspicious, and, losing our patience, impatiently turn around! Let us learn to ask this Sphinx some questions ourselves, for a change. Just *who* is it anyway who has been asking these questions? Just *what* is it in us that wants "to approach truth?" Indeed, we tarried a long time before the question of the cause of this will. And in the end we stopped altogether before the even more basic question. We asked "What is the value of this will?" Supposing we want truth: *why not rather* untruth? Uncertainty? Even Ignorance? The problem of the value of truth confronted us—or were we the ones who confronted the problems? Which of us is Oedipus? Which of us the Sphinx? It is a rendezvous of questions and question marks. It may be unbelievable, but it seems to us in the end as though the problem had never yet been posed—as though it were being seen, fixed, above all *risked*, for the first time. For there is a risk in posing it—perhaps no greater risk could be found.

2

How is it possible for anything to come out of its opposite? Truth, for example, out of error? Or the will to truth out of the will to deception? Or a selfless act out of self-interest? Or the pure sunny contemplation of a wise man out of covetousness? This sort of origin is impossible. Who dreams of it is a fool or worse; the things of highest value must have some other, *indigenous* origin; they cannot be derived from this ephemeral, seductive, deceptive, inferior world, this labyrinth of delusion and greed! Their basis must lie in the womb of Being, in the Eternal, in the hidden God, in the "Thing In Itself"—here, and nowhere else!—This type of judgment is the typical prejudice by which the metaphysicians of all time can be recognized. This type of valuation stands back of all their logical methods; this is the "faith" that enables them to struggle for what they call "knowing"—a something which at last they solemnly christen "truth." The basic faith of all metaphysicians is *faith in the antithetical nature of values.* It has never occurred to the most cautious of them, even though they had taken the vow to "doubt everything," to pause in doubt at the very threshold where doubt would have been most necessary. But we may indeed doubt: first, whether antitheses exist at all, and second, whether those popular valuations and value-antitheses upon which the metaphysicians have placed their stamp of approval are not perhaps merely superficial valuations, merely provisional perspectives—and perspectives from a tight corner at that, possibly from below, a "worm's eye view" so to speak. Admitting all the value accorded to the true, the truthful, the selfless, it is nonetheless possible that a higher value should be ascribed to appearance, to the will to deception, to self-interest, to greed—a higher value with respect to all life. Furthermore, it is quite possible that the very value of those good and honored things consists, in fact, in their insidious relatedness to these wicked, seemingly opposite things—it could be that they are inextricably bound up, entwined, perhaps even similar in their very nature. Perhaps! But who is willing to be troubled by such a perilous Perhaps? We must wait for a new species of philosopher to arrive, who will have some other, opposite tastes and inclinations than the previous ones. Philosophers of the Perilous Perhaps, in every sense! And seriously, I can see such new philosophers coming up over the horizon.

3

After keeping an eye on and reading between the lines of the philosophers for a long time, I find that I must tell myself the following: the largest part of conscious thinking must be considered an instinctual activity, even in the case of philosophical thinking. We must simply re-learn, as we have had to re-learn about heredity and "inborn" qualities. As little as the act of birth is of consequence in the whole process and progress of heredity, so little is consciousness in any decisive sense opposed to instinct. Most of the conscious thinking of a philosopher is secretly guided by his instincts and forced along certain lines. Even behind logic and its apparent sovereignty of development stand value judgments, or, to speak more plainly, physiological demands for preserving a certain type of life. Such as for example, that the definite is worth more than the indefinite, that appearance is less valuable than "the truth." Such valuations, all their regulative importance notwithstanding, can for *us* be only foreground-valuations, a definite type of ridiculous simplicity, possibly necessary for the preservation of the creature we happen to be. Assuming, to be sure, that man does not happen to be "the measure of all things". . . .

4

The falseness of a given judgment does not constitute an objection against it, so far as we are concerned. It is perhaps in this respect that our new language sounds strangest. The real question is how far a judgment furthers and maintains life, preserves a given type, possibly cultivates and trains a given type. We are, in fact, fundamentally inclined to maintain that the falsest judgments (to which belong the synthetic *a priori* judgments) are the most indispensable to us, that man cannot live without accepting the logical fictions as valid, without measuring reality against the purely invented world of the absolute, the immutable, without constantly falsifying the world by means of numeration. That getting along without false judgments would amount to getting along without life, negating life. To admit untruth as a necessary condition of life: this implies, to be sure, a perilous resistance against customary value-feelings. A philosophy that risks it nonetheless, if it did nothing else, would by this alone have taken its stand beyond good and evil.

5

What tempts us to look at all philosophers half suspiciously and half mockingly is not so much that we recognize again and again how innocent they are, how often and how easily they make mistakes and lose their way, in short their childishness and childlikeness—but rather that they are not sufficiently candid, though they make a great virtuous noisy to-do as soon as the problem of truthfulness is even remotely touched upon. Every one of them pretends that he has discovered and reached his opinions through the self-development of cold, pure, divinely untroubled dialectic (in distinction to the mystics of every rank who, more honest and fatuous, talk about "inspiration"), whereas, at bottom, a pre-conceived dogma, a notion, an "institution," or mostly a heart's desire, made abstract and refined, is defended by them with arguments sought after the fact. They are all of them lawyers (though wanting to be called anything but that), and for the most part quite sly defenders of their prejudices which they christen "truths"— *very* far removed they are from the courageous conscience which admits precisely this; very remote from the courageous good taste which makes sure that others understand—perhaps to warn an enemy or a friend, perhaps from sheer high spirits and self-mockery. The spectacle of old Kant's Tartuffery, as stiff as it is respectable, luring us onto the dialectical crooked paths which lead (or better, mislead) to his "categorical imperative"—this spectacle makes us, used to diversions as we are, smile. For we find no small entertainment in keeping our eye on the delicate tricks of ancient moralists and morality-preachers. Or consider that hocuspocus of mathematical form with which Spinoza masked and armor-plated as though in bronze his philosophy (or let us translate the word properly: "the love of *his own* wisdom")! He used it to intimidate at the very start the courageous attacker who might dare cast eyes on this invincible virgin and Pallas Athene— how much insecurity and vulnerability this masquerade of a sick recluse betrays!

6

Gradually I have come to realize what every great philosophy up to now has been: the personal confession of its originator, a type of involuntary and unaware memoirs; also that the moral (or amoral) intentions of each philosophy constitute the protoplasm from which each entire plant has grown. Indeed, one will do well (and wisely), if one wishes to explain to himself how on earth the more remote metaphysical assertions of a philosopher ever arose, to ask each time: What sort of morality is this (is *he*) aiming at? Thus I do not believe that a "desire for comprehension" is the father of philosophy, but rather that a quite different desire has here as elsewhere used comprehension (together with miscomprehension) as tools to serve its own ends. Anyone who looks at the basic desires of man with a view to finding out how well they have played their part in precisely this field as inspirational genii (or demons or hobgoblins) will note that they have all philosophized at one time or another. Each individual desire wants badly to represent itself as *the* final aim of existence and as rightful master of all the others. For each desire is autocratic and *as such* it attempts to philosophize. In the case of scholars, to be sure, the specifically "scientific" men, it may be different—"better" if you wish. They may really have something like a "desire for comprehension," some small independent clockwork mechanism which, when properly wound, works bravely on *without* involving the remaining desires of the scholars. The real "interests," therefore, of the scholars lie in quite another field—in their family, perhaps, or their livelihood, or in politics. It makes almost no difference, in fact, whether the little machine is employed in one place or another to serve science, and whether the "promising" young worker makes of himself a philologist or a mushroom-fancier or a chemist—his becoming this or that does not *characterize* him. Conversely, there is nothing impersonal whatever in the philosopher.

And particularly his morality testifies decidedly and decisively as to *who he is*—that is, what order of rank the innermost desires of his nature occupy.

Our whole modern world is caught in the net of Alexandrian culture and recognizes as its ideal the man of theory, equipped with the highest cognitive powers, working in the service of science, and whose archetype and progenitor is Socrates. All our pedagogic devices are oriented toward this ideal. Any type of existence that deviates from this model has a hard struggle and lives, at best, on sufferance. It is a rather frightening thought that for centuries the only form of educated man to be found was the scholar. Even our literary arts have been forced to develop out of learned imitations, and the important role rhyme plays in our poetry still betokens the derivation of our poetic forms from artificial experiments with a language not vernacular but properly learned. To any true Greek, that product of modern culture, *Faust*, would have seemed quite unintelligible, though we ourselves understand it well enough. We have only to place Faust, who storms unsatisfied through all the provinces of knowledge and is driven to make a bargain with the powers of darkness, beside Socrates in order to realize that modern man has begun to be aware of the limits of Socratic curiosity and to long, in the wide, waste ocean of knowledge, for a shore. Goethe once said to Eckermann, referring to Napoleon: "Yes indeed, my friend, there is also a productivity of actions." This *aperçu* suggests that for us moderns the man of action is something amazing and incredible, so that the wisdom of a Goethe was needed to find such a strange mode of existence comprehensible, even excusable.

We should acknowledge, then, that Socratic culture is rooted in an optimism which believes itself omnipotent. Nor should we be surprised when we see the fruits of such optimism fully matured, when a society that has been leavened through and through by such convictions begins to quake with extravagant bloatings and appetites, when the belief in general happiness and in the possibility of universal book knowledge becomes by degrees a peremptory demand for such an Alexandrian utopia and the advent of a Euripidean *deus ex machina*. One thing should be remembered: Alexandrian culture requires a slave class for its continued existence, but in its optimism it denies the necessity for such a class; therefore it courts disaster once the effect of its nice slogans concerning the dignity of man and the dignity of labor have worn thin. Nothing can be more terrible than a barbaric slave class that has learned to view its existence as an injustice and prepares to avenge not only its own wrongs but those of all past generations. Under such conditions, who would dare appeal confidently to our weary and etiolated religions, which have long since become "Brahmin" religions? Myth, the prerequisite of all religion, has been paralyzed everywhere, and theology has been invaded by that optimistic spirit which I have just stigmatized as the baneful virus of our society.

The blight which threatens theoretical culture has only begun to frighten modern man, and he is groping uneasily for remedies out of the storehouse of his experience, without having any real conviction that these remedies will prevail against disaster. In the meantime, there have arisen certain men of genius who, with admirable circumspection and consequence, have used the arsenal of science to demonstrate the limitations of science and of the cognitive faculty itself. They have authoritatively rejected science's claim to universal validity and to the attainment of universal goals and exploded for the first time the belief that man may plumb the universe by means of the law of causation. The extraordinary courage and wisdom of Kant and Schopenhauer have won the most difficult victory, that over the optimistic foundations of logic, which form the underpinnings of our culture. Whereas the current optimism had treated the universe as knowable, in the presumption of eternal truths, and space, time, and causality as absolute and universally valid laws, Kant showed how these supposed laws serve only to raise appearance—the work of Maya—to the status of true reality, thereby rendering impossible a genuine understanding of that reality: in the words of Schopenhauer, binding the dreamer even faster in sleep. This perception has initiated a culture which I dare describe as tragic. Its most important characteristic is that wisdom is put in the place of science as the highest goal. This wisdom, unmoved by the pleasant distractions of the sciences, fixes its gaze on the total constellation of the universe and tries to comprehend sympathetically the suffering of that universe as its own. Let us imagine a rising generation with undaunted eyes, with a heroic drive towards the unexplored; let us imagine the bold step of these St. Georges, their reckless pride as they turn their backs on all the valetudinarian doctrines of optimism, preparing to "dwell resolutely in the fullness of being": would it not be necessary for the tragic individual of such a culture, readied by his discipline for every contingency, every terror, to want a novel art of metaphysical solace as his Helena and to exclaim as Faust did:

> And shall not I, by mightiest desire,
> In living shape that precious form acquire?

Now that Socratic culture has been shaken from two sides and has begun to doubt its own infallibility (first, from fear of its own consequences, which it is just coming to realize, and second, because it is no longer as confident of the solidity of its foundation as it formerly was) it is sad to see how it runs eagerly to embrace one new shape after another, only to let go of it in horror, as Mephistophles did the seductive lamias. The man of theory, having begun to dread the consequences of his views, no longer dares commit himself freely to the icy flood of existence but runs nervously up and down the bank. He no longer wants to have anything entire with all the natural cruelty of things: to such an extent has the habit of optimism softened him. At the same time, he believes that a culture built on scientific principles must perish once it admits illogic, that is to say, refuses to face its consequences. Our art is a clear example of this universal misery: in vain do we imitate all the great creative periods and masters; in vain do we surround modern man with all of world literature and expect him to name its periods and styles as Adam did the beasts. He remains eternally hungry, the critic without strength or joy, the Alexandrian man who is at bottom a librarian and scholiast, blinding himself miserably over dusty books and typographical errors.

ALBERT CAMUS
The Fact of Absurdity

It happens that the stage sets collapse. Rising, streetcar, four hours in the office or the factory, meal, streetcar, four hours of work, meal, sleep, and Monday Tuesday Wednesday Thursday Friday and Saturday according to the same rhythm—this path is easily followed most of the time. But one day the "why" arises and everything begins in that weariness tinged with amazement. "Begins"—this is important. Weariness comes at the end of the acts of a mechanical life, but at the same time it inaugurates the impulse of consciousness. It awakens consciousness and provokes what follows. What follows is the gradual return into the chain or it is the definitive awakening. At the end of the awakening comes, in time, the consequence: suicide or recovery. In itself weariness has something sickening about it. Here, I must conclude that it is good. For everything begins with consciousness and nothing is worth anything except through it. There is nothing original about these remarks. But they are obvious; that is enough for a while, during a sketchy reconnaissance in the origins of the absurd. Mere "anxiety," as Heidegger says, is at the source of everything.

Likewise and during every day of an unillustrious life, time carries us. But a moment always comes when we have to carry it. We live on the future: "tomorrow," "later on," "when you have made your way," "you will understand when you are old enough." Such irrelevancies are wonderful, for, after all, it's a matter of dying. Yet a day comes when a man notices or says that he is thirty. Thus he asserts his youth. But simultaneously he situates himself in relation to time. He takes his place in it. He admits that he stands at a certain point on a curve that he acknowledges having to travel to its end. He belongs to time, and by the horror that seizes him, he recognizes his worst enemy. Tomorrow, he was longing for tomorrow, whereas everything in him ought to reject it. That revolt of the flesh is the absurd.[1]

A step lower and strangeness creeps in: perceiving that the world is "dense," sensing to what a degree a stone is foreign and irreducible to us, with what intensity nature or a landscape can negate us. At the heart of all beauty lies something inhuman, and these hills, the softness of the sky, the outline of these trees

[1] But not in the proper sense. This is not a definition, but rather an *enumeration* of the feelings that may admit of the absurd. Still, the enumeration finished, the absurd has nevertheless not been exhausted.

From *The Myth of Sisyphus* [1942], translated from the French by Justin O'Brien, New York, 1955, pp. 10-16. Copyright © 1955 by Alfred A. Knopf, Inc.; reprinted by permission of Random House, Alfred A. Knopf, Inc. and Hamish Hamilton Ltd.

at this very minute lose the illusory meaning with which we had clothed them, henceforth more remote than a lost paradise. The primitive hostility of the world rises up to face us across millennia. For a second we cease to understand it because for centuries we have understood in it solely the images and designs that we had attributed to it beforehand, because henceforth we lack the power to make use of that artifice. The world evades us because it becomes itself again. That stage scenery masked by habit becomes again what it is. It withdraws at a distance from us. Just as there are days when under the familiar face of a woman, we see as a stranger her we had loved months or years ago, perhaps we shall come even to desire what suddenly leaves us so alone. But the time has not yet come. Just one thing: that denseness and that strangeness of the world is the absurd.

Men, too, secrete the inhuman. At certain moments of lucidity, the mechanical aspect of their gestures, their meaningless pantomime makes silly everything that surrounds them. A man is talking on the telephone behind a glass partition; you cannot hear him, but you see his incomprehensible dumb show: you wonder why he is alive. This discomfort in the face of man's own inhumanity, this incalculable tumble before the image of what we are, this "nausea," as a writer of today calls it, is also the absurd. Likewise the stranger who at certain seconds comes to meet us in a mirror, the familiar and yet alarming brother we encounter in our own photographs is also the absurd.

I come at last to death and to the attitude we have toward it. On this point everything has been said and it is only proper to avoid pathos. Yet one will never be sufficiently surprised that everyone lives as if no one "knew." This is because in reality there is no experience of death. Properly speaking, nothing has been experienced but what has been lived and made conscious. Here, it is barely possible to speak of the experience of others' deaths. It is a substitute, an illusion, and it never quite convinces us. That melancholy convention cannot be persuasive. The horror comes in reality from the mathematical aspect of the event. If time frightens us, this is because it works out the problem and the solution comes afterward. All the pretty speeches about the soul will have their contrary convincingly proved, at least for a time. From this inert body on which a slap makes no mark the soul has disappeared. This elementary and definitive aspect of the adventure constitutes the absurd feeling. Under the fatal lighting of that destiny, its uselessness becomes evident. No code of ethics and no effort are justifiable *a priori* in the face of the cruel mathematics that command our condition.

Let me repeat: all this has been said over and over. I am limiting myself here to making a rapid classification and to pointing out these obvious themes. They run through all literatures and all philosophies. Everyday conversation feeds on them. There is no question of reinventing them. But it is essential to be sure of these facts in order to be able to question oneself subsequently on the primordial question. I am interested—let me repeat again—not so much in absurd discoveries as in their consequences. If one is assured of these facts, what is one to conclude, how far is one to go to elude nothing? Is one to die voluntarily or to hope in spite of everything? Beforehand, it is necessary to take the same rapid inventory on the plane of the intelligence.

The mind's first step is to distinguish what is true from what is false. However, as soon as thought reflects on itself, what it first discovers is a contradiction.

Useless to strive to be convincing in this case. Over the centuries no one has furnished a clearer and more elegant demonstration of the business than Aristotle: "The often ridiculed consequence of these opinions is that they destroy themselves. For by asserting that all is true we assert the truth of the contrary assertion and consequently the falsity of our own thesis (for the contrary assertion does not admit that it can be true). And if one says that all is false, that assertion is itself false. If we declare that solely the assertion opposed to ours is false or else that solely ours is not false, we are nevertheless forced to admit an infinite number of true or false judgments. For the one who expresses a true assertion proclaims simultaneously that it is true, and so on *ad infinitum*."

This vicious circle is but the first of a series in which the mind that studies itself gets lost in a giddy whirling. The very simplicity of these paradoxes makes them irreducible. Whatever may be the plays on words and the acrobatics of logic, to understand is, above all, to unify. The mind's deepest desire, even in its most elaborate operations, parallels man's unconscious feeling in the face of his universe: it is an insistence upon familiarity, an appetite for clarity. Understanding the world for a man is reducing it to the human, stamping it with his seal. The cat's universe is not the universe of the anthill. The truism "All thought is anthropomorphic" has no other meaning. Likewise, the mind that aims to understand reality can consider itself satisfied only by reducing it to terms of thought. If man realized that the universe like him can love and suffer, he would be reconciled. If thought discovered in the shimmering mirrors of phenomena eternal relations capable of summing them up and summing themselves up in a single principle, then would be seen an intellectual joy of which the myth of the blessed would be but a ridiculous imitation. That nostalgia for unity, that appetite for the absolute illustrates the essential impulse of the human drama. But the fact of that nostalgia's existence does not imply that it is to be immediately satisfied. For if, bridging the gulf that separates desire from conquest, we assert with Parmenides the reality of the One (whatever it may be), we fall into the ridiculous contradiction of a mind that asserts total unity and proves by its very assertion its own difference and the diversity it claimed to resolve. This other vicious circle is enough to stifle our hopes.

These are again truisms. I shall again repeat that they are not interesting in themselves but in the consequences that can be deduced from them. I know another truism: it tells me that man is mortal. One can nevertheless count the minds that have deduced the extreme conclusions from it. It is essential to consider as a constant point of reference in this essay the regular hiatus between what we fancy we know and what we really know, practical assent and simulated ignorance which allows us to live with ideas which, if we truly put them to the test, ought to upset our whole life. Faced with this inextricable contradiction of the mind, we shall fully grasp the divorce separating us from our own creations. So long as the mind keeps silent in the motionless world of its hopes, everything is reflected and arranged in the unity of its nostalgia. But with its first move this world cracks and tumbles: an infinite number of shimmering fragments is offered to the understanding. We must despair of ever reconstructing the familiar, calm surface which would give us peace of heart. After so many centuries of inquiries, so many abdications among thinkers, we are well aware that this is true for all our knowledge. With the exception of professional rationalists, today people despair of true knowledge. If the only significant history of human thought were to be written, it would have to be the history of its successive regrets and its impotences.

Of whom and of what indeed can I say: "I know that!" This heart within me I can feel, and I judge that it exists. This world I can touch, and I likewise judge that it exists. There ends all my knowledge, and the rest is construction. For if I try to seize this self of which I feel sure, if I try to define and to summarize it, it is nothing but water slipping through my fingers. I can sketch one by one all the aspects it is able to assume, all those likewise that have been attributed to it, this upbringing, this origin, this ardor or these silences, this nobility or this vileness. But aspects cannot be added up. This very heart which is mine will forever remain indefinable to me. Between the certainty I have of my existence and the content I try to give to that assurance, the gap will never be filled. Forever I shall be a stranger to myself. In psychology as in logic, there are truths but no truth. Socrates' "Know thyself" has as much value as the "Be virtuous" of our confessionals. They reveal a nostalgia at the same time as an ignorance. They are sterile exercises on great subjects. They are legitimate only in precisely so far as they are approximate.

And here are trees and I know their gnarled surface, water and I feel its taste. These scents of grass and stars at night, certain evenings when the heart relaxes—how shall I negate this world whose power and strength I feel? Yet all the knowledge on earth will give me nothing to assure me that this world is mine. You describe it to me and you teach me to classify it. You enumerate its laws and in my thirst for knowledge I admit that they are true. You take apart its mechanism and my hope increases. At the final stage you teach me that this wondrous and multicolored universe can be reduced to the atom and that the atom itself can be reduced to the electron. All this is good and I wait for you to continue. But you tell me of an invisible planetary system in which electrons gravitate around a nucleus. You explain this world to me with an image. I realize then that you have been reduced to poetry: I shall never know. Have I the time to become indignant? You have already changed theories. So that science that was to teach me everything ends up in a hypothesis, that lucidity founders in metaphor, that uncertainty is resolved in a work of art. What need had I of so many efforts? The soft lines of these hills and the hand of evening on this troubled heart teach me much more. I have returned to my beginning. I realize that if through science I can seize phenomena and enumerate them, I cannot, for all that, apprehend the world. Were I to trace its entire relief with my finger, I should not know any more. And you give me the choice between a description that is sure but that teaches me nothing and hypotheses that claim to teach me but that are not sure. A stranger to myself and to the world, armed solely with a thought that negates itself as soon as it asserts, what is this condition in which I can have peace only by refusing to know and to live, in which the appetite for conquest bumps into walls that defy its assaults? To will is to stir up paradoxes. Everything is ordered in such a way as to bring into being that poisoned peace produced by thoughtlessness, lack of heart, or fatal renunciations.

Hence the intelligence, too, tells me in its way that this world is absurd. Its contrary, blind reason, may well claim that all is clear; I was waiting for proof and longing for it to be right. But despite so many pretentious centuries and over the heads of so many eloquent and persuasive men, I know that is false. On this plane, at least, there is no happiness if I cannot know. That universal reason, practical or ethical, that determinism, those categories that explain everything are enough to make a decent man laugh. They have nothing to do with the mind. They negate its profound truth, which is to be enchained. In this unintelligible and limited universe, man's fate henceforth assumes its meaning. A horde of irrationals has sprung up and surrounds him until his ultimate end. In his recovered and now studied lucidity, the feeling of the absurd becomes clear and definite. I said that the world is absurd, but I was too hasty. This world in itself is not reasonable, that is all that can be said. But what is absurd is the confrontation of this irrational and the wild longing for clarity whose call echoes in the human heart. The absurd depends as much on man as on the world. For the moment it is all that links them together. It binds them one to the other as only hatred can weld two creatures together. This is all I can discern clearly in this measureless universe where my adventure takes place. Let us pause here. If I hold to be true that absurdity that determines my relationship with life, if I become thoroughly imbued with that sentiment that seizes me in face of the world's scenes, with that lucidity imposed on me by the pursuit of a science, I must sacrifice everything to these certainties and I must see them squarely to be able to maintain them. Above all, I must adapt my behavior to them and pursue them in all their consequences. I am speaking here of decency. But I want to know beforehand if thought can live in those deserts.

JEAN-PAUL SARTRE

Existence Precedes Essence

What . . . [all existentialists] have in common is simply the fact that they believe that *existence* comes before *essence*—or, if you will, that we must begin from the subjective. What exactly do we mean by that?

If one considers an article of manufacture—as, for example, a book or a paper-knife—one sees that it has been made by an artisan who had a conception of it; and he has paid attention, equally, to the conception of a paper-knife and to the pre-existent technique of production which is a part of that conception and is, at bottom, a formula. Thus the paper-knife is at the same time an article producible in a certain manner and one which, on the other hand, serves a definite purpose, for one cannot suppose that a man would produce a paper-knife without knowing what it was for. Let us say, then, of the paper-knife that its essence—that is to say the sum of the formulae and the qualities which made its production and its definition possible—precedes its existence. The presence of such-and-such a paper-knife or book is thus determined before my eyes. Here, then, we are viewing the world from a technical standpoint, and we can say that production precedes existence.

From *Existentialism and Humanism* [1946], translated from the French by Philip Mairet. Translation reprinted by permission of Methuen & Co. Ltd., London. Text reprinted by permission of The Philosophical Library, Inc., and Sanford Greenburger. Copyright 1947 by The Philosophical Library, Inc.

When we think of God as the creator, we are thinking of him, most of the time, as a supernal artisan. Whatever doctrine we may be considering, whether it be a doctrine like that of Descartes, or of Leibnitz himself, we always imply that the will follows, more or less, from the understanding or at least accompanies it, so that when God creates he knows precisely what he is creating. Thus, the conception of man in the mind of God is comparable to that of the paper-knife in the mind of the artisan: God makes man according to a procedure and a conception, exactly as the artisan manufactures a paper-knife, following a definition and a formula. Thus each individual man is the realization of a certain conception which dwells in the divine understanding. In the philosophic atheism of the eighteenth century, the notion of God is suppressed, but not, for all that, the idea that essence is prior to existence; something of that idea we still find everywhere, in Diderot, in Voltaire and even in Kant. Man possesses a human nature; that "human nature," which is the conception of human being, is found in every man; which means that each man is a particular example of a universal conception, the conception of Man. In Kant, this universality goes so far that the wild man of the woods, man in the state of nature and the bourgeois are all contained in the same definition and have the same fundamental qualities. Here again, the essence of man precedes that historic existence which we confront in experience.

Atheistic existentialism, of which I am a representative, declares with greater consistency that if God does not exist there is at least one being whose existence comes before its essence, a being which exists before it can be defined by any conception of it. That being is man or, as Heidegger has it, the human reality. What do we mean by saying that existence precedes essence? We mean that man first of all exists, encounters himself, surges up in the world—and defines himself afterwards. If man as the existentialist sees him is not definable, it is because to begin with he is nothing. He will not be anything until later, and then he will be what he makes of himself. Thus, there is no human nature, because there is no God to have a conception of it. Man simply is. Not that he is simply what he conceives himself to be, but he is what he wills, and as he conceives himself after already existing—as he wills to be after that leap towards existence. Man is nothing else but that which he makes of himself. That is the first principle of existentialism.

SØREN KIERKEGAARD

Choice

Now in case a man were able to maintain himself upon the pinnacle of the instant of choice, in case he could cease to be a man, in case he were in his inmost

From *Either/Or* [1843], translated from the Danish by Walter Lowrie, Princeton, 1949, Vol. II, pp. 138-9, 141, 142-3, 189-91, 194-5. Copyright 1944 by Princeton University Press; reprinted by permission of the Princeton University Press.
From *Journals*, ed. and translated by Alexander Dru, London and New York, 1938, pp. 372-3; reprinted by permission of Alexander Dru.

nature only an airy thought, in case personality meant nothing more than to be a kobold, which takes part, indeed, in the movements but nevertheless remains unchanged; in case such were the situation, it would be foolish to say that it might ever be too late for a man to choose, for in a deeper sense there could be no question of a choice. The choice itself is decisive for the content of the personality, through the choice the personality immerses itself in the thing chosen, and when it does not choose it withers away in consumption. For an instant it is so, for an instant it may seem as if the things between which a choice is to be made lie outside of the chooser, that he stands in no relationship to it, that he can preserve a state of indifference over against it. This is the instant of deliberation, but this, like the Platonic instant, has no existence, least of all in the abstract sense in which you would hold it fast, and the longer one stares at it the less it exists. That which has to be chosen stands in the deepest relationship to the chooser, and when it is a question of a choice involving a life problem the individual must naturally be living in the meantime, and hence, it comes about that the longer he postpones the choice the easier it is for him to alter its character, notwithstanding that he is constantly deliberating and deliberating and believes that thereby he is holding the alternatives distinctly apart. When life's either/or is regarded in this way one is not easily tempted to jest with it. One sees, then, that the inner drift of the personality leaves no time for thought experiments, that it constantly hastens onward and in one way or another posits this alternative or that, making the choice more difficult the next instant because what has thus been posited must be revoked. Think of the captain on his ship at the instant when it has to come about. He will perhaps be able to say, "I can either do this or that"; but in case he is not a pretty poor navigator, he will be aware at the same time that the ship is all the while making its usual headway, and that therefore it is only an instant when it is indifferent whether he does this or that. So it is with a man. If he forgets to take account of the headway, there comes at last an instant when there no longer is any question of an either/or, not because he has chosen but because he has neglected to choose, which is equivalent to saying, because others have chosen for him, because he has lost his self.

You will perceive also in what I have just been saying how essentially my view of choice differs from yours (if you can properly be said to have any view), for yours differs precisely in the fact that it prevents you from choosing. For me the instant of choice is very serious, not so much on account of the rigorous cogitation involved in weighing the alternatives, not on account of the multiplicity of thoughts which attach themselves to every link in the chain, but rather because there is danger afoot, danger that the next instant it may not be equally in my power to choose, that something already has been lived which must be lived over again. For to think that for an instant one can keep one's personality a blank, or that strictly speaking one can break off and bring to a halt the course of the personal life, is a delusion. The personality is already interested in the choice before one chooses, and when the choice is postponed the personality chooses unconsciously, or the choice is made by obscure powers within it. So when at last the choice is made one discovers (unless, as I remarked before, the personality has been completely volatilized) that there is something which must be done over again, something which must be revoked, and this is often very difficult. We read in fairy tales about human beings whom mermaids and mermen enticed into their power by means of demoniac music. In order to break the enchantment it was necessary in the fairy tale for the person who was under the spell to play the same piece of music backwards without making a single mistake. This is very profound, but very difficult to perform, and yet so it is: the errors one has taken into oneself one must eradicate in this way, and every time one makes a mistake one must begin all over. Therefore, it is important to choose and to choose in time. You, on the contrary, have another method. . . .

Your choice is an aesthetic choice, but an aesthetic choice is no choice. The act of choosing is essentially a proper and stringent expression of the ethical. Whenever in a stricter sense there is question of an either/or, one can always be sure that the ethical is involved. The only absolute either/or is the choice between good and evil, but that is also absolutely ethical. The aesthetic choice is either entirely immediate and to that extent no choice, or it loses itself in the multifarious. Thus, when a young girl follows the choice of her heart, this choice, however beautiful it may be, is in the strictest sense no choice, since it is entirely immediate. When a man deliberates aesthetically upon a multitude of life's problems, as you did in the foregoing, he does not easily get one either/or, but a whole multiplicity, because the self-determining factor in the choice is not ethically accentuated, and because when one does not choose absolutely one chooses only for the moment, and therefore can choose something different the next moment. The ethical choice is therefore in a certain sense much easier, much simpler, but in another sense it is infinitely harder. He who would define his life task ethically has ordinarily not so considerable a selection to choose from; on the other hand, the act of choice has far more importance for him. If you will understand me aright, I should like to say that in making a choice it is not so much a question of choosing the right as of the energy, the earnestness, the pathos with which one chooses. Thereby the personality announces its inner infinity, and thereby, in turn, the personality is consolidated. Therefore, even if a man were to choose the wrong, he will nevertheless discover, precisely by reason of the energy with which he chose, that he had chosen the wrong. For the choice being made with the whole inwardness of his personality, his nature is purified and he himself brought into immediate relation to the eternal Power whose omnipresence interpenetrates the whole of existence. This transfiguration, this higher consecration, is never attained by that man who chooses merely aesthetically. The rhythm in that man's soul, in spite of all its passion, is only a *spiritus lenis.* . . .

So then, one either has to live aesthetically or one has to live ethically. In this alternative, as I have said, there is not yet in the strictest sense any question of a choice; for he who lives aesthetically does not choose, and he who after the ethical has manifested itself to him chooses the aesthetical is not living aesthetically, for he is sinning and is subject to ethical determinants even though his life may be described as unethical. Lo, this is, as it were, a *character indelebilis* impressed upon the ethical, that though it modestly places itself on a level with the aesthetical, it is nevertheless that which makes the choice a choice. And this is the pitiful thing to one who contemplates human life, that so many live on in a quiet state of perdition; they outlive themselves, not in the sense that the content of life is successively unfolding and now is possessed in this expanded state, but they live their lives, as it were, outside of themselves, they vanish like shadows, their immortal soul is blown away, and they are not alarmed by the problem of its immortality, for they are already in a state of dissolution before they die. They do not live aesthetically, but neither has the ethical manifested itself in its entirety, so they have not exactly rejected it either, they therefore are not sinning, except in so far as it is sin not to be either one thing or the other; neither are they ever in doubt about their immortality, for he who deeply and sincerely is in doubt of it on his own behalf will surely find the right. *On his own behalf,* I say, and surely it is high time to utter a warning against the great-hearted, heroic objectivity with which many thinkers think on behalf of others and not on their own behalf. If one would call this which I here require selfishness, I would reply that this comes from the fact that people have no conception of what this "self" is, and that it would be of very little use to a man if he were to gain the whole world and lose himself, and that it must necessarily be a poor proof which does not first of all convince the man who presents it.

My either/or does not in the first instance denote the choice between good and evil; it denotes the choice whereby one chooses good *and* evil/or excludes them. Here the question is under what determinants one would contemplate the whole of existence and would himself live. That the man who chooses good and evil chooses the good is indeed true, but this becomes evident only afterwards; for the aesthetical is not the evil but neutrality, and that is the reason why I affirmed that it is the ethical which constitutes the choice. It is, therefore, not so much a question of choosing between willing the good *or* the evil, as of choosing to will, but by this in turn the good and the evil are posited. He who chooses the ethical chooses the good, but here the good is entirely abstract, only its being is posited, and hence it does not follow by any means that the chooser cannot in turn choose the evil, in spite of the fact that he chose the good. Here you see again how important it is that a choice be made, and that the crucial thing is not deliberation but the baptism of the will which lifts up the choice into the ethical. . . .

But what is it I choose? Is it this thing or that? No, for I choose absolutely, and the absoluteness of my choice is expressed precisely by the fact that I have not chosen to choose this or that. I choose the absolute. And what is the absolute? It is I myself in my eternal validity. Anything else but myself I never can choose as the absolute, for if I choose something else, I choose it as a finite thing and so do not choose it absolutely. Even the Jew who chose God did not choose absolutely, for he chose, indeed, the absolute, but did not choose it absolutely, and thereby it ceased to be the absolute and became a finite thing.

But what, then, is this self of mine? If I were required to define this, my first answer would be: It is the most abstract of all things, and yet at the same time it is the most concrete—it is freedom. Permit me at this point to make a little psychological observation. One often hears people give vent to their discontent with life, and often hears them express their wishes. Picture to yourself such a bungler —let us skip over the wishes which illuminate nothing because they have to do with the entirely accidental. He wishes: Would that I had that man's intelligence, or that man's talent, etc.—yea, to go to the extremest point, would that I had that man's firmness. Such wishes one hears frequently, but have you ever heard a man seriously express the wish that he might become another man? This is so far from being the case that it is precisely characteristic of the individuals we call unfortunate that for the most part they cling tightly to their own selves, that in spite of all their sufferings they would not for all the world be anybody else.

And the reason for this is that such individuals are very close to the truth and feel the eternal validity of their personality, not in its blessings but in its bane, even though they have refrained from giving voice to this perfectly abstract expression for the gladness of being themselves rather than anybody else. But then, that man of the many wishes thinks constantly that he would remain himself although everything were to be changed. So there is something in him which is absolute in relation to everything else, something whereby he is the man he is, even though the alteration he would accomplish by his wish were the greatest possible. That he is mistaken I shall show later, but here I would merely find the most abstract expression for this "self" which makes him the man he is. And this is nothing other than freedom. It would actually be possible in this way to produce a highly plausible proof for the eternal validity of the personality. Yea, even a suicide does not really desire to do away with his self, he too wishes, he wishes another form for his self, and therefore one may find a suicide who was in the highest degree convinced of the immortality of the soul but whose whole being was so entangled that by this step he expected to find the absolute form for his spirit.

The reason, however, why it seems to an individual as if he might constantly be changed and yet remain the same (as if his inmost nature were an algebraic sign which could signify anything whatever) is to be found in the fact that he is not correctly situated, has not chosen himself, has no conception of such a thing; and yet even in his lack of understanding there is implied a recognition of the eternal validity of the personality. He, on the other hand, who is correctly situated has a different experience. He chooses himself, not in a finite sense (for then this "self" would be something finite along with other things fin te), but in an absolute sense; and yet, in fact, he chooses himself and not another. This self which he then chooses is infinitely concrete, for it is in fact himself, and yet it is absolutely distinct from his former self, for he has chosen it absolutely. This self did not exist previously, for it came into existence by means of the choice, and yet it did exist, for it was in fact "himself."

In this case choice performs at one and the same time the two dialectical movements: that which is chosen does not exist and comes into existence with the choice; that which is chosen exists, otherwise there would not be a choice. For in case what I chose did not exist but absolutely came into existence with the choice, I would not be choosing, I would be creating; but I do not create myself, I choose myself. Therefore, while nature is created out of nothing, while I myself as an immediate personality am created out of nothing, as a free spirit I am born of the principle of contradiction, or born by the fact that I choose myself. . . .

But he who has now infinitely chosen himself—can he say, "Now I possess myself, I require nothing more, and to all the changes of the world I oppose the proud thought: I am the man I am"? By no manner of means! In case a man were to express himself thus he would easily see that he was on a wrong path. The fundamental error would, in that case, too, lie in the fact that in the strictest sense he had not chosen himself. He had chosen himself maybe, but outside himself. He had interpreted quite abstractly what it is to choose and had not grasped himself in his concretion, he had not chosen in such a way that by the choice he became himself, became invested with his self; he had chosen himself from necessity, not with freedom; aesthetically he had taken in vain the ethical choice. The more significant the result which is to issue from the choice, the more dangerous are the byways, and here there appears a dreadful byway. When the individual has grasped himself in his eternal validity this overwhelms him by its fullness. The temporal vanishes from before his eyes. At the first instant this fills him with indescribable bliss and gives him a sense of absolute security. If then he begins to gaze upon this bliss, the temporal advances its claim. This is scorned. What the temporal can give, the more or the less which now presents itself, is so very unimportant in comparison with what he eternally possesses. Everything comes with him to a standstill, he has, as it were, reached eternity before the time. He relapses into contemplation, he gazes at himself, but this gaze cannot fill up the time. Then it appears to him that time, that the temporal, is his ruin; he demands a more perfect form of existence, and at this point there comes to evidence a fatigue, an apathy, which resembles the languor which is the attendant of pleasure. This apathy may rest so broodingly upon a man that suicide appears to him the only way of escape. No power can wrest from him his self, the only power is time, but neither can that wrest from him his self; it checks him and delays, it arrests the embrace of the spirit with which he grasps his self. He has not chosen himself; like Narcissus he has fallen in love with himself. Such a situation has certainly ended not infrequently in suicide.

The error lies in the fact that he has not chosen in the right way, not simply in the sense that he had no eye for his error, but that he has seen himself under the category of necessity—himself, this personality, with all these manifold characteristics, he has seen as part and parcel of the world-process, he has seen this self confronted by the eternal Power the fire of which pervades it without consuming it. But he has not seen himself in his freedom, has not chosen himself with freedom. If he does that, then the very instant he chooses himself he is in motion; concrete as his self is, he has nevertheless chosen himself in accordance with his possibility, in repentance he has ransomed himself for the sake of remaining in his freedom, but he can remain in his freedom only by constantly realizing it. He, therefore, who has chosen himself is *eo ipso* active.

What a curious, yet profound turn of phrase which makes it possible to say: in this case there is no question of a *choice*—I choose this and this. To continue: Christianity says to a man: you shall choose the one essential thing but in such a way that there is no question of a choice—if you drivel on any longer then you do not in fact choose the one essential thing; like the Kingdom of God it must be chosen *first*.

So there is consequently something in regard to which there may not be, and in thought cannot be a choice, and nevertheless it is a choice. Consequently, the very fact that in this case there is no *choice* expresses the tremendous passion or intensity with which it must be *chosen*. Could there be a clearer expression of the fact that the liberty of choice is only a qualified form of freedom? . . . However astonishing it may seem, one is therefore obliged to say that only "fear and trembling," only constraint, can help a man to freedom. Because "fear and trembling" and compulsion can master him in such a way that there is no longer any question of choice—and then one chooses the right thing. At the hour of death most people choose the right thing.

Now how are the sciences to help? Simply not at all, in no way whatsoever. They reduce everything to calm and objective observation—with the result that freedom is an inexplicable something. Scientifically Spinoza is the only one who is consistent.

The problem is the same as with belief and speculation, and as Johannes Climacus has said, it is like sawing: in one case it means making oneself objectively light, in the other case making oneself subjectively heavy—and people want to saw in and out at the same time. Freedom really only *exists* because the same instant it (freedom of choice) exists it rushes with infinite speed to bind itself unconditionally by choosing resignation, the choice of which it is true that in it there is no question of a choice.

The inconceivable marvel of the omnipotence of love is that God can really grant so much to man, that almost like a lover he can say of himself: "will you have me or not," and so wait one second for the answer.

But alas, man is not so purely spirit. It seems to him that since the choice is left to him he can take time and *first of all* think the matter over *seriously*. What a miserable anti-climax. "Seriousness" simply means to choose God at once and "first." In that way man is left juggling with a phantom: freedom of choice—with the question whether he does or does not possess it etc. And it even becomes scientific. He does not notice that he has thus suffered the loss of his freedom. For a time perhaps he delights in the thought of freedom until it changes again, and he becomes doubtful whether he is free or not. Then he loses his freedom of choice. He confuses everything by his faulty tactics (militarily speaking). By directing his mind towards "freedom of choice" instead of choosing he loses both freedom and freedom of choice. Nor can he ever recover it by the use of thought alone. If he is to recover his freedom it can only be through an intensified "fear and trembling" brought forth by the thought of having lost it.

The most tremendous thing which has been granted to man is: the choice, freedom. And if you desire to save it and preserve it there is only one way: in the very same second unconditionally and in complete resignation to give it back to God, and yourself with it. If the sight of what is granted to you tempts you, and if you give way to the temptation and look with egoistic desire upon the freedom of choice, then you lose your freedom. And your punishment is: to go on in a kind of confusion priding yourself on having—freedom of choice, but woe upon you, that is your judgment: You have freedom of choice, you say, and still you have not chosen God. Then you will grow ill, freedom of choice will become your *idée fixe*, till at last you will be like the rich man who imagines that he is poor, and will die of want: you sigh that you have lost your freedom of choice—and your fault is only that you do not grieve deeply enough or you would find it again.

Choice in a World without God

Man will only attain existence when he is what he purposes to be. Not, however, what he may wish to be. For what we usually understand by wishing or willing is a conscious decision taken—much more often than not—after we have made ourselves what we are. I may wish to join a party, to write a book or to marry—but in such a case what is usually called my will is probably a manifestation of a prior and more spontaneous decision. If, however, it is true that existence is prior to essence, man is responsible for what he is. Thus, the first effect of existentialism is that it puts every man in possession of himself as he is, and places the entire responsibility for his existence squarely upon his own shoulders. And, when we say that man is responsible for himself, we do not mean that he is responsible only for his own individuality, but that he is responsible for all men. The word "subjectivism" is to be understood in two senses, and our adversaries play upon only one of them. Subjectivism means, on the one hand, the freedom of the individual subject and, on the other, that man cannot pass beyond human subjectivity. It is the latter which is the deeper meaning of existentialism. When we say that man chooses himself, we do mean that every one of us must choose himself; but by that we also mean that in choosing for himself he chooses for all men. For in effect, of all the actions a man may take in order to create himself as he wills to be, there is not one which is not creative, at the same time, of an image of man such as he believes he ought to be. To choose between this or that is at the same time to affirm the value of that which is chosen; for we are unable ever to choose the worse. What we choose is always the better; and nothing can be better for us unless it is better for all. If, moreover, existence precedes essence and we will to exist at the same time as we fashion our image, that image is valid for all and for the entire epoch in which we find ourselves. Our resonsibility is thus much greater than we had supposed, for it concerns mankind as a whole. If I am a worker, for instance, I may choose to join a Christian rather than a Communist trade union. And if, by that membership, I choose to signify that resignation is, after all, the attitude that best becomes a man, that man's kingdom is not upon this earth, I do not commit myself alone to that view. Resignation is my will for everyone, and my action is, in consequence, a commitment on behalf of all mankind. Or if, to take a more personal case, I decide to marry and to have children, even though this decision proceeds simply from my situation, from my passion or my desire, I am thereby committing not only myself, but humanity as a whole, to the practice of monogamy. I am thus responsible for myself and for all men, and I am creating a certain image of man as I would have him to be. In fashioning myself I fashion man.

This may enable us to understand what is meant by such terms—perhaps a little grandiloquent—as anguish, abandonment and despair. As you will soon see, it is very simple. First, what do we mean by anguish? The existentialist frankly

From *Existentialism and Humanism* [1946], translated from the French by Philip Mairet. Translation reprinted by permission of Methuen & Co. Ltd., London. Text reprinted by permission of The Philosophical Library, Inc., and Sanford Greenburger. Copyright 1947 by the Philosophical Library, Inc.

states that man is in anguish. His meaning is as follows—When a man commits himself to anything, fully realizing that he is not only choosing what he will be, but is thereby at the same time a legislator deciding for the whole of mankind— in such a moment a man cannot escape from the sense of complete and profound responsibility. There are many, indeed, who show no such anxiety. But we affirm that they are merely disguising their anguish or are in flight from it. Certainly, many people think that in what they are doing they commit no one but themselves to anything: and if you ask them, "What would happen if everyone did so?" they shrug their shoulders and reply, "Everyone does not do so." But in truth, one ought always to ask oneself what would happen if everyone did as one is doing; nor can one escape from that disturbing thought except by a kind of self-deception. The man who lies in self-excuse, by saying "Everyone will not do it" must be ill at ease in his conscience, for the act of lying implies the universal value which it denies. By its very disguise his anguish reveals itself. This is the anguish that Kierkegaard called "the anguish of Abraham." You know the story: An angel commanded Abraham to sacrifice his son: and obedience was obligatory, if it really was an angel who had appeared and said, "Thou, Abraham, shalt sacrifice thy son." But anyone in such a case would wonder, first, whether it was indeed an angel and secondly, whether I am really Abraham. Where are the proofs? A certain mad woman who suffered from hallucinations said that people were telephoning to her, and giving her orders. The doctor asked, "But who is it that speaks to you?" She replied: "He says it is God." And what, indeed, could prove to her that it was God? If an angel appears to me, what is the proof that it is an angel; or, if I hear voices, who can prove that they proceed from heaven and not from hell, or from my own subconsciousness or some pathological condition? Who can prove that they are really addressed to me?

Who, then, can prove that I am the proper person to impose, by my own choice, my conception of man upon mankind? I shall never find any proof whatever; there will be no sign to convince me of it. If a voice speaks to me, it is still I myself who must decide whether the voice is or is not that of an angel. If I regard a certain course of action as good, it is only I who choose to say that it is good and not bad. There is nothing to show that I am Abraham: nevertheless I also am obliged at every instant to perform actions which are examples. Everything happens to every man as though the whole human race had its eyes fixed upon what he is doing and regulated its conduct accordingly. So every man ought to say, "Am I really a man who has the right to act in such a manner that humanity regulates itself by what I do?" If a man does not say that, he is dissembling his anguish. Clearly, the anguish with which we are concerned here is not one that could lead to quietism or inaction. It is anguish pure and simple, of the kind well known to all those who have borne responsibilities. When, for instance, a military leader takes upon himself the responsibility for an attack and sends a number of men to their death, he chooses to do it and at bottom he alone chooses. No doubt he acts under a higher command, but its orders, which are more general, require interpretation by him and upon that interpretation depends the life of ten, fourteen or twenty men. In making the decision, he cannot but feel a certain anguish. All leaders know that anguish. It does not prevent their acting, on the contrary it is the very condition of their action, for the action presupposes that there is a plurality of possibilities, and in choosing one of these, they realize that it has value only because it is chosen. Now it is anguish of that kind which existentialism describes, and moreover, as we shall see, makes explicit through direct responsibility towards other men who are concerned. Far from being a screen which could separate us from action, it is a condition of action itself.

And when we speak of "abandonment"—a favorite word of Heidegger—we only mean to say that God does not exist, and that it is necessary to draw the consequences of his absence right to the end. The existentialist is strongly opposed to a certain type of secular moralism which seeks to suppress God at the least possible expense. Towards 1880, when the French professors endeavored to formulate a secular morality, they said something like this:—God is a useless and costly hypothesis, so we will do without it. However, if we are to have morality, a society and a law-abiding world, it is essential that certain values should be taken seriously; they must have an *a priori* existence ascribed to them. It must be considered obligatory *a priori* to be honest, not to lie, not to beat one's wife, to bring up children and so forth; so we are going to do a little work on this subject, which will enable us to show that these values exist all the same, inscribed in an intelligible heaven although, of course, there is no God. In other words—and this is, I believe, the purport of all that we in France call radicalism—nothing will be changed if God does not exist; we shall rediscover the same norms of honesty, progress and humanity, and we shall have disposed of God as an out-of-date hypothesis which will die away quietly of itself. The existentialist, on the contrary, finds it extremely embarrassing that God does not exist, for there disappears with Him all possibility of finding values in an intelligible heaven. There can no longer be any good *a priori*, since there is no infinite and perfect consciousness to think it. It is nowhere written that "the good" exists, that one must be honest or must not lie, since we are now upon the plane where there are only men. Dostoevsky once wrote "If God did not exist, everything would be permitted"; and that, for existentialism, is the starting point. Everything is indeed permitted if God does not exist, and man is in consequence forlorn, for he cannot find anything to depend upon either within or outside himself. He discovers forthwith, that he is without excuse. For if indeed existence precedes essence, one will never be able to explain one's action by reference to a given and specific human nature; in other words, there is no determinism—man is free, man *is* freedom. Nor, on the other hand, if God does not exist, are we provided with any values or commands that could legitimize our behavior. Thus we have neither behind us, nor before us in a luminous realm of values, any means of justification or excuse. We are left alone, without excuse. That is what I mean when I say that man is condemned to be free. Condemned, because he did not create himself, yet is nevertheless at liberty, and from the moment that he is thrown into this world he is responsible for everything he does. The existentialist does not believe in the power of passion. He will never regard a grand passion as a destructive torrent upon which a man is swept into certain actions as by fate, and which, therefore, is an excuse for them. He thinks that man is responsible for his passion. Neither will an existentialist think that a man can find help through some sign being vouchsafed upon earth for his orientation: for he thinks that the man himself interprets the sign as he chooses. He thinks that every man, without any support or help whatever, is condemned at every instant to invent man. As Ponge has written in a very fine article, "Man is the future of man." That is exactly true.

Only, if one took this to mean that the future is laid up in Heaven, that God knows what it is, it would be false, for then it would no longer even be a future. If, however, it means that, whatever man may now appear to be, there is a future to be fashioned, a virgin future that awaits him—then it is a true saying. But in the present one is forsaken.

MARTIN HEIDEGGER

Dread Reveals Nothing

Does there ever occur in human existence a mood of this kind, through which we are brought face to face with Nothing itself?

This may and actually does occur, albeit rather seldom and for moments only, in the key-mood of dread (*Angst*). By "dread" we do not mean "anxiety" (*Aengstlichkeit*), which is common enough and is akin to nervousness (*Furchtsamkeit*)—a mood that comes over us only too easily. Dread differs absolutely from fear (*Furcht*). We are always *afraid* of this or that definite thing, which threatens us in this or that definite way. "Fear of" is generally "fear about" something. Since fear has this characteristic limitation—"of" and "about"—the man who is afraid, the nervous man, is always bound by the thing he is afraid of or by the state in which he finds himself. In his efforts to save himself from this "something" he becomes uncertain in relation to other things; in fact, he "loses his bearings" generally.

In dread no such confusion can occur. It would be truer to say that dread is pervaded by a peculiar kind of peace. And although dread is always "dread of," it is not dread of this or that. "Dread of" is always a dreadful feeling "about"— but not about this or that. The indefiniteness of *what* we dread is not just lack of definition: it represents the essential impossibility of defining the "what." The indefiniteness is brought out in an illustration familiar to everybody.

In dread, as we say, "one feels something uncanny." What is this "something" (*es*) and this "one"? We are unable to say what gives "one" that uncanny feeling. "One" just feels it generally (*im Ganzen*). All things, and we with them, sink into a sort of indifference. But not in the sense that everything simply disappears; rather, in the very act of drawing away from us everything turns towards us. This withdrawal of what-is-in-totality, which then crowds round us in dread, this is what oppresses us. There is nothing to hold on to. The only thing that remains and overwhelms us whilst what-is slips away, is this "nothing."

Dread reveals Nothing.

In dread we are "in suspense" (*wir schweben*). Or, to put it more precisely, dread holds us in suspense because it makes what-is-in-totality slip away from us. Hence we too, as existents in the midst of what-is, slip away from ourselves along

From "What Is Metaphysics?" [1929], *Existence and Being*, translated from the German by R. F. C. Hull and Alan Crick, London, 1959, pp. 365-7; reprinted by permission of the publisher, Vision Press Ltd., London.

with it. For this reason it is not "you" or "I" that has the uncanny feeling, but "one." In the trepidation of this suspense where there is nothing to hold on to, pure *Da-sein* is all that remains.

Dread strikes us dumb. Because what-is-in-totality slips away and thus forces Nothing to the fore, all affirmation (lit. "Is"-saying: *"Ist"-Sagen*) fails in the face of it. The fact that when we are caught in the uncanniness of dread we often try to break the empty silence by words spoken at random, only proves the presence of Nothing. We ourselves confirm that dread reveals Nothing—when we have got over our dread. In the lucid vision which supervenes while yet the experience is fresh in our memory we must needs say that what we were afraid of was "actually" (*eigentlich*: also "authentic") Nothing. And indeed Nothing itself, Nothing as such, was there.

SØREN KIERKEGAARD
Dread as Education toward Faith

In one of Grimm's Fairy Tales there is the story of a youth who went out in search of adventures for the sake of learning what it is to fear or be in dread. We will let that adventurer go his way without troubling ourselves to learn whether in the course of it he encountered the dreadful. On the other hand I would say that learning to know dread is an adventure which every man has to affront if he would not go to perdition either by not having known dread or by sinking under it. He therefore who has learned rightly to be in dread has learned the most important thing.

If a man were a beast or an angel, he would not be able to be in dread. Since he is a synthesis he can be in dread, and the greater the dread, the greater the man. This, however, is not affirmed in the sense in which men commonly understand dread, as related to something outside a man, but in the sense that man himself produces dread. Only in this sense can we interpret the passage where it is said of Christ that he was in dread [*ængstes*] even unto death, and the place also where he says to Judas, "What thou doest, do quickly." Not even the terrible word upon which even Luther dreaded to preach, "My God, my God, why hast thou forsaken me?"—not even this expresses suffering so strongly. For this word indicates a situation in which Christ actually is; the former sayings indicate a relation to a situation which is not yet actual.

Dread is the possibility of freedom. Only this dread is by the aid of faith absolutely educative, laying bare as it does all finite aims and discovering all their deceptions. And no Grand Inquisitor has in readiness such terrible tortures as has dread, and no spy knows how to attack more artfully the man he suspects, choosing the instant when he is weakest, nor knows how to lay traps where he will be

From *The Concept of Dread* [1844], translated from the Danish by Walter Lowrie, Princeton, 1944, pp. 139-42. Copyright 1944 by Princeton University Press; reprinted by permission of the Princeton University Press.

caught and ensnared, as dread knows how, and no sharpwitted judge knows how to interrogate, to examine the accused, as dread does, which never lets him escape, neither by diversion nor by noise, neither at work nor at play, neither by day nor by night.

He who is educated by dread is educated by possibility, and only the man who is educated by possibility is educated in accordance with his infinity. Possibility is therefore the heaviest of all categories. One often hears, it is true, the opposite affirmed, that possibility is so light but reality is heavy. But from whom does one hear such talk? From a lot of miserable men who never have known what possibility is, and who, since reality showed them that they were not fit for anything and never would be, mendaciously bedizened a possibility which was so beautiful, so enchanting; and the only foundation of this possibility was a little youthful tomfoolery of which they might rather have been ashamed. Therefore by this possibility which is said to be light one commonly understands the possibility of luck, good fortune, etc. But this is not possibility, it is a mendacious invention which human depravity falsely embellishes in order to have reason to complain of life, of providence, and as a pretext for being self-important. No, in possibility everything is possible, and he who truly was brought up by possibility has comprehended the dreadful as well as the smiling. When such a person, therefore, goes out from the school of possibility, and knows more thoroughly than a child knows the alphabet that he can demand of life absolutely nothing, and that terror, perdition, annihilation, dwell next door to every man, and has learned the profitable lesson that every dread which alarms [ængste] may the next instant become a fact, he will then interpret reality differently, he will extol reality, and even when it rests upon him heavily he will remember that after all it is far, far lighter than the possibility was. Only thus can possibility educate; for finiteness and the finite relationships in which the individual is assigned a place, whether it be small and commonplace or world-historical, educate only finitely, and one can always talk them around, always get a little more out of them, always chaffer, always escaped a little way from them, always keep a little apart, always prevent oneself from learning absolutely from them; and if one is to learn absolutely, the individual must in turn have the possibility in himself and himself fashion that from which he is to learn, even though the next instant it does not recognize that it was fashioned by him, but absolutely takes the power from him.

But in order that the individual may thus absolutely and infinitely be educated by possibility, he must be honest towards possibility and must have faith. By faith I mean what Hegel in his fashion calls very rightly "the inward certainty which anticipates infinity." When the discoveries of possibility are honestly administered, possibility will then disclose all finitudes and idealize them in the form of infinity in the individual who is overwhelmed by dread, until in turn he is victorious by the anticipation of faith.

What I say here appears perhaps to many an obscure and foolish saying, since they even boast of never having been in dread. To this I would reply that doubtless one should not be in dread of men, of finite things, but that only the man who has gone through the dread of possibility is educated to have no dread —not because he avoids the dreadful things of life, but because they always are weak in comparison with those of possibility. If on the other hand the speaker means that the great thing about him is that he has never been in dread, then I shall gladly initiate him into my explanation, that this comes from the fact that he is spirit-less.

If the individual cheats the possibility by which he is to be educated, he never reaches faith; his faith remains the shrewdness of finitude, as his school was that of finitude. But men cheat possibility in every way—if they did not, one has only to stick one's head out of the window, and one would see enough for possibility to begin its exercises forthwith. There is an engraving by Chadowiecki which represents the surrender of Calais as viewed by the four temperaments, and the theme of the artist was to let the various impressions appear mirrored in the faces which express the various temperaments. The most commonplace life has events enough, no doubt, but the question is whether the possibility in the individuality is honest towards itself. It is recounted of an Indian hermit who for two years had lived upon dew, that he came once to the city, tasted wine, and then became addicted to drink. This story, like every other of the sort, can be understood in many ways, one can make it comic, one can make it tragic; but the man who is educated by possibility has more than enough to occupy him in such a story. Instantly he is absolutely identified with that unfortunate man, he knows no finite evasion by which he might escape. Now the dread of possibility holds him as its prey, until it can deliver him saved into the hands of faith. In no other place does he find repose, for every other point of rest is mere nonsense, even though in men's eyes it is shrewdness. This is the reason why possibility is so absolutely educative. No man has ever become so unfortunate in reality that there was not some little residue left to him, and, as common sense observes quite truly, if a man is canny, he will find a way. But he who went through the curriculum of misfortune offered by possibility lost everything, absolutely everything, in a way that no one has lost it in reality. If in this situation he did not behave falsely towards possibility, if he did not attempt to talk around the dread which would save him, then he received everything back again, as in reality no one ever did even if he received everything double, for the pupil of possibility received infinity, whereas the soul of the other expired in the finite. No one ever sank so deep in reality that he could not sink deeper, or that there might not be one or another sunk deeper than he. But he who sank in the possibility has an eye too dizzy to see the measuring rod which Tom, Dick, and Harry hold out as a straw to the drowning man; his ear is closed so that he cannot hear what the market price for men is in his day, cannot hear that he is just as good as most of them. He sank absolutely, but then in turn he floated up from the depth of the abyss, lighter now than all that is oppressive and dreadful in life. Only I do not deny that he who is educated by possibility is exposed—not to the danger of bad company and dissoluteness of various sorts, as are those who are educated by the finite, but—to one danger of downfall, and that is self-slaughter. If at the beginning of his education he misunderstands the anguish of dread, so that it does not lead him to faith but away from faith, then he is lost. On the other hand, he who is educated by possibility remains with dread, does not allow himself to be deceived by its countless counterfeits, he recalls the past precisely; then at last the attacks of dread, though they are fearful, are not such that he flees from them. For him dread becomes a serviceable spirit which against its will leads him whither he would go. Then when it announces itself, when it craftily insinuates that it has invented a new instrument of torture far more terrible than anything employed before, he does not recoil, still less does he attempt to hold it off with clamor and noise, but he bids it welcome, he hails it solemnly, as Socrates solemnly flourished the poisoned goblet, he shuts himself up with it, he says, as a patient says to the surgeon when a painful operation is about to being, "Now I am ready." Then dread enters into his soul and searches it thoroughly, constraining out of him all the finite and the petty, and leading him hence whither he would go.

JEAN-PAUL SARTRE

Authenticity

One can judge a man by saying that he deceives himself. Since we have defined the situation of man as one of free choice, without excuse and without help, any man who takes refuge behind the excuse of his passions, or by inventing some deterministic doctrine, is a self-deceiver. One may object: "But why should he not choose to deceive himself?" I reply that it is not for me to judge him morally, but I define his self-deception as an error. Here one cannot avoid pronouncing a judgment of truth. The self-deception is evidently a falsehood, because it is a dissimulation of man's complete liberty of commitment. Upon this same level, I say that it is also a self-deception if I choose to declare that certain values are incumbent upon me; I am in contradiction with myself if I will these values and at the same time say that they impose themselves upon me. If anyone says to me, "And what if I wish to deceive myself?" I answer, "There is no reason why you should not, but I declare that you are doing so, and that the attitude of strict consistency alone is that of good faith." Furthermore, I can pronounce a moral judgment. For I declare that freedom, in respect of concrete circumstances, can have no other end and aim but itself; and when once a man has seen that values depend upon himself, in that state of forsakenness he can will only one thing, and that is freedom as the foundation of all values. That does not mean that he wills it in the abstract: it simply means that the actions of men of good faith have, as their ultimate significance, the quest of freedom itself as such. A man who belongs to some communist or revolutionary society wills certain concrete ends, which imply the will to freedom, but that freedom is willed in community. We will freedom for freedom's sake, in and through particular circumstances. And in thus willing freedom, we discover that it depends entirely upon the freedom of others and that the freedom of others depends upon our own. Obviously, freedom as the definition of a man does not depend upon others, but as soon as there is a commitment, I am obliged to will the liberty of others at the same time as my own. I cannot make liberty my aim unless I make that of others equally my aim. Consequently, when I recognize, as entirely authentic, that man

From *Existentialism and Humanism* [1946], translated from the French by Philip Mairet. Translation reprinted by permission of Methuen & Co. Ltd., London. Text reprinted by permission of The Philosophical Library, Inc., and Sanford Greenburger. Copyright 1947 by the Philosophical Library, Inc.

is a being whose existence precedes his essence, and that he is a free being who cannot, in any circumstances, but will his freedom, at the same time I realize that I cannot not will the freedom of others. Thus, in the name of that will to freedom which is implied in freedom itself, I can form judgments upon those who seek to hide from themselves the wholly voluntary nature of their existence and its complete freedom. Those who hide from this total freedom, in a guise of solemnity or with deterministic excuses, I shall call cowards. Others, who try to show that their existence is necessary, when it is merely an accident of the appearance of the human race on earth—I shall call scum. But neither cowards nor scum can be identified except upon the plane of strict authenticity. Thus, although the content of morality is variable, a certain form of this morality is universal. Kant declared that freedom is a will both to itself and to the freedom of others. Agreed: but he thinks that the formal and the universal suffice for the constitution of a morality. We think, on the contrary, that principles that are too abstract break down when we come to defining action. To take once again the case of that student; by what authority, in the name of what golden rule of morality, do you think he could have decided, in perfect peace of mind, either to abandon his mother or to remain with her? There are no means of judging. The content is always concrete, and therefore unpredictable; it has always to be invented. The one thing that counts, is to know whether the invention is made in the name of freedom.

ALBERT CAMUS
Absurd Freedom

Now the main thing is done, I hold certain facts from which I cannot separate. What I know, what is certain, what I cannot deny, what I cannot reject—this is what counts. I can negate everything of that part of me that lives on vague nostalgias, except this desire for unity, this longing to solve, this need for clarity and cohesion. I can refute everything in this world surrounding me that offends or enraptures me, except this chaos, this sovereign chance and this divine equivalence which springs from anarchy. I don't know whether this world has a meaning that transcends it. But I know that I do not know that meaning and that it is impossible for me just now to know it. What can a meaning outside my condition mean to me? I can understand only in human terms. What I touch, what resists me—that is what I understand. And these two certainties—my appetite for the absolute and for unity and the impossibility of reducing this world to a rational and reasonable principle—I also know that I cannot reconcile them. What other truth can I admit without lying, without bringing in a hope I lack and which means nothing within the limits of my condition?

If I were a tree among trees, a cat among animals, this life would have a meaning, or rather this problem would not arise, for I should belong to this world. I should *be* this world to which I am now opposed by my whole consciousness and my whole insistence upon familiarity. This ridiculous reason is what sets me in opposition to all creation. I cannot cross it out with a stroke of the pen. What I believe to be true I must therefore preserve. What seems to me so obvious, even against me, I must support. And what constitutes the basis of that conflict, of that break between the world and my mind, but the awareness of it? If therefore I want to preserve it, I can through a constant awareness, ever revived, ever alert. This is what, for the moment, I must remember. At this moment the absurd, so obvious and yet so hard to win, returns to a man's life and finds its home there. At this moment, too, the mind can leave the arid, dried-up path of lucid effort. That path now emerges in daily life. It encounters the world of the anonymous impersonal pronoun "one," but henceforth man enters in with his revolt and his lucidity. He has forgotten how to hope. This hell of the present is his Kingdom at last. All problems recover their sharp edge. Abstract evidence retreats before

From *The Myth of Sisyphus* [1942], translated from the French by Justin O'Brien, New York, 1955, pp. 38-48, 88-91. Copyright © 1955 by Alfred A. Knopf, Inc.; reprinted by permission of Random House, Alfred A. Knopf, Inc. and Hamish Hamilton Ltd.

the poetry of forms and colors. Spiritual conflicts become embodied and return to the abject and magnificent shelter of man's heart. None of them is settled. But all are transfigured. Is one going to die, escape by the leap, rebuild a mansion of ideas and forms to one's own scale? Is one, on the contrary, going to take up the heart-rending and marvelous wager of the absurd? Let's make a final effort in this regard and draw all our conclusions. The body, affection, creation, action, human nobility will then resume their places in this mad world. At last man will again find there the wine of the absurd and the bread of indifference on which he feeds his greatness.

Let us insist again on the method: it is a matter of persisting. At a certain point on his path the absurd man is tempted. History is not lacking in either religions or prophets, even without gods. He is asked to leap. All he can reply is that he doesn't fully understand, that it is not obvious. Indeed, he does not want to do anything but what he fully understands. He is assured that this is the sin of pride, but he does not understand the notion of sin; that perhaps hell is in store, but he has not enough imagination to visualize that strange future; that he is losing immortal life, but that seems to him an idle consideration. An attempt is made to get him to admit his guilt. He feels innocent. To tell the truth, that is all he feels—his irreparable innocence. This is what allows him everything. Hence, what he demands of himself is to live *solely* with what he knows, to accommodate himself to what is, and to bring in nothing that is not certain. He is told that nothing is. But this at least is a certainty. And it is with this that he is concerned: he wants to find out if it is possible to live *without appeal*.

Now I can broach the notion of suicide. It has already been felt what solution might be given. At this point the problem is reversed. It was previously a question of finding out whether or not life had to have a meaning to be lived. It now becomes clear, on the contrary, that it will be lived all the better if it has no meaning. Living an experience, a particular fate, is accepting it fully. Now, no one will live this fate, knowing it to be absurd, unless he does everything to keep before him that absurd brought to light by consciousness. Negating one of the terms of the opposition on which he lives amounts to escaping it. To abolish conscious revolt is to elude the problem. The theme of permanent revolution is thus carried into individual experience. Living is keeping the absurd alive. Keeping it alive is, above all, contemplating it. Unlike Eurydice, the absurd dies only when we turn away from it. One of the only coherent philosophical positions is thus revolt. It is a constant confrontation between man and his own obscurity. It is an insistence upon an impossible transparency. It challenges the world anew every second. Just as danger provided man the unique opportunity of seizing awareness, so metaphysical revolt extends awareness to the whole of experience. It is that constant presence of man in his own eyes. It is not aspiration, for it is devoid of hope. That revolt is the certainty of a crushing fate, without the resignation that ought to accompany it.

This is where it is seen to what a degree absurd experience is remote from suicide. It may be thought that suicide follows revolt—but wrongly. For it does not represent the logical outcome of revolt. It is just the contrary by the consent it presupposes. Suicide, like the leap, is acceptance at its extreme. Everything is over and man returns to his essential history. His future, his unique and dreadful future—he sees and rushes toward it. In its way, suicide settles the absurd. It engulfs the absurd in the same death. But I know that in order to keep alive, the absurd cannot be settled. It escapes suicide to the extent that it is simultaneously awareness and rejection of death. It is, at the extreme limit of the condemned man's last thought, that shoelace that despite everything he sees a few yards away, on the very brink of his dizzying fall. The contrary of suicide, in fact, is the man condemned to death.

That revolt gives life its value. Spread out over the whole length of a life, it restores its majesty to that life. To a man devoid of blinders, there is no finer sight than that of the intelligence at grips with a reality that transcends it. The sight of human pride is unequaled. No disparagement is of any use. That discipline that the mind imposes on itself, that will conjured up out of nothing, that face-to-face struggle have something exceptional about them. To impoverish that reality whose inhumanity constitutes man's majesty is tantamount to impoverishing him himself. I understand then why the doctrines that explain everything to me also debilitate me at the same time. They relieve me of the weight of my own life, and yet I must carry it alone. At this juncture, I cannot conceive that a skeptical metaphysics can be joined to an ethics of renunciation.

Consciousness and revolt, these rejections are the contrary of renunciation. Everything that is indomitable and passionate in a human heart quickens them, on the contrary, with its own life. It is essential to die unreconciled and not of one's own free will. Suicide is a repudiation. The absurd man can only drain everything to the bitter end, and deplete himself. The absurd is his extreme tension, which he maintains constantly by solitary effort, for he knows that in that consciousness and in that day-to-day revolt he gives proof of his only truth, which is defiance. This is a first consequence.

If I remain in that prearranged position which consists in drawing all the conclusions (and nothing else) involved in a newly discovered notion, I am faced with a second paradox. In order to remain faithful to that method, I have nothing to do with the problem of metaphysical liberty. Knowing whether or not man is free doesn't interest me. I can experience only my own freedom. As to it, I can have no general notions, but merely a few clear insights. The problem of "freedom as such" has no meaning. For it is linked in quite a different way with the problem of God. Knowing whether or not man is free involves whether he can have a master. The absurdity peculiar to this problem comes from the fact that the very notion that makes the problem of freedom possible also takes away all its meaning. For in the presence of God there is less a problem of freedom than a problem of evil. You know the alternative: either we are not free and God the all-powerful is responsible for evil. Or we are free and responsible but God is not all-powerful. All the scholastic subtleties have neither added anything to nor subtracted anything from the acuteness of this paradox.

This is why I cannot get lost in the glorification or the mere definition of a notion which eludes me and loses its meaning as soon as it goes beyond the frame of reference of my individual experience. I cannot understand what kind of freedom would be given me by a higher being. I have lost the sense of hierarchy. The only conception of freedom I can have is that of the prisoner or the individual in the midst of the State. The only one I know is freedom of thought and action.

Now if the absurd cancels all my chances of eternal freedom, it restores and magnifies, on the other hand, my freedom of action. That privation of hope and future means an increase in man's availability.

Before encountering the absurd, the everyday man lives with aims, a concern for the future or for justification (with regard to whom or what is not the question). He weighs his chances, he counts on "someday," his retirement or the labor of his sons. He still thinks that something in his life can be directed. In truth, he acts as if he were free, even if all the facts make a point of contradicting that liberty. But after the absurd, everything is upset. That idea that "I am," my way of acting as if everything has a meaning (even if, on occasion, I said that nothing has)—all that is given the lie in vertiginous fashion by the absurdity of a possible death. Thinking of the future, establishing aims for oneself, having preferences—all this presupposes a belief in freedom, even if one occasionally ascertains that one doesn't feel it. But at that moment I am well aware that that higher liberty, that freedom *to be*, which alone can serve as basis for a truth, does not exist. Death is there as the only reality. After death the chips are down. I am not even free, either, to perpetuate myself, but a slave, and, above all, a slave without hope of an eternal revolution, without recourse to contempt. And who without revolution and without contempt can remain a slave? What freedom can exist in the fullest sense without assurance of eternity?

But at the same time the absurd man realizes that hitherto he was bound to that postulate of freedom on the illusion of which he was living. In a certain sense, that hampered him. To the extent to which he imagined a purpose to his life, he adapted himself to the demands of a purpose to be achieved and became the slave of his liberty. Thus I could not act otherwise than as the father (or the engineer or the leader of a nation, or the post-office sub-clerk) that I am preparing to be. I think I can choose to be that rather than something else. I think so unconsciously, to be sure. But at the same time I strengthen my postulate with the beliefs of those around me, with the presumptions of my human environment (others are so sure of being free, and that cheerful mood is so contagious!). However far one may remain from any presumption, moral or social, one is partly influenced by them and even, for the best among them (there are good and bad presumptions), one adapts one's life to them. Thus the absurd man realizes that he was not really free. To speak clearly, to the extent to which I hope, to which I worry about a truth that might be individual to me, about a way of being or creating, to the extent to which I arrange my life and prove thereby that I accept its having a meaning, I create for myself barriers between which I confine my life. I do like so many bureaucrats of the mind and heart who only fill me with disgust and whose only vice, I now see clearly, is to take man's freedom seriously.

The absurd enlightens me on this point: there is no future. Henceforth this is the reason for my inner freedom. I shall use two comparisons here. Mystics, to begin with, find freedom in giving themselves. By losing themselves in their god, by accepting his rules, they become secretly free. In spontaneously accepted slavery they recover a deeper independence. But what does that freedom mean? It may be said, above all, that they *feel* free with regard to themselves, and not so much free as liberated. Likewise, completely turned toward death (taken here as the most obvious absurdity), the absurd man feels released from everything outside that passionate attention crystallizing in him. He enjoys a freedom with regard to common rules. It can be seen at this point that the initial themes of existential philosophy keep their entire value. The return to consciousness, the escape from everyday sleep represent the first steps of absurd freedom. But it is existential *preaching* that is alluded to, and with it that spiritual leap which basically escapes consciousness. In the same way (this is my second comparison) the slaves of antiquity did not belong to themselves. But they knew that freedom which consists in not feeling responsible.[1] Death, too, has patrician hands which, while crushing, also liberate.

Losing oneself in that bottomless certainty, feeling henceforth sufficiently remote from one's own life to increase it and take a broad view of it—this involves the principle of a liberation. Such new independence has a definite time limit, like any freedom of action. It does not write a check on eternity. But it takes the place of the illusions of *freedom*, which all stopped with death. The divine availability of the condemned man before whom the prison doors open in a certain early dawn, that unbelievable disinterestedness with regard to everything except for the pure flame of life—it is clear that death and the absurd are here the principles of the only reasonable freedom: that which a human heart can experience and live. This is a second consequence. The absurd man thus catches sight of a burning and frigid, transparent and limited universe in which nothing is possible but everything is given, and beyond which all is collapse and nothingness. He can then decide to accept such a universe and draw from it his strength, his refusal to hope, and the unyielding evidence of a life without consolation.

But what does life mean in such a universe? Nothing else for the moment but indifference to the future and a desire to use up everything that is given. Belief in the meaning of life always implies a scale of values, a choice, our preferences. Belief in the absurd, according to our definitions, teaches the contrary. But this is worth examining.

Knowing whether or not one can live *without appeal* is all that interests me. I do not want to get out of my depth. This aspect of life being given me, can I adapt myself to it? Now, faced with this particular concern, belief in the absurd is tantamount to substituting the quantity of experiences for the quality. If I convince myself that this life has no other aspect than that of the absurd, if I feel that its whole equilibrium depends on that perpetual opposition between my conscious revolt and the darkness in which it struggles, if I admit that my freedom has no meaning except in relation to its limited fate, then I must say that what counts is not the best living but the most living. It is not up to me to wonder if this is vulgar or revolting, elegant or deplorable. Once and for all, value judgments are discarded here in favor of factual judgments. I have merely to draw the conclusions from what I can see and to risk nothing that is hypothetical. Supposing that living in this way were not honorable, then true propriety would command me to be dishonorable.

The most living; in the broadest sense, that rule means nothing. It calls for definition. It seems to begin with the fact that the notion of quantity has not been sufficiently explored. For it can account for a large share of human experience. A man's rule of conduct and his scale of values have no meaning except

[1] I am concerned here with a factual comparison, not with an apology of humility. The absurd man is the contrary of the reconciled man.

through the quantity and variety of experiences he has been in a position to accumulate. Now, the conditions of modern life impose on the majority of men the same quantity of experiences and consequently the same profound experience. To be sure, there must also be taken into consideration the individual's spontaneous contribution, the "given" element in him. But I cannot judge of that, and let me repeat that my rule here is to get along with the immediate evidence. I see, then, that the individual character of a common code of ethics lies not so much in the ideal importance of its basic principles as in the norm of an experience that it is possible to measure. To stretch a point somewhat, the Greeks had the code of their leisure just as we have the code of our eight-hour day. But already many men among the most tragic cause us to foresee that a longer experience changes this table of values. They make us imagine that adventurer of the everyday who through mere quantity of experiences would break all records (I am purposely using this sports expression) and would thus win his own code of ethics. Yet let's avoid romanticism and just ask ourselves what such an attitude may mean to a man with his mind made up to take up his bet and to observe strictly what he takes to be the rules of the game.

Breaking all the records is first and foremost being faced with the world as often as possible. How can that be done without contradictions and without playing on words? For on the one hand the absurd teaches that all experiences are unimportant, and on the other it urges toward the greatest quantity of experiences. How, then, can one fail to do as so many of those men I was speaking of earlier—choose the form of life that brings us the most possible of that human matter, thereby introducing a scale of values that on the other hand one claims to reject?

But again it is the absurd and its contradictory life that teaches us. For the mistake is thinking that that quantity of experiences depends on the circumstances of our life when it depends solely on us. Here we have to be over-simple. To two men living the same number of years, the world always provides the same sum of experiences. It is up to us to be conscious of them. Being aware of one's life, one's revolt, one's freedom, and to the maximum, is living, and to the maximum. Where lucidity dominates, the scale of values becomes useless. Let's be even more simple. Let us say that the sole obstacle, the sole deficiency to be made good, is constituted by premature death. Thus it is that no depth, no emotion, no passion, and no sacrifice could render equal in the eyes of the absurd man (even if he wished it so) a conscious life of forty years and a lucidity spread over sixty years. Madness and death are his irreparables. Man does not choose. The absurd and the extra life it involves *therefore do not depend on man's will*, but on its contrary, which is death. Weighing words carefully, it is altogether a question of luck. One just has to be able to consent to this. There will never be any substitute for twenty years of life and experience.

By what is an odd inconsistency in such an alert race, the Greeks claimed that those who died young were beloved of the gods. And that is true only if you are willing to believe that entering the ridiculous world of the gods is forever losing the purest of joys, which is feeling, and feeling on this earth. The present and the succession of presents before a constantly conscious soul is the ideal of the absurd man. But the word "ideal" rings false in this connection. It is not even his vocation, but merely the third consequence of his reasoning. Having started from an anguished awareness of the inhuman, the meditation on the absurd returns at the end of its itinerary to the very heart of the passionate flames of human revolt.

Thus I draw from the absurd three consequences, which are my revolt, my freedom, and my passion. By the mere activity of consciousness I transform into a rule of life what was an invitation to death—and I refuse suicide. I know, to be sure, the dull resonance that vibrates throughout these days. Yet I have but a word to say: that it is necessary. When Nietzsche writes: "It clearly seems that the chief thing in heaven and on earth is to *obey* at length and in a single direction: in the long run there results something for which it is worth the trouble of living on this earth as, for example, virtue, art, music, the dance, reason, the mind —something that transfigures, something delicate, mad, or divine," he elucidates the rule of a really distinguished code of ethics. But he also points the way of the absurd man. Obeying the flame is both the easiest and the hardest thing to do. However, it is good for man to judge himself occasionally. He is alone in being able to do so.

"Prayer," says Alain, "is when night descends over thought." "But the mind must meet the night," reply the mystics and the existentials. Yes, indeed, but not that night that is born under closed eyelids and through the mere will of man— dark, impenetrable night that the mind calls up in order to plunge into it. If it must encounter a night, let it be rather that of despair, which remains lucid— polar night, vigil of the mind, whence will arise perhaps that white and virginal brightness which outlines every object in the light of the intelligence. At that degree, equivalence encounters passionate understanding. Then it is no longer even a question of judging the existential leap. It resumes its place amid the age-old fresco of human attitudes. For the spectator, if he is conscious, that leap is still absurd. In so far as it thinks it solves the paradox, it reinstates it intact. On this score, it is stirring. On this score, everything resumes its place and the absurd world is reborn in all its splendor and diversity.

But it is bad to stop, hard to be satisfied with a single way of seeing, to go without contradiction, perhaps the most subtle of all spiritual forces. The preceding merely defines a way of thinking. But the point is to live.

The gods had condemned Sisyphus to ceaselessly rolling a rock to the top of a mountain, whence the stone would fall back of its own weight. They had thought with some reason that there is no more dreadful punishment than futile and hopeless labor.

If one believes Homer, Sisyphus was the wisest and most prudent of mortals. According to another tradition, however, he was disposed to practice the profession of highwayman. I see no contradiction in this. Opinions differ as to the reasons why he became the futile laborer of the underworld. To begin with, he is accused of a certain levity in regard to the gods. He stole their secrets. Ægina, the daughter of Æsopus, was carried off by Jupiter. The father was shocked by that disappearance and complained to Sisyphus. He, who knew of the abduction, offered to tell about it on condition that Æsopus would give water to the citadel of Corinth. To the celestial thunderbolts he preferred the benediction of water. He was punished for this in the underworld. Homer tells us also that Sisyphus had put Death in chains. Pluto could not endure the sight of his deserted, silent empire. He dispatched the god of war, who liberated Death from the hands of her conqueror.

It is said also that Sisyphus, being near to death, rashly wanted to test his wife's love. He ordered her to cast his unburied body into the middle of the public square. Sisyphus woke up in the underworld. And there, annoyed by an obedience so contrary to human love, he obtained from Pluto permission to return to earth in order to chastise his wife. But when he had seen again the face of this world, enjoyed water and sun, warm stones and the sea, he no longer wanted to go back to the infernal darkness. Recalls, signs of anger, warnings were of no avail. Many years more he lived facing the curve of the gulf, the sparkling sea, and the smiles of earth. A decree of the gods was necessary. Mercury came and seized the impudent man by the collar and, snatching him from his joys, led him forcibly back to the underworld, where his rock was ready for him.

You have already grasped that Sisyphus is the absurd hero. He *is*, as much through his passions as through his torture. His scorn of the gods, his hatred of death, and his passion for life won him that unspeakable penalty in which the whole being is exerted toward accomplishing nothing. This is the price that must be paid for the passions of this earth. Nothing is told us about Sisyphus in the underworld. Myths are made for the imagination to breathe life into them. As for this myth, one sees merely the whole effort of a body straining to raise the huge stone, to roll it and push it up a slope a hundred times over; one sees the face screwed up, the cheek tight against the stone, the shoulder bracing the clay-covered mass, the foot wedging it, the fresh start with arms outstretched, the wholly human security of two earth-clotted hands. At the very end of his long effort measured by skyless space and time without depth, the purpose is achieved. Then Sisyphus watches the stone rush down in a few moments toward that lower world whence he will have to push it up again toward the summit. He goes back down to the plain.

It is during that return, that pause, that Sisyphus interests me. A face that toils so close to stones is already stone itself! I see that man going back down with a heavy yet measured step toward the torment of which he will never know the end. That hour like a breathing-space which returns as surely as his suffering, that is the hour of consciousness. At each of those moments when he leaves the heights and gradually sinks toward the lairs of the gods, he is superior to his fate. He is stronger than his rock.

If this myth is tragic, that is because its hero is conscious. Where would his torture be, indeed, if at every step the hope of succeeding upheld him? The workman of today works every day in his life at the same tasks, and this fate is no less absurd. But it is tragic only at the rare moments when it becomes conscious. Sisyphus, proletarian of the gods, powerless and rebellious, knows the whole extent of his wretched condition: it is what he thinks of during his descent. The lucidity that was to constitute his torture at the same time crowns his victory. There is no fate that cannot be surmounted by scorn.

If the descent is thus sometimes performed in sorrow, it can also take place in joy. This word is not too much. Again I fancy Sisyphus returning toward his rock, and the sorrow was in the beginning. When the images of earth cling too tightly to memory, when the call of happiness becomes too insistent, it happens that melancholy rises in man's heart: this is the rock's victory, this is the rock itself. The boundless grief is too heavy to bear. These are our nights of Gethsemane. But crushing truths perish from being acknowledged. Thus, Œdipus at the outset obeys fate without knowing it. But from the moment he knows, his tragedy begins. Yet at the same moment, blind and desperate, he realizes that the only bond linking him to the world is the cool hand of a girl. Then a tremendous remark rings out: "Despite so many ordeals, my advanced age and the nobility of my soul make me conclude that all is well." Sophocles' Œdipus, like Dostoevsky's Kirilov, thus gives the recipe for the absurd victory. Ancient wisdom confirms modern heroism.

One does not discover the absurd without being tempted to write a manual of happiness. "What! by such narrow ways—?" There is but one world, however. Happiness and the absurd are two sons of the same earth. They are inseparable. It would be a mistake to say that happiness necessarily spring from the absurd discovery. It happens as well that the feeling of the absurd springs from happiness. "I conclude that all is well," says Œdipus, and that remark is sacred. It echoes in the wild and limited universe of man. It teaches that all is not, has not been, exhausted. It drives out of this world a god who had come into it with dissatisfaction and a preference for futile sufferings. It makes of fate a human matter, which must be settled among men.

All Sisyphus' silent joy is contained therein. His fate belongs to him. His rock is his thing. Likewise, the absurd man, when he contemplates his torment, silences all the idols. In the universe suddenly restored to its silence, the myriad wondering little voices of the earth rise up. Unconscious, secret calls, invitations from all the faces, they are the necessary reverse and price of victory. There is no sun without shadow, and it is essential to know the night. The absurd man says yes and his effort will henceforth be unceasing. If there is a personal fate, there is no higher destiny, or at least there is but one which he concludes is inevitable and despicable. For the rest, he knows himself to be the master of his days. At that subtle moment when man glances backward over his life, Sisyphus returning toward his rock, in that slight pivoting he contemplates that series of unrelated actions which becomes his fate, created by him, combined under his memory's eye and soon sealed by his death. Thus, convinced of the wholly human origin of all that is human, a blind man eager to see who knows that the night has no end, he is still on the go. The rock is still rolling.

I leave Sisyphus at the foot of the mountain! One always finds one's burden again. But Sisyphus teaches the higher fidelity that negates the gods and raises rocks. He too concludes that all is well. This universe henceforth without a master seems to him neither sterile nor futile. Each atom of that stone, each mineral flake of that night-filled mountain, in itself forms a world. The struggle itself toward the heights is enough to fill a man's heart. One must imagine Sisyphus happy.

Commitment

As for "despair," the meaning of this expression is extremely simple. It merely means that we limit ourselves to a reliance upon that which is within our wills, or within the sum of the probabilities which render our action feasible. Whenever one wills anything, there are always these elements of probability. If I am counting upon a visit from a friend, who may be coming by train or by tram, I presuppose that the train will arrive at the appointed time, or that the tram will not be derailed. I remain in the realm of possibilities; but one does not rely upon any possibilities beyond those that are strictly concerned in one's action. Beyond the point at which the possibilities under consideration cease to affect my action, I ought to disinterest myself. For there is no God and no prevenient design, which can adapt the world and all its possibilities to my will. When Descartes said, "Conquer yourself rather than the world," what he meant was, at bottom, the same—that we should act without hope.

Marxists, to whom I have said this, have answered: "Your action is limited, obviously, by your death; but you can rely upon the help of others. That is, you can count both upon what the others are doing to help you elsewhere, as in China and in Russia, and upon what they will do later, after your death, to take up your action and carry it forward to its final accomplishment which will be the revolution. Moreover you must rely upon this; not to do so is immoral." To this I rejoin, first, that I shall always count upon my comrades-in-arms in the struggle, in so far as they are committed, as I am, to a definite, common cause; and in the unity of a party or a group which I can more or less control—that is, in which I am enrolled as a militant and whose movements at every moment are known to me. In that respect, to rely upon the unity and the will of the party is exactly like my reckoning that the train will run to time or that the tram will not be derailed. But I cannot count upon men whom I do not know, I cannot base my confidence upon human goodness or upon man's interest in the good of society, seeing that man is free and that there is no human nature which I can take as foundational. I do not know where the Russian revolution will lead. I can admire it and take it as an example in so far as it is evident, today, that the proletariat plays a part in Russia which it has attained in no other nation. But I cannot affirm that this will necessarily lead to the triumph of the proletariat: I must confine myself to what I can see. Nor can I be sure that comrades-in-arms will take up my work after my death and carry it to the maximum perfection, seeing that those men are free agents and will freely decide, tomorrow, what man is then to be. Tomorrow, after my death, some men may decide to establish Fascism, and the others may be so cowardly or so slack as to let them do so. If so, Fascism will then be the truth of man, and so much the worse for us. In reality, things will be such as men have decided they shall be. Does that mean that I should abandon myself to quietism? No. First I ought to commit myself and then act my commitment, according to

From *Existentialism and Humanism* [1946], translated from the French by Philip Mairet. Translation reprinted by permission of Methuen & Co. Ltd., London. Text reprinted by permission of The Philosophical Library, Inc., and Sanford Greenburger. Copyright 1947 by the Philosophical Library, Inc.

the time-honored formula that "one need not hope in order to undertake one's work." Nor does this mean that I should not belong to a party, but only that I should be without illusion and that I should do what I can. For instance, if I ask myself "Will the social ideal as such, ever become a reality?" I cannot tell, I only know that whatever may be in my power to make it so, I shall do; beyond that, I can count upon nothing.

Quietism is the attitude of people who say, "let others do what I cannot do." The doctrine I am presenting before you is precisely the opposite of this, since it declares that there is no reality except in action. It goes further, indeed, and adds, "Man is nothing else but what he purposes, he exists only in so far as he realizes himself, he is therefore nothing else but the sum of his actions, nothing else but what his life is." Hence we can well understand why some people are horrified by our teaching. For many have but one resource to sustain them in their misery, and that is to think, "Circumstances have been against me, I was worthy to be something much better than I have been. I admit I have never had a great love or a great friendship; but that is because I never met a man or a woman who were worthy of it; if I have not written any very good books, it is because I had not the leisure to do so; or, if I have had no children to whom I could devote myself it is because I did not find the man I could have lived with. So there remains within me a wide range of abilities, inclinations and potentialities, unused but perfectly viable, which endow me with a worthiness that could never be inferred from the mere history of my actions." But in reality and for the existentialist, there is no love apart from the deeds of love; no potentiality of love other than that which is manifested in loving; there is no genius other than that which is expressed in works of art. The genius of Proust is the totality of the works of Proust; the genius of Racine is the series of his tragedies, outside of which there is nothing. Why should we attribute to Racine the capacity to write yet another tragedy when that is precisely what he did not write? In life, a man commits himself, draws his own portrait and there is nothing but that portrait. No doubt this thought may seem comfortless to one who has not made a success of his life. On the other hand, it puts everyone in a position to understand that reality alone is reliable; that dreams, expectations and hopes serve to define a man only as deceptive dreams, abortive hopes, expectations unfulfilled; that is to say, they define him negatively, not positively. Nevertheless, when one says, "You are nothing else but what you live," it does not imply that an artist is to be judged solely by his works of art, for a thousand other things contribute no less to his definition as a man. What we mean to say is that a man is no other than a series of undertakings, that he is the sum, the organization, the set of relations that constitute these undertakings.

In the light of all this, what people reproach us with is not, after all, our pessimism, but the sternness of our optimism. If people condemn our works of fiction, in which we describe characters that are base, weak, cowardly and sometimes even frankly evil, it is not only because those characters are base, weak, cowardly or evil. For suppose that, like Zola, we showed that the behavior of these characters was caused by their heredity, or by the action of their environment upon them, or by determining factors, psychic or organic. People would be reassured, they would say, "You see, that is what we are like, no one can do anything about it." But the existentialist, when he portrays a coward, shows him as responsible for his cowardice. He is not like that on account of a cowardly heart or lungs or cerebrum, he has not become like that through his physiological organism; he is like that because he has made himself into a coward by his actions. There is no such thing as a cowardly temperament. There are nervous temperaments; there is what is called impoverished blood, and there are also rich temperaments. But the man whose blood is poor is not a coward for all that, for what produces cowardice is the act of giving up or giving way; and a temperament is not an action. A coward is defined by the deed that he has done. What people feel obscurely, and with horror, is that the coward as we present him is guilty of being a coward. What people would prefer would be to be born either a coward or a hero. One of the charges most often laid against the *Chemins de la Liberté* is something like this—"But, after all, these people being so base, how can you make them into heroes?" That objection is really rather comic, for it implies that people are born heroes: and that is, at bottom, what such people would like to think. If you are born cowards, you can be quite content, you can do nothing about it and you will be cowards all your lives whatever you do; and if you are born heroes you can again be quite content; you will be heroes all your lives, eating and drinking heroically. Whereas the existentialist says that the coward makes himself cowardly, the hero makes himself heroic; and that there is always a possibility for the coward to give up cowardice and for the hero to stop being a hero. What counts is the total commitment, and it is not by a particular case or particular action that you are committed altogether.

SØREN KIERKEGAARD

Faith by Virtue of the Absurd

In connection with the aesthetic and the intellectual, to ask whether this or that is real, whether it really has happened, is a misunderstanding. So to ask betrays a failure to conceive the aesthetic and the intellectual ideality as a possibility, and forgets that to determine a scale of values for the aesthetic and the intellectual in this manner, is like ranking sensation higher than thought. Ethically it is correct to put the question: "Is it real?" But it is important to note that this holds true only when the individual subject asks this question of himself, and concerning his own reality. He can apprehend the ethical reality of another only by thinking it, and hence as a possibility. . . .

The mode of apprehension of the truth is precisely the truth. It is therefore

From *Concluding Unscientific Postscript* [1844], translated from the Danish by Dorothy Swenson and Walter Lowrie, Princeton, 1941, pp. 286-8, 290-91. Copyright 1941 by Princeton University Press; reprinted by permission of the Princeton University Press.
From *Journals*, ed. and translated by Alexander Dru, London and New York, 1938, pp. 291-2, 237-8; reprinted by permission of Alexander Dru.
From *Fear and Trembling* [1857], translated from the Danish by Walter Lowrie, Princeton, 1941, pp. 18-30. Copyright 1941 by Princeton University Press; reprinted by permission of the Princeton University Press.

untrue to answer a question in a medium in which the question cannot arise. So for example, to explain reality within the medium of the possible, or to distinguish between possibility and reality within possibility. By refraining from raising the question of reality from the aesthetic or intellectual point of view, but asking this question only ethically, and here again only in the interest of one's own reality, each individual will be isolated and compelled to exist for himself. . . . To be concerned ethically about another's reality is also a misunderstanding, since the only question of reality that is ethically pertinent, is the question of one's own reality. Here we may clearly note the difference that exists between faith *sensu strictissimo* on the one hand (referring as it does to the historical, and the realms of the aesthetic, the intellectual) and the ethical on the other. To ask with infinite interest about a reality which is not one's own, is faith, and this constitutes a paradoxical relationship to the paradoxical. Aesthetically it is impossible to raise such a question except in thoughtlessness, since possibility is aesthetically higher than reality. Nor is it possible to raise such a question ethically, since the sole ethical interest is the interest in one's own reality. The analogy between faith and the ethical is found in the infinite interest, which suffices to distinguish the believer absolutely from an aesthetician or a thinker. But the believer differs from the ethicist in being infinitely interested in the reality of another (in the fact, for example, that God has existed in time). . . .

A believer is one who is infinitely interested in another's reality. This is a decisive criterion for faith, and the interest in question is not just a little curiosity, but an absolute dependence upon faith's object.

The object of faith is the reality of another, and the relationship is one of infinite interest. The object of faith is not a doctrine, for then the relationship would be intellectual, and it would be of importance not to botch it, but to realize the maximum intellectual relationship. The object of faith is not a teacher with a doctrine; for when a teacher has a doctrine, the doctrine is *eo ipso* more important than the teacher, and the relationship is again intellectual, and it again becomes important not to botch it, but to realize the maximum intellectual relationship. The object of faith is the reality of the teacher, that the teacher really exists. The answer of faith is therefore unconditionally yes or no. For it does not concern a doctrine, as to whether the doctrine is true or not; it is the answer to a question concerning a fact: "Do you or do you not suppose that he has really existed?" And the answer, it must be noted, is with infinite passion. In the case of a human being, it is thoughtlessness to lay so great and infinite a stress on the question whether he has existed or not. If the object of faith is a human being, therefore, the whole proposal is the vagary of a stupid person, who has not even understood the spirit of the intellectual and the aesthetic. The object of faith is hence the reality of the God-man in the sense of his existence. But existence involves first and foremost particularity, and this is why thought must abstract from existence, because the particular cannot be thought, but only the universal. The object of faith is thus God's reality in existence as a particular individual, the fact that God has existed as an individual human being.

Christianity is no doctrine concerning the unity of the divine and the human, or concerning the identity of subject and object; nor is it any other of the logical transcriptions of Christianity. If Christianity were a doctrine, the relationship to it would not be one of faith, for only an intellectual type of relationship can correspond to a doctrine. Christianity is therefore not a doctrine, but the fact that God has existed.

The realm of faith is thus not a class for numbskulls in the sphere of the intellectual, or an asylum for the feeble-minded. Faith constitutes a sphere all by itself, and every misunderstanding of Christianity may at once be recognized by its transforming it into a doctrine, transferring it to the sphere of the intellectual. The maximum of attainment within the sphere of the intellectual, namely, to realize an entire indifference as to the reality of the teacher, is in the sphere of faith at the opposite end of the scale. The maximum of attainment within the sphere of faith is to become infinitely interested in the reality of the teacher.

If I really have powers of reflection and am in a situation in which I have to act decisively—what then? My powers of reflection will show me exactly as many possibilities *pro* as *contra*. The meaning of which is that I, like all men, shall be pleased to observe that there is a providence, guidance, a God, and that my powers of reflection, or those of any man, only enable one to learn and become aware of that fact; that here, if I may so express myself, is where one pays the turnpike money. Now what is it that I have come up against? The *absurd*. And what is the *absurd*? It is, as may quite easily be seen, that I, a rational being, must act in a case where my reason, my powers of reflection, tell me: you can just as well do the one thing as the other, that is to say where my reason and reflection say: you cannot act—and yet here is where I have to act. But that is the case every time I have to act really decisively; because I am then caught up in an infinite passion, and that is just where the incongruity between action and reflection becomes evident. In the routine of everyday I do not notice the secret of reflection, and so imagine that I am acting upon reflection in spite of the fact that nothing is more impossible—because reflection is the equilibrium of possibilities.

The absurd, or to act by virtue of the absurd, is to act upon faith, trusting in God. It is perfectly simple. I must act, but reflection has closed the road, so I take one of the possibilities and turn to God saying: This is what I do, bless my actions, I cannot do otherwise because I am brought to a standstill by my powers of reflection.

Everyone will experience this, whether his power of reflection is great or small. The nature of reflection is the same, though it is different in degree in different individuals. But the reason why it is so seldom seen is because the individual is seldom so introspective. When the difficulty arises he turns to another for advice, who gives him his reflections, and so he can act. . . .

There is nothing more impossible, or more self-contradictory than to act (decisively, infinitely) by virtue of reflection. If anyone asserts that they have done so they only give themselves away and show that either they have no powers of reflection (because the reflection which has not a *pro* for every *contra* is not reflection at all, the essence of it being its duality) or else that they do not know what it means to act. . . .

I understand more and more that Christianity is really too holy for us men. Only think what it means to dare to believe that God came into the world, and for my sake too. It almost sounds as though it were the most blasphemous presumption that a man should presume to believe such a thing. If it were not God himself who had said it—if a man had hit upon that idea in order to show how important man is to God: yes, of all blasphemies it would be the most terrible. It is therefore not invented in order to show how important man is to God—but in order to show how infinite is the love of God. For it is certainly infinite that he should care for a sparrow, but for the sake of a sinner (and a sinner is even less than a sparrow) to let himself be born and die: oh, infinite love.

NB. NB.

May 11. The majority of men (if they find that from their earliest years it is their lot to bear one suffering or another, one cross or another, one of those sad limitations of the soul) begin by hoping, or as they say, believing that things will go better, that God will make things all right etc., and then at length, when no change occurs they come little by little to rely upon the help of eternity *i.e.* they resign themselves and find strength in contenting themselves with the eternal.— The deeper nature, or he whom God has fashioned on a more eternal plan begins at once by understanding that this is a thing he must bear as long as he lives, he dares not require of God such an extraordinary paradoxical help. But God is perfect love just the same, nothing is more certain to him. So he is resigned and inasmuch as the eternal lies close to him he thus finds repose, blessedly assured all the while that God is love. But he must put up with suffering. Then in the course of time, when he becomes more concrete in the actuality of life, comes more and more to himself as a temporal being, when time and its succession exercises its power over him, when in spite of all his effort it becomes so difficult to live on with the assistance of only the eternal, when he becomes a human being in a humbler sense or learns what it means to be human (for in his resignation he is still too ideal or too abstract, for which reason also there is something of despair in such resignation):—then the possibility of faith presents itself to him in this form: whether he will believe by virtue of the absurd that God will help him temporally. (Here lie all the paradoxes.) So the forgiveness of sin also means to be helped temporally, otherwise it is mere resignation, which can endure to bear the punishment, though still convinced that God is love. But belief in the forgiveness of sins means to believe that here in time the sin is forgotten by God, that it is really true that God forgets. . . .

Humanly speaking Job's wife was, in a sense, right. For humanly it is indeed a great additional burden to be exhausted, while one suffers, with the thought that God is nevertheless love. That is enough to send one mad—and, humanly, it is much easier to despair and so make an end.

In suffering and tribulation there are really certain situations in which, humanly speaking, the thought of God and that he is nevertheless love, makes the suffering far more exhausting. In such cases faith is being tried and love put to the test, to see whether one really loves God, really cannot do without him. Humanly speaking one who suffered and was tried thus would be justified in saying: it would all be less painful to me if I did not at the same time have the idea of God. For either one suffers at the thought that God the all-powerful, who could so easily help, leaves one helpless, or else one suffers because one's reason is crucified by the thought that God is love all the same and that what happens to one is for one's good. Humanly speaking it is terrible only to have an opinion and a scrap of understanding about that which one should, so it would seem, be able to judge: one's own suffering—to be even less than a sparrow. Despair makes everything easier because it is an undisturbed agreement with oneself that the suffering is unbearable. The further effort which the idea of God demands of us is to have to understand that suffering must not only be borne but that it is a good, a gift of the God of love. Take this case! When a man who causes another man suffering and himself wishes to be cruel, adds: this is cruelty—that is some relief. But if, when he causes pain he says: this is kindness—that is enough to send one mad, humanly speaking.

Yet this is only a tribulation, which may be terrible enough as long as it lasts. But it is blessed to endure with God. In the first case the only thing is to call immediately upon one's idea of God, and that brings relief. In the second case (and this is the real tribulation) it seems that the idea of God itself increases the suffering. Then one must continue to endure it in faith. If you do not lose hold of God you will ultimately find blessed agreement with God that the suffering was kindness. For God wishes to be right, unconditionally; oh, but the highest blessedness is to put God in the right precisely when, humanly speaking, there seems almost to be an objection to be brought against him. God wishes to be believed, unconditionally; but one who is infinite cannot but put the price of faith infinitely high. Oh, but it is blessed to believe, and the higher the price the greater the happiness; the dearer you buy, the happier you will be. It would be sad and would make one ashamed to have bought the highest of all things for little or dirt cheap, if that were possible. Even a lover speaks in the same way, he is not happy to have bought his beloved cheap, the more he pays the happier he is, the price itself is his joy. Yet in love there is always the possibility that in the end the price will interest him even more than his beloved; where faith is concerned that is impossible.

No, not one shall be forgotten who was great in the world. But each was great in his own way, and each in proportion to the greatness of that which he *loved*. For he who loved himself became great by himself, and he who loved other men became great by his selfless devotion, but he who loved God became greater than all. Everyone shall be remembered, but each became great in proportion to his *expectation*. One became great by expecting the possible, another by expecting the eternal, but he who expected the impossible became greater than all. Everyone shall be remembered, but each was great in proportion to the greatness of that with which he *strove*. For he who strove with the world became great by overcoming the world, and he who strove with himself became great by overcoming himself, but he who strove with God became greater than all. So there was strife in the world, man against man, one against a thousand, but he who strove with God was greater than all. So there was strife upon earth: there was one who overcame all by his power, and there was one who overcame God by his impotence. There was one who relied upon himself and gained all, there was one who secure in his strength sacrificed all, but he who believed God was greater than all. There was one who was great by reason of his power, and one who was great by reason of his wisdom, and one who was great by reason of his hope, and one who was great by reason of his love; but Abraham was greater than all, great by reason of his power whose strength is impotence, great by reason of his wisdom whose secret is foolishness, great by reason of his hope whose form is madness, great by reason of the love which is hatred of oneself.

By faith Abraham went out from the land of his fathers and became a sojourner in the land of promise. He left one thing behind, took one thing with him: he left his earthly understanding behind and took faith with him—otherwise he would not have wandered forth but would have thought this unreasonable. By faith he was a stranger in the land of promise, and there was nothing to recall what was dear to him, but by its novelty everything tempted his soul to melancholy yearning—and yet he was God's elect, in whom the Lord was well pleased! Yea, if he had been disowned, cast off from God's grace, he could have comprehended it better; but now it was like a mockery of him and of his faith. There was in the world one too who lived in banishment from the fatherland he loved. He is not forgotten, nor his Lamentations when he sorrowfully sought and found what he had lost. There is no song of Lamentations by Abraham. It is human to lament, human to weep with them that weep, but it is greater to believe, more blessed to contemplate the believer.

By faith Abraham received the promise that in his seed all races of the world would be blessed. Time passed, the possibility was there, Abraham believed; time passed, it became unreasonable, Abraham believed. There was in the world one who had an expectation, time passed, the evening drew nigh, he was not paltry enough to have forgotten his expectation, therefore he too shall not be forgotten. Then he sorrowed, and sorrow did not deceive him as life had done, it did for him all it could, in the sweetness of sorrow he possessed his delusive expectation. It is human to sorrow, human to sorrow with them that sorrow, but it is greater to believe, more blessed to contemplate the believer. There is no song of Lamentations by Abraham. He did not mournfully count the days while time passed, he did not look at Sarah with a suspicious glance, wondering whether she were growing old, he did not arrest the course of the sun, that Sarah might not grow old, and his expectation with her. He did not sing lullingly before Sarah his mournful lay. Abraham became old, Sarah became a laughingstock in the land, and yet he was God's elect and inheritor of the promise that in his seed all the races of the world would be blessed. So were it not better if he had not been God's elect? What is it to be God's elect? It is to be denied in youth the wishes of youth, so as with great pains to get them fulfilled in old age. But Abraham believed and held fast the expectation. If Abraham had wavered, he would have given it up. If he had said to God, "Then perhaps it is not after all Thy will that it should come to pass, so I will give up the wish. It was my only wish, it was my bliss. My soul is sincere, I hide no secret malice because Thou didst deny it to me"—he would not have been forgotten, he would have saved many by his example, yet he would not be the father of faith. For it is great to give up one's wish, but it is greater to hold it fast after having given it up, it is great to grasp the eternal, but it is greater to hold fast to the temporal after having given it up.

Then came the fulness of time. If Abraham had not believed, Sarah surely would have been dead of sorrow, and Abraham, dulled by grief, would not have understood the fulfilment but would have smiled at it as at a dream of youth. But Abraham believed, therefore he was young; for he who always hopes for the best becomes old, and he who is always prepared for the worst grows old early, but he who believes preserves an eternal youth. Praise therefore to that story! For Sarah, though stricken in years, was young enough to desire the pleasure of motherhood, and Abraham, though gray-haired, was young enough to wish to be a father. In an outward respect the marvel consists in the fact that it came to pass according to their expectation, in a deeper sense the miracle of faith consists in the fact that Abraham and Sarah were young enough to wish, and that faith had preserved their wish and therewith their youth. He accepted the fulfilment of the promise, he accepted it by faith, and it came to pass according to the promise and according to his faith—for Moses smote the rock with his rod, but he did not believe.

Then there was joy in Abraham's house, when Sarah became a bride on the day of their golden wedding.

But it was not to remain thus. Still once more Abraham was to be tried. He had fought with that cunning power which invents everything, with that alert enemy which never slumbers, with that old man who outlives all things—he had fought with Time and preserved his faith. Now all the terror of the strife was concentrated in one instant. "And God tempted Abraham and said unto him, Take Isaac, thine only son, whom thou lovest, and get thee into the land of Moriah, and offer him there for a burnt offering upon the mountain which I will show thee."

So all was lost—more dreadfully than if it had never come to pass! So the Lord was only making sport of Abraham! He made miraculously the preposterous actual, and now in turn He would annihilate it. It was indeed foolishness, but Abraham did not laugh at it like Sarah when the promise was announced. All was lost! Seventy years of faithful expectation, the brief joy at the fulfilment of faith. Who then is he that plucks away the old man's staff, who is it that requires that he himself shall break it? Who is he that would make a man's gray hairs comfortless, who is it that requires that he himself shall do it? Is there no compassion for the venerable oldling, none for the innocent child? And yet Abraham was God's elect, and it was the Lord who imposed the trial. All would now be lost. The glorious memory to be preserved by the human race, the promise in Abraham's seed—this was only a whim, a fleeting thought which the Lord had had, which Abraham should now obliterate. That glorious treasure which was just as old as faith in Abraham's heart, many, many years older than Isaac, the fruit of Abraham's life, sanctified by prayers, matured in conflict—the blessing upon Abraham's lips, this fruit was now to be plucked prematurely and remain without significance. For what significance had it when Isaac was to be sacrificed? That sad and yet blissful hour when Abraham was to take leave of all that was dear to him, when yet once more he was to lift up his head, when his countenance would shine like that of the Lord, when he would concentrate his whole soul in a blessing which was potent to make Isaac blessed all his days—this time would not come! For he would indeed take leave of Isaac, but in such a way that he himself would remain behind; death would separate them, but in such a way that Isaac remained its prey. The old man would not be joyful in death as he laid his hands in blessing upon Isaac, but he would be weary of life as he laid violent hands upon Isaac. And it was God who tried him. Yea, woe, woe unto the messenger who had come before Abraham with such tidings! Who would have ventured to be the emissary of this sorrow? But it was God who tried Abraham.

Yet Abraham believed, and believed for this life. Yea, if his faith had been only for a future life, he surely would have cast everything away in order to hasten out of this world to which he did not belong. But Abraham's faith was not of this sort, if there be such a faith; for really this is not faith but the furthest possibility of faith which has a presentiment of its object at the extremest limit of the horizon, yet is separated from it by a yawning abyss within which despair carries on its game. But Abraham believed precisely for this life, that he was to grow old in the land, honored by the people, blessed in his generation, remembered forever in Isaac, his dearest thing in life, whom he embraced with a love for which it would be a poor expression to say that he loyally fulfilled the father's duty of loving the son, as indeed is evinced in the words of the summons, "the son whom thou lovest." Jacob had twelve sons, and one of them he loved; Abraham had only one, the son whom he loved.

Yet Abraham believed and did not doubt, he believed the preposterous. If Abraham had doubted—then he would have done something else, something glorious; for how could Abraham do anything but what is great and glorious! He would have marched up to Mount Moriah, he would have cleft the fire-wood, lit the pyre, drawn the knife—he would have cried out to God, "Despise not this sacrifice, it is not the best thing I possess, that I know well, for what is an old man in comparison with the child of promise; but it is the best I am able to give Thee. Let Isaac never come to know this, that he may console himself with his youth." He would have plunged the knife into his own breast. He would have been admired in the world, and his name would not have been forgotten; but it is one thing to be admired, and another to be the guiding star which saves the anguished.

But Abraham believed. He did not pray for himself, with the hope of moving the Lord—it was only when the righteous punishment was decreed upon Sodom and Gomorrha that Abraham came forward with his prayers.

We read in those holy books: "And God tempted Abraham, and said unto him, Abraham, Abraham, where art thou? And he said, Here am I." Thou to whom my speech is addressed, was such the case with thee? When afar off thou didst see the heavy dispensation of providence approaching thee, didst thou not say to the mountains, Fall on me, and to the hills, Cover me? Or if thou wast stronger, did not thy foot move slowly along the way, longing as it were for the old path? When a call was issued to thee, didst thou answer, or didst thou not answer perhaps in a low voice, whisperingly? Not so Abraham: joyfully, buoyantly, confidently, with a loud voice, he answered, "Here am I." We read further: "And Abraham rose early in the morning"—as though it were to a festival, so he hastened, and early in the morning he had come to the place spoken of, to Mount Moriah. He said nothing to Sarah, nothing to Eleazar. Indeed who could understand him? Had not the temptation by its very nature exacted of him an oath of silence? He cleft the wood, he bound Isaac, he lit the pyre, he drew the knife. My hearer, there was many a father who believed that with his son he lost everything that was dearest to him in the world, that he was deprived of every hope for the future, but yet there was none that was the child of promise in the sense that Isaac was for Abraham. There was many a father who lost his child; but then it was God, it was the unalterable, the unsearchable will of the Almighty, it was His hand took the child. Not so with Abraham. For him was reserved a harder trial, and Isaac's fate was laid along with the knife in Abraham's hand. And there he stood, the old man, with his only hope! But he did not doubt, he did not look anxiously to the right or to the left, he did not challenge heaven with his prayers. He knew that it was God the Almighty who was trying him, he knew that it was the hardest sacrifice that could be required of him; but he knew also that no sacrifice was too hard when God required it—and he drew the knife.

Who gave strength to Abraham's arm? Who held his right hand up so that it did not fall limp at his side? He who gazes at this becomes paralyzed. Who gave strength to Abraham's soul, so that his eyes did not grow dim, so that he saw neither Isaac nor the ram? He who gazes at this becomes blind.—And yet rare enough perhaps is the man who becomes paralyzed and blind, still more rare one who worthily recounts what happened. We all know it—it was only a trial.

If Abraham when he stood upon Mount Moriah had doubted, if he had gazed about him irresolutely, if before he drew the knife he had by chance discovered the ram, if God had permitted him to offer it instead of Isaac—then he would have betaken himself home, everything would have been the same, he has Sarah, he retained Isaac, and yet how changed! For his retreat would have been a flight, his salvation an accident, his reward dishonor, his future perhaps perdition. Then he would have borne witness neither to his faith nor to God's grace, but would have testified only how dreadful it is to march out to Mount Moriah. Then Abraham would not have been forgotten, nor would Mount Moriah, this mountain would then be mentioned, not like Ararat where the Ark landed, but would be spoken of as a consternation, because it was here that Abraham doubted.

Venerable Father Abraham! In marching home from Mount Moriah thou hadst no need of a panegyric which might console thee for thy loss; for thou didst gain all and didst retain Isaac. Was it not so? Never again did the Lord take him from thee, but thou didst sit at table joyfully with him in thy tent, as thou dost in the beyond to all eternity. Venerable Father Abraham! Thousands of years have run their course since those days, but thou hast need of no tardy lover to snatch the memorial of thee from the power of oblivion, for every language calls thee to remembrance—and yet thou dost reward thy lover more gloriously than does any other; hereafter thou dost make him blessed in thy bosom; here thou dost enthral his eyes and his heart by the marvel of thy deed. Venerable Father Abraham! Second Father of the human race! Thou who first wast sensible of and didst first bear witness to that prodigious passion which disdains the dreadful conflict with the rage of the elements and with the powers of creation in order to strive with God; thou who first didst know that highest passion, the holy, pure and humble expression of the divine madness which the pagans admired—forgive him who would speak in praise of thee, if he does not do it fittingly. He spoke humbly, as if it were the desire of his own heart, he spoke briefly, as it becomes him to do, but he will never forget that thou hadst need of a hundred years to obtain a son of old age against expectation, that thou didst have to draw the knife before retaining Isaac; he will never forget that in a hundred and thirty years thou didst not get further than to faith.

KARL JASPERS

The Will To Communicate

We have seen in the past decade an impotent and fruitless restriction of truth to the so-called rational truth which is only speciously rational, and then we have seen an equally fruitless rejection of reason into which the reliance upon an insufficiently understood reason easily turns. But the philosophy which today is called Existenz-philosophy in this light is not on the side of the chaotic and irrational movements, but rather should be seen as a counterblow to them; and the chaotic and ruinous can just as easily appear in the deceptive garments of rationality as in a frank irrationalism. In Existenz-philosophy, out of the decisiveness of our fundamental bases, the clarity of a life related to Transcendence should again become communicable in thought, as a philosophizing with which we actually live.

To ask again in the contemporary philosophic situation, what is philosophy? what will become of philosophy? means that we think we are in fact at an end. Hegel was the end of Western philosophy, of objective, confident, absolute rationality, and recent philosophizing in the manner of Hegel is a contemporary knowledge about the totality of a past reality. Kierkegaard and Nietzsche exhausted the possibilities of questioning, the questioning by exceptions in endless reflection standing outside communication, alone with God or nothingness. The study in their principles of both sorts of termination has become the condition, not only of acquiring the intellectual means for philosophizing, but also essentially of avoiding superficial and easy affirmations of nothingness, and of coming inwardly in one's own experience to the point where one really knows that here he can go no further. In fact we are not standing before nothingness, but rather, as always where men are living, before our fundamental bases. From such experience the new philosophizing grows of whose potentialities we shall now sketch a picture.

Philosophy after Kierkegaard and Nietzsche can no longer bring its thought into a single, complete system to be brought out as a presentation derived from its principles. It is a question of letting those principles themselves become effective. The problem for us is to philosophize without being exceptions, but with our eyes on the exception.

The truth in the exception for us is that it poses a perpetual question without which we would sink back into the more or less crude platitudes of a self-satisfaction which is no longer thinking radically. Through a knowledge of exceptions, our souls instead of incapsulating themselves in narrowness can remain open to

From *Reason and Existenz* [1935], translated from the German by William Earle, New York, 1955, pp. 128-9. Copyright 1955 by The Noonday Press, Inc.; reprinted by permission of Noonday Press, Inc. and Routledge & Kegan Paul Ltd.
From *The Perennial Scope of Philosophy* [1948], translated from the German by Ralph Manheim, New York, 1949, pp. 46-9; reprinted by permission of Philosophical Library, New York.
From "On My Philosophy" [1941], translated from the German by Felix Kaufmann, in *Existentialism from Dostoevsky to Sartre*, ed. Walter Kaufmann, New York, 1956, pp. 146-8. Copyright © 1956 by the World Publishing Company; reprinted by permission of Meridian Books.

the possible truth and reality which can speak even in despair, suicide, in the passion toward Night, in every form of negative resolution. To see rationally what is counter-rational shows us not only the possibility of a positive side in the negative, but also the ground on which we ourselves stand. An indispensable approach to the truth would be lost without the exceptions. Their earnestness and absoluteness overpower us as standards although we do not follow them in their content. That we owe something new to Kierkegaard and Nietzsche—the possibility of laying the deepest foundations—and yet that we do not follow them in their essential decisions, makes up the difficulty of our philosophical situation.

The philosophizing which owes its impulse to them will, in opposition to their lack of communication, be a communicative philosophizing (or it would be labor lost, since the exception can not be repeated). Against the negative, unlimited radicality of the exception, it will be bound in the communicability of all modes of the Encompassing. Against their risks of worldlessness, it will not only be a weakening, but issue forth from a will to connection in communication as an historical task.

Reason forbids fixation in any truth-meaning that does not embrace all truth. It forbids resignation, it forbids us to lose ourselves in blind alleys, it forbids us to content ourselves with limited solutions, however seductive, it forbids us to forget or pass anything by, whether it is reality or value or possibility. Reason urges us to leave nothing out of account, to relate ourselves with everything that is, to seek beyond all limits what is and should be, to encompass even antinomies, and always apprehend the whole, to apprehend every possible harmony.

But then again reason strives to effect the necessary break-through in every totality. It forbids definitive harmony. It goes to the extreme to apprehend authentic being.

Its root is not a destructive will, such as is manifested in the relativism of intellectual sophistry, but openness to the infinity of meaningful contents. To doubt is imperative to it, but it doubts in order to gain pure truth. The understanding, as unanchored thought, is nihilistic; reason, as grounded in existence, is salvation from nihilism, because it preserves the confidence that through its movement in conjunction with the understanding, it will, amid the conflicts, divisions, and abysses of the concrete world, regain in the end its certitude of transcendence.

Reason is the Comprehensive in us; it does not flow from the primal source of being, but is an instrument of existence. It is the existential absolute that serves to actualize the primal source and bring it to the widest manifestation.

There is something like a climate of reason. The passion for the open works in cool clarity. The rational man lives resolutely out of the root of his own historical soil, and at the same time he gives himself to every mode of historicity which he encounters, in order to penetrate to the depth of the world's historicity, through which alone a sympathetic understanding of everything becomes possible. From this develops what was also the motive force from the outset—the love of being, of everything existent as existent in its transparency, thanks to which its relations to the primal source become visible. Reason enriches man by sharpening his hearing, increases his capacity for communication, makes him capable of change through new experience, but while doing all this it remains essentially one, unswerving in its faith, living in actually efficacious memory of everything that was once real to it.

He who engages in philosophy cannot sufficiently praise reason, to which he owes all his achievements. Reason is the bond that unites all the modes of the Comprehensive. It allows no existent to separate itself absolutely, to sink into isolation, to be reduced to nothingness by fragmentation. Nothing must be lost. Where reason is effective, that which is strives for unification. A universal fellowship arises, in which men are open to all things and everything concerns them. Reason quickens dormant springs, frees what is hidden, makes possible authentic struggles. It presses toward the One that is all, it does away with the delusions that fixate the One prematurely, incompletely, in partisanship.

Reason demands boundless *communication*, it is itself the total will to communicate. Because, in time, we cannot have objective possession of a truth that is the eternal truth, and because being-there is possible only with other being-there, and existence can come into its own only with other existence, communication is the form in which truth is revealed in time.

The great seductions are: through belief in God to withdraw from men; through supposed knowledge of the absolute truth to justify one's isolation; through supposed possession of being itself to fall into a state of complacency that is in truth lovelessness. And to these may be added the assertion that every man is a self-contained monad, that no one can emerge from himself, that communication is a delusion.

In opposition to these stands philosophical faith, which may also be called faith in communication. For it upholds these two propositions: Truth is what joins us together; and, truth has its origin in communication. The only reality with which man can reliably and in self-understanding ally himself in the world, is his fellow man. At all the levels of communication among men, companions in fate lovingly find the road to the truth. This road is lost to the man who shuts himself off from others in stubborn self-will, who lives in a shell of solitude.

The philosophical mood arose from the experience of insufficiency in communication. Occupation with mere objects which does not lead somehow to communication seemed wrong to me. Solitary devotion to nature—this deep experience of the universe in the landscape and in the physical nearness to its shapes and elements, this source of strength for the soul—could seem like a wrong done to other human beings, if it became a means of avoiding them, and like a wrong done to myself, if it tempted me to a secluded self-sufficiency in nature. Solitude in nature can indeed be a wonderful source of *self-being*; but whoever remains solitary in nature is liable to impoverish his self-being and to lose it in the end. To be near to nature in the beautiful world around me therefore became questionable when it did not lead back to community with humanity and serve this community as background and as language. Subsequently the question "What do they mean for communication?" passed through my philosophizing with respect to all thought, all experience, and all subject-matters. Are they apt to promote communication or to impede it? Are they tempters to solitude or heralds of communication?

This led to the basic philosophical questions: How is communication possible? What forms of communication can be accomplished? What is their relation to each other? In what sense are solitude and the strength to be able to be alone sources of communication? The answers are given, especially in the second volume of my *Philosophy*, in terms of concrete representations—by psychological means—and their principles will be treated in my *Logic*.

The thesis of my philosophizing is: The individual cannot become human by himself. Self-being is only real in communication with another self-being. Alone, I sink into gloomy isolation—only in community with others can I be revealed in the act of mutual discovery. My own freedom can only exist if the other is also free. Isolated or self-isolating Being remains mere potentiality or disappears into nothingness. All institutions that maintain soothing contact between men under unexpressed conditions and within unadmitted limits are certainly indispensable for communal existence; but beyond that they are pernicious, because they veil the truth in the manifestation of human Existenz with illusory contentment. . . .

The cogent correctness of the sciences is but a small part of truth. This correctness, in its universal validity, does not unite us completely as real human beings, but only as intellectual beings. It unites us in the object that is understood, in the particular, but not in the totality. Admittedly, men can be true friends through scientific research, by means of the ideas that are realized in this process, and the impulses towards Existenz that make their appearance in it. But the correctness of scientific knowledge unites all intellectual beings in their equality, as it were, as replaceable points, not, in its essence, as human beings.

To the intellect all else, in comparison with what is correct, counts only as feeling, subjectivity, instinct. In this division, apart from the bright world of the intellect, there is only the irrational, in which is lumped together, according to the point of view, what is despised or desired. The impulse which pursues real truth by thought springs from the dissatisfaction with what is merely correct. The division, spoken of previously, paralyzes this impulse; it causes man to oscillate between the dogmatism of the intellect that transcends its limits and, as it were, the rapture of the vital, the chance of the moment, life. The soul becomes impoverished in all the multiplicity of disparate experience. Then truth disappears from the field of vision and is replaced by a variety of opinions which are hung on the skeleton of a supposedly rational pattern. Truth is infinitely *more* than scientific correctness.

Communication, too, points to this *more*. Communication is the path to truth in all its forms. Thus the intellect finds clarity only in discussion. How man as an existent, as spirit, as Existenz, is or can be in communication—that is what allows all other truth to appear.

JEAN-PAUL SARTRE

The Common Condition of Man

Our point of departure is, indeed, the subjectivity of the individual, and that for strictly philosophic reasons. It is not because we are bourgeois, but because we seek to base our teaching upon the truth, and not upon a collection of fine theories, full of hope but lacking real foundations. And at the point of departure there cannot be any other truth than this, *I think, therefore I am,* which is the absolute truth of consciousness as it attains to itself. Every theory which begins with man, outside of this moment of self-attainment, is a theory which thereby suppresses the truth, for outside of the Cartesian *cogito,* all objects are no more than probable, and any doctrine of probabilities which is not attached to a truth will crumble into nothing. In order to define the probable one must possess the true. Before there can be any truth whatever, then, there must be an absolute truth, and there is such a truth which is simple, easily attained and within the reach of everybody; it consists in one's immediate sense of one's self.

In the second place, this theory alone is compatible with the dignity of man, it is the only one which does not make man into an object. All kinds of materialism lead one to treat every man including oneself as an object—that is, as a set of pre-determined reactions, in no way different from the patterns of qualities and phenomena which constitute a table, or a chair or a stone. Our aim is precisely to establish the human kingdom as a pattern of values in distinction from the material world. But the subjectivity which we thus postulate as the standard of truth is no narrowly individual subjectivism, for as we have demonstrated, it is not only one's own self that one discovers in the *cogito,* but those of others too. Contrary to the philosophy of Descartes, contrary to that of Kant, when we say "I think" we are attaining to ourselves in the presence of the other, and we are just as certain of the other as we are of ourselves. Thus the man who discovers himself directly in the *cogito* also discovers all the others, and discovers them as the condition of his own existence. He recognizes that he cannot be anything (in the sense in which one says one is spiritual, or that one is wicked or jealous) unless others recognize him as such. I cannot obtain any truth whatsoever about myself, except through the mediation of another. The other is indispensable to my existence, and equally so to any knowledge I can have of myself. Under these conditions, the intimate discovery of myself is at the same time the revelation of the other as a freedom which confronts mine, and which cannot think or will without doing so either for or against me. Thus, at once, we find ourselves in a world which is, let us say, that of "inter-subjectivity." It is in this world that man has to decide what he is and what others are.

Furthermore, although it is impossible to find in each and every man a universal essence that can be called human nature, there is nevertheless a human universality of *condition.* It is not by chance that the thinkers of today are so much more ready to speak of the condition than of the nature of man. By his condition they understand, with more or less clarity, all the *limitations* which *a priori* define man's fundamental situation in the universe. His historical situations are variable: man may be born a slave in a pagan society, or may be a feudal baron, or a proletarian. But what never vary are the necessities of being in the world, of having to labor and to die there. These limitations are neither subjective nor objective, or rather there is both a subjective and an objective aspect of them. Objective, because we meet with them everywhere and they are everywhere recognizable: and subjective because they are *lived* and are nothing if man does not live them—if, that is to say, he does not freely determine himself and his existence in relation to them. And, diverse though man's purposes may be, at least none of them is wholly foreign to me, since every human purpose presents itself as an attempt either to surpass these limitations, or to widen them, or else to deny or to accommodate oneself to them. Consequently every purpose, however individual it may be, is of universal value. Every purpose, even that of a Chinese, an Indian or a Negro, can be understood by a European. To say it can be understood, means that the European of 1945 may be striving out of a certain situation towards the same limitations in the same way, and that he may reconceive in himself the purpose of the Chinese, of the Indian or the African. In every purpose there is universality, in this sense that every purpose is comprehensible to every man. Not that this or that purpose defines man for ever, but that it may be entertained again and again. There is always some way of understanding an idiot, a child, a primitive man or a foreigner if one has sufficient information. In this sense we may say that there is a human universality, but it is not something given; it is being perpetually made. I make this universality in choosing myself; I also make it by understanding the purpose of any other man, of whatever epoch. This absoluteness of the act of choice does not alter the relativity of each epoch.

What is at the very heart and center of existentialism, is the absolute character of the free commitment, by which every man realizes himself in realizing a type of humanity—a commitment always understandable, to no matter whom in no matter what epoch—and its bearing upon the relativity of the cultural pattern which may result from such absolute commitment. One must observe equally the relativity of Cartesianism and the absolute character of the Cartesian commitment. In this sense you may say, if you like, that every one of us makes the absolute by breathing, by eating, by sleeping or by behaving in any fashion whatsoever. There is no difference between free being—being as self-committal, as existence choosing its essence—and absolute being. And there is no difference whatever between being as an absolute, temporarily localized—that is, localized in history—and universally intelligible being. . . .

Man is all the time outside of himself: it is in projecting and losing himself beyond himself that he makes man to exist; and, on the other hand, it is by pursuing transcendent aims that he himself is able to exist. Since man is thus self-surpassing, and can grasp objects only in relation to his self-surpassing, he is himself the heart and center of his transcendence. There is no other universe except the human universe, the universe of human subjectivity. This relation of transcendence as constitutive of man (not in the sense that God is transcendent, but in the sense of self-surpassing) with subjectivity (in such a sense that man is not shut up in himself but forever present in a human universe)—it is this that we call existential humanism. This is humanism, because we remind man that there is no legislator but himself; that he himself, thus abandoned, must decide for himself; also because we show that it is not by turning back upon himself, but always by seeking, beyond himself, an aim which is one of liberation or of some particular realization, that man can realize himself as truly human.

MARTIN BUBER

The Primary Words

To man the world is twofold, in accordance with his twofold attitude.

The attitude of man is twofold, in accordance with the twofold nature of the primary words which he speaks.

The primary words are not isolated words, but combined words.

The one primary word is the combination I-Thou.

The other primary word is the combination I-It; wherein, without a change in the primary word, one of the words He and She can replace It.

Hence the I of man is also twofold.

For the I of the primary word I-Thou is a different I from that of the primary word I-It.

Primary words do not signify things, but they intimate relations.

Primary words do not describe something that might exist independently of them, but being spoken they bring about existence.

Primary words are spoken from the being.

If Thou is said, the I of the combination I-Thou is said along with it.

If It is said, the I of the combination I-It is said along with it.

The primary word I-Thou can only be spoken with the whole being.

The primary word I-It can never be spoken with the whole being.

There is no I taken in itself, but only the I of the primary word I-Thou and the I of the primary word I-It.

When a man says I he refers to one or other of these. The I to which he refers is present when he says I. Further, when he says Thou or It, the I of one of the two primary words is present.

The existence of I and the speaking of I are one and the same thing.

When a primary word is spoken the speaker enters the word and takes his stand in it.

The life of human beings is not passed in the sphere of transitive verbs alone. It does not exist in virtue of activities alone which have some thing for their object.

From I and Thou [1923], translated from the German by Ronald Gregor Smith, Edinburgh and New York, 1937, pp. 3-10, 16-18, 56-9; reprinted by permission of Charles Scribner's Sons and T. and T. Clark, Publishers, Edinburgh.

I perceive something. I am sensible of something. I imagine something. I will something. I feel something. I think something. The life of human beings does not consist of all this and the like alone.

This and the like together establish the realm of *It*.

But the realm of *Thou* has a different basis.

When *Thou* is spoken, the speaker has no thing for his object. For where there is a thing there is another thing. Every *It* is bounded by others; *It* exists only through being bounded by others. But when *Thou* is spoken, there is no thing. *Thou* has no bounds.

When *Thou* is spoken, the speaker has no *thing*; he has indeed nothing. But he takes his stand in relation.

It is said that man experiences his world. What does that mean?

Man travels over the surface of things and experiences them. He extracts knowledge about their constitution from them: he wins an experience from them. He experiences what belongs to the things.

But the world is not presented to man by experiences alone. These present him only with a world composed of *It* and *He* and *She* and *It* again.

I experience something.—If we add "inner" to "outer" experiences, nothing in the situation is changed. We are merely following the uneternal division that springs from the lust of the human race to whittle away the secret of death. Inner things or outer things, what are they but things and things!

I experience something.—If we add "secret" to "open" experiences, nothing in the situation is changed. How self-confident is that wisdom which perceives a closed compartment in things, reserved for the initiate and manipulated only with the key. O secrecy without a secret! O accumulation of information! It, always It!

The man who experiences has no part in the world. For it is "in him" and not between him and the world that the experience arises.

The world has no part in the experience. It permits itself to be experienced, but has no concern in the matter. For it does nothing to the experience, and the experience does nothing to it.

As experience, the world belongs to the primary word *I-It*.

The primary word *I-Thou* establishes the world of relation.

The spheres in which the world of relation arises are three.

First, our life with nature. There the relation sways in gloom, beneath the level of speech. Creatures live and move over against us, but cannot come to us, and when we address them as *Thou*, our words cling to the threshold of speech.

Second, our life with men. There the relation is open and in the form of speech. We can give and accept the *Thou*.

Third, our life with intelligible forms. There the relation is clouded, yet it discloses itself; it does not use speech, yet begets it. We perceive no *Thou*, but none the less we feel we are addressed and we answer—forming, thinking, acting. We speak the primary word with our being, though we cannot utter *Thou* with our lips.

But with what right do we draw what lies outside speech into relation with the world of the primary word?

In every sphere in its own way, through each process of becoming that is present to us we look out toward the fringe of the eternal *Thou*; in each we are aware of a breath from the eternal *Thou*; in each *Thou* we address the eternal *Thou*.

I consider a tree.

I can look on it as a picture: stiff column in a shock of light, or splash of green shot with the delicate blue and silver of the background.

I can perceive it as movement: flowing veins on clinging, pressing pith, suck of the roots, breathing of the leaves, ceaseless commerce with earth and air—and the obscure growth itself.

I can classify it in a species and study it as a type in its structure and modes of life.

I can subdue its actual presence and form so sternly that I recognise it only as an expression of law—of the laws in accordance with which a constant opposition of forces is continually adjusted, or of those in accordance with which the component substances mingle and separate.

I can dissipate it and perpetuate it in number, in pure numerical relation.

In all this the tree remains my object, occupies space and time, and has its nature and constitution.

It can, however, also come about, if I have both will and grace, that in considering the tree I become bound up in relation to it. The tree is now no longer *It*. I have been seized by the power of exclusiveness.

To effect this it is not necessary for me to give up any of the ways in which I consider the tree. There is nothing from which I would have to turn my eyes away in order to see, and no knowledge that I would have to forget. Rather is everything, picture and movement, species and type, law and number, indivisibly united in this event.

Everything belonging to the tree is in this: its form and structure, its colours and chemical composition, its intercourse with the elements and with the stars, are all present in a single whole.

The tree is no impression, no play of my imagination, no value depending on my mood; but it is bodied over against me and has to do with me, as I with it— only in a different way.

Let no attempt be made to sap the strength from the meaning of the relation: relation is mutual.

The tree will have a consciousness, then, similar to our own? Of that I have no experience. But do you wish, through seeming to succeed in it with yourself, once again to disintegrate that which cannot be disintegrated? I encounter no soul or dryad of the tree, but the tree itself.

If I face a human being as my *Thou*, and say the primary word *I-Thou* to him, he is not a thing among things, and does not consist of things.

This human being is not *He* or *She*, bounded from every other *He* and *She*, a specific point in space and time within the net of the world; nor is he a nature able to be experienced and described, a loose bundle of named qualities. But with no neighbour, and whole in himself, he is *Thou* and fills the heavens. This does not mean that nothing exists except himself. But all else lives in *his* light.

Just as the melody is not made up of notes nor the verse of words nor the statue of lines, but they must be tugged and dragged till their unity has been scattered into these many pieces, so with the man to whom I say *Thou*. I can take out from him the colour of his hair, or of his speech, or of his goodness. I must continually do this. But each time I do it he ceases to be *Thou*.

And just as prayer is not in time but time in prayer, sacrifice not in space but space in sacrifice, and to reverse the relation is to abolish the reality, so with the man to whom I say *Thou*. I do not meet with him at some time and place or other. I can set him in a particular time and place; I must continually do it: but I set only a *He* or a *She*, that is an *It*, no longer my *Thou*.

So long as the heaven of *Thou* is spread out over me the winds of causality cower at my heels, and the whirlpool of fate stays its course.

I do not experience the man to whom I say *Thou*. But I take my stand in relation to him, in the sanctity of the primary word. Only when I step out of it do I experience him once more. In the act of experience *Thou* is far away.

Even if the man to whom I say *Thou* is not aware of it in the midst of his experience, yet relation may exist. For *Thou* is more than *It* realises. No deception penetrates here; here is the cradle of the Real Life.

This is the eternal source of art: a man is faced by a form which desires to be made through him into a work. This form is no offspring of his soul, but is an appearance which steps up to it and demands of it the effective power. The man is concerned with an act of his being. If he carries it through, if he speaks the primary word out of his being to the form which appears, then the effective power streams out, and the work arises.

The act includes a sacrifice and a risk. This is the sacrifice: the endless possibility that is offered up on the altar of the form. For everything which just this moment in play ran through the perspective must be obliterated; nothing of that may penetrate the work. The exclusiveness of what is facing it demands that it be so. This is the risk: the primary word can only be spoken with the whole being. He who gives himself to it may withhold nothing of himself. The work does not suffer me, as do the tree and the man, to turn aside and relax in the world of *It*; but it commands. If I do not serve it aright it is broken, or it breaks me.

I can neither experience nor describe the form which meets me, but only body it forth. And yet I behold it, splendid in the radiance of what confronts me, clearer than all the clearness of the world which is experienced. I do not behold it as a thing among the "inner" things nor as an image of my "fancy," but as that which exists in the present. If test is made of its objectivity the form is certainly not "there." Yet what is actually so much present as it is? And the relation in which I stand to it is real, for it affects me, as I affect it.

To produce is to draw forth, to invent is to find, to shape is to discover. In bodying forth I disclose. I lead the form across—into the world of *It*. The word produced is a thing among things, able to be experienced and described as a sum of qualities. But from time to time it can face the receptive beholder in its whole embodied form.

—You speak of love as though it were the only relation between men. But properly speaking, can you take it even only as an example, since there is such a thing as hate?

—So long as love is "blind," that is, so long as it does not see a *whole* being, it is not truly under the sway of the primary word of relation. Hate is by nature blind. Only a part of a being can be hated. He who sees a whole being and is compelled to reject it is no longer in the kingdom of hate, but is in that of human restriction of the power to say *Thou*. He finds himself unable to say the primary word to the other human being confronting him. This word consistently involves an affirmation of the being addressed. He is therefore compelled to reject either the other or himself. At this barrier the entering on a relation recognises its relativity, and only simultaneously with this will the barrier be raised.

Yet the man who straightforwardly hates is nearer to relation than the man without hate and love.

But this is the exalted melancholy of our fate, that every *Thou* in our world must become an *It*. It does not matter how exclusively present the *Thou* was in the direct relation. As soon as the relation has been worked out or has been permeated with a means, the *Thou* becomes an object among objects—perhaps the chief, but still one of them, fixed in its size and its limits. In the work of art realisation in one sense means loss of reality in another. Genuine contemplation is over in a short time; now the life in nature, that first unlocked itself to me in the mystery of mutual action, can again be described, taken to pieces, and classified—the meeting-point of manifold systems of laws. And love itself cannot persist in direct relation. It endures, but in interchange of actual and potential being. The human being who was even now single and unconditioned, not something lying to hand, only present, not able to be experienced, only able to be fulfilled, has now become again a *He* or a *She*, a sum of qualities, a given quantity with a certain shape. Now I may take out from him again the colour of his hair or of his speech or of his goodness. But so long as I can do this he is no more my *Thou* and cannot yet be my *Thou* again.

Every *Thou* in the world is by its nature fated to become a thing, or continually to re-enter into the condition of things. In objective speech it would be said that every thing in the world, either before or after becoming a thing, is able to appear to an *I* as its *Thou*. But objective speech snatches only at a fringe of real life.

The *It* is the eternal chrysalis, the *Thou* the eternal butterfly—except that situations do not always follow one another in clear succession, but often there is a happening profoundly twofold, confusedly entangled.

The quasi-biological and quasi-historical thought of to-day, however different the aims of each, have worked together, to establish a more tenacious and oppressive belief in fate than has ever before existed. The might of *karma* or of the stars no longer controls inevitably the lot of man; many powers claim the mastery, but rightly considered most of our contemporaries believe in a mixture of them, just as the late Romans believed in a mixture of gods. This is made easier by the nature of the claim. Whether it is the "law of life" of a universal struggle in which all must take part or renounce life, or the "law of the soul" which completely builds up the psychical person from innate habitual instincts, or the "social law" of an irresistible social process to which will and consciousness may only be accompaniments, or the "cultural law" of an unchangeably uniform coming and going of historical structures—whatever form it takes, it always means that man is set in the frame of an inescapable happening that he cannot, or can only in his frenzy, resist. Consecration in the mysteries brought freedom from the compulsion of the stars, and brahman-sacrifice with its accompanying knowledge brought freedom from the compulsion of *karma*: in both salvation was represented. But the composite god tolerates no belief in release. It is considered folly to imagine any freedom; there is only a choice, between resolute, and hopeless rebellious, slavery. And no matter how much is said, in all these laws, of teleological development and organic growth, at the basis of them all lies possession by process, that is by unlimited causality. The dogma of gradual process is the abdication of man before the exuberant world of *It*. He misuses the name of destiny: destiny is not a dome pressed tightly down on the world of men; no one meets it but he who went out from freedom. But the dogma of process leaves no room for freedom, none for its most real revelation of all, whose calm strength changes the face of the earth—reversal. This dogma does not know the man who through reversal surmounts the universal struggle, tears to pieces the web of habitual instincts, raises the class ban, and stirs, rejuvenates, and transforms the stable structures of history. This dogma allows you in its game only the choice to observe the rules or to retire: but the man who is realising reversal overthrows the pieces. The dogma is always willing to allow you to fulfil its limitation with your life and "to remain free" in your soul; but the man who is realising reversal looks on this freedom as the most ignominious bondage.

The only thing that can become fate for a man is belief in fate; for this suppresses the movement of reversal.

Belief in fate is mistaken from the beginning. All consideration in terms of process is merely an ordering of pure "having become," of the separated world-event, of objectivity as though it were history; the presence of the *Thou*, the becoming out of solid connexion, is inaccessible to it. It does not know the reality of spirit; its scheme is not valid for spirit. Prediction from objectivity is valid only for the man who does not know presentness. He who is overcome by the world of *It* is bound to see, in the dogma of immutable process, a truth that clears a way through the exuberant growth; in very truth this dogma enslaves him only the more deeply to the world of *It*. But the world of *Thou* is not closed. He who goes out to it with concentrated being and risen power to enter into relation becomes aware of freedom. And to be freed from belief that there is no freedom is indeed to be free.

As power over the incubus is obtained by addressing it with its real name, so the world of *It*, which a moment ago was stretched in its uncanniness before the puny strength of men, is bound to yield to the man who knows it for what it really is—severance and alienation of that out of whose abundance, when it streams close at hand, every earthly *Thou* is met, and of that which, though seeming at times great and fearful like the mother-god, yet always had a motherly air.

—But how can the man in whose being lurks a ghost, the *I* emptied of reality, muster the strength to address the incubus by name? How can the ruined power in a being to enter into relation be raised again, when an active ghost tramples continually on the ruins? How does a being gather itself together, that is madly and unceasingly hunted in an empty circle by the separated *I*? How may a man who lives in arbitrary self-will become aware of freedom?

—As freedom and destiny, so arbitrary self-will and fate belong together. But freedom and destiny are solemnly promised to one another and linked together in meaning; while arbitrary self-will and fate, soul's spectre and world's nightmare, endure one another, living side by side and avoiding one another, without connexion or conflict, in meaninglessness—till in an instant there is confused shock of glance on glance, and confession of their non-salvation breaks from them. How much eloquent and ingenious spirituality is expended to-day in the effort to avert, or at least to veil, this event!

KARL JASPERS

The Encompassing

In order to see most clearly into what is true and real, into what is no longer fastened to any particular thing or colored by any particular atmosphere, we must push into the widest range of the possible. And then we experience the following: everything that is an object for us, even though it be the greatest, is still always within another, is not yet all. Wherever we arrive, the horizon which includes the attained itself goes further and forces us to give up any final rest. We can secure no standpoint from which a closed whole of Being would be surveyable, nor any sequence of standpoints through whose totality Being would be given even indirectly.

We always live and think within a horizon. But the very fact that it is a horizon indicates something further which again surrounds the given horizon. From this situation arises the question about the Encompassing. The Encompassing is not a horizon within which every determinate mode of Being and truth emerges for us, but rather that within which every particular horizon is enclosed as in something absolutely comprehensive which is no longer visible as a horizon at all. . . .

The Encompassing appears and disappears for us in two opposed perspectives: either as Being itself, in and through which we are—or else as the Encompassing

From *Reason and Existenz* [1935], translated from the German by William Earle, New York, 1955, pp. 51-2, 75-6. Copyright 1955 by The Noonday Press, Inc.; reprinted by permission of Noonday Press, Inc. and Routledge & Kegan Paul Ltd.
From "On My Philosophy" [1941], translated from the German by Felix Kaufmann, in *Existentialism from Dostoevsky to Sartre*, ed. Walter Kaufmann, New York, 1956, pp. 141-2. Copyright © 1956 by The World Publishing Company, reprinted by permission of Meridian Books.

which we ourselves are, and in which every mode of Being appears to us. The latter would be as the medium or condition under which all Being appears as Being for us. In neither case is the Encompassing the sum of some provisional kinds of being, a part of whose contents we know, but rather it is the whole as the most extreme, self-supporting ground of Being, whether it is Being in itself, or Being as it is for us.

All of our natural knowledge and dealings with things lies between these final and no longer conditioned bases of encompassing Being. The Encompassing never appears as an object in experience, nor as an explicit theme of thinking, and therefore might seem to be empty. But precisely here is where the possibility for our deepest insight into Being arises, whereas all other knowledge about Being is merely knowledge of particular, individual being. . . .

The purpose and therefore the meaning of a philosophical idea is not the cognition of an object, but rather an alteration of our consciousness of Being and of our inner attitude toward things.

Understanding the meaning of the Encompassing has the significance of creating a possibility. The philosopher therein says to himself: preserve the open space of the Encompassing! Do not lose yourself in what is merely known! Do not let yourself become separated from Transcendence!

In thinking about temporal existence, one must continually run through the circuit of the modes of the Encompassing. We can remain static in none of its modes. Each demands the others. The loss of one mode lets all the others become false. The philosopher seeks to omit none. . . .

The open space of such philosophizing becomes a danger unless one keeps in steady consciousness one's potential Existenz: there is a danger that one may see oneself as lost through abstract thinking on the whole range of things. Genuine thinking about the Encompassing, however, is reflected back from the total range of revealed directions ever so much more decisively onto the concrete historicity of my own present. Now for the first time it is possible to be in the present without disappearing into the restrictions of the unthinking, the blind, and the unrelated. Now also it is possible to grasp the whole spaciousness of Being without losing oneself in the void of the mere universal of the understanding, in the meaningless facticity of empirical existence, or in some empty beyond. For the determinateness of the historical depths is bound up with the openness of unlimited ranges of Being, and the truth of one's own bases with their relation to the ungrounded openness of Being, Existenz with reason. The more unrestrictedly I penetrate by thought into the depths, the truer my love becomes in its historical present. Hölderlin said: "Who has thought about the deepest, loves what is most alive."

Man can seek the path of his truth in unfanatical absoluteness, in a decisiveness which remains open.

In the world *man* alone is the reality which is accessible to me. Here is presence, nearness, fullness, life. Man is the place at which and through which everything that is real exists for us at all. To fail to be human would mean to slip into nothingness. What man is and can become is a fundamental question for man.

Man, however, is not a self-sufficient separate entity, but is constituted by the things he makes his own. In every form of his being man is related to something other than himself: as a being to his world, as consciousness to objects, as spirit to the idea of whatever constitutes totality, as Existenz to Transcendence. Man always becomes man by devoting himself to this other. Only through his absorption in the world of Being, in the immeasurable space of objects, in ideas, in Transcendence, does he become real to himself. If he makes himself the immediate object of his efforts he is on his last and perilous path; for it is possible that in doing so he will lose the Being of the other and then no longer find anything in himself. If man wants to grasp himself directly, he ceases to understand himself, to know who he is and what he should do.

This confusion was intensified as a result of the process of education in the nineteenth century. The wealth of knowledge of everything that was produced a state in which it seemed that man could gain mastery over all Being without yet being anything himself. This happened because he no longer devoted himself to the thing as it was, but made it a function of his education. Where humanity founds itself only on itself, it is experienced again that it has no ground beneath it.

The question about humanity is pushed forward. It no longer suffices to ask beyond oneself with Kant "What may I hope?" Man strives more decisively than ever for a certainty that he lacks, for the certainty that there is that which is eternal, that there is a Being through which alone he himself is. If the Deity is, then all hope is possible.

Hence the question "What is man?" must be complemented by the essential question whether and what Transcendence (Deity) is. The thesis becomes possible: Transcendence alone is the real Being. That the Deity is suffices. To be certain of that is the only thing that matters. Everything else follows from that. Man is not worth considering. In the Deity alone there is reality, truth, and the immutability of being itself. In the Deity there is peace, as well as the origin and aim of man who, by himself, is nothing, and what he is he is only in relation to the Deity.

But time and again it is seen: for us the Deity, if it exists, is only as it appears to us in the world, as it speaks to us in the language of man and the world. It exists for us only in the way in which it assumes concrete shape, which by human measure and thought always serves to hide it at the same time. Only in ways that man can grasp does the Deity appear.

Thus it is seen that it is wrong to play off against each other the question about man and the question about the Deity. Although in the world only man is reality for us that does not preclude that precisely the quest for man leads to Transcendence. That the Deity alone is truly reality does not preclude that this reality is accessible to us only in the world; as it were, as an image in the mirror of man, because something of the Deity must be in him for him to be able to respond to the Deity. Thus the theme of philosophy is oriented, in polar alternation, in two directions: *deum et animam scire cupio* [I desire knowledge of God and the soul].

Recollection of Being

Metaphysics . . . speaks continually and in the most various ways of Being. Metaphysics gives, and seems to confirm, the appearance that it asks and answers the question concerning Being. In fact, metaphysics never answers the question concerning the truth of Being, for it never asks this question. Metaphysics does not ask this question because it thinks of Being only by representing beings as beings. It means all beings as a whole, although it speaks of Being. It refers to Being and means beings as beings. From its beginning to its completion, the propositions of metaphysics have been strangely involved in a persistent confusion of beings and Being. This confusion, to be sure, must be considered an event and not a mere mistake. It cannot by any means be charged to a mere negligence of thought or a carelessness of expression. Owing to this persistent confusion, the claim that metaphysics poses the question of Being lands us in utter error.

Due to the manner in which it thinks of beings, metaphysics almost seems to be, without knowing it, the barrier which keeps man from the original involvement of Being in human nature.

What if the absence of this involvement and the oblivion of this absence determined the entire modern age? What if the absence of Being abandoned man more and more exclusively to beings, leaving him forsaken and far from any involvement of Being in his nature, while this forsakenness itself remained veiled? What if this were the case—and had been the case for a long time now? What if there were signs that this oblivion will become still more decisive in the future?

Would there still be occasion for a thoughtful person to give himself arrogant airs in view of this fateful withdrawal with which Being presents us? Would there still be occasion, if this should be our situation, to deceive ourselves with pleasant phantasms and to indulge, of all things, in an artificially induced elation? If the oblivion of Being which has been described here should be real, would there not be occasion enough for a thinker who recalls Being to experience a genuine horror? What more can his thinking do than to endure in dread this fateful withdrawal, while first of all facing up to the oblivion of Being? But how could thought achieve this as long as its fatefully granted dread seems to it no more than a mood of depression? What does such dread, which is fated by Being, have to do with psychology or psychoanalysis?

Suppose that the overcoming of metaphysics involved the endeavor to commence with a regard for the oblivion of Being—the attempt to learn to develop such a regard, in order to experience this oblivion and to absorb this experience into the involvement of Being in man, and to preserve it there: then, in the distress of the oblivion of Being, the question "What is metaphysics?" might well become the most necessary necessity for thought.

Thus everything depends on this: that our thinking should become more thoughtful in its season. This is achieved when our thinking, instead of imple-

From "The Way Back into the Ground of Metaphysics" [1949], translated from the German by Walter Kaufmann, in *Existentialism from Dostoevsky to Sartre*, New York, 1956, pp. 211-12. Copyright © 1956 by The World Publishing Company; reprinted by permission of Meridian Books.

menting a higher degree of exertion, is directed toward a different point of origin. The thinking which is posited by beings as such, and therefore representational and illuminating in that way, must be supplanted by a different kind of thinking which is brought to pass by Being itself and, therefore, responsive to Being.

9
FAITH

Christianity and Christendom
WILLIAM BLAKE: The Lord's Prayer Modernized
SØREN KIERKEGAARD: A Hypocritical Generation
F. M. DOSTOEVSKY: Christ and the Grand Inquisitor

Deified Man
WILLIAM BLAKE: God in Man
FRIEDRICH NIETZSCHE: The Death of God and the Antichrist

Poetized Religion
MATTHEW ARNOLD: The Finer Spirit of Knowledge
GEORGE SANTAYANA: An Allegory of Human Life

Paganized Christianity
D. H. LAWRENCE: The Resurrection of the Body
ANDRÉ GIDE: Salvation on Earth

Orthodoxy
PAUL CLAUDEL: The Errors of André Gide
CHARLES BAUDELAIRE: Man Become God
JACQUES MARITAIN: The Errors of Modern Rationalism
T. E. HULME: The Modern Confusion of Categories
KARL BARTH: The One and Only God

The State of Doubt
PAUL TILLICH: The Meaning of Meaninglessness

Introduction

The declining authority of the Christian churches, with the decline of individual Christian faith, is a cultural fact that weighs heavily upon the modern consciousness. Responses to it are often indirect and only half intended, as in the quasi-religious vocabulary that enters into some of the most thoroughly secularized modern writing. More conscious and well-defined responses have been extremely varied. There have been attempts to turn the discrediting of public Christian institutions into a renascence of personal Christian belief; there have been reinterpretations of Christian doctrine and of the meaning of religion in general; and there have been embattled declarations of orthodoxy.

For Blake and Kierkegaard, both devout in their very different ways, the prime enemy of faith is not the professed atheist but the unconscious one. Religious institutions, simply as such, are anti-religious: the conventional believer clings to his church in proportion to his own lack of real faith and his secret commitment to an irreligious secular world. Blake ridicules the nominal Christian whose recital of the Lord's Prayer is actually a worship of material power. Kierkegaard flails at the hypocrites of "Christendom"—his word for the publicly established play-acting that supplants private acts of devotion. Both of these kinds of religious decadence—materialism and mumbo-jumbo—enter into Dostoevsky's horrific image of the Grand Inquisitor. In Ivan's story of the Inquisitor in *The Brothers Karamazov*, Dostoevsky ironically permits an eloquent and sophisticated exponent of "Christendom" to defend his improvements upon Christianity. The Inquisitor explains to Christ, who has miraculously appeared in Spain, that men cannot endure the burden of personal faith. The freedom and responsibility of faith, which were what Christ offered them, have turned out to be beyond their powers; they require a secular institution to provide them with bodily food, to tyrannize over their consciences, to satisfy their craving for tangible signs of grace. The Grand Inquisitor stands not only for the Church as a worldly institution but also for all forms of secular rationalism, whether authoritarian or ostensibly liberal and humanitarian. Through him Dostoevsky frames the issues clearly: spiritual freedom or enslavement to the things of this world, religion or the disappearance of religion in a specious substitute.[1]

While Dostoevsky's alternative to secularized Christianity is a return to a primitive Christian experience of suffering and love, Blake calls for an explosive release of human poetic and prophetic genius, which he holds to be the real divinity. But the divine man is not the natural man. Nature is in league with the "corporeal" eye to conceal from us the spiritual world that we would otherwise see. The visionary imagination, independent of physical nature and the organs of sense, is the divinity in man. It is universally creative and subversive of codified morals, a kind of spiritual energy, and it is one with Christ. Like Christ, human genius is the eternal redeemer; like the eternal poetic power, Christ acts from impulse rather than from rules. Faith in Christ as the best of men is for Blake faith in the imagination as the best of man; there is no other God.[2]

Blake's revision of Christianity is so extreme that at many points he moves close to Nietzsche, who rejects Christianity entirely. Nietzsche would doubtless say that Blake is using an outmoded language to express an entirely new sense of human life, for his own starting point is the psychological fact that "God is dead"—that we no longer think in terms of a supernatural divinity, though many are not yet aware of this revolutionary change. The creative will of man has displayed itself in the destruction of the idea of God; now it must go on to destroy its own limitations and strive to project the Superman out of itself. The lingering on of Christianity is the great obstacle to human self-creation and the coming of the higher man. This particular religion is, and has always been, especially perverted. It suppresses instinctual life, exults in pity and passivity instead of the active will to power; its god is simply nonentity enthroned. Yet Nietzsche, the "hyperborean" prophet of the Superman, is himself full of religious fervor, and the Christian yearning for a savior reappears, strangely altered, in his dream of human self-overcoming. If Blake approaches Nietzsche to the extent that his God becomes Man, Nietzsche approaches Blake to the extent that his Superman becomes the image of a redeeming God.[3]

Arnold's idea of a "poetic" religion is based on a less exalted view of both poetry and religion than Blake entertains; and though he perceives, like Nietzsche, that the idea of God can no longer be invoked in the old way, he has no faith in a creative human will that is virtually divine. Religion, which once purported to be fact, is now only feeling, and it merges into another realm of objectless feelings—the realm of poetry. Art is thus the stronghold of rootless values, whether aesthetic or religious and moral, in a valueless

[1] For related selections from Blake, see Sections 1, 5, and 6; from Kierkegaard, Sections 7 and 8; from Dostoevsky, Sections 2 and 7. Compare the selection from Berdyaev in Section 4.

[2] Tolstoy's ethical art, based on brotherhood in God (Section 2), is a different form of the religion of humanity. Close to Tolstoy is the outlook of George Sand (Section 2).

[3] For related selections from Nietzsche, see Sections 1, 4, 5, 7, and 8.

world of sceptical science. But only by holding to such feelings of value can we remain human, and in this sense both poetry and religion are for the first time coming into their own. In a similar vein, Santayana looks back upon the original triumph of Christianity over paganism and declares that it was really an aesthetic triumph. Even in its heyday, the Christian revelation moved men because it was a masterful piece of imagery, a language that supremely revealed man to himself. Freed of all claims to extra-human reference, poetry and religion can be seen to have their function as "the moral autobiography of man."[4]

Writers like Lawrence and Gide also humanize and poetize religion, but they give a special turn to these strategies: they attempt to reinterpret Christ in a pre-Christian mode. They revive the pagan nature-worship that was long ago caught up into Christianity and transformed by it. This is their way of fixing upon the imaginative and vital energy celebrated by Blake and Nietzsche. Lawrence reports that two of the major Christian images—the Crucifixion and the Virgin Mother—have wholly lost their efficacy for the generation after the First World War. What is now relevant is the image of the Resurrection, and not of resurrection in heaven but of resurrection on earth, the pagan spring. Christ risen in the flesh is Lawrence's emblem for a triumph of the natural body and the instinctual and emotional life over the modern death-world of money and machines. That this is the essential Christ, according to Gide, is what Nietzsche failed to understand when he condemned Christianity. Gide undertakes his own exegesis of the Gospels in order to show that Christ proclaimed not an other-worldly salvation, but eternal life in this world. The true Christian, who has been submerged by the official creeds, is the joyful natural man.[5]

Paul Claudel, who strove for years to bring Gide around to orthodox Christianity, not only declares that Gide's idea of a "pagan sanctity" is a mockery of faith but also insists on the necessity of public Christian institutions. Art and beauty divorced from service of the Christian community are corrupt; individual speculation divorced from the service of God is sinful pride. Claudel speaks from the security of his own righteous life, but much the same orthodoxy is echoed by Baudelaire out of the depths of his despair. Baudelaire pictures the modern individualist as a nervous, cultivated, sensitive, but unproductive being whose aspirations, no better than hashish fantasies, become so megalomaniac as to make him believe in his own godhead.

More systematically, Maritain passes a sweeping judgment on modern secularism. It is heresy, and the root of the heresy lies in the philosophic

[4] Both the Blakean divine imagination and the poetized religion of Arnold and Santayana are related to the symbolist religion of art (Section 1). See especially the selections from Flaubert, Mallarmé, Rilke, Auden, and Stevens in that section and Flaubert's reply to George Sand in Section 2. Santayana's version of poetic religion comes close to some of the concepts of literary myth illustrated in Section 6.

[5] For related selections from Lawrence, see Sections 3, 5, and 7; from Gide, Sections 1, 3, and 7.

dream of Descartes—a dream of the self-intoxicated human reason. Cartesian rationalism is disjunctive, splitting up the world at every turn: God and man, mind and nature, thought and feeling.[6] Its aim has been to achieve human power, but its actual result has been ruinous in every dimension of life. To dissociate man from God, even with no anti-religious intent, is a self-defeating maneuver. It perverts the mind into a mere instrument working upon a mechanical nature; it desiccates the processes of thought and leaves the untended feelings to run riot. Only by virtue of man's metaphysical striving toward a transcendent God and by virtue of divine grace can there be any unity in the world or any worth in its various aspects. Reason alone cannot create a reasonable world. T. E. Hulme would agree, but with quite a different emphasis: he would want to add that there is no possibility of unity in earthly existence. While Maritain writes from a Catholic standpoint, Hulme's attitude is essentially Protestant. For him, the errors of modernism began not so much in Cartesian reason as in the Renaissance dream of universal harmony. Since the Renaissance, men have been trying to override the intrinsic oppositions between divinity and organic life, life and inorganic matter. A principle of discontinuity must be enforced; otherwise we mechanize life (the heresy of a misapplied physical science) or we vitalize God (the heretical religion of nature). In particular, Hulme would combat the modern confusion of the divine absolute with the fluid, merely relative world of organic things.[7] He foresees an abstract, highly stylized art, which will make use of inorganic forms to suggest the divinity beyond organic life.

Among modern theologians, Karl Barth is perhaps the most uncompromising in his determination to make no concessions whatsoever to secularism. He denounces all secularist influences as false gods, and he propounds the one God, the transcendent lawgiver, of a radical Protestant orthodoxy. The ideas and ideals that preoccupy us are simply idols, worshipped in the universities that are their appointed temples. In striking contrast to Barth, Paul Tillich would incorporate the entire burden of modern faithlessness within the Christian faith. He considers the sense of absurdity recorded by the existentialists to be a true gauge of the modern spirit,[8] and he holds that Christianity must build upon it rather than brush it aside. Religious meaning, in Tillich's theology, necessarily involves religious doubt, the experience of non-meaning; it is not static but dynamic, not a result but a process. For him, being includes non-being, and through non-being reveals itself; similarly, faith reveals itself through despair and the surmounting of despair.[9]

[6] Compare Whitehead's attack on Cartesian rationalism (Section 3).
[7] See "Organicism" in Section 3 and Hegel's immanent Spirit (Section 4).
[8] See the selections from Camus and Sartre in Section 8.
[9] Tillich recalls Kierkegaard's emphasis on the process or striving of faith, while Barth's doctrine is cognate to Kierkegaard's insistence on the wholly transcendent object of faith. Compare the selections from Kierkegaard in Section 8.

WILLIAM BLAKE

The Lord's Prayer Modernized

Doctor Thornton's Tory Translation, Translated out of its disguise in the Classical & Scotch languages into the vulgar English.

Our Father Augustus Ceasar, who art in these thy Substantial Astronomical Telescopic Heavens, Holiness to thy Name or Title, & reverence to thy Shadow. Thy Kingship come upon Earth first & then in Heaven. Give us day by day our Real Taxed Substantial Money bought Bread; deliver from the Holy Ghost whatever cannot be Taxed; for all is debts & Taxes between Caesar & us & one another; lead us not to read the Bible, but let our Bible be Virgil & Shakespeare; & deliver us from Poverty in Jesus, that Evil One. For thine is the Kingship, [or] Allegoric Godship, & the Power, or War, & the Glory, or Law, Ages after Ages in thy descendants; for God is only an Allegory of Kings & nothing Else.

Amen.

"Annotations to Dr. Thornton's 'New Translation of the Lord's Prayer'" [1827], *Complete Writings*, ed. Geoffrey Keynes, London, 1957, pp. 788-9; reprinted by permission of the Nonesuch Press.

SØREN KIERKEGAARD

A Hypocritical Generation

And now for the words of Christ to which I refer.

They are found in Matthew 23:29-33; Luke 11:47, 48; and they read as follows:

> Woe unto you, scribes and Pharisees, hypocrites! for ye build the sepulchers of the prophets and garnish the tombs of the righteous, and say, if we had been in the days of our fathers, we should not have

From Attack upon "Christendom" [1854-55], translated from the Danish by Walter Lowrie, Princeton, 1944, pp. 120-23. Copyright 1944 by Princeton University Press; reprinted by permission of the Princeton University Press.

been partakers with them in the blood of the prophets. Wherefore ye witness to yourselves, that ye are sons of them that slew the prophets. Fill up then the measure of your fathers. Ye serpents, ye offspring of vipers, how shall ye escape the judgment of hell?

Woe unto you! for ye build the tombs of the prophets, and your fathers killed them. So ye are witnesses and consent unto the works of your fathers: for they killed them, and ye build their tombs.

But what then is "Christendom"? Is not "Christendom" the most colossal attempt at serving God, not by following Christ, as He required, and suffering for the doctrine, but instead of that, by "building the sepulchers of the prophets and garnishing the tombs of the righteous" and saying, "If we had been in the days of our fathers, we should not have been partakers with them in the blood of the prophets"?

It is of this sort of divine service I used the expression that, in comparison with the Christianity of the New Testament, it is playing Christianity. The expression is essentially true and characterizes the thing perfectly. For what does it mean to play, when one reflects how the word must be understood in this connection? It means to imitate, to counterfeit, a danger when there is no danger, and to do it in such a way that the more art is applied to it, the more delusive the pretense is that the danger is present. So it is that soldiers play war on the parade grounds: there is no danger, one only pretends that there is, and the art essentially consists in making everything deceptive, just as if it were a matter of life and death. And thus Christianity is played in "Christendom." Artists in dramatic costumes make their appearance in artistic buildings—there really is no danger at all, anything but that: the teacher is a royal functionary, steadily promoted, making a career—and now he dramatically plays Christianity, in short, he plays comedy. He lectures about renunciation, but he himself is being steadily promoted; he teaches all that about despising worldly titles and rank, but he himself is making a career; he describes the glorious ones ("the prophets") who were killed, and the constant refrain is: If we had been in the days of our fathers, we should not have been partakers with them in the blood of the prophets—we who build their sepulchers and garnish their tombs. So they will not go so far even as to do what I have constantly, insistently and imploringly proposed, that they should at least be so truthful as to admit that they are not a bit better than those who killed the prophets. No, they take advantage of the circumstance that they are not in fact contemporary with them to assert mendaciously of themselves that they are far, far better than those who killed the prophets, entirely different beings from those monsters —they in fact build the sepulchers of the men so unjustly killed and garnish their tombs.

However, this expression, "to play Christianity," could not be used by the Authoritative Teacher; He has a different way of talking about it.

Christ calls it (O give heed!), He calls it "hypocrisy." And not only that, but He says (now shudder!), He says that this guilt of hypocrisy is as great, precisely as great a crime as that of killing the prophets, so it is blood-guilt. Yea, if one could question Him, He would perhaps make answer that this guilt of hypocrisy, precisely because it is adroitly hidden and deliberately carried on through a whole lifetime, is a greater crime than theirs who in an outburst of rage killed the prophets.

This then is the judgment, Christ's judgment upon "Christendom." Shudder; for if you do not, you are implicated in it. It is so deceptive: must not we be nice people, true Christians, we who build the sepulchers of the prophets and garnish the tombs of the righteous, must not we be nice people, especially in comparison with those monsters who killed them? And besides, what else shall we do? We surely cannot do more than be willing to give of our money to build churches, etc., not be stingy with the priest, and go ourselves to hear him. The New Testament answers: What thou shalt do is to follow Christ, to suffer, suffer for the doctrine; the divine service thou wouldst like to carry on is hypocrisy; what the priests, with family, live on is that thou art a hypocrite, or they live by making thee a hypocrite, by keeping thee a hypocrite.

"Your fathers killed them, and ye build their tombs: so ye are witnesses and consent unto the works of your fathers." Luke 11:48.

Yes, Sunday Christianity and the huge gang of tradesmen-priests may indeed become furious at such a speech, which with one single word closes all their shops, quashes all this royally authorized trade, and not only that, but warns against their divine worship as against blood-guilt.

However, it is Christ who speaks. So profoundly does hypocrisy inhere in human nature that just when the natural man feels at his best, has got a divine worship fixed up entirely to his own liking, Christ's judgment is heard: This is hypocrisy, it is blood-guilt. It is not true that while on weekdays thy life is worldliness, the good thing about thee is that after all on Sundays thou goest to church, the church of official Christianity. No, no, official Christianity is much worse than all thy weekday worldliness, it is hypocrisy, it is blood-guilt.

At the bottom of "Christendom" there is this truth, that man is a born hypocrite. The Christianity of the New Testament was truth. But man shrewdly and knavishly invented a new kind of Christianity which builds the sepulchers of the prophets and garnishes the tombs of the righteous, and says, "If we had been in the days of our fathers." And this is what Christ calls blood-guilt.

What Christianity wants is . . . the following of Christ. What man does not want is suffering, least of all the kind of suffering which is properly the Christian sort, suffering at the hands of men. So he dispenses with "following," and consequently with suffering, the peculiarly Christian suffering, and then builds the sepulchers of the prophets. That is one thing. And then he says, lyingly before God, to himself and to others, that he is better than those who killed the prophets. That is the second thing. Hypocrisy first and hypocrisy last—and according to the judgment of Christ . . . blood-guilt.

Imagine that the people are assembled in a church in Christendom, and Christ suddenly enters the assembly. What dost thou think He would do?

He would turn upon the *teachers* (for of the *congregation* He would judge as He did of yore, that they were led astray), He would turn upon them who "walk in long robes," tradesmen, jugglers, who have made God's house, if not a den of robbers, at least a shop, a peddler's stall, and would say, "Ye hypocrites, ye serpents, ye generation of vipers"; and likely as of yore He would make a whip of small cords and drive them out of the temple.

Thou who readest this, if thou knowest nothing more about Christianity than is to be learned from the Sunday twaddle—I am thoroughly prepared for thee to be shocked at me, as though I were guilty of the cruelest mockery of God by representing Christ in this way, "putting such words into his mouth: serpents, generation of vipers. That is so dreadful. These indeed are words one never hears from the mouth of a cultivated person; and to make Him repeat them several times, that is so dreadfully common; and to turn Christ into a man who uses violence."

My friend, thou canst look it up in the New Testament. But when what has to be attained by preaching and teaching Christianity is an agreeable, a pleasurable life in a position of prestige, then the picture of Christ must be altered considerably. As for "garnishing"—no, there will be no sparing on that: gold, diamonds, rubies, etc. No, the priest is glad to see that and makes men believe that this is Christianity. But severity, the severity which is inseparable from the seriousness of eternity, that must go. Christ thus becomes a languishing figure, the impersonation of insipid human kindliness.

F. M. DOSTOEVSKY

Christ and the Grand Inquisitor

"Even this must have a preface—that is, a literary preface," laughed Ivan, "and I am a poor hand at making one. You see, my action takes place in the sixteenth century, and at that time, as you probably learned at school, it was customary in poetry to bring down heavenly powers on earth. Not to speak of Dante, in France, clerks, as well as the monks in the monasteries, used to give regular performances in which the Madonna, the saints, the angels, Christ, and God Himself were brought on the stage. In those days it was done in all simplicity. In Victor Hugo's *Notre Dame de Paris* an edifying and gratuitous spectacle was provided for the people in the Hôtel de Ville of Paris in the reign of Louis XI in honour of the birth of the dauphin. It was called *Le bon jugement de la très sainte et gracieuse Vierge Marie*, and she appears herself on the stage and pronounces her *bon jugement*. Similar plays, chiefly from the Old Testament, were occasionally performed in Moscow too, up to the times of Peter the Great. But besides plays there were all sorts of legends and ballads scattered about the world, in which the saints and angels and all the powers of Heaven took part when required. In our monasteries the monks busied themselves in translating, copying, and even composing such poems—and even under the Tatars. There is, for instance, one such poem (of course, from the Greek), 'The Wanderings of Our Lady through Hell,' with descriptions as bold as Dante's. Our Lady visits Hell, and the Archangel Michael leads her through the torments. She sees the sinners and their punishments. There she sees among others one noteworthy set of sinners in a burning lake; some of

From *The Brothers Karamazov* [1880], translated from the Russian by Constance Garnett, first published in London by Heinemann in 1912, pp. 259-71; reprinted by permission of The Macmillan Company and William Heinemann Ltd.

them sink to the bottom of the lake so that they can't swim out, and 'these God forgets'—an expression of extraordinary depth and force. And so Our Lady, shocked and weeping, falls before the throne of God and begs for mercy for all in Hell—for all she has seen there, indiscriminately. Her conversation with God is immensely interesting. She beseeches Him, she will not desist, and when God points to the hands and feet of her Son, nailed to the Cross, and asks: 'How can I forgive His tormentors?' she bids all the saints, all the martyrs, all the angels and archangels to fall down with her and pray for mercy on all without distinction. It ends by her winning from God a respite of suffering every year from Good Friday till Trinity day, and the sinners at once raise a cry of thankfulness from Hell, chanting: 'Thou art just, O Lord, in this judgment.' Well, my poem would have been of that kind if it had appeared at that time. He comes on the scene in my poem, but He says nothing, only appears and passes on. Fifteen centuries have passed since He promised to come in His glory, fifteen centuries since His prophet wrote, 'Behold, I come quickly'; 'Of that day and that hour knoweth no man, neither the Son, but the Father,' as He Himself predicted on earth. But humanity awaits him with the same faith and with the same love. Oh, with greater faith, for it is fifteen centuries since man has ceased to see signs from Heaven.

> No signs from Heaven come to-day
> To add to what the heart doth say.

There was nothing left but faith in what the heart doth say. It is true there were many miracles in those days. There were saints who performed miraculous cures; some holy people, according to their biographies, were visited by the Queen of Heaven herself. But the devil did not slumber, and doubts were already arising among men of the truth of these miracles. And just then there appeared in the north of Germany a terrible new heresy. 'A huge star like to a torch' (that is, to a church) 'fell on the sources of the waters and they became bitter.' These heretics began blasphemously denying miracles. But those who remained faithful were all the more ardent in their faith. The tears of humanity rose up to Him as before, awaited His coming, loved Him, hoped for Him, yearned to suffer and die for Him as before. And so many ages mankind had prayed with faith and fervour: 'O Lord our God, hasten Thy coming,' so many ages called upon Him, that in His infinite mercy He deigned to come down to His servants. Before that day He had come down, He had visited some holy men, martyrs and hermits, as is written in their 'Lives.' Among us, Tyutchev, with absolute faith in the truth of his words, bore witness that:

> Bearing the Cross, in slavish dress
> Weary and worn, the Heavenly King
> Our mother, Russia, came to bless,
> And through our land went wandering.

And that certainly was so, I assure you.

"And behold, He deigned to appear for a moment to the people, to the tortured, suffering people, sunk in iniquity but loving Him like children. My story is laid in Spain, in Seville, in the most terrible time of the Inquisition, when fires were lighted every day to the glory of God, and 'in the splendid *auto de fé* the wicked heretics were burnt.' Oh, of course, this was not the coming in which He will appear according to His promise at the end of time in all His heavenly glory, and which will be sudden 'as lightning flashing from east to west.' No, He visited His children only for a moment, and there where the flames were crackling round the heretics. In His infinite mercy He came once more among men in that human shape in which He walked among men for three years fifteen centuries ago. He came down to the 'hot pavements' of the southern town in which on the day before almost a hundred heretics had, *ad majorem gloriam Dei*, been burnt by the cardinal, the Grand Inquisitor, in a magnificent *auto de fé*, in the presence of the king, the court, the knights, the cardinals, the most charming ladies of the court, and the whole population of Seville.

"He came softly, unobserved, and yet, strange to say, everyone recognised Him. That might be one of the best passages in the poem. I mean, why they recognised Him. The people are irresistibly drawn to Him, they surround Him, they flock about Him, follow Him. He moves silently in their midst with a gentle smile of infinite compassion. The sun of love burns in His heart, light and power shine from His eyes, and their radiance, shed on the people, stirs their hearts with responsive love. He holds out His hands to them, blesses them, and a healing virtue comes from contact with Him, even with His garments. An old man in the crowd, blind from childhood, cries out, 'O Lord, heal me and I shall see Thee!' and, as it were, scales fall from his eyes and the blind man sees Him. The crowd weeps and kisses the earth under His feet. Children throw flowers before Him, sing, and cry hosannah. 'It is He—it is He!' all repeat. 'It must be He, it can be no one but Him!' He stops at the steps of the Seville cathedral at the moment when the weeping mourners are bringing in a little open white coffin. In it lies a child of seven, the only daughter of a prominent citizen. The dead child lies hidden in flowers. 'He will raise your child,' the crowd shouts to the weeping mother. The priest, coming to meet the coffin, looks perplexed, and frowns, but the mother of the dead child throws herself at His feet with a wail. 'If it is Thou, raise my child!' she cries holding out her hands to Him. The procession halts, the coffin is laid on the steps at His feet. He looks with compassion, and His lips once more softly pronounce, 'Maiden, arise!' and the maiden arises. The little girl sits up in the coffin and looks round, smiling with wide-open wondering eyes, holding a bunch of white roses they had put in her hand.

"There are cries, sobs, confusion among the people, and at that moment the cardinal himself, the Grand Inquisitor, passes by the cathedral. He is an old man, almost ninety, tall and erect, with a withered face and sunken eyes, in which there is still a gleam of light. He is not dressed in his gorgeous cardinal's robes, as he was the day before, when he was burning the enemies of the Roman Church —at that moment he was wearing his coarse, old, monk's cassock. At a distance behind him come his gloomy assistants and slaves and the 'holy guard.' He stops at the sight of the crowd and watches it from a distance. He sees everything; he sees them set the coffin down at His feet, sees the child rise up, and his face darkens. He knits his thick grey brows and his eyes gleam with a sinister fire. He holds out his finger and bids the guards take Him. And such is his power, so completely are the people cowed into submission and trembling obedience to him, that the crowd immediately make way for the guards, and in the midst of death-like silence they lay hands on Him and lead Him away. The crowd instantly bows down to the earth, like one man, before the old inquisitor. He blesses the people in silence and passes on. The guards lead their prisoner to the close, gloomy vaulted prison in the ancient palace of the Holy Inquisition and shut Him in it. The day passes and is followed by the dark, burning 'breathless' night of Seville. The air is 'fragrant with laurel and lemon.' In the pitch darkness the iron door of the prison is suddenly opened and the Grand Inquisitor himself comes in with a light in his hand. He is alone; the door is closed at once behind him. He stands in the doorway and for a minute or two gazes into His face. At last he goes up slowly, sets the light on the table and speaks.

" 'Is it Thou? Thou?' but receiving no answer, he adds at once: 'Don't answer, be silent. What canst Thou say, indeed? I know too well what Thou wouldst say. And Thou hast no right to add anything to what Thou hadst said of old. Why, then, art Thou come to hinder us? For Thou hast come to hinder us, and Thou knowest that. But dost Thou know what will be to-morrow? I know not who Thou art and care not to know whether it is Thou or only a semblance of Him, but to-morrow I shall condemn Thee and burn Thee at the stake as the worst of heretics. And the very people who have to-day kissed Thy feet, to-morrow at the faintest sign from me will rush to heap up the embers of Thy fire. Knowest Thou that? Yes, maybe Thou knowest it,' he added with thoughtful penetration, never for a moment taking his eyes off the Prisoner."

"I don't quite understand, Ivan. What does it mean?" Alyosha, who had been listening in silence, said with a smile. "Is it simply a wild fantasy, or a mistake on the part of the old man—some impossible *quid pro quo?*"

"Take it as the last," said Ivan, laughing, "if you are so corrupted by modern realism and can't stand anything fantastic. If you like it to be a case of mistaken identity, let it be so. It is true," he went on laughing, "the old man was ninety, and he might well be crazy over his set idea. He might have been struck by the appearance of the Prisoner. It might, in fact, be simply his ravings, the delusion of an old man of ninety, over-excited by the *auto de fé* of a hundred heretics the day before. But does it matter to us, after all, whether it was a mistake of identity or a wild fantasy? All that matters is that the old man should speak out, should speak openly of what he has thought in silence for ninety years."

"And the Prisoner too is silent? Does He look at him and not say a word?"

"That's inevitable in any case," Ivan laughed again. "The old man has told Him He hasn't the right to add anything to what He has said of old. One may say it is the most fundamental feature of Roman Catholicism, in my opinion at least. 'All has been given by Thee to the Pope,' they say, 'and all, therefore, is still in the Pope's hands, and there is no need for Thee to come now at all. Thou must not meddle for the time, at least.' That's how they speak and write too—the Jesuits, at any rate. I have read it myself in the works of their theologians. 'Hast Thou the right to reveal to us one of the mysteries of that world from which Thou hast come?' my old man asks Him, and answers the question for Him. 'No, Thou hast not; that Thou mayest not add to what has been said of old, and mayest not take from men the freedom which Thou didst exalt when Thou wast on earth. Whatsoever Thou revealest anew will encroach on men's freedom of faith; for it will be manifest as a miracle, and the freedom of their faith was dearer to Thee than anything in those days fifteen hundred years ago. Didst Thou not often say then, "I will make you free"? But now Thou hast seen these "free" men,' the old man adds suddenly, with a pensive smile. 'Yes, we've paid dearly for it,' he goes on, looking sternly at Him, 'but at last we have completed that work in Thy name. For fifteen centuries we have been wrestling with Thy freedom, but now it is ended and over for good. Dost Thou not believe that it's over for good? Thou lookest meekly at me and deignest not even to be wroth with me. But let me tell Thee that now, to-day, people are more persuaded than ever that they have perfect freedom, yet they have brought their freedom to us and laid it humbly at our feet. But that has been our doing. Was this what Thou didst? Was this Thy freedom?' "

"I don't understand again," Alyosha broke in. "Is he ironical, is he jesting?"

"Not a bit of it! He claims it as a merit for himself and his Church that at last they have vanquished freedom and have done so to make men happy. 'For now' (he is speaking of the Inquisition, of course) 'for the first time it has become possible to think of the happiness of men. Man was created a rebel; and how can rebels be happy? Thou wast warned,' he says to Him. 'Thou hast had no lack of admonitions and warnings, but Thou didst not listen to those warnings; Thou didst reject the only way by which men might be made happy. But, fortunately, departing Thou didst hand on the work to us. Thou hast promised, Thou hast established by Thy word, Thou hast given to us the right to bind and to unbind, and now, of course, Thou canst not think of taking it away. Why, then, hast Thou come to hinder us?' "

"And what's the meaning of 'no lack of admonitions and warnings'?" asked Alyosha.

"Why, that's the chief part of what the old man must say."

" 'The wise and dread Spirit, the spirit of self-destruction and non-existence,' the old man goes on, 'the great spirit talked with Thee in the wilderness, and we are told in the books that he "tempted" Thee. Is that so? And could anything truer be said than what he revealed to Thee in three questions and what Thou didst reject, and what in the books is called "the temptation"? And yet if there has ever been on earth a real stupendous miracle, it took place on that day, on the day of the three temptations. The statement of those three questions was itself the miracle. If it were possible to imagine simply for the sake of argument that those three questions of the dread spirit had perished utterly from the books, and that we had to restore them and to invent them anew, and to do so had gathered together all the wise men of the earth—rulers, chief priests, learned men, philosophers, poets—and had set them the task to invent three questions, such as would not only fit the occasion but express in three words, three human phrases, the whole future history of the world and of humanity—dost Thou believe that all the wisdom of the earth united could have invented anything in depth and force equal to the three questions which were actually put to Thee then by the wise and mighty spirit in the wilderness? From those questions alone, from the miracle of their statement, we can see that we have here to do not with the fleeting human intelligence but with the absolute and eternal. For in those three questions the whole subsequent history of mankind is, as it were, brought together into one whole, and foretold, and in them are united all the unsolved historical contradictions of human nature. At the time it could not be so clear, since the future was unknown; but now that fifteen hundred years have passed, we see that everything in those three questions was so justly divined and foretold, and has been so truly fulfilled, that nothing can be added to them or taken from them.

" 'Judge Thyself who was right—Thou or he who questioned Thee then? Remember the first question; its meaning, in other words, was this: "Thou wouldst go into the world, and art going with empty hands, with some promise of freedom which men in their simplicity and their natural unruliness cannot even understand, which they fear and dread—for nothing has ever been more insupportable for a man and a human society than freedom. But seest Thou these stones in this parched and barren wilderness? Turn them into bread, and mankind will run after Thee like a flock of sheep, grateful and obedient, though for ever trembling, lest Thou withdraw Thy hand and deny them Thy bread." But Thou wouldst not deprive man of freedom and didst reject the offer, thinking, what is that freedom worth, if obedience is bought with bread? Thou didst reply that man lives not by bread alone. But dost Thou know that for the sake of that earthly bread the spirit of the earth will rise up against Thee and will strive with Thee and overcome Thee, and all will follow him, crying, "Who can compare with this beast? He has given us fire from heaven!" Dost Thou know that the ages will pass, and humanity will proclaim by the lips of their sages that there is no crime, and therefore no sin; there is only hunger? "Feed men, and then ask of them virtue!" that's what they'll write on the banner, which they will raise against Thee, and with which they will destroy Thy temple. Where Thy temple stood will rise a new building; the terrible tower of Babel will be built again, and though, like the one of old, it will not be finished, yet Thou mightest have prevented that new tower and have cut short the sufferings of men for a thousand years; for they will come back to us after a thousand years of agony with their tower. They will seek us again, hidden underground in the catacombs, for we shall be again persecuted and tortured. They will find us and cry to us, "Feed us, for those who have promised us fire from heaven haven't given it!" And then we shall finish building their tower, for he finishes the building who feeds them. And we alone shall feed them in Thy name, declaring falsely that it is Thy name. Oh, never, never can they feed themselves without us! No science will give them bread so long as they remain free. In the end they will lay their freedom at our feet, and say to us, "Make us your slaves, but feed us." They will understand themselves, at least, that freedom and bread enough for all are inconceivable together, for never, never will they be able to share between them! They will be convinced, too, that they can never be free, for they are weak, vicious, worthless and rebellious. Thou didst promise them the bread of Heaven, but, I repeat again, can it compare with earthly bread in the eyes of the weak, ever-sinful and ignoble race of man? And if for the sake of the bread of Heaven thousands and tens of thousands shall follow Thee, what is to become of the millions and tens of thousands of millions of creatures who will not have the strength to forgo the earthly bread for the sake of the heavenly? Or dost Thou care only for the tens of thousands of the great and strong, while the millions, numerous as the sands of the sea, who are weak but love Thee, must exist only for the sake of the great and strong? No, we care for the weak too. They are sinful and rebellious, but in the end they too will become obedient. They will marvel at us and look on us as gods, because we are ready to endure the freedom which they have found so dreadful and to rule over them—so awful it will seem to them to be free. But we shall tell them that we are Thy servants and rule them in Thy name. We shall deceive them again, for we will not let Thee come to us again. That deception will be our suffering, for we shall be forced to lie.

" 'This is the significance of the first question in the wilderness, and this is what Thou hast rejected for the sake of that freedom which Thou hast exalted above everything. Yet in this question lies hid the great secret of this world. Choosing "bread," Thou wouldst have satisfied the universal and everlasting craving of humanity—to find someone to worship. So long as man remains free he strives for nothing so incessantly and so painfully as to find someone to worship. But man seeks to worship what is established beyond dispute, so that all men would agree at once to worship it. For these pitiful creatures are concerned not only to find what one or the other can worship, but to find something that all would believe in and worship; what is essential is that all may be *together* in it. This craving for *community* of worship is the chief misery of every man individually and of all humanity from the beginning of time. For the sake of common worship they've slain each other with the sword. They have set up gods and challenged one another, "Put away your gods and come and worship ours, or we will kill you and your gods!" And so it will be to the end of the world, even when gods disappear from the earth; they will fall down before idols just the same. Thou didst know, Thou couldst not but have known, this fundamental secret of human nature, but Thou didst reject the one infallible banner which was offered Thee to make all men bow down to Thee alone—the banner of earthly bread; and Thou hast rejected it for the sake of freedom and the bread of Heaven. Behold what Thou didst further. And all again in the name of freedom! I tell Thee that man is tormented by no greater anxiety than to find someone quickly to whom he can hand over that gift of freedom with which the ill-fated creature is born. But only one who can appease their conscience can take over their freedom. In bread there was offered Thee an invincible banner; give bread, and man will worship thee, for nothing is more certain than bread. But if someone else gains possession of his conscience—oh! then he will cast away Thy bread and follow after him who has ensnared his conscience. In that Thou wast right. For the secret of man's being is not only to live but to have something to live for. Without a stable conception of the object of life, man would not consent to go on living, and would rather destroy himself than remain on earth, though he had bread in abundance. That is true. But what happened? Instead of taking men's freedom from them, Thou didst make it greater than ever! Didst Thou forget that man prefers peace, and even death, to freedom of choice in the knowledge of good and evil? Nothing is more seductive for man than his freedom of conscience, but nothing is a greater cause of suffering. And behold, instead of giving a firm foundation for setting the conscience of man at rest for ever, Thou dist choose all that is exceptional, vague and enigmatic; Thou didst choose what was utterly beyond the strength of men, acting as though Thou didst not love them at all—Thou who didst come to give Thy life for them! Instead of taking possession of men's freedom, Thou didst increase it, and burdened the spiritual kingdom of mankind with its sufferings for ever. Thou didst desire man's free love, that he should follow Thee freely, enticed and taken captive by Thee. In place of the rigid ancient law, man must hereafter with free heart decide for himself what is good and what is evil, having only Thy image before him as his guide. But didst Thou not know that he would at last reject even Thy image and Thy truth, if he is weighed down with the fearful burden of free choice? They will cry aloud at last that the truth is not in Thee, for they could not have been left in greater confusion and suffering than Thou hast caused, laying upon them so many cares and unanswerable problems.

" 'So that, in truth, Thou didst Thyself lay the foundation for the destruction of Thy kingdom, and no one is more to blame for it. Yet what was offered Thee? There are three powers, three powers alone, able to conquer and to hold captive for ever the conscience of these impotent rebels for their happiness—those forces are miracle, mystery and authority. Thou hast rejected all three and hast set the example for doing so. When the wise and dread spirit set Thee on the pinnacle of the temple and said to Thee, "If Thou wouldst know whether Thou art the Son of God then cast Thyself down, for it is written: the angels shall hold him up lest he fall and bruise himself, and Thou shalt know then whether Thou art the Son of God and shalt prove then how great is Thy faith in Thy Father." But Thou didst refuse and wouldst not cast Thyself down. Oh! of course, Thou didst proudly and well, like God; but the weak, unruly race of men, are they gods? Oh, Thou didst know then that in taking one step, in making one movement to cast Thyself down, Thou wouldst be tempting God and have lost all Thy faith in Him, and wouldst have been dashed to pieces against that earth which Thou didst come to save. And the wise spirit that tempted Thee would have rejoiced. But I ask again, are there many like Thee? And couldst Thou believe for one moment that men, too, could face such a temptation? Is the nature of men such, that they can reject miracle, and at the great moments of their life, the moments of their deepest, most agonising spiritual difficulties, cling only to the free verdict of the heart? Oh, Thou didst know that Thy deed would be recorded in books, would be handed down to remote times and the utmost ends of the earth, and Thou didst hope that man, following Thee, would cling to God and not ask for a miracle. But Thou didst not know that when man rejects miracle he rejects God too; for man seeks not so much God as the miraculous. And as man cannot bear to be without the miraculous, he will create new miracles of his own for himself, and will worship deeds of sorcery and witchcraft, though he might be a hundred times over a rebel, heretic and infidel. Thou didst not come down from the Cross when they shouted to Thee, mocking and reviling Thee, "Come down from the Cross and we will believe that Thou art He." Thou didst not come down, for again Thou wouldst not enslave man by a miracle, and didst crave faith given freely, not based on miracle. Thou didst crave for free love and not the base raptures of the slave before the might that has overawed him for ever. But Thou didst think too highly of men therein, for they are slaves, of course, though rebellious by nature. Look round and judge; fifteen centuries have passed, look upon them. Whom hast Thou raised up to Thyself? I swear, man is weaker and baser by nature than Thou hast believed him! Can he, can he do what Thou didst? By showing him so much respect, Thou didst, as it were, cease to feel for him, for Thou didst ask far too much from him—Thou who hast loved him more than Thyself! Respecting him less, Thou wouldst have asked less of him. That would have been more like love, for his burden would have been lighter. He is weak and vile. What though he is everywhere now rebelling against our power, and proud of his rebellion? It is the pride of a child and a schoolboy. They are little children rioting and barring out the teacher at school. But their childish delight will end; it will cost them dear. They will cast down temples and drench the earth with blood. But they will see at last, the foolish children, that, though they are rebels, they are impotent rebels, unable to keep up their own rebellion. Bathed in their foolish tears, they will recognise at last that He who created them rebels must have meant to mock at them. They will say this in despair, and their utterance will be a blasphemy which will make them more unhappy still, for man's nature cannot bear blasphemy, and in the end always avenges it on itself. And so unrest, confusion and unhappiness—that is the present lot of man after Thou didst bear so much for their freedom! Thy great prophet tells, in vision and in image, that he saw all those who took part in the first resurrection and that there were of each tribe twelve thousand. But if there were so many of them, they must have been not men but gods. They had borne Thy cross, they had endured scores of years in the barren, hungry wilderness, living upon locusts and roots—and Thou mayest indeed point with pride at those children of freedom, of free love, of free and splendid sacrifice for Thy name. But remember that they were only some thousands; and what of the rest? And how are the other weak ones to blame, because they could not endure what the strong have endured? How is the weak soul to blame that it is unable to receive such terrible gifts? Canst Thou have simply come to the elect and for the elect? But if so, it is a mystery and we cannot understand it. And if it is a mystery, we too have a right to preach a mystery, and to teach them that it's not the free judgment of their hearts, not love that matters, but a mystery which they must follow blindly, even against their conscience. So we have done. We have corrected Thy work and have founded it upon *miracle, mystery* and *authority*. And men rejoiced that they were again led like sheep, and that the terrible gift that had brought them such suffering was, at last, lifted from their hearts. Were we right teaching them this? Speak! Did we not love mankind, so meekly acknowledging their feebleness, lovingly lightening their burden, and permitting their weak nature even sin with our sanction? Why hast Thou come now to hinder us? And why dost Thou look silently and searchingly at me with Thy mild eyes? Be angry. I don't want Thy love, for I love Thee not. And what use is it for me to hide anything from Thee? Don't I know to Whom I am speaking? All that I can say is known to Thee already. And is it for me to conceal from Thee our mystery? Perhaps it is Thy will to hear it from my lips. Listen, then. We are not working with Thee but with *him*—that is our mystery. It's long—eight centuries—since we have been on *his* side and not on Thine. Just eight centuries ago we took from him what Thou didst reject with scorn, that last gift he offered Thee, showing Thee all the kingdoms of the earth. We took from him Rome and the sword of Caesar, and proclaimed ourselves sole rulers of the earth, though hitherto we have not been able to complete our work. But whose fault is that? Oh, the work is only beginning, but it has begun. It has long to await completion and the earth has yet much to suffer, but we shall triumph and shall be Caesars, and then we shall plan the universal happiness of man. But Thou mightest have taken even then the sword of Caesar. Why didst Thou reject that last gift? Hadst Thou accepted that last counsel of the mighty spirit, Thou wouldst have accomplished all that man seeks on earth—that is, someone to worship, someone to keep his conscience, and some means of uniting all in one unanimous and harmonious ant-heap, for the craving for universal unity is the third and last anguish of men. Mankind as a whole has always striven to organise a universal state. There have been many great nations with great histories, but the more highly they were developed the more unhappy they were, for they felt more acutely than other people the craving for world-wide union. The great conquerors, Timours and Ghenghis Khans, whirled like hurricanes over the face of the earth striving to subdue its people, and they too were but the unconscious expression of the same craving for universal unity. Hadst Thou taken the world and Caesar's purple, Thou wouldst have founded the universal state and have given universal peace. For who can rule men if not he who holds their conscience and their bread in his hands? We have taken the sword of Caesar, and in taking it, of course have rejected Thee and followed *him*. Oh, ages are yet to come of the confusion of free thought, of their science and cannibalism. For having begun to build their tower of Babel without us, they will end, of course, with cannibalism. But then the beast will crawl to us and lick our feet and spatter them with tears of blood. And we shall sit upon the beast and raise the cup, and on it will be written, "Mystery." But then, and only then, the reign of peace and happiness will come for men. Thou art proud of Thine elect, but Thou hast only the elect, while we give rest to all. And besides, how many of those elect, those mighty ones who could become elect, have grown weary waiting for Thee, and have transferred and will transfer the powers of their spirit and the warmth of their heart to the other camp, and end by raising their *free* banner against Thee! Thou didst Thyself lift up that banner. But with us all will be happy and will no more rebel nor destroy one another as under Thy freedom. Oh, we shall persuade them that they will only become free when they renounce their freedom to us and submit to us. And shall we be right or shall we be lying? They will be convinced that we are right, for they will remember the horrors of slavery and confusion to which Thy freedom brought them. Freedom, free thought and science will lead them into such straits and will bring them face to face with such marvels and insoluble mysteries, that some of them, the fierce and rebellious, will destroy themselves; others, rebellious but weak, will destroy one another, while the rest, weak and unhappy, will crawl fawning to our feet and whine to us: "Yes, you were right, you alone possess His mystery, and we come back to you, save us from ourselves!"

" 'Receiving bread from us, they will see clearly that we take the bread made by their hands from them, to give it to them, without any miracle. They will see that we do not change the stones to bread, but in truth they will be more thankful for taking it from our hands than for the bread itself! For they will remember only too well that in old days, without our help, even the bread they made turned to stones in their hands, while since they have come back to us, the very stones have turned to bread in their hands. Too, too well will they know the value of complete submission! And until men know that, they will be unhappy. Who is most to blame for their not knowing it, speak? Who scattered the flock and sent it astray on unknown paths? But the flock will come together again and will submit once more, and then it will be once for all. Then we shall give them the quiet humble happiness of weak creatures such as they are by nature. Oh, we shall persuade them at last not to be proud, for Thou didst lift them up and thereby taught them to be proud. We shall show them that they are weak, that they are only pitiful children, but that childlike happiness is the sweetest of all. They will become timid and will look to us and huddle close to us in fear, as chicks to the hen. They will marvel at us and will be awestricken before us, and will be proud at our being so powerful and clever, that we have been able to subdue such a turbulent flock of thousands of millions. They will tremble impotently before our wrath, their minds will grow fearful, they will be quick to shed tears like women and children, but they will be just as ready at a sign from us to pass to laughter and rejoicing, to happy mirth and childish song. Yes, we shall set them to work, but in their leisure hours we shall make their life like a child's game, with children's songs and innocent dance. Oh, we shall allow them every sin, they are weak and helpless, and they will love us like children because we allow them to sin. We shall tell them that every sin will be expiated, if it is done with our permission, that we allow them to sin because we love them, and the punishment for these sins we take upon ourselves. And we shall take it upon ourselves, and they will adore us as their saviours who have taken on themselves their sins before God. And they will have no secrets from us. We shall allow or forbid them to live with their wives and mistresses, to have or not to have children—according to whether they have been obedient or disobedient—and they will submit to us gladly and cheerfully. The most painful secrets of their conscience, all, all they will bring to us, and we shall have an answer for all. And they will be glad to believe our answer, for it will save them from the great anxiety and terrible agony they endure at present in making a free decision for themselves. And all will be happy, all the millions of creatures except the hundred thousand who rule over them. For only we, we who guard the mystery, shall be unhappy. There will be thousands of millions of happy babes, and a hundred thousand sufferers who have taken upon themselves the curse of the knowledge of good and evil. Peacefully they will die, peacefully they will expire in Thy name, and beyond the grave they will find nothing but death. But we shall keep the secret, and for their happiness we shall allure them with the reward of heaven and eternity. Though if there were anything in the other world, it certainly would not be for such as they. It is prophesied that Thou wilt come again in victory, Thou wilt come with Thy chosen, the proud and strong, but we will say that they have only saved themselves, but we have saved all. We are told that the harlot who sits upon the beast, and holds in her hands the *mystery*, shall be put to shame, that the weak will rise up again, and will rend her royal purple and will strip naked her loathsome body. But then I will stand up and point out to Thee the thousand millions of happy children who have known no sin. And we who have taken their sins upon us for their happiness will stand up before Thee and say: "Judge us if Thou canst and darest." Know that I fear Thee not. Know that I too have been in the wilderness, I too have lived on roots and locusts, I too prized the freedom with which Thou hast blessed men, and I too was striving to stand among Thy elect, among the strong and powerful, thirsting "to make up the number." But I awakened and would not serve madness. I turned back and joined the ranks of those *who have corrected Thy work*. I left the proud and went back to the humble, for the happiness of the humble. What I say to Thee will come to pass, and our dominion will be built up. I repeat, to-morrow Thou shalt see that obedient flock who at a sign from me will hasten to heap up the hot cinders about the pile on which I shall burn Thee for coming to hinder us. For if anyone has ever deserved our fires, it is Thou. To-morrow I shall burn Thee. Dixi.' "

Ivan stopped. He was carried away as he talked and spoke with excitement; when he had finished, he suddenly smiled.

Alyosha had listened in silence; towards the end he was greatly moved and seemed several times on the point of interrupting, but restrained himself. Now his words came with a rush.

"But . . . that's absurd!" he cried, flushing. "Your poem is in praise of Jesus, not in blame of Him—as you meant it to be. And who will believe you about freedom? Is that the way to understand it? That's not the idea of it in the Orthodox Church . . . That's Rome, and not even the whole of Rome, it's false— those are the worst of the Catholics, the Inquisitors, the Jesuits! . . . And there could not be such a fantastic creature as your Inquisitor. What are these sins of mankind they take on themselves? Who are these keepers of the mystery who have taken some curse upon themselves for the happiness of mankind? When have they been seen? We know the Jesuits, they are spoken ill of, but surely they are not what you describe? They are not that at all, not at all. . . . They are simply the Romish army for the earthly sovereignty of the world in the future, with the Pontiff of Rome for Emperor . . . that's their ideal, but there's no sort of mystery or lofty melancholy about it. . . . It's simple lust of power, of filthy earthly gain, of domination—something like a universal serfdom with them as masters—that's all they stand for. They don't even believe in God, perhaps. Your suffering inquisitor is a mere fantasy."

"Stay, stay," laughed Ivan, 'how hot you are! A fantasy, you say, let it be so! Of course it's a fantasy. But allow me to say: do you really think that the Roman Catholic movement of the last centuries is actually nothing but the lust of power, of filthy earthly gain? Is that Father Païssy's teaching?"

"No, no, on the contrary, Father Païssy did once say something rather the same as you . . . but of course it's not the same, not a bit the same," Alyosha hastily corrected himself.

"A precious admission, in spite of your 'not a bit the same.' I ask you why your Jesuits and Inquisitors have united simply for vile material gain? Why can there not be among them one martyr oppressed by great sorrow and loving humanity? You see, only suppose that there was one such man among all those who desire nothing but filthy material gain—if there's only one like my old inquisitor, who had himself eaten roots in the desert and made frenzied efforts to subdue his flesh to make himself free and perfect. But yet all his life he loved humanity, and suddenly his eyes were opened, and he saw that it is no great moral blessedness to attain perfection and freedom, if at the same time one gains the conviction that millions of God's creatures have been created as a mockery, that they will never be capable of using their freedom, that these poor rebels can never turn into giants to complete the tower, that it was not for such geese that the great idealist dreamt his dream of harmony. Seeing all that he turned back and joined—the clever people. Surely that could have happened?"

"Joined whom, what clever people?" cried Alyosha, completely carried **away.**

"They have no such great cleverness and no mysteries and secrets. . . . Perhaps nothing but Atheism, that's all their secret. Your inquisitor does not believe in God, that's his secret!"

"What if it is so? At last you have guessed it. It's perfectly true, it's true that that's the whole secret, but isn't that suffering, at least for a man like that, who has wasted his whole life in the desert and yet could not shake off his incurable love of humanity? In his old age he reached the clear conviction that nothing but the advice of the great dread spirit could build up any tolerable sort of life for the feeble, unruly, 'incomplete, empirical creatures created in jest.' And so, convinced of this, he sees that he must follow the council of the wise spirit, the dread spirit of death and destruction, and therefore accept lying and deception, and lead men consciously to death and destruction, and yet deceive them all the way so that they may not notice where they are being led, that the poor blind creatures may at least, on the way, think themselves happy. And note, the deception is in the name of Him in Whose ideal the old man had so fervently believed all his life long. Is not that tragic? And if only one such stood at the head of the whole army 'filled with the lust of power only for the sake of filthy gain'—would not one such be enough to make a tragedy? More than that, one such standing at the head is enough to create the actual leading idea of the Roman Church, with all its armies and Jesuits, its highest idea. I tell you frankly that I firmly believe that there has always been such a man among those who stood at the head of the movement. Who knows, there may have been some such even among the Roman Popes. Who knows, perhaps the spirit of that accursed old man who loves mankind so obstinately in his own way, is to be found even now in a whole multitude of such old men, existing not by chance but by agreement, as a secret league formed long ago for the guarding of the mystery, to guard it from the weak and the unhappy, so as to make them happy. No doubt it is so, and so it must be indeed. I fancy that even among the Masons there's something of the same mystery at the bottom, and that that's why the Catholics so detest the Masons as their rivals breaking up the unity of the idea, while it is so essential that there should be one flock and one shepherd. . . . But from the way I defend my idea I might be an author impatient of your criticism. Enough of it."

"You are perhaps a Mason yourself!" broke suddenly from Alyosha. "You don't believe in God," he added, speaking this time very sorrowfully. He fancied besides that his brother was looking at him ironically. "How does your poem end?" he asked, suddenly looking down. "Or was it the end?"

"I meant to end it like this. When the Inquisitor ceased speaking he waited some time for his Prisoner to answer him. His silence weighed down upon him. He saw that the Prisoner had listened intently all the time, looking gently in his face and evidently not wishing to reply. The old man longed for Him to say something, however bitter and terrible. But He suddenly approached the old man in silence and softly kissed him on his bloodless aged lips. That was all his answer. The old man shuddered. His lips moved. He went to the door, opened it, and said to Him: 'Go, and come no more . . . come not at all, never, never!' And he let Him out into the dark alleys of the town. The Prisoner went away."

"And the old man?"

"The kiss glows in his heart, but the old man adheres to his idea."

WILLIAM BLAKE

God in Man

THERE IS NO NATURAL RELIGION [FIRST SERIES]

The *Argument.* Man has no notion of moral fitness but from Education. Naturally he is only a natural organ subject to Sense.

I. Man cannot naturally Perceive but through his natural or bodily organs.

II. Man by his reasoning power can only compare & judge of what he has already perceiv'd.

III. From a perception of only 3 senses or 3 elements none could deduce a fourth or fifth.

IV. None could have other than natural or organic thoughts if he had none but organic perceptions.

V. Man's desires are limited by his perceptions, none can desire what he has not perceiv'd.

VI. The desires & perceptions of man, untaught by any thing but organs of sense, must be limited to objects of sense.

Conclusion. If it were not for the Poetic or Prophetic character the Philosophic & Experimental would soon be at the ratio of all things, & stand still, unable to do other than repeat the same dull round over again.

THERE IS NO NATURAL RELIGION [SECOND SERIES]

I. Man's perceptions are not bounded by organs of perception; he perceives more than sense (tho' ever so acute) can discover.

II. Reason, or the ratio of all we have already known, is not the same that it shall be when we know more.

III. [This proposition has been lost.]

IV. The bounded is loathed by its possessor. The same dull round, even of a universe, would soon become a mill with complicated wheels.

V. If the many become the same as the few when possess'd, More! More! is the cry of a mistaken soul; less than All cannot satisfy Man.

From "There Is No Natural Religion" [1788], "All Religions Are One" [1788], and "The Marriage of Heaven and Hell" [1790-93], *Complete Writings,* ed. Geoffrey Keynes, London, 1957, pp. 97-8, 158; reprinted by permission of the Nonesuch Press.

vi. If any could desire what he is incapable of possessing, despair must be his eternal lot.

vii. The desire of Man being Infinite, the possession is Infinite & himself Infinite.

Application. He who sees the Infinite in all things, sees God. He who sees the Ratio only, sees himself only.

Therefore God becomes as we are, that we may be as he is.

ALL RELIGIONS ARE ONE

The Voice of one crying in the Wilderness

The *Argument.* As the true method of knowledge is experiment, the true faculty of knowing must be the faculty which experiences. This faculty I treat of.

Principle 1st. That the Poetic Genius is the true Man, and that the body or outward form of Man is derived from the Poetic Genius. Likewise that the forms of all things are derived from their Genius, which by the Ancients was call'd an Angel & Spirit & Demon.

Principle 2d. As all men are alike in outward form, So (and with the same infinite variety) all are alike in the Poetic Genius.

Principle 3d. No man can think, write, or speak from his heart, but he must intend truth. Thus all sects of Philosophy are from the Poetic Genius adapted to the weaknesses of every individual.

Principle 4th. As none by traveling over known lands can find out the unknown, So from already acquired knowledge Man could not acquire more: therefore an universal Poetic Genius exists.

Principle 5th. The Religions of all Nations are derived from each Nation's different reception of the Poetic Genius, which is every where call'd the Spirit of Prophecy.

Principle 6th. The Jewish & Christian Testaments are An original derivation from the Poetic Genius; this is necessary from the confined nature of bodily sensation.

Principle 7th. As all men are alike (tho' infinitely various), So all Religions &, as all similars, have one source.

The true Man is the source, he being the Poetic Genius.

The ancient Poets animated all sensible objects with Gods or Geniuses, calling them by the names and adorning them with the properties of woods, rivers, mountains, lakes, cities, nations, and whatever their enlarged & numerous senses could perceive.

And particularly they studied the genius of each city & country, placing it under its mental deity;

Till a system was formed, which some took advantage of, & enslav'd the vulgar by attempting to realize or abstract the mental deities from their objects: thus began Priesthood;

Choosing forms of worship from poetic tales.

And at length they pronounc'd that the Gods had order'd such things.

Thus men forgot that All deities reside in the human breast. . . .

Once I saw a Devil in a flame of fire, who arose before an Angel that sat on a cloud, and the Devil utter'd these words:

"The worship of God is: Honouring his gifts in other men, each according to his genius, and loving the greatest men best: those who envy or calumniate great men hate God; for there is no other God."

The Angel hearing this became almost blue; but mastering himself he grew yellow, & at last white, pink, & smiling, and then replied:

"Thou Idolater! is not God One? & is not he visible in Jesus Christ? and has not Jesus Christ given his sanction to the law of ten commandments? and are not all other men fools, sinners, & nothings?"

The Devil answer'd: "bray a fool in a morter with wheat, yet shall not his folly be beaten out of him; if Jesus Christ is the greatest man, you ought to love him in the greatest degree; now hear how he has given his sanction to the law of ten commandments: did he not mock at the sabbath, and so mock the sabbath's God? murder those who were murder'd because of him? turn away the law from the woman taken in adultery? steal the labor of others to support him? bear false witness when he omitted making a defence before Pilate? covet when he pray'd for his disciples, and when he bid them shake off the dust of their feet against such as refused to lodge them? I tell you, no virtue can exist without breaking these ten commandments. Jesus was all virtue, and acted from impulse, not from rules."

When he had so spoken, I beheld the Angel, who stretched out his arms, embracing the flame of fire, & he was consumed and arose as Elijah.

Note: This Angel, who is now become a Devil, is my particular friend; we often read the Bible together in its infernal or diabolical sense, which the world shall have if they behave well.

I have also The Bible of Hell, which the world shall have whether they will or no.

FRIEDRICH NIETZSCHE

The Death of God and the Antichrist

Have you not heard of that madman who lit a lantern in the bright morning hours, ran to the market-place, and cried incessantly: "I am looking for God! I am looking for God!" As many of those who did not believe in God were standing together there, he excited considerable laughter. Have you lost him, then? said

From *The Gay Science* [1882], translated from the German by R. J. Hollingdale, in Introduction to *Thus Spoke Zarathustra*, 1961, pp. 9-10; and from Hollingdale's translation of *Thus Spoke Zarathustra* [1885], pp. 109-12. Reprinted by permission of Penguin Books Inc.

From *The Antichrist* [1895], translated from the German by Walter Kaufmann, *The Portable Nietzsche*, New York, 1954, pp. 569-74, 581-5; reprinted by permission of The Viking Press Inc.

one. Did he lose his way like a child? said another. Or is he hiding? Is he afraid of us? Has he gone on a voyage? or emigrated? Thus they shouted and laughed. The madman sprang into their midst and pierced them with his glances.

"Where has God gone?" he cried. "I shall tell you. *We have killed him—you and I.* We are all his murderers. But how have we done this? How were we able to drink up the sea? Who gave us the sponge to wipe away the entire horizon? What did we do when we unchained this earth from its sun? Whither is it moving now? Whither are we moving now? Away from all suns? Are we not perpetually falling? Backward, sideward, forward, in all directions? Is there any up or down left? Are we not straying as through an infinite nothing? Do we not feel the breath of empty space? Has it not become colder? Is not more and more night coming on all the time? Must not lanterns be lit in the morning? Do we not hear anything yet of the noise of the gravediggers who are burying God? Do we not smell anything yet of God's decomposition? Gods too decompose. God is dead. God remains dead. And we have killed him. How shall we, the murderers of all murderers, console ourselves? That which was holiest and mightiest of all that the world has yet possessed has bled to death under our knives. Who will wipe this blood off us? With what water could we purify ourselves? What festivals of atonement, what sacred games shall we need to invent? Is not the greatness of this deed too great for us? Must not we ourselves become gods simply to seem worthy of it? There has never been a greater deed; and whoever shall be born after us—for the sake of this deed he shall be part of a higher history than all history hitherto."

Here the madman fell silent and again regarded his listeners; and they too were silent and stared at him in astonishment. At last he threw his lantern to the ground, and it broke and went out. "I come too early," he said then; "my time has not come yet. This tremendous event is still on its way, still travelling—it has not yet reached the ears of men. Lightning and thunder require time, the light of the stars requires time, deeds require time even after they are done, before they can be seen and heard. This deed is still more distant from them than the most distant stars—*and yet they have done it themselves.*"

It has been related further that on that same day the madman entered divers churches and there sang a *requiem aeternam deo.* Led out and quietened, he is said to have retorted each time: "What are these churches now if they are not the tombs and sepulchres of God?"

The figs are falling from the trees, they are fine and sweet; and as they fall their red skins split. I am a north wind to ripe figs.

Thus, like figs, do these teachings fall to you, my friends: now drink their juice and eat their sweet flesh! It is autumn all around and clear sky and afternoon.

Behold, what abundance is around us! And it is fine to gaze out upon distant seas from the midst of superfluity.

Once you said "God" when you gazed upon distant seas; but now I have taught you to say "Superman."

God is a supposition; but I want your supposing to reach no further than your creating will.

Could you *create* a god?—So be silent about all gods! But you could surely create the Superman.

Perhaps not you yourselves, my brothers! But you could transform yourselves into forefathers and ancestors of the Superman: and let this be your finest creating!

God is a supposition: but I want your supposing to be bounded by conceivability.

Could you *conceive* a god?—But may the will to truth mean this to you: that everything shall be transformed into the humanly-conceivable, the humanly-evident, the humanly-palpable! You should follow your own senses to the end!

And you yourselves should create what you have hitherto called the World: the World should be formed in your image by your reason, your will, and your love! And truly, it will be to your happiness, you enlightened men!

And how should you endure life without this hope, you enlightened men? Neither in the incomprehensible nor in the irrational can you be at home.

But to reveal my heart entirely to you, friends: *if* there were gods, how could I endure not to be a god! *Therefore* there are no gods.

I, indeed, drew that conclusion; but now it draws me.

God is a supposition: but who could imbibe all the anguish of this supposition without dying? Shall the creator be robbed of his faith and the eagle of his soaring into the heights?

God is a thought that makes all that is straight crooked and all that stands giddy. What? Would time be gone and all that is transitory only a lie?

To think this is giddiness and vertigo to the human frame, and vomiting to the stomach: truly, I call it the giddy sickness to suppose such a thing.

I call it evil and misanthropic, all this teaching about the one and the perfect and the unmoved and the sufficient and the intransitory.

All that is intransitory—that is but an image! And the poets lie too much.

But the best images and parables should speak of time and becoming: they should be a eulogy and a justification of all transitoriness.

Creation—that is the great redemption from suffering, and life's easement. But that the creator may exist, that itself requires suffering and much transformation.

Yes, there must be much bitter dying in your life, you creators! Thus you are advocates and justifiers of all transitoriness.

For the creator himself to be the child new-born he must also be willing to be the mother and endure the mother's pain.

Truly, I have gone my way through a hundred souls and through a hundred cradles and birth-pangs. I have taken many departures, I know the heart-breaking last hours.

But my creative will, my destiny, wants it so. Or, to speak more honestly: my will wants precisely such a destiny.

All *feeling* suffers in me and is in prison: but my *willing* always comes to me as my liberator and bringer of joy.

Willing liberates: that is the true doctrine of will and freedom—thus Zarathustra teaches you.

No more to will and no more to evaluate and no more to create! ah, that this great lassitude may ever stay far from me!

In knowing and understanding, too, I feel only my will's delight in begetting and becoming; and if there be innocence in my knowledge it is because will to begetting is in it.

This will lured me away from God and gods; for what would there be to create if gods—existed!

But again and again it drives me to mankind, my ardent, creative will; thus it drives the hammer to the stone.

Ah, you men, I see an image sleeping in the stone, the image of my visions! Ah, that it must sleep in the hardest, ugliest stone!

Now my hammer rages fiercely against its prison. Fragments fly from the stone: what is that to me?

I will complete it: for a shadow came to me—the most silent, the lightest of all things once came to me!

The beauty of the Superman came to me as a shadow. Ah, my brothers! What are the gods to me now!

Thus spoke Zarathustra.

Let us face ourselves. We are Hyperboreans; we know very well how far off we live. "Neither by land nor by sea will you find the way to the Hyperboreans"—Pindar already knew this about us. Beyond the north, ice, and death—*our* life, *our* happiness. We have discovered happiness, we know the way, we have found the exit out of the labyrinth of thousands of years. Who *else* has found it? Modern man perhaps? "I have got lost; I am everything that has got lost," sighs modern man.

This modernity was our sickness: lazy peace, cowardly compromise, the whole virtuous uncleanliness of the modern Yes and No. This tolerance and *largeur* of the heart, which "forgives" all because it "understands" all, is *sirocco* for us. Rather live in the ice than among modern virtues and other south winds!

We were intrepid enough, we spared neither ourselves nor others; but for a long time we did not know where to turn with our intrepidity. We became gloomy, we were called fatalists. Our *fatum*—the abundance, the tension, the damming of strength. We thirsted for lightning and deeds and were most remote from the happiness of the weakling, "resignation." In our atmosphere was a thunderstorm; the nature we are became dark—*for we saw no way.* Formula for our happiness: a Yes, a No, a straight line, a goal. . . .

What is good? Everything that heightens the feeling of power in man, the will to power, power itself.

What is bad? Everything that is born of weakness.

What is happiness? The feeling that power is *growing*, that resistance is overcome.

Not contentedness but more power; not peace but war; not virtue but fitness (Renaissance virtue, *virtù*, virtue that is moraline[1]-free).

The weak and the failures shall perish: first principle of *our* love of man. And they shall even be given every possible assistance.

[1] The coinage of a man who neither smoked nor drank coffee. [TRANSLATOR'S NOTE.]

What is more harmful than any vice? Active pity for all the failures and all the weak: Christianity. . . .

The problem I thus pose is not what shall succeed mankind in the sequence of living beings (man is an *end*), but what type of man shall be *bred*, shall be *willed*, for being higher in value, worthier of life, more certain of a future.

Even in the past this higher type has appeared often—but as a fortunate accident, as an exception, never as something *willed*. In fact, this has been the type most dreaded—almost *the* dreadful—and from dread the opposite type was willed, bred, and *attained*: the domestic animal, the herd animal, the sick human animal —the Christian. . . .

Christianity should not be beautified and embellished: it has waged deadly war against this higher type of man; it has placed all the basic instincts of this type under the ban; and out of these instincts it has distilled evil and the Evil One: the strong man as the typically reprehensible man, the "reprobate." Christianity has sided with all that is weak and base, with all failures; it has made an ideal of whatever *contradicts* the instinct of the strong life to preserve itself; it has corrupted the reason even of those strongest in spirit by teaching men to consider the supreme values of the spirit as something sinful, as something that leads into error—as temptations. The most pitiful example: the corruption of Pascal, who believed in the corruption of his reason through original sin when it had in fact been corrupted only by his Christianity. . . .

Christianity is called the religion of *pity*. Pity stands opposed to the tonic emotions which heighten our vitality: it has a depressing effect. We are deprived of strength when we feel pity. That loss of strength which suffering as such inflicts on life is still further increased and multiplied by pity. Pity makes suffering contagious. Under certain circumstances, it may engender a total loss of life and vitality out of all proportion to the magnitude of the cause (as in the case of the death of the Nazarene). That is the first consideration, but there is a more important one.

Suppose we measure pity by the value of the reactions it usually produces; then its perilous nature appears in an even brighter light. Quite in general, pity crosses the law of development, which is the law of *selection*. It preserves what is ripe for destruction; it defends those who have been disinherited and condemned by life; and by the abundance of the failures of all kinds which it keeps alive, it gives life itself a gloomy and questionable aspect.

Some have dared to call pity a virtue (in every *noble* ethic it is considered a weakness); and as if this were not enough, it has been made *the* virtue, the basis and source of all virtues. To be sure—and one should always keep this in mind— this was done by a philosophy that was nihilistic and had inscribed the *negation of life* upon its shield. Schopenhauer was consistent enough: pity negates life and renders it *more deserving of negation*.

Pity is the *practice* of nihilism. To repeat: this depressive and contagious instinct crosses those instincts which aim at the preservation of life and at the enhancement of its value. It multiplies misery and conserves all that is miserable, and is thus a prime instrument of the advancement of decadence: pity persuades men to *nothingness!* Of course, one does not say "nothingness" but "beyond" or "God," or *"true* life," or Nirvana, salvation, blessedness.

This innocent rhetoric from the realm of the religious-moral idiosyncrasy appears much less innocent as soon as we realize which tendency it is that here shrouds itself in sublime words: *hostility against life.* Schopenhauer was hostile to life; therefore pity became a virtue for him.

Aristotle, as is well known, considered pity a pathological and dangerous condition, which one would be well advised to attack now and then with a purge: he understood tragedy as a purge. From the standpoint of the instinct of life, a remedy certainly seems necessary for such a pathological and dangerous accumulation of pity as is represented by the case of Schopenhauer (and unfortunately by our entire literary and artistic decadence from St. Petersburg to Paris, from Tolstoi to Wagner)—to puncture it and make it *burst.*

In our whole unhealthy modernity there is nothing more unhealthy than Christian pity. To be physicians *here,* to be inexorable *here,* to wield the scalpel *here*—that is *our* part, that is *our* love of man, that is how *we* are philosophers, we *Hyperboreans.* . . .

In Christianity neither morality nor religion has even a single point of contact with reality. Nothing but imaginary *causes* ("God," "soul," "ego," "spirit," "free will"—for that matter, "unfree will"), nothing but imaginary *effects* ("sin," "redemption," "grace," "punishment," "forgiveness of sins"). Intercourse between imaginary *beings* ("God," "spirits," "souls"); an imaginary *natural* science (anthropocentric; no trace of any concept of natural causes); an imaginary *psychology* (nothing but self-misunderstandings, interpretations of agreeable or disagreeable general feelings—for example, of the states of the *nervus sympathicus*—with the aid of the sign language of the religio-moral idiosyncrasy: "repentance," "pangs of conscience," "temptation by the devil," "the presence of God"); an imaginary *teleology* ("the kingdom of God," "the Last Judgment," "eternal life").

This *world of pure fiction* is vastly inferior to the world of dreams insofar as the latter *mirrors* reality, whereas the former falsifies, devalues, and negates reality. Once the concept of "nature" had been invented as the opposite of "God," "natural" had to become a synonym of "reprehensible": this whole world of fiction is rooted in *hatred* of the natural (of reality!); it is the expression of a profound vexation at the sight of reality.

But this explains everything. Who alone has good reason to lie his way out of reality? He who suffers from it. But to suffer from reality is to be a piece of reality that has come to grief. The preponderance of feelings of displeasure over feelings of pleasure is the cause of this fictitious morality and religion; but such a preponderance provides the very formula for decadence. . . .

A critique of the *Christian conception of God* forces us to the same conclusion. A people that still believes in itself retains its own god. In him it reveres the conditions which let it prevail, its virtues: it projects its pleasure in itself, its feeling of power, into a being to whom one may offer thanks. Whoever is rich wants to give of his riches; a proud people needs a god: it wants to *sacrifice.* Under such conditions, religion is a form of thankfulness. Being thankful for himself, man needs a god. Such a god must be able to help and to harm, to be friend and enemy—he is admired whether good or destructive. The *anti-natural* castration of a god, to make him a god of the good alone, would here be contrary to everything desirable. The evil god is needed no less than the good god: after all, we do not owe our own existence to tolerance and humanitarianism.

What would be the point of a god who knew nothing of wrath, revenge, envy, scorn, cunning, and violence? who had perhaps never experienced the delightful *ardeurs* of victory and annihilation? No one would understand such a god: why have him then?

To be sure, when a people is perishing, when it feels how its faith in the future and its hope of freedom are waning irrevocably, when submission begins to appear to it as the prime necessity and it becomes aware of the virtues of the subjugated as the conditions of self-preservation, then its god *has to* change too. Now he becomes a sneak, timid and modest; he counsels "peace of soul," hate-no-more, forbearance, even "love" of friend and enemy. He moralizes constantly, he crawls into the cave of every private virtue, he becomes god for everyman, he becomes a private person,[2] a cosmopolitan.

Formerly, he represented a people, the strength of a people, everything aggressive and power-thirsty in the soul of a people; now he is merely the good god.

Indeed, there is no other alternative for gods: *either* they are the will to power, and they remain a people's gods, *or* the incapacity for power, and then they necessarily become *good.* . . .

Wherever the will to power declines in any form, there is invariably also a physiological retrogression, decadence. The deity of decadence, gelded in his most virile virtues and instincts, becomes of necessity the god of the physiologically retrograde, of the weak. Of course, they do not *call* themselves the weak; they call themselves "the good."

No further hint is required to indicate the moments in history at which the dualistic fiction of a good and an evil god first became possible. The same instinct which prompts the subjugated to reduce their god to the "good-in-itself" also prompts them to eliminate all the good qualities from the god of their conquerors; they take revenge on their masters by turning their god into the *devil.* The *good* god and the devil—both abortions of decadence.

How can anyone today still submit to the simplicity of Christian theologians to the point of insisting with them that the development of the conception of God from the "God of Israel," the god of a people, to the Christian God, the quintessence of everything good, represents *progress?* Yet even Renan does this. As if Renan had the right to be simple-minded! After all, the opposite stares you in the face. When the presuppositions of *ascending* life, when everything strong, brave, masterful, and proud is eliminated from the conception of God; when he degenerates step by step into a mere symbol, a staff for the weary, a sheet-anchor for the drowning; when he becomes the god of the poor, the sinners, and the sick par excellence, and the attribute "Savior" or "Redeemer" remains in the end as the one essential attribute of divinity—just *what* does such a transformation signify? what, such a *reduction* of the divine?

To be sure, "the kingdom of God" has thus been enlarged. Formerly he had

2 Literal translation of the *Greek idiotes.* [TRANSLATOR'S NOTE.]

only his people, his "chosen" people. Then he, like his people, became a wanderer and went into foreign lands; and ever since, he has not settled down anywhere—until he finally came to feel at home anywhere, this great cosmopolitan—until "the great numbers" and half the earth were on his side. Nevertheless, the god of "the great numbers," the democrat among the gods, did not become a proud pagan god: he remained a Jew, he remained a god of nooks, the god of all the dark corners and places, of all the unhealthy quarters the world over!

His world-wide kingdom is, as ever, an underworld kingdom, a hospital, a *souterrain* kingdom, a ghetto kingdom. And he himself: so pale, so weak, so decadent. Even the palest of the pale were able to master him: our honorable metaphysicians, those concept-albinos. They spun their webs around him until, hypnotized by their motions, he himself became a spider, another metaphysician. Now he, in turn, spun the world out of himself—*sub specie Spinozae*. Now he transfigured himself into something even thinner and paler; he became an "ideal," he became "pure spirit," the "Absolute," the "thing-in-itself." The deterioration of a god: God became the "thing-in-itself." . . .

The Christian conception of God—God as god of the sick, God as a spider, God as spirit—is one of the most corrupt conceptions of the divine ever attained on earth. It may even represent the low-water mark in the descending development of divine types. God degenerated into the *contradiction* of life, instead of being its transfiguration and eternal Yes! God as the declaration of war against life, against nature, against the will to live! God—the formula for every slander against "this world," for every lie about the "beyond"! God—the deification of nothingness, the will to nothingness pronounced holy!

MATTHEW ARNOLD
The Finer Spirit of Knowledge

"The future of poetry is immense, because in poetry, where it is worthy of its high destinies, our race, as time goes on, will find an ever surer and surer stay. There is not a creed which is not shaken, not an accredited dogma which is not shown to be questionable, not a received tradition which does not threaten to dissolve. Our religion has materialised itself in the fact, in the supposed fact; it has attached its emotion to the fact, and now the fact is failing it. But for poetry the idea is everything; the rest is a world of illusion, of divine illusion. Poetry attaches its emotion to the idea; the idea *is* the fact. The strongest part of our religion to-day is its unconscious poetry."

Let me be permitted to quote these words of my own, as uttering the thought which should, in my opinion, go with us and govern us in all our study of poetry. . . . We should conceive of poetry worthily, and more highly than it has been the custom to conceive of it. We should conceive of it as capable of higher uses, and called to higher destinies, than those which in general men have assigned to it hitherto. More and more mankind will discover that we have to turn to poetry to interpret life for us, to console us, to sustain us. Without poetry, our science will appear incomplete; and most of what now passes with us for religion and philosophy will be replaced by poetry. Science, I say, will appear incomplete without it. For finely and truly does Wordsworth call poetry "the impassioned expression which is in the countenance of all science"; and what is a countenance without its expression? Again, Wordsworth finely and truly calls poetry "the breath and finer spirit of all knowledge": our religion, parading evidences such as those on which the popular mind relies now; our philosophy, pluming itself on its reasonings about causation and finite and infinite being; what are they but the shadows and dreams and false shows of knowledge? The day will come when we shall wonder at ourselves for having trusted to them, for having taken them seriously; and the more we perceive their hollowness, the more we shall prize "the breath and finer spirit of knowledge" offered to us by poetry.

From "The Study of Poetry," *Essays in Criticism,* Second Series, New York and London, 1888, pp. 1-3.
From "Literature and Science," *Discourses in America,* New York and London, 1885, pp. 15-18.

913

Professor Huxley holds up to scorn mediæval education, with its neglect of the knowledge of nature, its poverty even of literary studies, its formal logic devoted to "showing how and why that which the Church said was true must be true." But the great mediæval Universities were not brought into being, we may be sure, by the zeal for giving a jejune and contemptible education. Kings have been their nursing fathers, and queens have been their nursing mothers, but not for this. The mediæval Universities came into being, because the supposed knowledge, delivered by Scripture and the Church, so deeply engaged men's hearts, by so simply, easily, and powerfully relating itself to their desire for conduct, their desire for beauty. All other knowledge was dominated by this supposed knowledge and was subordinated to it, because of the surpassing strength of the hold which it gained upon the affections of men, by allying itself profoundly with their sense for conduct, their sense for beauty.

But now, says Professor Huxley, conceptions of the universe fatal to the notions held by our forefathers have been forced upon us by physical science. Grant to him that they are thus fatal, that the new conceptions must and will soon become current everywhere, and that every one will finally perceive them to be fatal to the beliefs of our forefathers. The need of humane letters, as they are truly called, because they serve the paramount desire in men that good should be for ever present to them,—the need of humane letters, to establish a relation between the new conceptions, and our instinct for beauty, our instinct for conduct, is only the more visible. The Middle Age could do without humane letters, as it could do without the study of nature, because its supposed knowledge was made to engage its emotions so powerfully. Grant that the supposed knowledge disappears, its power of being made to engage the emotions will of course disappear along with it,—but the emotions themselves, and their claim to be engaged and satisfied, will remain. Now if we find by experience that humane letters have an undeniable power of engaging the emotions, the importance of humane letters in a man's training becomes not less, but greater, in proportion to the success of modern science in extirpating what it calls "mediæval thinking."

GEORGE SANTAYANA

An Allegory of Human Life

What overcame the world, because it was what the world desired, was not a moral reform—for that was preached by every sect; not an ascetic regimen—for that was practised by heathen gymnosophists and Pagan philosophers; not brotherly love within the Church—for the Jews had and have that at least in equal measure; but what overcame the world was what Saint Paul said he would always preach: Christ and him crucified. Therein was a new poetry, a new ideal, a new God. Therein was the transcript of the real experience of humanity, as men found

From "The Poetry of Christian Dogma," *Interpretations of Poetry and Religion,* New York, 1900, pp. 85-94.

it in their inmost souls and as they were dimly aware of it in universal history. The moving power was a fable—for who stopped to question whether its elements were historical, if only its meaning were profound and its inspiration contagious? This fable had points of attachment to real life in a visible brotherhood and in an extant worship, as well as in the religious past of a whole people. At the same time it carried the imagination into a new sphere; it sanctified the poverty and sorrow at which Paganism had shuddered; it awakened tenderer emotions, revealed more human objects of adoration, and furnished subtler instruments of grace. It was a whole world of poetry descended among men, like the angels at the Nativity, doubling, as it were, their habitation, so that they might move through supernatural realms in the spirit while they walked the earth in the flesh. The consciousness of new loves, new duties, fresh consolations, and luminous unutterable hopes accompanied them wherever they went. They stopped willingly in the midst of their business for recollection, like men in love; they sought to stimulate their imaginations, to focus, as it were, the long vistas of an invisible landscape.

If the importunity of affairs or of ill-subdued passions disturbed that dream, they could still return to it at leisure in the solitude of some shrine or under the spell of some canticle or of some sacramental image; and meantime they could keep their faith in reserve as their secret and their resource. The longer the vision lasted and the steadier it became, the more closely, of course, was it intertwined with daily acts and common affections; and as real life gradually enriched that vision with its suggestions, so religion in turn gradually coloured common life with its unearthly light. In the saint, in the soul that had become already the perpetual citizen of that higher sphere, nothing in this world remained without reference to the other, nor was anything done save for a supernatural end. Thus the redemption was actually accomplished and the soul was lifted above the conditions of this life, so that death itself could bring but a slight and unessential change of environment.

Morbid as this species of faith may seem, visionary as it certainly was, it is not to be confused with an arbitrary madness or with personal illusions. Two circumstances raised this imaginative piety to a high dignity and made it compatible with great accomplishments, both in thought and in action. In the first place the religious world constituted a system complete and consistent within itself. There was occasion within it for the exercise of reason, for the awakening and discipline of emotion, for the exertion of effort. As music, for all that it contains nothing of a material or practical nature, offers a field for the development of human faculty and presents laws and conditions which, within its sphere, must be obeyed and which reward obedience with the keenest and purest pleasures; so a supernatural religion, when it is traditional and systematic like Christianity, offers another world, almost as vast and solid as the real one, in which the soul may develop. In entering it we do not enter a sphere of arbitrary dreams, but a sphere of law where learning, experience, and happiness may be gained. There is more method, more reason, in such madness than in the sanity of most people. The world of the Christian imagination was eminently a field for moral experience; moral ideas were there objectified into supernatural forces, and instead of being obscured as in the real world by irrational accidents formed an intelligible cosmos, vast, massive, and steadfast. For this reason the believer in any adequate and mature supernatural religion clings to it with such strange tenacity and regards it as his highest heritage, while the outsider, whose imagination speaks another language or is dumb altogether, wonders how so wild a fiction can take root in a reasonable mind.

The other circumstance that ennobled the Christian system was that all its parts had some significance and poetic truth, although they contained, or needed to contain, nothing empirically real. The system was a great poem which, besides being well constructed in itself, was allegorical of actual experience, and contained, as in a hieroglyph, a very deep knowledge of the world and of the human mind. For what was the object that unfolded itself before the Christian imagination, the vision that converted and regenerated the world? It was a picture of human destiny. It was an epic, containing, as it were, the moral autobiography of man. The object of Pagan religion and philosophy had been a picture of the material cosmos, conceived as a vast animal and inhabited by a multitude of individual spirits. Even the Neo-Platonists thought of nothing else, much as they might multiply abstract names for its principles and fancifully confuse them with the spheres. It was always a vast, living, physical engine, a cosmos of life in which man had a determinate province. His spirit, losing its personality, might be absorbed into the ethereal element from which it came; but this emanation and absorption was itself an unchanging process, the systole and diastole of the universal heart. Practical religion consisted in honouring the nearest gods and accepting from them man's apportioned goods, not without looking, perhaps, with a reverence that needed no ritual, to the enveloping whole that prescribed to gods and men their respective functions. Thus even Neo-Platonism represented man as a minor incident in the universe, supernatural though that universe might be. The spiritual spheres were only the invisible repetitions of the visible, as the Platonic ideas from the beginning had been only a dialectic reduplication of the objects in this world. It was against this allotment that the soul was rebelling. It was looking for a deliverance that should be not so much the consciousness of something higher as the hope of something better.

Now, the great characteristic of Christianity, inherited from Judaism, was that its scheme was historical. Not existences but events were the subject of its primary interest. It presented a story, not a cosmology. It was an epic in which there was, of course, superhuman machinery, but of which the subject was man, and, notable circumstance, the Hero was a man as well. Like Buddhism, it gave the highest honour to a man who could lead his fellow-men to perfection. What had previously been the divine reality—the engine of Nature—now became a temporary stage, built for the exigencies of a human drama. What had been before a detail of the edifice—the life of man—now became the argument and purpose of the whole creation. Notable transformation, on which the philosopher cannot meditate too much.

Was Christianity right in saying that the world was made for man? Was the account it adopted of the method and causes of Creation conceivably correct? Was the garden of Eden a historical reality, and were the Hebrew prophecies announcements of the advent of Jesus Christ? Did the deluge come because of man's wickedness, and will the last day coincide with the dramatic dénouement of the Church's history? In other words, is the spiritual experience of man the explanation of the universe? Certainly not, if we are thinking of a scientific, not of a poetical explanation. As a matter of fact, man is a product of laws which must also destroy him, and which, as Spinoza would say, infinitely exceed him in their scope and power. His welfare is indifferent to the stars, but dependent on them. And yet that counter-Copernican revolution accomplished by Christianity—a revolution which Kant should hardly have attributed to himself—which put man in the centre of the universe and made the stars circle about him, must have some kind of justification. And indeed its justification (if we may be so brief on so great a subject) is that what is false in the science of facts may be true in the science of values. While the existence of things must be understood by referring them to their causes, which are mechanical, their functions can only be explained by what is interesting in their results, in other words, by their relation to human nature and to human happiness.

The Christian drama was a magnificent poetic rendering of this side of the matter, a side which Socrates had envisaged by his admirable method, but which now flooded the consciousness of mankind with torrential emotions. Christianity was born under an eclipse, when the light of Nature was obscured; but the star that intercepted that light was itself luminous, and shed on succeeding ages a moonlike radiance, paler and sadder than the other, but no less divine, and meriting no less to be eternal. Man now studied his own destiny, as he had before studied the sky, and the woods, and the sunny depths of water; and as the earlier study produced in his soul—*anima naturaliter poeta*—the images of Zeus, Pan, and Nereus, so the later study produced the images of Jesus and of Mary, of Heaven and Hell, of miracles and sacraments. The observation was no less exact, the translation into poetic images no less wonderful here than there. To trace the endless transfiguration, with all its unconscious ingenuity and harmony, might be the theme of a fascinating science. Let not the reader fancy that in Christianity everything was settled by records and traditions. The idea of Christ himself had to be constructed by the imagination in response to moral demands, tradition giving only the barest external points of attachment. The facts were nothing until they became symbols; and nothing could turn them into symbols except an eager imagination on the watch for all that might embody its dreams.

The crucifixion, for example, would remain a tragic incident without further significance, if we regard it merely as a historical fact; to make it a religious mystery, an idea capable of converting the world, the moral imagination must transform it into something that happens for the sake of the soul, so that each believer may say to himself that Christ so suffered for the love of him. And such a thought is surely the objectification of an inner impulse; the idea of Christ becomes something spiritual, something poetical. What literal meaning could there be in saying that one man or one God died for the sake of each and every other individual? By what effective causal principle could their salvation be thought to necessitate his death, or his death to make possible their salvation? By an ὕστερον πρότερον natural to the imagination; for in truth the matter is reversed. Christ's death is a symbol of human life. Men could "believe in" his death, because it was a figure and premonition of the burden of their experience. That is why, when some Apostle told them the story, they could say to him: "Sir, I perceive that thou art a prophet: thou hast told me all things whatsoever I have felt." Thus the central fact of all Christ's history, narrated by every Evangelist, could still be nothing but a painful incident, as unessential to the Christian religion as the death of Socrates to the Socratic philosophy, were it not transformed by the imagination of the believer into the counterpart of his own moral need. Then, by ceasing to be viewed as a historical fact, the death of Christ becomes a religious inspiration. The whole of Christian doctrine is thus religious and efficacious only when it becomes poetry, because only then is it the felt counterpart of personal experience and a genuine expansion of human life.

D. H. LAWRENCE

The Resurrection of the Body

The risen lord, the risen lord
has risen in the flesh,
and treads the earth to feel the soil
though his feet are still nesh.

The Churches loudly assert: We preach Christ crucified!—But in so doing, they preach only half of the Passion, and do only half their duty. The Creed says: "Was crucified, dead, and buried . . . the third day He rose again from the dead." And again, "I believe in the resurrection of the body . . ." So that to preach Christ Crucified is to preach half the truth. It is the business of the Church to preach Christ born among men—which is Christmas; Christ crucified, which is Good Friday; and Christ Risen, which is Easter. And after Easter, till November and All Saints, and till Annunciation, the year belongs to the Risen Lord: that is, all the full-flowering spring, all summer, and the autumn of wheat and fruit, all belong to Christ Risen.

But the Churches insist on Christ Crucified, and rob us of the blossom and fruit of the year. The Catholic Church, which has given us our images, has given us the Christ-child, in the lap of woman, and again, Christ Crucified: then the Mass, the mystery of atonement through sacrifice. Yet all this is really preparatory, these are the preparatory stages of the real living religion. The Christ-child, enthroned in the lap of the Mother, is obviously only a preparatory image, to prepare us for Christ the Man. Yet a vast mass of Christians stick there.

What we have to remember is that the great religious images are only images of our own experiences, or of our own state of mind and soul. In the Catholic countries, where the Madonna-and-Child image overwhelms everything else, the man visions himself all the time as a child, a Christ-Child, standing on the lap of a virgin mother. Before the war, if an Italian hurt himself, or suddenly fell into distress, his immediate cry was: *O mamma mia! mamma mia!—Oh, mother, mother!*—The same was true of many Englishmen. And what does this mean? It means that the man sees himself as a child, the innocent saviour-child enthroned on the lap of the all-pitying virgin mother. He lives according to this image of

From "The Risen Lord" [1929], *Assorted Articles*, New York and London, 1930, pp. 105-17; reprinted by permission of Random House, Alfred A. Knopf, Inc., William Heinemann Ltd., Lawrence Pollinger Ltd. and the Estate of the late Mrs. Frieda Lawrence.

himself—the image of the guileless "good" child sheltered in the arms of an all-sheltering mother—until the image breaks in his heart.

And during the war, this image broke in the hearts of most men, though not in the hearts of their women. During the war, the man who suffered most bitterly suffered beyond the help of wife or mother, and no wife nor mother nor sister nor any beloved could save him from the guns. This fact went home in his heart, and broke the image of mother and Christ-child, and left in its place the image of Christ crucified.

It was not so, of course, for the woman. The image did not break for her. She visioned herself still as the all-pitying, all-sheltering Madonna, on whose lap the man was enthroned, as in the old pictures, like a Christ-child. And naturally the woman did not want to abandon this vision of herself. It gave her her greatest significance; and the greatest power. Break the image, and her significance and her power were gone. But the men came back from the war and denied the image—for them it was broken. So she fought to maintain it, the great vision of man, the Christ-child, enthroned in the lap of the all-pitying virginal woman. And she fought in vain, though not without disastrous result.

For the vision of the all-pitying and all-helpful Madonna was shattered in the hearts of men, during the war. The all-pitying and all-helpful Woman actually did not, whether she could or not, prevent the guns from blowing to pieces the men who called upon her. So her image collapsed, and with it the image of the Christ-child. For the man who went through the war the resultant image inevitably was Christ Crucified, Christ tortured on the Cross. And Christ Crucified is essentially womanless.

True, many of the elderly men who never went through the war still insist on the Christ-child business, and most of the elderly women insist on their benevolent Madonna supremacy. But it is in vain. The guns broke the image in the hearts of middle-aged men, and the young were born, or are come to real consciousness, after the image was already smashed.

So there we are! We have three great image-divisions among men and women to-day. We have the old and the elderly, who never were exposed to the guns, still fatuously maintaining that man is the Christ-child and woman the infallible safeguard from all evil and all danger. It is fatuous, because it absolutely didn't work. Then we have the men of middle age, who were all tortured and virtually put to death by the war. They accept Christ Crucified as their image, are essentially womanless, and take the great cry: *Consummatum est!—It is finished!*—as their last word.—Thirdly, we have the young, who never went through the war. They have no illusions about it, however, and the death-cry of their elder generation: *It is finished!* rings cold through their blood. They cannot answer. They cannot even scoff. It is no joke, and never will be a joke.

And yet, neither of the great images is *their* image. They cannot accept the child-and-mother position which the old buffers still pose in. They cannot accept the Christ Crucified finality of the generations immediately ahead. For they, the young, came into the field of life after the death-cry *Consummatum est!* had rung through the world, and while the body, so to speak, was being put into the tomb. By the time the young came on to the stage, Calvary was empty, the tombs were closed, the women had lost for ever the Christ-child and the virgin savour, and it was altogether the day after, cold, bleak, empty, blank, meaningless, almost silly.

The young came into life, and found everything finished. Everywhere the empty crosses, everywhere the closed tombs, everywhere the manless, bitter or over-assertive woman, everywhere the closed grey disillusion of Christ Crucified, dead, and buried, those grey empty days between Good Friday and Easter.

And the Churches, instead of preaching the Risen Lord, go on preaching the Christ-child and Christ Crucified. Now man cannot live without some vision of himself. But still less can he live with a vision that is not true to his inner experience and inner feeling. And the vision of Christ-Child and Christ Crucified are both untrue to the inner experience and feeling of the young. They don't feel that way. They show the greatest forbearance and tolerance of their elders, for whom the two images *are* livingly true. But for the post-war young, neither the Christ-child nor Christ Crucified means much.

I doubt whether the Protestant Churches, which supported the war, will ever have the faith and the power of life to take the great step onwards, and preach Christ Risen. The Catholic Church might. In the countries of the Mediterranean, Easter has always been the greatest of the holy days, the gladdest and holiest, not Christmas, the birth of the Child. Easter, Christ Risen, the Risen Lord, this, to the old faith, is still the first day in the year. The Easter festivities are the most joyful, the Easter processions the finest, the Easter ceremonies the most splendid. In Sicily the women take into church the saucers of growing corn, the green blades rising tender and slim like green light, in little pools, filling round the altar. It is Adonis. It is the re-born year. It is Christ Risen. It is the Risen Lord. And in the warm south still a great joy floods the hearts of the people on Easter Sunday. They feel it, they feel it everywhere. The Lord is risen. The Lord of the rising wheat and the plum blossoms is warm and kind upon earth again, after having been done to death by the evil and the jealous ones.

The Roman Catholic Church may still unfold this part of the Passion fully, and make men happy again. For Resurrection is indeed the consummation of all the passion. Not even Atonement, the being at one with Christ through partaking in His sacrifice, consummates the Passion finally. For even after Atonement, men still must live, and must go forward with the vision. After we share in the body of Christ, we rise with Him in the body. And that is the final vision that has been blurred to all the Churches.

Christ risen in the flesh! We must accept the image complete, if we accept it at all. We must take the mystery in its fulness and in fact. It is only the image of our own experience. Christ rises, when He rises from the dead, in the flesh, not merely as spirit. He rises with hands and feet, as Thomas knew for certain: and if with hands and feet, then with lips and stomach and genitals of a man. Christ risen, and risen in the whole of His flesh, not with some left out.

Christ risen in the full flesh! What for? It is here the gospels are all vague and faltering, and the Churches leave us in the lurch. Christ risen in the flesh in order to lurk obscurely for six weeks on earth, then be taken vaguely up into heaven in a cloud? Flesh, solid flesh, feet and bowels and teeth and eyes of a man, taken up into heaven in a cloud, and never put down again?

It is the only part of the great mystery which is all wrong. The virgin birth, the

baptism, the temptation, the teaching, Gethsemane, the betrayal, the crucifixion, the burial and the resurrection, these are all true according to our inward
experience. They are what men and women go through, in their different ways.
But floated up into heaven as flesh-and-blood, and never set down again—this
nothing in all our experience will ever confirm. If aeroplanes take us up, they
bring us down, or let us down. Flesh and blood belong to the earth, and only to
the earth. We know it.

And Jesus was risen flesh-and-blood. He rose a man on earth to live on earth.
The greatest test was still before him: His life as a man on earth. Hitherto He
had been a sacred child, a teacher, a messiah, but never a full man. Now, risen
from the dead, He rises to be a man on earth, and live His life of the flesh, the
great life, among other men. This is the image of our inward state to-day.

This is the image of the young: the Risen Lord. The teaching is over, the
crucifixion is over, the sacrifice is made, the salvation is accomplished. Now
comes the true life, man living his full life on earth, as flowers live their full life,
without rhyme or reason except the magnificence of coming forth into fulness.

If Jesus rose from the dead in triumph, a man on earth triumphant in renewed
flesh, triumphant over the mechanical anti-life convention of Jewish priests, Roman despotism, and universal money-lust; triumphant above all over His own self-
absorption, self-consciousness, self-importance; triumphant and free as a man in
full flesh and full, final experience, even the accomplished acceptance of His own
death; a man at last full and free in flesh and soul, a man at one with death:
then He rose to become at one with life, to live the great life of the flesh and
the soul together, as peonies or foxes do, in their lesser way. If Jesus rose as a full
man, in full flesh and soul, then He rose to take a woman to Himself, to live with
her, and to know the tenderness and blossoming of the twoness with her; He
who had been hitherto so limited to His oneness, or His universality, which is the
same thing. If Jesus rose in the full flesh, He rose to know the tenderness of a
woman, and the great pleasure of her, and to have children by her. He rose to
know the responsibility and the peculiar delight of children, and also the exasperation and nuisance of them. If Jesus rose as a full man, in the flesh, He rose
to have friends, to have a man-friend whom He would hold sometimes to His
breast, in strong affection, and who would be dearer to Him than a brother, just
out of the sheer mystery of sympathy. And how much more wonderful, this, than
having disciples! If Jesus rose a full man in the flesh, He rose to do His share in
the world's work, something He really liked doing. And if He remembered His
first life, it would neither be teaching nor preaching, but probably carpentering
again, with joy, among the shavings. If Jesus rose a full man in the flesh, He rose
to continue His fight with the hard-boiled conventionalists like Roman judges
and Jewish priests and money-makers of every sort. But this time, it would no
longer be the fight of self-sacrifice that would end in crucifixion. This time it
would be a freed man fighting to shelter the rose of life from being trampled on
by the pigs. This time, if Satan attempted temptation in the wilderness, the Risen
Lord would answer: Satan, your silly temptations no longer tempt me. Luckily, I
have died to that sort of self-importance and self-conceit. But let me tell you
something, old man! Your name's Satan, isn't it? And your name is Mammon?
You are the selfish hog that's got hold of all the world, aren't you? Well, look
here, my boy, I'm going to take it all from you, so don't worry. The world and

the power and the riches thereof, I'm going to take them all from you, Satan or Mammon or whatever your name is. Because you don't know how to use them. The earth is the Lord's, and the fulness thereof, and it's going to be. Men have risen from the dead and learned not to be so greedy and self-important. We left most of that behind in the late tomb. Men have risen beyond you, Mammon, they are your risen lords. And so, you hook-nosed, glisten-eyed, ugly, money-smelling anachronism, you've got to get out. Men have not died and risen again for nothing. Whom do you think the earth belong to, you stale old rat? The earth is the Lord's and is given to the men who have died and had the power to rise again. The earth is given to the men who have risen from the dead, risen, you old grabber, and when did you ever rise? Never! So go you down to oblivion, and give your place to the risen men, and the women of the risen men. For man has been dispossessed of the full earth and the earth's fulness long enough. And the poor women, they have been shoved about manless and meaningless long enough. The earth is the Lord's and the fulness thereof, and I, the Risen Lord, am here to take possession. For now I am fully a man, and free above all from my own self-importance. I want life, and the pure contact with life. What are riches, and glory, and honour, and might, and power, to me who have died and lost my self-importance? That's why I am going to take them all from you, Mammon, because I care nothing about them. I am going to destroy all your values, Mammon; all your money values and conceit values, I am going to destroy them all.

Because only life is lovely, and you, Mammon, prevent life. I love to see a squirrel peep round a tree; and left to you, Mammon, there will soon be no squirrels to peep. I love to hear a man singing a song to himself, and if it is an old, improper song, about the fun between lads and girls, I like it all the better. But you, beastly mealy-mouthed Mammon, you would arrest any lad that sings a gay song. I love the movement of life, and the beauty of life, O Mammon, since I am risen, I love the beauty of life intensely; columbine flowers, for example, the way they dangle, or the delicate way a young girl sits and wonders, or the rage with which a man turns and kicks a fool dog that suddenly attacks him—beautiful that, the swift fierce turn and lunge of a kick, then the quivering pause for the next attack; or even the slightly silly glow that comes over some men as they are getting tipsy—it still is a glow, beautiful; or the swift look a woman fetches me, when she would really like me to go off with her, but she is troubled; or the real compassion I saw a woman express for a man who slipped and wrenched his foot: life, the beauty, the beauty of life! But that which is anti-life, Mammon, like you, and money, and machines, and prostitution, and all that tangled mass of self-importance and greediness and self-conscious conceit which adds up to Mammon, I hate it. I hate it, Mammon, I hate you and am going to push you off the face of the earth, Mammon, you great mob-thing, fatal to men.

Salvation on Earth

I cannot set up against Christ that proud and jealous resistance of Nietzsche. When he speaks of Christ, his marvelous perspicacity seems to me to fail him; yes, truly, he seems to me to accept an already second-hand and distorted image of Christ, and, in order to oppose him better, to hold Christ responsible for all the clouds and all the shadows projected on this earth by the sorry misinterpretation of his words.

I feel in Christ's teaching as much emancipatory power as in Nietzsche's; as much opposition between the value of the individual and the state, or civilization, or "Cæsar"; as much abnegation and joy. What am I saying: as much? I discover still more, and a more profound and more secret opposition; more assured and, hence, calmer; more complete and, hence, less tense, in the Gospel of Christ than in the Gospel of Zarathustra. Nietzsche is much closer to Christ than was Goethe, for instance (or Hölderlin), in whom I feel the pagan values of ancient Greece standing quite naïvely and spontaneously in opposition to the truly Christian values (I mean: those of Christ himself and not of the Church); much closer than he knew himself or was willing to admit. This is also, indeed, why the things it pleases Nietzsche to discover in Greece are that very dissatisfaction and that sacred disequilibrium in which Christianity will find its authorization, its motivation, its *raison d'être*. What he sees in Greek culture is Dionysus, whereas Goethe is on the side of Apollo. It belonged to Nietsche to rediscover under the winding-sheets and resuscitate a true Christ, but, rather than rally to Him whose teaching surpassed his own, Nietzsche thought to increase his stature by opposing Him. He resolutely misunderstands Christ; but for this misunderstanding, which is to be his springboard, the Church is, even more than he, responsible; by annexing, by trying (in vain moreover) to assimilate Christ, instead of assimilating herself to Him, she cripples Him more—and it is this crippled Christ that Nietzsche is fighting.

Numquid et vos seducti estis?
(John, vii, 47)
Numquid et tu Galilæus? . . .
(John, vii, 52)[1]

What do I care about the controversies and quibbles of the doctors? In the name of science they can deny the miracles; in the name of philosophy, the doctrine; and in the name of history, the facts. They can cast doubt on His every existence, and through philological criticism throw suspicion on the authenticity of the texts. It even pleases me that they should succeed in doing so, for my faith in no wise depends on that.

[1] "Are ye also deceived?" and "Art thou also of Galilee?"

From *Journals*, Vol. III [1937], p. 370, and from "Numquid et tu . . . ," *Journals*, Vol. II [1916-19], pp. 169-70, 170-71, 172-3, 184-5, 185-6, translated from the French by Justin O'Brien, New York, 1947-51. Copyright 1947, 1948, 1949, 1951, 1956 by Alfred A. Knopf, Inc.; reprinted by permission of Random House, Alfred A. Knopf, Inc. and Martin Secker & Warburg Ltd.

I hold this little book in my hand, and no argument either suppresses it or takes it away from me; I hold it fast and can read it when I will. Wherever I open it, it shines in quiet divine fashion, and anything that can be brought against it will do nothing against that. This is where Christ escapes the very ones who have come to lay hold of him, and not through cunning or force; and where they, back among the chief priests, when the chief priests and Pharisees ask them: *Why have ye not brought him?—Quare non adduxistis illum?*—reply: *Nunquam sic locutus est homo.—Never man spake thus—sicut hic homo—like this man.* (*John, vii, 46.*)

I read, in the preface to the Gospels in my Vulgate, that if "instead of making of the apostles witnesses who are reporting what they have seen and heard, one tried to make of them, as the rationalists suppose, writers who are inventing what they say, it would be appropriate to say with Rousseau that the inventor is much more surprising than the hero." I did not know that Rousseau had said that, but I think it also, and that it is not so much a question of believing in the words of Christ because Christ is the Son of God as of understanding that he is the Son of God because his word is divine and infinitely above everything that the art and wisdom of man offer us.

This divinity is enough for me. My mind and heart are satisfied with this proof. Anything you contribute in addition obscures it.

It is because Christ is the Son of God, they have said, that we must believe in his words. And others came who ceased to bear his words in mind because they did not admit that Jesus was the Son of God.

O Lord, it is not because I have been told that you were the Son of God that I listen to your word; but your word is beautiful beyond any human word, and that is how I recognize that you are the Son of God.

It is true, this opening of the Epistle to the Romans is confused, full of repetitions, annoying to anyone who is not aware of the pathetic effort of the apostle to bring forth so novel a truth, which he feels with all his soul, and not confusedly, but which eludes his grasp and wrestles with him like an angel and struggles.

Not the law but grace. It is the emancipation in love—and the progress through love to an exquisite and perfect obedience.

One must feel here the effort of the tender young Christian doctrine to burst the tight swaddling-clothes of Semitism that enfold it. This cannot be fully understood before having first grasped the Jewish spirit.

For I was alive without the law once: but when the commandment came, sin revived, and I died.

To be sure, it is only too easy to distort the meaning of this extraordinary word and to lend to St. Paul an intention that was never his. However, if one grants that the law precedes grace, cannot one admit a state of innocence preceding the law? *For I was alive without the law once.* This sentence is lighted up and filled, despite St. Paul, with a fearful significance.

Except a man be born again.[2]

[2] This line appears in English in the original.

See everything with novelty; is it not true that the Kingdom of God is nothing else? The innocence of the little child: *If you do not become like unto these—these* little children who *are naked and feel no shame.*

For I was alive without the law once. Oh, to achieve that state of second innocence, that pure and laughing rapture!

The Christian artist is not he who paints saints and angels, any more than edifying subjects; but rather he who puts into practice the words of Christ—and I am amazed that no one has ever sought to bring out the *æsthetic* truth of the Gospels.

Oh, to be born again! To forget what other men have written, have painted, have thought, and what one has thought oneself. To be born anew.

Et nunc . . .

It is *in eternity* that right now one must live. And it is right *now* that one must live in eternity.

What care I for eternal life without awareness at every instant of the duration?

Just as Jesus said: *I AM the way, the truth,* He says: *I am the resurrection and the life.*

Eternal life is not only to come. It is right now wholly present in us; we live it from the moment that we consent to die to ourselves, to obtain from ourselves this renunciation which permits resurrection in eternity. *He that hateth his life in this world shall keep it unto eternal life.* (John, xii, 25.)

Once more, there is neither prescription nor command here. Simply it is the secret of the higher felicity that Christ, as everywhere else in the Gospels, reveals to us.

If ye know these things, happy are ye, says Christ later. (John, xiii, 17.) Not: *Ye shall be happy*—but: *happy ARE ye.* It is right now and immediately that we can share in felicity.

What tranquillity! Here truly time stops. Here breathes the Eternal. We enter into the Kingdom of God.

One of the gravest misunderstandings of the spirit of Christ comes from the confusion frequently established in the Christian's mind between future life and eternal life.

The eternal life that Christ offers, and in which all his teaching invites us to share, that eternal life has nothing future about it. It is not beyond death that it awaits us; and indeed, if we do not attain it at once, there is no hope that we may ever achieve it. . . . The words of Christ are divinely luminous and it has taken nothing less than all the ingenuity of man to dim or change the obvious meaning. But they shine anew for whoever rereads them with a new heart, with a childlike spirit.

It is to eternal life, it is to participate at once in the eternity of life, it is to enter the kingdom of God that Christ invites Nicodemus when He says to him: *Except a man be born again, he cannot see the kingdom of God—for whosoever shall seek to save his life shall lose it,* but whosoever is born again, whosoever surrenders up his life to be reborn, whosoever renounces himself to follow *Him,* makes his soul truly living, is reborn to eternal life and enters the Kingdom of God.

And is this not likewise what Christ teaches, on the edge of the well, to the woman of Samaria: *But whosoever drinketh of the water that I shall give him shall never thirst?* . . .

But the hour cometh, AND NOW IS, says Christ right after this. *Venit hora,* ET NUNC EST. Whoever waits for that hour beyond death waits for it in vain. From the very hour at which you are born again, from the very moment at which you drink of this water, you enter the Kingdom of God, you share in eternal life. *Verily, verily, I say unto you,* Christ repeats everywhere, *He that heareth my word and believeth on him that sent me* HATH (not: *will have,* but *already has*) EVERLASTING LIFE . . . *he is passed from death unto life. Transiit a morte in vitam.* (John, v, 24.)

PAUL CLAUDEL
The Errors of André Gide

7th November 1905,
The Feast of the Immaculate Conception

My dear Friend,

As for what people call "Art" and "Beauty," I had rather that they perished a thousand times over than that we should prefer such creatures to their Creator and the futile constructions of our imagination to the reality in which alone we may find delight. What is it that St. John condemns, under the name of the three Concupiscences,—the preferring of things for their own sake, and the considering of them as nothing more than that, and the liking of them for what they are not, that is to say, for what is no part of the Eternal Being, instead of for what makes them eternally the creatures of their Creator, sustained by the working of this glorious goodness? Can't you see the basis of a whole art, brilliant and generous, in that chapter in *Proverbs* when the Spirit of God moves over chaos in sublime liberty? What is art, if not an exclamation and an acclamation, a counting and a conferring of Graces, like the Canticle of the young men in the fiery furnace, like St. Francis of Assisi's Canticle of the Sun? More than that—a sort of mimicry of the Word that creates, the Word that is "poetry," a repeating of the *Fiat* which brought everything about? What sort of a thing is modern art, from which everything of real substance has been taken away, and with it that powerful source of youth inherent only in the heavenly *naturalness* that animates Homeric poetry, for example? How should we prefer these enormous gardens which we work with our hands, like Cain the first of all farmers, to the Paradise which Our Lord has bounded by four rivers?

We cannot all become Saints, but it is our duty to do what we can, in all honesty, every moment of our lives; and, to speak the truth, it is in this alone that sanctity consists—in a filial submission of our will to the Will of our heavenly father. How then can you speak of a pagan sanctity,—that is to say, of an execrable pride, of the spiritual gormandizing of a creation that has turned in upon itself and revels in its strength and beauty, as if it were itself responsible for their

Letter to André Gide [1905], *Correspondence, 1899-1926, between Paul Claudel and André Gide*, ed. by Robert Millet and translated from the French by John Russell, New York, 1952, pp. 42-4. Copyright 1952 by Pantheon Books; reprinted by permission of Pantheon Books.

creation? All that comes not from the source is corruption and uncleanliness. It is for you, my dear Gide, to realize the stage which you have reached in your life, to have no illusions as to the demands of the voice which summons you, to gauge the obstacles which stand in your way, and to see whether, in respect of absolute Truth, you are still in that state of *invincible ignorance* which alone excuses the schismatic and the procrastinator. It is before God that you have to examine yourself in the sincerity of your own conscience.

I read yesterday a book which made me shudder—Philippe's *Bubu de Mont-parnasse*. What a hell it is that surrounds us! Evil has always the same face, and as I followed this coarse and touching story there came to my mind memories of that hideous Paganism, as the black historians of Rome describe it—Sejanus' daughter, of whom I spoke to you yesterday, that beast Nero, an "artist" after the heart of the iniquitous Renan, slavering over the victims of the arena, Batavia slavered over by Germanicus, and children and young girls sent by the hundreds to the brothels of Rome.—What a responsibility for us! You know that there are two sorts of duties—the duties of charity and the duties of justice. The duties of charity are to intervene to the limits of our strength in the necessities of our neighbour (*prochain, proximus*: he who is nearest). The duties of justice, which are still more binding, are founded on that great truth of the division of labour, which obtains throughout the whole of Christian society. Others have to bake our bread, slaughter beasts for us, and so on. And we also—it is of supreme importance—we also must shoulder, as good founders of families, the burden which is laid upon us of being such-and-such a flower or fruit. When we appear before God's tribunal, let us hope not to hear the appalling clamour of those unhappy multitudes, those submerged myriads who will give evidence against us and say: "O Lord, we others were born to ignorance, poverty, crime, and servitude. But look at those who were rich, whose parents were people of honesty and good character, who enjoyed leisure, education, and wide knowledge. We do not reproach them for not coming to our aid, for having left us, their brothers and Thy children, in our ghastly twilight. But let them be judged. What have they done with the rare and exceptional gifts which were accorded to them? Were these simply given in order that they could have a more amusing time? Or become artists and dilettantes? How have they fulfilled the mission which was given them before Thee, in our name and in our stead,—in the name of ourselves, the miserable legion of the lost and the drowned?" What a responsibility for us writers, above all, who are the leaders of men and the directors of their souls! The mere fact of our enlightenment makes us spread light all about us. We are delegated by the rest of the world to the way of knowledge and truth, and there is no other truth but Christ, who is the Way and the Life, and the duty of knowing and serving Him lies more heavily on us than upon others, and lies upon us with a terrible urgency. May you grasp all this in a generous spirit, my dear Gide, and may this festival of Christmas, which once witnessed the great compassion of God towards myself when in the half-darkness of Notre-Dame He came and took a poor child by the hand—may this festival not pass without giving me the joy of breaking the bread of the Saints and the Strong with a brother.

P. CLAUDEL.

Man Become God

It is time to say farewell to all these conjuror's tricks, to these great puppets born of the fumes of infantile brains. Have we not something graver to discuss: the effects of hashish upon human sentiments—its *moral* effects, in short?

Hitherto I have merely been compiling an abridged monograph on the intoxication itself; I have confined myself to emphasising its main features, especially the material ones. But what will seem more important, I think, to a man of spiritual discernment is to understand the poison's action upon man's spiritual part—the enlargement, distortion and exaggeration of his normal sentiments and moral perceptions until they present, in this unusual atmosphere, a real phenomenon of refraction. . . .

The English frequently use, when speaking of opium-eaters, terms that will seem excessive only to innocents who know nothing of the horrors of this downfall: "enchained," "fettered," "enslaved." Chains, indeed, in comparison with which all other chains—those of duty or lawless passion—are ribbons of gauze, spider's webs! An appalling thing, the marriage of a man to himself! . . .

I propose, in this last section of my essay to describe and analyse the moral ravages caused by this dangerous and delightful course of exercise: ravages so great, and a danger so profound, that those who return from the fight only lightly injured seem to me like brave men who have escaped from the cave of a multiform Proteus; like Orpheuses victorious over Hell.

You may regard such words, if you wish, as an exaggerated metaphor; but I shall assert that the stimulant poisons are, in my opinion, not only one of the most terrible and surest means at the disposal of the Prince of Darkness for the recruitment and subjugation of deplorable humanity, but actually one of his most perfect embodiments.

At this point, in order to lessen my task and clarify my analysis, I shall cease compiling disparate anecdotes, and instead assemble a mass of observations around a single fictitious individual. I must therefore create for this purpose a personality of my own choosing . . . something analogous to what the eighteenth century called "the man of sensibility" and the Romantics "the misunderstood genius"; or what families and the mass of citizenry today generally stigmatise as "an original."

A temperament half nervous and half choleric—such is the one most favourable to the evolutions of the intoxication that we are discussing. Let us add to this a cultivated mind, practised in the study of form and colour; and a tender heart, wearied by unhappiness but still ready for rejuvenescence. We shall even, if you insist, go so far as to admit the presence of certain old weaknesses, and—as their inevitable consequence, in an easily excitable nature—moments of what may or may not be positive remorse, but is at least a regret for profaned and ill-spent time. We may usefully add a taste for metaphysics and an acquaintance with

From "The Poem of Hashish" [1860], *My Heart Laid Bare and Other Writings*, ed. by Peter Quennell and translated from the French by Norman Cameron, London, 1950, pp. 105, 106, 107-8, 108-9, 114-15, 117-18; reprinted by permission of George Weidenfeld & Nicolson Ltd.

the various basic theories of philosophy concerning human destiny; also that love of virtue—abstract virtue, either stoical or mystical—which is advocated, in all the books that nowadays provide the spiritual nourishment of adolescence, as the highest summit that a noble soul can attain. If we add to all this a great subtlety of the senses—which I have omitted as supererogatory—I think that I have assembled all the general elements common to the man of sensibility in our time: what might be called "the ordinary sort of eccentric."

Let us now see what happens to such a personality when driven to desperate extremes by hashish. Let us follow the procession of the human imagination to its last and most magnificent altar, to the individual's belief in his own godhead. . . .

There is no sort of combination of the sentiments to which the pliable love of a slave to hashish cannot lend itself. A pleasant sense of giving protection, a feeling of ardent and devoted fatherliness, can be mingled with a disgraceful sensuality, for which hashish will always find excuse and absolution.

It goes still further. Let us suppose that the subject has committed faults which have left traces of bitterness in his soul; that he is a husband or lover who, in his normal state, must feel regret whenever he contemplates a somewhat stormy past. Now this bitterness can be changed to sweetness; the need for pardon makes the imagination more adroit, more suppliant; and remorse itself—in this diabolic drama, which takes the form of a long monologue—can be a stimulant, powerfully rekindling the heart's enthusiasm.

Yes, remorse! Was I wrong in saying that to a truly philosophic mind hashish must seem that perfect instrument of Satan? Remorse, that odd ingredient of pleasure, is soon drowned in the delicious contemplation of remorse, in a sort of voluptuous self-analysis; and this analysis is so rapid that man—this devil by nature, to use the Swedenborgian phrase—does not realise how involuntary it is, or how, second by second, he is approaching perfect diabolism. He *admires* his remorse, he glories in himself, even as his freedom slips away.

So by this time my hypothetical man, this soul of my choosing, has reached the pitch of joy and serenity at which he is *compelled* to admire himself. Every contradiction effaces itself, all the problems of philosophy become crystal-clear, or at least appear to be so. Everything is a matter for rejoicing. The fullness of his life at this moment inspires him with a disproportionate pride. A voice speaks within him (alas! it is his own), saying to him: "You are now entitled to consider yourself superior to all men; nobody knows, or could understand, all that you think and feel; men would be incapable even of appreciating the benevolence with which they inspire you. You are a king unrecognised by the passers-by, a king who lives in the solitude of his own certainty. But what do you care? Do you not possess that sovereign pride which so ennobles the soul?" . . .

Shall I continue the analysis of this conquering monomania? Shall I explain how, under the dominion of the poison, our man soon makes himself the centre of the universe? How he becomes a living and outrageous personification of the proverb which says that desire knows no barriers? He believes in his own virtue and genius: can the end not be guessed? All surrounding objects are so many suggestions provoking in him a world of thought, all more highly coloured, more vivid and more subtle than ever before and clad in a veneer of magic. "These magnificent cities," he tells himself, "with their superb buildings echelonned as if on a stage—these handsome ships swaying on the waters of the harbour in nostalgic idleness, seeming to express my very thought: 'When shall we set out for happiness?'—these museums crammed with lively shapes and intoxicating colours—these libraries where all the works of Science and the dreams of the Muses are assembled—these massed instruments speaking with a single voice—these enchanting women, made still more charming by the science of self-adornment and the demureness of their glances—all these things were created for me, for me, for me! For me humanity has worked, been martyrised and immolated—to provide pasture, pabulum to my implacable appetite for emotion, knowledge and beauty!"

Let us hasten on and cut the story short. Nobody will be surprised that a final, supreme thought bursts from the dreamer's brain: "I have become God!"; that a wild and ardent shout breaks from his bosom with such force, such projectile power that, if the wishes and beliefs of a drunken man had any effective virtue, this shout would bowl over the angels scattered on the paths of Heaven: "I am a God!"

Soon, however, this hurricane of pride dies down into a weather of calm, silent, restful beatitude. All creation is richly coloured, as if illumined by a sulphurous dawn. If by chance a vague memory slips into the soul of the deplorable ecstatic: "Might there not be another God?" you may be sure that he will squarely confront that other, discuss his intentions and face him without terror.

JACQUES MARITAIN
The Errors of Modern Rationalism

[Descartes] constantly broke up the harmonies of philosophia perennis into two antinomic errors, each one disguising the other. He needs God as the guarantor of science; therefore he betakes himself to Him by the quickest route, one which most resembles an intuition: to know that He exists and that He guarantees the human order. Reassured of it as a practical man, he loses interest in God; it is the world which interests him now. He turns aside religiously from God. Too exalted a God! Too sublime. Let us pay our respects to the Creator with despatch. And now, bring on the world. If reason were to linger over things divine, it could only be in order to submit them to itself, since to know, for Cartesian reasoning, is to subjugate the object. A sacred flight precipitates it toward things below.

And this is what matters to us: the overturning of the intellectual order, the inversion of the impulse of knowledge, for which Descartes is doubtless not the first one responsible, but as it were the prince and legislator. Metaphysics is reduced to a justification of science; it has as its aim to make physics possible.

Aristotle said that there is more joy in knowing divine things imperfectly and obscurely than in knowing perfectly the things proportioned to our minds. And

From The Dream of Descartes [1931], translated from the French by M. L. Anderson, New York, 1944, pp. 176-84; reprinted by permission of Philosophical Library, New York.

thus the nature of our intellect is to drag itself along toward divine things. Descartes on the contrary, boasted of devoting only a very few hours a year to metaphysical thoughts. In his eyes, it is important "to have thoroughly understood once in one's life the principles of metaphysics," but "it would be very harmful to occupy one's understanding in meditating upon them, because it would then be unable to attend to the functions of the imagination and the senses as well." Cartesian understanding does not drag itself along toward things divine, it settles comfortably in worldly things. Cartesian science is by essence a rich man's, a propertied man's science. What is, first of all, important to him is not the dignity of the object, even though it be obtained only through certainly not luxurious means—what is important to him is the perfection of the means, it is the comfort of clear ideas.

With regard to what is inferior to man, to the world of corporeal nature, Cartesian intellect claims to understand everything exposed to the core, through the substance, through the essence itself. Matter lies naked before it as before the angels. The mathematical knowledge of nature, for Descartes, is not what it is in reality, a certain interpretation of phenomena, invaluable moreover, but which does not answer questions bearing upon the first principles of things. This knowledge is, for him, the revelation of the very essence of things. These are analyzed exhaustively by geometric extension and local movement. The whole of physics, that is, the whole of the philosophy of nature, is nothing but geometry.

Thus Cartesian evidence goes straight to mechanicism. It mechanizes nature, it does violence to it; it annihilates everything which causes things to symbolize with the spirit, to partake of the genius of the Creator, to speak to us. The universe becames dumb.

And why all this? What is the end of all our effort to know? It is a practical end: to become, as Descartes puts it in the *Discourse on Method*, *masters and possessors of nature*. To desire to dominate and utilize material nature is a good thing! But once the direction of knowledge was reversed, as I remarked a while back, this practical domination of created force was to become two centuries after Descartes, the final aim of civilization—and that is a very great evil.

The cultural significance of rationalism thus becomes clearly apparent to us. It implies an anthropocentric naturalism of wisdom; and what optimism! It is a doctrine of necessary progress, of salvation by science and by reason; I mean, temporal and worldly salvation of humanity by reason alone, which, thanks to the principles of Descartes, will lead man to felicity, to "that highest degree of wisdom in which the sovereign good of human life consists" (he wrote it himself in the preface to the French translation of the *Principles*)—in giving man full mastery over nature and over his nature; and, as the Hegelians were to add two centuries later, over his history. As if reason by itself alone was capable of making men act reasonably and of securing the good of peoples! There is no worse delusion.

On the balance-sheet we should inscribe; rupture of the impulse which was directing all the labor of human science towards the eternal, toward conversation with the three divine Persons—upsetting of the élan of knowledge. Knowledge does not aspire to do more than give man the means of domesticating matter.

The sole retreat remaining for the spiritual will be science's reflection upon itself. And doubtless, that is indeed something of spiritual but of an autophagous spiritual. To delude oneself with the thought that the idealistic ruminating of physics and mathematics is enough to force the gates to the kingdom of God, to introduce man to wisdom and to freedom, to transform him into a fire of love burning for all eternity, is psychological childishness and metaphysical humbug. Man becomes spiritualized only by joining with a spiritual and eternal living One. There is only one spiritual life which does not mislead—that which the Holy Spirit bestows. Rationalism is the death of spirituality.

Then it is through the experience of sin, of suffering and despair that in the nineteenth century we will see spirituality reawaken in the wilderness: through a Baudelaire, a Rimbaud. An ambiguous spirituality, good for heaven if grace takes hold of it, good for hell if pride interferes. Many of our contemporaries will seek nourishment for their souls in anti-reason, and below reason, nourishment which should be sought only above reason. And to have led so many reasoning animals around to a hatred of reason is another of rationalism's misdeeds.

It remains for us to consider rapidly a third aspect of Descartes' doctrine—the one which concerns human nature.

Cartesian dualism breaks man up into two complete substances, joined to one another no one knows how: on the one hand, the body which is only geometric extension; on the other, the soul which is only thought—an angel inhabiting a machine and directing it by means of the pineal gland. . . .

Thought side. We know the effects of the triumph of this dualism in the second half of the seventeenth century: a theoretical contempt of the body and the senses; nothing worthwhile but pure thought. That means, in fact, the triumph of artificial thought and of false intellectualism; for human intellection is living and fresh only when it is centered upon the vigilance of sense perception. The natural roots of our knowledge being cut, a general drying-up in philosophy and culture resulted, a drought for which romantic tears were later to provide only an insufficient remedy.

In the second place, a complete disregard of the affective life. Feeling is no longer anything more than a confused idea. The existence of love and of will as forming a distinct world, having its own life and its own laws in the heaven of the soul, is radically misunderstood. Affectivity will have its revenge. Take for example the present tendencies of psychology, which would submerge everything under affectivism and instinctivism.

In the third place, for Cartesian civilization, man is only thought. "I, that is to say, my thought," said the philosopher. Man has lost his body. Alas! The body has not let go of him. Only the ascetics have the means of scorning the body. The Cartesian contempt for the body is a theorist's illusion. In the end, Freud will turn up with his great sadistic lyricism and claim to reduce man to sexuality and the instinct of death.

Body side. I was saying that the Cartesian man had lost his body: he has delivered it over to the universal mechanism, to the energies of matter regarded as forming a closed world. What have been the results?

First of all, man's body ceases to be regarded as human by essence. Cartesian physicians, iatromechanists or iatrochemists, treat it as an automaton or as a retort. And, in a general way, medicine tends to forget that it is dealing with a being whose life is not only corporeal, but moral and spiritual as well.

This observation ought to be generalized: we leave Descartes himself then, but not the Cartesian spirit. Let us say that in the modern world, everything which is amenable to any technique whatever in human life tends to resolve itself into a closed world, separate, independent. Things like politics and economics in particular will become contrivances removed from the specific regulation of the human good; they will cease to be, as the ancients wished, subordinated intrinsically and of themselves, to ethics. With greater reason, speculative science and art, which do not appertain of themselves to the domain of ethics, will impose on man a law which is not his own.

Here is man then, the centre of the world, of a world inhuman in every respect, pressing in upon him. Nothing in human life is any longer made to man's measure, to the rhythm of the human heart. The forces he has unleashed, split him asunder.

He wishes to reign nevertheless, and more than ever—and over his own nature. But how? By technique alone—that is, by means extraneous to himself. Thus we arrive at the great dispute of our age, freedom by technique versus freedom by self-determination.

I should like to put it in this way: there are two ways of looking at man's mastery of himself. Man can become master of his nature by imposing the law of reason—of reason aided by grace—on the universe of his own inner energies. That work, which in itself is a construction in love, requires that our branches be pruned to bear fruit: a process called *mortification*. Such a morality is an ascetic morality.

What rationalism claims to impose upon us today is an entirely different morality, anti-ascetic, exclusively technological. An appropriate technique should permit us to rationalize human life, *i.e.*, to satisfy our desires with the least possible inconvenience, without any interior reform of ourselves. What such a morality subjects to reason are material forces and agents exterior to man, instruments of human life; it is not man, nor human life as such. It does not free man, it weakens him, it disarms him, it renders him a slave to all the atoms of the universe, and especially to his own misery and egoism. What remains of man? A consumer crowned by science. This is the final gift, the twentieth century gift of the Cartesian reform.

Technique is good—mechanics is good. I disapprove of the spirit of archaism which would suppress the machine and technique. But if mechanics and technique are not mastered, subjected by force to the good of man, that is to say entirely and rigorously subordinated to religious ethics and made instruments of an ascetic morality, humanity is literally lost.

How then shall we characterize the cultural significance of Cartesian dualism? To sum up the preceding observations, let us say that this dualism carries along with it both an anthropocentric angelism and materialism of civilization. On the balance-sheet must be written: division of man, rupture of the human life. They began by putting the human self above everything else, an angelic self—nay, a divine self. It is so perfectly one that no plurality of powers or of faculties is to be distinguished in it! Its substance is the very act of thinking.

This Cartesian man, naturally good in so far as he is reason, will later become the man of Rousseau, naturally good in so far as he is sentiment and instinct, and whom social life and reflection corrupt. He has no further need to perfect himself, to build himself up by his virtues, he has only to blossom forth, to display himself by virtue of sincerity. It is as though one were to tell a fertilized egg to be sincere and not to have the hypocrisy to construct its form by its own efforts, through a host of morphogenetic choices and differentiations which cruelly limit its availability.

Reflection has progressed prodigiously. Never has man more carefully scrutinized his innermost recesses. Never has he experienced so heart-rending a nostalgia for freedom. Yet how is he truly to know freedom? His own personality escapes him, he is a prey to that duality characterized so well by Nicolas Berdiaev in the most thoughtful pages of his book on Dostoievsky.

T. E. HULME

The Modern Confusion of Categories

One of the main achievements of the nineteenth century was the elaboration and universal application of the principle of *continuity*. The destruction of this conception is, on the contrary, an urgent necessity of the present.

Originally urged only by the few, it has spread—implicit in the popular conception of evolution—till it has attained the status of a category. We now absorb it unconsciously from an environment already completely soaked in it; so that we regard it not as a principle in the light of which certain regions of fact can be conveniently ordered, but as an inevitable constituent of reality itself. When any fact seems to contradict this principle, we are inclined to deny that the fact really exists. We constantly tend to think that the discontinuities in nature are only *apparent*, and that a fuller investigation would reveal the underlying continuity. This shrinking from a *gap* or jump in nature has developed to a degree which paralyses any objective perception, and prejudices our seeing things as they really are. For an objective view of reality we must make use both of the categories of continuity and discontinuity. Our principal concern then at the present moment should be the re-establishment of the temper or disposition of mind which can look at a *gap* or chasm without shuddering.

I am not concerned in these notes, however, with gaps in nature, in the narrow sense of the word. I am thinking rather of general theories about the nature of reality. One of the results of the temper of mind I have just discussed is that any general theories of this kind which assert the existence of absolute gaps between one region of reality and another, are at once almost instinctively felt to be inadmissible. Now the method of criticism I wish to employ here is based on the fact that most of the errors in certain subjects spring from an almost instinctive attempt on our part to gloze over and disguise a particular *discontinuity* in the nature of reality. It was then necessary first of all to deal with the source of this

From "Humanism and the Religious Attitude," *Speculations*, ed. by Herbert Read, New York and London, 1924, pp. 3-11; reprinted by permission of Routledge & Kegan Paul Ltd.

instinctive behaviour, by pointing out the arbitrary character of the principle of continuity.

What is this Method? It is only possible here to describe it quite abstractly, leaving the details till later. Certain regions of reality differ not relatively but absolutely. There exists between them a real discontinuity. As the mind looks on discontinuity with horror it has attempted to exhibit these opposed things as differing only in degree, as if there is in reality a continuous scale leading from one to the other. From this springs a whole mass of confused thinking in religion and ethics. If we first of all form a clear conception of the nature of a discontinuity, of a chasm, and form in ourselves the temper of mind which can support this opposition without irritation, we shall then have in our hands an instrument which may shatter all this confused thinking, and enable us to form accurate ideas on these subjects. In this way a flood of light may be thrown on old controversies.

A necessary preliminary to this, however, must be some account of the nature of the particular absolute discontinuity that I want to use.

In order to simplify matters, it may be useful here to give the exposition a kind of geometrical character. Let us assume that reality is divided into three regions, separated from one another by absolute divisions, by real discontinuities. (1) The inorganic world, of mathematical and physical science, (2) the organic world, dealt with by biology, psychology and history, and (3) the world of ethical and religious values. Imagine these three regions as three zones marked out on a flat surface by two concentric circles. The outer zone is the world of physics, the inner that of religion and ethics, the intermediate one that of life. The outer and inner regions have certain characteristics in common. They have both an *absolute* character, and knowledge about them can legitimately be called absolute knowledge. The intermediate region of life is, on the other hand, essentially relative; it is dealt with by *loose* sciences like biology, psychology and history. A muddy mixed zone then lies between two absolutes. To make the image a more faithful representation one would have to imagine the extreme zones partaking of the perfection of geometrical figures, while the middle zone was covered with some confused muddy substance.

I am afraid I shall have to abandon this model, for to make it represent faithfully what I want, I shall have to add a further complication. There must be an *absolute* division between each of the three regions, a kind of *chasm*. There must be no continuity, no bridge leading from one to the other. It is these *discontinuities* that I want to discuss here.

A convenient way of realising the nature of these divisions is to consider the movement away from materialism, at the end of the nineteenth century. In the middle period of the century, the predominant popular view entirely ignored the division between the inner and outer zones, and tended to treat them as one. There was no separating chasm and the two were muddled together. Vital phenomena were only extremely complicated forms of mechanical change. (Cf. Spencer's Biology and the entirely mechanical view involved in the definition of life as adaptation to environment.) Then you get the movement represented in very different ways by Nitszsche, Dilthey, and Bergson, which clearly recognised the chasm between the two worlds of life and matter. Vital events are not completely *determined* and mechanical. It will always be impossible to describe them completely in terms of the laws of physics. This was not merely a local reaction against a local false doctrine. It contained an original element. This movement made the immense step forward involved in treating life, almost for the first time, as a unity, as something positive, a kind of stream overflowing, or at any rate not entirely enclosed, in the boundaries of the physical and spatial world. "In dein Auge schaute ich, O Leben," etc.

So far so good. But the same movement that recognises the existence of the first absolute chasm (between the physical and the vital), proceeds to ignore the second, that between biology and the ethical, religious values. Having made this immense step away from materialism, it believes itself adequately equipped for a statement of all the ideal values. It does not distinguish different levels of the non-material. All that is non-material, must it thinks be *vital*. The momentum of its escape from mechanism carries it on to the attempt to restate the whole of religion in terms of vitalism. This is ridiculous. Biology is not theology, nor can God be defined in terms of "life" or "progress." Modernism entirely misunderstands the nature of religion. But the last twenty years have produced masses of writing on this basis, and in as far as thought to-day is not materialistic, it tends to be exclusively of this kind.

It is easy to understand why the absolute division between the inorganic and the organic is so much more easily recognised than the second division. For the first falls easily into line with humanism, while the second breaks the whole Renaissance tradition.

It is necessary, however, that this second absolute difference should also be understood. It is necessary to realise that there is an absolute, and not a relative, difference between humanism (which we can take to be the highest expression of the vital), and the religious spirit. The *divine* is not *life* at its intensest. It contains in a way an almost *anti-vital* element; quite different of course from the non-vital character of the outside physical region. The questions of Original Sin, of chastity, of the motives behind Buddhism, etc., all part of the very essence of the religious spirits, are quite incomprehensible for humanism. The difference is seen perhaps most obviously in art. At the Renaissance, there were many pictures with religious subjects, but no religious art in the proper sense of the word. All the emotions expressed are perfectly human ones. Those who choose to think that religious emotion is only the highest form of the emotions that fall inside the humanist ideology, may call this religious art, but they will be wrong. When the intensity of the religious attitude finds proper expression in art, then you get a very different result. Such expression springs not from a delight in life but from a feeling for certain absolute values, which are entirely independent of vital things. The disgust with the trivial and accidental characteristics of living shapes, the searching after an austerity, a monumental stability and permanence, a perfection and rigidity, which vital things can never have, leads to the use of forms which can almost be called *geometrical*. (Cf. Byzantine, Egyptian and early Greek art.) If we think of physical science as represented by geometry, then instead of saying that the modern progress away from materialism has been from physics through vitalism to the absolute values of religion, we might say that it is from *geometry through life and back to geometry*. It certainly seems as if the extreme regions had resemblances not shared by the middle region. This is because they are both, in different ways, absolute.

We can repeat this in a more summary form. Two sets of errors spring from the attempt to treat different regions of reality as if they were alike. (1) The attempt to introduce the *absolute* of mathematical physics into the essentially relative middle zone of life leads to the *mechanistic* view of the world. (2) The attempt to explain the *absolute* of religious and ethical values in terms of the categories appropriate to the essentially relative and non-absolute vital zone, leads to the entire misunderstanding of these values, and to the creation of a series of mixed or bastard phenomena, which will be the subject of these notes. (Cf. Romanticism in literature, Relativism in ethics, Idealism in philosophy, and Modernism in religion.)

To say that these bastard phenomena are the result of the shrinking from discontinuity would be an entirely inadequate account of the matter. They spring from a more positive cause, the inability of the prevailing ideology to understand the nature of this absolute. But they are certainly shaped by this instinctive effort to dig away at the edges of the precipice, which really separates two regions of reality, until it is transformed into a slope leading gradually from one to the other.

Romanticism, for example, confuses both human and divine things, but not clearly separating them. The main thing with which it can be reproached is that it blurs the clear outlines of human relations—whether in political thought or in the literary treatment of sex—by introducing in them the *Perfection* that properly belongs to the non-human.

The method I wish to pursue then is this. In dealing with these confused phenomena, to hold the real nature of the *absolute discontinuity* between vital and religious things constantly before the mind; and thus to clearly separate those things, which are in reality separate. I believe this to be a very fertile method, and that it is possible by using it, not only to destroy all these bastard phenomena, but also to recover the real significance of many things which it seems absolutely impossible for the "modern" mind to understand.

KARL BARTH

The One and Only God

> We confesse and acknawledge ane onelie God, to whom only we must cleave, whom onelie we must serve, whom onelie we must worship, and in whom onelie we must put our trust.

I

"We confesse and acknawledge God . . . ." So begins the Scottish Confession. Who or what lies hidden behind this word "God"—a word with which indeed

From *The Knowledge of God and the Service of God,* translated from the German by J. L. M. Haire and Ian Henderson, London, 1938, pp. 13-21; reprinted by permission of Hodder and Stoughton Ltd. and Curtis Brown Ltd.

we are only too familiar? All confessions of all churches and religions purport to treat of "God." What is conceived by all other "believers," past, present and future, whatever the manner, place and date of their belief, is certainly not what the Scottish Confession means by the object of its profession. The Confession does not *conceive* its object at all, it *acknowledges* it: "We confesse and acknawledge." And before we have time to ask it how and where it acknowledges God, it has already singled out a part of this knowledge of God,—or should we not rather say the whole of it?—and placed it before us in the words "We confesse and acknawledge *ane onelie* God." It thus puts to us, so to speak, the counter question whether we ourselves do not acknowledge this same one and only God, and whether we have not long known how and where He, the one and only God, was to be acknowledged. But a Confession cannot wait for the assent of its hearers. *This*, it says, *this* is God, the one and only God, "to whom only we must cleave, whom onelie we must serve, whom onelie we must worship, and in whom onelie we must put our trust." The note struck here is characteristic of all confessions of the Reformed church; the French and Dutch confessions for instance begin in an exactly similar way. Yet this note is struck with special emphasis in the Scottish Confession, and we shall meet it time and again in our text.

It will repay us to halt here for a moment and to consider this phrase "ane onelie God" carefully. It is not an innovation or a discovery of the sixteenth century which is put forward here, but it is certainly a renewal, a rediscovery and a restoration of knowledge long forgotten and denied. The voice of the Old Testament becomes articulate here once more, "Here, O Israel, Jahweh our God is Jahweh the one and only God" (Deut. 6, 4). The voice of the New Testament becomes audible too, "We know that there is none other God but one" (1 Cor. 8, 4). So, too, the voice of the early church: "Deus si non unus est, non est" (Tert. *adv. Marc.* 1, 3). Therefore to speak of God is to speak of the one and only God. To know God means to know the one and only God. To serve God means to serve the *one and only* God. This is what Reformed teaching brings to light again. In and along with everything else which it says, it says this also.

In saying this what does Reformed teaching mean? It does not mean that God alone exists. It does not deny the world. It denies neither its variety nor its unity in itself, neither its splendour nor its fearful secrets, neither the profundity of nature nor the profundity of spirit. The world *exists*, but the world does not exist alone. And if the world does not exist alone, because it exists through God and therefore as having God behind, above and before it, as Him without whom it would not exist, so God does not exist alone, because the world exists through Him. It exists through Him, Who, without the world, would yet be in Himself no less what He is. The difference in the relation between them is this—God exists along with the world as its free creator, whereas the world exists along with God as the creation founded on His freedom. By recognising this difference we recognise God as the one and only God. At the conclusion of our confession we find the invocation, "Arise, O Lord, and let thy enimies be confounded . . ." Knowledge of the one and only God becomes possible and real, because this does happen, because God does "arise" and makes Himself visible in the world and distinguishes Himself *from* the world as its creator, thereby making the world visible and distinguishing it as His creation. Whatever the world may be as a whole and whatever separate entity may exist within the world—be it its final grounds and principles—this is not creative in the way in which God is creative, nor free as God is free, nor Lord as He is Lord. For it exists through God and, unlike God, does not possess its specific existence in itself. "We acknawledge ane onelie God"—that is the description of how we know the One Who becomes knowable in this distinction, consummated by Him Himself. Our knowledge will only be able to follow the drawing of this distinction. "Arise, O Lord." Our thought in so far as it follows this "arising" attains to this knowledge of God, and can attain to this knowledge alone. "We acknowledge ane onelie God"—this is no mere part of the knowledge of God, but rightly understood is itself the sum of all true knowledge of God and for that reason this sentence may legitimately stand at the head of the confession.

II

Let us, in the first place, make clear to ourselves the far-reaching importance of this sentence. I repeat, it does not mean the negation, the denial or the depreciation of that which is not God. But it does mean that this latter factor is criticised, *limited* and made *relative*. It says precisely that this factor is not God. Whatever else it may be, only illegitimately can it conduct itself as God, and only illegitimately can it be regarded and treated as God. Whatever else it may be, we are free to abandon it; we are not compelled to serve it or worship it and we cannot in any sense or on any account put our hope of salvation in it. The greatness, beauty and importance which it may have in itself and also for us within the world is indisputable. That is expressly acknowledged in the New Testament passage previously cited, "There are (in heaven and on earth) gods many and lords many" (1 Cor. 8, 5). But these are gods so-called ($\lambda\epsilon\gamma\acute{o}\mu\epsilon\nu o\iota$ $\theta\epsilon o\acute{\iota}$) and the knowledge of the one and only God means that they are unmasked as such.

The god "so-called," which the proposition about the "ane onelie God" was designed to combat, is above all *man himself*. We cannot help seeing this to-day even more clearly than was possible in the sixteenth century before the Cartesian revolution had taken place. It is man's self-assertion which is the source of the possible or actual denial of the one and only God—not perhaps in the form that man denies the existence of the one and only God but very simply in the form that he identifies himself with the one and only God. Man can regard himself and treat himself as the measure of all things, just as if he were Creator or free or Lord like Him to whom he owes his being. He can therefore think that he dare not abandon himself but must serve and worship himself, and that he can therefore put his hope of salvation in himself. Without denying God, man can consider himself as having power over God. And not only can man do that, but he actually does it. Eritis sicut Deus. This voice was heard and obeyed by man long before the time of Descartes. Now the knowledge of the one and only God means the *limiting* of this human self-assertion. "We acknawledge ane onelie God" means simply, we men are not gods or are merely gods so-called or make-believe gods. We are forced to retire within the bounds of our own creatureliness and our own human nature. The modern world has failed to hear the warning of the Reformed confession precisely at this point and has thought fit to exchange the mediæval conception of the world as geocentric for the much more naïve conception of the world as anthropocentric.

The gods so-called, which the proposition about the "ane onelie God" was designed to combat, are, however, also the gods and godheads of all the human ideologies and mythologies, philosophies and religions. With the well-known ambition of a devoted father, man decks the children of his self-assertion with the same authority with which he has previously decked himself. These are the systems by means of which he proposes—at least in phantasy and fancy—to exercise his divine freedom and lordship. They might also be described as costumes, each one more beautiful than the other, which man dons in turn in his role as the one and only reality. And just as fathers must sometimes accommodate themselves to their children, and just as each costume constrains the actor to adopt a definite attitude, so the systems woven in man's phantasy and fancy come to possess and keep a definite power over him. His conception of the world and thus his world become full of ideas and principles, points of view scientific, ethical and æsthetic, axioms, self-evident truths social and political, certainties conservative and revolutionary. They exercise so real a dominion and they bear so definitely the character of gods and godheads, that not infrequently devotion to them actually crystallises into mythologies and religions. (Universities are the temples of these religions.) But each one of these claims at the moment to be the one and only reality with monopoly over all systems. It is now considered impossible to abandon them either. Service and honour are offered them also and it is believed that the hope of salvation should be put in them. To recognise the one and only God means to make all these systems relative. "We acknawledge ane onelie God" means that the principles and objects of these systems, whatever they may be, are in reality no gods or at best gods so-called. Are they to be annihilated? Perhaps not at all, perhaps not yet. But the end of their authority is within sight. When the knowledge of God becomes manifest, they can no longer possess ultimate credibility, and real, serious and solemn reverence cannot be shown them any longer. "What askest thou Me concerning the good? One is good" (Matt. 19, 17). "The destruction of the gods" comes down upon them then. In any case they can henceforward prolong their existence only as symbols and hypotheses, perhaps as angels or as demons, perhaps only as ghosts and comical figures. This makes clear to us how it was possible for the early Christians to have been accused of atheism, and the Christian church would be in a better position if she had remained suspect of atheism in this sense of the word in modern times as well. All that we can say is that this is not the case. The church has much rather played a most lively part in the game of dressing up in different costumes a mere counterfeit of the one and only reality.

III

Knowledge of the truly one and only God gains this meaning when it is brought about by this truly one and only God Himself. God is the one and only One and proves Himself to be such by His being both the Author of His own Being and the source of all knowledge of Himself. In both these respects He differs from everything in the world. A God who could be known otherwise than through Himself, i.e. otherwise than through His revelation of Himself, would have already betrayed, eo ipso, that He was not the one and only one and so was not God. He would have betrayed Himself to be one of those principles underlying human systems and finally identical with man himself. But the *Confessio* speaks not of one of those principles nor of man but of God, and therefore of One through whom all things exist, and who wills to be known through no one except through Himself.

There exists a conception of the *unity* of all being in its totality. All human thought takes this into account. And this conception can even gain remarkable depth and richness by means of the conception of the *uniqueness* (the one-and-onlyness) of all being in its individuality. All human thought has taken this also into account from the start. We may adopt this hypothesis of the one, and we may recognise and formulate this cosmic problem of the one as such. Yet in doing so we have done absolutely nothing that would have even a distant connection with the knowledge of God. The secret fire of all or almost all philosophies and religions is kindled by the charm of the idea of mathematical unity, intensified by the charm of the principle of individuality—not to speak of the fire which political domination has needed, whenever the world or a part of it has been ripe for such a domination. But a wrong is done and a strange fire is brought to the altar, if men seek to kindle the fire of the knowledge of God by this charm—and from time to time the Fathers did do this. Thomas Aquinas's sentence that "Deus non est in aliquo genere" (*Sum. Theol.* 1, Ques. 3, Art. 5) must be rigorously applied to the genus "unity" or "uniqueness" (one-and-onlyness) also. What falls under this genus is as such not God, even if it were the ultimate and highest conceivable or perceptible unity of the world. The God of Mohammed is an idol like all other idols, and it is an optical illusion to characterise Christianity along with Islam as a "monotheistic" religion.

True knowledge of the one and only God, knowledge of Him in the sense of our Confession, is based on the fact that the one and only God makes Himself known. Everything is through Him Himself or is not at all. He makes Himself known through Himself by distinguishing Himself *in* the world *from* the world. Otherwise He cannot be known at all. He can be known, because He arises—"Arise, O Lord"—in human form and therefore in a way that is visible and audible for us, i.e. as the eternal Son of God in the flesh, the one and only God in Whom we have been called to believe, Jesus Christ.

PAUL TILLICH
The Meaning of Meaninglessness

Twentieth-century man has lost a meaningful world and a self which lives in meanings out of a spiritual center. The man-created world of objects has drawn into itself him who created it and who now loses his subjectivity in it. He has sacrificed himself to his own productions. But man still is aware of what he has lost or is continuously losing. He is still man enough to experience his dehumanization as despair. He does not know a way out but he tries to save his humanity by expressing the situation as without an "exit." He reacts with the courage of despair, the courage to take his despair upon himself and to resist the radical threat of nonbeing by the courage to be as oneself. Every analyst of present-day Existentialist philosophy, art, and literature can show their ambiguous structure: the meaninglessness which drives to despair, a passionate denunciation of this situation, and the successful or unsuccessful attempt to take the anxiety of meaninglessness into the courage to be as oneself.

It is not astonishing that those who are unshaken in their courage to be as a part, either in its collectivist or in its conformist form, are disturbed by the expressions of the Existentialist courage of despair. They are unable to understand what is happening in our period. They are unable to distinguish the genuine from the neurotic anxiety in Existentialism. They attack as a morbid longing for negativity what in reality is courageous acceptance of the negative. They call decay what is actually the creative expression of decay. They reject as meaningless the meaningful attempt to reveal the meaninglessness of our situation. It is not the ordinary difficulty of understanding those who break new ways in thinking and artistic expression which produces the widespread resistance to recent Existentialism but the desire to protect a self-limiting courage to be as a part. Somehow one feels that this is not a true safety; one has to suppress inclinations to accept the Existentialist visions, one even enjoys them if they appear in the theater or in novels, but one refuses to take them seriously, that is as revelations of one's own existential meaninglessness and hidden despair. The violent reactions against modern art in collectivist (Nazi, Communist) as well as conformist (American democratic) groups show that they feel seriously threatened by it. But one does not feel spiritually threatened by something which is not an element of onself. And since it is a symptom of the neurotic character to resist non-

From *The Courage To Be*, New Haven, 1952, pp. 139-41, 142-3, 174-6, 178-81, 190; reprinted by permission of the Yale University Press.

being by reducing being, the Existentialist could reply to the frequent reproach that he is neurotic by showing the neurotic defense mechanisms of the anti-Existentialist desire for traditional safety.

There should be no question of what Christian theology has to do in this situation. It should decide for truth against safety, even if the safety is consecrated and supported by the churches. Certainly there is a Christian conformism, from the beginning of the Church on, and there is a Christian collectivism—or at least semicollectivism, in several periods of Church history. But this should not induce Christian theologians to identify Christian courage with the courage to be as a part. They should realize that the courage to be as onself is the necessary corrective to the courage to be as a part—even if they rightly assume that neither of these forms of the courage to be gives the final solution. . . .

The courage of despair, the experience of meaninglessness, and the self-affirmation in spite of them are manifest in the Existentialists of the 20th century. Meaninglessness is the problem of all of them. The anxiety of doubt and meaninglessness is, as we have seen, the anxiety of our period. The anxiety of fate and death and the anxiety of guilt and condemnation are implied but they are not decisive. When Heidegger speaks about the anticipation of one's own death it is not the question of immortality which concerns him but the question of what the anticipation of death means for the human situation. When Kierkegaard deals with the problem of guilt it is not the theological question of sin and forgiveness that moves him but the question of what the possibility of personal existence is in the light of personal guilt. The problem of meaning troubles recent Existentialists even when they speak of finitude and guilt.

The decisive event which underlies the search for meaning and the despair of it in the 20th century is the loss of God in the 19th century. Feuerbach explained God away in terms of the infinite desire of the human heart; Marx explained him away in terms of an ideological attempt to rise above the given reality; Nietzsche as a weakening of the will to live. The result is the pronouncement "God is dead," and with him the whole system of values and meanings in which one lived. This is felt both as a loss and as a liberation. It drives one either to nihilism or to the courage which takes nonbeing into itself. There is probably nobody who has influenced modern Existentialism as much as Nietzsche and there is probably nobody who has presented the will to be oneself more consistently and more absurdly. In him the feeling of meaninglessness became despairing and self-destructive.

On this basis Existentialism, that is the great art, literature, and philosophy of the 20th century, reveals the courage to face things as they are and to express the anxiety of meaninglessness. It is creative courage which appears in the creative expressions of despair. . . .

How is the courage to be possible if all the ways to create it are barred by the experience of their ultimate insufficiency? If life is as meaningless as death, if guilt is as questionable as perfection, if being is no more meaningful than nonbeing, on what can one base the courage to be?

There is an inclination in some Existentialists to answer these questions by a leap from doubt to dogmatic certitude, from meaninglessness to a set of symbols in which the meaning of a special ecclesiastical or political group is embodied. This leap can be interpreted in different ways. It may be the expression of a desire for safety; it may be as arbitrary as, according to Existentialist principles, every decision is; it may be the feeling that the Christian message is the answer to the questions raised by an analysis of human existence; it may be a genuine conversion, independent of the theoretical situation. In any case it is not a solution of the problem of radical doubt. It gives the courage to be to those who are converted but it does not answer the question as to how such a courage is possible in itself. The answer must accept, as its precondition, the state of meaninglessness. It is not an answer if it demands the removal of this state; for that is just what cannot be done. He who is in the grip of doubt and meaninglessness cannot liberate himself from this grip; but he asks for an answer which is valid within and not outside the situation of his despair. He asks for the ultimate foundation of what we have called the "courage of despair." There is only one possible answer, if one does not try to escape the question: namely that the acceptance of despair is in itself faith and on the boundary line of the courage to be. In this situation the meaning of life is reduced to despair about the meaning of life. But as long as this despair is an act of life it is positive in its negativity. Cynically speaking, one could say that it is true to life to be cynical about it. Religiously speaking, one would say that one accepts oneself as accepted in spite of one's despair about the meaning of this acceptance. The paradox of every radical negativity, as long as it is an active negativity, is that it must affirm itself in order to be able to negate itself. No actual negation can be without an implicit affirmation. The hidden pleasure produced by despair witnesses to the paradoxical character of self-negation. The negative lives from the positive it negates.

The faith which makes the courage of despair possible is the acceptance of the power of being, even in the grip of nonbeing. Even in the despair about meaning being affirms itself through us. The act of accepting meaninglessness is in itself a meaningful act. It is an act of faith. We have seen that he who has the courage to affirm his being in spite of fate and guilt has not removed them. He remains threatened and hit by them. But he accepts his acceptance by the power of being-itself in which he participates and which gives him the courage to take the anxieties of fate and guilt upon himself. The same is true of doubt and meaninglessness. The faith which creates the courage to take them into itself has no special content. It is simply faith, undirected, absolute. It is undefinable, since everything defined is dissolved by doubt and meaninglessness. Nevertheless, even absolute faith is not an eruption of subjective emotions or a mood without objective foundation. . . .

The courage to be in all its forms has, by itself, revelatory character. It shows the nature of being, it shows that the self-affirmation of being is an affirmation that overcomes negation. In a metaphorical statement (and every assertion about being-itself is either metaphorical or symbolic) one could say that being includes nonbeing but nonbeing does not prevail against it. "Including" is a spatial metaphor which indicates that being embraces itself and that which is opposed to it, nonbeing. Nonbeing belongs to being, it cannot be separated from it. We could not even think "being" without a double negation: being must be thought as the negation of the negation of being. This is why we describe being best by the metaphor "power of being." Power is the possibility a being has to actualize itself against the resistance of other beings. If we speak of the power of being-itself we indicate that being affirms itself against nonbeing. In our discussion of courage

and life we have mentioned the dynamic understanding of reality by the philosophers of life. Such an understanding is possible only if one accepts the view that
nonbeing belongs to being, that being could not be the ground of life without
nonbeing. The self-affirmation of being without nonbeing would not even be self-
affirmation but an immovable self-identity. Nothing would be manifest, nothing
expressed, nothing revealed. But nonbeing drives being out of its seclusion, it
forces it to affirm itself dynamically. Philosophy has dealt with the dynamic self-
affirmation of being-itself wherever it spoke dialectically, notably in Neoplaton-
ism, Hegel, and the philosophers of life and process. Theology has done the same
whenever it took the idea of the living God seriously, most obviously in the trini-
tarian symbolization of the inner life of God. Spinoza, in spite of his static definition of substance (which is his name for the ultimate power of being), unites
philosophical and mystical tendencies when he speaks of the love and knowledge
with which God loves and knows himself through the love and knowledge of
finite beings. Nonbeing (that in God which makes his self-affirmation dynamic)
opens up the divine self-seclusion and reveals him as power and love. Nonbeing
makes God a living God. Without the No he has to overcome in himself and in
his creature, the divine Yes to himself would be lifeless. There would be no revelation of the ground of being, there would be no life.

But where there is nonbeing there is finitude and anxiety. If we say that nonbeing belongs to being-itself, we say that finitude and anxiety belong to being-
itself. Wherever philosophers or theologians have spoken of the divine blessedness
they have implicitly (and sometimes explicitly) spoken of the anxiety of finitude
which is eternally taken into the blessedness of the divine infinity. The infinite
embraces itself and the finite, the Yes includes itself and the No which it takes
into itself, blessedness comprises itself and the anxiety of which it is the conquest.
All this is implied if one says that being includes nonbeing and that through
nonbeing it reveals itself. It is a highly symbolic language which must be used at
this point. But its symbolic character does not diminish its truth; on the contrary, it is a condition of its truth. To speak unsymbolically about being-itself
is untrue.

The divine self-affirmation is the power that makes the self-affirmation of the
finite being, the courage to be, possible. Only because being-itself has the character of self-affirmation in spite of nonbeing is courage possible. Courage participates in the self-affirmation of being-itself, it participates in the power of being
which prevails against nonbeing. He who receives this power in an act of mystical or personal or absolute faith is aware of the source of his courage to be.

Man is not necessarily aware of this source. In situations of cynicism and indifference he is not aware of it. But it works in him as long as he maintains the
courage to take his anxiety upon himself. In the act of the courage to be the
power of being is effective in us, whether we recognize it or not. Every act of
courage is a manifestation of the ground of being, however questionable the content of the act may be. The content may hide or distort true being, the courage
in it reveals true being. Not arguments but the courage to be reveals the true nature of being-itself. By affirming our being we participate in the self-affirmation of
being-itself. There are no valid arguments for the "existence" of God, but there
are acts of courage in which we affirm the power of being, whether we know it or
not. If we know it, we accept acceptance consciously. If we do not know it, we

nevertheless accept it and participate in it. And in our acceptance of that which we do not know the power of being is manifest to us. Courage has revealing power, the courage to be is the key to being-itself. . . . The courage to take the anxiety of meaninglessness upon oneself is the boundary line up to which the courage to be can go. Beyond it is mere nonbeing. Within it all forms of courage are re-established in the power of the God above the God of theism. *The courage to be is rooted in the God who appears when God has disappeared in the anxiety of doubt.*

953